Joseph P. Cain

JOHN KEATS
PERCY BYSSHE SHELLEY

THE COMPLETE POEMS OF
JOHN KEATS
AND
PERCY BYSSHE SHELLEY

WITH THE EXPLANATORY NOTES
OF SHELLEY'S POEMS BY MRS. SHELLEY

THE MODERN LIBRARY

NEW YORK

Distributed in Canada
by Random House of Canada Limited, Toronto.

THE MODERN LIBRARY
is published by
RANDOM HOUSE, INC.

New York, New York

Manufactured in the United States of America

ꞇ̠ English poetry.
19th century.
ae Shelley, Percy Bysshe,
1792- 1822.

CONTENTS

CONTENTS

POEMS
PUBLISHED IN 1817

DEDICATION

GLORY and loveliness have pass'd away;
  For if we wander out in early morn,
  No wreathed incense do we see upborne
Into the east, to meet the smiling day:
No crowd of nymphs soft voic'd and young, and gay,   5
  In woven baskets bringing ears of corn,
  Roses, and pinks, and violets, to adorn
The shrine of Flora in her early May.
But there are left delights as high as these,
  And I shall ever bless my destiny,
That in a time, when under pleasant trees
  Pan is no longer sought, I feel a free,
A leafy luxury, seeing I could please
  With these poor offerings, a man like thee.

POEMS

"Places of nestling green for Poets made."
Story of Rimini.

I STOOD tip-toe upon a little hill,
The air was cooling, and so very still,
That the sweet buds which with a modest pride
Pull droopingly, in slanting curve aside,
Their scantly leav'd, and finely tapering stems,
Had not yet lost those starry diadems
Caught from the early sobbing of the morn.
The clouds were pure and white as flocks new shorn,
And fresh from the clear brook; sweetly they slept
On the blue fields of heaven, and then there crept   10
A little noiseless noise among the leaves,
Born of the very sigh that silence heaves:
For not the faintest motion could be seen
Of all the shades that slanted o'er the green.
There was wide wand'ring for the greediest eye,
To peer about upon variety;
Far round the horizon's crystal air to skim,
And trace the dwindled edgings of its brim;
To picture out the quaint, and curious bending
Of a fresh woodland alley, never ending;   20
Or by the bowery clefts, and leafy shelves,
Guess where the jaunty streams refresh themselves.
I gazed awhile, and felt as light, and free
As though the fanning wings of Mercury
Had play'd upon my heels: I was light-hearted,
And many pleasures to my vision started;
So I straightway began to pluck a posey
Of luxuries bright, milky, soft and rosy.

A bush of May flowers with the bees about them;
Ah, sure no tasteful nook would be without them;   30
And let a lush laburnum oversweep them,
And let long grass grow round the roots to keep them
Moist, cool and green; and shade the violets,
That they may bind the moss in leafy nets.
A filbert hedge with wild briar overtwined,
And clumps of woodbine taking the soft wind

1

Upon their summer thrones; there too should be
The frequent chequer of a youngling tree,
That with a score of light green brethren shoots
From the quaint mossiness of aged roots: 40
Round which is heard a spring-head of clear waters
Babbling so wildly of its lovely daughters
The spreading blue-bells: it may haply mourn
That such fair clusters should be rudely torn
From their fresh beds, and scattered thoughtlessly
By infant hands, left on the path to die.

Open afresh your round of starry folds,
Ye ardent marigolds!
Dry up the moisture from your golden lids,
For great Apollo bids   50
That in these days your praises should be sung
On many harps, which he has lately strung;
And when again your dewiness he kisses,
Tell him, I have you in my world of blisses:
So haply when I rove in some far vale,
His mighty voice may come upon the gale.

Here are sweet peas, on tip-toe for a flight:
With wings of gentle flush o'er delicate white,
And taper fingers catching at all things,
To bind them all about with tiny rings.   60

Linger awhile upon some bending planks
That lean against a streamlet's rushy banks,
And watch intently Nature's gentle doings:
They will be found softer than ring-dove's cooings.
How silent comes the water round that bend;
Not the minutest whisper does it send
To the o'erhanging sallows: blades of grass
Slowly across the chequer'd shadows pass.

Why, you might read two sonnets, ere they reach
To where the hurrying freshnesses aye preach   70
A natural sermon o'er their pebbly beds;
Where swarms of minnows show their little heads,
Staying their wavy bodies 'gainst the streams,
To taste the luxury of sunny beams
Temper'd with coolness. How they ever wrestle
With their own sweet delight, and ever nestle
Their silver bellies on the pebbly sand.
If you but scantily hold out the hand,
That very instant not one will remain;

But turn your eye, and they are there again.
The ripples seem right glad to reach those cresses,
And cool themselves among the em'rald tresses;
The while they cool themselves, they freshness give,
And moisture, that the bowery green may live:
So keeping up an interchange of favours,
Like good men in the truth of their behaviours.
Sometimes goldfinches one by one will drop
From low hung branches; little space they stop;
But sip, and twitter, and their feathers sleek;
Then off at once, as in a wanton freak: 90
Or perhaps, to show their black, and golden wings,
Pausing upon their yellow flutterings.
Were I in such a place, I sure should pray
That naught less sweet, might call my thoughts away,
Than the soft rustle of a maiden's gown
Fanning away the dandelion's down;
Than the light music of her nimble toes
Patting against the sorrel as she goes.
How she would start, and blush, thus to be caught
Playing in all her innocence of thought.   100
O let me lead her gently o'er the brook,
Watch her half-smiling lips, and downward look;
O let me for one moment touch her wrist;
Let me one moment to her breathing list;
And as she leaves me may she often turn
Her fair eyes looking through her locks auburne.
What next? A tuft of evening primroses,
O'er which the mind may hover till it dozes;
O'er which it well might take a pleasant sleep,
But that 'tis ever startled by the leap   110
Of buds into ripe flowers; or by the flitting
Of diverse moths, that aye their rest are quitting;
Or by the moon lifting her silver rim
Above a cloud, and with a gradual swim
Coming into the blue with all her light.
O Maker of sweet poets, dear delight
Of this fair world, and all its gentle livers;
Spangler of clouds, halo of crystal rivers,
Mingler with leaves, and dew and tumbling streams,
Closer of lovely eyes to lovely dreams,   120
Lover of loneliness, and wandering,
Of upcast eye, and tender pondering!
Thee must I praise above all other glories
That smile us on to tell delightful stories.
For what has made the sage or poet write
But the fair paradise of Nature's light?

In the calm grandeur of a sober line,
We see the waving of the mountain pine;
And when a tale is beautifully staid,
We feel the safety of a hawthorn glade: 130
When it is moving on luxurious wings,
The soul is lost in pleasant smotherings:
Fair dewy roses brush against our faces,
And flowering laurels spring from diamond vases;
O'er head we see the jasmine and sweet briar,
And bloomy grapes laughing from green attire;
While at our feet, the voice of crystal bubbles
Charms us at once away from all our troubles:
So that we feel uplifted from the world,
Walking upon the white clouds wreath'd and curl'd.
So felt he, who first told, how Psyche went   141
On the smooth wind to realms of wonderment;
What Psyche felt, and Love, when their full lips
First touch'd; what amorous, and fondling nips
They gave each other's cheeks; with all their sighs,
And how they kist each other's tremulous eyes:
The silver lamp,—the ravishment,—the wonder—
The darkness,—loneliness,—the fearful thunder;
Their woes gone by, and both to heaven upflown,
To bow for gratitude before Jove's throne.   150
So did he feel, who pull'd the boughs aside,
That we might look into a forest wide,
To catch a glimpse of Fauns, and Dryades
Coming with softest rustle through the trees;
And garlands woven of flowers wild, and sweet,
Upheld on ivory wrists, or sporting feet:
Telling us how fair, trembling Syrinx fled
Arcadian Pan, with such a fearful dread.
Poor nymph,—poor Pan,—how he did weep to find,
Naught but a lovely sighing of the wind   160
Along the reedy stream; a half-heard strain,
Full of sweet desolation—balmy pain.

What first inspired a bard of old to sing
Narcissus pining o'er the untainted spring?
In some delicious ramble, he had found
A little space, with boughs all woven round;
And in the midst of all, a clearer pool
Than e'er reflected in its pleasant cool,
The blue sky here, and there, serenely peeping
Through tendril wreaths fantastically creeping.   170
And on the bank a lonely flower he spied,
A meek and forlorn flower, with naught of pride,

Drooping its beauty o'er the watery clearness,
To woo its own sad image into nearness:
Deaf to light Zephyrus it would not move;
But still would seem to droop, to pine, to love.
So while the poet stood in this sweet spot,
Some fainter gleamings o'er his fancy shot;
Nor was it long ere he had told the tale
Of young Narcissus, and sad Echo's bale.   180

Where had he been, from whose warm head out-flew
That sweetest of all songs, that ever new,
That aye refreshing, pure deliciousness,
Coming ever to bless
The wanderer by moonlight? to him bringing
Shapes from the invisible world, unearthly singing
From out the middle air, from flowery nests,
And from the pillowy silkiness that rests
Full in the speculation of the stars.
Ah! surely he had burst our mortal bars;   190
Into some wond'rous region he had gone,
To search for thee, divine Endymion!

He was a Poet, sure a lover too,
Who stood on Latmus' top, what time there blew
Soft breezes from the myrtle vale below;
And brought in faintness solemn, sweet, and slow
A hymn from Dian's temple; while upswelling,
The incense went to her own starry dwelling.
But though her face was clear as infant's eyes,
Though she stood smiling o'er the sacrifice,   200
The Poet wept at her so piteous fate,
Wept that such beauty should be desolate:
So in fine wrath some golden sounds he won,
And gave meek Cynthia her Endymion.

Queen of the wide air; thou most lovely queen
Of all the brightness that mine eyes have seen!
As thou exceedest all things in thy shine,
So every tale, does this sweet tale of thine.
O for three words of honey, that I might
Tell but one wonder of thy bridal night!   210

Where distant ships do seem to show their keels,
Phoebus awhile delay'd his mighty wheels,
And turn'd to smile upon thy bashful eyes,
Ere he his unseen pomp would solemnize.
The evening weather was so bright, and clear,

That men of health were of unusual cheer;
Stepping like Homer at the trumpet's call,
Or young Apollo on the pedestal:
And lovely women were as fair and warm,
As Venus looking sideways in alarm.   220
The breezes were ethereal, and pure,
And crept through half-closed lattices to cure
The languid sick; it cool'd their fever'd sleep,
And soothed them into slumbers full and deep.
Soon they awoke clear eyed: nor burnt with thirsting,
Nor with hot fingers, nor with temples bursting:
And springing up, they met the wond'ring sight
Of their dear friends, nigh foolish with delight;
Who feel their arms, and breasts, and kiss and stare,
And on their placid foreheads part the hair.   230
Young men, and maidens at each other gaz'd
With hands held back, and motionless, amaz'd
To see the brightness in each other's eyes;
And so they stood, fill'd with a sweet surprise,
Until their tongues were loos'd in poesy.
Therefore no lover did of anguish die:
But the soft numbers, in that moment spoken,
Made silken ties, that never may be broken.
Cynthia! I cannot tell the greater blisses,
That follow'd thine, and thy dear shepherd's kisses: 240
Was there a poet born?—but now no more,
My wand'ring spirit must no further soar.—

SPECIMEN OF AN INDUCTION TO A POEM

Lo! I must tell a tale of chivalry;
For large white plumes are dancing in mine eye.
Not like the formal crest of latter days:
But bending in a thousand graceful ways;
So graceful, that it seems no mortal hand,
Or e'en the touch of Archimago's wand,
Could charm them into such an attitude.
We must think rather, that in playful mood,
Some mountain breeze had turn'd its chief delight,
To show this wonder of its gentle might.   10
Lo! I must tell a tale of chivalry;
For while I muse, the lance points slantingly
Athwart the morning air: some lady sweet,
Who cannot feel for cold her tender feet,
From the worn top of some old battlement
Hails it with tears, her stout defender sent:

And from her own pure self no joy dissembling,
Wraps round her ample robe with happy trembling.
Sometimes, when the good Knight his rest would take,
It is reflected, clearly, in a lake,   20
With the young ashen boughs, 'gainst which it rests,
And th' half seen mossiness of linnets' nests.
Ah! shall I ever tell its cruelty,
When the fire flashes from a warrior's eye,
And his tremendous hand is grasping it,
And his dark brow for very wrath is knit?
Or when his spirit, with more calm intent,
Leaps to the honors of a tournament,
And makes the gazers round about the ring
Stare at the grandeur of the ballancing?   30
No, no! this is far off:—then how shall I
Revive the dying tones of minstrelsy,
Which linger yet about long gothic arches,
In dark green ivy, and among wild larches?
How sing the splendour of the revelries,
When butts of wine are drunk off to the lees?
And that bright lance, against the fretted wall,
Beneath the shade of stately banneral,
Is slung with shining cuirass, sword, and shield?
Where ye may see a spur in bloody field.   40
Light-footed damsels move with gentle paces
Round the wide hall, and show their happy faces;
Or stand in courtly talk by fives and sevens:
Like those fair stars that twinkle in the heavens.
Yet must I tell a tale of chivalry:
Or wherefore comes that steed so proudly by?
Wherefore more proudly does the gentle knight,
Rein in the swelling of his ample might?

Spenser! thy brows are arched, open, kind,
And come like a clear sun-rise to my mind;   50
And always does my heart with pleasure dance,
When I think on thy noble countenance:
Where never yet was aught more earthly seen
Than the pure freshness of thy laurels green.
Therefore, great bard, I not so fearfully
Call on thy gentle spirit to hover nigh
My daring steps: or if thy tender care,
Thus startled unaware,
Be jealous that the foot of other wight
Should madly follow that bright path of light   60
Trac'd by thy lov'd Libertas; he will speak,
And tell thee that my prayer is very meek;

That I will follow with due reverence,
And start with awe at mine own strange pretence.
Him thou wilt hear; so I will rest in hope
To see wide plains, fair trees and lawny slope:
The morn, the eve, the light, the shade, the flowers;
Clear streams, smooth lakes, and overlooking towers.

CALIDORE

A FRAGMENT

YOUNG Calidore is paddling o'er the lake;
His healthful spirit eager and awake
To feel the beauty of a silent eve,
Which seem'd full loth this happy world to leave;
The light dwelt o'er the scene so lingeringly.
He bares his forehead to the cool blue sky,
And smiles at the far clearness all around,
Until his heart is well nigh over wound,
And turns for calmness to the pleasant green
Of easy slopes, and shadowy trees that lean   10
So elegantly o'er the waters' brim
And show their blossoms trim.
Scarce can his clear and nimble eye-sight follow
The freaks, and dartings of the black-wing'd swallow,
Delighting much, to see it half at rest,
Dip so refreshingly its wings, and breast
'Gainst the smooth surface, and to mark anon,
The widening circles into nothing gone.

And now the sharp keel of his little boat
Comes up with ripple, and with easy float,   20
And glides into a bed of water lillies:
Broad leav'd are they and their white canopies
Are upward turn'd to catch the heavens' dew.
Near to a little island's point they grew;
Whence Calidore might have the goodliest view
Of this sweet spot of earth. The bowery shore
Went off in gentle windings to the hoar
And light blue mountains: but no breathing man
With a warm heart, and eye prepared to scan
Nature's clear beauty, could pass lightly by   30
Objects that look'd out so invitingly
On either side. These, gentle Calidore
Greeted, as he had known them long before.
The sidelong view of swelling leafiness,

Which the glad setting sun, in gold doth dress;
Whence ever, and anon the jay outsprings,
And scales upon the beauty of its wings.
The lonely turret, shatter'd, and outworn,
Stands venerably proud; too proud to mourn
Its long lost grandeur: fir trees grow around,   40
Aye dropping their hard fruit upon the ground.
The little chapel with the cross above
Upholding wreaths of ivy; the white dove,
That on the window spreads his feathers light,
And seems from purple clouds to wing its flight.
Green tufted islands casting their soft shades
Across the lake; sequester'd leafy glades,
That through the dimness of their twilight show
Large dock leaves, spiral foxgloves, or the glow
Of the wild cat's eyes, or the silvery stems   50
Of delicate birch trees, or long grass which hems
A little brook. The youth had long been viewing
These pleasant things, and heaven was bedewing
The mountain flowers, when his glad senses caught
A trumpet's silver voice. Ah! it was fraught
With many joys for him: the warder's ken
Had found white coursers prancing in the glen:
Friends very dear to him he soon will see;
So pushes off his boat most eagerly,
And soon upon the lake he skims along,   60
Deaf to the nightingale's first under-song;
Nor minds he the white swans that dream so sweetly:
His spirit flies before him so completely.

And now he turns a jutting point of land,
Whence may be seen the castle gloomy, and grand:
Nor will a bee buzz round two swelling peaches,
Before the point of his light shallop reaches
Those marble steps that through the water dip:
Now over them he goes with hasty trip,
And scarcely stays to ope the folding doors: 70
Anon he leaps along the oaken floors
Of halls and corridors.
Delicious sounds! those little bright-eyed things
That float about the air on azure wings,
Had been less heartfelt by him than the clang
Of clattering hoofs; into the court he sprang,
Just as two noble steeds, and palfreys twain,
Were slanting out their necks with loosened rein;
While from beneath the threat'ning portcullis
They brought their happy burthens. What a kiss,   80

What gentle squeeze he gave each lady's hand!
How tremblingly their delicate ankles spann'd!
Into how sweet a trance his soul was gone,
While whisperings of affection
Made him delay to let their tender feet
Come to the earth; with an incline so sweet
From their low palfreys o'er his neck they bent:
And whether there were tears of languishment,
Or that the evening dew had pearl'd their tresses
He feels a moisture on his cheek, and blesses   90
With lips that tremble, and with glistening eye,
All the soft luxury
That nestled in his arms. A dimpled hand,
Fair as some wonder out of fairy land,
Hung from his shoulder like the drooping flowers
Of whitest Cassia, fresh from summer showers:
And this he fondled with his happy cheek
As if for joy he would no further seek;
When the kind voice of good Sir Clerimond
Came to his ear, like something from beyond   100
His present being; so he gently drew
His warm arms, thrilling now with pulses new,
From their sweet thrall, and forward meekly bending,
Thank'd heaven that his joy was never ending;
While 'gainst his forehead he devoutly press'd
A hand heaven made to succour the distress'd;
A hand that from the world's bleak promontory
Had lifted Calidore for deeds of Glory.

Amid the pages, and the torches' glare,
There stood a knight, patting the flowing hair   110
Of his proud horse's mane: he was withal
A man of elegance, and stature tall:
So that the waving of his plumes would be
High as the berries of a wild ash tree,
Or as the winged cap of Mercury.
His armour was so dexterously wrought
In shape, that sure no living man had thought
It hard, and heavy steel: but that indeed
It was some glorious form, some splendid weed,
In which a spirit new come from the skies   120
Might live, and show itself to human eyes.
'Tis the far-fam'd, the brave Sir Gondibert,
Said the good man to Calidore alert;
While the young warrior with a step of grace
Came up,—a courtly smile upon his face,
And mailed hand held out, ready to greet

The large-eyed wonder, and ambitious heat
Of the aspiring boy; who as he led
Those smiling ladies, often turn'd his head
To admire the visor arch'd so gracefully   130
Over a knightly brow; while they went by
The lamps that from the high roof'd hall were pendent,
And gave the steel a shining quite transcendent.

Soon in a pleasant chamber they are seated;
The sweet-lipp'd ladies have already greeted
All the green leaves that round the window clamber,
To show their purple stars, and bells of amber.
Sir Gondibert has doff'd his shining steel,
Gladdening in the free, and airy feel
Of a light mantle; and while Clerimond   140
Is looking round about him with a fond,
And placid eye, young Calidore is burning
To hear of knightly deeds, and gallant spurning
Of all unworthiness; and how the strong of arm
Kept off dismay, and terror, and alarm
From lovely women: while brimful of this,
He gave each damsel's hand so warm a kiss,
And had such manly ardour in his eye,
That each at other look'd half staringly;
And then their features started into smiles   150
Sweet as blue heavens o'er enchanted isles.

Softly the breezes from the forest came,
Softly they blew aside the taper's flame;
Clear was the song from Philomel's far bower;
Grateful the incense from the lime-tree flower;
Mysterious, wild, the far heard trumpet's tone;
Lovely the moon in ether, all alone:
Sweet too the converse of these happy mortals,
As that of busy spirits when the portals
Are closing in the west; or that soft humming   160
We hear around when Hesperus is coming.
Sweet be their sleep. * * * * * * * * *

TO SOME LADIES

WHAT though while the wonders of nature exploring,
    I cannot your light, mazy footsteps attend;
Nor listen to accents, that almost adoring,
    Bless Cynthia's face, the enthusiast's friend·

Yet over the steep, whence the mountain stream rushes,
    With you, kindest friends, in idea I muse;
Mark the clear tumbling crystal, its passionate gushes,
    In spray that the wild flower kindly bedews.

Why linger you so, the wild labyrinth strolling?
    Why breathless, unable your bliss to declare?   **10**
Ah! you list to the nightingale's tender condoling,
    Responsive to sylphs, in the moon-beamy air.

'Tis morn, and the flowers with dew are yet drooping,
    I see you are treading the verge of the sea:
And now! ah, I see it—you just now are stooping
    To pick up the keep-sake intended for me.

If a cherub, on pinions of silver descending,
    Had brought me a gem from the fret-work of heaven;
And smiles, with his star-cheering voice sweetly blending,
    The blessings of Tighe had melodiously given;   **20**

It had not created a warmer emotion
    Than the present, fair nymphs, I was blest with from you,
Than the shell, from the bright golden sands of the ocean
    Which the emerald waves at your feet gladly threw.

For, indeed, 'tis a sweet and peculiar pleasure
    (And blissful is he who such happiness finds),
To possess but a span of the hour of leisure,
    In elegant, pure, and aerial minds.

ON RECEIVING A CURIOUS SHELL, AND A COPY OF VERSES

FROM THE SAME LADIES

Hast thou from the caves of Golconda, a gem
    Pure as the ice-drop that froze on the mountain?
Bright as the humming-bird's green diadem,
    When it flutters in sun-beams that shine through a fountain?

Hast thou a goblet for dark sparkling wine?
    That goblet right heavy, and massy, and gold?
And splendidly mark'd with the story divine
    Of Armida the fair, and Rinaldo the bold?

Hast thou a steed with a mane richly flowing?
    Hast thou a sword that thine enemy's smart is?   **10**
Hast thou a trumpet rich melodies blowing?
    And wear'st thou the shield of the fam'd Britomartis?

What is it that hangs from thy shoulder, so brave,
    Embroider'd with many a spring peering flower?
Is it a scarf that thy fair lady gave?
    And hastest thou now to that fair lady's bower?

Ah! courteous Sir Knight, with large joy thou art crown'd;
    Full many the glories that brighten thy youth!
I will tell thee my blisses, which richly abound
    In magical powers to bless, and to sooth.   **20**

On this scroll thou seest written in characters fair
    A sun-beamy tale of a wreath, and a chain;
And, warrior, it nurtures the property rare
    Of charming my mind from the trammels of pain.

This canopy mark: 'tis the work of a fay;
    Beneath its rich shade did King Oberon languish,
When lovely Titania was far, far away,
    And cruelly left him to sorrow, and anguish.

There, oft would he bring from his soft sighing lute
    Wild strains to which, spell-bound, the nightingales listen'd;   **30**
The wondering spirits of heaven were mute,
    And tears 'mong the dewdrops of morning oft glisten'd.

In this little dome, all those melodies strange,
    Soft, plaintive, and melting, for ever will sigh;
Nor e'er will the notes from their tenderness change;
    Nor e'er will the music of Oberon die.

So, when I am in a voluptuous vein,
    I pillow my head on the sweets of the rose,
And list to the tale of the wreath, and the chain,
    Till its echoes depart; then I sink to repose.   **40**

Adieu, valiant Eric! with joy thou art crown'd;
    Full many the glories that brighten thy youth,
I too have my blisses, which richly abound
    In magical powers, to bless and to sooth.

TO * * * *

[GEORGIANA AUGUSTA WYLIE, AFTERWARDS
MRS. GEORGE KEATS]

HADST thou liv'd in days of old,
O what wonders had been told
Of thy lively countenance,
And thy humid eyes that dance
In the midst of their own brightness;
In the very fane of lightness.
Over which thine eyebrows, leaning,
Picture out each lovely meaning:
In a dainty bend they lie,
Like to streaks across the sky,
Or the feathers from a crow,
Fallen on a bed of snow.
Of thy dark hair that extends
Into many graceful bends:
As the leaves of Hellebore
Turn to whence they sprung before
And behind each ample curl
Peeps the richness of a pearl.
Downward too flows many a tress
With a glossy waviness;
Full, and round like globes that rise
From the censer to the skies
Through sunny air. Add too, the sweetness
Of thy honey'd voice; the neatness
Of thine ankle lightly turn'd:
With those beauties, scarce discern'd,
Kept with such sweet privacy,
That they seldom meet the eye
Of the little loves that fly
Round about with eager pry.
Saving when, with freshening lave,
Thou dipp'st them in the taintless wave;
Like twin water lillies, born
In the coolness of the morn.
O, if thou hadst breathed then,
Now the Muses had been ten.
Couldst thou wish for lineage higher
Than twin sister of Thalia?
At least for ever, evermore,
Will I call the Graces four.

Hadst thou liv'd when chivalry
Lifted up her lance on high,
Tell me what thou wouldst have been?
Ah! I see the silver sheen
Of thy broider'd, floating vest
Cov'ring half thine ivory breast;
Which, O heavens! I should see,
But that cruel destiny
Has placed a golden cuirass there;
Keeping secret what is fair.   50
Like sunbeams in a cloudlet nested
Thy locks in knightly casque are rested:
O'er which bend four milky plumes
Like the gentle lilly's blooms
Springing from a costly vase.
See with what a stately pace
Comes thine alabaster steed;
Servant of heroic deed!
O'er his loins, his trappings glow
Like the northern lights on snow.   60
Mount his back! thy sword unsheath!
Sign of the enchanter's death;
Bane of every wicked spell;
Silencer of dragon's yell.
Alas! thou this wilt never do:
Thou art an enchantress too,
And wilt surely never spill
Blood of those whose eyes can kill.

TO HOPE

When by my solitary hearth I sit,
    And hateful thoughts enwrap my soul in gloom;
When no fair dreams before my 'mind's eye' flit,
    And the bare heath of life presents no bloom;
        Sweet Hope, ethereal balm upon me shed,
        And wave thy silver pinions o'er my head.

Whene'er I wander, at the fall of night,
    Where woven boughs shut out the moon's bright ray,
Should sad Despondency my musings fright,
    And frown, to drive fair Cheerfulness away,   10
        Peep with the moon-beams through the leafy roof
        And keep that fiend Despondence far aloof.

Should Disappointment, parent of Despair,
  Strive for her son to seize my careless heart;
When, like a cloud, he sits upon the air,
  Preparing on his spell-bound prey to dart:
    Chace him away, sweet Hope, with visage bright,
    And fright him as the morning frightens night!

Whene'er the fate of those I hold most dear
  Tells to my fearful breast a tale of sorrow,
O bright-eyed Hope, my morbid fancy cheer;
  Let me awhile thy sweetest comforts borrow:
    Thy heaven-born radiance around me shed,
    And wave thy silver pinions o'er my head!

Should e'er unhappy love my bosom pain,
  From cruel parents, or relentless fair;
O let me think it is not quite in vain
  To sigh out sonnets to the midnight air!
    Sweet Hope, ethereal balm upon me shed,
    And wave thy silver pinions o'er my head!

In the long vista of the years to roll,
  Let me not see our country's honour fade:
O let me see our land retain her soul,
  Her pride, her freedom; and not freedom's shade.
    From thy bright eyes unusual brightness shed—
    Beneath thy pinions canopy my head!

Let me not see the patriot's high bequest,
  Great Liberty! how great in plain attire!
With the base purple of a court oppress'd,
  Bowing her head, and ready to expire:
    But let me see thee stoop from heaven on wings
    That fill the skies with silver glitterings!

And as, in sparkling majesty, a star
  Gilds the bright summit of some gloomy cloud;
Brightening the half veil'd face of heaven afar:
  So, when dark thoughts my boding spirit shroud,
    Sweet Hope, celestial influence round me shed,
    Waving thy silver pinions o'er my head.

February, 1815.

IMITATION OF SPENSER

* * * * * * *

Now Morning from her orient chamber came,
And her first footsteps touch'd a verdant hill;
Crowning its lawny crest with amber flame,
Silv'ring the untainted gushes of its rill;
Which, pure from mossy beds, did down distill,
And after parting beds of simple flowers,
By many streams a little lake did fill,
Which round its marge reflected woven bowers,
And, in its middle space, a sky that never lowers.

There the king-fisher saw his plumage bright   10
Vieing with fish of brilliant dye below;
Whose silken fins, and golden scales' light
Cast upward, through the waves, a ruby glow:
There saw the swan his neck of arched snow,
And oar'd himself along with majesty;
Sparkled his jetty eyes; his feet did show
Beneath the waves like Afric's ebony,
And on his back a fay reclined voluptuously.

Ah! could I tell the wonders of an isle
That in that fairest lake had placed been,   20
I could e'en Dido of her grief beguile;
Or rob from aged Lear his bitter teen:
For sure so fair a place was never seen,
Of all that ever charm'd romantic eye:
It seem'd an emerald in the silver sheen
Of the bright waters; or as when on high,
Through clouds of fleecy white, laughs the cœrulean sky.

And all around it dipp'd luxuriously
Slopings of verdure through the glossy tide,
Which, as it were in gentle amity,   30
Rippled delighted up the flowery side;
As if to glean the ruddy tears, it tried,
Which fell profusely from the rose-tree stem!
Haply it was the workings of its pride,
In strife to throw upon the shore a gem
Outvieing all the buds in Flora's diadem.

* * * * * * *

[EDMONTON.]

WOMAN! when I behold thee flippant, vain,
　　Inconstant, childish, proud, and full of fancies;
　　Without that modest softening that enhances
The downcast eye, repentant of the pain
That its mild light creates to heal again:
　　E'en then, elate, my spirit leaps, and prances,
　　E'en then my soul with exultation dances

For that to love, so long, I've dormant lain:
But when I see thee meek, and kind, and tender,
　　Heavens! how desperately do I adore
Thy winning graces;—to be thy defender
　　I hotly burn—to be a Calidore—
A very Red Cross Knight—a stout Leander—
Might I be loved by thee like these of yore.

Light feet, dark violet eyes, and parted hair;
　　Soft dimpled hands, white neck, and creamy breast,
　　Are things on which the dazzled senses rest
Till the fond, fixed eyes, forget they stare.
From such fine pictures, heavens! I cannot dare
　　To turn my admiration, though unpossess'd
　　They be of what is worthy,—though not drest
In lovely modesty, and virtues rare.
Yet these I leave as thoughtless as a lark;
　　These lures I straight forget,—e'en ere I dine,
Or thrice my palate moisten: but when I mark
　　Such charms with mild intelligences shine,
My ear is open like a greedy shark,
　　To catch the tunings of a voice divine.

Ah! who can e'er forget so fair a being?
　　Who can forget her half retiring sweets?
　　God! she is like a milk-white lamb that bleats
For man's protection. Surely the All-seeing,
Who joys to see us with his gifts agreeing,
　　Will never give him pinions, who intreats
　　Such innocence to ruin,—who vilely cheats
A dove-like bosom. In truth there is no freeing
One's thoughts from such a beauty; when I hear
　　A lay that once I saw her hand awake,
Her form seems floating palpable, and near;
　　Had I e'er seen her from an arbour take
A dewy flower, oft would that hand appear,
　　And o'er my eyes the trembling moisture shake.

10

20

30

40

EPISTLES

TO GEORGE FELTON MATHEW

SWEET are the pleasures that to verse belong,
And doubly sweet a brotherhood in song;
Nor can remembrance, Mathew! bring to view
A fate more pleasing, a delight more true
Than that in which the brother Poets joy'd,
Who with combined powers, their wit employ'd
To raise a trophy to the drama's muses.
The thought of this great partnership diffuses
Over the genius loving heart, a feeling
Of all that's high, and great, and good, and healing

Too partial friend! fain would I follow thee   **11**
Past each horizon of fine poesy;
Fain would I echo back each pleasant note
As o'er Sicilian seas, clear anthems float
'Mong the light skimming gondolas far parted,
Just when the sun his farewell beam has darted:
But 'tis impossible; far different cares
Beckon me sternly from soft 'Lydian airs,'
And hold my faculties so long in thrall,
That I am oft in doubt whether at all   **20**
I shall again see Phœbus in the morning:
Or flush'd Aurora in the roseate dawning!
Or a white Naiad in a rippling stream;
Or a rapt seraph in a moonlight beam;
Or again witness what with thee I've seen,
The dew by fairy feet swept from the green,
After a night of some quaint jubilee
Which every elf and fay had come to see:
When bright processions took their airy march
Beneath the curved moon's triumphal arch.   **30**
But might I now each passing moment give
To the coy muse, with me she would not live
In this dark city, nor would condescend
'Mid contradictions her delights to lend.
Should e'er the fine-eyed maid to me be kind,
Ah! surely it must be whene'er I find
Some flowery spot, sequester'd, wild, romantic,
That often must have seen a poet frantic;
Where oaks that erst the Druid knew, are growing,

And flowers, the glory of one day, are blowing;
Where the dark-leav'd laburnum's drooping clusters
Reflect athwart the stream their yellow lustres,
And intertwined the cassia's arms unite,
With its own drooping buds, but very white.
Where on one side are covert branches hung,
'Mong which the nightingales have always sung
In leafy quiet: where to pry, aloof,
Atween the pillars of the sylvan roof,
Would be to find where violet beds were nestling,
And where the bee with cowslip bells was wrestling.
There must be too a ruin dark, and gloomy,
To say 'joy not too much in all that's bloomy.'

Yet this is vain—O Mathew lend thy aid
To find a place where I may greet the maid—
Where we may soft humanity put on,
And sit, and rhyme and think on Chatterton;
And that warm-hearted Shakespeare sent to meet him
Four laurell'd spirits, heaven-ward to intreat him.
With reverence would we speak of all the sages
Who have left streaks of light athwart their ages:
And thou shouldst moralize on Milton's blindness,
And mourn the fearful dearth of human kindness
To those who strove with the bright golden wing
Of genius, to flap away each sting
Thrown by the pitiless world. We next could tell
Of those who in the cause of freedom fell;
Of our own Alfred, of Helvetian Tell;
Of him whose name to ev'ry heart's a solace,
High-minded and unbending William Wallace.
While to the rugged north our musing turns
We well might drop a tear for him, and Burns.
Felton! without incitements such as these,
How vain for me the niggard Muse to tease:
For thee, she will thy every dwelling grace,
And make 'a sun-shine in a shady place:'
For thou wast once a flowret blooming wild,
Close to the source, bright, pure, and undefil'd,
Whence gush the streams of song: in happy hour
Came chaste Diana from her shady bower,
Just as the sun was from the east uprising;
And, as for him some gift she was devising,
Beheld thee, pluck'd thee, cast thee in the stream
To meet her glorious brother's greeting beam.
I marvel much that thou hast never told
How, from a flower, into a fish of gold

Apollo chang'd thee; how thou next didst seem
A black-eyed swan upon the widening stream;
And when thou first didst in that mirror trace
The placid features of a human face:
That thou hast never told thy travels strange,   90
And all the wonders of the mazy range
O'er pebbly crystal, and o'er golden sands;
Kissing thy daily food from Naiad's pearly hands.

    November, 1815.

TO MY BROTHER GEORGE

FULL many a dreary hour have I past,
My brain bewilder'd, and my mind o'ercast
With heaviness; in seasons when I've thought
No spherey strains by me could e'er be caught
From the blue dome, though I to dimness gaze
On the far depth where sheeted lightning plays;
Or, on the wavy grass outstretch'd supinely,
Pry 'mong the stars, to strive to think divinely:
That I should never hear Apollo's song,
Though feathery clouds were floating all along   10
The purple west, and, two bright streaks between,
The golden lyre itself were dimly seen:
That the still murmur of the honey bee
Would never teach a rural song to me:
That the bright glance from beauty's eyelids slanting
Would never make a lay of mine enchanting,
Or warm my breast with ardour to unfold
Some tale of love and arms in time of old.

But there are times, when those that love the bay,
Fly from all sorrowing far, far away;   20
A sudden glow comes on them, naught they see
In water, earth, or air, but poesy.
It has been said, dear George, and true I hold it,
(For knightly Spenser to Libertas told it,)
That when a Poet is in such a trance,
In air he sees white coursers paw, and prance,
Bestridden of gay knights, in gay apparel,
Who at each other tilt in playful quarrel,
And what we, ignorantly, sheet-lightning call,
Is the swift opening of their wide portal,   30
When the bright warder blows his trumpet clear,
Whose tones reach naught on earth but Poet's ear.

When these enchanted portals open wide,
And through the light the horsemen swiftly glide,
The Poet's eye can reach those golden halls,
And view the glory of their festivals:
Their ladies fair, that in the distance seem
Fit for the silv'ring of a seraph's dream;
Their rich brimm'd goblets, that incessant run
Like the bright spots that move about the sun;
And, when upheld, the wine from each bright jar
Pours with the lustre of a falling star.
Yet further off, are dimly seen their bowers,
Of which, no mortal eye can reach the flowers;
And 'tis right just, for well Apollo knows
'Twould make the Poet quarrel with the rose.
All that's reveal'd from that far seat of blisses,
Is, the clear fountains' interchanging kisses,
As gracefully descending, light and thin,
Like silver streaks across a dolphin's fin,
When he upswimmeth from the coral caves,
And sports with half his tail above the waves.

These wonders strange he sees, and many more,
Whose head is pregnant with poetic lore.
Should he upon an evening ramble fare
With forehead to the soothing breezes bare,
Would he naught see but the dark, silent blue
With all its diamonds trembling through and through?
Or the coy moon, when in the waviness
Of whitest clouds she does her beauty dress,
And staidly paces higher up, and higher,
Like a sweet nun in holy-day attire?
Ah, yes! much more would start into his sight—
The revelries, and mysteries of night:
And should I ever see them, I will tell you
Such tales as needs must with amazement spell you.

These are the living pleasures of the bard:
But richer far posterity's award.
What does he murmur with his latest breath,
While his proud eye looks through the film of death?
"What though I leave this dull, and earthly mould,
Yet shall my spirit lofty converse hold
With after times.—The patriot shall feel
My stern alarum, and unsheath his steel:
Or, in the senate thunder out my numbers
To startle princes from their easy slumbers.

The sage will mingle with each moral theme
My happy thoughts sententious; he will teem
With lofty periods when my verses fire him,
And then I'll stoop from heaven to inspire him.   80
Lays have I left of such a dear delight
That maids will sing them on their bridal night.
Gay villagers, upon a morn of May,
When they have tired their gentle limbs with play,
And form'd a snowy circle on the grass,
And plac'd in midst of all that lovely lass
Who chosen is their queen,—with her fine head
Crowned with flowers purple, white, and red:
For there the lilly, and the musk-rose, sighing,
Are emblems true of hapless lovers dying: 90
Between her breasts, that never yet felt trouble,
A bunch of violets full blown, and double,
Serenely sleep:—she from a casket takes
A little book,—and then a joy awakes
About each youthful heart,—with stifled cries,
And rubbing of white hands, and sparkling eyes:
For she's to read a tale of hopes, and fears;
One that I foster'd in my youthful years:
The pearls, that on each glist'ning circlet sleep,
Gush ever and anon with silent creep,   100
Lured by the innocent dimples.   To sweet rest
Shall the dear babe, upon its mother's breast,
Be lull'd with songs of mine. Fair world, adieu!
Thy dales, and hills, are fading from my view:
Swiftly I mount, upon wide spreading pinions,
Far from the narrow bounds of thy dominions.
Full joy I feel, while thus I cleave the air,
That my soft verse will charm thy daughters fair,
And warm thy sons!" Ah, my dear friend and brother,
Could I, at once, my mad ambition smother,   110
For tasting joys like these, sure I should be
Happier, and dearer to society.
At times, 'tis true, I've felt relief from pain
When some bright thought has darted through my brain:
Through all that day I've felt a greater pleasure
Than if I'd brought to light a hidden treasure.
As to my sonnets, though none else should heed them,
I feel delighted, still, that you should read them.
Of late, too, I have had much calm enjoyment,   119
Stretch'd on the grass at my best lov'd employment
Of scribbling lines for you. These things I thought
While, in my face, the freshest breeze I caught.

E'en now I'm pillow'd on a bed of flowers
That crowns a lofty clift, which proudly towers
Above the ocean-waves. The stalks, and blades,
Chequer my tablet with their quivering shades.
On one side is a field of drooping oats,
Through which the poppies show their scarlet coats;
So pert and useless, that they bring to mind
The scarlet coats that pester human-kind.   130
And on the other side, outspread, is seen
Ocean's blue mantle streak'd with purple, and green.
Now 'tis I see a canvass'd ship, and now
Mark the bright silver curling round her prow.
I see the lark down-dropping to his nest,
And the broad winged sea-gull never at rest;
For when no more he spreads his feathers free,
His breast is dancing on the restless sea.
Now I direct my eyes into the west,
Which at this moment is in sun-beams drest: 140
Why westward turn? 'Twas but to say adieu!
'Twas but to kiss my hand, dear George, to you!

    [MARGATE] *August*, 1816.

TO CHARLES COWDEN CLARKE

OFT have you seen a swan superbly frowning,
And with proud breast his own white shadow crowning;
He slants his neck beneath the waters bright
So silently, it seems a beam of light
Come from the galaxy: anon he sports,—
With outspread wings the Naiad Zephyr courts,
Or ruffles all the surface of the lake
In striving from its crystal face to take
Some diamond water drops, and them to treasure
In milky nest, and sip them off at leisure.   10
But not a moment can he there insure them,
Nor to such downy rest can he allure them;
For down they rush as though they would be free,
And drop like hours into eternity.
Just like that bird am I in loss of time,
Whene'er I venture on the stream of rhyme;
With shatter'd boat, oar snapt, and canvass rent
I slowly sail, scarce knowing my intent;
Still scooping up the water with my fingers,
In which a trembling diamond never lingers.   20
By this, friend Charles, you may full plainly see
Why I have never penn'd a line to thee:

Because my thoughts were never free, and clear,
And little fit to please a classic ear;
Because my wine was of too poor a savour
For one whose palate gladdens in the flavour
Of sparkling Helicon:—small good it were
To take him to a desert rude, and bare,
Who had on Baiæ's shore reclin'd at ease,
While Tasso's page was floating in a breeze   30
That gave soft music from Armida's bowers,
Mingled with fragrance from her rarest flowers:
Small good to one who had by Mulla's stream
Fondled the maidens with the breasts of cream;
Who had beheld Belphœbe in a brook,
And lovely Una in a leafy nook,
And Archimago leaning o'er his book:
Who had of all that's sweet tasted, and seen,
From silv'ry ripple, up to beauty's queen;
From the sequester'd haunts of gay Titania,   40
To the blue dwelling of divine Urania:
One, who, of late, had ta'en sweet forest walks
With him who elegantly chats and talks—
The wrong'd Libertas,—who has told you stories
Of laurel chaplets, and Apollo's glories;
Of troops chivalrous prancing through a city,
And tearful ladies made for love, and pity:
With many else which I have never known.
Thus have I thought; and days on days have flown
Slowly, or rapidly—unwilling still   50
For you to try my dull, unlearned quill.
Nor should I now, but that I've known you long;
That you first taught me all the sweets of song:
The grand, the sweet, the terse, the free, the fine;
What swell'd with pathos, and what right divine:
Spenserian vowels that elope with ease,
And float along like birds o'er summer seas;
Miltonian storms. and more, Miltonian tenderness;
Michael in arms, and more, meek Eve's fair slenderness.
Who read for me the sonnet swelling loudly   60
Up to its climax and then dying proudly?
Who found for me the grandeur of the ode,
Growing, like Atlas, stronger from its load?
Who let me taste that more than cordial dram,
The sharp, the rapier-pointed epigram?
Show'd me that epic was of all the king,
Round, vast, and spanning all like Saturn's ring?
You too upheld the veil from Clio's beauty,
And pointed out the patriot's stern duty:

The might of Alfred, and the shaft of Tell;   70
The hand of Brutus, that so grandly fell
Upon a tyrant's head. Ah! had I never seen,
Or known your kindness, what might I have been?
What my enjoyments in my youthful years,
Bereft of all that now my life endears?
And can I e'er these benefits forget?
And can I e'er repay the friendly debt?
No, doubly no;—yet should these rhymings please,
I shall roll on the grass with two-fold ease:
For I have long time been my fancy feeding   80
With hopes that you would one day think the reading
Of my rough verses not an hour misspent;
Should it e'er be so, what a rich content!
Some weeks have pass'd since last I saw the spires
In lucent Thames reflected:—warm desires
To see the sun o'erpeep the eastern dimness,
And morning shadows streaking into slimness
Across the lawny fields, and pebbly water;
To mark the time as they grow broad, and shorter;
To feel the air that plays about the hills,   90
And sips its freshness from the little rills;
To see high, golden corn wave in the light
When Cynthia smiles upon a summer's night,
And peers among the cloudlets jet and white,
As though she were reclining in a bed
Of bean blossoms, in heaven freshly shed.
No sooner had I stepp'd into these pleasures
Than I began to think of rhymes and measures:
The air that floated by me seem'd to say
"Write! thou wilt never have a better day."   100
And so I did. When many lines I'd written,
Though with their grace I was not oversmitten,
Yet, as my hand was warm, I thought I'd better
Trust to my feelings, and write you a letter.
Such an attempt required an inspiration
Of a peculiar sort,—a consummation;—
Which, had I felt, these scribblings might have been
Verses from which the soul would never wean:
But many days have passed since last my heart
Was warm'd luxuriously by divine Mozart;   110
By Arne delighted, or by Handel madden'd;
Or by the song of Erin pierc'd and sadden'd:
What time you were before the music sitting,
And the rich notes to each sensation fitting.
Since I have walk'd with you through shady lanes
That freshly terminate in open plains,

And revel'd in a chat that ceased not
When at night-fall among your books we got:
No, nor when supper came, nor after that,—
Nor when reluctantly I took my hat;   120
No, nor till cordially you shook my hand
Mid-way between our homes:—your accents bland
Still sounded in my ears, when I no more
Could hear your footsteps touch the grav'ly floor.
Sometimes I lost them, and then found again;
You chang'd the footpath for the grassy plain.
In those still moments I have wish'd you joys
That well you know to honour:—"Life's very toys
"With him," said I, "will take a pleasant charm;
"It cannot be that aught will work him harm."   130
These thoughts now come o'er me with all their might:—
Again I shake your hand,—friend Charles, good night.

    September, 1816.

SONNETS

I

TO MY BROTHER GEORGE

MANY the wonders I this day have seen:
    The sun, when first he kist away the tears
    That fill'd the eyes of morn;—the laurell'd peers
Who from the feathery gold of evening lean;—
The ocean with its vastness, its blue green,
    Its ships, its rocks, its caves, its hopes, its fears,—
    Its voice mysterious, which whoso hears
Must think on what will be, and what has been.
E'en now, dear George, while this for you I write,
    Cynthia is from her silken curtains peeping   10
So scantly, that it seems her bridal night,
    And she her half-discover'd revels keeping.
But what, without the social thought of thee,
Would be the wonders of the sky and sea?

II

TO * * * * * *

HAD I a man's fair form, then might my sighs
    Be echoed swiftly through that ivory shell
    Thine ear, and find thy gentle heart; so well
Would passion arm me for the enterprise:
But ah! I am no knight whose foeman dies;
    No cuirass glistens on my bosom's swell;
    I am no happy shepherd of the dell
Whose lips have trembled with a maiden's eyes.
Yet must I dote upon thee,—call thee sweet,
    Sweeter by far than Hybla's honied roses   10
        When steep'd in dew rich to intoxication.
Ah! I will taste that dew, for me 'tis meet,
    And when the moon her pallid face discloses,
        I'll gather some by spells, and incantation.

III

WRITTEN ON THE DAY THAT MR. LEIGH HUNT LEFT PRISON

WHAT though, for showing truth to flatter'd state,
    Kind Hunt was shut in prison, yet has he,
    In his immortal spirit, been as free

As the sky-searching lark, and as elate.
Minion of grandeur! think you he did wait?
  Think you he naught but prison walls did see,
  Till, so unwilling, thou unturn'dst the key?
Ah, no! far happier, nobler was his fate!
In Spenser's halls he stray'd, and bowers fair,
  Culling enchanted flowers; and he flew   10
With daring Milton through the fields of air:
  To regions of his own his genius true
Took happy flights. Who shall his fame impair
  When thou art dead, and all thy wretched crew?

IV

How many bards gild the lapses of time!
  A few of them have ever been the food
  Of my delighted fancy,—I could brood
Over their beauties, earthly, or sublime:
And often, when I sit me down to rhyme,
  These will in throngs before my mind intrude:
  But no confusion, no disturbance rude
Do they occasion; 'tis a pleasing chime.
So the unnumber'd sounds that evening store;   9
The songs of birds—the whisp'ring of the leaves—
  The voice of waters—the great bell that heaves
With solemn sound,—and thousand others more,
  That distance of recognizance bereaves,
Make pleasing music, and not wild uproar.

V

TO A FRIEND WHO SENT ME SOME ROSES

As late I rambled in the happy fields,
  What time the sky-lark shakes the tremulous dew
  From his lush clover covert;—when anew
Adventurous knights take up their dinted shields:
I saw the sweetest flower wild nature yields,
  A fresh-blown musk-rose; 'twas the first that threw
  Its sweets upon the summer: graceful it grew
As is the wand that queen Titania wields.
And, as I feasted on its fragrancy,
  I thought the garden-rose it far excell'd: 10
But when, O Wells! thy roses came to me
  My sense with their deliciousness was spell'd:
Soft voices had they, that with tender plea
  Whisper'd of peace, and truth, and friendliness unquell'd.
    June 29, 1816.

VI

TO G. A. W.

[Georgiana Augusta Wylie]

Nymph of the downward smile and sidelong glance,
    In what diviner moments of the day
    Art thou most lovely?—when gone far astray
Into the labyrinths of sweet utterance,
Or when serenely wand'ring in a trance
    Of sober thought?—or when starting away
    With careless robe to meet the morning ray
Thou spar'st the flowers in thy mazy dance?
Haply 'tis when thy ruby lips part sweetly,
    And so remain, because thou listenest:
But thou to please wert nurtured so completely
    That I can never tell what mood is best.
I shall as soon pronounce which Grace more neatly
    Trips it before Apollo than the rest.

10

VII

O Solitude! if I must with thee dwell,
    Let it not be among the jumbled heap
    Of murky buildings; climb with me the steep,—
Nature's observatory—whence the dell,
Its flowery slopes, its river's crystal swell,
    May seem a span; let me thy vigils keep
    'Mongst boughs pavillion'd, where the deer's swift leap
Startles the wild bee from the fox-glove bell.
But though I'll gladly trace these scenes with thee,
    Yet the sweet converse of an innocent mind,
    Whose words are images of thoughts refin'd,
Is my soul's pleasure; and it sure must be
    Almost the highest bliss of human-kind,
When to thy haunts two kindred spirits flee.

10

VIII

TO MY BROTHERS

Small, busy flames play through the fresh laid coals,
    And their faint cracklings o'er our silence creep
    Like whispers of the household gods that keep
A gentle empire o'er fraternal souls.
And while. for rhymes, I search around the poles,

Your eyes are fix'd, as in poetic sleep,
Upon the lore so voluble and deep,
That aye at fall of night our care condoles.
This is your birth-day Tom, and I rejoice
    That thus it passes smoothly, quietly.   10
Many such eves of gently whisp'ring noise
    May we together pass, and calmly try
What are this world's true joys,—ere the great voice,
    From its fair face, shall bid our spirits fly.
    November 18, 1816.

IX

KEEN, fitful gusts are whisp'ring here and there
    Among the bushes half leafless, and dry;
    The stars look very cold about the sky,
And I have many miles on foot to fare.
Yet feel I little of the cool bleak air,
    Or of the dead leaves rustling drearily,
    Or of those silver lamps that burn on high,
Or of the distance from home's pleasant lair:
For I am brimfull of the friendliness
    That in a little cottage I have found;   10
Of fair-hair'd Milton's eloquent distress,
    And all his love for gentle Lycid drown'd;
Of lovely Laura in her light green dress,
    And faithful Petrarch gloriously crown'd.

X

To one who has been long in city pent,
    'Tis very sweet to look into the fair
    And open face of heaven,—to breathe a prayer
Full in the smile of the blue firmament.
Who is more happy, when, with heart's content,
    Fatigued he sinks into some pleasant lair
    Of wavy grass, and reads a debonair
And gentle tale of love and languishment?
Returning home at evening, with an ear
    Catching the notes of Philomel,—an eye   10
Watching the sailing cloudlet's bright career,
    He mourns that day so soon has glided by:
E'en like the passage of an angel's tear
    That falls through the clear ether silently.

XI

ON FIRST LOOKING INTO CHAPMAN'S HOMER

MUCH have I travell'd in the realms of gold,
    And many goodly states and kingdoms seen;
    Round many western islands have I been
Which bards in fealty to Apollo hold.
Oft of one wide expanse had I been told
    That deep-brow'd Homer ruled as his demesne;
    Yet did I never breathe its pure serene
Till I heard Chapman speak out loud and bold:
Then felt I like some watcher of the skies
    When a new planet swims into his ken;   10
Or like stout Cortez when with eagle eyes
    He star'd at the Pacific—and all his men
Look'd at each other with a wild surmise—
    Silent, upon a peak in Darien.

XII

ON LEAVING SOME FRIENDS AT AN EARLY HOUR

GIVE me a golden pen, and let me lean
    On heap'd up flowers, in regions clear, and far;
    Bring me a tablet whiter than a star,
Or hand of hymning angel, when 'tis seen
The silver strings of heavenly harp atween:
    And let there glide by many a pearly car,
    Pink robes, and wavy hair, and diamond jar,
And half discovered wings, and glances keen.
The while let music wander round my ears,
    And as it reaches each delicious ending,   10
        Let me write down a line of glorious tone,
And full of many wonders of the spheres:
    For what a height my spirit is contending!
    'Tis not content so soon to be alone.

XIII

ADDRESSED TO HAYDON

HIGHMINDEDNESS, a jealousy for good,
    A loving-kindness for the great man's fame,
    Dwells here and there with people of no name,
In noisome alley, and in pathless wood:
And where we think the truth least understood,

Oft may be found a "singleness of aim,"
That ought to frighten into hooded shame
A money-mong'ring, pitiable brood.
How glorious this affection for the cause
   Of stedfast genius, toiling gallantly!   **10**
What when a stout unbending champion awes
   Envy, and Malice to their native sty?
Unnumber'd souls breathe out a still applause,
   Proud to behold him in his country's eye.

XIV

ADDRESSED TO THE SAME

GREAT spirits now on earth are sojourning;
   He of the cloud, the cataract, the lake,
   Who on Helvellyn's summit, wide awake,
Catches his freshness from Archangel's wing:
He of the rose, the violet, the spring,
   The social smile, the chain for Freedom's sake:
   And lo!—whose stedfastness would never take
A meaner sound than Raphael's whispering.
And other spirits there are standing apart
   Upon the forehead of the age to come;   **10**
These, these will give the world another heart,
   And other pulses. Hear ye not the hum
Of mighty workings?——
   Listen awhile, ye nations, and be dumb.

XV

ON THE GRASSHOPPER AND CRICKET

THE poetry of earth is never dead:
   When all the birds are faint with the hot sun,
   And hide in cooling trees, a voice will run
From hedge to hedge about the new-mown mead;
That is the Grasshopper's—he takes the lead
   In summer luxury,—he has never done
   With his delights; for when tired out with fun
He rests at ease beneath some pleasant weed.
The poetry of earth is ceasing never:
   On a lone winter evening, when the frost   **10**
     Has wrought a silence, from the stove there shrills
The Cricket's song, in warmth increasing ever,
   And seems to one in drowsiness half lost,
     The Grasshopper's among some grassy hills.
December 30, 1816.

XVI

TO KOSCIUSKO

Good Kosciusko, thy great name alone
　　Is a full harvest whence to reap high feeling;
　　It comes upon us like the glorious pealing
Of the wide spheres—an everlasting tone.
And now it tells me, that in worlds unknown,
　　The names of heroes, burst from clouds concealing,
　　And change to harmonies, for ever stealing
Through cloudless blue, and round each silver throne.
It tells me too, that on a happy day,
　　When some good spirit walks upon the earth,　　　　10
　　　Thy name with Alfred's, and the great of yore
　　Gently commingling, gives tremendous birth
To a loud hymn, that sounds far, far away
　　　To where the great God lives for evermore.
　　　December, 1816.

XVII

Happy is England! I could be content
　　To see no other verdure than its own;
　　To feel no other breezes than are blown
Through its tall woods with high romances blent:
Yet do I sometimes feel a languishment
　　For skies Italian, and an inward groan
　　To sit upon an Alp as on a throne,
And half forget what world or worldling meant.
Happy is England, sweet her artless daughters;
　　Enough their simple loveliness for me,　　　　10
　　　Enough their whitest arms in silence clinging:
　　Yet do I often warmly burn to see
　　　Beauties of deeper glance, and hear their singing,
And float with them about the summer waters.

SLEEP AND POETRY

"As I lay in my bed slepe full unmete
"Was unto me, but why that I ne might
"Rest I ne wist, for there n'as erthly wight
"(As I suppose) had more of hertis ese
"Than I, for I n'ad sicknesse nor diese."

CHAUCER.

WHAT is more gentle than a wind in summer?
What is more soothing than the pretty hummer
That stays one moment in an open flower,
And buzzes cheerily from bower to bower?
What is more tranquil than a musk-rose blowing
In a green island, far from all men's knowing?
More healthful than the leafiness of dales?
More secret than a nest of nightingales?
More serene than Cordelia's countenance?
More full of visions than a high romance?   10
What, but thee Sleep? Soft closer of our eyes!
Low murmurer of tender lullabies!
Light hoverer around our happy pillows!
Wreather of poppy buds, and weeping willows!
Silent entangler of a beauty's tresses!
Most happy listener! when the morning blesses
Thee for enlivening all the cheerful eyes
That glance so brightly at the new sun-rise.

But what is higher beyond thought than thee?
Fresher than berries of a mountain tree?   20
More strange, more beautiful, more smooth, more regal,
Than wings of swans, than doves, than dim-seen eagle?
What is it? And to what shall I compare it?
It has a glory, and naught else can share it:
The thought thereof is awful, sweet, and holy,
Chasing away all worldliness and folly;
Coming sometimes like fearful claps of thunder,
Or the low rumblings earth's regions under;
And sometimes like a gentle whispering
Of all the secrets of some wond'rous thing   30
That breathes about us in the vacant air;
So that we look around with prying stare,
Perhaps to see shapes of light, aerial limning,
And catch soft floatings from a faint-heard hymning;
To see the laurel wreath, on high suspended,
That is to crown our name when life is ended.

35

Sometimes it gives a glory to the voice,
And from the heart up-springs, rejoice! rejoice!
Sounds which will reach the Framer of all things,
And die away in ardent mutterings.   40

No one who once the glorious sun has seen,
And all the clouds, and felt his bosom clean
For his great Maker's presence, but must know
What 'tis I mean, and feel his being glow:
Therefore no insult will I give his spirit,
By telling what he sees from native merit.

O Poesy! for thee I hold my pen
That am not yet a glorious denizen
Of thy wide heaven—Should I rather kneel
Upon some mountain-top until I feel   50
A glowing splendour round about me hung,
And echo back the voice of thine own tongue?
O Poesy! for thee I grasp my pen
That am not yet a glorious denizen
Of thy wide heaven; yet, to my ardent prayer,
Yield from thy sanctuary some clear air,
Smooth'd for intoxication by the breath
Of flowering bays, that I may die a death
Of luxury, and my young spirit follow
The morning sun-beams to the great Apollo   60
Like a fresh sacrifice; or, if I can bear
The o'erwhelming sweets, 'twill bring to me the fair
Visions of all places: a bowery nook
Will be elysium—an eternal book
Whence I may copy many a lovely saying
About the leaves, and flowers—about the playing
Of nymphs in woods, and fountains; and the shade
Keeping a silence round a sleeping maid;
And many a verse from so strange influence
That we must ever wonder how, and whence   70
It came. Also imaginings will hover
Round my fire-side, and haply there discover
Vistas of solemn beauty, where I'd wander
In happy silence, like the clear Meander
Through its lone vales; and where I found a spot
Of awfuller shade, or an enchanted grot,
Or a green hill o'erspread with chequer'd dress
Of flowers, and fearful from its loveliness,
Write on my tablets all that was permitted,
All that was for our human senses fitted.   80

Then the events of this wide world I'd seize
Like a strong giant, and my spirit teaze
Till at its shoulders it should proudly see
Wings to find out an immortality.

Stop and consider! life is but a day;
A fragile dew-drop on its perilous way
From a tree's summit; a poor Indian's sleep
While his boat hastens to the monstrous steep
Of Montmorenci. Why so sad a moan?
Life is the rose's hope while yet unblown;   90
The reading of an ever-changing tale;
The light uplifting of a maiden's veil;
A pigeon tumbling in clear summer air;
A laughing school-boy, without grief or care,
Riding the springy branches of an elm.

O for ten years, that I may overwhelm
Myself in poesy; so I may do the deed
That my own soul has to itself decreed.
Then will I pass the countries that I see
In long perspective, and continually   100
Taste their pure fountains. First the realm I'll pass
Of Flora, and old Pan: sleep in the grass,
Feed upon apples red, and strawberries,
And choose each pleasure that my fancy sees;
Catch the white-handed nymphs in shady places,
To woo sweet kisses from averted faces,—
Play with their fingers, touch their shoulders white
Into a pretty shrinking with a bite
As hard as lips can make it: till agreed,
A lovely tale of human life we'll read.   110
And one will teach a tame dove how it best
May fan the cool air gently o'er my rest;
Another, bending o'er her nimble tread,
Will set a green robe floating round her head,
And still will dance with ever varied ease,
Smiling upon the flowers and the trees:
Another will entice me on, and on
Through almond blossoms and rich cinnamon;
Till in the bosom of a leafy world
We rest in silence, like two gems upcurl'd   120
In the recesses of a pearly shell.

And can I ever bid these joys farewell?
Yes, I must pass them for a nobler life,
Where I may find the agonies, the strife

Of human hearts: for lo! I see afar,
O'ersailing the blue cragginess, a car
And steeds with streamy manes—the charioteer
Looks out upon the winds with glorious fear:
And now the numerous tramplings quiver lightly
Along a huge cloud's ridge; and now with sprightly
Wheel downward come they into fresher skies,   131
Tipt round with silver from the sun's bright eyes.
Still downward with capacious whirl they glide;
And now I see them on the green-hill's side
In breezy rest among the nodding stalks.
The charioteer with wond'rous gesture talks
To the trees and mountains; and there soon appear
Shapes of delight, of mystery, and fear,
Passing along before a dusky space
Made by some mighty oaks: as they would chace   140
Some ever-fleeting music on they sweep.
Lo! how they murmur, laugh, and smile, and weep:
Some with upholden hand and mouth severe;
Some with their faces muffled to the ear
Between their arms; some, clear in youthful bloom,
Go glad and smilingly athwart the gloom;
Some looking back, and some with upward gaze;
Yes, thousands in a thousand different ways
Flit onward—now a lovely wreath of girls
Dancing their sleek hair into tangled curls;   150
And now broad wings. Most awfully intent
The driver of those steeds is forward bent,
And seems to listen: O that I might know
All that he writes with such a hurrying glow.

The visions all are fled—the car is fled
Into the light of heaven, and in their stead
A sense of real things comes doubly strong,
And, like a muddy stream, would bear along
My soul to nothingness: but I will strive
Against all doubtings, and will keep alive   160
The thought of that same chariot, and the strange
Journey it went.

               Is there so small a range
In the present strength of mankind, that the high
Imagination cannot freely fly
As she was wont of old? prepare her steeds,
Paw up against the light, and do strange deeds
Upon the clouds? Has she not shown us all?
From the clear space of ether, to the small

Breath of new buds unfolding? From the meaning
Of Jove's large eye-brow, to the tender greening   170
Of April meadows? Here her altar shone,
E'en in this isle; and who could paragon
The fervid choir that lifted up a noise
Of harmony, to where it aye will poise
Its mighty self of convoluting sound,
Huge as a planet, and like that roll round,
Eternally around a dizzy void?
Ay, in those days the Muses were nigh cloy'd
With honours; nor had any other care
Than to sing out and soothe their wavy hair.   180

Could all this be forgotten? Yes, a schism
Nurtured by foppery and barbarism,
Made great Apollo blush for this his land.
Men were thought wise who could not understand
His glories: with a puling infant's force
They sway'd about upon a rocking horse,
And thought it Pegasus. Ah dismal soul'd!
The winds of heaven blew, the ocean roll'd
Its gathering waves—ye felt it not. The blue
Bared its eternal bosom, and the dew   190
Of summer nights collected still to make
The morning precious: beauty was awake!
Why were ye not awake? But ye were dead
To things ye knew not of,—were closely wed
To musty laws lined out with wretched rule
And compass vile: so that ye taught a school
Of dolts to smooth, inlay, and clip, and fit,
Till, like the certain wands of Jacob's wit,
Their verses tallied. Easy was the task:
A thousand handicraftsmen wore the mask   200
Of Poesy. Ill-fated, impious race!
That blasphemed the bright Lyrist to his face,
And did not know it,—no, they went about,
Holding a poor, decrepid standard out
Mark'd with most flimsy mottos, and in large
The name of one Boileau!

                              O ye whose charge
It is to hover round our pleasant hills!
Whose congregated majesty so fills
My boundly reverence, that I cannot trace
Your hallowed names, in this unholy place,   210
So near those common folk; did not their shames
Affright you? Did our old lamenting Thames

Delight you? Did ye never cluster round
Delicious Avon, with a mournful sound,
And weep? Or did ye wholly bid adieu
To regions where no more the laurel grew?
Or did ye stay to give a welcoming
To some lone spirits who could proudly sing
Their youth away, and die? 'Twas even so:
But let me think away those times of woe: 220
Now 'tis a fairer season; ye have breathed
Rich benedictions o'er us; ye have wreathed
Fresh garlands: for sweet music has been heard
In many places;—some has been upstirr'd
From out its crystal dwelling in a lake,
By a swan's ebon bill; from a thick brake,
Nested and quiet in a valley mild,
Bubbles a pipe; fine sounds are floating wild
About the earth: happy are ye and glad.   229

These things are doubtless: yet in truth we've had
Strange thunders from the potency of song;
Mingled indeed with what is sweet and strong,
From majesty: but in clear truth the themes
Are ugly clubs, the Poets' Polyphemes
Disturbing the grand sea. A drainless shower
Of light is poesy; 'tis the supreme of power;
'Tis might half slumb'ring on its own right arm.
The very archings of her eye-lids charm
A thousand willing agents to obey,
And still she governs with the mildest sway: 240
But strength alone though of the Muses born
Is like a fallen angel: trees uptorn,
Darkness, and worms, and shrouds, and sepulchres
Delight it; for it feeds upon the burrs,
And thorns of life; forgetting the great end
Of poesy, that it should be a friend
To soothe the cares, and lift the thoughts of man.

Yet I rejoice: a myrtle fairer than
E'er grew in Paphos, from the bitter weeds
Lifts its sweet head into the air, and feeds   250
A silent space with ever sprouting green.
All tenderest birds there find a pleasant screen,
Creep through the shade with jaunty fluttering,
Nibble the little cupped flowers and sing.
Then let us clear away the choking thorns
From round its gentle stem; let the young fawns,

Yeaned in after times, when we are flown,
Find a fresh sward beneath it, overgrown
With simple flowers: let there nothing be
More boisterous than a lover's bended knee;   260
Nought more ungentle than the placid look
Of one who leans upon a closed book;
Nought more untranquil than the grassy slopes
Between two hills. All hail delightful hopes!
As she was wont, th' imagination
Into most lovely labyrinths will be gone,
And they shall be accounted poet kings
Who simply tell the most heart-easing things.
O may these joys be ripe before I die.

Will not some say that I presumptuously   270
Have spoken? that from hastening disgrace
'Twere better far to hide my foolish face?
That whining boyhood should with reverence bow
Ere the dread thunderbolt could reach? How!
If I do hide myself, it sure shall be
In the very fane, the light of Poesy:
If I do fall, at least I will be laid
Beneath the silence of a poplar shade;
And over me the grass shall be smooth shaven;
And there shall be a kind memorial graven.   280
But off Despondence! miserable bane!
They should not know thee, who athirst to gain
A noble end, are thirsty every hour.
What though I am not wealthy in the dower
Of spanning wisdom; though I do not know
The shiftings of the mighty winds that blow
Hither and thither all the changing thoughts
Of man: though no great minist'ring reason sorts
Out the dark mysteries of human souls
To clear conceiving: yet there ever rolls   290
A vast idea before me, and I glean
Therefrom my liberty; thence too I've seen
The end and aim of Poesy. 'Tis clear
As anything most true; as that the year
Is made of the four seasons—manifest
As a large cross, some old cathedral's crest,
Lifted to the white clouds. Therefore should I
Be but the essence of deformity,
A coward, did my very eye-lids wink
At speaking out what I have dared to think.   300
Ah! rather let me like a madman run
Over some precipice; let the hot sun

Melt my Dedalian wings, and drive me down
Convuls'd and headlong! Stay! an inward frown
Of conscience bids me be more calm awhile.
An ocean dim, sprinkled with many an isle,
Spreads awfully before me. How much toil!
How many days! what desperate turmoil!
Ere I can have explored its widenesses.
Ah, what a task! upon my bended knees,   310
I could unsay those—no, impossible!
Impossible!

    For sweet relief I'll dwell
On humbler thoughts, and let this strange assay
Begun in gentleness die so away.
E'en now all tumult from my bosom fades:
I turn full hearted to the friendly aids
That smooth the path of honour; brotherhood,
And friendliness the nurse of mutual good.
The hearty grasp that sends a pleasant sonnet
Into the brain ere one can think upon it;   320
The silence when some rhymes are coming out;
And when they're come, the very pleasant rout:
The message certain to be done to-morrow.
'Tis perhaps as well that it should be to borrow
Some precious book from out its snug retreat,
To cluster round it when we next shall meet.
Scarce can I scribble on; for lovely airs
Are fluttering round the room like doves in pairs;
Many delights of that glad day recalling,
When first my senses caught their tender falling.   330
And with these airs come forms of elegance
Stooping their shoulders o'er a horse's prance,
Careless, and grand—fingers soft and round
Parting luxuriant curls;—and the swift bound
Of Bacchus from his chariot, when his eye
Made Ariadne's cheek look blushingly.
Thus I remember all the pleasant flow
Of words at opening a portfolio.

Things such as these are ever harbingers
To trains of peaceful images: the stirs   340
Of a swan's neck unseen among the rushes:
A linnet starting all about the bushes:
A butterfly, with golden wings broad parted,
Nestling a rose, convuls'd as though it smarted
With over pleasure—many, many more,
Might I indulge at large in all my store

Of luxuries: yet I must not forget
Sleep, quiet with his poppy coronet:
For what there may be worthy in these rhymes
I partly owe to him: and thus, the chimes   350
Of friendly voices had just given place
To as sweet a silence, when I 'gan retrace
The pleasant day, upon a couch at ease.
It was a poet's house who keeps the keys
Of pleasure's temple. Round about were hung
The glorious features of the bards who sung
In other ages—cold and sacred busts
Smiled at each other. Happy he who trusts
To clear Futurity his darling fame!
Then there were fauns and satyrs taking aim   360
At swelling apples with a frisky leap
And reaching fingers, 'mid a luscious heap
Of vine-leaves. Then there rose to view a fane
Of liny marble, and thereto a train
Of nymphs approaching fairly o'er the sward:
One, loveliest, holding her white hand toward
The dazzling sun-rise: two sisters sweet
Bending their graceful figures till they meet
Over the trippings of a little child:
And some are hearing, eagerly, the wild   370
Thrilling liquidity of dewy piping.
See, in another picture, nymphs are wiping
Cherishingly Diana's timorous limbs;—
A fold of lawny mantle dabbling swims
At the bath's edge, and keeps a gentle motion
With the subsiding crystal: as when ocean
Heaves calmly its broad swelling smoothness o'er
Its rocky marge, and balances once more
The patient weeds; that now unshent by foam
Feel all about their undulating home.   380

Sappho's meek head was there half smiling down
At nothing; just as though the earnest frown
Of over thinking had that moment gone
From off her brow, and left her all alone.
Great Alfred's too, with anxious, pitying eyes,
As if he always listened to the sighs
Of the goaded world; and Kosciusko's worn
By horrid suffrance—mightily forlorn.
Petrarch, outstepping from the shady green,
Starts at the sight of Laura; nor can wean   390
His eyes from her sweet face. Most happy they!
For over them was seen a free display

Of out-spread wings, and from between them shone
The face of Poesy: from off her throne
She overlook'd things that I scarce could tell.
The very sense of where I was might well
Keep Sleep aloof: but more than that there came
Thought after thought to nourish up the flame
Within my breast; so that the morning light
Surprised me even from a sleepless night;
And up I rose refresh'd, and glad, and gay,
Resolving to begin that very day
These lines; and howsoever they be done,
I leave them as a father does his son.

40

ENDYMION

A POETIC ROMANCE

INSCRIBED

TO THE MEMORY

OF

THOMAS CHATTERTON

1818

PREFACE

KNOWING within myself the manner in which this Poem has been produced, it is not without a feeling of regret that I make it public.

What manner I mean, will be quite clear to the reader, who must soon perceive great inexperience, immaturity, and every error denoting a feverish attempt, rather than a deed accomplished. The two first books, and indeed the two last, I feel sensible are not of such completion as to warrant their passing the press; nor should they if I thought a year's castigation would do them any good;—it will not: the foundations are too sandy. It is just that this youngster should die away: a sad thought for me, if I had not some hope that while it is dwindling I may be plotting, and fitting myself for verses fit to live.

This may be speaking too presumptuously, and may deserve a punishment: but no feeling man will be forward to inflict it: he will leave me alone, with the conviction that there is not a fiercer hell than the failure in a great object. This is not written with the least atom of purpose to forestall criticisms of course, but from the desire I have to conciliate men who are competent to look, and who do look with a zealous eye, to the honour of English literature.

The imagination of a boy is healthy, and the mature imagination of a man is healthy; but there is a space of life between, in which the soul is in a ferment, the character undecided, the way of life uncertain, the ambition thick-sighted: thence proceeds mawkishness, and all the thousand bitters which those men I speak of must necessarily taste in going over the following pages.

I hope I have not in too late a day touched the beautiful mythology of Greece, and dulled its brightness: for I wish to try once more, before I bid it farewell.

[TEIGNMOUTH] April 10, 1818.

ENDYMION:

BOOK I

A THING of beauty is a joy for ever:
Its loveliness increases; it will never
Pass into nothingness; but still will keep
A bower quiet for us, and a sleep
Full of sweet dreams, and health, and quiet breathing.
Therefore, on every morrow, are we wreathing
A flowery band to bind us to the earth,
Spite of despondence, of the inhuman dearth
Of noble natures, of the gloomy days,
Of all the unhealthy and o'er-darkened ways   10
Made for our searching: yes, in spite of all,
Some shape of beauty moves away the pall
From our dark spirits. Such the sun, the moon,
Trees old, and young, sprouting a shady boon
For simple sheep; and such are daffodils
With the green world they live in; and clear rills
That for themselves a cooling covert make
'Gainst the hot season; the mid forest brake,
Rich with a sprinkling of fair musk-rose blooms:
And such too is the grandeur of the dooms   20
We have imagined for the mighty dead;
All lovely tales that we have heard or read:
An endless fountain of immortal drink,
Pouring unto us from the heaven's brink.

Nor do we merely feel these essences
For one short hour; no, even as the trees
That whisper round a temple become soon
Dear as the temple's self, so does the moon,
The passion poesy, glories infinite,
Haunt us till they become a cheering light   30
Unto our souls, and bound to us so fast,
That, whether there be shine, or gloom o'ercast,
They always must be with us, or we die.

Therefore, 'tis with full happiness that I
Will trace the story of Endymion.
The very music of the name has gone

47

Into my being, and each pleasant scene
Is growing fresh before me as the green
Of our own vallies: so I will begin
Now while I cannot hear the city's din;   40
Now while the early budders are just new,
And run in mazes of the youngest hue
About old forests; while the willow trails
Its delicate amber; and the dairy pails
Bring home increase of milk. And, as the year
Grows lush in juicy stalks, I'll smoothly steer
My little boat, for many quiet hours,
With streams that deepen freshly into bowers.
Many and many a verse I hope to write,
Before the daisies, vermeil rimm'd and white,   50
Hide in deep herbage; and ere yet the bees
Hum about globes of clover and sweet peas,
I must be near the middle of my story.
O may no wintry season, bare and hoary,
See it half finish'd: but let Autumn bold,
With universal tinge of sober gold,
Be all about me when I make an end.
And now at once, adventuresome, I send
My herald thought into a wilderness:
There let its trumpet blow, and quickly dress   60
My uncertain path with green, that I may speed
Easily onward, thorough flowers and weed.

Upon the sides of Latmos was outspread
A mighty forest; for the moist earth fed
So plenteously all weed-hidden roots
Into o'er-hanging boughs, and precious fruits.
And it had gloomy shades, sequestered deep,
Where no man went; and if from shepherd's keep
A lamb stray'd far a-down those inmost glens,
Never again saw he the happy pens   70
Whither his brethren, bleating with content,
Over the hills at every nightfall went.
Among the shepherds, 'twas believed ever,
That not one fleecy lamb which thus did sever
From the white flock, but pass'd unworried
By angry wolf, or pard with prying head,
Until it came to some unfooted plains
Where fed the herds of Pan: aye great his gains
Who thus one lamb did lose. Paths there were many,
Winding through palmy fern, and rushes fenny,   80
And ivy banks; all leading pleasantly
To a wide lawn, whence one could only see

Stems thronging all around between the swell
Of turf and slanting branches: who could tell
The freshness of the space of heaven above,
Edg'd round with dark tree tops? through which a dove
Would often beat its wings, and often too
A little cloud would move across the blue.

Full in the middle of this pleasantness
There stood a marble altar, with a tress   90
Of flowers budded newly; and the dew
Had taken fairy phantasies to strew
Daisies upon the sacred sward last eve,
And so the dawned light in pomp receive.
For 'twas the morn: Apollo's upward fire
Made every eastern cloud a silvery pyre
Of brightness so unsullied, that therein
A melancholy spirit well might win
Oblivion, and melt out his essence fine
Into the winds: rain-scented eglantine   100
Gave temperate sweets to that well-wooing sun;
The lark was lost in him; cold springs had run
To warm their chilliest bubbles in the grass;
Man's voice was on the mountains; and the mass
Of nature's lives and wonders puls'd tenfold,
To feel this sun-rise and its glories old.

Now while the silent workings of the dawn
Were busiest, into that self-same lawn
All suddenly, with joyful cries, there sped
A troop of little children garlanded;   110
Who gathering round the altar, seem'd to pry
Earnestly round as wishing to espy
Some folk of holiday: nor had they waited
For many moments, ere their ears were sated
With a faint breath of music, which ev'n then
Fill'd out its voice, and died away again.
Within a little space again it gave
Its airy swellings, with a gentle wave,
To light-hung leaves, in smoothest echoes breaking
Through copse-clad vallies,—ere their death, o'ertaking
The surgy murmurs of the lonely sea.   121

And now, as deep into the wood as we
Might mark a lynx's eye, there glimmered light
Fair faces and a rush of garments white,
Plainer and plainer showing, till at last
Into the widest alley they all past,

Making directly for the woodland altar.
O kindly muse! let not my weak tongue faulter
In telling of this goodly company,
Of their old piety, and of their glee: 130
But let a portion of ethereal dew
Fall on my head, and presently unmew
My soul; that I may dare, in wayfaring,
To stammer where old Chaucer us'd to sing.

Leading the way, young damsels danced along,
Bearing the burden of a shepherd song;
Each having a white wicker over brimm'd
With April's tender younglings: next, well trimm'd,
A crowd of shepherds with as sunburnt looks
As may be read of in Arcadian books;   140
Such as sat listening round Apollo's pipe,
When the great deity, for earth too ripe,
Let his divinity o'erflowing die
In music, through the vales of Thessaly:
Some idly trail'd their sheep-hooks on the ground,
And some kept up a shrilly mellow sound
With ebon-tipped flutes: close after these,
Now coming from beneath the forest trees,
A venerable priest full soberly,
Begirt with ministring looks: alway his eye   150
Stedfast upon the matted turf he kept,
And after him his sacred vestments swept.
From his right hand there swung a vase, milk-white,
Of mingled wine, out-sparkling generous light;
And in his left he held a basket full
Of all sweet herbs that searching eye could cull:
Wild thyme, and valley-lillies whiter still
Than Leda's love, and cresses from the rill.
His aged head, crowned with beechen wreath,
Seem'd like a poll of ivy in the teeth   160
Of winter hoar. Then came another crowd
Of shepherds, lifting in due time aloud
Their share of the ditty. After them appear'd,
Up-followed by a multitude that rear'd
Their voices to the clouds, a fair wrought car
Easily rolling so as scarce to mar
The freedom of three steeds of dapple brown:
Who stood therein did seem of great renown
Among the throng. His youth was fully blown,
Showing like Ganymede to manhood grown;   170
And, for those simple times, his garments were
A chieftain king's: beneath his breast, half bare,

Was hung a silver bugle, and between
His nervy knees there lay a boar-spear keen.
A smile was on his countenance; he seem'd,
To common lookers on, like one who dream'd
Of idleness in groves Elysian:
But there were some who feelingly could scan
A lurking trouble in his nether lip,
And see that oftentimes the reins would slip   180
Through his forgotten hands: then would they sigh,
And think of yellow leaves, of owlets' cry,
Of logs piled solemnly.—Ah, well-a-day,
Why should our young Endymion pine away!

Soon the assembly, in a circle rang'd,
Stood silent round the shrine: each look was chang'd
To sudden veneration: women meek
Beckon'd their sons to silence; while each cheek
Of virgin bloom paled gently for slight fear.
Endymion too, without a forest peer,   190
Stood, wan, and pale, and with an awed face,
Among his brothers of the mountain chace.
In midst of all, the venerable priest
Eyed them with joy from greatest to the least,
And, after lifting up his aged hands,
Thus spake he: "Men of Latmos! shepherd bands!
Whose care it is to guard a thousand flocks:
Whether descended from beneath the rocks
That overtop your mountains; whether come
From vallies where the pipe is never dumb;   200
Or from your swelling downs, where sweet air stirs
Blue hare-bells lightly, and where prickly furze
Buds lavish gold; or ye, whose precious charge
Nibble their fill at ocean's very marge,
Whose mellow reeds are touch'd with sounds forlorn
By the dim echoes of Old Triton's horn:
Mothers and wives! who day by day prepare
The scrip, with needments, for the mountain air;
And all ye gentle girls who foster up
Udderless lambs, and in a little cup   210
Will put choice honey for a favoured youth:
Yea, every one attend! for in good truth
Our vows are wanting to our great god Pan.
Are not our lowing heifers sleeker than
Night-swollen mushrooms? Are not our wide plains
Speckled with countless fleeces? Have not rains
Green'd over April's lap? No howling sad
Sickens our fearful ewes; and we have had

Great bounty from Endymion our lord.
The earth is glad: the merry lark has pour'd   220
His early song against yon breezy sky,
That spreads so clear o'er our solemnity."

Thus ending, on the shrine he heap'd a spire
Of teeming sweets, enkindling sacred fire;
Anon he stain'd the thick and spongy sod
With wine, in honour of the shepherd-god.
Now while the earth was drinking it, and while
Bay leaves were crackling in the fragrant pile,
And gummy frankincense was sparkling bright
'Neath smothering parsley, and a hazy light   230
Spread greyly eastward, thus a chorus sang:

"O THOU, whose mighty palace roof doth hang
From jagged trunks, and overshadoweth
Eternal whispers, glooms, the birth, life, death
Of unseen flowers in heavy peacefulness;
Who lov'st to see the hamadryads dress
Their ruffled locks where meeting hazels darken;
And through whole solemn hours dost sit, and hearken
The dreary melody of bedded reeds—
In desolate places, where dank moisture breeds   240
The pipy hemlock to strange overgrowth;
Bethinking thee, how melancholy loth
Thou wast to lose fair Syrinx—do thou now,
By thy love's milky brow!
By all the trembling mazes that she ran,
Hear us, great Pan!

"O thou, for whose soul-soothing quiet, turtles
Passion their voices cooingly 'mong myrtles,
What time thou wanderest at eventide
Through sunny meadows, that outskirt the side   250
Of thine enmossed realms: O thou, to whom
Broad leaved fig trees even now foredoom
Their ripen'd fruitage; yellow girted bees
Their golden honeycombs; our village leas
Their fairest blossom'd beans and poppied corn;
The chuckling linnet its five young unborn,
To sing for thee; low creeping strawberries
Their summer coolness; pent up butterflies
Their freckled wings; yea, the fresh budding year
All its completions—be quickly near,   260
By every wind that nods the mountain pine,
O forester divine!

"Thou, to whom every faun and satyr flies
For willing service; whether to surprise
The squatted hare while in half sleeping fit;
Or upward ragged precipices flit
To save poor lambkins from the eagle's maw;
Or by mysterious enticement draw
Bewildered shepherds to their path again;
Or to tread breathless round the frothy main,   270
And gather up all fancifullest shells
For thee to tumble into Naiads' cells,
And, being hidden, laugh at their out-peeping;
Or to delight thee with fantastic leaping,
The while they pelt each other on the crown
With silvery oak apples, and fir cones brown—
By all the echoes that about thee ring,
Hear us, O satyr king!

"O Hearkener to the loud clapping shears
While ever and anon to his shorn peers   280
A ram goes bleating: Winder of the horn,
When snouted wild-boars routing tender corn
Anger our huntsmen: Breather round our farms,
To keep off mildews, and all weather harms:
Strange ministrant of undescribed sounds,
That come a swooning over hollow grounds,
And wither drearily on barren moors:
Dread opener of the mysterious doors
Leading to universal knowledge—see,
Great son of Dryope,   290
The many that are come to pay their vows
With leaves about their brows!

"Be still the unimaginable lodge
For solitary thinkings; such as dodge
Conception to the very bourne of heaven,
Then leave the naked brain: be still the leaven,
That spreading in this dull and clodded earth
Gives it a touch ethereal—a new birth:
Be still a symbol of immensity;
A firmament reflected in a sea;   300
An element filling the space between;
An unknown—but no more: we humbly screen
With uplift hands our foreheads, lowly bending,
And giving out a shout most heaven rending,
Conjure thee to receive our humble Pæan,
Upon thy Mount Lycean!"

Éven while they brought the burden to a close,
A shout from the whole multitude arose,
That lingered in the air like dying rolls
Of abrupt thunder, when Ionian shoals   310
Of dolphins bob their noses through the brine.
Meantime, on shady levels, mossy fine,
Young companies nimbly began dancing
To the swift treble pipe, and humming string.
Aye, those fair living forms swam heavily
To tunes forgotten—out of memory:
Fair creatures! whose young children's children bred
Thermopylæ its heroes—not yet dead,
But in old marbles ever beautiful.
High genitors, unconscious did they cull   320
Time's sweet first-fruits—they danc'd to weariness,
And then in quiet circles did they press
The hillock turf, and caught the latter end
Of some strange history, potent to send
A young mind from its bodily tenement.
Or they might watch the quoit-pitchers, intent
On either side; pitying the sad death
Of Hyacinthus, when the cruel breath
Of Zephyr slew him,—Zephyr penitent,
Who now, ere Phœbus mounts the firmament,   330
Fondles the flower amid the sobbing rain.
The archers too, upon a wider plain,
Beside the feathery whizzing of the shaft,
And the dull twanging bowstring, and the raft
Branch down sweeping from a tall ash top,
Call'd up a thousand thoughts to envelope
Those who would watch. Perhaps, the trembling knee
And frantic gape of lonely Niobe,
Poor, lonely Niobe! when her lovely young
Were dead and gone, and her caressing tongue   340
Lay a lost thing upon her paly lip,
And very, very deadliness did nip
Her motherly cheeks. Arous'd from this sad mood
By one, who at a distance loud halloo'd,
Uplifting his strong bow into the air,
Many might after brighter visions stare:
After the Argonauts, in blind amaze
Tossing about on Neptune's restless ways,
Until, from the horizon's vaulted side,
There shot a golden splendour far and wide,   350
Spangling those million poutings of the brine
With quivering ore: 'twas even an awful shine

From the exaltation of Apollo's bow;
A heavenly beacon in their dreary woe.
Who thus were ripe for high contemplating,
Might turn their steps towards the sober ring
Where sat Endymion and the aged priest
'Mong shepherds gone in eld, whose looks increas'd
The silvery setting of their mortal star.
There they discours'd upon the fragile bar   360
That keeps us from our homes ethereal;
And what our duties there: to nightly call
Vesper, the beauty-crest of summer weather;
To summon all the downiest clouds together
For the sun's purple couch; to emulate
In minist'ring the potent rule of fate
With speed of fire-tail'd exhalations;
To tint her pallid cheek with bloom, who cons
Sweet poesy by moonlight: besides these,
A world of other unguess'd offices.   370
Anon they wander'd, by divine converse,
Into Elysium; vieing to rehearse
Each one his own anticipated bliss.
One felt heart-certain that he could not miss
His quick gone love, among fair blossom'd boughs,
Where every zephyr-sigh pouts, and endows
Her lips with music for the welcoming.
Another wish'd, mid that eternal spring,
To meet his rosy child, with feathery sails,
Sweeping, eye-earnestly, through almond vales: 380
Who, suddenly, should stoop through the smooth wind,
And with the balmiest leaves his temples bind;
And, ever after, through those regions be
His messenger, his little Mercury.
Some were athirst in soul to see again
Their fellow huntsmen o'er the wide champaign
In times long past; to sit with them, and talk
Of all the chances in their earthly walk;
Comparing, joyfully, their plenteous stores
Of happiness, to when upon the moors,   390
Benighted, close they huddled from the cold,
And shar'd their famish'd scrips. Thus all out-told
Their fond imaginations,—saving him
Whose eyelids curtain'd up their jewels dim,
Endymion: yet hourly had he striven
To hide the cankering venom, that had riven
His fainting recollections. Now indeed
His senses had swoon'd off: he did not heed

The sudden silence, or the whispers low,
Or the old eyes dissolving at his woe,   400
Or anxious calls, or close of trembling palms,
Or maiden's sigh, that grief itself embalms:
But in the self-same fixed trance he kept,
Like one who on the earth had never stept.
Aye, even as dead-still as a marble man,
Frozen in that old tale Arabian.

Who whispers him so pantingly and close?
Peona, his sweet sister: of all those,
His friends, the dearest. Hushing signs she made,
And breath'd a sister's sorrow to persuade   410
A yielding up, a cradling on her care.
Her eloquence did breathe away the curse:
She led him, like some midnight spirit nurse
Of happy changes in emphatic dreams,
Along a path between two little streams,—
Guarding his forehead, with her round elbow,
From low-grown branches, and his footsteps slow
From stumbling over stumps and hillocks small;
Until they came to where these streamlets fall,
With mingled bubblings and a gentle rush,   420
Into a river, clear, brimful, and flush
With crystal mocking of the trees and sky.
A little shallop, floating there hard by,
Pointed its beak over the fringed bank;
And soon it lightly dipt, and rose, and sank,
And dipt again, with the young couple's weight,—
Peona guiding, through the water straight,
Towards a bowery island opposite;
Which gaining presently, she steered light
Into a shady, fresh, and ripply cove,   430
Where nested was an arbour, overwove
By many a summer's silent fingering;
To whose cool bosom she was used to bring
Her playmates, with their needle broidery,
And minstrel memories of times gone by.

So she was gently glad to see him laid
Under her favourite bower's quiet shade,
On her own couch, new made of flower leaves,
Dried carefully on the cooler side of sheaves
When last the sun his autumn tresses shook,   440
And the tann'd harvesters rich armfuls took.
Soon was he quieted to slumbrous rest:
But, ere it crept upon him, he had prest

Peona's busy hand against his lips,
And still, a sleeping, held her finger-tips
In tender pressure. And as a willow keeps
A patient watch over the stream that creeps
Windingly by it, so the quiet maid
Held her in peace: so that a whispering blade
Of grass, a wailful gnat, a bee bustling   450
Down in the blue-bells, or a wren light rustling
Among sere leaves and twigs, might all be heard.

    O magic sleep! O comfortable bird,
That broodest o'er the troubled sea of the mind
Till it is hush'd and smooth! O unconfin'd
Restraint! imprisoned liberty! great key
To golden palaces, strange minstrelsy,
Fountains grotesque, new trees, bespangled caves,
Echoing grottos, full of tumbling waves
And moonlight; aye, to all the mazy world   460
Of silvery enchantment!—who, upfurl'd
Beneath thy drowsy wing a triple hour,
But renovates and lives?—Thus, in the bower,
Endymion was calm'd to life again.
Opening his eyelids with a healthier brain,
He said: "I feel this thine endearing love
All through my bosom: thou art as a dove
Trembling its closed eyes and sleeked wings
About me; and the pearliest dew not brings
Such morning incense from the fields of May,   470
As do those brighter drops that twinkling stray
From those kind eyes,—the very home and haunt
Of sisterly affection. Can I want
Aught else, aught nearer heaven, than such tears?
Yet dry them up, in bidding hence all fears
That, any longer, I will pass my days
Alone and sad. No, I will once more raise
My voice upon the mountain-heights; once more
Make my horn parley from their foreheads hoar:
Again my trooping hounds their tongues shall loll   480
Around the breathed boar: again I'll poll
The fair-grown yew tree, for a chosen bow:
And, when the pleasant sun is getting low,
Again I'll linger in a sloping mead
To hear the speckled thrushes, and see feed
Our idle sheep. So be thou cheered sweet,
And, if thy lute is here, softly intreat
My soul to keep in its resolved course."

Hereat Peona, in their silver source,
Shut her pure sorrow drops with glad exclaim,   490
And took a lute, from which there pulsing came
A lively prelude, fashioning the way
In which her voice should wander. 'Twas a lay
More subtle cadenced, more forest wild
Than Dryope's lone lulling of her child;
And nothing since has floated in the air
So mournful strange. Surely some influence rare
Went, spiritual, through the damsel's hand;
For still, with Delphic emphasis, she spann'd
The quick invisible strings, even though she saw   500
Endymion's spirit melt away and thaw
Before the deep intoxication.
But soon she came, with sudden burst, upon
Her self-possession—swung the lute aside,
And earnestly said: "Brother, 'tis vain to hide
That thou dost know of things mysterious,
Immortal, starry; such alone could thus
Weigh down thy nature. Hast thou sinn'd in aught
Offensive to the heavenly powers? Caught
A Paphian dove upon a message sent?   510
Thy deathful bow against some deer-herd bent
Sacred to Dian? Haply, thou hast seen
Her naked limbs among the alders green;
And that, alas, is death. No, I can trace
Something more high perplexing in thy face!"

Endymion look'd at her, and press'd her hand,
And said, "Art thou so pale, who wast so bland
And merry in our meadows? How is this?
Tell me thine ailment: tell me all amiss!—
Ah! thou hast been unhappy at the change   520
Wrought suddenly in me. What indeed more strange?
Or more complete to overwhelm surmise?
Ambition is so sluggard: 'tis no prize,
That toiling years would put within my grasp,
That I have sighed for: with so deadly gasp
No man e'er panted for a mortal love.
So all have set my heavier grief above
These things which happen. Rightly have they done:
I, who still saw the horizontal sun
Heave his broad shoulder o'er the edge of the world,   53
Out-facing Lucifer, and then had hurl'd
My spear aloft, as signal for the chace—
I, who, for very sport of heart, would race

With my own steed from Araby; pluck down
A vulture from his towery perching; frown
A lion into growling, loth retire—
To lose, at once, all my toil-breeding fire,
And sing thus low! but I will ease my breast
Of secret grief, here in this bowery nest.

"This river does not see the naked sky,   540
Till it begins to progress silverly
Around the western border of the wood,
Whence, from a certain spot, its winding flood
Seems at the distance like a crescent moon:
And in that nook, the very pride of June,
Had I been used to pass my weary eves;
The rather for the sun unwilling leaves
So dear a picture of his sovereign power,
And I could witness his most kingly hour,
When he doth tighten up the golden reins,   550
And paces leisurely down amber plains
His snorting four. Now when his chariot last
Its beams against the zodiac-lion cast,
There blossom'd suddenly a magic bed
Of sacred ditamy, and poppies red:
At which I wondered greatly, knowing well
That but one night had wrought this flowery spell;
And, sitting down close by, began to muse
What it might mean. Perhaps, thought I, Morpheus,
In passing here, his owlet pinions shook;   560
Or, it may be, ere matron Night uptook
Her ebon urn, young Mercury, by stealth,
Had dipt his rod in it: such garland wealth
Came not by common growth. Thus on I thought,
Until my head was dizzy and distraught.
Moreover, through the dancing poppies stole
A breeze, most softly lulling to my soul;
And shaping visions all about my sight
Of colours, wings, and bursts of spangly light;
The which became more strange, and strange, and dim,
And then were gulph'd in a tumultuous swim: 571
And then I fell asleep. Ah, can I tell
The enchantment that afterwards befel?
Yet it was but a dream: yet such a dream
That never tongue, although it overteem
With mellow utterance, like a cavern spring,
Could figure out and to conception bring
All I beheld and felt. Methought I lay
Watching the zenith, where the milky way

Among the stars in virgin splendour pours;   580
And travelling my eye, until the doors
Of heaven appear'd to open for my flight,
I became loth and fearful to alight
From such high soaring by a downward glance:
So kept me stedfast in that airy trance,
Spreading imaginary pinions wide.
When, presently, the stars began to glide,
And faint away, before my eager view:
At which I sigh'd that I could not pursue,
And dropt my vision to the horizon's verge;   590
And lo! from opening clouds, I saw emerge
The loveliest moon, that ever silver'd o'er
A shell for Neptune's goblet: she did soar
So passionately bright, my dazzled soul
Commingling with her argent spheres did roll
Through clear and cloudy, even when she went
At last into a dark and vapoury tent—
Whereat, methought, the lidless-eyed train
Of planets all were in the blue again.
To commune with those orbs, once more I rais'd   600
My sight right upward: but it was quite dazed
By a bright something, sailing down apace,
Making me quickly veil my eyes and face:
Again I look'd, and, O ye deities,
Who from Olympus watch our destinies!
Whence that completed form of all completeness?
Whence came that high perfection of all sweetness?
Speak, stubborn earth, and tell me where, O where
Hast thou a symbol of her golden hair?
Not oat-sheaves drooping in the western sun;   610
Not—thy soft hand, fair sister! let me shun
Such follying before thee—yet she had,
Indeed, locks bright enough to make me mad;
And they were simply gordian'd up and braided,
Leaving, in naked comeliness, unshaded,
Her pearl round ears, white neck, and orbed brow;
The which were blended in, I know not how,
With such a paradise of lips and eyes,
Blush-tinted cheeks, half smiles, and faintest sighs,
That, when I think thereon, my spirit clings   62(
And plays about its fancy, till the stings
Of human neighbourhood envenom all.
Unto what awful power shall I call?
To what high fane?—Ah! see her hovering feet,
More bluely vein'd, more soft, more whitely sweet

Than those of sea-born Venus, when she rose
From out her cradle shell. The wind out-blows
Her scarf into a fluttering pavillion;
'Tis blue, and over-spangled with a million
Of little eyes, as though thou wert to shed,   630
Over the darkest, lushest blue-bell bed,
Handfuls of daisies."—"Endymion, how strange!
Dream within dream!"—"She took an airy range,
And then, towards me, like a very maid,
Came blushing, waning, willing, and afraid,
And press'd me by the hand: Ah! 'twas too much;
Methought I fainted at the charmed touch,
Yet held my recollection, even as one
Who dives three fathoms where the waters run
Gurgling in beds of coral: for anon,   640
I felt upmounted in that region
Where falling stars dart their artillery forth,
And eagles struggle with the buffeting north
That ballances the heavy meteor-stone;—
Felt too, I was not fearful, nor alone,
But lapp'd and lull'd along the dangerous sky.
Soon, as it seem'd, we left our journeying high,
And straightway into frightful eddies swoop'd;
Such as aye muster where grey time has scoop'd
Huge dens and caverns in a mountain's side: 650
There hollow sounds arous'd me, and I sigh'd
To faint once more by looking on my bliss—
I was distracted; madly did I kiss
The wooing arms which held me, and did give
My eyes at once to death: but 'twas to live,
To take in draughts of life from the gold fount
Of kind and passionate looks; to count, and count
The moments, by some greedy help that seem'd
A second self, that each might be redeem'd
And plunder'd of its load of blessedness.   660
Ah, desperate mortal! I e'en dar'd to press
Her very cheek against my crowned lip,
And, at that moment, felt my body dip
Into a warmer air: a moment more,
Our feet were soft in flowers. There was store
Of newest joys upon that alp. Sometimes
A scent of violets, and blossoming limes,
Loiter'd around us; then of honey cells,
Made delicate from all white-flower bells;
And once, above the edges of our nest,   670
An arch face peep'd,—an Oread as I guess'd.

"Why did I dream that sleep o'er-power'd me
In midst of all this heaven? Why not see,
Far off, the shadows of his pinions dark,
And stare them from me? But no, like a spark
That needs must die, although its little beam
Reflects upon a diamond, my sweet dream
Fell into nothing—into stupid sleep.
And so it was, until a gentle creep,
A careful moving caught my waking ears,
And up I started: Ah! my sighs, my tears,   680
My clenched hands;—for lo! the poppies hung
Dew-dabbled on their stalks, the ouzel sung
A heavy ditty, and the sullen day
Had chidden herald Hesperus away,
With leaden looks: the solitary breeze
Bluster'd, and slept, and its wild self did teaze
With wayward melancholy; and I thought,
Mark me, Peona! that sometimes it brought
Faint fare-thee-wells, and sigh-shrilled adieus!—   690
Away I wander'd—all the pleasant hues
Of heaven and earth had faded: deepest shades
Were deepest dungeons: heaths and sunny glades
Were full of pestilent light; our taintless rills
Seem'd sooty, and o'er-spread with upturn'd gills
Of dying fish; the vermeil rose had blown
In frightful scarlet, and its thorns out-grown
Like spiked aloe. If an innocent bird
Before my heedless footsteps stirr'd, and stirr'd
In little journeys, I beheld in it   700
A disguis'd demon, missioned to knit
My soul with under darkness; to entice
My stumblings down some monstrous precipice:
Therefore I eager followed, and did curse
The disappointment. Time, that aged nurse,
Rock'd me to patience. Now, thank gentle heaven!
These things, with all their comfortings, are given
To my down-sunken hours, and with thee,
Sweet sister, help to stem the ebbing sea
Of weary life."
                        Thus ended he, and both   710
Sat silent: for the maid was very loth
To answer; feeling well that breathed words
Would all be lost, unheard, and vain as swords
Against the enchased crocodile, or leaps
Of grasshoppers against the sun. She weeps,
And wonders; struggles to devise some blame;
To put on such a look as would say, *Shame*

On this poor weakness! but, for all her strife,
She could as soon have crush'd away the life   719
From a sick dove. At length, to break the pause,
She said with trembling chance: "Is this the cause?
This all? Yet it is strange, and sad, alas!
That one who through this middle earth should pass
Most like a sojourning demi-god, and leave
His name upon the harp-string, should achieve
No higher bard than simple maidenhood,
Singing alone, and fearfully,—how the blood
Left his young cheek; and how he used to stray
He knew not where; and how he would say, *nay,*
If any said 'twas love: and yet 'twas love;   730
What could it be but love? How a ring-dove
Let fall a sprig of yew tree in his path;
And how he died: and then, that love doth scathe,
The gentle heart, as northern blasts do roses;
And then the ballad of his sad life closes
With sighs, and an alas!—Endymion!
Be rather in the trumpet's mouth,—anon
Among the winds at large—that all may hearken!
Although, before the crystal heavens darken,
I watch and dote upon the silver lakes   740
Pictur'd in western cloudiness, that takes
The semblance of gold rocks and bright gold sands,
Islands, and creeks, and amber-fretted strands
With horses prancing o'er them, palaces
And towers of amethyst,—would I so teaze
My pleasant days, because I could not mount
Into those regions? The Morphean fount
Of that fine element that visions, dreams,
And fitful whims of sleep are made of, streams
Into its airy channels with so subtle,   750
So thin a breathing, not the spider's shuttle,
Circled a million times within the space
Of a swallow's nest-door, could delay a trace,
A tinting of its quality: how light
Must dreams themselves be; seeing they're more slight
Than the mere nothing that engenders them!
Then wherefore sully the entrusted gem
Of high and noble life with thoughts so sick?
Why pierce high-fronted honour to the quick
For nothing but a dream?" Hereat the youth   760
Look'd up: a conflicting of shame and ruth
Was in his plaited brow: yet, his eyelids
Widened a little, as when Zephyr bids

A little breeze to creep between the fans
Of careless butterflies: amid his pains
He seemed to taste a drop of manna-dew,
Full palatable; and a colour grew
Upon his cheek, while thus he lifeful spake.

"Peona! ever have I long'd to slake
My thirst for the world's praises: nothing base,　　770
No merely slumberous phantasm, could unlace
The stubborn canvas for my voyage prepar'd—
Though now 'tis tatter'd; leaving my bark bar'd
And sullenly drifting: yet my higher hope
Is of too wide, too rainbow-large a scope,
To fret at myriads of earthly wrecks.
Wherein lies happiness? In that which becks
Our ready minds to fellowship divine,
A fellowship with essence; till we shine,
Full alchemiz'd, and free of space. Behold　　780
The clear religion of heaven! Fold
A rose leaf round thy finger's taperness,
And soothe thy lips: hist, when the airy stress
Of music's kiss impregnates the free winds,
And with a sympathetic touch unbinds
Æolian magic from their lucid wombs:
Then old songs waken from enclouded tombs;
Old ditties sigh above their father's grave;
Ghosts of melodious prophecyings rave
Round every spot where trod Apollo's foot;　　790
Bronze clarions awake, and faintly bruit,
Where long ago a giant battle was;
And, from the turf, a lullaby doth pass
In every place where infant Orpheus slept.
Feel we these things?—that moment have we stept
Into a sort of oneness, and our state
Is like a floating spirit's. But there are
Richer entanglements, enthralments far
More self-destroying, leading, by degrees,
To the chief intensity: the crown of these　　800
Is made of love and friendship, and sits high
Upon the forehead of humanity.
All its more ponderous and bulky worth
Is friendship, whence there ever issues forth
A steady splendour; but at the tip-top,
There hangs by unseen film, an orbed drop
Of light, and that is love: its influence,
Thrown in our eyes, genders a novel sense,

At which we start and fret; till in the end,
Melting into its radiance, we blend,   810
Mingle, and so become a part of it,—
Nor with aught else can our souls interknit
So wingedly: when we combine therewith,
Life's self is nourish'd by its proper pith,
And we are nurtured like a pelican brood.
Aye, so delicious is the unsating food,
That men, who might have tower'd in the van
Of all the congregated world, to fan
And winnow from the coming step of time
All chaff of custom, wipe away all slime   820
Left by men-slugs and human serpentry,
Have been content to let occasion die,
Whilst they did sleep in love's elysium.
And, truly, I would rather be struck dumb,
Than speak against this ardent listlessness:
For I have ever thought that it might bless
The world with benefits unknowingly;
As does the nightingale, upperched high,
And cloister'd among cool and bunched leaves—
She sings but to her love, nor e'er conceives   830
How tiptoe Night holds back her dark-grey hood.
Just so may love, although 'tis understood
The mere commingling of passionate breath,
Produce more than our searching witnesseth:
What I know not: but who, of men, can tell
That flowers would bloom, or that green fruit would swell
To melting pulp, that fish would have bright mail,
The earth its dower of river, wood, and vale,
The meadows runnels, runnels pebble-stones,
The seed its harvest, or the lute its tones,   840
Tones ravishment, or ravishment its sweet
If human souls did never kiss and greet?

    "Now, if this earthly love has power to make
Men's being mortal, immortal; to shake
Ambition from their memories, and brim
Their measure of content: what merest whim,
Seems all this poor endeavour after fame,
To one, who keeps within his stedfast aim
A love immortal, an immortal too.
Look not so wilder'd; for these things are true,   850
And never can be born of atomies
That buzz about our slumbers, like brain-flies,
Leaving us fancy-sick. No, no, I'm sure,
My restless spirit never could endure

To breed so long upon one luxury,
Unless it did, though fearfully, espy
A hope beyond the shadow of a dream.
My sayings will the less obscured seem,
When I have told thee how my waking sight
Has made me scruple whether that same night   860
Was pass'd in dreaming. Hearken, sweet Peona!
Beyond the matron-temple of Latona,
Which we should see but for these darkening boughs,
Lies a deep hollow, from whose ragged brows
Bushes and trees do lean all round athwart
And meet so nearly, that with wings outraught,
And spreaded tail, a vulture could not glide
Past them, but he must brush on every side.
Some moulder'd steps lead into this cool cell,
Far as the slabbed margin of a well,   870
Whose patient level peeps its crystal eye
Right upward, through the bushes, to the sky.
Oft have I brought thee flowers, on their stalks set
Like vestal primroses, but dark velvet
Edges them round, and they have golden pits:
'Twas there I got them, from the gaps and slits
In a mossy stone, that sometimes was my seat,
When all above was faint with mid-day heat.
And there in strife no burning thoughts to heed,
I'd bubble up the water through a reed;   880
So reaching back to boy-hood: make me ships
Of moulted feathers, touchwood, alder chips,
With leaves stuck in them; and the Neptune be
Of their petty ocean. Oftener, heavily,
When love-lorn hours had left me less a child,
I sat contemplating the figures wild
Of o'er-head clouds melting the mirror through.
Upon a day, while thus I watch'd, by flew
A cloudy Cupid, with his bow and quiver;
So plainly character'd, no breeze would shiver   890
The happy chance: so happy, I was fain
To follow it upon the open plain,
And, therefore, was just going; when, behold!
A wonder, fair as any I have told—
The same bright face I tasted in my sleep,
Smiling in the clear well. My heart did leap
Through the cool depth.—It moved as if to flee—
I started up, when lo! refreshfully,
There came upon my face in plenteous showers   895
Dew-drops, and dewy buds, and leaves, and flowers,

Wrapping all objects from my smothered sight,
Bathing my spirit in a new delight.
Aye, such a breathless honey-feel of bliss
Alone preserved me from the drear abyss
Of death, for the fair form had gone again.
Pleasure is oft a visitant; but pain
Clings cruelly to us, like the gnawing sloth
On the deer's tender haunches: late, and loth,
'Tis scar'd away by slow returning pleasure.
How sickening, how dark the dreadful leisure   910
Of weary days, made deeper exquisite,
By a fore-knowledge of unslumbrous night!
Like sorrow came upon me, heavier still,
Than when I wander'd from the poppy hill:
And a whole age of lingering moments crept
Sluggishly by, ere more contentment swept
Away at once the deadly yellow spleen.
Yes, thrice have I this fair enchantment seen;
Once more been tortured with renewed life.
When last the wintry gusts gave over strife   920
With the conquering sun of spring, and left the skies
Warm and serene, but yet with moistened eyes
In pity of the shatter'd infant buds,—
That time thou didst adorn, with amber studs,
My hunting cap, because I laugh'd and smil'd,
Chatted with thee, and many days exil'd
All torment from my breast;—'twas even then.
Straying about, yet, coop'd up in the den
Of helpless discontent,—hurling my lance
From place to place, and following at chance,   930
At last, by hap, through some young trees it struck,
And, plashing among bedded pebbles, stuck
In the middle of a brook,—whose silver ramble
Down twenty little falls, through reeds and bramble,
Tracing along, it brought me to a cave,
Whence it ran brightly forth, and white did lave
The nether sides of mossy stones and rock,—
'Mong which it gurgled blythe adieus, to mock
its own sweet grief at parting. Overhead,   939
Hung a lush screen of drooping weeds, and spread
Thick, as to curtain up some wood-nymph's home.
"Ah! impious mortal, whither do I roam?"
Said I, low voic'd: "Ah, whither! 'Tis the grot
"Of Proserpine, when Hell, obscure and hot,
"Doth her resign; and where her tender hands
"She dabbles, on the cool and sluicy sands:

"Or 'tis the cell of Echo, where she sits,
"And babbles thorough silence, till her wits
"Are gone in tender madness, and anon,
"Faints into sleep, with many a dying tone   950
"Of sadness. O that she would take my vows,
"And breathe them sighingly among the boughs,
"To sue her gentle ears for whose fair head,
"Daily, I pluck sweet flowerets from their bed,
"And weave them dyingly—send honey-whispers
"Round every leaf, that all those gentle lispers
"May sigh my love unto her pitying!
"O charitable Echo! hear, and sing
"This ditty to her!—tell her"—so I stay'd
My foolish tongue, and listening, half afraid,   960
Stood stupefied with my own empty folly,
And blushing for the freaks of melancholy.
Salt tears were coming, when I heard my name
Most fondly lipp'd, and then these accents came:
"Endymion! the cave is secreter
"Than the isle of Delos. Echo hence shall stir
"No sighs but sigh-warm kisses, or light noise
"Of thy combing hand, the while it travelling cloys
"And trembles through my labyrinthine hair."
At that oppress'd I hurried in.—Ah! where   970
Are those swift moments? Whither are they fled?
I'll smile no more, Peona; nor will wed
Sorrow the way to death; but patiently
Bear up against it: so farewell, sad sigh;
And come instead demurest meditation,
To occupy me wholly, and to fashion
My pilgrimage for the world's dusky brink.
No more will I count over, link by link,
My chain of grief: no longer strive to find
A half-forgetfulness in mountain wind   980
Blustering about my ears: aye, thou shalt see,
Dearest of sisters, what my life shall be;
What a calm round of hours shall make my days.
There is a paly flame of hope that plays
Where'er I look: but yet, I'll say 'tis naught—
And here I bid it die. Have not I caught,
Already, a more healthy countenance?
By this the sun is setting; we may chance
Meet some of our near-dwellers with my car."

This said, he rose, faint-smiling like a star   990
Through autumn mists, and took Peona's hand:
They stept into the boat, and launch'd from land.

BOOK II

O SOVEREIGN power of love! O grief! O balm!
All records, saving thine, come cool, and calm,
And shadowy, through the mist of passed years:
For others, good or bad, hatred and tears
Have become indolent; but touching thine,
One sigh doth echo, one poor sob doth pine,
One kiss brings honey-dew from buried days.
The woes of Troy, towers smothering o'er their blaze,
Stiff-holden shields, far-piercing spears, keen blades,
Struggling, and blood, and shrieks—all dimly fades
Into some backward corner of the brain;   11
Yet, in our very souls, we feel amain
The close of Troilus and Cressid sweet.
Hence, pageant history! hence, gilded cheat!
Swart planet in the universe of deeds!
Wide sea, that one continuous murmur breeds
Along the pebbled shore of memory!
Many old rotten-timber'd boats there be
Upon thy vaporous bosom, magnified
To goodly vessels; many a sail of pride,   20
And golden keel'd, is left unlaunch'd and dry.
But wherefore this? What care, though owl did fly
About the great Athenian admiral's mast?
What care, though striding Alexander past
The Indus with his Macedonian numbers?
Though old Ulysses tortured from his slumbers
The glutted Cyclops, what care?—Juliet leaning
Amid her window-flowers,—sighing,—weaning
Tenderly her fancy from its maiden snow,
Doth more avail than these: the silver flow   30
Of Hero's tears, the swoon of Imogen,
Fair Pastorella in the bandit's den,
Are things to brood on with more ardency
Than the death-day of empires. Fearfully
Must such conviction come upon his head,
Who, thus far, discontent, has dared to tread,
Without one muse's smile, or kind behest,
The path of love and poesy. But rest,
In chaffing restlessness, is yet more drear
Than to be crush'd, in striving to uprear   40
Love's standard on the battlements of song.
So once more days and nights aid me along,
Like legion'd soldiers.

Brain-sick shepherd prince,
What promise hast thou faithful guarded since
The day of sacrifice? Or, have new sorrows
Come with the constant dawn upon thy morrows?
Alas! 'tis his old grief. For many days,
Has he been wandering in uncertain ways:
Through wilderness, and woods of mossed oaks;
Counting his woe-worn minutes, by the strokes   50
Of the lone woodcutter; and listening still,
Hour after hour, to each lush-leav'd rill.
Now he is sitting by a shady spring,
And elbow-deep with feverous fingering
Stems the upbursting cold: a wild rose tree
Pavillions him in bloom, and he doth see
A bud which snares his fancy: lo! but now
He plucks it, dips its stalk in the water: how!
It swells, it buds, it flowers beneath his sight;
And, in the middle, there is softly pight   60
A golden butterfly; upon whose wings
There must be surely character'd strange things,
For with wide eye he wonders, and smiles oft.

    Lightly this little herald flew aloft,
Follow'd by glad Endymion's clasped hands:
Onward it flies. From languor's sullen bands
His limbs are loos'd, and eager, on he hies
Dazzled to trace it in the sunny skies.
It seem'd he flew, the way so easy was;
And like a new-born spirit did he pass   70
Through the green evening quiet in the sun,
O'er many a heath, through many a woodland dun,
Through buried paths, where sleepy twilight dreams
The summer time away. One track unseams
A wooded cleft, and, far away, the blue
Of ocean fades upon him; then, anew,
He sinks adown a solitary glen,
Where there was never sound of mortal men,
Saving, perhaps, some snow-light cadences
Melting to silence, when upon the breeze   80
Some holy bark let forth an anthem sweet,
To cheer itself to Delphi. Still his feet
Went swift beneath the merry-winged guide,
Until it reach'd a splashing fountain's side
That, near a cavern's mouth, for ever pour'd
Unto the temperate air: then high it soar'd,
And, downward, suddenly began to dip,
As if, athirst with so much toil, 'twould sip

The crystal spout-head: so it did, with touch
Most delicate, as though afraid to smutch   90
Even with mealy gold the waters clear.
But, at that very touch, to disappear
So fairy-quick, was strange! Bewildered,
Endymion sought around, and shook each bed
Of covert flowers in vain; and then he flung
Himself along the grass. What gentle tongue,
What whisperer disturb'd his gloomy rest?
It was a nymph uprisen to the breast
In the fountain's pebbly margin, and she stood
'Mong lillies, like the youngest of the brood.   100
To him her dripping hand she softly kist,
And anxiously began to plait and twist
Her ringlets round her fingers, saying: "Youth!
Too long, alas, hast thou starv'd on the ruth,
The bitterness of love: too long indeed,
Seeing thou art so gentle. Could I weed
Thy soul of care, by heavens, I would offer
All the bright riches of my crystal coffer
To Amphitrite; all my clear-eyed fish,
Golden, or rainbow-sided, or purplish,   110
Vermilion-tail'd, or finn'd with silvery gauze;
Yea, or my veined pebble-floor, that draws
A virgin light to the deep; my grotto-sands
Tawny and gold, ooz'd slowly from far lands
By my diligent springs; my level lillies, shells,
My charming rod, my potent river spells;
Yes, every thing, even to the pearly cup
Meander gave me,—for I bubbled up
To fainting creatures in a desert wild.
But woe is me, I am but as a child   120
To gladden thee; and all I dare to say,
Is, that I pity thee; that on this day
I've been thy guide; that thou must wander far
In other regions, past the scanty bar
To mortal steps, before thou can'st be ta'en
From every wasting sigh, from every pain,
Into the gentle bosom of thy love.
Why it is thus, one knows in heaven above:
But, a poor Naiad, I guess not. Farewell!
I have a ditty for my hollow cell."   130

    Hereat, she vanished from Endymion's gaze,
Who brooded o'er the water in amaze:
The dashing fount pour'd on, and where its pool
Lay, half asleep, in grass and rushes cool,

Quick waterflies and gnats were sporting still,
And fish were dimpling, as if good nor ill
Had fallen out that hour. The wanderer,
Holding his forehead, to keep off the burr
Of smothering fancies, patiently sat down;
And, while beneath the evening's sleepy frown   140
Glow-worms began to trim their starry lamps,
Thus breath'd he to himself: "Whoso encamps
To take a fancied city of delight,
O what a wretch is he! and when 'tis his,
After long toil and travelling, to miss
The kernel of his hopes, how more than vile:
Yet, for him there's refreshment even in toil;
Another city doth he set about,
Free from the smallest pebble-bead of doubt
That he will seize on trickling honey-combs: 150
Alas, he finds them dry; and then he foams,
And onward to another city speeds.
But this is human life: the war, the deeds,
The disappointment, the anxiety,
Imagination's struggles, far and nigh,
All human; bearing in themselves this good,
That they are still the air, the subtle food,
To make us feel existence, and to show
How quiet death is. Where soil is men grow,
Whether to weeds or flowers; but for me,   160
There is no depth to strike in: I can see
Naught earthly worth my compassing; so stand
Upon a misty, jutting head of land—
Alone? No, no; and by the Orphean lute,
When mad Eurydice is listening to't;
I'd rather stand upon this misty peak,
With not a thing to sigh for, or to seek,
But the soft shadow of my thrice-seen love,
Than be—I care not what. O meekest dove
Of heaven! O Cynthia, ten-times bright and fair!
From thy blue throne, now filling all the air,   170
Glance but one little beam of temper'd light
Into my bosom, that the dreadful might
And tyranny of love be somewhat scar'd!
Yet do not so, sweet queen; one torment spar'd,
Would give a pang to jealous misery,
Worse than the torment's self: but rather tie
Large wings upon my shoulders, and point out
My love's far dwelling. Though the playful rout
Of Cupids shun thee, too divine art thou,   180
Too keen in beauty, for thy silver prow

Not to have dipp'd in love's most gentle stream,
O be propitious, nor severely deem
My madness impious; for, by all the stars
That tend thy bidding, I do think the bars
That kept my spirit in are burst—that I
Am sailing with thee through the dizzy sky!
How beautiful thou art! The world how deep!
How tremulous-dazzlingly the wheels sweep
Around their axle! Then these gleaming reins,   190
How lithe! When this thy chariot attains
Its airy goal, haply some bower veils
Those twilight eyes? Those eyes!—my spirit fails—
Dear goddess, help! or the wide-gaping air
Will gulph me—help!"—At this with madden'd stare,
And lifted hands, and trembling lips he stood;
Like old Deucalion mountain'd o'er the flood,
Or blind Orion hungry for the morn.
And, but from the deep cavern there was borne
A voice, he had been froze to senseless stone;   200
Nor sigh of his, nor plaint, nor passion'd moan
Had more been heard. Thus swell'd it forth: "Descend,
Young mountaineer! descend where alleys bend
Into the sparry hollows of the world!
Oft hast thou seen bolts of the thunder hurl'd
As from thy threshold; day by day hast been
A little lower than the chilly sheen
Of icy pinnacles, and dipp'dst thine arms
Into the deadening ether that still charms
Their marble being: now, as deep profound   210
As those are high, descend! He ne'er is crown'd
With immortality, who fears to follow
Where airy voices lead: so through the hollow,
The silent mysteries of earth, descend!"

He heard but the last words, nor could contend
One moment in reflection: for he fled
Into the fearful deep, to hide his head
From the clear moon, the trees, and coming madness.

'Twas far too strange, and wonderful for sadness;
Sharpening, by degrees, his appetite   220
To dive into the deepest. Dark, nor light,
The region; nor bright, nor sombre wholly,
But mingled up; a gleaming melancholy;
A dusky empire and its diadems;
One faint eternal eventide of gems.

Aye, millions sparkled on a vein of gold,
Along whose track the prince quick footsteps told,
With all its lines abrupt and angular:
Out-shooting sometimes, like a meteor-star,
Through a vast antre; then the metal woof,   230
Like Vulcan's rainbow, with some monstrous roof
Curves hugely: now, far in the deep abyss,
It seems an angry lightning, and doth hiss
Fancy into belief: anon it leads
Through winding passages, where sameness breeds
Vexing conceptions of some sudden change;
Whether to silver grots, or giant range
Of sapphire columns, or fantastic bridge
Athwart a flood of crystal. On a ridge
Now fareth he, that o'er the vast beneath   240
Towers like an ocean-cliff, and whence he seeth
A hundred waterfalls, whose voices come
But as the murmuring surge. Chilly and numb
His bosom grew, when first he, far away
Descried an orbed diamond, set to fray
Old darkness from his throne: 'twas like the sun
Uprisen o'er chaos: and with such a stun
Came the amazement, that, absorb'd in it,
He saw not fiercer wonders—past the wit
Of any spirit to tell, but one of those   250
Who, when this planet's sphering time doth close,
Will be its high remembrancers: who they?
The mighty ones who have made eternal day
For Greece and England. While astonishment
With deep-drawn sighs was quieting, he went
Into a marble gallery, passing through
A mimic temple, so complete and true
In sacred custom, that he well nigh fear'd
To search it inwards; whence far off appear'd,
Through a long pillar'd vista, a fair shrine,   260
And just beyond, on light tiptoe divine,
A quiver'd Dian. Stepping awfully,
The youth approach'd; oft turning his veil'd eye
Down sidelong aisles, and into niches old.
And when, more near against the marble cold
He had touch'd his forehead, he began to thread
All courts and passages, where silence dead
Rous'd by his whispering footsteps murmured faint:
And long he travers'd to and fro, to acquaint
Himself with every mystery, and awe;   270
Till, weary, he sat down before the maw

Of a wide outlet, fathomless and dim,
To wild uncertainty and shadows grim.
There, when new wonders ceas'd to float before,
And thoughts of self came on, how crude and sore
The journey homeward to habitual self!
A mad-pursuing of the fog-born elf,
Whose flitting lantern, through rude nettle-briar,
Cheats us into a swamp, into a fire,
Into the bosom of a hated thing.   280

What misery most drowningly doth sing
In lone Endymion's ear, now he has raught
The goal of consciousness? Ah, 'tis the thought,
The deadly feel of solitude: for lo!
He cannot see the heavens, nor the flow
Of rivers, nor hill-flowers running wild
In pink and purple chequer, nor, up-pil'd,
The cloudy rack slow journeying in the west,
Like herded elephants; nor felt, nor prest
Cool grass, nor tasted the fresh slumberous air;   290
But far from such companionship to wear
An unknown time, surcharg'd with grief, away,
Was now his lot. And must he patient stay,
Tracing fantastic figures with his spear?
"No!" exclaim'd he, "why should I tarry here?"
No! loudly echoed times innumerable.
At which he straightway started, and 'gan tell
His paces back into the temple's chief;
Warming and glowing strong in the belief
Of help from Dian: so that when again   300
He caught her airy form, thus did he plain,
Moving more near the while: "O Haunter chaste
Of river sides, and woods, and heathy waste,
Where with thy silver bow and arrows keen
Art thou now forested? O woodland Queen,
What smoothest air thy smoother forehead woos?
Where dost thou listen to the wide halloos
Of thy disparted nymphs? Through what dark tree
Glimmers thy crescent? Wheresoe'er it be,
'Tis in the breath of heaven: thou dost taste   310
Freedom as none can taste it, nor dost waste
Thy loveliness in dismal elements;
But, finding in our green earth sweet contents,
There livest blissfully. Ah, if to thee
It feels Elysian, how rich to me,
An exil'd mortal, sounds its pleasant name!
Within my breast there lives a choking flame—

O let me cool't the zephyr-boughs among!
A homeward fever parches up my tongue—
O let me slake it at the running springs!   320
Upon my ear a noisy nothing rings—
O let me once more hear the linnet's note!
Before mine eyes thick films and shadows float—
O let me 'noint them with the heaven's light!
Dost thou now lave thy feet and ankles white?
O think how sweet to me the freshening sluice!
Dost thou now please thy thirst with berry-juice?
O think how this dry palate would rejoice!
If in soft slumber thou dost hear my voice,
O think how I should love a bed of flowers!—   330
Young goddess! let me see my native bowers!
Deliver me from this rapacious deep!"

    Thus ending loudly, as he would o'erleap
His destiny, alert he stood: but when
Obstinate silence came heavily again,
Feeling about for its old couch of space
And airy cradle, lowly bow'd his face
Desponding, o'er the marble floor's cold thrill.
But 'twas not long; for, sweeter than the rill
To its old channel, or a swollen tide   340
To margin sallows, were the leaves he spied,
And flowers, and wreaths, and ready myrtle crowns
Up heaping through the slab: refreshment drowns
Itself, and strives its own delights to hide—
Nor in one spot alone; the floral pride
In a long whispering birth enchanted grew
Before his footsteps; as when heav'd anew
Old ocean rolls a lengthened wave to the shore,
Down whose green back the short-liv'd foam, all hoar,
Bursts gradual, with a wayward indolence.   350

    Increasing still in heart, and pleasant sense,
Upon his fairy journey on he hastes;
So anxious for the end, he scarcely wastes
One moment with his hand among the sweets:
Onward he goes—he stops—his bosom beats
As plainly in his ear, as the faint charm
Of which the throbs were born. This still alarm,
This sleepy music, forc'd him walk tiptoe:
For it came more softly than the east could blow
Arion's magic to the Atlantic isles;   360
Or than the west, made jealous by the smiles

Of thron'd Apollo, could breathe back the lyre
To seas Ionian and Tyrian.

O did he ever live, that lonely man,
Who lov'd—and music slew not? 'Tis the pest
Of love, that fairest joys give most unrest;
That things of delicate and tenderest worth
Are swallow'd all, and made a seared dearth,
By one consuming flame: it doth immerse
And suffocate true blessings in a curse.   370
Half-happy, by comparison of bliss,
Is miserable. 'Twas even so with this
Dew-dropping melody, in the Carian's ear;
First heaven, then hell, and then forgotten clear,
Vanish'd in elemental passion.

And down some swart abysm he had gone,
Had not a heavenly guide benignant led
To where thick myrtle branches, 'gainst his head
Brushing, awakened: then the sounds again
Went noiseless as a passing noontide rain   380
Over a bower, where little space he stood;
For as the sunset peeps into a wood
So saw he panting light, and towards it went
Through winding alleys; and lo, wonderment!
Upon soft verdure saw, one here, one there,
Cupids a slumbering on their pinions fair.

After a thousand mazes overgone,
At last, with sudden step, he came upon
A chamber, myrtle wall'd, embowered high,
Full of light, incense, tender minstrelsy,   390
And more of beautiful and strange beside:
For on a silken couch of rosy pride,
In midst of all, there lay a sleeping youth
Of fondest beauty; fonder, in fair sooth,
Than sighs could fathom, or contentment reach:
And coverlids gold-tinted like the peach,
Or ripe October's faded marigolds,
Fell sleek about him in a thousand folds—
Not hiding up an Apollonian curve
Of neck and shoulder, nor the tenting swerve   400
Of knee from knee, nor ankles pointing light;
But rather, giving them to the filled sight
Officiously. Sideway his face repos'd
On one white arm, and tenderly unclos'd,

By tenderest pressure, a faint damask mouth
To slumbery pout; just as the morning south
Disparts a dew-lipp'd rose. Above his head,
Four lilly stalks did their white honours wed
To make a coronal; and round him grew
All tendrils green, of every bloom and hue,   410
Together intertwin'd and trammell'd fresh:
The vine of glossy sprout; the ivy mesh,
Shading its Ethiop berries; and woodbine,
Of velvet leaves and bugle-blooms divine;
Convolvulus in streaked vases flush;
The creeper, mellowing for an autumn blush;
And virgin's bower, trailing airily;
With others of the sisterhood. Hard by,
Stood serene Cupids watching silently.
One, kneeling to a lyre, touch'd the strings,   420
Muffling to death the pathos with his wings;
And, ever and anon, uprose to look
At the youth's slumber; while another took
A willow-bough, distilling odorous dew,
And shook it on his hair; another flew
In through the woven roof, and fluttering-wise
Rain'd violets upon his sleeping eyes.

At these enchantments, and yet many more,
The breathless Latmian wonder'd o'er and o'er;
Until, impatient in embarrassment,   430
He forthright pass'd, and lightly treading went
To that same feather'd lyrist, who straightway,
Smiling, thus whisper'd: "Though from upper day
Thou art a wanderer, and thy presence here
Might seem unholy, be of happy cheer!
For 'tis the nicest touch of human honour,
When some ethereal and high-favouring donor
Presents immortal bowers to mortal sense;
As now 'tis done to thee, Endymion. Hence
Was I in no wise startled. So recline   440
Upon these living flowers. Here is wine,
Alive with sparkles—never, I aver,
Since Ariadne was a vintager,
So cool a purple: taste these juicy pears,
Sent me by sad Vertumnus, when his fears
Were high about Pomona: here is cream,
Deepening to richness from a snowy gleam;
Sweeter than that nurse Amalthea skimm'd
For the boy Jupiter: and here, undimm'd

By any touch, a bunch of blooming plums 450
Ready to melt between an infant's gums:
And here is manna pick'd from Syrian trees,
In starlight, by the three Hesperides.
Feast on, and meanwhile I will let thee know
Of all these things around us." He did so,
Still brooding o'er the cadence of his lyre;
And thus: "I need not any hearing tire
By telling how the sea-born goddess pin'd
For a mortal youth, and how she strove to bind
Him all in all unto her doting self, 460
Who would not be so prison'd? but, fond elf,
He was content to let her amorous plea
Faint through his careless arms; content to see
An unseiz'd heaven dying at his feet;
Content, O fool! to make a cold retreat,
When on the pleasant grass such love, lovelorn,
Lay sorrowing; when every tear was born
Of diverse passion; when her lips and eyes
Were clos'd in sullen moisture, and quick sighs
Came vex'd and pettish through her nostrils small.
Hush! no exclaim—yet, justly mightst thou call
Curses upon his head.—I was half glad 472
But my poor mistress went distract and mad,
When the boar tusk'd him: so away she flew
To Jove's high throne, and by her plainings drew
Immortal tear-drops down the thunderer's beard;
Whereon, it was decreed he should be rear'd
Each summer time to life. Lo! this is he,
That same Adonis, safe in the privacy
Of this still region all his winter-sleep. 480
Aye, sleep; for when our love-sick queen did weep
Over his waned corse, the tremulous shower
Heal'd up the wound, and, with a balmy power,
Medicined death to a lengthened drowsiness:
The which she fills with visions, and doth dress
In all this quiet luxury; and hath set
Us young immortals, without any let,
To watch his slumber through. 'Tis well nigh pass'd,
Even to a moment's filling up, and fast
She scuds with summer breezes, to pant through 490
The first long kiss, warm firstling, to renew
Embower'd sports in Cytherea's isle.
Look! how those winged listeners all this while
Stand anxious: see! behold!"—This clamant word
Broke through the careful silence; for they heard

A rustling noise of leaves, and out there flutter'd
Pigeons and doves: Adonis something mutter'd
The while one hand, that erst upon his thigh
Lay dormant, mov'd convuls'd and gradually
Up to his forehead. Then there was a hum   500
Of sudden voices, echoing, "Come! come!
Arise! awake! Clear summer has forth walk'd
Unto the clover-sward, and she has talk'd
Full soothingly to every nested finch:
Rise, Cupids! or we'll give the blue-bell pinch
To your dimpled arms. Once more sweet life begin!"
At this, from every side they hurried in,
Rubbing their sleepy eyes with lazy wrists,
And doubling over head their little fists
In backward yawns. But all were soon alive: 510
For as delicious wine doth, sparkling, dive
In nectar'd clouds and curls through water fair,
So from the arbour roof down swell'd an air
Odorous and enlivening; making all
To laugh, and play, and sing, and loudly call
For their sweet queen: when lo! the wreathed green
Disparted, and far upward could be seen
Blue heaven, and a silver car, air-borne,
Whose silent wheels, fresh wet from clouds of morn,
Spun off a drizzling dew,—which falling chill   520
On soft Adonis' shoulders, made him still
Nestle and turn uneasily about.
Soon were the white doves plain, with neck stretch'd out,
And silken traces lighten'd in descent;
And soon, returning from love's banishment,
Queen Venus leaning downward open arm'd:
Her shadow fell upon his breast, and charm'd
A tumult to his heart, and a new life
Into his eyes. Ah, miserable strife,
But for her comforting! unhappy sight,   530
But meeting her blue orbs! Who, who can write
Of these first minutes? The unchariest muse
To embracements warm as theirs makes coy excuse.

     O it has ruffled every spirit there,
Saving Love's self, who stands superb to share
The general gladness: awfully he stands;
A sovereign quell is in his waving hands;
No sight can bear the lightning of his bow;
His quiver is mysterious, none can know   53
What themselves think of it; from forth his eyes
There darts strange light of varied hues and dies:

A scowl is sometimes on his brow, but who
Look full upon it feel anon the blue
Of his fair eyes run liquid through their souls.
Endymion feels it, and no more controls
The burning prayer within him; so, bent low,
He had begun a plaining of his woe.
But Venus, bending forward, said: "My child,
Favour this gentle youth; his days are wild
With love—he—but alas! too well I see   550
Thou know'st the deepness of his misery.
Ah, smile not so, my son: I tell thee true,
That when through heavy hours I used to rue
The endless sleep of this new-born Adon',
This stranger aye I pitied. For upon
A dreary morning once I fled away
Into the breezy clouds, to weep and pray
For this my love: for vexing Mars had teaz'd
Me even to tears: thence, when a little eas'd,
Down-looking, vacant, through a hazy wood,   560
I saw this youth as he despairing stood:
Those same dark curls blown vagrant in the wind;
Those same full fringed lids a constant blind
Over his sullen eyes: I saw him throw
Himself on wither'd leaves, even as though
Death had come sudden; for no jot he mov'd,
Yet mutter'd wildly. I could hear he lov'd
Some fair immortal, and that his embrace
Had zoned her through the night. There is no trace
Of this in heaven: I have mark'd each cheek,   570
And find it is the vainest thing to seek;
And that of all things 'tis kept secretest.
Endymion! one day thou wilt be blest:
So still obey the guiding hand that fends
Thee safely through these wonders for sweet ends.
'Tis a concealment needful in extreme;
And if I guess'd not so, the sunny beam
Thou shouldst mount up to with me. Now adieu!
Here must we leave thee."—At these words upflew
The impatient doves, uprose the floating car,   580
Up went the hum celestial. High afar
The Latmian saw them minish into naught;
And, when all were clear vanish'd, still he caught
A vivid lightning from that dreadful bow.
When all was darkened, with Ætnean throe
The earth clos'd—gave a solitary moan—
And left him once again in twilight lone.

He did not rave, he did not stare aghast,
For all those visions were o'ergone, and past,
And he in loneliness: he felt assur'd
Of happy times, when all he had endur'd
Would seem a feather to the mighty prize.
So, with unusual gladness, on he hies
Through caves, and palaces of mottled ore,
Gold dome, and crystal wall, and turquoise floor,
Black polish'd porticos of awful shade,
And, at the last, a diamond balustrade,
Leading afar past wild magnificence,
Spiral through ruggedest loopholes, and thence
Stretching across a void, then guiding o'er   600
Enormous chasms, where, all foam and roar,
Streams subterranean teaze their granite beds;
Then heighten'd just above the silvery heads
Of a thousand fountains, so that he could dash
The waters with his spear; but at the splash,
Done heedlessly, those spouting columns rose
Sudden a poplar's height, and 'gan to enclose
His diamond path with fretwork, streaming round
Alive, and dazzling cool, and with a sound,
Haply, like dolphin tumults, when sweet shells   610
Welcome the float of Thetis. Long he dwells
On this delight; for, every minute's space,
The streams with changed magic interlace:
Sometimes like delicatest lattices,
Cover'd with crystal vines; then weeping trees.
Moving about as in a gentle wind,
Which, in a wink, to watery gauze refin'd,
Pour'd into shapes of curtain'd canopies,
Spangled, and rich with liquid broideries
Of flowers, peacocks, swans, and naiads fair.   620
Swifter than lightning went these wonders rare;
And then the water, into stubborn streams
Collecting, mimick'd the wrought oaken beams,
Pillars, and frieze, and high fantastic roof,
Of those dusk places in times far aloof
Cathedrals call'd. He bade a loth farewell
To these founts Protean, passing gulph, and dell,
And torrent, and ten thousand jutting shapes,
Half seen through deepest gloom, and grisly gapes,
Blackening on every side, and overhead   630
A vaulted dome like Heaven's, far bespread
With starlight gems: aye, all so huge and strange,
The solitary felt a hurried change

Working within him into something dreary,—
Vex'd like a morning eagle, lost, and weary,
And purblind amid foggy, midnight wolds.
But he revives at once· for who beholds
New sudden things, nor casts his mental slough?
Forth from a rugged arch, in the dusk below,
Came mother Cybele! alone—alone—   640
In sombre chariot; dark foldings thrown
About her majesty, and front death-pale,
With turrets crown'd. Four maned lions hale
The sluggish wheels; solemn their toothed maws,
Their surly eyes brow-hidden, heavy paws
Uplifted drowsily, and nervy tails
Cowering their tawny brushes. Silent sails
This shadowy queen athwart, and faints away
In another gloomy arch.

                Wherefore delay,
Young traveller, in such a mournful place?   650
Art thou wayworn, or canst not further trace
The diamond path? And does it indeed end
Abrupt in middle air? Yet earthward bend
Thy forehead, and to Jupiter cloud-borne
Call ardently! He was indeed wayworn;
Abrupt, in middle air, his way was lost;
To cloud-borne Jove he bowed, and there crost
Towards him a large eagle, 'twixt whose wings,
Without one impious word, himself he flings,
Committed to the darkness and the gloom: 660
Down, down, uncertain to what pleasant doom,
Swift as a fathoming plummet down he fell
Through unknown things; till exhaled asphodel,
And rose, with spicy fannings interbreath'd,
Came swelling forth where little caves were wreath'd
So thick with leaves and mosses, that they seem'd
Large honeycombs of green, and freshly teem'd
With airs delicious. In the greenest nook
The eagle landed him, and farewell took.

  It was a jasmine bower, all bestrown   670
With golden moss. His every sense had grown
Ethereal for pleasure; 'bove his head
Flew a delight half-graspable; his tread
Was Hesperean; to his capable ears
Silence was music from the holy spheres;
A dewy luxury was in his eyes;
The little flowers felt his pleasant sighs

And stirr'd them faintly. Verdant cave and cell
He wander'd through, oft wondering at such swell
Of sudden exaltation: but, "Alas!"   680
Said he, "will all this gush of feeling pass
Away in solitude? And must they wane,
Like melodies upon a sandy plain,
Without an echo? Then shall I be left
So sad, so melancholy, so bereft!
Yet still I feel immortal! O my love,
My breath of life, where art thou? High above,
Dancing before the morning gates of heaven?
Or keeping watch among those starry seven,
Old Atlas' children? Art a maid of the waters,   690
One of shell-winding Triton's bright-hair'd daughters?
Or art, impossible! a nymph of Dian's,
Weaving a coronal of tender scions
For very idleness? Where'er thou art,
Methinks it now is at my will to start
Into thine arms; to scare Aurora's train,
And snatch thee from the morning; o'er the main
To scud like a wild bird, and take thee off
From thy sea-foamy cradle; or to doff
Thy shepherd vest, and woo thee mid fresh leaves.   700
No, no, too eagerly my soul deceives
Its powerless self: I know this cannot be.
O let me then by some sweet dreaming flee
To her entrancements: hither sleep awhile!
Hither most gentle sleep! and soothing foil
For some few hours the coming solitude."

    Thus spake he, and that moment felt endued
With power to dream deliciously; so wound
Through a dim passage, searching till he found
The smoothest mossy bed and deepest, where   710
He threw himself, and just into the air
Stretching his indolent arms, he took, O bliss!
A naked waist: "Fair Cupid, whence is this?"
A well-known voice sigh'd, "Sweetest, here am I!"
At which soft ravishment, with doting cry
They trembled to each other.—Helicon!
O fountain'd hill! Old Homer's Helicon!
That thou wouldst spout a little streamlet o'er
These sorry pages; then the verse would soar
And sing above this gentle pair, like lark   720
Over his nested young: but all is dark
Around thine aged top, and thy clear fount
Exhales in mists to heaven. Aye, the count

Of mighty Poets is made up; the scroll
Is folded by the Muses; the bright roll
Is in Apollo's hand: our dazed eyes
Have seen a new tinge in the western skies:
The world has done its duty. Yet, oh yet,
Although the sun of poesy is set,
These lovers did embrace, and we must weep   730
That there is no old power left to steep
A quill immortal in their joyous tears.
Long time ere silence did their anxious fears
Question that thus it was; long time they lay
Fondling and kissing every doubt away;
Long time ere soft caressing sobs began
To mellow into words, and then there ran
Two bubbling springs of talk from their sweet lips.
"O known Unknown! from whom my being sips
Such darling essence, wherefore may I not   740
Be ever in these arms? in this sweet spot
Pillow my chin for ever? ever press
These toying hands and kiss their smooth excess?
Why not for ever and for ever feel
That breath about my eyes? Ah, thou wilt steal
Away from me again, indeed, indeed—
Thou wilt be gone away, and wilt not heed
My lonely madness. Speak, delicious fair!
Is—is it to be so? No! Who will dare
To pluck thee from me? And, of thine own will,   750
Full well I feel thou wouldst not leave me. Still
Let me entwine thee surer, surer—now
How can we part? Elysium! who art thou?
Who, that thou canst not be for ever here,
Or lift me with thee to some starry sphere?
Enchantress! tell me by this soft embrace,
By the most soft completion of thy face,
Those lips, O slippery blisses, twinkling eyes,
And by these tenderest, milky sovereignties—
These tenderest, and by the nectar-wine,   760
The passion"————"O dov'd Ida the divine!
Endymion! dearest! Ah, unhappy me!
His soul will 'scape us—O felicity!
How he does love me! His poor temples beat
To the very tune of love—how sweet, sweet, sweet.
Revive, dear youth, or I shall faint and die;
Revive, or these soft hours will hurry by
In tranced dulness; speak, and let that spell
Affright this lethargy! I cannot quell

Its heavy pressure, and will press at least 770
My lips to thine, that they may richly feast
Until we taste the life of love again.
What! dost thou move? dost kiss? O bliss! O pain!
I love thee, youth, more than I can conceive;
And so long absence from thee doth bereave
My soul of any rest: yet must I hence:
Yet, can I not to starry eminence
Uplift thee; nor for very shame can own
Myself to thee: Ah, dearest, do not groan
Or thou wilt force me from this secrecy, 780
And I must blush in heaven. O that I
Had done 't already; that the dreadful smiles
At my lost brightness, my impassion'd wiles,
Had waned from Olympus' solemn height,
And from all serious Gods; that our delight
Was quite forgotten, save of us alone!
And wherefore so ashamed? 'Tis but to atone
For endless pleasure, by some coward blushes:
Yet must I be a coward!—Horror rushes
Too palpable before me—the sad look 790
Of Jove—Minerva's start—no bosom shook
With awe of purity—no Cupid pinion
In reverence vailed—my crystalline dominion
Half lost, and all old hymns made nullity!
But what is this to love? O I could fly
With thee into the ken of heavenly powers,
So thou wouldst thus, for many sequent hours,
Press me so sweetly. Now I swear at once
That I am wise, that Pallas is a dunce—
Perhaps her love like mine is but unknown— 800
O I do think that I have been alone
In chastity: yes, Pallas has been sighing,
While every eve saw me my hair uptying
With fingers cool as aspen leaves. Sweet love,
I was as vague as solitary dove,
Nor knew that nests were built. Now a soft kiss—
Aye, by that kiss, I vow an endless bliss,
An immortality of passion's thine:
Ere long I will exalt thee to the shine
Of heaven ambrosial; and we will shade 810
Ourselves whole summers by a river glade;
And I will tell thee stories of the sky,
And breathe thee whispers of its minstrelsy.
My happy love will overwing all bounds!
O let me melt into thee; let the sounds

Of our close voices marry at their birth;
Let us entwine hoveringly—O dearth
Of human words! roughness of mortal speech!
Lispings empyrean will I sometime teach
Thine honied tongue—lute-breathings, which I gasp
To have thee understand, now while I clasp   821
Thee thus, and weep for fondness—I am pain'd,
Endymion: woe! woe! is grief contain'd
In the very deeps of pleasure, my sole life?"—
Hereat, with many sobs, her gentle strife
Melted into a languor. He return'd
Entranced vows and tears.

                  Ye who have yearn'd
With too much passion, will here stay and pity,
For the mere sake of truth; as 'tis a ditty
Not of these days, but long ago 'twas told   830
By a cavern wind unto a forest old;
And then the forest told it in a dream
To a sleeping lake, whose cool and level gleam
A poet caught as he was journeying
To Phœbus' shrine; and in it he did fling
His weary limbs, bathing an hour's space,
And after, straight in that inspired place
He sang the story up into the air,
Giving it universal freedom. There
Has it been ever sounding for those ears   840
Whose tips are glowing hot. The legend cheers
Yon centinel stars; and he who listens to it
Must surely be self-doom'd or he will rue it:
For quenchless burnings come upon the heart,
Made fiercer by a fear lest any part
Should be engulphed in the eddying wind.
As much as here is penn'd doth always find
A resting place, thus much comes clear and plain;
Anon the strange voice is upon the wane—
And 'tis but echo'd from departing sound,   850
That the fair visitant at last unwound
Her gentle limbs, and left the youth asleep.—
Thus the tradition of the gusty deep.

   Now turn we to our former chroniclers.—
Endymion awoke, that grief of hers
Sweet paining on his ear: he sickly guess'd
How lone he was once more, and sadly press'd
His empty arms together, hung his head,
And most forlorn upon that widow'd bed

Sat silently. Love's madness he had known:
Often with more than tortured lion's groan
Moanings had burst from him; but now that rage
Had pass'd away: no longer did he wage
A rough-voic'd war against the dooming stars.
No, he had felt too much for such harsh jars:
The lyre of his soul Æolian tun'd
Forgot all violence, and but commun'd
With melancholy thought: O he had swoon'd
Drunken from pleasure's nipple; and his love   870
Henceforth was dove-like.—Loth was he to move
From the imprinted couch, and when he did,
'Twas with slow, languid paces, and face hid
In muffling hands. So temper'd, out he stray'd
Half seeing visions that might have dismay'd
Alecto's serpents; ravishments more keen
Than Hermes' pipe, when anxious he did lean
Over eclipsing eyes: and at the last
It was a sounding grotto, vaulted, vast,
O'er studded with a thousand, thousand pearls,
And crimson mouthed shells with stubborn curls,   880
Of every shape and size, even to the bulk
In which whales arbour close, to brood and sulk
Against an endless storm. Moreover too,
Fish-semblances, of green and azure hue,
Ready to snort their streams. In this cool wonder
Endymion sat down, and 'gan to ponder
On all his life: his youth, up to the day
When 'mid acclaim, and feasts, and garlands gay,
He stept upon his shepherd throne: the look
Of his white palace in wild forest nook,   890
And all the revels he had lorded there:
Each tender maiden whom he once thought fair,
With every friend and fellow-woodlander—
Pass'd like a dream before him. Then the spur
Of the old bards to mighty deeds: his plans
To nurse the golden age 'mong shepherd clans:
That wondrous night: the great Pan-festival:
His sister's sorrow; and his wanderings all,
Until into the earth's deep maw he rush'd:
Then all its buried magic, till it flush'd   900
High with excessive love. "And now," thought he,
"How long must I remain in jeopardy
Of blank amazements that amaze no more?
Now I have tasted her sweet soul to the core
All other depths are shallow: essences,
Once spiritual, are like muddy lees,

Meant but to fertilize my earthly root,
And make my branches lift a golden fruit
Into the bloom of heaven: other light,
Though it be quick and sharp enough to blight   910
The Olympian eagle's vision, is dark,
Dark as the parentage of chaos. Hark!
My silent thoughts are echoing from these shells;
Or they are but the ghosts, the dying swells
Of noises far away?—list!"—Hereupon
He kept an anxious ear. The humming tone
Came louder, and behold, there as he lay,
On either side outgush'd, with misty spray,
A copious spring; and both together dash'd
Swift, mad, fantastic round the rocks, and lash'd   920
Among the conchs and shells of the lofty grot,
Leaving a trickling dew. At last they shot
Down from the ceiling's height, pouring a noise
As of some breathless racers whose hopes poize
Upon the last few steps, and with spent force
Along the ground they took a winding course.
Endymion follow'd—for it seem'd that one
Ever pursued, the other strove to shun—
Follow'd their languid mazes, till well nigh
He had left thinking of the mystery,—   930
And was now rapt in tender hoverings
Over the vanish'd bliss. Ah! what is it sings
His dream away? What melodies are these?
They sound as through the whispering of trees,
Not native in such barren vaults. Give ear!

"O Arethusa, peerless nymph! why fear
Such tenderness as mine? Great Dian, why,
Why didst thou hear her prayer? O that I
Were rippling round her dainty fairness now,
Circling about her waist, and striving how   940
To entice her to a dive! then stealing in
Between her luscious lips and eyelids thin.
O that her shining hair was in the sun,
And I distilling from it thence to run
In amorous rillets down her shrinking form!
To linger on her lilly shoulders, warm
Between her kissing breasts, and every charm
Touch raptur'd!—See how painfully I flow:
Fair maid, be pitiful to my great woe.
Stay, stay thy weary course, and let me lead   950
A happy wooer, to the flowery mead

Where all that beauty snar'd me."—"Cruel god,
Desist! or my offended mistress' nod
Will stagnate all thy fountains:—teaze me not
With syren words—Ah, have I really got
Such power to madden thee? And is it true—
Away, away, or I shall dearly rue
My very thoughts: in mercy then away,
Kindest Alpheus, for should I obey
My own dear will, 'twould be a deadly bane.   960
O, Oread-Queen! would that thou hadst a pain
Like this of mine, then would I fearless turn
And be a criminal. Alas, I burn,
I shudder—gentle river, get thee hence.
Alpheus! thou enchanter! every sense
Of mine was once made perfect in these woods.
Fresh breezes, bowery lawns, and innocent floods,
Ripe fruits, and lonely couch, contentment gave;
But ever since I heedlessly did lave
In thy deceitful stream, a panting glow   970
Grew strong within me: wherefore serve me so,
And call it love? Alas, 'twas cruelty.
Not once more did I close my happy eye
Amid the thrushes' song. Away! Avaunt!
O 'twas a cruel thing."—"Now thou dost taunt
So softly, Arethusa, that I think
If thou wast playing on my shady brink,
Thou wouldst bathe once again. Innocent maid!
Stifle thine heart no more; nor be afraid
Of angry powers: there are deities   980
Will shade us with their wings. Those fitful sighs
'Tis almost death to hear: O let me pour
A dewy balm upon them!—fear no more,
Sweet Arethusa! Dian's self must feel
Sometime these very pangs. Dear maiden, steal
Blushing into my soul, and let us fly
These dreary caverns for the open sky.
I will delight thee all my winding course,
From the green sea up to my hidden source
About Arcadian forests; and will show   990
The channels where my coolest waters flow
Through mossy rocks; where, 'mid exuberant green,
I roam in pleasant darkness, more unseen
Than Saturn in his exile; where I brim
Round flowery islands, and take thence a skim
Of mealy sweets, which myriads of bees
Buzz from their honey'd wings: and thou shouldst please

Thyself to choose the richest, where we might
Be incense-pillow'd every summer night.
Doff all sad fears, thou white deliciousness, 1000
And let us be thus comforted; unless
Thou couldst rejoice to see my hopeless stream
Hurry distracted from Sol's temperate beam,
And pour to death along some hungry sands."—
"What can I do, Alpheus? Dian stands
Severe before me: persecuting fate!
Unhappy Arethusa! thou wast late
A huntress free in"—At this, sudden fell
Those two sad streams adown a fearful dell.
The Latmian listen'd, but he heard no more, 1010
Save echo, faint repeating o'er and o'er
The name of Arethusa. On the verge
Of that dark gulph he wept, and said: "I urge
Thee, gentle Goddess of my pilgrimage,
By our eternal hopes, to soothe, to assuage,
If thou art powerful, these lovers' pains;
And make them happy in some happy plains."

He turn'd—there was a whelming sound—he slept,
There was a cooler light; and so he kept
Towards it by a sandy path, and lo! 1020
More suddenly than doth a moment go,
The visions of the earth were gone and fled—
He saw the giant sea above his head.

BOOK III

THERE are who lord it o'er their fellow-men
With most prevailing tinsel: who unpen
Their baaing vanities, to browse away
The comfortable green and juicy hay
From human pastures; or, O torturing fact!
Who, through an idiot blink, will see unpack'd
Fire-branded foxes to sear up and singe
Our gold and ripe-ear'd hopes. With not one tinge
Of sanctuary splendour, not a sight
Able to face an owl's, they still are dight 10
By the blear-eyed nations in empurpled vests,
And crowns, and turbans. With unladen breasts,
Save of blown self-applause, they proudly mount
To their spirit's perch, their being's high account,
Their tiptop nothings, their dull skies, their thrones—
Amid the fierce intoxicating tones

Of trumpets, shoutings, and belabour'd drums,
And sudden cannon. Ah! how all this hums,
In wakeful ears, like uproar past and gone—
Like thunder clouds that spake to Babylon,   20
And set those old Chaldeans to their tasks.—
Are then regalities all gilded masks?
No, there are throned seats unscalable
But by a patient wing, a constant spell,
Or by ethereal things that, unconfin'd,
Can make a ladder of the eternal wind,
And poize about in cloudy thunder-tents
To watch the abysm-birth of elements.
Aye, 'bove the withering of old-lipp'd Fate
A thousand Powers keep religious state,   30
In water, fiery realm, and airy bourne;
And, silent as a consecrated urn,
Hold sphery sessions for a season due.
Yet few of these far majesties, ah, few!
Have bared their operations to this globe—
Few, who with gorgeous pageantry enrobe
Our piece of heaven—whose benevolence
Shakes hand with our own Ceres; every sense
Filling with spiritual sweets to plenitude,
As bees gorge full their cells. And, by the feud   40
'Twixt Nothing and Creation, I here swear,
Eterne Apollo! that thy Sister fair
Is of all these the gentlier-mightiest.
When thy gold breath is misting in the west,
She unobserved steals unto her throne,
And there she sits most meek and most alone;
As if she had not pomp subservient;
As if thine eye, high Poet! was not bent
Towards her with the Muses in thine heart;
As if the ministring stars kept not apart,   50
Waiting for silver-footed messages.
O Moon! the oldest shades 'mong oldest trees
Feel palpitations when thou lookest in:
O Moon! old boughs lisp forth a holier din
The while they feel thine airy fellowship.
Thou dost bless every where, with silver lip
Kissing dead things to life. The sleeping kine,
Couch'd in thy brightness, dream of fields divine:
Innumerable mountains rise, and rise,
Ambitious for the hallowing of thine eyes;   60
And yet thy benediction passeth not
One obscure hiding-place, one little spot

Where pleasure may be sent: the nested wren
Has thy fair face within its tranquil ken,
And from beneath a sheltering ivy leaf
Takes glimpses of thee; thou art a relief
To the poor patient oyster, where it sleeps
Within its pearly house.—The mighty deeps,
The monstrous sea is thine—the myriad sea!
O Moon! far-spooming Ocean bows to thee,   70
And Tellus feels his forehead's cumbrous load.

      Cynthia! where art thou now? What far abode
Of green or silvery bower doth enshrine
Such utmost beauty? Alas, thou dost pine
For one as sorrowful: thy cheek is pale
For one whose cheek is pale: thou dost bewail
His tears, who weeps for thee. Where dost thou sigh?
Ah! surely that light peeps from Vesper's eye,
Or what a thing is love! 'Tis She, but lo!
How chang'd, how full of ache, how gone in woe!   80
She dies at the thinnest cloud; her loveliness
Is wan on Neptune's blue: yet there's a stress
Of love-spangles, just off yon cape of trees,
Dancing upon the waves, as if to please
The curly foam with amorous influence.
O, not so idle: for down-glancing thence
She fathoms eddies, and runs wild about
O'erwhelming water-courses; scaring out
The thorny sharks from hiding-holes, and fright'ning
Their savage eyes with unaccustom'd lightning.   90
Where will the splendour be content to reach?
O love! how potent hast thou been to teach
Strange journeyings! Wherever beauty dwells,
In gulph or aerie, mountains or deep dells,
In light, in gloom, in star or blazing sun,
Thou pointest out the way, and straight 'tis won.
Amid his toil thou gav'st Leander breath;
Thou leddest Orpheus through the gleams of death;
Thou madest Pluto bear thin element;
And now, O winged Chieftain! thou hast sent   100
A moon-beam to the deep, deep water-world,
To find Endymion.

                    On gold sand impearl'd
With lilly shells, and pebbles milky white,
Poor Cynthia greeted him, and sooth'd her light
Against his pallid face: he felt the charm
To breathlessness, and suddenly a warm

Of his heart's blood: 'twas very sweet; he stay'd
His wandering steps, and half-entranced laid
His head upon a tuft of straggling weeds,
To taste the gentle moon, and freshening beads,   110
Lash'd from the crystal roof by fishes' tails.
And so he kept, until the rosy veils
Mantling the east, by Aurora's peering hand
Were lifted from the water's breast, and fann'd
Into sweet air; and sober'd morning came
Meekly through billows:—when like taper-flame
Left sudden by a dallying breath of air,
He rose in silence, and once more 'gan fare
Along his fated way.

               Far had he roam'd,
With nothing save the hollow vast, that foam'd,   120
Above, around, and at his feet; save things
More dead than Morpheus' imaginings:
Old rusted anchors, helmets, breast-plates large
Of gone sea-warriors; brazen beaks and targe;
Rudders that for a hundred years had lost
The sway of human hand; gold vase emboss'd
With long-forgotten story, and wherein
No reveller had ever dipp'd a chin
But those of Saturn's vintage; mouldering scrolls,
Writ in the tongue of heaven, by those souls   130
Who first were on the earth; and sculptures rude
In ponderous stone, developing the mood
Of ancient Nox;—then skeletons of man,
Of beast, behemoth, and leviathan,
And elephant, and eagle, and huge jaw
Of nameless monster. A cold leaden awe
These secrets struck into him; and unless
Dian had chaced away that heaviness,
He might have died: but now, with cheered feel,
He onward kept; wooing these thoughts to steal   140
About the labyrinth in his soul of love.

  "What is there in thee, Moon! that thou shouldst move
My heart so potently? When yet a child
I oft have dried my tears when thou hast smil'd.
Thou seem'dst my sister: hand in hand we went
From eve to morn across the firmament.
No apples would I gather from the tree,
Till thou hadst cool'd their cheeks deliciously:
No tumbling water ever spake romance,
But when my eyes with thine thereon could dance: 150

No woods were green enough, no bower divine,
Until thou liftedst up thine eyelids fine:
In sowing time ne'er would I dibble take,
Or drop a seed, till thou wast wide awake;
And, in the summer tide of blossoming,
No one but thee hath heard me blythly sing
And mesh my dewy flowers all the night.
No melody was like a passing spright
If it went not to solemnize thy reign.
Yes, in my boyhood, every joy and pain   160
By thee were fashion'd to the self-same end;
And as I grew in years, still didst thou blend
With all my ardours: thou wast the deep glen;
Thou wast the mountain-top—the sage's pen—
The poet's harp—the voice of friends—the sun;
Thou wast the river—thou wast glory won;
Thou wast my clarion's blast—thou wast my steed—
My goblet full of wine—my topmost deed:—
Thou wast the charm of women, lovely Moon!
O what a wild and harmonized tune   170
My spirit struck from all the beautiful!
On some bright essence could I lean, and lull
Myself to immortality: I prest
Nature's soft pillow in a wakeful rest.
But, gentle Orb! there came a nearer bliss—
My strange love came—Felicity's abyss!
She came, and thou didst fade, and fade away—
Yet not entirely; no, thy starry sway
Has been an under-passion to this hour.
Now I begin to feel thine orby power   180
Is coming fresh upon me: O be kind,
Keep back thine influence, and do not blind
My sovereign vision.—Dearest love, forgive
That I can think away from thee and live!—
Pardon me, airy planet, that I prize
One thought beyond thine argent luxuries!
How far beyond!" At this a surpris'd start
Frosted the springing verdure of his heart;
For as he lifted up his eyes to swear
How his own goddess was past all things fair,   190
He saw far in the concave green of the sea
An old man sitting calm and peacefully.
Upon a weeded rock this old man sat,
And his white hair was awful, and a mat
Of weeds were cold beneath his cold thin feet;
And, ample as the largest winding-sheet,

A cloak of blue wrapp'd up his aged bones,
O'erwrought with symbols by the deepest groans
Of ambitious magic: every ocean-form
Was woven in with black distinctness; storm,   200
And calm, and whispering, and hideous roar,
Quicksand, and whirlpool, and deserted shore,
Were emblem'd in the woof; with every shape
That skims, or dives, or sleeps, 'twixt cape and cape.
The gulphing whale was like a dot in the spell,
Yet look upon it, and 'twould size and swell
To its huge self; and the minutest fish
Would pass the very hardest gazer's wish,
And show his little eye's anatomy.
Then there was pictur'd the regality   .   210
Of Neptune; and the sea nymphs round his state,
In beauteous vassalage, look up and wait.
Beside this old man lay a pearly wand,
And in his lap a book, the which he conn'd
So stedfastly, that the new denizen
Had time to keep him in amazed ken,
To mark these shadowings, and stand in awe.

The old man rais'd his hoary head and saw
The wilder'd stranger—seeming not to see,
His features were so lifeless. Suddenly   220
He woke as from a trance; his snow-white brows
Went arching up, and like two magic ploughs
Furrow'd deep wrinkles in his forehead large,
Which kept as fixedly as rocky marge,
Till round his wither'd lips had gone a smile.
Then up he rose, like one whose tedious toil
Had watch'd for years in forlorn hermitage,
Who had not from mid-life to utmost age
Eas'd in one accent his o'er-burden'd soul,
Even to the trees. He rose: he grasp'd his stole,
With convuls'd clenches waving it abroad,   23
And in a voice of solemn joy, that aw'd
Echo into oblivion, he said:—

"Thou art the man! Now shall I lay my head
In peace upon my watery pillow: now
Sleep will come smoothly to my weary brow.
O Jove! I shall be young again, be young!
O shell-borne Neptune, I am pierc'd and stung
With new-born life! What shall I do? Where go,
When I have cast this serpent-skin of woe?—   24

I'll swim to the syrens, and one moment listen
Their melodies, and see their long hair glisten;
Anon upon that giant's arm I'll be,
That writhes about the roots of Sicily:
To northern seas I'll in a twinkling sail,
And mount upon the snortings of a whale
To some black cloud; thence down I'll madly sweep
On forked lightning, to the deepest deep,
Where through some sucking pool I will be hurl'd
With rapture to the other side of the world!   250
O, I am full of gladness! Sisters three,
I bow full hearted to your old decree!
Yes, every god be thank'd, and power benign,
For I no more shall wither, droop, and pine.
Thou art the man!" Endymion started back
Dismay'd; and, like a wretch from whom the rack
Tortures hot breath, and speech of agony,
Mutter'd: "What lonely death am I to die
In this cold region? Will he let me freeze,
And float my brittle limbs o'er polar seas?   260
Or will he touch me with his searing hand,
And leave a black memorial on the sand?
Or tear me piece-meal with a bony saw,
And keep me as a chosen food to draw
His magian fish through hated fire and flame?
O misery of hell! resistless, tame,
Am I to be burnt up? No, I will shout,
Until the gods through heaven's blue look out!—
O Tartarus! but some few days agone
Her soft arms were entwining me, and on   270
Her voice I hung like fruit among green leaves:
Her lips were all my own, and—ah, ripe sheaves
Of happiness! ye on the stubble droop,
But never may be garner'd. I must stoop
My head, and kiss death's foot. Love! love, farewell!
Is there no hope from thee? This horrid spell
Would melt at thy sweet breath.—By Dian's hind
Feeding from her white fingers, on the wind
I see thy streaming hair! and now, by Pan,
I care not for this old mysterious man!"   280

    He spoke, and walking to that aged form,
Look'd high defiance. Lo! his heart 'gan warm
With pity, for the grey-hair'd creature wept.
Had he then wrong'd a heart where sorrow kept?
Had he, though blindly contumelious, brought
Rheum to kind eyes, a sting to humane thought,

Convulsion to a mouth of many years?
He had in truth; and he was ripe for tears.
The penitent shower fell, as down he knelt
Before that care-worn sage, who trembling felt   290
About his large dark locks, and faultering spake:

"Arise, good youth, for sacred Phœbus' sake!
I know thine inmost bosom, and I feel
A very brother's yearning for thee steal
Into mine own: for why? thou openest
The prison gates that have so long opprest
My weary watching. Though thou know'st it not,
Thou art commission'd to this fated spot
For great enfranchisement. O weep no more;
I am a friend to love, to loves of yore: 300
Aye, hadst thou never lov'd an unknown power,
I had been grieving at this joyous hour.
But even now most miserable old,
I saw thee, and my blood no longer cold
Gave mighty pulses: in this tottering case
Grew a new heart, which at this moment plays
As dancingly as thine. Be not afraid,
For thou shalt hear this secret all display'd,
Now as we speed towards our joyous task."

So saying, this young soul in age's mask   310
Went forward with the Carian side by side:
Resuming quickly thus; while ocean's tide
Hung swollen at their backs, and jewel'd sands
Took silently their foot-prints.
                                "My soul stands
Now past the midway from mortality,
And so I can prepare without a sigh
To tell thee briefly all my joy and pain.
I was a fisher once, upon this main,
And my boat danc'd in every creek and bay;
Rough billows were my home by night and day,—
The sea-gulls not more constant; for I had   321
No housing from the storm and tempests mad,
But hollow rocks,—and they were palaces
Of silent happiness, of slumberous ease:
Long years of misery have told me so.
Aye, thus it was one thousand years ago.
One thousand years!—Is it then possible
To look so plainly through them? to dispel
A thousand years with backward glance sublime?
To breathe away as 'twere all scummy slime   330

From off a crystal pool, to see its deep,
And one's own image from the bottom peep?
Yes: now I am no longer wretched thrall,
My long captivity and moanings all
Are but a slime, a thin-pervading scum,
The which I breathe away, and thronging come
Like things of yesterday my youthful pleasures.

"I touch'd no lute, I sang not, trod no measures:
I was a lonely youth on desert shores.
My sports were lonely, 'mid continuous roars,   340
And craggy isles, and sea-mew's plaintive cry
Plaining discrepant between sea and sky.
Dolphins were still my playmates; shapes unseen
Would let me feel their scales of gold and green,
Nor be my desolation; and, full oft,
When a dread waterspout had rear'd aloft
Its hungry hugeness, seeming ready ripe
To burst with hoarsest thunderings, and wipe
My life away like a vast sponge of fate,
Some friendly monster, pitying my sad state,   350
Has dived to its foundations, gulph'd it down,
And left me tossing safely. But the crown
Of all my life was utmost quietude:
More did I love to lie in cavern rude,
Keeping in wait whole days for Neptune's voice,
And if it came at last, hark, and rejoice!
There blush'd no summer eve but I would steer
My skiff along green shelving coasts, to hear
The shepherd's pipe come clear from aery steep,
Mingled with ceaseless bleatings of his sheep: 360
And never was a day of summer shine,
But I beheld its birth upon the brine:
For I would watch all night to see unfold
Heaven's gates, and Æthon snort his morning gold
Wide o'er the swelling streams: and constantly
At brim of day-tide, on some grassy lea,
My nets would be spread out, and I at rest.
The poor folk of the sea-country I blest
With daily boon of fish most delicate:
They knew not whence this bounty, and elate   370
Would strew sweet flowers on a sterile beach.

"Why was I not contented? Wherefore reach
At things which, but for thee, O Latmian!
Had been my dreary death? Fool! I began

To feel distemper'd longings: to desire
The utmost privilege that ocean's sire
Could grant in benediction: to be free
Of all his kingdom. Long in misery
I wasted, ere in one extremest fit
I plung'd for life or death. To interknit   380
One's senses with so dense a breathing stuff
Might seem a work of pain; so not enough
Can I admire how crystal-smooth it felt,
And buoyant round my limbs. At first I dwelt
Whole days and days in sheer astonishment;
Forgetful utterly of self-intent;
Moving but with the mighty ebb and flow.
Then, like a new fledg'd bird that first doth show
His spreaded feathers to the morrow chill,
I tried in fear the pinions of my will.   390
'Twas freedom! and at once I visited
The ceaseless wonders of this ocean-bed.
No need to tell thee of them, for I see
That thou hast been a witness—it must be—
For these I know thou canst not feel a drouth,
By the melancholy corners of that mouth.
So I will in my story straightway pass
To more immediate matter. Woe, alas!
That love should be my bane! Ah, Scylla fair!
Why did poor Glaucus ever—ever dare   400
To sue thee to his heart? Kind stranger-youth!
I lov'd her to the very white of truth,
And she would not conceive it. Timid thing!
She fled me swift as sea-bird on the wing,
Round every isle, and point, and promontory,
From where large Hercules wound up his story
Far as Egyptian Nile. My passion grew
The more, the more I saw her dainty hue
Gleam delicately through the azure clear:
Until 'twas too fierce agony to bear;   410
And in that agony, across my grief
It flash'd, that Circe might find some relief—
Cruel enchantress! So above the water
I rear'd my head, and look'd for Phœbus' daughter.
Æxa's isle was wondering at the moon:—
It seem'd to whirl around me, and a swoon
Left me dead-drifting to that fatal power.

"When I awoke, 'twas in a twilight bower;
Just when the light of morn, with hum of bees,
Stole through its verdurous matting of fresh trees.

How sweet, and sweeter; for I heard a lyre,   421
And over it a sighing voice expire.
It ceased—I caught light footsteps; and anon
The fairest face that morn e'er look'd upon
Push'd through a screen of roses. Starry Jove!
With tears, and smiles, and honey-words she wove
A net whose thraldom was more bliss than all
The range of flower'd Elysium. Thus did fall
The dew of her rich speech: "Ah! Art awake?
"O let me hear thee speak, for Cupid's sake!   430
"I am so oppress'd with joy! Why, I have shed
"An urn of tears, as though thou wert cold dead;
"And now I find thee living, I will pour
"From these devoted eyes their silver store,
"Until exhausted of the latest drop,
"So it will pleasure thee, and force thee stop
"Here, that I too may live: but if beyond
"Such cool and sorrowful offerings, thou art fond
"Of soothing warmth, of dalliance supreme;
"If thou art ripe to taste a long love dream;   440
"If smiles, if dimples, tongues for ardour mute,
"Hang in thy vision like a tempting fruit,
"O let me pluck it for thee." Thus she link'd
Her charming syllables, till indistinct
Their music came to my o'er-sweeten'd soul;
And then she hover'd over me, and stole
So near, that if no nearer it had been
This furrow'd visage thou hadst never seen.

"Young man of Latmos! thus particular
Am I, that thou may'st plainly see how far   450
This fierce temptation went: and thou may'st not
Exclaim, How then, was Scylla quite forgot?

"Who could resist? Who in this universe?
She did so breathe ambrosia; so immerse
My fine existence in a golden clime.
She took me like a child of suckling time,
And cradled me in roses. Thus condemn'd,
The current of my former life was stemm'd,
And to this arbitrary queen of sense
I bow'd a tranced vassal: nor would thence   460
Have mov'd, even though Amphion's harp had woo'd
Me back to Scylla o'er the billows rude.
For as Apollo each eve doth devise
A new appareling for western skies;

So every eve, nay every spendthrift hour
Shed balmy consciousness within that bower.
And I was free of haunts umbrageous;
Could wander in the mazy forest-house
Of squirrels, foxes shy, and antler'd deer,
And birds from coverts innermost and drear   470
Warbling for very joy melliflous sorrow—
To me new born delights!
                               "Now let me borrow,
For moments few, a temperament as stern
As Pluto's sceptre, that my words not burn
These uttering lips, while I in calm speech tell
How specious heaven was changed to real hell.

"One morn she left me sleeping: half awake
I sought for her smooth arms and lips, to slake
My greedy thirst with nectarous camel-draughts;
But she was gone. Whereat the barbed shafts   480
Of disappointment stuck in me so sore,
That out I ran and search'd the forest o'er.
Wandering about in pine and cedar gloom
Damp awe assail'd me; for there 'gan to boom
A sound of moan, an agony of sound,
Sepulchral from the distance all around.
Then came a conquering earth-thunder, and rumbled
That fierce complain to silence: while I stumbled
Down a precipitous path, as if impell'd.
I came to a dark valley.—Groanings swell'd   490
Poisonous about my ears, and louder grew,
The nearer I approach'd a flame's gaunt blue,
That glar'd before me through a thorny brake.
This fire, like the eye of gordian snake,
Bewitch'd me towards; and I soon was near
A sight too fearful for the feel of fear:
In thicket hid I curs'd the haggard scene—
The banquet of my arms, my arbour queen,
Seated upon an uptorn forest root;
And all around her shapes, wizard and brute,   500
Laughing and wailing, groveling, serpenting,
Showing tooth, tusk, and venom-bag, and sting!
O such deformities! Old Charon's self,
Should he give up awhile his penny pelf,
And take a dream 'mong rushes Stygian,
It could not be so phantasied. Fierce, wan,
And tyrannizing was the lady's look,
As over them a gnarled staff she shook.

Oft-times upon the sudden she laugh'd out,
And from a basket emptied to the rout   510
Clusters of grapes, the which they raven'd quick
And roar'd for more; with many a hungry lick
About their shaggy jaws. Avenging, slow,
Anon she took a branch of mistletoe,
And emptied on't a black dull-gurgling phial:
Groan'd one and all, as if some piercing trial
Was sharpening for their pitiable bones.
She lifted up the charm: appealing groans
From their poor breasts went sueing to her ear
In vain; remorseless as an infant's bier   520
She whisk'd against their eyes the sooty oil.
Whereat was heard a noise of painful toil,
Increasing gradual to a tempest rage,
Shrieks, yells, and groans of torture-pilgrimage;
Until their grieved bodies 'gan to bloat
And puff from the tail's end to stifled throat:
Then was appalling silence: then a sight
More wildering than all that hoarse affright;
For the whole herd, as by a whirlwind writhen,
Went through the dismal air like one huge Python
Antagonizing Boreas,—and so vanish'd.   531
Yet there was not a breath of wind: she banish'd
These phantoms with a nod. Lo! from the dark
Came waggish fauns, and nymphs, and satyrs stark,
With dancing and loud revelry,—and went
Swifter than centaurs after rapine bent.—
Sighing an elephant appear'd and bow'd
Before the fierce witch, speaking thus aloud
In human accent: "Potent goddess! chief
"Of pains resistless! make my being brief,   540
"Or let me from this heavy prison fly:
"Or give me to the air, or let me die!
"I sue not for my happy crown again;
"I sue not for my phalanx on the plain;
"I sue not for my lone, my widow'd wife;
"I sue not for my ruddy drops of life,
"My children fair, my lovely girls and boys!
"I will forget them; I will pass these joys;
"Ask nought so heavenward, so too—too high:
"Only I pray, as fairest boon, to die,   550
"Or be deliver'd from this cumbrous flesh,
"From this gross, detestable, filthy mesh,
"And merely given to the cold bleak air.
"Have mercy, Goddess! Circe, feel my prayer!"

"That curst magician's name fell icy numb
Upon my wild conjecturing: truth had come
Naked and sabre-like against my heart.
I saw a fury whetting a death-dart;
And my slain spirit, overwrought with fright,
Fainted away in that dark lair of night.   560
Think, my deliverer, how desolate
My waking must have been! disgust, and hate,
And terrors manifold divided me
A spoil amongst them. I prepar'd to flee
Into the dungeon core of that wild wood:
I fled three days—when lo! before me stood
Glaring the angry witch. O Dis, even now,
A clammy dew is beading on my brow,
At mere remembering her pale laugh, and curse.
"Ha! ha! Sir Dainty! there must be a nurse   570
"Made of rose leaves and thistledown, express,
"To cradle thee my sweet, and lull thee: yes,
"I am too flinty-hard for thy nice touch:
"My tenderest squeeze is but a giant's clutch.
"So, fairy-thing, it shall have lullabies
"Unheard of yet: and it shall still its cries
"Upon some breast more lilly-feminine.
"Oh, no—it shall not pine, and pine, and pine
"More than one pretty, trifling thousand years;
"And then 'twere pity, but fate's gentle shears   580
"Cut short its immortality. Sea-flirt!
"Young dove of the waters! truly I'll not hurt
"One hair of thine: see how I weep and sigh,
"That our heart-broken parting is so nigh.
"And must we part? Ah, yes, it must be so.
"Yet ere thou leavest me in utter woe,
"Let me sob over thee my last adieus,
"And speak a blessing: Mark me! Thou hast thews
"Immortal, for thou art of heavenly race:
"But such a love is mine, that here I chace   590
"Eternally away from thee all bloom
"Of youth, and destine thee towards a tomb.
"Hence shalt thou quickly to the watery vast;
"And there, ere many days be overpast,
"Disabled age shall seize thee; and even then
"Thou shalt not go the way of aged men;
"But live and wither, cripple and still breathe
"Ten hundred years: which gone, I then bequeath
"Thy fragile bones to unknown burial.
"Adieu, sweet love, adieu!"—As shot stars fall,

She fled ere I could groan for mercy. Stung
And poison'd was my spirit: despair sung
A war-song of defiance 'gainst all hell.
A hand was at my shoulder to compel
My sullen steps; another 'fore my eyes
Moved on with pointed finger. In this guise
Enforced, at the last by ocean's foam
I found me; by my fresh, my native home.
Its tempering coolness, to my life akin,
Came salutary as I waded in;   610
And, with a blind voluptuous rage, I gave
Battle to the swollen billow-ridge, and drave
Large froth before me, while there yet remain'd
Hale strength, nor from my bones all marrow drain'd.

"Young lover, I must weep—such hellish spite
With dry cheek who can tell? While thus my might
Proving upon this element, dismay'd,
Upon a dead thing's face my hand I laid;
I look'd—'twas Scylla! Cursed, cursed Circe!
O vulture-witch, hast never heard of mercy?   620
Could not thy harshest vengeance be content,
But thou must nip this tender innocent
Because I lov'd her?—Cold, O cold indeed
Were her fair limbs, and like a common weed
The sea-swell took her hair. Dead as she was
I clung about her waist, nor ceas'd to pass
Fleet as an arrow through unfathom'd brine,
Until there shone a fabric crystalline,
Ribb'd and inlaid with coral, pebble, and pearl.
Headlong I darted; at one eager swirl   630
Gain'd its bright portal, enter'd, and behold!
'Twas vast, and desolate, and icy-cold;
And all around—But wherefore this to thee
Who in few minutes more thyself shalt see?—
I left poor Scylla in a niche and fled.
My fever'd parchings up, my scathing dread
Met palsy half way: soon these limbs became
Gaunt, wither'd, sapless, feeble, cramp'd, and lame.

"Now let me pass a cruel, cruel space,
Without one hope, without one faintest trace   640
Of mitigation, or redeeming bubble
Of colour'd phantasy; for I fear 'twould trouble
Thy brain to loss of reason: and next tell
How a restoring chance came down to quell
One half of the witch in me.

"On a day,
Sitting upon a rock above the spray,
I saw grow up from the horizon's brink
A gallant vessel: soon she seem'd to sink
Away from me again, as though her course
Had been resum'd in spite of hindering force—   650
So vanish'd: and not long, before arose
Dark clouds, and muttering of winds morose.
Old Æolus would stifle his mad spleen,
But could not: therefore all the billows green
Toss'd up the silver spume against the clouds.
The tempest came: I saw that vessel's shrouds
In perilous bustle; while upon the deck
Stood trembling creatures. I beheld the wreck;
The final gulphing; the poor struggling souls:
I heard their cries amid loud thunder-rolls.   660
O they had all been sav'd but crazed eld
Annull'd my vigorous cravings: and thus quell'd
And curb'd, think on't, O Latmian! did I sit
Writhing with pity, and a cursing fit
Against that hell-born Circe. The crew had gone,
By one and one, to pale oblivion;
And I was gazing on the surges prone,
With many a scalding tear and many a groan,
When at my feet emerg'd an old man's hand,
Grasping this scroll, and this same slender wand.   670
I knelt with pain—reach'd out my hand—had grasp'd
These treasures—touch'd the knuckles—they unclasp'd—
I caught a finger: but the downward weight
O'erpowered me—it sank. Then 'gan abate
The storm, and through chill aguish gloom outburst
The comfortable sun. I was athirst
To search the book, and in the warming air
Parted its dripping leaves with eager care.
Strange matters did it treat of, and drew on
My soul page after page, till well-nigh won   680
Into forgetfulness; when, stupefied,
I read these words, and read again, and tried
My eyes against the heavens, and read again.
O what a load of misery and pain
Each Atlas-line bore off!—a shine of hope
Came gold around me, cheering me to cope
Strenuous with hellish tyranny. Attend!
For thou hast brought their promise to an end.

"In wide sea there lives a forlorn wretch,
Doom'd with enfeebled carcase to outstretch   690

His loath'd existence through ten centuries,
And then to die alone. Who can devise
A total opposition? No one. So
One million times ocean must ebb and flow,
And he oppressed. Yet he shall not die,
These things accomplish'd:—If he utterly
Scans all the depths of magic, and expounds
The meanings of all motions, shapes and sounds;
If he explores all forms and substances
Straight homeward to their symbol-essences;   700
He shall not die. Moreover, and in chief,
He must pursue this task of joy and grief
Most piously;—all lovers tempest-tost,
And in the savage overwhelming lost,
He shall deposit side by side, until
Time's creeping shall the dreary space fulfil:
Which done, and all these labours ripened,
A youth, by heavenly power lov'd and led,
Shall stand before him; whom he shall direct
How to consummate all. The youth elect   710
Must do the thing, or both will be destroy'd."—

"Then," cried the young Endymion, overjoy'd,
"We are twin brothers in this destiny!
Say, I intreat thee, what achievement high
Is, in this restless world, for me reserv'd.
What! if from thee my wandering feet had swerv'd,
Had we both perish'd?"—"Look!" the sage replied,
"Dost thou not mark a gleaming through the tide,
Of diverse brilliances? 'tis the edifice
I told thee of, where lovely Scylla lies;   720
And where I have enshrined piously
All lovers, whom fell storms have doom'd to die
Throughout my bondage." Thus discoursing, on
They went till unobscur'd the porches shone;
Which hurrying they gain'd, and enter'd straight.
Sure never since king Neptune held his state
Was seen such wonder underneath the stars.
Turn to some level plain where haughty Mars
Has legion'd all his battle; and behold
How every soldier, with firm foot, doth hold   730
His even breast: see, many steeled squares,
And rigid ranks of iron—whence who dares
One step? Imagine further, line by line,
These warrior thousands on the field supine:—
So in that crystal place, in silent rows,
Poor lovers lay at rest from joys and woes.—

The stranger from the mountains, breathless, trac'd
Such thousands of shut eyes in order plac'd;
Such ranges of white feet, and patient lips
All ruddy,—for here death no blossom nips.   740
He mark'd their brows and foreheads; saw their hair
Put sleekly on one side with nicest care;
And each one's gentle wrists, with reverence,
Put cross-wise to its heart.

              "Let us commence,"
Whisper'd the guide, stuttering with joy, "even now."
He spake, and, trembling like an aspen-bough,
Began to tear his scroll in pieces small,
Uttering the while some mumblings funeral.
He tore it into pieces small as snow
That drifts unfeather'd when bleak northerns blow;
And having done it, took his dark blue cloak   751
And bound it round Endymion: then struck
His wand against the empty air times nine.—
"What more there is to do, young man, is thine:
But first a little patience; first undo
This tangled thread, and wind it to a clue.
Ah, gentle! 'tis as weak as spider's skein;
And shouldst thou break it—What, is it done so clean?
A power overshadows thee! O, brave!
The spite of hell is tumbling to its grave.   760
Here is a shell; 'tis pearly blank to me,
Nor mark'd with any sign or charactery—
Canst thou read aught? O read for pity's sake!
Olympus! we are safe! Now, Carian, break
This wand against yon lyre on the pedestal."

'Twas done: and straight with sudden swell and fall
Sweet music breath'd her soul away, and sigh'd
A lullaby to silence.—"Youth! now strew
These minced leaves on me, and passing through
Those files of dead, scatter the same around,   770
And thou wilt see the issue."—'Mid the sound
Of flutes and viols, ravishing his heart,
Endymion from Glaucus stood apart,
And scatter'd in his face some fragments light.
How lightning-swift the change! a youthful wight
Smiling beneath a coral diadem,
Out-sparkling sudden like an upturn'd gem,
Appear'd, and, stepping to a beauteous corse,
Kneel'd down beside it, and with tenderest force
Press'd its cold hand, and wept,—and Scylla sigh'd!
Endymion, with quick hand, the charm applied—   781

The nymph arose: he left them to their joy,
And onward went upon his high employ,
Showering those powerful fragments on the dead.
And, as he pass'd, each lifted up his head,
As doth a flower at Apollo's touch.
Death felt it to his inwards: 'twas too much:
Death fell a weeping in his charnel-house.
The Latmian persever'd along, and thus
All were re-animated. There arose   790
A noise of harmony, pulses and throes
Of gladness in the air—while many, who
Had died in mutual arms devout and true,
Sprang to each other madly; and the rest
Felt a high certainty of being blest.
They gaz'd upon Endymion. Enchantment
Grew drunken, and would have its head and bent.
Delicious symphonies, like airy flowers,
Budded, and swell'd, and, full-blown, shed full showers
Of light, soft, unseen leaves of sounds divine.   800
The two deliverers tasted a pure wine
Of happiness, from fairy-press ooz'd out.
Speechless they eyed each other, and about
The fair assembly wander'd to and fro,
Distracted with the richest overflow
Of joy that ever pour'd from heaven.

                                    ——"Away!"
Shouted the new born god; "Follow, and pay
Our piety to Neptunus supreme!"—
Then Scylla, blushing sweetly from her dream,
They led on first, bent to her meek surprise,   810
Through portal columns of a giant size,
Into the vaulted, boundless emerald.
Joyous all follow'd as the leader call'd,
Down marble steps; pouring as easily
As hour-glass sand,—and fast, as you might see
Swallows obeying the south summer's call,
Or swans upon a gentle waterfall.

    Thus went that beautiful multitude, nor far,
Ere from among some rocks of glittering spar,
Just within ken, they saw descending thick   820
Another multitude. Whereat more quick
Moved either host. On a wide sand they met,
And of those numbers every eye was wet;
For each their old love found. A murmuring rose,
Like what was never heard in all the throes

Of wind and waters: 'tis past human wit
To tell; 'tis dizziness to think of it.

   This mighty consummation made, the host
Mov'd on for many a league; and gain'd, and lost
Huge sea-marks; vanward swelling in array,   830
And from the rear diminishing away,—
Till a faint dawn surpris'd them. Glaucus cried,
"Behold! behold, the palace of his pride!
God Neptune's palaces!" With noise increas'd,
They shoulder'd on towards that brightening east.
At every onward step proud domes arose
In prospect,—diamond gleams, and golden glows
Of amber 'gainst their faces levelling.
Joyous, and many as the leaves in spring,
Still onward; still the splendour gradual swell'd.   840
Rich opal domes were seen, on high upheld
By jasper pillars, letting through their shafts
A blush of coral. Copious wonder-draughts
Each gazer drank; and deeper drank more near:
For what poor mortals fragment up, as mere
As marble was there lavish, to the vast
Of one fair palace, that far far surpass'd,
Even for common bulk, those olden three,
Memphis, and Babylon, and Nineveh.

   As large, as bright, as colour'd as the bow   850
Of Iris, when unfading it doth show
Beyond a silvery shower, was the arch
Through which this Paphian army took its march,
Into the outer courts of Neptune's state:
Whence could be seen, direct, a golden gate,
To which the leaders sped; but not half raught
Ere it burst open swift as fairy thought,
And made those dazzled thousands veil their eyes
Like callow eagles at the first sunrise.
Soon with an eagle nativeness their gaze   860
Ripe from hue-golden swoons took all the blaze,
And then, behold! large Neptune on his throne
Of emerald deep: yet not exalt alone;
At his right hand stood winged Love, and on
His left sat smiling Beauty's paragon.

   Far as the mariner on highest mast
Can see all round upon the calmed vast,
So wide was Neptune's hall: and as the blue
Doth vault the waters, so the waters drew

Their doming curtains, high, magnificent,   870
Aw'd from the throne aloof;—and when storm-rent
Disclos'd the thunder-gloomings in Jove's air;
But sooth'd as now, flash'd sudden everywhere,
Noiseless, sub-marine cloudlets, glittering
Death to a human eye: for there did spring
From natural west, and east, and south, and north,
A light as of four sunsets, blazing forth
A gold-green zenith 'bove the Sea-God's head.
Of lucid depth the floor, and far outspread
As breezeless lake, on which the slim canoe   880
Of feather'd Indian darts about, as through
The delicatest air: air verily,
But for the portraiture of clouds and sky:
This palace floor breath-air,—but for the amaze
Of deep-seen wonders motionless,—and blaze
Of the dome pomp, reflected in extremes,
Globing a golden sphere.

                They stood in dreams
Till Triton blew his horn. The palace rang;
The Nereids danc'd; the Syrens faintly sang;
And the great Sea-King bow'd his dripping head.   890
Then Love took wing, and from his pinions shed
On all the multitude a nectarous dew.
The ooze-born Goddess beckoned and drew
Fair Scylla and her guides to conference;
And when they reach'd the throned eminence
She kist the sea-nymph's cheek,—who sat her down
A toying with the doves. Then,—"Mighty crown
And sceptre of this kingdom!" Venus said,
"Thy vows were on a time to Nais paid:
Behold!"— Two copious tear-drops instant fell   900
From the God's large eyes; he smil'd delectable,
And over Glaucus held his blessing hands.—
"Endymion! Ah! still wandering in the bands
Of love? Now this is cruel. Since the hour
I met thee in earth's bosom, all my power
Have I put forth to serve thee. What, not yet
Escap'd from dull mortality's harsh net?
A little patience, youth! 'twill not be long,
Or I am skilless quite: an idle tongue,
A humid eye, and steps luxurious,   910
Where these are new and strange, are ominous.
Aye, I have seen these signs in one of heaven,
When others were all blind: and were I given

To utter secrets, haply I might say
Some pleasant words:—but Love will have his day.
So wait awhile expectant. Pr'ythee soon,
Even in the passing of thine honey-moon,
Visit thou my Cythera: thou wilt find
Cupid well-natured, my Adonis kind;
And pray persuade with thee—Ah, I have done,
All blisses be upon thee, my sweet son!"—   921
Thus the fair goddess: While Endymion
Knelt to receive those accents halcyon.

Meantime a glorious revelry began
Before the Water-Monarch. Nectar ran
In courteous fountains to all cups outreach'd;
And plunder'd vines, teeming exhaustless, pleach'd
New growth about each shell and pendent lyre;
The which, in disentangling for their fire,
Pull'd down fresh foliage and coverture   930
For dainty toying. Cupid, empire-sure,
Flutter'd and laugh'd, and oft-times through the throng
Made a delighted way. Then dance, and song,
And garlanding grew wild; and pleasure reign'd.
In harmless tendril they each other chain'd,
And strove who should be smother'd deepest in
Fresh crush of leaves.

                   O 'tis a very sin
For one so weak to venture his poor verse
In such a place as this. O do not curse,
High Muses! let him hurry to the ending.   940

     All suddenly were silent. A soft blending
Of dulcet instruments came charmingly;
And then a hymn.

               "KING of the stormy sea!
Brother of Jove, and co-inheritor
Of elements! Eternally before
Thee the waves awful bow. Fast, stubborn rock,
At thy fear'd trident shrinking, doth unlock
Its deep foundations, hissing into foam.
All mountain-rivers, lost in the wide home
Of thy capacious bosom, ever flow.   950
Thou frownest, and old Æolus thy foe
Skulks to his cavern, 'mid the gruff complaint
Of all his rebel tempests. Dark clouds faint

When, from thy diadem, a silver gleam
Slants over blue dominion. Thy bright team
Gulphs in the morning light, and scuds along
To bring thee nearer to that golden song
Apollo singeth, while his chariot
Waits at the doors of heaven. Thou art not   960
For scenes like this: an empire stern hast thou;
And it hath furrow'd that large front: yet now,
As newly come of heaven, dost thou sit
To blend and interknit
Subdued majesty with this glad time.
O shell-borne King sublime!
We lay our hearts before thee evermore—
We sing, and we adore!

   "Breathe softly, flutes;
Be tender of your strings, ye soothing lutes;
Nor be the trumpet heard! O vain, O vain;   970
Not flowers budding in an April rain,
Nor breath of sleeping dove, nor river's flow,—
No, nor the Æolian twang of Love's own bow,
Can mingle music fit for the soft ear
Of goddess Cytherea!
Yet deign, white Queen of Beauty, thy fair eyes
On our souls' sacrifice.

   "Bright-winged Child!
Who has another care when thou hast smil'd?
Unfortunates on earth, we see at last   980
All death-shadows, and glooms that overcast
Our spirits, fann'd away by thy light pinions.
O sweetest essence! sweetest of all minions!
God of warm pulses, and dishevell'd hair,
And panting bosoms bare!
Dear unseen light in darkness! eclipser
Of light in light! delicious poisoner!
Thy venom'd goblet will we quaff until
We fill—we fill!
And by thy Mother's lips————"

                Was heard no more   990
For clamour, when the golden palace door
Opened again, and from without, in shone
A new magnificence. On oozy throne
Smooth-moving came Oceanus the old,
To take a latest glimpse at his sheep-fold,
Before he went into his quiet cave
To muse for ever—Then a lucid wave,

Scoop'd from its trembling sisters of mid-sea,
Afloat, and pillowing up the majesty
Of Doris, and the Ægean seer, her spouse—   1000
Next, on a dolphin, clad in laurel boughs,
Theban Amphion leaning on his lute:
His fingers went across it—All were mute
To gaze on Amphitrite, queen of pearls,
And Thetis pearly too.—

                         The palace whirls
Around giddy Endymion; seeing he
Was there far strayed from mortality.
He could not bear it—shut his eyes in vain;
Imagination gave a dizzier pain.
"O I shall die! sweet Venus, be my stay!   1010
Where is my lovely mistress? Well-away!
I die—I hear her voice—I feel my wing—"
At Neptune's feet he sank. A sudden ring
Of Nereids were about him, in kind strife
To usher back his spirit into life:
But still he slept. At last they interwove
Their cradling arms, and purpos'd to convey
Towards a crystal bower far away.

    Lo! while slow carried through the pitying crowd,
To his inward senses these words spake aloud;   1020
Written in star-light on the dark above:
Dearest Endymion! my entire love!
How have I dwelt in fear of fate: 'tis done—
Immortal bliss for me too hast thou won.
Arise then! for the hen-dove shall not hatch
Her ready eggs, before I'll kissing snatch
Thee into endless heaven. Awake! awake!

    The youth at once arose: a placid lake
Came quiet to his eyes; and forest green,
Cooler than all the wonders he had seen,   1030
Lull'd with its simple song his fluttering breast.
How happy once again in grassy nest!

BOOK IV

MUSE of my native land! loftiest Muse!
O first-born on the mountains! by the hues
Of heaven on the spiritual air begot:
Long didst thou sit alone in northern grot,

While yet our England was a wolfish den;
Before our forests heard the talk of men;
Before the first of Druids was a child;—
Long didst thou sit amid our regions wild
Rapt in a deep prophetic solitude.
There came an eastern voice of solemn mood:—   10
Yet wast thou patient. Then sang forth the Nine,
Apollo's garland:—yet didst thou divine
Such home-bred glory, that they cry'd in vain,
"Come hither, Sister of the Island!" Plain
Spake fair Ausonia; and once more she spake
A higher summons:—still didst thou betake
Thee to thy native hopes. O thou hast won
A full accomplishment! The thing is done,
Which undone, these our latter days had risen
On barren souls. Great Muse, thou know'st what prison,
Of flesh and bone, curbs, and confines, and frets   21
Our spirit's wings: despondency besets
Our pillows; and the fresh to-morrow morn
Seems to give forth its light in very scorn
Of our dull, uninspired, snail-paced lives.
Long have I said, how happy he who shrives
To thee! But then I thought on poets gone,
And could not pray:—nor could I now—so on
I move to the end in lowliness of heart.——

    "Ah, woe is me! that I should fondly part   30
From my dear native land! Ah, foolish maid!
Glad was the hour, when, with thee, myriads bade
Adieu to Ganges and their pleasant fields!
To one so friendless the clear freshet yields
A bitter coolness; the ripe grape is sour:
Yet I would have, great gods! but one short hour
Of native air—let me but die at home."

    Endymion to heaven's airy dome
Was offering up a hecatomb of vows,
When these words reach'd him. Whereupon he bows   41
His head through thorny-green entanglement
Of underwood, and to the sound is bent,
Anxious as hind towards her hidden fawn.

    "Is no one near to help me? No fair dawn
Of life from charitable voice? No sweet saying
To set my dull and sadden'd spirit playing?

No hand to toy with mine? No lips so sweet
That I may worship them? No eyelids meet
To twinkle on my bosom? No one dies
Before me, till from these enslaving eyes   50
Redemption sparkles!—I am sad and lost."

    Thou, Carian lord, hadst better have been tost
Into a whirlpool. Vanish into air,
Warm mountaineer! for canst thou only bear
A woman's sigh alone and in distress?
See not her charms! Is Phœbe passionless?
Phœbe is fairer far—O gaze no more:—
Yet if thou wilt behold all beauty's store,
Behold her panting in the forest grass!
Do not those curls of glossy jet surpass   60
For tenderness the arms so idly lain
Amongst them? Feelest not a kindred pain,
To see such lovely eyes in swimming search
After some warm delight, that seems to perch
Dovelike in the dim cell lying beyond
Their upper lids?—Hist!

                "O for Hermes' wand,
To touch this flower into human shape!
That woodland Hyacinthus could escape
From his green prison, and here kneeling down
Call me his queen, his second life's fair crown!   70
Ah me, how I could love!—My soul doth melt
For the unhappy youth—Love! I have felt
So faint a kindness, such a meek surrender
To what my own full thoughts had made too tender,
That but for tears my life had fled away!—
Ye deaf and senseless minutes of the day,
And thou, old forest, hold ye this for true,
There is no lightning, no authentic dew
But in the eye of love: there's not a sound,
Melodious howsoever, can confound   80
The heavens and earth in one to such a death
As doth the voice of love: there's not a breath
Will mingle kindly with the meadow air,
Till it has panted round, and stolen a share
Of passion from the heart!"—

                    Upon a bough
He leant, wretched. He surely cannot now
Thirst for another love: O impious,
That he can ever dream upon it thus!—

Thought he, "Why am I not as are the dead,
Since to a woe like this I have been led   90
Through the dark earth, and through the wondrous sea?
Goddess! I love thee not the less: from thee
By Juno's smile I turn not—no, no, no—
While the great waters are at ebb and flow.—
I have a triple soul! O fond pretence—
For both, for both my love is so immense,
I feel my heart is cut for them in twain."

   And so he groan'd, as one by beauty slain.
The lady's heart beat quick, and he could see
Her gentle bosom heave tumultuously.   100
He sprang from his green covert: there she lay,
Sweet as a muskrose upon new-made hay;
With all her limbs on tremble, and her eyes
Shut softly up alive. To speak he tries.
"Fair damsel, pity me! forgive that I
Thus violate thy bower's sanctity!
O pardon me, for I am full of grief—
Grief born of thee, young angel! fairest thief!
Who stolen hast away the wings wherewith
I was to top the heavens. Dear maid, sith   110
Thou art my executioner, and I feel
Loving and hatred, misery and weal,
Will in a few short hours be nothing to me,
And all my story that much passion slew me;
Do smile upon the evening of my days:
And, for my tortur'd brain begins to craze,
Be thou my nurse; and let me understand
How dying I shall kiss that lilly hand.—
Dost weep for me? Then should I be content.
Scowl on, ye fates! until the firmament   120
Outblackens Erebus, and the full-cavern'd earth
Crumbles into itself. By the cloud girth
Of Jove, those tears have given me a thirst
To meet oblivion."—As her heart would burst
The maiden sobb'd awhile, and then replied:
"Why must such desolation betide
As that thou speak'st of? Are not these green nooks
Empty of all misfortune? Do the brooks
Utter a gorgon voice? Does yonder thrush,
Schooling its half-fledg'd little ones to brush   130
About the dewy forest, whisper tales?—
Speak not of grief, young stranger, or cold snails

Will slime the rose to night. Though if thou wilt,
Methinks 'twould be a guilt—a very guilt—
Not to companion thee, and sigh away
The light—the dusk—the dark—till break of day!"
"Dear lady," said Endymion, " 'tis past:
I love thee! and my days can never last.
That I may pass in patience still speak:
Let me have music dying, and I seek   140
No more delight—I bid adieu to all.
Didst thou not after other climates call,
And murmur about Indian streams?"—Then she,
Sitting beneath the midmost forest tree,
For pity sang this roundelay————

"O Sorrow,
Why dost borrow
The natural hue of health, from vermeil lips?—
To give maiden blushes
To the white rose bushes?   150
Or is't thy dewy hand the daisy tips?

"O Sorrow,
Why dost borrow
The lustrous passion from a falcon-eye?—
To give the glow-worm light?
Or, on a moonless night,
To tinge, on syren shores, the salt sea-spry?

"O Sorrow,
Why dost borrow
The mellow ditties from a mourning tongue?—   160
To give at evening pale
Unto the nightingale,
That thou mayst listen the cold dews among?

"O Sorrow,
Why dost borrow
Heart's lightness from the merriment of May?—
A lover would not tread
A cowslip on the head,
Though he should dance from eve till peep of day—
Nor any drooping flower   170
Held sacred for thy bower,
Wherever he may sport himself and play.

      "To Sorrow,
      I bade good-morrow,
And thought to leave her far away behind;
      But cheerly, cheerly,
      She loves me dearly;
She is so constant to me, and so kind:
      I would deceive her
      And so leave her,   180
But ah! she is so constant and so kind.

"Beneath my palm trees, by the river side,
I sat a weeping: in the whole world wide
There was no one to ask me why I wept,—
      And so I kept
Brimming the water-lily cups with tears
      Cold as my fears.

"Beneath my palm trees, by the river side,
I sat a weeping: what enamour'd bride,
Cheated by shadowy wooer from the clouds,   190
      But hides and shrouds
Beneath dark palm trees by a river side?

"And as I sat, over the light blue hills
There came a noise of revellers: the rills
Into the wide stream came of purple hue—
      'Twas Bacchus and his crew!
The earnest trumpet spake, and silver thrills
From kissing cymbals made a merry din—
      'Twas Bacchus and his kin!
Like to a moving vintage down they came,   200
Crown'd with green leaves, and faces all on flame;
All madly dancing through the pleasant valley,
      To scare thee, Melancholy!
O then, O then, thou wast a simple name!
And I forgot thee, as the berried holly
By shepherds is forgotten, when, in June,
Tall chestnuts keep away the sun and moon: —
      I rush'd into the folly!

"Within his car, aloft, young Bacchus stood,
Trifling his ivy-dart, in dancing mood,   210
      With sidelong laughing;
And little rills of crimson wine imbrued
His plump white arms, and shoulders, enough white
      For Venus' pearly bite:

And near him rode Silenus on his ass,
Pelted with flowers as he on did pass
    Tipsily quaffing.

"Whence came ye, merry Damsels! whence came ye!
So many, and so many, and such glee?
Why have ye left your bowers desolate,   220
    Your lutes, and gentler fate?—
'We follow Bacchus! Bacchus on the wing,
    A conquering!
Bacchus, young Bacchus! good or ill betide,
We dance before him thorough kingdoms wide:—
Come hither, lady fair, and joined be
    To our wild minstrelsy!'

"Whence came ye, jolly Satyrs! whence came ye!
So many, and so many, and such glee?
Why have ye left your forest haunts, why left   230
    Your nuts in oak-tree cleft?—
'For wine, for wine we left our kernel tree;
For wine we left our heath, and yellow brooms,
    And cold mushrooms;
For wine we follow Bacchus through the earth;
Great God of breathless cups and chirping mirth!-
Come hither, lady fair, and joined be
    To our mad minstrelsy!'

"Over wide streams and mountains great we went,
And, save when Bacchus kept his ivy tent,
Onward the tiger and the leopard pants,   24
    With Asian elephants:
Onward these myriads—with song and dance,
With zebras striped, and sleek Arabians' prance,
Web-footed alligators, crocodiles,
Bearing upon their scaly backs, in files,
Plump infant laughers mimicking the coil
Of seamen, and stout galley-rowers' toil:
With toying oars and silken sails they glide,   2!
    Nor care for wind and tide.

"Mounted on panthers' furs and lions' manes,
From rear to van they scour about the plains;
A three days' journey in a moment done:
And always, at the rising of the sun,
About the wilds they hunt with spear and horn,
    On spleenful unicorn.

"I saw Osirian Egypt kneel adown
    Before the vine-wreath crown!
I saw parch'd Abyssinia rouse and sing
    To the silver cymbals' ring!   260
I saw the whelming vintage hotly pierce
    Old Tartary the fierce!
The kings of Inde their jewel-sceptres vail,
And from their treasures scatter pearled hail;
Great Brahma from his mystic heaven groans,
    And all his priesthood moans;
Before young Bacchus' eye-wink turning pale.—
Into these regions came I following him,
Sick hearted, weary—so I took a whim
To stray away into these forests drear   270
    Alone, without a peer:
And I have told thee all thou mayest hear.

     "Young stranger!
     I've been a ranger
In search of pleasure throughout every clime:
    Alas, 'tis not for me!
    Bewitch'd I sure must be,
To lose in grieving all my maiden prime.

     "Come then, Sorrow!
     Sweetest Sorrow!   280
Like an own babe I nurse thee on my breast:
    I thought to leave thee
    And deceive thee,
But now of all the world I love thee best.

     "There is not one,
     No, no, not one
But thee to comfort a poor lonely maid:
    Thou art her mother,
    And her brother,
Her playmate, and her wooer in the shade."   290

O what a sigh she gave in finishing,
And look, quite dead to every worldly thing!
Endymion could not speak, but gazed on her;
And listened to the wind that now did stir
About the crisped oaks full drearily,
Yet with as sweet a softness as might be
Remember'd from its velvet summer song.
At last he said: "Poor lady, how thus long

Have I been able to endure that voice?
Fair Melody! kind Syren! I've no choice;   300
I must be thy sad servant evermore:
I cannot choose but kneel here and adore.
Alas, I must not think—by Phœbe, no!
Let me not think, soft Angel! shall it be so?
Say, beautifullest, shall I never think?
O thou could'st foster me beyond the brink
Of recollection! make my watchful care
Close up its bloodshot eyes, nor see despair!
Do gently murder half my soul, and I
Shall feel the other half so utterly!—   310
I'm giddy at that cheek so fair and smooth;
O let it blush so ever! let it soothe
My madness! let it mantle rosy-warm
With the tinge of love, panting in safe alarm.—
This cannot be thy hand, and yet it is;
And this is sure thine other softling—this
Thine own fair bosom, and I am so near!
Wilt fall asleep? O let me sip that tear!
And whisper one sweet word that I may know
This is this world—sweet dewy blossom!"—*Woe!*   320
Woe! Woe to that Endymion! Where is he?—
Even these words went echoing dismally
Through the wide forest—a most fearful tone,
Like one repenting in his latest moan;
And while it died away a shade pass'd by,
As of a thunder cloud. When arrows fly
Through the thick branches, poor ring-doves sleek forth
Their timid necks and tremble; so these both
Leant to each other trembling, and sat so
Waiting for some destruction—when lo,   330
Foot-feather'd Mercury appear'd sublime
Beyond the tall tree tops; and in less time
Than shoots the slanted hail-storm, down he dropt
Towards the ground; but rested not, nor stopt
One moment from his home: only the sward
He with his wand light touch'd, and heavenward
Swifter than sight was gone—even before
The teeming earth a sudden witness bore
Of his swift magic. Diving swans appear
Above the crystal circlings white and clear;   340
And catch the cheated eye in wide surprise,
How they can dive in sight and unseen rise—
So from the turf outsprang two steeds jet-black,
Each with large dark blue wings upon his back.

The youth of Caria plac'd the lovely dame
On one, and felt himself in spleen to tame
The other's fierceness. Through the air they flew,
High as the eagles. Like two drops of dew
Exhal'd to Phœbus' lips, away they are gone,
Far from the earth away—unseen, alone,   350
Among cool clouds and winds, but that the free,
The buoyant life of song can floating be
Above their heads, and follow them untir'd.—
Muse of my native land, am I inspir'd?
This is the giddy air, and I must spread
Wide pinions to keep here; nor do I dread
Or height, or depth, or width, or any chance
Precipitous: I have beneath my glance
Those towering horses and their mournful freight.
Could I thus sail, and see, and thus await   360
Fearless for power of thought, without thine aid?—

There is a sleepy dusk, an odorous shade
From some approaching wonder, and behold
Those winged steeds, with snorting nostrils bold
Snuff at its faint extreme, and seem to tire,
Dying to embers from their native fire!

There curl'd a purple mist around them; soon,
It seem'd as when around the pale new moon
Sad Zephyr droops the clouds like weeping willow:
'Twas Sleep slow journeying with head on pillow.   370
For the first time, since he came nigh dead born
From the old womb of night, his cave forlorn
Had he left more forlorn; for the first time,
He felt aloof the day and morning's prime—
Because into his depth Cimmerian
There came a dream, showing how a young man,
Ere a lean bat could plump its wintery skin,
Would at high Jove's empyreal footstool win
An immortality, and how espouse
Jove's daughter, and be reckon'd of his house.   380
Now was he slumbering towards heaven's gate,
That he might at the threshold one hour wait
To hear the marriage melodies, and then
Sink downward to his dusky cave again.
His litter of smooth semilucent mist,
Diversely ting'd with rose and amethyst,
Puzzled those eyes that for the centre sought;
And scarcely for one moment could be caught

His sluggish form reposing motionless.
Those two on winged steeds, with all the stress   390
Of vision search'd for him, as one would look
Athwart the sallows of a river nook
To catch a glance at silver-throated eels,—
Or from old Skiddaw's top, when fog conceals
His rugged forehead in a mantle pale,
With an eye-guess towards some pleasant vale
Descry a favourite hamlet faint and far.

These raven horses, though they foster'd are
Of earth's splenetic fire, dully drop
Their full-vein'd ears, nostrils blood wide, and stop;   400
Upon the spiritless mist have they outspread
Their ample feathers, are in slumber dead,—
And on those pinions, level in mid air,
Endymion sleepeth and the lady fair.
Slowly they sail, slowly as icy isle
Upon a calm sea drifting: and meanwhile
The mournful wanderer dreams. Behold! he walks
On heaven's pavement; brotherly he talks
To divine powers: from his hand full fain
Juno's proud birds are pecking pearly grain: 410
He tries the nerve of Phœbus' golden bow,
And asketh where the golden apples grow:
Upon his arm he braces Pallas' shield,
And strives in vain to unsettle and wield
A Jovian thunderbolt: arch Hebe brings
A full-brimm'd goblet, dances lightly, sings
And tantalizes long; at last he drinks,
And lost in pleasure at her feet he sinks,
Touching with dazzled lips her starlight hand.
He blows a bugle,—an ethereal band   420
Are visible above: the Seasons four,—
Green-kyrtled Spring, flush Summer, golden store
In Autumn's sickle, Winter frosty hoar,
Join dance with shadowy Hours; while still the blast,
In swells unmitigated, still doth last
To sway their floating morris. "Whose is this?
Whose bugle?" he inquires; they smile—"O Dis!
Why is this mortal here? Dost thou not know
Its mistress' lips? Not thou?—'Tis Dian's: lo!
She rises crescented!" He looks, 'tis she,   430
His very goddess: good-bye earth, and sea,
And air, and pains, and care, and suffering;
Good-bye to all but love! Then doth he spring

Towards her, and awakes—and, strange, o'erhead,
Of those same fragrant exhalations bred,
Beheld awake his very dream: the gods
Stood smiling; merry Hebe laughs and nods;
And Phœbe bends towards him crescented.
O state perplexing! On the pinion bed,
Too well awake, he feels the panting side   440
Of his delicious lady. He who died
For soaring too audacious in the sun,
When that same treacherous wax began to run,
Felt not more tongue-tied than Endymion.
His heart leapt up as to its rightful throne,
To that fair shadow'd passion puls'd its way—
Ah, what perplexity! Ah, well a day!
So fond, so beauteous was his bed-fellow,
He could not help but kiss her: then he grew
Awhile forgetful of all beauty save   450
Young Phœbe's, golden hair'd; and so 'gan crave
Forgiveness: yet he turn'd once more to look
At the sweet sleeper,—all his soul was shook,—
She press'd his hand in slumber; so once more
He could not help but kiss her and adore.
At this the shadow wept, melting away.
The Latmian started up: "Bright goddess, stay!
Search my most hidden breast! By truth's own tongue,
I have no dædale heart: why is it wrung
To desperation? Is there nought for me,   460
Upon the bourne of bliss, but misery?"

    These words awoke the stranger of dark tresses:
Her dawning love-look rapt Endymion blesses
With 'haviour soft. Sleep yawn'd from underneath.
"Thou swan of Ganges, let us no more breathe
This murky phantasm! thou contented seem'st
Pillow'd in lovely idleness, nor dream'st
What horrors may discomfort thee and me.
Ah, shouldst thou die from my heart-treachery!—
Yet did she merely weep—her gentle soul   470
Hath no revenge in it: as it is whole
In tenderness, would I were whole in love!
Can I prize thee, fair maid, all price above,
Even when I feel as true as innocence?
I do, I do.—What is this soul then? Whence
Came it? It does not seem my own, and I
Have no self-passion or identity.
Some fearful end must be: where, where is it?
By Nemesis, I see my spirit flit

Alone about the dark—Forgive me, sweet: 480
Shall we away?" He rous'd the steeds: they beat
Their wings chivalrous into the clear air,
Leaving old Sleep within his vapoury lair.

The good-night blush of eve was waning slow,
And Vesper, risen star, began to throe
In the dusk heavens silverly, when they
Thus sprang direct towards the Galaxy.
Nor did speed hinder converse soft and strange—
Eternal oaths and vows they interchange,
In such wise, in such temper, so aloof   490
Up in the winds, beneath a starry roof,
So witless of their doom, that verily
'Tis well nigh past man's search their hearts to see;
Whether they wept, or laugh'd, or griev'd, or toy'd—
Most like with joy gone mad, with sorrow cloy'd.

Full facing their swift flight, from ebon streak,
The moon put forth a little diamond peak,
No bigger than an unobserved star,
Or tiny point of fairy scymetar;
Bright signal that she only stoop'd to tie   500
Her silver sandals, ere deliciously
She bow'd into the heavens her timid head.
Slowly she rose, as though she would have fled,
While to his lady meek the Carian turn'd,
To mark if her dark eyes had yet discern'd
This beauty in its birth—Despair! despair!
He saw her body fading gaunt and spare
In the cold moonshine. Straight he seiz'd her wrist;
It melted from his grasp: her hand he kiss'd,
And, horror! kiss'd his own—he was alone.   510
Her steed a little higher soar'd, and then
Dropt hawkwise to the earth.

                      There lies a den,
Beyond the seeming confines of the space
Made for the soul to wander in and trace
Its own existence, of remotest glooms.
Dark regions are around it, where the tombs
Of buried griefs the spirit sees, but scarce
One hour doth linger weeping, for the pierce
Of new-born woe it feels more inly smart:
And in these regions many a venom'd dart   520
At random flies; they are the proper home
Of every ill: the man is yet to come

Who hath not journeyed in this native hell.
But few have ever felt how calm and well
Sleep may be had in that deep den of all.
There anguish does not sting; nor pleasure pall:
Woe-hurricanes beat ever at the gate,
Yet all is still within and desolate.
Beset with plainful gusts, within ye hear
No sound so loud as when on curtain'd bier   530
The death-watch tick is stifled. Enter none
Who strive therefore on the sudden it is won.
Just when the sufferer begins to burn,
Then it is free to him; and from an urn,
Still fed by melting ice, he takes a draught—
Young Semele such richness never quaft
In her maternal longing! Happy gloom!
Dark Paradise! where pale becomes the bloom
Of health by due; where silence dreariest
Is most articulate; where hopes infest;   540
Where those eyes are the brightest far that keep
Their lids shut longest in a dreamless sleep.
O happy spirit-home! O wondrous soul!
Pregnant with such a den to save the whole
In thine own depth. Hail, gentle Carian!
For, never since thy griefs and woes began,
Hast thou felt so content: a grievous feud
Hath led thee to this Cave of Quietude.
Aye, his lull'd soul was there, although upborne
With dangerous speed: and so he did not mourn
Because he knew not whither he was going.   551
So happy was he, not the aerial blowing
Of trumpets at clear parley from the east
Could rouse from that fine relish, that high feast.
They stung the feather'd horse: with fierce alarm
He flapp'd towards the sound. Alas, no charm
Could lift Endymion's head, or he had view'd
A skyey mask, a pinion'd multitude,—
And silvery was its passing: voices sweet
Warbling the while as if to lull and greet   560
The wanderer in his path. Thus warbled they,
While past the vision went in bright array.

    "Who, who from Dian's feast would be away?
For all the golden bowers of the day
Are empty left? Who, who away would be
From Cynthia's wedding and festivity?
Not Hesperus: lo! upon his silver wings
He leans away for highest heaven and sings,

Snapping his lucid fingers merrily!—
Ah, Zephyrus! art here, and Flora too!   570
Ye tender bibbers of the rain and dew,
Young playmates of the rose and daffodil,
Be careful, ere ye enter in, to fill
          Your baskets high
With fennel green, and balm, and golden pines,
Savory, latter-mint, and columbines,
Cool parsley, basil sweet, and sunny thyme;
Yea, every flower and leaf of every clime,
All gather'd in the dewy morning: hie
          Away! fly, fly!—   580
Crystalline brother of the belt of heaven,
Aquarius! to whom king Jove has given
Two liquid pulse streams 'stead of feather'd wings,
Two fan-like fountains,—thine illuminings
          For Dian play:
Dissolve the frozen purity of air;
Let thy white shoulders silvery and bare
Show cold through watery pinions; make more bright
The Star-Queen's crescent on her marriage night:
          Haste, haste away!—   590
Castor has tamed the planet Lion, see!
And of the Bear has Pollux mastery:
A third is in the race! who is the third
Speeding away swift as the eagle bird?
          The ramping Centaur!
The Lion's mane's on end: the Bear how fierce!
The Centaur's arrow ready seems to pierce
Some enemy: far forth his bow is bent
Into the blue of heaven. He'll be shent,
          Pale unrelentor,   600
When he shall hear the wedding lutes a playing.—
Andromeda! sweet woman! why delaying
So timidly among the stars: come hither!
Join this bright throng, and nimbly follow whither
          They all are going.
Danae's Son, before Jove newly bow'd,
Has wept for thee, calling to Jove aloud.
Thee, gentle lady, did he disenthral:
Ye shall for ever live and love, for all
          Thy tears are flowing.—   61
By Daphne's fright, behold Apollo!—"
                                        More
Endymion heard not: down his steed him bore,
Prone to the green head of a misty hill.

His first touch of the earth went nigh to kill.
"Alas!" said he, "were I but always borne
Through dangerous winds, had but my footsteps worn
A path in hell, for ever would I bless
Horrors which nourish an uneasiness
For my own sullen conquering: to him
Who lives beyond earth's boundary, grief is dim,
Sorrow is but a shadow: now I see   621
The grass; I feel the solid ground—Ah, me!
It is thy voice—divinest! Where?—who? who
Left thee so quiet on this bed of dew?
Behold upon this happy earth we are;
Let us aye love each other; let us fare
On forest-fruits, and never, never go
Among the abodes of mortals here below,
Or be by phantoms duped. O destiny!
Into a labyrinth now my soul would fly,   630
But with thy beauty will I deaden it.
Where didst thou melt to? By thee will I sit
For ever: let our fate stop here—a kid
I on this spot will offer: Pan will bid
Us live in peace, in love and peace among
His forest wildernesses. I have clung
To nothing, lov'd a nothing, nothing seen
Or felt but a great dream! O I have been
Presumptuous against love, against the sky,
Against all elements, against the tie   640
Of mortals each to each, against the blooms
Of flowers, rush of rivers, and the tombs
Of heroes gone! Against his proper glory
Has my own soul conspired: so my story
Will I to children utter, and repent.
There never liv'd a mortal man, who bent
His appetite beyond his natural sphere,
But starv'd and died. My sweetest Indian, here,
Here will I kneel, for thou redeemed hast
My life from too thin breathing: gone and past   650
Are cloudy phantasms. Caverns lone, farewell!
And air of visions, and the monstrous swell
Of visionary seas! No, never more
Shall airy voices cheat me to the shore
Of tangled wonder, breathless and aghast.
Adieu, my daintiest Dream! although so vast
My love is still for thee. The hour may come
When we shall meet in pure elysium.
On earth I may not love thee; and therefore
Doves will I offer up, and sweetest store   660

All through the teeming year: so thou wilt shine
On me, and on this damsel fair of mine,
And bless our silver lives. My Indian bliss!
My river-lilly bud! one human kiss!
One sign of real breath—one gentle squeeze,
Warm as a dove's nest among summer trees,
And warm with dew at ooze from living blood!
Whither didst melt? Ah, what of that!—all good
We'll talk about—no more of dreaming.—Now,
Where shall our dwelling be? Under the brow   670
Of some steep mossy hill, where ivy dun
Would hide us up, although spring leaves were none;
And where dark yew trees, as we rustle through,
Will drop their scarlet berry cups of dew?
O thou wouldst joy to live in such a place;
Dusk for our loves, yet light enough to grace
Those gentle limbs on mossy bed reclin'd:
For by one step the blue sky shouldst thou find,
And by another, in deep dell below,
See, through the trees, a little river go   680
All in its mid-day gold and glimmering.
Honey from out the gnarled hive I'll bring,
And apples, wan with sweetness, gather thee,—
Cresses that grow where no man may them see,
And sorrel untorn by the dew-claw'd stag:
Pipes will I fashion of the syrinx flag,
That thou mayst always know whither I roam,
When it shall please thee in our quiet home
To listen and think of love. Still let me speak;
Still let me dive into the joy I seek,—   690
For yet the past doth prison me. The rill,
Thou haply mayst delight in, will I fill
With fairy fishes from the mountain tarn,
And thou shalt feed them from the squirrel's barn.
Its bottom will I strew with amber shells,
And pebbles blue from deep enchanted wells.
Its sides I'll plant with dew-sweet eglantine,
And honeysuckles full of clear bee-wine.
I will entice this crystal rill to trace
Love's silver name upon the meadow's face.   700
I'll kneel to Vesta, for a flame of fire;
And to god Phœbus, for a golden lyre;
To Empress Dian, for a hunting spear;
To Vesper, for a taper silver-clear,
That I may see thy beauty through the night;
To Flora, and a nightingale shall light

Tame on thy finger; to the River-gods,
And they shall bring thee taper fishing-rods
Of gold, and lines of Naiads' long bright tress.
Heaven shield thee for thine utter loveliness!   710
Thy mossy footstool shall the altar be
'Fore which I'll bend, bending, dear love, to thee:
Those lips shall be my Delphos, and shall speak
Laws to my footsteps, colour to my cheek,
Trembling or stedfastness to this same voice,
And of three sweetest pleasurings the choice:
And that affectionate light, those diamond things,
Those eyes, those passions, those supreme pearl springs,
Shall be my grief, or twinkle me to pleasure.
Say, is not bliss within our perfect seisure?   720
O that I could not doubt!"
                                  The mountaineer
Thus strove by fancies vain and crude to clear
His briar'd path to some tranquillity.
It gave bright gladness to his lady's eye,
And yet the tears she wept were tears of sorrow;
Answering thus, just as the golden morrow
Beam'd upward from the vallies of the east:
"O that the flutter of this heart had ceas'd,
Or the sweet name of love had pass'd away.
Young feather'd tyrant! by a swift decay   730
Wilt thou devote this body to the earth:
And I do think that at my very birth
I lisp'd thy blooming titles inwardly;
For at the first, first dawn and thought of thee,
With uplift hands I blest the stars of heaven.
Art thou not cruel? Ever have I striven
To think thee kind, but ah, it will not do!
When yet a child, I heard that kisses drew
Favour from thee, and so I kisses gave
To the void air, bidding them find out love: 740
But when I came to feel how far above
All fancy, pride, and fickle maidenhood,
All earthly pleasure, all imagin'd good,
Was the warm tremble of a devout kiss,—
Even then, that moment, at the thought of this,
Fainting I fell into a bed of flowers,
And languish'd there three days. Ye milder powers,
Am I not cruelly wrong'd? Believe, believe
Me, dear Endymion, were I to weave
With my own fancies garlands of sweet life,   750
Thou shouldst be one of all. Ah, bitter strife!

I may not be thy love: I am forbidden—
Indeed I am—thwarted, affrighted, chidden,
By things I trembled at, and gorgon wrath.
Twice hast thou ask'd whither I went: henceforth
Ask me no more! I may not utter it,
Nor may I be thy love. We might commit
Ourselves at once to vengeance; we might die;
We might embrace and die: voluptuous thought!
Enlarge not to my hunger, or I'm caught   760
In trammels of perverse deliciousness.
No, no, that shall not be: thee will I bless,
And bid a long adieu."

                    The Carian
No word return'd: both lovelorn, silent, wan,
Into the vallies green together went.
Far wandering, they were perforce content
To sit beneath a fair lone beechen tree;
Nor at each other gaz'd, but heavily
Por'd on its hazle cirque of shedded leaves.

     Endymion! unhappy! it nigh grieves   770
Me to behold thee thus in last extreme:
Ensky'd ere this, but truly that I deem
Truth the best music in a first-born song.
Thy lute-voic'd brother will I sing ere long,
And thou shalt aid—hast thou not aided me?
Yes, moonlight Emperor! felicity
Has been thy meed for many thousand years;
Yet often have I, on the brink of tears,
Mourn'd as if yet thou wert a forester;—
Forgetting the old tale.

                    He did not stir   780
His eyes from the dead leaves, or one small pulse
Of joy he might have felt. The spirit culls
Unfaded amaranth, when wild it strays
Through the old garden-ground of boyish days.
A little onward ran the very stream
By which he took his first soft poppy dream;
And on the very bark 'gainst which he leant
A crescent he had carv'd, and round it spent
His skill in little stars. The teeming tree
Had swollen and green'd the pious charactery,   790
But not ta'en out. Why, there was not a slope
Up which he had not fear'd the antelope;
And not a tree, beneath whose rooty shade
He had not with his tamed leopards play'd:

Nor could an arrow light, or javelin,
Fly in the air where his had never been—
And yet he knew it not.

                 O treachery!
Why does his lady smile, pleasing her eye
With all his sorrowing? He sees her not.
But who so stares on him? His sister sure!
Peona of the woods!—Can she endure—
Impossible—how dearly they embrace!
His lady smiles; delight is in her face;
It is no treachery.

                 "Dear brother mine!
Endymion, weep not so! Why shouldst thou pine
When all great Latmos so exalt will be?
Thank the great gods, and look not bitterly;
And speak not one pale word, and sigh no more.
Sure I will not believe thou hast such store
Of grief, to last thee to my kiss again.
Thou surely canst not bear a mind in pain,
Come hand in hand with one so beautiful.
Be happy both of you! for I will pull
The flowers of autumn for your coronals.
Pan's holy priest for young Endymion calls;
And when he is restor'd, thou, fairest dame,
Shalt be our queen. Now, is it not a shame
To see ye thus,—not very, very sad?
Perhaps ye are too happy to be glad:
O feel as if it were a common day;
Free-voic'd as one who never was away.
No tongue shall ask, whence come ye? but ye shall
Be gods of your own rest imperial.
Not even I, for one whole month, will pry
Into the hours that have pass'd us by,
Since in my arbour I did sing to thee.
O Hermes! on this very night will be
A hymning up to Cynthia, queen of light;
For the soothsayers old saw yesternight
Good visions in the air,—whence will befal,
As say these sages, health perpetual
To shepherds and their flocks; and furthermore,
In Dian's face they read the gentle lore:
Therefore for her these vesper-carols are.
Our friends will all be there from nigh and far.
Many upon thy death have ditties made;
And many, even now, their foreheads shade
With cypress, on a day of sacrifice.
New singing for our maids shalt thou devise,

     800

     810

     820

     830

And pluck the sorrow from our huntsmen's brows.   840
Tell me, my lady-queen, how to espouse
This wayward brother to his rightful joys!
His eyes are on thee bent, as thou didst poize
His fate most goddess-like. Help me, I pray,
To lure—Endymion, dear brother, say
What ails thee?" He could bear no more, and so
Bent his soul fiercely like a spiritual bow,
And twang'd it inwardly, and calmly said:
"I would have thee my only friend, sweet maid!
My only visitor! not ignorant though,   850
That those deceptions which for pleasure go
'Mong men, are pleasures real as real may be:
But there are higher ones I may not see,
If impiously an earthly realm I take.
Since I saw thee, I have been wide awake
Night after night, and day by day, until
Of the empyrean I have drunk my fill.
Let it content thee, Sister, seeing me
More happy than betides mortality.
A hermit young, I'll live in mossy cave,   860
Where thou alone shalt come to me, and lave
Thy spirit in the wonders I shall tell.
Through me the shepherd realm shall prosper well;
For to thy tongue will I all health confide.
And, for my sake, let this young maid abide
With thee as a dear sister. Thou alone,
Peona, mayst return to me. I own
This may sound strangely: but when, dearest girl,
Thou seest it for my happiness, no pearl
Will trespass down those cheeks. Companion fair!   870
Wilt be content to dwell with her, to share
This sister's love with me?" Like one resign'd
And bent by circumstance, and thereby blind
In self-commitment, thus that meek unknown:
"Aye, but a buzzing by my ears has flown,
Of jubilee to Dian:—truth I heard?
Well then, I see there is no little bird,
Tender soever, but is Jove's own care.
Long have I sought for rest, and, unaware,
Behold I find it! so exalted too!   880
So after my own heart! I knew, I knew
There was a place untenanted in it:
In that same void white Chastity shall sit,
And monitor me nightly to lone slumber.
With sanest lips I vow me to the number

Of Dian's sisterhood; and, kind lady,
With thy good help, this very night shall see
My future days to her fane consecrate."

As feels a dreamer what doth most create
His own particular fright, so these three felt: 890
Or like one who, in after ages, knelt
To Lucifer or Baal, when he'd pine
After a little sleep: or when in mine
Far under-ground, a sleeper meets his friends
Who know him not. Each diligently bends
Towards common thoughts and things for very fear;
Striving their ghastly malady to cheer,
By thinking it a thing of yes and no,
That housewives talk of. But the spirit-blow
Was struck, and all were dreamers. At the last   900
Endymion said: "Are not our fates all cast?
Why stand we here? Adieu, ye tender pair!
Adieu!" Whereat those maidens, with wild stare,
Walk'd dizzily away. Pained and hot
His eyes went after them, until they got
Near to a cypress grove, whose deadly maw,
In one swift moment, would what then he saw
Engulph for ever. "Stay!" he cried, "ah, stay!
Turn, damsels! hist! one word I have to say.
Sweet Indian, I would see thee once again.   910
It is a thing I dote on: so I'd fain,
Peona, ye should hand in hand repair
Into those holy groves, that silent are
Behind great Dian's temple. I'll be yon,
At vesper's earliest twinkle—they are gone—
But once, once, once again—" At this he press'd
His hands against his face, and then did rest
His head upon a mossy hillock green,
And so remain'd as he a corpse had been
All the long day; save when he scantly lifted   920
His eyes abroad, to see how shadows shifted
With the slow move of time,—sluggish and weary
Until the poplar tops, in journey dreary,
Had reach'd the river's brim. Then up he rose,
And, slowly as that very river flows,
Walk'd towards the temple grove with this lament:
"Why such a golden eve? The breeze is sent
Careful and soft, that not a leaf may fall
Before the serene father of them all
Bows down his summer head below the west.   930
Now am I of breath, speech, and speed possest,

But at the setting I must bid adieu
To her for the last time. Night will strew
On the damp grass myriads of lingering leaves,
And with them shall I die; nor much it grieves
To die, when summer dies on the cold sward.
Why, I have been a butterfly, a lord
Of flowers, garlands, love-knots, silly posies,
Groves, meadows, melodies, and arbour roses;
My kingdom's at its death, and just it is   940
That I should die with it: so in all this
We miscall grief, bale, sorrow, heartbreak, woe.
What is there to plain of? By Titan's foe
I am but rightly serv'd." So saying, he
Tripp'd lightly on, in sort of deathful glee;
Laughing at the clear stream and setting sun,
As though they jests had been: nor had he done
His laugh at nature's holy countenance,
Until that grove appear'd, as if perchance,
And then his tongue with sober seemlihed   950
Gave utterance as he enter'd: "Ha! I said,
King of the butterflies; but by this gloom,
And by old Rhadamanthus' tongue of doom,
This dusk religion, pomp of solitude,
And the Promethean clay by thief endued,
By old Saturnus' forelock, by his head
Shook with eternal palsy, I did wed
Myself to things of light from infancy;
And thus to be cast out, thus lorn to die,
Is sure enough to make a mortal man   960
Grow impious." So he inwardly began
On things for which no wording can be found;
Deeper and deeper sinking, until drown'd
Beyond the reach of music: for the choir
Of Cynthia he heard not, though rough briar
Nor muffling thicket interpos'd to dull
The vesper hymn, far swollen, soft and full,
Through the dark pillars of those sylvan aisles.
He saw not the two maidens, nor their smiles,
Wan as primroses gather'd at midnight   970
By chilly finger'd spring. "Unhappy wight!
Endymion!" said Peona, "we are here!
What wouldst thou ere we all are laid on bier?"
Then he embrac'd her, and his lady's hand
Press'd, saying: "Sister, I would have command,
If it were heaven's will, on our sad fate."
At which that dark-eyed stranger stood elate

And said, in a new voice, but sweet as love,
To Endymion's amaze: "By Cupid's dove,
And so thou shalt! and by the lilly truth   980
Of my own breast thou shalt, beloved youth!"
And as she spake, into her face there came
Light, as reflected from a silver flame:
Her long black hair swell'd ampler, in display
Full golden; in her eyes a brighter day
Dawn'd blue and full of love. Aye, he beheld
Phœbe, his passion! joyous she upheld
Her lucid bow, continuing thus: "Drear, drear
Has our delaying been; but foolish fear
Withheld me first; and then decrees of fate;   990
And then 'twas fit that from this mortal state
Thou shouldst, my love, by some unlook'd for change
Be spiritualiz'd. Peona, we shall range
These forests, and to thee they safe shall be
As was thy cradle; hither shalt thou flee
To meet us many a time." Next Cynthia bright
Peona kiss'd, and bless'd with fair good night:
Her brother kiss'd her too, and knelt adown
Before his goddess, in a blissful swoon.
She gave her fair hands to him, and behold,   1000
Before three swiftest kisses he had told,
They vanish'd far away!—Peona went
Home through the gloomy wood in wonderment.

                    THE END

LAMIA,

ISABELLA,

THE EVE OF ST. AGNES,

AND

OTHER POEMS.

1820.

ADVERTISEMENT

IF any apology be thought necessary for the appearance of the unfinished poem of HYPERION, the publishers beg to state that they alone are responsible, as it was printed at their particular request, and contrary to the wish of the author. The poem was intended to have been of equal length with ENDYMION, but the reception given to that work discouraged the author from proceeding.

FLEET STREET, *June* 26, 1820.

LAMIA

PART I

Upon a time, before the faery broods
Drove Nymph and Satyr from the prosperous woods,
Before king Oberon's bright diadem,
Sceptre, and mantle, clasp'd with dewy gem,
Frighted away the Dryads and the Fauns
From rushes green, and brakes, and cowslip'd lawns,
The ever-smitten Hermes empty left
His golden throne, bent warm on amorous theft:
From high Olympus had he stolen light,
On this side of Jove's clouds, to escape the sight   10
Of his great summoner, and made retreat
Into a forest on the shores of Crete.
For somewhere in that sacred island dwelt
A nymph, to whom all hoofed Satyrs knelt;
At whose white feet the languid Tritons poured
Pearls, while on land they wither'd and adored.
Fast by the springs where she to bathe was wont,
And in those meads where sometime she might haunt,
Were strewn rich gifts, unknown to any Muse,
Though Fancy's casket were unlock'd to choose.   20
Ah, what a world of love was at her feet!
So Hermes thought, and a celestial heat
Burnt from his winged heels to either ear,
That from a whiteness, as the lilly clear,
Blush'd into roses 'mid his golden hair,
Fallen in jealous curls about his shoulders bare.

From vale to vale, from wood to wood, he flew,
Breathing upon the flowers his passion new,
And wound with many a river to its head,   29
To find where this sweet nymph prepar'd her secret bed:
In vain; the sweet nymph might nowhere be found,
And so he rested, on the lonely ground,
Pensive, and full of painful jealousies
Of the Wood-Gods, and even the very trees.
There as he stood, he heard a mournful voice,
Such as once heard, in gentle heart, destroys
All pain but pity: thus the lone voice spake:
"When from this wreathed tomb shall I awake!

"When move in a sweet body fit for life,
"And love, and pleasure, and the ruddy strife   40
"Of hearts and lips! Ah, miserable me!"
The God, dove-footed, glided silently
Round bush and tree, soft-brushing, in his speed,
The taller grasses and full-flowering weed,
Until he found a palpitating snake,
Bright, and cirque-couchant in a dusky brake.

     She was a gordian shape of dazzling hue,
Vermilion-spotted, golden, green, and blue;
Striped like a zebra, freckled like a pard,
Eyed like a peacock, and all crimson barr'd;   50
And full of silver moons, that, as she breathed,
Dissolv'd, or brighter shone, or interwreathed
Their lustres with the gloomier tapestries—
So rainbow-sided, touch'd with miseries,
She seem'd, at once, some penanced lady elf,
Some demon's mistress, or the demon's self.
Upon her crest she wore a wannish fire
Sprinkled with stars, like Ariadne's tiar:
Her head was serpent, but ah, bitter-sweet!   59
She had a woman's mouth with all its pearls complete:
And for her eyes: what could such eyes do there
But weep, and weep, that they were born so fair?
As Proserpine still weeps for her Sicilian air.
Her throat was serpent, but the words she spake
Came, as through bubbling honey, for Love's sake,
And thus; while Hermes on his pinions lay,
Like a stoop'd falcon ere he takes his prey.

     "Fair Hermes, crown'd with feathers, fluttering light,
"I had a splendid dream of thee last night:
"I saw thee sitting, on a throne of gold,   70
"Among the Gods, upon Olympus old,
"The only sad one; for thou didst not hear
"The soft, lute-finger'd Muses chaunting clear,
"Nor even Apollo when he sang alone,
"Deaf to his throbbing throat's long, long melodious moan.
"I dreamt I saw thee, robed in purple flakes,
"Break amorous through the clouds, as morning breaks,
"And, swiftly as a bright Phœbean dart,
"Strike for the Cretan isle; and here thou art!
"Too gentle Hermes, hast thou found the maid?"
Whereat the star of Lethe not delay'd   81
His rosy eloquence, and thus inquired:

"Thou smooth-lipp'd serpent, surely high inspired!
"Thou beauteous wreath, with melancholy eyes,
"Possess whatever bliss thou canst devise,
"Telling me only where my nymph is fled,—
"Where she doth breathe!" "Bright planet, thou hast said,"
Return'd the snake, "but seal with oaths, fair God!"
"I swear," said Hermes, "by my serpent rod,
"And by thine eyes, and by thy starry crown!"   90
Light flew his earnest words, among the blossoms blown.
Then thus again the brilliance feminine:
"Too frail of heart! for this lost nymph of thine,
"Free as the air, invisibly, she strays
"About these thornless wilds; her pleasant days
"She tastes unseen; unseen her nimble feet
"Leave traces in the grass and flowers sweet;
"From weary tendrils, and bow'd branches green,
"She plucks the fruit unseen, she bathes unseen:
"And by my power is her beauty veil'd   100
"To keep it unaffronted, unassail'd
"By the love-glances of unlovely eyes,
"Of Satyrs, Fauns, and blear'd Silenus' sighs.
"Pale grew her immortality, for woe
"Of all these lovers, and she grieved so
"I took compassion on her, bade her steep
"Her hair in weïrd syrops, that would keep
"Her loveliness invisible, yet free
"To wander as she loves, in liberty.
"Thou shalt behold her, Hermes, thou alone,   110
"If thou wilt, as thou swearest, grant my boon!"
Then, once again, the charmed God began
An oath, and through the serpent's ears it ran
Warm, tremulous, devout, psalterian.
Ravish'd, she lifted her Circean head,
Blush'd a live damask, and swift-lisping said,
"I was a woman, let me have once more
"A woman's shape, and charming as before.
"I love a youth of Corinth—O the bliss!
"Give me my woman's form, and place me where he is.
"Stoop, Hermes, let me breathe upon thy brow,   121
"And thou shalt see thy sweet nymph even now."
The God on half-shut feathers sank serene,
She breath'd upon his eyes, and swift was seen
Of both the guarded nymph near-smiling on the green.
It was no dream; or say a dream it was,
Real are the dreams of Gods, and smoothly pass

Their pleasures in a long immortal dream.
One warm, flush'd moment, hovering, it might seem
Dash'd by the wood-nymph's beauty, so he burn'd;   130
Then, lighting on the printless verdure, turn'd
To the swoon'd serpent, and with languid arm,
Delicate, put to proof the lythe Caducean charm.
So done, upon the nymph his eyes he bent
Full of adoring tears and blandishment,
And towards her stept: she, like a moon in wane,
Faded before him, cower'd, nor could restrain
Her fearful sobs, self-folding like a flower
That faints into itself at evening hour:
But the God fostering her chilled hand,   140
She felt the warmth, her eyelids open'd bland,
And, like new flowers at morning song of bees,
Bloom'd, and gave up her honey to the lees.
Into the green-recessed woods they flew;
Nor grew they pale, as mortal lovers do.

    Left to herself, the serpent now began
To change; her elfin blood in madness ran,
Her mouth foam'd and the grass, therewith besprent,
Wither'd at dew so sweet and virulent;
Her eyes in torture fix'd, and anguish drear,   150
Hot, glaz'd, and wide, with lid-lashes all sear,
Flash'd phosphor and sharp sparks, without one cooling tear.
The colours all inflam'd throughout her train,
She writh'd about, convulsed with scarlet pain:
A deep volcanian yellow took the place
Of all her milder-mooned body's grace;
And, as the lava ravishes the mead,
Spoilt all her silver mail, and golden brede;
Made gloom of all her frecklings, streaks and bars,
Eclips'd her crescents, and lick'd up her stars: 160
So that, in moments few, she was undrest
Of all her sapphires, greens, and amethyst,
And rubious-argent: of all these bereft,
Nothing but pain and ugliness were left.
Still shone her crown; that vanish'd, also she
Melted and disappear'd as suddenly;
And in the air, her new voice luting soft,
Cried, "Lycius! gentle Lycius!"—Borne aloft
With the bright mists about the mountains hoar
These words dissolv'd: Crete's forests heard no more.

    Whither fled Lamia, now a lady bright,   171
A full-born beauty new and exquisite?

She fled into that valley they pass o'er
Who go to Corinth from Cenchreas' shore;
And rested at the foot of those wild hills,
The rugged founts of the Peræan rills,
And of that other ridge whose barren back
Stretches, with all its mist and cloudy rack,
South-westward to Cleone. There she stood
About a young bird's flutter from a wood,   180
Fair, on a sloping green of mossy tread,
By a clear pool, wherein she passioned
To see herself escap'd from so sore ills,
While her robes flaunted with the daffodils.

Ah, happy Lycius!—for she was a maid
More beautiful than ever twisted braid,
Or sigh'd, or blush'd, or on spring-flowered lea
Spread a green kirtle to the minstrelsy:
A virgin purest lipp'd, yet in the lore
Of love deep learned to the red heart's core: 190
Not one hour old, yet of sciential brain
To unperplex bliss from its neighbour pain;
Define their pettish limits, and estrange
Their points of contact, and swift counterchange;
Intrigue with the specious chaos, and dispart
Its most ambiguous atoms with sure art;
As though in Cupid's college she had spent
Sweet days a lovely graduate, still unshent,
And kept his rosy terms in idle languishment.

Why this fair creature chose so faerily   200
By the wayside to linger, we shall see;
But first 'tis fit to tell how she could muse
And dream, when in the serpent prison-house,
Of all she list, strange or magnificent:
How, ever, where she will'd, her spirit went;
Whether to faint Elysium, or where
Down through tress-lifting waves the Nereids fair
Wind into Thetis' bower by many a pearly stair;
Or where God Bacchus drains his cups divine,
Stretch'd out, at ease, beneath a glutinous pine;   210
Or where in Pluto's gardens palatine
Mulciber's columns gleam in far piazzian line.
And sometimes into cities she would send
Her dream, with feast and rioting to blend;
And once, while among mortals dreaming thus,
She saw the young Corinthian Lycius
Charioting foremost in the envious race,

Like a young Jove with calm uneager face,
And fell into a swooning love of him.
Now on the moth-time of that evening dim   220
He would return that way, as well she knew,
To Corinth from the shore; for freshly blew
The eastern soft wind, and his galley now
Grated the quaystones with her brazen prow
In port Cenchreas, from Egina isle
Fresh anchor'd; whither he had been awhile
To sacrifice to Jove, whose temple there
Waits with high marble doors for blood and incense rare.
Jove heard his vows, and better'd his desire;
For by some freakful chance he made retire   230
From his companions, and set forth to walk,
Perhaps grown wearied of their Corinth talk:
Over the solitary hills he fared,
Thoughtless at first, but ere eve's star appeared
His phantasy was lost, where reason fades,
In the calm'd twilight of Platonic shades.
Lamia beheld him coming, near, more near—
Close to her passing, in indifference drear,
His silent sandals swept the mossy green;
So neighbour'd to him, and yet so unseen   240
She stood: he pass'd, shut up in mysteries,
His mind wrapp'd like his mantle, while her eyes
Follow'd his steps, and her neck regal white
Turn'd—syllabling thus, "Ah, Lycius bright,
"And will you leave me on the hills alone?
"Lycius, look back! and be some pity shown."
He did; not with cold wonder fearingly,
But Orpheus-like at an Eurydice;
For so delicious were the words she sung,
It seem'd he had lov'd them a whole summer long: 250
And soon his eyes had drunk her beauty up,
Leaving no drop in the bewildering cup,
And still the cup was full,—while he, afraid
Lest she should vanish ere his lip had paid
Due adoration, thus began to adore;
Her soft look growing coy, she saw his chain so sure:
"Leave thee alone! Look back! Ah, Goddess, see
"Whether my eyes can ever turn from thee!
"For pity do not this sad heart belie—
"Even as thou vanishest so shall I die.   260
"Stay! though a Naiad of the rivers, stay!
"To thy far wishes will thy streams obey:
"Stay! though the greenest woods be thy domain,
"Alone they can drink up the morning rain:

"Though a descended Pleiad, will not one
"Of thine harmonious sisters keep in tune
"Thy spheres, and as thy silver proxy shine?
"So sweetly to these ravish'd ears of mine
"Came thy sweet greeting, that if thou shouldst fade
"Thy memory will waste me to a shade:—   270
"For pity do not melt!"—"If I should stay,"
Said Lamia, "here, upon this floor of clay,
"And pain my steps upon these flowers too rough,
"What canst thou say or do of charm enough
"To dull the nice remembrance of my home?
"Thou canst not ask me with thee here to roam
"Over these hills and vales, where no joy is,—
"Empty of immortality and bliss!
"Thou art a scholar, Lycius, and must know
"That finer spirits cannot breathe below   280
"In human climes, and live: Alas! poor youth,
"What taste of purer air hast thou to soothe
"My essence? What serener palaces,
"Where I may all my many senses please,
"And by mysterious sleights a hundred thirsts appease?
"It cannot be—Adieu!" So said, she rose
Tiptoe with white arms spread. He, sick to lose
The amorous promise of her lone complain,
Swoon'd, murmuring of love, and pale with pain.
The cruel lady, without any show   290
Of sorrow for her tender favourite's woe,
But rather, if her eyes could brighter be,
With brighter eyes and slow amenity,
Put her new lips to his, and gave afresh
The life she had so tangled in her mesh:
And as he from one trance was wakening
Into another, she began to sing,
Happy in beauty, life, and love, and every thing,
A song of love, too sweet for earthly lyres,
While, like held breath, the stars drew in their panting fires.
And then she whisper'd in such trembling tone,   301
As those who, safe together met alone
For the first time through many anguish'd days,
Use other speech than looks; bidding him raise
His drooping head, and clear his soul of doubt,
For that she was a woman, and without
Any more subtle fluid in her veins
Than throbbing blood, and that the self-same pains
Inhabited her frail-strung heart as his.
And next she wonder'd how his eyes could miss   310

Her face so long in Corinth, where, she said,
She dwelt but half retir'd, and there had led
Days happy as the gold coin could invent
Without the aid of love; yet in content
Till she saw him, as once she pass'd him by,
Where 'gainst a column he lent thoughtfully
At Venus' temple porch, 'mid baskets heap'd
Of amorous herbs and flowers, newly reap'd
Late on that eve, as 'twas the night before
The Adonian feast; whereof she saw no more,   320
But wept alone those days, for why should she adore?
Lycius from death awoke into amaze,
To see her still, and singing so sweet lays;
Then from amaze into delight he fell
To hear her whisper woman's lore so well;
And every word she spake entic'd him on
To unperplex'd delight and pleasure known.
Let the mad poets say whate'er they please
Of the sweets of Faeries, Peris, Goddesses,
There is not such a treat among them all,   330
Haunters of cavern, lake, and waterfall,
As a real woman, lineal indeed
From Pyrrha's pebbles or old Adam's seed.
Thus gentle Lamia judg'd, and judg'd aright,
That Lycius could not love in half a fright,
So threw the goddess off, and won his heart
More pleasantly by playing woman's part,
With no more awe than what her beauty gave,
That, while it smote, still guaranteed to save.
Lycius to all made eloquent reply,   340
Marrying to every word a twinborn sigh;
And last, pointing to Corinth, ask'd her sweet,
If 'twas too far that night for her soft feet.
The way was short, for Lamia's eagerness
Made, by a spell, the triple league decrease
To a few paces; not at all surmised
By blinded Lycius, so in her comprized.
They pass'd the city gates, he knew not how,
So noiseless, and he never thought to know.

As men talk in a dream, so Corinth all,   350
Throughout her palaces imperial,
And all her populous streets and temples lewd,
Mutter'd, like tempest in the distance brew'd,
To the wide-spreaded night above her towers.
Men, women, rich and poor, in the cool hours,

Shuffled their sandals o'er the pavement white,
Companion'd or alone; while many a light
Flared, here and there, from wealthy festivals,
And threw their moving shadows on the walls,
Or found them cluster'd in the corniced shade   360
Of some arch'd temple door, or dusky colonnade.

Muffling his face, of greeting friends in fear,
Her fingers he press'd hard, as one came near
With curl'd gray beard, sharp eyes, and smooth bald crown,
Slow-stepp'd, and robed in philosophic gown:
Lycius shrank closer, as they met and past,
Into his mantle, adding wings to haste,
While hurried Lamia trembled: "Ah," said he,
"Why do you shudder, love, so ruefully?
"Why does your tender palm dissolve in dew?"—
"I'm wearied," said fair Lamia: "tell me who   371
"Is that old man? I cannot bring to mind
"His features:—Lycius! wherefore did you blind
"Yourself from his quick eyes?" Lycius replied,
" 'Tis Apollonius sage, my trusty guide
"And good instructor; but to-night he seems
"The ghost of folly haunting my sweet dreams."

While yet he spake they had arrived before
A pillar'd porch, with lofty portal door,
Where hung a silver lamp, whose phosphor glow
Reflected in the slabbed steps below,   381
Mild as a star in water; for so new,
And so unsullied was the marble's hue,
So through the crystal polish, liquid fine,
Ran the dark veins, that none but feet divine
Could e'er have touch'd there. Sounds Æolian
Breath'd from the hinges, as the ample span
Of the wide doors disclos'd a place unknown
Some time to any, but these two alone,
And a few Persian mutes, who that same year   396
Were seen about the markets: none knew where
They could inhabit; the most curious
Were foil'd, who watch'd to trace them to their house:
And but the flitter-winged verse must tell,
For truth's sake, what woes afterwards befel,
'Twould humour many a heart to leave them thus,
Shut from the busy world of more incredulous.

PART II

LOVE in a hut, with water and a crust,
Is—Love, forgive us!—cinders, ashes, dust;
Love in a palace is perhaps at last
More grievous torment than a hermit's fast:—
That is a doubtful tale from faery land,
Hard for the non-elect to understand.
Had Lycius liv'd to hand his story down,
He might have given the moral a fresh frown,
Or clench'd it quite: but too short was their bliss
To breed distrust and hate, that make the soft voice hiss.
Beside, there, nightly, with terrific glare,   11
Love, jealous grown of so complete a pair,
Hover'd and buzz'd his wings, with fearful roar,
Above the lintel of their chamber door,
And down the passage cast a glow upon the floor.

For all this came a ruin: side by side
They were enthroned, in the even tide,
Upon a couch, near to a curtaining
Whose airy texture, from a golden string,
Floated into the room, and let appear   20
Unveil'd the summer heaven, blue and clear,
Betwixt two marble shafts:—there they reposed,
Where use had made it sweet, with eyelids closed,
Saving a tythe which love still open kept,
That they might see each other while they almost slept;
When from the slope side of a suburb hill,
Deafening the swallow's twitter, came a thrill
Of trumpets—Lycius started—the sounds fled,
But left a thought, a buzzing in his head.
For the first time, since first he harbour'd in   30
That purple-lined palace of sweet sin,
His spirit pass'd beyond its golden bourn
Into the noisy world almost forsworn.
The lady, ever watchful, penetrant,
Saw this with pain, so arguing a want
Of something more, more than her empery
Of joys; and she began to moan and sigh
Because he mused beyond her, knowing well
That but a moment's thought is passion's passing bell.
"Why do you sigh, fair creature?" whisper'd he:
"Why do you think?" return'd she tenderly: 41
"You have deserted me;—where am I now?
"Not in your heart while care weighs on your brow:

"No, no, you have dismiss'd me; and I go
"From your breast houseless: aye, it must be so."
He answer'd, bending to her open eyes,
Where he was mirror'd small in paradise,
"My silver planet, both of eve and morn!
"Why will you plead yourself so sad forlorn,
"While I am striving how to fill my heart   50
"With deeper crimson, and a double smart?
"How to entangle, trammel up and snare
"Your soul in mine, and labyrinth you there
"Like the hid scent in an unbudded rose?
"Aye, a sweet kiss—you see your mighty woes.
"My thoughts! shall I unveil them? Listen then!
"What mortal hath a prize, that other men
"May be confounded and abash'd withal,
"But lets it sometimes pace abroad majestical,
"And triumph, as in thee I should rejoice   60
"Amid the hoarse alarm of Corinth's voice.
"Let my foes choke, and my friends shout afar,
"While through the thronged streets your bridal car
"Wheels round its dazzling spokes."—The lady's cheek
Trembled; she nothing said, but, pale and meek,
Arose and knelt before him, wept a rain
Of sorrows at his words; at last with pain
Beseeching him, the while his hand she wrung,
To change his purpose. He thereat was stung,
Perverse, with stronger fancy to reclaim   70
Her wild and timid nature to his aim:
Besides, for all his love, in self despite,
Against his better self, he took delight
Luxurious in her sorrows, soft and new.
His passion, cruel grown, took on a hue
Fierce and sanguineous as 'twas possible
In one whose brow had no dark veins to swell.
Fine was the mitigated fury, like
Apollo's presence when in act to strike
The serpent—Ha, the serpent! certes, she   80
Was none. She burnt, she lov'd the tyranny,
And, all subdued, consented to the hour
When to the bridal he should lead his paramour.
Whispering in midnight silence, said the youth,
"Sure some sweet name thou hast, though, by my truth,
"I have not ask'd it, ever thinking thee
"Not mortal, but of heavenly progeny,
"As still I do. Hast any mortal name,
"Fit appellation for this dazzling frame?

"Or friends or kinsfolk on the citied earth,   90
"To share our marriage feast and nuptial mirth?"
"I have no friends," said Lamia, "no, not one;
"My presence in wide Corinth hardly known:
"My parents' bones are in their dusty urns
"Sepulchred, where no kindled incense burns,
"Seeing all their luckless race are dead, save me,
"And I neglect the holy rite for thee.
"Even as you list invite your many guests;
"But if, as now it seems, your vision rests
"With any pleasure on me, do not bid   100
"Old Apollonius—from him keep me hid."
Lycius, perplex'd at words so blind and blank,
Made close inquiry; from whose touch she shrank,
Feigning a sleep; and he to the dull shade
Of deep sleep in a moment was betray'd.

It was the custom then to bring away
The bride from home at blushing shut of day,
Veil'd, in a chariot, heralded along
By strewn flowers, torches, and a marriage song,
With other pageants: but this fair unknown   110
Had not a friend. So being left alone,
(Lycius was gone to summon all his kin)
And knowing surely she could never win
His foolish heart from its mad pompousness,
She set herself, high-thoughted, how to dress
The misery in fit magnificence.
She did so, but 'tis doubtful how and whence
Came, and who were her subtle servitors.
About the halls, and to and from the doors,
There was a noise of wings, till in short space   120
The glowing banquet-room shone with wide-arched grace.
A haunting music, sole perhaps and lone
Supportress of the faery-roof, made moan
Throughout, as fearful the whole charm might fade.
Fresh carved cedar, mimicking a glade
Of palm and plantain, met from either side,
High in the midst, in honour of the bride:
Two palms and then two plantains, and so on,
From either side their stems branch'd one to one
All down the aisled place; and beneath all   130
There ran a stream of lamps straight on from wall to wall.
So canopied, lay an untasted feast
Teeming with odours. Lamia, regal drest,
Silently paced about, and as she went,
In pale contented sort of discontent,

Mission'd her viewless servants to enrich
The fretted splendour of each nook and niche.
Between the tree-stems, marbled plain at first,
Came jasper pannels; then, anon, there burst
Forth creeping imagery of slighter trees,   140
And with the larger wove in small intricacies.
Approving all, she faded at self-will,
And shut the chamber up, close, hush'd and still,
Complete and ready for the revels rude,
When dreadful guests would come to spoil her solitude.

    The day appear'd, and all the gossip rout.
O senseless Lycius! Madman! wherefore flout
The silent-blessing fate, warm cloister'd hours,
And show to common eyes these secret bowers?
The herd approach'd; each guest, with busy brain.   151
Arriving at the portal, gaz'd amain,
And enter'd marveling: for they knew the street,
Remember'd it from childhood all complete
Without a gap, yet ne'er before had seen
That royal porch, that high-built fair demesne;
So in they hurried all, maz'd, curious and keen:
Save one, who look'd thereon with eye severe,
And with calm-planted steps walk'd in austere;
'Twas Apollonius: something too he laugh'd,   160
As though some knotty problem, that had daft
His patient thought, had now begun to thaw,
And solve and melt:—'twas just as he foresaw.

    He met within the murmurous vestibule
His young disciple. "'Tis no common rule,
Lycius," said he, "for uninvited guest
"To force himself upon you, and infest
"With an unbidden presence the bright throng
"Of younger friends; yet must I do this wrong,
"And you forgive me." Lycius blush'd, and led
The old man through the inner doors broad-spread;   171
With reconciling words and courteous mien
Turning into sweet milk the sophist's spleen.

    Of wealthy lustre was the banquet-room,
Fill'd with pervading brilliance and perfume:
Before each lucid pannel fuming stood
A censer fed with myrrh and spiced wood,
Each by a sacred tripod held aloft,
Whose slender feet wide-swerv'd upon the soft

Wool-woofed carpets: fifty wreaths of smoke
From fifty censers their light voyage took   180
To the high roof, still mimick'd as they rose
Along the mirror'd walls by twin-clouds odorous.
Twelve sphered tables, by silk seats insphered,
High as the level of a man's breast rear'd
On libbard's paws, upheld the heavy gold
Of cups and goblets, and the store thrice told
Of Ceres' horn, and, in huge vessels, wine
Come from the gloomy tun with merry shine.
Thus loaded with a feast the tables stood,
Each shrining in the midst the image of a God.   190

    When in an antichamber every guest
Had felt the cold full sponge to pleasure press'd,
By minist'ring slaves, upon his hands and feet,
And fragrant oils with ceremony meet
Pour'd on his hair, they all mov'd to the feast
In white robes, and themselves in order placed
Around the silken couches, wondering
Whence all this mighty cost and blaze of wealth could spring.

    Soft went the music the soft air along,
While fluent Greek a vowel'd undersong   200
Kept up among the guests, discoursing low
At first, for scarcely was the wine at flow;
But when the happy vintage touch'd their brains,
Louder they talk, and louder come the strains
Of powerful instruments:—the gorgeous dyes,
The space, the splendour of the draperies,
The roof of awful richness, nectarous cheer,
Beautiful slaves, and Lamia's self, appear,
Now, when the wine has done its rosy deed,
And every soul from human trammels freed,   210
No more so strange; for merry wine, sweet wine,
Will make Elysian shades not too fair, too divine.
Soon was God Bacchus at meridian height;
Flush'd were their cheeks, and bright eyes double bright:
Garlands of every green, and every scent
From vales deflower'd, or forest-trees branch-rent,
In baskets of bright osier'd gold were brought
High as the handles heap'd, to suit the thought
Of every guest; that each, as he did please,
Might fancy-fit his brows, silk-pillow'd at his ease.   220

    What wreath for Lamia? What for Lycius?
What for the sage, old Apollonius?

Upon her aching forehead be there hung
The leaves of willow and of adder's tongue;
And for the youth, quick, let us strip for him
The thyrsus, that his watching eyes may swim
Into forgetfulness; and, for the sage,
Let spear-grass and the spiteful thistle wage
War on his temples. Do not all charms fly
At the mere touch of cold philosophy?   230
There was an awful rainbow once in heaven:
We know her woof, her texture; she is given
In the dull catalogue of common things.
Philosophy will clip an Angel's wings,
Conquer all mysteries by rule and line,
Empty the haunted air, and gnomed mine—
Unweave a rainbow, as it erewhile made
The tender-person'd Lamia melt into a shade.

By her glad Lycius sitting, in chief place,
Scarce saw in all the room another face,   240
Till, checking his love trance, a cup he took
Full brimm'd, and opposite sent forth a look
'Cross the broad table, to beseech a glance
From his old teacher's wrinkled countenance,
And pledge him. The bald-head philosopher
Had fix'd his eye, without a twinkle or stir
Full on the alarmed beauty of the bride,
Brow-beating her fair form, and troubling her sweet pride.
Lycius then press'd her hand, with devout touch,
As pale it lay upon the rosy couch: 250
'Twas icy, and the cold ran through his veins;
Then sudden it grew hot, and all the pains
Of an unnatural heat shot to his heart.
"Lamia, what means this? Wherefore dost thou start?
"Know'st thou that man?" Poor Lamia answer'd not.
He gaz'd into her eyes, and not a jot
Own'd they the lovelorn piteous appeal:
More, more he gaz'd: his human senses reel:
Some hungry spell that loveliness absorbs;
There was no recognition in those orbs.   260
"Lamia!" he cried—and no soft-toned reply.
The many heard, and the loud revelry
Grew hush; the stately music no more breathes;
The myrtle sicken'd in a thousand wreaths.
By faint degrees, voice, lute, and pleasure ceased;
A deadly silence step by step increased,
Until it seem'd a horrid presence there,
And not a man but felt the terror in his hair.

"Lamia!" he shriek'd; and nothing but the shriek
With its sad echo did the silence break.   270
"Begone, foul dream!" he cried, gazing again
In the bride's face, where now no azure vein
Wander'd on fair-spaced temples; no soft bloom
Misted the cheek; no passion to illume
The deep-recessed vision:—all was blight;
Lamia, no longer fair, there sat a deadly white.
"Shut, shut those juggling eyes, thou ruthless man!
"Turn them aside, wretch! or the righteous ban
"Of all the Gods, whose dreadful images
"Here represent their shadowy presences,   280
"May pierce them on the sudden with the thorn
"Of painful blindness; leaving thee forlorn,
"In trembling dotage to the feeblest fright
"Of conscience, for their long offended might,
"For all thine impious proud-heart sophistries,
"Unlawful magic, and enticing lies.
"Corinthians! look upon that grey-beard wretch!
"Mark how, possess'd, his lashless eyelids stretch
"Around his demon eyes! Corinthians, see!
"My sweet bride withers at their potency."   290
"Fool!" said the sophist, in an under-tone
Gruff with contempt; which a death-nighing moan
From Lycius answer'd, as heart-struck and lost,
He sank supine beside the aching ghost.
"Fool! Fool!" repeated he, while his eyes still
Relented not, nor mov'd; "from every ill
"Of life have I preserv'd thee to this day,
"And shall I see thee made a serpent's prey?"
Then Lamia breath'd death breath; the sophist's eye,
Like a sharp spear, went through her utterly,   300
Keen, cruel, perceant, stinging: she, as well
As her weak hand could any meaning tell,
Motion'd him to be silent; vainly so,
He look'd and look'd again a level—No!
"A serpent!" echoed he; no sooner said,
Than with a frightful scream she vanished:
And Lycius' arms were empty of delight,
As were his limbs of life, from that same night.
On the high couch he lay!—his friends came round—
Supported him—no pulse, or breath they found,   310
And, in its marriage robe, the heavy body wound.

ISABELLA;

OR

THE POT OF BASIL

A Story from Boccaccio

I

FAIR Isabel, poor simple Isabel!
    Lorenzo, a young palmer in Love's eye!
They could not in the self-same mansion dwell
    Without some stir of heart, some malady;
They could not sit at meals but feel how well
    It soothed each to be the other by;
They could not, sure, beneath the same roof sleep
But to each other dream, and nightly weep.

II

With every morn their love grew tenderer,
    With every eve deeper and tenderer still;
He might not in house, field, or garden stir,
    But her full shape would all his seeing fill;
And his continual voice was pleasanter
    To her, than noise of trees or hidden rill;
Her lute-string gave an echo of his name,
She spoilt her half-done broidery with the same.

III

He knew whose gentle hand was at the latch
    Before the door had given her to his eyes;
And from her chamber-window he would catch
    Her beauty farther than the falcon spies;
And constant as her vespers would he watch,
    Because her face was turn'd to the same skies;
And with sick longing all the night outwear,
To hear her morning-step upon the stair.

IV

A whole long month of May in this sad plight
    Made their cheeks paler by the break of June:
"To-morrow will I bow to my delight,
    "To-morrow will I ask my lady's boon."—

"O may I never see another night,
   "Lorenzo, if thy lips breathe not love's tune." —
So spake they to their pillows; but, alas,
Honeyless days and days did he let pass;

V

Until sweet Isabella's untouched cheek
   Fell sick within the rose's just domain,
Fell thin as a young mother's, who doth seek
   By every lull to cool her infant's pain:
"How ill she is," said he, "I may not speak,
   "And yet I will, and tell my love all plain:
"If looks speak love-laws, I will drink her tears,
"And at the least 'twill startle off her cares."

VI

So said he one fair morning, and all day
   His heart beat awfully against his side;
And to his heart he inwardly did pray
   For power to speak; but still the ruddy tide
Stifled his voice, and puls'd resolve away—
   Fever'd his high conceit of such a bride,
Yet brought him to the meekness of a child:
Alas! when passion is both meek and wild!

VII

So once more he had wak'd and anguished
   A dreary night of love and misery,
If Isabel's quick eye had not been wed
   To every symbol on his forehead high;
She saw it waxing very pale and dead,
   And straight all flush'd; so, lisped tenderly,
"Lorenzo!"—here she ceas'd her timid quest,
But in her tone and look he read the rest.

VIII

"O Isabella, I can half perceive
   "That I may speak my grief into thine ear;
"If thou didst ever anything believe,
   "Believe how I love thee, believe how near
"My soul is to its doom: I would not grieve
   "Thy hand by unwelcome pressing, would not fear
"Thine eyes by gazing; but I cannot live
"Another night, and not my passion shrive.

IX

"Love! thou art leading me from wintry cold,
    "Lady! thou leadest me to summer clime,
"And I must taste the blossoms that unfold
    "In its ripe warmth this gracious morning time."
So said, his erewhile timid lips grew bold,
    And poesied with hers in dewy rhyme:
Great bliss was with them, and great happiness
Grew, like a lusty flower in June's caress.

X

Parting they seem'd to tread upon the air,
    Twin roses by the zephyr blown apart
Only to meet again more close, and share
    The inward fragrance of each other's heart.
She, to her chamber gone, a ditty fair
    Sang, of delicious love and honey'd dart;
He with light steps went up a western hill,
And bade the sun farewell, and joy'd his fill.

XI

All close they met again, before the dusk
    Had taken from the stars its pleasant veil,
All close they met, all eves, before the dusk
    Had taken from the stars its pleasant veil,
Close in a bower of hyacinth and musk,
    Unknown of any, free from whispering tale.
Ah! better had it been for ever so,
Than idle ears should pleasure in their woe.

XII

Were they unhappy then?—It cannot be—
    Too many tears for lovers have been shed,
Too many sighs give we to them in fee,
    Too much of pity after they are dead,
Too many doleful stories do we see,
    Whose matter in bright gold were best be read;
Except in such a page where Theseus' spouse
Over the pathless waves towards him bows.

XIII

But, for the general award of love,
    The little sweet doth kill much bitterness;
Though Dido silent is in under-grove,
    And Isabella's was a great distress,

Though Young Lorenzo in warm Indian clove
　　Was not embalm'd, this truth is not the less—
Even bees, the little almsmen of spring-bowers,
Know there is richest juice in poison-flowers.

XIV

With her two brothers this fair lady dwelt,
　　Enriched from ancestral merchandize,
And for them many a weary hand did swelt
　　In torched mines and noisy factories
And many once proud-quiver'd loins did melt
　　In blood from stinging whip;—with hollow eyes
Many all day in dazzling river stood,
To take the rich-ored driftings of the flood.

XV

For them the Ceylon diver held his breath,
　　And went all naked to the hungry shark;
For them his ears gush'd blood; for them in death
　　The seal on the cold ice with piteous bark
Lay full of darts; for them alone did seethe
　　A thousand men in troubles wide and dark:
Half-ignorant, they turn'd an easy wheel,
That set sharp racks at work, to pinch and peel.

XVI

Why were they proud? Because their marble founts
　　Gush'd with more pride than do a wretch's tears?—
Why were they proud? Because fair orange-mounts
　　Were of more soft ascent than lazar stairs?—
Why were they proud? Because red-lin'd accounts
　　Were richer than the songs of Grecian years?—
Why were they proud? again we ask aloud,
Why in the name of Glory were they proud?

XVII

Yet were these Florentines as self-retired
　　In hungry pride and gainful cowardice,
As two close Hebrews in that land inspired,
　　Paled in and vineyarded from beggar-spies;
The hawks of ship-mast forests—the untired
　　And pannier'd mules for ducats and old lies—
Quick cat's-paws on the generous stray-away,—
Great wits in Spanish, Tuscan, and Malay.

XVIII

How was it these same ledger-men could spy
    Fair Isabella in her downy nest?
How could they find out in Lorenzo's eye
    A straying from his toil? Hot Egypt's pest
Into their vision covetous and sly!
    How could these money-bags see east and west?—
Yet so they did—and every dealer fair
Must see behind, as doth the hunted hare.

XIX

O eloquent and famed Boccaccio!
    Of thee we now should ask forgiving boon,
And of thy spicy myrtles as they blow,
    And of thy roses amorous of the moon,
And of thy lillies, that do paler grow
    Now they can no more hear thy ghittern's tune,
For venturing syllables that ill beseem
The quiet glooms of such a piteous theme.

XX

Grant thou a pardon here, and then the tale
    Shall move on soberly, as it is meet;
There is no other crime, no mad assail
    To make old prose in modern rhyme more sweet:
But it is done—succeed the verse or fail—
    To honour thee, and thy gone spirit greet;
To stead thee as a verse in English tongue,
An echo of thee in the north-wind sung.

XXI

These brethren having found by many signs
    What love Lorenzo for their sister had,
And how she lov'd him too, each unconfines
    His bitter thoughts to other, well nigh mad
That he, the servant of their trade designs,
    Should in their sister's love be blithe and glad,
When 'twas their plan to coax her by degrees
To some high noble and his olive-trees.

XXII

And many a jealous conference had they,
    And many times they bit their lips alone,
Before they fix'd upon a surest way
    To make the youngster for his crime atone;

And at the last, these men of cruel clay
    Cut Mercy with a sharp knife to the bone;
For they resolved in some forest dim
To kill Lorenzo, and there bury him.

XXIII

So on a pleasant morning, as he leant
    Into the sun-rise, o'er the balustrade
Of the garden-terrace, towards him they bent
    Their footing through the dews; and to him said,
"You seem there in the quiet of content,
    "Lorenzo, and we are most loth to invade
"Calm speculation; but if you are wise,
"Bestride your steed while cold is in the skies.

XXIV

"To-day we purpose, aye, this hour we mount
    "To spur three leagues towards the Apennine;
"Come down, we pray thee, ere the hot sun count
    "His dewy rosary on the eglantine."
Lorenzo, courteously as he was wont,
    Bow'd a fair greeting to these serpents' whine;
And went in haste, to get in readiness,
With belt, and spur, and bracing huntsman's dress.

XXV

And as he to the court-yard pass'd along,
    Each third step did he pause, and listen'd oft
If he could hear his lady's matin-song,
    Or the light whisper of her footstep soft;
And as he thus over his passion hung,
    He heard a laugh full musical aloft;
When, looking up, he saw her features bright
Smile through an in-door lattice, all delight.

XXVI

"Love, Isabel!" said he, "I was in pain
    "Lest I should miss to bid thee a good morrow:
"Ah! what if I should lose thee, when so fain
    "I am to stifle all the heavy sorrow
"Of a poor three hours' absence? but we'll gain
    "Out of the amorous dark what day doth borrow.
"Good bye! I'll soon be back."—"Good bye!" said she:—
And as he went she chanted merrily.

XXVII

So the two brothers and their murder'd man
   Rode past fair Florence, to where Arno's stream
Gurgles through straiten'd banks, and still doth fan
   Itself with dancing bulrush, and the bream
Keeps head against the freshets. Sick and wan
   The brothers' faces in the ford did seem,
Lorenzo's flush with love.—They pass'd the water
Into a forest quiet for the slaughter.

XXVIII

There was Lorenzo slain and buried in,
   There in that forest did his great love cease;
Ah! when a soul doth thus its freedom win,
   It aches in loneliness—is ill at peace
As the break-covert blood-hounds of such sin:
   They dipp'd their swords in the water, and did tease
Their horses homeward, with convulsed spur,
Each richer by his being a murderer.

XXIX

They told their sister how, with sudden speed,
   Lorenzo had ta'en ship for foreign lands,
Because of some great urgency and need
   In their affairs, requiring trusty hands.
Poor Girl! put on thy stifling widow's weed,
   And 'scape at once from Hope's accursed bands;
To-day thou wilt not see him, nor to-morrow,
And the next day will be a day of sorrow.

XXX

She weeps alone for pleasures not to be;
   Sorely she wept until the night came on,
And then, instead of love, O misery!
   She brooded o'er the luxury alone:
His image in the dusk she seem'd to see,
   And to the silence made a gentle moan,
Spreading her perfect arms upon the air,
And on her couch low murmuring "Where? O where?"

XXXI

But Selfishness, Love's cousin, held not long
   Its fiery vigil in her single breast;
She fretted for the golden hour, and hung
   Upon the time with feverish unrest—

Not long—for soon into her heart a throng
  Of higher occupants, a richer zest,
Came tragic; passion not to be subdued,
And sorrow for her love in travels rude.

XXXII

In the mid days of autumn, on their eves
  The breath of Winter comes from far away,
And the sick west continually bereaves
  Of some gold tinge, and plays a roundelay
Of death among the bushes and the leaves,
  To make all bare before he dares to stray
From his north cavern. So sweet Isabel
By gradual decay from beauty fell,

XXXIII

Because Lorenzo came not. Oftentimes
  She ask'd her brothers, with an eye all pale,
Striving to be itself, what dungeon climes
  Could keep him off so long? They spake a tale
Time after time, to quiet her. Their crimes
  Came on them, like a smoke from Hinnom's vale;
And every night in dreams they groan'd aloud,
To see their sister in her snowy shroud.

XXXIV

And she had died in drowsy ignorance,
  But for a thing more deadly dark than all;
It came like a fierce potion, drunk by chance,
  Which saves a sick man from the feather'd pall
For some few gasping moments; like a lance,
  Waking an Indian from his cloudy hall
With cruel pierce, and bringing him again
Sense of the gnawing fire at heart and brain.

XXXV

It was a vision.—In the drowsy gloom,
  The dull of midnight, at her couch's foot
Lorenzo stood, and wept: the forest tomb
  Had marr'd his glossy hair which once could shoot
Lustre into the sun, and put cold doom
  Upon his lips, and taken the soft lute
From his lorn voice, and past his loamed ears
Had made a miry channel for his tears.

XXXVI

Strange sound it was, when the pale shadow spake;
  For there was striving, in its piteous tongue,
To speak as when on earth it was awake,
  And Isabella on its music hung:
Languor there was in it, and tremulous shake,
  As in a palsied Druid's harp unstrung;
And through it moan'd a ghostly under-song,
Like hoarse night-gusts sepulchral briars among.

XXXVII

Its eyes, though wild, were still all dewy bright
  With love, and kept all phantom fear aloof
From the poor girl by magic of their light,
  The while it did unthread the horrid woof
Of the late darken'd time,—the murderous spite
  Of pride and avarice,—the dark pine roof
In the forest,—and the sodden turfed dell,
Where, without any word, from stabs he fell.

XXXVIII

Saying moreover, "Isabel, my sweet!
  "Red whortle-berries droop above my head,
"And a large flint-stone weighs upon my feet;
  "Around me beeches and high chestnuts shed
"Their leaves and prickly nuts; a sheep-fold bleat
  "Comes from beyond the river to my bed:
"Go, shed one tear upon my heather-bloom,
"And it shall comfort me within the tomb.

XXXIX

"I am a shadow now, alas! alas!
  "Upon the skirts of human-nature dwelling
"Alone: I chant alone the holy mass,
  "While little sounds of life are round me knelling,
"And glossy bees at noon do fieldward pass,
  "And many a chapel bell the hour is telling,
"Paining me through: those sounds grow strange to me,
"And thou art distant in Humanity.

XL

"I know what was, I feel full well what is,
  "And I should rage, if spirits could go mad;
"Though I forget the taste of earthly bliss,
  "That paleness warms my grave, as though I had

"A Seraph chosen from the bright abyss
  "To be my spouse: thy paleness makes me glad;
"Thy beauty grows upon me, and I feel
"A greater love through all my essence steal."

XLI

The Spirit mourn'd "Adieu!"—dissolv'd and left
  The atom darkness in a slow turmoil;
As when of healthful midnight sleep bereft,
  Thinking on rugged hours and fruitless toil,
We put our eyes into a pillowy cleft,
  And see the spangly gloom froth up and boil:
It made sad Isabella's eyelids ache,
And in the dawn she started up awake;

XLII

"Ha! ha!" said she, "I knew not this hard life,
  "I thought the worst was simple misery;
"I thought some Fate with pleasure or with strife
  "Portion'd us—happy days, or else to die;
"But there is crime—a brother's bloody knife!
  "Sweet Spirit, thou hast school'd my infancy:
"I'll visit thee for this, and kiss thine eyes,
"And greet thee morn and even in the skies."

XLIII

When the full morning came, she had devised
  How she might secret to the forest hie;
How she might find the clay, so dearly prized,
  And sing to it one latest lullaby;
How her short absence might be unsurmised,
  While she the inmost of the dream would try.
Resolv'd, she took with her an aged nurse,
And went into that dismal forest-hearse.

XLIV

See, as they creep along the river side,
  How she doth whisper to that aged Dame,
And, after looking round the champaign wide,
  Shows her a knife.—"What feverous hectic flame
"Burns in thee, child?—What good can thee betide,
  "That thou should'st smile again?"—The evening came,
And they had found Lorenzo's earthy bed;
The flint was there, the berries at his head.

XLV

Who hath not loiter'd in a green church-yard,
    And let his spirit, like a demon-mole,
Work through the clayey soil and gravel hard,
    To see scull, coffin'd bones, and funeral stole;
Pitying each form that hungry Death hath marr'd,
    And filling it once more with human soul?
Ah! this is holiday to what was felt
When Isabella by Lorenzo knelt.

XLVI

She gaz'd into the fresh-thrown mould, as though
    One glance did fully all its secrets tell;
Clearly she saw, as other eyes would know
    Pale limbs at bottom of a crystal well;
Upon the murderous spot she seem'd to grow,
    Like to a native lilly of the dell:
Then with her knife, all sudden, she began
To dig more fervently than misers can.

XLVII

Soon she turn'd up a soiled glove, whereon
    Her silk had play'd in purple phantasies,
She kiss'd it with a lip more chill than stone,
    And put it in her bosom, where it dries
And freezes utterly unto the bone
    Those dainties made to still an infant's cries:
Then 'gan she work again; nor stay'd her care,
But to throw back at times her veiling hair.

XLVIII

That old nurse stood beside her wondering,
    Until her heart felt pity to the core
At sight of such a dismal labouring,
    And so she kneeled, with her locks all hoar,
And put her lean hands to the horrid thing:
    Three hours they labour'd at this travail sore;
At last they felt the kernel of the grave,
And Isabella did not stamp and rave.

XLIX

Ah! wherefore all this wormy circumstance?
    Why linger at the yawning tomb so long?
O for the gentleness of old Romance,
    The simple plaining of a minstrel's song!

Fair reader, at the old tale take a glance,
  For here, in truth, it doth not well belong
To speak:—O turn thee to the very tale,
And taste the music of that vision pale.

L

With duller steel than the Perséan sword
  They cut away no formless monster's head,
But one, whose gentleness did well accord
  With death, as life. The ancient harps have said,
Love never dies, but lives, immortal Lord:
  If Love impersonate was ever dead,
Pale Isabella kiss'd it, and low moan'd.
'Twas love; cold,—dead indeed, but not dethroned.

LI

In anxious secrecy they took it home,
  And then the prize was all for Isabel:
She calm'd its wild hair with a golden comb,
  And all around each eye's sepuchral cell
Pointed each fringed lash; the smeared loam
  With tears, as chilly as a dripping well,
She drench'd away:—and still she comb'd, and kept
Sighing all day—and still she kiss'd, and wept.

LII

Then in a silken scarf,—sweet with the dews
  Of precious flowers pluck'd in Araby,
And divine liquids come with odorous ooze
  Through the cold serpent-pipe refreshfully,—
She wrapp'd it up; and for its tomb did choose
  A garden-pot, wherein she laid it by,
And cover'd it with mould, and o'er it set
Sweet Basil, which her tears kept ever wet.

LIII

And she forgot the stars, the moon, and sun,
  And she forgot the blue above the trees,
And she forgot the dells where waters run,
  And she forgot the chilly autumn breeze;
She had no knowledge when the day was done,
  And the new morn she saw not: but in peace
Hung over her sweet Basil evermore,
And moisten'd it with tears unto the core.

LIV

And so she ever fed it with thin tears,
  Whence thick, and green, and beautiful it grew,
So that it smelt more balmy than its peers
  Of Basil-tufts in Florence; for it drew
Nurture besides, and life, from human fears,
  From the fast mouldering head there shut from view:
So that the jewel, safely casketed,
Came forth, and in perfumed leafits spread.

LV

O Melancholy, linger here awhile!
  O Music, Music, breathe despondingly!
O Echo, Echo, from some sombre isle,
  Unknown, Lethean, sigh to us—O sigh!
Spirits in grief, lift up your heads, and smile;
  Lift up your heads, sweet Spirits, heavily,
And make a pale light in your cypress glooms,
Tinting with silver wan your marble tombs.

LVI

Moan hither, all ye syllables of woe,
  From the deep throat of sad Melpomene!
Through bronzed lyre in tragic order go,
  And touch the strings into a mystery;
Sound mournfully upon the winds and low;
  For simple Isabel is soon to be
Among the dead: She withers, like a palm
Cut by an Indian for its juicy balm.

LVII

O leave the palm to wither by itself;
  Let not quick Winter chill its dying hour!—
It may not be—those Baälites of pelf,
  Her brethren, noted the continual shower
From her dead eyes; and many a curious elf,
  Among her kindred, wonder'd that such dower
Of youth and beauty should be thrown aside
By one mark'd out to be a Noble's bride.

LVIII

And, furthermore, her brethren wonder'd much
  Why she sat drooping by the Basil green,
And why it flourish'd, as by magic touch;
  Greatly they wonder'd what the thing might mean:

They could not surely give belief, that such
   A very nothing would have power to wean
Her from her own fair youth, and pleasures gay,
And even remembrance of her love's delay.

LIX

Therefore they watch'd a time when they might sift
   This hidden whim; and long they watch'd in vain;
For seldom did she go to chapel-shrift,
   And seldom felt she any hunger-pain;
And when she left, she hurried back, as swift
   As bird on wing to breast its eggs again;
And, patient as a hen-bird, sat her there
Beside her Basil, weeping through her hair.

LX

Yet they contriv'd to steal the Basil-pot,
   And to examine it in secret place;
The thing was vile with green and livid spot,
   And yet they knew it was Lorenzo's face:
The guerdon of their murder they had got,
   And so left Florence in a moment's space,
Never to turn again.—Away they went,
With blood upon their heads, to banishment.

LXI

O Melancholy, turn thine eyes away!
   O Music, Music, breathe despondingly!
O Echo, Echo, on some other day,
   From isles Lethean, sigh to us—O sigh!
Spirits of grief, sing not your "Well-a-way!"
   For Isabel, sweet Isabel, will die;
Will die a death too lone and incomplete,
Now they have ta'en away her Basil sweet.

LXII

Piteous she look'd on dead and senseless things,
   Asking for her lost Basil amorously;
And with melodious chuckle in the strings
   Of her lorn voice, she oftentimes would cry
After the Pilgrim in his wanderings,
   To ask him where her Basil was; and why
'Twas hid from her: "For cruel 'tis," said she,
"To steal my Basil-pot away from me."

LXIII

And so she pined, and so she died forlorn,
　　Imploring for her Basil to the last.
No heart was there in Florence but did mourn
　　In pity of her love, so overcast.
And a sad ditty of this story born
　　From mouth to mouth through all the country pass'd:
Still is the burthen sung—"O cruelty,
"To steal my Basil-pot away from me!"

THE EVE OF ST. AGNES

I

St. Agnes' Eve—Ah, bitter chill it was!
The owl, for all his feathers, was a-cold;
The hare limp'd trembling through the frozen grass,
And silent was the flock in woolly fold:
Numb were the Beadsman's fingers, while he told
His rosary, and while his frosted breath,
Like pious incense from a censer old,
Seem'd taking flight for heaven, without a death,
Past the sweet Virgin's picture, while his prayer he saith.

II

His prayer he saith, this patient, holy man;
Then takes his lamp, and riseth from his knees,
And back returneth, meagre, barefoot, wan,
Along the chapel aisle by slow degrees:
The sculptur'd dead, on each side, seem to freeze,
Emprison'd in black, purgatorial rails:
Knights, ladies, praying in dumb orat'ries,
He passeth by; and his weak spirit fails
To think how they may ache in icy hoods and mails.

III

Northward he turneth through a little door,
And scarce three steps, ere Music's golden tongue
Flatter'd to tears this aged man and poor;
But no—already had his deathbell rung:
The joys of all his life were said and sung:
His was harsh penance on St. Agnes' Eve:
Another way he went, and soon among
Rough ashes sat he for his soul's reprieve,
And all night kept awake, for sinners' sake to grieve.

IV

That ancient Beadsman heard the prelude soft;
And so it chanc'd, for many a door was wide,
From hurry to and fro. Soon, up aloft,
The silver, snarling trumpets 'gan to chide:

The level chambers, ready with their pride,
Were glowing to receive a thousand guests:
The carved angels, ever eager-eyed,
Star'd, where upon their heads the cornice rests,
With hair blown back, and wings put cross-wise on their breasts.

V

At length burst in the argent revelry,
With plume, tiara, and all rich array,
Numerous as shadows haunting faerily
The brain, new stuff'd, in youth, with triumphs gay
Of old romance. These let us wish away,
And turn, sole-thoughted, to one Lady there,
Whose heart had brooded, all that wintry day,
On love, and wing'd St. Agnes' saintly care,
As she had heard old dames full many times declare.

VI

They told her how, upon St. Agnes' Eve,
Young virgins might have visions of delight,
And soft adorings from their loves receive
Upon the honey'd middle of the night,
If ceremonies due they did aright;
As, supperless to bed they must retire,
And couch supine their beauties, lilly white;
Nor look behind, nor sideways, but require
Of Heaven with upward eyes for all that they desire.

VII

Full of this whim was thoughtful Madeline:
The music, yearning like a God in pain,
She scarcely heard: her maiden eyes divine,
Fix'd on the floor, saw many a sweeping train
Pass by—she heeded not at all: in vain
Came many a tiptoe, amorous cavalier,
And back retir'd; not cool'd by high disdain,
But she saw not: her heart was otherwhere:
She sigh'd for Agnes' dreams, the sweetest of the year.

VIII

She danc'd along with vague, regardless eyes,
Anxious her lips, her breathing quick and short:
The hallow'd hour was near at hand: she sighs
Amid the timbrels, and the throng'd resort

Of whisperers in anger, or in sport;
'Mid looks of love, defiance, hate, and scorn,
Hoodwink'd with faery fancy; all amort,
Save to St. Agnes and her lambs unshorn,
And all the bliss to be before to-morrow morn.

IX

So, purposing each moment to retire,
She linger'd still. Meantime, across the moors,
Had come young Porphyro, with heart on fire
For Madeline. Beside the portal doors,
Buttress'd from moonlight, stands he, and implores
All saints to give him sight of Madeline,
But for one moment in the tedious hours,
That he might gaze and worship all unseen;
Perchance speak, kneel, touch, kiss—in sooth such things
        have been.

X

He ventures in: let no buzz'd whisper tell:
All eyes be muffled, or a hundred swords
Will storm his heart, Love's fev'rous citadel:
For him, those chambers held barbarian hordes,
Hyena foemen, and hot-blooded lords,
Whose very dogs would execrations howl
Against his lineage: not one breast affords
Him any mercy, in that mansion foul,
Save one old beldame, weak in body and in soul.

XI

Ah, happy chance! the aged creature came,
Shuffling along with ivory-headed wand,
To where he stood, hid from the torch's flame,
Behind a broad hall-pillar, far beyond
The sound of merriment and chorus bland:
He startled her; but soon she knew his face,
And grasp'd his fingers in her palsied hand,
Saying, "Mercy, Porphyro! hie thee from this place:
"They are all here to-night, the whole blood-thirsty race!

XII

·"Get hence! get hence! there's dwarfish Hildebrand;
"He had a fever late, and in the fit
"He cursed thee and thine, both house and land:
"Then there's that old Lord Maurice, not a whit

"More tame for his gray hairs—Alas me! flit!
"Flit like a ghost away."—"Ah, Gossip dear,
"We're safe enough; here in this arm-chair sit,
"And tell me how"—"Good Saints! not here, not here;
"Follow me, child, or else these stones will be thy bier."

XIII

He follow'd through a lowly arched way,
Brushing the cobwebs with his lofty plume,
And as she mutter'd "Well-a—well-a-day!"
He found him in a little moonlight room,
Pale, lattic'd, chill, and silent as a tomb.
"Now tell me where is Madeline," said he,
"O tell me, Angela, by the holy loom
"Which none but secret sisterhood may see,
"When they St. Agnes' wool are weaving piously."

XIV

"St. Agnes! Ah! it is St. Agnes' Eve—
"Yet men will murder upon holy days:
"Thou must hold water in a witch's sieve,
"And be liege-lord of all the Elves and Fays,
"To venture so: it fills me with amaze
"To see thee, Porphyro!—St. Agnes' Eve!
"God's help! my lady fair the conjuror plays
"This very night: good angels her deceive!
"But let me laugh awhile, I've mickle time to grieve."

XV

Feebly she laugheth in the languid moon,
While Porphyro upon her face doth look,
Like puzzled urchin on an aged crone
Who keepeth clos'd a wond'rous riddle-book,
As spectacled she sits in chimney nook.
But soon his eyes grew brilliant, when she told
His lady's purpose; and he scarce could brook
Tears, at the thought of those enchantments cold,
And Madeline asleep in lap of legends old.

XVI

Sudden a thought came like a full-blown rose,
Flushing his brow, and in his pained heart
Made purple riot: then doth he propose
A stratagem, that makes the beldame start:

"A cruel man and impious thou art:
"Sweet lady, let her pray, and sleep, and dream
"Alone with her good angels, far apart
"From wicked men like thee. Go, go!—I deem
"Thou canst not surely be the same that thou didst seem."

XVII

"I will not harm her, by all saints I swear,"
Quoth Porphyro: "O may I ne'er find grace
"When my weak voice shall whisper its last prayer,
"If one of her soft ringlets I displace,
"Or look with ruffian passion in her face:
"Good Angela, believe me by these tears;
"Or I will, even in a moment's space,
"Awake, with horrid shout, my foemen's ears,
"And beard them, though they be more fang'd than wolves
      and bears."

XVIII

"Ah! why wilt thou affright a feeble soul?
"A poor, weak, palsy-stricken, churchyard thing,
"Whose passing-bell may ere the midnight toll;
"Whose prayers for thee, each morn and evening,
"Were never miss'd."—Thus plaining, doth she bring
A gentler speech from burning Porphyro;
So woful, and of such deep sorrowing,
That Angela gives promise she will do
Whatever he shall wish, betide her weal or woe.

XIX

Which was, to lead him, in close secrecy,
Even to Madeline's chamber, and there hide
Him in a closet, of such privacy
That he might see her beauty unespied,
And win perhaps that night a peerless bride,
While legion'd faeries pac'd the coverlet,
And pale enchantment held her sleepy-eyed.
Never on such a night have lovers met,
Since Merlin paid his Demon all the monstrous debt.

XX

"It shall be as thou wishest," said the Dame:
"All cates and dainties shall be stored there
"Quickly on this feast-night: by the tambour frame
"Her own lute thou wilt see: no time to spare,

"For I am slow and feeble, and scarce dare
"On such a catering trust my dizzy head.
"Wait here, my child, with patience; kneel in prayer
"The while: Ah! thou must needs the lady wed,
"Or may I never leave my grave among the dead."

XXI

So saying, she hobbled off with busy fear.
The lover's endless minutes slowly pass'd;
The dame return'd, and whisper'd in his ear
To follow her; with aged eyes aghast
From fright of dim espial. Safe at last,
Through many a dusky gallery, they gain
The maiden's chamber, silken, hush'd, and chaste;
Where Porphyro took covert, pleas'd amain.
His poor guide hurried back with agues in her brain.

XXII

Her falt'ring hand upon the balustrade,
Old Angela was feeling for the stair,
When Madeline, St. Agnes' charmed maid,
Rose, like a mission'd spirit, unaware:
With silver taper's light, and pious care,
She turn'd, and down the aged gossip led
To a safe level matting. Now prepare,
Young Porphyro, for gazing on that bed;
She comes, she comes again, like ring-dove fray'd and fled.

XXIII

Out went the taper as she hurried in;
Its little smoke, in pallid moonshine, died:
She clos'd the door, she panted, all akin
To spirits of the air, and visions wide:
No uttered syllable, or, woe betide!
But to her heart, her heart was voluble,
Paining with eloquence her balmy side;
As though a tongueless nightingale should swell
Her throat in vain, and die, heart-stifled, in her dell.

XXIV

A casement high and triple-arch'd there was,
All garlanded with carven imag'ries
Of fruits, and flowers, and bunches of knot-grass,
And diamonded with panes of quaint device,

Innumerable of stains and splendid dyes,
As are the tiger-moth's deep-damask'd wings;
And in the midst, 'mong thousand heraldries,
And twilight saints, and dim emblazonings,
A shielded scutcheon blush'd with blood of queens and kings.

XXV

Full on this casement shone the wintry moon,
And threw warm gules on Madeline's fair breast,
As down she knelt for heaven's grace and boon;
Rose-bloom fell on her hands, together prest,
And on her silver cross soft amethyst,
And on her hair a glory, like a saint:
She seem'd a splendid angel, newly drest,
Save wings, for heaven:—Porphyro grew faint:
She knelt, so pure a thing, so free from mortal taint.

XXVI

Anon his heart revives: her vespers done,
Of all its wreathed pearls her hair she frees;
Unclasps her warmed jewels one by one;
Loosens her fragrant boddice; by degrees
Her rich attire creeps rustling to her knees:
Half-hidden, like a mermaid in sea-weed,
Pensive awhile she dreams awake, and sees,
In fancy, fair St. Agnes in her bed,
But dares not look behind, or all the charm is fled.

XXVII

Soon, trembling in her soft and chilly nest,
In sort of wakeful swoon, perplex'd she lay,
Until the poppied warmth of sleep oppress'd
Her soothed limbs, and soul fatigued away;
Flown, like a thought, until the morrow-day;
Blissfully haven'd both from joy and pain;
Clasp'd like a missal where swart Paynims pray;
Blinded alike from sunshine and from rain,
As though a rose should shut, and be a bud again.

XXVIII

Stol'n to this paradise, and so entranced,
Porphyro gazed upon her empty dress,
And listen'd to her breathing, if it chanced
To wake into a slumberous tenderness;

Which when he heard, that minute did he bless,
And breath'd himself: then from the closet crept,
Noiseless as fear in a wide wilderness,
And over the hush'd carpet, silent, stept,
And 'tween the curtains peep'd, where, lo!—how fast she slept.

XXIX

Then by the bed-side, where the faded moon
Made a dim, silver twilight, soft he set
A table, and, half anguish'd, threw thereon
A cloth of woven crimson, gold, and jet:—
O for some drowsy Morphean amulet!
The boisterous, midnight, festive clarion,
The kettle-drum, and far-heard clarinet,
Affray his ears, though but in dying tone:—
The hall door shuts again, and all the noise is gone.

XXX

And still she slept an azure-lidded sleep,
In blanched linen, smooth, and lavender'd,
While he from forth the closet brought a heap
Of candied apple, quince, and plum, and gourd;
With jellies soother than the creamy curd,
And lucent syrops, tinct with cinnamon;
Manna and dates, in argosy transferr'd
From Fez; and spiced dainties, every one,
From silken Samarcand to cedar'd Lebanon.

XXXI

These delicates he heap'd with glowing hand
On golden dishes and in baskets bright
Of wreathed silver: sumptuous they stand
In the retired quiet of the night,
Filling the chilly room with perfume light.—
"And now, my love, my seraph fair, awake!
"Thou art my heaven, and I thine eremite:
"Open thine eyes, for meek St. Agnes' sake,
"Or I shall drowse beside thee, so my soul doth ache."

XXXII

Thus whispering, his warm, unnerved arm
Sank in her pillow. Shaded was her dream
By the dusk curtains:—'twas a midnight charm
Impossible to melt as iced stream·

The lustrous salvers in the moonlight gleam;
Broad golden fringe upon the carpet lies:
It seem'd he never, never could redeem
From such a stedfast spell his lady's eyes;
So mus'd awhile, entoil'd in woofed phantasies.

XXXIII

Awakening up, he took her hollow lute,—
Tumultuous,—and, in chords that tenderest be,
He play'd an ancient ditty, long since mute,
In Provence call'd, "La belle dame sans mercy:"
Close to her ear touching the melody;—
Wherewith disturb'd, she utter'd a soft moan:
He ceased—she panted quick—and suddenly
Her blue affrayed eyes wide open shone:
Upon his knees he sank, pale as smooth-sculptured stone.

XXXIV

Her eyes were open, but she still beheld,
Now wide awake, the vision of her sleep:
There was a painful change, that nigh expell'd
The blisses of her dream so pure and deep
At which fair Madeline began to weep,
And moan forth witless words with many a sigh;
While still her gaze on Porphyro would keep;
Who knelt, with joined hands and piteous eye,
Fearing to move or speak, she look'd so dreamingly.

XXXV

"Ah, Porphyro!" said she, "but even now
"Thy voice was at sweet tremble in mine ear,
"Made tuneable with every sweetest vow;
"And those sad eyes were spiritual and clear:
"How chang'd thou art! how pallid, chill, and drear!
"Give me that voice again, my Porphyro,
"Those looks immortal, those complainings dear!
"Oh, leave me not in this eternal woe,
"For if thou diest, my Love, I know not where to go."

XXXVI

Beyond a mortal man impassion'd far
At these voluptuous accents, he arose,
Ethereal, flush'd, and like a throbbing star
Seen mid the sapphire heaven's deep repose;

Into her dream he melted, as the rose
Blendeth its odour with the violet,—
Solution sweet: meantime the frost-wind blows
Like Love's alarum pattering the sharp sleet
Against the window-panes; St. Agnes' moon hath set.

XXXVII

'Tis dark: quick pattereth the flaw-blown sleet:
"This is no dream, my bride, my Madeline!"
'Tis dark: the iced gusts still rave and beat:
"No dream, alas! alas! and woe is mine!
"Porphyro will leave me here to fade and pine.—
"Cruel! what traitor could thee hither bring?
"I curse not, for my heart is lost in thine,
"Though thou forsakest a deceived thing;—
"A dove forlorn and lost with sick unpruned wing."

XXXVIII

"My Madeline! sweet dreamer! lovely bride!
"Say, may I be for aye thy vassal blest?
"Thy beauty's shield, heart-shap'd and vermeil dyed?
"Ah, silver shrine, here will I take my rest
"After so many hours of toil and quest,
"A famish'd pilgrim,—sav'd by miracle.
"Though I have found, I will not rob thy nest
"Saving of thy sweet self; if thou think'st well
"To trust, fair Madeline, to no rude infidel.

XXXIX

"Hark! 'tis an elfin-storm from faery land,
"Of haggard seeming, but a boon indeed:
"Arise—arise! the morning is at hand;—
"The bloated wassaillers will never heed:—
"Let us away, my love, with happy speed;
"There are no ears to hear, or eyes to see,—
"Drown'd all in Rhenish and the sleepy mead:
"Awake! arise! my love, and fearless be,
"For o'er the southern moors I have a home for thee."

XL

She hurried at his words, beset with fears,
For there were sleeping dragons all around,
At glaring watch, perhaps, with ready spears—
Down the wide stairs a darkling way they found.—

In all the house was heard no human sound.
A chain-droop'd lamp was flickering by each door;
The arras, rich with horseman, hawk, and hound,
Flutter'd in the besieging wind's uproar;
And the long carpets rose along the gusty floor.

XLI

They glide, like phantoms, into the wide hall;
Like phantoms, to the iron porch, they glide;
Where lay the Porter, in uneasy sprawl,
With a huge empty flaggon by his side:
The wakeful bloodhound rose, and shook his hide,
But his sagacious eye an inmate owns:
By one, and one, the bolts full easy slide;—
The chains lie silent on the footworn stones;—
The key turns, and the door upon its hinges groans.

XLII

And they are gone: aye, ages long ago
These lovers fled away into the storm.
That night the Baron dreamt of many a woe,
And all his warrior-guests, with shade and form
Of witch, and demon, and large coffin-worm,
Were long be-nightmar'd. Angela the old
Died palsy-twitch'd, with meagre face deform;
The Beadsman, after thousand aves told,
For aye unsought-for slept among his ashes cold.

POEMS

ODE TO A NIGHTINGALE

I

My heart aches, and a drowsy numbness pains
  My sense, as though of hemlock I had drunk,
Or emptied some dull opiate to the drains
  One minute past, and Lethe-wards had sunk:
'Tis not through envy of thy happy lot,
  But being too happy in thine happiness,—
    That thou, light-winged Dryad of the trees,
      In some melodious plot
  Of beechen green, and shadows numberless,
    Singest of summer in full-throated ease.

II

O, for a draught of vintage! that hath been
  Cool'd a long age in the deep-delved earth,
Tasting of Flora and the country green,
  Dance, and Provençal song, and sunburnt mirth!
O for a beaker full of the warm South,
  Full of the true, the blushful Hippocrene,
    With beaded bubbles winking at the brim,
      And purple-stained mouth;
  That I might drink, and leave the world unseen,
    And with thee fade away into the forest dim:

III

Fade far away, dissolve, and quite forget
  What thou among the leaves hast never known,
The weariness, the fever, and the fret
  Here, where men sit and hear each other groan;
Where palsy shakes a few, sad, last gray hairs,
  Where youth grows pale, and spectre-thin, and dies;
    Where but to think is to be full of sorrow
      And leaden-eyed despairs,
  Where Beauty cannot keep her lustrous eyes,
    Or new Love pine at them beyond to-morrow.

IV

Away! away! for I will fly to thee,
   Not charioted by Bacchus and his pards,
But on the viewless wings of Poesy,
   Though the dull brain perplexes and retards:
Already with thee! tender is the night,
   And haply the Queen-Moon is on her throne,
      Cluster'd around by all her starry Fays;
         But here there is no light,
Save what from heaven is with the breezes blown
   Through verdurous glooms and winding mossy ways.

V

I cannot see what flowers are at my feet,
   Nor what soft incense hangs upon the boughs,
But, in embalmed darkness, guess each sweet
   Wherewith the seasonable month endows
The grass, the thicket, and the fruit-tree wild;
   White hawthorn, and the pastoral eglantine;
      Fast fading violets cover'd up in leaves;
         And mid-May's eldest child,
The coming musk-rose, full of dewy wine,
   The murmurous haunt of flies on summer eves.

VI

Darkling I listen; and, for many a time
   I have been half in love with easeful Death,
Call'd him soft names in many a mused rhyme,
   To take into the air my quiet breath;
Now more than ever seems it rich to die,
   To cease upon the midnight with no pain,
      While thou art pouring forth thy soul abroad
         In such an ecstasy!
Still wouldst thou sing, and I have ears in vain—
   To thy high requiem become a sod.

VII

Thou wast not born for death, immortal Bird!
   No hungry generations tread thee down;
The voice I hear this passing night was heard
   In ancient days by emperor and clown:
Perhaps the self-same song that found a path
   Through the sad heart of Ruth, when, sick for home,
      She stood in tears amid the alien corn;
         The same that oft-times hath

Charm'd magic casements, opening on the foam
    Of perilous seas, in faery lands forlorn.

VIII

Forlorn! the very word is like a bell
    To toll me back from thee to my sole self!
Adieu! the fancy cannot cheat so well
    As she is fam'd to do, deceiving elf.
Adieu! adieu! thy plaintive anthem fades
    Past the near meadows, over the still stream,
        Up the hill-side; and now 'tis buried deep
            In the next valley-glades:
    Was it a vision, or a waking dream?
    Fled is that music:—Do I wake or sleep?

ODE ON A GRECIAN URN

I

THOU still unravish'd bride of quietness,
    Thou foster-child of silence and slow time,
Sylvan historian, who canst thus express
    A flowery tale more sweetly than our rhyme:
What leaf-fring'd legend haunts about thy shape
    Of deities or mortals, or of both,
        In Tempe or the dales of Arcady?
    What men or gods are these? What maidens loth?
What mad pursuit? What struggle to escape?
        What pipes and timbrels? What wild ecstasy?

II

Heard melodies are sweet, but those unheard
    Are sweeter; therefore, ye soft pipes, play on;
Not to the sensual ear, but, more endear'd,
    Pipe to the spirit ditties of no tone:
Fair youth, beneath the trees, thou canst not leave
    Thy song, nor ever can those trees be bare;
        Bold Lover, never, never canst thou kiss,
Though winning near the goal—yet, do not grieve;
    She cannot fade, though thou hast not thy bliss,
        For ever wilt thou love, and she be fair!

III

Ah, happy, happy boughs! that cannot shed
    Your leaves, nor ever bid the Spring adieu;
And, happy melodist, unwearied,
    For ever piping songs for ever new;

More happy love! more happy, happy love!
  For ever warm and still to be enjoy'd,
    For ever panting, and for ever young;
All breathing human passion far above,
  That leaves a heart high-sorrowful and cloy'd,
    A burning forehead, and a parching tongue.

IV

Who are these coming to the sacrifice?
  To what green altar, O mysterious priest,
Lead'st thou that heifer lowing at the skies,
  And all her silken flanks with garlands drest?
What little town by river or sea shore,
  Or mountain-built with peaceful citadel,
    Is emptied of this folk, this pious morn?
And, little town, thy streets for evermore
  Will silent be; and not a soul to tell
    Why thou art desolate, can e'er return.

V

O Attic shape! Fair attitude! with brede
  Of marble men and maidens overwrought,
With forest branches and the trodden weed;
  Thou, silent form, dost tease us out of thought
As doth eternity: Cold Pastoral!
  When old age shall this generation waste,
    Thou shalt remain, in midst of other woe
Than ours, a friend to man, to whom thou say'st,
  "Beauty is truth, truth beauty,"—that is all
    Ye know on earth, and all ye need to know.

ODE TO PSYCHE

O GODDESS! hear these tuneless numbers, wrung
  By sweet enforcement and remembrance dear,
And pardon that thy secrets should be sung
  Even into thine own soft-conched ear:
Surely I dreamt to-day, or did I see
  The winged Psyche with awaken'd eyes?
I wander'd in a forest thoughtlessly,
  And, on the sudden, fainting with surprise,
Saw two fair creatures, couched side by side
  In deepest grass, beneath the whisp'ring roof
  Of leaves and trembled blossoms, where there ran
    A brooklet, scarce espied: **10**

'Mid hush'd, cool-rooted flowers, fragrant-eyed,
  Blue, silver-white, and budded Tyrian,
They lay calm-breathing on the bedded grass;
  Their arms embraced, and their pinions too;
  Their lips touch'd not, but had not bade adieu,
As if disjoined by soft-handed slumber,
And ready still past kisses to outnumber
  At tender eye-dawn of aurorean love: 20
    The winged boy I knew;
  But who wast thou, O happy, happy dove?
    His Psyche true!

O latest born and loveliest vision far
  Of all Olympus' faded hierarchy!
Fairer than Phœbe's sapphire-region'd star,
  Or Vesper, amorous glow-worm of the sky;
Fairer than these, though temple thou hast none,
  Nor altar heap'd with flowers;
Nor virgin-choir to make delicious moan   30
    Upon the midnight hours;
No voice, no lute, no pipe, no incense sweet
  From chain-swung censer teeming;
No shrine, no grove, no oracle, no heat
  Of pale-mouth'd prophet dreaming.

O brightest! though too late for antique vows,
  Too, too late for the fond believing lyre,
When holy were the haunted forest boughs,
  Holy the air, the water, and the fire;
Yet even in these days so far retir'd   40
  From happy pieties, thy lucent fans,
  Fluttering among the faint Olympians,
I see, and sing, by my own eyes inspir'd.
So let me be thy choir, and make a moan
    Upon the midnight hours;
Thy voice, thy lute, thy pipe, thy incense sweet
  From swinged censer teeming;
Thy shrine, thy grove, thy oracle, thy heat
  Of pale-mouth'd prophet dreaming.

Yes, I will be thy priest, and build a fane   50
  In some untrodden region of my mind,
Where branched thoughts, new grown with pleasant pain,
  Instead of pines shall murmur in the wind:
Far, far around shall those dark-cluster'd trees
  Fledge the wild-ridged mountains steep by steep;

And there by zephyrs, streams, and birds, and bees,
  The moss-lain Dryads shall be lull'd to sleep;
And in the midst of this wide quietness
A rosy sanctury will I dress

With the wreath'd trellis of a working brain,   60
  With buds, and bells, and stars without a name,
With all the gardener Fancy e'er could feign,
  Who breeding flowers, will never breed the same:
And there shall be for thee all soft delight
  That shadowy thought can win,
A bright torch, and a casement ope at night,
  To let the warm Love in!

FANCY

EVER let the fancy roam,
Pleasure never is at home:
At a touch sweet Pleasure melteth,
Like to bubbles when rain pelteth;
Then let winged Fancy wander
Through the thought still spread beyond her:
Open wide the mind's cage-door,
She'll dart forth, and cloudward soar.
O sweet Fancy! let her loose;
Summer's joys are spoilt by use,   10
And the enjoying of the Spring
Fades as does its blossoming;
Autumn's red-lipp'd fruitage too,
Blushing through the mist and dew,
Cloys with tasting: What do then?
Sit thee by the ingle, when
The sear faggot blazes bright,
Spirit of a winter's night;
When the soundless earth is muffled,
And the caked snow is shuffled   20
From the ploughboy's heavy shoon;
When the Night doth meet the Noon
In a dark conspiracy
To banish Even from her sky.
Sit thee there, and send abroad,
With a mind self-overaw'd,
Fancy, high-commission'd:—send her!
She has vassals to attend her:
She will bring, in spite of frost,
Beauties that the earth hath lost;   30

She will bring thee, all together,
All delights of summer weather;
All the buds and bells of May,
From dewy sward or thorny spray;
All the heaped Autumn's wealth,
With a still, mysterious stealth:
She will mix these pleasures up
Like three fit wines in a cup,
And thou shalt quaff it:—thou shalt hear
Distant harvest-carols clear;   40
Rustle of the reaped corn;
Sweet birds antheming the morn:
And, in the same moment—hark!
'Tis the early April lark,
Or the rooks, with busy caw,
Foraging for sticks and straw.
Thou shalt, at one glance, behold
The daisy and the marigold;
White-plum'd lillies, and the first
Hedge-grown primrose that hath burst;   50
Shaded hyacinth, alway
Sapphire queen of the mid-May;
And every leaf, and every flower
Pearled with the self-same shower.
Thou shalt see the field-mouse peep
Meagre from its celled sleep;
And the snake all winter-thin
Cast on sunny bank its skin;
Freckled nest-eggs thou shalt see
Hatching in the hawthorn tree,   60
When the hen-bird's wing doth rest
Quiet on her mossy nest;
Then the hurry and alarm
When the bee-hive casts its swarm;
Acorns ripe down-pattering,
While the autumn breezes sing.

Oh, sweet Fancy! let her loose;
Every thing is spoilt by use:
Where's the cheek that doth not fade,
Too much gaz'd at? Where's the maid   70
Whose lip mature is ever new?
Where's the eye, however blue,
Doth not weary? Where's the face
One would meet in every place?
Where's the voice, however soft,
One would hear so very oft?

At a touch sweet Pleasure melteth
Like to bubbles when rain pelteth.
Let, then, winged Fancy find
Thee a mistress to thy mind: 80
Dulcet-eyed as Ceres' daughter,
Ere the God of Torment taught her
How to frown and how to chide;
With a waist and with a side
White as Hebe's, when her zone
Slipt its golden clasp, and down
Fell her kirtle to her feet,
While she held the goblet sweet,
And Jove grew languid.—Break the mesh
Of the Fancy's silken leash;   90
Quickly break her prison-string
And such joys as these she'll bring.—
Let the winged Fancy roam,
Pleasure never is at home.

ODE

*[Written on the blank page before Beaumont and Fletcher's Tragi-
Comedy "The Fair Maid of the Inn."]*

BARDS of Passion and of Mirth,
Ye have left your souls on earth!
Have ye souls in heaven too,
Double lived in regions new?
Yes, and those of heaven commune
With the spheres of sun and moon;
With the noise of fountains wound'rous,
And the parle of voices thund'rous;
With the whisper of heaven's trees
And one another, in soft ease   10

Seated on Elysian lawns
Brows'd by none but Dian's fawns;
Underneath large blue-bells tented,
Where the daisies are rose-scented,
And the rose herself has got
Perfume which on earth is not;
Where the nightingale doth sing
Not a senseless, tranced thing,
But divine melodious truth;
Philosophic numbers smooth;   20
Tales and golden histories
Of heaven and its mysteries.

Thus ye live on high, and then
On the earth ye live again;
And the souls ye left behind you
Teach us, here, the way to find you,
Where your other souls are joying,
Never slumber'd, never cloying.
Here, your earth-born souls still speak
To mortals, of their little week;   30
Of their sorrows and delights;
Of their passions and their spites;
Of their glory and their shame;
What doth strengthen and what maim.
Thus ye teach us, every day,
Wisdom, though fled far away.

Bards of Passion and of Mirth,
Ye have left your souls on earth!
Ye have souls in heaven too,
Double-lived in regions new!   40

LINES ON THE MERMAID TAVERN

SOULS of Poets dead and gone,
What Elysium have ye known,
Happy field or mossy cavern,
Choicer than the Mermaid Tavern?
Have ye tippled drink more fine
Than mine host's Canary wine?
Or are fruits of Paradise
Sweeter than those dainty pies
Of venison? O generous food!
Drest as though bold Robin Hood   10
Would, with his maid Marian,
Sup and bowse from horn and can.

I have heard that on a day
Mine host's sign-board flew away,
Nobody knew whither, till
An astrologer's old quill
To a sheepskin gave the story,
Said he saw you in your glory,
Underneath a new old sign
Sipping beverage divine,   20
And pledging with contented smack
The Mermaid in the Zodiac.

Souls of Poets dead and gone,
What Elysium have ye known,
Happy field or mossy cavern,
Choicer than the Mermaid Tavern?

ROBIN HOOD

TO A FRIEND

No! those days are gone away,
And their hours are old and gray,
And their minutes buried all
Under the down-trodden pall
Of the leaves of many years:
Many times have winter's shears,
Frozen North, and chilling East,
Sounded tempests to the feast
Of the forest's whispering fleeces,
Since men knew nor rent nor leases.   10

No, the bugle sounds no more,
And the twanging bow no more;
Silent is the ivory shrill
Past the heath and up the hill;
There is no mid-forest laugh,
Where lone Echo gives the half
To some wight, amaz'd to hear
Jesting, deep in forest drear.

On the fairest time of June
You may go, with sun or moon,   20
Or the seven stars to light you,
Or the polar ray to right you;
But you never may behold
Little John, or Robin bold;
Never one, of all the clan,
Thrumming on an empty can
Some old hunting ditty, while
He doth his green way beguile
To fair hostess Merriment,
Down beside the pasture Trent;   30
For he left the merry tale
Messenger for spicy ale.

Gone, the merry morris din;
Gone, the song of Gamelyn;
Gone, the tough-belted outlaw
Idling in the "grenè shawe";
All are gone away and past!
And if Robin should be cast
Sudden from his turfed grave,
And if Marian should have   40
Once again her forest days,
She would weep, and he would craze:
He would swear, for all his oaks,
Fall'n beneath the dockyard strokes,
Have rotted on the briny seas;
She would weep that her wild bees
Sang not to her—strange! that honey
Can't be got without hard money!

So it is: yet let us sing,
Honour to the old bow-string!   50
Honour to the bugle-horn!
Honour to the woods unshorn!
Honour to the Lincoln green!
Honour to the archer keen!
Honour to tight little John,
And the horse he rode upon!
Honour to bold Robin Hood,
Sleeping in the underwood!
Honour to maid Marian,
And to all the Sherwood-clan!   60
Though their days have hurried by
Let us two a burden try.

TO AUTUMN

I

Season of mists and mellow fruitfulness,
  Close bosom-friend of the maturing sun;
Conspiring with him how to load and bless
  With fruit the vines that round the thatch-eves run;
To bend with apples the moss'd cottage-trees,
  And fill all fruit with ripeness to the core;
    To swell the gourd, and plump the hazel shells
  With a sweet kernel; to set budding more,
And still more, later flowers for the bees,
Until they think warm days will never cease,
  For Summer has o'er-brimm'd their clammy cells.

II

Who hath not seen thee oft amid thy store?
  Sometimes whoever seeks abroad may find
Thee sitting careless on a granary floor,
  Thy hair soft-lifted by the winnowing wind;
Or on a half-reap'd furrow sound asleep,
  Drows'd with the fume of poppies, while thy hook
    Spares the next swath and all its twined flowers:
And sometimes like a gleaner thou dost keep
  Steady thy laden head across a brook;
  Or by a cyder-press, with patient look,
    Thou watchest the last oozings hours by hours.

III

Where are the songs of Spring? Ay, where are they?
  Think not of them, thou hast thy music too,—
While barred clouds bloom the soft-dying day,
  And touch the stubble-plains with rosy hue;
Then in a wailful choir the small gnats mourn
  Among the river sallows, borne aloft
    Or sinking as the light wind lives or dies;
And full-grown lambs loud bleat from hilly bourn;
  Hedge-crickets sing; and now with treble soft
  The red-breast whistles from a garden-croft;
    And gathering swallows twitter in the skies.

ODE ON MELANCHOLY

I

No, no, go not to Lethe, neither twist
  Wolf's bane, tight-rooted, for its poisonous wine;
Nor suffer thy pale forehead to be kiss'd
  By nightshade, ruby grape of Proserpine;
Make not your rosary of yew-berries,
  Nor let the beetle, nor the death-moth be
    Your mournful Psyche, nor the downy owl
A partner in your sorrow's mysteries;
  For shade to shade will come too drowsily,
    And drown the wakeful anguish of the soul.

II

But when the melancholy fit shall fall
  Sudden from heaven like a weeping cloud,
That fosters the droop-headed flowers all,
  And hides the green hill in an April shroud;

Then glut thy sorrow on a morning rose,
　　Or on the rainbow of the salt sand-wave,
　　Or on the wealth of globed peonies;
Or if thy mistress some rich anger shows,
　　Emprison her soft hand, and let her rave,
　　　　And feed deep, deep upon her peerless eyes.

III

She dwells with Beauty—Beauty that must die;
　　And Joy, whose hand is ever at his lips
Bidding adieu; and aching Pleasure nigh,
　　Turning to Poison while the bee-mouth sips:
Ay, in the very temple of delight
　　Veil'd Melancholy has her sovran shrine,
　　　　Though seen of none save him whose strenuous tongue
Can burst Joy's grape against his palate fine;
His soul shall taste the sadness of her might,
　　And be among her cloudy trophies hung.

HYPERION

A FRAGMENT

BOOK I

DEEP in the shady sadness of a vale
Far sunken from the healthy breath of morn,
Far from the fiery noon, and eve's one star,
Sat gray-hair'd Saturn, quiet as a stone,
Still as the silence round about his lair;
Forest on forest hung about his head
Like cloud on cloud. No stir of air was there,
Not so much life as on a summer's day
Robs not one light seed from the feather'd grass,
But where the dead leaf fell, there did it rest. 10
A stream went voiceless by, still deadened more
By reason of his fallen divinity
Spreading a shade: the Naiad 'mid her reeds
Press'd her cold finger closer to her lips.

Along the margin-sand large foot-marks went,
No further than to where his feet had stray'd,
And slept there since. Upon the sodden ground
His old right hand lay nerveless, listless, dead,
Unsceptred; and his realmless eyes were closed;
While his bow'd head seem'd list'ning to the Earth,
His ancient mother, for some comfort yet. 21

It seem'd no force could wake him from his place;
But there came one, who with a kindred hand
Touch'd his wide shoulders, after bending low
With reverence, though to one who knew it not.
She was a Goddess of the infant world;
By her in stature the tall Amazon
Had stood a pigmy's height: she would have ta'en
Achilles by the hair and bent his neck;
Or with a finger stay'd Ixion's wheel. 30
Her face was large as that of Memphian sphinx,
Pedestal'd haply in a palace court,
When sages look'd to Egypt for their lore.

But oh! how unlike marble was that face:
How beautiful, if sorow had not made
Sorrow more beautiful than Beauty's self.
There was a listening fear in her regard,
As if calamity had but begun;
As if the vanward clouds of evil days
Had spent their malice, and the sullen rear   40
Was with its stored thunder labouring up.
One hand she press'd upon that aching spot
Where beats the human heart, as if just there,
Though an immortal, she felt cruel pain:
The other upon Saturn's bended neck
She laid, and to the level of his ear
Leaning with parted lips, some words she spake
In solemn tenour and deep organ tone:
Some mourning words. which in our feeble tongue
Would come in these ʌike accents; O how frail   50
To that large utterance of the early Gods!
"Saturn, look up!—though wherefore, poor old King?
"I have no comfort for thee, no not one:
"I cannot say, 'O wherefore sleepest thou?'
"For heaven is parted from thee, and the earth
"Knows thee not, thus afflicted, for a God;
"And ocean too, with all its solemn noise,
"Has from thy sceptre pass'd; and all the air
"Is emptied of thine hoary majesty.
"Thy thunder, conscious of the new command,   60
"Rumbles reluctant o'er our fallen house;
"And thy sharp lightning in unpractis'd hands
"Scorches and burns our once serene domain.
"O aching time! O moments big as years!
"All as ye pass swell out the monstrous truth,
"And press it so upon our weary griefs
"That unbelief has not a space to breathe.
"Saturn, sleep on:—O thoughtless, why did I
"Thus violate thy slumbrous solitude?
"Why should I ope thy melancholy eyes?   70
"Saturn, sleep on! while at thy feet I weep."

    As when, upon a tranced summer-night,
Those green-rob'd senators of mighty woods,
Tall oaks, branch-charmed by the earnest stars,
Dream, and so dream all night without a stir,
Save from one gradual solitary gust
Which comes upon the silence, and dies off,
As if the ebbing air had but one wave;
So came these words and went; the while in tears

She touch'd her fair large forehead to the ground,
Just where her falling hair might be outspread   81
A soft and silken mat for Saturn's feet.
One moon, with alteration slow, had shed
Her silver seasons four upon the night,
And still these two were postured motionless,
Like natural sculpture in cathedral cavern;
The frozen God still couchant on the earth,
And the sad Goddess weeping at his feet:
Until at length old Saturn lifted up
His faded eyes, and saw his kingdom gone,   90
And all the gloom and sorrow of the place,
And that fair kneeling Goddess; and then spake,
As with a palsied tongue, and while his beard
Shook horrid with such aspen-malady:
"O tender spouse of gold Hyperion,
"Thea, I feel thee ere I see thy face;
"Look up, and let me see our doom in it;
"Look up, and tell me if this feeble shape
"Is Saturn's; tell me, if thou hear'st the voice
"Of Saturn; tell me, if this wrinkling brow,   100
"Naked and bare of its great diadem,
"Peers like the front of Saturn. Who had power
"To make me desolate? whence came the strength?
"How was it nurtur'd to such bursting forth,
"While Fate seem'd strangled in my nervous grasp?
"But it is so; and I am smother'd up,
"And buried from all godlike exercise
"Of influence benign on planets pale,
"Of admonitions to the winds and seas,
"Of peaceful sway above man's harvesting,   110
"And all those acts which Deity supreme
"Doth ease its heart of love in.—I am gone
"Away from my own bosom: I have left
"My strong identity, my real self,
"Somewhere between the throne, and where I sit
"Here on this spot of earth. Search, Thea, search!
"Open thine eyes eterne, and sphere them round
"Upon all space: space starr'd, and lorn of light;
"Space region'd with life-air; and barren void;
"Spaces of fire, and all the yawn of hell.—   120
"Search, Thea, search! and tell me, if thou seest
"A certain shape or shadow, making way
"With wings or chariot fierce to repossess
"A heaven he lost erewhile: it must—it must
"Be of ripe progress—Saturn must be King.
"Yes, there must be a golden victory;

"There must be Gods thrown down, and trumpets blown
"Of triumph calm, and hymns of festival
"Upon the gold clouds metropolitan,
"Voices of soft proclaim, and silver stir   130
"Of strings in hollow shells; and there shall be
"Beautiful things made new, for the surprise
"Of the sky-children; I will give command:
"Thea! Thea! Thea! where is Saturn?"

          This passion lifted him upon his feet,
And made his hands to struggle in the air,
His Druid locks to shake and ooze with sweat,
His eyes to fever out, his voice to cease.
He stood, and heard not Thea's sobbing deep;
A little time, and then again he snatch'd   140
Utterance thus.—"But cannot I create?
"Cannot I form? Cannot I fashion forth
"Another world, another universe,
"To overbear and crumble this to naught?
"Where is another chaos? Where?"—That word
Found way unto Olympus, and made quake
The rebel three.—Thea was startled up,
And in her bearing was a sort of hope,
As thus she quick-voic'd spake, yet full of awe.
"This cheers our fallen house: come to our friends,   150
"O Saturn! come away, and give them heart;
"I know the covert, for thence came I hither."
Thus brief; then with beseeching eyes she went
With backward footing through the shade a space:
He follow'd, and she turn'd to lead the way
Through aged boughs, that yielded like the mist
Which eagles cleave upmounting from their nest.

          Meanwhile in other realms big tears were shed,
More sorrow like to this, and such like woe,
Too huge for mortal tongue or pen of scribe: 160
The Titans fierce, self-hid, or prison-bound,
Groan'd for the old allegiance once more,
And listen'd in sharp pain for Saturn's voice.
But one of the whole mammoth-brood still kept
His sov'reignty, and rule, and majesty;—
Blazing Hyperion on his orbed fire
Still sat, still snuff'd the incense, teeming up
From man to the sun's God; yet unsecure:
For as among us mortals omens drear
Fright and perplex, so also shuddered he—   170
Not at dog's howl, or gloom-bird's hated screech,

Or the familiar visiting of one
Upon the first toll of his passing-bell,
Or prophesyings of the midnight lamp;
But horrors, portion'd to a giant nerve,
Oft made Hyperion ache. His palace bright
Bastion'd with pyramids of glowing gold,
And touch'd with shade of bronzed obelisks,
Glar'd a blood-red through all its thousand courts,
Arches, and domes, and fiery galleries;   180
And all its curtains of Aurorian clouds
Flush'd angerly: while sometimes eagles' wings,
Unseen before by Gods or wondering men,
Darken'd the place; and neighing steeds were heard,
Not heard before by Gods or wondering men.
Also, when he would taste the spicy wreaths
Of incense, breath'd aloft from sacred hills,
Instead of sweets, his ample palate took
Savour of poisonous brass and metal sick:
And so, when harbour'd in the sleepy west,   190
After the full completion of fair day,—
For rest divine upon exalted couch
And slumber in the arms of melody,
He pac'd away the pleasant hours of ease
With stride colossal, on from hall to hall;
While far within each aisle and deep recess,
His winged minions in close clusters stood,
Amaz'd and full of fear; like anxious men
Who on wide plains gather in panting troops,
When earthquakes jar their battlements and towers.   200
Even now, while Saturn, rous'd from icy trance,
Went step for step with Thea through the woods,
Hyperion, leaving twilight in the rear,
Came slope upon the threshold of the west;
Then, as was wont, his palace-door flew ope
In smoothest silence, save what solemn tubes,
Blown by the serious Zephyrs, gave of sweet
And wandering sounds, slow-breathed melodies;
And like a rose in vermeil tint and shape,
In fragrance soft, and coolness to the eye,   210
That inlet to severe magnificence
Stood full blown, for the God to enter in.

He enter'd, but he enter'd full of wrath;
His flaming robes stream'd out beyond his heels,
And gave a roar, as if of earthly fire,
That scar'd away the meek ethereal Hours
And made their dove-wings tremble. On he flared,

From stately nave to nave, from vault to vault,
Through bowers of fragrant and enwreathed light,   220
And diamond-paved lustrous long arcades,
Until he reach'd the great main cupola;
There standing fierce beneath, he stamped his foot,
And from the basements deep to the high towers
Jarr'd his own golden region; and before
The quavering thunder thereupon had ceas'd,
His voice leapt out, despite of godlike curb,
To this result: "O dreams of day and night!
"O monstrous forms! O effigies of pain!
"O spectres busy in a cold, cold gloom!
"O lank-ear'd Phantoms of black-weeded pools!   230
"Why do I know ye? why have I seen ye? why
"Is my eternal essence thus distraught
"To see and to behold these horrors new?
"Saturn is fallen, am I too to fall?
"Am I to leave this haven of my rest,
"This cradle of my glory, this soft clime,
"This calm luxuriance of blissful light,
"These crystalline pavilions, and pure fanes,
"Of all my lucent empire? It is left
"Deserted, void, nor any haunt of mine.   240
"The blaze, the splendour, and the symmetry,
"I cannot see—but darkness, death and darkness.
"Even here, into my centre of repose,
"The shady visions come to domineer,
"Insult, and blind, and stifle up my pomp.—
"Fall!—No, by Tellus and her briny robes!
"Over the fiery frontier of my realms
"I will advance a terrible right arm
"Shall scare that infant thunderer, rebel Jove,
"And bid old Saturn take his throne again."—   250
He spake, and ceas'd, the while a heavier threat
Held struggle with his throat but came not forth;
For as in theatres of crowded men
Hubbub increases more they call out "Hush!"
So at Hyperion's words the Phantoms pale
Bestirr'd themselves, thrice horrible and cold;
And from the mirror'd level where he stood
A mist arose, as from a scummy marsh.
At this, through all his bulk an agony
Crept gradual, from the feet unto the crown,   260
Like a lithe serpent vast and muscular
Making slow way, with head and neck convuls'd
From over-strained might. Releas'd, he fled
To the eastern gates, and full six dewy hours

Before the dawn in season due should blush,
He breath'd fierce breath against the sleepy portals,
Clear'd them of heavy vapours, burst them wide
Suddenly on the ocean's chilly streams.
The planet orb of fire, whereon he rode
Each day from east to west the heavens through,   270
Spun round in sable curtaining of clouds;
Not therefore veiled quite, blindfold, and hid,
But ever and anon the glancing spheres,
Circles, and arcs, and broad-belting colure,
Glow'd through, and wrought upon the muffling dark
Sweet-shaped lightnings from the nadir deep
Up to the zenith,—hieroglyphics old
Which sages and keen-eyed astrologers
Then living on the earth, with labouring thought
Won from the gaze of many centuries: 280
Now lost, save what we find on remnants huge
Of stone, or marble swart; their import gone,
Their wisdom long since fled.—Two wings this orb
Possess'd for glory, two fair argent wings,
Ever exalted at the God's approach:
And now, from forth the gloom their plumes immense
Rose, one by one, till all outspreaded were;
While still the dazzling globe maintain'd eclipse,
Awaiting for Hyperion's command.
Fain would he have commanded, fain took throne   290
And bid the day begin, if but for change.
He might not:—No, though a primeval God:
The sacred seasons might not be disturb'd.
Therefore the operations of the dawn
Stay'd in their birth, even as here 'tis told.
Those silver wings expanded sisterly,
Eager to sail their orb; the porches wide
Open'd upon the dusk demesnes of night;
And the bright Titan, phrenzied with new woes,
Unus'd to bend, by hard compulsion bent   300
His spirit to the sorrow of the time;
And all along a dismal rack of clouds,
Upon the boundaries of day and night,
He stretch'd himself in grief and radiance faint.
There as he lay, the Heaven with its stars
Look'd down on him with pity, and the voice
Of Cœlus, from the universal space,
Thus whisper'd low and solemn in his ear.
"O brightest of my children dear, earth-born
"And sky-engendered, Son of Mysteries   310
"All unrevealed even to the powers

"Which met at thy creating; at whose joys
"And palpitations sweet, and pleasures soft,
"I, Cœlus, wonder, how they came and whence;
"And at the fruits thereof what shapes they be,
"Distinct, and visible; symbols divine,
"Manifestations of that beauteous life
"Diffus'd unseen throughout eternal space:
"Of these new-form'd art thou, oh brightest child!
"Of these, thy brethren and the Goddesses!   320
"There is sad feud among ye, and rebellion
"Of son against his sire. I saw him fall,
"I saw my first-born tumbled from his throne!
"To me his arms were spread, to me his voice
"Found way from forth the thunders round his head!
"Pale wox I, and in vapours hid my face.
"Art thou, too, near such doom? vague fear there is:
"For I have seen my sons most unlike Gods.
"Divine ye were created, and divine
"In sad demeanour, solemn, undisturb'd,   330
"Unruffled, like high Gods, ye liv'd and ruled:
"Now I behold in you fear, hope, and wrath;
"Actions of rage and passion; even as
"I see them, on the mortal world beneath,
"In men who die.—This is the grief, O Son!
"Sad sign of ruin, sudden dismay, and fall!
"Yet do thou strive; as thou art capable,
"As thou canst move about, an evident God;
"And canst oppose to each malignant hour
"Ethereal presence:—I am but a voice;   340
"My life is but the life of winds and tides,
"No more than winds and tides can I avail:—
"But thou canst.—Be thou therefore in the van
"Of circumstance; yea, seize the arrow's barb
"Before the tense string murmur.—To the earth!
"For there thou wilt find Saturn, and his woes.
"Meantime I will keep watch on thy bright sun,
"And of thy seasons be a careful nurse."—
Ere half this region-whisper had come down,
Hyperion arose, and on the stars   350
Lifted his curved lids, and kept them wide
Until it ceased; and still he kept them wide:
And still they were the same bright, patient stars.
Then with a slow incline of his broad breast,
Like to a diver in the pearly seas,
Forward he stoop'd over the airy shore,
And plung'd all noiseless into the deep night.

HYPERION. BOOK II

JUST at the self-same beat of Time's wide wings
Hyperion slid into the rustled air,
And Saturn gain'd with Thea that sad place
Where Cybele and the bruised Titans mourn'd.
It was a den where no insulting light
Could glimmer on their tears; where their own groans
They felt, but heard not, for the solid roar
Of thunderous waterfalls and torrents hoarse,
Pouring a constant bulk, uncertain where.
Crag jutting forth to crag, and rocks that seem'd   10
Ever as if just rising from a sleep,
Forehead to forehead held their monstrous horns;
And thus in thousand hugest phantasies
Made a fit roofing to this nest of woe.
Instead of thrones, hard flint they sat upon,
Couches of rugged stone, and slaty ridge
Stubborn'd with iron. All were not assembled:
Some chain'd in torture, and some wandering.
Cœus, and Gyges, and Briareüs,
Typhon, and Dolor, and Porphyrion,   20
With many more, the brawniest in assault,
Were pent in regions of laborious breath;
Dungeon'd in opaque element, to keep
Their clenched teeth still clench'd, and all their limbs
Lock'd up like veins of metal, crampt and screw'd;
Without a motion, save of their big hearts
Heaving in pain, and horribly convuls'd
With sanguine feverous boiling gurge of pulse,
Mnemosyne was straying in the world;
Far from her moon had Phœbe wandered;   30
And many else were free to roam abroad,
But for the main, here found they covert drear.
Scarce images of life, one here, one there,
Lay vast and edgeways; like a dismal cirque
Of Druid stones, upon a forlorn moor,
When the chill rain begins at shut of eve,
In dull November, and their chancel vault,
The Heaven itself, is blinded throughout night.
Each one kept shroud, nor to his neighbour gave
Or word, or look, or action of despair.   40
Creüs was one; his ponderous iron mace
Lay by him, and a shatter'd rib of rock
Told of his rage, ere he thus sank and pined.
Iäpetus another; in his grasp,

A serpent's plashy neck; its barbed tongue
Squeez'd from the gorge, and all its uncurl'd length
Dead; and because the creature could not spit
Its poison in the eyes of conquering Jove.
Next Cottus: prone he lay, chin uppermost,
As though in pain; for still upon the flint   50
He ground severe his skull, with open mouth
And eyes at horrid working. Nearest him
Asia, born of most enormous Caf,
Who cost her mother Tellus keener pangs,
Though feminine, than any of her sons:
More thought than woe was in her dusky face,
For she was prophesying of her glory;
And in her wide imagination stood
Palm-shaded temples, and high rival fanes,
By Oxus or in Ganges' sacred isles.   60
Even as Hope upon her anchor leans,
So leant she, not so fair, upon a tusk
Shed from the broadest of her elephants.
Above her, on a crag's uneasy shelve,
Upon his elbow rais'd, all prostrate else,
Shadow'd Enceladus; once tame and mild
As grazing ox unworried in the meads;
Now tiger-passion'd, lion-thoughted, wroth,
He meditated, plotted, and even now
Was hurling mountains in that second war,   70
Not long delay'd, that scar'd the younger Gods
To hide themselves in forms of beast and bird.
Not far hence Atlas; and beside him prone
Phorcus, the sire of Gorgons. Neighbour'd close
Oceanus, and Tethys, in whose lap
Sobb'd Clymene among her tangled hair.
In midst of all lay Themis, at the feet
Of Ops the queen all clouded round from sight;
No shape distinguishable, more than when
Thick night confounds the pine-tops with the clouds:
And many else whose names may not be told.   81
For when the Muse's wings are air-ward spread,
Who shall delay her flight? And she must chaunt
Of Saturn, and his guide, who now had climb'd
With damp and slippery footing from a depth
More horrid still. Above a sombre cliff
Their heads appear'd, and up their stature grew
Till on the level height their steps found ease:
Then Thea spread abroad her trembling arms
Upon the precincts of this nest of pain,   90
And sidelong fix'd her eye on Saturn's face:

There saw she direst strife; the supreme God
At war with all the frailty of grief,
Of rage, of fear, anxiety, revenge,
Remorse, spleen, hope, but most of all despair.
Against these plagues he strove in vain; for Fate
Had pour'd a mortal oil upon his head,
A disanointing poison: so that Thea,
Affrighted, kept her still, and let him pass
First onwards in, among the fallen tribe.　　　　　100

　　As with us mortal men, the laden heart
Is persecuted more, and fever'd more,
When it is nighing to the mournful house
Where other hearts are sick of the same bruise;
So Saturn, as he walk'd into the midst,
Felt faint, and would have sunk among the rest,
But that he met Enceladus's eye,
Whose mightiness, and awe of him, at once
Came like an inspiration; and he shouted,
"Titans, behold your God!" at which some groan'd;
Some started on their feet; some also shouted;　　　111
Some wept, some wail'd, all bow'd with reverence:
And Ops, uplifting her black folded veil,
Show'd her pale cheeks, and all her forehead wan,
Her eye-brows thin and jet, and hollow eyes.
There is a roaring in the bleak-grown pines
When Winter lifts his voice; there is a noise
Among immortals when a God gives sign,
With hushing finger, how he means to load
His tongue with the full weight of utterless thought,
With thunder, and with music, and with pomp:　　　121
Such noise is like the roar of bleak-grown pines:
Which, when it ceases in this mountain'd world,
No other sound succeeds; but ceasing here,
Among these fallen, Saturn's voice therefrom
Grew up like organ, that begins anew
Its strain, when other harmonies, stopt short,
Leave the dinn'd air vibrating silverly.
Thus grew it up—"Not in my own sad breast,
"Which is its own great judge and searcher out,
"Can I find reason why ye should be thus:　　　131
"Not in the legends of the first of days,
"Studied from that old spirit-leaved book
"Which starry Uranus with finger bright
"Sav'd from the shores of darkness, when the waves
"Low-ebb'd still hid it up in shallow gloom;—
"And the which book ye know I ever kept

"For my firm-based footstool:—Ah, infirm!
"Not there, nor in sign, symbol, or portent
"Of element, earth, water, air, and fire,—   140
"At war, at peace, or inter-quarreling
"One against one, or two, or three, or all
"Each several one against the other three,
"As fire with air loud warring when rain-floods
"Drown both, and press them both against earth's face,
"Where, finding sulphur, a quadruple wrath
"Unhinges the poor world;—not in that strife,
"Wherefrom I take strange lore, and read it deep,
"Can I find reason why ye should be thus:
"No, no-where can unriddle, though I search,   150
"And pore on Nature's universal scroll
"Even to swooning, why ye, Divinities,
"The first-born of all shap'd and palpable Gods,
"Should cower beneath what, in comparison,
"Is untremendous might. Yet ye are here,
"O'erwhelm'd, and spurn'd, and batter'd, ye are here!
"O Titans, shall I say, 'Arise!'—Ye groan:
"Shall I say 'Crouch!'—Ye groan. What can I then?
"O Heaven wide! O unseen parent dear!
"What can I? Tell me, all ye brethren Gods,   160
"How we can war, how engine our great wrath!
"O speak your counsel now, for Saturn's ear
"Is all a-hunger'd. Thou, Oceanus,
"Ponderest high and deep; and in thy face
"I see, astonied, that severe content
"Which comes of thought and musing: give us help!"

   So ended Saturn; and the God of the Sea,
Sophist and sage, from no Athenian grove,
But cogitation in his watery shades,
Arose, with locks not oozy, and began,   170
In murmurs, which his first-endeavouring tongue
Caught infant-like from the far-foamed sands.
"O ye, whom wrath consumes! who, passion-strung,
"Writhe at defeat, and nurse your agonies!
"Shut up your senses, stifle up your ears,
"My voice is not a bellows unto ire.
"Yet listen, ye who will, whilst I bring proof
"How ye, perforce, must be content to stoop:
"And in the proof much comfort will I give,
"If ye will take that comfort in its truth.   180
"We fall by course of Nature's law, not force
"Of thunder, or of Jove. Great Saturn, thou
"Hast sifted well the atom-universe;

"But for this reason, that thou art the King,
"And only blind from sheer supremacy,
"One avenue was shaded from thine eyes,
"Through which I wandered to eternal truth.
"And first, as thou wast not the first of powers,
"So art thou not the last; it cannot be:
"Thou art not the beginning nor the end.   190
"From chaos and parental darkness came
"Light, the first fruits of that intestine broil,
"That sullen ferment, which for wondrous ends
"Was ripening in itself. The ripe hour came,
"And with it light, and light, engendering
"Upon its own producer, forthwith touch'd
"The whole enormous matter into life.
"Upon that very hour, our parentage,
"The Heavens and the Earth, were manifest:
"Then thou first born, and we the giant race,   200
"Found ourselves ruling new and beauteous realms.
"Now comes the pain of truth, to whom 'tis pain;
"O folly! for to bear all naked truths,
"And to envisage circumstance, all calm,
"That is the top of sovereignty. Mark well!
"As Heaven and Earth are fairer, fairer far
"Than Chaos and blank Darkness, though once chiefs;
"And as we show beyond that Heaven and Earth
"In form and shape compact and beautiful,
"In will, in action free, companionship,   210
"And thousand other signs of purer life;
"So on our heels a fresh perfection treads,
"A power more strong in beauty, born of us
"And fated to excel us, as we pass
"In glory that old Darkness: nor are we
"Thereby more conquer'd, than by us the rule
"Of shapeless Chaos. Say, doth the dull soil
"Quarrel with the proud forests it hath fed,
"And feedeth still, more comely than itself?
"Can it deny the chiefdom of green groves?   220
"Or shall the tree be envious of the dove
"Because it cooeth, and hath snowy wings
"To wander wherewithal and find its joys?
"We are such forest-trees, and our fair boughs
"Have bred forth, not pale solitary doves,
"But eagles golden-feather'd, who do tower
"Above us in their beauty, and must reign
"In right thereof; for 'tis the eternal law
"That first in beauty should be first in might:
"Yea, by that law, another race may drive   230

"Our conquerors to mourn as we do now.
"Have ye beheld the young God of the Seas,
"My dispossessor? Have ye seen his face?
"Have ye beheld his chariot, foam'd along
"By noble winged creatures he hath made?
"I saw him on the calmed waters scud,
"With such a glow of beauty in his eyes,
"That it enforc'd me to bid sad farewell
"To all my empire: farewell sad I took,
"And hither came, to see how dolorous fate   240
"Had wrought upon ye; and how I might best
"Give consolation in this woe extreme.
"Receive the truth, and let it be your balm."

Whether through poz'd conviction, or disdain,
They guarded silence, when Oceanus
Left murmuring, what deepest thought can tell?
But so it was, none answer'd for a space.
Save one whom none regarded, Clymene;
And yet she answer'd not, only complain'd,
With hectic lips, and eyes up-looking mild,   250
Thus wording timidly among the fierce:
"O Father, I am here the simplest voice,
"And all my knowledge is that joy is gone,
"And this thing woe crept in among our hearts,
"There to remain for ever, as I fear:
"I would not bode of evil, if I thought
"So weak a creature could turn off the help
"Which by just right should come of mighty Gods;
"Yet let me tell my sorrow, let me tell
"Of what I heard, and how it made me weep,   260
"And know that we had parted from all hope.
"I stood upon a shore, a pleasant shore,
"Where a sweet clime was breathed from a land
"Of fragrance, quietness, and trees, and flowers.
"Full of calm joy it was, as I of grief;
"Too full of joy and soft delicious warmth;
"So that I felt a movement in my heart
"To chide, and to reproach that solitude
"With songs of misery, music of our woes;
"And sat me down, and took a mouthed shell   270
"And murmur'd into it, and made melody—
"O melody no more! for while I sang,
"And with poor skill let pass into the breeze
"The dull shell's echo, from a bowery strand
"Just opposite, an island of the sea,
"There came enchantment with the shifting wind,

"That did both drown and keep alive my ears.
"I threw my shell away upon the sand,
"And a wave fill'd it, as my sense was fill'd
"With that new blissful golden melody.   280
"A living death was in each gush of sounds,
"Each family of rapturous hurried notes,
"That fell, one after one, yet all at once,
"Like pearl beads dropping sudden from their string:
"And then another, then another strain,
"Each like a dove leaving its olive perch,
"With music wing'd instead of silent plumes,
"To hover round my head, and make me sick
"Of joy and grief at once. Grief overcame,
"And I was stopping up my frantic ears,   290
"When, past all hindrance of my trembling hands,
"A voice came sweeter, sweeter than all tune,
"And still it cried, 'Apollo! young Apollo!
" 'The morning-bright Apollo! young Apollo!'
"I fled, it follow'd me, and cried 'Apollo!'
"O Father, and O Brethren, had ye felt
"Those pains of mine; O Saturn, hadst thou felt,
"Ye would not call this too indulged tongue
"Presumptuous, in thus venturing to be heard."

So far her voice flow'd on, like timorous brook   300
That, lingering along a pebbled coast,
Doth fear to meet the sea: but sea it met,
And shudder'd; for the overwhelming voice
Of huge Enceladus swallow'd it in wrath:
The ponderous syllables, like sullen waves
In the half-glutted hollows of reef-rocks,
Came booming thus, while still upon his arm
He lean'd; not rising, from supreme contempt.
"Or shall we listen to the over-wise,
"Or to the over-foolish, Giant-Gods?   310
"Not thunderbolt on thunderbolt, till all
"That rebel Jove's whole armoury were spent,
"Not world on world upon these shoulders piled,
"Could agonize me more than baby-words
"In midst of this dethronement horrible.
"Speak! roar! shout! yell! ye sleepy Titans all.
"Do ye forget the blows, the buffets vile?
"Are ye not smitten by a youngling arm?
"Dost thou forget, sham Monarch of the Waves,
"Thy scalding in the seas? What, have I rous'd   320
"Your spleens with so few simple words as these?
"O joy! for now I see ye are not lost:

"O joy! for now I see a thousand eyes
"Wide-glaring for revenge!"—As this he said,
He lifted up his stature vast, and stood,
Still without intermission speaking thus:
"Now ye are flames, I'll tell you how to burn,
"And purge the ether of our enemies;
"How to feed fierce the crooked stings of fire,
"And singe away the swollen clouds of Jove,   330
"Stifling that puny essence in its tent.
"O let him feel the evil he hath done;
"For though I scorn Oceanus's lore,
"Much pain have I for more than loss of realms:
"The days of peace and slumberous calm are fled;
"Those days, all innocent of scathing war,
"When all the fair Existences of heaven
"Came open-eyed to guess what we would speak:—
"That was before our brows were taught to frown,
"Before our lips knew else but solemn sounds;   340
"That was before we knew the winged thing,
"Victory, might be lost, or might be won.
"And be ye mindful that Hyperion,
"Our brightest brother, still is undisgraced—
"Hyperion, lo! his radiance is here!"

   All eyes were on Enceladus's face,
And they beheld, while still Hyperion's name
Flew from his lips up to the vaulted rocks,
A pallid gleam across his features stern:
Not savage, for he saw full many a God   350
Wroth as himself. He look'd upon them all,
And in each face he saw a gleam of light,
But splendider in Saturn's, whose hoar locks
Shone like the bubbling foam about a keel
When the prow sweeps into a midnight cove.
In pale and silver silence they remain'd,
Till suddenly a splendour, like the morn,
Pervaded all the beetling gloomy steeps,
All the sad spaces of oblivion,
And every gulf, and every chasm old,   360
And every height, and every sullen depth,
Voiceless, or hoarse with loud tormented streams:
And all the everlasting cataracts,
And all the headlong torrents far and near,
Mantled before in darkness and huge shade,
Now saw the light and made it terrible.
It was Hyperion:—a granite peak
His bright feet touch'd, and there he stay'd to view

The misery his brilliance had betray'd
To the most hateful seeing of itself.   370
Golden his hair of short Numidian curl,
Regal his shape majestic, a vast shade
In midst of his own brightness, like the bulk
Of Memnon's image at the set of sun
To one who travels from the dusking East:
Sighs, too, as mournful as that Memnon's harp
He utter'd, while his hands contemplative
He press'd together, and in silence stood.
Despondence seiz'd again the fallen Gods
At sight of the dejected King of Day,   380
And many hid their faces from the light:
But fierce Enceladus sent forth his eyes
Among the brotherhood; and, at their glare,
Uprose Iäpetus, and Creüs, too,
And Phorcus, sea-born, and together strode
To where he towered on his eminence.
There those four shouted forth old Saturn's name;
Hyperion from the peak loud answered, "Saturn!"
Saturn sat near the Mother of the Gods,
In whose face was no joy, though all the Gods   390
Gave from their hollow throats the name of "Saturn!"

HYPERION. BOOK III

THUS in alternate uproar and sad peace,
Amazed were those Titans utterly.
O leave them, Muse! O leave them to their woes;
For thou art weak to sing such tumults dire:
A solitary sorrow best befits
Thy lips, and antheming a lonely grief.
Leave them, O Muse! for thou anon wilt find
Many a fallen old Divinity
Wandering in vain about bewildered shores.
Meantime touch piously the Delphic harp,   10
And not a wind of heaven but will breathe
In aid soft warble from the Dorian flute;
For lo! 'tis for the Father of all verse.
Flush every thing that hath a vermeil hue,
Let the rose glow intense and warm the air,
And let the clouds of even and of morn
Float in voluptuous fleeces o'er the hills;
Let the red wine within the goblet boil,
Cold as a bubbling well; let faint-lipp'd shells,
On sands, or in great deeps, vermilion turn   20
Through all their labyrinths; and let the maid

Blush keenly, as with some warm kiss surpris'd.
Chief isle of the embowered Cyclades,
Rejoice, O Delos, with thine olives green,
And poplars, and lawn-shading palms, and beech,
In which the Zephyr breathes the loudest song,
And hazels thick, dark-stemm'd beneath the shade:
Apollo is once more the golden theme!
Where was he, when the Giant of the Sun
Stood bright, amid the sorrow of his peers?   30
Together had he left his mother fair
And his twin-sister sleeping in their bower,
And in the morning twilight wandered forth
Beside the osiers of a rivulet,
Full ankle-deep in lillies of the vale.
The nightingale had ceas'd, and a few stars
Were lingering in the heavens, while the thrush
Began calm-throated. Throughout all the isle
There was no covert, no retired cave
Unhaunted by the murmurous noise of waves,   40
Though scarcely heard in many a green recess.
He listen'd, and he wept, and his bright tears
Went trickling down the golden bow he held.
Thus with half-shut suffused eyes he stood,
While from beneath some cumbrous boughs hard by
With solemn step an awful Goddess came,
And there was purport in her looks for him,
Which he with eager guess began to read
Perplex'd, the while melodiously he said:
"How cam'st thou over the unfooted sea?   50
"Or hath that antique mien and robed form
"Mov'd in these vales invisible till now?
"Sure I have heard those vestments sweeping o'er
"The fallen leaves, when I have sat alone
"In cool mid-forest. Surely I have traced
"The rustle of those ample skirts about
"These grassy solitudes, and seen the flowers
"Lift up their heads, as still the whisper pass'd.
"Goddess! I have beheld those eyes before,
"And their eternal calm, and all that face,   60
"Or I have dream'd."—"Yes," said the supreme shape,
"Thou hast dream'd of me; and awaking up
"Didst find a lyre all golden by thy side,
"Whose strings touch'd by thy fingers, all the vast
"Unwearied ear of the whole universe
"Listen'd in pain and pleasure at the birth
"Of such new tuneful wonder. Is't not strange
"That thou shouldst weep, so gifted? Tell me, youth,

"What sorrow thou canst feel; for I am sad
"When thou dost shed a tear: explain thy griefs
"To one who in this lonely isle hath been   **71**
"The watcher of thy sleep and hours of life,
"From the young day when first thy infant hand
"Pluck'd witless the weak flowers, till thine arm
"Could bend that bow heroic to all times.
"Show thy heart's secret to an ancient Power
"Who hath forsaken old and sacred thrones
"For prophecies of thee, and for the sake
"Of loveliness new born."—Apollo then,
With sudden scrutiny and gloomless eyes,   **80**
Thus answer'd, while his white melodious throat
Throbb'd with the syllables.—"Mnemosyne!
"Thy name is on my tongue, I know not how;
"Why should I tell thee what thou so well seest?
"Why should I strive to show what from thy lips
"Would come no mystery? For me, dark, dark,
"And painful vile oblivion seals my eyes:
"I strive to search wherefore I am so sad,
"Until a melancholy numbs my limbs;
"And then upon the grass I sit, and moan,   **90**
"Like one who once had wings.—O why should I
"Feel curs'd and thwarted, when the liegeless air
"Yields to my step aspirant? why should I
"Spurn the green turf as hateful to my feet?
"Goddess benign, point forth some unknown thing:
"Are there not other regions than this isle?
"What are the stars? There is the sun, the sun!
"And the most patient brilliance of the moon!
"And stars by thousands! Point me out the way
"To any one particular beauteous star,   **100**
"And I will flit into it with my lyre,
"And make its silvery splendour pant with bliss.
"I have heard the cloudy thunder: Where is power?
"Whose hand, whose essence, what divinity
"Makes this alarum in the elements,
"While I here idle listen on the shores
"In fearless yet in aching ignorance?
"O tell me, lonely Goddess, by thy harp,
"That waileth every morn and eventide,
"Tell me why thus I rave, about these groves!   **11◦**
"Mute thou remainest—mute! yet I can read
"A wondrous lesson in thy silent face:
"Knowledge enormous makes a God of me.
"Names, deeds, grey legends, dire events, rebellions,
"Majesties, sovran voices, agonies,

"Creations and destroyings, all at once
"Pour into the wide hollows of my brain,
"And deify me, as if some blithe wine
"Or bright elixir peerless I had drunk,
"And so become immortal."—Thus the God,   120
While his enkindled eyes, with level glance
Beneath his white soft temples, stedfast kept
Trembling with light upon Mnemosyne.
Soon wild commotions shook him, and made flush
All the immortal fairness of his limbs;
Most like the struggle at the gate of death;
Or liker still to one who should take leave
Of pale immortal death, and with a pang
As hot as death's is chill, with fierce convulse
Die into life: so young Apollo anguish'd: 130
His very hair, his golden tresses famed
Kept undulation round his eager neck.
During the pain Mnemosyne upheld
Her arms as one who prophesied.—At length
Apollo shriek'd;—and lo! from all his limbs
Celestial   *   *   *   *   *   *   *
*   *   *   *   *   *   *   *   *

THE END

POSTHUMOUS

AND

FUGITIVE POEMS

POSTHUMOUS AND FUGITIVE POEMS

ON DEATH

I

Can death be sleep, when life is but a dream,
  And scenes of bliss pass as a phantom by?
The transient pleasures as a vision seem,
  And yet we think the greatest pain's to die.

II

How strange it is that man on earth should roam,
  And lead a life of woe, but not forsake
His rugged path; nor dare he view alone
  His future doom which is but to awake.

WOMEN, WINE, AND SNUFF

Give me women, wine and snuff
Until I cry out "hold, enough!"
You may do so sans objection
Till the day of resurrection;
For bless my beard they aye shall be
My beloved Trinity.

FILL FOR ME A BRIMMING BOWL

Fill for me a brimming bowl
And let me in it drown my soul:
But put therein some drug, designed
To Banish Women from my mind:
For I want not the stream inspiring
That fills the mind with—fond desiring,
But I want as deep a draught
As e'er from Lethe's wave was quaff'd;
From my despairing heart to charm
The Image of the fairest form
That e'er my reveling eyes beheld,
That e'er my wandering fancy spell'd.
In vain! away I cannot chace
The melting softness of that face,

The beaminess of those bright eyes,
That breast—earth's only Paradise.
My sight will never more be blest;
For all I see has lost its zest:
Nor with delight can I explore
The Classic page, or Muse's lore.   20
Had she but known how beat my heart,
And with one smile reliev'd its smart
I should have felt a sweet relief,
I should have felt "the joy of grief."
Yet as the Tuscan mid the snow
Of Lapland thinks on sweet Arno,
Even so for ever shall she be
The Halo of my Memory.

August, 1814.

SONNET

ON PEACE

O PEACE! and dost thou with thy presence bless
   The dwellings of this war-surrounded Isle;
Soothing with placid brow our late distress,
   Making the triple kingdom brightly smile?
Joyful I hail thy presence; and I hail
   The sweet companions that await on thee;
Complete my joy—let not my first wish fail,
   Let the sweet mountain nymph thy favourite be,
With England's happiness proclaim Europa's Liberty.
O Europe! let not sceptred tyrants see   10
   That thou must shelter in thy former state;
Keep thy chains burst, and boldly say thou art free;
   Give thy kings law—leave not uncurbed the great;
   So with the horrors past thou'lt win thy happier fate!

SONNET TO BYRON

BYRON! how sweetly sad thy melody!
   Attuning still the soul to tenderness,
   As if soft Pity, with unusual stress,
Had touch'd her plaintive lute, and thou, being by,
Hadst caught the tones, nor suffer'd them to die.
   O'ershadowing sorrow doth not make thee less
   Delightful: thou thy griefs dost dress
With a bright halo, shining beamily,
As when a cloud the golden moon doth veil,
   Its sides are ting'd with a resplendent glow,   10

Through the dark robe oft amber rays prevail,
    And like fair veins in sable marble flow;
Still warble, dying swan! still tell the tale,
    The enchanting tale, the tale of pleasing woe.

SONNET TO CHATTERTON

O CHATTERTON! how very sad thy fate!
    Dear child of sorrow—son of misery!
    How soon the film of death obscur'd that eye,
Whence Genius mildly flash'd, and high debate.
How soon that voice, majestic and elate,
    Melted in dying numbers! Oh! how nigh
    Was night to thy fair morning. Thou didst die
A half-blown flow'ret which cold blasts amate.
But this is past: thou art among the stars
    Of highest Heaven: to the rolling spheres   10
Thou sweetly singest: naught thy hymning mars,
    Above the ingrate world and human fears.
On earth the good man base detraction bars
    From thy fair name, and waters it with tears.

SONNET TO SPENSER

SPENSER! a jealous honourer of thine,
    A forester deep in thy midmost trees,
Did last eve ask my promise to refine
    Some English that might strive thine ear to please.
But Elfin Poet 'tis impossible
    For an inhabitant of wintry earth
To rise like Phœbus with a golden quill
    Fire-wing'd and make a morning in his mirth.
It is impossible to escape from toil
    O' the sudden and receive thy spiriting: 10
The flower must drink the nature of the soil
    Before it can put forth its blossoming:
Be with me in the summer days and I
Will for thine honour and his pleasure try.

ODE TO APOLLO

IN thy western halls of gold
    When thou sittest in thy state,
Bards, that erst sublimely told
    Heroic deeds, and sang of fate,
With fervour seize their adamantine lyres,
Whose chords are solid rays, and twinkle radiant fires.

Here Homer with his nervous arms
    Strikes the twanging harp of war,
And even the western splendour warms,
    While the trumpets sound afar: 10
But, what creates the most intense surprise,
His soul looks out through renovated eyes.

Then, through thy Temple wide, melodious swells
    The sweet majestic tone of Maro's lyre:
The soul delighted on each accent dwells,—
    Enraptur'd dwells,—not daring to respire,
The while he tells of grief around a funeral pyre.

'Tis awful silence then again;
    Expectant stand the spheres;
    Breathless the laurel'd peers,   20
Nor move, till ends the lofty strain,
    Nor move till Milton's tuneful thunders cease,
And leave once more the ravish'd heavens in peace.

Thou biddest Shakspeare wave his hand,
    And quickly forward spring
The Passions—a terrific band—
    And each vibrates the string
That with its tyrant temper best accords,
While from their Master's lips pour forth the inspiring words.

A silver trumpet Spenser blows,   30
    And, as its martial notes to silence flee,
From a virgin chorus flows
    A hymn in praise of spotless Chastity.
'Tis still! Wild warblings from the Æolian lyre
Enchantment softly breathe, and tremblingly expire.

Next thy Tasso's ardent numbers
    Float along the pleased air,
Calling youth from idle slumbers,
    Rousing them from Pleasure's lair:—
Then o'er the strings his fingers gently move,
And melt the soul to pity and to love.   41

But when *Thou* joinest with the Nine,
And all the powers of song combine,
    We listen here on earth:
The dying tones that fill the air,
And charm the ear of evening fair,
From thee, great God of Bards, receive their heavenly birth

SONNET

TO A YOUNG LADY WHO SENT ME A LAUREL CROWN

FRESH morning gusts have blown away all fear
    From my glad bosom,—now from gloominess
    I mount for ever—not an atom less
Than the proud laurel shall content my bier.
No! by the eternal stars! or why sit here
    In the Sun's eye, and 'gainst my temples press
    Apollo's very leaves, woven to bless
By thy white fingers and thy spirit clear.
Lo! who dares say, "Do this"? Who dares call down
    My will from its high purpose? Who say, "Stand,"
Or "Go"? This mighty moment I would frown
    On abject Cæsars—not the stoutest band
Of mailed heroes should tear off my crown:
    Yet would I kneel and kiss thy gentle hand!

ON RECEIVING A LAUREL CROWN FROM LEIGH HUNT

MINUTES are flying swiftly, and as yet
    Nothing unearthly has enticed my brain
    Into a delphic Labyrinth—I would fain
Catch an unmortal thought to pay the debt
I owe to the kind Poet who has set
    Upon my ambitious head a glorious gain.
    Two bending laurel Sprigs—'tis nearly pain
To be conscious of such a Coronet.
Still time is fleeting, and no dream arises
    Gorgeous as I would have it—only I see
A Trampling down of what the world most prizes
    Turbans and Crowns, and blank regality;
And then I run into most wild surmises
    Of all the many glories that may be.

10

SONNET

TO THE LADIES WHO SAW ME CROWN'D

WHAT is there in the universal Earth
    More lovely than a Wreath from the bay tree?
    Haply a Halo round the Moon—a glee
Circling from three sweet pair of Lips in Mirth;
And haply you will say the dewy birth
    Of morning Roses—ripplings tenderly
    Spread by the Halcyon's breast upon the Sea—

But these Comparisons are nothing worth—
Then is there nothing in the world so fair?
   The silvery tears of April?—Youth of May?   **10**
Or June that breathes out life for butterflies?
   No—none of these can from my favourite bear
Away the Palm—yet shall it ever pay
   Due Reverence to your most sovereign eyes.

HYMN TO APOLLO

      God of the golden bow,
        And of the golden lyre,
      And of the golden hair,
        And of the golden fire,
          Charioteer
          Of the patient year,
        Where—where slept thine ire,
When like a blank idiot I put on thy wreath,
        Thy laurel, thy glory,
        The light of thy story,   **10**
Or was I a worm—too low crawling, for death?
      O Delphic Apollo!

      The Thunderer grasp'd and grasp'd,
        The Thunderer frown'd and frown'd;
      The eagle's feathery mane
        For wrath became stiffen'd—the sound
          Of breeding thunder
          Went drowsily under,
        Muttering to be unbound.
O why didst thou pity, and for a worm   **20**
        Why touch thy soft lute
        Till the thunder was mute,
Why was not I crush'd—such a pitiful germ?
      O Delphic Apollo!

      The Pleiades were up,
        Watching the silent air;
      The seeds and roots in the Earth
        Were swelling for summer fare;
          The Ocean, its neighbour,
          Was at its old labour,   **30**
        When, who—who did dare
To tie, like a madman, thy plant round his brow,
        And grin and look proudly,
        And blaspheme so loudly,
And live for that honour, to stoop to thee now?
      O Delphic Apollo!

SONNET

As from the darkening gloom a silver dove
 Upsoars, and darts into the Eastern light,
 On pinions that naught moves but pure delight,
So fled thy soul into the realms above,
Regions of peace and everlasting love;
 Where happy spirits, crown'd with circlets bright
 Of starry beam, and gloriously bedight,
Taste the high joy none but the blest can prove.
There thou or joinest the immortal quire
 In melodies that even Heaven fair   **10**
Fill with superiour bliss, or, at desire
 Of the omnipotent Father, cleavest the air
On holy message sent—What pleasures higher?
 Wherefore does any grief our joy impair?

STANZAS TO MISS WYLIE

O COME Georgiana! the rose is full blown,
The riches of Flora are lavishly strown,
The air is all softness, and crystal the streams,
The West is resplendently clothed in beams.
O come! let us haste to the freshening shades,
The quaintly carv'd seats, and the opening glades;
Where the faeries are chanting their evening hymns,
And in the last sun-beam the sylph lightly swims.
And when thou art weary I'll find thee a bed,
Of mosses and flowers to pillow thy head: **10**
And there Georgiana I'll sit at thy feet,
While my story of love I enraptur'd repeat.
So fondly I'll breathe, and so softly I'll sigh,
Thou wilt think that some amorous Zephyr is nigh:
Yet no—as I breathe I will press thy fair knee,
And then thou wilt know that the sigh comes from me.
Ah! why dearest girl should we lose all these blisses?
That mortal's a fool who such happiness misses:
So smile acquiescence, and give me thy hand,
With love-looking eyes, and with voice sweetly bland. **20**

SONNET

OH! how I love, on a fair summer's eve,
 When streams of light pour down the golden west,
 And on the balmy zephyrs tranquil rest
The silver clouds, far—far away to leave
All meaner thoughts, and take a sweet reprieve.

From little cares; to find, with easy quest,
A fragrant wild, with Nature's beauty drest,
And there into delight my soul deceive.
There warm my breast with patriotic lore,
    Musing on Milton's fate—on Sydney's bier—   10
    Till their stern forms before my mind arise:
Perhaps on wing of Poesy upsoar,
    Full often dropping a delicious tear,
    When some melodious sorrow spells mine eyes.

SONNET

BEFORE he went to feed with owls and bats
    Nebuchadnezzar had an ugly dream,
    Worse than an Hus'if's when she thinks her cream
Made a Naumachia for mice and rats.
So scared, he sent for that "Good King of Cats"
    Young Daniel, who soon did pluck away the beam
    From out his eye, and said he did not deem
The sceptre worth a straw—his Cushions old door-mats.
A horrid nightmare similar somewhat
    Of late has haunted a most motley crew,   10
    Most loggerheads and Chapmen—we are told
That any Daniel tho' he be a sot
    Can make the lying lips turn pale of hue
    By belching out "ye are that head of Gold."

SONNET

WRITTEN IN DISGUST OF VULGAR SUPERSTITION

THE church bells toll a melancholy round,
    Calling the people to some other prayers,
    Some other gloominess, more dreadful cares,
More hearkening to the sermon's horrid sound.
Surely the mind of man is closely bound
    In some black spell; seeing that each one tears
    Himself from fireside joys, and Lydian airs,
And converse high of those with glory crown'd.
Still, still they toll, and I should feel a damp,—
    A chill as from a tomb, did I not know   10
That they are dying like an outburnt lamp;
    That 'tis their sighing, wailing ere they go
    Into oblivion;—that fresh flowers will grow,
And many glories of immortal stamp.

SONNET

AFTER dark vapours have oppress'd our plains
  For a long dreary season, comes a day
  Born of the gentle South, and clears away
From the sick heavens all unseemly stains.
The anxious month, relieved of its pains,
  Takes as a long-lost right the feel of May;
  The eyelids with the passing coolness play
Like rose leaves with the drip of Summer rains.
The calmest thoughts come round us; as of leaves
  Budding—fruit ripening in stillness—Autumn suns
Smiling at eve upon the quiet sheaves—   **11**
Sweet Sappho's cheek—a smiling infant's breath—
  The gradual sand that through an hour-glass runs—
A woodland rivulet—a Poet's death.

SONNET

[Written at the end of "The Floure and the Lefe"]

THIS pleasant tale is like a little copse:
  The honied lines do freshly interlace
  To keep the reader in so sweet a place,
So that he here and there full-hearted stops;
And oftentimes he feels the dewy drops
  Come cool and suddenly against his face,
  And by the wandering melody may trace
Which way the tender-legged linnet hops.
Oh! what a power hath white Simplicity!
  What mighty power has this gentle story!   **10**
  I that for ever feel athirst for glory
Could at this moment be content to lie
  Meekly upon the grass, as those whose sobbings
  Were heard of none beside the mournful robins.

TWO SONNETS

I

TO HAYDON, WITH A SONNET WRITTEN ON SEEING THE ELGIN MARBLES

HAYDON! forgive me that I cannot speak
  Definitively on these mighty things;
  Forgive me that I have not Eagle's wings—
That what I want I know not where to seek:
And think that I would not be over meek

In rolling out upfollow'd thunderings,
Even to the steep of Heliconian springs,
Were I of ample strength for such a freak—
Think too, that all those numbers should be thine;
    Whose else? In this who touch thy vesture's hem?
For when men star'd at what was most divine   11
    With browless idiotism—o'erwise phlegm—
Thou hadst beheld the Hesperean shine
    Of their star in the East, and gone to worship them.

II

ON SEEING THE ELGIN MARBLES

My spirit is too weak—mortality
    Weighs heavily on me like unwilling sleep,
    And each imagin'd pinnacle and steep
Of godlike hardship, tells me I must die
Like a sick Eagle looking at the sky.
    Yet 'tis a gentle luxury to weep
    That I have not the cloudy winds to keep,
Fresh for the opening of the morning's eye.
Such dim-conceived glories of the brain
    Bring round the heart an undescribable feud;
So do these wonders a most dizzy pain,   11
    That mingles Grecian grandeur with the rude
Wasting of old Time—with a billowy main—
    A sun—a shadow of a magnitude.

SONNET

ON A PICTURE OF LEANDER

Come hither all sweet maidens soberly,
    Down-looking aye, and with a chasten'd light,
    Hid in the fringes of your eyelids white,
And meekly let your fair hands joined be,
As if so gentle that ye could not see,
    Untouch'd, a victim of your beauty bright,
    Sinking away to his young spirit's night,—
Sinking bewilder'd 'mid the dreary sea:
'Tis young Leander toiling to his death;
    Nigh swooning, he doth purse his weary lips   10
        For Hero's cheek, and smiles against her smile.
    O horrid dream! see how his body dips
        Dead-heavy; arms and shoulders gleam awhile:
He's gone: up bubbles all his amorous breath!

TO ———

THINK not of it, sweet one, so;—
  Give it not a tear;
Sigh thou mayst, and bid it go
  Any, any where.

Do not look so sad, sweet one,—
  Sad and fadingly;
Shed one drop, then it is gone,
  O 'twas born to die.

Still so pale? then dearest weep;   10
  Weep, I'll count the tears,
And each one shall be a bliss
  For thee in after years.

Brighter has it left thine eyes
  Than a sunny rill;
And thy whispering melodies
  Are tenderer still.

Yet—as all things mourn awhile
  At fleeting blisses,
Let us too! but be our dirge   20
  A dirge of kisses.

LINES

I

UNFELT, unheard, unseen,
I've left my little queen,
Her languid arms in silver slumber lying:
  Ah! through their nestling touch,
  Who—who could tell how much
There is for madness—cruel, or complying?

II

Those faery lids how sleek!
Those lips how moist!—they speak,
In ripest quiet, shadows of sweet sounds:
  Into my fancy's ear
  Melting a burden dear,
How "Love doth know no fullness nor no bounds."

III

True!—tender monitors!
I bend unto your laws:
This sweetest day for dalliance was born!
So, without more ado,
I'll feel my heaven anew,
For all the blushing of the hasty morn.

SONNET

ON THE SEA

IT keeps eternal whisperings around
  Desolate shores, and with its mighty swell
  Gluts twice ten thousand Caverns, till the spell
Of Hecate leaves them their old shadowy sound.
Often 'tis in such gentle temper found,
  That scarcely will the very smallest shell
  Be mov'd for days from where it sometime fell,
When last the winds of Heaven were unbound.
Oh ye! who have your eye-balls vex'd and tir'd,
  Feast them upon the wideness of the Sea;   10
    Oh ye! whose ears are dinn'd with uproar rude,
Or fed too much with cloying melody—
    Sit ye near some old Cavern's Mouth, and brood
Until ye start, as if the sea-nymphs quir'd!

SONNET

ON LEIGH HUNT'S POEM "THE STORY OF RIMINI"

WHO loves to peer up at the morning sun,
  With half-shut eyes and comfortable cheek,
  Let him, with this sweet tale, full often seek
For meadows where the little rivers run;
Who loves to linger with that brightest one
  Of Heaven—Hesperus—let him lowly speak
  These numbers to the night, and starlight meek,
Or moon, if that her hunting be begun.
He who knows these delights, and too is prone
  To moralize upon a smile or tear,   10
Will find at once a region of his own,
  A bower for his spirit, and will steer
To alleys where the fir-tree drops its cone.
  Where robins hop, and fallen leaves are sear

ON OXFORD

A PARODY

I

THE Gothic looks solemn,
The plain Doric column
Supports an old Bishop and Crosier;
The mouldering arch,
Shaded o'er by a larch
Stands next door to Wilson the Hosier.

II

Vice—that is, by turns,—
O'er pale faces mourns
The black tassell'd trencher and common hat;
The Chantry boy sings,
The Steeple-bell rings,
And as for the Chancellor—*dominat.*

III

There are plenty of trees,
And plenty of ease,
And plenty of fat deer for Parsons;
And when it is venison,
Short is the benison,—
Then each on a leg or thigh fastens.

THE POET

A FRAGMENT

WHERE's the Poet? show him! show him,
Muses nine! that I may know him!
'Tis the man who with a man
Is an equal, be he King,
Or poorest of the beggar-clan,
Or any other wondrous thing
A man may be 'twixt ape and Plato;
'Tis the man who with a bird,
Wren or Eagle, finds his way to
All its instincts; he hath heard
The Lion's roaring, and can tell
What his horny throat expresseth,
And to him the Tiger's yell
Comes articulate and presseth
On his ear like mother-tongue.

10

MODERN LOVE

AND what is love? It is a doll dress'd up
For idleness to cosset, nurse, and dandle;
A thing of soft misnomers, so divine
That silly youth doth think to make itself
Divine by loving, and so goes on
Yawning and doting a whole summer long,
Till Miss's comb is made a pearl tiara,
And common Wellingtons turn Romeo boots;
Then Cleopatra lives at number seven,
And Antony resides in Brunswick Square.   10
Fools! if some passions high have warm'd the world,
If Queens and Soldiers have play'd deep for hearts,
It is no reason why such agonies
Should be more common than the growth of weeds.
Fools! make me whole again that weighty pearl
The Queen of Egypt melted, and I'll say
That ye may love in spite of beaver hats.

THE CASTLE BUILDER

FRAGMENTS OF A DIALOGUE

CASTLE BUILDER

*   *   *   *   *   *   *

IN short, convince you that however wise
You may have grown from Convent libraries,
I have, by many yards at least, been carding
A longer skein of wit in Convent garden.

BERNARDINE

A very Eden that same place must be!
Pray what demesne? Whose Lordship's legacy?
What, have you convents in that Gothic Isle?
Pray pardon me, I cannot help but smile.
*   *   *   *   *   *   *

CASTLE BUILDER

Sir, Convent Garden is a monstrous beast
From morning, four o'clock, to twelve at noon,   10
It swallows cabbages without a spoon,
And then, from twelve till two, this Eden made is
A promenade for cooks and ancient ladies;

And then for supper, 'stead of soup and poaches,
It swallows chairmen, damns, and Hackney coaches.
In short, Sir, 'tis a very place for monks,
For it containeth twenty thousand punks,
Which any man may number for his sport,
By following fat elbows up a court.

*   *   *   *   *   *   *

In such like nonsense would I pass an hour   20
With random Friar, or Rake upon his tour,
Or one of few of that imperial host
Who came unmaimed from the Russian frost

*   *   *   *   *   *   *

To-night I'll have my friar—let me think
About my room,—I'll have it in the pink;
It should be rich and sombre, and the moon,
Just in its mid-life in the midst of June,
Should look thro' four large windows and display
Clear, but for gold-fish vases in the way,
Their glassy diamonding on Turkish floor;   30
The tapers keep aside, an hour and more,
To see what else the moon alone can show;
While the night-breeze doth softly let us know
My terrace is well bower'd with oranges.
Upon the floor the dullest spirit sees
A guitar-ribband and a lady's glove
Beside a crumple-leaved tale of love;
A tambour-frame, with Venus sleeping there,
All finish'd but some ringlets of her hair;
A viol-bow, strings torn, cross-wise upon   40
A glorious folio of Anacreon;
A skull upon a mat of roses lying,
Ink'd purple with a song concerning dying;
An hour-glass on the turn, amid the trails
Of passion-flower;—just in time there sails
A cloud across the moon,—the lights bring in!
And see what more my phantasy can win.
It is a gorgeous room, but somewhat sad;
The draperies are so, as tho' they had
Been made for Cleopatra's winding-sheet;   50
And opposite the stedfast eye doth meet
A spacious looking-glass, upon whose face,
In letters raven-sombre, you may trace
Old "Mene, Mene, Tekel, Upharsin."
Greek busts and statuary have ever been
Held, by the finest spirits, fitter far
Than vase grotesque and Siamesian jar;

Therefore 'tis sure a want of Attic taste
That I should rather love a Gothic waste
Of eyesight on cinque-coloured potter's clay,   60
Than on the marble fairness of old Greece.
My table-coverlits of Jason's fleece
And black Numidian sheep-wool should be wrought,
Gold, black, and heavy, from the Lama brought.
My ebon sofas should delicious be
With down from Leda's cygnet progeny.
My pictures all Salvator's, save a few
Of Titian's portraiture, and one, though new,
Of Haydon's in its fresh magnificence.
My wine—O good! 'tis here at my desire,   70
And I must sit to supper with my friar.

*   *   *   *   *   *   *

A SONG OF OPPOSITES

"Under the flag
Of each his faction, they to battle bring
Their embryon atoms."—MILTON.

WELCOME joy, and welcome sorrow,
    Lethe's weed and Hermes' feather;
Come to-day, and come to-morrow,
    I do love you both together!
    I love to mark sad faces in fair weather;
And hear a merry laugh amid the thunder;
    Fair and foul I love together.
Meadows sweet where flames are under,
And a giggle at a wonder;
Visage sage at pantomime;   10
Funeral, and steeple-chime;
Infant playing with a skull;
Morning fair, and shipwreck'd hull;
Nightshade with the woodbine kissing;
Serpents in red roses hissing;
Cleopatra regal-dress'd
With the aspic at her breast;
Dancing music, music sad,
Both together, sane and mad;
Muses bright and muses pale;   20
Sombre Saturn, Momus hale;—
Laugh and sigh, and laugh again;
Oh the sweetness of the pain!
Muses bright, and muses pale,
Bare your faces of the veil;

Let me see; and let me write
Of the day, and of the night—
Both together:—let me slake
All my thirst for sweet heart-ache!
Let my bower be of yew,   30
Interwreath'd with myrtles new;
Pines and lime-trees full in bloom,
And my couch a low grass-tomb.

SONNET

TO A CAT

CAT! who hast pass'd thy grand climacteric,
  How many mice and rats hast in thy days
  Destroy'd?—How many tit bits stolen? Gaze
With those bright languid segments green, and prick
Those velvet ears—but pr'ythee do not stick
  Thy latent talons in me—and upraise
  Thy gentle mew—and tell me all thy frays
Of fish and mice, and rats and tender chick.
Nay, look not down, nor lick thy dainty wrists—
  For all the wheezy asthma,—and for all   10
Thy tail's tip is nick'd off—and though the fists
  Of many a maid have given thee many a maul,
Still is that fur as soft as when the lists
  In youth thou enter'dst on glass bottled wall.

LINES ON SEEING A LOCK OF MILTON'S HAIR

CHIEF of organic numbers!
  Old Scholar of the Spheres!
Thy spirit never slumbers,
  But rolls about our ears,
For ever, and for ever!
O what a mad endeavour
    Worketh he,
Who to thy sacred and ennobled hearse
Would offer a burnt sacrifice of verse
    And melody.   1(

How heavenward thou soundest,
  Live Temple of sweet noise,
And Discord unconfoundest,
  Giving Delight new joys,
And Pleasure nobler pinions!
O, where are thy dominions?

Lend thine ear
To a young Delian oath,—aye, by thy soul,
By all that from thy mortal lips did roll,
And by the kernel of thine earthly love,   20
Beauty, in things on earth, and things above
              I swear!

       When every childish fashion
          Has vanish'd from my rhyme,
       Will I, grey-gone in passion,
             Leave to an after-time,
             Hymning and harmony
Of thee, and of thy works, and of thy life;
But vain is now the burning and the strife,
Pangs are in vain, until I grow high-rife   30
             With old Philosophy,
And mad with glimpses of futurity!

For many years my offering must be hush'd;
   When I do speak, I'll think upon this hour,
Because I feel my forehead hot and flush'd,
   Even at the simplest vassal of thy power,—
             A lock of thy bright hair,—
             Sudden it came,
And I was startled, when I caught thy name
             Coupled so unaware;   40
Yet, at the moment, temperate was my blood.
I thought I had beheld it from the flood.

SONNET

ON SITTING DOWN TO READ KING LEAR ONCE AGAIN

O GOLDEN tongued Romance, with serene lute!
   Fair plumed Syren, Queen of far-away!
   Leave melodizing on this wintry day,
Shut up thine olden pages, and be mute:
Adieu! for, once again, the fierce dispute
   Betwixt damnation and impassion'd clay
   Must I burn through; once more humbly assay
The bitter-sweet of this Shakespearian fruit:
Chief Poet! and ye clouds of Albion,
   Begetters of our deep eternal theme!   10
When through the old oak Forest I am gone,
   Let me not wander in a barren dream,
But, when I am consumed in the fire,
Give me new Phœnix wings to fly at my desire.

SONNET

WHEN I have fears that I may cease to be
   Before my pen has glean'd my teeming brain,
Before high-piled books, in charactery,
   Hold like rich garners the full ripen'd grain;
When I behold, upon the night's starr'd face,
   Huge cloudy symbols of a high romance,
And think that I may never live to trace
   Their shadows, with the magic hand of chance;
And when I feel, fair creature of an hour,
   That I shall never look upon thee more,   10
Never have relish in the faery power
   Of unreflecting love;—then on the shore
Of the wide world I stand alone, and think
Till love and fame to nothingness do sink.

SHARING EVE'S APPLE

I

O BLUSH not so! O blush not so!
   Or I shall think you knowing;
And if you smile the blushing while,
   Then maidenheads are going.

II

There's a blush for won't, and a blush for shan't,
   And a blush for having done it:
There's a blush for thought and a blush for naught,
   And a blush for just begun it.

III

O sigh not so! O sigh not so!
   For it sounds of Eve's sweet pippin;
By these loosen'd lips you have tasted the pips
   And fought in an amorous nipping.

IV

Will you play once more at nice-cut-core,
   For it only will last our youth out,
And we have the prime of the kissing time,
   We have not one sweet tooth out.

V

There's a sigh for yes, and a sigh for no,
And a sigh for I can't bear it!
O what can be done, shall we stay or run?
O cut the sweet apple and share it!

A DRAUGHT OF SUNSHINE

Hence Burgundy, Claret, and Port,
    Away with old Hock and Madeira,
Too earthly ye are for my sport;
    There's a beverage brighter and clearer.
Instead of a pitiful rummer,
My wine overbrims a whole summer;
        My bowl is the sky,
        And I drink at my eye,
        Till I feel in the brain
        A Delphian pain—   10
Then follow, my Caius! then follow:
        On the green of the hill
        We will drink our fill
        Of golden sunshine,
        Till our brains intertwine
With the glory and grace of Apollo!
        God of the Meridian,
            And of the East and West,
        To thee my soul is flown,
            And my body is earthward press'd.—   20
It is an awful mission,
A terrible division;
And leaves a gulph austere
To be fill'd with worldly fear.
Aye, when the soul is fled
To high above our head,
Affrighted do we gaze
After its airy maze,
As doth a mother wild,
When her young infant child   30
Is in an eagle's claws—
And is not this the cause
Of madness?—God of Song,
Thou bearest me along
Through sights I scarce can bear:
O let me, let me share

With the hot lyre and thee,
The staid Philosophy.
Temper my lonely hours,
And let me see thy bowers   40
More unalarm'd!

SONNET

TO THE NILE

SON of the old moon-mountains African!
  Chief of the Pyramid and Crocodile!
  We call thee fruitful, and, that very while,
A desert fills our seeing's inward span;
Nurse of swart nations since the world began,
  Art thou so fruitful? or dost thou beguile
  Such men to honour thee, who, worn with toil,
Rest for a space 'twixt Cairo and Decan?
O may dark fancies err! they surely do;
  'Tis ignorance that makes a barren waste   10
Of all beyond itself, thou dost bedew
  Green rushes like our rivers, and dost taste
The pleasant sun-rise, green isles hast thou too,
  And to the sea as happily dost haste.

SONNET

TO A LADY SEEN FOR A FEW MOMENTS AT VAUXHALL

TIME's sea hath been five years at its slow ebb,
  Long hours have to and fro let creep the sand,
Since I was tangled in thy beauty's web,
  And snared by the ungloving of thine hand.
And yet I never look on midnight sky,
  But I behold thine eyes' well memory'd light;
I cannot look upon the rose's dye,
  But to thy cheek my soul doth take its flight.
I cannot look on any budding flower,
  But my fond ear, in fancy at thy lips   10
And hearkening for a love-sound, doth devour
  Its sweets in the wrong sense:—Thou dost eclipse
Every delight with sweet remembering,
  And grief unto my darling joys dost bring

SONNET

WRITTEN IN ANSWER TO A SONNET ENDING THUS:—

> Dark eyes are dearer far
> Than those that mock the hyacinthine bell—
>   By J. H. REYNOLDS.

BLUE! 'Tis the life of heaven,—the domain
    Of Cynthia,—the wide palace of the sun,—
The tent of Hesperus, and all his train,—
    The bosomer of clouds, gold, grey and dun.
Blue! 'Tis the life of waters:—Ocean
    And all its vassal streams, pools numberless,
May rage, and foam, and fret, but never can
    Subside, if not to dark blue nativeness.
Blue! Gentle cousin of the forest-green,
    Married to green in all the sweetest flowers,—   **10**
Forget-me-not,—the Blue bell,—and, that Queen
    Of secrecy, the Violet: what strange powers
Hast thou, as a mere shadow! But how great,
When in an Eye thou art, alive with fate!

SONNET

TO JOHN HAMILTON REYNOLDS

O THAT a week could be an age, and we
    Felt parting and warmth meeting every week,
Then one poor year a thousand years would be,
    The flush of welcome ever on the cheek:
So could we live long life in little space,
    So time itself would be annihilate,
So a day's journey in oblivious haze
    To serve our joys would lengthen and dilate.
O to arrive each Monday morn from Ind!
    To land each Tuesday from the rich Levant!   **10**
In little time a host of joys to bind,
    And keep our souls in one eternal pant!
This morn, my friend, and yester-evening taught
Me how to harbour such a happy thought.

WHAT THE THRUSH SAID

LINES FROM A LETTER TO JOHN HAMILTON REYNOLDS

O THOU whose face hath felt the Winter's wind,
    Whose eye has seen the snow-clouds hung in mist,

And the black elm tops 'mong the freezing stars,
To thee the spring will be a harvest-time.
O thou, whose only book has been the light
Of supreme darkness which thou feddest on
Night after night when Phœbus was away,
To thee the Spring shall be a triple morn.
O fret not after knowledge—I have none,
And yet my song comes native with the warmth.
O fret not after knowledge—I have none,   11
And yet the Evening listens. He who saddens
At thought of idleness cannot be idle,
And he's awake who thinks himself asleep.

SONNET

THE HUMAN SEASONS

Four seasons fill the measure of the year;
    There are four seasons in the mind of man:
He has his lusty Spring, when fancy clear
    Takes in all beauty with an easy span:
He has his Summer, when luxuriously
    Spring's honied cud of youthful thought he loves
To ruminate, and by such dreaming nigh
    His nearest unto heaven: quiet coves
His soul has in its Autumn, when his wings
    He furleth close; contented so to look   10
On mists in idleness—to let fair things
    Pass by unheeded as a threshold brook.
He has his Winter too of pale misfeature,
Or else he would forego his mortal nature.

EXTRACTS FROM AN OPERA

O! were I one of the Olympian twelve,
Their godships should pass this into a law,—
That when a man doth set himself in toil
After some beauty veiled far away,
Each step he took should make his lady's hand
More soft, more white, and her fair cheek more fair;
And for each briar-berry he might eat,
A kiss should bud upon the tree of love,
And pulp and ripen richer every hour,
To melt away upon the traveller's lips.   10

*   *   *   *   *   *

DAISY'S SONG

I

The sun, with his great eye,
Sees not so much as I;
And the moon, all silver-proud,
Might as well be in a cloud.

II

And O the spring—the spring!
I lead the life of a king!
Couch'd in the teeming grass,
I spy each pretty lass.

III

I look where no one dares,
And I stare where no one stares,
And when the night is nigh,
Lambs bleat my lullaby.

*   *   *   *   *   *

FOLLY'S SONG

When wedding fiddles are a-playing,
    Huzza for folly O!
And when maidens go a-maying,
    Huzza, &c.
When a milk-pail is upset,
    Huzza, &c.
And the clothes left in the wet,
    Huzza, &c.
When the barrel's set abroach,
    Huzza, &c.
When Kate Eyebrow keeps a coach,
    Huzza, &c.
When the pig is over-roasted,
    Huzza, &c.
And the cheese is over-toasted,
    Huzza, &c.
When Sir Snap is with his lawyer,
    Huzza, &c.
And Miss Chip has kissed the sawyer,
    Huzza, &c.

*   *   *   *   *   *

10

20

Oh, I am frighten'd with most hateful thoughts!
Perhaps her voice is not a nightingale's,
Perhaps her teeth are not the fairest pearl;
Her eye-lashes may be, for aught I know,
Not longer than the May-fly's small fan-horns;
There may not be one dimple on her hand;
And freckles many; ah! a careless nurse,
In haste to teach the little thing to walk,
May have crumpt up a pair of Dian's legs,
And warpt the ivory of a Juno's neck.

* * * * * * *

SONG

I

The stranger lighted from his steed,
    And ere he spake a word,
He seiz'd my lady's lilly hand,
    And kiss'd it all unheard.

II

The stranger walk'd into the hall,
    And ere he spake a word,
He kissed my lady's cherry lips,
    And kiss'd 'em all unheard.

III

The stranger walk'd into the bower,—
    But my lady first did go,—
Aye hand in hand into the bower,
    Where my lord's roses blow.

IV

My lady's maid had a silken scarf,
    And a golden ring had she,
And a kiss from the stranger, as off he went
    Again on his fair palfrey.

* * * * *

Asleep! O sleep a little while, white pearl!
And let me kneel, and let me pray to thee,
And let me call Heaven's blessing on thine eyes,
And let me breathe into the happy air,
That doth enfold and touch thee all about,
Vows of my slavery, my giving up,
My sudden adoration, my great love!

FAERY SONGS

I

SHED no tear—O shed no tear!
The flower will bloom another year.
Weep no more—O weep no more!
Young buds sleep in the root's white core.
Dry your eyes—O dry your eyes,
For I was taught in Paradise
To ease my breast of melodies—
      Shed no tear.

Overhead—look overhead
'Mong the blossoms white and red—   **10**
Look up, look up—I flutter now
On this flush pomegranate bough—
See me—'tis this silvery bill
Ever cures the good man's ill—
Shed no tear—O shed no tear!
The flower will bloom another year.
Adieu—Adieu—I fly, adieu,
I vanish in the heaven's blue—
      Adieu, Adieu!

II

Ah! woe is me! poor silver-wing!
  That I must chant thy lady's dirge,
And death to this fair haunt of spring,
  Of melody, and streams of flowery verge,—
Poor silver-wing! ah! woe is me!
      That I must see
These blossoms snow upon thy lady's pall!
  Go, pretty page! and in her ear
  Whisper that the hour is near!
  Softly tell her not to fear   **10**
Such calm favonian burial!
  Go, pretty page! and soothly tell,—
  The blossoms hang by a melting spell,
And fall they must, ere a star wink thrice
      Upon her closed eyes,
That now in vain are weeping their last tears,
  At sweet life leaving, and these arbours green,—
Rich dowry from the Spirit of the Spheres,—
      Alas! poor Queen!

SONNET

TO HOMER

STANDING aloof in giant ignorance,
  Of thee I hear and of the Cyclades,
As one who sits ashore and longs perchance
  To visit dolphin-coral in deep seas.
So thou wast blind;—but then the veil was rent,
  For Jove uncurtain'd Heaven to let thee live,
And Neptune made for thee a spumy tent,
  And Pan made sing for thee his forest-hive;
Aye on the shores of darkness there is light,
  And precipices show untrodden green,   10
There is a budding morrow in midnight,
  There is a triple sight in blindness keen;
Such seeing hadst thou, as it once befel
To Dian, Queen of Earth, and Heaven, and Hell.

SONG

[*Written on a blank page in Beaumont and Fletcher's Works, between* *"Cupid's Revenge" and "The Two Noble Kinsmen"*]

I

SPIRIT here that reignest!
Spirit here that painest!
Spirit here that burnest!
Spirit here that mournest!
    Spirit, I bow
    My forehead low,
  Enshaded with thy pinions.
    Spirit, I look
    All passion-struck
  Into thy pale dominions.

II

Spirit here that laughest!
Spirit here that quaffest!
Spirit here that dancest!
Noble soul that prancest!
    Spirit, with thee
    I join in the glee
  A-nudging the elbow of Momus.
    Spirit, I flush
    With a Bacchanal blush
  Just fresh from the Banquet of Comus.

TEIGNMOUTH

"SOME DOGGEREL" SENT IN A LETTER TO B. R. HAYDON

I

Here all the summer could I stay,
    For there's Bishop's teign
    And King's teign
And Coomb at the clear teign head—
    Where close by the stream
    You may have your cream
All spread upon barley bread.

II

    There's arch Brook
    And there's larch Brook
Both turning many a mill;
    And cooling the drouth
    Of the salmon's mouth,
And fattening his silver gill.

III

    There is Wild wood,
    A Mild hood
To the sheep on the lea o' the down,
    Where the golden furze,
    With its green, thin spurs,
Doth catch at the maiden's gown.

IV

    There is Newton marsh
    With its spear grass harsh—
A pleasant summer level
    Where the maidens sweet
    Of the Market Street,
Do meet in the dusk to revel.

V

    There's the Barton rich
    With dyke and ditch
And hedge for the thrush to live in
    And the hollow tree
    For the buzzing bee
And a bank for the wasp to hive in.

VI

And O, and O
The daisies blow
And the primroses are waken'd,
And violets white
Sit in silver plight,
And the green bud's as long as the spike end.

VII

Then who would go
Into dark Soho,
And chatter with dack'd hair'd critics,
When he can stay
For the new-mown hay,
And startle the dappled Prickets?

THE DEVON MAID

STANZAS SENT IN A LETTER TO B. R. HAYDON

I

WHERE be ye going, you Devon Maid?
And what have ye there in the Basket?
Ye tight little fairy just fresh from the dairy,
Will ye give me some cream if I ask it?

II

I love your Meads, and I love your flowers,
And I love your junkets mainly,
But 'hind the door I love kissing more,
O look not so disdainly.

III

I love your hills, and I love your dales,
And I love your flocks a-bleating—
But O, on the heather to lie together,
With both our hearts a-beating!

IV

I'll put your Basket all safe in a nook,
Your shawl I hang up on the willow,
And we will sigh in the daisy's eye
And kiss on a grass green pillow.

EPISTLE TO JOHN HAMILTON REYNOLDS

DEAR Reynolds! as last night I lay in bed,
There came before my eyes that wonted thread
Of shapes, and shadows, and remembrances,
That every other minute vex and please:
Things all disjointed come from north and south,—
Two Witch's eyes above a Cherub's mouth,
Voltaire with casque and shield and habergeon,
And Alexander with his nightcap on;
Old Socrates a-tying his cravat,
And Hazlitt playing with Miss Edgeworth's cat; 10
And Junius Brutus, pretty well so so,
Making the best of's way towards Soho.

Few are there who escape these visitings,—
Perhaps one or two whose lives have patent wings,
And thro' whose curtains peeps no hellish nose,
No wild-boar tushes, and no Mermaid's toes;
But flowers bursting out with lusty pride,
And young Æolian harps personified;
Some Titian colours touch'd into real life,—
The sacrifice goes on; the pontiff knife 20
Gleams in the Sun, the milk-white heifer lows,
The pipes go shrilly, the libation flows:
A white sail shows above the green-head cliff,
Moves round the point, and throws her anchor stiff;
The mariners join hymn with those on land.

You know the Enchanted Castle,—it doth stand
Upon a rock, on the border of a Lake,
Nested in trees, which all do seem to shake
From some old magic-like Urganda's Sword.
O Phœbus! that I had thy sacred word 30
To show this Castle, in fair dreaming wise,
Unto my friend, while sick and ill he lies!

You know it well enough, where it doth seem
A mossy place, a Merlin's Hall, a dream;
You know the clear Lake, and the little Isles,
The mountains blue, and cold near neighbour rills,
All which elsewhere are but half animate;
There do they look alive to love and hate,
To smiles and frowns; they seem a lifted mound
Above some giant, pulsing underground. 40

Part of the Building was a chosen See,
Built by a banish'd Santon of Chaldee;
The other part, two thousand years from him,
Was built by Cuthbert de Saint Aldebrim;
Then there's a little wing, far from the Sun,
Built by a Lapland Witch turn'd maudlin Nun;
And many other juts of aged stone
Founded with many a mason-devil's groan.

The doors all look as if they op'd themselves,
The windows as if latch'd by Fays and Elves,   50
And from them comes a silver flash of light,
As from the westward of a Summer's night;
Or like a beauteous woman's large blue eyes
Gone mad thro' olden songs and poesies.

See! what is coming from the distance dim!
A golden Galley all in silken trim!
Three rows of oars are lightening, moment whiles,
Into the verd'rous bosoms of those isles;
Towards the shade, under the Castle wall,
It comes in silence,—now 'tis hidden all.   60
The Clarion sounds, and from a Postern-gate
An echo of sweet music doth create
A fear in the poor Herdsman, who doth bring
His beasts to trouble the enchanted spring,—
He tells of the sweet music, and the spot,
To all his friends, and they believe him not.

O that our dreamings all, of sleep or wake,
Would all their colours from the sunset take:
From something of material sublime,
Rather than shadow our own soul's day-time   70
In the dark void of night. For in the world
We jostle,—but my flag is not unfurl'd
On the Admiral-staff,—and so philosophize
I dare not yet! Oh, never will the prize,
High reason, and the love of good and ill,
Be my award! Things cannot to the will
Be settled, but they tease us out of thought;
Or is it that imagination brought
Beyond its proper bound, yet still confin'd,
Lost in a sort of Purgatory blind,   80
Cannot refer to any standard law
Of either earth or heaven? It is a flaw
In happiness, to see beyond our bourn,—
It forces us in summer skies to mourn,
It spoils the singing of the Nightingale.

Dear Reynolds! I have a mysterious tale,
And cannot speak it: the first page I read
Upon a Lampit rock of green sea-weed
Among the breakers; 'twas a quiet eve,
The rocks were silent, the wide sea did weave   90
An untumultuous fringe of silver foam
Along the flat brown sand; I was at home
And should have been most happy,—but I saw
Too far into the sea, where every maw
The greater on the less feeds evermore.—
But I saw too distinct into the core
Of an eternal fierce destruction,
And so from happiness I far was gone.
Still am I sick of it, and tho', to-day,
I've gather'd young spring-leaves, and flowers gay
Of periwinkle and wild strawberry,   101
Still do I that most fierce destruction see,—
The Shark at savage prey,—the Hawk at pounce,—
The gentle Robin, like a Pard or Ounce,
Ravening a worm,—Away, ye horrid moods!
Moods of one's mind! You know I hate them well.
You know I'd sooner be a clapping Bell
To some Kamtschatcan Missionary Church,
Than with these horrid moods be left i' the lurch.

DAWLISH FAIR

OVER the Hill and over the Dale,
     And over the Bourne to Dawlish,
Where ginger-bread wives have a scanty sale,
     And ginger-bread nuts are smallish.

FRAGMENT OF AN ODE TO MAIA, WRITTEN ON MAY DAY, 1818

MOTHER of Hermes! and still youthful Maia!
     May I sing to thee
As thou wast hymned on the shores of Baiæ?
     Or may I woo thee
In earlier Sicilian? or thy smiles
Seek as they once were sought, in Grecian isles,
By bards who died content on pleasant sward,
     Leaving great verse unto a little clan?
O, give me their old vigour, and unheard
     Save of the quiet Primrose, and the span   10

> Of heaven and few ears,
> Rounded by thee, my song should die away
> Content as theirs,
> Rich in the simple worship of a day.

ACROSTIC

GEORGIANA AUGUSTA KEATS

GIVE me your patience Sister while I frame
Exact in Capitals your golden name
Or sue the fair Apollo and he will
Rouse from his heavy slumber and instil
Great love in me for thee and Poesy.
Imagine not that greatest mastery
And kingdom over all the Realms of verse
Nears more to Heaven in aught than when we nurse
And surety give to love and Brotherhood.

Anthropophagi in Othello's mood;   10
Ulysses stormed, and his enchanted belt
Glow with the Muse, but they are never felt
Unbosom'd so and so eternal made,
Such tender incense in their Laurel shade,
To all the regent sisters of the Nine
As this poor offering to you, sister mine.

Kind sister! aye, this third name says you are;
Enchanted has it been the Lord knows where.
And may it taste to you like good old wine,
Take you to real happiness and give   20
Sons, daughters and a home like honied hive.

SONNET

ON VISITING THE TOMB OF BURNS

THE town, the churchyard, and the setting sun,
    The clouds, the trees, the rounded hills all seem,
    Though beautiful, cold—strange—as in a dream,
I dreamed long ago, now new begun.
The short-liv'd, paly Summer is but won
    From Winter's ague, for one hour's gleam;
    Though sapphire-warm, their stars do never beam:
All is cold Beauty; pain is never done:

For who has mind to relish, Minos-wise,
  The Real of Beauty, free from that dead hue
    Sickly imagination and sick pride
Cast wan upon it! Burns! with honour due
  I oft have honour'd thee. Great shadow, hide
Thy face; I sin against thy native skies.

MEG MERRILIES

I

OLD MEG she was a Gipsy,
  And liv'd upon the Moors:
Her bed it was the brown heath turf,
  And her house was out of doors.

II

Her apples were swart blackberries,
  Her currants pods o' broom;
Her wine was dew of the wild white rose,
  Her book a churchyard tomb.

III

Her Brothers were the craggy hills,
  Her Sisters larchen trees—
Alone with her great family
  She liv'd as she did please.

IV

No breakfast had she many a morn,
  No dinner many a noon,
And 'stead of supper she would stare
  Full hard against the Moon.

V

But every morn of woodbine fresh
  She made her garlanding,
And every night the dark glen Yew
  She wove, and she would sing.

VI

And with her fingers old and brown
  She plaited Mats o' Rushes,
And gave them to the Cottagers
  She met among the Bushes.

VII

Old Meg was brave as Margaret Queen
    And tall as Amazon:
And old red blanket cloak she wore;
    A chip hat had she on.
God rest her aged bones somewhere—
    She died full long agone!

A SONG ABOUT MYSELF

FROM A LETTER TO FANNY KEATS

I

THERE was naughty Boy,
    A naughty boy was he,
He would not stop at home,
    He could not quiet be—
        He took
        In his Knapsack
        A Book
        Full of vowels
        And a shirt
        With some towels—
        A slight cap
        For night cap—
        A hair brush,
        Comb ditto,
        New Stockings
        For old ones
        Would split O!
        This Knapsack
        Tight at's back
        He rivetted close
    And followed his Nose
        To the North,
        To the North,
    And follow'd his nose
        To the North.

        An ink stand
        In his hand
        And a pen
        Big as ten
        In the other.
        And away
        In a Pother
        He ran
        To the mountains
        And fountains
        And ghostes
        And Postes
        And witches
        And ditches
        And wrote
        In his coat
        When the weather
        Was cool,
        Fear of gout,
        And without
        When the weather
        Was warm—
        Och the charm
        When we choose
    To follow one's nose
        To the north,
        To the north,
    To follow one's nose
        To the north!

II

There was a naughty boy
    And a naughty boy was he,
For nothing would he do
    But scribble poetry—
        He took

III

There was a naughty boy
    And a naughty boy was he,
He kept little fishes
    In washing tubs three

In spite
Of the might
Of the Maid
Nor afraid
Of his Granny-good—
He often would
Hurly burly
Get up early
And go
By hook or crook
To the brook
And bring home
Miller's thumb,
Tittlebat
Not over fat,
Minnows small
As the stall
Of a glove,
Not above
The size
Of a nice
Little Baby's
Little fingers—
O he made
'Twas his trade
Of Fish a pretty Kettle
A Kettle—
A Kettle

Of Fish a pretty Kettle
A Kettle!

IV

There was a naughty Boy,
And a naughty Boy was he,
He ran away to Scotland
The people for to see—
Then he found
That the ground
Was as hard,
That a yard
Was as long,
That a song
Was as merry,
That a cherry
Was as red—
That lead
Was as weighty,
That fourscore
Was as eighty,
That a door
Was as wooden
As in England—
So he stood in his shoes
And he wonder'd,
He wonder'd,
He stood in his shoes
And he wonder'd.

A GALLOWAY SONG

FROM A LETTER TO TOM KEATS

AH! ken ye what I met the day
   Out oure the Mountains
A coming down by craggi[e]s grey
   And mossie fountains—
A [h] goud hair'd Marie yeve I pray
   Ane minute's guessing—
For that I met upon the way
   Is past expressing.
As I stood where a rocky brig
   A torrent crosses
I spied upon a misty rig
   A troup o' Horses—

And as they trotted down the glen
 I sped to meet them
To see if I might know the Men
 To stop and greet them.
First Willie on his sleek mare came
 At canting gallop
His long hair rustled like a flame
 On board a shallop.   20
Then came his brother Rab and then
 Young Peggy's mither
And Peggy too—adown the glen
 They went togither—
I saw her wrappit in her hood
 Fra wind and raining—
Her cheek was flush wi' timid blood
 Twixt growth and waning—
She turn'd her dazed head full oft
 For there her Brithers   30
Came riding with her Bridegroom soft
 And mony ithers.
Young Tam came up an' eyed me quick
 With reddened cheek—
Braw Tam was daffed like a chick—
 He coud na speak—
Ah Marie they are all gane hame
 Through blustering weather
An' every heart is full on flame
 An' light as feather.   40
Ah! Marie they are all gone hame
 Fra happy wedding,
Whilst I—Ah is it not a shame?
 Sad tears am shedding.

SONNET

TO AILSA ROCK

Hearken, thou craggy ocean pyramid!
 Give answer from thy voice, the sea-fowls' screams!
 When were thy shoulders mantled in huge streams?
When, from the sun, was thy broad forehead hid?
How long is't since the mighty power bid
 Thee heave to airy sleep from fathom dreams?
 Sleep in the lap of thunder or sunbeams,
Or when grey clouds are thy cold coverlid.
Thou answer'st not; for thou art dead asleep;
 Thy life is but two dead eternities—   10

The last in air, the former in the deep;
   First with the whales, last with the eagle-skies—
Drown'd wast thou till an earthquake made thee steep,
   Another cannot wake thy giant size.

SONNET

WRITTEN IN THE COTTAGE WHERE BURNS WAS BORN

THIS mortal body of a thousand days
   Now fills, O Burns, a space in thine own room,
Where thou didst dream alone on budded bays,
   Happy and thoughtless of thy day of doom!
My pulse is warm with thine own Barley-bree,
   My head is light with pledging a great soul,
My eyes are wandering, and I cannot see,
   Fancy is dead and drunken at its goal;
Yet can I stamp my foot upon thy floor,
   Yet can I ope thy window-sash to find   10
The meadow thou hast tramped o'er and o'er,—
   Yet can I think of thee till thought is blind,—
Yet can I gulp a bumper to thy name,—
   O smile among the shades, for this is fame!

LINES WRITTEN IN THE HIGHLANDS AFTER A VISIT TO BURNS'S COUNTRY

THERE is a charm in footing slow across a silent plain,
Where patriot battle has been fought, where glory had the gain;
There is a pleasure on the heath where Druids old have been,
Where mantles grey have rustled by and swept the nettles green;
There is a joy in every spot made known by times of old,
New to the feet, although each tale a hundred times be told;
There is a deeper joy than all, more solemn in the heart,
More parching to the tongue than all, of more divine a smart,
When weary steps forget themselves upon a pleasant turf,
Upon hot sand, or flinty road, or sea-shore iron scurf,   10
Toward the castle or the cot, where long ago was born
One who was great through mortal days, and died of fame unshorn,
Light heather-bells may tremble then, but they are far away;
Wood-lark may sing from sandy fern,—the Sun may hear his lay;
Runnels may kiss the grass on shelves and shallows clear,
But their low voices are not heard, though come on travels drear;
Blood-red the Sun may set behind black mountain peaks;
Blue tides may sluice and drench their time in caves and weedy creeks;
Eagles may seem to sleep wing-wide upon the air;
Ring-doves may fly convuls'd across to some high-cedar'd lair;   20

But the forgotten eye is still fast lidded to the ground,
As Palmer's, that with weariness, mid-desert shrine hath found.
At such a time the soul's a child, in childhood is the brain;
Forgotten is the worldly heart—alone, it beats in vain.—
Aye, if a madman could have leave to pass a healthful day
To tell his forehead's swoon and faint when first began decay,
He might make tremble many a one whose spirit had gone forth
To find a Bard's low cradle-place about the silent North!
Scanty the hour and few the steps beyond the bourn of care,
Beyond the sweet and bitter world,—beyond it unaware! 30
Scanty the hour and few the steps, because a longer stay
Would bar return, and make a man forget his mortal way:
O horrible! to lose the sight of well remember'd face,
Of Brother's eyes, of Sister's brow—constant to every place;
Filling the air, as on we move, with portraiture intense;
More warm than those heroic tints that pain a painter's sense,
When shapes of old come striding by, and visages of old,
Locks shining black, hair scanty grey, and passions manifold.
No, no, that horror cannot be, for at the cable's length
Man feels the gentle anchor pull and gladdens in its strength:— 40
One hour, half-idiot, he stands by mossy waterfall,
But in the very next he reads his soul's memorial:—
He reads it on the mountain's height, where chance he may sit down
Upon rough marble diadem—that hill's eternal crown.
Yet be his anchor e'er so fast, room is there for a prayer
That man may never lose his mind on mountains black and bare;
That he may stray league after league some great birthplace to find
And keep his vision clear from speck, his inward sight unblind.

THE GADFLY

FROM A LETTER TO TOM KEATS

I

ALL gentle folks who owe a grudge
 To any living thing
Open your ears and stay your
  t[r]udge
Whilst I in dudgeon sing.

II

The Gadfly he hath stung me
 sore—
 O may he ne'er sting you!
But we have many a horrid bore
 He may sting black and blue.

III

Has any here an old grey Mare
 With three legs all her store,
O put it to her Buttocks bare
 And straight she'll run on four.

IV

Has any here a Lawyer suit
 Of Seventeen-Forty-Three,
Take Lawyer's nose and put it to't
 And you the end will see.

V

Is there a Man in Parliament
    Dum[b-]founder'd in his
        speech,
O let his neighbour make a rent
    And put one in his breech.

VI

O Lowther how much better thou
    Hadst figur'd t'other day
When to the folks thou mad'st a
        bow
    And hadst no more to say

VII

If lucky Gadfly had but ta'en
    His seat   *   *   *
And put thee to a little pain
    To save thee from a worse.

VIII

Better than Southey it had been,
    Better than Mr. D——,
Better than Wordsworth too, I
        ween,
    Better than Mr. V——.

IX

Forgive me pray good people all
    For deviating so—
In spirit sure I had a call—
    And now I on will go.

X

Has any here a daughter fair
    Too fond of reading novels,
Too apt to fall in love with care
    And charming Mister Lovels,

XI

O put a Gadfly to that thing
    She keeps so white and pert—
I mean the finger for the ring,
    And it will breed a wort.

XII

Has any here a pious spouse
    Who seven times a day
Scolds as King David pray'd, to
        chouse
    And have her holy way—

XIII

O let a Gadfly's little sting
    Persuade her sacred tongue
That noises are a common thing
    But that her bell has rung.

XIV

And as this is the summum bo-
    num of all conquering,
I leave "withouten wordes mo"
    The Gadfly's little sting.

SONNET

ON HEARING THE BAG-PIPE AND SEEING "THE STRANGER" PLAYED AT INVERARY

Of late two dainties were before me plac'd
Sweet, holy, pure, sacred and innocent,
    From the ninth sphere to me benignly sent
That Gods might know my own particular taste.
First the soft Bag-pipe mourn'd with zealous haste.

The Stranger next with head on bosom bent
Sigh'd; rueful again the piteous Bag-pipe went,
Again the Stranger sighings fresh did waste.
O Bag-pipe thou didst steal my heart away—
   O Stranger thou my nerves from Pipe didst charm—
O Bag-pipe thou didst re-assert thy sway—   11
   Again thou Stranger gav'st me fresh alarm—
Alas! I could not choose. Ah! my poor heart,
Mum chance art thou with both oblig'd to part.

STAFFA

Not Aladdin magian
Ever such a work began;
Not the wizard of the Dee
Ever such a dream could see;
Not St. John, in Patmos' Isle,
In the passion of his toil,
When he saw the churches seven,
Golden aisl'd, built up in heaven,
Gaz'd at such a rugged wonder.
As I stood its roofing under,   10
Lo! I saw one sleeping there,
On the marble cold and bare.
While the surges wash'd his feet,
And his garments white did beat
Drench'd about the sombre rocks,
On his neck his well-grown locks,
Lifted dry above the main,
Were upon the curl again.
"What is this? and what art thou?"
Whisper'd I, and touch'd his brow;   20
"What art thou? and what is this?"
Whisper'd I, and strove to kiss
The spirit's hand, to wake his eyes;
Up he started in a trice:
"I am Lycidas," said he,
"Fam'd in funeral minstrelsy!
This was architectur'd thus
By the great Oceanus!—
Here his mighty waters play
Hollow organs all the day;   30
Here by turns his dolphins all,
Finny palmers great and small,
Come to pay devotion due—
Each a mouth of pearls must strew.

Many a mortal of these days,
Dares to pass our sacred ways,
Dares to touch audaciously
This Cathedral of the Sea!
I have been the pontiff-priest   40
Where the waters never rest,
Where a fledgy sea-bird choir
Soars for ever; holy fire
I have hid from mortal man;
Proteus is my Sacristan.
But the dulled eye of mortal
Hath pass'd beyond the rocky portal;
So for ever will I leave
Such a taint, and soon unweave
All the magic of the place."

* * * * *

So saying, with a Spirit's glance   50
He dived!

SONNET

WRITTEN UPON THE TOP OF BEN NEVIS

READ me a lesson, Muse, and speak it loud
 Upon the top of Nevis, blind in mist!
I look into the chasms, and a shroud
 Vapourous doth hide them,—just so much I wist
Mankind do know of hell; I look o'erhead,
 And there is sullen mist,—even so much
Mankind can tell of heaven; mist is spread
 Before the earth, beneath me,—even such,
Even so vague is man's sight of himself!
 Here are the craggy stones beneath my feet,—   10
Thus much I know that, a poor witless elf,
 I tread on them,—that all my eye doth meet
Is mist and crag, not only on this height,
But in the world of thought and mental might!

BEN NEVIS

A DIALOGUE

[PERSONS: MRS. CAMERON AND BEN NEVIS]

MRS. C.

UPON my life Sir Nevis I am pique'd
That I have so far panted tugg'd and reek'd
To do an hono[u]r to your old bald pate

And now am sitting on you just to bate,
Without your paying me one compliment.
Alas 'tis so with all, when our intent
Is plain, and in the eye of all Mankind
We fair ones show a preference, too blind!
You Gentle man immediately turn tail—
O let me then my hapless fate bewail!   10
Ungrateful Baldpate, have I not disdain'd
The pleasant Valleys—have I not, madbrain'd,
Deserted all my Pickles and preserves,
My China closet too—with wretched Nerves
To boot—say, wretched ingrate, have I not
Le[f]t my soft cushion chair and caudle pot?
'Tis true I had no corns—no! thank the fates,
My Shoemaker was always Mr. Bates.
And if not Mr. Bates why I'm not old!
Still dumb, ungrateful Nevis—still so cold!   20

Here the Lady took some more w[h]iskey and was putting even
more to her lips when she dashed [it] to the Ground for the
Mountain began to grumble—which continued for a few minutes
before he thus began,

BEN NEVIS

What whining bit of tongue and Mouth thus dares
Disturb my slumber of a thousand years?
Even so long my sleep has been secure—
And to be so awaked I'll not endure.
Oh pain—for since the Eagle's earliest scream
I've had a dam[n]'d confounded ugly dream,
A Nightmare sure. What, Madam, was it you?
It cannot be! My old eyes are not true!
Red-Crag, my Spectacles! Now let me see!
Good Heavens, Lady, how the gemini   30
Did you get here? O I shall split my sides!
I shall earthquake——

MRS. C.

Sweet Nevis, do not quake, for though I love
You[r] honest Countenance all things above,
Truly I should not like to be convey'd
So far into your Bosom—gentle Maid
Loves not too rough a treatment, gentle Sir—
Pray thee be calm and do not quake nor stir,
No not a Stone, or I shall go in fits—

BEN NEVIS

I must—I shall—I meet not such tit bits—   40
I meet not such sweet creatures every day—
By my old night-cap, night-cap night and day,
I must have one sweet Buss—I must and shall!
Red-Crag!—What, Madam, can you then repent
Of all the toil and vigour you have spent
To see Ben Nevis and to touch his nose?
Red-Crag, I say! O I must have them close!
Red-Crag, there lies beneath my farthest toe
A vein of Sulphur—go dear Red-Crag, go—
And rub your flinty back against it—budge!   50
Dear Madam, I must kiss you, faith I must!
I must Embrace you with my dearest gust!
Block-head, d'ye hear—Block-head, I'll make her feel—
There lies beneath my east leg's northern heel
A cave of young earth dragons—well, my boy,
Go thither quick and so complete my joy;
Take you a bundle of the largest pines
And when the sun on fiercest Phosphor shines
Fire them and ram them in the Dragon's nest,
Then will the dragons fry and fizz their best   60
Until ten thousand now no bigger than
Poor Al[l]igators—poor things of one span—
Will each one swell to twice ten times the size
Of northern whale—then for the tender prize—
The moment then—for then will Red-Crag rub
His flinty back—and I shall kiss and snub
And press my dainty morsel to my breast.
Block-head, make haste!
              O Muses weep the rest—
The Lady fainted and he thought her dead
So pulled the clouds again about his head   70
And went to sleep again—soon she was rous'd
By her affrighted servants—next day hous'd
Safe on the lowly ground she bless'd her fate
That fainting fit was not delayed too late.

TRANSLATION FROM A SONNET OF RONSARD

Nature withheld Cassandra in the skies,
   For more adornment, a full thousand years;
She took their cream of Beauty's fairest dyes,
   And shap'd and tinted her above all Peers:
Meanwhile Love kept her dearly with his wings,
   And underneath their shadow fill'd her eyes

With such a richness that the cloudy Kings
Of high Olympus utter'd slavish sighs.
When from the Heavens I saw her first descend,
My heart took fire, and only burning pains,   10
They were my pleasures—they my Life's sad end;
Love pour'd her beauty into my warm veins . . .

      *   *   *   *   *   *   *
      *   *   *   *   *   *   *

A PROPHECY: TO GEORGE KEATS IN AMERICA

'TIS the witching hour of night,
Orbed is the moon and bright,
And the stars they glisten, glisten,
Seeming with bright eyes to listen—
    For what listen they?
For a song and for a charm,
See they glisten in alarm,
And the moon is waxing warm
    To hear what I shall say.
Moon! keep wide thy golden ears—   10
Hearken, stars! and hearken, spheres!—
Hearken, thou eternal sky!
I sing an infant's lullaby,
    A pretty lullaby.
Listen, listen, listen, listen,
Glisten, glisten, glisten, glisten,
    And hear my lullaby!
Though the rushes that will make
Its cradle still are in the lake—
Though the linen that will be   20
Its swathe, is on the cotton tree—
Though the woollen that will keep
It warm, is on the silly sheep—
Listen, starlight, listen, listen,
Glisten, glisten, glisten, glisten,
    And hear my lullaby!
Child, I see thee! Child, I've found thee
Midst of the quiet all around thee!
Child, I see thee! Child, I spy thee!
And thy mother sweet is nigh thee!   30
Child, I know thee! Child no more,
But a Poet evermore!
See, see, the lyre, the lyre,
In a flame of fire,
Upon the little cradle's top

Flaring, flaring, flaring,
Past the eyesight's bearing.
Awake it from its sleep,
And see if it can keep
Its eyes upon the blaze— 40
　　Amaze, amaze!
It stares, it stares, it stares,
It dares what no one dares!
It lifts its little hand into the flame
Unharm'd, and on the strings
Paddles a little tune, and sings,
With dumb endeavour sweetly—
Bard art thou completely!
　　Little child
　　O' th' western wild, 50
Bard art thou completely!
Sweetly with dumb endeavour,
A Poet now or never,
　　Little child
　　O' th' western wild,
A Poet now or never!

STANZAS

I

In a drear-nighted December,
　　Too happy, happy tree,
Thy branches ne'er remember
　　Their green felicity:
The north cannot undo them,
With a sleety whistle through them;
Nor frozen thawings glue them
　　From budding at the prime.

II

In a drear-nighted December,
　　Too happy, happy brook,
Thy bubblings ne'er remember
　　Apollo's summer look;
But with a sweet forgetting,
They stay their crystal fretting,
Never, never petting
　　About the frozen time.

III

Ah! would 'twere so with many
    A gentle girl and boy!
But were there ever any
    Writh'd not at passed joy?
To know the change and feel it,
When there is none to heal it,
Nor numbed sense to steel it,
    Was never said in rhyme.

SPENSERIAN STANZA

*[Written at the close of Canto II, Book V, of
"The Faerie Queene"]*

In after-time, a sage of mickle lore
Yclep'd Typographus, the Giant took,
And did refit his limbs as heretofore,
And made him read in many a learned book,
And into many a lively legend look;
Thereby in goodly themes so training him,
That all his brutishness he quite forsook,
When, meeting Artegall and Talus grim,
The one he struck stone-blind, the other's eyes wox dim.

THE EVE OF SAINT MARK

Upon a Sabbath-day it fell:
Twice holy was the Sabbath-bell,
That call'd the folk to evening prayer;
The city streets were clean and fair
From wholesome drench of April rains;
And, on the western window panes,
The chilly sunset faintly told
Of unmatur'd green vallies cold,
Of the green thorny bloomless hedge,
Of rivers new with spring-tide sedge,   10
Of primroses by shelter'd rills,
And daisies on the aguish hills.
Twice holy was the Sabbath-bell:
The silent streets were crowded well
With staid and pious companies,
Warm from their fire-side orat'ries;
And moving, with demurest air,
To even-song, and vesper prayer.
Each arched porch, and entry low,
Was fill'd with patient folk and slow,   20

With whispers hush, and shuffling feet,
While play'd the organ loud and sweet.

The bells had ceas'd, the prayers begun,
And Bertha had not yet half done
A curious volume, patch'd and torn,
That all day long, from earliest morn,
Had taken captive her two eyes,
Among its golden broideries;
Perplex'd her with a thousand things,—
The stars of Heaven, and angels' wings,   30
Martyrs in a fiery blaze,
Azure saints in silver rays,
Moses' breastplate, and the seven
Candlesticks John saw in Heaven,
The winged Lion of Saint Mark,
And the Covenantal Ark,
With its many mysteries,
Cherubim and golden mice.

Bertha was a maiden fair,
Dwelling in the old Minster-square;   40
From her fire-side she could see,
Sidelong, its rich antiquity,
Far as the Bishop's garden-wall;
Where sycamores and elm-trees tall,
Full-leav'd, the forest had outstript,
By no sharp north-wind ever nipt,
So shelter'd by the mighty pile.
Bertha arose, and read awhile,
With forehead 'gainst the window-pane.
Again she try'd, and then again,   50
Until the dusk eve left her dark
Upon the legend of St. Mark.
From plaited lawn-frill, fine and thin,
She lifted up her soft warm chin,
With aching neck and swimming eyes,
And daz'd with saintly imageries.

All was gloom, and silent all,
Save now and then the still foot-fall
Of one returning homewards late,
Past the echoing minster-gate.   60

The clamorous daws, that all the day
Above tree-tops and towers play,
Pair by pair had gone to rest,
Each in its ancient belfry-nest,

Where asleep they fall betimes,
To music of the drowsy chimes.

All was silent, all was gloom,
Abroad and in the homely room:
Down she sat, poor cheated soul!
And struck a lamp from the dismal coal;   70
Lean'd forward, with bright drooping hair
And slant book, full against the glare.
Her shadow, in uneasy guise,
Hover'd about, a giant size,
On ceiling-beam and old oak chair,
The parrot's cage, and panel square;
And the warm angled winter screen,
On which were many monsters seen,
Call'd doves of Siam, Lima mice,
And legless birds of Paradise,   80
Macaw, and tender Avadavat,
And silken-furr'd Angora cat.
Untir'd she read, her shadow still
Glower'd about, as it would fill
The room with wildest forms and shades,
As though some ghostly queen of spades
Had come to mock behind her back,
And dance, and ruffle her garments black.
Untir'd she read the legend page,
Of holy Mark, from youth to age,   90
On land, on sea, in pagan chains,
Rejoicing for his many pains.
Sometimes the learned eremite,
With golden star, or dagger bright,
Referr'd to pious poesies
Written in smallest crow-quill size
Beneath the text; and thus the rhyme
Was parcell'd out from time to time:
——"Als writith he of swevenis,
Men han beforene they wake in bliss,   100
Whanne that hir friendes thinke hem bound
In crimped shroude farre under grounde;
And how a litling child mote be
A saint er its nativitie,
Gif that the modre (God her blesse!)
Kepen in solitarinesse,
And kissen devoute the holy croce.
Of Goddess love, and Sathan's force,—
He writith; and thinges many mo:
Of swiche thinges I may not show.   110

Bot I must tellen verilie
Somdel of Saintè Cicilie,
And chieflie what he auctorethe
Of Saintè Markis life and dethe:"

At length her constant eyelids come
Upon the fervent martyrdom;
Then lastly to his holy shrine,
Exalt amid the tapers' shine
At Venice,—-

ODE TO FANNY

I

PHYSICIAN Nature! let my spirit blood!
O ease my heart of verse and let me rest;
Throw me upon thy Tripod, till the flood
    Of stifling numbers ebbs from my full breast.
A theme! a theme! great nature! give a theme;
        Let me begin my dream.
I come—I see thee, as thou standest there,
Beckon me not into the wintry air.

II

Ah! dearest love, sweet home of all my fears,
    And hopes, and joys, and panting miseries,—
To-night, if I may guess, thy beauty wears
        A smile of such delight,
        As brilliant and as bright,
    As when with ravished, aching, vassal eyes,
        Lost in soft amaze,
        I gaze, I gaze!

III

Who now, with greedy looks, eats up my feast?
    What stare outfaces now my silver moon!
Ah! keep that hand unravished at the least;
        Let, let, the amorous burn—
        But, pr'ythee, do not turn
    The current of your heart from me so soon.
        O! save, in charity,
        The quickest pulse for me.

IV

Save it for me, sweet love! though music breathe
　Voluptuous visions into the warm air;
Though swimming through the dance's dangerous
　　　　wreath,
　　　　　Be like an April day,
　　　　　Smiling and cold and gay,
　A temperate lilly, temperate as fair;
　　　　　Then, Heaven! there will be
　　　　　A warmer June for me.

V

Why, this—you'll say, my Fanny! is not true:
　Put your soft hand upon your snowy side,
Where the heart beats: confess—'tis nothing new—
　　　　　Must not a woman be
　　　　　A feather on the sea,
　Sway'd to and fro by every wind and tide?
　　　　　Of as uncertain speed
　　　　　As blow-ball from the mead?

VI

I know it—and to know it is despair
　To one who loves you as I love, sweet Fanny!
Whose heart goes fluttering for you every where,
　　　　　Nor, when away you roam,
　　　　　Dare keep its wretched home,
　Love, love alone, his pains severe and many:
　　　　　Then, loveliest! keep me free,
　　　　　From torturing jealousy.

VII

Ah! if you prize my subdued soul above
　The poor, the fading, brief, pride of an hour;
Let none profane my Holy See of love,
　　　　　Or with a rude hand break
　　　　　The sacramental cake:
　Let none else touch the just new-budded flower;
　　　　　If not—may my eyes close,
　　　　　Love! on their lost repose.

SONNET

TO SLEEP

O SOFT embalmer of the still midnight,
　　Shutting, with careful fingers and benign,
Our gloom-pleas'd eyes, embower'd from the light,
　　Enshaded in forgetfulness divine:
O soothest Sleep! if so it please thee, close
　　In midst of this thine hymn my willing eyes,
Or wait the "Amen," ere thy poppy throws
　　Around my bed its lulling charities.
Then save me, or the passed day will shine
Upon my pillow, breeding many woes,—　　　　　　10
　　Save me from curious Conscience, that still lords
Its strength for darkness, burrowing like a mole;
　　Turn the key deftly in the oiled wards,
And seal the hushed Casket of my Soul.

SONG

I

HUSH, hush! tread softly! hush, hush my dear!
　　All the house is asleep, but we know very well
That the jealous, the jealous old bald-pate may hear,
　　Tho' you've padded his night-cap—O sweet Isabel!
　　　Tho' your feet are more light than a Fairy's feet,
　　　Who dances on bubbles where brooklets meet,—
Hush, hush! soft tiptoe! hush, hush my dear!
For less than a nothing the jealous can hear.

II

No leaf doth tremble, no ripple is there
　　On the river,—all's still, and the night's sleepy eye
Closes up, and forgets all its Lethean care,
　　Charm'd to death by the drone of the humming Mayfly;
　　　And the Moon, whether prudish or complaisant,
　　　Has fled to her bower, well knowing I want
No light in the dusk, no torch in the gloom,
But my Isabel's eyes, and her lips pulp'd with bloom.

III

Lift the latch! ah gently! ah tenderly—sweet!
　　We are dead if that latchet gives one little clink!
Well done—now those lips, and a flowery seat—
　　The old man may sleep, and the planets may wink;

The shut rose shall dream of our loves, and awake
Full blown, and such warmth for the morning's take,
The stock-dove shall hatch her soft brace and shall coo,
While I kiss to the melody, aching all through!

SONG

I HAD a dove and the sweet dove died;
  And I have thought it died of grieving:
O, what could it grieve for? Its feet were tied,
  With a silken thread of my own hand's weaving;
Sweet little red feet! why should you die—
Why should you leave me, sweet bird! why?
You liv'd alone in the forest-tree,
Why, pretty thing! would you not live with me?
I kiss'd you oft and gave you white peas;
Why not live sweetly, as in the green trees?   10

ODE ON INDOLENCE

"They toil not, neither do they spin."

I

ONE morn before me were three figures seen,
  With bowed necks, and joined hands, side-faced;
And one behind the other stepp'd serene,
  In placid sandals, and in white robes graced;
They pass'd, like figures on a marble urn,
  When shifted round to see the other side;
    They came again; as when the urn once more
Is shifted round, the first seen shades return;
  And they were strange to me, as may betide
    With vases, to one deep in Phidian lore.

II

How is it, Shadows! that I knew ye not?
  How came ye muffled in so hush a mask?
Was it a silent deep-disguised plot
  To steal away, and leave without a task
My idle days? Ripe was the drowsy hour;
  The blissful cloud of summer-indolence
    Benumb'd my eyes; my pulse grew less and less;
Pain had no sting, and pleasure's wreath no flower:
  O, why did ye not melt, and leave my sense
    Unhaunted quite of all but—nothingness?

III

A third time pass'd they by, and, passing, turn'd
    Each one the face a moment whiles to me;
Then faded, and to follow them I burn'd
    And ach'd for wings because I knew the three;
The first was a fair Maid, and Love her name;
    The second was Ambition, pale of cheek,
        And ever watchful with fatigued eye;
The last, whom I love more, the more of blame
    Is heap'd upon her, maiden most unmeek,—
        I knew to be my demon Poesy.

IV

They faded, and, forsooth! I wanted wings:
    O folly! What is love! and where is it?
And for that poor Ambition! it springs
    From a man's little heart's short fever-fit;
For Poesy!—no,—she has not a joy,—
    At least for me,—so sweet as drowsy noons,
        And evenings steep'd in honied indolence;
O, for an age so shelter'd from annoy,
    That I may never know how change the moons,
        Or hear the voice of busy common-sense!

V

And once more came they by;—alas! wherefore?
    My sleep had been embroider'd with dim dreams;
My soul had been a lawn besprinkled o'er
    With flowers, and stirring shades, and baffled beams:
The morn was clouded, but no shower fell,
    Tho' in her lids hung the sweet tears of May;
        The open casement press'd a new-leav'd vine,
    Let in the budding warmth and throstle's lay;
O Shadows! 'twas a time to bid farewell!
    Upon your skirts had fallen no tears of mine.

VI

So, ye three Ghosts, adieu! Ye cannot raise
    My head cool-bedded in the flowery grass;
For I would not be dieted with praise,
    A pet-lamb in a sentimental farce!
Fade softly from my eyes, and be once more
    In masque-like figures on the dreamy urn;
        Farewell! I yet have visions for the night,
And for the day faint visions there is store;
        Vanish, ye Phantoms! from my idle spright,
    Into the clouds, and never more return!

SONNET

Why did I laugh to-night? No voice will tell:
  No God, no Demon of severe response,
Deigns to reply from heaven or from Hell.
  Then to my human heart I turn at once.
Heart! Thou and I are here sad and alone;
  I say, why did I laugh! O mortal pain!
O Darkness! Darkness! ever must I moan,
  To question Heaven and Hell and Heart in vain.
Why did I laugh? I know this Being's lease,
  My fancy to its utmost blisses spreads;   10
Yet would I on this very midnight cease,
  And the world's gaudy ensigns see in shreds;
Verse, Fame, and Beauty are intense indeed,
But Death intenser—Death is Life's high meed.

SONNET

A DREAM, AFTER READING DANTE'S EPISODE OF PAULO AND FRANCESCA

As Hermes once took to his feathers light,
  When lulled Argus, baffled, swoon'd and slept,
So on a Delphic reed, my idle spright
  So play'd, so charm'd, so conquer'd, so bereft
The dragon-world of all its hundred eyes;
  And, seeing it asleep, so flew away—
Not to pure Ida with its snow-cold skies,
  Nor unto Tempe where Jove griev'd a day;
But to that second circle of sad hell,
  Where 'mid the gust, the whirlwind, and the flaw
Of rain and hail-stones, lovers need not tell   11
  Their sorrows. Pale were the sweet lips I saw,
Pale were the lips I kiss'd, and fair the form
I floated with, about that melancholy storm.

AN EXTEMPORE

FROM A LETTER TO GEORGE KEATS AND HIS WIFE

When they were come into the Faery's Court
They rang—no one at home—all gone to sport
And dance and kiss and love as faeries do
For Fa[e]ries be as humans, lovers true—
Amid the woods they were, so lone and wild,
Where even the Robin feels himself exil'd
And where the very brooks as if afraid
Hurry along to some less magic shade.

"No one at home!" the fretful princess cried
"And all for nothing such a dre[a]ry ride,   10
And all for nothing my new diamond cross,
No one to see my Persian feathers toss,
No one to see my Ape, my Dwarf, my Fool,
Or how I pace my Otaheitan mule.
Ape, Dwarf and Fool, why stand you gaping there?
Burst the door open, quick—or I declare
I'll switch you soundly and in pieces tear."
The Dwarf began to tremble and the Ape
Star'd at the Fool, the Fool was all agape,
The Princess grasp'd her switch, but just in time   20
The dwarf with piteous face began to rhyme.
"O mighty Princess did you ne'er hear tell
What your poor servants know but too too well?
Know you the three great crimes in faery land?
The first, alas! poor Dwarf, I understand—
I made a whipstock of a faery's wand—
The next is snoring in their company—
The next, the last, the direst of the three
Is making free when they are not at home.
I was a Prince—a baby prince—my doom   30
You see, I made a whipstock of a wand—
My top has henceforth slept in faery land.
He was a Prince, the Fool, a grown up Prince,
But he has never been a King's son since
He fell a-snoring at a faery Ball—
Your poor Ape was a prince and he, poor thing,
Picklock'd a faery's boudour—now no king,
But ape—so pray your highness stay awhile;
'Tis sooth indeed, we know it to our sorrow—
Persist and *you* may be an ape tomorrow—   40
While the Dwarf spake the Princess all for spite
Peal'd [*sic*] the brown hazel twig to lilly white,
Clench'd her small teeth, and held her lips apart,
Try'd to look unconcern'd with beating heart.
They saw her highness had made up her mind
And quaver'd like the reeds before the wind,
And they had had it, but, O happy chance!
The Ape for very fear began to dance
And grin'd as all his ugliness did ache—
She staid her vixen fingers for his sake,   50
He was so very ugly: then she took
Her pocket glass mirror and began to look
First at herself and [then] at him and then
She smil'd at her own beauteous face again.

Yet for all this—for all her pretty face
She took it in her head to see the place.
Women gain little from experience
Either in Lovers, husbands or expense.
The more the beauty, the more fortune too,
Beauty before the wide world never knew. 60
So each fair reasons—tho' it oft miscarries.
She thought *her* pretty face would please the fa[e]ries.
"My darling Ape I won't whip you today—
Give me the Picklock, sirrah, and go play."
They all three wept—but counsel was as vain
As crying cup biddy to drops of rain.
Yet lingeringly did the sad Ape forth draw
The Picklock from the Pocket in his Jaw.
The Princess took it and dismounting straight
Trip'd in blue silver'd slippers to the gate 70
And touch'd the wards, the Door full cou[r]teou[s]ly
Opened—she enter'd with her servants three.
Again it clos'd and there was nothing seen
But the Mule grazing on the herbage green.

End of Canto xii

Canto the xiii

The Mule no sooner saw himself alone
Than he prick'd up his Ears—and said "well done!
At least, unhappy Prince, I may be free—
No more a Princess shall side-saddle me.
O King of Otaheitè—tho' a Mule
'Aye every inch a King'—tho' 'Fortune's fool'— 80
Well done—for by what Mr. Dwarfy said
I would not give a sixpence for her head."
Even as he spake he trotted in high glee
To the knotty side of an old Pollard tree
And rub['d] his sides against the mossed bark
Till his Girths burst and left him naked stark
Except his Bridle—how get rid of that,
Buckled and tied with many a twist and plait?
At last it struck him to pretend to sleep
And then the thievish Monkeys down would creep 90
And filch the unpleasant trammels quite away.
No sooner thought of than adown he lay,
Sham'd a good snore—the Monkey-men descended
And whom they thought to injure they befriended.
They hung his Bridle on a topmost bough
And of[f] he went, run, trot, or anyhow —
    Brown is gone to bed—and I am tired of rhyming . . .

SPENSERIAN STANZAS
ON CHARLES ARMITAGE BROWN

I

He is to weet a melancholy carle:
Thin in the waist, with bushy head of hair,
As hath the seeded thistle when in parle
It holds the Zephyr, ere it sendeth fair
Its light balloons into the summer air;
Thereto his beard had not begun to bloom,
No brush had touch'd his chin or razor sheer;
No care had touch'd his cheek with mortal doom,
But new he was and bright as scarf from Persian loom.

II

Ne cared he for wine, or half-and-half
Ne cared he for fish or flesh or fowl,
And sauces held he worthless as the chaff;
He 'sdeigned the swine-head at the wassail-bowl;
Ne with lewd ribbalds sat he cheek by jowl;
Ne with sly Lemans in the scorner's chair;
But after water-brooks this Pilgrim's soul
Panted, and all his food was woodland air
Though he would oft-times feast on gilliflowers rare.

III

The slang of cities in no wise he knew,
Tipping the wink to him was heathen Greek;
He sipp'd no olden Tom or ruin blue,
Or nantz or cherry-brandy drank full meek
By many a damsel hoarse and rouge of cheek;
Nor did he know each aged watchman's beat,
Nor in obscured purlieus would he seek
For curled Jewesses, with ankles neat,
Who as they walk abroad make tinkling with their feet.

TWO OR THREE

FROM A LETTER TO HIS SISTER

Two or three Posies
With two or three simples—
Two or three Noses
With two or three pimples—
Two or three wise men

And two or three ninny's—
Two or three purses
And two or three guineas—
Two or three raps
At two or three doors—   10
Two or three naps
Of two or three hours—
Two or three Cats
And two or three mice—
Two or three sprats
At a very great price—
Two or three sandies
And two or three tabbies—
Two or three dandies
And two Mrs. [Abbeys]   mum!   20
Two or three Smiles
And two or three frowns—
Two or three Miles
To two or three towns—
Two or three pegs
For two or three bonnets—
Two or three dove eggs
To hatch into sonnets.

LA BELLE DAME SANS MERCI

I

Ah, what can ail thee, wretched wight,
  Alone and palely loitering;
The sedge is wither'd from the lake,
  And no birds sing.

II

Ah, what can ail thee, wretched wight,
  So haggard and so woe-begone?
The squirrel's granary is full,
  And the harvest's done.

III

I see a lilly on thy brow,
  With anguish moist and fever dew;
And on thy cheek a fading rose
  Fast withereth too.

IV

I met a lady in the meads
　Full beautiful, a faery's child;
Her hair was long, her foot was light,
　And her eyes were wild.

V

I set her on my pacing steed,
　And nothing else saw all day long;
For sideways would she lean, and sing
　A faery's song.

VI

I made a garland for her head,
　And bracelets too, and fragrant zone;
She look'd at me as she did love,
　And made sweet moan.

VII

She found me roots of relish sweet,
　And honey wild, and manna dew;
And sure in language strange she said,
　I love thee true.

VIII

She took me to her elfin grot,
　And there she gaz'd and sighed deep,
And there I shut her wild sad eyes—
　So kiss'd to sleep.

IX

And there we slumber'd on the moss,
　And there I dream'd, ah woe betide,
The latest dream I ever dream'd
　On the cold hill side.

X

I saw pale kings, and princes too,
　Pale warriors, death-pale were they all;
Who cry'd—"La belle Dame sans merci
　Hath thee in thrall!"

XI

I saw their starv'd lips in the gloam
  With horrid warning gaped wide,
And I awoke, and found me here
  On the cold hill side.

XII

And this is why I sojourn here
  Alone and palely loitering,
Though the sedge is wither'd from the lake,
  And no birds sing.

SONG OF FOUR FAERIES,

FIRE, AIR, EARTH, AND WATER,

SALAMANDER, ZEPHYR, DUSKETHA, AND BREAMA

SALAMANDER

HAPPY, happy glowing fire!

ZEPHYR

Fragrant air! delicious light!

DUSKETHA

Let me to my glooms retire!

BREAMA

I to green-weed rivers bright!

SALAMANDER

Happy, happy glowing fire!
Dazzling bowers of soft retire,
Ever let my nourish'd wing,
Like a bat's, still wandering,
Faintless fan your fiery spaces,
Spirit sole in deadly places.
In unhaunted roar and blaze,
Open eyes that never daze,
Let me see the myriad shapes
Of men, and beasts, and fish, and apes,
Portray'd in many a fiery den,
And wrought by spumy bitumen.

10

On the deep intenser roof,
Arched every way aloof,
Let me breathe upon their skies,
And anger their live tapestries;
Free from cold, and every care,
Of chilly rain, and shivering air.

20

ZEPHYR

Spirit of Fire! away! away!
Or your very roundelay
Will sear my plumage newly budded
From its quilled sheath, all studded
With the self-same dews that fell
On the May-grown Asphodel.
Spirit of Fire—away! away!

BREAMA

Spirit of Fire—away! away!
Zephyr, blue-eyed Faery, turn,
And see my cool sedge-bury'd urn,
Where it rests its mossy brim
'Mid water-mint and cresses dim;
And the flowers, in sweet troubles,
Lift their eyes above the bubbles,
Like our Queen, when she would please
To sleep, and Oberon *will* teaze.
Love me, blue-eyed Faery, true!
Soothly I am sick for you.

30

40

ZEPHYR

Gentle Breama! by the first
Violet young nature nurst,
I will bathe myself with thee,
So you sometimes follow me
To my home, far, far, in west,
Beyond the nimble-wheeled quest
Of the golden-browed sun:
Come with me, o'er tops of trees,
To my fragrant palaces.
Where they ever floating are
Beneath the cherish of a star
Call'd Vesper, who with silver veil
Ever hides his brilliance pale,
Ever gently-drows'd doth keep
Twilight for the Fayes to sleep.

50

Fear not that your watery hair
Will thirst in drouthy ringlets there;
Clouds of stored summer rains
Thou shalt taste, before the stains
Of the mountain soil they take,   60
And too unlucent for thee make.
I love thee, crystal Faery, true!
Sooth I am as sick for you!

SALAMANDER

Out, ye aguish Faeries, out!
Chilly lovers, what a rout
Keep ye with your frozen breath,
Colder than the mortal death.
Adder-eyed Dusketha, speak,
Shall we leave these, and go seek
In the earth's wide entrails old   70
Couches warm as their's are cold?
O for a fiery gloom and thee,
Dusketha, so enchantingly
Freckle-wing'd and lizard-sided!

DUSKETHA

By thee, Sprite, will I be guided!
I care not for cold or heat;
Frost and flame, or sparks, or sleet,
To my essence are the same;—
But I honour more the flame.
Sprite of Fire, I follow thee   80
Wheresoever it may be,
To the torrid spouts and fountains,
Underneath earth-quaked mountains;
Or, at thy supreme desire,
Touch the very pulse of fire
With my bare unlidded eyes.

SALAMANDER

Sweet Dusketha! paradise!
Off, ye icy Spirits, fly!
Frosty creatures of the sky!

DUSKETHA

Breathe upon them, fiery sprite!   90

ZEPHYR AND BREAMA

Away! away to our delight!

SALAMANDER

Go, feed on icicles, while we
Bedded in tongue-flames will be.

DUSKETHA

Lead me to those feverous glooms,
Sprite of Fire!

BREAMA

　　　　Me to the blooms,
Blue-eyed Zephyr, of those flowers
Far in the west where the May-cloud lowers;
And the beams of still Vesper, when winds are all wist,
Are shed thro' the rain and the milder mist,
And twilight your floating bowers.　　　　　　　　100

TWO SONNETS ON FAME

I

FAME, like a wayward Girl, will still be coy
　　To those who woo her with too slavish knees,
But makes surrender to some thoughtless Boy,
　　And dotes the more upon a heart at ease;
She is a Gipsey, will not speak to those
　　Who have not learnt to be content without her;
A Jilt, whose ear was never whisper'd close,
　　Who thinks they scandal her who talk about her;
A very Gipsey is she, Nilus-born,
　　Sister-in-law to jealous Potiphar;　　　　　　　10
Ye love-sick Bards, repay her scorn for scorn,
　　Ye Artists lovelorn, madmen that ye are!
Make your best bow to her and bid adieu,
Then, if she likes it, she will follow you.

II

"You cannot eat your cake and have it too."—*Proverb*.

How fever'd is the man, who cannot look
　　Upon his mortal days with temperate blood,
Who vexes all the leaves of his life's book,
　　And robs his fair name of its maidenhood;
It is as if the rose should pluck herself,
　　Or the ripe plum finger its misty bloom,
As if a Naiad, like a meddling elf,
　　Should darken her pure grot with muddy gloom,

But the rose leaves herself upon the briar,
   For winds to kiss and grateful bees to feed,   **10**
And the ripe plum still wears its dim attire,
     The undisturbed lake has crystal space,
     Why then should man, teasing the world for grace,
   Spoil his salvation for a fierce miscreed?

SONNET

ON THE SONNET

IF by dull rhymes our English must be chain'd,
And, like Andromeda, the Sonnet sweet
Fetter'd, in spite of pained loveliness,
Let us find, if we must be constrain'd,
Sandals more interwoven and complete
To fit the naked foot of Poesy:
Let us inspect the Lyre, and weigh the stress
Of every chord, and see what may be gain'd
By ear industrious, and attention meet;
Misers of sound and syllable, no less   **10**
Than Midas of his coinage, let us be
Jealous of dead leaves in the bay wreath crown;
So, if we may not let the Muse be free,
She will be bound with garlands of her own.

APOLLO AND THE GRACES

WRITTEN TO THE TUNE OF THE AIR IN "DON GIOVANNI"

APOLLO

   WHICH of the fairest three
   To-day will ride with me?
My steeds are all pawing at the threshold of the morn:
   Which of the fairest three
   To-day will ride with me
Across the gold Autumn's whole Kingdom of corn?

THE GRACES *all answer*

   I will, I— I— I—
   O young Apollo let me fly
     Along with thee,
   I will—I, I, I,
     The many wonders see   **10**
   I— I— I— I—
And thy lyre shall never have a slackened string:
     I, I, I, I,
Thro' the golden day will sing.

YOU SAY YOU LOVE

I

You say you love; but with a voice
    Chaster than a nun's, who singeth
The soft Vespers to herself
    While the chime-bell ringeth—
        O love me truly!

II

You say you love; but with a smile
    Cold as sunrise in September,
As you were Saint Cupid's nun,
    And kept his weeks of Ember.
        O love me truly!

III

You say you love—but then your lips
    Coral tinted teach no blisses,
More than coral in the sea—
    They never pout for kisses—
        O love me truly!

IV

You say you love; but then your hand
    No soft squeeze for squeeze returneth,
It is like a statue's dead—
    While mine to passion burneth—
        O love me truly!

V

O breathe a word or two of fire!
    Smile, as if those words should burn me,
Squeeze as lovers should—O kiss
    And in thy heart inurn me!
        O love me truly!

OTHO THE GREAT

A TRAGEDY

IN FIVE ACTS

DRAMATIS PERSONÆ

OTHO THE GREAT, *Emperor of Germany.*
LUDOLPH, *his Son.*
CONRAD, *Duke of Franconia.*
ALBERT, *a Knight, favoured by Otho.*
SIGIFRED, *an Officer, friend of Ludolph.*
THEODORE, ⎱ *Officers.*
GONFRED, ⎰
ETHELBERT, *an Abbot.*
GERSA, *Prince of Hungary.*
An Hungarian Captain.
Physician.
Page.
Nobles, Knights, Attendants, and Soldiers.
ERMINIA, *Niece of Otho.*
AURANTHE, *Conrad's Sister.*
Ladies and Attendants.

SCENE.   *The Castle of Friedburg, its vicinity, and the Hungarian Camp.*

TIME.   *One Day.*

OTHO THE GREAT

ACT I

Scene I.—*An Apartment in the Castle. Enter* Conrad.

Conrad. So, I am safe emerged from these broils!
Amid the wreck of thousands I am whole;
For every crime I have a laurel-wreath,
For every lie a lordship. Nor yet has
My ship of fortune furl'd her silken sails,—
Let her glide on! This danger'd neck is saved,
By dexterous policy, from the rebel's axe;
And of my ducal palace not one stone
Is bruised by the Hungarian petards.
Toil hard, ye slaves, and from the miser-earth   10
Bring forth once more my bullion, treasured deep,
With all my jewell'd salvers, silver and gold,
And precious goblets that make rich the wine.
But why do I stand babbling to myself?
Where is Auranthe? I have news for her
Shall—

Enter Auranthe.

Auranthe. Conrad! what tidings? Good, if I may guess
From your alert eyes and high-lifted brows.
What tidings of the battle? Albert? Ludolph? Otho?
Conrad. You guess aright. And, sister, slurring o'er   20
Our by-gone quarrels, I confess my heart
Is beating with a child's anxiety,
To make our golden fortune known to you.
Auranthe. So serious?
Conrad.   Yes, so serious, that before
I utter even the shadow of a hint
Concerning what will make that sin-worn cheek
Blush joyous blood through every lineament,
You must make here a solemn vow to me.
Auranthe. I prythee, Conrad, do not overact
The hypocrite—what vow would you impose?
Conrad. Trust me for once,—that you may be assur'd   31
'Tis not confiding to a broken reed,
A poor Court-bankrupt, outwitted and lost,
Revolve these facts in your acutest mood,

287

In such a mood as now you listen to me:—
A few days since, I was an open rebel
Against the Emperor, had suborn'd his son,
Drawn off his nobles to revolt, and shown
Contented fools causes for discontent
Fresh hatch'd in my ambition's eagle nest—
So thriv'd I as a rebel, and behold   40
Now I am Otho's favourite, his dear friend,
His right hand, his brave Conrad.

    Auranthe.   I confess
You have intrigued with these unsteady times
To admiration; but to be a favourite—

    Conrad. I saw my moment. The Hungarians,
Collected silently in holes and corners,
Appear'd, a sudden host, in the open day.
I should have perish'd in our empire's wreck,
But, calling interest loyalty, swore faith
To most believing Otho; and so help'd   50
His blood-stain'd ensigns to the victory
In yesterday's hard fight, that it has turn'd
The edge of his sharp wrath to eager kindness.

    Auranthe. So far yourself. But what is this to me
More than that I am glad? I gratulate you.

    Conrad. Yes, sister, but it does regard you greatly,
Nearly, momentously,—aye, painfully!
Make me this vow—

    Auranthe.   Concerning whom or what?

    Conrad. Albert!

    Auranthe.   I would inquire somewhat of him:
You had a letter from me touching him?   60
No treason 'gainst his head in deed or word!
Surely you spar'd him at my earnest prayer?
Give me the letter—it should not exist!

    Conrad. At one pernicious charge of the enemy,
I, for a moment-whiles, was prisoner ta'en
And rifled,—stuff! the horses' hoofs have minc'd it!

    Auranthe. He is alive?

    Conrad.   He is! but here make oath
To alienate him from your scheming brain,
Divorce him from your solitary thoughts,
And cloud him in such utter banishment,   70
That when his person meets again your eye,
Your vision shall quite lose its memory,
And wander past him as through vacancy.

    Auranthe. I'll not be perjured.

    Conrad.   No, nor great, nor mighty;
You would not wear a crown, or rule a kingdom.

To you it is indifferent.

    Auranthe.   What means this?

    Conrad. You'll not be perjured! Go to Albert then,
That camp-mushroom—dishonour of our house.
Go, page his dusty heels upon a march,
Furbish his jingling baldric while he sleeps,   80
And share his mouldy ration in a siege.
Yet stay,—perhaps a charm may call you back,
And make the widening circlets of your eyes
Sparkle with healthy fevers.—The Emperor
Hath given consent that you should marry Ludolph!

    Auranthe. Can it be, brother? For a golden crown
With a queen's awful lips I doubly thank you!
This is to wake in Paradise! Farewell
Thou clod of yesterday—'twas not myself!
Not till this moment did I ever feel   90
My spirit's faculties! I'll flatter you
For this, and be you ever proud of it;
Thou, Jove-like, struck'dst thy forehead,
And from the teeming marrow of thy brain
I spring complete Minerva! But the prince—
His highness Ludolph—where is he?

    Conrad.   I know not:
When, lackeying my counsel at a beck,
The rebel lords, on bended knees, received
The Emperor's pardon, Ludolph kept aloof,
Sole, in a stiff, fool-hardy, sulky pride;   100
Yet, for all this, I never saw a father
In such a sickly longing for his son.
We shall soon see him, for the Emperor
He will be here this morning.

    Auranthe.   That I heard
Among the midnight rumours from the camp.

    Conrad. You give up Albert to me?

    Auranthe.   Harm him not!
E'en for his highness Ludolph's sceptry hand,
I would not Albert suffer any wrong.

    Conrad. Have I not laboured, plotted—?

    Auranthe.   See you spare him: 110
Nor be pathetic, my kind benefactor,
On all the many bounties of your hand,—
'Twas for yourself you laboured—not for me!
Do you not count, when I am queen, to take
Advantage of your chance discoveries
Of my poor secrets, and so hold a rod
Over my life?

Conrad.   Let not this slave—this villain—
Be cause of feud between us. See! he comes!
Look, woman, look, your Albert is quite safe!
In haste it seems. Now shall I be in the way,
And wish'd with silent curses in my grave,   120
Or side by side with 'whelmed mariners.

Enter ALBERT.

Albert. Fair on your graces fall this early morrow!
So it is like to do, without my prayers,
For your right noble names, like favourite tunes,
Have fall'n full frequent from our Emperor's lips,
High commented with smiles.
     Auranthe.   Noble Albert!
     Conrad (aside).   Noble!
     Auranthe. Such salutation argues a glad heart
In our prosperity. We thank you, sir.
     Albert. Lady! O, would to Heaven your poor servant
Could do you better service than mere words!   130
But I have other greeting than mine own,
From no less man than Otho, who has sent
This ring as pledge of dearest amity;
'Tis chosen I hear from Hymen's jewel'ry,
And you will prize it, lady, I doubt not,
Beyond all pleasures past, and all to come.
To you great duke—
     Conrad.   To me! What of me, ha?
     Albert. What pleas'd your grace to say?
     Conrad.   Your message, sir!
     Albert. You mean not this to me?
     Conrad.   Sister, this way;
For there shall be no "gentle Alberts" now,   [*Aside.*
No "sweet Auranthes!"   141

[*Exeunt* CONRAD *and* AURANTHE.

Albert (solus). The duke is out of temper; if he knows
More than a brother of a sister ought,
I should not quarrel with his peevishness.
Auranthe—Heaven preserve her always fair!—
Is in the heady, proud, ambitious vein;
I bicker not with her,—bid her farewell!
She has taken flight from me, then let her soar, —
He is a fool who stands at pining gaze!
But for poor Ludolph, he is food for sorrow: 150
No levelling bluster of my licens'd thoughts,
No military swagger of my mind,
Can smother from myself the wrong I've done him,—

Without design, indeed,—yet it is so,—
And opiate for the conscience have I none!   [*Exit.*

SCENE II.—*The Court-yard of the Castle.*

Martial Music. Enter, from the outer gate, OTHO, *Nobles, Knights, and Attendants. The Soldiers halt at the gate, with Banners in sight.*

Otho. Where is my noble herald?

Enter CONRAD, *from the Castle, attended by two Knights and Servants.* ALBERT *following.*

Well, hast told
Auranthe our intent imperial?
Lest our rent banners, too o' the sudden shown,
Should fright her silken casements, and dismay
Her household to our lack of entertainment.
A victory!
   Conrad. God save illustrious Otho!
   Otho. Aye, Conrad, it will pluck out all grey hairs;
It is the best physician for the spleen;
The courtliest inviter to a feast;
The subtlest excuser of small faults;   10
And a nice judge in the age and smack of wine.

Enter, from the Castle, AURANTHE, *followed by Pages holding up her robes, and a train of Women. She kneels.*

Hail my sweet hostess! I do thank the stars,
Or my good soldiers, or their ladies' eyes,
That, after such a merry battle fought,
I can, all safe in body and in soul,
Kiss your fair hand and lady fortune's too.
My ring! now, on my life, it doth rejoice
These lips to feel 't on this soft ivory!
Keep it, my brightest daughter; it may prove
The little prologue to a line of kings.   20
I strove against thee and my hot-blood son,
Dull blockhead that I was to be so blind,
But now my sight is clear; forgive me, lady.
   Auranthe. My lord, I was a vassal to your frown,
And now your favour makes me but more humble;
In wintry winds the simple snow is safe,
But fadeth at the greeting of the sun:
Unto thine anger I might well have spoken,
Taking on me a woman's privilege,
But this so sudden kindness makes me dumb.   30
   Otho. What need of this? Enough, if you will be
A potent tutoress to my wayward boy,
And teach him, what it seems his nurse could not.

To say, for once, I thank you. Sigifred!
   Albert. He has not yet return'd, my gracious liege.
   Otho. What then! No tidings of my friendly Arab?
   Conrad. None, mighty Otho.

                 [*To one of his Knights, who goes out.*

                     Send forth instantly
An hundred horsemen from my honoured gates,
To scour the plains and search the cottages.
Cry a reward, to him who shall first bring   40
News of that vanished Arabian,
A full-heap'd helmet of the purest gold.
   Otho. More thanks, good Conrad; for, except my son's,
There is no face I rather would behold
Than that same quick-eyed pagan's. By the saints,
This coming night of banquets must not light
Her dazzling torches; nor the music breathe
Smooth, without clashing cymbal, tones of peace
And in-door melodies; nor the ruddy wine
Ebb spouting to the lees; if I pledge not,   50
In my first cup, that Arab!
   Albert.   Mighty Monarch,
I wonder not this stranger's victor-deeds
So hang upon your spirit. Twice in the fight
It was my chance to meet his olive brow,
Triumphant in the enemy's shatter'd rhomb;
And, to say truth, in any Christian arm
I never saw such prowess.
   Otho.   Did you ever?
O, 'tis a noble boy!—tut!—what do I say?
I mean a triple Saladin, whose eyes,
When in the glorious scuffle they met mine,   60
Seem'd to say—"Sleep, old man, in safety sleep;
I am the victory!"
   Conrad.   Pity he's not here.
   Otho. And my son too, pity he is not here.
Lady Auranthe, I would not make you blush,
But can you give a guess where Ludolph is?
Know you not of him?
   Auranthe.   Indeed, my liege, no secret—
   Otho. Nay, nay, without more words, dost know of him?
   Auranthe. I would I were so over-fortunate,
Both for his sake and mine, and to make glad
A father's ears with tidings of his son.   70
   Otho. I see 'tis like to be a tedious day.
Were Theodore and Gonfred and the rest
Sent forth with my commands?

Albert.   Aye, my lord.

Otho. And no news! No news! 'Faith! 'tis very strange
He thus avoids us. Lady, is't not strange?
Will he be truant to you too? It is a shame.

Conrad. Will 't please your highness enter, and accept
The unworthy welcome of your servant's house?
Leaving your cares to one whose diligence
May in few hours make pleasures of them all.   80

Otho. Not so tedious, Conrad. No, no, no,—
I must see Ludolph or the— What's that shout!

Voices without. Huzza! huzza! Long live the Emperor!

Other Voices. Fall back! Away there!

Otho.   Say, what noise is that?

[ALBERT *advancing from the back of the Stage, whither he had
    hastened on hearing the cheers of the soldiery.*

Albert. It is young Gersa, the Hungarian prince,
Pick'd like a red stag from the fallow herd
Of prisoners. Poor prince, forlorn he steps,
Slow, and demure, and proud in his despair.
If I may judge by his so tragic bearing,
His eye not downcast, and his folded arm,   90
He doth this moment wish himself asleep
Among his fallen captains on yon plains.

Enter GERSA, *in chains, and guarded.*

Otho. Well said, Sir Albert.

Gersa.   Not a word of greeting,
No welcome to a princely visitor,
Most mighty Otho? Will not my great host
Vouchsafe a syllable, before he bids
His gentlemen conduct me with all care
To some securest lodgings?—cold perhaps!

Otho. What mood is this? Hath fortune touch'd thy brain?

Gersa. O kings and princes of this fev'rous world,
What abject things, what mockeries must ye be,   101
What nerveless minions of safe palaces!
When here, a monarch, whose proud foot is used
To fallen princes' necks, as to his stirrup,
Must needs exclaim that I am mad forsooth,
Because I cannot flatter with bent knees
My conqueror!

Otho.   Gersa, I think you wrong me:
I think I have a better fame abroad.

Gersa. I prythee mock me not with gentle speech,
But, as a favour, bid me from thy presence;   110
Let me no longer be the wondering food

Of all these eyes; prythee command me hence!
   Otho. Do not mistake me, Gersa. That you may not,
Come, fair Auranthe, try if your soft hands
Can manage those hard rivets to set free
So brave a prince and soldier.
   Auranthe (*sets him free*).   Welcome task!
   Gersa. I am wound up in deep astonishment!
Thank you, fair lady. Otho! emperor!
You rob me of myself; my dignity
Is now your infant; I am a weak child.   120
   Otho. Give me your hand, and let this kindly grasp
Live in our memories.
   Gersa.   In mine it will.
I blush to think of my unchasten'd tongue;
But I was haunted by the monstrous ghost
Of all our slain battalions. Sire, reflect,
And pardon you will grant, that, at this hour,
The bruised remnants of our stricken camp
Are huddling undistinguish'd my dear friends,
With common thousands, into shallow graves.
   Otho. Enough, most noble Gersa. You are free
To cheer the brave remainder of your host   131
By your own healing presence, and that too,
Not as their leader merely, but their king;
For, as I hear, the wily enemy,
Who eas'd the crownet from your infant brows,
Bloody Taraxa, is among the dead.
   Gersa. Then I retire, so generous Otho please,
Bearing with me a weight of benefits
Too heavy to be borne.
   Otho.   It is not so;
Still understand me, King of Hungary,   140
Nor judge my open purposes awry.
Though I did hold you high in my esteem
For your self's sake, I do not personate
The stage-play emperor to entrap applause,
To set the silly sort o' the world agape,
And make the politic smile; no, I have heard
How in the Council you condemn'd this war,
Urging the perfidy of broken faith,—
For that I am your friend.
   Gersa.   If ever, sire,
You are mine enemy, I dare here swear   150
'Twill not be Gersa's fault. Otho, farewell!
   Otho. Will you return, Prince, to our banqueting?
   Gersa. As to my father's board I will return.
   Otho. Conrad, with all due ceremony, give

The prince a regal escort to his camp;
Albert, go thou and bear him company.
Gersa, farewell!
    Gersa.   All happiness attend you!
    Otho. Return with what good speed you may; for soon
We must consult upon our terms of peace.

           [*Exeunt* GERSA *and* ALBERT *with others.*

And thus a marble column do I build   160
To prop my empire's dome. Conrad, in thee
I have another stedfast one, to uphold
The portals of my state; and, for my own
Pre-eminence and safety, I will strive
To keep thy strength upon its pedestal.
For, without thee, this day I might have been
A show-monster about the streets of Prague,
In chains, as just now stood that noble prince:
And then to me no mercy had been shown,
For when the conquer'd lion is once dungeon'd, 170
Who lets him forth again? or dares to give
An old lion sugar-cates of mild reprieve?
Not to thine ear alone I make confession,
But to all here, as, by experience,
I know how the great basement of all power
Is frankness, and a true tongue to the world;
And how intriguing secrecy is proof
Of fear and weakness, and a hollow state.
Conrad, I owe thee much.
    Conrad.   To kiss that hand,
My emperor, is ample recompense,   180
For a mere act of duty.
    Otho.   Thou art wrong;
For what can any man on earth do more?
We will make trial of your house's welcome,
My bright Auranthe!
    Conrad.   How is Friedburg honoured!

Enter ETHELBERT *and six Monks.*

    Ethelbert. The benison of heaven on your head,
Imperial Otho!
    Otho.   Who stays me? Speak! Quick!
    Ethelbert. Pause but one moment, mighty conqueror
Upon the threshold of this house of joy.
    Otho. Pray, do not prose, good Ethelbert, but speak
What is your purpose.   190
    Ethelbert. The restoration of some captive maids,
Devoted to Heaven's pious ministries,

Who, being driven from their religious cells,
And kept in thraldom by our enemy,
When late this province was a lawless spoil,
Still weep amid the wild Hungarian camp,
Though hemm'd around by thy victorious arms.
   Otho. Demand the holy sisterhood in our name
From Gersa's tents. Farewell, old Ethelbert.   199
   Ethelbert. The saints will bless you for this pious care.
   Otho. Daughter, your hand; Ludolph's would fit it best.
   Conrad. Ho! let the music sound!

[*Music.* ETHELBERT *raises his hands, as in benediction of* OTHO.
Exeunt severally. The scene closes on them.

SCENE III.—*The Country, with the Castle in the distance.*

Enter LUDOLPH *and* SIGIFRED.

   Ludolph. You have my secret; let it not be breath'd.
   Sigifred. Still give me leave to wonder that the Prince
Ludolph and the swift Arab are the same;
Still to rejoice that 'twas a German arm
Death doing in a turban'd masquerade.
   Ludolph. The Emperor must not know it, Sigifred.
   Sigifred. I prythee, why? What happier hour of time
Could thy pleas'd star point down upon from heaven
With silver index, bidding thee make peace?
   Ludolph. Still it must not be known, good Sigifred;
The star may point oblique.   11
   Sigifred.   If Otho knew
His son to be that unknown Mussulman
After whose spurring heels he sent me forth,
With one of his well-pleas'd Olympian oaths,
The charters of man's greatness, at this hour
He would be watching round the castle walls,
And, like an anxious warder, strain his sight
For the first glimpse of such a son return'd—
Ludolph, that blast of the Hungarians,
That Saracenic meteor of the fight,   20
That silent fury, whose fell Scymitar
Kept danger all aloof from Otho's head,
And left him space for wonder.
   Ludolph.   Say no more.
Not as a swordsman would I pardon claim,
But as a son. The bronz'd centurion,
Long toil'd in foreign wars, and whose high deeds
Are shaded in a forest of tall spears,
Known only to his troop, hath greater plea

Of favour with my sire than I can have.   29
   Sigifred. My lord, forgive me that I cannot see
How this proud temper with clear reason squares.
What made you then, with such an anxious love,
Hover around that life, whose bitter days
You vext with bad revolt? Was 't opium,
Or the mad-fumed wine? Nay, do not frown,
I rather would grieve with you than upbraid.
   Ludolph. I do believe you. No, 'twas not to make
A father his son's debtor, or to heal
His deep heart-sickness for a rebel child.
'Twas done in memory of my boyish days,   40
Poor cancel for his kindness to my youth,
For all his calming of my childish griefs,
And all his smiles upon my merriment.
No, not a thousand foughten fields could sponge
Those days paternal from my memory,
Though now upon my head he heaps disgrace.
   Sigifred. My Prince, you think too harshly—
   Ludolph.   Can I so?
Hath he not gall'd my spirit to the quick?
And with a sullen rigour obstinate
Pour'd out a phial of wrath upon my faults?   50
Hunted me as the Tartar does the boar,
Driven me to the very edge o' the world,
And almost put a price upon my head?
   Sigifred. Remember how he spar'd the rebel lords.
   Ludolph. Yes, yes, I know he hath a noble nature
That cannot trample on the fallen. But his
Is not the only proud heart in his realm.
He hath wrong'd me, and I have done him wrong;
He hath lov'd me, and I have shown him kindness;
We should be almost equal.
   Sigifred.   Yet, for all this,   60
I would you had appear'd among those lords,
And ta'en his favour.
   Ludolph.   Ha! till now I thought
My friend had held poor Ludolph's honour dear.
What! would you have me sue before his throne
And kiss the courtier's missal, its silk steps?
Or hug the golden housings of his steed,
Amid a camp, whose steeled swarms I dar'd
But yesterday? And, at the trumpet sound,
Bow like some unknown mercenary's flag,
And lick the soiled grass? No, no, my friend,   70
I would not, I, be pardon'd in the heap,
And bless indemnity with all that scum,—

Those men I mean, who on my shoulders propp'd
Their weak rebellion, winning me with lies,
And pitying forsooth my many wrongs;
Poor self-deceived wretches, who must think
Each one himself a king in embryo,
Because some dozen vassals cry'd—my lord!
Cowards, who never knew their little hearts,
Till flurried danger held the mirror up,   80
And then they own'd themselves without a blush,
Curling, like spaniels, round my father's feet.
Such things deserted me and are forgiven,
While I, least guilty, am an outcast still,
And will be, for I love such fair disgrace.
   Sigifred. I know the clear truth; so would Otho see,
For he is just and noble. Fain would I
Be pleader for you—
   Ludolph.   He'll hear none of it;
You know his temper, hot, proud, obstinate;
Endanger not yourself so uselessly.   90
I will encounter his thwart spleen myself,
To-day, at the Duke Conrad's, where he keeps
His crowded state after the victory.
There will I be, a most unwelcome guest,
And parley with him, as a son should do,
Who doubly loathes a father's tyranny;
Tell him how feeble is that tyranny;
How the relationship of father and son
Is no more valid than a silken leash
Where lions tug adverse, if love grow not   100
From interchanged love through many years.
Aye, and those turreted Franconian walls,
Like to a jealous casket, hold my pearl—
My fair Auranthe! Yes, I will be there.
   Sigifred. Be not so rash; wait till his wrath shall pass,
Until his royal spirit softly ebbs
Self-influenced; then, in his morning dreams
He will forgive thee, and awake in grief
To have not thy good morrow.
   Ludolph.   Yes, to-day
I must be there, while her young pulses beat   110
Among the new-plum'd minions of the war.
Have you seen her of late? No? Auranthe,
Franconia's fair sister, 'tis I mean.
She should be paler for my troublous days—
And there it is—my father's iron lips
Have sworn divorcement 'twixt me and my right.
   Sigifred (aside). Auranthe! I had hop'd this whim had pass'd.

Ludolph. And, Sigifred, with all his love of justice,
When will he take that grandchild in his arms,
That, by my love I swear, shall soon be his?   120
This reconcilement is impossible,
For see—but who are these?
  Sigifred.   They are messengers
From our great emperor; to you, I doubt not,
For couriers are abroad to seek you out.

    Enter THEODORE *and* GONFRED.

 Theodore. Seeing so many vigilant eyes explore
The province to invite your highness back
To your high dignities, we are too happy.
  Gonfred. We have no eloquence to colour justly
The emperor's anxious wishes.
  Ludolph.   Go. I follow you.

     [*Exeunt* THEODORE *and* GONFRED.

I play the prude: it is but venturing—   130
Why should he be so earnest? Come, my friend,
Let us to Friedburg castle.

ACT II

SCENE I.—*An Ante-chamber in the Castle.*

Enter LUDOLPH *and* SIGIFRED.

 Ludolph. No more advices, no more cautioning:
I leave it all to fate—to any thing!
I cannot square my conduct to time, place,
Or circumstances; to me 'tis all a mist!
  Sigifred. I say no more.
  Ludolph.   It seems I am to wait
Here in the ante-room;—that may be a trifle.
You see now how I dance attendance here,
Without that tyrant temper, you so blame,
Snapping the rein. You have medicin'd me
With good advices; and I here remain,   10
In this most honourable ante-room,
Your patient scholar.
  Sigifred.   Do not wrong me, Prince.
By Heavens, I'd rather kiss Duke Conrad's slipper,
When in the morning he doth yawn with pride,
Than see you humbled but a half-degree!
Truth is, the Emperor would fain dismiss
The nobles ere he sees you.

Enter GONFRED *from the Council-room.*

Ludolph.   Well, sir! What?
Gonfred. Great honour to the Prince! The Emperor,
Hearing that his brave son had re-appeared,
Instant dismiss'd the Council from his sight,   20
As Jove fans off the clouds. Even now they pass.

                                          [*Exit.*

Enter the Nobles from the Council-room. They cross the stage,
   bowing with respect to LUDOLPH, *he frowning on them.*
   CONRAD *follows. Exeunt Nobles.*

Ludolph. Not the discoloured poisons of a fen,
Which he who breathes feels warning of his death,
Could taste so nauseous to the bodily sense,
As these prodigious sycophants disgust
The soul's fine palate.
Conrad.   Princely Ludolph, hail!
Welcome, thou younger sceptre to the realm!
Strength to thy virgin crownet's golden buds,
That they, against the winter of thy sire,
May burst, and swell, and flourish round thy brows,   30
Maturing to a weighty diadem!
Yet be that hour far off; and may he live,
Who waits for thee, as the chapp'd earth for rain.
Set my life's star! I have lived long enough,
Since under my glad roof, propitiously,
Father and son each other re-possess.
Ludolph. Fine wording, Duke! but words could never yet
Forestall the fates; have you not learnt that yet?
Let me look well: your features are the same;
Your gait the same; your hair of the same shade;   40
As one I knew some passed weeks ago,
Who sung far different notes into mine ears.
I have mine own particular comments on 't;
You have your own, perhaps.
Conrad.   My gracious Prince,
All men may err. In truth I was deceived
In your great father's nature, as you were.
Had I known that of him I have since known,
And what you soon will learn, I would have turn'd
My sword to my own throat, rather than held
Its threatening edge against a good King's quiet: 50
Or with one word fever'd you, gentle Prince,
Who seem'd to me, as rugged times then went,
Indeed too much oppress'd. May I be bold

To tell the Emperor you will haste to him?
Ludolph. Your Dukedom's privilege will grant so much.

[*Exit* CONRAD

He's very close to Otho, a tight leech!
Your hand—I go. Ha! here the thunder comes
Sullen against the wind! If in two angry brows
My safety lies, then Sigifred, I'm safe.

Enter OTHO *and* CONRAD.

Otho. Will you make Titan play the lackey-page   60
To chattering pigmies? I would have you know
That such neglect of our high Majesty
Annuls all feel of kindred. What is son,—
Or friend,—or brother,—or all ties of blood,—
When the whole kingdom, centred in ourself,
Is rudely slighted? Who am I to wait?
By Peter's chair! I have upon my tongue
A word to fright the proudest spirit here!—
Death!—and slow tortures to the hardy fool,
Who dares take such large charter from our smiles!   70
Conrad, we would be private. Sigifred!
Off! And none pass this way on pain of death!

[*Exeunt* CONRAD *and* SIGIFRED.

Ludolph. This was but half expected, my good sire,
Yet I am griev'd at it, to the full height,
As though my hopes of favour had been whole.
Otho. How you indulge yourself! What can you hope for?
Ludolph. Nothing, my liege; I have to hope for nothing.
I come to greet you as a loving son,
And then depart, if I may be so free,
Seeing that blood of yours in my warm veins   80
Has not yet mitigated into milk.
Otho. What would you, sir?
Ludolph.   A lenient banishment;
So please you let me unmolested pass
This Conrad's gates, to the wide air again.
I want no more. A rebel wants no more.
Otho. And shall I let a rebel loose again
To muster kites and eagles 'gainst my head?
No, obstinate boy, you shall be kept cag'd up,
Serv'd with harsh food, with scum for Sunday-drink.
Ludolph. Indeed!
Otho.   And chains too heavy for your life:
I'll choose a gaoler, whose swart monstrous face   91
Shall be a hell to look upon, and she—

Ludolph.   Ha!
Otho. Shall be your fair Auranthe.
Ludolph.   Amaze! Amaze!
Otho. To-day you marry her.
Ludolph.   This is a sharp jest!
Otho. No. None at all. When have I said a lie?
Ludolph. If I sleep not, I am a waking wretch.
Otho. Not a word more. Let me embrace my child.
Ludolph. I dare not. 'Twould pollute so good a father!
O heavy crime! that your son's blinded eyes
Could not see all his parent's love aright,   100
As now I see it. Be not kind to me—
Punish me not with favour.
          Otho.   Are you sure,
Ludolph, you have no saving plea in store?
     Ludolph. My father, none!
     Otho.   Then you astonish me.
     Ludolph. No, I have no plea. Disobedience,
Rebellion, obstinacy, blasphemy,
Are all my counsellors. If they can make
My crooked deeds show good and plausible,
Then grant me loving pardon, but not else,
Good Gods! not else, in any way, my liege!   110
     Otho. You are a most perplexing, noble boy.
     Ludolph. You not less a perplexing noble father.
     Otho. Well, you shall have free passport through the gates.
Farewell!
     Ludolph. Farewell! and by these tears believe,
And still remember, I repent in pain
All my misdeeds!
     Otho.   Ludolph, I will! I will!
But, Ludolph, ere you go, I would enquire
If you, in all your wandering, ever met
A certain Arab haunting in these parts.
     Ludolph. No, my good lord, I cannot say I did.   120
     Otho. Make not your father blind before his time;
Nor let these arms paternal hunger more
For an embrace, to dull the appetite
Of my great love for thee, my supreme child!
Come close, and let me breathe into thine ear.
I knew you through disguise. You are the Arab!
You can't deny it.   [*Embracing him*.
     Ludolph.   Happiest of days!
     Otho. We'll make it so.
     Ludolph.   'Stead of one fatted calf
Ten hecatombs shall bellow out their last,
Smote 'twixt the horns by the death-stunning mace   13

Of Mars, and all the soldiery shall feast
Nobly as Nimrod's masons, when the towers
Of Nineveh new kiss'd the parted clouds!
  Otho. Large as a God speak out, where all is thine.
  Ludolph. Aye, father, but the fire in my sad breast
Is quench'd with inward tears! I must rejoice
For you, whose wings so shadow over me
In tender victory, but for myself
I still must mourn. The fair Auranthe mine!
Too great a boon! I prythee let me ask   140
What more than I know of could so have changed
Your purpose touching her?
  Otho.   At a word, this:
In no deed did you give me more offense
Than your rejection of Erminia.
To my appalling, I saw too good proof
Of your keen-eyed suspicion,—she is naught!
  Ludolph. You are convinc'd?
  Otho.   Aye, spite of her sweet looks.
O, that my brother's daughter should so fall!
Her fame has pass'd into the grosser lips
Of soldiers in their cups.
  Ludolph.   'Tis very sad.   150
  Otho. No more of her. Auranthe—Ludolph, come!
This marriage be the bond of endless peace!   [*Exeunt.*

SCENE II.—*The Entrance of* GERSA'S *Tent in the Hungarian Camp.*

Enter ERMINIA.

  Erminia. Where! where! where shall I find a messenger?
A trusty soul? A good man in the camp?
Shall I go myself? Monstrous wickedness!
O cursed Conrad! devilish Auranthe!
Here is proof palpable as the bright sun!
O for a voice to reach the Emperor's ears!

[*Shouts in the Camp.*

Enter an HUNGARIAN CAPTAIN.

  Captain. Fair prisoner, hear you those joyous shouts?
The king—aye, now our king,—but still your slave,
Young Gersa, from a short captivity
Has just return'd. He bids me say, bright Dame,   10
That even the homage of his ranged chiefs
Cures not his keen impatience to behold
Such beauty once again. What ails you, lady?
  Erminia. Say, is not that a German, yonder? There!
  Captain. Methinks by his stout bearing he should be—

Yes—'tis one Albert; a brave German knight,
And much in the emperor's favour.
    Erminia.   I would fain
Enquire of friends and kinsfolk; how they fared
In these rough times. Brave soldier, as you pass
To royal Gersa with my humble thanks,   20
Will you send yonder knight to me?
      Captain.   I will.   [*Exit*.
    Ermina. Yes, he was ever known to be a man
Frank, open, generous; Albert I may trust.
O proof! proof! proof! Albert's an honest man;
Not Ethelbert the monk, if he were here,
Would I hold more trustworthy. Now!

                Enter ALBERT.
    Albert.   Good Gods!
Lady Erminia! are you prisoner
In this beleaguer'd camp? Or are you here
Of your own will? You pleas'd to send for me.
By Venus, 'tis a pity I knew not   30
Your plight before, and, by her Son, I swear
To do you every service you can ask.
What would the fairest—?
    Erminia.   Albert, will you swear?
    Albert. I have. Well?
    Erminia.   Albert, you have fame to lose.
If men, in court and camp, lie not outright,
You should be, from a thousand, chosen forth
To do an honest deed. Shall I confide—?
    Albert. Aye, anything to me, fair creature. Do;
Dictate my task. Sweet woman,—
    Erminia.   Truce with that.
You understand me not; and, in your speech,   40
I see how far the slander is abroad.
Without proof could you think me innocent?
    Albert. Lady, I should rejoice to know you so.
    Erminia. If you have any pity for a maid,
Suffering a daily death from evil tongues;
Any compassion for that Emperor's niece,
Who, for your bright sword and clear honesty,
Lifted you from the crowd of common men
Into the lap of honour;—save me, knight!
    Albert. How? Make it clear; if it be possible,   50
I, by the banner of Saint Maurice, swear
To right you.
    Erminia. Possible!—Easy. O my heart!
This letter's not so soil'd but you may read it;—

Possible! There—that letter! Read—read it.

[Gives him a letter.

Albert (*reading*). "To the Duke Conrad.—Forget the threat you
made at parting, and I will forget to send the Emperor letters and
papers of your's I have become possessed of. His life is no trifle to
me; his death you shall find none to yourself." (*Speaks to himself:*) 'Tis me—my life that's pleaded for! (*Reads.*) "He, for his
own sake, will be dumb as the grave. Erminia has my shame fix'd
upon her, sure as a wen. We are safe.

AURANTHE."

A she-devil! A dragon! I her imp!
Fire of Hell! Auranthe—lewd demon!
Where got you this? Where? When?
    Erminia. I found it in the tent, among some spoils
Which, being noble, fell to Gersa's lot.
Come in, and see.   *[They go in and return.*
    Albert.   Villainy! Villainy!
Conrad's sword, his corslet, and his helm,   70
And his letter. Caitiff, he shall feel—
    Erminia. I see you are thunderstruck. Haste, haste away!
    Albert. O I am tortured by this villainy.
    Erminia. You needs must be. Carry it swift to Otho;
Tell him, moreover, I am prisoner
Here in this camp, where all the sisterhood,
Forc'd from their quiet cells, are parcell'd out
For slaves among these Huns. Away! Away!
    Albert. I am gone.
    Erminia.   Swift be your steed! Within this hour
The Emperor will see it.
    Albert.   Ere I sleep: 80
That I can swear.   *[Hurries out.*
    Gersa (*without*). Brave captains! thanks. Enough
Of loyal homage now!

Enter GERSA.

    Erminia.   Hail, royal Hun!
    Gersa. What means this, fair one? Why in such alarm?
Who was it hurried by me so distract?
It seem'd you were in deep discourse together;
Your doctrine has not been so harsh to him
As to my poor deserts. Come, come, be plain.
I am no jealous fool to kill you both,
Or, for such trifles, rob the adorned world
Of such a beauteous vestal.
    Erminia.   I grieve, my Lord,   90
To hear you condescend to ribald phrase.
    Gersa. This is too much! Hearken, my lady pure!

Erminia. Silence! and hear the magic of a name—
Erminia! I am she,—the Emperor's niece!
Prais'd be the Heavens, I now dare own myself!
   Gersa. Erminia! Indeed! I've heard of her.
Prythee, fair lady, what chance brought you here?
   Erminia. Ask your own soldiers.
   Gersa.   And you dare own your name.
For loveliness you may—and for the rest
My vein is not censorious.
   Erminia.   Alas! poor me!   100
'Tis false indeed.
   Gersa.   Indeed you are too fair:
The swan, soft leaning on her fledgy breast,
When to the stream she launches, looks not back
With such a tender grace; nor are her wings
So white as your soul is, if that but be
Twin-picture to your face. Erminia!
To-day, for the first day, I am a king,
Yet would I give my unworn crown away
To know you spotless.
   Erminia.   Trust me one day more,
Generously, without more certain guarantee,   110
Than this poor face you deign to praise so much;
After that, say and do whate'er you please.
If I have any knowledge of you, sir,
I think, nay I am sure, you will grieve much
To hear my story. O be gentle to me,
For I am sick and faint with many wrongs,
Tir'd out, and weary-worn with contumelies.
   Gersa. Poor lady!

Enter ETHELBERT.

   Erminia.   Gentle Prince, 'tis false indeed.
Good morrow, holy father! I have had
Your prayers, though I look'd for you in vain.   120
   Ethelbert. Blessings upon you, daughter! Sure you look
Too cheerful for these foul pernicious days.
Young man, you heard this virgin say 'twas false,
'Tis false, I say. What! can you not employ
Your temper elsewhere, 'mong these burly tents,
But you must taunt this dove, for she hath lost
The Eagle Otho to beat off assault?
Fie! fie! But I will be her guard myself;
In the Emperor's name. I here demand of you
Herself, and all her sisterhood. She false!   130
   Gersa. Peace! peace, old man! I cannot think she is.
   Ethelbert. Whom I have known from her first infancy,

Baptiz'd her in the bosom of the Church,
Watch'd her, as anxious husbandmen the grain,
From the first shoot till the unripe mid-May,
Then to the tender ear of her June days,
Which, lifting sweet abroad its timid green,
Is blighted by the touch of calumny;
You cannot credit such a monstrous tale.

   Gersa. I cannot. Take her. Fair Erminia,   140
I follow you to Friedburg,—is't not so?
   Erminia. Aye, so we purpose.
   Ethelbert.   Daughter, do you so?
How's this? I marvel! Yet you look not mad.
   Erminia. I have good news to tell you, Ethelbert.
   Gersa. Ho! ho, there! Guards!
Your blessing, father! Sweet Erminia,
Believe me, I am well nigh sure—
   Erminia.   Farewell!
Short time will show.   [*Enter Chiefs.*
               Yes, father Ethelbert,
I have news precious as we pass along.
   Ethelbert. Dear daughter, you shall guide me.   149
   Erminia.   To no ill.
   Gersa. Command an escort to the Friedburg lines.
                        [*Exeunt Chiefs.*
Pray let me lead. Fair lady, forget not
Gersa, how he believ'd you innocent.
I follow you to Friedburg with all speed.   [*Exeunt.*

ACT III.

SCENE I.—*The Country.*

Enter ALBERT.

   Albert. O that the earth were empty, as when Cain
Had no perplexity to hide his head!
Or that the sword of some brave enemy
Had put a sudden stop to my hot breath,
And hurl'd me down the illimitable gulph
Of times past, unremember'd! Better so
Than thus fast-limed in a cursed snare,
The white limbs of a wanton. This the end
Of an aspiring life! My boyhood past
In feud with wolves and bears, when no eye saw
The solitary warfare, fought for love   11
Of honour 'mid the growling wilderness.
My sturdier youth, maturing to the sword,
Won by the syren-trumpets, and the ring

Of shields upon the pavement, when bright-mail'd
Henry the Fowler pass'd the streets of Prague.
Was't to this end I louted and became
The menial of Mars, and held a spear
Sway'd by command, as corn is by the wind?
Is it for this, I now am lifted up   20
By Europe's throned Emperor, to see
My honour be my executioner,—
My love of fame, my prided honesty
Put to the torture for confessional?
Then the damn'd crime of blurting to the world
A woman's secret!—Though a fiend she be,
Too tender of my ignominious life;
But then to wrong the generous Emperor
In such a searching point, were to give up
My soul for foot-ball at Hell's holiday!   30
I must confess,—and cut my throat,—to-day?
To-morrow? Ho! some wine!

Enter SIGIFRED.

Sigifred.   A fine humour—
Albert. Who goes there? Count Sigifred? Ha! Ha!
Sigifred. What, man, do you mistake the hollow sky
For a throng'd tavern,—and these stubbed trees
For old serge hangings,—me, your humble friend,
For a poor waiter? Why, man, how you stare!
What gipsies have you been carousing with?
No, no more wine; methinks you've had enough.
Albert. You well may laugh and banter. What a fool
An injury may make of a staid man!   41
You shall know all anon.
Sigifred.   Some tavern brawl?
Albert. 'Twas with some people out of common reach;
Revenge is difficult.
Sigifred.   I am your friend;
We meet again to-day, and can confer
Upon it. For the present I'm in haste.
Albert. Whither?
Sigifred.   To fetch King Gersa to the feast.
The Emperor on this marriage is so hot,
Pray Heaven it end not in apoplexy!
The very porters, as I pass'd the doors,   50
Heard his loud laugh, and answer'd in full choir.
I marvel, Albert, you delay so long
From those bright revelries; go, show yourself,
You may be made a duke.
Albert.   Aye, very like:

Pray, what day has his Highness fix'd upon?

Sigifred. For what?

Albert.   The marriage. What else can I mean?

Sigifred. To-day! O, I forgot, you could not know;
The news is scarce a minute old with me.

Albert. Married to-day! To-day! You did not say so?

Sigifred. Now, while I speak to you, their comely heads   60
Are bow'd before the mitre.

Albert.   O! Monstrous!

Sigifred. What is this?

Albert.   Nothing, Sigifred. Farewell!
We'll meet upon our subject. Farewell, count!

                                                     [*Exit.*

Sigifred. Is this clear-headed Albert? He brain-turn'd!
'Tis as portentous as a meteor.   [*Exit.*

SCENE II.—*An Apartment in the Castle.*

Enter, as from the Marriage, OTHO, LUDOLPH, AURANTHE, CONRAD.
        Nobles, Knights, Ladies, &c. Music.

Otho. Now, Ludolph! Now, Auranthe! Daughter fair!
What can I find to grace your nuptial day
More than my love, and these wide realms in fee?

Ludolph. I have too much.

Auranthe.   And I, my liege, by far.

Ludolph. Auranthe! I have! O, my bride, my love!
Not all the gaze upon us can restrain
My eyes, too long poor exiles from thy face,
From adoration, and my foolish tongue
From uttering soft responses to the love
I see in thy mute beauty beaming forth!   10
Fair creature, bless me with a single word!
All mine!

Auranthe. Spare, spare me, my Lord! I swoon else.

Ludolph. Soft beauty! by to-morrow I should die,
Wert thou not mine.   [*They talk apart.*

First Lady.   How deep she has bewitch'd him!

First Knight. Ask you for her recipe for love philtres.

Second Lady. They hold the Emperor in admiration.

Otho. If ever king was happy, that am I!
What are the cities 'yond the Alps to me,
The provinces about the Danube's mouth,
The promise of fair soil beyond the Rhone;   20
Or routing out of Hyperborean hordes,
To those fair children, stars of a new age?
Unless perchance I might rejoice to win
This little ball of earth, and chuck it them

To play with!

Auranthe. Nay, my Lord, I do not know.

Ludolph. Let me not famish.

Otho (*to Conrad*).   Good Franconia,
You heard what oath I sware, as the sun rose,
That unless Heaven would send me back my son,
My Arab,—no soft music should enrich
The cool wine, kiss'd off with a soldier's smack;
Now all my empire, barter'd for one feast,
Seems poverty.

Conrad.   Upon the neighbour-plain
The heralds have prepar'd a royal lists;
Your knights, found war-proof in the bloody field,
Speed to the game.

Otho.   Well, Ludolph, what say you?

Ludolph. My lord!

Otho.   A tourney?

Conrad.   Or, if't please you best—

Ludolph. I want no more!

First Lady.   He soars!

Second Lady.   Past all reason.

Ludolph. Though heaven's choir
Should in a vast circumference descend
And sing for my delight, I'd stop my ears!
Though bright Apollo's car stood burning here,
And he put out an arm to bid me mount,
His touch an immortality, not I!
This earth, this palace, this room, Auranthe!

Otho. This is a little painful; just too much.
Conrad, if he flames longer in this wise,
I shall believe in wizard-woven loves
And old romances; but I'll break the spell.
Ludolph!

Conrad. He will be calm, anon.

Ludolph.   You call'd?
Yes, yes, yes, I offend. You must forgive me;
Not being quite recover'd from the stun
Of your large bounties. A tourney, is it not?

        [*A senet heard faintly.*

Conrad. The trumpets reach us.

Ethelbert (*without*).   On your peril, sirs,
Detain us!

First Voice (*without*). Let not the abbot pass.

Second Voice (*without*).   No,
On your lives!

First Voice (*without*). Holy Father, you must not.

Ethelbert (*without*). Otho!

30

40

50

Otho.   Who calls on Otho?
Ethelbert (without).   Ethelbert!
Otho. Let him come in.

Enter ETHELBERT *leading in* ERMINIA.

                      Thou cursed abbot, why
Hast brought pollution to our holy rites?
Hast thou no fear of hangman, or the faggot?   59
    Ludolph. What portent—what strange prodigy is this?
    Conrad. Away!
    Ethelbert.   You, Duke?
    Erminia.   Albert has surely fail'd me!
Look at the Emperor's brow upon me bent!
    Ethelbert. A sad delay!
    Conrad.   Away, thou guilty thing!
    Ethelbert. You again, Duke? Justice, most mighty Otho!
You—go to your sister there and plot again,
A quick plot, swift as thought to save your heads;
For lo! the toils are spread around your den,
The word is all agape to see dragg'd forth
Two ugly monsters.
    Ludolph.   What means he, my lord?
    Conrad. I cannot guess.
    Ethelbert.   Best ask your lady sister,   70
Whether the riddle puzzles her beyond
The power of utterance.
    Conrad.   Foul barbarian, cease;
The Princess faints!
    Ludolph.   Stab him! O, sweetest wife!
                      [*Attendants bear off* AURANTHE.
    Erminia. Alas!
    Ethelbert.   Your wife?
    Ludolph.   Aye, Satan! does that yerk ye?
    Ethelbert. Wife! so soon!
    Ludolph.   Aye, wife! Oh, impudence!
Thou bitter mischief! Venomous mad priest!
How dar'st thou lift those beetle brows at me?
Me—the prince Ludolph, in this presence here,
Upon my marriage-day, and scandalize
My joys with such opprobrious surprise?   80
Wife! Why dost linger on that syllable,
As if it were some demon's name pronounc'd
To summon harmful lightning, and make roar
The sleepy thunder? Hast no sense of fear?
No ounce of man in thy mortality?
Tremble! for, at my nod, the sharpen'd axe
Will make thy bold tongue quiver to the roots,

Those grey lids wink, and thou not know it more!

Ethelbert. O, poor deceived Prince! I pity thee!

Great Otho! I claim justice—

 Ludolph.   Thou shalt hav 't!   91

Thine arms from forth a pulpit of hot fire

Shall sprawl distracted! O that that dull cowl

Were some most sensitive portion of thy life,

That I might give it to my hounds to tear!

Thy girdle some fine zealous-pained nerve

To girth my saddle! And those devil's beads

Each one a life, that I might, every day,

Crush one with Vulcan's hammer!

 Otho.   Peace, my son;

You far outstrip my spleen in this affair.

Let us be calm, and hear the abbot's plea   100

For this intrusion.

 Ludolph.   I am silent, sire.

 Otho. Conrad, see all depart not wanted here.

         [*Exeunt Knights, Ladies, &c.*

Ludolph, be calm. Ethelbert, peace awhile.

This mystery demands an audience

Of a just judge, and that will Otho be.

 Ludolph. Why has he time to breathe another word?

 Otho. Ludolph, old Ethelbert, be sure, comes not

To beard us for no cause; he's not the man

To cry himself up an ambassador

Without credentials.

 Ludolph.   I'll chain up myself.   110

 Otho. Old Abbot, stand here forth. Lady Erminia,

Sit. And now, Abbot! what have you to say?

Our ear is open. First we here denounce

Hard penalties against thee, if't be found

The cause for which you have disturb'd us here,

Making our bright hours muddy, be a thing

Of little moment.

 Ethelbert.   See this innocent!

Otho! thou father of the people call'd,

Is her life nothing? Her fair honour nothing?

Her tears from matins until even-song   120

Nothing? Her burst heart nothing? Emperor!

Is this your gentle niece—the simplest flower

Of the world's herbal—this fair lily blanch'd

Still with the dews of piety, this meek lady

Here sitting like an angel newly-shent,

Who veils its snowy wings and grows all pale,—

Is she nothing?

 Otho.   What more to the purpose, abbot?

Ludolph. Whither is he winding?
Conrad.   No clue yet!
Ethelbert. You have heard, my Liege, and so, no
    doubt, all here,
Foul, poisonous, malignant whisperings;   130
Nay open speech, rude mockery grown common,
Against the spotless nature and clear fame
Of the princess Erminia, your niece.
I have intruded here thus suddenly,
Because I hold those base weeds, with tight hand,
Which now disfigure her fair growing stem,
Waiting but for your sign to pull them up
By the dark roots, and leave her palpable,
To all men's sight, a Lady, innocent.
The ignominy of that whisper'd tale   140
About a midnight gallant, seen to climb
A window to her chamber neighbour'd near,
I will from her turn off, and put the load
On the right shoulders; on that wretch's head,
Who, by close stratagems, did save herself,
Chiefly by shifting to this lady's room
A rope-ladder for false witness.
    Ludolph.   Most atrocious!
Otho. Ethelbert, proceed.
    Ethelbert.   With sad lips I shall:
For in the healing of one wound, I fear
To make a greater. His young highness here   150
To-day was married.
    Ludolph.   Good.
    Ethelbert.   Would it were good!
Yet why do I delay to spread abroad
The names of those two vipers, from whose jaws
A deadly breath went forth to taint and blast
This guileless lady?
    Otho.   Abbot, speak their names.
Ethelbert. A minute first. It cannot be—but may
I ask, great judge, if you to-day have put
A letter by unread?
    Otho.   Does 't end in this?
Conrad. Out with their names!
    Ethelbert.   Bold sinner, say you so?
Ludolph. Out, tedious monk!
    Otho.   Confess, or by the wheel—
Ethelbert. My evidence cannot be far away;   161
And, though it never come, be on my head
The crime of passing an attaint upon
The slanderers of this virgin.

Ludolph.   Speak aloud!
Ethelbert. Auranthe, and her brother there.
Conrad.   Amaze!
Ludolph. Throw them from the windows!
Otho. Do what you will!
Ludolph.   What shall I do with **them?**
Something of quick dispatch, for should she hear,
My soft Auranthe, her sweet mercy would
Prevail against my fury. Damned priest!   170
What swift death wilt thou die? As to the lady
I touch her not.
     Ethelbert.   Illustrious Otho, stay!
An ample store of misery thou hast,
Choak not the granary of thy noble mind
With more bad bitter grain, too difficult
A cud for the repentance of a man
Grey-growing. To thee only I appeal,
Not to thy noble son, whose yeasting youth
Will clear itself, and crystal turn again.
A young man's heart, by Heaven's blessing, is   180
A wide world, where a thousand new-born hopes
Empurple fresh the melancholy blood:
But an old man's is narrow, tenantless
Of hopes, and stuff'd with many memories,
Which, being pleasant, ease the heavy pulse—
Painful, clog up and stagnate. Weigh this matter
Even as a miser balances his coin;
And, in the name of mercy, give command
That your knight Albert be brought here before you.
He will expound this riddle; he will show   190
A noon-day proof of bad Auranthe's guilt.
     Otho. Let Albert straight be summon'd.

                           [*Exit one of the Nobles.*

    Ludolph.   Impossible!
I cannot doubt—I will not—no—to doubt
Is to be ashes!—wither'd up to death!
     Otho. My gentle Ludolph, harbour not a fear;
You do yourself much wrong.
     Ludolph.   O, wretched dolt!
Now, when my foot is almost on thy neck,
Wilt thou infuriate me? Proof! thou fool!
Why wilt thou teaze impossibility
With such a thick-skull'd persevering suit?   200
Fanatic obstinacy! Prodigy!
Monster of folly! Ghost of a turn'd brain!
You puzzle me,—you haunt me,—when I dream

Of you my brain will split! Bald sorcerer!
Juggler! May I come near you? On my soul
I know not whether to pity, curse, or laugh.

Enter ALBERT, *and the Nobleman.*

Here, Albert, this old phantom wants a proof!
Give him his proof! A camel's load of proofs!
  Otho. Albert, I speak to you as to a man
Whose words once utter'd pass like current gold;   210
And therefore fit to calmly put a close
To this brief tempest. Do you stand possess'd
Of any proof against the honourableness
Of Lady Auranthe, our new-spoused daughter?
  Albert. You chill me with astonishment. How's this?
My Liege, what proof should I have 'gainst a fame
Impossible of slur?   [OTHO *rises.*
  Erminia.   O wickedness!
  Ethelbert. Deluded monarch, 'tis a cruel lie.
  Otho. Peace, rebel-priest!
  Conrad.   Insult beyond credence!
  Erminia. Almost a dream!
  Ludolph.   We have awaken'd from   220
A foolish dream that from my brow hath wrung
A wrathful dew. O folly! why did I
So act the lion with this silly gnat?
Let them depart. Lady Erminia!
I ever griev'd for you, as who did not?
But now you have, with such a brazen front,
So most maliciously, so madly striven
To dazzle the soft moon, when tenderest clouds
Should be unloop'd around to curtain her;
I leave you to the desert of the world   230
Almost with pleasure. Let them be set free
For me! I take no personal revenge
More than against a nightmare, which a man
Forgets in the new dawn.

                           [*Exit* LUDOLPH.

  Otho. Still in extremes! No, they must not be loose.
  Ethelbert. Albert, I must suspect thee of a crime
So fiendish—
  Otho.   Fear'st thou not my fury, monk?
Conrad, be they in your sure custody
Till we determine some fit punishment.
It is so mad a deed, I must reflect   240
And question them in private; for perhaps,
By patient scrutiny, we may discover

Whether they merit death, or should be placed
In care of the physicians.

                 [Exeunt OTHO *and Nobles,* ALBERT *following.*

   Conrad. My guards, ho!

   Erminia.   Albert, wilt thou follow there?
Wilt thou creep dastardly behind his back,
And slink away from a weak woman's eye?
Turn, thou court-Janus! thou forget'st thyself;
Here is the Duke, waiting with open arms,

                            [Enter Guards.

To thank thee; here congratulate each other;   250
Wring hands; embrace; and swear how lucky 'twas
That I, by happy chance, hit the right man
Of all the world to trust in.

   Albert.   Trust! to me!

   Conrad (aside). He is the sole one in this mystery.

   Erminia. Well, I give up, and save my prayers for Heaven!
You, who could do this deed, would ne'er relent,
Though, at my words, the hollow prison-vaults
Would groan for pity.

   Conrad.   Manacle them both!

   Ethelbert. I know it—it must be—I see it all!
Albert, thou art the minion!

   Erminia.   Ah! too plain—   260

   Conrad. Silence! Gag up their mouths! I cannot bear
More of this brawling. That the Emperor
Had plac'd you in some other custody!
Bring them away.

                       [Exeunt all but ALBERT.

   Albert. Though my name perish from the book of honour,
Almost before the recent ink is dry,
And be no more remember'd after death,
Than any drummer's in the muster-roll;
Yet shall I season high my sudden fall
With triumph o'er that evil-witted duke!   270
He shall feel what it is to have the hand
Of a man drowning, on his hateful throat.

              Enter GERSA *and* SIGIFRED.

   Gersa. What discord is at ferment in this house?

   Sigifred. We are without conjecture; not a soul
We met could answer any certainty.

   Gersa. Young Ludolph, like a fiery arrow, shot
By us.

   Sigifred. The Emperor, with cross'd arms, in thought.

   Gersa. In one room music, in another sadness,
Perplexity every where!

Albert.   A trifle more!
Follow; your presences will much avail   280
To tune our jarred spirits. I'll explain.   [*Exeunt.*

ACT IV.

SCENE I.—AURANTHE'S *Apartment.*

AURANTHE *and* CONRAD *discovered.*

Conrad. Well, well, I know what ugly jeopardy
We are cag'd in; you need not pester that
Into my ears. Prythee, let me be spared
A foolish tongue, that I may bethink me
Of remedies with some deliberation.
You cannot doubt but 'tis in Albert's power
To crush or save us?
        Auranthe.   No, I cannot doubt.
He has, assure yourself, by some strange means,
My secret; which I ever hid from him,
Knowing his mawkish honesty.
        Conrad.   Curs'd slave!   10
Auranthe. Ay, I could almost curse him now myself.
Wretched impediment! Evil genius!
A glue upon my wings, that cannot spread,
When they should span the provinces! A snake,
A scorpion, sprawling on the first gold step,
Conducting to the throne, high canopied.
        Conrad. You would not hear my council, when his life
Might have been trodden out, all sure and hush'd;
Now the dull animal forsooth must be
Intreated, managed! When can you contrive   20
The interview he demands?
        Auranthe.   As speedily
It must be done as my brib'd woman can
Unseen conduct him to me; but I fear
'Twill be impossible, while the broad day
Comes through the panes with persecuting glare.
Methinks, if 't now were night I could intrigue
With darkness, bring the stars to second me,
And settle all this trouble.
        Conrad.   Nonsense! Child!
See him immediately; why not now?
        Auranthe. Do you forget that even the senseless door-posts   30
Are on the watch and gape through all the house?
How many whispers there are about,
Hungry for evidence to ruin me;
Men I have spurn'd, and women I have taunted?

Besides, the foolish prince sends, minute whiles,
His pages—so they tell me—to enquire
After my health, entreating, if I please,
To see me.
    Conrad.   Well, suppose this Albert here;
What is your power with him?
    Auranthe.   He should be
My echo, my taught parrot! but I fear   40
He will be cur enough to bark at me;
Have his own say; read me some silly creed
'Bout shame and pity.
    Conrad.   What will you do then?
    Auranthe. What I shall do, I know not: what I would
Cannot be done; for see, this chamber-floor
Will not yield to the pick-axe and the spade,—
Here is no quiet depth of hollow ground.
    Conrad. Sister, you have grown sensible and wise,
Seconding, ere I speak it, what is now,
I hope, resolv'd between us.
    Auranthe.   Say, what is 't?   50
    Conrad. You need not be his sexton too: a man
May carry that with him shall make him die
Elsewhere,—give that to him; pretend the while
You will to-morrow succumb to his wishes,
Be what they may, and send him from the Castle
On some fool's errand; let his latest groan
Frighten the wolves!
    Auranthe.   Alas! he must not die!
    Conrad. Would you were both hears'd up in stifling lead!
Detested—
    Auranthe. Conrad, hold! I would not bear
The little thunder of your fretful tongue,   60
Tho' I alone were taken in these toils,
And you could free me; but remember, sir,
You live alone in my security:
So keep your wits at work, for your own sake,
Not mine, and be more mannerly.
    Conrad.   Thou wasp!
If my domains were emptied of these folk,
And I had thee to starve—
    Auranthe.   O, marvellous!
But Conrad, now be gone; the Host is look'd for;
Cringe to the Emperor, entertain the Lords,
And, do ye mind, above all things, proclaim   70
My sickness, with a brother's sadden'd eye,
Condoling with Prince Ludolph. In fit time
Return to me.

Conrad.   I leave you to your thoughts.   [*Exit.*

Auranthe (*sola*). Down, down, proud temper! down,
      Auranthe's pride!
Why do I anger him when I should kneel?
Conrad! Albert! help! help! What can I do?
O wretched woman! lost, wreck'd, swallow'd up,
Accursed, blasted! O, thou golden Crown,
Orbing along the serene firmament
Of a wide empire, like a glowing moon;   80
And thou, bright sceptre! lustrous in my eyes,—
There—as the fabled fair Hesperian tree,
Bearing a fruit more precious! graceful thing,
Delicate, godlike, magic! must I leave
Thee to melt in the visionary air,
Ere, by one grasp, this common hand is made
Imperial? I do not know the time
When I have wept for sorrow; but methinks
I could now sit upon the ground, and shed
Tears, tears of misery. O, the heavy day!   90
How shall I bear my life till Albert comes?
Ludolph! Erminia! Proofs! O heavy day!
Bring me some mourning weeds, that I may 'tire
Myself, as fits one wailing her own death:
Cut off these curls, and brand this lilly hand,
And throw these jewels from my loathing sight,—
Fetch me a missal, and a string of beads,—
A cup of bitter'd water, and a crust,—
I will confess, O holy Abbot—How!
What is this? Auranthe! thou fool, dolt,   100
Whimpering idiot! up! up! act and quell!
I am safe! Coward! why am I in fear?
Albert! he cannot stickle, chew the cud
In such a fine extreme,—impossible!
Who knocks?   [*Goes to the Door, listens, and opens it.*

Enter ALBERT.

Albert, I have been waiting for you here
With such an aching heart, such swooning throbs
On my poor brain, such cruel—cruel sorrow,
That I should claim your pity! Art not well?
      Albert. Yes, lady, well.
      Auranthe.   You look not so, alas!   110
But pale, as if you brought some heavy news.
      Albert. You know full well what makes me look so pale.
      Auranthe. No! Do I? Surely I am still to learn
Some horror; all I know, this present, is
I am near hustled to a dangerous gulph,

Which you can save me from,—and therefore safe,
So trusting in thy love; that should not make
Thee pale, my Albert.
    Albert.   It doth make me freeze.
    Auranthe. Why should it, love?
    Albert.   You should not ask me that,
But make your own heart monitor, and save   120
Me the great pain of telling. You must know.
    Auranthe. Something has vexed you, Albert. There are times
When simplest things put on a sombre cast;
A melancholy mood will haunt a man,
Until most easy matters take the shape
Of unachievable tasks; small rivulets
Then seem impassable.
    Albert.   Do not cheat yourself
With hope that gloss of words, or suppliant action,
Or tears, or ravings, or self-threaten'd death,
Can alter my resolve.
    Auranthe.   You make me tremble;   130
Not so much at your threats, as at your voice.
Untun'd. and harsh, and barren of all love.
    Albert. You suffocate me! Stop this devil's parley,
And listen to me; know me once for all.
    Auranthe. I thought I did. Alas! I am deceiv'd.
    Albert. No, you are not deceiv'd. You took me for
A man detesting all inhuman crime;
And therefore kept from me your demon's plot
Against Erminia. Silent? Be so still;
For ever! Speak no more; but hear my words,
Thy fate. Your safety I have bought to-day   141
By blazoning a lie, which in the dawn
I'll expiate with truth.
    Auranthe.   O cruel traitor!
    Albert. For I would not set eyes upon thy shame;
I would not see thee dragg'd to death by the hair,
Penanc'd, and taunted on a scaffolding!
To-night, upon the skirts of the blind wood
That blackens northward of these horrid towers,
I wait for you with horses. Choose your fate.
Farewell.
    Auranthe. Albert, you jest; I'm sure you must.
You, an ambitious Soldier! I, a Queen,   151
One who could say,—Here, rule these Provinces!
Take tribute from those cities for thyself!
Empty these armouries, these treasuries,
Muster thy warlike thousands at a nod!
Go! conquer Italy!

Albert.   Auranthe, you have made
The whole world chaff to me. Your doom is fix'd.

Auranthe. Out, villain! dastard!

Albert.   Look there to the door!
Who is it?

Auranthe. Conrad, traitor!

Albert.   Let him in.

Enter CONRAD.

Do not affect amazement, hypocrite,   160
At seeing me in this chamber.

Conrad.   Auranthe?

Albert. Talk not with eyes, but speak your curses out
Against me, who would sooner crush and grind
A brace of toads, than league with them to oppress
An innocent lady, gull an Emperor,
More generous to me than autumn's sun
To ripening harvests.

Auranthe.   No more insult, sir!

Albert. Aye, clutch your scabbard; but, for prudence sake,
Draw not the sword; 'twould make an uproar, Duke,
You would not hear the end of. At nightfall   170
Your lady sister, if I guess aright,
Will leave this busy castle. You had best
Take farewell too of worldly vanities.

Conrad. Vassal!

Albert.   To-morrow, when the Emperor sends
For loving Conrad, see you fawn on him.
Good even!

Auranthe. You'll be seen!

Albert.   See the coast clear then.

Auranthe (as he goes). Remorseless Albert! Cruel,
    cruel wretch!

                                        [*She lets him out.*

Conrad. So, we must lick the dust?

Auranthe.   I follow him.

Conrad. How? Where? The plan of your escape?

Auranthe.   He waits   180
For me with horses by the forest-side,
Northward.

Conrad. Good, good! he dies. You go, say you?

Auranthe. Perforce.

Conrad.   Be speedy, darkness! Till that comes,
Fiends keep you company!   [*Exit.*

Auranthe.   And you! And you!
And all men! Vanish!

                                        [*Retires to an inner Apartment.*

Scene II.—*An Apartment in the Castle.*

Enter Ludolph *and* Page.

Page. Still very sick, my Lord; but now I went
Knowing my duty to so good a Prince;
And there her women in a mournful throng
Stood in the passage whispering: if any
Mov'd 'twas with careful steps and hush'd as death;
They bid me stop.
  Ludolph.   Good fellow, once again
Make soft enquiry; prythee be not stay'd
By any hindrance, but with gentlest force
Break through her weeping servants, till thou com'st
E'en to her chamber door, and there, fair boy,   10
If with thy mother's milk thou hast suck'd in
Any diviner eloquence; woo her ears
With plaints for me more tender than the voice
Of dying Echo, echoed.
  Page.   Kindest master!
To know thee sad thus, will unloose my tongue
In mournful syllables. Let but my words reach
Her ears and she shall take them coupled with
Moans from my heart and sighs not counterfeit.
May I speed better!   [*Exit Page.*
  Ludolph.   Auranthe! My Life!
Long have I lov'd thee, yet till now not lov'd: 20
Remembering, as I do, hard-hearted times
When I had heard even of thy death perhaps,
And thoughtless, suffered to pass alone
Into Elysium! now I follow thee
A substance or a shadow, wheresoe'er
Thou leadest me,—whether thy white feet press,
With pleasant weight, the amorous-aching earth,
Or thro' the air thou pioneerest me,
A shade! Yet sadly I predestinate!
O unbenignest Love, why wilt thou let   30
Darkness steal out upon the sleepy world
So wearily; as if night's chariot wheels
Were clog'd in some thick cloud. O, changeful Love,
Let not her steeds with drowsy-footed pace
Pass the high stars, before sweet embassage
Comes from the pillow'd beauty of that fair
Completion of all delicate nature's wit.
Pout her faint lips anew with rubious health
And with thine infant fingers lift the fringe
Of her sick eyelids; that those eyes may glow 40

With wooing light upon me, ere the Morn
Peers with disrelish, grey, barren, and cold.

Enter GERSA *and Courtiers.*

Otho calls me his Lion—should I blush
To be so tam'd, so——
 Gersa.   Do me the courtesy
Gentlemen to pass on.
 Courtier.   We are your servants.

          [Exeunt Courtiers.

 Ludolph. It seems then, Sir, you have found out the man
You would confer with; me?
 Gersa.   If I break not
Too much upon your thoughtful mood, I will
Claim a brief while your patience.
 Ludolph.   For what cause
Soe'er I shall be honour'd.
 Gersa. I not less.   50
 Ludolph. What may it be? No trifle can take place
Of such deliberate prologue, serious 'haviour.
But be it what it may I cannot fail
To listen with no common interest—
For though so new your presence is to me,
I have a soldier's friendship for your fame—
Please you explain.
 Gersa. As thus—for, pardon me,
I cannot in plain terms grossly assault
A noble nature; and would faintly sketch
What your quick apprehension will fill up   60
So finely I esteem you.
 Ludolph.   I attend—
 Gersa. Your generous Father, most illustrious Otho,
Sits in the Banquet room among his chiefs—
His wine is bitter, for you are not there—
His eyes are fix'd still on the open doors,
And every passer in he frowns upon
Seeing no Ludolph comes.
 Ludolph.   I do neglect—
 Gersa. And for your absence, may I guess the cause?
 Ludolph. Stay there! no—guess? more princely you must be—
Than to make guesses at me. 'Tis enough,   70
I'm sorry I can hear no more.
 Gersa.   And I
As griev'd to force it on you so abrupt;
Yet one day you must know a grief whose sting
Will sharpen more the longer 'tis conceal'd.
 Ludolph. Say it at once, sir, dead, dead, is she dead?

Gersa. Mine is a cruel task: she is not dead—
And would for your sake she were innocent—

Ludolph. Thou liest! thou amazest me beyond
All scope of thought; convulsest my heart's blood
To deadly churning—Gersa you are young   80
As I am; let me observe you face to face;
Not grey-brow'd like the poisonous Ethelbert,
No rheumed eyes, no furrowing of age,
No wrinkles where all vices nestle in
Like crannied vermin—no, but fresh and young
And hopeful featur'd. Ha! by heaven you weep
Tears, human tears—Do you repent you then
Of a curs'd torturer's office! Why shouldst join—
Tell me, the league of Devils? Confess—confess
The Lie.—

Gersa. Lie!—but begone all ceremonious points   90
Of honour battailous. I could not turn
My wrath against thee for the orbed world.

Ludolph. Your wrath, weak boy? Tremble at mine unless
Retraction follow close upon the heels
Of that late stounding insult: why has my sword
Not done already a sheer judgment on thee?
Despair, or eat thy words. Why, thou wast nigh
Whimpering away my reason: hark ye, Sir,
It is no secret;—that Erminia,
Erminia, Sir, was hidden in your tent;   100
O bless'd asylum! comfortable home!
Begone, I pity thee, thou art a Gull—
Erminia's last new puppet—

Gersa.   Furious fire!
Thou mak'st me boil as hot as thou canst flame!
And in thy teeth I give thee back the lie!
Thou liest! Thou, Auranthe's fool, a wittol——

Ludolph. Look! look at this bright sword;
There is no part of it to the very hilt
But shall indulge itself about thine heart—
Draw—but remember thou must cower thy plumes,   110
As yesterday the Arab made thee stoop—

Gersa. Patience! not here, I would not spill thy blood
Here underneath this roof where Otho breathes,
Thy father—almost mine—

Ludolph.   O faltering coward—

Re-enter PAGE.

Stay, stay, here is one I have half a word with—
Well—What ails thee child?

Page.   My lord,

Ludolph.   Good fellow!
Page. They are fled!
Ludolph.   They—who?
Page.   When anxiously
I hasten'd back, your grieving messenger,
I found the stairs all dark, the lamps extinct,
And not a foot or whisper to be heard.   120
I thought her dead, and on the lowest step
Sat listening; when presently came by
Two muffled up,—one sighing heavily,
The other cursing low, whose voice I knew
For the Duke Conrad's. Close I follow'd them
Thro' the dark ways they chose to the open air;
And, as I follow'd, heard my lady speak.
     Ludolph. Thy life answers the truth!
     Page.   The chamber's empty!
Ludolph. As I will be of mercy! So, at last,
This nail is in my temples!
     Gersa.   Be calm in this.   130
Ludolph. I am.
     Gersa.   And Albert too has disappear'd;
Ere I met you, I sought him everywhere;
You would not hearken.
     Ludolph.   Which way went they, boy?
Gersa. I'll hunt with you.
     Ludolph.   No, no, no. My senses are
Still whole. I have surviv'd. My arm is strong—
My appetite sharp—for revenge! I'll no sharer
In my feast; my injury is all my own,
And so is my revenge, my lawful chattels!
Terrier, ferret them out! Burn—burn the witch!
Trace me their footsteps! Away!   140
                                        [*Exeunt.*

ACT V.

SCENE I.—*A part of the Forest.*

Enter CONRAD *and* AURANTHE.

Auranthe. Go no further; not a step more; thou art
A master-plague in the midst of miseries.
Go—I fear thee. I tremble every limb,
Who never shook before. There's moody death
In thy resolved looks—Yes, I could kneel
To pray thee far away. Conrad, go, go—
There! yonder underneath the boughs I see
Our horses!

Conrad. Aye, and the man.
Auranthe.   Yes, he is there.
Go, go,—no blood, no blood; go, gentle Conrad!
Conrad. Farewell!
Auranthe.   Farewell, for this Heaven pardon you.   10

[*Exit* AURANTHE.

Conrad. If he survive one hour, then may I die
In unimagined tortures—or breathe through
A long life in the foulest sink of the world!
He dies—'tis well she do not advertise
The caitiff of the cold steel at his back.

[*Exit* CONRAD.

Enter LUDOLPH *and* PAGE.

Ludolph. Miss'd the way, boy, say not that on your peril!
Page. Indeed, indeed I cannot trace them further.
Ludolph. Must I stop here? Here solitary die?
Stifled beneath the thick oppressive shade
Of these dull boughs,—this oven of dark thickets,—   20
Silent,—without revenge?—pshaw!—bitter end,—
A bitter death,—a suffocating death,—
A gnawing—silent—deadly, quiet death!
Escap'd?—fled?—vanish'd? melted into air?
She's gone! I cannot clutch her! no revenge!
A muffled death, ensnar'd in horrid silence!
Suck'd to my grave amid a dreamy calm!
O, where is that illustrious noise of war,
To smother up this sound of labouring breath,
This rustle of the trees!

[AURANTHE *shrieks at a distance.*

Page.   My Lord, a noise!   30
This way—hark!
Ludolph.   Yes, yes! A hope! A music!
A glorious clamour! How I live again!

[*Exeunt.*

SCENE II.—*Another part of the Forest.*

Enter ALBERT (*wounded*).

Albert. O for enough life to support me on
To Otho's feet—

Enter LUDOLPH.

Ludolph.   Thrice villainous, stay there!
Tell me where that detested woman is
Or this is through thee!
Albert.   My good Prince, with me
The sword has done its worst; not without worst

Done to another—Conrad has it home—
I see you know it all—
    Ludolph.   Where is his sister?

AURANTHE *rushes in.*

Auranthe. Albert!
Ludolph. Ha! There! there!—He is the paramour!—
There—hug him—dying! O, thou innocence,
Shrine him and comfort him at his last gasp,   10
Kiss down his eyelids! Was he not thy love?
Wilt thou forsake him at his latest hour?
Keep fearful and aloof from his last gaze,
His most uneasy moments, when cold death
Stands with the door ajar to let him in?
    Albert. O that that door with hollow slam would close
Upon me sudden, for I cannot meet,
In all the unknown chambers of the dead,
Such horrors———
    Ludolph.   Auranthe! what can he mean?
What horrors? Is it not a joyous time?   20
Am I not married to a paragon
"Of personal beauty and untainted soul"?
A blushing fair-eyed Purity! A Sylph,
Whose snowy timid hand has never sin'd
Beyond a flower pluck'd, white as itself?
Albert, you do insult my Bride—your Mistress—
To talk of horrors on our wedding night.
    Albert. Alas! poor Prince, I would you knew my heart.
'Tis not so guilty—
    Ludolph.   Hear you he pleads not guilty—
You are not? or if so what matters it?   30
You have escap'd me,—free as the dusk air—
Hid in the forest—safe from my revenge;
I cannot catch you—You should laugh at me,
Poor cheated Ludolph,—make the forest hiss
With jeers at me—You tremble; faint at once,
You will come to again. O Cockatrice,
I have you. Whither wander those fair eyes
To entice the Devil to your help, that he
May change you to a Spider, so to crawl
Into some cranny to escape my wrath?   40
    Albert. Sometimes the counsel of a dying man
Doth operate quietly when his breath is gone—
Disjoin those hands—part—part, do not destroy
Each other—forget her—our miseries
Are equal shar'd, and mercy is—
    Ludolph.   A boon

When one can compass it. Auranthe, try
Your oratory—your breath is not so hitch'd—
Aye, stare for help—

[ALBERT *groans and dies.*

                    There goes a spotted soul
Howling in vain along the hollow night—
Hear him—he calls you—Sweet Auranthe, come!   50
   Auranthe. Kill me.
   Ludolph.   No! What? upon our Marriage-night!
The earth would shudder at so foul a deed—
A fair Bride, a sweet Bride, an innocent Bride!
No, we must revel it, as 'tis in use
In times of delicate brilliant ceremony:
Come, let me lead you to our halls again—
Nay, linger not—make no resistance sweet—
Will you—Ah wretch, thou canst not, for I have
The strength of twenty lions 'gainst a lamb—
Now one adieu for Albert—come away.—   60

[*Exeunt.*

SCENE III.—*An inner Court of the Castle.*

Enter SIGIFRED, GONFRED, *and* THEODORE *meeting.*

   Theodore. Was ever such a night?
   Sigifred.   What horrors more?
Things unbeliev'd one hour, so strange they are,
The next hour stamps with credit.
   Theodore.   Your last news?
   Gonfred. After the Page's story of the death
Of Albert and Duke Conrad?
   Sigifred.   And the return
Of Ludolph with the Princess.
   Gonfred.   No more save
Prince Gersa's freeing Abbot Ethelbert,
And the sweet lady, fair Erminia,
From prison.
   Theodore. Where are they now? hast yet heard?
   Gonfred. With the sad Emperor they are closeted;
I saw the three pass slowly up the stairs,   11
The lady weeping, the old Abbot cowl'd.
   Sigifred. What next?
   Thedore.   I ache to think on't.
   Gonfred.   'Tis with fate.
   Theodore. One while these proud towers are hush'd as death.
   Gonfred. The next our poor Prince fills the arched rooms
With ghastly ravings.

Sigifred.   I do fear his brain.
Gonfred. I will see more. Bear you so stout a heart?

> [*Exeunt into the Castle.*

SCENE IV.—*A Cabinet, opening towards a Terrace.*

OTHO, ERMINIA, ETHELBERT, *and a Physician, discovered.*

Otho. O, my poor Boy! my Son! my Son! My Ludolph!
Have ye no comfort for me, ye Physicians
Of the weak Body and Soul?
    Ethelbert.   'Tis not the Medicine
Either of heaven or earth can cure unless
Fit time be chosen to administer—
    Otho. A kind forbearance, holy Abbot—come
Erminia, here sit by me, gentle Girl;
Give me thy hand—hast thou forgiven me?
    Erminia. Would I were with the saints to pray for you!   9
    Otho. Why will ye keep me from my darling child?
    Physician. Forgive me, but he must not see thy face—
    Otho. Is then a father's countenance a Gorgon?
Hath it not comfort in it? Would it not
Console my poor Boy, cheer him, heal his spirits?
Let me embrace him, let me speak to him—
I will—who hinders me? Who's Emperor?
    Physician. You may not, Sire—'twould overwhelm him quite,
He is so full of grief and passionate wrath,
Too heavy a sigh would kill him—or do worse.
He must be sav'd by fine contrivances—   20
And most especially we must keep clear
Out of his sight a Father whom he loves—
His heart is full, it can contain no more,
And do its ruddy office.
    Ethelbert.   Sage advice;
We must endeavour how to ease and slacken
The tight-wound energies of his despair,
Not make them tenser—
    Otho.   Enough! I hear, I hear.
Yet you were about to advise more—I listen.
    Ethelbert. This learned doctor will agree with me,
That not in the smallest point should he be thwarted
Or gainsaid by one word—his very motions,   31
Nods, becks and hints, should be obey'd with care,
Even on the moment: so his troubled mind
May cure itself—
    Physician.   There is no other means.
    Otho. Open the door: let's hear if all is quiet—
    Physician. Beseech you, Sire, forbear.

Erminia.   Do, do.

Otho. .   I command!

Open it straight—hush!—quiet—my lost Boy!
My miserable Child!

    Ludolph (*indistinctly without*). Fill, fill my goblet,—
Here's a health!

    Erminia.   O, close the door!

    Otho. Let, let me hear his voice; this cannot last—
And fain would I catch up his dying words   41
Though my own knell they be—this cannot last—
O let me catch his voice—for lo! I hear
This silence whisper me that he is dead!
It is so. Gersa?

Enter GERSA.

    Physician. Say, how fares the prince?

    Gersa. More calm—his features are less wild and flush'd—
Once he complain'd of weariness—

    Physician.   Indeed!
'Tis good—'tis good—let him.but fall asleep,
That saves him.

    Otho.   Gersa, watch him like a child—   49
Ward him from harm—and bring me better news—

    Physician. Humour him to the height. I fear to go;
For should he catch a glimpse of my dull garb,
It might affright him—fill him with suspicion
That we believe him sick, which must not be—

    Gersa. I will invent what soothing means I can.

                                     [*Exit* GERSA.

    Physician. This should cheer up your Highness—weariness
Is a good symptom, and most favourable—
It gives me pleasant hopes. Please you walk forth
Onto the Terrace; the refreshing air
Will blow one half of your sad doubts away.   60

                                         [*Exeunt.*

SCENE V.—*A Banqueting Hall, brilliantly illuminated, and set forth
with all costly magnificence, with Supper-tables, laden with services
of Gold and Silver. A door in the back scene, guarded by two Soldiers. Lords, Ladies, Knights, Gentlemen, &c., whispering sadly,
and ranging themselves; part entering and part discovered.*

    First Knight. Grievously are we tantaliz'd, one and all—
Sway'd here and there, commanded to and fro
As though we were the shadows of a dream
And link'd to a sleeping fancy. What do we here?

    Gonfred. I am no Seer—you know we must obey

The prince from A to Z—though it should be
To set the place in flames. I pray hast heard
Where the most wicked Princess is?
    First Knight.   There, Sir,
In the next room—have you remark'd those two
Stout soldiers posted at the door?
    Gonfred.   For what?   10
                                 [They whisper.

    First Lady. How ghast a train!
    Second Lady. Sure this should be some splendid burial.
    First Lady. What fearful whispering! See, see,—Gersa there.

Enter GERSA.

    Gersa. Put on your brightest looks; smile if you can;
Behave as all were happy; keep your eyes
From the least watch upon him; if he speaks
To any one, answer collectedly,
Without surprise, his questions, howe'er strange.
Do this to the utmost,—though, alas! with me
The remedy grows hopeless! Here he comes,—   20
Observe what I have said,—show no surprise.

Enter LUDOLPH, *followed by* SIGIFRED *and Page.*

    Ludolph. A splendid company! rare beauties here!
I should have Orphean lips, and Plato's fancy,
Amphion's utterance, toned with his lyre,
Or the deep key of Jove's sonorous mouth,
To give fit salutation. Methought I heard,
As I came in, some whispers,—what of that?
'Tis natural men should whisper; at the kiss
Of Psyche given by Love, there was a buzz
Among the gods!—and silence is as natural.   30
These draperies are fine, and, being a mortal,
I should desire no better; yet, in truth,
There must be some superiour costliness,
Some wider-domed high magnificence!
I would have, as a mortal I may not,
Hanging of heaven's clouds, purple and gold,
Slung from the spheres; gauzes of silver mist,
Loop'd up with cords of twisted wreathed light,
And tassell'd round with weeping meteors!
These pendent lamps and chandeliers are bright   40
As earthly fires from dull dross can be cleansed;
Yet could my eyes drink up intenser beams
Undazzled,—this is darkness,—when I close
These lids, I see far fiercer brilliances,—
Skies full of splendid moons, and shooting stars,

And spouting exhalations, diamond fires,
And panting fountains quivering with deep glows!
Yes—this is dark—is it not dark?

    Sigifred.   My Lord,
'Tis late; the lights of festival are ever
Quench'd in the morn.

    Ludolph.   'Tis not to-morrow then?   50
    Sigifred. 'Tis early dawn.
    Gersa.   Indeed full time we slept;
Say you so, Prince?

    Ludolph.   I say I quarrell'd with you;
We did not tilt each other,—that's a blessing,—
Good gods! no innocent blood upon my head!

    Sigifred. Retire, Gersa!
    Ludolph.   There should be three more here:
For two of them, they stay away perhaps,
Being gloomy-minded, haters of fair revels,—
They know their own thoughts best.

                             As for the third,
Deep blue eyes—semi-shaded in white lids,
Finish'd with lashes fine for more soft shade,   60
Completed by her twin-arch'd ebon brows—
White temples of exactest elegance,
Of even mould felicitous and smooth—
Cheeks fashion'd tenderly on either side,
So perfect, so divine that our poor eyes
Are dazzled with the sweet proportioning,
And wonder that 'tis so,—the magic chance!
Her nostrils, small, fragrant, faery-delicate;
Her lips—I swear no human bones e'er wore
So taking a disguise—you shall behold her!   70
We'll have her presently; aye, you shall see her,
And wonder at her, friends, she is so fair—
She is the world's chief Jewel, and by heaven
She's mine by right of marriage—she is mine!
Patience, good people, in fit time I send
A Summoner—she will obey my call,
Being a wife most mild and dutiful.
First I would hear what music is prepared
To herald and receive her—let me hear!

    Sigifred. Bid the musicians soothe him tenderly.   80
                       [*A soft strain of Music.*

    Ludolph. Ye have none better—no—I am content;
'Tis a rich sobbing melody, with reliefs
Full and majestic; it is well enough,
And will be sweeter, when ye see her pace
Sweeping into this presence, glisten'd o'er

With emptied caskets, and her train upheld
By ladies, habited in robes of lawn,
Sprinkled with golden crescents; (others bright
In silks, with spangles shower'd,) and bow'd to
By Duchesses and pearled Margravines—   90
Sad, that the fairest creature of the earth—
I pray you mind me not—'tis sad, I say,
That the extremest beauty of the world
Should so entrench herself away from me,
Behind a barrier of engender'd guilt!
    Second Lady. Ah! what a moan!
    First Knight.   Most piteous indeed!
    Ludolph. She shall be brought before this company,
And then—then—
    First Lady.   He muses.
    Gersa.   O, Fortune, where will this end?
    Sigifred. I guess his purpose! Indeed he must not have
That pestilence brought in,—that cannot be,   100
There we must stop him.
    Gersa.   I am lost! Hush, hush!
He is about to rave again.
    Ludolph. A barrier of guilt! I was the fool.
She was the cheater! Who's the cheater now,
And who the fool? The entrapp'd, the caged fool,
The bird-lim'd raven? She shall croak to death
Secure! Methinks I have her in my fist,
To crush her with my heel! Wait, wait! I marvel
My father keeps away: good friend, ah! Sigifred!
Do bring him to me—and Erminia   110
I fain would see before I sleep—and Ethelbert,
That he may bless me, as I know he will
Though I have curs'd him.
    Sigifred.   Rather suffer me
To lead you to them—
    Ludolph.   No, excuse me, no—
The day is not quite done—go bring them hither.

                           [*Exit* SIGIFRED.

Certes, a father's smile should, like sunlight,,
Slant on my sheafed harvest of ripe bliss—
Besides, I thirst to pledge my lovely Bride
In a deep goblet: let me see—what wine?
The strong Iberian juice, or mellow Greek?   120
Or pale Calabrian? Or the Tuscan grape?
Or of old Ætna's pulpy wine presses,
Black stain'd with the fat vintage, as it were
The purple slaughter-house, where Bacchus' self
Prick'd his own swollen veins? Where is my Page?

Page.   Here, here!
Ludolph. Be ready to obey me; anon thou shalt
Bear a soft message for me—for the hour
Draws near when I must make a winding up
Of bridal Mysteries—a fine-spun vengeance!
Carve it on my Tomb, that when I rest beneath   130
Men shall confess—This Prince was gull'd and cheated,
But from the ashes of disgrace he rose
More than a fiery Phœnix—and did burn
His ignominy up in purging fires—
Did I not send, Sir, but a moment past,
For my Father?
  Gersa.   You did.
  Ludolph.   Perhaps 'twould be
Much better he came not.
  Gersa.   He enters now!

Enter OTHO, ERMINIA, ETHELBERT, SIGIFRED, *and Physician.*

  Ludolph. O thou good Man, against whose sacred head
I was a mad conspirator, chiefly too
For the sake of my fair newly wedded wife,   140
Now to be punish'd, do not look so sad!
Those charitable eyes will thaw my heart,
Those tears will wash away a just resolve,
A verdict ten times sworn! Awake—awake—
Put on a judge's brow, and use a tongue
Made iron-stern by habit! Thou shalt see
A deed to be applauded, 'scribed in gold!
Join a loud voice to mine, and so denounce
What I alone will execute!
  Otho.   Dear son,
What is it? By your father's love, I sue   150
That it be nothing merciless!
  Ludolph.   To that demon?
Not so! No! She is in temple-stall
Being garnish'd for the sacrifice, and I,
The Priest of Justice, will immolate her
Upon the altar of wrath! She stings me through!—
Even as the worm doth feed upon the nut,
So she, a scorpion, preys upon my brain!
I feel her gnawing here! Let her but vanish,
Then, father, I will lead your legions forth,
Compact in steeled squares, and speared files,   160
And bid our trumpets speak a fell rebuke
To nations drows'd in peace!
  Otho.   To-morrow, Son,
Be your word law—forget to-day—

Ludolph. I will
When I have finish'd it—now! now! I'm pight,
Tight-footed for the deed!
    Erminia. Alas! Alas!
    Ludolph. What Angel's voice is that? Erminia!
Ah! gentlest creature, whose sweet innocence
Was almost murder'd; I am penitent,
Wilt thou forgive me? And thou, holy Man,
Good Ethelbert, shall I die in peace with you?   170
    Erminia. Die, my lord!
    Ludolph. I feel it possible.
    Otho. Physician?
    Physician. I fear me he is past my skill.
    Otho. Not so!
    Ludolph. I see it, I see it—I have been wandering—
Half-mad—not right here—I forget my purpose.
Bestir, bestir, Auranthe! ha! ha! ha!
Youngster! Page! go bid them drag her to me!
Obey! This shall finish it!   *[Draws a dagger.*
    Otho. O my Son! my Son!
    Sigifred. This must not be—stop there!
    Ludolph. Am I obey'd?
A little talk with her—no harm—haste! haste!
    [Exit Page.
    180
Set her before me—never fear I can strike.
    Several Voices. My Lord! My Lord!
    Gersa. Good Prince!
    Ludolph. Why do ye trouble me? out—out—out away!
There she is! take that! and that! no, no—
That's not well done—Where is she?
    *The doors open. Enter Page. Several women are seen grouped
about* AURANTHE *in the inner room.*
    Page. Alas! My Lord, my Lord! they cannot move her!
Her arms are stiff,—her fingers clench'd and cold—
    Ludolph. She's dead!
    [Staggers and falls into their arms.
    Ethelbert. Take away the dagger.
    Gersa. Softly; so!
    Otho. Thank God for that!
    Sigifred. I fear it could not harm him.
    Gersa. No!—brief be his anguish!
    Ludolph. She's gone—I am content—Nobles, good night!   190
We are all weary—faint—set ope the doors—
I will to bed!—To-morrow—
    [Dies.

THE CURTAIN FALLS.

KING STEPHEN

A FRAGMENT OF A TRAGEDY

WRITTEN IN NOVEMBER 1819

KING STEPHEN

A FRAGMENT OF A TRAGEDY

ACT I.

SCENE I.—*Field of Battle.*

Alarum. Enter King STEPHEN, *Knights, and Soldiers.*

Stephen. If shame can on a soldier's vein-swoll'n front
Spread deeper crimson than the battle's toil,
Blush in your casing helmets! for see, see!
Yonder my chivalry, my pride of war,
Wrench'd with an iron hand from firm array,
Are routed loose about the plashy meads,
Of honour forfeit. O that my known voice
Could reach your dastard ears, and fright you more!
Fly, cowards, fly! Glocester is at your backs!
Throw your slack bridles o'er the flurried manes,   10
Ply well the rowel with faint trembling heels,
Scampering to death at last!
    First Knight.   The enemy
Bears his flaunt standard close upon their rear.
    Second Knight. Sure of a bloody prey, seeing the fens
Will swamp them girth-deep.
    Stephen.   Over head and ears,
No matter! 'Tis a gallant enemy;
How like a comet he goes streaming on.
But we must plague him in the flank,—hey, friends?
We are well breathed,—follow!
      Enter Earl BALDWIN *and Soldiers, as defeated.*
    Stephen.   De Redvers!
What is the monstrous bugbear that can fright   20
Baldwin?
    Baldwin. No scare-crow, but the fortunate star
Of boisterous Chester, whose fell truncheon now
Points level to the goal of victory.
This way he comes, and if you would maintain
Your person unaffronted by vile odds,

339

Take horse, my Lord.
   Stephen.   And which way spur for life?
Now I thank Heaven I am in the toils,
That soldiers may bear witness how my arm
Can burst the meshes. Not the eagle more
Loves to beat up against a tyrannous blast,   30
Than I to meet the torrent of my foes.
This is a brag,—be 't so,—but if I fall,
Carve it upon my 'scutcheon'd sepulchre.
On, fellow soldiers! Earl of Redvers, back!
Not twenty Earls of Chester shall brow-beat
The diadem.   [*Exeunt. Alarum.*

Scene II.—*Another part of the Field.*

Trumpets sounding a Victory. Enter Glocester, *Knights, and Forces.*

   Glocester. Now may we lift our bruised vizors up,
And take the flattering freshness of the air,
While the wide din of battle dies away
Into times past, yet to be echoed sure
In the silent pages of our chroniclers.
   First Knight. Will Stephen's death be mark'd there, my good
     Lord,
Or that we gave him lodging in yon towers?
   Glocester. Fain would I know the great usurper's fate.

Enter two Captains severally.

   First Captain. My Lord!
   Second Captain.   Most noble Earl!
   First Captain.   The King—
   Second Captain. The Empress greets—
   Glocester. What of the King?
   First Captain.   He sole and lone maintains   10
A hopeless bustle mid our swarming arms,
And with a nimble savageness attacks,
Escapes, makes fiercer onset, then anew
Eludes death, giving death to most that dare
Trespass within the circuit of his sword!
He must by this have fallen. Baldwin is taken;
And for the Duke of Bretagne, like a stag
He flies, for the Welsh beagles to hunt down.
God save the Empress!
   Glocester.   Now our dreaded Queen:
What message from her Highness?
   Second Captain.   Royal Maud   20
From the throng'd towers of Lincoln hath look'd down,
Like Pallas from the walls of Ilion,

And seen her enemies havock'd at her feet.
She greets most noble Glocester from her heart,
Intreating him, his captains, and brave knights,
To grace a banquet. The high city gates
Are envious which shall see your triumph pass;
The streets are full of music.

Enter Second Knight.

Glocester.   Whence come you?
Second Knight. From Stephen, my good Prince,—Stephen!
      Stephen!   29
Glocester. Why do you make such echoing of his name?
Second Knight. Because I think, my lord, he is no man,
But a fierce demon, 'nointed safe from wounds,
And misbaptized with a Christian name.
Glocester. A mighty soldier!—Does he still hold out?
Second Knight. He shames our victory. His valour still
Keeps elbow-room amid our eager swords,
And holds our bladed falchions all aloof—
His gleaming battle-axe being slaughter-sick,
Smote on the morion of a Flemish knight,
Broke short in his hand; upon the which he flung
The heft away with such a vengeful force,   41
It paunch'd the Earl of Chester's horse, who then
Spleen-hearted came in full career at him.
Glocester. Did no one take him at a vantage then?
Second Knight. Three then with tiger leap upon him flew,
Whom, with his sword swift-drawn and nimbly held,
He stung away again, and stood to breathe,
Smiling. Anon upon him rush'd once more
A throng of foes, and in this renew'd strife,
My sword met his and snapp'd off at the hilts.   50
Glocester. Come, lead me to this Mars—and let us move
In silence, not insulting his sad doom
With clamorous trumpets. To the Empress bear
My salutation as befits the time.

          [*Exeunt* GLOCESTER *and Forces.*

SCENE III.—*The Field of Battle. Enter* STEPHEN *unarmed.*

   Stephen. Another sword! And what if I could seize
One from Bellona's gleaming armoury,
Or choose the fairest of her sheaved spears!
Where are my enemies? Here, close at hand,
Here come the testy brood. O for a sword!
I'm faint—a biting sword! A noble sword!
A hedge-stake—or a ponderous stone to hurl
With brawny vengeance, like the labourer Cain.
Come on! Farewell my kingdom, and all hail

Thou superb, plum'd, and helmeted renown,
All hail—I would not truck this brilliant day
To rule in Pylos with a Nestor's beard—
Come on!

Enter DE KAIMS *and Knights, &c.*

De Kaims. Is 't madness, or a hunger after death,
That makes thee thus unarm'd throw taunts at us?
Yield, Stephen, or my sword's point dip in
The gloomy current of a traitor's heart.
 Stephen. Do it, De Kaims, I will not budge an inch.
 De Kaims. Yes, of thy madness thou shalt take the meed.
 Stephen. Darest thou?
 De Kaims.   How dare, against a man disarm'd?
 Stephen. What weapons has the lion but himself?
Come not near me, De Kaims, for by the price   21
Of all the glory I have won this day,
Being a king, I will not yield alive
To any but the second man of the realm,
Robert of Glocester.
 De Kaims.   Thou shalt vail to me.
 Stephen. Shall I, when I have sworn against it, sir?
Thou think'st it brave to take a breathing king,
That, on a court-day bow'd to haughty Maud,
The awed presence-chamber may be bold
To whisper, there's the man who took alive   30
Stephen—me—prisoner. Certes, De Kaims,
The ambition is a noble one.
 De Kaims.   'Tis true,
And, Stephen, I must compass it.
 Stephen.   No, no,
Do not tempt me to throttle you on the gorge,
Or with my gauntlet crush your hollow breast,
Just when your knighthood is grown ripe and full
For lordship.
 A Soldier. Is an honest yeoman's spear
Of no use at a need? Take that.
 Stephen.   Ah, dastard!
 De Kaims. What, you are vulnerable! my prisoner!
 Stephen. No, not yet. I disclaim it, and demand
Death as a sovereign right unto a king
Who 'sdains to yield to any but his peer,
If not in title, yet in noble deeds,
The Earl of Glocester. Stab to the hilts, De Kaims,
For I will never by mean hands be led
From this so famous field. Do ye hear! Be quick!

[Trumpets. Enter the Earl of CHESTER *and Knights.*

SCENE IV.—*A Presence Chamber. Queen* MAUD *in a Chair of State, the Earls of* GLOCESTER *and* CHESTER, *Lords, Attendants.*

Maud. Glocester, no more: I will behold that Boulogne:
Set him before me. Not for the poor sake
Of regal pomp and a vain-glorious hour,
As thou with wary speech, yet near enough,
Hast hinted.

 Glocester. Faithful counsel have I given;
If wary, for your Highness' benefit.

 Maud. The Heavens forbid that I should not think so,
For by thy valour have I won this realm,
Which by thy wisdom I will ever keep.
To sage advisers let me ever bend   10
A meek attentive ear, so that they treat
Of the wide kingdom's rule and government,
Not trenching on our actions personal.
Advis'd, not school'd, I would be; and henceforth
Spoken to in clear, plain, and open terms,
Not side-ways sermon'd at.

 Glocester.   Then, in plain terms,
Once more for the fallen king—

 Maud.   Your pardon, Brother,
I would no more of that; for, as I said,
'Tis not for worldly pomp I wish to see
The rebel, but as dooming judge to give   20
A sentence something worthy of his guilt.

 Glocester. If't must be so, I'll bring him to your presence.

             [Exit GLOCESTER.

 Maud. A meaner summoner might do as well—
My Lord of Chester, is 't true what I hear
Of Stephen of Boulogne, our prisoner,
That he, as a fit penance for his crimes,
Eats wholesome, sweet, and palatable food
Off Glocester's golden dishes—drinks pure wine,
Lodgest soft?

 Chester. More than that, my gracious Queen,
Has anger'd me. The noble Earl, methinks,   30
Full soldier as he is, and without peer
In counsel, dreams too much among his books.
It may read well, but sure 'tis out of date
To play the Alexander with Darius.

 Maud. Truth! I think so. By Heavens it shall not last!

 Chester. It would amaze your Highness now to mark
How Glocester overstrains his courtesy
To that crime-loving rebel, that Boulogne—

Maud. That ingrate!

Chester.   For whose vast ingratitude   40
To our late sovereign lord, your noble sire,
The generous Earl condoles in his mishaps,
And with a sort of lackeying friendliness,
Talks off the mighty frowning from his brow,
Woos him to hold a duet in a smile,
Or, if it please him, play an hour at chess—

Maud. A perjured slave!

Chester.   And for his perjury,
Glocester has fit rewards—nay, I believe,
He sets his bustling household's wits at work
For flatteries to ease this Stephen's hours,
And make a heaven of his purgatory;   50
Adorning bondage with the pleasant gloss
Of feasts and music, and all idle shows
Of indoor pageantry; while syren whispers,
Predestin'd for his ear, 'scape as half-check'd
From lips the courtliest and the rubiest
Of all the realm, admiring of his deeds.

Maud. A frost upon his summer!

Chester.   A queen's nod
Can make his June December. Here he comes.

POEMS

WRITTEN LATE IN 1819

POEMS WRITTEN LATE IN 1819

A PARTY OF LOVERS:

"A few Nonsense Verses" sent in a Letter to George Keats.

PENSIVE they sit, and roll their languid eyes,
Nibble their toast and cool their tea with sighs;
Or else forget the purpose of the night,
Forget their tea, forget their appetite.
See, with cross'd arms they sit—Ah! happy crew,
The fire is going out and no one rings
For coals, and therefore no coals Betty brings.
A fly is in the milk-pot. Must he die
Circled by a humane society?
No, no; there, Mr. Werter takes his spoon,
Inserts it, dips the handle, and lo! soon
The little straggler, sav'd from perils dark,
Across the teaboard draws a long wet mark.

Romeo! Arise, take snuffers by the handle,
There's a large cauliflower in each candle.
A winding sheet—ah, me! I must away
To No. 7, just beyond the circus gay.
Alas, my friend, your coat sits very well;
Where may your Tailor live? I may not tell.
O pardon me. I'm absent now and then.
Where *might* my Tailor live? I say again
I cannot tell, let me no more be teazed;
He lives in Wapping, might live where he pleased.

SONNET

THE day is gone, and all its sweets are gone!
　Sweet voice, sweet lips, soft hand, and softer breast,
Warm breath, light whisper, tender semi-tone.
　Bright eyes, accomplish'd shape, and lang'rous waist!
Faded the flower and all its budded charms,
　Faded the sight of beauty from my eyes,
Faded the shape of beauty from my arms,
　Faded the voice, warmth, whiteness, paradise—

Vanish'd unseasonably at shut of eve,
  When the dusk holiday— or holinight
Of fragrant-curtain'd love begins to weave
  The woof of darkness thick, for hid delight;
But, as I've read love's missal through to-day,
He'll let me sleep, seeing I fast and pray.

LINES TO FANNY

WHAT can I do to drive away
Remembrance from my eyes? for they have seen,
Aye, an hour ago, my brilliant Queen!
Touch has a memory. O say, love, say,
What can I do to kill it and be free
In my old liberty?
When every fair one that I saw was fair,
Enough to catch me in but half a snare,
Not keep me there:
When, howe'er poor or particolour'd things,
My muse had wings,
And ever ready was to take her course
Whither I bent her force,
Unintellectual, yet divine to me;—
Divine, I say!—What sea-bird o'er the sea
Is a philosopher the while he goes
Winging along where the great water throes?

   How shall I do
   To get anew
Those moulted feathers, and so mount once more
   Above, above
   The reach of fluttering Love,
And make him cower lowly while I soar?
Shall I gulp wine? No, that is vulgarism,
A heresy and schism,
   Foisted into the canon law of love;—
No,—wine is only sweet to happy men;
   More dismal cares
   Seize on me unawares,—
Where shall I learn to get my peace again?
To banish thoughts of that most hateful land,
Dungeoner of my friends, that wicked strand
Where they were wreck'd and live a wrecked life;
That monstrous region, whose dull rivers pour,
Ever from their sordid urns unto the shore,
Unown'd of any weedy-haired gods;
Whose winds, all zephyrless, hold scourging rods,

Iced in the great lakes, to afflict mankind;
Whose rank-grown forests, frosted, black, and blind,
Would fright a Dryad; whose harsh herbag'd meads
Make lean and lank the starv'd ox while he feeds;
There bad flowers have no scent, birds no sweet song,
And great unerring Nature once seems wrong.   43

O, for some sunny spell
To dissipate the shadows of this hell!
Say they are gone,—with the new dawning light
Steps forth my lady bright!
O, let me once more rest
My soul upon that dazzling breast!
Let once again these aching arms be plac'd,   50
The tender gaolers of thy waist!
And let me feel that warm breath here and there
To spread a rapture in my very hair,—
O, the sweetness of the pain!
Give me those lips again!
Enough! Enough! it is enough for me
To dream of thee!

SONNET

TO FANNY

I CRY your mercy—pity—love!—aye, love!
    Merciful love that tantalizes not,
One-thoughted, never-wandering, guileless love,
    Unmask'd, and being seen—without a blot!
O! let me have thee whole,—all—all—be mine!
    That shape, that fairness, that sweet minor zest
Of love, your kiss,—those hands, those eyes divine,
    That warm, white, lucent, million-pleasured breast,—
Yourself—your soul—in pity give me all,
    Withhold no atom's atom or I die,   10
Or living on perhaps, your wretched thrall,
    Forget, in the mist of idle misery,
Life's purposes,—the palate of my mind
Losing its gust, and my ambition blind!

THE FALL OF HYPERION

A DREAM

AN ATTEMPT MADE AT THE END OF 1819 TO
RECONSTRUCT THE POEM

THE FALL OF HYPERION

A DREAM

[CANTO I]

FANATICS have their dreams, wherewith they weave
A paradise for a sect; the savage too
From forth the loftiest fashion of his sleep
Guesses at Heaven; pity these have not
Trac'd upon vellum or wild Indian leaf
The shadows of melodious utterance.
But bare of laurel they live, dream, and die;
For Poesy alone can tell her dreams,
With the fine spell of words alone can save
Imagination from the sable chain   10
And dumb enchantment. Who alive can say,
"Thou art no Poet—may'st not tell thy dreams?"
Since every man whose soul is not a clod
Hath visions, and would speak, if he had loved,
And been well nurtured in his mother tongue.
Whether the dream now purpos'd to rehearse
Be poet's or fanatic's will be known
When this warm scribe my hand is in the grave.

Methought I stood where trees of every clime,
Palm, myrtle, oak, and sycamore, and beech,   20
With plantain, and spice-blossoms, made a screen;
In neighbourhood of fountains (by the noise
Soft-showering in my ears), and, (by the touch
Of scent,) not far from roses. Turning round
I saw an arbour with a drooping roof
Of trellis vines, and bells, and larger blooms,
Like floral censers, swinging light in air;
Before its wreathed doorway, on a mound
Of moss, was spread a feast of summer fruits,
Which, nearer seen, seem'd refuse of a meal   30
By angel tasted or our Mother Eve;
For empty shells were scattered on the grass,
And grape-stalks but half bare, and remnants more,
Sweet-smelling, whose pure kinds I could not know.
Still was more plenty than the fabled horn
Thrice emptied could pour forth, at banqueting

For Proserpine return'd to her own fields,
Where the white heifers low. And appetite
More yearning than on Earth I ever felt
Growing within, I ate deliciously;   40
And, after not long, thirsted, for thereby
Stood a cool vessel of transparent juice
Sipp'd by the wander'd bee, the which I took,
And, pledging all the mortals of the world,
And all the dead whose names are in our lips,
Drank. That full draught is parent of my theme.
No Asian poppy nor elixir fine
Of the soon-fading jealous Caliphat;
No poison gender'd in close monkish cell,
To thin the scarlet conclave of old men,   50
Could so have rapt unwilling life away.
Among the fragrant husks and berries crush'd,
Upon the grass I struggled hard against
The domineering potion; but in vain:
The cloudy swoon came on, and down I sank,
Like a Silenus on an antique vase.
How long I slumber'd 'tis a chance to guess.
When sense of life return'd, I started up
As if with wings; but the fair trees were gone,
The mossy mound and arbour were no more: 60
I look'd around upon the carved sides
Of an old sanctuary with roof august,
Builded so high, it seem'd that filmed clouds
Might spread beneath, as o'er the stars of heaven;
So old the place was, I remember'd none
The like upon the Earth: what I had seen
Of grey cathedrals, buttress'd walls, rent towers,
The superannuations of sunk realms,
Or Nature's rocks toil'd hard in waves and winds,
Seem'd but the faulture of decrepit things   70
To that eternal domed Monument.—
Upon the marble at my feet there lay
Store of strange vessels and large draperies,
Which needs had been of dyed asbestos wove,
Or in that place the moth could not corrupt,
So white the linen, so, in some, distinct
Ran imageries from a sombre loom.
All in a mingled heap confus'd there lay
Robes, golden tongs, censer and chafing-dish,
Girdles, and chains, and holy jewelries.   80

Turning from these with awe, once more I rais'd
My eyes to fathom the space every way;

The embossed roof, the silent massy range
Of columns north and south, ending in mist
Of nothing, then to eastward, where black gates
Were shut against the sunrise evermore.—
Then to the west I look'd, and saw far off
An image, huge of feature as a cloud,
At level of whose feet an altar slept,
To be approach'd on either side by steps,   90
And marble balustrade, and patient travail
To count with toil the innumerable degrees.
Towards the altar sober-paced I went,
Repressing haste, as too unholy there;
And, coming nearer, saw beside the shrine
One minist'ring; and there arose a flame.—
When in mid-way the sickening East wind
Shifts sudden to the south, the small warm rain
Melts out the frozen incense from all flowers,
And fills the air with so much pleasant health   100
That even the dying man forgets his shroud;—
Even so that lofty sacrificial fire,
Sending forth Maian incense, spread around
Forgetfulness of everything but bliss,
And clouded all the altar with soft smoke;
From whose white fragrant curtains thus I heard
Language pronounc'd: "If thou canst not ascend
"These steps, die on that marble where thou art.
"Thy flesh, near cousin to the common dust,
"Will parch for lack of nutriment—thy bones   110
"Will wither in few years, and vanish so
"That not the quickest eye could find a grain
"Of what thou now art on that pavement cold.
"The sands of thy short life are spent this hour,
"And no hand in the universe can turn
"Thy hourglass, if these gummed leaves be burnt
"Ere thou canst mount up these immortal steps."
I heard, I look'd: two senses both at once,
So fine, so subtle, felt the tyranny
Of that fierce threat and the hard task proposed.   120
Prodigious seem'd the toil; the leaves were yet
Burning—when suddenly a palsied chill
Struck from the paved level up my limbs,
And was ascending quick to put cold grasp
Upon those streams that pulse beside the throat:
I shriek'd, and the sharp anguish of my shriek
Stung my own ears—I strove hard to escape
The numbness; strove to gain the lowest step.
Slow, heavy, deadly was my pace: the cold

Grew stifling, suffocating, at the heart;
And when I clasp'd my hands I felt them not.
One minute before death, my iced foot touch'd
The lowest stair; and as it touch'd, life seem'd
To pour in at the toes: I mounted up,
As once fair angels on a ladder flew
From the green turf to Heaven—"Holy Power,"
Cried I, approaching near the horned shrine,
"What am I that should so be saved from death?
"What am I that another death come not
"To choke my utterance sacrilegious, here?"   140
Then said the veiled shadow—"Thou hast felt
"What 'tis to die and live again before
"Thy fated hour, that thou hadst power to do so
"Is thy own safety; thou hast dated on
Thy doom."—"High Prophetess," said I, "purge off,
Benign, if so it please thee, my mind's film."—
"None can usurp this height," return'd that shade,
"But those to whom the miseries of the world
"Are misery, and will not let them rest.
"All else who find a haven in the world,   150
"Where they may thoughtless sleep away their days,
"If by a chance into this fane they come,
"Rot on the pavement where thou rottedst half."—
"Are there not thousands in the world," said I,
Encourag'd by the sooth voice of the shade,
"Who love their fellows even to the death,
"Who feel the giant agony of the world,
"And more, like slaves to poor humanity,
"Labour for mortal good? I sure should see
"Other men here; but I am here alone."   160
"Those whom thou spak'st of are no vision'ries,"
Rejoin'd that voice—"They are no dreamers weak,
"They seek no wonder but the human face;
"No music but a happy-noted voice—
"They come not here, they have no thought to come—
"And thou art here, for thou art less than they—
"What benefit canst thou, or all thy tribe,
"To the great world? Thou art a dreaming thing,
"A fever of thyself—think of the Earth;
"What bliss even in hope is there for thee?   170
"What haven? every creature hath its home;
"Every sole man hath days of joy and pain,
"Whether his labours be sublime or low—
"The pain alone; the joy alone; distinct:
"Only the dreamer venoms all his days,
"Bearing more woe than all his sins deserve.

"Therefore, that happiness be somewhat shar'd,
"Such things as thou art are admitted oft
"Into like gardens thou didst pass erewhile,
"And suffer'd in these temples: for that cause   180
"Thou standest safe beneath this statue's knees."
"That I am favour'd for unworthiness,
"By such propitious parley medicin'd
"In sickness not ignoble, I rejoice,
"Aye, and could weep for love of such award."
So answer'd I, continuing, "If it please,
"Majestic shadow, tell me: sure not all
"Those melodies sung into the World's ear
"Are useless: sure a poet is a sage;
"A humanist, physician to all men.   190
"That I am none I feel, as vultures feel
"They are no birds when eagles are abroad.
"What am I then: Thou spakest of my tribe:
"What tribe?" The tall shade veil'd in drooping white
Then spake, so much more earnest, that the breath
Moved the thin linen folds that drooping hung
About a golden censer from the hand
Pendent—"Art thou not of the dreamer tribe?
"The poet and the dreamer are distinct,
"Diverse, sheer opposite, antipodes.   200
"The one pours out a balm upon the World,
"The other vexes it." Then shouted I
Spite of myself, and with a Pythia's spleen
"Apollo! faded! O far flown Apollo!
"Where is thy misty pestilence to creep
"Into the dwellings, through the door crannies
"Of all mock lyrists, large self worshipers
"And careless Hectorers in proud bad verse.
"Though I breathe death with them it will be life
"To see them sprawl before me into graves.   210
"Majestic shadow, tell me where I am,
"Whose altar this; for whom this incense curls;
"What image this whose face I cannot see,
"For the broad marble knees; and who thou art,
"Of accent feminine so courteous?"

        Then the tall shade, in drooping linens veil'd
Spoke out, so much more earnest, that her breath
Stirr'd the thin folds of gauze that drooping hung
About a golden censer from her hand
Pendent; and by her voice I knew she shed   220
Long-treasured tears. "This temple, sad and lone,
"Is all spar'd from the thunder of a war

"Foughten long since by giant hierarchy
"Against rebellion: this old image here,
"Whose carved features wrinkled as he fell,
"Is Saturn's; I Moneta, left supreme
"Sole Priestess of this desolation."—
I had no words to answer, for my tongue,
Useless, could find about its roofed home
No syllable of a fit majesty   230
To make rejoinder to Moneta's mourn.
There was a silence, while the altar's blaze
Was fainting for sweet food: I look'd thereon,
And on the paved floor, where nigh were piled
Faggots of cinnamon, and many heaps
Of other crisped spice-wood—then again
I look'd upon the altar, and its horns
Whiten'd with ashes, and its lang'rous flame,
And then upon the offerings again;
And so by turns—till sad Moneta cried,   240
"The sacrifice is done, but not the less
"Will I be kind to thee for thy good will.
"My power, which to me is still a curse,
"Shall be to thee a wonder; for the scenes
"Still swooning vivid through my globed brain,
"With an electral changing misery,
"Thou shalt with these dull mortal eyes behold,
"Free from all pain, if wonder pain thee not."
As near as an immortal's sphered words
Could to a mother's soften, were these last: 250
And yet I had a terror of her robes,
And chiefly of the veils, that from her brow
Hung pale, and curtain'd her in mysteries,
That made my heart too small to hold its blood.
This saw that Goddess, and with sacred hand
Parted the veils. Then saw I a wan face,
Not pin'd by human sorrows, but bright-blanch'd
By an immortal sickness which kills not;
It works a constant change, which happy death
Can put no end to; deathwards progressing   260
To no death was that visage; it had past
The lilly and the snow; and beyond these
I must not think now, though I saw that face—
But for her eyes I should have fled away.
They held me back, with a benignant light,
Soft mitigated by divinest lids
Half-closed, and visionless entire they seem'd
Of all external things;—they saw me not,
But in blank splendour, beam'd like the mild moon,

Who comforts those she sees not, who knows not
What eyes are upward cast. As I had found   271
A grain of gold upon a mountain's side,
And twing'd with avarice strain'd out my eyes
To search its sullen entrails rich with ore,
So at the view of sad Moneta's brow,
I ask'd to see what things the hollow brain
Behind environed: what high tragedy
In the dark secret chambers of her skull
Was acting, that could give so dread a stress
To her cold lips, and fill with such a light   280
Her planetary eyes; and touch her voice
With such a sorrow—"Shade of Memory!"—
Cried I, with act adorant at her feet,
"By all the gloom hung round thy fallen house,
"By this last temple, by the golden age,
"By great Apollo, thy dear Foster Child,
"And by thyself, forlorn divinity,
"The pale Omega of a withered race,
"Let me behold, according as thou saidst,
"What in thy brain so ferments to and fro!"   290
No sooner had this conjuration pass'd
My devout lips, than side by side we stood
(Like a stunt bramble by a solemn pine)
Deep in the shady sadness of a vale,
Far sunken from the healthy breath of morn,
Far from the fiery noon and eve's one star.
Onward I look'd beneath the gloomy boughs,
And saw, what first I thought an image huge,
Like to the image pedestal'd so high
In Saturn's temple. Then Moneta's voice   300
Came brief upon mine ear—"So Saturn sat
When he had lost his Realms—" whereon there grew
A power within me of enormous ken
To see as a god sees, and take the depth
Of things as nimbly as the outward eye
Can size and shape pervade. The lofty theme
At those few words hung vast before my mind,
With half-unravel'd web. I set myself
Upon an eagle's watch, that I might see,
And seeing ne'er forget. No stir of life   310
Was in this shrouded vale, not so much air
As in the zoning of a summer's day
Robs not one light seed from the feather'd grass,
But where the dead leaf fell there did it rest:
A stream went voiceless by, still deaden'd more
By reason of the fallen divinity

Spreading more shade; the Naiad 'mid her reeds
Prest her cold finger closer to her lips.

Along the margin-sand large footmarks went
No farther than to where old Saturn's feet   320
Had rested, and there slept, how long a sleep!
Degraded, cold, upon the sodden ground
His old right hand lay nerveless, listless, dead,
Unsceptred; and his realmless eyes were clos'd,
While his bow'd head seem'd listening to the Earth,
His ancient mother, for some comfort yet.

It seem'd no force could wake him from his place;
But there came one who, with a kindred hand
Touch'd his wide shoulders after bending low
With reverence, though to one who knew it not.   330
Then came the griev'd voice of Mnemosyne,
And griev'd I hearken'd. "That divinity
"Whom thou saw'st step from yon forlornest wood,
"And with slow pace approach our fallen King,
"Is Thea, softest-natur'd of our Brood."
I mark'd the Goddess in fair statuary
Surpassing wan Moneta by the head,
And in her sorrow nearer woman's tears.
There was a listening fear in her regard,
As if calamity had but begun;   340
As if the vanward clouds of evil days
Had spent their malice, and the sullen rear
Was with its stored thunder labouring up.
One hand she press'd upon that aching spot
Where beats the human heart, as if just there,
Though an immortal, she felt cruel pain;
The other upon Saturn's bended neck
She laid, and to the level of his hollow ear
Leaning with parted lips, some words she spake
In solemn tenor and deep organ tune;   350
Some mourning words, which in our feeble tongue
Would come in this-like accenting; how frail
To that large utterance of the early Gods!

"Saturn! look up—and for what, poor lost King?
"I have no comfort for thee; no not one;
"I cannot say, wherefore thus sleepest thou?
"For Heaven is parted from thee, and the Earth
"Knows thee not, so afflicted, for a God;
"And Ocean too, with all its solemn noise,
"Has from thy sceptre pass'd, and all the air   360

"Is emptied of thine hoary majesty:
"Thy thunder, captious at the new command,
"Rumbles reluctant o'er our fallen house;
"And thy sharp lightning, in unpracticed hands,
"Scorches and burns our once serene domain.
"With such remorseless speed still come new woes,
"That unbelief has not a space to breathe.
"Saturn! sleep on:—Me thoughtless, why should I
"Thus violate thy slumbrous solitude?
"Why should I ope thy melancholy eyes?   370
"Saturn, sleep on, while at thy feet I weep."

        As when upon a tranced summer-night
Forests, branch-charmed by the earnest stars,
Dream, and so dream all night without a noise,
Save from one gradual solitary gust,
Swelling upon the silence; dying off;
As if the ebbing air had but one wave;
So came these words, and went; the while in tears
She prest her fair large forehead to the earth,   379
Just where her fallen hair might spread in curls,
A soft and silken mat for Saturn's feet.
Long, long these two were postured motionless,
Like sculpture builded-up upon the grave
Of their own power. A long awful time
I look'd upon them: still they were the same;
The frozen God still bending to the earth,
And the sad Goddess weeping at his feet,
Moneta silent. Without stay or prop,
But my own weak mortality, I bore
The load of this eternal quietude,   390
The unchanging gloom, and the three fixed shapes
Ponderous upon my senses, a whole moon.
For by my burning brain I measured sure
Her silver seasons shedded on the night,
And every day by day methought I grew
More gaunt and ghostly.—Oftentimes I pray'd
Intense, that Death would take me from the Vale
And all its burthens—gasping with despair
Of change, hour after hour I curs'd myself;
Until old Saturn rais'd his faded eyes,   400
And look'd around and saw his kingdom gone,
And all the gloom and sorrow of the place,
And that fair kneeling Goddess at his feet.
As the moist scent of flowers, and grass, and leaves,
Fills forest dells with a pervading air,
Known to the woodland nostril, so the words

Of Saturn fill'd the mossy glooms around,
Even to the hollows of time-eaten oaks,
And to the windings of the foxes' hole,
With sad low tones, while thus he spake, and sent
Strange musings to the solitary Pan.
"Moan, brethren, moan; for we are swallow'd up
"And buried from all Godlike exercise
"Of influence benign on planets pale,
"And peaceful sway above man's harvesting,   415
"And all those acts which Deity supreme
"Doth ease its heart of love in. Moan and wail,
"Moan, brethren, moan; for lo, the rebel spheres
"Spin round, the stars their ancient courses keep,
"Clouds still with shadowy moisture haunt the earth,
"Still suck their fill of light from sun and moon;
"Still buds the tree, and still the sea-shores murmur;
"There is no death in all the Universe,   423
"No smell of death—there shall be death—Moan, moan,
"Moan, Cybele, moan; for thy pernicious Babes
"Have changed a god into an aching Palsy.
"Moan, brethren, moan, for I nave no strength left,
"Weak as the reed—weak—feeble as my voice—
"O, O, the pain, the pain of feebleness.
"Moan, moan, for still I thaw—or give me help;
"Throw down those imps, and give me victory.   431
"Let me hear other groans, and trumpets blown
"Of triumph calm, and hymns of festival,
"From the gold peaks of Heaven's high-piled clouds;
"Voices of soft proclaim, and silver stir
"Of strings in hollow shells; and there shall be
"Beautiful things made new for the surprise
"Of the sky-children." So he feebly ceas'd,
With such a poor and sickly sounding pause,
Methought I heard some old man of the earth   440
Bewailing earthly loss; nor could my eyes
And ears act with that pleasant unison of sense
Which marries sweet sound with the grace of form.
And dolorous accent from a tragic harp
With large-limb'd visions.—More I scrutinized:
Still fix'd he sat beneath the sable trees,
Whose arms spread straggling in wild serpent forms,
With leaves all hush'd; his awful presence there
(Now all was silent) gave a deadly lie
To what I erewhile heard—only his lips   450
Trembled amid the white curls of his beard.
They told the truth, though, round, the snowy locks
Hung nobly, as upon the face of heaven

A mid-day fleece of clouds. Thea arose,
And stretched her white arm through the hollow dark,
Pointing some whither: whereat he too rose
Like a vast giant, seen by men at sea
To grow pale from the waves at dull midnight.
They melted from my sight into the woods;
Ere I could turn, Moneta cried, "These twain
"Are speeding to the families of grief,
"Where roof'd in by black rocks they waste, in pain
"And darkness, for no hope."—And she spake on,
As ye may read who can unwearied pass
Onward from th' Antichamber of this dream,
Where even at the open doors awhile
I must delay, and glean my memory
Of her high phrase:—perhaps no further dare.

END OF CANTO I

CANTO II

"MORTAL, that thou may'st understand aright,
"I humanize my sayings to thine ear,
"Making comparisons of earthly things;
"Or thou might'st better listen to the wind,
"Whose language is to thee a barren noise,
"Though it blows legend-laden thro' the trees.—
"In melancholy realms big tears are shed,
"More sorrow like to this, and such like woe,
"Too huge for mortal tongue, or pen of scribe.
"The Titans fierce, self hid or prison bound,
"Groan for the old allegiance once more,
"Listening in their doom for Saturn's voice.
"But one of our whole eagle-brood still keeps
"His sov'reignty, and rule, and majesty;
"Blazing Hyperion on his orbed fire
"Still sits, still snuffs the incense teeming up
"From Man to the Sun's God: yet unsecure.
"For as upon the earth dire prodigies
"Fright and perplex, so also shudders he:
"Nor at dog's howl or gloom-bird's Even screech,
"Or the familiar visitings of one
"Upon the first toll of his passing bell:
"But horrors, portioned to a giant nerve,
"Make great Hyperion ache. His palace bright,
"Bastion'd with pyramids of glowing gold,
"And touch'd with shade of bronzed obelisks,
"Glares a blood-red thro' all the thousand courts,

"Arches, and domes, and fiery galleries:
"And all its curtains of Aurorian clouds
"Flush angerly; when he would taste the wreaths   30
"Of incense breathed aloft from sacred hills,
"Instead of sweets, his ample palate takes
"Savour of poisonous brass and metals sick.
"Wherefore when harbour'd in the sleepy West,
"After the full completion of fair day,
"For rest divine upon exalted couch
"And slumber in the arms of melody,
"He paces through the pleasant hours of ease
"With strides colossal, on from hall to hall;
"While far within each aisle and deep recess   40
"His winged minions in close clusters stand
"Amaz'd, and full of fear; like anxious men,
"Who on a wide plain gather in sad troops,
"When earthquakes jar their battlements and towers.
"Even now, while Saturn, roused from icy trance,
"Goes, step for step, with Thea from yon woods,
"Hyperion, leaving twilight in the rear,
"Is sloping to the threshold of the West.—
"Thither we tend."—Now in clear light I stood,
Reliev'd from the dusk vale. Mnemosyne   50
Was sitting on a square-edg'd polish'd stone,
That in its lucid depth reflected pure
Her priestess-garments.—My quick eyes ran on
From stately nave to nave, from vault to vault,
Through bow'rs of fragrant and enwreathed light
And diamond-paved lustrous long arcades.
Anon rush'd by the bright Hyperion;
His flaming robes stream'd out beyond his heels,
And gave a roar, as if of earthly fire,
That scared away the meek ethereal hours,   60
And made their dove-wings tremble. On he flared.

THE CAP AND BELLS

OR THE JEALOUSIES

A FAERY TALE—UNFINISHED

THE CAP AND BELLS

OR THE JEALOUSIES

I

In midmost Ind, beside Hydaspes cool,
There stood, or hover'd, tremulous in the air,
A faery city, 'neath the potent rule
Of Emperor Elfinan; fam'd ev'rywhere
For love of mortal women, maidens fair,
Whose lips were solid, whose soft hands were made
Of a fit mould and beauty, ripe and rare,
To pamper his slight wooing, warm yet staid:
He lov'd girls smooth as shades, but hated a mere shade.

II

This was a crime forbidden by the law;
And all the priesthood of his city wept,
For ruin and dismay they well foresaw,
If impious prince no bound or limit kept,
And faery Zendervester overstept;
They wept, he sin'd, and still he would sin on,
They dreamt of sin, and he sin'd while they slept;
In vain the pulpit thunder'd at the throne,
Caricature was vain, and vain the tart lampoon.

III

Which seeing, his high court of parliament
Laid a remonstrance at his Highness' feet,
Praying his royal senses to content
Themselves with what in faery land was sweet,
Befitting best that shade with shade should meet:
Whereat, to calm their fears, he promis'd soon
From mortal tempters all to make retreat,—
Aye, even on the first of the new moon,
An immaterial wife to espouse as heaven's boon.

367

IV

Meantime he sent a fluttering embassy
To Pigmio, of Imaus sovereign,
To half beg, and half demand, respectfully,
The hand of his fair daughter Bellanaine;
An audience had, and speeching done, they gain
Their point, and bring the weeping bride away;
Whom, with but one attendant, safely lain
Upon their wings, they bore in bright array,
While little harps were touch'd by many a lyric fay.

V

As in old pictures tender cherubim
A child's soul thro' the sapphir'd canvas bear,
So, thro' a real heaven, on they swim
With the sweet princess on her plumag'd lair,
Speed giving to the winds her lustrous hair;
And so she journey'd, sleeping or awake,
Save when, for healthful exercise and air,
She chose to *promener à l'aile*, or take
A pigeon's somerset, for sport or change's sake.

VI

"Dear Princess, do not whisper me so loud,"
Quoth Corallina, nurse and confidant,
"Do not you see there, lurking in a cloud,
Close at your back, that sly old Crafticant?
He hears a whisper plainer than a rant:
Dry up your tears, and do not look so blue;
He's Elfinan's great state-spy militant,
His running, lying, flying foot-man too,—
Dear mistress, let him have no handle against you!

VII

"Show him a mouse's tail, and he will guess,
With metaphysic swiftness, at the mouse;
Show him a garden, and with speed no less,
He'll surmise sagely of a dwelling house,
And plot, in the same minute, how to chouse
The owner out of it; show him a"— "Peace!
Peace! nor contrive thy mistress' ire to rouse!"
Return'd the Princess, "my tongue shall not cease
Till from this hated match I get a free release.

VIII

"Ah, beauteous mortal!" "Hush!" quoth **Coralline,**
"Really you must not talk of him, indeed."
"You hush!" replied the mistress, with a shine
Of anger in her eyes, enough to breed
In stouter hearts than nurse's fear and dread:
'Twas not the glance itself made nursey flinch,
But of its threat she took the utmost heed;
Not liking in her heart an hour-long pinch,
Or a sharp needle run into her back an inch.

IX

So she was silenc'd, and fair Bellanaine,
Writhing her little body with ennui,
Continued to lament and to complain,
That Fate, cross-purposing, should let her be
Ravish'd away far from her dear countree;
That all her feelings should be set at naught,
In trumping up this match so hastily,
With lowland blood; and lowland blood she thought
Poison, as every staunch true-born Imaian ought.

X

Sorely she griev'd, and wetted three or four
White Provence rose-leaves with her faery tears,
But not for this cause;—alas! she had more
Bad reasons for her sorrow, as appears
In the fam'd memoirs of a thousand years,
Written by Crafticant, and published
By Parpaglion and Co., (those sly compeers
Who rak'd up ev'ry fact against the dead,)
In Scarab Street, Panthea, at the Jubal's Head.

XI

Where, after a long hypercritic howl
Against the vicious manners of the age
He goes on to expose, with heart and soul,
What vice in this or that year was the rage,
Backbiting all the world in every page;
With special strictures on the horrid crime,
(Section'd and subsection'd with learning sage,)
Of faeries stooping on their wings sublime
To kiss a mortal's lips, when such were in their prime.

XII

Turn to the copious index, you will find
Somewhere in the column, headed letter B,
The name of Bellanaine, if you're not blind;
Then pray refer to the text, and you will see
An article made up of calumny
Against this highland princess, rating her
For giving way, so over fashionably,
To this new-fangled vice, which seems a burr
Stuck in his moral throat, no coughing e'er could stir.

XIII

There he says plainly that she lov'd a man!
That she around him flutter'd, flirted, toy'd,
Before her marriage with great Elfinan;
That after marriage too, she never joy'd
In husband's company, but still employ'd
Her wits to 'scape away to Angle-land;
Where liv'd the youth, who worried and annoy'd
Her tender heart, and its warm ardours fann'd
To such a dreadful blaze, her side would scorch her hand.

XIV

But let us leave this idle tittle-tattle
To waiting-maids, and bed-room coteries,
Nor till fit time against her fame wage battle.
Poor Elfinan is very ill at ease,
Let us resume his subject if you please:
For it may comfort and console him much
To rhyme and syllable his miseries;
Poor Elfinan! whose cruel fate was such,
He sat and curs'd a bride he knew he could not touch.

XV

Soon as (according to his promises)
The bridal embassy had taken wing,
And vanish'd, bird-like, o'er the suburb trees,
The Emperor, empierc'd with the sharp sting
Of love, retired, vex'd and murmuring
Like any drone shut from the fair bee-queen,
Into his cabinet, and there did fling
His limbs upon a sofa, full of spleen,
And damn'd his House of Commons, in complete chagrin.

XVI

"I'll trounce some of the members," cried the Prince,
"I'll put a mark against some rebel names,
I'll make the Opposition-benches wince,
I'll show them very soon, to all their shames,
What 'tis to smother up a Prince's flames;
That ministers should join in it, I own,
Surprises me!—they too at these high games!
Am I an Emperor? Do I wear a crown?
Imperial Elfinan, go hang thyself or drown!

XVII

"I'll trounce 'em!—there's the square-cut chancellor,
His son shall never touch that bishopric;
And for the nephew of old Palfior,
I'll show him that his speech has made me sick,
And give the colonelcy to Phalaric;
The tiptoe marquis, moral and gallant,
Shall lodge in shabby taverns upon tick;
And for the Speaker's second cousin's aunt,
She sha'n't be maid of honour,—by heaven that she sha'n't!

XVIII

"I'll shirk the Duke of A.; I'll cut his brother;
I'll give no garter to his eldest son;
I won't speak to his sister or his mother!
The Viscount B. shall live at cut-and-run;
But how in the world can I contrive to stun
That fellow's voice, which plagues me worse than any,
That stubborn fool, that impudent state-dun,
Who sets down ev'ry sovereign as a zany,—
That vulgar commoner, Esquire Biancopany?

XIX

"Monstrous affair! Pshaw! pah! what ugly minx
Will they fetch from Imaus for my bride?
Alas! my wearied heart within me sinks,
To think that I must be so near allied
To a cold dullard fay,—ah, woe betide!
Ah, fairest of all human loveliness!
Sweet Bertha! what crime can it be to glide
About the fragrant pleatings of thy dress,
Or kiss thine eyes, or count thy locks, tress after tress?"

XX

So said, one minute's while his eyes remain'd
Half lidded, piteous, languid, innocent;
But, in a wink, their splendour they regain'd,
Sparkling revenge with amorous fury blent.
Love thwarted in bad temper oft has vent:
He rose, he stampt his foot, he rang the bell,
And order'd some death-warrants to be sent
For signature:—somewhere the tempest fell,
As many a poor felon does not live to tell.

XXI

"At the same time Eban,"—(this was his page,
A fay of colour, slave from top to toe,
Sent as a present, while yet under age,
From the Viceroy of Zanguebar,—wise, slow,
His speech, his only words were "yes" and "no,"
But swift of look, and foot, and wing was he,—)
"At the same time, Eban, this instant go
To Hum the soothsayer, whose name I see
Among the fresh arrivals in our empery.

XXII

"Bring Hum to me! But stay—here, take my ring,
The pledge of favour, that he not suspect
Any foul play, or awkward murdering,
Tho' I have bowstrung many of his sect;
Throw in a hint, that if he should neglect
One hour, the next shall see him in my grasp,
And the next after that shall see him neck'd,
Or swallow'd by my hunger-starved asp,—
And mention ('tis as well) the torture of the wasp."

XXIII

These orders given, the Prince, in half a pet,
Let o'er the silk his propping elbow slide,
Caught up his little legs, and, in a fret,
Fell on the sofa on his royal side.
The slave retreated backwards, humble-eyed,
And with a slave-like silence clos'd the door,
And to old Hum thro' street and alley hied;
He "knew the city," as we say, of yore,
And for short cuts and turns, was nobody knew more.

XXIV

It was the time when wholesale houses close
Their shutters with a moody sense of wealth,
But retail dealers, diligent, let loose
The gas (objected to on score of health),
Convey'd in little solder'd pipes by stealth,
And make it flare in many a brilliant form,
That all the powers of darkness it repell'th,
Which to the oil-trade doth great scaith and harm,
And supersedeth quite the use of the glow-worm.

XXV

Eban, untempted by the pastry-cooks,
(Of pastry he got store within the palace,)
With hasty steps, wrapp'd cloak, and solemn looks,
Incognito upon his errand sallies,
His smelling-bottle ready for the allies;
He pass'd the Hurdy-gurdies with disdain,
Vowing he'd have them sent aboard the gallies;
Just as he made his vow, it 'gan to rain,
Therefore he call'd a coach, and bade it drive amain.

XXVI

"I'll pull the string," said he, and further said,
"Polluted Jarvey! Ah, thou filthy hack!
Whose springs of life are all dried up and dead,
Whose linsey-woolsey lining hangs all slack,
Whose rug is straw, whose wholeness is a crack;
And evermore thy steps go clatter-clitter;
Whose glass once up can never be got back,
Who prov'st, with jolting arguments and bitter,
That 'tis of modern use to travel in a litter.

XXVII

"Thou inconvenience! thou hungry crop
For all corn! thou snail-creeper to and fro,
Who while thou goest ever seem'st to stop,
And fiddle-faddle standest while you go;
I' the morning, freighted with a weight of woe,
Unto some lazar-house thou journeyest,
And in the evening tak'st a double row
Of dowdies, for some dance or party drest,
Besides the goods meanwhile thou movest east and west.

XXVIII

"By thy ungallant bearing and sad mien,
An inch appears the utmost thou couldst budge;
Yet at the slightest nod, or hint, or sign,
Round to the curb-stone patient dost thou trudge,
School'd in a beckon, learned in a nudge,
A dull-eyed Argus watching for a fare;
Quiet and plodding, thou dost bear no grudge
To whisking Tilburies, or Phaetons rare,
Curricles, or Mail-coaches, swift beyond compare."

XXIX

Philosophizing thus, he pull'd the check,
And bade the Coachman wheel to such a street,
Who, turning much his body, more his neck,
Louted full low, and hoarsely did him greet:
"Certes, Monsieur were best take to his feet,
Seeing his servant can no further drive
For press of coaches, that to-night here meet
Many as bees about a straw-capp'd hive,
When first for April honey into faint flowers they dive."

XXX

Eban then paid his fare, and tiptoe went
To Hum's hotel; and, as he on did pass
With head inclin'd, each dusky lineament
Show'd in the pearl-pav'd street, as in a glass;
His purple vest, that ever peeping was
Rich from the fluttering crimson of his cloak,
His silvery trowsers, and his silken sash
Tied in a burnish'd knot, their semblance took
Upon the mirror'd walls, wherever he might look.

XXXI

He smil'd at self, and, smiling, show'd his teeth,
And seeing his white teeth, he smil'd the more;
Lifted his eye-brows, spurn'd the path beneath,
Show'd teeth again, and smil'd as heretofore,
Until he knock'd at the magician's door;
Where, till the porter answer'd, might be seen,
In the clear panel more he could adore,—
His turban wreath'd of gold, and white, and green,
Mustachios, ear-ring, nose-ring, and his sabre keen.

XXXII

"Does not your master give a rout to-night?"
Quoth the dark page. "Oh, no!" return'd the Swiss,
"Next door but one to us, upon the right,
The *Magazin des Modes* now open is
Against the Emperor's wedding;—and, sir, this
My master finds a monstrous horrid bore;
As he retir'd, an hour ago I wis,
With his best beard and brimstone, to explore
And cast a quiet figure in his second floor.

XXXIII

"Gad! he's oblig'd to stick to business!
For chalk, I hear, stands at a pretty price;
And as for aqua vitæ—there's a mess!
The *dentes sapientiæ* of mice,
Our barber tells me too, are on the rise,—
Tinder's a lighter article,—nitre pure
Goes off like lightning,—grains of Paradise
At an enormous figure!—stars not sure!—
Zodiac will not move without a sly douceur!

XXXIV

"Venus won't stir a peg without a fee,
And master is too partial, *entre nous,*
To"— "Hush—hush!" cried Eban, "sure that is he
Coming down stairs,—by St. Bartholomew!
As backwards as he can,—is 't something new?
Or is 't his custom, in the name of fun?"
"He always comes down backward, with one shoe"—
Return'd the porter—"off, and one shoe on,
Like, saving shoe for sock or stocking, my man John!"

XXXV

It was indeed the great Magician,
Feeling, with careful toe, for every stair,
And retrograding careful as he can,
Backwards and downwards from his own two pair:
"Salpietro!" exclaim'd Hum, "is the dog there?
He's always in my way upon the mat!"
"He's in the kitchen, or the Lord knows where,"—
Replied the Swiss,—"the nasty, yelping brat!"
"Don't beat him!" return'd Hum, and on the floor came pat.

XXXVI

Then facing right about, he saw the Page,
And said: "Don't tell me what you want, Eban;
The Emperor is now in a huge rage,—
'Tis nine to one he'll give you the rattan!
Let us away!" Away together ran
The plain-dress'd sage and spangled blackamoor,
Nor rested till they stood to cool, and fan,
And breathe themselves at the Emperor's chamber door,
When Eban thought he heard a soft imperial snore.

XXXVII

"I thought you guess'd, foretold, or prophesied,
That 's Majesty was in a raving fit?"
"He dreams," said Hum, "or I have ever lied,
That he is tearing you, sir, bit by bit."
"He's not asleep, and you have little wit,"
Replied the page: "that little buzzing noise,
Whate'er your palmistry may make of it,
Comes from a play-thing of the Emperor's choice,
From a Man-Tiger-Organ, prettiest of his toys."

XXXVIII

Eban then usher'd in the learned Seer:
Elfinan's back was turn'd, but, ne'ertheless,
Both, prostrate on the carpet, ear by ear,
Crept silently, and waited in distress,
Knowing the Emperor's moody bitterness;
Eban especially, who on the floor 'gan
Tremble and quake to death,—he feared less
A dose of senna-tea or nightmare Gorgon
Than the Emperor when he play'd on his Man-Tiger-Organ.

XXXIX

They kiss'd nine times the carpet's velvet face
Of glossy silk, soft, smooth, and meadow-green,
Where the close eye in deep rich fur might trace
A silver tissue, scantly to be seen,
As daisies lurk'd in June-grass, buds in treen;
Sudden the music ceased, sudden the hand
Of majesty, by dint of passion keen,
Doubled into a common fist, went grand,
And knock'd down three cut glasses, and his best ink-stand.

XL

Then turning round, he saw those trembling two:
"Eban," said he, "as slaves should taste the fruits
Of diligence, I shall remember you
To-morrow, or the next day, as time suits,
In a finger conversation with my mutes,—
Begone!—for you, Chaldean! here remain!
Fear not, quake not, and as good wine recruits
A conjurer's spirits, what cup will you drain?
Sherry in silver, hock in gold, or glass'd champagne?"

XLI

"Commander of the Faithful!" answer'd Hum,
"In preference to these, I'll merely taste
A thimble-full of old Jamaica rum."
"A simple boon!" said Elfinan; "thou may'st
Have Nantz, with which my morning-coffee's lac'd."
"I'll have a glass of Nantz, then," said the Seer,—
"Made racy—(sure my boldness is misplac'd!)—
With the third part—(yet that is drinking dear!)—
Of the least drop of *crème de citron,* crystal clear."

XLII

"I pledge you, Hum! and pledge my dearest love,
My Bertha!" "Bertha! Bertha!" cried the sage,
"I know a many Berthas!" "Mine's above
All Berthas!" sighed the Emperor. "I engage,"
Said Hum, "in duty, and in vassalage,
To mention all the Berthas in the Earth;—
There's Bertha Watson,—and Miss Bertha Page,—
This fam'd for languid eyes, and that for mirth,—
There's Bertha Blount of York,—and Bertha Knox of Perth."

XLIII

"You seem to know"—"I do know," answer'd Hum,
"Your Majesty's in love with some fine girl
Named Bertha; but her surname will not come,
Without a little conjuring." "'Tis Pearl,
'Tis Bertha Pearl that makes my brains so whirl;
And she is softer, fairer than her name!"
"Where does she live?" ask'd Hum. "Her fair locks curl
So brightly, they put all our fays to shame!—
Live?—O! at Canterbury, with her old grand-dame."

XLIV

"Good! good!" cried Hum, "I've known her from a child!
She is a changeling of my management;
She was born at midnight in an Indian wild;
Her mother's screams with the striped tiger's blent,
While the torch-bearing slaves a halloo sent
Into the jungles; and her palanquin,
Rested amid the desert's dreariment,
Shook with her agony, till fair were seen
The little Bertha's eyes oped on the stars serene."

XLV

"I can't say," said the monarch; "that may be
Just as it happen'd, true or else a bam!
Drink up your brandy, and sit down by me,
Feel, feel my pulse, how much in love I am;
And if your science is not all a sham,
Tell me some means to get the lady here."
"Upon my honour!" said the son of Cham,
"She is my dainty changeling, near and dear,
Although her story sounds at first a little queer."

XLVI

"Convey her to me, Hum, or by my crown,
My sceptre, and my cross-surmounted globe,
I'll knock you"—"Does your majesty mean—*down?*
No, no, you never could my feelings probe
To such a depth!" The Emperor took his robe,
And wept upon its purple palatine,
While Hum continued, shamming half a sob,—
"In Canterbury doth your lady shine?
But let me cool your brandy with a little wine."

XLVII

Whereat a narrow Flemish glass he took,
That once belong'd to Admiral de Witt,
Admir'd it with a connoisseuring look,
And with the ripest claret crowned it,
And, ere one lively bead could burst and flit,
He turn'd it quickly, nimbly upside down,
His mouth being held conveniently fit
To catch the treasure: "Best in all the town!"
He said, smack'd his moist lips, and gave a pleasant frown.

XLVIII

"Ah! good my Prince, weep not!" And then again
He fill'd a bumper. "Great Sire, do not weep!
Your pulse is shocking, but I'll ease your pain."
"Fetch me that Ottoman, and prithee keep
Your voice low," said the Emperor; "and steep
Some lady's-fingers nice in Candy wine;
And prithee, Hum, behind the screen do peep
For the rose-water vase, magician mine!
And sponge my forehead,—so my love doth make me pine.

XLIX

"Ah, cursed Bellanaine!" "Don't think of her,"
Rejoin'd the Mago, "but on Bertha muse;
For, by my choicest best barometer,
You shall not throttled be in marriage noose;
I've said it, Sire; you only have to choose
Bertha or Bellanaine." So saying, he drew
From the left pocket of his threadbare hose,
A sampler hoarded slyly, good as new,
Holding it by his thumb and finger full in view.

L

"Sire, this is Bertha Pearl's neat handy-work,
Her *name*, see here, *Midsummer, ninety-one*."
Elfinan snatch'd it with a sudden jerk,
And wept as if he never would have done,
Honouring with royal tears the poor homespun;
Whereon were broider'd tigers with black eyes,
And long-tail'd pheasants, and a rising sun,
Plenty of posies, great stags, butterflies
Bigger than stags,—a moon,—with other mysteries.

LI

The monarch handled o'er and o'er again
These day-school hieroglyphics with a sigh;
Somewhat in sadness, but pleas'd in the main,
Till this oracular couplet met his eye
Astounded—*Cupid I, do thee defy!*
It was too much. He shrunk back in his chair,
Grew pale as death, and fainted—very nigh!
"Pho! nonsense!" exclaim'd Hum, "now don't despair;
She does not mean it really. Cheer up hearty there!

LII

"And listen to my words. You say you won't,
On any terms, marry Miss Bellanaine;
It goes against your conscience—good! Well, don't.
You say you love a mortal. I would fain
Persuade your honour's highness to refrain
From peccadilloes. But, Sire, as I say,
What good would that do? And, to be more plain,
You would do me a mischief some odd day,
Cut off my ears and hands, or head too, by my fay!

LIII

"Besides, manners forbid that I should pass any
Vile strictures on the conduct of a prince
Who should indulge his genius, if he has any,
Not, like a subject, foolish matters mince.
Now I think on 't, perhaps I could convince
Your Majesty there is no crime at all
In loving pretty little Bertha, since
She's very delicate,—not over tall,—
A fairy's hand, and in the waist, why—very small."

LIV

"Ring the repeater, gentle Hum!" " 'Tis five,"
Said gentle Hum; "the nights draw in apace;
The little birds I hear are all alive;
I see the dawning touch'd upon your face;
Shall I put out the candles, please your Grace?"
"Do put them out, and, without more ado,
Tell me how I may that sweet girl embrace,—
How you can bring her to me." "That's for you,
Great Emperor! to adventure, like a lover true."

LV

"I fetch her!"—"Yes, an 't like your Majesty;
And as she would be frighten'd wide awake
To travel such a distance through the sky,
Use of some soft manœuvre you must make,
For your convenience, and her dear nerves' sake;
Nice way would be to bring her in a swoon,
Anon, I'll tell what course were best to take;
You must away this morning." "Hum! so soon?"
"Sire, you must be in Kent by twelve o'clock at noon."

LVI

At this great Cæsar started on his feet,
Lifted his wings and stood attentive-wise.
"Those wings to Canterbury you must beat,
If you hold Bertha as a worthy prize.
Look in the Almanack—*Moore* never lies—
April the twenty-fourth—this coming day,
Now breathing its new bloom upon the skies,
Will end in St. Mark's Eve;—you must away,
For on that eve alone can you the maid convey."

LVII

Then the magician solemnly 'gan frown,
So that his frost-white eyebrows, beetling low,
Shaded his deep-green eyes, and wrinkles brown
Plaited upon his furnace-scorched brow:
Forth from the hood that hung his neck below,
He lifted a bright casket of pure gold,
Touch'd a spring-lock, and there in wool, or snow
Charm'd into ever-freezing, lay an old
And legend-leaved book, mysterious to behold.

LVIII

"Take this same book,—it will not bite you, Sire;
There, put it underneath your royal arm;
Though it's a pretty weight it will not tire,
But rather on your journey keep you warm:
This is the magic, this the potent charm,
That shall drive Bertha to a fainting fit!
When the time comes, don't feel the least alarm,
Uplift her from the ground, and swiftly flit
Back to your palace, where I wait for guerdon fit."

LIX

"What shall I do with this same book?" "Why merely
Lay it on Bertha's table, close beside
Her work-box, and 'twill help your purpose dearly;
I say no more." "Or good or ill betide,
Through the wide air to Kent this morn I glide!"
Exclaim'd the Emperor. "When I return,
Ask what you will,—I'll give you my new bride!
And take some more wine, Hum;—O Heavens! I burn
To be upon the wing! Now, now, that minx I spurn!"

LX

"Leave her to me," rejoin'd the magian:
"But how shall I account, illustrious fay!
For thine imperial absence? Pho! I can
Say you are very sick, and bar the way
To your so loving courtiers for one day;
If either of their two archbishops' graces
Should talk of extreme unction, I shall say
You do not like cold pig with Latin phrases,
Which never should be used but in alarming cases."

LXI

"Open the window, Hum; I'm ready now!"
"Zooks!" exclaim'd Hum, as up the sash he drew,
"Behold, your Majesty, upon the brow
Of yonder hill, what crowds of people!" "Whew!
The monster's always after something new,"
Return'd his Highness, "they are piping hot
To see my pigsny Bellanaine. Hum! do
Tighten my belt a little,—so, so,—not
Too tight,—the book!—my wand!—so, nothing is forgot."

LXII

"Wounds! how they shout!" said Hum, "and there,—see, see!
The Ambassadors return'd from Pigmio!
The morning's very fine,—uncommonly!
See, past the skirts of yon white cloud they go,
Tinging it with soft crimsons! Now below
The sable-pointed heads of firs and pines
They dip, move on, and with them moves a glow
Along the forest side! Now amber lines
Reach the hill top, and now throughout the valley shines."

LXIII

"Why, Hum, you're getting quite poetical!
Those *nows* you managed in a special style."
"If ever you have leisure, Sire, you shall
See scraps of mine will make it worth your while,
Tit-bits for Phœbus!—yes, you well may smile.
Hark! Hah! the bells!" "A little further yet,
Good Hum, and let me view this mighty coil."
Then the great Emperor full graceful set
His elbow for a prop, and snuff'd his mignonnette.

LXIV

The morn is full of holiday; loud bells
With rival clamours ring from every spire;
Cunningly-station'd music dies and swells
In echoing places; when the winds respire,
Light flags stream out like gauzy tongues of fire;
A metropolitan murmur, lifeful, warm,
Comes from the northern suburbs; rich attire
Freckles with red and gold the moving swarm;
While here and there clear trumpets blow a keen alarm.

LXV

And now the fairy escort was seen clear,
Like the old pageant of Aurora's train,
Above a pearl-built minster, hovering near;
First wily Crafticant, the chamberlain,
Balanc'd upon his grey-grown pinions twain,
His slender wand officially reveal'd;
Then black gnomes scattering sixpences like rain;
Then pages three and three; and next, slave-held,
The Imaian 'scutcheon bright,—one mouse in argent field.

LXVI

Gentlemen pensioners next; and after them,
A troop of winged Janizaries flew;
Then Slaves, as presents bearing many a gem;
Then twelve physicians fluttering two and two;
And next a chaplain in a cassock new;
Then Lords in waiting; then (what head not reels
For pleasure?)—the fair Princess in full view,
Borne upon wings,—and very pleas'd she feels
To have such splendour dance attendance at her heels.

LXVII

For there was more magnificence behind:
She wav'd her handkerchief. "Ah, very grand!"
Cried Elfinan, and clos'd the window-blind;
"And, Hum, we must not shilly-shally stand,—
Adieu! adieu! I'm off for Angle-land!
I say, old Hocus, have you such a thing
About you,—feel your pockets, I command,—
I want, this instant, an invisible ring,—
Thank you, old mummy!—now securely I take wing."

LXVIII

Then Elfinan swift vaulted from the floor,
And lighted graceful on the window-sill;
Under one arm the magic book he bore,
The other he could wave about at will;
Pale was his face, he still look'd very ill:
He bow'd at Bellanaine, and said—"Poor Bell!
Farewell! farewell! and if for ever! still
For ever fare thee well!"—and then he fell
A laughing!—snapp'd his fingers!—shame it is to tell!

LXIX

"By'r Lady! he is gone!" cries Hum, "and I—
(I own it)—have made too free with his wine;
Old Crafticant will smoke me. By the bye—
This room is full of jewels as a mine,—
Dear valuable creatures, how ye shine!
Sometime to-day I must contrive a minute,
If Mercury propitiously incline,
To examine his scrutoire, and see what's in it,
For of superfluous diamonds I as well may thin it.

LXX

"The Emperor's horrid bad; yes, that's my cue!"
Some histories say that this was Hum's last speech;
That, being fuddled, he went reeling through
The corridor, and scarce upright could reach
The stair-head; that being glutted as a leech,
And us'd, as we ourselves have just now said,
To manage stairs reversely, like a peach
Too ripe, he fell, being puzzled in his head
With liquor and the staircase: verdict—*found stone dead.*

LXXI

This as a falsehood Crafticanto treats;
And as his style is of strange elegance,
Gentle and tender, full of soft conceits,
(Much like our Boswell's,) we will take a glance
At his sweet prose, and, if we can, make dance
His woven periods into careless rhyme;
O, little faery Pegasus! rear—prance—
Trot round the quarto—ordinary time!
March, little Pegasus, with pawing hoof sublime!

LXXII

Well, let us see,—*tenth book and chapter nine,*—
Thus Crafticant pursues his diary:—
" 'Twas twelve o'clock at night, the weather fine,
Latitude thirty-six; our scouts descry
A flight of starlings making rapidly
Towards Thibet. Mem.:—birds fly in the night;
From twelve to half-past—wings not fit to fly
For a thick fog—the Princess sulky quite
Call'd for an extra shawl, and gave her nurse a bite.

LXXIII

"Five minutes before one—brought down a moth
With my new double-barrel—stew'd the thighs
And made a very tolerable broth—
Princess turn'd dainty;—to our great surprise,
Alter'd her mind, and thought it very nice:
Seeing her pleasant, tried her with a pun,
She frown'd; a monstrous owl across us flies
About this time,—a sad old figure of fun;
Bad omen—this new match can't be a happy one.

LXXIV

"From two till half-past, dusky way we made,
Above the plains of Gobi,—desert, bleak;
Beheld afar off, in the hooded shade
Of darkness, a great mountain (strange to speak),
Spitting, from forth its sulphur-baken peak,
A fan-shap'd burst of blood-red, arrowy fire,
Turban'd with smoke, which still away did reek,
Solid and black from that eternal pyre,
Upon the laden wind that scantly could respire.

LXXV

"Just upon three o'clock a falling star
Created an alarm among our troop,
Kill'd a man-cook, a page, and broke a jar,
A tureen, and three dishes, at one swoop,
Then passing by the Princess, singed her hoop:
Could not conceive what Coralline was at,
She clapp'd her hands three times and cried out 'Whoop!'
Some strange Imaian custom. A large bat
Came sudden 'fore my face, and brush'd against my hat.

LXXVI

"Five minutes thirteen seconds after three,
Far in the west a mighty fire broke out,
Conjectur'd, on the instant, it might be
The city of Balk—'twas Balk beyond all doubt:
A Griffin, wheeling here and there about,
Kept reconnoitring us—doubled our guard—
Lighted our torches, and kept up a shout,
Till he sheer'd off—the Princess very scar'd—
And many on their marrow-bones for death prepar'd.

LXXVII

"At half-past three arose the cheerful moon—
Bivouack'd for four minutes on a cloud—
Where from the earth we heard a lively tune
Of tambourines and pipes, serene and loud,
While on a flowery lawn a brilliant crowd
Cinque-parted danc'd, some half asleep reposed
Beneath the green-fan'd cedars, some did shroud
In silken tents, and 'mid light fragrance dozed,
Or on the open turf their soothed eyelids closed.

LXXVIII

"Dropp'd my gold watch, and kill'd a kettledrum—
It went for apoplexy—foolish folks!—
Left it to pay the piper—a good sum—
(I've got a conscience, maugre people's jokes;)
To scrape a little favour 'gan to coax
Her Highness' pug-dog—got a sharp rebuff—
She wish'd a game at whist—made three revokes—
Turn'd from myself, her partner, in a huff;
His majesty will know her temper time enough.

LXXIX

"She cried for chess—I play'd a game with her—
Castled her king with such a vixen look,
It bodes ill to his Majesty—(refer
To the second chapter of my fortieth book,
And see what hoity-toity airs she took).
At half-past four the morn essay'd to beam—
Saluted, as we pass'd, an early rook—
The Princess fell asleep, and, in her dream,
Talk'd of one Master Hubert, deep in her esteem.

LXXX

"About this time,—making delightful way,—
Shed a quill-feather from my larboard wing—
Wish'd, trusted, hop'd 'twas no sign of decay—
Thank heaven, I'm hearty yet!—'twas no such thing:—
At five the golden light began to spring,
With fiery shudder through the bloomed east;
At six we heard Panthea's churches ring—
The city all her unhiv'd swarms had cast,
To watch our grand approach, and hail us as we pass'd.

LXXXI

"As flowers turn their faces to the sun,
So on our flight with hungry eyes they gaze,
And, as we shap'd our course, this, that way run,
With mad-cap pleasure, or hand-clasp'd amaze;
Sweet in the air a mild-ton'd music plays,
And progresses through its own labyrinth;
Buds gather'd from the green spring's middle-days,
They scatter'd,—daisy, primrose, hyacinth,—
Or round white columns wreath'd from capital to plinth.

LXXXII

"Onward we floated o'er the panting streets,
That seem'd throughout with upheld faces paved;
Look where we will, our bird's-eye vision meets
Legions of holiday; bright standards waved,
And fluttering ensigns emulously craved
Our minute's glance; a busy thunderous roar,
From square to square, among the buildings raved,
As when the sea, at flow, gluts up once more
The craggy hollowness of a wild reefed shore.

LXXXIII

"And 'Bellanaine for ever!' shouted they,
While that fair Princess, from her winged chair,
Bow'd low with high demeanour, and, to pay
Their new-blown loyalty with guerdon fair,
Still emptied, at meet distance, here and there,
A plenty horn of jewels. And here I
(Who wish to give the devil her due) declare
Against that ugly piece of calumny,
Which calls them Highland pebble-stones not worth a fly.

LXXXIV

"Still 'Bellanaine!' they shouted, while we glide
'Slant to a light Ionic portico,
The city's delicacy, and the pride
Of our Imperial Basilic; a row
Of lords and ladies, on each hand, make show
Submissive of knee-bent obeisance,
All down the steps; and, as we enter'd, lo!
The strangest sight—the most unlook'd-for chance—
All things turn'd topsy-turvy in a devil's dance.

LXXXV

" 'Stead of his anxious Majesty and court
At the open doors, with wide saluting eyes,
Congées and scape-graces of every sort,
And all the smooth routine of gallantries,
Was seen, to our immoderate surprise,
A motley crowd thick gather'd in the hall,
Lords, scullions, deputy-scullions, with wild cries
Stunning the vestibule from wall to wall,
Where the Chief Justice on his knees and hands doth crawl.

LXXXVI

"Counts of the palace, and the state purveyor
Of moth's-down, to make soft the royal beds,
The Common Council and my fool Lord Mayor
Marching a-row, each other slipshod treads;
Powder'd bag-wigs and ruffy-tuffy heads
Of cinder wenches meet and soil each other;
Toe crush'd with heel ill-natur'd fighting breeds,
Frill-rumpling elbows brew up many a bother,
And fists in the short ribs keep up the yell and pother.

LXXXVII

"A Poet, mounted on the Court-Clown's back,
Rode to the Princess swift with spurring heels,
And close into her face, with rhyming clack,
Began a Prothalamion;—she reels,
She falls, she faints! while laughter peals
Over her woman's weakness. 'Where!' cried I,
'Where is his Majesty?' No person feels
Inclin'd to answer; wherefore instantly
I plung'd into the crowd to find him or to die.

LXXXVIII

"Jostling my way I gain'd the stairs, and ran
To the first landing, where, incredible!
I met, far gone in liquor, that old man,
That vile impostor Hum,——"
                    So far so well,—
For we have prov'd the Mago never fell
Down stairs on Crafticanto's evidence;
And therefore duly shall proceed to tell,
Plain in our own original mood and tense,
The sequel of this day, though labour 'tis immense!

*   *   *   *

LINES SUPPOSED TO HAVE BEEN ADDRESSED
TO FANNY BRAWNE

THIS living hand, now warm and capable
Of earnest grasping, would, if it were cold
And in the icy silence of the tomb,
So haunt thy days and chill thy dreaming nights
That thou would[st] wish thine own heart dry of blood
So in my veins red life might stream again,
And thou be conscience-calm'd—see here it is—
I hold it towards you.

SONNET

*Written on a Blank Page in Shakespeare's Poems,
facing "A Lover's Complaint"*

BRIGHT star, would I were stedfast as thou art—
    Not in lone splendour hung aloft the night
And watching, with eternal lids apart,
    Like nature's patient, sleepless Eremite,
The moving waters at their priestlike task
    Of pure ablution round earth's human shores,
Or gazing on the new soft-fallen mask
    Of snow upon the mountains and the moors—
No—yet still stedfast, still unchangeable,
    Pillow'd upon my fair love's ripening breast,
To feel for ever its soft fall and swell,
    Awake for ever in a sweet unrest,
Still, still to hear her tender-taken breath,
And so live ever—or else swoon to death.

10

INDEX OF TITLES

INDEX OF FIRST LINES

395

THE COMPLETE
POETICAL WORKS OF
PERCY BYSSHE SHELLEY

PREFACE BY MRS. SHELLEY

TO FIRST COLLECTED EDITION, 1839

OBSTACLES have long existed to my presenting the public with a perfect edition of Shelley's Poems. These being at last happily removed, I hasten to fulfil an important duty,—that of giving the productions of a sublime genius to the world, with all the correctness possible, and of, at the same time, detailing the history of those productions, as they sprang, living and warm, from his heart and brain. I abstain from any remark on the occurrences of his private life, except inasmuch as the passions which they engendered inspired his poetry. This is not the time to relate the truth; and I should reject any colouring of the truth. No account of these events has ever been given at all approaching reality in their details, either as regards himself or others; nor shall I further allude to them than to remark that the errors of action committed by a man as noble and generous as Shelley, may, as far as he only is concerned, be fearlessly avowed by those who loved him, in the firm conviction that, were they judged impartially, his character would stand in fairer and brighter light than that of any contemporary. Whatever faults he had ought to find extenuation among his fellows, since they prove him to be human; without them, the exalted nature of his soul would have raised him into something divine.

The qualities that struck any one newly introduced to Shelley were,—First, a gentle and cordial goodness that animated his intercourse with warm affection and helpful sympathy. The other, the eagerness and ardour with which he was attached to the cause of human happiness and improvement; and the fervent eloquence with which he discussed such subjects. His conversation was marked by its happy abundance, and the beautiful language in which he clothed his poetic ideas and philosophical notions. To defecate life of its misery and its evil was the ruling passion of his soul; he dedicated to it every power of his mind, every pulsation of his heart. He looked on political freedom as the direct agent to effect the happiness of mankind; and thus any new-sprung hope of liberty inspired a joy and an exultation more intense and wild than he could have felt for any personal advantage. Those who have never experienced the workings of passion on general and unselfish subjects cannot understand this; and it must be difficult of comprehension to the younger generation rising around, since they cannot remember the scorn and hatred with wnich the partisans of reform were regarded some few years ago, nor the persecutions to which they were exposed. He had been from youth the victim of the state of feeling inspired by the reaction of the French Revolution; and believing firmly in the justice and excellence of his views, it cannot be wondered that a nature as sensitive, as impetuous, and as generous as his, should put its whole force into the attempt to alleviate for others the evils of those systems from which he had himself suffered. Many advantages

iii

attended his birth; he spurned them all when balanced with what he considered his duties. He was generous to imprudence, devoted to heroism.

These characteristics breathe throughout his poetry. The struggle for human weal; the resolution firm to martyrdom; the impetuous pursuit, the glad triumph in good; the determination not to despair;—such were the features that marked those of his works which he regarded with most complacency, as sustained by a lofty subject and useful aim.

In addition to these, his poems may be divided into two classes,—the purely imaginative, and those which sprang from the emotions of his heart. Among the former may be classed the *Witch of Atlas, Adonais,* and his latest composition, left imperfect, the *Triumph of Life.* In the first of these particularly he gave the reins to his fancy, and luxuriated in every idea as it rose; in all there is that sense of mystery which formed an essential portion of his perception of life—a clinging to the subtler inner spirit, rather than to the outward form—a curious and metaphysical anatomy of human passion and perception.

The second class is, of course, the more popular, as appealing at once to emotions common to us all; some of these rest on the passion of love; others on grief and despondency; others on the sentiments inspired by natural objects. Shelley's conception of love was exalted, absorbing, allied to all that is purest and noblest in our nature, and warmed by earnest passion; such it appears when he gave it a voice in verse. Yet he was usually averse to expressing these feelings, except when highly idealized; and many of his more beautiful effusions he had cast aside unfinished, and they were never seen by me till after I had lost him. Others, as for instance *Rosalind and Helen* and *Lines written among the Euganean Hills,* I found among his papers by chance; and with some difficulty urged him to complete them. There are others, such as the *Ode to the Skylark* and *The Cloud,* which, in the opinion of many critics, bear a purer poetical stamp than any other of his productions. They were written as his mind prompted: listening to the carolling of the bird, aloft in the azure sky of Italy; or marking the cloud as it sped across the heavens, while he floated in his boat on the Thames.

No poet was ever warmed by a more genuine and unforced inspiration. His extreme sensibility gave the intensity of passion to his intellectual pursuits; and rendered his mind keenly alive to every perception of outward objects, as well as to his internal sensations. Such a gift is, among the sad vicissitudes of human life, the disappointments we meet, and the galling sense of our own mistakes and errors, fraught with pain; to escape from such, he delivered up his soul to poetry, and felt happy when he sheltered himself, from the influence of human sympathies, in the wildest regions of fancy. His imagination has been termed too brilliant, his thoughts too subtle. He loved to idealize reality; and this is a taste shared by few. We are willing to have our passing whims exalted into passions, for this gratifies our vanity; but few of us understand or sympathize with the endeavour to ally the love of abstract beauty, and adoration of abstract good, the τὸ ἀγαθὸν καὶ τὸ καλόν of the Socratic philosophers, with our sympathies with our kind. In this, Shelley resembled Plato; both taking more delight in the abstract and the ideal than in the special and tangible. This did not result from imitation; for it was not till Shelley resided in Italy that he made Plato his study. He then translated his *Symposium* and his *Ion;* and the English language boasts of no more brilliant composition than Plato's Praise of Love translated by Shelley. To return to his own poetry. The luxury of imagination, which sought nothing beyond itself (as a child burdens itself with spring flowers, thinking of no use beyond the enjoyment of gathering them), often showed itself in his verses: they will be only appreciated by minds which have resemblance to his own; and the mystic subtlety of many of his thoughts will share the same fate. The metaphysical strain that characterizes much of what he has written was, indeed, the portion of his works to which, apart from those whose scope was to awaken mankind to aspirations for what he considered the true and good, he was himself particularly attached. There is much, however, that speaks to the many. When he would consent to dismiss these huntings after the obscure (which, entwined with his nature as they were, he did with difficulty), no poet ever expressed in sweeter, more heart-reaching, or more passionate verse, the gentler or more forcible emotions of the soul.

A wise friend once wrote to Shelley: 'You are still very young, and in certain essential respects you do not yet sufficiently perceive that you are so.' It is seldom that the young know what youth is, till they have got beyond its period; and time was not given him to attain this knowledge. It must be remembered that there is the stamp of such inexperience on all he wrote; he had not completed his nine-and-twentieth year when he died. The calm of middle life did not add the seal of the virtues which adorn maturity to those generated by the vehement spirit of youth. Through life also he was a martyr to ill-health, and constant pain wound up his nerves to a pitch of susceptibility that rendered his views of life different from those of a man in the enjoyment of healthy sensations. Perfectly gentle and forbearing in manner, he suffered a good deal of internal irritability, or rather excitement, and his fortitude to bear was almost always on the stretch; and thus, during a short life, he had gone through more experience of sensation than many whose existence is protracted. 'If I die to-morrow,' he said, on the eve of his unanticipated death, 'I have lived to be older than my father.' The weight of thought and feeling burdened him heavily; you read his sufferings in his attenuated frame, while you perceived the mastery he held over them in his animated countenance and brilliant eyes.

He died, and the world showed no outward sign. But his influence over mankind, though slow in growth, is fast augmenting; and, in the ameliorations that have taken place in the political state of his country, we may trace in part the operation of his arduous struggles. His spirit gathers peace in its new state from the sense that, though late, his exertions were not made in vain, and in the progress of the liberty he so fondly loved.

He died, and his place, among those who knew him intimately, has never been filled up. He walked beside them like a spirit of good to comfort and benefit—to enlighten the darkness of life with irradiations of genius, to cheer it with his sympathy and love. Any one, once attached to Shelley, must feel all other affections, however true and fond, as wasted on barren soil in comparison. It is our best consolation to know that such a pure-minded and exalted being was once among us, and now exists where we hope one day to join him;—although the intolerant, in their blindness, poured down anathemas, the Spirit of Good, who can judge the heart, never rejected him.

In the notes appended to the poems I have endeavoured to narrate the origin and history of each. The loss of nearly all letters and papers which refer to his early life renders the execution more imperfect than it would otherwise have been. I have, however, the liveliest recollection of all that was done and said during the period of my knowing him. Every impression is as clear as if stamped yesterday, and I have no apprehension of any mistake in my statements as far as they go. In other respects I am indeed incompetent: but I feel the importance of the task, and regard it as my most sacred duty. I endeavour to fulfil it in a manner he would himself approve; and hope, in this publication, to lay the first stone of a monument due to Shelley's genius, his sufferings, and his virtues:

> Se al seguir son tarda,
> Forse avverrà che 'l bel nome gentile
> Consacrerò con questa stanca penna.

POSTSCRIPT IN SECOND EDITION OF 1839

In revising this new edition, and carefully consulting Shelley's scattered and confused papers, I found a few fragments which had hitherto escaped me, and was enabled to complete a few poems hitherto left unfinished. What at one time escapes the searching eye, dimmed by its own earnestness, becomes clear at a future period. By the aid of a friend, I also present some poems complete and correct which hitherto have been defaced by various mistakes and omissions. It was suggested that the poem *To the Queen of my Heart* was falsely attributed to Shelley. I certainly find no trace of it among his papers; and, as those of his intimate friends whom I have consulted never heard of it, I omit it.

Two poems are added of some length, *Swellfoot the Tyrant* and *Peter Bell the Third*. I have mentioned the circumstances under which they were written in the notes; and need only add that they are conceived in a very different spirit from Shelley's usual compositions. They are specimens of the burlesque and fanciful; but, although they adopt a familiar style and homely imagery, there shine through the radiance of the poet's imagination the earnest views and opinions of the politician and the moralist.

At my request the publisher has restored the omitted passages of *Queen Mab*. I now present this edition as a complete collection of my husband's poetical works, and I do not foresee that I can hereafter add to or take away a word or line.

PUTNEY, *November* 6, 1839.

PREFACE BY MRS. SHELLEY
TO THE VOLUME OF POSTHUMOUS POEMS
PUBLISHED IN 1824

In nobil sangue vita umile e queta,
Ed in alto intelletto un puro core;
Frutto senile in sul giovenil fiore,
E in aspetto pensoso anima lieta.—PETRARCA.

IT had been my wish, on presenting the public with the Posthumous Poems of Mr. Shelley, to have accompanied them by a biographical notice; as it appeared to me that at this moment a narration of the events of my husband's life would come more gracefully from other hands than mine, I applied to Mr. Leigh Hunt. The distinguished friendship that Mr. Shelley felt for him, and the enthusiastic affection with which Mr. Leigh Hunt clings to his friend's memory, seemed to point him out as the person best calculated for such an undertaking. His absence from this country, which prevented our mutual explanation, has unfortunately rendered my scheme abortive. I do not doubt but that on some other occasion he will pay this tribute to his lost friend, and sincerely regret that the volume which I edit has not been honoured by its insertion.

The comparative solitude in which Mr. Shelley lived was the occasion that he was personally known to few; and his fearless enthusiasm in the cause which he considered the most sacred upon earth, the improvement of the moral and physical state of mankind, was the chief reason why he, like other illustrious reformers, was pursued by hatred and calumny. No man was ever more devoted than he to the endeavour of making those around him happy; no man ever possessed friends more unfeignedly attached to him. The ungrateful world did not feel his loss, and the gap it made seemed to close as quickly over his memory as the murderous sea above his living frame. Hereafter men will lament that his transcendent powers of intellect were extinguished before they had bestowed on them their choicest treasures. To his friends his loss is irremediable: the wise, the brave, the gentle, is gone for ever! He is to them as a bright vision, whose radiant track, left behind in the memory, is worth all the realities that society can afford. Before the critics contradict me, let them appeal to any one who had ever known him. To see him was to love him: and his presence, like Ithuriel's spear, was alone sufficient to disclose the falsehood of the tale which his enemies whispered in the ear of the ignorant world.

His life was spent in the contemplation of Nature, in arduous study, or in acts of kindness and affection. He was an elegant scholar and a profound metaphysician; without possessing much scientific knowledge, he was unrivalled in the justness and extent of his observations on natural objects; he knew every plant by its name, and was familiar with the history and habits of every production of the earth; he could interpret without a fault each appearance in the sky; and the varied phenomena of heaven and earth filled him with deep emotion. He made his study and reading-room of the shadowed copse, the stream, the lake, and the water-fall. Ill health and continual pain preyed upon his powers; and the soli-tude in which we lived, particularly on our first arrival in Italy, although congenial to his feelings, must frequently have weighed upon his spirits; those beautiful and affecting *Lines written in Dejection near Naples* were composed at such an interval; but, when in health, his spirits were buoyant and youthful to an extraordinary degree.

Such was his love for Nature that every page of his poetry is associated, in the minds of his friends, with the loveliest scenes of the countries which he inhabited. In early life he visited the most beautiful parts of this country and Ireland. Afterwards the Alps of Switzerland became his in-spirers. *Prometheus Unbound* was written among the deserted and flower-grown ruins of Rome; and, when he made his home under the Pisan hills, their roofless recesses harboured him as he composed the *Witch of Atlas, Adonais,* and *Hellas.* In the wild but beautiful Bay of Spezzia, the winds and waves which he loved became his playmates. His days were chiefly spent on the water; the management of his boat, its alterations and im-provements, were his principal occupation. At night, when the unclouded moon shone on the calm sea, he often went alone in his little shallop to the rocky caves that bordered it, and, sitting beneath their shelter, wrote the *Triumph of Life,* the last of his productions. The beauty but strangeness of this lonely place, the refined pleasure which he felt in the companion-ship of a few selected friends, our entire sequestration from the rest of the world, all contributed to render this period of his life one of con-tinued enjoyment. I am convinced that the two months we passed there were the happiest which he had ever known: his health even rapidly im-proved, and he was never better than when I last saw him, full of spirits and joy, embark for Leghorn, that he might there welcome Leigh Hunt to Italy. I was to have accompanied him; but illness confined me to my room, and thus put the seal on my misfortune. His vessel bore out of sight with a favouring wind, and I remained awaiting his return by the breakers of that sea which was about to engulf him.

He spent a week at Pisa, employed in kind offices toward his friend, and enjoying with keen delight the renewal of their intercourse. He then embarked with Mr. Williams, the chosen and beloved sharer of his pleas-ures and of his fate, to return to us. We waited for them in vain; the sea by its restless moaning seemed to desire to inform us of what we would not learn:—but a veil may well be drawn over such misery. The real anguish of those moments transcended all the fictions that the most glowing imagination ever portrayed; our seclusion, the savage nature of the inhabitants of the surrounding villages, and our immediate vicinity to the troubled sea, combined to imbue with strange horror our days of uncertainty. The truth was at last known,—a truth that made our loved and lovely Italy appear a tomb, its sky a pall. Every heart echoed the deep lament, and my only consolation was in the praise and earnest love that each voice bestowed and each countenance demonstrated for him we had lost,—not, I fondly hope, for ever; his unearthly and elevated nature is a pledge of the continuation of his being, although in an altered form. Rome received his ashes; they are deposited beneath its weed-grown wall, and 'the world's sole monument' is enriched by his remains.

I must add a few words concerning the contents of this volume. *Julian and Maddalo,* the *Witch of Atlas,* and most of the *Translations,* were written some years ago; and, with the exception of the *Cyclops,* and the Scenes from the *Magico Prodigioso,* may be considered as having received the author's ultimate corrections. The *Triumph of Life* was his last work, and was left in so unfinished a state that I arranged it in its present form with great difficulty. All his poems which were scattered in periodical works are collected in this volume, and I have added a reprint of *Alastor, or the Spirit of Solitude*: the difficulty with which a copy can be obtained is the cause of its republication. Many of the Miscellaneous Poems, written on the spur of the occasion, and never retouched, I found among his manuscript books, and have carefully copied. I have subjoined, whenever I have been able, the date of their composition.

I do not know whether the critics will reprehend the insertion of some of the most imperfect among them; but I frankly own that I have been more actuated by the fear lest any monument of his genius should escape me than the wish of presenting nothing but what was complete to the fastidious reader. I feel secure that the lovers of Shelley's poetry (who know how, more than any poet of the present day, every line and word he wrote is instinct with peculiar beauty) will pardon and thank me: I consecrate this volume to them.

The size of this collection has prevented the insertion of any prose pieces. They will hereafter appear in a separate publication.

MARY W. SHELLEY.

LONDON, *June* 1, 1824.

CONTENTS

CONTENTS

ALASTOR

OR

THE SPIRIT OF SOLITUDE

PREFACE

THE poem entitled Alastor may be considered as allegorical of one of the most interesting situations of the human mind. It represents a youth of uncorrupted feelings and adventurous genius led forth by an imagination inflamed and purified through familiarity with all that is excellent and majestic, to the contemplation of the universe. He drinks deep of the fountains of knowledge, and is still insatiate. The magnificence and beauty of the external world sinks profoundly into the frame of his conceptions, and affords to their modifications a variety not to be exhausted. So long as it is possible for his desires to point towards objects thus infinite and unmeasured, he is joyous, and tranquil, and self-possessed. But the period arrives when these objects cease to suffice. His mind is at length suddenly awakened and thirsts for intercourse with an intelligence similar to itself. He images to himself the Being whom he loves. Conversant with speculations of the sublimest and most perfect natures, the vision in which he embodies his own imaginations unites all of wonderful, or wise, or beautiful, which the poet, the philosopher, or the lover could depicture. The intellectual faculties, the imagination, the functions of sense, have their respective requisitions on the sympathy of corresponding powers in other human beings. The Poet is represented as uniting these requisitions, and attaching them to a single image. He seeks in vain for a prototype of his conception. Blasted by his disappointment, he descends to an untimely grave.

The picture is not barren of instruction to actual men. The Poet's self-centred seclusion was avenged by the furies of an irresistible passion pursuing him to speedy ruin. But that Power which strikes the luminaries of the world with sudden darkness and extinction, by awakening them to too exquisite a perception of its influences, dooms to a slow and poisonous decay those meaner spirits that dare to abjure its dominion. Their destiny is more abject and inglorious as their delinquency is more contemptible and pernicious. They who, deluded by no generous error, instigated by no sacred thirst of doubtful knowledge, duped by no illustrious superstition, loving nothing on this earth, and cherishing no hopes beyond, yet keep aloof from sympathies with their kind, rejoicing neither in human joy nor mourning with human grief; these, and such as they, have their apportioned curse. They languish, because none feel with them their common nature. They are morally dead. They are neither friends, nor lovers, nor fathers, nor citizens of the world, nor benefactors of their country. Among those who attempt to exist without human sympathy, the pure and tender-hearted perish through the intensity and passion of their search after its communities, when the vacancy of their spirit suddenly makes itself felt. All else, selfish, blind, and torpid, are those unforeseeing multitudes who constitute, together with their own, the lasting misery and loneliness of the world. Those who love not their fellow-beings live unfruitful lives, and prepare for their old age a miserable grave.

> "The good die first,
> And those whose hearts are dry as summer dust.
> Burn to the socket!"

December 14, 1815.

Nondum amabam, et amare amabam, quaerebam quid amarem, amans amare.
                                            The Confessions of St. Augustine.

EARTH, ocean, air, belovèd brotherhood!
If our great Mother has imbued my soul
With aught of natural piety to feel
Your love, and recompense the boon with mine;
If dewy morn, and odorous noon, and even,   5
With sunset and its gorgeous ministers,
And solemn midnight's tingling silentness;
If autumn's hollow sighs in the sere wood,
And winter robing with pure snow and crowns
Of starry ice the grey grass and bare boughs;   10
If spring's voluptuous pantings when she breathes
Her first sweet kisses, have been dear to me;
If no bright bird, insect, or gentle beast
I consciously have injured, but still loved
And cherished these my kindred; then forgive   15
This boast, belovèd brethren, and withdraw
No portion of your wonted favour now!

Mother of this unfathomable world!
Favour my solemn song, for I have loved
Thee ever, and thee only; I have watched   20
Thy shadow, and the darkness of thy steps,
And my heart ever gazes on the depth
Of thy deep mysteries. I have made my bed
In charnels and on coffins, where black death
Keeps record of the trophies won from thee,   25
Hoping to still these obstinate questionings
Of thee and thine, by forcing some lone ghost

Thy messenger, to render up the tale
Of what we are. In lone and silent hours,
When night makes a weird sound of its own stillness,
Like an inspired and desperate alchymist   31
Staking his very life on some dark hope,
Have I mixed awful talk and asking looks
With my most innocent love, until strange tears
Uniting with those breathless kisses, made   35
Such magic as compels the charmèd night
To render up thy charge: . . . and, though ne'er yet
Thou hast unveiled thy inmost sanctuary,
Enough from incommunicable dream,
And twilight phantasms, and deep noon-day thought, 40
Has shone within me, that serenely now
And moveless, as a long-forgotten lyre
Suspended in the solitary dome
Of some mysterious and deserted fane,
I wait thy breath, Great Parent, that my strain   45
May modulate with murmurs of the air,
And motions of the forests and the sea,
And voice of living beings, and woven hymns
Of night and day, and the deep heart of man.

There was a Poet whose untimely tomb   50
No human hands with pious reverence reared,
But the charmed eddies of autumnal winds
Built o'er his mouldering bones a pyramid
Of mouldering leaves in the waste wilderness:—
A lovely youth,—no mourning maiden decked   55
With weeping flowers, or votive cypress wreath,
The lone couch of his everlasting sleep:—
Gentle, and brave, and generous,—no lorn bard
Breathed o'er his dark fate one melodious sigh:
He lived, he died, he sung, in solitude.   60
Strangers have wept to hear his passionate notes,
And virgins, as unknown he passed, have pined
And wasted for fond love of his wild eyes.
The fire of those soft orbs has ceased to burn,
And Silence, too enamoured of that voice,   65
Locks its mute music in her rugged cell.

By solemn vision, and bright silver dream,
His infancy was nurtured. Every sight
And sound from the vast earth and ambient air,
Sent to his heart its choicest impulses.   70
The fountains of divine philosophy
Fled not his thirsting lips, and all of great,

Or good, or lovely, which the sacred past
In truth or fable consecrates, he felt
And knew. When early youth had passed, he left   75
His cold fireside and alienated home
To seek strange truths in undiscovered lands.
Many a wide waste and tangled wilderness
Has lured his fearless steps; and he has bought
With his sweet voice and eyes, from savage men,   80
His rest and food. Nature's most secret steps
He like her shadow has pursued, where'er
The red volcano overcanopies
Its fields of snow and pinnacles of ice
With burning smoke, or where bitumen lakes   85
On black bare pointed islets ever beat
With sluggish surge, or where the secret caves
Rugged and dark, winding among the springs
Of fire and poison, inaccessible
To avarice or pride, their starry domes   90
Of diamond and of gold expand above
Numberless and immeasurable halls,
Frequent with crystal column, and clear shrines
Of pearl, and thrones radiant with chrysolite.
Nor had that scene of ampler majesty   95
Than gems or gold, the varying roof of heaven
And the green earth lost in his heart its claims
To love and wonder; he would linger long
In lonesome vales, making the wild his home,
Until the doves and squirrels would partake   100
From his innocuous hand his bloodless food,
Lured by the gentle meaning of his looks,
And the wild antelope, that starts whene'er
The dry leaf rustles in the brake, suspend
Her timid steps to gaze upon a form   105
More graceful than her own.
                                        His wandering step
Obedient to high thoughts, has visited
The awful ruins of the days of old:
Athens, and Tyre, and Balbec, and the waste
Where stood Jersualem, the fallen towers   110
Of Babylon, the eternal pyramids,
Memphis and Thebes, and whatsoe'er of strange
Sculptured on alabaster obelisk,
Or jasper tomb, or mutilated sphynx,
Dark Æthiopia in her desert hills   115
Conceals. Among the ruined temples there,
Stupendous columns, and wild images
Of more than man, where marble daemons watch

The Zodiac's brazen mystery, and dead men
Hang their mute thoughts on the mute walls around,   120
He lingered, poring on memorials
Of the world's youth, through the long burning day
Gazed on those speechless shapes, nor, when the moon
Filled the mysterious halls with floating shades
Suspended he that task, but ever gazed   125
And gazed, till meaning on his vacant mind
Flashed like strong inspiration, and he saw
The thrilling secrets of the birth of time.

Meanwhile an Arab maiden brought his food,
Her daily portion, from her father's tent,   130
And spread her matting for his couch, and stole
From duties and repose to tend his steps:—
Enamoured, yet not daring for deep awe
To speak her love:—and watched his nightly sleep,
Sleepless herself, to gaze upon his lips   135
Parted in slumber, whence the regular breath
Of innocent dreams arose: then, when red morn
Made paler the pale moon, to her cold home
Wildered, and wan, and panting, she returned.

The Poet wandering on, through Arabie   140
And Persia, and the wild Carmanian waste,
And o'er the aërial mountains which pour down
Indus and Oxus from their icy caves,
In joy and exultation held his way;
Till in the vale of Cashmire, far within   145
Its loneliest dell, where odorous plants entwine
Beneath the hollow rocks a natural bower,
Beside a sparkling rivulet he stretched
His languid limbs. A vision on his sleep
There came, a dream of hopes that never yet   150
Had flushed his cheek. He dreamed a veilèd maid
Sate near him, talking in low solemn tones.
Her voice was like the voice of his own soul
Heard in the calm of thought; its music long,
Like woven sounds of streams and breezes, held   155
His inmost sense suspended in its web
Of many-coloured woof and shifting hues.
Knowledge and truth and virtue were her theme,
And lofty hopes of divine liberty,
Thoughts the most dear to him, and poesy,   160
Herself a poet. Soon the solemn mood
Of her pure mind kindled through all her frame
A permeating fire: wild numbers then

She raised, with voice stifled in tremulous sobs
Subdued by its own pathos: her fair hands   165
Were bare alone, sweeping from some strange harp
Strange symphony, and in their branching veins
The eloquent blood told an ineffable tale.
The beating of her heart was heard to fill
The pauses of her music, and her breath   170
Tumultuously accorded with those fits
Of intermitted song. Sudden she rose,
As if her heart impatiently endured
Its bursting burthen: at the sound he turned,
And saw by the warm light of their own life   175
Her glowing limbs beneath the sinuous veil
Of woven wind, her outspread arms now bare,
Her dark locks floating in the breath of night,
Her beamy bending eyes, her parted lips
Outstretched, and pale, and quivering eagerly.   180
His strong heart sunk and sickened with excess
Of love. He reared his shuddering limbs and quelled
His gasping breath, and spread his arms to meet
Her panting bosom: . . . she drew back a while,
Then, yielding to the irresistible joy,   185
With frantic gesture and short breathless cry
Folded his frame in her dissolving arms.
Now blackness veiled his dizzy eyes, and night
Involved and swallowed up the vision; sleep,
Like a dark flood suspended in its course,   190
Rolled back its impulse on his vacant brain.

Roused by the shock he started from his trance—
The cold white light of morning, the blue moon
Low in the west, the clear and garish hills,
The distinct valley and the vacant woods,   195
Spread round him where he stood. Whither have fled
The hues of heaven that canopied his bower
Of yesternight? The sounds that soothed his sleep,
The mystery and the majesty of Earth,
The joy, the exultation? His wan eyes   200
Gaze on the empty scene as vacantly
As ocean's moon looks on the moon in heaven.
The spirit of sweet human love has sent
A vision to the sleep of him who spurned
Her choicest gifts. He eagerly pursues   205
Beyond the realms of dream that fleeting shade;
He overleaps the bounds. Alas! Alas!
Were limbs, and breath, and being intertwined
Thus treacherously? Lost, lost, for ever lost,

In the wide pathless desert of dim sleep,   210
That beautiful shape! Does the dark gate of death
Conduct to thy mysterious paradise,
O Sleep? Does the bright arch of rainbow clouds,
And pendent mountains seen in the calm lake,
Lead only to a black and watery depth,   215
While death's blue vault, with loathliest vapours hung,
Where every shade which the foul grave exhales
Hides its dead eye from the detested day,
Conducts, O Sleep, to thy delightful realms?
This doubt with sudden tide flowed on his heart,   220
The insatiate hope which it awakened, stung
His brain even like despair.
                              While daylight held
The sky, the Poet kept mute conference
With his still soul. At night the passion came,
Like the fierce fiend of a distempered dream,   225
And shook him from his rest, and led him forth
Into the darkness.—As an eagle grasped
In folds of the green serpent, feels her breast
Burn with the poison, and precipitates
Through night and day, tempest, and calm, and cloud,
Frantic with dizzying anguish, her blind flight   231
O'er the wide aëry wilderness: thus driven
By the bright shadow of that lovely dream,
Beneath the cold glare of the desolate night,
Through tangled swamps and deep precipitous dells,   235
Startling with careless step the moonlight snake,
He fled. Red morning dawned upon his flight,
Shedding the mockery of its vital hues
Upon his cheek of death. He wandered on
Till vast Aornos seen from Petra's steep   240
Hung o'er the low horizon like a cloud;
Through Balk, and where the desolated tombs
Of Parthian kings scatter to every wind
Their wasting dust, wildly he wandered on,
Day after day a weary waste of hours,   245
Bearing within his life the brooding care
That ever fed on its decaying flame.
And now his limbs were lean; his scattered hair
Sered by the autumn of strange suffering
Sung dirges in the wind; his listless hand   250
Hung like dead bone within its withered skin;
Life, and the lustre that consumed it, shone
As in a furnace burning secretly
From his dark eyes alone. The cottagers,
Who ministered with human charity   255

His human wants, beheld with wondering awe
Their fleeting visitant. The mountaineer,
Encountering on some dizzy precipice
That spectral form, deemed that the Spirit of wind
With lightning eyes, and eager breath, and feet   260
Disturbing not the drifted snow, had paused
In its career: the infant would conceal
His troubled visage in his mother's robe
In terror at the glare of those wild eyes,
To remember their strange light in many a dream   265
Of after-times; but youthful maidens, taught
By nature, would interpret half the woe
That wasted him, would call him with false names
Brother, and friend, would press his pallid hand
At parting, and watch, dim through tears, the path   270
Of his departure from their father's door.

    At length upon the lone Chorasmian shore
He paused, a wide and melancholy waste
Of putrid marshes. A strong impulse urged
His steps to the sea-shore. A swan was there,   27{
Beside a sluggish stream among the reeds.
It rose as he approached, and with strong wings
Scaling the upward sky, bent its bright course
High over the immeasurable main.
His eyes pursued its flight.—'Thou hast a home,   280
Beautiful bird; thou voyagest to thine home,
Where thy sweet mate will twine her downy neck
With thine, and welcome thy return with eyes
Bright in the lustre of their own fond joy.
And what am I that I should linger here,   285
With voice far sweeter than thy dying notes,
Spirit more vast than thine, frame more attuned
To beauty, wasting these surpassing powers
In the deaf air, to the blind earth, and heaven
That echoes not my thoughts?' A gloomy smile   290
Of desperate hope wrinkled his quivering lips.
For sleep, he knew, kept most relentlessly
Its precious charge, and silent death exposed,
Faithless perhaps as sleep, a shadowy lure,
With doubtful smile mocking its own strange charms.

    Startled by his own thoughts he looked around.   296
There was no fair fiend near him, not a sight
Or sound of awe but in his own deep mind.
A little shallop floating near the shore
Caught the impatient wandering of his gaze.   300

It had been long abandoned, for its sides
Gaped wide with many a rift, and its frail joints
Swayed with the undulations of the tide.
A restless impulse urged him to embark
And meet lone Death on the drear ocean's waste;　　　305
For well he knew that mighty Shadow loves
The slimy caverns of the populous deep.

The day was fair and sunny, sea and sky
Drank its inspiring radiance, and the wind
Swept strongly from the shore, blackening the waves.
Following his eager soul, the wanderer　　　311
Leaped in the boat, he spread his cloak aloft
On the bare mast, and took his lonely seat,
And felt the boat speed o'er the tranquil sea
Like a torn cloud before the hurricane.　　　315

As one that in a silver vision floats
Obedient to the sweep of odorous winds
Upon resplendent clouds, so rapidly
Along the dark and ruffled waters fled
The straining boat.—A whirlwind swept it on,　　　320
With fierce gusts and precipitating force,
Through the white ridges of the cha-fèd sea.
The waves arose. Higher and higher still
Their fierce necks writhed beneath the tempest's scourge
Like serpents struggling in a vulture's grasp.　　　325
Calm and rejoicing in the fearful war
Of wave ruining on wave, and blast on blast
Descending, and black flood on whirlpool driven
With dark obliterating course, he sate:
As if their genii were the ministers　　　330
Appointed to conduct him to the light
Of those belovèd eyes the Poet sate
Holding the steady helm. Evening came on,
The beams of sunset hung their rainbow hues
High 'mid the shifting domes of sheeted spray　　　335
That canopied his path o'er the waste deep;
Twilight, ascending slowly from the east,
Entwined in duskier wreaths her braided locks
O'er the fair front and radiant eyes of day;
Night followed, clad with stars. On every side　　　340
More horribly the multitudinous streams
Of ocean's mountainous waste to mutual war
Rushed in dark tumult thundering, as to mock
The calm and spangled sky. The little boat
Still fled before the storm; still fled, like foam　　　345

Down the steep cataract of a wintry river;
Now pausing on the edge of the riven wave;
Now leaving far behind the bursting mass
That fell, convulsing ocean: safely fled—
As if that frail and wasted human form,   350
Had been an elemental god.

                    At midnight
The moon arose: and lo! the ethereal cliffs
Of Caucasus, whose icy summits shone
Among the stars like sunlight, and around
Whose caverned base the whirlpools and the waves   355
Bursting and eddying irresistibly
Rage and resound for ever.—Who shall save?—
The boat fled on,—the boiling torrent drove,—
The crags closed round with black and jagged arms,
The shattered mountain overhung the sea,   360
And faster still, beyond all human speed,
Suspended on the sweep of the smooth wave,
The little boat was driven. A cavern there
Yawned, and amid its slant and winding depths
Ingulfed the rushing sea. The boat fled on   365
With unrelaxing speed.—'Vision and Love!'
The Poet cried aloud, 'I have beheld
The path of thy departure. Sleep and death
Shall not divide us long!'

                    The boat pursued
The windings of the cavern. Daylight shone   370
At length upon that gloomy river's flow;
Now, where the fiercest war among the waves
Is calm, on the unfathomable stream
The boat moved slowly. Where the mountain, riven,
Exposed those black depths to the azure sky,   375
Ere yet the flood's enormous volume fell
Even to the base of Caucasus, with sound
That shook the everlasting rocks, the mass
Filled with one whirlpool all that ample chasm;
Stair above stair the eddying waters rose,   380
Circling immeasurably fast, and laved
With alternating dash the gnarled roots
Of mighty trees, that stretched their giant arms
In darkness over it. I' the midst was left,
Reflecting, yet distorting every cloud,   385
A pool of treacherous and tremendous calm.
Seized by the sway of the ascending stream,
With dizzy swiftness, round, and round, and round,
Ridge after ridge the straining boat arose,

Till on the verge of the extremest curve, 390
Where, through an opening of the rocky bank,
The waters overflow, and a smooth spot
Of glassy quiet mid those battling tides
Is left, the boat paused shuddering.—Shall it sink
Down the abyss? Shall the reverting stress 395
Of that resistless gulf embosom it?
Now shall it fall?—A wandering stream of wind,
Breathed from the west, has caught the expanded sail,
And, lo! with gentle motion, between banks
Of mossy slope, and on a placid stream, 400
Beneath a woven grove it sails, and, hark!
The ghastly torrent mingles its far roar,
With the breeze murmuring in the musical woods.
Where the embowering trees recede, and leave
A little space of green expanse, the cove 405
Is closed by meeting banks, whose yellow flowers
For ever gaze on their own drooping eyes,
Reflected in the crystal calm. The wave
Of the boat's motion marred their pensive task,
Which nought but vagrant bird, or wanton wind, 410
Or falling spear-grass, or their own decay
Had e'er disturbed before. The Poet longed
To deck with their bright hues his withered hair,
But on his heart its solitude returned,
And he forbore. Not the strong impulse hid 415
In those flushed cheeks, bent eyes, and shadowy frame
Had yet performed its ministry: it hung
Upon his life, as lightning in a cloud
Gleams, hovering ere it vanish, ere the floods
Of night close over it.
              The noonday sun 420
Now shone upon the forest, one vast mass
Of mingling shade, whose brown magnificence
A narrow vale embosoms. There, huge caves,
Scooped in the dark base of their aëry rocks
Mocking its moans, respond and roar for ever. 425
The meeting boughs and implicated leaves
Wove twilight o'er the Poet's path, as led
By love, or dream, or god, or mightier Death,
He sought in Nature's dearest haunt, some bank,
Her cradle, and his sepulchre. More dark 430
And dark the shades accumulate. The oak,
Expanding its immense and knotty arms,
Embraces the light beech. The pyramids
Of the tall cedar overarching, frame
Most solemn domes within, and far below, 435

Like clouds suspended in an emerald sky,
The ash and the acacia floating hang
Tremulous and pale. Like restless serpents, clothed
In rainbow and in fire, the parasites,
Starred with ten thousand blossoms, flow around   440
The grey trunks, and, as gamesome infants' eyes,
With gentle meanings, and most innocent wiles,
Fold their beams round the hearts of those that love,
These twine their tendrils with the wedded boughs
Uniting their close union; the woven leaves   445
Make net-work of the dark blue light of day,
And the night's noontide clearness, mutable
As shapes in the weird clouds. Soft mossy lawns
Beneath these canopies extend their swells,
Fragrant with perfumed herbs, and eyed with blooms   450
Minute yet beautiful. One darkest glen
Sends from its woods of musk-rose, twined with jasmine,
A soul-dissolving odour, to invite
To some more lovely mystery. Through the dell,
Silence and Twilight here, twin-sisters, keep   455
Their noonday watch, and sail among the shades,
Like vaporous shapes half seen; beyond, a well,
Dark, gleaming, and of most translucent wave,
Images all the woven boughs above,
And each depending leaf, and every speck   460
Of azure sky, darting between their chasms;
Nor aught else in the liquid mirror laves
Its portraiture, but some inconstant star
Between one foliaged lattice twinkling fair,
Or, painted bird, sleeping beneath the moon,   465
Or gorgeous insect floating motionless,
Unconscious of the day, ere yet his wings
Have spread their glories to the gaze of noon.

Hither the Poet came. His eyes beheld
Their own wan light through the reflected lines   470
Of his thin hair, distinct in the dark depth
Of that still fountain; as the human heart,
Gazing in dreams over the gloomy grave,
Sees its own treacherous likeness there. He heard
The motion of the leaves, the grass that sprung   475
Startled and glanced and trembled even to feel
An unaccustomed presence, and the sound
Of the sweet brook that from the secret springs
Of that dark fountain rose. A Spirit seemed
To stand beside him—clothed in no bright robes   480
Of shadowy silver or enshrining light.

Borrowed from aught the visible world affords
Of grace, or majesty, or mystery;—
But, undulating woods, and silent well,
And leaping rivulet, and evening gloom   485
Now deepening the dark shades, for speech assuming,
Held commune with him, as if he and it
Were all that was,—only . . . when his regard
Was raised by intense pensiveness, . . . two eyes,
Two starry eyes, hung in the gloom of thought,   490
And seemed with their serene and azure smiles
To beckon him.

          Obedient to the light
That shone within his soul, he went, pursuing
The windings of the dell.—The rivulet
Wanton and wild, through many a green ravine   495
Beneath the forest flowed. Sometimes it fell
Among the moss with hollow harmony
Dark and profound. Now on the polished stones
It danced; like childhood laughing as it went:
Then, through the plain in tranquil wanderings crept, 500
Reflecting every herb and drooping bud
That overhung its quietness.—'O stream!
Whose source is inaccessibly profound,
Whither do thy mysterious waters tend?
Thou imagest my life. Thy darksome stillness,   505
Thy dazzling waves, thy loud and hollow gulfs,
Thy searchless fountain, and invisible course
Have each their type in me; and the wide sky,
And measureless ocean may declare as soon
What oozy cavern or what wandering cloud   510
Contains thy waters, as the universe
Tell where these living thoughts reside, when stretched
Upon thy flowers my bloodless limbs shall waste
I' the passing wind!'

          Beside the grassy shore
Of the small stream he went; he did impress   515
On the green moss his tremulous step, that caught
Strong shuddering from his burning limbs. As one
Roused by some joyous madness from the couch
Of fever, he did move; yet, not like him,
Forgetful of the grave, where, when the flame   520
Of his frail exultation shall be spent,
He must descend. With rapid steps he went
Beneath the shade of trees, beside the flow
Of the wild babbling rivulet; and now

The forest's solemn canopies were changed 525
For the uniform and lightsome evening sky.
Grey rocks did peep from the spare moss, and stemmed
The struggling brook: tall spires of windlestrae
Threw their thin shadows down the rugged slope,
And nought but gnarled roots of ancient pines 530
Branchless and blasted, clenched with grasping roots
The unwilling soil. A gradual change was here,
Yet ghastly. For, as fast years flow away,
The smooth brow gathers, and the hair grows thin
And white, and where irradiate dewy eyes 535
Had shone, gleam stony orbs:—so from his steps
Bright flowers departed, and the beautiful shade
Of the green groves, with all their odorous winds
And musical motions. Calm, he still pursued
The stream, that with a larger volume now 540
Rolled through the labyrinthine dell; and there
Fretted a path through its descending curves
With its wintry speed. On every side now rose
Rocks, which, in unimaginable forms,
Lifted their black and barren pinnacles 545
In the light of evening, and, its precipice
Obscuring the ravine, disclosed above,
Mid toppling stones, black gulfs and yawning caves,
Whose windings gave ten thousand various tongues
To the loud stream. Lo! where the pass expands 550
Its stony jaws, the abrupt mountain breaks,
And seems, with its accumulated crags,
To overhang the world: for wide expand
Beneath the wan stars and descending moon
Islanded seas, blue mountains, mighty streams, 555
Dim tracts and vast, robed in the lustrous gloom
Of leaden-coloured even, and fiery hills
Mingling their flames with twilight, on the verge
Of the remote horizon. The near scene,
In naked and severe simplicity, 560
Made contrast with the universe. A pine,
Rock-rooted, stretched athwart the vacancy
Its swinging boughs, to each inconstant blast
Yielding one only response, at each pause
In most familiar cadence, with the howl 565
The thunder and the hiss of homeless streams
Mingling its solemn song, whilst the broad river,
Foaming and hurrying o'er its rugged path,
Fell into that immeasurable void
Scattering its waters to the passing winds. 570

Yet the grey precipice and solemn pine
And torrent, were not all;—one silent nook
Was there. Even on the edge of that vast mountain,
Upheld by knotty roots and fallen rocks,
It overlooked in its serenity   575
The dark earth, and the bending vault of stars.
It was a tranquil spot, that seemed to smile
Even in the lap of horror. Ivy clasped
The fissured stones with its entwining arms,
And did embower with leaves for ever green,   580
And berries dark, the smooth and even space
Of its inviolated floor, and here
The children of the autumnal whirlwind bore,
In wanton sport, those bright leaves, whose decay,
Red, yellow, or ethereally pale,   585
Rivals the pride of summer. 'Tis the haunt
Of every gentle wind, whose breath can teach
The wilds to love tranquillity. One step,
One human step alone, has ever broken
The stillness of its solitude:—one voice   590
Alone inspired its echoes;—even that voice
Which hither came, floating among the winds,
And led the loveliest among human forms
To make their wild haunts the depository
Of all the grace and beauty that endued   595
Its motions, render up its majesty,
Scatter its music on the unfeeling storm,
And to the damp leaves and blue cavern mould,
Nurses of rainbow flowers and branching moss,
Commit the colours of that varying cheek,   600
That snowy breast, those dark and drooping eyes.

The dim and hornèd moon hung low, and poured
A sea of lustre on the horizon's verge
That overflowed its mountains. Yellow mist
Filled the unbounded atmosphere, and drank   605
Wan moonlight even to fulness: not a star
Shone, not a sound was heard; the very winds,
Danger's grim playmates, on that precipice
Slept, clasped in his embrace.—O, storm of death!
Whose sightless speed divides this sullen night: 610
And thou, colossal Skeleton, that, still
Guiding its irresistible career
In thy devastating omnipotence,
Art king of this frail world, from the red field
Of slaughter, from the reeking hospital,   615
The patriot's sacred couch, the snowy bed

Of innocence, the scaffold and the throne,
A mighty voice invokes thee. Ruin calls
His brother Death. A rare and regal prey
He hath prepared, prowling around the world;   620
Glutted with which thou mayst repose, and men
Go to their graves like flowers or creeping worms,
Nor ever more offer at thy dark shrine
The unheeded tribute of a broken heart.

When on the threshold of the green recess   625
The wanderer's footsteps fell, he knew that death
Was on him. Yet a little, ere it fled,
Did he resign his high and holy soul
To images of the majestic past,
That paused within his passive being now,   630
Like winds that bear sweet music, when they breathe
Through some dim latticed chamber. He did place
His pale lean hand upon the rugged trunk
Of the old pine. Upon an ivied stone
Reclined his languid head, his limbs did rest,   635
Diffused and motionless, on the smooth brink
Of that obscurest chasm;—and thus he lay,
Surrendering to their final impulses
The hovering powers of life. Hope and despair,
The torturers, slept; no mortal pain or fear   640
Marred his repose, the influxes of sense,
And his own being unalloyed by pain,
Yet feebler and more feeble, calmly fed
The stream of thought, till he lay breathing there
At peace, and faintly smiling:—his last sight   645
Was the great moon, which o'er the western line
Of the wide world her mighty horn suspended,
With whose dun beams inwoven darkness seemed
To mingle. Now upon the jagged hills
It rests, and still as the divided frame   650
Of the vast meteor sunk, the Poet's blood,
That ever beat in mystic sympathy
With nature's ebb and flow, grew feebler still:
And when two lessening points of light alone
Gleamed through the darkness, the alternate gasp   655
Of his faint respiration scarce did stir
The stagnate night:—till the minutest ray
Was quenched, the pulse yet lingered in his heart.
It paused—it fluttered. But when heaven remained
Utterly black, the murky shades involved   660
An image, silent, cold, and motionless,
As their own voiceless earth and vacant air.

Even as a vapour fed with golden beams
That ministered on sunlight, ere the west
Eclipses it, was now that wondrous frame—   665
No sense, no motion, no divinity—
A fragile lute, on whose harmonious strings
The breath of heaven did wander—a bright stream
Once fed with many-voicèd waves—a dream
Of youth, which night and time have quenched for ever,
Still, dark, and dry, and unremembered now.   671
  O, for Medea's wondrous alchemy,
Which wheresoe'er it fell made the earth gleam
With bright flowers, and the wintry boughs exhale
From vernal blooms fresh fragrance! O, that God,   675
Profuse of poisons, would concede the chalice
Which but one living man has drained, who now,
Vessel of deathless wrath, a slave that feels
No proud exemption in the blighting curse
He bears, over the world wanders for ever,   680
Lone as incarnate death! O, that the dream
Of dark magician in his visioned cave,
Raking the cinders of a crucible
For life and power, even when his feeble hand
Shakes in its last decay, were the true law   685
Of this so lovely world! But thou art fled
Like some frail exhalation; which the dawn
Robes in its golden beams,—ah! thou hast fled!
The brave, the gentle, and the beautiful,
The child of grace and genius. Heartless things   690
Are done and said i' the world, and many worms
And beasts and men live on, and mighty Earth
From sea and mountain, city and wilderness,
In vesper low or joyous orison,
Lifts still its solemn voice:—but thou art fled—   695
Thou canst no longer know or love the shapes
Of this phantasmal scene, who have to thee
Been purest ministers, who are, alas!
Now thou art not. Upon those pallid lips
So sweet even in their silence, on those eyes   700
That image sleep in death, upon that form
Yet safe from the worm's outrage, let no tear
Be shed—not even in thought. Nor, when those hues
Are gone, and those divinest lineaments,
Worn by the senseless wind, shall live alone   705
In the frail pauses of this simple strain,
Let not high verse, mourning the memory
Of that which is no more, or painting's woe
Or sculpture, speak in feeble imagery

Their own cold powers. Art and eloquence,   710
And all the shows o' the world are frail and vain
To weep a loss that turns their lights to shade.
It is a woe too 'deep for tears,' when all
Is reft at once, when some surpassing Spirit,
Whose light adorned the world around it, leaves   715
Those who remain behind, not sobs or groans,
The passionate tumult of a clinging hope;
But pale despair and cold tranquillity,
Nature's vast frame, the web of human things,
Birth and the grave, that are not as they were.   720

NOTE ON ALASTOR, BY MRS. SHELLEY

Alastor is written in a very different tone from *Queen Mab*. In the latter, Shelley poured out all the cherished speculations of his youth—all the irrepressible emotions of sympathy, censure, and hope, to which the present suffering, and what he considers the proper destiny, of his fellow-creatures, gave birth. *Alastor*, on the contrary, contains an individual interest only. A very few years, with their attendant events, had checked the ardour of Shelley's hopes, though he still thought them well grounded, and that to advance their fulfilment was the noblest task man could achieve.

This is neither the time nor place to speak of the misfortunes that chequered his life. It will be sufficient to say that, in all he did, he at the time of doing it believed himself justified to his own conscience; while the various ills of poverty and loss of friends brought home to him the sad realities of life. Physical suffering had also considerable influence in causing him to turn his eyes inward; inclining him rather to brood over the thoughts and emotions of his own soul than to glance abroad, and to make, as in *Queen Mab*, the whole universe the object and subject of his song. In the Spring of 1815 an eminent physician pronounced that he was dying rapidly of a consumption; abscesses were formed on his lungs, and he suffered acute spasms. Suddenly a complete change took place; and, though through life he was a martyr to pain and debility, every symptom of pulmonary disease vanished. His nerves, which nature had formed sensitive to an unexampled degree, were rendered still more susceptible by the state of his health.

As soon as the peace of 1814 had opened the Continent, he went abroad. He visited some of the more magnificent scenes of Switzerland, and returned to England from Lucerne, by the Reuss and the Rhine. The river-navigation enchanted him. In his favourite poem of *Thalaba*, his imagination had been excited by a description of such a voyage. In the summer of 1815, after a tour along the southern coast of Devonshire and a visit to Clifton, he rented a house on Bishopgate Heath, on the borders of Windsor Forest, where he enjoyed several months of comparative health and tranquil happiness. The later summer months were

warm and dry. Accompanied by a few friends, he visited the source of
the Thames, making a voyage in a wherry from Windsor to Cricklade.
His beautiful stanzas in the churchyard of Lechlade were written on
that occasion. *Alastor* was composed on his return. He spent his days
under the oak-shades of Windsor Great Park; and the magnificent wood
land was a fitting study to inspire the various descriptions of forest-
scenery we find in the poem.

None of Shelley's poems is more characteristic than this. The solemn
spirit that reigns throughout, the worship of the majesty of nature, the
broodings of a poet's heart in solitude—the mingling of the exulting joy
which the various aspects of the visible universe inspires with the sad
and struggling pangs which human passion imparts—give a touching
interest to the whole. The death which he had often contemplated during
the last months as certain and near he here represented in such colours
as had, in his lonely musings, soothed his soul to peace. The versification
sustains the solemn spirit which breathes throughout: it is peculiarly
melodious. The poem ought rather to be considered didactic than narrative: it was the outpouring of his own emotions, embodied in the purest
form he could conceive, painted in the ideal hues which his brilliant
imagination inspired, and softened by the recent anticipation of death.

THE DAEMON OF THE WORLD

A FRAGMENT

PART I

Nec tantum prodere vati,
Quantum scire licet. Venit aetas omnis in unam
Congeriem, miserumque premunt tot saecula pectus.
LUCAN, *Phars.* v. 176.

How wonderful is Death,
Death and his brother Sleep!
One pale as yonder wan and hornèd moon,
With lips of lurid blue,
The other glowing like the vital morn,   5
When throned on ocean's wave
It breathes over the world:
Yet both so passing strange and wonderful!

Hath then the iron-sceptred Skeleton,
Whose reign is in the tainted sepulchres,   10
To the hell dogs that couch beneath his throne
Cast that fair prey? Must that divinest form,
Which love and admiration cannot view
Without a beating heart, whose azure veins

Steal like dark streams along a field of snow,   15
Whose outline is as fair as marble clothed
In light of some sublimest mind, decay?
    Nor putrefaction's breath
Leave aught of this pure spectacle
    But loathsomeness and ruin?—   20
    Spare aught but a dark theme,
On which the lightest heart might moralize?
Or is it but that downy-wingèd slumbers
Have charmed their nurse coy Silence near her lids
    To watch their own repose?   25
    Will they, when morning's beam
    Flows through those wells of light,
Seek far from noise and day some western cave,
Where woods and streams with soft and pausing winds
    A lulling murmur weave?—   30
    Ianthe doth not sleep
    The dreamless sleep of death:
Nor in her moonlight chamber silently
Doth Henry hear her regular pulses throb,
    Or mark her delicate cheek   35
With interchange of hues mock the broad moon,
    Outwatching weary night,
    Without assured reward.
    Her dewy eyes are closed;
On their translucent lids, whose texture fine   40
Scarce hides the dark blue orbs that burn below
    With unapparent fire,
    The baby Sleep is pillowed:
    Her golden tresses shade
    The bosom's stainless pride,   45
Twining like tendrils of the parasite
    Around a marble column.

    Hark! whence that rushing sound?
    'Tis like a wondrous strain that sweeps
    Around a lonely ruin   50
When west winds sigh and evening waves respond
    In whispers from the shore:
'Tis wilder than the unmeasured notes
Which from the unseen lyres of dells and groves
    The genii of the breezes sweep.   55
Floating on waves of music and of light,
The chariot of the Daemon of the World
    Descends in silent power:
Its shape reposed within: slight as some cloud
That catches but the palest tinge of day   60

When evening yields to night,
Bright as that fibrous woof when stars indue
    Its transitory robe.
Four shapeless shadows bright and beautiful
Draw that strange car of glory, reins of light   65
Check their unearthly speed; they stop and fold
    Their wings of braided air:
The Daemon leaning from the ethereal car
    Gazed on the slumbering maid.
Human eye hath ne'er beheld   70
A shape so wild, so bright, so beautiful,
As that which o'er the maiden's charmèd sleep
    Waving a starry wand,
    Hung like a mist of light.
Such sounds as breathed around like odorous winds
    Of wakening spring arose,   76
Filling the chamber and the moonlight sky.
Maiden, the world's supremest spirit
    Beneath the shadow of her wings
Folds all thy memory doth inherit   80
    From ruin of divinest things,
      Feelings that lure thee to betray,
      And light of thoughts that pass away.

For thou hast earned a mighty boon,
    The truths which wisest poets see   85
Dimly, thy mind may make its own,
    Rewarding its own majesty,
      Entranced in some diviner mood
      Of self-oblivious solitude.

Custom, and Faith, and Power thou spurnest;   90
    From hate and awe thy heart is free;
Ardent and pure as day thou burnest,
    For dark and cold mortality
      A living light, to cheer it long,
      The watch-fires of the world among.   95

Therefore from nature's inner shrine,
    Where gods and fiends in worship bend,
Majestic spirit, be it thine
    The flame to seize, the veil to rend,
      Where the vast snake Eternity   100
      In charmèd sleep doth ever lie.

All that inspires thy voice of love,
    Or speaks in thy unclosing eyes,
Or through thy frame doth burn or move,
    Or think, or feel, awake, arise!   105

Spirit, leave for mine and me
Earth's unsubstantial mimicry!

It ceased, and from the mute and moveless frame
    A radiant spirit arose,
All beautiful in naked purity.   110
Robed in its human hues it did ascend,
Disparting as it went the silver clouds,
It moved towards the car, and took its seat
    Beside the Daemon shape.

Obedient to the sweep of aëry song,   115
    The mighty ministers
Unfurled their prismy wings.
    The magic car moved on;
The night was fair, innumerable stars
    Studded heaven's dark blue vault;   120
    The eastern wave grew pale
    With the first smile of morn.
    The magic car moved on.
From the swift sweep of wings
The atmosphere in flaming sparkles flew;   125
    And where the burning wheels
Eddied above the mountain's loftiest peak
    Was traced a line of lightning.
Now far above a rock the utmost verge
    Of the wide earth it flew,   130
The rival of the Andes, whose dark brow
    Frowned o'er the silver sea.

Far, far below the chariot's stormy path,
    Calm as a slumbering babe,
    Tremendous ocean lay.   135
Its broad and silent mirror gave to view
    The pale and waning stars,
    The chariot's fiery track,
    And the grey light of morn
    Tingeing those fleecy clouds   140
That cradled in their folds the infant dawn.
    The chariot seemed to fly
Through the abyss of an immense concave,
Radiant with million constellations, tinged
    With shades of infinite colour,   145
    And semicircled with a belt
    Flashing incessant meteors.

    As they approached their goal,
The wingèd shadows seemed to gather speed.
The sea no longer was distinguished; earth   150

Appeared a vast and shadowy sphere, suspended
   In the black concave of heaven
     With the sun's cloudless orb,
     Whose rays of rapid light
Parted around the chariot's swifter course,   155
And fell like ocean's feathery spray
     Dashed from the boiling surge
     Before a vessel's prow.

     The magic car moved on.
     Earth's distant orb appeared   160
The smallest light that twinkles in the heavens,
     Whilst round the chariot's way
Innumerable systems widely rolled,
     And countless spheres diffused
       An ever varying glory.   165
It was a sight of wonder! Some were horned,
And like the moon's argentine crescent hung
In the dark dome of heaven; some did shed
A clear mild beam like Hesperus, while the sea
Yet glows with fading sunlight; others dashed   170
Athwart the night with trains of bickering fire,
Like spherèd worlds to death and ruin driven;
Some shone like stars, and as the chariot passed
     Bedimmed all other light.

     Spirit of Nature! here   175
In this interminable wilderness
Of worlds, at whose involved immensity
     Even soaring fancy staggers,
     Here is thy fitting temple.
     Yet not the lightest leaf   180
That quivers to the passing breeze
     Is less instinct with thee,—
     Yet not the meanest worm,
That lurks in graves and fattens on the dead,
     Less shares thy eternal breath.   185
     Spirit of Nature! thou
Imperishable as this glorious scene,
     Here is thy fitting temple.

If solitude hath ever led thy steps
To the shore of the immeasurable sea,   190
     And thou hast lingered there
     Until the sun's broad orb
Seemed resting on the fiery line of ocean,
Thou must have marked the braided webs of gold
     That without motion hang   195

Over the sinking sphere:
Thou must have marked the billowy mountain clouds,
Edged with intolerable radiancy,
    Towering like rocks of jet
    Above the burning deep: 200
    And yet there is a moment
    When the sun's highest point
Peers like a star o'er ocean's western edge,
When those far clouds of feathery purple gleam
Like fairy lands girt by some heavenly sea: 205
Then has thy rapt imagination soared
Where in the midst of all existing things
The temple of the mightiest Daemon stands.

    Yet not the golden islands
That gleam amid yon flood of purple light,   210
    Nor the feathery curtains
That canopy the sun's resplendent couch,
    Nor the burnished ocean waves
    Paving that gorgeous dome,
    So fair, so wonderful a sight   215
As the eternal temple could afford.
The elements of all that human thought
Can frame of lovely or sublime, did join
To rear the fabric of the fane, nor aught
Of earth may image forth its majesty.   220
Yet likest evening's vault that faëry hall,
As heaven low resting on the wave it spread
    Its floors of flashing light,
    Its vast and azure dome;
And on the verge of that obscure abyss   225
Where crystal battlements o'erhang the gulf
Of the dark world, ten thousand spheres diffuse
Their lustre through its adamantine gates.

    The magic car no longer moved;
    The Daemon and the Spirit   230
    Entered the eternal gates.
    Those clouds of aëry gold
    That slept in glittering billows
    Beneath the azure canopy,
With the ethereal footsteps trembled not;   235
    While slight and odorous mists
Floated to strains of thrilling melody
Through the vast columns and the pearly shrines.

    The Daemon and the Spirit
Approached the overhanging battlement,   240

Below lay stretched the boundless universe!
    There, far as the remotest line
That limits swift imagination's flight,
Unending orbs mingled in mazy motion,   245
    Immutably fulfilling
    Eternal Nature's law.
    Above, below, around,
    The circling systems formed
    A wilderness of harmony,
    Each with undeviating aim   250
In eloquent silence through the depths of space
    Pursued its wondrous way.—

Awhile the Spirit paused in ecstasy.
Yet soon she saw, as the vast spheres swept by,
Strange things within their belted orbs appear.   255
Like animated frenzies, dimly moved
Shadows, and skeletons, and fiendly shapes,
Thronging round human graves, and o'er the dead
Sculpturing records for each memory
In verse, such as malignant gods pronounce,   260
Blasting the hopes of men, when heaven and hell
Confounded burst in ruin o'er the world:
And they did build vast trophies, instruments
Of murder, human bones, barbaric gold,
Skins torn from living men, and towers of skulls   265
With sightless holes gazing on blinder heaven,
Mitres, and crowns, and brazen chariots stained
With blood, and scrolls of mystic wickedness,
The sanguine codes of venerable crime.
The likeness of a thronèd king came by,   270
When these had passed, bearing upon his brow
A threefold crown; his countenance was calm,
His eye severe and cold; but his right hand
Was charged with bloody coin, and he did gnaw
By fits, with secret smiles, a human heart   275
Concealed beneath his robe; and motley shapes,
A multitudinous throng, around him knelt,
With bosoms bare, and bowed heads, and false looks
Of true submission, as the sphere rolled by.
Brooking no eye to witness their foul shame,   280
Which human hearts must feel, while human tongues
Tremble to speak, they did rage horribly,
Breathing in self-contempt fierce blasphemies
Against the Daemon of the World, and high
Hurling their armèd hands where the pure Spirit,   285
Serene and inaccessibly secure,

Stood on an isolated pinnacle,
The flood of ages combating below,
The depth of the unbounded universe
    Above, and all around   290
Necessity's unchanging harmony.

PART II

O HAPPY Earth! reality of Heaven!
To which those restless powers that ceaselessly
Throng through the human universe aspire;
Thou consummation of all mortal hope!   295
Thou glorious prize of blindly-working will!
Whose rays, diffused throughout all space and time,
Verge to one point and blend for ever there:
Of purest spirits thou pure dwelling-place!
Where care and sorrow, impotence and crime,   300
Languor, disease, and ignorance dare not come:
O happy Earth, reality of Heaven!

    Genius has seen thee in her passionate dreams,
And dim forebodings of thy loveliness,
Haunting the human heart, have there entwined   305
Those rooted hopes, that the proud Power of Evil
Shall not for ever on this fairest world
Shake pestilence and war, or that his slaves
With blasphemy for prayer, and human blood
For sacrifice, before his shrine for ever   310
In adoration bend, or Erebus
With all its banded fiends shall not uprise
To overwhelm in envy and revenge
The dauntless and the good, who dare to hurl
Defiance at his throne, girt tho' it be   315
With Death's omnipotence. Thou hast beheld
His empire, o'er the present and the past;
It was a desolate sight—now gaze on mine,
Futurity. Thou hoary giant Time,
Render thou up thy half-devoured babes,—   320
And from the cradles of eternity,
Where millions lie lulled to their portioned sleep
By the deep murmuring stream of passing things,
Tear thou that gloomy shroud.—Spirit, behold
Thy glorious destiny!

               The Spirit saw   325
The vast frame of the renovated world
Smile in the lap of Chaos, and the sense

Of hope thro' her fine texture did suffuse
Such varying glow, as summer evening casts
On undulating clouds and deepening lakes.   330
Like the vague sighings of a wind at even,
That wakes the wavelets of the slumbering sea
And dies on the creation of its breath,
And sinks and rises, fails and swells by fits,
Was the sweet stream of thought that with wild motion
Flowed o'er the Spirit's human sympathies.   336
The mighty tide of thought had paused awhile,
Which from the Daemon now like Ocean's stream
Again began to pour.—

          To me is given
The wonders of the human world to keep—   340
Space, matter, time and mind—let the sight
Renew and strengthen all thy failing hope.
All things are recreated, and the flame
Of consentaneous love inspires all life:
The fertile bosom of the earth gives suck   345
To myriads, who still grow beneath her care,
Rewarding her with their pure perfectness:
The balmy breathings of the wind inhale
Her virtues, and diffuse them all abroad:
Health floats amid the gentle atmosphere,   350
Glows in the fruits, and mantles on the stream;
No storms deform the beaming brow of heaven,
Nor scatter in the freshness of its pride
The foliage of the undecaying trees;
But fruits are ever ripe, flowers ever fair,   355
And Autumn proudly bears her matron grace,
Kindling a flush on the fair cheek of Spring,
Whose virgin bloom beneath the ruddy fruit
Reflects its tint and blushes into love.

  The habitable earth is full of bliss;   360
Those wastes of frozen billows that were hurled
By everlasting snow-storms round the poles,
Where matter dared not vegetate nor live,
But ceaseless frost round the vast solitude
Bound its broad zone of stillness, are unloosed;   365
And fragrant zephyrs there from spicy isles
Ruffle the placid ocean-deep, that rolls
Its broad, bright surges to the sloping sand,
Whose roar is wakened into echoings sweet
To murmur through the heaven-breathing groves   370
And melodise with man's blest nature there.

The vast tract of the parched and sandy waste
Now teems with countless rills and shady woods,
Corn-fields and pastures and white cottages;
And where the startled wilderness did hear   375
A savage conqueror stained in kindred blood,
Hymning his victory, or the milder snake
Crushing the bones of some frail antelope
Within his brazen folds—the dewy lawn,
Offering sweet incense to the sunrise, smiles   380
To see a babe before his mother's door,
Share with the green and golden basilisk
That comes to lick his feet, his morning's meal.

Those trackless deeps, where many a weary sail
Has seen, above the illimitable plain,   385
Morning on night and night on morning rise,
Whilst still no land to greet the wanderer spread
Its shadowy mountains on the sunbright sea,
Where the loud roarings of the tempest-waves
So long have mingled with the gusty wind   390
In melancholy loneliness, and swept
The desert of those ocean solitudes,
But vocal to the sea-bird's harrowing shriek,
The bellowing monster, and the rushing storm,
Now to the sweet and many-mingling sounds   395
Of kindliest human impulses respond:
Those lonely realms bright garden-isles begem,
With lightsome clouds and shining seas between,
And fertile valleys, resonant with bliss,
Whilst green woods overcanopy the wave,   400
Which like a toil-worn labourer leaps to shore,
To meet the kisses of the flowerets there.

Man chief perceives the change, his being notes
The gradual renovation, and defines
Each movement of its progress on his mind.   405
Man, where the gloom of the long polar night
Lowered o'er the snow-clad rocks and frozen soil,
Where scarce the hardiest herb that braves the frost
Basked in the moonlight's ineffectual glow,   409
Shrank with the plants, and darkened with the night;
Nor where the tropics bound the realms of day
With a broad belt of mingling cloud and flame,
Where blue mists through the unmoving atmosphere
Scattered the seeds of pestilence, and fed
Unnatural vegetation, where the land   415
Teemed with all earthquake, tempest and disease,

Was man a nobler being; slavery
Had crushed him to his country's blood-stained dust.

Even where the milder zone afforded man
A seeming shelter, yet contagion there,   420
Blighting his being with unnumbered ills,
Spread like a quenchless fire; nor truth availed
Till late to arrest its progress, or create
That peace which first in bloodless victory waved
Her snowy standard o'er this favoured clime: 425
There man was long the train-bearer of slaves,
The mimic of surrounding misery,
The jackal of ambition's lion-rage,
The bloodhound of religion's hungry zeal.

Here now the human being stands adorning   430
This loveliest earth with taintless body and mind;
Blest from his birth with all bland impulses,
Which gently in his noble bosom wake
All kindly passions and all pure desires.
Him, still from hope to hope the bliss pursuing,   435
Which from the exhaustless lore of human weal
Dawns on the virtuous mind, the thoughts that rise
In time-destroying infiniteness gift
With self-enshrined eternity, that mocks
The unprevailing hoariness of age,   440
And man, once fleeting o'er the transient scene
Swift as an unremembered vision, stands
Immortal upon earth: no longer now
He slays the beast that sports around his dwelling
And horribly devours its mangled flesh,   445
Or drinks its vital blood, which like a stream
Of poison thro' his fevered veins did flow
Feeding a plague that secretly consumed
His feeble frame, and kindling in his mind
Hatred, despair, and fear and vain belief,   450
The germs of misery, death, disease, and crime.
No longer now the wingèd habitants,
That in the woods their sweet lives sing away,
Flee from the form of man; but gather round,
And prune their sunny feathers on the hands   455
Which little children stretch in friendly sport
Towards these dreadless partners of their play.
All things are void of terror: man has lost
His desolating privilege, and stands
An equal amidst equals: happiness   460
And science dawn though late upon the earth;

Peace cheers the mind, health renovates the frame;
Disease and pleasure cease to mingle here,
Reason and passion cease to combat there;
Whilst mind unfettered o'er the earth extends   465
Its all-subduing energies, and wields
The sceptre of a vast dominion there.

Mild is the slow necessity of death:
The tranquil spirit fails beneath its grasp,
Without a groan, almost without a fear,   470
Resigned in peace to the necessity,
Calm as a voyager to some distant land,
And full of wonder, full of hope as he.
The deadly germs of languor and disease
Waste in the human frame, and Nature gifts   475
With choicest boons her human worshippers.
How vigorous now the athletic form of age!
How clear its open ana unwrinkled brow!
Where neither avarice, cunning, pride, or care,
Had stamped the seal of grey deformity   480
On all the mingling lineaments of time.
How lovely the intrepid front of youth!
How sweet the smiles of taintless infancy.

Within the massy prison's mouldering courts,
Fearless and free the ruddy children play,   485
Weaving gay chaplets for their innocent brows
With the green ivy and the red wall-flower,
That mock the dungeon's unavailing gloom;
The ponderous chains, and gratings of strong iron,
There rust amid the accumulated ruins   490
Now mingling slowly with their native earth:
There the broad beam of day, which feebly once
Lighted the cheek of lean captivity
With a pale and sickly glare, now freely shines
On the pure smiles of infant playfulness: 495
No more the shuddering voice of hoarse despair
Peals through the echoing vaults, but soothing notes
Of Ivy-fingered winds and gladsome birds
And merriment are resonant around.

The fanes of Fear and Falsehood hear no more   500
The voice that once waked multitudes to war
Thundering thro' all their aisles: but now respond
To the death dirge of the melancholy wind:
It were a sight of awfulness to see
The works of faith and slavery, so vast,   505

So sumptuous, yet withal so perishing!
Even as the corpse that rests beneath their wall.
A thousand mourners deck the pomp of death
To-day, the breathing marble glows above
To decorate its memory, and tongues   510
Are busy of its life: to-morrow, worms
In silence and in darkness seize their prey.
These ruins soon leave not a wreck behind:
Their elements, wide-scattered o'er the globe,
To happier shapes are moulded, and become   51̈
Ministrant to all blissful impulses:
Thus human things are perfected, and earth,
Even as a child beneath its mother's love,
Is strengthened in all excellence, and grows
Fairer and nobler with each passing year.   52υ

Now Time his dusky pennons o'er the scene
Closes in steadfast darkness, and the past
Fades from our charmèd sight. My task is done:
Thy lore is learned. Earth's wonders are thine own,
With all the fear and all the hope they bring.   52̈
My spells are past: the present now recurs.
Ah me! a pathless wilderness remains
Yet unsubdued by man's reclaiming hand.

Yet, human Spirit, bravely hold thy course,
Let virtue teach thee firmly to pursue   530
The gradual paths of an aspiring change:
For birth and life and death, and that strange state
Before the naked powers that thro' the world
Wander like winds have found a human home,
All tend to perfect happiness, and urge   535
The restless wheels of being on their way,
Whose flashing spokes, instinct with infinite life,
Bicker and burn to gain their destined goal:
For birth but wakes the universal mind
Whose mighty streams might else in silence flow   540
Thro' the vast world, to individual sense
Of outward shows, whose unexperienced shape
New modes of passion to its frame may lend;
Life is its state of action, and the store
Of all events is aggregated there   545
That variegate the eternal universe;
Death is a gate of dreariness and gloom,
That leads to azure isles and beaming skies
And happy regions of eternal hope.
Therefore, O Spirit! fearlessly bear on: 550

Though storms may break the primrose on its stalk,
Though frosts may blight the freshness of its bloom,
Yet spring's awakening breath will woo the earth,
To feed with kindliest dews its favourite flower,
That blooms in mossy banks and darksome glens,   555
Lighting the green wood with its sunny smile.

Fear not then, Spirit, death's disrobing hand,
So welcome when the tyrant is awake,
So welcome when the bigot's hell-torch flares;
'Tis but the voyage of a darksome hour,   560
The transient gulf-dream of a startling sleep.
For what thou art shall perish utterly,
But what is thine may never cease to be;
Death is no foe to virtue: earth has seen
Love's brightest roses on the scaffold bloom,   565
Mingling with freedom's fadeless laurels there,
And presaging the truth of visioned bliss.
Are there not hopes within thee, which this scene
Of linked and gradual being has confirmed?
Hopes that not vainly thou, and living fires   570
Of mind as radiant and as pure as thou,
Have shone upon the paths of men—return,
Surpassing Spirit, to that world, where thou
Art destined an eternal war to wage
With tyranny and falsehood, and uproot   575
The germs of misery from the human heart.
Thine is the hand whose piety would soothe
The thorny pillow of unhappy crime,
Whose impotence an easy pardon gains,
Watching its wanderings as a friend's disease: 580
Thine is the brow whose mildness would defy
Its fiercest rage, and brave its sternest will,
When fenced by power and master of the world.
Thou art sincere and good; of resolute mind,
Free from heart-withering custom's cold control,   585
Of passion lofty, pure and unsubdued.
Earth's pride and meanness could not vanquish thee,
And therefore art thou worthy of the boon
Which thou hast now received: virtue shall keep
Thy footsteps in the path that thou hast trod,   590
And many days of beaming hope shall bless
Thy spotless life of sweet and sacred love.
Go, happy one, and give that bosom joy
    Whose sleepless spirit waits to catch
    Light, life and rapture from thy smile.   595

The Daemon called its wingèd ministers.
Speechless with bliss the Spirit mounts the car,
That rolled beside the crystal battlement,
Bending her beamy eyes in thankfulness.
   The burning wheels inflame   600
The steep descent of Heaven's untrodden way.
   Fast and far the chariot flew:
   The mighty globes that rolled
Around the gate of the Eternal Fane
Lessened by slow degrees, and soon appeared   605
Such tiny twinkles as the planet orbs
That ministering on the solar power
With borrowed light pursued their narrower way.
   Earth floated then below:
   The chariot paused a moment;   610
   The Spirit then descended:
   And from the earth departing
   The shadows with swift wings
Speeded like thought upon the light of Heaven.

   The Body and the Soul united then,   615
A gentle start convulsed Ianthe's frame:
Her veiny eyelids quietly unclosed;
Moveless awhile the dark blue orbs remained:
She looked around in wonder and beheld
Henry, who kneeled in silence by her couch,   620
Watching her sleep with looks of speechless love,
   And the bright beaming stars
   That through the casement shone.

THE REVOLT OF ISLAM

A POEM IN TWELVE CANTOS

‘’Οσαις δὲ βροτὸν ἔθνος ἀγλαίαις ἀπιόμεσθα
   περαίνει πρὸς ἔσχατον
πλόον’ ναυσὶ δ’ οὔτε πεζὸς ἰὼν ἄν εὕροις
ἐς ‘Υπερβορέων ἀγῶνα θαυματὰν ὁδόν.
                              Πινδ. Πυθ. x.

PREFACE

THE Poem which I now present to the world is an attempt from which
I scarcely dare to expect success, and in which a writer of established
fame might fail without disgrace. It is an experiment on the temper of the
public mind, as to how far a thirst for a happier condition of moral and
political society survives, among the enlightened and refined, the tempests

which have shaken the age in which we live. I have sought to enlist the harmony of metrical language, the ethereal combinations of the fancy, the rapid and subtle transitions of human passion, all those elements which essentially compose a Poem, in the cause of a liberal and comprehensive morality; and in the view of kindling within the bosoms of my readers a virtuous enthusiasm for those doctrines of liberty and justice, that faith and hope in something good, which neither violence nor misrepresentation nor prejudice can ever totally extinguish among mankind.

For this purpose I have chosen a story of human passion in its most universal character, diversified with moving and romantic adventures, and appealing, in contempt of all artificial opinions or institutions, to the common sympathies of every human breast. I have made no attempt to recommend the motives which I would substitute for those at present governing mankind, by methodical and systematic argument. I would only awaken the feelings, so that the reader should see the beauty of true virtue, and be incited to those inquiries which have led to my moral and political creed, and that of some of the sublimest intellects in the world. The Poem therefore (with the exception of the first canto, which is purely introductory) is narrative, not didactic. It is a succession of pictures illustrating the growth and progress of individual mind aspiring after excellence, and devoted to the love of mankind; its influence in refining and making pure the most daring and uncommon impulses of the imagination, the understanding, and the senses; its impatience at 'all the oppressions which are done under the sun'; its tendency to awaken public hope, and to enlighten and improve mankind; the rapid effects of the application of that tendency; the awakening of an immense nation from their slavery and degradation to a true sense of moral dignity and freedom; the bloodless dethronement of their oppressors, and the unveiling of the religious frauds by which they had been deluded into submission; the tranquillity of successful patriotism, and the universal toleration and benevolence of true philanthropy; the treachery and barbarity of hired soldiers; vice not the object of punishment and hatred, but kindness and pity; the faithlessness of tyrants; the confederacy of the Rulers of the World, and the restoration of the expelled Dynasty by foreign arms; the massacre and extermination of the Patriots, and the victory of established power; the consequences of legitimate despotism, —civil war, famine, plague, superstition, and an utter extinction of the domestic affections; the judicial murder of the advocates of Liberty; the temporary triumph of oppression, that secure earnest of its final and inevitable fall; the transient nature of ignorance and error, and the eternity of genius and virtue. Such is the series of delineations of which the Poem consists. And, if the lofty passions with which it has been my scope to distinguish this story shall not excite in the reader a generous impulse, an ardent thirst for excellence, an interest profound and strong such as belongs to no meaner desires, let not the failure be imputed to a natural unfitness for human sympathy in these sublime and animating themes. It is the business of the Poet to communicate to others the pleasure and the enthusiasm arising out of those images and feelings in the vivid presence of which within his own mind consists at once his inspiration and his reward.

The panic which, like an epidemic transport, seized upon all classes of men during the excesses consequent upon the French Revolution, is gradually giving place to sanity. It has ceased to be believed that whole generations of mankind ought to consign themselves to a hopeless inheritance of ignorance and misery, because a nation of men who had been dupes and slaves for centuries were incapable of conducting themselves with the wisdom and tranquillity of freemen so soon as some of their fetters were partially loosened. That their conduct could not have been marked by any other characters than ferocity and thoughtlessness is the historical fact from which liberty derives all its recommendations, and falsehood the worst features of its deformity. There is a reflux in the tide of human things which bears the shipwrecked hopes of men into a secure haven after the storms are past. Methinks, those who now live have survived an age of despair.

The French Revolution may be considered as one of those manifestations of a general state of feeling among civilised mankind produced by a defect of correspondence between the knowledge existing in society and the improvement or gradual abolition of political institutions. The year 1788 may be assumed as the epoch of one of the most important crises produced by this feeling. The sympathies connected with that event extended to every bosom. The most generous and amiable natures were those which participated the most extensively in these sympathies. But such a degree of unmingled good was expected as it was impossible to realise. If the Revolution had been in every respect prosperous, then misrule and superstition would lose half their claims to our abhorrence, as fetters which the captive can unlock with the slightest motion of his fingers, and which do not eat with poisonous rust into the soul. The revulsion occasioned by the atrocities of the demagogues, and the re-establishment of successive tyrannies in France, was terrible, and felt in the remotest corner of the civilised world. Could they listen to the plea of reason who had groaned under the calamities of a social state according to the provisions of which one man riots in luxury whilst another famishes for want of bread? Can he who the day before was a trampled slave suddenly become liberal-minded, forbearing, and independent? This is the consequence of the habits of a state of society to be produced by resolute perseverance and indefatigable hope, and long-suffering and long-believing courage, and the systematic efforts of generations of men of intellect and virtue. Such is the lesson which experience teaches now. But, on the first reverses of hope in the progress of French liberty, the sanguine eagerness for good overleaped the solution of these questions, and for a time extinguished itself in the unexpectedness of their result. Thus, many of the most ardent and tender-hearted of the worshippers of public good have been morally ruined by what a partial glimpse of the events they deplored appeared to show as the melancholy desolation of all their cherished hopes. Hence gloom and misanthropy have become the characteristics of the age in which we live, the solace of a disappointment that unconsciously finds relief only in the wilful exaggeration of its own despair. This influence has tainted the literature of the age with the hopelessness of the minds from which it flows. Metaphysics,[1] and inquiries into moral and political science, have become little else than vain attempts to revive exploded superstitions, or sophisms like those [2] of Mr. Malthus, calculated to lull the oppressors of mankind into a security of everlasting triumph. Our works of fiction and poetry have been overshadowed by the same infectious gloom. But mankind appear to me to be emerging from their trance. I am aware, methinks, of a slow, gradual, silent change. In that belief I have composed the following Poem.

I do not presume to enter into competition with our greatest contemporary Poets. Yet I am unwilling to tread in the footsteps of any who have preceded me. I have sought to avoid the imitation of any style of language or versification peculiar to the original minds of which it is the character; designing that, even if what I have produced be worthless, it should still be properly my own. Nor have I permitted any system relating to mere words to divert the attention of the reader, from whatever interest I may have succeeded in creating, to my own ingenuity in contriving to disgust them according to the rules of criticism. I have simply clothed my thoughts in what appeared to me the most obvious and appropriate language. A person familiar with nature, and with the most celebrated productions of the human mind, can scarcely err in following the instinct, with respect to selection of language, produced by that familiarity.

There is an education peculiarly fitted for a Poet, without which genius and sensibility can hardly fill the circle of their capacities. No education, indeed, can entitle to this appellation a dull and unobservant mind, or one, though neither dull nor unobservant, in which the channels of communication between thought and expression have been obstructed or closed. How far it is my fortune to belong to either of the latter classes I cannot know. I aspire to be something better. The circumstances of my accidental education have been favourable to this ambition. I have been familiar from boyhood with mountains and lakes and the sea, and the solitude of forests: Danger, which sports upon the brink of precipices, has been my playmate. I have trodden the glaciers of the Alps, and lived under the eye of Mont Blanc. I have been a wanderer among distant fields. I have sailed down mighty rivers, and seen the sun rise and set, and the stars come forth, whilst I have sailed night and day down a

[1] I ought to except Sir W. Drumond's *Academical Questions;* a volume of very acute and powerful metaphysical criticism.

[2] It is remarkable, as a symptom of the revival of public hope, that Mr. Malthus has assigned, in the later editions of his work, an indefinite dominion to moral restraint over the principle of population. This concession answers all the inferences from his doctrine unfavourable to human improvement, and reduces the *Essay on Population* to a commentary illustrative of the unanswerableness of *Political Justice.*

rapid stream among mountains. I have seen populous cities, and have watched the passions which rise and spread, and sink and change, amongst assembled multitudes of men. I have seen the theatre of the more visible ravages of tyranny and war; cities and villages reduced to scattered groups of black and roofless houses, and the naked inhabitants sitting famished upon their desolated thresholds. I have conversed with living men of genius. The poetry of ancient Greece and Rome, and modern Italy, and our own country, has been to me, like external nature, a passion and an enjoyment. Such are the sources from which the materials for the imagery of my Poem have been drawn. I have considered Poetry in its most comprehensive sense; and have read the Poets and the Historians and the Metaphysicians [1] whose writings have been accessible to me, and have looked upon the beautiful and majestic scenery of the earth, as common sources of those elements which it is the province of the Poet to embody and combine. Yet the experience and the feelings to which I refer do not in themselves constitute men Poets, but only prepares them to be the auditors of those who are. How far I shall be found to possess that more essential attribute of Poetry, the power of awakening in others sensations like those which animate my own bosom, is that which, to speak sincerely, I know not; and which, with an acquiescent and contented spirit, I expect to be taught by the effect which I shall produce upon those whom I now address.

I have avoided, as I have said before, the imitation of any contemporary style. But there must be a resemblance, which does not depend upon their own will, between all the writers of any particular age. They cannot escape from subjection to a common influence which arises out of an infinite combination of circumstances belonging to the times in which they live; though each is in a degree the author of the very influence by which his being is thus pervaded. Thus, the tragic poets of the age of Pericles; the Italian revivers of ancient learning; those mighty intellects of our own country that succeeded the Reformation, the translators of the Bible, Shakespeare, Spenser, the dramatists of the reign of Elizabeth, and Lord Bacon [2]; the colder spirits of the interval that succeeded;—all resemble each other, and differ from every other in their several classes. In this view of things, Ford can no more be called the imitator of Shakespeare than Shakespeare the imitator of Ford. There were perhaps few other points of resemblance between these two men than that which the universal and inevitable influence of their age produced. And this is an influence which neither the meanest scribbler nor the sublimest genius of any era can escape; and which I have not attempted to escape.

I have adopted the stanza of Spenser (a measure inexpressibly beautiful), not because I consider it a finer model of poetical harmony than the

[1] In this sense there may be such a thing as perfectibility in works of fiction, notwithstanding the concession often made by the advocates of human improvement, that perfectibility is a term applicable only to science.

[2] Milton stands alone in the age which he illumined.

blank verse of Shakespeare and Milton, but because in the latter there is no shelter for mediocrity; you must either succeed or fail. This perhaps an aspiring spirit should desire. But I was enticed also by the brilliancy and magnificence of sound which a mind that has been nourished upon musical thoughts can produce by a just and harmonious arrangement of the pauses of this measure. Yet there will be found some instances where I have completely failed in this attempt; and one, which I here request the reader to consider as an erratum, where there is left, most inadvertently, an alexandrine in the middle of a stanza.

But in this as in every other respect I have written fearlessly. It is the misfortune of this age that its Writers, too thoughtless of immortality, are exquisitely sensible to temporary praise or blame. They write with the fear of Reviews before their eyes. This system of criticism sprang up in that torpid interval when Poetry was not. Poetry, and the art which professes to regulate and limit its powers, cannot subsist together. Longinus could not have been the contemporary of Homer, nor Boileau of Horace. Yet this species of criticism never presumed to assert an understanding of its own: it has always, unlike true science, followed, not preceded, the opinion of mankind, and would even now bribe with worthless adulation some of our greatest Poets to impose gratuitous fetters on their own imaginations, and become unconscious accomplices in the daily murder of all genius either not so aspiring or not so fortunate as their own. I have sought therefore to write, as I believe that Homer, Shakespeare, and Milton, wrote, with an utter disregard of anonymous censure. I am certain that calumny and misrepresentation, though it may move me to compassion, cannot disturb my peace. I shall understand the expressive silence of those sagacious enemies who dare not trust themselves to speak. I shall endeavour to extract, from the midst of insult and contempt and maledictions, those admonitions which may tend to correct whatever imperfections such censurers may discover in this my first serious appeal to the Public. If certain Critics were as clear-sighted as they are malignant, how great would be the benefit to be derived from their virulent writings! As it is, I fear I shall be malicious enough to be amused with their paltry tricks and lame invectives. Should the Public judge that my composition is worthless, I shall indeed bow before the tribunal from which Milton received his crown of immortality; and shall seek to gather, if I live, strength from that defeat, which may nerve me to some new enterprise of thought which may *not* be worthless. I cannot conceive that Lucretius, when he meditated that poem whose doctrines are yet the basis of our metaphysical knowledge, and whose eloquence has been the wonder of mankind, wrote in awe of such censure as the hired sophists of the impure and superstitious noblemen of Rome might affix to what he should produce. It was at the period when Greece was led captive, and Asia made tributary to the Republic, fast verging itself to slavery and ruin, that a multitude of Syrian captives, bigoted to the worship of their obscene Ashtaroth, and the unworthy successors of Socrates and Zeno, found there a precarious subsistence by administering, under the name of freedmen, to the vices and vanities of the great. These wretched men were skilled to plead, with a superficial but plausible set of sophisms, in favour of that contempt for virtue which is the portion of slaves, and that faith in portents, the most fatal substitute for benevolence in the imaginations of men, which, arising from the enslaved communities of the East, then first began to overwhelm the western nations in its stream. Were these the kind of men whose disapprobation the wise and lofty-minded Lucretius should have regarded with a salutary awe? The latest and perhaps the meanest of those who follow in his footsteps would disdain to hold life on such conditions.

The Poem now presented to the Public occupied little more than six months in the composition. That period has been devoted to the task with unremitting ardour and enthusiasm. I have exercised a watchful and earnest criticism on my work as it grew under my hands. I would willingly have sent it forth to the world with that perfection which long labour and revision is said to bestow. But I found that, if I should gain something in exactness by this method, I might lose much of the newness and energy of imagery and language as it flowed fresh from my mind. And, although the mere composition occupied no more than six months, the thoughts thus arranged were slowly gathered in as many years.

I trust that the reader will carefully distinguish between those opinions which have a dramatic propriety in reference to the characters which they are designed to elucidate, and such as are properly my own. The erroneous and degrading idea which men have conceived of a Supreme Being, for instance, is spoken against, but not the Supreme Being itself. The belief which some superstitious persons whom I have brought upon the stage entertain of the Deity, as injurious to the character of his benevolence, is widely different from my own. In recommending also a great and important change in the spirit which animates the social institutions of mankind, I have avoided all flattery to those violent and malignant passions of our nature which are ever on the watch to mingle with and to alloy the most beneficial innovations. There is no quarter given to Revenge, or Envy, or Prejudice. Love is celebrated everywhere as the sole law which should govern the moral world.

DEDICATION

> There is no danger to a man, that knows
> What life and death is: there's not any law
> Exceeds his knowledge; neither is it lawful
> That he should stoop to any other law.—CHAPMAN.

TO MARY — —

I

So now my summer task is ended, Mary,
  And I return to thee, mine own heart's home;
As to his Queen some victor Knight of Faëry,
  Earning bright spoils for her enchanted dome;

Nor thou disdain, that ere my fame become 5
A star among the stars of mortal night,
 If it indeed may cleave its natal gloom,
 Its doubtful promise thus I would unite
With thy belovèd name, thou Child of love and light.

II

The toil which stole from thee so many an hour, 10
 Is ended,—and the fruit is at thy feet!
No longer where the woods to frame a bower
 With interlacèd branches mix and meet,
 Or where with sound like many voices sweet,
Waterfalls leap among wild islands green, 15
 Which framed for my lone boat a lone retreat
Of moss-grown trees and weeds, shall I be seen:
But beside thee, where still my heart has ever been.

III

Thoughts of great deeds were mine, dear Friends, when first
 The clouds which wrap this world from youth did pass. 20
I do remember well the hour which burst
 My spirit's sleep: a fresh May-dawn it was,
 When I walked forth upon the glittering grass,
And wept, I knew not why; until there rose
 From the near schoolhouse, voices, that, alas! 25
Were but one echo from a world of woes—
The harsh and grating strife of tyrants and of foes.

IV

And then I clasped my hands and looked around—
 —But none was near to mock my streaming eyes,
Which poured their warm drops on the sunny ground— 30
 So, without shame, I spake:—'I will be wise,
 And just, and free, and mild, if in me lies
Such power, for I grow weary to behold
 The selfish and the strong still tyrannise
Without reproach or check.' I then controlled 35
My tears, my heart grew calm, and I was meek and bold.

V

And from that hour did I with earnest thought
 Heap knowledge from forbidden mines of lore,
Yet nothing that my tyrants knew or taught
 I cared to learn, but from that secret store 40

Wrought linkèd armour for my soul, before
It might walk forth to war among mankind;
  Thus power and hope were strengthened more and more
Within me, till there came upon my mind
A sense of loneliness, a thirst with which I pined.   45

VI

Alas, that love should be a blight and snare
  To those who seek all sympathies in one!—
Such once I sought in vain; then black despair,
  The shadow of a starless night, was thrown
  Over the world in which I moved alone:—   50
Yet never found I one not false to me,
  Hard hearts, and cold, like weights of icy stone
Which crushed and withered mine, that could not be
Aught but a lifeless clod, until revived by thee.

VII

Thou Friend, whose presence on my wintry heart   55
  Fell, like bright Spring upon some herbless plain;
How beautiful and calm and free thou wert
  In thy young wisdom, when the mortal chain
  Of Custom thou didst burst and rend in twain,
And walked as free as light the clouds among,   60
  Which many an envious slave then breathed in vain
From his dim dungeon, and my spirit sprung
To meet thee from the woes which had begirt it long!

VIII

No more alone through the world's wilderness,
  Although I trod the paths of high intent,   65
I journeyed now: no more companionless,
  Where solitude is like despair, I went.—
  There is the wisdom of a stern content
When Poverty can blight the just and good,
  When Infamy dares mock the innocent,   70
And cherished friends turn with the multitude
To trample: this was ours, and we unshaken stood!

IX

Now has descended a serener hour,
  And with inconstant fortune, friends return;
Though suffering leaves the knowledge and the power   75
  Which says:—Let scorn be not repaid with scorn.

And from thy side two gentle babes are born
  To fill our home with smiles, and thus are we
    Most fortunate beneath life's beaming morn;
And these delights, and thou, have been to me   80
The parents of the Song I consecrate to thee.

X

Is it, that now my inexperienced fingers
  But strike the prelude of a loftier strain?
Or, must the lyre on which my spirit lingers
    Soon pause in silence, ne'er to sound again,   85
    Though it might shake the Anarch Custom's reign,
And charm the minds of men to Truth's own sway
  Holier than was Amphion's? I would fain
Reply in hope—but I am worn away,
And Death and Love are yet contending for their prey.   90

XI

And what art thou? I know, but dare not speak:
  Time may interpret to his silent years.
Yet in the paleness of thy thoughtful cheek,
    And in the light thine ample forehead wears,
    And in thy sweetest smiles, and in thy tears,   95
And in thy gentle speech, a prophecy
  Is whispered, to subdue my fondest fears:
And through thine eyes, even in thy soul I see
A lamp of vestal fire burning internally.

XII

They say that thou wert lovely from thy birth,   100
  Of glorious parents, thou aspiring Child.
I wonder not—for One then left this earth
    Whose life was like a setting planet mild,
    Which clothed thee in the radiance undefiled
Of its departing glory; still her fame   105
    Shines on thee, through the tempests dark and wild
Which shake these latter days; and thou canst claim
The shelter, from thy Sire, of an immortal name.

XIII

One voice came forth from many a mighty spirit,
  Which was the echo of three thousand years;   110
And the tumultuous world stood mute to hear it,
  As some lone man who in a desert hears

The music of his home:—unwonted fears
Fell on the pale oppressors of our race,
    And Faith, and Custom, and low-thoughted cares,   115
Like thunder-stricken dragons, for a space
Left the torn human heart, their food and dwelling-place.

XIV

Truth's deathless voice pauses among mankind!
    If there must be no response to my cry—
If men must rise and stamp with fury blind   120
On his pure name who loves them,—thou and I,
    Sweet friend! can look from our tranquillity
Like lamps into the world's tempestuous night,—
    Two tranquil stars, while clouds are passing by
Which wrap them from the foundering seaman's sight,   125
That burn from year to year with unextinguished light.

CANTO I

I

When the last hope of trampled France had failed
    Like a brief dream of unremaining glory,
From visions of despair I rose, and scaled
    The peak of an aëreal promontory,   130
    Whose caverned base with the vexed surge was hoary;
And saw the golden dawn break forth, and waken
    Each cloud, and every wave:—but transitory
The calm: for sudden, the firm earth was shaken,
As if by the last wreck its frame were overtaken.   135

II

So as I stood, one blast of muttering thunder
    Burst in far peals along the waveless deep,
When, gathering fast, around, above, and under,
    Long trains of tremulous mist began to creep,
    Until their complicating lines did steep   140
The orient sun in shadow:—not a sound
    Was heard; one horrible repose did keep
The forests and the floods, and all around
Darkness more dread than night was poured upon the ground.

III

Hark! 'tis the rushing of a wind that sweeps   145
    Earth and the ocean. See! the lightnings yawn
Deluging Heaven with fire, and the lashed deeps
    Glitter and boil beneath: it rages on,

One mighty stream, whirlwind and waves upthrown,
Lightning, and hail, and darkness eddying by.   150
    There is a pause—the sea-birds, that were gone
Into their caves to shriek, come forth, to spy
What calm has fall'n on earth, what light is in the sky.

IV

For, where the irresistible storm had cloven
    That fearful darkness, the blue sky was seen   155
Fretted with many a fair cloud interwoven
    Most delicately, and the ocean green,
    Beneath that opening spot of blue serene,
Quivered like burning emerald: calm was spread
    On all below; but far on high, between   160
Earth and the upper air, the vast clouds fled,
Countless and swift as leaves on autumn's tempest shed.

V

For ever, as the war became more fierce
    Between the whirlwinds and the rack on high,
That spot grew more serene; blue light did pierce   165
    The woof of those white clouds, which seem to lie
    Far, deep, and motionless; while through the sky
The pallid semicircle of the moon
    Passed on, in slow and moving majesty;
Its upper horn arrayed in mists, which soon   170
But slowly fled, like dew beneath the beams of noon.

VI

I could not choose but gaze; a fascination
    Dwelt in that moon, and sky, and clouds, which drew
My fancy thither, and in expectation
    Of what I knew not, I remained:—the hue   175
    Of the white moon, amid that heaven so blue,
Suddenly stained with shadow did appear;
    A speck, a cloud, a shape, approaching grew,
Like a great ship in the sun's sinking sphere
Beheld afar at sea, and swift it came anear.   180

VII

Even like a bark, which from a chasm of mountains,
    Dark, vast, and overhanging, on a river
Which there collects the strength of all its fountains,
    Comes forth, whilst with the speed its frame doth quiver,

Sails, oars, and stream, tending to one endeavour; 185
So, from that chasm of light a wingèd Form
  On all the winds of heaven approaching ever
Floated, dilating as it came: the storm
Pursued it with fierce blasts, and lightnings swift and warm.

VIII

A course precipitous, of dizzy speed, 190
  Suspending thought and breath; a monstrous sight!
For in the air do I behold indeed
  An Eagle and a Serpent wreathed in fight:—
  And now relaxing its impetuous flight,
Before the aëreal rock on which I stood, 195
  The Eagle, hovering, wheeled to left and right,
And hung with lingering wings over the flood,
And startled with its yells the wide air's solitude.

IX

A shaft of light upon its wings descended,
  And every golden feather gleamed therein— 200
Feather and scale, inextricably blended.
  The Serpent's mailed and many-coloured skin
  Shone through the plumes its coils were twined within
By many a swoln and knotted fold, and high
  And far, the neck, receding lithe and thin, 205
Sustained a crested head, which warily
Shifted and glanced before the Eagle's steadfast eye.

X

Around, around, in ceaseless circles wheeling
  With clang of wings and scream, the Eagle sailed
Incessantly—sometimes on high concealing 210
  Its lessening orbs, sometimes as if it failed,
  Drooped through the air; and still it shrieked and wailed,
And casting back its eager head, with beak
  And talon unremittingly assailed
The wreathèd Serpent, who did ever seek 215
Upon his enemy's heart a mortal wound to wreak.

XI

What life, what power, was kindled and arose
  Within the sphere of that appalling fray!
For, from the encounter of those wondrous foes,
  A vapour like the sea's suspended spray 220

Hung gathered: in the void air, far away,
Floated the shattered plumes; bright scales did leap,
Where'er the Eagle's talons made their way,
Like sparks into the darkness;—as they sweep,
Blood stains the snowy foam of the tumultuous deep.   225

XII

Swift chances in that combat—many a check,
  And many a change, a dark and wild turmoil;
Sometimes the Snake around his enemy's neck
  Locked in stiff rings his adamantine coil,
  Until the Eagle, faint with pain and toil,   230
Remitted his strong flight, and near the sea
  Languidly fluttered, hopeless so to foil
His adversary, who then reared on high
His red and burning crest, radiant with victory.

XIII

Then on the white edge of the bursting surge,   235
  Where they had sunk together, would the Snake
Relax his suffocating grasp, and scourge
  The wind with his wild writhings; for to break
  That chain of torment, the vast bird would shake
The strength of his unconquerable wings   240
  As in despair, and with his sinewy neck,
Dissolve in sudden shock those linkèd rings,
Then soar—as swift as smoke from a volcano springs.

XIV

Wile baffled wile, and strength encountered strength,
  Thus long, but unprevailing:—the event   245
Of that portentous fight appeared at length:
  Until the lamp of day was almost spent
  It had endured, when lifeless, stark, and rent,
Hung high that mighty Serpent, and at last
  Fell to the sea, while o'er the continent,   250
With clang of wings and scream the Eagle passed,
Heavily borne away on the exhausted blast.

XV

And with it fled the tempest, so that ocean
  And earth and sky shone through the atmosphere—
Only, 'twas strange to see the red commotion   255
  Of waves like mountains o'er the sinking sphere

    Of sunset sweep, and their fierce roar to hear
      Amid the calm: down the steep path I wound
    To the sea-shore—the evening was most clear
    And beautiful, and there the sea I found   260
Calm as a cradled child in dreamless slumber bound.

XVI

    There was a Woman, beautiful as morning,
      Sitting beneath the rocks, upon the sand
    Of the waste sea—fair as one flower adorning
      An icy wilderness—each delicate hand   265
      Lay crossed upon her bosom, and the band
    Of her dark hair had fall'n, and so she sate
      Looking upon the waves; on the bare strand
    Upon the sea-mark a small boat did wait,
Fair as herself, like Love by Hope left desolate.   270

XVII

    It seemed that this fair Shape had looked upon
      That unimaginable fight, and now
    That her sweet eyes were weary of the sun,
      As brightly it illustrated her woe;
      For in the tears which silently to flow   275
    Paused not, its lustre hung: she watching aye
      The foam-wreaths which the faint tide wove below
    Upon the spangled sands, groaned heavily,
And after every groan looked up over the sea.

XVIII

    And when she saw the wounded Serpent make   280
      His path between the waves, her lips grew pale,
    Parted, and quivered; the tears ceased to break
      From her immovable eyes; no voice of wail
      Escaped her; but she rose, and on the gale
    Loosening her star-bright robe and shadowy hair   285
      Poured forth her voice; the caverns of the vale
    That opened to the ocean, caught it there,
And filled with silver sounds the overflowing air.

XIX

    She spake in language whose strange melody
      Might not belong to earth. I hear, alone,   290
    What made its music more melodious be,
      The pity and the love of every tone;

But to the Snake those accents sweet were known
His native tongue and hers; nor did he beat
   The hoar spray idly then, but winding on   295
Through the green shadows of the waves that meet
Near to the shore, did pause beside her snowy feet.

XX

Then on the sands the Woman sate again,
   And wept and clasped her hands, and all between,
Renewed the unintelligble strain   300
   Of her melodious voice and eloquent mien;
   And she unveiled her bosom, and the green
And glancing shadows of the sea did play
   O'er its marmoreal depth:—one moment seen,
For ere the next, the Serpent did obey   305
Her voice, and, coiled in rest in her embrace it lay.

XXI

Then she arose, and smiled on me with eyes
   Serene yet sorrowing, like that planet fair,
While yet the daylight lingereth in the skies
   Which cleaves with arrowy beams the dark-red air,   310
   And said: 'To grieve is wise, but the despair
Was weak and vain which led thee here from sleep:
   This shalt thou know, and more, if thou dost dare
With me and with this Serpent, o'er the deep,
A voyage divine and strange, companionship to keep.'   315

XXII

Her voice was like the wildest, saddest tone,
   Yet sweet, of some loved voice heard long ago.
I wept. 'Shall this fair woman all alone,
   Over the sea with that fierce Serpent go?
   His head is on her heart, and who can know   320
How soon he may devour his feeble prey?'—
   Such were my thoughts, when the tide gan to flow;
And that strange boat like the moon's shade did sway
Amid reflected stars that in the waters lay:—

XXIII

A boat of rare device, which had no sail   325
   But its own curvèd prow of thin moonstone,
Wrought like a web of texture fine and frail,
   To catch those gentlest winds which are not known

To breathe, but by the steady speed alone
With which it cleaves the sparkling sea; and now   330
   We are embarked—the mountains hang and frown
Over the starry deep that gleams below,
A vast and dim expanse, as o'er the waves we go.

XXIV

And as we sailed, a strange and awful tale
   That Woman told, like such mysterious dream   335
As makes the slumberer's cheek with wonder pale!
   'Twas midnight, and around, a shoreless stream,
   Wide ocean rolled, when that majestic theme
Shrined in her heart found utterance, and she bent
   Her looks on mine; those eyes a kindling beam   340
Of love divine into my spirit sent,
And ere her lips could move, made the air eloquent.

XXV

'Speak not to me, but hear! Much shalt thou learn,
   Much must remain unthought, and more untold,
In the dark Future's ever-flowing urn: 345
   Know then, that from the depth of ages old,
   Two Powers o'er mortal things dominion hold
Ruling the world with a divided lot,
   Immortal, all-pervading, manifold,
Twin Genii, equal Gods—when life and thought   350
Sprang forth, they burst the womb of inessential Nought.

XXVI

'The earliest dweller of the world, alone,
   Stood on the verge of chaos. Lo! afar
O'er the wide wild abyss two meteors shone,
   Sprung from the depth of its tempestuous jar: 355
   A blood-red Comet and the Morning Star
Mingling their beams in combat—as he stood,
   All thoughts within his mind waged mutual war,
In dreadful sympathy—when to the flood
That fair Star fell, he turned and shed his brother's blood.

XXVII

'Thus evil triumphed, and the Spirit of evil,   361
   One Power of many shapes which none may know,
One Shape of many names; the Fiend did revel
   In victory, reigning o'er a world of woe,

For the new race of man went to and fro,   365
Famished and homeless, loathed and loathing, wild,
And hating good—for his immortal foe,
He changed from starry shape, beauteous and mild,
To a dire Snake, with man and beast unreconciled.

XXVIII

'The darkness lingering o'er the dawn of things,   370
    Was Evil's breath and life; this made him strong
To soar aloft with overshadowing wings;
    And the great Spirit of Good did creep among
    The nations of mankind, and every tongue
Cursed and blasphemed him as he passed; for none   375
    Knew good from evil, though their names were hung
In mockery o'er the fane where many a groan,
As King, and Lord, and God, the conquering Fiend did own,—

XXIX

'The Fiend, whose name was Legion; Death, Decay,
    Earthquake and Blight, and Want, and Madness pale,
Wingèd and wan diseases, an array   381
    Numerous as leaves that strew the autumnal gale;
    Poison, a snake in flowers, beneath the veil
Of food and mirth hiding his mortal head;
    And, without whom all these might nought avail,   385
Fear, Hatred, Faith, and Tyranny, who spread
Those subtle nets which snare the living and the dead.

XXX

'His spirit is their power, and they his slaves
    In air, and light, and thought, and language, dwell;
And keep their state from palaces to graves,   390
    In all resorts of men—invisible,
    But when, in ebon mirror, Nightmare fell
To tyrant or impostor bids them rise,
    Black-wingèd demon forms—whom, from the hell,
His reign and dwelling beneath nether skies,   395
He loosens to their dark and blasting ministries.

XXXI

'In the world's youth his empire was as firm
    As its foundations . . . Soon the Spirit of Good,
Though in the likeness of a loathsome worm,
    Sprang from the billows of the formless flood,   400

Which shrank and fled; and with that Fiend of blood
Renewed the doubtful war . . . Thrones then first shook,
And earth's immense and trampled multitude
In hope on their own powers began to look,
And Fear, the demon pale, his sanguine shrine forsook.   405

XXXII

'Then Greece arose, and to its bards and sages,
   In dream, the golden-pinioned Genii came,
Even where they slept amid the night of ages,
   Steeping their hearts in the divinest flame
      Which thy breath kindled, Power of holiest name!   410
And oft in cycles since, when darkness gave
   New weapons to thy foe, their sunlike fame
Upon the combat shone—a light to save,
Like Paradise spread forth beyond the shadowy grave.

XXXIII

'Such is this conflict—when mankind doth strive   415
   With its oppressors in a strife of blood,
Or when free thoughts, like lightnings, are alive,
   And in each bosom of the multitude
   Justice and truth with Custom's hydra brood
Wage silent war; when Priests and Kings dissemble   420
   In smiles or frowns their fierce disquietude,
When round pure hearts a host of hopes assemble,
The Snake and Eagle meet—the world's foundations tremble!

XXXIV

'Thou hast beheld that fight—when to thy home
   Thou dost return, steep not its hearth in tears;   425
Though thou may'st hear that earth is now become
   The tyrant's garbage, which to his compeers,
   The vile reward of their dishonoured years,
He will dividing give.—The victor Fiend,
   Omnipotent of yore, now quails, and fears   430
His triumph dearly won, which soon will lend
An impulse swift and sure to his approaching end.

XXXV

List, stranger, list, mine is an human form,
   Like that thou wearest—touch me—shrink not now!
My hand thou feel'st is not a ghost's, but warm   435
   With human blood.—'Twas many years ago,

Since first my thirsting soul aspired to know
The secrets of this wondrous world, when deep
My heart was pierced with sympathy, for woe
Which could not be mine own—and thought did keep,
In dream, unnatural watch beside an infant's sleep.   441

XXXVI

'Woe could not be mine own, since far from men
I dwelt, a free and happy orphan child,
By the sea-shore, in a deep mountain-glen;
And near the waves, and through the forests wild,   445
I roamed, to storm and darkness reconciled:
For I was calm while tempest shook the sky:
But when the breathless heavens in beauty smiled,
I wept, sweet tears, yet too tumultuously
For peace, and clasped my hands aloft in ecstasy.   450

XXXVII

'These were forebodings of my fate—before
A woman's heart beat in my virgin breast,
It had been nurtured in divinest lore:
A dying poet gave me books, and blessed
With wild but holy talk the sweet unrest   455
In which I watched him as he died away—
A youth with hoary hair—a fleeting guest
Of our lone mountains: and this lore did sway
My spirit like a storm, contending there alway.

XXXVIII

'Thus the dark tale which history doth unfold   460
I knew, but not, methinks, as others know,
For they weep not; and Wisdom had unrolled
The clouds which hide the gulf of mortal woe,—
To few can she that warning vision show—
For I loved all things with intense devotion;   465
So that when Hope's deep source in fullest flow,
Like earthquake did uplift the stagnant ocean
Of human thoughts—mine shook beneath the wide emotion.

XXXIX

'When first the living blood through all these veins
Kindled a thought in sense, great France sprang forth,
And seized, as if to break, the ponderous chains   471
Which bind in woe the nations of the earth.

I saw, and started from my cottage-hearth;
And to the clouds and waves in tameless gladness,
   Shrieked, till they caught immeasurable mirth—   475
And laughed in light and music: soon, sweet madness
Was poured upon my heart, a soft and thrilling sadness.

XL

'Deep slumber fell on me:—my dreams were fire—
   Soft and delightful thoughts did rest and hover
Like shadows o'er my brain; and strange desire,   480
   The tempest of a passion, raging over
   My tranquil soul, its depths with light did cover,—
Which passed; and calm, and darkness, sweeter far,
   Came—then I loved; but not a human lover!
For when I rose from sleep, the Morning Star   485
Shone through the woodbine-wreaths which round my casement
   were.

XLI

'Twas like an eye which seemed to smile on me.
   I watched, till by the sun made pale, it sank
Under the billows of the heaving sea;
   But from its beams deep love my spirit drank,   490
   And to my brain the boundless world now shrank
Into one thought—one image—yes, for ever!
   Even like the dayspring, poured on vapours dank,
The beams of that one Star did shoot and quiver
Through my benighted mind—and were extinguished never.

XLII

'The day passed thus: at night, methought in dream   496
   A shape of speechless beauty did appear:
It stood like light on a careering stream
   Of golder. clouds which shook the atmosphere;
   A wingèd youth, his radiant brow did wear   500
The Morning Star: a wild dissolving bliss
   Over my frame he breathed, approaching near,
And bent his eyes of kindling tenderness
Near mine, and on my lips impressed a lingering kiss,—

XLIII

'And said: "A Spirit loves thee, mortal maiden,   505
   How wilt thou prove thy worth?" Then joy and sleep
Together fled, my soul was deeply laden,
   And to the shore I went to muse and weep;

But as I moved, over my heart did creep
A joy less soft, but more profound and strong 510
Than my sweet dream; and it forbade to keep
The path of the sea-shore: that Spirit's tongue
Seemed whispering in my heart, and bore my steps along.

XLIV

'How, to that vast and peopled city led,
Which was a field of holy warfare then, 515
I walked among the dying and the dead,
And shared in fearless deeds with evil men,
Calm as an angel in the dragon's den—
How I braved death for liberty and truth,
And spurned at peace, and power, and fame—and when
Those hopes had lost the glory of their youth, 521
How sadly I returned—might move the hearer's ruth:

XLV

'Warm tears throng fast! the tale may not be said—
Know then, that when this grief had been subdued,
I was not left, like others, cold and dead; 525
The Spirit whom I loved, in solitude
Sustained his child: the tempest-shaken wood,
The waves, the fountains, and the hush of night—
These were his voice, and well I understood
His smile divine, when the calm sea was bright 530
With silent stars, and Heaven was breathless with delight.

XLVI

'In lonely glens, amid the roar of rivers,
When the dim nights were moonless, have I known
Joys which no tongue can tell; my pale lip quivers
When thought revisits them:—know thou alone, 535
That after many wondrous years were flown,
I was awakened by a shriek of woe;
And over me a mystic robe was thrown,
By viewless hands, and a bright Star did glow
Before my steps—the Snake then met his mortal foe.' 540

XLVII

'Thou fearest not then the Serpent on thy heart?'
'Fear it!' she said, with brief and passionate cry,
And spake no more: that silence made me start—
I looked, and we were sailing pleasantly,

Swift as a cloud between the sea and sky; 545
Beneath the rising moon seen far away,
    Mountains of ice, like sapphire, piled on high,
    Hemming the horizon round, in silence lay
On the still waters—these we did approach alway.

XLVIII

And swift and swifter grew the vessel's motion, 550
    So that a dizzy trance fell on my brain—
Wild music woke me: we had passed the ocean
    Which girds the pole, Nature's remotest reign—
    And we glode fast o'er a pellucid plain
Of waters, azure with the noontide day. 555
    Ethereal mountains shone around—a Fane
    Stood in the midst, girt by green isles which lay
On the blue sunny deep, resplendent far away.

XLIX

It was a Temple, such as mortal hand
    Has never built, nor ecstasy, nor dream 560
Reared in the cities of enchanted land:
    'Twas likest Heaven, ere yet day's purple stream
    Ebbs o'er the western forest, while the gleam
Of the unrisen moon among the clouds
    Is gathering—when with many a golden beam 565
The thronging constellations rush in crowds,
Paving with fire the sky and the marmoreal floods.

L

Like what may be conceived of this vast dome,
    When from the depths which thought can seldom pierce
Genius beholds it rise, his native home. 570
    Girt by the deserts of the Universe;
    Yet, nor in painting's light, or mightier verse,
Or sculpture's marble language, can invest
    That shape to mortal sense—such glooms immerse
That incommunicable sight, and rest 575
Upon the labouring brain and overburdened breast.

LI

Winding among the lawny islands fair,
    Whose blosmy forests starred the shadowy deep,
The wingless boat paused where an ivory stair
    Its fretwork in the crystal sea did steep, 580

Encircling that vast Fane's aërial heap:
We disembarked, and through a portal wide
     We passed—whose roof of moonstone carved, did keep
A glimmering o'er the forms on every side,
Sculptures like life and thought; immovable, deep-eyed.   585

LII

We came to a vast hall, whose glorious roof
     Was diamond, which had drank the lightning's sheen
In darkness, and now poured it through the woof
     Of spell-inwoven clouds hung there to screen
     Its blinding splendour—through such veil was seen   590
That work of subtlest power, divine and rare;
     Orb above orb, with starry shapes between,
And hornèd moons, and meteors strange and fair,
On night-black columns poised—one hollow hemisphere!

LIII

Ten thousand columns in that quivering light   595
     Distinct—between whose shafts wound far away
The long and labyrinthine aisles—more bright
     With their own radiance than the Heaven of Day;
     And on the jasper walls around, there lay
Paintings, the poesy of mightiest thought,   600
     Which did the Spirit's history display;
A tale of passionate change, divinely taught,
Which, in their wingèd dance, unconscious Genii wrought.

LIV

Beneath, there sate on many a sapphire throne,
     The Great, who had departed from mankind,   605
A mighty Senate;—some, whose white hair shone
     Like mountain snow, mild, beautiful, and blind;
     Some, female forms, whose gestures beamed with mind;
And ardent youths, and children bright and fair;
     And some had lyres whose strings were intertwined   610
With pale and clinging flames, which ever there
Waked faint yet thrilling sounds that pierced the crystal air.

LV

One seat was vacant in the midst, a throne,
     Reared on a pyramid like sculptured flame,
Distinct with circling steps which rested on   615
     Their own deep fire—soon as the Woman came

Into that hall, she shrieked the Spirit's name
And fell; and vanished slowly from the sight.
Darkness arose from her dissolving frame,
Which gathering, filled that dome of woven light,   620
Blotting its spherèd stars with supernatural night.

LVI

Then first, two glittering lights were seen to glide
In circles on the amethystine floor,
Small serpent eyes trailing from side to side,
Like meteors on a river's grassy shore,   625
They round each other rolled, dilating more
And more—then rose, commingling into one,
One clear and mighty planet hanging o'er
A cloud of deepest shadow, which was thrown
Athwart the glowing steps and the crystalline throne.   630

LVII

The cloud which rested on that cone of flame
Was cloven; beneath the planet sate a Form,
Fairer than tongue can speak or thought may frame,
The radiance of whose limbs rose-like and warm
Flowed forth, and did with softest light inform   631
The shadowy dome, the sculptures, and the state
Of those assembled shapes—with clinging charm
Sinking upon their hearts and mine. He sate
Majestic, yet most mild—calm, yet compassionate.

LVIII

Wonder and joy a passing faintness threw   640
Over my brow—a hand supported me,
Whose touch was magic strength: an eye of blue
Looked into mine, like moonlight, soothingly;
And a voice said.—'Thou must a listener be
This day—two mighty Spirits now return,   645
Like birds of calm, from the world's raging sea,
They pour fresh light from Hope's immortal urn;
A tale of human power—despair not—list and learn!'

LIX

I looked, and lo! one stood forth eloquently,
His eyes were dark and deep, and the clear brow   650
Which shadowed them was like the morning sky,
The cloudless Heaven of Spring, when in their flow

Through the bright air, the soft winds as they blow
Wake the green world—his gestures did obey
    The oracular mind that made his features glow,   655
And where his curvèd lips half-open lay,
Passion's divinest stream had made impetuous way.

LX

Beneath the darkness of his outspread hair
    He stood thus beautiful: but there was One
Who sate beside him like his shadow there,   660
    And held his hand—far lovelier—she was known
    To be thus fair, by the few lines alone
Which through her floating locks and gathered cloak,
    Glances of soul-dissolving glory, shone:—
None else beheld her eyes—in him they woke   665
Memories which found a tongue as thus he silence broke.

CANTO II

I

THE starlight smile of children, the sweet looks
    Of women, the fair breast from which I fed,
The murmur of the unreposing brooks,
    And the green light which, shifting overhead,   670
    Some tangled bower of vines around me shed,
The shells on the sea-sand, and the wild flowers,
    The lamplight through the rafters cheerly spread,
And on the twining flax—in life's young hours
These sights and sounds did nurse my spirit's folded powers.

II

In Argolis, beside the echoing sea,   676
    Such impulses within my mortal frame
Arose, and they were dear to memory,
    Like tokens of the dead:—but others came
    Soon, in another shape: the wondrous fame   680
Of the past world, the vital words and deeds
    Of minds whom neither time nor change can tame,
Traditions dark and old, whence evil creeds
Start forth, and whose dim shade a stream of poison feeds.

III

I heard, as all have heard, the various story   685
    Of human life, and wept unwilling tears.
Feeble historians of its shame and glory,
    False disputants on all its hopes and fears,

Victims who worshipped ruin,—chroniclers
Of daily scorn, and slaves who loathed their state   690
Yet, flattering power, had given its ministers
A throne of judgement in the grave:—'twas fate,
That among such as these my youth should seek its mate.

IV

The land in which I lived, by a fell bane
   Was withered up. Tyrants dwelt side by side,   695
And stabled in our homes,—until the chain
   Stifled the captive's cry, and to abide
   That blasting curse men had no shame—all vied
In evil, slave and despot; fear with lust
   Strange fellowship through mutual hate had tied,   700
Like two dark serpents tangled in the dust,
Which on the paths of men their mingling poison thrust.

V

Earth, our bright home, its mountains and its waters,
   And the ethereal shapes which are suspended
Over its green expanse, and those fair daughters,   705
   The clouds, of Sun and Ocean, who have blended
   The colours of the air since first extended
It cradled the young world, none wandered forth
   To see or feel: a darkness had descended
On every heart: the light which shows its worth,   710
Must among gentle thoughts and fearless take its birth.

VI

This vital world, this home of happy spirits,
   Was as a dungeon to my blasted kind;
All that despair from murdered hope inherits
   They sought, and in their helpless misery blind,   715
   A deeper prison and heavier chains did find,
And stronger tyrants:—a dark gulf before,
   The realm of a stern Ruler, yawned; behind,
Terror and Time conflicting drove, and bore
On their tempestuous flood the shrieking wretch from shore.

VII

Out of that Ocean's wrecks had Guilt and Woe   721
   Framed a dark dwelling for their homeless thought,
And, starting at the ghosts which to and fro
   Glide o'er its dim and gloomy strand, had brought

The worship thence which they each other taught.   725
Well might men loathe their life, well might they turn
    Even to the ills again from which they sought
Such refuge after death!—well might they learn
    To gaze on this fair world with hopeless unconcern!

VIII

For they all pined in bondage; body and soul,   730
    Tyrant and slave, victim and torturer, bent
Before one Power, to which supreme control
    Over their will by their own weakness lent,
    Made all its many names omnipotent;
All symbols of things evil, all divine;   735
    And hymns of blood or mockery, which rent
The air from all its fanes, did intertwine
Imposture's impious toils round each discordant shrine.

IX

I heard, as all have heard, life's various story,
    And in no careless heart transcribed the tale;   740
But, from the sneers of men who had grown hoary
    In shame and scorn, from groans of crowds made pale
    By famine, from a mother's desolate wail
O'er her polluted child, from innocent blood
    Poured on the earth, and brows anxious and pale   745
With the heart's warfare; did I gather food
To feed my many thoughts: a tameless multitude!

X

I wandered through the wrecks of days departed
    Far by the desolated shore, when even
O'er the still sea and jagged islets darted   750
    The light of moonrise; in the northern Heaven,
    Among the clouds near the horizon driven,
The mountains lay beneath our planet pale;
    Around me, broken tombs and columns riven
Looked vast in twilight, and the sorrowing gale   755
Waked in those ruins gray its everlasting wail!

XI

I knew not who had framed these wonders then,
    Nor had I heard the story of their deeds;
But dwellings of a race of mightier men,
    And monuments of less ungentle creeds   760

Tell their own tale to him who wisely heeds
The language which they speak; and now, to me
The moonlight making pale the blooming weeds,
The bright stars shining in the breathless sea,
Interpreted those scrolls of mortal mystery. 765

XII

Such man has been, and such may yet become!
Ay, wiser, greater, gentler, even than they
Who on the fragments of yon shattered dome
Have stamped the sign of power—I felt the sway
Of the vast stream of ages bear away 770
My floating thoughts—my heart beat loud and fast—
Even as a storm let loose beneath the ray
Of the still moon, my spirit onward past
Beneath truth's steady beams upon its tumult cast.

XIII

It shall be thus no more! too long, too long, 775
Sons of the glorious dead, have ye lain bound
In darkness and in ruin!—Hope is strong,
Justice and Truth their wingèd child have found—
Awake! arise! until the mighty sound
Of your career shall scatter in its gust 780
The thrones of the oppressor, and the ground
Hide the last altar's unregarded dust,
Whose Idol has so long betrayed your impious trust!

XIV

It must be so—I will arise and waken
The multitude, and like a sulphurous hill, 785
Which on a sudden from its snows has shaken
The swoon of ages, it shall burst and fill
The world with cleansing fire: it must, it will—
It may not be restrained!—and who shall stand
Amid the rocking earthquake steadfast still, 790
But Laon? on high Freedom's desert land
A tower whose marble walls the leaguèd storms withstand!

XV

One summer night, in commune with the hope
Thus deeply fed, amid those ruins gray
I watched, beneath the dark sky's starry cope; 795
And ever from that hour upon me lay

The burden of this hope, and night or day,
    In vision or in dream, clove to my breast:
        Among mankind, or when gone far away
To the lone shores and mountains, 'twas a guest   800
Which followed where I fled, and watched when I did rest.

XVI

These hopes found words through which my spirit sought
    To weave a bondage of such sympathy,
As might create some response to the thought
        Which ruled me now—and as the vapours lie   805
        Bright in the outspread morning's radiancy,
So were these thoughts invested with the light
        Of language: and all bosoms made reply
On which its lustre streamed, whene'er it might
Through darkness wide and deep those trancèd spirits smite.

XVII

Yes, many an eye with dizzy tears was dim,   811
    And oft I thought to clasp my own heart's brother,
When I could feel the listener's senses swim,
        And hear his breath its own swift gaspings smother
        Even as my words evoked them—and another,   815
And yet another, I did fondly deem,
        Felt that we all were sons of one great mother;
And the cold truth such sad reverse did seem,
As to awake in grief from some delightful dream.

XVIII

Yes, oft beside the ruined labyrinth   820
    Which skirts the hoary caves of the green deep,
Did Laon and his friend, on one gray plinth,
        Round whose worn base the wild waves hiss and leap,
        Resting at eve, a lofty converse keep:
And that this friend was false, may now be said   825
        Calmly—that he like other men could weep
Tears which are lies, and could betray and spread
Snares for that guileless heart which for his own had bled.

XIX

Then, had no great aim recompensed my sorrow,
    I must have sought dark respite from its stress   830
In dreamless rest, in sleep that sees no morrow—
    For to tread life's dismaying wilderness

Without one smile to cheer, one voice to bless,
Amid the snares and scoffs of human kind,
Is hard—but I betrayed it not, nor less 835
With love that scorned return, sought to unbind
The interwoven clouds which make its wisdom blind.

XX

With deathless minds which leave where they have passed
A path of light, my soul communion knew;
Till from that glorious intercourse, at last, 840
As from a mine of magic store, I drew
Words which were weapons;—round my heart there grew
The adamantine armour of their power,
And from my fancy wings of golden hue
Sprang forth—yet not alone from wisdom's tower, 845
A minister of truth, these plumes young Laon bore.

XXI

An orphan with my parents lived, whose eyes
Were lodestars of delight, which drew me home
When I might wander forth; nor did I prize
Aught human thing beneath Heaven's mighty dome 850
Beyond this child: so when sad hours were come,
And baffled hope like ice still clung to me,
Since kin were cold, and friends had now become
Heartless and false, I turned from all, to be,
Cythna, the only source of tears and smiles to thee. 855

XXII

What wert thou then? A child most infantine,
Yet wandering far beyond that innocent age
In all but its sweet looks and mien divine:
Even then, methought, with the world's tyrant rage
A patient warfare thy young heart did wage, 860
When those soft eyes of scarcely conscious thought
Some tale, or thine own fancies, would engage
To overflow with tears, or converse fraught
With passion, o'er their depths its fleeting light had wrought.

XXIII

She moved upon this earth a shape of brightness, 865
A power, that from its objects scarcely drew
One impulse of her being—in her lightness
Most like some radiant cloud of morning dew,

Which wanders through the waste air's pathless blue,
To nourish some far desert: she did seem   870
    Beside me, gathering beauty as she grew,
Like the bright shade of some immortal dream
Which walks, when tempest sleeps, the wave of life's dark stream.

XXIV

As mine own shadow was this child to me,
    A second self, far dearer and more fair;   875
Which clothed in undissolving radiancy
    All those steep paths which languor and despair
    Of human things, had made so dark and bare,
But which I trod alone—nor, till bereft
    Of friends, and overcome by lonely care,   880
Knew I what solace for that loss was left,
Though by a bitter wound my trusting heart was cleft.

XXV

Once she was dear, now she was all I had
    To love in human life—this playmate sweet,
This child of twelve years old—so she was made   885
    My sole associate, and her willing feet
    Wandered with mine where earth and ocean meet,
Beyond the aëreal mountains whose vast cells
    The unreposing billows ever beat.
Through forests wide and old, and lawny dells   890
Where boughs of incense droop over the emerald wells.

XXVI

And warm and light I felt her clasping hand
    When twined in mine: she followed where I went,
Through the lone paths of our immortal land.
    It had no waste but some memorial lent   895
    Which strung me to my toil—some monument
Vital with mind: then, Cythna by my side,
    Until the bright and beaming day were spent,
Would rest, with looks entreating to abide,
Too earnest and too sweet ever to be denied.   900

XXVII

And soon I could not have refused her—thus
    For ever, day and night, we two were ne'er
Parted, but when brief sleep divided us:
    And when the pauses of the lulling air

Of noon beside the sea, had made a lair   905
For her soothed senses, in my arms she slept,
And I kept watch over her slumbers there,
While, as the shifting visions o'er her swept,
Amid her innocent rest by turns she smiled and wept.

XXVIII

And, in the murmur of her dreams was heard   910
    Sometimes the name of Laon:—suddenly
She would arise, and, like the secret bird
    Whom sunset wakens, fill the shore and sky
    With her sweet accents—a wild melody!
Hymns which my soul had woven to Freedom, strong   915
    The source of passion, whence they rose, to be;
Triumphant strains, which, like a spirit's tongue,
To the enchanted waves that child of glory sung—

XXIX

Her white arms lifted through the shadowy stream
    Of her loose hair—oh, excellently great   920
Seemed to me then my purpose, the vast theme
    Of those impassioned songs, when Cythna sate
    Amid the calm which rapture doth create
After its tumult, her heart vibrating,
    Her spirit o'er the ocean's floating state   925
From her deep eyes far wandering, on the wing
Of visions that were mine, beyond its utmost spring.

XXX

For, before Cythna loved it, had my song
    Peopled with thoughts the boundless universe,
A mighty congregation, which were strong   930
    Where'er they trod the darkness to disperse
    The cloud of that unutterable curse
Which clings upon mankind:—all things became
    Slaves to my holy and heroic verse,
Earth, sea and sky, the planets, life and fame   935
And fate, or whate'er else binds the world's wondrous frame.

XXXI

And this beloved child thus felt the sway
    Of my conceptions, gathering like a cloud
The very wind on which it rolls away:
    Hers too were all my thoughts, ere yet, endowed   940

With music and with light, their fountains flowed
In poesy; and her still and earnest face,
Pallid with feelings which intensely glowed
Within, was turned on mine with speechless grace,
Watching the hopes which there her heart had learned to trace.

XXXII

In me, communion with this purest being   946
    Kindled intenser zeal, and made me wise
In knowledge, which, in hers mine own mind seeing,
    Left in the human world few mysteries:
    How without fear of evil or disguise   950
Was Cythna!—what a spirit strong and mild,
    Which death, or pain or peril could despise,
Yet melt in tenderness! what genius wild
Yet mighty, was enclosed within one simple child!

XXXIII

New lore was this—old age, with its gray hair,   955
    And wrinkled legends of unworthy things,
And icy sneers, is nought: it cannot dare
    To burst the chains which life for ever flings
    On the entangled soul's aspiring wings,
So is it cold and cruel, and is made   960
    The careless slave of that dark power which brings
Evil, like blight, on man, who, still betrayed,
Laughs o'er the grave in which his living hopes are laid.

XXXIV

Nor are the strong and the severe to keep
    The empire of the world: thus Cythna taught   965
Even in the visions of her eloquent sleep,
    Unconscious of the power through which she wrought
    The woof of such intelligible thought,
As from the tranquil strength which cradled lay
    In her smile-peopled rest, my spirit sought   970
Why the deceiver and the slave has sway
O'er heralds so divine of truth's arising day.

XXXV

Within that fairest form, the female mind
    Untainted by the poison-clouds which rest
On the dark world, a sacred home did find: 975
    But else, from the wide earth's maternal breast,

Victorious Evil, which had dispossessed
All native power, had those fair children torn,
  And made them slaves to soothe his vile unrest,
  And minister to lust its joys forlorn,   980
Till they had learned to breathe the atmosphere of scorn.

XXXVI

This misery was but coldly felt, till she
  Became my only friend, who had endued
My purpose with a wider sympathy;
  Thus, Cythna mourned with me the servitude   985
  In which the half of humankind were mewed
Victims of lust and hate, the slaves of slaves,
  She mourned that grace and power were thrown as food
To the hyaena lust, who, among graves,
Over his loathèd meal, laughing in agony, raves.   990

XXXVII

And I, still gazing on that glorious child,
  Even as these thoughts flushed o'er her:—'Cythna sweet,
Well with the world art thou unreconciled;
  Never will peace and human nature meet
  Till free and equal man and woman greet   995
Domestic peace; and ere this power can make
  In human hearts its calm and holy seat,
This slavery must be broken'—as I spake,
From Cythna's eyes a light of exultation brake.

XXXVIII

She replied earnestly:—'It shall be mine,   1000
  This task, mine, Laon!—thou hast much to gain;
Nor wilt thou at poor Cythna's pride repine,
  If she should lead a happy female train
  To meet thee over the rejoicing plain,
When myriads at thy call shall throng around   1005
  The Golden City.'—Then the child did strain
My arm upon her tremulous heart, and wound
Her own about my neck, till some reply she found.

XXXIX

I smiled, and spake not.—'Wherefore dost thou smile
  At what I say? Laon, I am not weak,   1010
And though my cheek might become pale the while,
  With thee, if thou desirest, will I seek

Through their array of banded slaves to wreak
Ruin upon the tyrants. I had thought
   It was more hard to turn my unpractised cheek   1015
To scorn and shame, and this beloved spot
And thee, O dearest friend, to leave and murmur not.

XL

'Whence came I what I am? Thou, Laon, knowest
   How a young child should thus undaunted be;
Methinks, it is a power which thou bestowest,   1020
   Through which I seek, by most resembling thee,
   So to become most good and great and free,
Yet far beyond this Ocean's utmost roar
   In towers and huts are many like to me,
Who, could they see thine eyes, or feel such lore   1025
As I have learnt from them, like me would fear no more.

XLI

'Think'st thou that I shall speak unskilfully,
   And none will heed me? I remember now,
How once, a slave in tortures doomed to die,
   Was saved, because in accents sweet and low   1030
   He sung a song his Judge loved long ago,
As he was led to death.—All shall relent
   Who hear me—tears, as mine have flowed, shall flow,
Hearts beat as mine now beats, with such intent
As renovates the world; a will omnipotent!   1035

XLII

'Yes, I will tread Pride's golden palaces,
   Through Penury's roofless huts and squalid cells
Will I descend, where'er in abjectness
   Woman with some vile slave her tyrant dwells,
   There with the music of thine own sweet spells   1040
Will disenchant the captives, and will pour
   For the despairing, from the crystal wells
Of thy deep spirit, reason's mighty lore,
And power shall then abound, and hope arise once more.

XLIII

'Can man be free if woman be a slave?   1045
   Chain one who lives, and breathes this boundless air
To the corruption of a closèd grave!
   Can they whose mates are beasts, condemned to bear

Scorn, heavier far than toil or anguish, dare
To trample their oppressors? in their home   1050
    Among their babes, thou knowest a curse would wear
The shape of woman—hoary Crime would come
Behind, and Fraud rebuild religion's tottering dome.

XLIV

'I am a child:—I would not yet depart.
    When I go forth alone, bearing the lamp   1055
Aloft which thou hast kindled in my heart,
    Millions of slaves from many a dungeon damp
    Shall leap in joy, as the benumbing cramp
Of ages leaves their limbs—no ill may harm
    Thy Cythna ever—truth its radiant stamp   1060
Has fixed, as an invulnerable charm
Upon her children's brow, dark Falsehood to disarm.

XLV

'Wait yet awhile for the appointed day—
    Thou wilt depart, and I with tears stall stand
Watching thy dim sail skirt the ocean gray;   1065
    Amid the dwellers of this lonely land
    I shall remain alone—and thy command
Shall then dissolve the world's unquiet trance,
    And, multitudinous as the desert sand
Borne on the storm, its millions shall advance,   1070
Thronging round thee, the light of their deliverance.

XLVI

'Then, like the forests of some pathless mountain,
    Which from remotest glens two warring winds
Involve in fire which not the loosened fountain
    Of broadest floods might quench, shall all the kinds
    Of evil, catch from our uniting minds   1076
The spark which must consume them;—Cythna then
    Will have cast off the impotence that binds
Her childhood now, and through the paths of men
Will pass, as the charmed bird that haunts the serpent's den.

XLVII

'We part!—O Laon, I must dare nor tremble   1081
    To meet those looks no more!—Oh, heavy stroke!
Sweet brother of my soul! can I dissemble
    The agony of this thought?'—As thus she spoke

The gathered sobs her quivering accents broke,   1085
And in my arms she hid her beating breast.
I remained still for tears—sudden she woke
    As one awakes from sleep, and wildly pressed
My bosom, her whole frame impetuously possessed.

XLVIII

'We part to meet again—but yon blue waste,   1090
    Yon desert wide and deep holds no recess,
Within whose happy silence, thus embraced
    We might survive all ills in one caress:
    Nor doth the grave—I fear 'tis passionless—
Nor yon cold vacant Heaven:—we meet again   1095
    Within the minds of men, whose lips shall bless
Our memory, and whose hopes its light retain
When these dissevered bones are trodden in the plain.'

XLIX

I could not speak, though she had ceased, for now
    The fountains of her feeling, swift and deep,   1100
Seemed to suspend the tumult of their flow;
    So we arose, and by the starlight steep
    Went homeward—neither did we speak nor weep,
But, pale, were calm with passion—thus subdued
    Like evening shades that o'er the mountains creep,   1105
We moved towards our home; where, in this mood,
Each from the other sought refuge in solitude.

CANTO III

I

WHAT thoughts had sway o'er Cythna's lonely slumber
    That night, I know not; but my own did seem
As if they might ten thousand years outnumber   1110
    Of waking life, the visions of a dream
    Which hid in one dim gulf the troubled stream
Of mind; a boundless chaos wild and vast,
    Whose limits yet were never memory's theme:
And I lay struggling as its whirlwinds passed,   1115
Sometimes for rapture sick, sometimes for pain aghast.

II

Two hours, whose mighty circle did embrace
    More time than might make gray the infant world,
Rolled thus, a weary and tumultuous space:
    When the third came, like mist on breezes curled,   1120

From my dim sleep a shadow was unfurled:
Methought, upon the threshold of a cave
  I sate with Cythna; drooping briony, pearled
With dew from the wild streamlet's shattered wave,
Hung, where we sate to taste the joys which Nature gave.

III

We lived a day as we were wont to live,   1126
  But Nature had a robe of glory on,
And the bright air o'er every shape did weave
  Intenser hues, so that the herbless stone,
  The leafless bough among the leaves alone,   1130
Had being clearer than its own could be,
  And Cythna's pure and radiant self was shown,
In this strange vision, so divine to me,
That, if I loved before, now love was agony.

IV

Morn fled, noon came, evening, then night descended,
  And we prolonged calm talk beneath the sphere   1136
Of the calm moon—when suddenly was blended
  With our repose a nameless sense of fear;
  And from the cave behind I seemed to hear
Sounds gathering upwards!—accents incomplete,   1140
  And stifled shrieks,—and now, more near and near,
A tumult and a rush of thronging feet
The cavern's secret depths beneath the earth did beat.

V

The scene was changed, and away, away, away!
  Through the air and over the sea we sped,   1145
And Cythna in my sheltering bosom lay,
  And the winds bore me—through the darkness spread
  Around, the gaping earth then vomited
Legions of foul and ghastly shapes, which hung
  Upon my flight; and ever, as we fled,   1150
They plucked at Cythna—soon to me then clung
A sense of actual things those monstrous dreams among.

VI

And I lay struggling in the impotence
  Of sleep, while outward life had burst its bound,
Though, still deluded, strove the tortured sense   1155
  To its dire wanderings to adapt the sound

Which in the light of morn was poured around
  Our dwelling—breathless, pale, and unaware
  I rose, and all the cottage crowded found
  With armèd men, whose glittering swords were bare,   1160
And whose degraded limbs the tyrant's garb did wear.

VII

And, ere with rapid lips and gathered brow
  I could demand the cause—a feeble shriek—
It was a feeble shriek, faint, far and low,
  Arrested me—my mien grew calm and meek,   1165
  And grasping a small knife, I went to seek
That voice among the crowd—'twas Cythna's cry!
  Beneath most calm resolve did agony wreak
  Its whirlwind rage:—so I passed quietly
Till I beheld, where bound, that dearest child did lie.   1170

VIII

I started to behold her, for delight
  And exultation, and a joyance free,
Solemn, serene and lofty, filled the light
  Of the calm smile with which she looked on me:
  So that I feared some brainless ecstasy,   1175
Wrought from that bitter woe, had wildered her—
  'Farewell! farewell!' she said, as I drew nigh.
'At first my peace was marred by this strange stir,
Now I am calm as truth—its chosen minister.

IX

'Look not so, Laon—say farewell in hope,   1180
  These bloody men are but the slaves who bear
Their mistress to her task—it was my scope
  The slavery where they drag me now, to share,
  And among captives willing chains to wear
Awhile—the rest thou knowest—return, dear friend!   1185
  Let our first triumph trample the despair
Which would ensnare us now, for in the end,
In victory or in death our hopes and fears must blend.'

X

These words had fallen on my unheeding ear,
  Whilst I had watched the motions of the crew   1190
With seeming-careless glance; not many were
  Around her, for their comrades just withdrew

To guard some other victim—so I drew
My knife, and with one impulse, suddenly
   All unaware three of their number slew,   1195
And grasped a fourth by the throat, and with loud cry
My countrymen invoked to death or liberty!

XI

What followed then, I know not—for a stroke
  On my raised arm and naked head, came down,
Filling my eyes with blood—when I awoke,   1200
  I felt that they had bound me in my swoon,
  And up a rock which overhangs the town,
By the steep path were bearing me: below,
  The plain was filled with slaughter,—overthrown
The vineyards and the harvests, and the glow   1205
Of blazing roofs shone far o'er the white Ocean's flow.

XII

Upon that rock a mighty column stood,
  Whose capital seemed sculptured in the sky,
Which to the wanderers o'er the solitude
  Of distant seas, from ages long gone by,   1210
  Had made a landmark; o'er its height to fly
Scarcely the cloud, the vulture, or the blast,
  Has power—and when the shades of evening lie
On Earth and Ocean, its carved summits cast
The sunken daylight far through the aërial waste.   1215

XIII

They bore me to a cavern in the hill
  Beneath that column, and unbound me there:
And one did strip me stark; and one did fill
  A vessel from the putrid pool; one bare
  A lighted torch, and four with friendless care   1220
Guided my steps the cavern-paths along,
  Then up a steep and dark and narrow stair
We wound, until the torch's fiery tongue
Amid the gushing day beamless and pallid hung.

XIV

They raised me to the platform of the pile,   1225
  That column's dizzy height:—the grate of brass
Through which they thrust me, open stood the while,
  As to its ponderous and suspended mass,

With chains which eat into the flesh, alas!
With brazen links, my naked limbs they bound: 1230
   The grate, as they departed to repass,
With horrid clangour fell, and the far sound
Of their retiring steps in the dense gloom were drowned.

XV

The noon was calm and bright:—around that column
   The overhanging sky and circling sea   1235
Spread forth in silentness profound and solemn
   The darkness of brief frenzy cast on me,
   So that I knew not my own misery:
The islands and the mountains in the day
   Like clouds reposed afar; and I could see   1240
The town among the woods below that lay,
And the dark rocks which bound the bright and glassy bay.

XVI

It was so calm, that scarce the feathery weed
   Sown by some eagle on the topmost stone
Swayed in the air:—so bright, that noon did breed   1245
   No shadow in the sky beside mine own—
   Mine, and the shadow of my chain alone.
Below, the smoke of roofs involved in flame
   Rested like night, all else was clearly shown
In that broad glare, yet sound to me none came,   1250
But of the living blood that ran within my frame.

XVII

The peace of madness fled, and ah, too soon!
   A ship was lying on the sunny main,
Its sails were flagging in the breathless noon—
   Its shadow lay beyond—that sight again   1255
   Waked, with its presence, in my trancèd brain
The stings of a known sorrow, keen and cold:
   I knew that ship bore Cythna o'er the plain
Of waters, to her blighting slavery sold,
And watched it with such thoughts as must remain untold.

XVIII

I watched, until the shades of evening wrapped   1261
   Earth like an exhalation—then the bark
Moved, for that calm was by the sunset snapped.
   It moved a speck upon the Ocean dark:

Soon the wan stars came forth, and I could mark   1265
  Its path no more!—I sought to close mine eyes,
    But like the balls, their lids were stiff and stark;
  I would have risen, but ere that I could rise,
My parchèd skin was split with piercing agonies.

XIX

I gnawed my brazen chain, and sought to sever   1270
  Its adamantine links, that I might die:
O Liberty! forgive the base endeavour,
  Forgive me, if, reserved for victory,
    The Champion of thy faith e'er sought to fly.—
That starry night, with its clear silence, sent   1275
  Tameless resolve which laughed at misery
Into my soul—linkèd remembrance lent
To that such power, to me such a severe content.

XX

To breathe, to be, to hope, or to despair
  And die, I questioned not; nor, though the Sun   1280
Its shafts of agony kindling through the air
  Moved over me, nor though in evening dun,
    Or when the stars their visible courses run,
  Or morning, the wide universe was spread
    In dreary calmness round me, did I shun   1285
Its presence, nor seek refuge with the dead
From one faint hope whose flower a dropping poison shed.

XXI

Two days thus passed—I neither raved nor died—
  Thirst raged within me, like a scorpion's nest
Built in mine entrails; I had spurned aside   1290
  The water-vessel, while despair possessed
    My thoughts, and now no drop remained! The uprest
Of the third sun brought hunger—but the crust
  Which had been left, was to my craving breast
Fuel, not food. I chewed the bitter dust,   1295
And bit my bloodless arm, and licked the brazen rust.

XXII

My brain began to fail when the fourth morn
  Burst o'er the golden isles—a fearful sleep,
Which through the caverns dreary and forlorn
  Of the riven soul, sent its foul dreams to sweep   1300

With whirlwind swiftness—a fall far and deep,—
A gulf, a void, a sense of senselessness—
   These things dwelt in me, even as shadows keep
Their watch in some dim charnel's loneliness,
A shoreless sea, a sky sunless and planetless!   1305

XXIII

The forms which peopled this terrific trance
   I well remember—like a choir of devils,
Around me they involved a giddy dance;
   Legions seemed gathering from the misty levels
   Of Ocean, to supply those ceaseless revels,   1310
Foul, ceaseless shadows:—thought could not divide
   The actual world from these entangling evils,
Which so bemocked themselves, that I descried
All shapes like mine own self, hideously multiplied.

XXIV

The sense of day and night, of false and true,   1315
   Was dead within me. Yet two visions burst
That darkness—one, as since that hour I knew,
   Was not a phantom of the realms accursed,
   Where then my spirit dwelt—but of the first
I know not yet, was it a dream or no.   1320
   But both, though not distincter, were immersed
In hues which, when through memory's waste they flow,
Make their divided streams more bright and rapid now.

XXV

Methought that grate was lifted, and the seven
   Who brought me thither four stiff corpses bare,   1325
And from the frieze to the four winds of Heaven
   Hung them on high by the entangled hair:
   Swarthy were three—the fourth was very fair:
As they retired, the golden moon upsprung,
   And eagerly, out in the giddy air,   1330
Leaning that I might eat, I stretched and clung
Over the shapeless depth in which those corpses hung.

XXVI

A woman's shape, now lank and cold and blue,
   The dwelling of the many-coloured worm,
Hung there; the white and hollow cheek I drew   1335
   To my dry lips—what radiance did inform

Those horny eyes? whose was that withered form?
  Alas, alas! it seemed that Cythna's ghost
    Laughed in those looks, and that the flesh was warm
  Within my teeth!—A whirlwind keen as frost   1340
Then in its sinking gulfs my sickening spirit tossed.

XXVII

Then seemed it that a tameless hurricane
  Arose, and bore me in its dark career
Beyond the sun, beyond the stars that wane
  On the verge of formless space—it languished there, 1345
  And dying, left a silence lone and drear,
More horrible than famine:—in the deep
  The shape of an old man did then appear,
Stately and beautiful; that dreadful sleep
His heavenly smiles dispersed, and I could wake and weep.

XXVIII

And, when the blinding tears had fallen, I saw   1351
  That column, and those corpses, and the moon,
And felt the poisonous tooth of hunger gnaw
  My vitals, I rejoiced, as if the boon
  Of senseless death would be accorded soon;—   1355
When from that stony gloom a voice arose,
  Solemn and sweet as when low winds attune
The midnight pines; the grate did then unclose,
And on that reverend form the moonlight did repose.

XXIX

He struck my chains, and gently spake and smiled: 1360
  As they were loosened by that Hermit old,
Mine eyes were of their madness half beguiled,
  To answer those kind looks—he did enfold
  His giant arms around me, to uphold
My wretched frame, my scorchèd limbs he wound   1365
  In linen moist and balmy, and as cold
As dew to drooping leaves;—the chain, with sound
Like earthquake, through the chasm of that steep stair did bound,

XXX

As, lifting me, it fell!—What next I heard,
  Were billows leaping on the harbour-bar,   1370
And the shrill sea-wind, whose breath idly stirred
  My hair;—I looked abroad, and saw a star

Shining beside a sail, and distant far
That mountain and its column, the known mark
   Of those who in the wide deep wandering are,   1375
So that I feared some Spirit, fell and dark,
In trance had lain me thus within a fiendish bark.

XXXI

For now indeed, over the salt sea-billow
   I sailed: yet dared not look upon the shape
Of him who ruled the helm, although the pillow   1380
   For my light head was hollowed in his lap,
   And my bare limbs his mantle did enwrap,
Fearing it was a fiend: at last, he bent
   O'er me his aged face, as if to snap
Those dreadful thoughts the gentle grandsire bent,   1385
And to my inmost soul his soothing looks he sent.

XXXII

A soft and healing potion to my lips
   At intervals he raised—now looked on high,
To mark if yet the starry giant dips
   His zone in the dim sea—now cheeringly,   1390
   Though he said little, did he speak to me.
'It is a friend beside thee—take good cheer,
   Poor victim, thou art now at liberty!'
I joyed as those a human tone to hear,
Who in cells deep and lone have languished many a year.

XXXIII

A dim and feeble joy, whose glimpses oft   1396
   Were quenched in a relapse of wildering dreams,
Yet still methought we sailed, until aloft
   The stars of night grew pallid, and the beams
   Of morn descended on the ocean-streams,   1400
And still that aged man, so grand and mild,
   Tended me, even as some sick mother seems
To hang in hope over a dying child,
Till in the azure East darkness again was piled.

XXXIV

And then the night-wind steaming from the shore,   1405
   Sent odours dying sweet across the sea,
And the swift boat the little waves which bore,
   Were cut by its keen keel, though slantingly;

Soon I could hear the leaves sigh, and could see
The myrtle-blossoms starring the dim grove, 1410
    As past the pebbly beach the boat did flee
On sidelong wing, into a silent cove,
Where ebon pines a shade under the starlight wove.

CANTO IV

I

THE old man took the oars, and soon the bark
    Smote on the beach beside a tower of stone; 1415
It was a crumbling heap, whose portal dark
    With blooming ivy-trails was overgrown;
    Upon whose floor the spangling sands were strown,
And rarest sea-shells, which the eternal flood,
    Slave to the mother of the months, had thrown 1420
Within the walls of that gray tower, which stood
A changeling of man's art, nursed amid Nature's brood.

II

When the old man his boat had anchorèd,
    He wound me in his arms with tender care,
And very few, but kindly words he said, 1425
    And bore me through the tower adown a stair,
    Whose smooth descent some ceaseless step to wear
For many a year had fallen.—We came at last
    To a small chamber, which with mosses rare
Was tapestried, where me his soft hands placed 1430
Upon a couch of grass and oak-leaves interlaced.

III

The moon was darting through the lattices
    Its yellow light, warm as the beams of day—
So warm, that to admit the dewy breeze,
    The old man opened them; the moonlight lay 1435
    Upon a lake whose waters wove their play
Even to the threshold of that lonely home:
    Within was seen in the dim wavering ray
The antique sculptured roof, and many a tome
Whose lore had made that sage all that he had become.

IV

The rock-built barrier of the sea was past,— 1441
    And I was on the margin of a lake,
A lonely lake, amid the forests vast
    And snowy mountains:—did my spirit wake

From sleep as many-coloured as the snake   1445
    That girds eternity? in life and truth,
        Might not my heart its cravings ever slake?
Was Cythna then a dream, and all my youth,
And all its hopes and fears, and all its joy and ruth?

                              v

Thus madness came again,—a milder madness,   1450
    Which darkened nought but time's unquiet flow
With supernatural shades of clinging sadness;
    That gentle Hermit, in my helpless woe,
    By my sick couch was busy to and fro,
Like a strong spirit ministrant of good: 1455
    When I was healed, he led me forth to show
The wonders of his sylvan solitude,
And we together sate by that isle-fretted flood.

                             VI

He knew his soothing words to weave with skill
    From all my madness told; like mine own heart,   1460
Of Cythna would he question me, until
    That thrilling name had ceased to make me start,
    From his familiar lips—it was not art,
Of wisdom and of justice when he spoke—
    When mid soft looks of pity, there would dart   1465
A glance as keen as is the lightning's stroke
When it doth rive the knots of some ancestral oak.

                            VII

Thus slowly from my brain the darkness rolled,
    My thoughts their due array did re-assume
Through the enchantments of that Hermit old;   1470
    Then I bethought me of the glorious doom
    Of those who sternly struggle to relume
The lamp of Hope o'er man's bewildered lot,
    And, sitting by the waters, in the gloom
Of eve, to that friend's heart I told my thought—   1475
That heart which had grown old, but had corrupted not.

                           VIII

That hoary man had spent his livelong age
    In converse with the dead, who leave the stamp
Of ever-burning thoughts on many a page,
    When they are gone into the senseless damp   1480

Of graves;—his spirit thus became a lamp
Of splendour, like to those on which it fed:
    Through peopled haunts, the City and the Camp,
Deep thirst for knowledge had his footsteps led,
And all the ways of men among mankind he read.   1485

IX

But custom maketh blind and obdurate
    The loftiest hearts:—he had beheld the woe
In which mankind was bound, but deemed that fate
    Which made them abject, would preserve them so;
    And in such faith, some steadfast joy to know,   1490
He sought this cell: but when fame went abroad,
    That one in Argolis did undergo
Torture for liberty, and that the crowd
High truths from gifted lips had heard and understood;

X

And that the multitude was gathering wide,—   1495
    His spirit leaped within his aged frame,
In lonely peace he could no more abide,
    But to the land on which the victor's flame
    Had fed, my native land, the Hermit came:
Each heart was there a shield. and every tongue   1500
    Was as a sword, of truth—young Laon's name
Rallied their secret hopes, though tyrants sung
Hymns of triumphant joy our scattered tribes among.

XI

He came to the lone column on the rock,
    And with his sweet and mighty eloquence   1505
The hearts of those who watched it did unlock,
    And made them melt in tears of penitence.
    They gave him entrance free to bear me thence.
'Since this,' the old man said, 'seven years are spent,
    While slowly truth on thy benighted sense   1510
Has crept; the hope which wildered it has lent
Meanwhile, to me the power of a sublime intent.

XII

'Yes, from the records of my youthful state,
    And from the lore of bards and sages old,
From whatsoe'er my wakened thoughts create   1515
    Out of the hopes of thine aspirings bold,

Have I collected language to unfold
  Truth to my countrymen; from shore to shore
    Doctrines of human power my words have told,
They have been heard, and men aspire to more   1520
Than they have ever gained or ever lost of yore.

XIII

'In secret chambers parents read, and weep,
  My writings to their babes, no longer blind;
And young men gather when their tyrants sleep,
    And vows of faith each to the other bind;   1525
    And marriageable maidens, who have pined
With love, till life seemed melting through their look,
  A warmer zeal, a nobler hope now find;
And every bosom thus is rapt and shook,
Like autumn's myriad leaves in one swoln mountain-brook.

XIV

'The tyrants of the Golden City tremble   1531
  At voices which are heard about the streets,
The ministers of fraud can scarce dissemble
    The lies of their own heart; but when one meets
    Another at the shrine, he inly weets,   1535
Though he says nothing, that the truth is known;
  Murderers are pale upon the judgement-seats,
And gold grows vile even to the wealthy crone,
And laughter fills the Fane, and curses shake the Throne.

XV

'Kind thoughts, and mighty hopes, and gentle deeds   1540
  Abound, for fearless love, and the pure law
Of mild equality and peace, succeeds
    To faiths which long have held the world in awe,
    Bloody and false, and cold:—as whirlpools draw
All wrecks of Ocean to their chasm, the sway   1545
  Of thy strong genius, Laon, which foresaw
This hope, compels all spirits to obey,
Which round thy secret strength now throng in wide array.

XVI

'For I have been thy passive instrument'—
  (As thus the old man spake, his countenance   1550
Gleamed on me like a spirit's)—'thou hast lent
  To me, to all, the power to advance

Towards this unforeseen deliverance
From our ancestral chains—ay, thou didst rear
   That lamp of hope on high, which time nor chance 1555
Nor change may not extinguish, and my share
Of good, was o'er the world its gathered beams to bear.

XVII

'But I, alas! am both unknown and old,
   And though the woof of wisdom I know well
To dye in hues of language, I am cold 1560
   In seeming, and the hopes which inly dwell,
   My manners note that I did long repel;
But Laon's name to the tumultuous throng
   Were like the star whose beams the waves compel
And tempests, and his soul-subduing tongue 1565
Were as a lance to quell the mailèd crest of wrong.

XVIII

'Perchance blood need not flow, if thou at length
   Wouldst rise, perchance the very slaves would spare
Their brethren and themselves; great is the strength
   Of words—for lately did a maiden fair, 1570
   Who from her childhood has been taught to bear
The tyrant's heaviest yoke, arise, and make
   Her sex the law of truth and freedom hear,
And with these quiet words—"For thine own sake
I prithee spare me;"—did with ruth so take 1575

XIX

'All hearts, that even the torturer who had bound
   Her meek calm frame, ere it was yet impaled,
Loosened her, weeping then; nor could be found
   One human hand to harm her—unassailed
   Therefore she walks through the great City, veiled 1580
In virtue's adamantine eloquence,
   'Gainst scorn, and death and pain thus trebly mailed,
And blending, in the smiles of that defence,
The Serpent and the Dove, Wisdom and Innocence.

XX

'The wild-eyed women throng around her path: 1585
   From their luxurious dungeons, from the dust
Of meaner thralls, from the oppressor's wrath,
   Or the caresses of his sated lust

They congregate:—in her they put their trust;
The tyrants send their armèd slaves to quell   1590
    Her power;—they, even like a thunder-gust
Caught by some forest, bend beneath the spell
Of that young maiden's speech, and to their chiefs rebel.

XXI

'Thus she doth equal laws and justice teach
    To woman, outraged and polluted long;   1595
Gathering the sweetest fruit in human reach
    For those fair hands now free, while armèd wrong
    Trembles before her look, though it be strong;
Thousands thus dwell beside her, virgins bright,
    And matrons with their babes, a stately throng!   1600
Lovers renew the vows which they did plight
In early faith, and hearts long parted now unite,

XXII

'And homeless orphans find a home near her,
    And those poor victims of the proud, no less,
Fair wrecks, on whom the smiling world with stir,   1605
    Thrusts the redemption of its wickedness:—
    In squalid huts, and in its palaces
Sits Lust alone, while o'er the land is borne
    Her voice, whose awful sweetness doth repress
All evil, and her foes relenting turn,   1610
And cast the vote of love in hope's abandoned urn.

XXIII

'So in the populous City, a young maiden
    Has baffled Havoc of the prey which he
Marks as his own, whene'er with chains o'erladen
    Men make them arms to hurl down tyranny,—   1615
    False arbiter between the bound and free;
And o'er the land, in hamlets and in towns
    The multitudes collect tumultuously,
And throng in arms; but tyranny disowns
Their claim, and gathers strength around its trembling
        thrones.   1620

XXIV

'Blood soon, although unwillingly, to shed,
    The free cannot forbear—the Queen of Slaves,
The hoodwinked Angel of the blind and dead,
    Custom, with iron mace points to the graves

Where her own standard desolately waves   1625
Over the dust of Prophets and of Kings.
   Many yet stand in her array—"she paves
Her path with human hearts," and o'er it flings
The wildering gloom of her immeasurable wings.

XXV

'There is a plain beneath the City's wall,   1630
   Bounded by misty mountains, wide and vast,
Millions there lift at Freedom's thrilling call
   Ten thousand standards wide, they load the blast
   Which bears one sound of many voices past,
And startles on his throne their sceptred foe: 1635
   He sits amid his idle pomp aghast,
And that his power hath passed away, doth know—
Why pause the victor swords to seal his overthrow?

XXVI

'The tyrant's guards resistance yet maintain:
   Fearless, and fierce, and hard as beasts of blood,   1640
They stand a speck amid the peopled plain;
   Carnage and ruin have been made their food
   From infancy—ill has become their good,
And for its hateful sake their will has wove
   The chains which eat their hearts—the multitude   1645
Surrounding them, with words of human love,
Seek from their own decay their stubborn minds to move.

XXVII

'Over the land is felt a sudden pause,
   As night and day those ruthless bands around,
The watch of love is kept:—a trance which awes   1650
   The thoughts of men with hope—as, when the sound
   Of whirlwind, whose fierce blasts the waves and clouds confound,
Dies suddenly, the mariner in fear
   Feels silence sink upon his heart—thus bound,
The conquerors pause, and oh! may freemen ne'er   1655
Clasp the relentless knees of Dread the murderer!

XXVIII

'If blood be shed, 'tis but a change and choice
   Of bonds,—from slavery to cowardice
A wretched fall!—Uplift thy charmèd voice!
   Pour on those evil men the love that lies   1660

Hovering within those spirit-soothing eyes—
  Arise, my friend, farewell!'—As thus he spake,
From the green earth lightly I did arise,
  As one out of dim dreams that doth awake,
And looked upon the depth of that reposing lake.   1665

XXIX

I saw my countenance reflected there;—
  And then my youth fell on me like a wind
Descending on still waters—my thin hair
    Was prematurely gray, my face was lined
    With channels, such as suffering leaves behind,   1670
  Not age; my brow was pale, but in my cheek
    And lips a flush of gnawing fire did find
  Their food and dwelling; though mine eyes might speak
A subtle mind and strong within a frame thus weak.

XXX

And though their lustre now was spent and faded,   1675
    Yet in my hollow looks and withered mien
The likeness of a shape for which was braided
    The brightest woof of genius, still was seen—
    One who, methought, had gone from the world's scene,
  And left it vacant—'twas her lover's face—   1680
    It might resemble her—it once had been
  The mirror of her thoughts, and still the grace
Which her mind's shadow cast, left there a lingering trace.

XXXI

What then was I? She slumbered with the dead.
    Glory and joy and peace, had come and gone.   1685
Doth the cloud perish, when the beams are fled
    Which steeped its skirts in gold? or, dark and lone,
    Doth it not through the paths of night unknown,
  On outspread wings of its own wind upborne
    Pour rain upon the earth? The stars are shown,   1690
  When the cold moon sharpens her silver horn
Under the sea, and make the wide night not forlorn.

XXXII

Strengthened in heart, yet sad, that aged man
    I left, with interchange of looks and tears,
And lingering speech, and to the Camp began   1695
    My way. O'er many a mountain-chain which rears

Its hundred crests aloft, my spirit bears
My frame: o'er many a dale and many a moor,
And gaily now meseems serene earth wears
    The blosmy spring's star-bright investiture,   1700
A vision which aught sad from sadness might allure.

XXXIII

My powers revived within me, and I went
    As one whom winds waft o'er the bending grass,
Through many a vale of that broad continent.
    At night when I reposed, fair dreams did pass   1705
    Before my pillow;—my own Cythna was,
Not like a child of death, among them ever;
    When I arose from rest, a woful mass
That gentlest sleep seemed from my life to sever,
As if the light of youth were not withdrawn for ever.   1716

XXXIV

Aye as I went, that maiden who had reared
    The torch of Truth afar, of whose high deeds
The Hermit in his pilgrimage had heard,
    Haunted my thoughts.—Ah, Hope its sickness feeds
    With whatso'er it finds, or flowers or weeds!   1715
Could she be Cythna?—Was that corpse a shade
    Such as self-torturing thought from madness breeds?
Why was this hope not torture? Yet it made
A light around my steps which would not ever fade.

CANTO V

I

OVER the utmost hill at length I sped,   1720
    A snowy steep:—the moon was hanging low
Over the Asian mountains, and outspread
    The plain, the City, and the Camp below,
    Skirted the midnight Ocean's glimmering flow;
The City's moonlit spires and myriad lamps,   1725
    Like stars in a sublunar sky did glow,
And fires blazed far amid the scattered camps,
Like springs of flame, which burst where'er swift Earthquake
        stamps.

II

All slept but those in watchful arms who stood,
    And those who sate tending the beacon's light,   1730
And the few sounds from that vast multitude
    Made silence more profound.—Oh, what a might

Of human thought was cradled in that night!
How many hearts impenetrably veiled
    Beat underneath its shade, what secret fight   1735
Evil and good, in woven passions mailed,
Waged through that silent throng; a war that never failed!

III

And now the Power of Good held victory,
    So, through the labyrinth of many a tent,
Among the silent millions who did lie   1740
    In innocent sleep, exultingly I went;
    The moon had left Heaven desert now, but lent
From eastern morn the first faint lustre showed
    An armèd youth—over his spear he bent
His downward face.—'A friend!' I cried aloud,   1745
And quickly common hopes made freemen understood.

IV

I sate beside him while the morning beam
    Crept slowly over Heaven, and talked with him
Of those immortal hopes, a glorious theme!
    Which led us forth, until the stars grew dim: 1750
    And all the while, methought, his voice did swim
As if it drownèd in remembrance were
    Of thoughts which make the moist eyes overbrim:
At last, when daylight 'gan to fill the air,
He looked on me, and cried in wonder—'Thou art here!'   1755

V

Then, suddenly, I knew it was the youth
    In whom its earliest hopes my spirit found;
But envious tongues had stained his spotless truth,
    And thoughtless pride his love in silence bound,
    And shame and sorrow mine in toils had wound,   1760
Whilst he was innocent, and I deluded;
    The truth now came upon me, on the ground
Tears of repenting joy, which fast intruded,
Fell fast, and o'er its peace our mingling spirits brooded.

VI

Thus, while with rapid lips and earnest eyes   1765
    We talked, a sound of sweeping conflict spread
As from the earth did suddenly arise;
    From every tent roused by that clamour dread,

Our bands outsprung and seized their arms—we sped
Towards the sound: our tribes were gathering far.   1770
  Those sanguine slaves amid ten thousand dead
Stabbed in their sleep, trampled in treacherous war
The gentle hearts whose power their lives had sought to spare.

VII

Like rabid snakes, that sting some gentle child
  Who brings them food, when winter false and fair   1775
Allures them forth with its cold smiles, so wild
  They rage among the camp;—they overbear
  The patriot hosts—confusion, then despair
Descends like night—when 'Laon!' one did cry:
  Like a bright ghost from Heaven that shout did scare
The slaves, and widening through the vaulted sky,   1781
Seemed sent from Earth to Heaven in sign of victory.

VIII

In sudden panic those false murderers fled,
  Like insect tribes before the northern gale:
But swifter still, our hosts encompassèd   1785
  Their shattered ranks, and in a craggy vale,
  Where even their fierce despair might nought avail,
Hemmed them around!—and then revenge and fear
  Made the high virtue of the patriots fail:
One pointed on his foe the mortal spear—   1790
I rushed before its point, and cried, 'Forbear, forbear!'

IX

The spear transfixed my arm that was uplifted
  In swift expostulation, and the blood
Gushed round its point: I smiled, and—'Oh! thou gifted
  With eloquence which shall not be withstood,   1795
  Flow thus!'—I cried in joy, 'thou vital flood,
Until my heart be dry, ere thus the cause
  For which thou wert aught worthy be subdued—
Ah, ye are pale,—ye weep,—your passions pause,—
'Tis well! ye feel the truth of love's benignant laws.   1800

X

'Soldiers, our brethren and our friends are slain.
  Ye murdered them, I think, as they did sleep!
Alas, what have ye done? the slightest pain
  Which ye might suffer, there were eyes to weep,

But ye have quenched them—there were smiles to steep
    Your hearts in balm, but they are lost in woe;   1806
      And those whom love did set his watch to keep
    Around your tents, truth's freedom to bestow,
Ye stabbed as they did sleep—but they forgive ye now.

XI

'Oh wherefore should ill ever flow from ill,   1810
    And pain still keener pain for ever breed?
We all are brethren—even the slaves who kill
    For hire, are men; and to avenge misdeed
      On the misdoer, doth but Misery feed
With her own broken heart! O Earth, O Heaven!   1815
    And thou, dread Nature, which to every deed
    And all that lives or is, to be hath given,
Even as to thee have these done ill, and are forgiven!

XII

'Join then your hands and hearts, and let the past
    Be as a grave which gives not up its dead   1820
To evil thoughts.'—A film then overcast
    My sense with dimness, for the wound, which bled
    Freshly, swift shadows o'er mine eyes had shed.
When I awoke, I lay mid friends and foes,
    And earnest countenances on me shed   1825
The light of questioning looks, whilst one did close
My wound with balmiest herbs, and soothed me to repose;

XIII

And one whose spear had pierced me, leaned beside,
    With quivering lips and humid eyes;—and all
Seemed like some brothers on a journey wide   1830
    Gone forth, whom now strange meeting did befall
    In a strange land, round one whom they might call
Their friend, their chief, their father, for assay
    Of peril, which had saved them from the thrall
Of death, now suffering. Thus the vast array   1835
Of those fraternal bands were reconciled that day.

XIV

Lifting the thunder of their acclamation,
    Towards the City then the multitude,
And I among them, went in joy—a nation
    Made free by love;—a mighty brotherhood   1840

Linked by a jealous interchange of good;
A glorious pageant, more magnificent
    Than kingly slaves arrayed in gold and blood,
When they return from carnage, and are sent
In triumph bright beneath the populous battlement.   1845

XV

Afar, the city-walls were thronged on high,
    And myriads on each giddy turret clung,
And to each spire far lessening in the sky
    Bright pennons on the idle winds were hung;
    As we approached, a shout of joyance sprung   1850
At once from all the crowd, as if the vast
    And peopled Earth its boundless skies among
The sudden clamour of delight had cast,
When from before its face some general wreck had passed.

XVI

Our armies through the City's hundred gates   1855
    Were poured, like brooks which to the rocky lair
Of some deep lake, whose silence them awaits,
    Throng from the mountains when the storms are there
    And, as we passed through the calm sunny air
A thousand flower-inwoven crowns were shed,   1860
    The token flowers of truth and freedom fair,
And fairest hands bound them on many a head,
Those angels of love's heaven, that over all was spread.

XVII

I trod as one tranced in some rapturous vision:
    Those bloody bands so lately reconciled,   1865
Were, ever as they went, by the contrition
    Of anger turned to love, from ill beguiled,
    And every one on them more gently smiled,
Because they had done evil:—the sweet awe
    Of such mild looks made their own hearts grow mild,
And did with soft attraction ever draw   1871
Their spirits to the love of freedom's equal law.

XVIII

And they, and all, in one loud symphony
    My name with Liberty commingling, lifted,
'The friend and the preserver of the free!   1875
    The parent of this joy!' and fair eyes gifted

With feelings, caught from one who had uplifted
The light of a great spirit, round me shone;
And all the shapes of this grand scenery shifted
Like restless clouds before the steadfast sun,— 1880
Where was that Maid? I asked, but it was known of none.

XIX

Laone was the name her love had chosen,
For she was nameless, and her birth none knew:
Where was Laone now?—The words were frozen
Within my lips with fear; but to subdue 1885
Such dreadful hope, to my great task was due,
And when at length one brought reply, that she
To-morrow would appear, I then withdrew
To judge what need for that great throng might be,
For now the stars came thick over the twilight sea. 1890

XX

Yet need was none for rest or food to care,
Even though that multitude was passing great,
Since each one for the other did prepare
All kindly succour—Therefore to the gate
Of the Imperial House, now desolate, 1895
I passed, and there was found aghast, alone,
The fallen Tyrant!—Silently he sate
Upon the footstool of his golden throne,
Which, starred with sunny gems, in its own lustre shone.

XXI

Alone, but for one child, who led before him 1900
A graceful dance: the only living thing
Of all the crowd, which thither to adore him
Flocked yesterday, who solace sought to bring
In his abandonment!—She knew the King
Had praised her dance of yore, and now she wove 1905
Its circles, aye weeping and murmuring
Mid her sad task of unregarded love,
That to no smiles it might his speechless sadness move.

XXII

She fled to him, and wildly clasped his feet
When human steps were heard:—he moved nor spoke,
Nor changed his hue, nor raised his looks to meet 1911
The gaze of strangers—our loud entrance woke

The echoes of the hall, which circling broke
The calm of its recesses,—like a tomb
   Its sculptured walls vacantly to the stroke   1915
Of footfalls answered, and the twilight's gloom
Lay like a charnel's mist within the radiant dome.

XXIII

The little child stood up when we came nigh;
   Her lips and cheeks seemed very pale and wan,
But on her forehead, and within her eye   1920
   Lay beauty, which makes hearts that feed thereon
   Sick with excess of sweetness; on the throne
She leaned;—the King, with gathered brow, and lips
   Wreathed by long scorn, did inly sneer and frown
With hue like that when some great painter dips   1925
His pencil in the gloom of earthquake and eclipse.

XXIV

She stood beside him like a rainbow braided
   Within some storm, when scarce its shadows vast
From the blue paths of the swift sun have faded;
   A sweet and solemn smile, like Cythna's cast   1930
   One moment's light, which made my heart beat fast,
O'er that child's parted lips—a gleam of bliss,
   A shade of vanished days,—as the tears passed
Which wrapped it, even as with a father's kiss
I pressed those softest eyes in trembling tenderness.   1935

XXV

The sceptred wretch then from that solitude
   I drew, and, of his change compassionate,
With words of sadness soothed his rugged mood.
   But he, while pride and fear held deep debate,
   With sullen guile of ill-dissembled hate   1940
Glared on me as a toothless snake might glare:
   Pity, not scorn I felt, though desolate
The desolator now, and unaware
The curses which he mocked had caught him by the hair.

XXVI

I led him forth from that which now might seem   1945
   A gorgeous grave: through portals sculptured deep
With imagery beautiful as dream
   We went, and left the shades which tend on sleep

Over its unregarded gold to keep
Their silent watch.—The child trod faintingly,   1950
And as she went, the tears which she did weep
Glanced in the starlight; wildered seemèd she,
And when I spake, for sobs she could not answer me.

XXVII

At last the tyrant cried, 'She hungers, slave,
Stab her, or give her bread!'—It was a tone   1955
Such as sick fancies in a new-made grave
Might hear. I trembled, for the truth was known;
He with this child had thus been left alone,
And neither had gone forth for food,—but he
In mingled pride and awe cowered near his throne,
And she a nursling of captivity   1961
Knew nought beyond those walls, nor what such change might be.

XXVIII

And he was troubled at a charm withdrawn
Thus suddenly; that sceptres ruled no more—
That even from gold the dreadful strength was gone,   1965
Which once made all things subject to its power—
Such wonder seized him, as if hour by hour
The past had come again; and the swift fall
Of one so great and terrible of yore,
To desolateness, in the hearts of all   1970
Like wonder stirred, who saw such awful change befall.

XXIX

A mighty crowd, such as the wide land pours
Once in a thousand years, now gathered round
The fallen tyrant;—like the rush of showers
Of hail in spring, pattering along the ground,   1975
Their many footsteps fell, else came no sound
From the wide multitude: that lonely man
Then knew the burden of his change, and found,
Concealing in the dust his visage wan,
Refuge from the keen looks which through his bosom ran.

XXX

And he was faint withal: I sate beside him   1981
Upon the earth, and took that child so fair
From his weak arms, that ill might none betide him
Or her:—when food was brought to them, her share

To his averted lips the child did bear,   1985
  But, when she saw he had enough, she ate
    And wept the while;—the lonely man's despair
Hunger then overcame, and of his state
Forgetful, on the dust as in a trance he sate.

XXXI

Slowly the silence of the multitudes   1990
  Passed, as when far is heard in some lone dell
The gathering of a wind among the woods—
    'And he is fallen!' they cry, 'he who did dwell
    Like famine or the plague, or aught more fell
Among our homes, is fallen! the murderer   1995
  Who slaked his thirsting soul as from a well
Of blood and tears with ruin! he is here!
Sunk in a gulf of scorn from which none may him rear!'

XXXII

Then was heard—'He who judged let him be brought
  To judgement! blood for blood cries from the soil   2000
On which his crimes have deep pollution wrought!
    Shall Othman only unavenged despoil?
    Shall they who by the stress of grinding toil
Wrest from the unwilling earth his luxuries,
  Perish for crime, while his foul blood may boil,   2005
Or creep within his veins at will?—Arise!
And to high justice make her chosen sacrifice.'

XXXIII

'What do ye seek? what fear ye,' then I cried,
  Suddenly starting forth, 'that ye should shed
The blood of Othman?—if your hearts are tried   2010
    In the true love of freedom, cease to dread
    This one poor lonely man—beneath Heaven spread
In purest light above us all, through earth
  Maternal earth, who doth her sweet smiles shed
For all, let him go free; until the worth   2015
Of human nature win from these a second birth.

XXXIV

'What call ye *justice*? Is there one who ne'er
  In secret thought has wished another's ill?—
Are ye all pure? Let those stand forth who hear,
    And tremble not. Shall they insult and kill,   2020

If such they be? their mild eyes can they fill
With the false anger of the hypocrite?
    Alas, such were not pure,—the chastened will
    Of virtue sees that justice is the light
Of love, and not revenge, and terror and despite.'   2025

XXXV

The murmur of the people, slowly dying,
    Paused as I spake, then those who near me were,
Cast gentle looks where the lone man was lying
    Shrouding his head, which now that infant fair
    Clasped on her lap in silence;—through the air   2030
Sobs were then heard, and many kissed my feet
    In pity's madness, and to the despair
Of him whom late they cursed, a solace sweet
His very victims brought—soft looks and speeches meet.

XXXVI

Then to a home for his repose assigned,   2035
    Accompanied by the still throng he went
In silence, where, to soothe his rankling mind,
    Some likeness of his ancient state was lent;
    And if his heart could have been innocent
As those who pardoned him, he might have ended   2040
    His days in peace; but his straight lips were bent,
Men said, into a smile which guile portended,
A sight with which that child like hope with fear was blended.

XXXVII

'Twas midnight now, the eve of that great day
    Whereon the many nations at whose call   2045
The chains of earth like mist melted away,
    Decreed to hold a sacred Festival,
    A rite to attest the equality of all
Who live. So to their homes, to dream or wake
    All went. The sleepless silence did recall   2050
Laone to my thoughts, with hopes that make
The flood recede from which their thirst they seek to slake.

XXXVIII

The dawn flowed forth, and from its purple fountains
    I drank those hopes which make the spirit quail,
As to the plain between the misty mountains   2055
    And the great City, with a countenance pale

I went:—it was a sight which might avail
To make men weep exulting tears, for whom
  Now first from human power the reverend veil
Was torn, to see Earth from her general womb   2060
Pour forth her swarming sons to a fraternal doom:

XXXIX

To see, far glancing in the misty morning,
  The signs of that innumerable host,
To hear one sound of many made, the warning
  Of Earth to Heaven from its free children tossed,   2065
  While the eternal hills, and the sea lost
In wavering light, and, starring the blue sky
  The city's myriad spires of gold, almost
With human joy made mute society—
Its witnesses with men who must hereafter be.   2070

XL

To see, like some vast island from the Ocean,
  The Altar of the Federation rear
Its pile i' the midst; a work which the devotion
  Of millions in one night created there,
  Sudden, as when the moonrise makes appear   2075
Strange clouds in the east; a marble pyramid
  Distinct with steps: that mighty shape did wear
The light of genius; its still shadow hid
Far ships: to know its height the morning mists forbid!

XLI

To hear the restless multitudes for ever   2080
  Around the base of that great Altar flow,
As on some mountain-islet burst and shiver
  Atlantic waves; and solemnly and slow
  As the wind bore that tumult to and fro,
To feel the dreamlike music, which did swim   2085
  Like beams through floating clouds on waves below
Falling in pauses, from that Altar dim
As silver-sounding tongues breathed an aëreal hymn.

XLII

To hear, to see, to live, was on that morn
  Lethean joy! so that all those assembled   2090
Cast off their memories of the past outworn;
  Two only bosoms with their own life trembled,

And mine was one,—and we had both dissembled;
  So with a beating heart I went, and one,
    Who having much, covets yet more, resembled;   2095
  A lost and dear possession, which not won,
He walks in lonely gloom beneath the noonday sun.

XLIII

To the great Pyramid I came: its stair
  With female choirs was thronged: the loveliest
Among the free, grouped with its sculptures rare;   2100
  As I approached, the morning's golden mist,
  Which now the wonder-stricken breezes kissed
With their cold lips, fled, and the summit shone
  Like Athos seen from Samothracia, dressed
In earliest light, by vintagers, and one   2105
Sate there, a female Shape upon an ivory throne:

XLIV

A Form most like the imagined habitant
  Of silver exhalations sprung from dawn,
By winds which feed on sunrise woven, to enchant
  The faiths of men: all mortal eyes were drawn,   2110
  As famished mariners through strange seas gone
Gaze on a burning watch-tower, by the light
  Of those divinest lineaments—alone
With thoughts which none could share, from that fair sight
I turned in sickness, for a veil shrouded her countenance bright.

XLV

And, neither did I hear the acclamations,   2116
  Which from brief silence bursting, filled the air
With her strange name and mine, from all the nations
  Which we, they said, in strength had gathered there
  From the sleep of bondage; nor the vision fair   2120
Of that bright pageantry beheld,—but blind
  And silent, as a breathing corpse did fare,
Leaning upon my friend, till like a wind
To fevered cheeks, a voice flowed o'er my troubled mind.

XLVI

Like music of some minstrel heavenly-gifted,   2125
  To one whom fiends enthral, this voice to me;
Scarce did I wish her veil to be uplifted,
  I was so calm and joyous.—I could see

The platform where we stood, the statues three
Which kept their marble watch on that high shrine,   2130
    The multitudes, the mountains, and the sea;
As when eclipse hath passed, things sudden shine
To men's astonished eyes most clear and crystalline.

XLVII

At first Laone spoke most tremulously:
    But soon her voice the calmness which it shed   2135
Gathered, and—'Thou art whom I sought to see,
    And thou art our first votary here,' she said:
    'I had a dear friend once, but he is dead!—
And of all those on the wide earth who breathe,
    Thou dost resemble him alone—I spread   2140
This veil between us two, that thou beneath
Shouldst image one who may have been long lost in death.

XLVIII

'For this wilt thou not henceforth pardon me?
    Yes, but those joys which silence well requite
Forbid reply;—why men have chosen me   2145
    To be the Priestess of this holiest rite
    I scarcely know, but that the floods of light
Which flow over the world, have borne me hither
    To meet thee, long most dear; and now unite
Thine hand with mine, and may all comfort wither   2150
From both the hearts whose pulse in joy now beat together,

XLIX

'If our own will as others' law we bind,
    If the foul worship trampled here we fear;
If as ourselves we cease to love our kind!'—
    She paused, and pointed upwards—sculptured there   2155
    Three shapes around her ivory throne appear;
One was a Giant, like a child asleep
    On a loose rock, whose grasp crushed, as it were
In dream, sceptres and crowns; and one did keep
Its watchful eyes in doubt whether to smile or weep;   2160

L

A Woman sitting on the sculptured disk
    Of the broad earth, and feeding from one breast
A human babe and a young basilisk;
    Her looks were sweet as Heaven's when loveliest

In Autumn eves. The third Image was dressed   2165
  In white wings swift as clouds in winter skies;
    Beneath his feet, 'mongst ghastliest forms, repressed
Lay Faith, an obscene worm, who sought to rise,
While calmly on the Sun he turned his diamond eyes.

LI

Beside that Image then I sate, while she   2170
  Stood, mid the throngs which ever ebbed and flowed,
Like light amid the shadows of the sea
  Cast from one cloudless star, and on the crowd
  That touch which none who feels forgets, bestowed;
And whilst the sun returned the steadfast gaze   2175
  Of the great Image, as o'er Heaven it glode.
That rite had place; it ceased when sunset's blaze
Burned o'er the isles. All stood in joy and deep amaze—
  —When in the silence of all spirits there
Laone's voice was felt, and through the air   2180
Her thrilling gestures spoke, most eloquently fair:—

1

'Calm art thou as yon sunset! swift and strong
As new-fledged Eagles, beautiful and young,
That float among the blinding beams of morning;
  And underneath thy feet writhe Faith, and Folly,   2185
  Custom, and Hell, and mortal Melancholy—
Hark! the Earth starts to hear the mighty warning
    Of thy voice sublime and holy;
    Its free spirits here assembled,
      See thee, feel thee, know thee now,—   2190
    To thy voice their hearts have trembled
      Like ten thousand clouds which flow
      With one wide wind as it flies!—
Wisdom! thy irresistible children rise
To hail thee, and the elements they chain   2195
And their own will, to swell the glory of thy train.

2

'O Spirit vast and deep as Night and Heaven!
Mother and soul of all to which is given
The light of life, the loveliness of being,
  Lo! thou dost re-ascend the human heart,   2200
  Thy throne of power, almighty as thou wert
In dreams of Poets old grown pale by seeing
  The shade of thee:—now, millions start

To feel thy lightnings through them burning:
Nature, or God, or Love, or Pleasure,   2205
Or Sympathy the sad tears turning
To mutual smiles, a drainless treasure,
Descends amidst us;—Scorn, and Hate,
Revenge and Selfishness are desolate—
A hundred nations swear that there shall be   2210
Pity and Peace and Love, among the good and free!

3

'Eldest of things, divine Equality!
Wisdom and Love are but the slaves of thee,
The Angels of thy sway, who pour around thee
Treasures from all the cells of human thought,   2215
And from the Stars, and from the Ocean brought,
And the last living heart whose beatings bound thee:
The powerful and the wise had sought
Thy coming, thou in light descending
O'er the wide land which is thine own   2220
Like the Spring whose breath is blending
All blasts of fragrance into one,
Comest upon the paths of men!—
Earth bares her general bosom to thy ken,
And all her children here in glory meet   2225
To feed upon thy smiles, and clasp thy sacred feet.

4

'My brethren, we are free! the plains and mountains,
The gray sea-shore, the forests and the fountains,
Are haunts of happiest dwellers;—man and woman,
Their common bondage burst, may freely borrow   2230
From lawless love a solace for their sorrow;
For oft we still must weep, since we are human.
A stormy night's serenest morrow,
Whose showers are pity's gentle tears,
Whose clouds are smiles of those that die   2235
Like infants without hopes or fears,
And whose beams are joys that lie
In blended hearts, now holds dominion;
The dawn of mind, which upwards on a pinion
Borne, swift as sunrise, far illumines space,   2240
And clasps this barren world in its own bright embrace!

5

'My brethren, we are free! The fruits are glowing
Beneath the stars, and the night winds are flowing

O'er the ripe corn, the birds and beasts are dreaming—
   Never again may blood of bird or beast   2245
   Stain with its venomous stream a human feast,
To the pure skies in accusation steaming;
   Avenging poisons shall have ceased
   To feed disease and fear and madness,
      The dwellers of the earth and air   2250
   Shall throng around our steps in gladness
   Seeking their food or refuge there.
Our toil from thought all glorious forms shall cull,
To make this Earth, our home, more beautiful,
And Science, and her sister Poesy,   2255
Shall clothe in light the fields and cities of the free!

6

'Victory, Victory to the prostrate nations!
Bear witness Night, and ye mute Constellations
Who gaze on us from your crystalline cars!
   Thoughts have gone forth whose powers can sleep no more!
   Victory! Victory! Earth's remotest shore,   2261
Regions which groan beneath the Antarctic stars,
   The green lands cradled in the roar
   Of western waves, and wildernesses
      Peopled and vast, which skirt the oceans   2265
   Where morning dyes her golden tresses,
   Shall soon partake our high emotions:
   Kings shall turn pale! Almighty Fear
The Fiend-God, when our charmèd name he hear,
Shall fade like shadow from his thousand fanes,   2270
While Truth with Joy enthroned o'er his lost empire reigns!'

LII

Ere she had ceased, the mists of night entwining
   Their dim woof, floated o'er the infinite throng;
She, like a spirit through the darkness shining,
   In tones whose sweetness silence did prolong,   2275
   As if to lingering winds they did belong,
Poured forth her inmost soul: a passionate speech
   With wild and thrilling pauses woven among,
Which whoso heard, was mute, for it could teach
To rapture like her own all listening hearts to reach.   2280

LIII

Her voice was as a mountain-stream which sweeps
   The withered leaves of Autumn to the lake,
And in some deep and narrow bay then sleeps
   In the shadow of the shores; as dead leaves wake

Under the wave, in flowers and herbs which make   2285
Those green depths beautiful when skies are blue,
    The multitude so moveless did partake
Such living change, and kindling murmurs flew
As o'er that speechless calm delight and wonder grew.

LIV

Over the plain the throngs were scattered then   2290
    In groups around the fires, which from the sea
Even to the gorge of the first mountain-glen
    Blazed wide and far: the banquet of the free
    Was spread beneath many a dark cypress-tree,
Beneath whose spires, which swayed in the red flame,   2295
    Reclining, as they ate, of Liberty,
And Hope, and Justice, and Laone's name,
Earth's children did a woof of happy converse frame.

LV

Their feast was such as Earth, the general mother,
    Pours from her fairest bosom, when she smiles   2300
In the embrace of Autumn;—to each other
    As when some parent fondly reconciles
    Her warring children, she their wrath beguiles
With her own sustenance; they relenting weep:
    Such was this Festival, which from their isles   2305
And continents, and winds, and oceans deep,
All shapes might throng to share, that fly, or walk, or creep,—

LVI

Might share in peace and innocence, for gore
    Or poison none this festal did pollute,
But piled on high, an overflowing store   2310
    Of pomegranates, and citrons, fairest fruit,
    Melons, and dates, and figs, and many a root
Sweet and sustaining, and bright grapes ere yet
    Accursed fire their mild juice could transmute
Into a mortal bane, and brown corn set   2315
In baskets; with pure streams their thirsting lips they wet.

LVII

Laone had descended from the shrine,
    And every deepest look and holiest mind
Fed on her form, though now those tones divine
    Were silent as she passed; she did unwind   2320

Her veil, as with the crowds of her own kind
She mixed; some impulse made my heart refrain
From seeking her that night, so I reclined
Amidst a group, where on the utmost plain
A festal watchfire burned beside the dusky main.   2325

LVIII

And joyous was our feast; pathetic talk,
And wit, and harmony of choral strains,
While far Orion o'er the waves did walk
That flow among the isles, held us in chains
Of sweet captivity, which none disdains   2330
Who feels: but when his zone grew dim in mist
Which clothes the Ocean's bosom, o'er the plains
The multitudes went homeward, to their rest,
Which that delightful day with its own shadow blessed.

CANTO VI

I

BESIDE the dimness of the glimmering sea,   2335
Weaving swift language from impassioned themes,
With that dear friend I lingered, who to me
So late had been restored, beneath the gleams
Of the silver stars; and ever in soft dreams
Of future love and peace sweet converse lapped   2340
Our willing fancies, till the pallid beams
Of the last watchfire fell, and darkness wrapped
The waves, and each bright chain of floating fire was snapped;

II

And till we came even to the City's wall
And the great gate; then, none knew whence or why,
Disquiet on the multitudes did fall: 2346
And first, one pale and breathless passed us by,
And stared and spoke not;—then with piercing cry
A troop of wild-eyed women, by the shrieks
Of their own terror driven,—tumultuously   2350
Hither and thither hurrying with pale cheeks,
Each one from fear unknown a sudden refuge seeks—

III

Then, rallying cries of treason and of danger
Resounded: and—'They come! to arms! to arms!
The Tyrant is amongst us, and the stranger   2355
Comes to enslave us in his name! to arms!'

In vain: for Panic, the pale fiend who charms
    Strength to forswear her right, those millions swept
Like waves before the tempest—these alarms
    Came to me, as to know their cause I lept   2360
On the gate's turret, and in rage and grief and scorn I wept!

IV

For to the North I saw the town on fire,
    And its red light made morning pallid now,
Which burst over wide Asia;—louder, higher,
    The yells of victory and the screams of woe   2365
    I heard approach, and saw the throng below
Stream through the gates like foam-wrought waterfalls
    Fed from a thousand storms—the fearful glow
Of bombs flares overhead—at intervals
The red artillery's bolt mangling among them falls.   2370

V

And now the horsemen come—and all was done
    Swifter than I have spoken—I beheld
Their red swords flash in the unrisen sun.
    I rushed among the rout, to have repelled
    That miserable flight—one moment quelled   2375
By voice and looks and eloquent despair,
    As if reproach from their own hearts withheld
Their steps, they stood; but soon came pouring there
New multitudes, and did those rallied bands o'erbear.

VI

I strove, as, drifted on some cataract   2380
    By irresistible streams, some wretch might strive
Who hears its fatal roar:—the files compact
    Whelmed me, and from the gate availed to drive
    With quickening impulse, as each bolt did rive
Their ranks with bloodier chasm:—into the plain   238&
    Disgorged at length the dead and the alive
In one dread mass, were parted, and the stain
Of blood, from mortal steel fell o'er the fields like rain.

VII

For now the despot's bloodhounds with their prey
    Unarmed and unaware, were gorging deep   2390
Their gluttony of death; the loose array
    Of horsemen o'er the wide fields murdering sweep,

And with loud laughter for their tyrant reap
A harvest sown with other hopes, the while,
    Far overhead, ships from Propontis keep   2395
A killing rain of fire:—when the waves smile
As sudden earthquakes light many a volcano-isle,

VIII

Thus sudden, unexpected feast was spread
    For the carrion-fowls of Heaven.—I saw the sight—
I moved—I lived—as o'er the heaps of dead,   2400
    Whose stony eyes glared in the morning light
    I trod;—to me there came no thought of flight,
But with loud cries of scorn which whoso heard
    That dreaded death, felt in his veins the might
Of virtuous shame return, the crowd I stirred,   2405
And desperation's hope in many hearts recurred.

IX

A band of brothers gathering round me, made,
    Although unarmed, a steadfast front, and still
Retreating, with stern looks beneath the shade
    Of gathered eyebrows, did the victors fill   2410
    With doubt even in success; deliberate will
Inspired our growing troop, not overthrown
    It gained the shelter of a grassy hill,
And ever still our comrades were hewn down,
And their defenceless limbs beneath our footsteps strown.

X

Immovably we stood—in joy I found,   2416
    Beside me then, firm as a giant pine
Among the mountain-vapours driven around,
    The old man whom I loved—his eyes divine
    With a mild look of courage answered mine,   2420
And my young friend was near, and ardently
    His hand grasped mine a moment—now the line
Of war extended, to our rallying cry
As myriads flocked in love and brotherhood to die.

XI

For ever while the sun was climbing Heaven   2425
    The horseman hewed our unarmed myriads down
Safely, though when by thirst of carnage driven
    Too near, those slaves were swiftly overthrown

By hundreds leaping on them:—flesh and bone
Soon made our ghastly ramparts; then the shaft 2430
    Of the artillery from the sea was thrown
More fast and fiery, and the conquerors laughed
In pride to hear the wind our screams of torment waft.

XII

For on one side alone the hill gave shelter,
    So vast that phalanx of unconquered men, 2435
And there the living in the blood did welter
    Of the dead and dying, which, in that green glen,
    Like stifled torrents, made a plashy fen
Under the feet—thus was the butchery waged
    While the sun clomb Heaven's eastern steep—but when
It 'gan to sink—a fiercer combat raged, 2441
For in more doubtful strife the armies were engaged.

XIII

Within a cave upon the hill were found
    A bundle of rude pikes, the instrument
Of those who war but on their native ground 2445
    For natural rights: a shout of joyance sent
    Even from our hearts the wide air pierced and rent,
As those few arms the bravest and the best
    Seized, and each sixth, thus armed, did now present
A line which covered and sustained the rest, 2450
A confident phalanx, which the foe on every side invest.

XIV

That onset turned the foes to flight almost;
    But soon they saw their present strength, and knew
That coming night would to our resolute host
    Bring victory; so dismounting, close they drew 2455
    Their glittering files, and then the combat grew
Unequal but most horrible;—and ever
    Our myriads, whom the swift bolt overthrew,
Or the red sword, failed like a mountain-river
Which rushes forth in foam to sink in sands for ever. 2460

XV

Sorrow and shame, to see with their own kind
    Our human brethren mix, like beasts of blood,
To mutual ruin armed by one behind
    Who sits and scoffs!—That friend so mild and good,

Who like its shadow near my youth had stood,   2465
Was stabbed!—my old preserver's hoary hair
   With the flesh clinging to its roots, was strewed
Under my feet!—I lost all sense or care,
And like the rest I grew desperate and unaware.

XVI

The battle became ghastlier—in the midst   2470
   I paused, and saw, how ugly and how fell
O Hate! thou art, even when thy life thou shedd'st
   For love. The ground in many a little dell
   Was broken, up and down whose steeps befell
Alternate victory and defeat, and there   2475
   The combatants with rage most horrible
Strove, and their eyes started with cracking stare,
And impotent their tongues they lolled into the air,

XVII

Flaccid and foamy, like a mad dog's hanging;
   Want, and Moon-madness, and the pest's swift Bane   2480
When its shafts smite—while yet its bow is twanging—
   Have each their mark and sign—some ghastly stain;
   And this was thine, O War! of hate and pain
Thou loathèd slave. I saw all shapes of death
   And ministered to many, o'er the plain   2485
While carnage in the sunbeam's warmth did seethe,
Till twilight o'er the east wove her serenest wreath.

XVIII

The few who yet survived, resolute and firm
   Around me fought. At the decline of day
Winding above the mountain's snowy term   2490
   New banners shone: they quivered in the ray
   Of the sun's unseen orb—ere night the array
Of fresh troops hemmed us in—of those brave bands
   I soon survived alone—and now I lay
Vanquished and faint, the grasp of bloody hands   2495
I felt, and saw on high the glare of falling brands:

XIX

When on my foes a sudden terror came,
   And they fled, scattering—lo! with reinless speed
A black Tartarian horse of giant frame
   Comes trampling over the dead, the living bleed   2500

Beneath the hoofs of that tremendous steed,
  On which, like to an Angel, robed in white.
    Sate one waving a sword;—the hosts recede
And fly, as through their ranks with awful might,
Sweeps in the shadow of eve that Phantom swift and bright;

XX

And its path made a solitude.—I rose   2506
  And marked its coming: it relaxed its course
As it approached me, and the wind that flows
    Through night, bore accents to mine ear whose force
    Might create smiles in death—the Tartar horse   2510
Paused, and I saw the shape its might which swayed,
  And heard her musical pants, like the sweet source
Of waters in the desert, as she said,
'Mount with me, Laon, now!'—I rapidly obeyed.

XXI

Then: 'Away! away!' she cried, and stretched her sword
  As 'twere a scourge over the courser's head,   2516
And lightly shook the reins.—We spake no word,
  But like the vapour of the tempest fled
    Over the plain; her dark hair was dispread
Like the pine's locks upon the lingering blast;   2520
  Over mine eyes its shadowy strings it spread
Fitfully, and the hills and streams fled fast,
As o'er their glimmering forms the steed's broad shadow passed.

XXII

And his hoofs ground the rocks to fire and dust,
  His strong sides made the torrents rise in spray,   2525
And turbulence, as of a whirlwind's gust
  Surrounded us;—and still away! away!
    Through the desert night we sped, while she alway
Gazed on a mountain which we neared, whose crest,
  Crowned with a marble ruin, in the ray   2530
Of the obscure stars gleamed;—its rugged breast
The steed strained up, and then his impulse did arrest.

XXIII

A rocky hill which overhung the Ocean:—
  From that lone ruin, when the steed that panted
Paused, might be heard the murmur of the motion   2535
  Of waters, as in spots for ever haunted

By the choicest winds of Heaven, which are enchanted
   To music, by the wand of Solitude,
      That wizard wild, and the far tents implanted
   Upon the plain, be seen by those who stood   2540
Thence marking the dark shore of Ocean's curvèd flood.

XXIV

One moment these were heard and seen—another
   Passed; and the two who stood beneath that night,
Each only heard, or saw, or felt the other;
   As from the lofty steed she did alight,   2545
   Cythna, (for, from the eyes whose deepest light
Of love and sadness made my lips feel pale
   With influence strange of mournfullest delight,
My own sweet Cythna looked), with joy did quail,
And felt her strength in tears of human weakness fail.   2550

XXV

And for a space in my embrace she rested,
   Her head on my unquiet heart reposing,
While my faint arms her languid frame invested:
   At length she looked on me, and half unclosing
   Her tremulous lips, said: 'Friend, thy bands were losing
The battle, as I stood before the King   2556
   In bonds.—I burst them then, and swiftly choosing
The time, did seize a Tartar's sword, and spring
Upon his horse, and, swift as on the whirlwind's wing,

XXVI

'Have thou and I been borne beyond pursuer,   2560
   And we are here.'—Then turning to the steed,
She pressed the white moon on his front with pure
   And rose-like lips, and many a fragrant weed
   From the green ruin plucked, that he might feed;—
But I to a stone seat that Maiden led,   2565
   And kissing her fair eyes, said, 'Thou hast need
Of rest,' and I heaped up the courser's bed
In a green mossy nook, with mountain-flowers dispread.

XXVII

Within that ruin, where a shattered portal
   Looks to the eastern stars, abandoned now   2570
By man, to be the home of things immortal,
   Memories, like awful ghosts which come and go,

   And must inherit all he builds below,
When he is gone, a hall stood; o'er whose roof
   Fair clinging weeds with ivy pale did grow,   2575
   Clasping its gray rents with a verdurous woof,
A hanging dome of leaves, a canopy moon-proof.

XXVIII

The autumnal winds, as if spell-bound, had made
   A natural couch of leaves in that recess,
Which seasons none disturbed, but, in the shade   2580
   Of flowering parasites, did Spring love to dress
   With their sweet blooms the wintry loneliness
Of those dead leaves, shedding their stars, whene'er
   The wandering wind her nurslings might caress;
   Whose intertwining fingers ever there   2585
Made music wild and soft that filled the listening air.

XXIX

We know not where we go, or what sweet dream
   May pilot us through caverns strange and fair
Of far and pathless passion, while the stream
   Of life, our bark doth on its whirlpools bear,   2590
   Spreading swift wings as sails to the dim air;
Nor should we seek to know, so the devotion
   Of love and gentle thoughts be heard still there
Louder and louder from the utmost Ocean
Of universal life, attuning its commotion.   2595

XXX

To the pure all things are pure! Oblivion wrapped
   Our spirits, and the fearful overthrow
Of public hope was from our being snapped,
   Though linkèd years had bound it there; for now
   A power, a thirst, a knowledge, which below   2600
All thoughts, like light beyond the atmosphere,
   Clothing its clouds with grace, doth ever flow,
Came on us, as we sate in silence there,
Beneath the golden stars of the clear azure air:—

XXXI

In silence which doth follow talk that causes   2605
   The baffled heart to speak with sighs and tears,
When wildering passion swalloweth up the pauses
   Of inexpressive speech:—the youthful years

Which we together passed, their hopes and fears,
The blood itself which ran within our frames,   2610
That likeness of the features which endears
The thoughts expressed by them, our very names,
And all the wingèd hours which speechless memory claims,

XXXII

Had found a voice—and ere that voice did pass,
The night grew damp and dim, and through a rent   2615
Of the ruin where we sate, from the morass,
A wandering Meteor by some wild wind sent,
Hung high in the green dome, to which it lent
A faint and pallid lustre; while the song
Of blasts, in which its blue hair quivering bent,   2620
Strewed strangest sounds the moving leaves among;
A wondrous light, the sound as of a spirit's tongue.

XXXIII

The Meteor showed the leaves on which we sate,
And Cythna's glowing arms, and the thick ties
Of her soft hair, which bent with gathered weight   2625
My neck near hers, her dark and deepening eyes,
Which, as twin phantoms of one star that lies
O'er a dim well, move, though the star reposes,
Swam in our mute and liquid ecstasies,
Her marble brow, and eager lips, like roses,   2630
With their own fragrance pale, which Spring but half uncloses.

XXXIV

The Meteor to its far morass returned:
The beating of our veins one interval
Made still; and then I felt the blood that burned
Within her frame, mingle with mine, and fall   2635
Around my heart like fire; and over all
A mist was spread, the sickness of a deep
And speechless swoon of joy, as might befall
Two disunited spirits when they leap
In union from this earth's obscure and fading sleep.   2640

XXXV

Was it one moment that confounded thus
All thought, all sense, all feeling, into one
Unutterable power, which shielded us
Even from our own cold looks, when we had gone

Into a wide and wild oblivion   2645
Of tumult and of tenderness? or now
Had ages, such as make the moon and sun,
The seasons, and mankind their changes know,
Left fear and time unfelt by us alone below?

XXXVI

I know not. What are kisses whose fire clasps   2650
The failing heart in languishment, or limb
Twined within limb? or the quick dying gasps
Of the life meeting, when the faint eyes swim
Through tears of a wide mist boundless and dim,
In one caress? What is the strong control   2655
Which leads the heart that dizzy steep to climb,
Where far over the world those vapours roll,
Which blend two restless frames in one reposing soul?

XXXVII

It is the shadow which doth float unseen,
But not unfelt, o'er blind mortality,   2660
Whose divine darkness fled not, from that green
And lone recess, where lapped in peace did lie
Our linkèd frames till, from the changing sky,
That night and still another day had fled;
And then I saw and felt. The moon was high,   2665
And clouds, as of a coming storm, were spread
Under its orb,—loud winds were gathering overhead.

XXXVIII

Cythna's sweet lips seemed lurid in the moon,
Her fairest limbs with the night wind were chill,
And her dark tresses were all loosely strewn   2670
O'er her pale bosom:—all within was still,
And the sweet peace of joy did almost fill
The depth of her unfathomable look;—
And we sate calmly, though that rocky hill,
The waves contending in its caverns strook,   2675
For they foreknew the storm, and the gray ruin shook.

XXXIX

There we unheeding sate, in the communion
Of interchangèd vows, which, with a rite
Of faith most sweet and sacred, stamped our union.—
Few were the living hearts which could unite   2680

Like ours, or celebrate a bridal-night
With such close sympathies, for they had sprung
From linkèd youth, and from the gentle might
Of earliest love, delayed and cherished long,
Which common hopes and fears made, like a tempest, strong.

XL

And such is Nature's law divine, that those   2686
    Who grow together cannot choose but love,
If faith or custom do not interpose,
    Or common slavery mar what else might move
    All gentlest thoughts; as in the sacred grove   2690
Which shades the springs of Ethiopian Nile,
    That living tree, which, if the arrowy dove
Strike with her shadow, shrinks in fear awhile,
But its own kindred leaves clasps while the sunbeams smile;

XLI

And clings to them, when darkness may dissever   2695
    The close caresses of all duller plants
Which bloom on the wide earth—thus we for ever
    Were linked, for love had nursed us in the haunts
    Where knowledge, from its secret source enchants
Young hearts with the fresh music of its springing,   2700
    Ere yet its gathered flood feeds human wants,
As the great Nile feeds Egypt; ever flinging
Light on the woven boughs which o'er its waves are swinging.

XLII

The tones of Cythna's voice like echoes were
    Of those far murmuring streams; they rose and fell,
Mixed with mine own in the tempestuous air,—   2706
    And so we sate, until our talk befell
    Of the late ruin, swift and horrible,
And how those seeds of hope might yet be sown,
    Whose fruit is evil's mortal poison: well,   2710
For us, this ruin made a watch-tower lone,
But Cythna's eyes looked faint, and now two days were gone

XLIII

Since she had food:—therefore I did awaken
    The Tartar steed, who, from his ebon mane
Soon as the clinging slumbers he had shaken,   2715
    Bent his thin head to seek the brazen rein,

Following me obediently; with pain
Of heart, so deep and dread, that one caress,
     When lips and heart refuse to part again
Till they have told their fill, could scarce express   2720
The anguish of her mute and fearful tenderness,

XLIV

Cythna beheld me part, as I bestrode
     That willing steed—the tempest and the night,
Which gave my path its safety as I rode
     Down the ravine of rocks, did soon unite   2725
     The darkness and the tumult of their might
Borne on all winds.—Far through the streaming rain
     Floating at intervals the garments white
Of Cythna gleamed, and her voice once again
Came to me on the gust, and soon I reached the plain.   2730

XLV

I dreaded not the tempest, nor did he
     Who bore me, but his eyeballs wide and red
Turned on the lightning's cleft exultingly;
     And when the earth beneath his tameless tread,
     Shook with the sullen thunder, he would spread   2735
His nostrils to the blast, and joyously
     Mock the fierce peal with neighings;—thus we sped
O'er the lit plain, and soon I could descry
Where Death and Fire had gorged the spoil of victory.

XLVI

There was a desolate village in a wood   2740
     Whose bloom-inwoven leaves now scattering fed
The hungry storm; it was a place of blood,
     A heap of hearthless walls;—the flames were dead
     Within those dwellings now,—the life had fled
From all those corpses now,—but the wide sky   2745
     Flooded with lightning was ribbed overhead
By the black rafters, and around did lie
Women. and babes, and men, slaughtered confusedly.

XLVII

Beside the fountain in the market-place
     Dismounting, I beheld those corpses stare   2750
With horny eyes upon each other's face,
     And on the earth and on the vacant air,

And upon me, close to the waters where
I stooped to slake my thirst;—I shrank to taste,
   For the salt bitterness of blood was there;   2755
But tied the steed beside, and sought in haste
If any yet survived amid that ghastly waste.

XLVIII

No living thing was there beside one woman,
   Whom I found wandering in the streets, and she
Was withered from a likeness of aught human   2760
   Into a fiend, by some strange misery:
   Soon as she heard my steps she leaped on me,
And glued her burning lips to mine, and laughed
   With a loud, long, and frantic laugh of glee,
And cried, 'Now, Mortal, thou hast deeply quaffed   2765
The Plague's blue kisses—soon millions shall pledge the
      draught!

XLIX

'My name is Pestilence—this bosom dry,
   Once fed two babes—a sister and a brother—
When I came home, one in the blood did lie
   Of three death-wounds—the flames had ate the other!
   Since then I have no longer been a mother,   2771
But I am Pestilence;—hither and thither
   I flit about, that I may slay and smother:—
All lips which I have kissed must surely wither,
But Death's—if thou art he, we'll go to work together!   2775

L

'What seek'st thou here? The moonlight comes in flashes,—
   The dew is rising dankly from the dell—
'Twill moisten her! and thou shalt see the gashes
   In my sweet boy, now full of worms—but tell
   First what thou seek'st.'—'I seek for food.'—' 'Tis well,
Thou shalt have food; Famine, my paramour,   2781
   Waits for us at the feast—cruel and fell
Is Famine, but he drives not from his door
Those whom these lips have kissed, alone. No more, no more!'

LI

As thus she spake, she grasped me with the strength   2785
   Of madness, and by many a ruined hearth
She led, and over many a corpse:—at length
   We came to a lone hut where on the earth

Which made its floor, she in her ghastly mirth
Gathering from all those homes now desolate,   2790
   Had piled three heaps of loaves, making a dearth
Among the dead—round which she set in state
A ring of cold, stiff babes; silent and stark they sate.

LII

She leaped upon a pile, and lifted high
   Her mad looks to the lightning, and cried: 'Eat!   2795
Share the great feast—to-morrow we must die!'
   And then she spurned the loaves with her pale feet,
   Towards her bloodless guests;—that sight to meet,
Mine eyes and my heart ached, and but that she
   Who loved me, did with absent looks defeat   2800
Despair, I might have raved in sympathy;
But now I took the food that woman offered me;

LIII

And vainly having with her madness striven
   If I might win her to return with me,
Departed. In the eastern beams of Heaven   2805
   The lightning now grew pallid—rapidly,
   As by the shore of the tempestuous sea
The dark steed bore me, and the mountain gray
   Soon echoed to his hoofs, and I could see
Cythna among the rocks, where she alway   2810
Had sate, with anxious eyes fixed on the lingering day.

LIV

And joy was ours to meet: she was most pale,
   Famished, and wet and weary, so I cast
My arms around her, lest her steps should fail
   As to our home we went, and thus embraced,   2815
   Her full heart seemed a deeper joy to taste
Than e'er the prosperous know; the steed behind
   Trod peacefully along the mountain waste:
We reached our home ere morning could unbind
Night's latest veil, and on our bridal-couch reclined.   2820

LV

Her chilled heart having cherished in my bosom,
   And sweetest kisses past, we two did share
Our peaceful meal:—as an autumnal blossom
   Which spreads its shrunk leaves in the sunny air,

After cold showers, like rainbows woven there,   2825
  Thus in her lips and cheeks the vital spirit
    Mantled, and in her eyes, an atmosphere
Of health, and hope; and sorrow languished near it,
And fear, and all that dark despondence doth inherit.

CANTO VII

I

So we sate joyous as the morning ray   2830
  Which fed upon the wrecks of night and storm
Now lingering on the winds; light airs did play
  Among the dewy weeds, the sun was warm,
  And we sate linked in the inwoven charm
Of converse and caresses sweet and deep,   2835
  Speechless caresses, talk that might disarm
Time, though he wield the darts of death and sleep,
And those thrice mortal barbs in his own poison steep.

II

I told her of my sufferings and my madness,
  And how, awakened from that dreamy mood   2840
By Liberty's uprise, the strength of gladness
  Came to my spirit in my solitude;
  And all that now I was—while tears pursued
Each other down her fair and glistening cheek
  Fast as the thoughts which fed them, like a flood   2845
From sunbright dales; and when I ceased to speak,
Her accents soft and sweet the pausing air did wake.

III

She told me a strange tale of strange endurance,
  Like broken memories of many a heart
Woven into one; to which no firm assurance,   2850
  So wild were they, could her own faith impart.
  She said that not a tear did dare to start
From the swoln brain, and that her thoughts were firm
  When from all mortal hope she did depart,
Borne by those slaves across the Ocean's term,   2855
And that she reached the port without one fear infirm.

IV

One was she among many there, the thralls
  Of the cold Tyrant's cruel lust: and they
Laughed mournfully in those polluted halls;
  But she was calm and sad, musing alway   2860

On loftiest enterprise, till on a day
The Tyrant heard her singing to her lute
A wild, and sad, and spirit-thrilling lay,
Like winds that die in wastes—one moment mute
The evil thoughts it made, which did his breast pollute.   2865

V

Even when he saw her wondrous loveliness,
    One moment to great Nature's sacred power
He bent, and was no longer passionless;
    But when he bade her to his secret bower
    Be borne, a loveless victim, and she tore   2870
Her locks in agony, and her words of flame
    And mightier looks availed not; then he bore
Again his load of slavery, and became
A king, a heartless beast, a pageant and a name.

VI

She told me what a loathsome agony   2875
    Is that when selfishness mocks love's delight,
Foul as in dream's most fearful imagery
    To dally with the mowing dead—that night
    All torture, fear, or horror made seem light
Which the soul dreams or knows, and when the day   2880
    Shone on her awful frenzy, from the sight
Where like a Spirit in fleshly chains she lay
Struggling, aghast and pale the Tyrant fled away.

VII

Her madness was a beam of light, a power   2884
    Which dawned through the rent soul; and words it gave,
Gestures, and looks, such as in whirlwinds bore
    Which might not be withstood—whence none could save—
    All who approached their sphere,—like some calm wave
Vexed into whirlpools by the chasms beneath;
    And sympathy made each attendant slave   2890
Fearless and free, and they began to breathe
Deep curses, like the voice of flames far underneath.

VIII

The King felt pale upon his noonday throne:
    At night two slaves he to her chamber sent,—
One was a green and wrinkled eunuch, grown   2895
    From human shape into an instrument

Of all things ill—distorted, bowed and bent.
The other was a wretch from infancy
  Made dumb by poison; who nought knew or **meant**
But to obey: from the fire-isles came he,   2900
A diver lean and strong, of Oman's coral sea.

IX

They bore her to a bark, and the swift stroke
  Of silent rowers clove the blue moonlight seas,
Until upon their path the morning broke;
  They anchored then, where, be there calm or breeze, 2905
  The gloomiest of the drear Symplegades
Shakes with the sleepless surge;—the Ethiop there
  Wound his long arms around her, and with knees
Like iron clasped her feet, and plunged with her
Among the closing waves out of the boundless air.   2910

X

'Swift as an eagle stooping from the plain
  Of morning light, into some shadowy wood,
He plunged through the green silence of the main,
  Through many a cavern which the eternal flood
  Had scooped, as dark lairs for its monster brood; 2915
And among mighty shapes which fled in wonder,
  And among mightier shadows which pursued
His heels, he wound: until the dark rocks under
He touched a golden chain—a sound arose like thunder.

XI

'A stunning clang of massive bolts redoubling   2920
  Beneath the deep—a burst of waters driven
As from the roots of the sea, raging and bubbling:
  And in that roof of crags a space was riven
  Through which there shone the emerald beams of heaven,
Shot through the lines of many waves inwoven,   2925
  Like sunlight through acacia woods at even,
Through which, his way the diver having cloven,
Passed like a spark sent up out of a burning oven.

XII

'And then,' she said, 'he laid me in a cave
  Above the waters, by that chasm of sea,   2930
A fountain round and vast, in which the wave
  Imprisoned, boiled and leaped perpetually,

Down which, one moment resting, he did flee,
Winning the adverse depth; that spacious cell
   Like an hupaithric temple wide and high,   2935
Whose aëry dome is inaccessible,
Was pierced with one round cleft through which the sunbeams
      fell.

XIII

'Below, the fountain's brink was richly paven
   With the deep's wealth, coral, and pearl, and sand
Like spangling gold, and purple shells engraven   2940
   With mystic legends by no mortal hand,
   Left there, when thronging to the moon's command,
The gathering waves rent the Hesperian gate
   Of mountains, and on such bright floor did stand
Columns, and shapes like statues, and the state   2945
Of kingless thrones, which Earth did in her heart create.

XIV

'The fiend of madness which had made its prey
   Of my poor heart, was lulled to sleep awhile:
There was an interval of many a day,
   And a sea-eagle brought me food the while,   2950
   Whose nest was built in that untrodden isle,
And who, to be the gaoler had been taught
   Of that strange dungeon; as a friend whose smile
Like light and rest at morn and even is sought   2954
That wild bird was to me, till madness misery brought.

XV

'The misery of a madness slow and creeping,
   Which made the earth seem fire, the sea seem air,
And the white clouds of noon which oft were sleeping,
   In the blue heaven so beautiful and fair,
   Like hosts of ghastly shadows hovering there;   2960
And the sea-eagle looked a fiend, who bore
   Thy mangled limbs for food!—Thus all things were
Transformed into the agony which I wore
Even as a poisoned robe around my bosom's core.

XVI

'Again I knew the day and night fast fleeing,   2965
   The eagle, and the fountain, and the air;
Another frenzy came—there seemed a being
   Within me—a strange load my heart did bear.

As if some living thing had made its lair
Even in the fountains of my life:—a long   2970
    And wondrous vision wrought from my despair,
Then grew, like sweet reality among
Dim visionary woes, an unreposing throng.

XVII

'Methought I was about to be a mother—
    Month after month went by, and still I dreamed   2975
That we should soon be all to one another,
    I and my child; and still new pulses seemed
    To beat beside my heart, and still I deemed
There was a babe within—and, when the rain
    Of winter through the rifted cavern streamed,   2980
Methought, after a lapse of lingering pain,
I saw that lovely shape, which near my heart had lain.

XVIII

'It was a babe, beautiful from its birth,—
    It was like thee, dear love, its eyes were thine,
Its brow, its lips, and so upon the earth   2985
    It laid its fingers, as now rest on mine
    Thine own, belovèd!—'twas a dream divine;
Even to remember how it fled, how swift,
    How utterly, might make the heart repine,—
Though 'twas a dream.'—Then Cythna did uplift   2990
Her looks on mine, as if some doubt she sought to shift:

XIX

A doubt which would not flee, a tenderness
    Of questioning grief, a source of thronging tears:
Which having passed, as one whom sobs oppress
    She spoke: 'Yes, in the wilderness of years   2995
    Her memory, aye, like a green home appears;
She sucked her fill even at this breast, sweet love,
    For many month.. I had no mortal fears;
Methought I felt her lips and breath approve,—
It was a human thing which to my bosom clove.   3000

XX

'I watched the dawn of her first smiles, and soon
    When zenith-stars were trembling on the wave,
Or when the beams of the invisible moon,
    Or sun, from many a prism within the cave

Their gem-born shadows to the water gave,   3005
Her looks would hunt them, and with outspread hand,
    From the swift lights which might that fountain pave,
She would mark one, and laugh, when that command
Slighting, it lingered there, and could not understand.

XXI

'Methought her looks began to talk with me;   3010
    And no articulate sounds, but something sweet
Her lips would frame,—so sweet it could not be,
    That it was meaningless; her touch would meet
    Mine, and our pulses calmly flow and beat
In response while we slept; and on a day   3015
    When I was happiest in that strange retreat,
With heaps of golden shells we two did play,—
Both infants, weaving wings for time's perpetual way.

XXII

'Ere night, methought, her waning eyes were grown
    Weary with joy, and tired with our delight,   3020
We, on the earth, like sister twins lay down
    On one fair mother's bosom:—from that night
    She fled;—like those illusions clear and bright,
Which dwell in lakes, when the red moon on high
    Pause ere it wakens tempest;—and her flight,   3025
Though 'twas the death of brainless fantasy,
Yet smote my lonesome heart more than all misery.

XXIII

'It seemed that in the dreary night, the diver
    Who brought me thither, came again, and bore
My child away. I saw the waters quiver,   3030
    When he so swiftly sunk, as once before;
    Then morning came—it shone even as of yore,
But I was changed—the very life was gone
    Out of my heart—I wasted more and more,
Day after day, and sitting there alone,   3035
Vexed the inconstant waves with my perpetual moan.

XXIV

'I was no longer mad, and yet methought
    My breasts were swoln and changed:—in every vein
The blood stood still one moment, while that thought
    Was passing—with a gush of sickening pain   3040

It ebbed even to its withered springs again:
When my wan eyes in stern resolve I turned
  From that most strange delusion, which would fain
Have waked the dream for which my spirit yearned
With more than human love,—then left it unreturned.   3045

XXV

'So now my reason was restored to me
  I struggled with that dream, which, like a beast
Most fierce and beauteous, in my memory
  Had made its lair, and on my heart did feast;
  But all that cave and all its shapes, possessed   3050
By thoughts which could not fade, renewed each one
  Some smile, some look, some gesture which had blessed
Me heretofore: I, sitting there alone,
Vexed the inconstant waves with my perpetual moan.

XXVI

'Time passed, I know not whether months or years;
  For day, nor night, nor change of seasons made   3056
Its note, but thoughts and unavailing tears:
  And I became at last even as a shade,
  A smoke, a cloud on which the winds have preyed,
Till it be thin as air; until, one even,   3060
  A Nautilus upon the fountain played,
Spreading his azure sail where breath of Heaven
Descended not, among the waves and whirlpools driven.

XXVII

'And, when the Eagle came, that lovely thing,
  Oaring with rosy feet its silver boat,   3065
Fled near me as for shelter; on slow wing,
  The Eagle, hovering o'er his prey did float;
  But when he saw that I with fear did note
His purpose, proffering my own food to him,
  The eager plumes subsided on his throat—   3070
He came where that bright child of sea did swim,
And o'er it cast in peace his shadow broad and dim.

XXVIII

'This wakened me, it gave me human strength;
  And hope, I knew not whence or wherefore, rose,
But I resumed my ancient powers at length;   3075
  My spirit felt again like one of those

Like thine, whose fate it is to make the woes
Of humankind their prey—what was this cave?
 Its deep foundation no firm purpose knows
Immutable, resistless, strong to save,   3080
Like mind while yet it mocks the all-devouring grave.

XXIX

'And where was Laon? might my heart be dead,
 While that far dearer heart could move and be?
Or whilst over the earth the pall was spread,
 Which I had sworn to rend? I might be free,   3085
 Could I but win that friendly bird to me,
To bring me ropes; and long in vain I sought
 By intercourse of mutual imagery
Of objects, if such aid he could be taught;
But fruit, and flowers, and boughs, yet never ropes he brought.

XXX

'We live in our own world, and mine was made   3091
 From glorious fantasies of hope departed:
Aye we are darkened with their floating shade,
 Or cast a lustre on them—time imparted
 Such power to me—I became fearless-hearted,   3095
My eye and voice grew firm, calm was my mind,
 And piercing, like the morn, now it has darted
Its lustre on all hidden things, behind
Yon dim and fading clouds which load the weary wind.

XXXI

'My mind became the book through which I grew   3100
 Wise in all human wisdom, and its cave,
Which like a mine I rifled through and through,
 To me the keeping of its secrets gave—
 One mind, the type of all, the moveless wave
Whose calm reflects all moving things that are,   3105
 Necessity, and love, and life, the grave,
And sympathy, fountains of hope and fear;
Justice, and truth, and time, and the world's natural sphere.

XXXII

'And on the sand would I make signs to range
 These woofs, as they were woven, of my thought;   3110
Clear, elemental shapes, whose smallest change
 A subtler language within language wrought:

The key of truths which once were dimly taught
  In old Crotona;—and sweet melodies
    Of love, in that lorn solitude I caught   3115
From mine own voice in dream, when thy dear eyes
Shone through my sleep, and did that utterance harmonize.

XXXIII

'Thy songs were winds whereon I fled at will,
  As in a wingèd chariot, o'er the plain
    Of crystal youth; and thou wert there to fill   3120
  My heart with joy, and there we sate again
  On the gray margin of the glimmering main,
Happy as then but wiser far, for we
  Smiled on the flowery grave in which were lain
Fear, Faith, and Slavery; and mankind was free,   3125
Equal, and pure, and wise, in Wisdom's prophecy.

XXXIV

'For to my will my fancies were as slaves
  To do their sweet and subtile ministries;
And oft from that bright fountain's shadowy waves
  They would make human throngs gather and rise   3130
  To combat with my overflowing eyes,
And voice made deep with passion—thus I grew
  Familiar with the shock and the surprise
And war of earthly minds, from which I drew
The power which has been mine to frame their thoughts anew.

XXXV

'And thus my prison was the populous earth—   3136
  Where I saw—even as misery dreams of morn
Before the east has given its glory birth—
  Religion's pomp made desolate by the scorn
  Of Wisdom's faintest smile, and thrones, uptorn,   3140
And dwellings of mild people interspersed
  With undivided fields of ripening corn,
And love made free,—a hope which we have nursed
Even with our blood and tears,—until its glory burst.

XXXVI

'All is not lost! There is some recompense   3145
  For hope whose fountain can be thus profound,
Even thronèd Evil's splendid impotence,
  Girt by its hell of power, the secret sound

Of hymns to truth and freedom—the dread bound
Of life and death passed fearlessly and well,   3150
  Dungeons wherein the high resolve is found,
Racks which degraded woman's greatness tell,
And what may else be good and irresistible.

XXXVII

'Such are the thoughts which, like the fires that flare
  In storm-encompassed isles, we cherish yet   3155
In this dark ruin—such were mine even there;
  As in its sleep some odorous violet,
  While yet its leaves with nightly dews are wet,
Breathes in prophetic dreams of day's uprise,
  Or, as ere Scythian frost in fear has met   3160
Spring's messengers descending from the skies,
The buds foreknow their life—this hope must ever rise.

XXXVIII

'So years had passed, when sudden earthquake rent
  The depth of ocean, and the cavern cracked
With sound, as if the world's wide continent   3165
  Had fallen in universal ruin wracked:
  And through the cleft streamed in one cataract
The stifling waters—when I woke, the flood
  Whose banded waves that crystal cave had sacked
Was ebbing round me, and my bright abode   3170
Before me yawned—a chasm desert, and bare, and broad.

XXXIX

'Above me was the sky, beneath the sea:
  I stood upon a point of shattered stone,
And heard loose rocks rushing tumultuously
  With splash and shock into the deep—anon   3175
  All ceased, and there was silence wide and lone.
I felt that I was free! The Ocean-spray
  Quivered beneath my feet, the broad Heaven shone
Around, and in my hair the winds did play
Lingering as they pursued their unimpeded way.   3180

XL

'My spirit moved upon the sea like wind
  Which round some thymy cape will lag and hover,
Though it can wake the still cloud, and unbind
  The strength of tempest: day was almost over,

When through the fading light I could discover   3185
A ship approaching—its white sails were fed
    With the north wind—its moving shade did cover
The twilight deep;—the Mariners in dread
Cast anchor when they saw new rocks around them spread.

XLI

'And when they saw one sitting on a crag,   3190
    They sent a boat to me;—the Sailors rowed
In awe through many a new and fearful jag
    Of overhanging rock, through which there flowed
    The foam of streams that cannot make abode.
They came and questioned me, but when they heard   3195
    My voice, they became silent, and they stood
And moved as men in whom new love had stirred
Deep thoughts: so to the ship we passed without a word.

CANTO VIII

I

'I SATE beside the Steersman then, and gazing
    Upon the west, cried, "Spread the sails! Behold!   3200
The sinking moon is like a watch-tower blazing
    Over the mountains yet;—the City of Gold
    Yon Cape alone does from the sight withhold;
The stream is fleet—the north breathes steadily
    Beneath the stars, they tremble with the cold!   3205
Yet cannot rest upon the dreary sea!—
Haste, haste to the warm home of happier destiny!"

II

'The Mariners obeyed—the Captain stood
    Aloof, and, whispering to the Pilot, said,
"Alas, alas! I fear we are pursued   3210
    By wicked ghosts: a Phantom of the Dead,
    The night before we sailed, came to my bed
In dream, like that!" The Pilot then replied,
    "It cannot be—she is a human Maid—
Her low voice makes you weep—she is some bride,   3215
Or daughter of high birth—she can be nought beside."

III

'We passed the islets, borne by wind and stream,
    And as we sailed, the Mariners came near
And thronged around to listen;—in the gleam
    Of the pale moon I stood, as one whom fear   3220

May not attaint, and my calm voice did rear;
"Ye all are human—yon broad moon gives light
    To millions who the selfsame likeness wear,
Even while I speak—beneath this very night,   3224
Their thoughts flow on like ours, in sadness or delight.

IV

' "What dream ye? Your own hands have built an home,
    Even for yourselves on a beloved shore:
For some, fond eyes are pining till they come,
    How they will greet him when his toils are o'er,   3229
    And laughing babes rush from the well-known door!
Is this your care? ye toil for your own good—
    Ye feel and think—has some immortal power
Such purposes? or in a human mood,
Dream ye some Power thus builds for man in solitude?

V

' "What is that Power? Ye mock yourselves, and give
    A human heart to what ye cannot know: 3236
As if the cause of life could think and live!
    'Twere as if man's own works should feel, and show
    The hopes, and fears, and thoughts from which they flow,
And he be like to them! Lo! Plague is free   3240
    To waste, Blight, Poison, Earthquake, Hail, and Snow,
Disease, and Want, and worse Necessity
Of hate and ill, and Pride, and Fear, and Tyranny!

VI

' "What is that Power? Some moon-struck sophist stood
    Watching the shade from his own soul upthrown   3245
Fill Heaven and darken Earth, and in such mood
    The Form he saw and worshipped was his own,
    His likeness in the world's vast mirror shown;
And 'twere an innocent dream, but that a faith
    Nursed by fear's dew of poison, grows thereon,   3250
And that men say, that Power has chosen Death
On all who scorn its laws, to wreak immortal wrath.

VII

' "Men say that they themselves have heard and seen,
    Or known from others who have known such things,
A Shade, a Form, which Earth and Heaven between   3255
    Wields an invisible rod—that Priests and Kings,

Custom, domestic sway, ay, all that brings
Man's freeborn soul beneath the oppressor's heel,
Are his strong ministers, and that the stings
Of death will make the wise his vengeance feel,   3260
Though truth and virtue arm their hearts with tenfold steel.

VIII

" 'And it is said, this Power will punish wrong;
Yes, add despair to crime, and pain to pain!
And deepest hell, and deathless snakes among,
Will bind the wretch on whom is fixed a stain,   3265
Which, like a plague, a burden, and a bane,
Clung to him while he lived;—for love and hate,
Virtue and vice, they say are difference vain—
The will of strength is right—this human state
Tyrants, that they may rule, with lies thus desolate.   3270

IX

' "Alas, what strength? Opinion is more frail
Than yon dim cloud now fading on the moon
Even while we gaze, though it awhile avail
To hide the orb of truth—and every throne
Of Earth or Heaven, though shadow, rests thereon,   3275
One shape of many names:—for this ye plough
The barren waves of ocean, hence each one
Is slave or tyrant; all betray and bow,
Command, or kill, or fear, or wreak, or suffer woe.

X

' "Its names are each a sign which maketh holy   3280
All power—ay, the ghost, the dream, the shade
Of power—lust, falsehood, hate, and pride, and folly;
The pattern whence all fraud and wrong is made,
A law to which mankind has been betrayed;
And human love, is as the name well known   3285
Of a dear mother, whom the murderer laid
In bloody grave, and into darkness thrown,
Gathered her wildered babes around him as his own.

XI

' "O Love, who to the hearts of wandering men
Art as the calm to Ocean's weary waves!
Justice, or Truth, or Joy! those only can   3290
From slavery and religion's labyrinth caves

Guide us, as one clear star the seaman saves.
To give to all an equal share of good,
    To track the steps of Freedom, though through graves
    She pass, to suffer all in patient mood,   3296
To weep for crime, though stained with thy friend's dearest
        blood,—

XII

' "To feel the peace of self-contentment's lot,
    To own all sympathies, and outrage none,
And in the inmost bowers of sense and thought,   3300
    Until life's sunny day is quite gone down,
    To sit and smile with Joy, or, not alone,
To kiss salt tears from the worn cheek of Woe;
    To live, as if to love and live were one,—
This is not faith or law, nor those who bow   3305
To thrones on Heaven or Earth, such destiny may know.

XIII

' "But children near their parents tremble now,
    Because they must obey—one rules another,
And as one Power rules both high and low,
    So man is made the captive of his brother,   3310
    And Hate is throned on high with Fear her mother,
Above the Highest—and those fountain-cells,
    Whence love yet flowed when faith had choked all other,
Are darkened—Woman as the bond-slave dwells
Of man, a slave; and life is poisoned in its wells.   3315

XIV

' "Man seeks for gold in mines, that he may weave
    A lasting chain for his own slavery;—
In fear and restless care that he may live
    He toils for others, who must ever be
    The joyous thralls of like captivity;   3320
He murders, for his chiefs delight in ruin;
    He builds the altar, that its idol's fee
    May be his very blood; he is pursuing—
O, blind and willing wretch!—his own obscure undoing.

XV

' "Woman!—she is his slave, she has become   3325
    A thing I weep to speak—the child of scorn,
The outcast of a desolated home;
    Falsehood, and fear, and toil, like waves have worn

Channels upon her cheek, which smiles adorn,
As calm decks the false Ocean:—well ye know   3330
What Woman is, for none of Woman born,
Can choose but drain the bitter dregs of woe,
Which ever from the oppressed to the oppressors flow.

XVI

' "This need not be; ye might arise, and will
That gold should lose its power, and thrones their glory;
That love, which none may bind, be free to fill   3336
The world, like light; and evil faith, grown hoary
With crime, be quenched and die.—Yon promontory
Even now eclipses the descending moon!—
Dungeons and palaces are transitory—   3340
High temples fade like vapour—Man alone
Remains, whose will has power when all beside is gone.

XVII

' "Let all be free and equal!—From your hearts
I feel an echo; through my inmost frame
Like sweetest sound, seeking its mate, it darts—   3345
Whence come ye, friends? Alas, I cannot name
All that I read of sorrow, toil, and shame,
On your worn faces; as in legends old
Which make immortal the disastrous fame
Of conquerors and impostors false and bold,   3350
The discord of your hearts, I in your looks behold.

XVIII

' "Whence come ye, friends? from pouring human blood
Forth on the earth? Or bring ye steel and gold,
That Kings may dupe and slay the multitude?
Or from the famished poor, pale, weak, and cold,   3355
Bear ye the earnings of their toil? Unfold!
Speak! Are your hands in slaughter's sanguine hue
Stained freshly? have your hearts in guile grown old?
Know yourselves thus! ye shall be pure as dew,
And I will be a friend and sister unto you.   3360

XIX

' "Disguise it not—we have one human heart—
All mortal thoughts confess a common home:
Blush not for what may to thyself impart
Stains of inevitable crime: the doom

Is this, which has, or may, or must become 3365
Thine, and all humankind's. Ye are the spoil
  Which Time thus marks for the devouring tomb,
Thou and thy thoughts and they, and all the toil
Wherewith ye twine the rings of life's perpetual coil.

XX

' "Disguise it not—ye blush for what ye hate, 3370
  And Enmity is sister unto Shame;
Look on your mind—it is the book of fate—
  Ah! it is dark with many a blazoned name
  Of misery—all are mirrors of the same;
But the dark fiend who with his iron pen 3375
  Dipped in scorn's fiery poison, makes his fame
Enduring there, would o'er the heads of men
Pass harmless, if they scorned to make their hearts his den.

XXI

' "Yes, it is Hate—that shapeless fiendly thing
  Of many names, all evil, some divine, 3380
Whom self-contempt arms with a mortal sting;
  Which, when the heart its snaky folds entwine
  Is wasted quite, and when it doth repine
To gorge such bitter prey, on all beside
  It turns with ninefold rage, as with its twine 3385
When Amphisbæna some fair bird has tied,
Soon o'er the putrid mass he threats on every side.

XXII

' "Reproach not thine own soul, but know thyself,
  Nor hate another's crime, nor loathe thine own.
It is the dark idolatry of self, 3390
  Which, when our thoughts and actions once are gone,
  Demands that man should weep, and bleed, and groan;
O vacant expiation! Be at rest.—
  The past is Death's, the future is thine own;
And love and joy can make the foulest breast 3395
A paradise of flowers, where peace might build her nest.

XXIII

' "Speak thou! whence come ye?"—A Youth made reply:
  "Wearily, wearily o'er the boundless deep
We sail;—thou readest well the misery
  Told in these faded eyes, but much doth sleep 3400

Within, which there the poor heart loves to keep,
    Or dare not write on the dishonoured brow;
        Even from our childhood have we learned to steep
    The bread of slavery in the tears of woe,
And never dreamed of hope or refuge until now.   3405

XXIV

' "Yes—I must speak—my secret should have perished
    Even with the heart it wasted, as a brand
Fades in the dying flame whose life it cherished,
    But that no human bosom can withstand
    Thee, wondrous Lady, and the mild command   3410
Of thy keen eyes:—yes, we are wretched slaves,
    Who from their wonted loves and native land
Are reft, and bear o'er the dividing waves
The unregarded prey of calm and happy graves.

XXV

' "We drag afar from pastoral vales the fairest   3415
    Among the daughters of those mountains lone,
We drag them there, where all things best and rarest
    Are stained and trampled:—years have come and gone
    Since, like the ship which bears me, I have known
No thought;—but now the eyes of one dear Maid   3420
    On mine with light of mutual love have shone—
She is my life,—I am but as the shade
Of her,—a smoke sent up from ashes, soon to fade.

XXVI

' "For she must perish in the Tyrant's hall—
    Alas, alas!"—He ceased, and by the sail   3425
Sate cowering—but his sobs were heard by all,
    And still before the ocean and the gale
    The ship fled fast till the stars 'gan to fail,
And, round me gathered with mute countenance,
    The Seamen gazed, the Pilot, worn and pale   3430
With toil, the Captain with gray locks, whose glance
Met mine in restless awe—they stood as in a trance.

XXVII

' "Recede not! pause not now! Thou art grown old,
    But Hope will make thee young, for Hope and Youth
Are children of one mother, even Love—behold!   3435
    The eternal stars gaze on us! Is the truth

Within your soul? care for your own, or ruth
For others' sufferings? do ye thirst to bear
A heart which not the serpent Custom's tooth
May violate?—Be free! and even here,   3440
Swear to be firm till death!" They cried "We swear! We swear!"

XXVIII

'The very darkness shook, as with a blast
Of subterranean thunder, at the cry;
The hollow shore its thousand echoes cast
Into the night, as if the sea, and sky,   3445
And earth, rejoiced with new-born liberty,
For in that name they swore! Bolts were undrawn,
And on the deck, with unaccustomed eye
The captives gazing stood, and every one   3449
Shrank as the inconstant torch upon her countenance shone.

XXIX

'They were earth's purest children, young and fair,
With eyes the shrines of unawakened thought,
And brows as bright as Spring or Morning, ere
Dark time had there its evil legend wrought
In characters of cloud which wither not.—   3455
The change was like a dream to them; but soon
They knew the glory of their altered lot,
In the bright wisdom of youth's breathless noon,
Sweet talk, and smiles, and sighs, all bosoms did attune.

XXX

'But one was mute, her cheeks and lips most fair,   3460
Changing their hue like lilies newly blown,
Beneath a bright acacia's shadowy hair,
Waved by the wind amid the sunny noon,
Showed that her soul was quivering; and full soon
That Youth arose, and breathlessly did look   3465
On her and me, as for some speechless boon:
I smiled, and both their hands in mine I took,
And felt a soft delight from what their spirits shook.

CANTO IX

I

'THAT night we anchored in a woody bay,
And sleep no more around us dared to hover   3470
Than, when all doubt and fear has passed away,
It shades the couch of some unresting lover,

Whose heart is now at rest: thus night passed over
In mutual joy:—around, a forest grew
   Of poplar and dark oaks, whose shade did cover   3475
The waning stars pranked in the waters blue,
And trembled in the wind which from the morning flew.

II

'The joyous Mariners, and each free Maiden,
   Now brought from the deep forest many a bough,
With woodland spoil most innocently laden;   3480
   Soon wreaths of budding foliage seemed to flow
   Over the mast and sails, the stern and prow
Were canopied with blooming boughs,—the while
   On the slant sun's path o'er the waves we go
Rejoicing, like the dwellers of an isle   3485
Doomed to pursue those waves that cannot cease to smile.

III

'The many ships spotting the dark blue deep
   With snowy sails, fled fast as ours came nigh,
In fear and wonder; and on every steep
   Thousands did gaze, they heard the startling cry,   3490
   Like Earth's own voice lifted unconquerably
To all her children, the unbounded mirth,
   The glorious joy of thy name—Liberty!
They heard!—As o'er the mountains of the earth
From peak to peak leap on the beams of Morning's birth:

IV

'So from that cry over the boundless hills   3496
   Sudden was caught one universal sound,
Like a volcano's voice, whose thunder fills
   Remotest skies,—such glorious madness found
   A path through human hearts with stream which drowned
Its struggling fears and cares, dark Custom's brood;   3501
   They knew not whence it came, but felt around
A wide contagion poured—they called aloud
On Liberty—that name lived on the sunny flood.

V

'We reached the port.—Alas! from many spirits   3505
   The wisdom which had waked that cry, was fled,
Like the brief glory which dark Heaven inherits
   From the false dawn, which fades ere it is spread,

Upon the night's devouring darkness shed:
Yet soon bright day will burst—even like a chasm   3510
  Of fire, to burn the shrouds outworn and dead,
  Which wrap the world; a wide enthusiasm,
To cleanse the fevered world as with an earthquake's spasm!

VI

'I walked through the great City then, but free
  From shame or fear; those toil-worn Mariners   3515
And happy Maidens did encompass me;
  And like a subterranean wind that stirs
  Some forest among caves, the hopes and fears
From every human soul, a murmur strange
  Made as I passed: and many wept, with tears   3520
Of joy and awe, and wingèd thoughts did range,
And half-extinguished words, which prophesied of change.

VII

'For, with strong speech I tore the veil that hid
  Nature, and Truth, and Liberty, and Love,—
As one who from some mountain's pyramid   3525
  Points to the unrisen sun!—the shades approve
  His truth, and flee from every stream and grove.
Thus, gentle thoughts did many a bosom fill,—
  Wisdom, the mail of tried affections wove
For many a heart, and tameless scorn of ill,   3530
Thrice steeped in molten steel the unconquerable will.

VIII

'Some said I was a maniac wild and lost;
  Some, that I scarce had risen from the grave,
The Prophet's virgin bride, a heavenly ghost:—
  Some said, I was a fiend from my weird cave,   3535
  Who had stolen human shape, and o'er the wave,
The forest, and the mountain came;—some said
  I was the child of God, sent down to save
Women from bonds and death, and on my head
The burden of their sins would frightfully be laid.   3540

IX

'But soon my human words found sympathy
  In human hearts: the purest and the best,
As friend with friend, made common cause with me,
  And they were few, but resolute:—the rest,

Ere yet success the enterprise had blessed,   3545
  Leagued with me in their hearts;—their meals, their slumber,
    Their hourly occupations, were possessed
  By hopes which I had armed to overnumber
Those hosts of meaner cares, which life's strong wings encumber.

X

'But chiefly women, whom my voice did waken   3550
  From their cold, careless, willing slavery,
Sought me: one truth their dreary prison has shaken,—
  They looked around, and lo! they became free!
    Their many tyrants sitting desolately
In slave-deserted halls, could none restrain;   3555
  For wrath's red fire had withered in the eye,
Whose lightning once was death,—nor fear, nor gain
Could tempt one captive now to lock another's chain.

XI

'Those who were sent to bind me, wept, and felt
  Their minds outsoar the bonds which clasped them round,
Even as a waxen shape may waste and melt   3561
  In the white furnace; and a visioned swound,
    A pause of hope and awe the City bound,
Which, like the silence of a tempest's birth,
  When in its awful shadow it has wound   3565
The sun, the wind, the ocean, and the earth,
Hung terrible, ere yet the lightnings have leaped forth.

XII

'Like clouds inwoven in the silent sky,
  By winds from distant regions meeting there,
In the high name of truth and liberty,   3570
  Around the City millions gathered were,
    By hopes which sprang from many a hidden lair,—
Words which the lore of truth in hues of flame
  Arrayed, thine own wild songs which in the air
Like homeless odours floated, and the name   3575
Of thee, and many a tongue which thou hadst dipped in flame.

XIII

'The Tyrant knew his power was gone, but Fear,
  The nurse of Vengeance, bade him wait the event—
That perfidy and custom, gold and prayer,
  And whatsoe'er, when force is impotent,   3580

To fraud the sceptre of the world has lent,
Might, as he judged, confirm his failing sway.
Therefore throughout the streets, the Priests he sent
To curse the rebels.—To their gods did they
For Earthquake, Plague, and Want, kneel in the public way.

XIV

'And grave and hoary men were bribed to tell   3586
    From seats where law is made the slave of wrong,
How glorious Athens in her splendour fell,
    Because her sons were free,—and that among
    Mankind, the many to the few belong,   3590
By Heaven, and Nature, and Necessity.
    They said, that age was truth, and that the young
Marred with wild hopes the peace of slavery,
With which old times and men had quelled the vain and free.

XV

'And with the falsehood of their poisonous lips   3595
    They breathed on the enduring memory
Of sages and of bards a brief eclipse;
    There was one teacher, who necessity
    Had armed with strength and wrong against mankind,
His slave and his avenger aye to be;   3600
    That we were weak and sinful, frail and blind,
And that the will of one was peace, and we
Should seek for nought on earth but toil and misery—

XVI

' "For thus we might avoid the hell hereafter."
    So spake the hypocrites, who cursed and lied;   3605
Alas, their sway was past, and tears and laughter
    Clung to their hoary hair, withering the pride
    Which in their hollow hearts dared still abide;
And yet obscener slaves with smoother brow,
    And sneers on their strait lips, thin, blue and wide,   3610
Said, that the rule of men was over now,
And hence, the subject world to woman's will must bow;

XVII

'And gold was scattered through the streets, and wine
    Flowed at a hundred feasts within the wall.
In vain! the steady towers in Heaven did shine   3615
    As they were wont, nor at the priestly call

Left Plague her banquet in the Ethiop's hall,
  Nor Famine from the rich man's portal came,
    Where at her ease she ever preys on all
  Who throng to kneel for food: nor fear nor shame,   3620
Nor faith, nor discord, dimmed hope's newly kindled flame.

XVIII

'For gold was as a god whose faith began
  To fade, so that its worshippers were few,
    And Faith itself, which in the heart of man
      Gives shape, voice, name, to spectral Terror, knew   3625
      Its downfall, as the altars lonelier grew,
  Till the Priests stood alone within the fane;
    The shafts of falsehood unpolluting flew,
  And the cold sneers of calumny were vain,
The union of the free with discord's brand to stain.   3630

XIX

'The rest thou knowest.—Lo! we two are here—
  We have survived a ruin wide and deep—
  Strange thoughts are mine.—I cannot grieve or fear,
    Sitting with thee upon this lonely steep
    I smile, though human love should make me weep.   3635
  We have survived a joy that knows no sorrow,
    And I do feel a mighty calmness creep
  Over my heart, which can no longer borrow
Its hues from chance or change, dark children of to-morrow.

XX

'We know not what will come—yet Laon, dearest,   3640
  Cythna shall be the prophetess of Love,
  Her lips shall rob thee of the grace thou wearest,
    To hide thy heart, and clothe the shapes which rove
    Within the homeless Future's wintry grove;
  For I now, sitting thus beside thee, seem   3645
    Even with thy breath and blood to live and move,
  And violence and wrong are as a dream
Which rolls from steadfast truth, an unreturning stream.

XXI

'The blasts of Autumn drive the wingèd seeds
  Over the earth,—next come the snows, and rain,   3650
  And frosts, and storms, which dreary Winter leads
    Out of his Scythian cave, a savage train;

Behold! Spring sweeps over the world again,
  Shedding soft dews from her ethereal wings;
    Flowers on the mountains, fruits over the plain, 3655
  And music on the waves and woods she flings,
And love on all that lives, and calm on lifeless things.

XXII

'O Spring, of hope, and love, and youth, and gladness
    Wind-wingèd emblem! brightest, best and fairest!
  Whence comest thou, when, with dark Winter's sadness 3660
    The tears that fade in sunny smiles thou sharest?
    Sister of joy, thou art the child who wearest
  Thy mother's dying smile, tender and sweet;
    Thy mother Autumn, for whose grave thou bearest
  Fresh flowers, and beams like flowers, with gentle feet, 3665
Disturbing not the leaves which are her winding-sheet.

XXIII

'Virtue, and Hope, and Love, like light and Heaven,
    Surround the world.—We are their chosen slaves.
  Has not the whirlwind of our spirit driven
    Truth's deathless germs to thought's remotest caves? 3670
    Lo, Winter comes!—the grief of many graves,
  The frost of death, the tempest of the sword,
    The flood of tyranny, whose sanguine waves
  Stagnate like ice at Faith the enchanter's word,
And bind all human hearts in its repose abhorred. 3675

XXIV

'The seeds are sleeping in the soil: meanwhile
    The Tyrant peoples dungeons with his prey,
  Pale victims on the guarded scaffold smile
    Because they cannot speak; and, day by day,
    The moon of wasting Science wanes away 3680
  Among her stars, and in that darkness vast
    The sons of earth to their foul idols pray,
  And gray Priests triumph, and like blight or blast
A shade of selfish care o'er human looks is cast.

XXV

'This is the winter of the world;—and here 3685
    We die, even as the winds of Autumn fade,
  Expiring in the frore and foggy air.—
    Behold! Spring comes, though we must pass, who made

The promise of its birth,—even as the shade
Which from our death, as from a mountain, flings   3690
The future, a broad sunrise; thus arrayed
As with the plumes of overshadowing wings,
From its dark gulf of chains, Earth like an eagle springs.

XXVI

'O dearest love! we shall be dead and cold
Before this morn may on the world arise;   3695
Wouldst thou the glory of its dawn behold?
Alas! gaze not on me, but turn thine eyes
On thine own heart—it is a paradise
Which everlasting Spring has made its own,
And while drear Winter fills the naked skies,   3700
Sweet streams of sunny thought, and flowers fresh-blown,
Are there, and weave their sounds and odours into one.

XXVII

'In their own hearts the earnest of the hope
Which made them great, the good will ever find;
And though some envious shades may interlope   3705
Between the effect and it, One comes behind,
Who aye the future to the past will bind—
Necessity, whose sightless strength for ever
Evil with evil, good with good must wind
In bands of union, which no power may sever: 3710
They must bring forth their kind, and be divided never!

XXVIII

'The good and mighty of departed ages
Are in their graves, the innocent and free,
Heroes, and Poets, and prevailing Sages,
Who leave the vesture of their majesty   3715
To adorn and clothe this naked world;—and we
Are like to them—such perish, but they leave
All hope, or love, or truth, or liberty,
Whose forms their mighty spirits could conceive,
To be a rule and law to ages that survive.   3720

XXIX

'So be the turf heaped over our remains
Even in our happy youth, and that strange lot,
Whate'er it be, when in these mingling veins
The blood is still, be ours; let sense and thought

Pass from our being, or be numbered not
Among the things that are; let those who come
    Behind, for whom our steadfast will has bought
A calm inheritance, a glorious doom,
Insult with careless tread, our undivided tomb.

XXX

'Our many thoughts and deeds, our life and love,   3730
    Our happiness, and all that we have been,
Immortally must live, and burn and move,
    When we shall be no more;—the world has seen
    A type of peace; and—as some most serene
And lovely spot to a poor maniac's eye,   3735
    After long years, some sweet and moving scene
Of youthful hope, returning suddenly,
Quells his long madness—thus man shall remember thee.

XXXI

'And Calumny meanwhile shall feed on us,
    As worms devour the dead, and near the throne   3740
And at the altar, most accepted thus
    Shall sneers and curses be;—what we have done
    None shall dare vouch, though it be truly known;
That record shall remain, when they must pass
    Who built their pride on its oblivion;   3745
And fame, in human hope which sculptured was,
Survive the perished scrolls of unenduring brass.

XXXII

'The while we two, belovèd, must depart,
    And Sense and Reason, those enchanters fair,
Whose wand of power is hope, would bid the heart   3750
    That gazed beyond the wormy grave despair:
    These eyes, these lips, this blood, seems darkly there
To fade in hideous ruin; no calm sleep
    Peopling with golden dreams the stagnant air,
Seems our obscure and rotting eyes to steep   3755
In joy;—but senseless death—a ruin dark and deep!

XXXIII

'These are blind fancies—reason cannot know
    What sense can neither feel, nor thought conceive;
There is delusion in the world—and woe,
    And fear, and pain—we know not whence we live,   3760

Or why, or how, or what mute Power may give
Their being to each plant, and star, and beast,
Or even these thoughts.—Come near me! I do weave
A chain I cannot break—I am possessed
With thoughts too swift and strong for one lone human
  breast.   3765

XXXIV

'Yes, yes—thy kiss is sweet, thy lips are warm—
 O! willingly, belovèd, would these eyes,
Might they no more drink being from thy form,
 Even as to sleep whence we again arise,
 Close their faint orbs in death: I fear nor prize   3770
Aught that can now betide, unshared by thee—
 Yes, Love when Wisdom fails makes Cythna wise:
Darkness and death, if death be true, must be
Dearer than life and hope, if unenjoyed with thee.

XXXV

'Alas, our thoughts flow on with stream, whose waters
 Return not to their fountain—Earth and Heaven,   3776
The Ocean and the Sun, the Clouds their daughters,
 Winter, and Spring, and Morn, and Noon, and Even,
 All that we are or know, is darkly driven
Towards one gulf.—Lo! what a change is come   3780
 Since I first spake—but time shall be forgiven,
Though it change all but thee!'—She ceased—night's gloom
Meanwhile had fallen on earth from the sky's sunless dome.

XXXVI

Though she had ceased, her countenance uplifted
 To Heaven, still spake, with solemn glory bright;   3785
Her dark deep eyes, her lips, whose motions gifted
 The air they breathed with love, her locks undight.
 'Fair star of life and love,' I cried, 'my soul's delight,
Why lookest thou on the crystalline skies?
 O, that my spirit were yon Heaven of night,   3790
Which gazes on thee with its thousand eyes!'
She turned to me and smiled—that smile was Paradise!

CANTO X

I

WAS there a human spirit in the steed,
 That thus with his proud voice, ere night was gone,
He broke our linkèd rest? or do indeed   3795
 All living things a common nature own,

And thought erect an universal throne,
Where many shapes one tribute ever bear?
    And Earth, their mutual mother, does she groan
To see her sons contend? and makes she bare   3800
Her breast, that all in peace its drainless stores may share?

II

I have heard friendly sounds from many a tongue
    Which was not human—the lone nightingale
Has answered me with her most soothing song,
    Out of her ivy bower, when I sate pale   3805
    With grief, and sighed beneath; from many a dale
The antelopes who flocked for food have spoken
    With happy sounds, and motions, that avail
Like man's own speech; and such was now the token   3810
Of waning night, whose calm by that proud neigh was broken.

III

Each night, that mighty steed bore me abroad,
    And I returned with food to our retreat,
And dark intelligence; the blood which flowed
    Over the fields, had stained the courser's feet;
    Soon the dust drinks that bitter dew,—then meet   3815
The vulture, and the wild dog, and the snake,
    The wolf, and the hyæna gray, and eat
The dead in horrid truce: their throngs did make
Behind the steed, a chasm like waves in a ship's wake.

IV

For, from the utmost realms of earth, came pouring   3820
    The banded slaves whom every despot sent
At that throned traitor's summons; like the roaring
    Of fire, whose floods the wild deer circumvent
    In the scorched pastures of the South; so bent
The armies of the leaguèd Kings around   3825
    Their files of steel and flame;—the continent
Trembled, as with a zone of ruin bound,
Beneath their feet, the sea shook with their Navies' sound.

V

From every nation of the earth they came,
    The multitude of moving heartless things,   3830
Whom slaves call men: obediently they came,
    Like sheep whom from the fold the shepherd brings

To the stall, red with blood; their many kings
Led them, thus erring, from their native land;
    Tartar and Frank, and millions whom the wings   3835
    Of Indian breezes lull, and many a band
The Arctic Anarch sent, and Idumea's sand,

VI

Fertile in prodigies and lies;—so there
    Strange natures made a brotherhood of ill.
The desert savage ceased to grasp in fear   3840
    His Asian shield and bow, when, at the will
    Of Europe's subtler son, the bolt would kill
Some shepherd sitting on a rock secure;
    But smiles of wondering joy his face would fill,
And savage sympathy: those slaves impure,   3845
Each one the other thus from ill to ill did lure.

VII

For traitorously did that foul Tyrant robe
    His countenance in lies,—even at the hour
When he was snatched from death, then o'er the globe,
    With secret signs from many a mountain-tower,   3850
    With smoke by day, and fire by night, the power
Of Kings and Priests, those dark conspirators,
    He called:—they knew his cause their own, and swore
Like wolves and serpents to their mutual wars   3855
Strange truce, with many a rite which Earth and Heaven abhors.

VIII

Myriads had come—millions were on their way;
    The Tyrant passed, surrounded by the steel
Of hired assassins, through the public way,
    Choked with his country's dead:—his footsteps reel
    On the fresh blood—he smiles. 'Ay, now I feel   3860
I am a King in truth!' he said, and took
    His royal seat, and bade the torturing wheel
Be brought, and fire, and pincers, and the hook,
And scorpions; that his soul on its revenge might look.

IX

'But first, go slay the rebels—why return   3865
    The victor bands?' he said, 'millions yet live,
Of whom the weakest with one word might turn
    The scales of victory yet;—let none survive

But those within the walls—each fifth shall give
The expiation for his brethren here.—   3870
    Go forth, and waste and kill!'—'O king, forgive
My speech,' a soldier answered—'but we fear
The spirits of the night, and morn is drawing near;

X

'For we were slaying still without remorse,
    And now that dreadful chief beneath my hand   3875
Defenceless lay, when, on a hell-black horse,
    An Angel bright as day, waving a brand
    Which flashed among the stars, passed.'—'Dost thou stand
Parleying with me, thou wretch?' the king replied;
    'Slaves, bind him to the wheel; and of this band,   3880
Whoso will drag that woman to his side
That scared him thus, may burn his dearest foe beside;

XI

'And gold and glory shall be his.—Go forth!'
    They rushed into the plain.—Loud was the roar
Of their career: the horsemen shook the earth;   3885
    The wheeled artillery's speed the pavement tore;
    The infantry, file after file, did pour
Their clouds on the utmost hills. Five days they slew
    Among the wasted fields; the sixth saw gore
Stream through the city; on the seventh, the dew   3890
Of slaughter became stiff, and there was peace anew:

XII

Peace in the desert fields and villages,
    Between the glutted beasts and mangled dead!
Peace in the silent streets! save when the cries
    Of victims to their fiery judgement led,   3895
    Made pale their voiceless lips who seemed to dread
Even in their dearest kindred, lest some tongue
    Be faithless to the fear yet unbetrayed;
Peace in the Tyrant's palace, where the throng
Waste the triumphal hours in festival and song!   3900

XIII

Day after day the burning sun rolled on
    Over the death-polluted land—it came
Out of the east like fire, and fiercely shone
    A lamp of Autumn, ripening with its flame

The few lone ears of corn;—the sky became   3905
Stagnate with heat, so that each cloud and blast
    Languished and died,—the thirsting air did claim
All moisture, and a rotting vapour passed
From the unburied dead, invisible and fast.

XIV

First Want, then Plague came on the beasts; their food
    Failed, and they drew the breath of its decay.   3911
Millions on millions, whom the scent of blood
    Had lured, or who, from regions far away,
    Had tracked the hosts in festival array,
From their dark deserts; gaunt and wasting now,   3915
    Stalked like fell shades among their perished prey;
In their green eyes a strange disease did glow.
They sank in hideous spasm, or pains severe and slow.

XV

The fish were poisoned in the streams; the birds
    In the green woods perished; the insect race   3920
Was withered up; the scattered flocks and herds
    Who had survived the wild beasts' hungry chase
    Died moaning, each upon the other's face
In helpless agony gazing; round the City
    All night, the lean hyænas their sad case   3925
Like starving infants wailed; a woeful ditty!
And many a mother wept, pierced with unnatural pity.

XVI

Amid the aëreal minarets on high,
    The Ethiopian vultures fluttering fell
From their long line of brethren in the sky,   3930
    Startling the concourse of mankind.—Too well
    These signs the coming mischief did foretell:—
Strange panic first, a deep and sickening dread
    Within each heart, like ice, did sink and dwell,
A voiceless thought of evil, which did spread   3935
With the quick glance of eyes, like withering lightnings shed.

XVII

Day after day, when the year wanes, the frosts
    Strip its green crown of leaves, till all is bare;
So on those strange and congregated hosts
    Came Famine, a swift shadow, and the air   3940

Groaned with the burden of a new despair;
Famine, than whom Misrule no deadlier daughter
Feeds from her thousand breasts, though sleeping there
With lidless eyes, lie Faith, and Plague, and Slaughter,
A ghastly brood; conceived of Lethe's sullen water. 3945

XVIII

There was no food, the corn was trampled down,
The flocks and herds had perished; on the shore
The dead and putrid fish were ever thrown;
The deeps were foodless, and the winds no more
Creaked with the weight of birds, but, as before 3950
Those wingèd things sprang forth, were void of shade;
The vines and orchards, Autumn's golden store,
Were burned;—so that the meanest food was weighed
With gold, and Avarice died before the god it made.

XIX

There was no corn—in the wide market-place 3955
All loathliest things, even human flesh, was sold;
They weighed it in small scales—and many a face
Was fixed in eager horror then: his gold
The miser brought; the tender maid, grown bold
Through hunger, bared her scornèd charms in vain; 3960
The mother brought her eldest-born, controlled
By instinct blind as love, but turned again
And bade her infant suck, and died in silent pain.

XX

Then fell blue Plague upon the race of man.
'O, for the sheathèd steel, so late which gave 3965
Oblivion to the dead, when the streets ran
With brothers' blood! O, that the earthquake's grave
Would gape, or Ocean lift its stifling wave!'
Vain cries—throughout the streets, thousands pursued
Each by his fiery torture howl and rave, 3970
Or sit, in frenzy's unimagined mood,
Upon fresh heaps of dead; a ghastly multitude.

XXI

It was not hunger now, but thirst. Each well
Was choked with rotting corpses, and became
A cauldron of green mist made visible 3975
At sunrise. Thither still the myriads came,

Seeking to quench the agony of the flame,
Which raged like poison through their bursting veins;
Naked they were from torture, without shame,
Spotted with nameless scars and lurid blains,   3980
Childhood, and youth, and age, writhing in savage pains.

XXII

It was not thirst but madness! Many saw
   Their own lean image everywhere, it went
A ghastlier self beside them, till the awe
   Of that dread sight to self-destruction sent   3985
   Those shrieking victims; some, ere life was spent,
Sought, with a horrid sympathy, to shed
   Contagion on the sound; and others rent
Their matted hair, and cried aloud, 'We tread
On fire! the avenging Power his hell on earth has spread!'

XXIII

Sometimes the living by the dead were hid.   3991
   Near the great fountain in the public square,
Where corpses made a crumbling pyramid
   Under the sun, was heard one stifled prayer
   For life, in the hot silence of the air;   3995
And strange 'twas, amid that hideous heap to see
   Some shrouded in their long and golden hair,
As if not dead, but slumbering quietly
Like forms which sculptors carve, then love to agony.

XXIV

Famine had spared the palace of the king:—   4000
   He rioted in festival the while,
He and his guards and priests; but Plague did fling
   One shadow upon all. Famine can smile
   On him who brings it food, and pass, with guile
Of thankful falsehood, like a courtier gray,   4005
   The house-dog of the throne; but many a mile
Comes Plague, a wingèd wolf, who loathes alway
The garbage and the scum that strangers make her prey.

XXV

So, near the throne, amid the gorgeous feast,
   Sheathed in resplendent arms, or loosely dight   4010
To luxury, ere the mockery yet had ceased
   That lingered on his lips, the warrior's might

Was loosened, and a new and ghastlier night
In dreams of frenzy lapped his eyes; he fell
    Headlong, or with stiff eyeballs sate upright   4015
Among the guests, or raving mad, did tell
Strange truths; a dying seer of dark oppression's hell.

XXVI

The Princes and the Priests were pale with terror;
    That monstrous faith wherewith they ruled mankind,
Fell, like a shaft loosed by the bowman's error,   4020
    On their own hearts: they sought and they could find
    No refuge—'twas the blind who led the blind!
So, through the desolate streets to the high fane,
    The many-tongued and endless armies wind
In sad procession: each among the train   4025
To his own Idol lifts his supplications vain.

XXVII

'O God!' they cried, 'we know our secret pride
    Has scorned thee, and thy worship, and thy name;
Secure in human power we have defied
    Thy fearful might; we bend in fear and shame   4030
    Before thy presence; with the dust we claim
Kindred; be merciful, O King of Heaven!
    Most justly have we suffered for thy fame
Made dim, but be at length our sins forgiven,
Ere to despair and death thy worshippers be driven.   4035

XXVIII

'O King of Glory! thou alone hast power!
    Who can resist thy will? who can restrain
Thy wrath, when on the guilty thou dost shower
    The shafts of thy revenge, a blistering rain?
    Greatest and best, be merciful again!   4040
Have we not stabbed thine enemies, and made
    The Earth an altar, and the Heavens a fane,
Where thou wert worshipped with their blood, and laid
Those hearts in dust which would thy searchless works have
    weighed?

XXIX

'Well didst thou loosen on this impious City   4045
    Thine angels of revenge: recall them now;
Thy worshippers, abased, here kneel for pity,
    And bind their souls by an immortal vow:

We swear by thee! and to our oath do thou
   Give sanction, from thine hell of fiends and flame,   4050
     That we will kill with fire and torments slow,
     The last of those who mocked thy holy name,
And scorned the sacred laws thy prophets did proclaim.'

XXX

Thus they with trembling limbs and pallid lips
   Worshipped their own hearts' image, dim and vast,
Scared by the shade wherewith they would eclipse   4056
     The light of other minds;—troubled they passed
     From the great Temple;—fiercely still and fast
The arrows of the plague among them fell,
   And they on one another gazed aghast,   4060
And through the hosts contention wild befell,
As each of his own god the wondrous works did tell.

XXXI

And Oromaze, Joshua, and Mahomet,
   Moses and Buddh, Zerdusht, and Brahm, and Foh,
A tumult of strange names, which never met   4065
     Before, as watchwords of a single woe,
     Arose; each raging votary 'gan to throw
Aloft his armèd hands, and each did howl
   'Our God alone is God!'—and slaughter now
Would have gone forth, when from beneath a cowl   4070
A voice came forth, which pierced like ice through every soul.

XXXII

'Twas an Iberian Priest from whom it came,
   A zealous man, who led the legioned West,
With words which faith and pride had steeped in flame,
     To quell the unbelievers; a dire guest   4075
     Even to his friends was he, for in his breast
Did hate and guile lie watchful, intertwined,
   Twin serpents in one deep and winding nest;
He loathed all faith beside his own, and pined
To wreak his fear of Heaven in vengeance on mankind.

XXXIII

But more he loathed and hated the clear light   4081
   Of wisdom and free thought, and more did fear,
Lest, kindled once, its beams might pierce the night,
     Even where his Idol stood; for, far and near

Did many a heart in Europe leap to hear   4085
  That faith and tyranny were trampled down;
    Many a pale victim, doomed for truth to share
  The murderer's cell, or see, with helpless groan,
The priests his children drag for slaves to serve their own.

XXXIV

He dared not kill the infidels with fire   4090
  Or steel, in Europe; the slow agonies
Of legal torture mocked his keen desire:
  So he made truce with those who did despise
    The expiation, and the sacrifice,
That, though detested, Islam's kindred creed   4095
  Might crush for him those deadlier enemies;
For fear of God did in his bosom breed
A jealous hate of man, an unreposing need.

XXXV

'Peace! Peace!' he cried, 'when we are dead, the Day
  Of Judgement comes, and all shall surely know   4100
Whose God is God, each fearfully shall pay
  The errors of his faith in endless woe!
    But there is sent a mortal vengeance now
On earth, because an impious race had spurned
  Him whom we all adore,—a subtle foe,   4105
By whom for ye this dread reward was earned,
And kingly thrones, which rest on faith, nigh overturned.

XXXVI

'Think ye, because ye weep, and kneel, and pray,
  That God will lull the pestilence? It rose
Even from beneath his throne, where, many a day,   4110
  His mercy soothed it to a dark repose:
    It walks upon the earth to judge his foes;
And what are thou and I, that he should deign
  To curb his ghastly minister, or close
The gates of death, ere they receive the twain   4115
Who shook with mortal spells his undefended reign?

XXXVII

'Ay, there is famine in the gulf of hell,
  Its giant worms of fire for ever yawn.—
Their lurid eyes are on us! those who fell
  By the swift shafts of pestilence ere dawn,   4120

Are in their jaws! they hunger for the spawn
Of Satan, their own brethren, who were sent
To make our souls their spoil. See! see! they fawn
Like dogs, and they will sleep with luxury spent,
When those detested hearts their iron fangs have rent!　4125

XXXVIII

'Our God may then lull Pestilence to sleep:—
Pile high the pyre of expiation now,
A forest's spoil of boughs, and on the heap
Pour venomous gums, which sullenly and slow,
When touched by flame, shall burn, and melt, and flow,
A stream of clinging fire,—and fix on high　4131
A net of iron, and spread forth below
A couch of snakes, and scorpions, and the fry
Of centipedes and worms, earth's hellish progeny!

XXXIX

'Let Laon and Laone on that pyre,　4135
Linked tight with burning brass, perish!—then pray
That, with this sacrifice, the withering ire
Of Heaven may be appeased.' He ceased, and they
A space stood silent, as far, far away
The echoes of his voice among them died;　4140
And he knelt down upon the dust, alway
Muttering the curses of his speechless pride,
Whilst shame, and fear, and awe, the armies did divide.

XL

His voice was like a blast that burst the portal
Of fabled hell; and as he spake, each one　4145
Saw gape beneath the chasms of fire immortal,
And Heaven above seemed cloven, where, on a throne
Girt round with storms and shadows, sate alone
Their King and Judge—fear killed in every breast
All natural pity then, a fear unknown　4150
Before, and with an inward fire possessed,
They raged like homeless beasts whom burning woods invest.

XLI

'Twas morn.—At noon the public crier went forth,
Proclaiming through the living and the dead,
'The Monarch saith, that his great Empire's worth　4155
Is set on Laon and Laone's head:

He who but one yet living here can lead,
  Or who the life from both their hearts can wring,
    Shall be the kingdom's heir, a glorious meed!
But he who both alive can hither bring,   4160
The Princess shall espouse, and reign an equal King.'

XLII

Ere night the pyre was piled, the net of iron
  Was spread above, the fearful couch below;
It overtopped the towers that did environ
    That spacious square; for Fear is never slow   4165
    To build the thrones of Hate, her mate and foe,
So, she scourged forth the maniac multitude
    To rear this pyramid—tottering and slow,
Plague-stricken, foodless, like lean herds pursued
By gadflies, they have piled the heath, and gums, and wood.

XLIII

Night came, a starless and a moonless gloom.   4171
  Until the dawn, those hosts of many a nation
Stood round that pile, as near one lover's tomb
    Two gentle sisters mourn their desolation;
    And in the silence of that expectation,   4175
Was heard on high the reptiles' hiss and crawl—
    It was so deep—save when the devastation
Of the swift pest, with fearful interval,
Marking its path with shrieks, among the crowd would fall.

XLIV

Morn came,—among those sleepless multitudes,   4180
  Madness, and Fear, and Plague, and Famine still
Heaped corpse on corpse, as in autumnal woods
    The frosts of many a wind with dead leaves fill
    Earth's cold and sullen brooks; in silence, still
The pale survivors stood; ere noon, the fear   4185
    Of Hell became a panic, which did kill
Like hunger or disease, with whispers drear,
As 'Hush! hark! Come they yet? Just Heaven! thine hour is
    near!'

XLV

And Priests rushed through their ranks, some counterfeiting
  The rage they did inspire, some mad indeed   4190
With their own lies; they said their god was waiting
  To see his enemies writhe, and burn, and bleed,—

And that, till then, the snakes of Hell had need
  Of human souls:—three hundred furnaces
    Soon blazed through the wide City, where, with speed,
  Men brought their infidel kindred to appease   4196
God's wrath, and while they burned, knelt round on quivering
      knees.

XLVI

The noontide sun was darkened with that smoke,
  The winds of eve dispersed those ashes gray.
The madness which these rites had lulled, awoke   4200
    Again at sunset.—Who shall dare to say
  The deeds which night and fear brought forth, or weigh
In balance just the good and evil there?
    He might man's deep and searchless heart display,
And cast a light on those dim labyrinths, where   4205
Hope, near imagined chasms, is struggling with despair.

XLVII

'Tis said, a mother dragged three children then,
  To those fierce flames which roast the eyes in the head,
And laughed, and died; and that unholy men,
    Feasting like fiends upon the infidel dead,   4210
    Looked from their meal, and saw an Angel tread
The visible floor of Heaven, and it was she!
    And, on that night, one without doubt or dread
  Came to the fire, and said, 'Stop, I am he!
Kill me!'—They burned them both with hellish mockery.

XLVIII

And, one by one, that night, young maidens came,   4216
  Beauteous and calm, like shapes of living stone
Clothed in the light of dreams, and by the flame
    Which shrank as overgorged, they laid them down,
  And sung a low sweet song, of which alone   4220
One word was heard, and that was Liberty;
    And that some kissed their marble feet, with moan
Like love, and died; and then that they did die
With happy smiles, which sunk in white tranquillity.

CANTO XI

I

SHE saw me not—she heard me not— alone   4225
  Upon the mountain's dizzy brink she stood;
She spake not, breathed not, moved not—there was thrown
  Over her look, the shadow of a mood

Which only clothes the heart in solitude,
A thought of voiceless depth;—she stood alone,   4230
　　Above, the Heavens were spread;—below, the flood
Was murmuring in its caves;—the wind had blown
Her hair apart, through which her eyes and forehead shone.

II

A cloud was hanging o'er the western mountains;
　　Before its blue and moveless depth were flying   4235
Gray mists poured forth from the unresting fountains
　　Of darkness in the North:—the day was dying:—
　　Sudden, the sun shone forth, its beams were lying
Like boiling gold on Ocean, strange to see,
　　And on the shattered vapours, which defying   424?
The power of light in vain, tossed restlessly
In the red Heaven, like wrecks in a tempestuous sea.

III

It was a stream of living beams, whose bank
　　On either side by the cloud's cleft was made;
And where its chasms that flood of glory drank,   4245
　　Its waves gushed forth like fire, and as if swayed
　　By some mute tempest, rolled on *her*; the shade
Of her bright image floated on the river
　　Of liquid light, which then did end and fade—
Her radiant shape upon its verge did shiver;   4250
Aloft, her flowing hair like strings of flame did quiver.

IV

I stood beside her, but she saw me not—
　　She looked upon the sea, and skies, and earth;
Rapture, and love, and admiration wrought
　　A passion deeper far than tears, or mirth,   4255
　　Or speech, or gesture, or whate'er has birth
From common joy; which with the speechless feeling
　　That led her there united, and shot forth
From her far eyes a light of deep revealing,
All but her dearest self from my regard concealing.   4260

V

Her lips were parted, and the measured breath
　　Was now heard there;—her dark and intricate eyes
Orb within orb, deeper than sleep or death,
　　Absorbed the glories of the burning skies.

Which, mingling with her heart's deep ecstasies,   4265
Burst from her looks and gestures;—and a light
    Of liquid tenderness, like love, did rise
From her whole frame, an atmosphere which quite
Arrayed her in its beams, tremulous and soft and bright.

VI

She would have clasped me to her glowing frame;   4270
    Those warm and odorous lips might soon have shed
On mine the fragrance and the invisible flame
    Which now the cold winds stole;—she would have laid
    Upon my languid heart her dearest head;
I might have heard her voice, tender and sweet;   4275
    Her eyes mingling with mine, might soon have fed
My soul with their own joy.—One moment yet
I gazed—we parted then, never again to meet!

VII

Never but once to meet on Earth again!
    She heard me as I fled—her eager tone   4280
Sunk on my heart, and almost wove a chain
    Around my will to link it with her own,
    So that my stern resolve was almost gone.
'I cannot reach thee! whither dost thou fly?
    My steps are faint—Come back, thou dearest one—
Return, ah me! return!'—The wind passed by   4286
On which those accents died, faint, far, and lingeringly.

VIII

Woe! Woe! that moonless midnight!—Want and Pest
    Were horrible, but one more fell doth rear,
As in a hydra's swarming lair, its crest   4290
    Eminent among those victims—even the Fear
    Of Hell: each girt by the hot atmosphere
Of his blind agony, like a scorpion stung
    By his own rage upon his burning bier
Of circling coals of fire; but still there clung   4295
One hope, like a keen sword on starting threads uphung:

IX

Not death—death was no more refuge or rest;
    Not life—it was despair to be!—not sleep,
For fiends and chasms of fire had dispossessed
    All natural dreams: to wake was not to weep,   4300

But to gaze mad and pallid, at the leap
To which the Future, like a snaky scourge,
    Or like some tyrant's eye, which aye doth keep
    Its withering beam upon his slaves, did urge
Their steps; they heard the roar of Hell's sulphureous surge.

X

Each of that multitude, alone, and lost   4306
    To sense of outward things, one hope yet knew;
As on a foam-girt crag some seaman tossed
    Stares at the rising tide, or like the crew
    Whilst now the ship is splitting through and through;
Each, if the tramp of a far steed was heard,   4311
    Started from sick despair, or if there flew
One murmur on the wind, or if some word
Which none can gather yet, the distant crowd has stirred.

XI

Why became cheeks, wan with the kiss of death,   4315
    Paler from hope? they had sustained despair.
Why watched those myriads with suspended breath
    Sleepless a second night? they are not here,
    The victims, and hour by hour, a vision drear,
Warm corpses fall upon the clay-cold dead;   4320
    And even in death their lips are wreathed with fear.—
The crowd is mute and moveless—overhead
Silent Arcturus shines—'Ha! hear'st thou not the tread

XII

'Of rushing feet? laughter? the shout, the scream,
    Of triumph not to be contained? See! hark!   4325
They come, they come! give way!' Alas, ye deem
    Falsely—'tis but a crowd of maniacs stark
    Driven, like a troop of spectres, through the dark,
From the choked well, whence a bright death-fire sprung,
    A lurid earth-star, which dropped many a spark   4330
From its blue train, and spreading widely, clung
To their wild hair, like mist the topmost pines among.

XIII

And many, from the crowd collected there,
    Joined that strange dance in fearful sympathies;
There was the silence of a long despair,   4335
    When the last echo of those terrible cries

Came from a distant street, like agonies
  Stifled afar.—Before the Tyrant's throne
    All night his aged Senate sate, their eyes
      In stony expectation fixed; when one   4340
Sudden before them stood, a Stranger and alone.

XIV

Dark Priests and haughty Warriors gazed on him
  With baffled wonder, for a hermit's vest
Concealed his face; but, when he spake, his tone,
    Ere yet the matter did their thoughts arrest,—   4345
      Earnest, benignant, calm, as from a breast
Void of all hate or terror—made them start;
    For as with gentle accents he addressed
His speech to them, on each unwilling heart
Unusual awe did fall—a spirit-quelling dart.   4350

XV

'Ye Princes of the Earth, ye sit aghast
  Amid the ruin which yourselves have made,
Yes, Desolation heard your trumpet's blast,
    And sprang from sleep!—dark Terror has obeyed
      Your bidding—O, that I whom ye have made   4355
Your foe, could set my dearest enemy free
    From pain and fear! but evil casts a shade,
Which cannot pass so soon, and Hate must be
The nurse and parent still of an ill progeny.

XVI

'Ye turn to Heaven for aid in your distress;   4360
  Alas, that ye, the mighty and the wise,
Who, if ye dared, might not aspire to less
    Than ye conceive of power, should fear the lies
      Which thou, and thou, didst frame for mysteries
To blind your slaves:—consider your own thought,   4365
    An empty and a cruel sacrifice
Ye now prepare, for a vain idol wrought
Out of the fears and hate which vain desires have brought.

XVII

'Ye seek for happiness—alas, the day!
  Ye find it not in luxury nor in gold,   4370
Nor in the fame, nor in the envied sway
    For which, O willing slaves to Custom old,

Severe taskmistress! ye your hearts have sold.
    Ye seek for peace, and when ye die, to dream
      No evil dreams: all mortal things are cold   4375
    And senseless then; if aught survive, I deem
It must be love and joy, for they immortal seem.

XVIII

'Fear not the future, weep not for the past.
    O, could I win your ears to dare be now
Glorious, and great, and calm! that ye would cast   4380
    Into the dust those symbols of your woe,
      Purple, and gold, and steel! that ye would go
Proclaiming to the nations whence ye came.
    That Want, and Plague, and Fear, from slavery flow;
    And that mankind is free, and that the shame   4385
Of royalty and faith is lost in freedom's fame!

XIX

'If thus, 'tis well—if not, I come to say
    That Laon—' while the Stranger spoke, among
The Council sudden tumult and affray
    Arose, for many of those warriors young,   4390
    Had on his eloquent accents fed and hung
Like bees on mountain-flowers; they knew the truth,
    And from their thrones in vindication sprung;
The men of faith and law then without ruth
Drew forth their secret steel, and stabbed each ardent youth.

XX

They stabbed them in the back and sneered—a slave   4396
    Who stood behind the throne, those corpses drew
Each to its bloody, dark, and secret grave;
    And one more daring raised his steel anew
      To pierce the Stranger. 'What hast thou to do   4400
With me, poor wretch?'—Calm, solemn, and severe,
    That voice unstrung his sinews, and he threw
His dagger on the ground, and pale with fear,
Sate silently—his voice then did the Stranger rear.

XXI

'It doth avail not that I weep for ye—   4405
    Ye cannot change, since ye are old and gray,
And ye have chosen your lot—your fame must be
    A book of blood, whence in a milder day

Men shall learn truth, when ye are wrapped in clay:
   Now ye shall triumph. I am Laon's friend,   4410
     And him to your revenge will I betray,
So ye concede one easy boon. Attend!
For now I speak of things which ye can apprehend.

XXII

'There is a People mighty in its youth,
   A land beyond the Oceans of the West,   4415
Where, though with rudest rites, Freedom and Truth
   Are worshipped; from a glorious Mother's breast,
     Who, since high Athens fell, among the rest
Sate like the Queen of Nations, but in woe,
   By inbred monsters outraged and oppressed,   4420
Turns to her chainless child for succour now,
It draws the milk of Power in Wisdom's fullest flow.

XXIII

'That land is like an Eagle, whose young gaze
   Feeds on the noontide beam, whose golden plume
Floats moveless on the storm, and in the blaze   4425
   Of sunrise gleams when Earth is wrapped in gloom;
     An epitaph of glory for the tomb
Of murdered Europe may thy fame be made,
   Great People! as the sands shalt thou become;   4429
Thy growth is swift as morn, when night must fade;
The multitudinous Earth shall sleep beneath thy shade.

XXIV

'Yes, in the desert there is built a home
   For Freedom. Genius is made strong to rear
The monuments of man beneath the dome
   Of a new Heaven; myriads assemble there,   4435
     Whom the proud lords of man, in rage or fear,
Drive from their wasted homes: the boon I pray
   Is this—that Cythna shall be convoyed there—
Nay, start not at the name—America!
And then to you this night Laon will I betray.   4440

XXV

'With me do what you will. I am your foe!'
   The light of such a joy as makes the stare
Of hungry snakes like living emeralds glow,
   Shone in a hundred human eyes—'Where, where

Is Laon? Haste! fly! drag him swiftly here! 4445
We grant thy boon.'—'I put no trust in ye,
  Swear by the Power ye dread.'—'We swear, we swear!'
The Stranger threw his vest back suddenly,
And smiled in gentle pride, and said, 'Lo! I am he!'

CANTO XII

I

THE transport of a fierce and monstrous gladness 4450
  Spread through the multitudinous streets, fast flying
Upon the winds of fear; from his dull madness
  The starveling waked, and died in joy; the dying,
  Among the corpses in stark agony lying,
Just heard the happy tidings, and in hope 4455
  Closed their faint eyes; from house to house replying
With loud acclaim, the living shook Heaven's cope,
And filled the startled Earth with echoes: morn did ope

II

Its pale eyes then; and lo! the long array
  Of guards in golden arms, and Priests beside, 4460
Singing their bloody hymns, whose garbs betray
  The blackness of the faith it seems to hide;
  And see, the Tyrant's gem-wrought chariot glide
Among the gloomy cowls and glittering spears—
  A Shape of light is sitting by his side, 4465
A child most beautiful. I' the midst appears
Laon,—exempt alone from mortal hopes and fears.

III

His head and feet are bare, his hands are bound
  Behind and with heavy chains, yet none do wreak
Their scoffs on him, though myriads throng around; 4470
  There are no sneers upon his lip which speak
  That scorn or hate has made him bold; his cheek
Resolve has not turned pale,—his eyes are mild
  And calm, and, like the morn about to break,
Smile on mankind—his heart seems reconciled 4475
To all things and itself, like a reposing child.

IV

Tumult was in the soul of all beside,
  Ill joy, or doubt, or fear; but those who saw
Their tranquil victim pass, felt wonder glide
  Into their brain, and became calm with awe.— 4480

See, the slow pageant near the pile doth draw.
  A thousand torches in the spacious square,
    Borne by the ready slaves of ruthless law,
    Await the signal round: the morning fair
Is changed to a dim night by that unnatural glare.   4485

V

And see! beneath a sun-bright canopy,
  Upon a platform level with the pile,
    The anxious Tyrant sit, enthroned on high,
      Girt by the chieftains of the host; all smile
      In expectation, but one child: the while   4490
I, Laon, led by mutes, ascend my bier
  Of fire, and look around: each distant isle
Is dark in the bright dawn; towers far and near,
Pierce like reposing flames the tremulous atmosphere.

VI

There was such silence through the host, as when   4495
  An earthquake trampling on some populous town,
Has crushed ten thousand with one tread, and men
    Expect the second; all were mute but one,
    That fairest child, who, bold with love, alone
Stood up before the King, without avail,   4500
  Pleading for Laon's life—her stifled groan
Was heard—she trembled like one aspen pale
Among the gloomy pines of a Norwegian vale.

VII

What were his thoughts linked in the morning sun,
  Among those reptiles, stingless with delay,   4505
Even like a tyrant's wrath?—The signal-gun
    Roared—hark, again! In that dread pause he lay
    As in a quiet dream—the slaves obey—
A thousand torches drop,—and hark, the last
  Bursts on that awful silence; far away,   4510
Millions, with hearts that beat both loud and fast,
Watch for the springing flame expectant and aghast.

VIII

They fly—the torches fall—a cry of fear
  Has startled the triumphant!—they recede!
For ere the cannon's roar has died, they hear   4515
    The tramp of hoofs like earthquake, and a steed

Dark and gigantic, with the tempest's speed,
   Bursts through their ranks: a woman sits thereon,
     Fairer, it seems, than aught that earth can breed,
Calm, radiant, like the phantom of the dawn,   4520
A spirit from the caves of daylight wandering gone.

IX

All thought it was God's Angel come to sweep
   The lingering guilty to their fiery grave;
The Tyrant from his throne in dread did leap,—
     Her innocence his child from fear did save;   4525
     Scared by the faith they feigned, each priestly slave
Knelt for his mercy whom they served with blood,
   And, like the refluence of a mighty wave
Sucked into the loud sea, the multitude
With crushing panic, fled in terror's altered mood.   4530

X

They pause, they blush, they gaze,—a gathering shout
   Bursts like one sound from the ten thousand streams
Of a tempestuous sea:—that sudden rout
     One checked, who, never in his mildest dreams
     Felt awe from grace or loveliness, the seams   4535
Of his rent heart so hard and cold a creed
   Had seared with blistering ice—but he misdeems
That he is wise, whose wounds do only bleed
Inly for self—thus thought the Iberian Priest indeed,

XI

And others too, thought he was wise to see,   4540
   In pain, and fear, and hate, something divine;
In love and beauty, no divinity.—
     Now with a bitter smile, whose light did shine
     Like a fiend's hope upon his lips and eyne,
He said, and the persuasion of that sneer   4545
   Rallied his trembling comrades—'Is it mine
To stand alone, when kings and soldiers fear
A woman? Heaven has sent its other victim here.'

XII

'Were it not impious,' said the King, 'to break
   Our holy oath?'—'Impious to keep it, say!'   4550
Shrieked the exulting Priest—'Slaves, to the stake
   Bind her, and on my head the burden lay

Of her just torments:—at the Judgement Day
Will I stand up before the golden throne
  Of Heaven, and cry, "To thee did I betray   4555
An Infidel; but for me she would have known
Another moment's joy! the glory be thine own!"'

XIII

They trembled, but replied not, nor obeyed,
  Pausing in breathless silence. Cythna sprung
From her gigantic steed, who, like a shade   4560
  Chased by the winds, those vacant streets among
  Fled tameless, as the brazen rein she flung
Upon his neck, and kissed his moonèd brow.
  A piteous sight, that one so fair and young,
The clasp of such a fearful death should woo   4565
With smiles of tender joy as beamed from Cythna now.

XIV

The warm tears burst in spite of faith and fear
  From many a tremulous eye, but like soft dews
Which feed Spring's earliest buds, hung gathered there,
  Frozen by doubt,—alas! they could not choose   4570
  But weep; for when her faint limbs did refuse
To climb the pyre, upon the mutes she smiled;
  And with her eloquent gestures, and the hues
Of her quick lips, even as a weary child
Wins sleep from some fond nurse with its caresses mild,

XV

She won them, though unwilling, her to bind   4576
  Near me, among the snakes. When there had fled
One soft reproach that was most thrilling kind,
  She smiled on me, and nothing then we said,
  But each upon the other's countenance fed   4580
Looks of insatiate love; the mighty veil
  Which doth divide the living and the dead
Was almost rent, the world grew dim and pale,—
All light in Heaven or Earth beside our love did fail.—

XVI

Yet—yet—one brief relapse, like the last beam   4585
  Of dying flames, the stainless air around
Hung silent and serene—a blood-red gleam
  Burst upwards, hurling fiercely from the ground

The globèd smoke,—I heard the mighty sound
Of its uprise, like a tempestuous ocean;   4590
And through its chasms I saw, as in a swound,
The tyrant's child fall without life or motion
Before his throne, subdued by some unseen emotion.

XVII

And is this death?—The pyre has disappeared,
The Pestilence, the Tyrant, and the throng;   4595
The flames grow silent—slowly there is heard
The music of a breath-suspending song,
Which, like the kiss of love when life is young,
Steeps the faint eyes in darkness sweet and deep:
With ever-changing notes it floats along,   4600
Till on my passive soul there seemed to creep
A melody, like waves on wrinkled sands that leap.

XVIII

The warm touch of a soft and tremulous hand
Wakened me then; lo! Cythna sate reclined
Beside me, on the waved and golden sand   4605
Of a clear pool, upon a bank o'ertwined
With strange and star-bright flowers, which to the wind
Breathed divine odour; high above, was spread
The emerald heaven of trees of unknown kind,
Whose moonlike blooms and bright fruit overhead   4610
A shadow, which was light, upon the waters shed.

XIX

And round about sloped many a lawny mountain
With incense-bearing forests, and vast caves
Of marble radiance, to that mighty fountain;
And where the flood its own bright margin laves,   4615
Their echoes talk with its eternal waves,
Which, from the depths whose jaggèd caverns breed
Their unreposing strife, it lifts and heaves,—
Till through a chasm of hills they roll, and feed
A river deep, which flies with smooth but arrowy speed.

XX

As we sate gazing in a trance of wonder,   4621
A boat approached, borne by the musical air
Along the waves which sung and sparkled under
Its rapid keel—a wingèd shape sate there,

A child with silver-shining wings, so fair,   4625
  That as her bark did through the waters glide,
  The shadow of the lingering waves did wear
Light, as from starry beams; from side to side,
While veering to the wind her plumes the bark did guide.

XXI

The boat was one curved shell of hollow pearl,   4630
  Almost translucent with the light divine
Of her within; the prow and stern did curl
  Hornèd on high, like the young moon supine,
  When o'er dim twilight mountains dark with pine,
It floats upon the sunset's sea of beams,   4635
  Whose golden waves in many a purple line
Fade fast, till borne on sunlight's ebbing streams,
Dilating, on earth's verge the sunken meteor gleams.

XXII

Its keel has struck the sands beside our feet;—
  Then Cythna turned to me, and from her eyes   4640
Which swam with unshed tears, a look more sweet
  Than happy love, a wild and glad surprise,
  Glanced as she spake: 'Ay, this is Paradise
And not a dream, and we are all united!
  Lo, that is mine own child, who in the guise   4645
Of madness came, like day to one benighted
In lonesome woods: my heart is now too well requited!'

XXIII

And then she wept aloud, and in her arms
  Clasped that bright Shape, less marvellously fair
Than her own human hues and living charms;   4650
  Which, as she leaned in passion's silence there,
  Breathed warmth on the cold bosom of the air,
Which seemed to blush and tremble with delight;
  The glossy darkness of her streaming hair
Fell o'er that snowy child, and wrapped from sight   4655
The fond and long embrace which did their hearts unite.

XXIV

Then the bright child, the plumèd Seraph came,
  And fixed its blue and beaming eyes on mine,
And said, 'I was disturbed by tremulous shame
  When once we met, yet knew that I was thine   4660

From the same hour in which thy lips divine
Kindled a clinging dream within my brain,
 Which ever waked when I might sleep, to twine
Thine image with *her* memory dear—again
We meet; exempted now from mortal fear or pain.   4665

XXV

'When the consuming flames had wrapped ye round,
 The hope which I had cherished went away;
I fell in agony on the senseless ground,
 And hid mine eyes in dust, and far astray
 My mind was gone, when bright, like dawning day,
The Spectre of the Plague before me flew,   4671
 And breathed upon my lips, and seemed to say,
"They wait for thee, belovèd!"—then I knew
The death-mark on my breast, and became calm anew.

XXVI

'It was the calm of love—for I was dying.   4675
 I saw the black and half-extinguished pyre
In its own gray and shrunken ashes lying;
 The pitchy smoke of the departed fire
 Still hung in many a hollow dome and spire
Above the towers, like night; beneath whose shade   4680
 Awed by the ending of their own desire
The armies stood; a vacancy was made
In expectation's depth, and so they stood dismayed.

XXVII

'The frightful silence of that altered mood,
 The tortures of the dying clove alone,   4685
Till one uprose among the multitude,
 And said—"The flood of time is rolling on,
 We stand upon its brink, whilst *they* are gone
To glide in peace down death's mysterious stream.   4689
 Have ye done well? They moulder flesh and bone,
Who might have made this life's envenomed dream
A sweeter draught than ye will ever taste, I deem.

XXVIII

' "These perish as the good and great of yore
 Have perished, and their murderers will repent,—
Yes, vain and barren tears shall flow before   4695
 Yon smoke has faded from the firmament

Even for this cause, that ye who must lament
  The death of those that made this world so fair,
    Cannot recall them now; but there is lent
To man the wisdom of a high despair,   4700
When such can die, and he live on and linger here.

XXIX

' "Ay, ye may fear not now the Pestilence,
  From fabled hell as by a charm withdrawn;
All power and faith must pass, since calmly hence
  In pain and fire have unbelievers gone;   4705
    And ye must sadly turn away, and moan
In secret, to his home each one returning,
    And to long ages shall this hour be known;
And slowly shall its memory, ever burning,
Fill this dark night of things with an eternal morning.

XXX

' "For me the world is grown too void and cold,   4711
  Since Hope pursues immortal Destiny
With steps thus slow—therefore shall ye behold
  How those who love, yet fear not, dare to die;
    Tell to your children this!" Then suddenly   4715
He sheathed a dagger in his heart and fell;
  My brain grew dark in death, and yet to me
There came a murmur from the crowd, to tell
Of deep and mighty change which suddenly befell.

XXXI

'Then suddenly I stood, a wingèd Thought,   4720
  Before the immortal Senate, and the seat
Of that star-shining spirit, whence is wrought
  The strength of its dominion, good and great,
  The better Genius of this world's estate.
His realm around one mighty Fane is spread,   4725
  Elysian islands bright and fortunate,
Calm dwellings of the free and happy dead,
Where I am sent to lead!' These wingèd words she said,

XXXII

And with the silence of her eloquent smile,
  Bade us embark in her divine canoe;
Then at the helm we took our seat, the while   4730
  Above her head those plumes of dazzling hue

Into the winds' invisible stream she threw,
Sitting beside the prow: like gossamer
    On the swift breath of morn, the vessel flew   4735
O'er the bright whirlpools of that fountain fair,
Whose shores receded fast, whilst we seemed lingering there;

XXXIII

Till down that mighty stream, dark, calm, and fleet,
    Between a chasm of cedarn mountains riven,
Chased by the thronging winds whose viewless feet   4740
    As swift as twinkling beams, had, under Heaven,
    From woods and waves wild sounds and odours driven,
The boat fled visibly—three nights and days,
    Borne like a cloud through morn, and noon, and even,
We sailed along the winding watery ways   4745
Of the vast stream, a long and labyrinthine maze.

XXXIV

A scene of joy and wonder to behold
    That river's shapes and shadows changing ever,
When the broad sunrise filled with deepening gold
    Its whirlpools, where all hues did spread and quiver;
    And where melodious falls did burst and shiver   4751
Among rocks clad with flowers, the foam and spray
    Sparkled like stars upon the sunny river,
Or when the moonlight poured a holier day,
One vast and glittering lake around green islands lay.   4755

XXXV

Morn, noon, and even, that boat of pearl outran
    The streams which bore it, like the arrowy cloud
Of tempest, or the speedier thought of man,
    Which flieth forth and cannot make abode;
    Sometimes through forests, deep like night, we glode,
Between the walls of mighty mountains crowned   4761
    With Cyclopean piles, whose turrets proud,
The homes of the departed, dimly frowned
O'er the bright waves which girt their dark foundations round.

XXXVI

Sometimes between the wide and flowering meadows,
    Mile after mile we sailed, and 'twas delight   4766
To see far off the sunbeams chase the shadows
    Over the grass; sometimes beneath the night

Of wide and vaulted caves, whose roofs were bright
With starry gems, we fled, whilst from their deep   4770
    And dark-green chasms, shades beautiful and white,
    Amid sweet sounds across our path would sweep,
Like swift and lovely dreams that walk the waves of sleep.

XXXVII

And ever as we sailed, our minds were full
    Of love and wisdom, which would overflow   4775
In converse wild, and sweet, and wonderful,
    And in quick smiles whose light would come and go
    Like music o'er wide waves, and in the flow
Of sudden tears, and in the mute caress—
    For a deep shade was cleft, and we did know,   4780
That virtue, though obscured on Earth, not less
Survives all mortal change in lasting loveliness.

XXXVIII

Three days and nights we sailed, as thought and feeling
    Number delightful hours—for through the sky
The spherèd lamps of day and night, revealing   4785
    New changes and new glories, rolled on high,
    Sun, Moon, and moonlike lamps, the progeny
Of a diviner Heaven, serene and fair:
    On the fourth day, wild as a windwrought sea
The stream became, and fast and faster bare   4790
The spirit-wingèd boat, steadily speeding there.

XXXIX

Steady and swift, where the waves rolled like mountains
    Within the vast ravine, whose rifts did pour
Tumultuous floods from their ten thousand fountains,
    The thunder of whose earth-uplifting roar   4795
    Made the air sweep in whirlwinds from the shore,
Calm as a shade, the boat of that fair child
    Securely fled, that rapid stress before,
Amid the topmost spray, and sunbows wild,
Wreathed in the silver mist: in joy and pride we smiled.

XL

The torrent of that wide and raging river   4801
    Is passed, and our aëreal speed suspended.
We look behind; a golden mist did quiver
    Where its wild surges with the lake were blended,—

Our bark hung there, as on a line suspended   4805
Between two heavens,—that windless waveless lake
Which four great cataracts from four vales, attended
By mists, aye feed; from rocks and clouds they break,
And of that azure sea a silent refuge make.

XLI

Motionless resting on the lake awhile,   4810
  I saw its marge of snow-bright mountains rear
Their peaks aloft, I saw each radiant isle,
  And in the midst, afar, even like a sphere
  Hung in one hollow sky, did there appear
The Temple of the Spirit; on the sound   4815
  Which issued thence, drawn nearer and more near,
Like the swift moon this glorious earth around,
The charmèd boat approached, and there its haven found.

NOTE ON THE REVOLT OF ISLAM, BY MRS. SHELLEY

SHELLEY possessed two remarkable qualities of intellect—a brilliant
imagination, and a logical exactness of reason. His inclinations led him
(he fancied) almost alike to poetry and metaphysical discussions. I say
'he fancied,' because I believe the former to have been paramount, and
that it would have gained the mastery even had he struggled against it.
However, he said that he deliberated at one time whether he should dedicate himself to poetry or metaphysics; and, resolving on the former, he
educated himself for it, discarding in a great measure his philosophical
pursuits, and engaging himself in the study of the poets of Greece, Italy,
and England. To these may be added a constant perusal of portions of
the Old Testament—the Psalms, the Book of Job, the Prophet Isaiah,
and others, the sublime poetry of which filled him with delight.

As a poet, his intellect and compositions were powerfully influenced by
exterior circumstances, and especially by his place of abode. He was very
fond of travelling, and ill-health increased this restlessness. The sufferings occasioned by a cold English winter made him pine, especially when
our colder spring arrived, for a more genial climate. In 1816 he again
visited Switzerland, and rented a house on the banks of the Lake of
Geneva; and many a day, in cloud or sunshine, was passed alone in his
boat—sailing as the wind listed, or weltering on the calm waters. The
majestic aspect of Nature ministered such thoughts as he afterwards
enwove in verse. His lines on the Bridge of the Arve, and his *Hymn to
Intellectual Beauty*, were written at this time. Perhaps during this summer his genius was checked by association with another poet whose
nature was utterly dissimilar to his own, yet who, in the poem he wrote

at that time, gave tokens that he shared for a period the more abstract and etherealised inspiration of Shelley. The saddest events awaited his return to England; but such was his fear to wound the feelings of others that he never expressed the anguish he felt, and seldom gave vent to the indignation roused by the persecutions he underwent; while the course of deep unexpressed passion, and the sense of injury, engendered the desire to embody themselves in forms defecated of all the weakness and evil which cling to real life.

He chose therefore for his hero a youth nourished in dreams of liberty, some of whose actions are in direct opposition to the opinions of the world; but who is animated throughout by an ardent love of virtue, and a resolution to confer the boons of political and intellectual freedom on his fellow-creatures. He created for this youth a woman such as he delighted to imagine—full of enthusiasm for the same objects; and they both, with will unvanquished, and the deepest sense of the justice of their cause, met adversity and death. There exists in this poem a memorial of a friend of his youth. The character of the old man who liberates Laon from his tower-prison, and tends on him in sickness, is founded on that of Doctor Lind, who, when Shelley was at Eton, had often stood by to befriend and support him, and whose name he never mentioned without love and veneration.

During the year 1817 we were established at Marlow in Buckinghamshire. Shelley's choice of abode was fixed chiefly by this town being at no great distance from London, and its neighbourhood to the Thames. The poem was written in his boat, as it floated under the beech-groves of Bisham, or during wanderings in the neighbouring country, which is distinguished for peculiar beauty. The chalk hills break into cliffs that overhang the Thames, or form valleys clothed with beech; the wilder portion of the country is rendered beautiful by exuberant vegetation; and the cultivated part is peculiarly fertile. With all this wealth of Nature which, either in the form of gentlemen's parks or soil dedicated to agriculture, flourishes around, Marlow was inhabited (I hope it is altered now) by a very poor population. The women are lacemakers, and lose their health by sedentary labour, for which they were very ill paid. The Poor-laws ground to the dust not only the paupers, but those who had risen just above that state, and were obliged to pay poor-rates. The changes produced by peace following a long war, and a bad harvest, brought with them the most heart-rending evils to the poor. Shelley afforded what alleviation he could. In the winter, while bringing out his poem, he had a severe attack of ophthalmia, caught while visiting the poor cottages. I mention these things—for this minute and active sympathy with his fellow-creatures gives a thousandfold interest to his speculations, and stamps with reality his pleadings for the human race.

The poem, bold in its opinions and uncompromising in their expression, met with many censurers, not only among those who allow of no virtue but such as supports the cause they espouse, but even among those whose opinions were similar to his own. I extract a portion of a letter written in answer to one of these friends. It best details the impulses of Shelley's mind, and his motives: it was written with entire unreserve; and is therefore a precious monument of his own opinion of his powers, of the purity of his designs, and the ardour with which he clung, in adversity and through the valley of the shadow of death, to views from which he believed the permanent happiness of mankind must eventually spring.

'Marlow, Dec. 11, 1817.

'I have read and considered all that you say about my general powers, and the particular instance of the poem in which I have attempted to develop them. Nothing can be more satisfactory to me than the interest which your admonitions express. But I think you are mistaken in some points with regard to the peculiar nature of my powers, whatever be their amount. I listened with deference and self-suspicion to your censures of *The Revolt of Islam;* but the productions of mine which you commend hold a very low place in my own esteem; and this reassures me, in some degree at least. The poem was produced by a series of thoughts which filled my mind with unbounded and sustained enthusiasm. I felt the precariousness of my life, and I engaged in this task, resolved to leave some record of myself. Much of what the volume contains was written with the same feeling—as real, though not so prophetic—as the communications of a dying man. I never presumed indeed to consider it anything approaching to faultless; but, when I consider contemporary productions of the same apparent pretensions, I own I was filled with confidence. I felt that it was in many respects a genuine picture of my own mind. I felt that the sentiments were true, not assumed. And in this have I long believed that my power consists; in sympathy, and that part of the imagination which relates to sentiment and contemplation. I am formed, if for anything not in common with the herd of mankind, to apprehend minute and remote distinction of feeling, whether relative to external nature or the living beings which surround us, and to communicate the conceptions which result from considering either the moral or the material universe as a whole. Of course, I believe these faculties, which perhaps comprehend all that is sublime in man, to exist very imperfectly in my own mind. But, when you advert to my Chancery-paper, a cold, forced, unimpassioned, insignificant piece of cramped and cautious argument, and to the little scrap about *Mandeville,* which expressed my feelings indeed, but cost scarcely two minutes' thought to express, as specimens of my powers more favourable than that which grew as it were from "the agony and bloody sweat" of intellectual travail; surely I must feel that, in some manner, either I am mistaken in believing that I have any talent at all, or you in the selection of the specimens of it. Yet, after all, I cannot but be conscious, in much of what I write, of an absence of that tranquillity which is the attribute and accompaniment of power. This feeling alone would make your most kind and wise admonitions, on the subject of the economy of intellectual force, valuable to me. And, if I live, or if I see

any trust in coming years, doubt not but that I shall do something, whatever it may be, which a serious and earnest estimate of my powers will
suggest to me, and which will be in every respect accommodated to their
utmost limits.' [Shelley to Godwin.]

PRINCE ATHANASE [1]

A FRAGMENT

PART I

THERE was a youth, who, as with toil and travel,
Had grown quite weak and gray before his time;
Nor any could the restless griefs unravel

Which burned within him, withering up his prime
And goading him, like fiends, from land to land.   5
Not his the load of any secret crime,

For nought of ill his heart could understand,
But pity and wild sorrow for the same;—
Not his the thirst for glory or command,

Baffled with blast of hope-consuming shame;   10
Nor evil joys which fire the vulgar breast,
And quench in speedy smoke its feeble flame,

Had left within his soul their dark unrest:
Nor what religion fables of the grave
Feared he,—Philosophy's accepted guest.   15

For none than he a purer heart could have,
Or that loved good more for itself alone;
Of nought in heaven or earth was he the slave.

What sorrow, strange, and shadowy, and unknown,
Sent him, a hopeless wanderer, through mankind?—   20
If with a human sadness he did groan,

[1] The idea Shelley had formed of Prince Athanase was a good deal modelled
on *Alastor*. In the first sketch of the poem, he named it *Pandemos and Urania*.
Athanase seeks through the world the One whom he may love. He meets, in the
ship in which he is embarked, a lady who appears to him to embody his ideal of
love and beauty. But she proves to be Pandemos, or the earthly and unworthy
Venus; who, after disappointing his cherished dreams and hopes, deserts him.
Athanase, crushed by sorrow, pines and dies. 'On his deathbed, the lady who can
really reply to his soul comes and kisses his lips' (*The Deathbed of Athanase*).
The poet describes her [in the words of the final fragment, p. 185]. This slender
note is all we have to aid our imagination in shaping out the form of the poem,
such as its author imagined. [Mrs. Shelley's Note.]

He had a gentle yet aspiring mind;
Just, innocent, with varied learning fed;
And such a glorious consolation find

In others' joy, when all their own is dead: 25
He loved, and laboured for his kind in grief,
And yet, unlike all others, it is said

That from such toil he never found relief.
Although a child of fortune and of power,
Of an ancestral name the orphan chief,   30

His soul had wedded Wisdom, and her dower
Is love and justice, clothed in which he sate
Apart from men, as in a lonely tower,

Pitying the tumult of their dark estate.—
Yet even in youth did he not e'er abuse   35
The strength of wealth or thought, to consecrate

Those false opinions which the harsh rich use
To blind the world they famish for their pride;
Nor did he hold from any man his dues,

But, like a steward in honest dealings tried,   40
With those who toiled and wept, the poor and wise,
His riches and his cares he did divide.

Fearless he was, and scorning all disguise,
What he dared do or think, though men might start,
He spoke with mild yet unaverted eyes;   45

Liberal he was of soul, and frank of heart,
And to his many friends—all loved him well—
Whate'er he knew or felt he would impart,

If words he found those inmost thoughts to tell;
If not, he smiled or wept; and his weak foes   50
He neither spurned nor hated—though with fell

And mortal hate their thousand voices rose,
They passed like aimless arrows from his ear—
Nor did his heart or mind its portal close

To those, or them, or any, whom life's sphere   55
May comprehend within its wide array.
What sadness made that vernal spirit sere?—

He knew not. Though his life, day after day,
Was failing like an unreplenished stream,
Though in his eyes a cloud and burthen lay, 60

Through which his soul, like Vesper's serene beam
Piercing the chasms of ever rising clouds,
Shone, softly burning; though his lips did seem

Like reeds which quiver in impetuous floods;
And through his sleep, and o'er each waking hour, 65
Thoughts after thoughts, unresting multitudes,

Were driven within him by some secret power,
Which bade them blaze, and live, and roll afar,
Like lights and sounds, from haunted tower to tower

O'er castled mountains borne, when tempest's war 70
Is levied by the night-contending winds,
And the pale dalesmen watch with eager ear;—

Though such were in his spirit, as the fiends
Which wake and feed an everliving woe,—
What was this grief, which ne'er in other minds 75

A mirror found,—he knew not—none could know;
But on whoe'er might question him he turned
The light of his frank eyes, as if to show

He knew not of the grief within that burned,
But asked forbearance with a mournful look; 80
Or spoke in words from which none ever learned

The cause of his disquietude; or shook
With spasms of silent passion; or turned pale:
So that his friends soon rarely undertook

To stir his secret pain without avail;— 85
For all who knew and loved him then perceived
That there was drawn an adamantine veil

Between his heart and mind,—both unrelieved
Wrought in his brain and bosom separate strife.
Some said that he was mad, others believed 90

That memories of an antenatal life
Made this, where now he dwelt, a penal hell;
And others said that such mysterious grief

From God's displeasure, like a darkness, fell
On souls like his, which owned no higher law   95
Than love; love calm, steadfast, invincible

By mortal fear or supernatural awe;
And others,—' 'Tis the shadow of a dream
Which the veiled eye of Memory never saw,

'But through the soul's abyss, like some dark stream   100
Through shattered mines and caverns underground,
Rolls, shaking its foundations; and no beam

'Of joy may rise, but it is quenched and drowned
In the dim whirlpools of this dream obscure;
Soon its exhausted waters will have found   105

'A lair of rest beneath thy spirit pure,
O Athanase!—in one so good and great,
Evil or tumult cannot long endure.'

So spake they: idly of another's state
Babbling vain words and fond philosophy;   110
This was their consolation; such debate

Men held with one another; nor did he,
Like one who labours with a human woe,
Decline this talk: as if its theme might be

Another, not himself, he to and fro   115
Questioned and canvassed it with subtlest wit;
And none but those who loved him best could know

That which he knew not, how it galled and bit
His weary mind, this converse vain and cold;
For like an eyeless nightmare grief did sit   120

Upon his being; a snake which fold by fold
Pressed out the life of life, a clinging fiend
Which clenched him if he stirred with deadlier hold;—
And so his grief remained—let it remain—untold.[1]

[1] The Author was pursuing a fuller development of the ideal character of Athanase, when it struck him that in an attempt at extreme refinement and analysis, his
conceptions might be betrayed into assuming a morbid character. The reader
will judge whether he is a loser or gainer by the difference. [Shelley's Note.]

PART II

FRAGMENT I

PRINCE ATHANASE had one belovèd friend,   125
An old, old man, with hair of silver white,
And lips where heavenly smiles would hang and blend

With his wise words; and eyes whose arrowy light
Shone like the reflex of a thousand minds.
He was the last whom superstition's blight   130

Had spared in Greece—the blight that cramps and blinds,—
And in his olive bower at Œnoe
Had sate from earliest youth. Like one who finds

A fertile island in the barren sea,
One mariner who has survived his mates   135
Many a drear month in a great ship—so he

With soul-sustaining songs, and sweet debates
Of ancient lore, there fed his lonely being:—
'The mind becomes that which it contemplates.'—

And thus Zonoras, by forever seeing   140
Their bright creations, grew like wisest men;
And when he heard the crash of nations fleeing

A bloodier power than ruled thy ruins then,
O sacred Hellas! many weary years
He wandered, till the path of Laian's glen   145

Was grass-grown—and the unremembered tears
Were dry in Laian for their honoured chief,
Who fell in Byzant, pierced by Moslem spears:—

And as the lady looked with faithful grief
From her high lattice o'er the rugged path,   150
Where she once saw that horseman toil, with brief

And blighting hope, who with the news of death
Struck body and soul as with a mortal blight,
She saw between the chestnuts, far beneath,

An old man toiling up, a weary wight;   155
And soon within her hospitable hall
She saw his white hairs glittering in the light

Of the wood fire, and round his shoulders fall;
And his wan visage and his withered mien,
Yet calm and gentle and majestical.   160

And Athanase, her child, who must have been
Then three years old, sate opposite and gazed
In patient silence.

FRAGMENT II

Such was Zonoras; and as daylight finds
One amaranth glittering on the path of frost,   165
When autumn nights have nipped all weaker kinds,

Thus through his age, dark, cold, and tempest-tossed,
Shone truth upon Zonoras; and he filled
From fountains pure, nigh overgrown and lost,

The spirit of Prince Athanase, a child,   170
With soul-sustaining songs of ancient lore
And philosophic wisdom, clear and mild.

And sweet and subtle talk they evermore,
The pupil and the master, shared; until,
Sharing that undiminishable store,   175

The youth, as shadows on a grassy hill
Outrun the winds that chase them, soon outran
His teacher, and did teach with native skill

Strange truths and new to that experienced man;
Still they were friends, as few have ever been   180
Who mark the extremes of life's discordant span.

So in the caverns of the forest green,
Or on the rocks of echoing ocean hoar,
Zonoras and Prince Athanase were seen

By summer woodmen; and when winter's roar   185
Sounded o'er earth and sea its blast of war,
The Balearic fisher, driven from shore,

Hanging upon the peakèd wave afar,
Then saw their lamp from Laian's turret gleam,
Piercing the stormy darkness, like a star   190

Which pours beyond the sea one steadfast beam,
Whilst all the constellations of the sky
Seemed reeling through the storm ... They did but seem—

For, lo! the wintry clouds are all gone by,
And bright Arcturus through yon pines is glowing,   195
And far o'er southern waves, immovably

Belted Orion hangs—warm light is flowing
From the young moon into the sunset's chasm.—
'O, summer eve! with power divine, bestowing

'On thine own bird the sweet enthusiasm   200
Which overflows in notes of liquid gladness,
Filling the sky like light! How many a spasm

'Of fevered brains, oppressed with grief and madness,
Were lulled by thee, delightful nightingale,—
And these soft waves, murmuring a gentle sadness,—   205

'And the far sighings of yon piny dale
Made vocal by some wind we feel not here.—
I bear alone what nothing may avail

'To lighten—a strange load!'—No human ear
Heard this lament; but o'er the visage wan   210
Of Athanase, a ruffling atmosphere

Of dark emotion, a swift shadow, ran,
Like wind upon some forest-bosomed lake,
Glassy and dark.—And that divine old man

Beheld his mystic friend's whole being shake,   215
Even where its inmost depths were gloomiest—
And with a calm and measured voice he spake,

And, with a soft and equal pressure, pressed
That cold lean hand:—'Dost thou remember yet
When the curved moon then lingering in the west   220

'Paused, in yon waves her mighty horns to wet,
How in those beams we walked, half resting on the sea?
'Tis just one year—sure thou dost not forget—

'Then Plato's words of light in thee and me
Lingered like moonlight in the moonless east,   225
For we had just then read—thy memory

'IS faithful now—the story of the feast;
And Agathon and Diotima seemed
From death and dark forgetfulness released . . . . .'

FRAGMENT III

AND when the old man saw that on the green   230
Leaves of his opening   a blight had lighted
He said: 'My friend, one grief alone can wean

A gentle mind from all that once delighted:—
Thou lovest, and thy secret heart is laden
With feelings which should not be unrequited.'   235

And Athanase . . . then smiled, as one o'erladen
With iron chains might smile to talk (?) of bands
Twined round her lover's neck by some blithe maiden,
And said . . . . .

FRAGMENT IV

'TWAS at the season when the Earth upsprings   240
From slumber, as a spherèd angel's child,
Shadowing its eyes with green and golden wings,

Stands up before its mother bright and mild,
Of whose soft voice the air expectant seems—
So stood before the sun, which shone and smiled   245

To see it rise thus joyous from its dreams,
The fresh and radiant Earth. The hoary grove
Waxed green—and flowers burst forth like starry beams;—

The grass in the warm sun did start and move,
And sea-buds burst under the waves serene:—   250
How many a one, though none be near to love,

Loves then the shade of his own soul, half seen
In any mirror—or the spring's young minions,
The wingèd leaves amid the copses green;—

How many a spirit then puts on the pinions   255
Of fancy, and outstrips the lagging blast,
And his own steps—and over wide dominions

Sweeps in his dream-drawn chariot, far and fast,
More fleet than storms—the wide world shrinks below,
When winter and despondency are past.   260

FRAGMENT V

'Twas at this season that Prince Athanase
Passed the white Alps—those eagle-baffling mountains
Slept in their shrouds of snow;—beside the ways

The waterfalls were voiceless—for their fountains
Were changed to mines of sunless crystal now,   265
Or by the curdling winds—like brazen wings

Which clanged along the mountain's marble brow—
Warped into adamantine fretwork, hung
And filled with frozen light the chasms below.

Vexed by the blast, the great pines groaned and swung
Under their load of [snow]—   271

  .   .   .   .
    .   .   .   .

Such as the eagle sees, when ne dives down
From the gray deserts of wide air, [beheld]   275
[Prince] Athanase; and o'er his mien (?) was thrown

The shadow of that scene, field after field,
Purple and dim and wide . . . . .

FRAGMENT VI

Thou art the wine whose drunkenness is all
We can desire, O Love! and happy souls,   280
Ere from thy vine the leaves of autumn fall,

Catch thee, and feed from their o'erflowing bowls
Thousands who thirst for thine ambrosial dew;—
Thou art the radiance which where ocean rolls

Investeth it; and when the heavens are blue   285
Thou fillest them; and when the earth is fair
The shadow of thy moving wings imbue

Its deserts and its mountains, till they wear
Beauty like some light robe;—thou ever soarest
Among the towers of men, and as soft air   290

In spring, which moves the unawakened forest,
Clothing with leaves its branches bare and bleak,
Thou floatest among men; and aye implorest

That which from thee they should implore:—the weak
Alone kneel to thee, offering up the hearts   295
The strong have broken—yet where shall any seek

A garment whom thou clothest not? the darts
Of the keen winter storm, barbèd with frost,
Which, from the everlasting snow that parts

The Alps from Heaven, pierce some traveller lost   300
In the wide waved interminable snow
Ungarmented, ...

ANOTHER FRAGMENT (A)

YES, often when the eyes are cold and dry,
And the lips calm, the Spirit weeps within
Tears bitterer than the blood of agony   305

Trembling in drops on the discoloured skin
Of those who love their kind and therefore perish
In ghastly torture—a sweet medicine

Of peace and sleep are tears, and quietly
Them soothe from whose uplifted eyes they fall   310
But . . . . .

ANOTHER FRAGMENT (B)

HER hair was brown, her spherèd eyes were brown,
And in their dark and liquid moisture swam,
Like the dim orb of the eclipsèd moon;

Yet when the spirit flashed beneath, there came   315
The light from them, as when tears of delight
Double the western planet's serene flame.

ROSALIND AND HELEN

A MODERN ECLOGUE

ADVERTISEMENT

THE story of *Rosalind and Helen* is, undoubtedly, not an attempt in
the highest style of poetry. It is in no degree calculated to excite profound meditation; and if, by interesting the affections and amusing the
imagination, it awakens a certain ideal melancholy favourable to the
reception of more important impressions, it will produce in the reader all
that the writer experienced in the composition. I resigned myself, as I

wrote, to the impulse of the feelings which moulded the conception of the story; and this impulse determined the pauses of a measure, which only pretends to be regular inasmuch as it corresponds with, and expresses, the irregularity of the imaginations which inspired it.

I do not know which of the few scattered poems I left in England will be selected by my bookseller to add to this collection. One,[1] which I sent from Italy, was written after a day's excursion among those lovely mountains which surround what was once the retreat, and where is now the sepulchre, of Petrarch. If any one is inclined to condemn the insertion of the introductory lines, which image forth the sudden relief of a state of deep despondency by the radiant visions disclosed by the sudden burst of an Italian sunrise in autumn on the highest peak of those delightful mountains, I can only offer as my excuse, that they were not erased at the request of a dear friend, with whom added years of intercourse only add to my apprehension of its value, and who would have had more right than any one to complain, that she has not been able to extinguish in me the very power of delineating sadness.

NAPLES, *Dec.* 20, 1818.

ROSALIND, HELEN AND HER CHILD

Scene, the Shore of the Lake of Como

Helen. Come hither, my sweet
        Rosalind.
'Tis long since thou and I have
        met;
And yet methinks it were unkind
Those moments to forget.
Come sit by me. I see thee stand 5
By this lone lake, in this far land,
Thy loose hair in the light wind
        flying,
Thy sweet voice to each tone of
        even
United, and thine eyes replying
To the hues of yon fair heaven. 10
Come, gentle friend: wilt sit by me?
And be as thou wert wont to be
Ere we were disunited?
None doth behold us now: the
        power
That led us forth at this lone hour
Will be but ill requited   16
If thou depart in scorn: oh! come,
And talk of our abandoned home.

Remember, this is Italy,
And we are exiles. Talk with me 20
Of that our land, whose wilds and
        floods,
Barren and dark although they be,
Were dearer than these chestnut
        woods:
Those heathy paths, that inland
        stream,
And the blue mountains, shapes
        which seem   25
Like wrecks of childhood's sunny
        dream:
Which that we have abandoned
        now,
Weighs on the heart like that re-
        morse
Which altered friendship leaves. I
        seek   29
No more our youthful intercourse.
That cannot be! Rosalind, speak.
Speak to me. Leave me not.—When
        morn did come,

---

[1] 'Lines written among the Euganean Hills.'

When evening fell upon our com-
mon home,
When for one hour we parted,—
do not frown:
I would not chide thee, though thy
faith is broken:
But turn to me. Oh! by this cher-
ished token, 36
Of woven hair, which thou wilt not
disown,
Turn, as 'twere but the memory of
me,
And not my scornèd self who
prayed to thee.
   Rosalind. Is it a dream, or do I
see 40
And hear frail Helen? I would flee
Thy tainting touch; but former
years
Arise, and bring forbidden tears;
And my o'erburthened memory
Seeks yet its lost repose in thee. 45
I share thy crime. I cannot choose
But weep for thee: mine own
strange grief
But seldom stoops to such relief:
Nor ever did I love thee less,
Though mourning o'er thy wicked-
ness 50
Even with a sister's woe. I knew
What to the evil world is due,
And therefore sternly did refuse
To link me with the infamy
Of one so lost as Helen. Now 55
Bewildered by my dire despair,
Wondering I blush, and weep that
thou
Should'st love me still,—thou only!
—There,
Let us sit on that gray stone,
Till our mournful talk be done. 60
   Helen. Alas! not there; I cannot
bear
The murmur of this lake to hear.
A sound from there, Rosalind dear,
Which never yet I heard elsewhere
But in our native land, recurs, 65

Even here where now we meet. It
stirs
Too much of suffocating sorrow!
In the dell of yon dark chestnut
wood
Is a stone seat, a solitude
Less like our own. The ghost of
Peace 70
Will not desert this spot. To-
morrow,
If thy kind feelings should not
cease,
We may sit here.
   Rosalind. Thou lead, my sweet,
And I will follow.
   Henry.   'Tis Fenici's seat
Where you are going? This is not
the way, 75
Mamma; it leads behind those
trees that grow
Close to the little river.
   Helen.   Yes: I know:
I was bewildered. Kiss me, and be
gay,
Dear boy: why do you sob?
   Henry.   I do not know:
But it might break any one's heart
to see 80
You and the lady cry so bitterly.
   Helen. It is a gentle child, my
friend. Go home,
Henry, and play with Lilla till I
come.
We only cried with joy to see each
other;
We are quite merry now: Good-
night.
                The boy 85
Lifted a sudden look upon his
mother,
And in the gleam of forced and
hollow joy
Which lightened o'er her face,
laughed with the glee
Of light and unsuspecting infancy,
And whispered in her ear, 'Bring
home with you 90

That sweet strange lady-friend.'
 Then off he flew,
But stopped, and beckoned with
 a meaning smile,
Where the road turned. Pale Rosa-
 lind the while,
Hiding her face, stood weeping
 silently.

In silence then they took the way 95
Beneath the forest's solitude.
It was a vast and antique wood,
Thro' which they took their way;
And the gray shades of evening
O'er that green wilderness did
 fling   100
Still deeper solitude.
Pursuing still the path that wound
The vast and knotted trees around
Through which slow shades were
 wandering,
To a deep lawny dell they came,
To a stone seat beside a spring, 106
O'er which the columned wood did
 frame
A roofless temple, like the fane
Where, ere new creeds could faith
 obtain,
Man's early race once knelt be-
 neath   110
The overhanging deity.
O'er this fair fountain hung the sky,
Now spangled with rare stars. The
 snake,
The pale snake, that with eager
 breath
Creeps here his noontide thirst to
 slake,   115
Is beaming with many a mingled
 hue,
Shed from yon dome's eternal blue,
When he floats on that dark and
 lucid flood
In the light of his own loveliness;
And the birds that in the fountain
 dip   120

Their plumes, with fearless fellow-
 ship
Above and round him wheel and
 hover.
The fitful wind is heard to stir
One solitary leaf on high;
The chirping of the grasshopper 125
Fills every pause. There is emotion
In all that dwells at noontide here:
Then, through the intricate wild
 wood,
A maze of life and light and motion
Is woven. But there is stillness
 now: 130
Gloom, and the trance of Nature
 now:
The snake is in his cave asleep;
The birds are on the branches
 dreaming:
Only the shadows creep: 134
Only the glow-worm is gleaming:
Only the owls and the nightingales
Wake in this dell when daylight
 fails,
And gray shades gather in the
 woods:
And the owls have all fled far away
In a merrier glen to hoot and
 play,   140
For the moon is veiled and sleeping
 now.
The accustomed nightingale still
 broods
On her accustomed bough.
But she is mute; for her false mate
Has fled and left her desolate. 145

This silent spot tradition old
Had peopled with the spectral
 dead.
For the roots of the speaker's hair
 felt cold
And stiff, as with tremulous lips he
 told
That a hellish shape at midnight
 led   150

The ghost of a youth with hoary
 hair,
And sate on the seat beside him
 there,
Till a naked child came wandering
 by,
When the fiend would change to a
 lady fair!
A fearful tale! The truth was
 worse: 155
For here a sister and a brother
Had solemnized a monstrous curse,
Meeting in this fair solitude:
For beneath yon very sky,
Had they resigned to one another
Body and soul. The multitude: 161
Tracking them to the secret wood,
Tore limb from limb their innocent
 child,
And stabbed and trampled on its
 mother;
But the youth, for God's most holy
 grace,   165
A priest saved to burn in the
 market-place.

Duly at evening Helen came
To this lone silent spot,
From the wrecks of a tale of wilder
 sorrow
So much of sympathy to borrow   170
As soothed her own dark lot.
Duly each evening from her home,
With her fair child would Helen
 come
To sit upon that antique seat,   174
While the hues of day were pale;
And the bright boy beside her feet
Now lay, lifting at intervals
His broad blue eyes on her;
Now, where some sudden impulse
 calls
Following. He was a gentle boy   180
And in all gentle sports took
 joy;
Oft in a dry leaf for a boat,
With a small feather for a sail,

His fancy on that spring would
 float,   184
If some invisible breeze might stir
Its marble calm: and Helen smiled
Through tears of awe on the gay
 child,
To think that a boy as fair as he,
In years which never more may be,
By that same fount, in that same
 wood,   190
The like sweet fancies had pursued;
And that a mother, lost like her,
Had mournfully sate watching him.
Then all the scene was wont to swim
Through the mist of a burning
 tear.   195

For many months had Helen known
This scene; and now she thither
 turned
Her footsteps, not alone.
The friend whose falsehood she had
 mourned,
Sate with her on that seat of stone.
Silent they sate; for evening,   201
And the power its glimpses bring
Had, with one awful shadow,
 quelled
The passion of their grief. They
 sate
With linkèd hands, for unre-
 pelled   205
Had Helen taken Rosalind's.
Like the autumn wind, when it
 unbinds
The tangled locks of the night-
 shade's hair,
Which is twined in the sultry
 summer air
Round the walls of an outworn
 sepulchre,   210
Did the voice of Helen, sad and
 sweet,
And the sound of her heart that
 ever beat,
As with sighs and words she
 breathed on her,

Unbind the knots of her friend's
despair,
Till her thoughts were free to float
and flow;   215
And from her labouring bosom
now,
Like the bursting of a prisoned
flame,
The voice of a long pent sorrow
came.
      Rosalind. I saw the dark earth
fall upon
The coffin; and I saw the stone 220
Laid over him whom this cold
breast
Had pillowed to his nightly rest!
Thou knowest not, thou canst not
know
My agony. Oh! I could not weep:
The sources whence such blessings
flow   225
Were not to be approached by me!
But I could smile, and I could
sleep,
Though with a self-accusing heart.
In morning's light, in evening's
gloom,
I watched,—and would not thence
depart—   230
My husband's unlamented tomb.
My children knew their sire was
gone,
But when I told them,—'he is
dead,'—
They laughed aloud in frantic glee,
They clapped their hands and
leaped about,   235
Answering each other's ecstasy
With many a prank and merry
shout.
But I sate silent and alone,
Wrapped in the mock of mourning
weed.

They laughed, for he was dead:
but I   240
Sate with a hard and tearless eye,

And with a heart which would
deny
The secret joy it could not quell,
Low muttering o'er his loathèd
name;
Till from that self-contention
came   245
Remorse where sin was none; a hell
Which in pure spirits should not
dwell.
I'll tell thee truth. He was a man
Hard, selfish, loving only gold,
Yet full of guile: his pale eyes
ran   250
With tears, which each some false-
hood told,
And oft his smooth and bridled
tongue
Would give the lie to his flushing
cheek:
He was a coward to the strong:
He was a tyrant to the weak,   255
On whom his vengeance he would
wreak:
For scorn, whose arrows search the
heart,
From many a stranger's eye would
dart,
And on his memory cling, and fol-
low
His soul to its home so cold and
hollow.   260
He was a tyrant to the weak,
And we were such, alas the day!
Oft, when my little ones at play,
Were in youth's natural lightness
gay,
Or if they listened to some tale 265
Of travellers, or of fairy land,—
When the light from the wood-fire's
dying brand
Flashed on their faces,—if they
heard
Or thought they heard upon the
stair   269
His footstep, the suspended word
Died on my lips: we all grew pale:

The babe at my bosom was hushed
  with fear
If it thought it heard its father
  near;
And my two wild boys would near
  my knee
Cling, cowed and cowering fearfully.   275

I'll tell thee truth: I loved another.
His name in my ear was ever
  ringing,
His form to my brain was ever
  clinging:
Yet if some stranger breathed that
  name,
My lips turned white, and my heart
  beat fast: 280
My nights were once haunted by
  dreams of flame,
My days were dim in the shadow
  cast
By the memory of the same!
Day and night, day and night,
He was my breath and life and
  light,   285
For three short years, which soon
  were passed.
On the fourth, my gentle mother
Led me to the shrine, to be
His sworn bride eternally.
And now we stood on the altar
  stair,   290
When my father came from a dis-
  tant land,
And with a loud and fearful cry
Rushed between us suddenly.
I saw the stream of his thin gray
  hair,
I saw his lean and lifted hand,   295
And heard his words,—and live!
  Oh God!
Wherefore do I live?—'Hold,
  hold!'
He cried,—'I tell thee 'tis her
  brother!
Thy mother, boy, beneath the sod

Of yon churchyard rests in her
  shroud so cold: 300
I am now weak, and pale, and old:
We were once dear to one another,
I and that corpse! Thou art our
  child!'
Then with a laugh both long and
  wild   304
The youth upon the pavement fell:
They found him dead! All looked
  on me,
The spasms of my despair to see:
But I was calm. I went away:
I was clammy-cold like clay!   309
I did not weep: I did not speak:
But day by day, week after week,
I walked about like a corpse alive!
Alas! sweet friend, you must be-
  lieve
This heart is stone: it did not
  break.
My father lived a little while,   315
But all might see that he was dying,
He smiled with such a woeful smile!
When he was in the churchyard
  lying
Among the worms, we grew quite
  poor,
So that no one would give us
  bread: 320
My mother looked at me, and said
Faint words of cheer, which only
  meant
That she could die and be content;
So I went forth from the same
  church door
To another husband's bed.   325
And this was he who died at last,
When weeks and months and years
  had passed,
Through which I firmly did fulfil
My duties, a devoted wife,
With the stern step of vanquished
  will,   330
Walking beneath the night of life,
Whose hours extinguished, like
  slow rain

Falling for ever, pain by pain,
The very hope of death's dear rest;
Which, since the heart within my
        breast   335
Of natural life was dispossessed,
Its strange sustainer there had been.

Wher flowers were dead, and grass
        was green
Upon my mother's grave,—that
        mother
Whom to outlive, and cheer, and
        make   340
My wan eyes glitter for her sake,
Was my vowed task, the single
        care
Which once gave life to my de-
        spair,—
When she was a thing that did not
        stir
And the crawling worms were
        cradling her   345
To a sleep more deep and so more
        sweet
Than a baby's rocked on its nurse's
        knee,
I lived: a living pulse then beat
Beneath my heart that awakened
        me.
What was this pulse so warm and
        free?   350
Alas! I knew it could not be
My own dull blood: 'twas like a
        thought
Of liquid love, that spread and
        wrought
Under my bosom and in my brain,
And crept with the blood through
        every vein;   355
And hour by hour, day after day,
The wonder could not charm away,
But laid in sleep, my wakeful pain,
Until I knew it was a child,
And then I wept. For long, long
        years   360
These frozen eyes had shed no
        tears:

But now—'twas the season fair and
        mild
When April has wept itself to May:
I sate through the sweet sunny day
By my window bowered round with
        leaves,   365
And down my cheeks the quick
        tears fell
Like twinkling rain-drops from the
        eaves,
When warm spring showers are
        passing o'er:
O Helen, none can ever tell
The joy it was to weep once
        more!   370

I wept to think how hard it were
To kill my babe, and take from it
The sense of light, and the warm
        air,
And my own fond and tender care,
And love and smiles; ere I knew
        yet   375
That these for it might, as for me,
Be the masks of a grinning mock-
        ery.
And haply, I would dream, 'twere
        sweet
To feed it from my faded breast,
Or mark my own heart's restless
        beat   380
Rock it to its untroubled rest,
And watch the growing soul be-
        neath
Dawn in faint smiles; and hear its
        breath,
Half interrupted by calm sighs,
And search the depth of its fair
        eyes   385
For long departed memories!
And so I lived till that sweet load
Was lightened. Darkly forward
        flowed
The stream of years, and on it bore
Two shapes of gladness to my
        sight;   390
Two other babes, delightful more

In my lost soul's abandoned night,
Than their own country ships may
   be
Sailing towards wrecked mariners,
Who cling to the rock of a wintry
   sea.   395
For each, as it came, brought sooth-
   ing tears,
And a loosening warmth, as each
   one lay
Sucking the sullen milk away
About my frozen heart, did play,
And weaned it, oh how pain-
   fully!—   400
As they themselves were weaned
   each one
From that sweet food,—even from
   the thirst
Of death, and nothingness, and
   rest,
Strange inmate of a living breast!
Which all that I had undergone 405
Of grief and shame, since she, who
   first
The gates of that dark refuge
   closed,
Came to my sight, and almost burst
The seal of that Lethean spring;
But these fair shadows inter-
   posed: 410
For all delights are shadows now!
And from my brain to my dull brow
The heavy tears gather and flow:
I cannot speak: Oh let me weep!

The tears which fell from her wan
   eyes   415
Glimmered among the moonlight
   dew:
Her deep hard sobs and heavy sighs
Their echoes in the darkness threw.
When she grew calm, she thus did
   keep
The tenor of her tale:
               He died: 420
I know not how: he was not old,
If age be numbered by its years:

But he was bowed and bent with
   fears,
Pale with the quenchless thirst of
   gold,
Which, like fierce fever, left him
   weak;   425
And his strait lip and bloated cheek
Were warped in spasms by hollow
   sneers;
And selfish cares with barren
   plough,
Not age, had lined his narrow
   brow,
And foul and cruel thoughts, which
   feed   430
Upon the withering life within,
Like vipers on some poisonous
   weed.
Whether his ill were death or sin
None knew, until he died indeed,
And then men owned they were the
   same.   435

Seven days within my chamber lay
That corse, and my babes made
   holiday:
At last, I told them what is death:
The eldest, with a kind of shame,
Came to my knees with silent
   breath,   440
And sate awe-stricken at my feet;
And soon the others left their play,
And sate there too. It is unmeet
To shed on the brief flower of youth
The withering knowledge of the
   grave;   445
From me remorse then wrung that
   truth.
I could not bear the joy which gave
Too just a response to mine own.
In vain. I dared not feign a groan;
And in their artless looks I saw, 450
Between the mists of fear and awe,
That my own thought was theirs;
   and they
Expressed it not in words, but said,
Each in its heart, how every day

Will pass in happy work and play,
Now he is dead and gone away. 456

After the funeral all our kin
Assembled, and the will was read.
My friend, I tell thee, even the dead
Have strength, their putrid shrouds
        within,   460
To blast and torture. Those who
        live
Still fear the living, but a corse
Is merciless, and power doth give
To such pale tyrants half the spoil
He rends from those who groan and
        toil,   465
Because they blush not with re-
        morse
Among their crawling worms. Be-
        hold,
I have no child! my tale grows old
With grief, and staggers: let it
        reach
The limits of my feeble speech, 470
And languidly at length recline
On the brink of its own grave and
        mine.

Thou knowest what a thing is Pov-
        erty
Among the fallen on evil days:
'Tis Crime, and Fear, and In-
        famy,   475
And houseless Want in frozen ways
Wandering ungarmented, and Pain,
And, worse than all, that inward
        stain
Foul Self-contempt, which drowns
        in sneers
Youth's starlight smile, and makes
        its tears   480
First like hot gall, then dry for
        ever!
And well thou knowest a mother
        never
Could doom her children to this ill,
And well he knew the same. The
        will

Imported, that if e'er again   485
I sought my children to behold,
Or in my birthplace did remain
Beyond three days, whose hours
        were told,
They should inherit nought: and
        he,
To whom next came their patri-
        mony,   490
A sallow lawyer, cruel and cold,
Aye watched me, as the will was
        read,
With eyes askance, which sought
        to see
The secrets of my agony;
And with close lips and anxious
        brow   495
Stood canvassing still to and fro
The chance of my resolve, and all
The dead man's caution just did
        call;
For in that killing lie 'twas said—
'She is adulterous, and doth
        hold   500
In secret that the Christian creed
Is false, and therefore is much need
That I should have a care to save
My children from eternal fire.'
Friend, he was sheltered by the
        grave,   505
And therefore dared to be a liar!
In truth, the Indian on the pyre
Of her dead husband, half con-
        sumed,
As well might there be false, as I
To those abhorred embraces
        doomed,   510
Far worse than fire's brief agony.
As to the Christian creed, if true
Or false, I never questioned it:
I took it as the vulgar do:
Nor my vexed soul had leisure
        yet   515
To doubt the things men say, or
        deem
That they are other than they
        seem.

All present who those crimes did hear,
In feigned or actual scorn and fear,
Men, women, children, slunk away, 520
Whispering with self-contented pride,
Which half suspects its own base lie.
I spoke to none, nor did abide,
But silently I went my way,
Nor noticed I where joyously 525
Sate my two younger babes at play,
In the court-yard through which I passed;
But went with footsteps firm and fast
Till I came to the brink of the ocean green,
And there, a woman with gray hairs, 530
Who had my mother's servant been,
Kneeling, with many tears and prayers,
Made me accept a purse of gold,
Half of the earnings she had kept
To refuge her when weak and old. 535

With woe, which never sleeps or slept,
I wander now. 'Tis a vain thought—
But on yon alp, whose snowy head
'Mid the azure air is islanded,
(We see it o'er the flood of cloud, 540
Which sunrise from its eastern caves
Drives, wrinkling into golden waves,
Hung with its precipices proud,
From that gray stone where first we met)
There—now who knows the dead feel nought?— 545

Should be my grave; for he who yet
Is my soul's soul, once said:
    ' 'Twere sweet
'Mid stars and lightnings to abide,
And winds and lulling snows, that beat
With their soft flakes the mountain wide, 550
Where weary meteor lamps repose,
And languid storms their pinions close:
And all things strong and bright and pure,
And ever during, aye endure:
Who knows, if one were buried there, 555
But these things might our spirits make,
Amid the all-surrounding air,
Their own eternity partake?'
Then 'twas a wild and playful saying
At which I laughed, or seemed to laugh: 560
They were his words. now heed my praying,
And let them be my epitaph.
Thy memory for a term may be
My monument. Wilt remember me?
I know thou wilt, and canst forgive 565
Whilst in this erring world to live
My soul disdained not, that I thought
Its lying forms were worthy aught
And much less thee.
  Helen.   O speak not so,
But come to me and pour thy woe 570
Into this heart, full though it be,
Ay, overflowing with its own:
I thought that grief had severed me
From all beside who weep and groan;
Its likeness upon earth to be, 575

Its express image; but thou art
More wretched. Sweet! we will not
      part
Henceforth, if death be not divi-
      sion;
If so, the dead feel no contrition.
But wilt thou hear since last we
      parted   580
All that has left me broken hearted?
    Rosalind. Yes, speak. The faint-
      est stars are scarcely shorn
Of their thin beams by that delu-
      sive morn
Which sinks again in darkness, like
      the light
Of early love, soon lost in total
      night.   585
    Helen. Alas! Italian winds are
      mild,
But my bosom is cold—wintry
      cold—
When the warm air weaves, among
      the fresh leaves,
Soft music, my poor brain is
      wild,
And I am weak like a nursling
      child,   590
Though my soul with grief is gray
      and old.
    Rosalind. Weep not at thine own
      words, though they must
      make
Me weep. What is thy tale?
    Helen.   I fear 'twill shake
Thy gentle heart with tears. Thou
      well
Rememberest when we met no
      more,   595
And, though I dwelt with Lionel,
That friendless caution pierced me
      sore
With grief; a wound my spirit
      bore
Indignantly, but when he died
With him lay dead both hope and
      pride.   600
Alas! all hope is buried now.

But then men dreamed the agèd
      earth
Was labouring in that mighty birth,
Which many a poet and a sage
Has aye foreseen—the happy
      age   605
When truth and love shall dwell
      below
Among the works and ways of
      men;
Which on this world not power but
      will
Even now is wanting to fulfil.

Among mankind what thence be-
      fell   610
Of strife, how vain, is known too
      well;
When Liberty's dear paean fell
'Mid murderous howls. To Lionel,
Though of great wealth and line-
      age high,
Yet through those dungeon walls
      there came   615
Thy thrilling light, O Liberty!
And as the meteor's midnight
      flame
Startles the dreamer, sun-like truth
Flashed on his visionary youth,
And filled him, not with love, but
      faith,   620
And hope, and courage mute in
      death;
For love and life in him were
      twins,
Born at one birth: in every other
First life then love its course be-
      gins,
Though they be children of one
      mother;   625
And so through this dark world
      they fleet
Divided, till in death they meet:
But he loved all things ever. Then
He passed amid the strife of men,
And stood at the throne of armèd
      power   630

Pleading for a world of woe:
Secure as one on a rock-built tower
O'er the wrecks which the surge
    trails to and fro,
'Mid the passions wild of human
    kind
He stood, like a spirit calming
    them;   635
For, it was said, his words could
    bind
Like music the lulled crowd, and
    stem
That torrent of unquiet dream,
Which mortals truth and reason
    deem,
But is revenge and fear and
    pride.   640
Joyous he was; and hope and peace
On all who heard him did abide,
Raining like dew from his sweet
    talk,
As where the evening star may
    walk   644
Along the brink of the gloomy seas,
Liquid mists of splendour quiver.
His very gestures touched to tears
The unpersuaded tyrant, never
So moved before: his presence
    stung
The torturers with their victim's
    pain,   650
And none knew how; and through
    their ears,
The subtle witchcraft of his tongue
Unlocked the hearts of those who
    keep
Gold, the world's bond of slavery.
Men wondered, and some sneered
    to see   655
One sow what he could never reap:
For he is rich, they said, and
    young,
And might drink from the depths
    of luxury.
If he seeks Fame, Fame never
    crowned
The champion of a trampled creed:

If he seeks Power, Power is en-
    throned   661
'Mid ancient rights and wrongs, to
    feed
Which hungry wolves with praise
    and spoil,
Those who would sit near Power
    must toil;
And such, there sitting, all may
    see.   665
What seeks he? All that others seek
He casts away, like a vile weed
Which the sea casts unreturn-
    ingly.
That poor and hungry men should
    break
The laws which wreak them toil
    and scorn,   670
We understand; but Lionel
We know is rich and nobly born.
So wondered they: yet all men
    loved
Young Lionel, though few ap-
    proved;
All but the priests, whose hatred
    fell   675
Like the unseen blight of a smil-
    ing day,
The withering honey dew, which
    clings
Under the bright green buds of
    May,
Whilst they unfold their emerald
    wings:
For he made verses wild and queer
On the strange creeds priests hold
    so dear,   681
Because they bring them land and
    gold.
Of devils and saints and all such
    gear,
He made tales which whoso heard
    or read
Would laugh till he were almost
    dead.   685
So this grew a proverb: 'Don't get
    old

Till Lionel's "Banquet in Hell"
   you hear,
And then you will laugh yourself
   young again.'
So the priests hated him, and he
Repaid their hate with cheerful
   glee.   690

Ah, smiles and joyance quickly
   died,
For public hope grew pale and dim
In an altered time and tide,
And in its wasting withered him,
As a summer flower that blows too
   soon   695
Droops in the smile of the waning
   moon,
When it scatters through an April
   night
The frozen dews of wrinkling
   blight.
None now hoped more. Gray
   Power was seated 700
Safely on her ancestral throne; 700
And Faith, the Python, undefeated,
Even to its blood-stained steps
   dragged on
Her foul and wounded train, and
   men
Were trampled and deceived again,
And words and shows again could
   bind   705
The wailing tribes of human kind
In scorn and famine. Fire and
   blood
Raged round the raging multitude,
To fields remote by tyrants sent
To be the scornèd instrument 710
With which they drag from mines
   of gore
The chains their slaves yet ever
   wore:
And in the streets men met each
   other,
And by old altars and in halls,
And smiled again at festivals, 715

But each man found in his heart's
   brother
Cold cheer; for all, though half de-
   ceived,
The outworn creeds again believed,
And the same round anew began,
Which the weary world yet ever
   ran.   720
Many then wept, not tears, but
   gall
Within their hearts, like drops
   which fall
Wasting the fountain-stone away.
And in that dark and evil day
Did all desires and thoughts, that
   claim   725
Men's care—ambition, friendship,
   fame,
Love, hope, though hope was now
   despair—
Indue the colours of this change,
As from the all-surrounding air
The earth takes hues obscure and
   strange,   730
When storm and earthquake linger
   there.
And so, my friend, it then befell
To many, most to Lionel,
Whose hope was like the life of
   youth
Within him, and when dead, be-
   came   735
A spirit of unresting flame,
Which goaded him in his distress
Over the world's vast wilderness.
Three years he left his native land,
And on the fourth, when he re-
   turned,   740
None knew him: he was stricken
   deep
With some disease of mind, and
   turned
Into aught unlike Lionel.
On him, on whom, did he pause in
   sleep,   744
Serenest smiles were wont to keep,
And, did he wake, a wingèd band

Of bright persuasions, which had
    fed
On his sweet lips and liquid eyes,
Kept their swift pinions half out-
    spread,
To do on men his least com-
    mand;   750
On him, whom once 'twas paradise
Even to behold, now misery lay:
In his own heart 'twas merciless,
To all things else none may express
Its innocence and tenderness. 755

'Twas said that he had refuge
    sought
In love from his unquiet thought
In distant lands, and been deceived
By some strange show; for there
    were found,   759
Blotted with tears as those relieved
By their own words are wont to do,
These mournful verses on the
    ground,
By all who read them blotted too.

'How am I changed! my hopes
    were once like fire:
I loved, and I believed that life
    was love.   765
How am I lost! on wings of swift
    desire
Among Heaven's winds my spirit
    once did move.
I slept, and silver dreams did aye
    inspire
My liquid sleep: I woke, and did
    approve
All nature to my heart, and thought
    to make   770
A paradise of earth for one sweet
    sake.

'I love, but I believe in love no
    more.
I feel desire, but hope not. O, from
    sleep

Most vainly must my weary brain
    implore
Its long lost flattery now: I wake
    to weep,   775
And sit through the long day gnaw-
    ing the core
Of my bitter heart, and, like a
    miser, keep,
Since none in what I feel take pain
    or pleasure,
To my own soul its self-consuming
    treasure.'
He dwelt beside me near the
    sea: 780
And oft in evening did we meet,
When the waves, beneath the star-
    light, flee
O'er the yellow sands with silver
    feet,
And talked: our talk was sad and
    sweet,
Till slowly from his mien there
    passed   785
The desolation which it spoke;
And smiles,—as when the light-
    ning's blast
Has parched some heaven-delight-
    ing oak,
The next spring shows leaves pale
    and rare,   789
But like flowers delicate and fair,
On its rent boughs,—again arrayed
His countenance in tender light:
His words grew subtile fire, which
    made
The air his hearers breathed de-
    light:
His motions, like the winds, were
    free,   795
Which bend the bright grass grace-
    fully,
Then fade away in circlets faint:
And wingèd Hope, on which up-
    borne
His soul seemed hovering in his
    eyes,   799
Like some bright spirit newly born

Floating amid the sunny skies,
Sprang forth from his rent heart
anew.
Yet o'er his talk, and looks, and
mien,
Tempering their loveliness too
keen,
Past woe its shadow backward
threw,   805
Till like an exhalation, spread
From flowers half drunk with eve-
ning dew,
They did become infectious: sweet
And subtile mists of sense and
thought:
Which wrapped us soon, when we
might meet,   810
Almost from our own looks and
aught
The wide world holds. And so, his
mind
Was healed, while mine grew sick
with fear:
For ever now his health declined,
Like some frail bark which cannot
bear   815
The impulse of an altered wind,
Though prosperous: and my heart
grew full
'Mid its new joy of a new care:
For his cheek became, not pale, but
fair,
As rose-o'ershadowed lilies are;   820
And soon his deep and sunny hair,
In this alone less beautiful,
Like grass in tombs grew wild and
rare.
The blood in his translucent veins
Beat, not like animal life, but love
Seemed now its sullen springs to
move,   826
When life had failed, and all its
pains:
And sudden sleep would seize him
oft
Like death, so calm, but that a tear,
His pointed eyelashes between.   830

Would gather in the light serene
Of smiles, whose lustre bright and
soft
Beneath lay undulating there.
His breath was like inconstant
flame,
As eagerly it went and came;   835
And I hung o'er him in his sleep,
Till, like an image in the lake
Which rains disturb, my tears
would break
Then he would bid me not to
weep,   840
The shadow of that slumber deep:
And say with flattery false, yet
sweet,
That death and he could never
meet,
If I would never part with him.
And so we loved, and did unite
All that in us was yet divided: 845
For when he said, that many a rite,
By men to bind but once provided,
Could not be shared by him and
me,
Or they would kill him in their
glee,
I shuddered, and then laughing
said—   850
'We will have rites our faith to
bind,
But our church shall be the starry
night,
Our altar the grassy earth out-
spread,
And our priest the muttering
wind.'
'Twas sunset as I spoke: one
star   855
Had scarce burst forth, when from
afar
The ministers of misrule sent,
Seized upon Lionel, and bore
His chained limbs to a dreary
tower,
In the midst of a city vast and
wide

For he, they said, from his mind
    had bent   861
Against their gods keen blasphemy,
For which, though his soul must
    roasted be
In hell's red lakes immortally,
Yet even on earth must he abide 865
The vengeance of their slaves: a
    trial,
I think, men call it. What avail
Are prayers and tears, which chase
    denial
From the fierce savage, nursed in
    hate?
What the knit soul that pleading
    and pale   870
Makes wan the quivering cheek,
    which late
It painted with its own delight?
We were divided. As I could,
I stilled the tingling of my blood,
And followed him in their de-
    spite,   875
As a widow follows, pale and wild,
The murderers and corse of her
    only child;
And when we came to the prison
    door
And I prayed to share his dungeon
    floor
With prayers which rarely have
    been spurned,   880
And when men drove me forth
    and I
Stared with blank frenzy on the
    sky,
A farewell look of love he turned,
Half calming me; then gazed
    awhile,
As if thro' that black and massy
    pile,   885
And thro' the crowd around him
    there,
And thro' the dense and murky air,
And the thronged streets, he did
    espy
What poets know and prophesy;

And said, with voice that made
    them shiver   890
And clung like music in my brain,
And which the mute walls spoke
    again
Prolonging it with deepened
    strain:
'Fear not the tyrants shall rule for
    ever,
Or the priests of the bloody
    faith;   895
They stand on the brink of that
    mighty river,
Whose waves they have tainted
    with death:
It is fed from the depths of a thou-
    sand dells,
Around them it foams, and rages,
    and swells,
And their swords and their scep-
    tres I floating see,   900
Like wrecks in the surge of eter·
    nity.'

I dwelt beside the prison gate,
And the strange crowd that out and
    in
Passed, some, no doubt, with mine
    own fate,
Might have fretted me with its
    ceaseless din,   905
But the fever of care was louder
    within.
Soon, but too late, in penitence
Or fear, his foes released him
    thence:
I saw his thin and languid form,
As leaning on the jailor's arm, 910
Whose hardened eyes grew moist
    the while,
To meet his mute and faded
    smile,
And hear his words of kind fare·
    well,
He tottered forth from his damp
    cell.
Many had never wept before, 915

From whom fast tears then gushed
    and fell:
Many will relent no more,
Who sobbed like infants then: aye,
    all
Who thronged the prison's stony
    hall,
The rulers or the slaves of law, 920
Felt with a new surprise and awe
That they were human, till strong
    shame
Made them again become the same.
The prison blood-hounds, huge
    and grim,
From human looks the infection
    caught, 925
And fondly crouched and fawned
    on him;
And men have heard the prisoners
    say,
Who in their rotting dungeons lay,
That from that hour, throughout
    one day,
The fierce despair and hate which
    kept 930
Their trampled bosoms almost
    slept:
Where, like twin vultures, they
    hung feeding
On each heart's wound, wide torn
    and bleeding,—
Because their jailors' rule, they
    thought, 934
Grew merciful, like a parent's sway.

I know not how, but we were free:
And Lionel sate alone with me,
As the carriage drove thro' the
    streets apace;
And we looked upon each other's
    face;
And the blood in our fingers inter-
    twined 940
Ran like the thoughts of a single
    mind,
As the swift emotions went and
    came

Thro' the veins of each united
    frame.
So thro' the long long streets we
    passed
Of the million-peopled City vast;
Which is that desert, where each
    one 946
Seeks his mate yet is alone,
Beloved and sought and mourned
    of none;
Until the clear blue sky was seen,
And the grassy meadows bright
    and green, 950
And then I sunk in his embrace,
Enclosing there a mighty space
Of love: and so we travelled on
By woods, and fields of yellow
    flowers,
And towns, and villages, and tow-
    ers,
Day after day of happy hours. 956
It was the azure time of June,
When the skies are deep in the
    stainless noon,
And the warm and fitful breezes
    shake
The fresh green leaves of the hedge-
    row briar, 960
And there were odours then to
    make
The very breath we did respire
A liquid element, whereon
Our spirits, like delighted things
That walk the air on subtle wings,
Floated and mingled far away, 966
'Mid the warm winds of the sunny
    day.
And when the evening star came
    forth
Above the curve of the new bent
    moon,
And light and sound ebbed from
    the earth, 970
Like the tide of the full and weary
    sea
To the depths of its tranquillity,
Our natures to its own repose

Did the earth's breathless sleep at-
    tune:
Like flowers, which on each other
    close   975
Their languid leaves when day-
    light's gone,
We lay, till new emotions came,
Which seemed to make each mortal
    frame
One soul of interwoven flame,
A life in life, a second birth   980
In worlds diviner far than earth,
Which, like two strains of harmony
That mingle in the silent sky
Then slowly disunite, passed by
And left the tenderness of tears, 985
A soft oblivion of all fears,
A sweet sleep: so we travelled on
Till we came to the home of Lionel,
Among the mountains wild and
    lone,
Beside the hoary western sea,   990
Which near the verge of the echo-
    ing shore
The massy forest shadowed o'er.

The ancient steward, with hair all
    hoar,
As we alighted, wept to see
His master changed so fearfully;
And the old man's sobs did waken
    me   996
From my dream of unremaining
    gladness;
The truth flashed o'er me like quick
    madness
When I looked, and saw that there
    was death
On Lionel: yet day by day   1000
He lived, till fear grew hope and
    faith,
And in my soul I dared to say,
Nothing so bright can pass away:
Death is dark, and foul, and dull,
But he is—O how beautiful!   1005
Yet day by day he grew more
    weak.

And his sweet voice, when he might
    speak,
Which ne'er was loud, became more
    low;
And the light which flashed through
    his waxen cheek
Grew faint, as the rose-like hues
    which flow   1010
From sunset o'er the Alpine snow:
And death seemed not like death
    in him,
For the spirit of life o'er every limb
Lingered, a mist of sense and
    thought.
When the summer wind faint
    odours brought   1015
From mountain flowers, even as it
    passed
His cheek would change, as the
    noonday sea
Which the dying breeze sweeps fit-
    fully.
If but a cloud the sky o'ercast,
You might see his colour come and
    go,   1020
And the softest strain of music
    made
Sweet smiles, yet sad, arise and
    fade
Amid the dew of his tender eyes;
And the breath, with intermitting
    flow,
Made his pale lips quiver and part.
You might hear the beatings of his
    heart,   1026
Quick, but not strong; and with my
    tresses
When oft he playfully would bind
In the bowers of mossy lonelinesses
His neck, and win me so to mingle
In the sweet depth of woven ca-
    resses,
And our faint limbs were inter-
    twined,   1032
Alas! the unquiet life did tingle
From mine own heart through every
    vein,

Like a captive in dreams of liberty,
Who beats the walls of his stony
    cell.   1036
But his, it seemed already free,
Like the shadow of fire surround-
    ing me!
On my faint eyes and limbs did
    dwell
That spirit as it passed, till soon,
As a frail cloud wandering o'er the
    moon,   1041
Beneath its light invisible,
Is seen when it folds its gray wings
    again
To alight on midnight's dusky
    plain,
I lived and saw, and the gathering
    soul
Passed from beneath that strong
    control,   1046
And I fell on a life which was sick
    with fear
Of all the woe that now I bear.

Amid a bloomless myrtle wood,
On a green and sea-girt promon-
    tory,
Not far from where we dwelt, there
    stood   1051
In record of a sweet sad story,
An altar and a temple bright
Circled by steps, and o'er the gate
Was sculptured, 'To Fidelity;'   1055
And in the shrine an image sate,
All veiled: but there was seen the
    light
Of smiles, which faintly could
    express
A mingled pain and tenderness
Through that ethereal drapery. 1060
The left hand held the head, the
    right—
Beyond the veil, beneath the skin,
You might see the nerves quivering
    within—
Was forcing the point of a barbèd
    dart

Into its side-convulsing heart. 1065
An unskilled hand, yet one in-
    formed
With genius, had the marble
    warmed
With that pathetic life. This tale
It told: A dog had from the sea,
When the tide was raging fearfully,
Dragged Lionel's mother, weak and
    pale,   1071
Then died beside her on the sand,
And she that temple thence had
    planned;
But it was Lionel's own hand
Had wrought the image. Each new
    moon   1075
That lady did, in this lone fane,
The rites of a religion sweet,
Whose god was in her heart and
    brain;
The season's loveliest flowers were
    strewn
On the marble floor beneath her
    feet,
And she brought crowns of sea-
    buds white,   1081
Whose odour is so sweet and faint,
And weeds, like branching chryso-
    lite,
Woven in devices fine and quaint.
And tears from her brown eyes did
    stain   1085
The altar: need but look upon
That dying statue fair and wan,
If tears should cease, to weep again:
And rare Arabian odours came,
Through the myrtle copses steam-
    ing thence   1090
From the hissing frankincense,
Whose smoke, wool-white as ocean
    foam,
Hung in dense flocks beneath the
    dome—
That ivory dome, whose azure night
With golden stars, like heaven, was
    bright—   1095
O'er the split cedar's pointed flame;

And the lady's harp would kindle
    there
The melody of an old air,
Softer than sleep; the villagers
Mixed their religion up with hers,
And as they listened round, shed
    tears.   1101

One eve he led me to this fane:
Daylight on its last purple cloud
Was lingering gray, and soon her
    strain   1104
The nightingale began; now loud,
Climbing in circles the windless sky,
Now dying music; suddenly
'Tis scattered in a thousand notes,
And now to the hushed ear it floats
Like field smells known in in-
    fancy,   1110
Then failing, soothes the air again.
We sate within that temple lone,
Pavilioned round with Parian
    stone:
His mother's harp stood near, and
    oft
I had awakened music soft   1115
Amid its wires: the nightingale
Was pausing in her heaven-taught
    tale:
'Now drain the cup,' said Lionel,
'Which the poet-bird has crowned
    so well
With the wine of her bright and
    liquid song!   1120
Heardst thou not sweet words
    among
That heaven-resounding min-
    strelsy?
Heardst thou not, that those who
    die
Awaken in a world of ecstasy?
That love, when limbs are inter-
    woven,   1125
And sleep, when the night of life
    is cloven,
And thought, to the world's dim
    boundaries clinging,

And music, when one beloved is
    singing,
Is death? Let us drain right joy-
    ously
The cup which the sweet bird fills
    for me.'   1130
He paused, and to my lips he bent
His own: like spirit his words went
Through all my limbs with the
    speed of fire;
And his keen eyes, glittering
    through mine,
Filled   me   with   the   flame
    divine,   1135
Which in their orbs was burning
    far,
Like the light of an unmeasured
    star,
In the sky of midnight dark and
    deep:
Yes, 'twas his soul that did inspire
Sounds, which my skill could ne'er
    awaken;   1140
And first, I felt my fingers sweep
The harp, and a long quivering cry
Burst from my lips in symphony:
The dusk and solid air was shaken,
As swift and swifter the notes
    came   1145
From my touch, that wandered like
    quick flame,
And from my bosom, labouring
With some unutterable thing:
The awful sound of my own voice
    made
My faint lips tremble; in some
    mood   1150
Of wordless thought Lionel stood
So pale that even beside his cheek
The snowy column from its shade
Caught whiteness: yet his counte-
    nance
Raised upward, burned with radi-
    ance   1155
Of spirit-piercing joy, whose light,
Like the moon struggling through
    the night

Of whirlwind-rifted clouds, did
   break
With beams that might not be con-
   fined.
I paused, but soon his gestures
   kindled   1160
New power, as by the moving wind
The waves are lifted, and my song
To low soft notes now changed and
   dwindled,
And from the twinkling wires
   among,
My languid fingers drew and flung
Circles of life-dissolving sound, 1166
Yet faint; in aëry rings they bound
My Lionel, who, as every strain
Grew fainter but more sweet, his
   mien
Sunk with the sound relaxed-
   ly;   1170
And slowly now he turned to me,
As slowly faded from his face
That awful joy: with looks serene
He was soon drawn to my embrace,
And my wild song then died away
In murmurs: words I dare not say
We mixed, and on his lips mine fed
Till they methought felt still and
   cold:
'What is it with thee, love?' I said:
No word, no look, no motion! yes,
There was a change, but spare to
   guess,   1181
Nor let that moment's hope be told.
I looked, and knew that he was
   dead,
And fell, as the eagle on the plain
Falls when life deserts her
   brain,   1185
And the mortal lightning is veiled
   again.

O that I were now dead! but such
(Did they not, love, demand too
   much,
Those dying murmurs?) he forbade.

O that I once again were mad! 1190
And yet, dear Rosalind, not so,
For I would live to share thy woe.
Sweet boy, did I forget thee too?
Alas, we know not what we do
When we speak words.
         No memory more   1195
Is in my mind of that sea shore.
Madness came on me, and a troop
Of misty shapes did seem to sit
Beside me, on a vessel's poop,
And the clear north wind was driv-
   ing it.   1200
Then I heard strange tongues, and
   saw strange flowers,
And the stars methought grew un-
   like ours,
And the azure sky and the storm-
   less sea
Made me believe that I had died,
And waked in a world, which was
   to me   1205
Drear hell, though heaven to all
   beside:
Then a dead sleep fell on my mind,
Whilst animal life many long years
Had rescue from a chasm of tears;
And when I woke, I wept to
   find   1210
That the same lady, bright and
   wise,
With silver locks and quick brown
   eyes,
The mother of my Lionel,
Had tended me in my distress,
And died some months before. Nor
   less   1215
Wonder, but far more peace and joy
Brought in that hour my lovely
   boy;
For through that trance my soul
   had well
The impress of thy being kept;
And if I waked, or if I slept,   1220
No doubt, though memory faithless
   be,
Thy image ever dwelt on me;

And thus, O Lionel, like thee
Is our sweet child. 'Tis sure most
    strange
I knew not of so great a
    change,   1225
As that which gave him birth, who
    now
Is ˄ll the solace of my woe.

That Lionel great wealth had left
By will to me, and that of all
The ready lies of law bereft   1230
My child and me, might well befall.
But let me think not of the scorn,
Which from the meanest I have
    borne,
When, for my child's belovèd sake,
I mixed with slaves, to vindi-
    cate   1235
The very laws themselves do make:
Let me not say scorn is my fate,
Lest I be proud, suffering the same
With those who live in deathless
    fame.

She ceased.—'Lo, where red morn-
    ing thro' the woods   1240
Is burning o'er the dew;' said
    Rosalind.
And with these words they rose, and
    towards the flood
Of the blue lake, beneath the leaves
    now wind
With equal steps and fingers inter-
    twined:
Thence to a lonely dwelling, where
    the shore   1245
Is shadowed with deep rocks, and
    cypresses
Cleave with their dark green cones
    the silent skies,
And with their shadows the clear
    depths below,
And where a little terrace from its
    bowers,
Of blooming myrtle and faint
    lemon-flowers,   1250

Scatters its sense-dissolving fra-
    grance o'er
The liquid marble of the windless
    lake;
And where the agèd forest's limbs
    look hoar,
Under the leaves which their green
    garments make,
They come: 'tis Helen's home, and
    clean and white,   1255
Like one which tyrants spare on our
    own land
In some such solitude, its casements
    bright
Shone through their vine-leaves in
    the morning sun,
And even within 'twas scarce like
    Italy.
And when she saw how all things
    there were planned,   1260
As in an English home, dim
    memory
Disturbed poor Rosalind: she stood
    as one
Whose mind is where his body can-
    not be,
Till Helen led her where her child
    yet slept,
And said, 'Observe, that brow was
    Lionel's,   1265
Those lips were his, and so he ever
    kept
One arm in sleep, pillowing his head
    with it.
You cannot see his eyes, they are
    two wells
Of liquid love: let us not wake him
    yet.'
But Rosalind could bear no more,
    and wept   1270
A shower of burning tears, which
    fell upon
His face, and so his opening lashes
    shone
With tears unlike his own, as he did
    leap

In sudden wonder from his in-
    nocent sleep.

So Rosalind and Helen lived to-
    gether
Thenceforth, changed in all else,
    yet friends again,   1276
Such as they were, when o'er the
    mountain heather
They wandered in their youth,
    through sun and rain.
And after many years, for human
    things
Change even like the ocean and the
    wind,   1280
Her daughter was restored to
    Rosalind,
And in their circle thence some
    visitings
Of joy 'mid their new calm would
    intervene:
A lovely child she was, of looks
    serene,
And motions which o'er things in-
    different shed   1285
The grace and gentleness from
    whence they came.
And Helen's boy grew with her,
    and they fed
From the same flowers of thought,
    until each mind
Like springs which mingle in one
    flood became,
And in their union soon their
    parents saw   1290
The shadow of the peace denied to
    them.
And Rosalind, for when the living-
    stem
Is cankered in its heart, the tree
    must fall,
Died ere her time; and with deep
    grief and awe
The pale survivors followed her re-
    mains   1295
Beyond the region of dissolving
    rains,

Up the cold mountain she was wont
    to call
Her tomb; and on Chiavenna's
    precipice
They raised a pyramid of lasting
    ice,
Whose polished sides, ere day had
    yet begun,   1300
Caught the first glow of the unrisen
    sun,
The last, when it had sunk; and
    thro' the night
The charioteers of Arctos wheelèd
    round
Its glittering point, as seen from
    Helen's home,
Whose sad inhabitants each year
    would come,   1305
With willing steps climbing that
    rugged height,
And hang long locks of hair, and
    garlands bound
With amaranth flowers, which, in
    the clime's despite,
Filled the frore air with unaccus-
    tomed light:
Such flowers, as in the wintry
    memory bloom   1310
Of one friend left, adorned that
    frozen tomb.

Helen, whose spirit was of softer
    mould,
Whose sufferings too were less,
    Death slowlier led
Into the peace of his dominion
    cold:
She died among her kindred, being
    old.   1315
And know, that if love die not in
    the dead
As in the living, none of mortal
    kind
Are blest, as now Helen and Rosa-
    lind.

NOTE BY MRS. SHELLEY

Rosalind and Helen was begun at Marlow, and thrown aside—till I found it; and, at my request, it was completed. Shelley had no care for any of his poems that did not emanate from the depths of his mind and develop some high or abstruse truth. When he does touch on human life and the human heart, no pictures can be more faithful, more delicate, more subtle, or more pathetic. He never mentioned Love but he shed a grace borrowed from his own nature, that scarcely any other poet has bestowed, on that passion. When he spoke of it as the law of life, which inasmuch as we rebel against we err and injure ourselves and others, he promulgated that which he considered an irrefragable truth. In his eyes it was the essence of our being, and all woe and pain arose from the war made against it by selfishness, or insensibility, or mistake. By reverting in his mind to this first principle, he discovered the source of many emotions, and could disclose the secrets of all hearts; and his delineations of passion and emotion touch the finest chords of our nature.

Rosalind and Helen was finished during the summer of 1818, while we were at the baths of Lucca.

JULIAN AND MADDALO

A CONVERSATION

PREFACE

> The meadows with fresh streams, the bees with thyme,
> The goats with the green leaves of budding Spring,
> Are saturated not—nor Love with tears.—VIRGIL's *Gallus*.

COUNT MADDALO is a Venetian nobleman of ancient family and of great fortune, who, without mixing much in the society of his countrymen, resides chiefly at his magnificent palace in that city. He is a person of the most consummate genius, and capable, if he would direct his energies to such an end, of becoming the redeemer of his degraded country. But it is his weakness to be proud: he derives, from a comparison of his own extraordinary mind with the dwarfish intellects that surround him, an intense apprehension of the nothingness of human life. His passions and his powers are incomparably greater than those of other men; and, instead of the latter having been employed in curbing the former, they have mutually lent each other strength. His ambition preys upon itself, for want of objects which it can consider worthy of exertion. I say that Maddalo is proud, because I can find no other word to express the concentered and impatient feelings which consume him; but it is on his own hopes and affections only that he seems to trample, for in social life no human being can be more gentle, patient, and unassuming than Maddalo. He is cheerful, frank, and witty. His more serious conversation

is a sort of intoxication; men are held by it as by a spell. He has travelled
much; and there is an inexpressible charm in his relation of his adventures in different countries.

Julian is an Englishman of good family, passionately attached to those
philosophical notions which assert the power of man over his own mind,
and the immense improvements of which, by the extinction of certain
moral superstitions, human society may be yet susceptible. Without concealing the evil in the world, he is for ever speculating how good may be
made superior. He is a complete infidel, and a scoffer at all things reputed
holy; and Maddalo takes a wicked pleasure in drawing out his taunts
against religion. What Maddalo thinks on these matters is not exactly
known. Julian, in spite of his heterodox opinions, is conjectured by his
friends to possess some good qualities. How far this is possible the pious
reader will determine. Julian is rather serious.

Of the Maniac I can give no information. He seems, by his own
account, to have been disappointed in love. He was evidently a very cultivated and amiable person when in his right senses. His story, told at
length, might be like many other stories of the same kind: the unconnected exclamations of his agony will perhaps be found a sufficient
comment for the text of every heart.

> I RODE one evening with Count Maddalo
> Upon the bank of land which breaks the flow
> Of Adria towards Venice: a bare strand
> Of hillocks, heaped from ever-shifting sand,
> Matted with thistles and amphibious weeds,   5
> Such as from earth's embrace the salt ooze breeds,
> Is this; an uninhabited sea-side,
> Which the lone fisher, when his nets are dried,
> Abandons; and no other object breaks
> The waste, but one dwarf tree and some few stakes   10
> Broken and unrepaired, and the tide makes
> A narrow space of level sand thereon,
> Where 'twas our wont to ride while day went down.
> This ride was my delight. I love all waste
> And solitary places; where we taste   15
> The pleasure of believing what we see
> Is boundless, as we wish our souls to be:
> And such was this wide ocean, and this shore
> More barren than its billows; and yet more
> Than all, with a remembered friend I love   20
> To ride as then I rode;—for the winds drove
> The living spray along the sunny air
> Into our faces; the blue heavens were bare,
> Stripped to their depths by the awakening north;
> And. from the waves, sound like delight broke forth   25

Harmonising with solitude, and sent
Into our hearts aëreal merriment.
So, as we rode, we talked; and the swift thought,
Winging itself with laughter, lingered not,
But flew from brain to brain,—such glee was ours, 30
Charged with light memories of remembered hours,
None slow enough for sadness: till we came
Homeward, which always makes the spirit tame.
This day had been cheerful but cold, and now
The sun was sinking, and the wind also. 35
Our talk grew somewhat serious, as may be
Talk interrupted with such raillery
As mocks itself, because it cannot scorn
The thoughts it would extinguish:—'twas forlorn,
Yet pleasing, such as once, so poets tell, 40
The devils held within the dales of Hell
Concerning God, freewill and destiny:
Of all that earth has been or yet may be,
All that vain men imagine or believe,
Or hope can paint or suffering may achieve, 45
We descanted, and I (for ever still
Is it not wise to make the best of ill?)
Argued against despondency, but pride
Made my companion take the darker side.
The sense that he was greater than his kind 50
Had struck, methinks, his eagle spirit blind
By gazing on its own exceeding light.
Meanwhile the sun paused ere it should alight,
Over the horizon of the mountains:—Oh,
How beautiful is sunset, when the glow 55
Of Heaven descends upon a land like thee,
Thou Paradise of exiles, Italy!
Thy mountains, seas, and vineyards, and the towers
Of cities they encircle!—it was ours
To stand on thee, beholding it: and then, 60
Just where we had dismounted, the Count's men
Were waiting for us with the gondola.—
As those who pause on some delightful way
Though bent on pleasant pilgrimage, we stood
Looking upon the evening, and the flood 65
Which lay between the city and the shore,
Paved with the image of the sky . . . the hoar
And aëry Alps towards the North appeared
Through mist, an heaven-sustaining bulwark reared
Between the East and West; and half the sky 70
Was roofed with clouds of rich emblazonry

Dark purple at the zenith, which still grew
Down the steep West into a wondrous hue
Brighter than burning gold, even to the rent
Where the swift sun yet paused in his descent   75
Among the many-folded hills: they were
Those famous Euganean hills, which bear,
As seen from Lido thro' the harbour piles,
The likeness of a clump of peakèd isles—
And then—as if the Earth and Sea had been   80
Dissolved into one lake of fire, were seen
Those mountains towering as from waves of flame
Around the vaporous sun, from which there came
The inmost purple spirit of light, and made,
Their very peaks transparent. 'Ere it fade,'   85
Said my companion, 'I will show you soon
A better station'—so, o'er the lagune
We glided; and from that funereal bark
I leaned, and saw the city, and could mark
How from their many isles, in evening's gleam,   90
Its temples and its palaces did seem
Like fabrics of enchantment piled to Heaven.
I was about to speak, when—'We are even
Now at the point I meant,' said Maddalo,
And bade the gondolieri cease to row.   95
'Look, Julian, on the west, and listen well
If you hear not a deep and heavy bell.'
I looked, and saw between us and the sun
A building on an island; such a one
As age to age might add, for uses vile,   100
A windowless, deformed and dreary pile;
And on the top an open tower, where hung
A bell, which in the radiance swayed and swung;
We could just hear its hoarse and iron tongue:
The broad sun sunk behind it, and it tolled   105
In strong and black relief.—'What we behold
Shall be the madhouse and its belfry tower,'
Said Maddalo, 'and ever at this hour
Those who may cross the water, hear that bell
Which calls the maniacs, each one from his cell,   110
To vespers.'—'As much skill as need to pray
In thanks or hope for their dark lot have they
To their stern maker,' I replied. 'O ho!
You talk as in years past,' said Maddalo.
' 'Tis strange men change not. You were ever still   115
Among Christ's flock a perilous infidel,
A wolf for the meek lambs—if you can't swim
Beware of Providence.' I looked on him,

But the gay smile had faded in his eye.
'And such,'—he cried, 'is our mortality,   120
And this must be the emblem and the sign
Of what should be eternal and divine!—
And like that black and dreary bell, the soul,
Hung in a heaven-illumined tower, must toll
Our thoughts and our desires to meet below   125
Round the rent heart and pray—as madmen do
For what? they know not,—till the night of death
As sunset that strange vision, severeth
Our memory from itself, and us from all
We sought and yet were baffled.' I recall   130
The sense of what he said, although I mar
The force of his expressions. The broad star
Of day meanwhile had sunk behind the hill,
And the black bell became invisible,
And the red tower looked gray, and all between   135
The churches, ships and palaces were seen
Huddled in gloom;—into the purple sea
The orange hues of heaven sunk silently.
We hardly spoke, and soon the gondola
Conveyed me to my lodging by the way.   140
    The following morn was rainy, cold and dim:
Ere Maddalo arose, I called on him,
And whilst I waited with his child I played;
A lovelier toy sweet Nature never made,
A serious, subtle, wild, yet gentle being,   145
Graceful without design and unforeseeing,
With eyes—Oh speak not of her eyes!—which seem
Twin mirrors of Italian Heaven, yet gleam
With such deep meaning, as we never see
But in the human countenance: with me   150
She was a special favourite: I had nursed
Her fine and feeble limbs when she came first
To this bleak world; and she yet seemed to know
On second sight her ancient playfellow,
Less changed than she was by six months or so;   155
For after her first shyness was worn out
We sate there, rolling billiard balls about,
When the Count entered. Salutations past—
'The word you spoke last night might well have cast
A darkness on my spirit—if man be   160
The passive thing you say, I should not see
Much harm in the religions and old saws
(Tho' I may never own such leaden laws)
Which break a teachless nature to the yoke:
Mine is another faith'—thus much I spoke   165

And noting he replied not, added: 'See
This lovely child, blithe, innocent and free;
She spends a happy time with little care,
While we to such sick thoughts subjected are
As came on you last night—it is our will   170
That thus enchains us to permitted ill—
We might be otherwise—we might be all
We dream of happy, high, majestical.
Where is the love, beauty, and truth we seek
But in our mind? and if we were not weak   175
Should we be less in deed than in desire?'
'Ay, if we were not weak—and we aspire
How vainly to be strong!' said Maddalo:
'You talk Utopia.' 'It remains to know,'
I then rejoined, 'and those who try may find   180
How strong the chains are which our spirit bind;
Brittle perchance as straw . . . We are assured
Much may be conquered, much may be endured,
Of what degrades and crushes us. We know
That we have power over ourselves to do   185
And suffer—what, we know not till we try;
But something nobler than to live and die—
So taught those kings of old philosophy
Who reigned, before Religion made men blind;
And those who suffer with their suffering kind   190
Yet feel their faith, religion.' 'My dear friend,'
Said Maddalo, 'my judgement will not bend
To your opinion, though I think you might
Make such a system refutation-tight
As far as words go. I knew one like you   195
Who to this city came some months ago,
With whom I argued in this sort, and he
Is now gone mad,—and so he answered me,—
Poor fellow! but if you would like to go
We'll visit him, and his wild talk will show   200
How vain are such aspiring theories.'
'I hope to prove the induction otherwise,
And that a want of that true theory, still,
Which seeks a "soul of goodness" in things ill
Or in himself or others, has thus bowed   205
His being—there are some by nature proud,
Who patient in all else demand but this—
To love and be beloved with gentleness;
And being scorned, what wonder if they die
Some living death? this is not destiny   210
But man's own wilful ill.'
                              As thus I spoke

Servants announced the gondola, and we
Through the fast-falling rain and high-wrought sea
Sailed to the island where the madhouse stands.
We disembarked. The clap of tortured hands,   215
Fierce yells and howlings and lamentings keen,
And laughter where complaint had merrier been,
Moans, shrieks, and curses, and blaspheming prayers
Accosted us. We climbed the oozy stairs
Into an old courtyard. I heard on high,   220
Then, fragments of most touching melody,
But looking up saw not the singer there—
Through the black bars in the tempestuous air
I saw, like weeds on a wrecked palace growing,
Long tangled locks flung wildly forth, and flowing,   225
Of those who on a sudden were beguiled
Into strange silence, and looked forth and smiled
Hearing sweet sounds.—Then I: 'Methinks there were
A cure of these with patience and kind care,
If music can thus move . . . but what is he   230
Whom we seek here?' 'Of his sad history
I know but this,' said Maddalo: 'he came
To Venice a dejected man, and fame
Said he was wealthy, or he had been so;
Some thought the loss of fortune wrought him woe;   235
But he was ever talking in such sort
As you do—far more sadly—he seemed hurt,
Even as a man with his peculiar wrong,
To hear but of the oppression of the strong,
Or those absurd deceits (I think with you   240
In some respects, you know) which carry through
The excellent impostors of this earth
When they outface detection—he had worth,
Poor fellow! but a humorist in his way'—
'Alas, what drove him mad?' 'I cannot say: 245
A lady came with him from France, and when
She left him and returned, he wandered then
About yon lonely isles of desert sand
Till he grew wild—he had no cash or land
Remaining,—the police had brought him here—   250
Some fancy took him and he would not bear
Removal; so I fitted up for him
Those rooms beside the sea, to please his whim,
And sent him busts and books and urns for flowers,
Which had adorned his life in happier hours,   255
And instruments of music—you may guess
A stranger could do little more or less
For one so gentle and unfortunate:

And those are his sweet strains which charm the weight
From madmen's chains, and make this Hell appear   260
A heaven of sacred silence, hushed to hear.'—
'Nay, this was kind of you—he had no claim,
As the world says'—'None—but the very same
Which I on all mankind were I as he
Fallen to such deep reverse;—his melody   265
Is interrupted—now we hear the din
Of madmen, shriek on shriek, again begin;
Let us now visit him; after this strain
He ever communes with himself again,
And sees nor hears not any.' Having said   270
These words we called the keeper, and he led
To an apartment opening on the sea—
There the poor wretch was sitting mournfully
Near a piano, his pale fingers twined
One with the other, and the ooze and wind   275
Rushed through an open casement, and did sway
His hair, and starred it with the brackish spray;
His head was leaning on a music book,
And he was muttering, and his lean limbs shook;
His lips were pressed against a folded leaf   280
In hue too beautiful for health, and grief
Smiled in their motions as they lay apart—
As one who wrought from his own fervid heart
The eloquence of passion, soon he raised
His sad meek face and eyes lustrous and glazed   285
And spoke—sometimes as one who wrote, and thought
His words might move some heart that heeded not,
If sent to distant lands: and then as one
Reproaching deeds never to be undone
With wondering self-compassion; then his speech   290
Was lost in grief, and then his words came each
Unmodulated, cold, expressionless,—
But that from one jarred accent you might guess
It was despair made them so uniform:
And all the while the loud and gusty storm   295
Hissed through the window, and we stood behind
Stealing his accents from the envious wind
Unseen. I yet remember what he said
Distinctly: such impression his words made.

'Month after month,' he cried, 'to bear this load   300
And as a jade urged by the whip and goad
To drag life on, which like a heavy chain
Lengthens behind with many a link of pain!—
And not to speak my grief—O, not to dare

To give a human voice to my despair, 305
But live and move, and, wretched thing! smile on
As if I never went aside to groan,
And wear this mask of falsehood even to those
Who are most dear—not for my own repose—
Alas! no scorn or pain or hate could be 310
So heavy as that falsehood is to me—
But that I cannot bear more altered faces
Than needs must be, more changed and cold embraces,
More misery, disappointment, and mistrust
To own me for their father . . . Would the dust 315
Were covered in upon my body now!
That the life ceased to toil within my brow!
And then these thoughts would at the least be fled;
Let us not fear such pain can vex the dead.

'What Power delights to torture us? I know 320
That to myself I do not wholly owe
What now I suffer, though in part I may.
Alas! none strewed sweet flowers upon the way
Where wandering heedlessly, I met pale Pain
My shadow, which will leave me not again— 325
If I have erred, there was no joy in error,
But pain and insult and unrest and terror;
I have not as some do, bought penitence
With pleasure, and a dark yet sweet offence,
For them,—if love and tenderness and truth 330
Had overlived hope's momentary youth,
My creed should have redeemed me from repenting;
But loathèd scorn and outrage unrelenting
Met love excited by far other seeming
Until the end was gained . . . as one from dreaming 335
Of sweetest peace, I woke, and found my state
Such as it is.—
          'O Thou, my spirit's mate
Who, for thou art compassionate and wise,
Wouldst pity me from thy most gentle eyes
If this sad writing thou shouldst ever see— 340
My secret groans must be unheard by thee,
Thou wouldst weep tears bitter as blood to know
Thy lost friend's incommunicable woe.

'Ye few by whom my nature has been weighed
In friendship, let me not that name degrade 345
By placing on your hearts the secret load
Which crushes mine to dust. There is one road
To peace and that is truth, which follow ye!
Love sometimes leads astray to misery.

Yet think not though subdued—and I may well   350
Say that I am subdued—that the full Hell
Within me would infect the untainted breast
Of sacred nature with its own unrest;
As some perverted beings think to find
In scorn or hate a medicine for the mind   355
Which scorn or hate have wounded—O how vain!
The dagger heals not but may rend again . . .
Believe that I am ever still the same
In creed as in resolve, and what may tame
My heart, must leave the understanding free,   360
Or all would sink in this keen agony—
Nor dream that I will join the vulgar cry;
Or with my silence sanction tyranny;
Or seek a moment's shelter from my pain
In any madness which the world calls gain,   365
Ambition or revenge or thoughts as stern
As those which make me what I am; or turn
To avarice or misanthropy or lust . . .
Heap on me soon, O grave, thy welcome dust!
Till then the dungeon may demand its prey,   370
And Poverty and Shame may meet and say—
Halting beside me on the public way—
"That love-devoted youth is ours—let's sit
Beside him—he may live some six months yet."
Or the red scaffold as our country bends,   375
May ask some willing victim, or ye friends
May fall under some sorrow which this heart
Or hand may share or vanquish or avert;
I am prepared—in truth with no proud joy—
To do or suffer aught, as when a boy   380
I did devote to justice and to love
My nature, worthless now! . . .

                              'I must remove
A veil from my pent mind. 'Tis torn aside!
O, pallid as Death's dedicated bride,
Thou mockery which art sitting by my side,   385
Am I not wan like thee? at the grave's call
I haste, invited to thy wedding-ball
To greet the ghastly paramour, for whom
Thou hast deserted me . . . and made the tomb
Thy bridal bed . . . But I beside your feet   390
Will lie and watch ye from my winding sheet—
Thus . . . wide awake tho' dead . . . yet stay, O stay!
Go not so soon—I know not what I say—
Hear but my reasons . . I am mad, I fear,
My fancy is o'erwrought . . thou art not here . . .   395

Pale art thou, 'tis most true . . but thou art gone,
Thy work is finished . . . I am left alone!—

   .   .   .   .

  'Nay, was it I who wooed thee to this breast
Which, like a serpent, thou envenomest
As in repayment of the warmth it lent? 400
Didst thou not seek me for thine own content?
Did not thy love awaken mine? I thought
That thou wert she who said, "You kiss me not
Ever, I fear you do not love me now"—
In truth I loved even to my overthrow 405
Her, who would fain forget these words: but they
Cling to her mind, and cannot pass away.

   .   .   .   .

  'You say that I am proud—that when I speak
My lip is tortured with the wrongs which break
The spirit it expresses . . . Never one 410
Humbled himself before, as I have done!
Even the instinctive worm on which we tread
Turns, though it wound not—then with prostrate head
Sinks in the dusk and writhes like me—and dies?
No: wears a living death of agonies! 415
As the slow shadows of the pointed grass
Mark the eternal periods, his pangs pass
Slow, ever-moving,—making moments be
As mine seem—each an immortality!

   .   .   .   .

  'That you had never seen me—never heard 420
My voice, and more than all had ne'er endured
The deep pollution of my loathed embrace—
That your eyes ne'er had lied love in my face—
That, like some maniac monk, I had torn out
The nerves of manhood by their bleeding root 425
With mine own quivering fingers, so that ne'er
Our hearts had for a moment mingled there
To disunite in horror—these were not
With thee, like some suppressed and hideous thought
Which flits athwart our musings, but can find 430
No rest within a pure and gentle mind . . .
Thou sealedst them with many a bare broad word,
And searedst my memory o'er them,—for I heard
And can forget not . . . they were ministered
One after one, those curses. Mix them up 435
Like self-destroying poisons in one cup.

And they will make one blessing which thou ne'er
Didst imprecate for, on me,—death.

    .   .   .   .   ,   .   .

                                        'It were
A cruel punishment for one most cruel,
If such can love, to make that love the fuel   440
Of the mind's hell; hate, scorn, remorse, despair:
But *me*—whose heart a stranger's tear might wear
As water-drops the sandy fountain-stone,
Who loved and pitied all things, and could moan
For woes which others hear not, and could see   445
The absent with the glance of phantasy,
And with the poor and trampled sit and weep,
Following the captive to his dungeon deep;
Me—who am as a nerve o'er which do creep
The else unfelt oppressions of this earth,   450
And was to thee the flame upon thy hearth,
When all beside was cold—that thou on me
Shouldst rain these plagues of blistering agony—
Such curses are from lips once eloquent
With love's too partial praise—let none relent   455
Who intend deeds too dreadful for a name
Henceforth, if an example for the same
They seek . . . for thou on me lookedst so, and so—
And didst speak thus . . and thus . . . I live to show
How much men bear and die not!   460

    .   .   .   .

                                'Thou wilt tell,
With the grimace of hate, how horrible
It was to meet my love when thine grew less;
Thou wilt admire how I could e'er address
Such features to love's work . . . this taunt, though true,
(For indeed Nature nor in form nor hue   465
Bestowed on me her choicest workmanship)
Shall not be thy defence . . . for since thy lip
Met mine first, years long past, since thine eye kindled
With soft fire under mine, I have not dwindled
Nor changed in mind or body, or in aught   470
But as love changes what it loveth not
After long years and many trials.
                                'How vain
Are words! I thought never to speak again,
Not even in secret,—not to my own heart—
But from my lips the unwilling accents start,   475
And from my pen the words flow as I write,
Dazzling my eyes with scalding tears . . . my sight

ᴌs dim to see that charactered in vain
On this unfeeling leaf which burns the brain
And eats into it . . . blotting all things fair   480
And wise and good which time had written there.

'Those who inflict must suffer, for they see
The work of their own hearts, and this must be
Our chastisement or recompense—O child!
I would that thine were like to be more mild   485
For both our wretched sakes . . . for thine the most
Who feelest already all that thou hast lost
Without the power to wish it thine again;
And as slow years pass, a funereal train
Each with the ghost of some lost hope or friend   490
Following it like its shadow, wilt thou bend
No thought on my dead memory?
          .   .   .   .   .   ˎ   .   .

                              'Alas, love!
Fear me not . . . against thee I would not move
A finger in despite. Do I not live
That thou mayst have less bitter cause to grieve?   495
I give thee tears for scorn and love for hate;
And that thy lot may be less desolate
Than his on whom thou tramplest, I refrain
From that sweet sleep which medicines all pain.
Then, when thou speakest of me, never say   500
"He could forgive not." Here I cast away
All human passions, all revenge, all pride;
I think, speak, act no ill; I do but hide
Under these words, like embers, every spark
Of that which has consumed me—quick and dark   505
The grave is yawning . . . as its roof shall cover
My limbs with dust and worms under and over
So let Oblivion hide this grief . . . the air
Closes upon my accents, as despair
Upon my heart—let death upon despair!'   510

He ceased, and overcome leant back awhile,
Then rising, with a melancholy smile
Went to a sofa, and lay down, and slept
A heavy sleep, and in his dreams he wept
And muttered some familiar name, and we   515
Wept without shame in his society.
I think I never was impressed so much;
The man who were not, must have lacked a touch
Of human nature . . . then we lingered not,
Although our argument was quite forgot,   520

But calling the attendants, went to dine
At Maddalo's; yet neither cheer nor wine
Could give us spirits, for we talked of him
And nothing else, till daylight made stars dim;
And we agreed his was some dreadful ill   525
Wrought on him boldly, yet unspeakable,
By a dear friend; some deadly change in love
Of one vowed deeply which he dreamed not of;
For whose sake he, it seemed, had fixed a blot
Of falsehood on his mind which flourished not   530
But in the light of all-beholding truth;
And having stamped this canker on his youth
She had abandoned him—and how much more
Might be his woe, we guessed not—he had store
Of friends and fortune once, as we could guess   535
From his nice habits and his gentleness;
These were now lost . . . it were a grief indeed
If he had changed one unsustaining reed
For all that such a man might else adorn.
The colours of his mind seemed yet unworn;   540
For the wild language of his grief was high,
Such as in measure were called poetry;
And I remember one remark which then
Maddalo made. He said: 'Most wretched men
Are cradled into poetry by wrong,   545
They learn in suffering what they teach in song.'

    If I had been an unconnected man
I, from this moment, should have formed some plan
Never to leave sweet Venice,—for to me
It was delight to ride by the lone sea;   550
And then, the town is silent—one may write
Or read in gondolas by day or night,
Having the little brazen lamp alight,
Unseen, uninterrupted; books are there,
Pictures, and casts from all those statues fair   555
Which were twin-born with poetry, and all
We seek in towns, with little to recall
Regrets for the green country. I might sit
In Maddalo's great palace, and his wit
And subtle talk would cheer the winter night   560
And make me know myself, and the firelight
Would flash upon our faces, till the day
Might dawn and make me wonder at my stay:
But I had friends in London too: the chief
Attraction here, was that I sought relief   565

From the deep tenderness that maniac wrought
Within me—'twas perhaps an idle thought—
But I imagined that if day by day
I watched him, and but seldom went away,
And studied all the beatings of his heart   570
With zeal, as men study some stubborn art
For their own good, and could by patience find
An entrance to the caverns of his mind,
I might reclaim him from his dark estate:
In friendships I had been most fortunate—   575
Yet never saw I one whom I would call
More willingly my friend; and this was all
Accomplished not; such dreams of baseless good
Oft come and go in crowds or solitude
And leave no trace—but what I now designed   580
Made for long years impression on my mind.
The following morning, urged by my affairs,
I left bright Venice.

                    After many years
And many changes I returned; the name
Of Venice, and its aspect, was the same;   585
But Maddalo was travelling far away
Among the mountains of Armenia.
His dog was dead. His child had now become
A woman; such as it has been my doom
To meet with few,—a wonder of this earth,   590
Where there is little of transcendent worth,—
Like one of Shakespeare's women: kindly she,
And, with a manner beyond courtesy,
Received her father's friend; and when I asked
Of the lorn maniac, she her memory tasked,   595
And told as she had heard the mournful tale:
'That the poor sufferer's health began to fail
Two years from my departure, but that then
The lady who had left him, came again.
Her mien had been imperious, but she now   600
Looked meek—perhaps remorse had brought her low.
Her coming made him better, and they stayed
Together at my father's—for I played,
As I remember, with the lady's shawl—
I might be six years old—but after all   605
She left him' . . . 'Why, her heart must have been tough:
How did it end?' 'And was not this enough?
They met—they parted'—'Child, is there no more?'
'Something within that interval which bore
The stamp of *why* they parted, *how* they met: 610
Yet if thine agèd eyes disdain to wet

Those wrinkled cheeks with youth's remembered tears,
Ask me no more, but let the silent years
Be closed and cered over their memory
As yon mute marble where their corpses lie.'   615
I urged and questioned still, she told me how
All happened—but the cold world shall not know.

CANCELLED FRAGMENTS OF JULIAN AND MADDALO

'What think you the dead are?' 'Why, dust and clay,
What should they be?' ' 'Tis the last hour of day.
Look on the west, how beautiful it is   620
Vaulted with radiant vapours! The deep bliss
Of that unutterable light has made
The edges of that cloud   fade
Into a hue, like some harmonious thought,
Wasting itself on that which it had wrought,   625
Till it dies   and   between
The light hues of the tender, pure, serene,
And infinite tranquillity of heaven.
Ay, beautiful! but when not. . . .'

.   .   .   .

'Perhaps the only comfort which remains   630
Is the unheeded clanking of my chains,
The which I make, and call it melody.'

NOTE BY MRS. SHELLEY

FROM the Baths of Lucca, in 1818, Shelley visited Venice; and, circumstances rendering it eligible that we should remain a few weeks in the
neighbourhood of that city, he accepted the offer of Lord Byron, who lent
him the use of a villa he rented near Este; and he sent for his family from
Lucca to join him.

I Capuccini was a villa built on the site of a Capuchin convent, demol-
ished when the French suppressed religious houses; it was situated on the
very overhanging brow of a low hill at the foot of a range of higher ones.
The house was cheerful and pleasant; a vine-trellised walk, a *pergola*,
as it is called in Italian, led from the hall-door to a summer-house at the
end of the garden, which Shelley made his study, and in which he began
the *Prometheus;* and here also, as he mentions in a letter, he wrote *Julian
and Maddalo*. A slight ravine, with a road in its depth, divided the garden
from the hill, on which stood the ruins of the ancient castle of Este, whose
dark massive wall gave forth an echo, and from whose ruined crevices
owls and bats flitted forth at night, as the crescent moon sunk behind the
black and heavy battlements. We looked from the garden over the wide
plain of Lombardy, bounded to the west by the far Apennines, while to
the east the horizon was lost in misty distance. After the picturesque but

limited view of mountain, ravine, and chestnut-wood, at the Baths of Lucca, there was something infinitely gratifying to the eye in the wide range of prospect commanded by our new abode.

Our first misfortune, of the kind from which we soon suffered even more severely, happened here. Our little girl, an infant in whose small features I fancied that I traced great resemblance to her father, showed symptoms of suffering from the heat of the climate. Teething increased her illness and danger. We were at Este, and when we became alarmed, hastened to Venice for the best advice. When we arrived at Fusina, we found that we had forgotten our passport, and the soldiers on duty attempted to prevent our crossing the laguna; but they could not resist Shelley's impetuosity at such a moment. We had scarcely arrived at Venice before life fled from the little sufferer, and we returned to Este to weep her loss.

After a few weeks spent in this retreat, which was interspersed by visits to Venice, we proceeded southward.

PROMETHEUS UNBOUND

A LYRICAL DRAMA

IN FOUR ACTS

AUDISNE HAEC AMPHIARAE, SUB TERRAM ABDITE?

PREFACE

THE Greek tragic writers, in selecting as their subject any portion of their national history or mythology, employed in their treatment of it a certain arbitrary discretion. They by no means conceived themselves bound to adhere to the common interpretation or to imitate in story as in title their rivals and predecessors. Such a system would have amounted to a resignation of those claims to preference over their competitors which incited the composition. The Agamemnonian story was exhibited on the Athenian theatre with as many variations as dramas.

I have presumed to employ a similar licence. The *Prometheus Unbound* of Æschylus supposed the reconciliation of Jupiter with his victim as the price of the disclosure of the danger threatened to his empire by the consummation of his marriage with Thetis. Thetis, according to this view of the subject, was given in marriage to Peleus, and Prometheus, by the permission of Jupiter, delivered from his captivity by Hercules. Had I framed my story on this model, I should have done no more than have attempted to restore the lost drama of Æschylus; an ambition which, if my preference to this mode of treating the subject had incited me to cherish, the recollection of the high comparison such an attempt would challenge might well abate. But, in truth, I was averse from a catastrophe so feeble as that of reconciling the Champion with the Oppressor of man-kind. The moral interest of the fable, which is so powerfully sustained by the sufferings and endurance of Prometheus, would be annihilated if we could conceive of him as unsaying his high language and quailing before his successful and perfidious adversary. The only imaginary being resembling in any degree Prometheus, is Satan; and Prometheus is, in my judgement, a more poetical character than Satan, because, in addition to courage, and majesty, and firm and patient opposition to omnipotent force, he is susceptible of being described as exempt from the taints of ambition, envy, revenge, and a desire for personal aggrandisement, which, in the Hero of *Paradise Lost*, interfere with the interest. The character of Satan engenders in the mind a pernicious casuistry which leads us to weigh his faults with his wrongs, and to excuse the former because the latter exceed all measure. In the minds of those who consider that magnificent fiction with a religious feeling it engenders something worse. But Prometheus is, as it were, the type of the highest perfection of moral and intellectual nature, impelled by the purest and the truest motives to the best and noblest ends.

This Poem was chiefly written upon the mountainous ruins of the Baths of Caracalla, among the flowery glades, and thickets of odoriferous blossoming trees, which are extended in ever winding labyrinths upon its immense platforms and dizzy arches suspended in the air. The bright blue sky of Rome, and the effect of the vigorous awakening spring in that divinest climate, and the new life with which it drenches the spirits even to intoxication, were the inspiration of this drama.

The imagery which I have employed will be found, in many instances, to have been drawn from the operations of the human mind, or from those external actions by which they are expressed. This is unusual in modern poetry, although Dante and Shakespeare are full of instances of the same kind. Dante indeed more than any other poet, and with greater success. But the Greek poets, as writers to whom no resource of awakening the sympathy of their contemporaries was unknown, were in the habitual use of this power; and it is the study of their works (since a higher merit would probably be denied me) to which I am willing that my readers should impute this singularity.

One word is due in candour to the degree in which the study of contemporary writings may have tinged my composition, for such has been a topic of censure with regard to poems far more popular, and indeed more deservedly popular, than mine. It is impossible that any one who inhabits the same age with such writers as those who stand in the foremost ranks of our own, can conscientiously assure himself that his language and tone of thought may not have been modified by the study of the productions of those extraordinary intellects. It is true, that, not the spirit of their genius, but the forms in which it has manifested itself, are due less to the peculiarities of their own minds than to the peculiarity of the moral and intellectual condition of the minds among which they have been produced. Thus a number of writers possess the form, whilst they want the spirit of those whom, it is alleged, they imitate; because the former is the endowment of the age in which they live, and the latter must be the uncommunicated lightning of their own mind.

The peculiar style of intense and comprehensive imagery which distinguishes the modern literature of England, has not been, as a general power, the product of the imitation of any particular writer. The mass of capabilities remains at every period materially the same; the circumstances which awaken it to action perpetually change. If England were divided into forty republics, each equal in population and extent to Athens, there is no reason to suppose but that, under institutions not more perfect than those of Athens, each would produce philosophers and poets equal to those who (if we except Shakespeare) have never been surpassed. We owe the great writers of the golden age of our literature to that fervid awakening of the public mind which shook to dust the oldest and most oppressive form of the Christian religion. We owe Milton to the progress and development of the same spirit: the sacred Milton was, let it ever be remembered, a republican, and a bold inquirer into morals and religion. The great writers of our own age are, we have reason to suppose, the companions and forerunners of some unimagined change in our social condition or the opinions which cement it. The cloud of mind is discharging its collected lightning, and the equilibrium between institutions and opinions is now restoring, or is about to be restored.

As to imitation, poetry is a mimetic art. It creates, but it creates by combination and representation. Poetical abstractions are beautiful and new, not because the portions of which they are composed had no previous existence in the mind of man or in nature, but because the whole produced by their combination has some intelligible and beautiful analogy with those sources of emotion and thought, and with the contemporary condition of them: one great poet is a masterpiece of nature which another not only ought to study but must study. He might as wisely and as easily determine that his mind should no longer be the mirror of all that is lovely in the visible universe, as exclude from his contemplation the beautiful which exists in the writings of a great contemporary. The pretence of doing it would be a presumption in any but the greatest; the effect, even in him, would be strained, unnatural, and ineffectual. A poet is the combined product of such internal powers as modify the nature of others; and of such external influences as excite and sustain these powers; he is not one, but both. Every man's mind is, in this respect, modified by all the objects of nature and art; by every word and every suggestion which he ever admitted to act upon his consciousness; it is the mirror upon which all forms are reflected, and in which they compose one form. Poets, not otherwise than philosophers, painters, sculptors, and musicians, are, in one sense, the creators, and, in another, the creations, of their age. From this subjection the loftiest do not escape. There is a similarity between Homer and Hesiod, between Æschylus and Euripides, between Virgil and Horace, between Dante and Petrarch, between Shakespeare and Fletcher, between Dryden and Pope; each has a generic resemblance under which their specific distinctions are arranged. If this similarity be the result of imitation, I am willing to confess that I have imitated.

Let this opportunity be conceded to me of acknowledging that I have, what a Scotch philosopher characteristically terms, 'a passion for reforming the world:' what passion incited him to write and publish his book, he omits to explain. For my part I had rather be damned with Plato and Lord Bacon, than go to Heaven with Paley and Malthus. But it is a mistake to suppose that I dedicate my poetical compositions solely to the direct enforcement of reform, or that I consider them in any degree as containing a reasoned system on the theory of human life. Didactic poetry is my abhorrence; nothing can be equally well expressed in prose that is not tedious and supererogatory in verse. My purpose has hitherto been simply to familiarise the highly refined imagination of the more select classes of poetical readers with beautiful idealisms of moral excellence; aware that until the mind can love, and admire, and trust, and hope, and endure, reasoned principles of moral conduct are seeds cast upon the highway of life which the unconscious passenger tramples into dust, although they would bear the harvest of his happiness. Should I live to accomplish what I purpose, that is, produce a systematical history of what appear to me to be the genuine elements of human society, let not the advocates of injustice and superstition flatter themselves that I should take Æschylus rather than Plato as my model.

The having spoken of myself with unaffected freedom will need little apology with the candid; and let the uncandid consider that they injure me less than their own hearts and minds by misrepresentation. Whatever talents a person may possess to amuse and instruct others, be they ever so inconsiderable, he is yet bound to exert them: if his attempt be ineffectual, let the punishment of an unaccomplished purpose have been sufficient; let none trouble themselves to heap the dust of oblivion upon his efforts; the pile they raise will betray his grave which might otherwise have been unknown.

DRAMATIS PERSONÆ

PROMETHEUS.	APOLLO.	HERCULES.
DEMOGORGON.	MERCURY.	THE PHANTASM OF JUPITER.
JUPITER.	ASIA ⎱ Ocean-	THE SPIRIT OF THE EARTH.
THE EARTH.	PANTHEA ⎰ ides.	THE SPIRIT OF THE MOON.
OCEAN.	IONE	SPIRITS OF THE HOURS.

SPIRITS.   ECHOES.   FAUNS.   FURIES.

ACT I

SCENE.—*A Ravine of Icy Rocks in the Indian Caucasus.* PROMETHEUS *is discovered bound to the Precipice.* PANTHEA *and* IONE *are seated at his feet. Time, night. During the Scene, morning slowly breaks.*

Prometheus. Monarch of Gods and Dæmons, and all Spirits
But One, who throng those bright and rolling worlds
Which Thou and I alone of living things

Behold with sleepless eyes! regard this Earth
Made multitudinous with thy slaves, whom thou 5
Requitest for knee-worship, prayer, and praise,
And toil, and hecatombs of broken hearts,
With fear and self-contempt and barren hope.
Whilst me, who am thy foe, eyeless in hate,
Hast thou made reign and triumph, to thy scorn, 10
O'er mine own misery and thy vain revenge.
Three thousand years of sleep-unsheltered hours,
And moments aye divided by keen pangs
Till they seemed years, torture and solitude,
Scorn and despair,—these are mine empire:— 15
More glorious far than that which thou surveyest
From thine unenvied throne, O Mighty God!
Almighty, had I deigned to share the shame
Of thine ill tyranny, and hung not here
Nailed to this wall of eagle-baffling mountain, 20
Black, wintry, dead, unmeasured; without herb,
Insect, or beast, or shape or sound of life.
Ah me! alas, pain, pain ever, for ever!

No change, no pause, no hope! Yet I endure.
I ask the Earth, have not the mountains felt? 25
I ask yon Heaven, the all-beholding Sun,
Has it not seen? The Sea, in storm or calm,
Heaven's ever-changing Shadow, spread below,
Have its deaf waves not heard my agony?
Ah me! alas, pain, pain ever, for ever! 30

The crawling glaciers pierce me with the spears
Of their moon-freezing crystals, the bright chains
Eat with their burning cold into my bones.
Heaven's wingèd hound, polluting from thy lips
His beak in poison not his own, tears up 35
My heart; and shapeless sights come wandering by,
The ghastly people of the realm of dream,
Mocking me: and the Earthquake-fiends are charged
To wrench the rivets from my quivering wounds
When the rocks split and close again behind: 40
While from their loud abysses howling throng
The genii of the storm, urging the rage
Of whirlwind, and afflict me with keen hail.
And yet to me welcome is day and night,
Whether one breaks the hoar frost of the morn, 45
Or starry, dim, and slow, the other climbs
The leaden-coloured east; for then they lead
The wingless. crawling hours, one among whom
—As some dark Priest hales the reluctant victim—

Shall drag thee, cruel King, to kiss the blood 50
From these pale feet, which then might trample thee
If they disdained not such a prostrate slave.
Disdain! Ah no! I pity thee. What ruin
Will hunt thee undefended through wide Heaven!
How will thy soul, cloven to its depth with terror, 55
Gape like a hell within! I speak in grief,
Not exultation, for I hate no more,
As then ere misery made me wise. The curse
Once breathed on thee I would recall. Ye Mountains,
Whose many-voicèd Echoes, through the mist 60
Of cataracts, flung the thunder of that spell!
Ye icy Springs, stagnant with wrinkling frost,
Which vibrated to hear me, and then crept
Shuddering through India! Thou serenest Air,
Through which the Sun walks burning without beams!
And ye swift Whirlwinds, who on poisèd wings 66
Hung mute and moveless o'er yon hushed abyss,
As thunder, louder than your own, made rock
The orbèd world! If then my words had power,
Though I am changed so that aught evil wish 70
Is dead within; although no memory be
Of what is hate, let them not lose it now!
What was that curse? for ye all heard me speak.

    First Voice (from the Mountains).
Thrice three hundred thousand years
    O'er the Earthquake's couch we stood: 75
Oft, as men convulsed with fears,
    We trembled in our multitude.

    Second Voice (from the Springs).
Thunderbolts had parched our water,
    We had been stained with bitter blood,
And had run mute, 'mid shrieks of slaughter, 80
    Thro' a city and a solitude.

    Third Voice (from the Air).
I had clothed, since Earth uprose,
    Its wastes in colours not their own,
And oft had my serene repose
    Been cloven by many a rending groan. 85

    Fourth Voice (from the Whirlwinds).
We had soared beneath these mountains
    Unresting ages; nor had thunder,
Nor yon volcano's flaming fountains,
    Nor any power above or under
    Ever made us mute with wonder. 90

First Voice.

But never bowed our snowy crest
As at the voice of thine unrest.

Second Voice.

Never such a sound before
To the Indian waves we bore.
A pilot asleep on the howling sea   95
Leaped up from the deck in agony,
And heard, and cried, 'Ah, woe is me!'
And died as mad as the wild waves be.

Third Voice.

By such dread words from Earth to Heaven
My still realm was never riven: 100
When its wound was closed, there stood
Darkness o'er the day like blood.

Fourth Voice.

And we shrank back: for dreams of ruin
To frozen caves our flight pursuing
Made us keep silence—thus—and thus—   105
Though silence is as hell to us.

The Earth. The tongueless Caverns of the craggy hills
Cried, 'Misery!' then; the hollow Heaven replied,
'Misery!' And the Ocean's purple waves,
Climbing the land, howled to the lashing winds,   110
And the pale nations heard it, 'Misery!'
Prometheus. I heard a sound of voices: not the voice
Which I gave forth. Mother, thy sons and thou
Scorn him, without whose all-enduring will
Beneath the fierce omnipotence of Jove,   115
Both they and thou had vanished, like thin mist
Unrolled on the morning wind. Know ye not me,
The Titan? He who made his agony
The barrier to your else all-conquering foe?
Oh, rock-embosomed lawns, and snow-fed streams,   120
Now seen athwart frore vapours, deep below,
Through whose o'ershadowing woods I wandered once
With Asia, drinking life from her loved eyes;
Why scorns the spirit which informs ye, now
To commune with me? me alone, who checked,   125
As one who checks a fiend-drawn charioteer,
The falsehood and the force of him who reigns
Supreme, and with the groans of pining slaves
Fills your dim glens and liquid wildernesses:

Why answer ye not, still? Brethren!
 The Earth.   They dare not.   130
 Prometheus. Who dares? for I would hear that curse again.
Ha, what an awful whisper rises up!
'Tis scarce like sound: it tingles through the frame
As lightning tingles, hovering ere it strike.
Speak, Spirit! from thine inorganic voice   135
I only know that thou art moving near
And love. How cursed I him?
 The Earth.   How canst thou hear
Who knowest not the language of the dead?
 Prometheus. Thou art a living spirit, speak as they.
 The Earth. I dare not speak like life, lest Heaven's fell King
Should hear, and link me to some wheel of pain   141
More torturing than the one whereon I roll.
Subtle thou art and good, and though the Gods
Hear not this voice, yet thou art more than God,
Being wise and kind: earnestly hearken now.   145
 Prometheus. Obscurely through my brain, like shadows dim,
Sweep awful thoughts, rapid and thick. I feel
Faint, like one mingled in entwining love;
Yet 'tis not pleasure.
 The Earth.   No, thou canst not hear:
Thou art immortal, and this tongue is known   150
Only to those who die.
 Prometheus.   And what art thou,
O, melancholy Voice?
 The Earth.   I am the Earth,
Thy mother; she within whose stony veins,
To the last fibre of the loftiest tree
Whose thin leaves trembled in the frozen air,   155
Joy ran, as blood within a living frame,
When thou didst from her bosom, like a cloud
Of glory, arise, a spirit of keen joy!
And at thy voice her pining sons uplifted
Their prostrate brows from the polluting dust,   160
And our almighty Tyrant with fierce dread
Grew pale, until his thunder chained thee here.
Then, see those million worlds which burn and roll
Around us: their inhabitants beheld
My spherèd light wane in wide Heaven; the sea   165
Was lifted by strange tempest, and new fire
From earthquake-rifted mountains of bright snow
Shook its portentous hair beneath Heaven's frown;
Lightning and Inundation vexed the plains;
Blue thistles bloomed in cities; foodless toads   170
Within voluptuous chambers panting crawled:

When Plague had fallen on man, and beast, and worm,
And Famine; and black blight on herb and tree;
And in the corn, and vines, and meadow-grass,
Teemed ineradicable poisonous weeds   175
Draining their growth, for my wan breast was dry
With grief; and the thin air, my breath, was stained
With the contagion of a mother's hate
Breathed on her child's destroyer; ay, I heard
Thy curse, the which, if thou rememberest not,   180
Yet my innumerable seas and streams,
Mountains, and caves, and winds, and yon wide air,
And the inarticulate people of the dead,
Preserve, a treasured spell. We meditate
In secret joy and hope those dreadful words,   185
But dare not speak them.
  Prometheus.   Venerable mother!
All else who live and suffer take from thee
Some comfort; flowers, and fruits, and happy sounds,
And love, though fleeting; these may not be mine.
But mine own words, I pray, deny me not.   190
  The Earth. They shall be told. Ere Babylon was dust,
The Magus Zoroaster, my dead child,
Met his own image walking in the garden.
That apparition, sole of men, he saw.
For know there are two worlds of life and death: 195
One that which thou beholdest; but the other
Is underneath the grave, where do inhabit
The shadows of all forms that think and live
Till death unite them and they part no more;
Dreams and the light imaginings of men,   200
And all that faith creates or love desires,
Terrible, strange, sublime and beauteous shapes.
There thou art, and dost hang, a writhing shade,
'Mid whirlwind-peopled mountains; all the gods
Are there, and all the powers of nameless worlds,   205
Vast, sceptred phantoms; heroes, men, and beasts;
And Demogorgon, a tremendous gloom;
And he, the supreme Tyrant, on his throne
Of burning gold. Son, one of these shall utter
The curse which all remember. Call at will   210
Thine own ghost, or the ghost of Jupiter,
Hades or Typhon, or what mightier Gods
From all-prolific Evil, since thy ruin
Have sprung, and trampled on my prostrate sons.
Ask, and they must reply: so the revenge   215
Of the Supreme may sweep through vacant shades,
As rainy wind through the abandoned gate

Of a fallen palace.
    Prometheus.   Mother, let not aught
Of that which may be evil, pass again
My lips, or those of aught resembling me.   220
Phantasm of Jupiter, arise, appear!

Ione.

My wings are folded o'er mine ears:
    My wings are crossèd o'er mine eyes:
Yet through their silver shade appears,
    And through their lulling plumes arise,   225
A Shape, a throng of sounds;
    May it be no ill to thee
O thou of many wounds!
Near whom, for our sweet sister's sake,
Ever thus we watch and wake.   230

Panthea.

The sound is of whirlwind underground.
    Earthquake, and fire, and mountains cloven;
The shape is awful like the sound,
    Clothed in dark purple, star-inwoven.
A sceptre of pale gold   235
    To stay steps proud, o'er the slow cloud
His veinèd hand doth hold.
Cruel he looks, but calm and strong,
Like one who does, not suffers wrong.

Phantasm of Jupiter. Why have the secret powers
    of this strange world   240
Driven me, a frail and empty phantom, hither
On direst storms? What unaccustomed sounds
Are hovering on my lips, unlike the voice
With which our pallid race hold ghastly talk
In darkness? And, proud sufferer, who art thou?   245
    Prometheus. Tremendous Image, as thou art must be
He whom thou shadowest forth. I am his foe,
The Titan. Speak the words which I would hear,
Although no thought inform thine empty voice.
    The Earth. Listen! And though your echoes must be mute,
Gray mountains, and old woods, and haunted springs,   251
Prophetic caves, and isle-surrounding streams,
Rejoice to hear what yet ye cannot speak,
    Phantasm. A spirit seizes me and speaks within:
It tears me as fire tears a thunder-cloud.   255
    Panthea. See, how he lifts his mighty looks, the Heaven
Darkens above.

Ione.   He speaks! O shelter me!

Prometheus. I see the curse on gestures proud and cold,
And looks of firm defiance, and calm hate,
And such despair as mocks itself with smiles,   260
Written as on a scroll: yet speak: Oh, speak!

Phantasm.

> Fiend, I defy thee! with a calm, fixed mind,
>   All that thou canst inflict I bid thee do;
> Foul Tyrant both of Gods and Human-kind,
>   One only being shalt thou not subdue.   265
> Rain then thy plagues upon me here,
> Ghastly disease, and frenzying fear;
> And let alternate frost and fire
> Eat into me, and be thine ire
> Lightning, and cutting hail, and legioned forms   270
> Of furies, driving by upon the wounding storms.
>
> Ay, do thy worst. Thou art omnipotent.
>   O'er all things but thyself I gave thee power,
> And my own will. Be thy swift mischiefs sent
>   To blast mankind, from yon ethereal tower.   275
> Let thy malignant spirit move
> In darkness over those I love:
> On me and mine I imprecate
> The utmost torture of thy hate;
> And thus devote to sleepless agony,   280
> This undeclining head while thou must reign on high.
>
> But thou, who art the God and Lord: O, thou,
>   Who fillest with thy soul this world of woe,
> To whom all things of Earth and heaven do bow
>   In fear and worship: all-prevailing foe!   285
> I curse thee! let a sufferer's curse
> Clasp thee, his torturer, like remorse;
> Till thine Infinity shall be
> A robe of envenomed agony;
> And thine Omnipotence a crown of pain,   290
> To cling like burning gold round thy dissolving brain.
>
> Heap on thy soul, by virtue of this Curse,
>   Ill deeds, then be thou damned, beholding good;
> Both infinite as is the universe,
>   And thou, and thy self-torturing solitude.   295
> An awful image of calm power
> Though now thou sittest, let the hour
> Come, when thou must appear to be
> That which thou art internally;

And after many a false and fruitless crime 300
Scorn track thy lagging fall through boundless space
    and time.

Prometheus. Were these my words, O Parent?
The Earth.   They were thine.
Prometheus. It doth repent me: words are quick and vain;
Grief for awhile is blind, and so was mine.
I wish no living thing to suffer pain. 305

The Earth.

Misery, Oh misery to me,
That Jove at length should vanquish thee.
Wail, howl aloud, Land and Sea,
The Earth's rent heart shall answer ye.
Howl, Spirits of the living and the dead, 310
Your refuge, your defence lies fallen and vanquishèd.

First Echo.

Lies fallen and vanquishèd!

Second Echo.

Fallen and vanquishèd!

Ione.

Fear not: 'tis but some passing spasm,
    The Titan is unvanquished still. 315
But see, where through the azure chasm
    Of yon forked and snowy hill
Trampling the slant winds on high
    With golden-sandalled feet, that glow
Under plumes of purple dye, 320
Like rose-ensanguined ivory,
    A Shape comes now,
Stretching on high from his right hand
A serpent-cinctured wand.
Panthea. 'Tis Jove's world-wandering herald, Mercury. 325

Ione.

And who are those with hydra tresses
    And iron wings that climb the wind,
Whom the frowning God represses
    Like vapours steaming up behind,
Clanging loud, an endless crowd— 330

Panthea.

These are Jove's tempest-walking hounds,
Whom he gluts with groans and blood,

When charioted on sulphurous cloud
He bursts Heaven's bounds.

Ione.

Are they now led, from the thin dead   335
On new pangs to be fed?

Panthea.

The Titan looks as ever, firm, not proud.
First Fury. Ha! I scent life!
Second Fury.   Let me but look into his eyes!
Third Fury. The hope of torturing him smells like a heap
Of corpses, to a death-bird after battle.   340
First Fury. Darest thou delay, O Herald! take cheer, Hounds
Of Hell: what if the Son of Maia soon
Should make us food and sport—who can please long
The Omnipotent?
Mercury.   Back to your towers of iron,
And gnash, beside the streams of fire and wail,   345
Your foodless teeth. Geryon, arise! and Gorgon,
Chimæra, and thou Sphinx, subtlest of fiends
Who ministered to Thebes Heaven's poisoned wine,
Unnatural love, and more unnatural hate:
These shall perform your task.
First Fury.   Oh, mercy! mercy!   350
We die with our desire: drive us not back!
Mercury. Crouch then in silence.
                              Awful Sufferer!
To thee unwilling, most unwillingly
I come, by the great Father's will driven down,
To execute a doom of new revenge.   355
Alas! I pity thee, and hate myself
That I can do no more: aye from thy sight
Returning, for a season, Heaven seems Hell,
So thy worn form pursues me night and day,
Smiling reproach. Wise art thou, firm and good,   360
But vainly wouldst stand forth alone in strife
Against the Omnipotent; as yon clear lamps
That measure and divide the weary years
From which there is no refuge, long have taught
And long must teach. Even now thy Torturer arms   365
With the strange might of unimagined pains
The powers who scheme slow agonies in Hell,
And my commission is to lead them here,
Or what more subtle, foul, or savage fiends
People the abyss, and leave them to their task.   370
Be it not so! there is a secret known

To thee, and to none else of living things,
Which may transfer the sceptre of wide Heaven,
The fear of which perplexes the Supreme:
Clothe it in words, and bid it clasp his throne   375
In intercession; bend thy soul in prayer,
And like a suppliant in some gorgeous fane,
Let the will kneel within thy haughty heart:
For benefits and meek submission tame
The fiercest and the mightiest.
   Prometheus.   Evil minds   380
Change good to their own nature. I gave all
He has; and in return he chains me here
Years, ages, night and day: whether the Sun
Split my parched skin, or in the moony night
The crystal-wingèd snow cling round my hair: 385
Whilst my belovèd race is trampled down
By his thought-executing ministers.
Such is the tyrant's recompense: 'tis just:
He who is evil can receive no good;
And for a world bestowed, or a friend lost,   390
He can feel hate, fear, shame; not gratitude:
He but requites me for his own misdeed.
Kindness to such is keen reproach, which breaks
With bitter stings the light sleep of Revenge.
Submission, thou dost know I cannot try: 395
For what submission but that fatal word,
The death-seal of mankind's captivity,
Like the Sicilian's hair-suspended sword,
Which trembles o'er his crown, would he accept,
Or could I yield? Which yet I will not yield.   400
Let others flatter Crime, where it sits throned
In brief Omnipotence: secure are they:
For Justice, when triumphant, will weep down
Pity, not punishment, on her own wrongs,
Too much avenged by those who err. I wait,   405
Enduring thus, the retributive hour
Which since we spake is even nearer now.
But hark, the hell-hounds clamour: fear delay:
Behold! Heaven lowers under thy Father's frown.
  Mercury. Oh, that we might be spared: I to inflict   410
And thou to suffer! Once more answer me:
Thou knowest not the period of Jove's power?
  Prometheus. I know but this, that it must come.
  Mercury.   Alas!
Thou canst not count thy years to come of pain?
  Prometheus. They last while Jove must reign: nor
   more, nor less   415

Do I desire or fear.

Mercury.   Yet pause, and plunge
Into Eternity, where recorded time,
Even all that we imagine, age on age,
Seems but a point, and the reluctant mind
Flags wearily in its unending flight,   420
Till it sink, dizzy, blind, lost, shelterless;
Perchance it has not numbered the slow years
Which thou must spend in torture, unreprieved?

Prometheus. Perchance no thought can count them, yet
     they pass.

Mercury. If thou might'st dwell among the Gods the while
Lapped in voluptuous joy?

Prometheus.   I would not quit   426
This bleak ravine, these unrepentant pains.

Mercury. Alas! I wonder at, yet pity thee.

Prometheus. Pity the self-despising slaves of Heaven,
Not me, within whose mind sits peace serene,   430
As light in the sun, throned: how vain is talk!
Call up the fiends.

Ione.   O, sister, look! White fire
Has cloven to the roots yon huge snow-loaded cedar;
How fearfully God's thunder howls behind!

Mercury. I must obey his words and thine; alas!   435
Most heavily remorse hangs at my heart!

Panthea. See where the child of Heaven, with wingèd feet,
Runs down the slanted sunlight of the dawn.

Ione. Dear sister, close thy plumes over thine eyes
Lest thou behold and die: they come: they come   440
Blackening the birth of day with countless wings,
And hollow underneath, like death.

First Fury.   Prometheus!

Second Fury. Immortal Titan!

Third Fury.   Champion of Heaven's slaves!

Prometheus. He whom some dreadful voice invokes is here,
Prometheus, the chained Titan. Horrible forms,   445
What and who are ye? Never yet there came
Phantasms so foul through monster-teeming Hell
From the all-miscreative brain of Jove;
Whilst I behold such execrable shapes,
Methinks I grow like what I contemplate,   450
And laugh and stare in loathsome sympathy.

First Fury. We are the ministers of pain, and fear,
And disappointment, and mistrust, and hate,
And clinging crime; and as lean dogs pursue
Through wood and lake some struck and sobbing fawn,   455
We track all things that weep, and bleed, and live,

When the great King betrays them to our will.
    Prometheus. Oh! many fearful natures in one name,
I know ye; and these lakes and echoes know
The darkness and the clangour of your wings.   460
But why more hideous than your loathèd selves
Gather ye up in legions from the deep?
    Second Fury. We knew not that: Sisters, rejoice, rejoice!
    Prometheus. Can aught exult in its deformity?
    Second Fury. The beauty of delight makes lovers glad,   465
Gazing on one another: so are we.
As from the rose which the pale priestess kneels
To gather for her festal crown of flowers
The aëreal crimson falls, flushing her cheek,
So from our victim's destined agony   470
The shade which is our form invests us round,
Else we are shapeless as our mother Night.
    Prometheus. I laugh your power, and his who sent you here,
To lowest scorn. Pour forth the cup of pain.
    First Fury. Thou thinkest we will rend thee bone from bone,
And nerve from nerve, working like fire within?   476
    Prometheus. Pain is my element, as hate is thine;
Ye rend me now: I care not.
    Second Fury.   Dost imagine
We will but laugh into thy lidless eyes?
    Prometheus. I weigh not what ye do, but what ye suffer,   480
Being evil. Cruel was the power which called
You, or aught else so wretched, into light.
    Third Fury. Thou think'st we will live through thee, one
        by one,
Like animal life, and though we can obscure not
The soul which burns within, that we will dwell   485
Beside it, like a vain loud multitude
Vexing the self-content of wisest men:
That we will be dread thought beneath thy brain,
And foul desire round thine astonished heart,
And blood within thy labyrinthine veins   490
Crawling like agony?
    Prometheus.   Why, we are thus now;
Yet am I king over myself, and rule
The torturing and conflicting throngs within,
As Jove rules you when Hell grows mutinous.   494

Chorus of Furies.

From the ends of the earth, from the ends of the earth,
Where the night has its grave and the morning its birth,
        Come, come, come!
Oh, ye who shake hills with the scream of your mirth,

When cities sink howling in ruin; and ye
Who with wingless footsteps trample the sea,   500
And close upon Shipwreck and Famine's track,
Sit chattering with joy on the foodless wreck;
        Come, come, come!
    Leave the bed, low, cold, and red,
    Strewed beneath a nation dead;   505
    Leave the hatred, as in ashes
        Fire is left for future burning:
    It will burst in bloodier flashes
        When ye stir it, soon returning:
    Leave the self-contempt implanted   510
    In young spirits, sense-enchanted,
        Misery's yet unkindled fuel:
    Leave Hell's secrets half unchanted
        To the maniac dreamer; cruel
    More than ye can be with hate   515
        Is he with fear.
        Come, come, come!
We are steaming up from Hell's wide gate
And we burthen the blast of the atmosphere,
But vainly we toil till ye come here.   520

Ione. Sister, I hear the thunder of new wings.
Panthea. These solid mountains quiver with the sound
Even as the tremulous air: their shadows make
The space within my plumes more black than night.

First Fury.

    Your call was as a wingèd car   525
    Driven on whirlwinds fast and far;
    It rapped us from red gulfs of war.

Second Fury.

From wide cities, famine-wasted;

Third Fury.

Groans half heard, and blood untasted;

Fourth Fury.

    Kingly conclaves stern and cold,   530
    Where blood with gold is bought and sold;

Fifth Fury.

From the furnace, white and hot,
In which—

A Fury.

Speak not: whisper not:
I know all that ye would tell,
But to speak might break the spell   535
Which must bend the Invincible,
    The stern of thought;
He yet defies the deepest power of Hell.

A Fury.

Tear the veil!

Another Fury.

It is torn.

Chorus.

The pale stars of the morn
Shine on a misery, dire to be borne.   540
Dost thou faint, mighty Titan? We laugh thee to scorn.
Dost thou boast the clear knowledge thou waken'dst for man?
Then was kindled within him a thirst which outran
Those perishing waters; a thirst of fierce fever,
Hope, love, doubt, desire, which consume him for ever.   545
    One came forth of gentle worth
    Smiling on the sanguine earth;
    His words outlived him, like swift poison
        Withering up truth, peace, and pity.
    Look! where round the wide horizon   550
        Many a million-peopled city
    Vomits smoke in the bright air.
    Hark that outcry of despair!
    'Tis his mild and gentle ghost
        Wailing for the faith he kindled: 555
    Look again, the flames almost
        To a glow-worm's lamp have dwindled:
'The survivors round the embers
    Gather in dread.
                Joy, joy, joy!   560
Past ages crowd on thee, but each one remembers,
And the future is dark, and the present is spread
Like a pillow of thorns for thy slumberless head.

Semichorus I.

    Drops of bloody agony flow
    From his white and quivering brow.   565
    Grant a little respite now:
    See a disenchanted nation

Springs like day from desolation;
To Truth its state is dedicate,
And Freedom leads it forth, her mate; 570
A legioned band of linkèd brothers
Whom Love calls children—

Semichorus II.

'Tis another's:
See how kindred murder kin:
'Tis the vintage-time for death and sin:
Blood, like new wine, bubbles within: 575
Till Despair smothers
The struggling world, which slaves and tyrants win.
[*All the* Furies *vanish, except one.*

Ione. Hark, sister! what a low yet dreadful groan
Quite unsuppressed is tearing up the heart
Of the good Titan, as storms tear the deep, 580
And beasts hear the sea moan in inland caves.
Darest thou observe how the fiends torture him?
    Panthea. Alas! I looked forth twice, but will no more.
    Ione. What didst thou see?
    Panthea.   A woful sight: a youth
With patient looks nailed to a crucifix. 585
    Ione. What next?
    Panthea.   The heaven around, the earth below
Was peopled with thick shapes of human death,
All horrible, and wrought by human hands,
And some appeared the work of human hearts.
For men were slowly killed by frowns and smiles: 590
And other sights too foul to speak and live
Were wandering by. Let us not tempt worse fear
By looking forth: those groans are grief enough.
    Fury. Behold an emblem: those who do endure
Deep wrongs for man, and scorn, and chains, but heap 595
Thousandfold torment on themselves and him.
    Prometheus. Remit the anguish of that lighted stare;
Close those wan lips; let that thorn-wounded brow
Stream not with blood; it mingles with thy tears!
Fix, fix those tortured orbs in peace and death, 600
So thy sick throes shake not that crucifix,
So those pale fingers play not with thy gore.
O, horrible! Thy name I will not speak,
It hath become a curse. I see, I see
The wise, the mild, the lofty, and the just, 605
Whom thy slaves hate for being like to thee,
Some hunted by foul lies from their heart's home,
An early-chosen, late-lamented home;

As hooded ounces cling to the driven hind;
Some linked to corpses in unwholesome cells: 610
Some—Hear I not the multitude laugh loud?—
Impaled in lingering fire: and mighty realms
Float by my feet, like sea-uprooted isles,
Whose sons are kneaded down in common blood
By the red light of their own burning homes.   615
    Fury. Blood thou canst see, and fire; and canst hear groans;
Worse things, unheard, unseen, remain behind.
    Prometheus. Worse?
    Fury.   In each human heart terror survives
The ravin it has gorged: the loftiest fear
All that they would disdain to think were true: 620
Hypocrisy and custom make their minds
The fanes of many a worship, now outworn.
They dare not devise good for man's estate,
And yet they know not that they do not dare.
The good want power, but to weep barren tears.   625
The powerful goodness want: worse need for them.
The wise want love; and those who love want wisdom; .
And all best things are thus confused to ill.
Many are strong and rich, and would be just,
But live among their suffering fellow-men   630
As if none felt: they know not what they do.
    Prometheus. Thy words are like a cloud of wingèd snakes;
And yet I pity those they torture not.
    Fury. Thou pitiest them? I speak no more!   [*Vanishes.*
    Prometheus.   Ah woe!
Ah woe! Alas! pain, pain ever, for ever!   635
I close my tearless eyes, but see more clear
Thy works within my woe-illumèd mind,
Thou subtle tyrant! Peace is in the grave.
The grave hides all things beautiful and good:
I am a God and cannot find it there,   640
Nor would I seek it: for, though dread revenge,
This is defeat, fierce king, not victory.
The sights with which thou torturest gird my soul
With new endurance, till the hour arrives
When they shall be no types of things which are.   645
    Panthea. Alas! what sawest thou more?
    Prometheus.   There are two woes:
To speak, and to behold; thou spare me one.
Names are there, Nature's sacred watchwords, they
Were borne aloft in bright emblazonry;
The nations thronged around, and cried aloud,   650
As with one voice, Truth, liberty, and love!
Suddenly fierce confusion fell from heaven

Among them: there was strife, deceit, and fear:
Tyrants rushed in, and did divide the spoil.
This was the shadow of the truth I saw.   655
   The Earth. I felt thy torture, son; with such mixed joy
As pain and virtue give. To cheer thy state
I bid ascend those subtle and fair spirits,
Whose homes are the dim caves of human thought,
And who inhabit, as birds wing the wind,   660
Its world-surrounding aether: they behold
Beyond that twilight realm, as in a glass,
The future: may they speak comfort to thee!
   Panthea. Look, sister, where a troop of spirits gather,
Like flocks of clouds in spring's delightful weather,   665
Thronging in the blue air!
   Ione.   And see! more come,
Like fountain-vapours when the winds are dumb,
That climb up the ravine in scattered lines.
And, hark! is it the music of the pines?
Is it the lake? Is it the waterfall?   670
   Panthea. 'Tis something sadder, sweeter far than all.

Chorus of Spirits.

From unremembered ages we
Gentle guides and guardians be
Of heaven-oppressed mortality;
And we breathe, and sicken not,   675
The atmosphere of human thought:
Be it dim, and dank, and gray,
Like a storm-extinguished day,
Travelled o'er by dying gleams;
   Be it bright as all between   680
Cloudless skies and windless streams,
   Silent, liquid, and serene;
As the birds within the wind,
   As the fish within the wave,
As the thoughts of man's own mind   685
   Float through all above the grave;
We make there our liquid lair,
Voyaging cloudlike and unpent
Through the boundless element:
Thence we bear the prophecy   690
Which begins and ends in thee!

   Ione. More yet come, one by one: the air around them
Looks radiant as the air around a star.

First Spirit.

On a battle-trumpet's blast
I fled hither, fast, fast, fast, 695
'Mid the darkness upward cast.
From the dust of creeds outworn,
From the tyrant's banner torn,
Gathering 'round me, onward borne,
There was mingled many a cry— 700
Freedom! Hope! Death! Victory!
Till they faded through the sky;
And one sound, above, around,
One sound beneath, around, above,
Was moving; 'twas the soul of Love; 705
'Twas the hope, the prophecy,
Which begins and ends in thee.

Second Spirit.

A rainbow's arch stood on the sea,
Which rocked beneath, immovably;
And the triumphant storm did flee, 710
Like a conqueror, swift and proud,
Between, with many a captive cloud.
A shapeless, dark and rapid crowd,
Each by lightning riven in half:
I heard the thunder hoarsely laugh: 715
Mighty fleets were strewn like chaff
And spread beneath a hell of death
O'er the white waters. I alit
On a great ship lightning-split,
And speeded hither on the sigh 720
Of one who gave an enemy
His plank, then plunged aside to die.

Third Spirit.

I sate beside a sage's bed,
And the lamp was burning red
Near the book where he had fed, 725
When a Dream with plumes of flame,
To his pillow hovering came,
And I knew it was the same
Which had kindled long ago
Pity, eloquence, and woe; 730
And the world awhile below
Wore the shade, its lustre made.
It has borne me here as fleet
As Desire's lightning feet:

I must ride it back ere morrow, 735
Or the sage will wake in sorrow.

Fourth Spirit.

On a poet's lips I slept
Dreaming like a love-adept
In the sound his breathing kept;
Nor seeks nor finds he mortal blisses, 740
But feeds on the aëreal kisses
Of shapes that haunt thought's wildernesses.
He will watch from dawn to gloom
The lake-reflected sun illume
The yellow bees in the ivy-bloom, 745
Nor heed nor see, what things they be;
But from these create he can
Forms more real than living man,
Nurslings of immortality!
One of these awakened me, 750
And I sped to succour thee.

Ione.

Behold'st thou not two shapes from the east and west
Come, as two doves to one belovèd nest,
Twin nurslings of the all-sustaining air
On swift still wings glide down the atmosphere? 755
And, hark! their sweet, sad voices! 'tis despair
Mingled with love and then dissolved in sound.
Panthea. Canst thou speak, sister? all my words are drowned.
Ione. Their beauty gives me voice. See how they float
On their sustaining wings of skiey grain, 760
Orange and azure deepening into gold:
Their soft smiles light the air like a star's fire.

Chorus of Spirits.

Hast thou beheld the form of Love?

Fifth Spirit.

As over wide dominions
I sped, like some swift cloud that wings the wide air's wilder-
nesses,
That planet-crested shape swept by on lightning-braided pin-
ions,
Scattering the liquid joy of life from his ambrosial tresses:
His footsteps paved the world with light; but as I passed 'twas
fading, 767
And hollow Ruin yawned behind: great sages bound in mad-
ness,

And headless patriots, and pale youths who perished, unup-
braiding,
    Gleamed in the night. I wandered o'er, till thou, O King of
        sadness,   770
Turned by thy smile the worst I saw to recollected gladness.

Sixth Spirit.

Ah, sister! Desolation is a delicate thing:
    It walks not on the earth, it floats not on the air,
But treads with lulling footstep, and fans with silent wing
    The tender hopes which in their hearts the best and gentlest
        bear;   775
Who, soothed to false repose by the fanning plumes above
    And the music-stirring motion of its soft and busy feet,
Dream visions of aëreal joy, and call the monster, Love,
    And wake, and find the shadow Pain, as he whom now we
        greet.

Chorus.

    Though Ruin now Love's shadow be,   780
    Following him, destroyingly,
        On Death's white and wingèd steed,
    Which the fleetest cannot flee,
        Trampling down both flower and weed,
    Man and beast, and foul and fair,   785
    Like a tempest through the air;
    Thou shalt quell this horseman grim,
    Woundless though in heart or limb.

Prometheus. Spirits! how know ye this shall be?

Chorus.

    In the atmosphere we breathe,   790
    As buds grow red when the snow-storms flee,
        From Spring gathering up beneath,
    Whose mild winds shake the elder brake,
    And the wandering herdsmen know
    That the white-thorn soon will blow: 795
        Wisdom, Justice, Love, and Peace,
        When they struggle to increase,
        Are to us as soft winds be
        To shepherd boys, the prophecy
        Which begins and ends in thee.   800
Ione. Where are the Spirits fled?
    Panthea.   Only a sense
Remains of them, like the omnipotence
Of music, when the inspired voice and lute
Languish, ere yet the responses are mute.

Which through the deep and labyrinthine soul, 805
Like echoes through long caverns, wind and roll.

Prometheus. How fair these airborn shapes! and yet I feel
Most vain all hope but love; and thou art far,
Asia! who, when my being overflowed,
Wert like a golden chalice to bright wine 810
Which else had sunk into the thirsty dust.
All things are still: alas! how heavily
This quiet morning weighs upon my heart;
Though I should dream I could even sleep with grief
If slumber were denied not. I would fain 815
Be what it is my destiny to be,
The saviour and the strength of suffering man,
Or sink into the original gulf of things:
There is no agony, and no solace left;
Earth can console, Heaven can torment no more. 820

Panthea. Hast thou forgotten one who watches thee
The cold dark night, and never sleeps but when
The shadow of thy spirit falls on her?

Prometheus. I said all hope was vain but love: thou lovest.

Panthea. Deeply in truth; but the eastern star looks white,
And Asia waits in that far Indian vale, 826
The scene of her sad exile; rugged once
And desolate and frozen, like this ravine;
But now invested with fair flowers and herbs,
And haunted by sweet airs and sounds, which flow 830
Among the woods and waters, from the aether
Of her transforming presence, which would fade
If it were mingled not with thine. Farewell!

END OF THE FIRST ACT.

ACT II

Scene I.—*Morning. A lovely Vale in the Indian Caucasus.* Asia *alone.*

Asia. From all the blasts of heaven thou hast descended:
Yes, like a spirit, like a thought, which makes
Unwonted tears throng to the horny eyes,
And beatings haunt the desolated heart,
Which should have learnt repose: thou hast descended 5
Cradled in tempests; thou dost wake, O Spring!
O child of many winds! As suddenly
Thou comest as the memory of a dream,
Which now is sad because it hath been sweet;
Like genius, or like joy which riseth up 10
As from the earth, clothing with golden clouds
The desert of our life.

This is tne season, this the day, the hour;
At sunrise thou shouldst come, sweet sister mine,
Too long desired, too long delaying, come!   15
How like death-worms the wingless moments crawl!
The point of one white star is quivering still
Deep in the orange light of widening morn
Beyond the purple mountains: through a chasm
Of wind-divided mist the darker lake   20
Reflects it: now it wanes: it gleams again
As the waves fade, and as the burning threads
Of woven cloud unravel in pale air:
'Tis lost! and through yon peaks of cloud-like snow
The roseate sunlight quivers: hear I not   25
The Æolian music of her sea-green plumes
Winnowing the crimson dawn?   [PANTHEA *enters.*
                          I feel, I see
Those eyes which burn through smiles that fade in tears,
Like stars half quenched in mists of silver dew.
Belovèd and most beautiful, who wearest   30
The shadow of that soul by which I live,
How late thou art! the spherèd sun had climbed
The sea; my heart was sick with hope, before
The printless air felt thy belated plumes.

Panthea. Pardon, great Sister! but my wings were faint
With the delight of a remembered dream,   36
As are the noontide plumes of summer winds
Satiate with sweet flowers. I was wont to sleep
Peacefully, and awake refreshed and calm
Before the sacred Titan's fall, and thy   40
Unhappy love, had made, through use and pity,
Both love and woe familiar to my heart
As they had grown to thine: erewhile I slept
Under the glaucous caverns of old Ocean
Within dim bowers of green and purple moss,   45
Our young Ione's soft and milky arms
Locked then, as now, behind my dark, moist hair,
While my shut eyes and cheek were pressed within
The folded depth of her life-breathing bosom:
But not as now, since I am made the wind   50
Which fails beneath the music that I bear
Of thy most wordless converse; since dissolved
Into the sense with which love talks, my rest
Was troubled and yet sweet; my waking hours
Too full of care and pain.

  Asia.   Lift up thine eyes,   55
And let me read thy dream.

    Panthea   As I have said

With our sea-sister at his feet I slept.
The mountain mists, condensing at our voice
Under the moon, had spread their snowy flakes,
From the keen ice shielding our linkèd sleep.   60
Then two dreams came. One, I remember not.
But in the other his pale wound-worn limbs
Fell from Prometheus, and the azure night
Grew radiant with the glory of that form
Which lives unchanged within, and his voice fell   65
Like music which makes giddy the dim brain,
Faint with intoxication of keen joy:
'Sister of her whose footsteps pave the world
With loveliness—more fair than aught but her,
Whose shadow thou art—lift thine eyes on me.'   70
I lifted them: the overpowering light
Of that immortal shape was shadowed o'er
By love; which, from his soft and flowing limbs,
And passion-parted lips, and keen, faint eyes,
Steamed forth like vaporous fire; an atmosphere   75
Which wrapped me in its all-dissolving power,
As the warm aether of the morning sun
Wraps ere it drinks some cloud of wandering dew.
I saw not, heard not, moved not, only felt
His presence flow and mingle through my blood   80
Till it became his life, and his grew mine,
And I was thus absorbed, until it passed,
And like the vapours when the sun sinks down,
Gathering again in drops upon the pines,
And tremulous as they, in the deep night   85
My being was condensed; and as the rays
Of thought were slowly gathered, I could hear
His voice, whose accents lingered ere they died
Like footsteps of weak melody: thy name
Among the many sounds alone I heard   90
Of what might be articulate; though still
I listened through the night when sound was none.
Ione wakened then, and said to me:
'Canst thou divine what troubles me to-night?
I always knew what I desired before,   95
Nor ever found delight to wish in vain.
But now I cannot tell thee what I seek;
I know not; something sweet, since it is sweet
Even to desire; it is thy sport, false sister;
Thou hast discovered some enchantment old,   100
Whose spells have stolen my spirit as I slept
And mingled it with thine: for when just now
We kissed, I felt within thy parted lips

The sweet air that sustained me, and the warmth
Of the life-blood, for loss of which I faint,   105
Quivered between our intertwining arms.'
I answered not, for the Eastern star grew pale,
But fled to thee.
  Asia.   Thou speakest, but thy words
Are as the air: I feel them not: Oh, lift
Thine eyes, that I may read his written soul!   110
  Panthea. I lift them though they droop beneath the load
Of that they would express: what canst thou see
But thine own fairest shadow imaged there?
  Asia. Thine eyes are like the deep, blue, boundless heaven
Contracted to two circles underneath   115
Their long, fine lashes; dark, far, measureless,
Orb within orb, and line through line inwoven.
  Panthea. Why lookest thou as if a spirit passed?
  Asia. There is a change: beyond their inmost depth
I see a shade, a shape: 'tis He, arrayed   120
In the soft light of his own smiles, which spread
Like radiance from the cloud-surrounded moon.
Prometheus, it is thine! depart not yet!
Say not those smiles that we shall meet again
Within that bright pavilion which their beams   125
Shall build o'er the waste world? The dream is told.
What shape is that between us? Its rude hair
Roughens the wind that lifts it, its regard
Is wild and quick, yet 'tis a thing of air,
For through its gray robe gleams the golden dew   130
Whose stars the noon has quenched not.
  Dream.   Follow! Follow!
  Panthea. It is mine other dream.
  Asia.   It disappears.
  Panthea. It passes now into my mind. Methought
As we sate here, the flower-infolding buds
Burst on yon lightning-blasted almond-tree,   135
When swift from the white Scythian wilderness
A wind swept forth wrinkling the Earth with frost:
I looked, and all the blossoms were blown down;
But on each leaf was stamped, as the blue bells
Of Hyacinth tell Apollo's written grief,   140
O, FOLLOW, FOLLOW!
  Asia.   As you speak, your words
Fill, pause by pause, my own forgotten sleep
With shapes. Methought among these lawns together
We wandered, underneath the young gray dawn,
And multitudes of dense white fleecy clouds   145
Were wandering in thick flocks along the mountains

Shepherded by the slow, unwilling wind;
And the white dew on the new-bladed grass,
Just piercing the dark earth, hung silently;
And there was more which I remember not: 150
But on the shadows of the morning clouds,
Athwart the purple mountain slope, was written
FOLLOW, O, FOLLOW! as they vanished by;
And on each herb, from which Heaven's dew had fallen,
The like was stamped, as with a withering fire;   155
A wind arose among the pines; it shook
The clinging music from their boughs, and then
Low, sweet, faint sounds, like the farewell of ghosts,
Were heard: O, FOLLOW, FOLLOW, FOLLOW ME!
And then I said: 'Panthea, look on me.'   160
But in the depth of those belovèd eyes
Still I saw, FOLLOW, FOLLOW!
    Echo.   Follow, follow!
    Panthea. The crags, this clear spring morning, mock
        our voices
As they were spirit-tongued.
    Asia.   It is some being
Around the crags. What fine clear sounds! O, list!   165

             Echoes (unseen).
             Echoes we: listen!
             We cannot stay:
             As dew-stars glisten
                Then fade away—
                    Child of Ocean!   170

    Asia. Hark! Spirits speak. The liquid responses
Of their aëreal tongues yet sound.
    Panthea.   I hear.
                Echoes.
        O, follow, follow,
           As our voice recedeth
        Through the caverns hollow,   175
            Where the forest spreadeth;
              (*More distant.*)
          O, follow, follow!
        Through the caverns hollow,
    As the song floats thou pursue,
    Where the wild bee never flew,   180
Through the noontide darkness deep,
By the odour-breathing sleep
Of faint night flowers, and the waves
At the fountain-lighted caves,

While our music, wild and sweet,   185
Mocks thy gently falling feet,
    Child of Ocean!

Asia. Shall we pursue the sound? It grows more faint
And distant.
Panthea.   List! the strain floats nearer now.

            Echoes.

In the world unknown   190
    Sleeps a voice unspoken;
By thy step alone
    Can its rest be broken;
        Child of Ocean!

Asia. How the notes sink upon the ebbing wind!   195

            Echoes.

O, follow, follow!
    Through the caverns hollow,
As the song floats thou pursue,
By the woodland noontide dew;
By the forest, lakes, and fountains,   200
Through the many-folded mountains;
To the rents, and gulfs, and chasms,
Where the Earth reposed from spasms,
On the day when He and thou
Parted, to commingle now;   205
        Child of Ocean!

Asia. Come, sweet Panthea, link thy hand in mine,
And follow, ere the voices fade away.

SCENE II.—*A Forest, intermingled with Rocks and Caverns.* ASIA *and*
PANTHEA *pass into it. Two young Fauns are sitting on a Rock lis-*
tening.

       Semichorus I. of Spirits.

The path through which that lovely twain
    Have passed, by cedar, pine, and yew,
    And each dark tree that ever grew,
    Is curtained out from Heaven's wide blue;
Nor sun, nor moon, nor wind, nor rain,   5
    Can pierce its interwoven bowers,
    Nor aught, save where some cloud of dew,
Drifted along the earth-creeping breeze,
Between the trunks of the hoar trees,
    Hangs each a pearl in the pale flowers   10
    Of the green laurel, blown anew;
And bends, and then fades silently,
One frail and fair anemone:
Or when some star of many a one

That climbs and wanders through steep night,   15
Has found the cleft through which alone
Beams fall from high those depths upon
Ere it is borne away, away,
By the swift Heavens that cannot stay,
It scatters drops of golden light,   20
Like lines of rain that ne'er unite:
And the gloom divine is all around,
And underneath is the mossy ground.

Semichorus II.

There the voluptuous nightingales,
    Are awake through all the broad noonday.   25
When one with bliss or sadness fails,
        And through the windless ivy-boughs,
        Sick with sweet love, droops dying away
On its mate's music-panting bosom;
Another from the swinging blossom,   30
        Watching to catch the languid close
    Of the last strain, then lifts on high
    The wings of the weak melody,
'Till some new strain of feeling bear
    The song, and all the woods are mute;   35
When there is heard through the dim air
The rush of wings, and rising there
    Like many a lake-surrounded flute,
Sounds overflow the listener's brain
So sweet, that joy is almost pain.   40

Semichorus I.

There those enchanted eddies play
    Of echoes, music-tongued, which draw,
    By Demogorgon's mighty law,
    With melting rapture, or sweet awe,
All spirits on that secret way;   45
    As inland boats are driven to Ocean
Down streams made strong with mountain-thaw:
        And first there comes a gentle sound
        To those in talk or slumber bound,
        And wakes the destined soft emotion,—   50
Attracts, impels them; those who saw
    Say from the breathing earth behind
    There steams a plume-uplifting wind
Which drives them on their path, while they
    Believe their own swift wings and feet   55
The sweet desires within obey:
And so they float upon their way,

Until, still sweet, but loud and strong,
The storm of sound is driven along,
    Sucked up and hurrying: as they fleet   60
    Behind, its gathering billows meet
And to the fatal mountain bear
Like clouds amid the yielding air.
First Faun. Canst thou imagine where those spirits live
Which make such delicate music in the woods?   65
We haunt within the least frequented caves
And closest coverts, and we know these wilds,
Yet never meet them, though we hear them oft:
Where may they hide themselves?
    Second Faun.   'Tis hard to tell:
I have heard those more skilled in spirits say,   70
The bubbles, which the enchantment of the sun
Sucks from the pale faint water-flowers that pave
The oozy bottom of clear lakes and pools,
Are the pavilions where such dwell and float
Under the green and golden atmosphere   75
Which noontide kindles through the woven leaves;
And when these burst, and the thin fiery air,
The which they breathed within those lucent domes,
Ascends to flow like meteors through the night,
They ride on them, and rein their headlong speed,   80
And bow their burning crests, and glide in fire
Under the waters of the earth again.
    First Faun. If such live thus, have others other lives,
Under pink blossoms or within the bells
Of meadow flowers, or folded violets deep,   85
Or on their dying odours, when they die,
Or in the sunlight of the spherèd dew?
    Second Faun. Ay, many more which we may well divine.
But, should we stay to speak, noontide would come,
And thwart Silenus find his goats undrawn,   90
And grudge to sing those wise and lovely songs
Of Fate, and Chance, and God, and Chaos old,
And Love, and the chained Titan's woful doom,
And how he shall be loosed, and make the earth
One brotherhood: delightful strains which cheer   95
Our solitary twilights, and which charm
To silence the unenvying nightingales.

SCENE III.—*A Pinnacle of Rock among Mountains.*
ASIA *and* PANTHEA.

Panthea. Hither the sound has borne us—to the realm
Of Demogorgon, and the mighty portal,

Like a volcano's meteor-breathing chasm,
Whence the oracular vapour is hurled up
Which lonely men drink wandering in their youth,   5
And call truth, virtue, love, genius, or joy,
That maddening wine of life, whose dregs they drain
To deep intoxication; and uplift,
Like Mænads who cry loud, Evoe! Evoe!
The voice which is contagion to the world.   10
    Asia. Fit throne for such a Power! Magnificent!
How glorious art thou, Earth! And if thou be
The shadow of some spirit lovelier still,
Though evil stain its work, and it should be
Like its creation, weak yet beautiful,   15
I could fall down and worship that and thee.
Even now my heart adoreth: Wonderful!
Look, sister, ere the vapour dim thy brain:
Beneath is a wide plain of billowy mist,
As a lake, paving in the morning sky,   20
With azure waves which burst in silver light,
Some Indian vale. Behold it, rolling on
Under the curdling winds, and islanding
The peak whereon we stand, midway, around,
Encinctured by the dark and blooming forests,   25
Dim twilight-lawns, and stream-illumèd caves,
And wind-enchanted shapes of wandering mist;
And far on high the keen sky-cleaving mountains
From icy spires of sun-like radiance fling
The dawn, as lifted Ocean's dazzling spray,   30
From some Atlantic islet scattered up,
Spangles the wind with lamp-like water-drops.
The vale is girdled with their walls, a howl
Of cataracts from their thaw-cloven ravines,
Satiates the listening wind, continuous, vast,   35
Awful as silence. Hark! the rushing snow!
The sun-awakened avalanche! whose mass,
Thrice sifted by the storm, had gathered there
Flake after flake, in heaven-defying minds
As thought by thought is piled, till some great truth   40
Is loosened, and the nations echo round,
Shaken to their roots, as do the mountains now.
    Panthea. Look how the gusty sea of mist is breaking
In crimson foam, even at our feet! it rises
As Ocean at the enchantment of the moon   45
Round foodless men wrecked on some oozy isle.
    Asia. The fragments of the clouds are scattered up;
The wind that lifts them disentwines my hair;
Its billows now sweep o'er mine eyes; my brain

Grows dizzy; see'st thou shapes within the mist?   50
    Panthea. A countenance with beckoning smiles: there burns
An azure fire within its golden locks!
Another and another: hark! they speak!

          Song of Spirits.
        To the deep, to the deep,
               Down, down!   55
        Through the shade of sleep,
        Through the cloudy strife
        Of Death and of Life;
        Through the veil and the bar
        Of things which seem and are   60
    Even to the steps of the remotest throne,
               Down, down!

        While the sound whirls around,
               Down, down!
        As the fawn draws the hound,   65
        As the lightning the vapour,
        As a weak moth the taper;
        Death, despair; love, sorrow;
        Time both; to-day, to-morrow;
    As steel obeys the spirit of the stone,   70
               Down, down!

        Through the gray, void abysm,
               Down, down!
        Where the air is no prism,
        And the moon and stars are not,   75
        And the cavern-crags wear not
        The radiance of Heaven,
        Nor the gloom to Earth given,
    Where there is One pervading, One alone,
               Down, down!   80

        In the depth of the deep,
               Down, down!
        Like veiled lightning asleep,
        Like the spark nursed in embers,
        The last look Love remembers,   85
        Like a diamond, which shines
        On the dark wealth of mines,
    A spell is treasured but for thee alone.
               Down, down!

        We have bound thee, we guide thee;   90
               Down, down!

With the bright form beside thee;
Resist not the weakness,
Such strength is in meekness
That the Eternal, the Immortal,   95
Must unloose through life's portal
The snake-like Doom coiled underneath his throne
By that alone.

SCENE IV.—*The Cave of Demogorgon.* ASIA *and* PANTHEA.

Panthea. What veilèd form sits on that ebon throne?
Asia. The veil has fallen.
Panthea.   I see a mighty darkness
Filling the seat of power, and rays of gloom
Dart round, as light from the meridian sun.
—Ungazed upon and shapeless; neither limb,   5
Nor form, nor outline; yet we feel it is
A living Spirit.
Demogorgon. Ask what thou wouldst know.
Asia. What canst thou tell?
Demogorgon.   All things thou dar'st demand.
Asia. Who made the living world?
Demogorgon.   God.
Asia.   Who made all
That it contains? thought, passion, reason, will,   10
Imagination?
Demogorgon. God: Almighty God.
Asia. Who made that sense which, when the winds of Spring
In rarest visitation, or the voice
Of one belovèd heard in youth alone,
Fills the faint eyes with falling tears which dim   15
The radiant looks of unbewailing flowers,
And leaves this peopled earth a solitude
When it returns no more?
Demogorgon.   Merciful God.
Asia. And who made terror, madness, crime, remorse,
Which from the links of the great chain of things,   20
To every thought within the mind of man
Sway and drag heavily, and each one reels
Under the load towards the pit of death;
Abandoned hope, and love that turns to hate;
And self-contempt, bitterer to drink than blood;   25
Pain, whose unheeded and familiar speech
Is howling, and keen shrieks, day after day;
And Hell, or the sharp fear of Hell?
Demogorgon.   He reigns.
Asia. Utter his name: a world pining in pain

Asks but his name: curses shall drag him down.   30
   Demogorgon. He reigns.
   Asia.   I feel, I know it: who?
   Demogorgon.   He reigns.
   Asia. Who reigns? There was the Heaven and Earth at first,
And Light and Love; then Saturn, from whose throne
Time fell, an envious shadow: such the state
Of the earth's primal spirits beneath his sway,   35
As the calm joy of flowers and living leaves
Before the wind or sun has withered them
And semivital worms; but he refused
The birthright of their being, knowledge, power,
The skill which wields the elements, the thought   40
Which pierces this dim universe like light,
Self-empire, and the majesty of love;
For thirst of which they fainted. Then Prometheus
Gave wisdom, which is strength, to Jupiter,
And with this law alone, 'Let man be free,'   45
Clothed him with the dominion of wide Heaven.
To know nor faith, nor love, nor law; to be
Omnipotent but friendless is to reign;
And Jove now reigned; for on the race of man
First famine, and then toil, and then disease,   50
Strife, wounds, and ghastly death unseen before,
Fell; and the unseasonable seasons drove
With alternating shafts of frost and fire,
Their shelterless, pale tribes to mountain caves:
And in their desert hearts fierce wants he sent,   55
And mad disquietude, and shadows idle
Of unreal good, which levied mutual war,
So ruining the lair wherein they raged.
Prometheus saw, and waked the legioned hopes
Which sleep within folded Elysian flowers,   60
Nepenthe, Moly, Amaranth, fadeless blooms,
That they might hide with thin and rainbow wings
The shape of Death; and Love he sent to bind
The disunited tendrils of that vine
Which bears the wine of life, the human heart;   65
And he tamed fire which like some beast of prey,
Most terrible, but lovely, played beneath
The frown of man; and tortured to his will
Iron and gold, the slaves and signs of power,
And gems and poisons, and all subtlest forms   70
Hidden beneath the mountains and the waves.
He gave man speech, and speech created thought,
Which is the measure of the universe;
And Science struck the thrones of earth and heaven,

Which shook, but fell not; and the harmonious mind   75
Poured itself forth in all-prophetic song;
And music lifted up the listening spirit
Until it walked, exempt from mortal care,
Godlike, o'er the clear billows of sweet sound;
And human hands first mimicked and then mocked,   80
With moulded limbs more lovely than its own,
The human form, till marble grew divine;
And mothers, gazing, drank the love men see
Reflected in their race, behold, and perish.
He told the hidden power of herbs and springs,   85
And Disease drank and slept. Death grew like sleep.
He taught the implicated orbits woven
Of the wide-wandering stars; and how the sun
Changes his lair, and by what secret spell
The pale moon is transformed, when her broad eye   90
Gazes not on the interlunar sea:
He taught to rule, as life directs the limbs,
The tempest-wingèd chariots of the Ocean,
And the Celt knew the Indian. Cities then
Were built, and through their snow-like columns flowed
The warm winds, and the azure aether shone,   96
And the blue sea and shadowy hills were seen.
Such, the alleviations of his state,
Prometheus gave to man, for which he hangs
Withering in destined pain: but who rains down   100
Evil, the immedicable plague, which, while
Man looks on his creation like a God
And sees that it is glorious, drives him on,
The wreck of his own will, the scorn of earth,
The outcast, the abandoned, the alone?   105
Not Jove: while yet his frown shook Heaven, ay, when
His adversary from adamantine chains
Cursed him, he trembled like a slave. Declare
Who is his master? Is he too a slave?
    Demogorgon. All spirits are enslaved which serve things evil:
Thou knowest if Jupiter be such or no.   111
    Asia. Whom calledst thou God?
    Demogorgon.   I spoke but as ye speak,
For Jove is the supreme of living things.
    Asia. Who is the master of the slave?
    Demogorgon.   If the abysm
Could vomit forth its secrets. . . . But a voice   113
Is wanting, the deep truth is imageless;
For what would it avail to bid thee gaze
On the revolving world? What to bid speak
Fate, Time, Occasion, Chance, and Change? To these

All things are subject but eternal Love.   120
    Asia. So much I asked before, and my heart gave
The response thou hast given; and of such truths
Each to itself must be the oracle.
One more demand; and do thou answer me
As mine own soul would answer, did it know   125
That which I ask. Prometheus shall arise
Henceforth the sun of this rejoicing world:
When shall the destined hour arrive?
    Demogorgon.   Behold!
    Asia. The rocks are cloven, and through the purple night
I see cars drawn by rainbow-wingèd steeds   130
Which trample the dim winds: in each there stands
A wild-eyed charioteer urging their flight.
Some look behind, as fiends pursued them there,
And yet I see no shapes but the keen stars:
Others, with burning eyes, lean forth, and drink   135
With eager lips the wind of their own speed,
As if the thing they loved fled on before,
And now, even now, they clasped it. Their bright locks
Stream like a comet's flashing hair: they all
Sweep onward.
    Demogorgon. These are the immortal Hours,   140
Of whom thou didst demand. One waits for thee.
    Asia. A spirit with a dreadful countenance
Checks its dark chariot by the craggy gulf.
Unlike thy brethren, ghastly charioteer,
Who art thou? Whither wouldst thou bear me? Speak!   145
    Spirit. I am the shadow of a destiny
More dread than is my aspect: ere yon planet
Has set, the darkness which ascends with me
Shall wrap in lasting night heaven's kingless throne.
    Asia. What meanest thou?
    Panthea.   That terrible shadow floats
Up from its throne, as may the lurid smoke   151
Of earthquake-ruined cities o'er the sea.
Lo! it ascends the car; the coursers fly
Terrified: watch its path among the stars
Blackening the night!
    Asia.   Thus I am answered: strange!   155
    Panthea. See, near the verge, another chariot stays;
An ivory shell inlaid with crimson fire,
Which comes and goes within its sculptured rim
Of delicate strange tracery; the young spirit
That guides it has the dove-like eyes of hope;   160
How its soft smiles attract the soul! as light
Lures wingèd insects through the lampless air.

Spirit.

My coursers are fed with the lightning,
  They drink of the whirlwind's stream,
And when the red morning is bright'ning   165
  They bathe in the fresh sunbeam;
  They have strength for their swiftness I deem,
Then ascend with me, daughter of Ocean.

I desire: and their speed makes night kindle;
  I fear: they outstrip the Typhoon;   170
Ere the cloud piled on Atlas can dwindle
  We encircle the earth and the moon:
  We shall rest from long labours at noon:
Then ascend with me, daughter of Ocean.

SCENE V.—*The Car pauses within a Cloud on the top of a snowy
Mountain.* ASIA, PANTHEA, *and the* SPIRIT OF THE HOUR.

Spirit.

On the brink of the night and the morning
  My coursers are wont to respire;
But the Earth has just whispered a warning
  That their flight must be swifter than fire:
  They shall drink the hot speed of desire!   5

Asia. Thou breathest on their nostrils, but my breath
Would give them swifter speed.
    Spirit.   Alas! it could not.
    Panthea. Oh Spirit! pause, and tell whence is the light
Which fills this cloud? the sun is yet unrisen.
    Spirit. The sun will rise not until noon. Apollo   10
Is held in heaven by wonder; and the light
Which fills this vapour, as the aëreal hue
Of fountain-gazing roses fills the water,
Flows from thy mighty sister.
    Panthea.   Yes, I feel—
    Asia. What is it with thee, sister? Thou art pale.   15
    Panthea. How thou art changed! I dare not look on thee;
I feel but see thee not. I scarce endure
The radiance of thy beauty. Some good change
Is working in the elements, which suffer
Thy presence thus unveiled. The Nereids tell   20
That on the day when the clear hyaline
Was cloven at thine uprise, and thou didst stand
Within a veinèd shell, which floated on
Over the calm floor of the crystal sea,

Among the Ægean isles, and by the shores   25
Which bear thy name; love, like the atmosphere
Of the sun's fire filling the living world,
Burst from thee, and illumined earth and heaven
And the deep ocean and the sunless caves
And all that dwells within them; till grief cast   30
Eclipse upon the soul from which it came:
Such art thou now; nor is it I alone,
Thy sister, thy companion, thine own chosen one,
But the whole world which seeks thy sympathy.
Hearest thou not sounds i' the air which speak the love   35
Of all articulate beings? Feelest thou not
The inanimate winds enamoured of thee? List!   [*Music.*
    Asia. Thy words are sweeter than aught else but his
Whose echoes they are: yet all love is sweet,
Given or returned. Common as light is love,   40
And its familiar voice wearies not ever.
Like the wide heaven, the all-sustaining air,
It makes the reptile equal to the God:
They who inspire it most are fortunate,
As I am now; but those who feel it most   45
Are happier still, after long sufferings,
As I shall soon become.
    Panthea.   List! Spirits speak.

Voices in the Air, singing.

    Life of Life! thy lips enkindle
      With their love the breath between them;
    And thy smiles before they dwindle   50
      Make the cold air fire; then screen them
    In those looks, where whoso gazes
    Faints, entangled in their mazes.

    Child of Light! thy limbs are burning
      Through the vest which seems to hide them;   55
    As the radiant lines of morning
      Through the clouds ere they divide them;
    And this atmosphere divinest
    Shrouds thee wheresoe'er thou shinest.

    Fair are others; none beholds thee,   60
      But thy voice sounds low and tender
    Like the fairest, for it folds thee
      From the sight, that liquid splendour,
    And all feel, yet see thee never,
    As I feel now, lost for ever!   65

Lamp of Earth! where'er thou movest
   Its dim shapes are clad with brightness,
And the souls of whom thou lovest
   Walk upon the winds with lightness,
Till they fail, as I am failing,   70
Dizzy, lost, yet unbewailing!

Asia.

My soul is an enchanted boat,
   Which, like a sleeping swan, doth float
Upon the silver waves of thy sweet singing;
   And thine doth like an angel sit   75
   Beside a helm conducting it,
Whilst all the winds with melody are ringing.
   It seems to float ever, for ever,
   Upon that many-winding river,
   Between mountains, woods, abysses,   80
A paradise of wildernesses!
Till, like one in slumber bound,
Borne to the ocean, I float down, around,
Into a sea profound, of ever-spreading sound:

   Meanwhile thy spirit lifts its pinions   85
   In music's most serene dominions;
Catching the winds that fan that happy heaven.
   And we sail on, away, afar,
   Without a course, without a star,
But, by the instinct of sweet music driven;   90
   Till through Elysian garden islets
   By thee, most beautiful of pilots,
   Where never mortal pinnace glided,
   The boat of my desire is guided:
Realms where the air we breathe is love,   95
Which in the winds and on the waves doth move,
Harmonizing this earth with what we feel above.

   We have passed Age's icy caves,
   And Manhood's dark and tossing waves,
And Youth's smooth ocean, smiling to betray: 100
   Beyond the glassy gulfs we flee
   Of shadow-peopled Infancy,
Through Death and Birth, to a diviner day;
   A paradise of vaulted bowers,
   Lit by downward-gazing flowers,   105
   And watery paths that wind between
   Wildernesses calm and green.

Peopled by shapes too bright to see,
And rest, having beheld; somewhat like thee;
Which walk upon the sea, and chant melodiously!   110

END OF THE SECOND ACT.

ACT III

SCENE I.—*Heaven.* JUPITER *on his Throne;* THETIS *and the other
Deities assembled.*

Jupiter. Ye congregated powers of heaven, who share
The glory and the strength of him ye serve,
Rejoice! henceforth I am omnipotent.
All else had been subdued to me; alone
The soul of man, like unextinguished fire,   5
Yet burns towards heaven with fierce reproach, and doubt,
And lamentation, and reluctant prayer,
Hurling up insurrection, which might make
Our antique empire insecure, though built
On eldest faith, and hell's coeval, fear;   10
And though my curses through the pendulous air,
Like snow on herbless peaks, fall flake by flake,
And cling to it; though under my wrath's night
It climbs the crags of life, step after step,
Which wound it, as ice wounds unsandalled feet,   15
It yet remains supreme o'er misery,
Aspiring, unrepressed, yet soon to fall:
Even now have I begotten a strange wonder,
That fatal child, the terror of the earth,
Who waits but till the destined hour arrive,   20
Bearing from Demogorgon's vacant throne
The dreadful might of ever-living limbs
Which clothed that awful spirit unbeheld,
To redescend, and trample out the spark.
Pour forth heaven's wine, Idæan Ganymede,   25
And let it fill the Dædal cups like fire,
And from the flower-inwoven soil divine
Ye all-triumphant harmonies arise,
As dew from earth under the twilight stars:
Drink! be the nectar circling through your veins   30
The soul of joy, ye ever-living Gods,
Till exultation burst in one wide voice
Like music from Elysian winds.
                     And thou
Ascend beside me, veilèd in the light
Of the desire which makes thee one with me,   35
Thetis. bright image of eternity!

When thou didst cry, 'Insufferable might!
God! Spare me! I sustain not the quick flames,
The penetrating presence; all my being,
Like him whom the Numidian seps did thaw   40
Into a dew with poison, is dissolved,
Sinking through its foundations:' even then
Two mighty spirits, mingling, made a third
Mightier than either, which, unbodied now,
Between us floats, felt, although unbeheld,   45
Waiting the incarnation, which ascends.
(Hear ye the thunder of the fiery wheels
Griding the winds?) from Demogorgon's throne.
Victory! victory! Feel'st thou not, O world,
The earthquake of his chariot thundering up   50
Olympus?

[*The Car of the* HOUR *arrives.* DEMOGORGON *descends,*
and moves towards the Throne of JUPITER.

Awful shape, what art thou? Speak!
Demogorgon. Eternity. Demand no direr name.
Descend, and follow me down the abyss.
I am thy child, as thou wert Saturn's child;
Mightier than thee: and we must dwell together   55
Henceforth in darkness. Lift thy lightnings not.
The tyranny of heaven none may retain,
Or reassume, or hold, succeeding thee:
Yet if thou wilt, as 'tis the destiny
Of trodden worms to writhe till they are dead,   60
Put forth thy might.
      Jupiter.   Detested prodigy!
Even thus beneath the deep Titanian prisons
I trample thee! thou lingerest?
                          Mercy! mercy!
No pity, no release, no respite! Oh,
That thou wouldst make mine enemy my judge,   65
Even where he hangs, seared by my long revenge,
On Caucasus! he would not doom me thus.
Gentle, and just, and dreadless, is he not
The monarch of the world? What then art thou?
No refuge! no appeal!
                    Sink with me then,   70
We two will sink on the wide waves of ruin,
Even as a vulture and a snake outspent
Drop, twisted in inextricable fight,
Into a shoreless sea. Let hell unlock
Its mounded oceans of tempestuous fire,   75
And whelm on them into the bottomless void

This desolated world, and thee, and me,
The conqueror and the conquered, and the wreck
Of that for which they combated.
                                        Ai! Ai!
The elements obey me not. I sink   80
Dizzily down, ever, for ever, down.
And, like a cloud, mine enemy above
Darkens my fall with victory! Ai, Ai!

SCENE II.—*The Mouth of a great River in the Island Atlantis.* OCEAN *is
discovered reclining near the Shore;* APOLLO *stands beside him.*

Ocean. He fell, thou sayest, beneath his conqueror's frown?
Apollo. Ay, when the strife was ended which made dim
The orb I rule, and shook the solid stars,
The terrors of his eye illumined heaven
With sanguine light, through the thick ragged skirts   5
Of the victorious darkness, as he fell:
Like the last glare of day's red agony,
Which, from a rent among the fiery clouds,
Burns far along the tempest-wrinkled deep.
    Ocean. He sunk to the abyss? To the dark void?   10
    Apollo. An eagle so caught in some bursting cloud
On Caucasus, his thunder-baffled wings
Entangled in the whirlwind, and his eyes
Which gazed on the undazzling sun, now blinded
By the white lightning, while the ponderous hail   15
Beats on his struggling form, which sinks at length
Prone, and the aëreal ice clings over it.
    Ocean. Henceforth the fields of heaven-reflecting sea
Which are my realm, will heave, unstained with blood,
Beneath the uplifting winds, like plains of corn   20
Swayed by the summer air; my streams will flow
Round many-peopled continents, and round
Fortunate isles; and from their glassy thrones
Blue Proteus and his humid nymphs shall mark
The shadow of fair ships, as mortals see   25
The floating bark of the light-laden moon
With that white star, its sightless pilot's crest,
Borne down the rapid sunset's ebbing sea;
Tracking their path no more by blood and groans,
And desolation, and the mingled voice   30
Of slavery and command; but by the light
Of wave-reflected flowers, and floating odours,
And music soft, and mild, free, gentle voices,
And sweetest music, such as spirits love.
    Apollo. And I shall gaze not on the deeds which make   35

My mind obscure with sorrow, as eclipse
Darkens the sphere I guide; but list, I hear
The small, clear, silver lute of the young Spirit
That sits i' the morning star.
    Ocean.   Thou must away;
Thy steeds will pause at even, till when farewell: 40
The loud deep calls me home even now to feed it
With azure calm out of the emerald urns
Which stand for ever full beside my throne.
Behold the Nereids under the green sea,
Their wavering limbs borne on the wind-like stream,   45
Their white arms lifted o'er their streaming hair
With garlands pied and starry sea-flower crowns,
Hastening to grace their mighty sister's joy.
                     [*A sound of waves is heard.*
It is the unpastured sea hungering for calm.
Peace, monster; I come now. Farewell.
    Apollo.   Farewell.   50

SCENE III.—*Caucasus.* PROMETHEUS, HERCULES, IONE, *the* EARTH, SPIRITS, ASIA, *and* PANTHEA, *borne in the Car with the* SPIRIT OF THE HOUR. HERCULES *unbinds* PROMETHEUS, *who descends.*

    Hercules. Most glorious among Spirits, thus doth strength
To wisdom, courage, and long-suffering love,
And thee, who art the form they animate,
Minister like a slave.
    Prometheus.   Thy gentle words
Are sweeter even than freedom long desired   5
And long delayed.
                 Asia, thou light of life,
Shadow of beauty unbeheld: and ye,
Fair sister nymphs, who made long years of pain
Sweet to remember, through your love and care:
Henceforth we will not part. There is a cave,   10
All overgrown with trailing odorous plants,
Which curtain out the day with leaves and flowers,
And paved with veinèd emerald, and a fountain
Leaps in the midst with an awakening sound.
From its curved roof the mountain's frozen tears   15
Like snow, or silver, or long diamond spires,
Hang downward, raining forth a doubtful light:
And there is heard the ever-moving air,
Whispering without from tree to tree, and birds,
And bees; and all around are mossy seats,   20
And the rough walls are clothed with long soft grass;
A simple dwelling, which shall be our own:

Where we will sit and talk of time and change,
As the world ebbs and flows, ourselves unchanged.
What can hide man from mutability?   25
And if ye sigh, then I will smile; and thou,
Ione, shalt chant fragments of sea-music,
Until I weep, when ye shall smile away
The tears she brought, which yet were sweet to shed.
We will entangle buds and flowers and beams   30
Which twinkle on the fountain's brim, and make
Strange combinations out of common things,
Like human babes in their brief innocence;
And we will search, with looks and words of love,
For hidden thoughts, each lovelier than the last,   35
Our unexhausted spirits; and like lutes
Touched by the skill of the enamoured wind,
Weave harmonies divine, yet ever new,
From difference sweet where discord cannot be;
And hither come, sped on the charmèd winds,   40
Which meet from all the points of heaven, as bees
From every flower aëreal Enna feeds,
At their known island-homes in Himera,
The echoes of the human world, which tell
Of the low voice of love, almost unheard,   45
And dove-eyed pity's murmured pain, and music,
Itself the echo of the heart, and all
That tempers or improves man's life, now free;
And lovely apparitions,—dim at first,
Then radiant, as the mind, arising bright   50
From the embrace of beauty (whence the forms
Of which these are the phantoms) casts on them
The gathered rays which are reality—
Shall visit us, the progeny immortal
Of Painting, Sculpture, and rapt Poesy,   55
And arts, though unimagined, yet to be.
The wandering voices and the shadows these
Of all that man becomes, the mediators
Of that best worship love, by him and us
Given and returned; swift shapes and sounds, which grow
More fair and soft as man grows wise and kind,   61
And, veil by veil, evil and error fall:
Such virtue has the cave and place around.
                        [*Turning to the* SPIRIT OF THE HOUR.
For thee, fair Spirit, one toil remains. Ione,
Give her that curvèd shell, which Proteus old   65
Made Asia's nuptial boon, breathing within it
A voice to be accomplished, and which thou
Didst hide in grass under the hollow rock.

Ione. Thou most desired Hour, more loved and lovely
Than all thy sisters, this is the mystic shell;   70
See the pale azure fading into silver
Lining it with a soft yet glowing light:
Looks it not like lulled music sleeping there?
    Spirit. It seems in truth the fairest shell of Ocean:
Its sound must be at once both sweet and strange.   75
    Prometheus. Go, borne over the cities of mankind
On whirlwind-footed coursers: once again
Outspeed the sun around the orbèd world;
And as thy chariot cleaves the kindling air,
Thou breathe into the many-folded shell,   80
Loosening its mighty music; it shall be
As thunder mingled with clear echoes: then
Return; and thou shalt dwell beside our cave.
And thou, O, Mother Earth!—
    The Earth.   I hear, I feel;
Thy lips are on me, and their touch runs down   85
Even to the adamantine central gloom
Along these marble nerves; 'tis life, 'tis joy,
And through my withered, old, and icy frame
The warmth of an immortal youth shoots down
Circling. Henceforth the many children fair   90
Folded in my sustaining arms; all plants,
And creeping forms, and insects rainbow-winged,
And birds, and beasts, and fish, and human shapes,
Which drew disease and pain from my wan bosom,
Draining the poison of despair, shall take   95
And interchange sweet nutriment; to me
Shall they become like sister-antelopes
By one fair dam, snow-white and swift as wind,
Nursed among lilies near a brimming stream.
The dew-mists of my sunless sleep shall float   100
Under the stars like balm: night-folded flowers
Shall suck unwithering hues in their repose:
And men and beasts in happy dreams shall gather
Strength for the coming day, and all its joy:
And death shall be the last embrace of her   105
Who takes the life she gave, even as a mother
Folding her child, says, 'Leave me not again.'
    Asia. Oh, mother! wherefore speak the name of death?
Cease they to love, and move, and breathe, and speak,
Who die?
    The Earth. It would avail not to reply: 110
Thou art immortal, and this tongue is known
But to the uncommunicating dead.
Death is the veil which those who live call life:

They sleep, and it is lifted: and meanwhile
In mild variety the seasons mild　　　　　　　115
With rainbow-skirted showers, and odorous winds,
And long blue meteors cleansing the dull night,
And the life-kindling shafts of the keen sun's
All-piercing bow, and the dew-mingled rain
Of the calm moonbeams, a soft influence mild,　120
Shall clothe the forests and the fields, ay, even
The crag-built deserts of the barren deep,
With ever-living leaves, and fruits, and flowers.
And thou! There is a cavern where my spirit
Was panted forth in anguish whilst thy pain　　125
Made my heart mad, and those who did inhale it
Became mad too, and built a temple there,
And spoke, and were oracular, and lured
The erring nations round to mutual war,
And faithless faith, such as Jove kept with thee;　130
Which breath now rises, as amongst tall weeds
A violet's exhalation, and it fills
With a serener light and crimson air
Intense, yet soft, the rocks and woods around;
It feeds the quick growth of the serpent vine,　135
And the dark linkèd ivy tangling wild,
And budding, blown, or odour-faded blooms
Which star the winds with points of coloured light,
As they rain through them, and bright golden globes
Of fruit, suspended in their own green heaven,　140
And through their veinèd leaves and amber stems
The flowers whose purple and translucid bowls
Stand ever mantling with aëreal dew,
The drink of spirits: and it circles round,
Like the soft waving wings of noonday dreams,　145
Inspiring calm and happy thoughts, like mine,
Now thou art thus restored. This cave is thine.
Arise! Appear!
　　　　　　　[A SPIRIT *rises in the likeness of a winged child.*
　　　　　This is my torch-bearer;
Who let his lamp out in old time with gazing
On eyes from which he kindled it anew　　　　150
With love, which is as fire, sweet daughter mine,
For such is that within thine own. Run, wayward,
And guide this company beyond the peak
Of Bacchic Nysa, Mænad-haunted mountain,
And beyond Indus and its tribute rivers,　　　155
Trampling the torrent streams and glassy lakes
With feet unwet, unwearied, undelaying,
And up the green ravine, across the vale,

Beside the windless and crystalline pool,
Where ever lies, on unerasing waves,   160
The image of a temple, built above,
Distinct with column, arch, and architrave,
And palm-like capital, and over-wrought,
And populous with most living imagery,
Praxitelean shapes, whose marble smiles   165
Fill the hushed air with everlasting love.
It is deserted now, but once it bore
Thy name, Prometheus; there the emulous youths
Bore to thy honour through the divine gloom
The lamp which was thine emblem; even as those   170
Who bear the untransmitted torch of hope
Into the grave, across the night of life,
As thou hast borne it most triumphantly
To this far goal of Time. Depart, farewell.
Beside that temple is the destined cave.   175

SCENE IV.—*A Forest. In the Background a Cave.* PROMETHEUS, ASIA,
PANTHEA, IONE, *and the* SPIRIT OF THE EARTH.

Ione. Sister, it is not earthly: how it glides
Under the leaves! how on its head there burns
A light, like a green star, whose emerald beams
Are twined with its fair hair! how, as it moves,
The splendour drops in flakes upon the grass!   5
Knowest thou it?
        Panthea.   It is the delicate spirit
That guides the earth through heaven. From afar
The populous constellations call that light
The loveliest of the planets; and sometimes
It floats along the spray of the salt sea,   10
Or makes its chariot of a foggy cloud,
Or walks through fields or cities while men sleep,
Or o'er the mountain tops, or down the rivers,
Or through the green waste wilderness, as now,
Wondering at all it sees. Before Jove reigned   15
It loved our sister Asia, and it came
Each leisure hour to drink the liquid light
Out of her eyes, for which it said it thirsted
As one bit by a dipsas, and with her
It made its childish confidence, and told her   20
All it had known or seen, for it saw much,
Yet idly reasoned what it saw; and called her—
For whence it sprung it knew not, nor do I—
Mother, dear mother.

The Spirit of the Earth (running to Asia). Mother, dearest
    mother;
May I then talk with thee as I was wont?   25
May I then hide my eyes in thy soft arms,
After thy looks have made them tired of joy?
May I then play beside thee the long noons,
When work is none in the bright silent air?
    Asia. I love thee, gentlest being, and henceforth   30
Can cherish thee unenvied: speak, I pray:
Thy simple talk once solaced, now delights.
    Spirit of the Earth. Mother, I am grown wiser, though a child
Cannot be wise like thee, within this day;
And happier too; happier and wiser both.   35
Thou knowest that toads, and snakes, and loathly worms,
And venomous and malicious beasts, and boughs
That bore ill berries in the woods, were ever
An hindrance to my walks o'er the green world:
And that, among the haunts of humankind,   40
Hard-featured men, or with proud, angry looks,
Or cold, staid gait, or false and hollow smiles,
Or the dull sneer of self-loved ignorance,
Or other such foul masks, with which ill thoughts
Hide that fair being whom we spirits call man;   45
And women too, ugliest of all things evil,
(Though fair, even in a world where thou art fair,
When good and kind, free and sincere like thee),
When false or frowning made me sick at heart
To pass them, though they slept, and I unseen.   50
Well, my path lately lay through a great city
Into the woody hills surrounding it:
A sentinel was sleeping at the gate:
When there was heard a sound, so loud, it shook
The towers amid the moonlight, yet more sweet   55
Than any voice but thine, sweetest of all;
A long, long sound, as it would never end:
And all the inhabitants leaped suddenly
Out of their rest, and gathered in the streets,
Looking in wonder up to Heaven, while yet   60
The music pealed along. I hid myself
Within a fountain in the public square,
Where I lay like the reflex of the moon
Seen in a wave under green leaves; and soon
Those ugly human shapes and visages   65
Of which I spoke as having wrought me pain,
Passed floating through the air, and fading still
Into the winds that scattered them; and those
From whom they passed seemed mild and lovely forms

After some foul disguise had fallen, and all   70
Were somewhat changed, and after brief surprise
And greetings of delighted wonder, all
Went to their sleep again: and when the dawn
Came, wouldst thou think that toads, and snakes, and efts,
Could e'er be beautiful? yet so they were,   75
And that with little change of shape or hue:
All things had put their evil nature off:
I cannot tell my joy, when o'er a lake
Upon a drooping bough with nightshade twined,
I saw two azure halcyons clinging downward   80
And thinning one bright bunch of amber berries,
With quick long beaks, and in the deep there lay
Those lovely forms imaged as in a sky;
So, with my thoughts full of these happy changes,
We meet again, the happiest change of all.   85
    Asia. And never will we part, till thy chaste sister
Who guides the frozen and inconstant moon
Will look on thy more warm and equal light
Till her heart thaw like flakes of April snow
And love thee.
    Spirit of the Earth. What; as Asia loves Prometheus?   90
    Asia. Peace, wanton, thou art yet not old enough.
Think ye by gazing on each other's eyes
To multiply your lovely selves, and fill
With sph, erèd fires the interlunar air?
    Spirit of the Earth. Nay, mother, while my sister trims her lamp
'Tis hard I should go darkling.
    Asia.   Listen; look!   96
                                [*The* SPIRIT OF THE HOUR *enters.*
    Prometheus. We feel what thou hast heard and seen: yet speak.
    Spirit of the Hour. Soon as the sound had ceased whose thunder
        filled
The abysses of the sky and the wide earth,
There was a change: the impalpable thin air   100
And the all-circling sunlight were transformed,
As if the sense of love dissolved in them
Had folded itself round the spherèd world.
My vision then grew clear, and I could see
Into the mysteries of the universe: 105
Dizzy as with delight I floated down,
Winnowing the lightsome air with languid plumes,
My coursers sought their birthplace in the sun,
Where they henceforth will live exempt from toil,
Pasturing flowers of vegetable fire;   110
And where my moonlike car will stand within
A temple, gazed upon by Phidian forms

Of thee, and Asia, and the Earth, and me,
And you fair nymphs looking the love we feel,—
In memory of the tidings it has borne,—   115
Beneath a dome fretted with graven flowers,
Poised on twelve columns of resplendent stone,
And open to the bright and liquid sky.
Yoked to it by an amphisbaenic snake
The likeness of those wingèd steeds will mock   120
The flight from which they find repose. Alas,
Whither has wandered now my partial tongue
When all remains untold which ye would hear?
As I have said, I floated to the earth:
It was, as it is still, the pain of bliss   125
To move, to breathe, to be; I wandering went
Among the haunts and dwellings of mankind,
And first was disappointed not to see
Such mighty change as I had felt within
Expressed in outward things; but soon I looked,   130
And behold, thrones were kingless, and men walked
One with the other even as spirits do,
None fawned, none trampled; hate, disdain, or fear,
Self-love or self-contempt, on human brows
No more inscribed, as o'er the gate of hell,   135
'All hope abandon ye who enter here;'
None frowned, none trembled, none with eager fear
Gazed on another's eye of cold command,
Until the subject of a tyrant's will
Became, worse fate, the abject of his own,   140
Which spurred him, like an outspent horse, to death.
None wrought his lips in truth-entangling lines
Which smiled the lie his tongue disdained to speak;
None, with firm sneer, trod out in his own heart
The sparks of love and hope till there remained   145
Those bitter ashes, a soul self-consumed,
And the wretch crept a vampire among men,
Infecting all with his own hideous ill;
None talked that common, false, cold, hollow talk
Which makes the heart deny the *yes* it breathes,   150
Yet question that unmeant hypocrisy
With such a self-mistrust as has no name.
And women, too, frank, beautiful, and kind
As the free heaven which rains fresh light and dew
On the wide earth, past; gentle radiant forms,   155
From custom's evil taint exempt and pure;
Speaking the wisdom once they could not think,
Looking emotions once they feared to feel,
And changed to all which once they dared not be,

Yet being now, made earth like heaven; nor pride,   160
Nor jealousy, nor envy, nor ill shame,
The bitterest of those drops of treasured gall,
Spoilt the sweet taste of the nepenthe, love.

Thrones, altars, judgement-seats, and prisons; wherein,
And beside which, by wretched men were borne   165
Sceptres, tiaras, swords, and chains, and tomes
Of reasoned wrong, glozed on by ignorance,
Were like those monstrous and barbaric shapes,
The ghosts of a no-more-remembered fame,
Which, from their unworn obelisks, look forth   170
In triumph o'er the palaces and tombs
Of those who were their conquerors: mouldering round,
These imaged to the pride of kings and priests
A dark yet mighty faith, a power as wide
As is the world it wasted, and are now   175
But an astonishment; even so the tools
And emblems of its last captivity,
Amid the dwellings of the peopled earth,
Stand, not o'erthrown, but unregarded now.
And those foul shapes, abhorred by god and man,—   180
Which, under many a name and many a form
Strange, savage, ghastly, dark and execrable,
Were Jupiter, the tyrant of the world;
And which the nations, panic-stricken, served
With blood, and hearts broken by long hope, and love
Dragged to his altars soiled and garlandless,   186
And slain amid men's unreclaiming tears,
Flattering the thing they feared, which fear was hate,—
Frown, mouldering fast, o'er their abandoned shrines:
The painted veil, by those who were, called life,   190
Which mimicked, as with colours idly spread,
All men believed or hoped, is torn aside;
The loathsome mask has fallen, the man remains
Sceptreless, free, uncircumscribed, but man
Equal, unclassed, tribeless, and nationless,   195
Exempt from awe, worship, degree, the king
Over himself; just, gentle, wise: but man
Passionless?——no, yet free from guilt or pain,
Which were, for his will made or suffered them,
Nor yet exempt, though ruling them like slaves,   200
From chance, and death, and mutability,
The clogs of that which else might oversoar
The loftiest star of unascended heaven,
Pinnacled dim in the intense inane.

           END OF THE THIRD ACT.

ACT IV

Scene.—*A Part of the Forest near the Cave of* Prometheus. Panthea
and Ione *are sleeping: they awaken gradually during the first Song.*

Voice of unseen Spirits.

The pale stars are gone!
For the sun, their swift shepherd,   3
To their folds them compelling,
In the depths of the dawn,
Hastes, in meteor-eclipsing array, and they flee   5
Beyond his blue dwelling,
As fawns flee the leopard.
But where are ye?

A Train of dark Forms and Shadows passes by confusedly, singing.

Here, oh, here:
We bear the bier   10
Of the Father of many a cancelled year
Spectres we
Of the dead Hours be,
We bear Time to his tomb in eternity.

Strew, oh, strew   15
Hair, not yew!
Wet the dusty pall with tears, not dew!
Be the faded flowers
Of Death's bare bowers
Spread on the corpse of the King of Hours!   20

Haste, oh, haste!
As shades are chased,
Trembling, by day, from heaven's blue waste.
We melt away,
Like dissolving spray,   25
From the children of a diviner day,
With the lullaby
Of winds that die
On the bosom of their own harmony!

Ione.

What dark forms were they?   30

Panthea.

The past Hours weak and gray,
With the spoil which their toil
Raked together
From the conquest but One could foil.

Ione.

Have they passed?

Panthea.

           They have passed;   35
They outspeeded the blast,
While 'tis said, they are fled:

Ione.

Whither, oh, whither?

Panthea.

To the dark, to the past, to the dead.

Voice of unseen Spirits.

Bright clouds float in heaven,   40
Dew-stars gleam on earth,
Waves assemble on ocean,
They are gathered and driven
By the storm of delight, by the panic of glee!
   They shake with emotion,   45
   They dance in their mirth.
      But where are ye?

The pine boughs are singing
Old songs with new gladness,
The billows and fountains   50
Fresh music are flinging,
Like the notes of a spirit from land and from sea;
   The storms mock the mountains
   With the thunder of gladness.
      But where are ye?   55

Ione. What charioteers are these?
Panthea.   Where are their chariots?

Semichorus of Hours.

The voice of the Spirits of Air and of Earth
  Have drawn back the figured curtain of sleep
Which covered our being and darkened our birth
  In the deep.

A Voice.

In the deep?

Semichorus II.

> Oh, below tho doop.   60

Semichorus I.

An hundred ages we had been kept
  Cradled in visions of hate and care,
And each one who waked as his brother slept,
  Found the truth—

Semichorus II.

> Worse than his visions were!

Semichorus I.

We have heard the lute of Hope in sleep;   65
  We have known the voice of Love in dreams;
We have felt the wand of Power, and leap—

Semichorus II.

As the billows leap in the morning beams!

Chorus.

Weave the dance on the floor of the breeze,
  Pierce with song heaven's silent light,   70
Enchant the day that too swiftly flees,
  To check its flight ere the cave of Night.

Once the hungry Hours were hounds
  Which chased the day like a bleeding deer,
And it limped and stumbled with many wounds   75
  Through the nightly dells of the desert year.

But now, oh weave the mystic measure
  Of music, and dance, and shapes of light,
Let the Hours, and the spirits of might and pleasure,
  Like the clouds and sunbeams, unite.

A Voice.

> Unite!   80
Panthea. See, where the Spirits of the human mind
Wrapped in sweet sounds, as in bright veils, approach.

Chorus of Spirits.

> We join the throng
> Of the dance and the song,
> By the whirlwind of gladness borne along;   85

As the flying-fish leap
From the Indian deep,
And mix with the sea-birds, half asleep.

Chorus of Hours.

Whence come ye, so wild and so fleet,
For sandals of lightning are on your feet,   90
And your wings are soft and swift as thought,
And your eyes are as love which is veilèd not?

Chorus of Spirits.

We come from the mind
Of human kind
Which was late so dusk, and obscene, and blind,   95
Now 'tis an ocean
Of clear emotion,
A heaven of serene and mighty motion.

From that deep abyss
Of wonder and bliss,   100
Whose caverns are crystal palaces;
From those skiey towers
Where Thought's crowned powers
Sit watching your dance, ye happy Hours!

From the dim recesses   105
Of woven caresses,
Where lovers catch ye by your loose tresses
From the azure isles,
Where sweet Wisdom smiles,
Delaying your ships with her siren wiles.   110

From the temples high
Of Man's ear and eye,
Roofed over Sculpture and Poesy;
From the murmurings
Of the unsealed springs   115
Where Science bedews her Dædal wings.

Years after years,
Through blood, and tears,
And a thick hell of hatreds, and hopes, and fears;
We waded and flew,   120
And the islets were few
Where the bud-blighted flowers of happiness grew.

Our feet now, every palm,
Are sandalled with calm,
And the dew of our wings is a rain of balm;   125

And, beyond our eyes,
The human love lies
Which makes all it gazes on Paradise.

Chorus of Spirits and Hours.

Then weave the web of the mystic measure;
From the depths of the sky and the ends of the earth,
Come, swift Spirits of might and of pleasure,   131
Fill the dance and the music of mirth,
As the waves of a thousand streams rush by
To an ocean of splendour and harmony!

Chorus of Spirits.

Our spoil is won,   135
Our task is done,
We are free to dive, or soar, or run;
Beyond and around,
Or within the bound
Which clips the world with darkness round.   140

We'll pass the eyes
Of the starry skies
Into the hoar deep to colonize;
Death, Chaos, and Night,
From the sound of our flight,   145
Shall flee, like mist from a tempest's might.

And Earth, Air, and Light,
And the Spirit of Might,
Which drives round the stars in their fiery flight;
And Love, Thought, and Breath,   150
The powers that quell Death,
Wherever we soar shall assemble beneath.

And our singing shall build
In the void's loose field
A world for the Spirit of Wisdom to wield;   155
We will take our plan
From the new world of man,
And our work shall be called the Promethean.

Chorus of Hours.

Break the dance, and scatter the song;
Let some depart, and some remain.   160

Semichorus I.

We, beyond heaven, are driven along:

Semichorus II.

Us the enchantments of earth retain:

Semichorus I.

Ceaseless, and rapid, and fierce, and free,
With the Spirits which build a new earth and sea,
And a heaven where yet heaven could never be. 165

Semichorus II.

Solemn, and slow, and serene, and bright,
Leading the Day and outspeeding the Night,
With the powers of a world of perfect light.

Semichorus I.

We whirl, singing loud, round the gathering sphere,
Till the trees, and the beasts, and the clouds appear 170
From its chaos made calm by love, not fear.

Semichorus II.

We encircle the ocean and mountains of earth,
And the happy forms of its death and birth
Change to the music of our sweet mirth.

Chorus of Hours and Spirits.

Break the dance, and scatter the song, 175
  Let some depart, and some remain,
Wherever we fly we lead along
In leashes, like starbeams, soft yet strong,
  The clouds that are heavy with love's sweet rain.

Panthea. Ha! they are gone!
Ione.   Yet feel you no delight 180
From the past sweetness?
    Panthea.   As the bare green hill
When some soft cloud vanishes into rain,
Laughs with a thousand drops of sunny water
To the unpavilioned sky!
    Ione.   Even whilst we speak
New notes arise. What is that awful sound? 185
    Panthea. 'Tis the deep music of the rolling world
Kindling within the strings of the waved air
Æolian modulation.
    Ione.   Listen too,
How every pause is filled with under-notes,
Clear, silver, icy, keen, awakening tones, 190

Which pierce the sense, and live within the soul,
As the sharp stars pierce winter's crystal air
And gaze upon themselves within the sea.
    Panthea. But see where through two openings in the forest
Which hanging branches overcanopy,   195
And where two runnels of a rivulet,
Between the close moss violet-inwoven,
Have made their path of melody, like sisters
Who part with sighs that they may meet in smiles,
Turning their dear disunion to an isle   200
Of lovely grief, a wood of sweet sad thoughts;
Two visions of strange radiance float upon
The ocean-like enchantment of strong sound,
Which flows intenser, keener, deeper yet
Under the ground and through the windless air.   205
    Ione. I see a chariot like that thinnest boat,
In which the Mother of the Months is borne
By ebbing light into her western cave.
When she upsprings from interlunar dreams;
O'er which is curved an orblike canopy   210
Of gentle darkness, and the hills and woods,
Distinctly seen through that dusk aëry veil,
Regard like shapes in an enchanter's glass;
Its wheels are solid clouds, azure and gold,
Such as the genii of the thunderstorm   215
Pile on the floor of the illumined sea
When the sun rushes under it; they roll
And move and grow as with an inward wind;
Within it sits a wingèd infant, white
Its countenance, like the whiteness of bright snow,   220
Its plumes are as feathers of sunny frost,
Its limbs gleam white, through the wind-flowing folds
Of its white robe, woof of ethereal pearl.
Its hair is white, the brightness of white light
Scattered in strings; yet its two eyes are heavens   225
Of liquid darkness, which the Deity
Within seems pouring, as a storm is poured
From jaggèd clouds, out of their arrowy lashes,
Tempering the cold and radiant air around,
With fire that is not brightness; in its hand   230
It sways a quivering moonbeam, from whose point
A guiding power directs the chariot's prow
Over its wheelèd clouds, which as they roll
Over the grass, and flowers, and waves, wake sounds,
Sweet as a singing rain of silver dew.   235
    Panthea. And from the other opening in the wood
Rushes, with loud and whirlwind harmony,

A sphere, which is as many thousand spheres,
Solid as crystal, yet through all its mass
Flow, as through empty space, music and light: 240
Ten thousand orbs involving and involved,
Purple and azure, white, and green, and golden,
Sphere within sphere; and every space between
Peopled with unimaginable shapes,
Such as ghosts dream dwell in the lampless deep,   245
Yet each inter-transpicuous, and they whirl
Over each other with a thousand motions,
Upon a thousand sightless axles spinning,
And with the force of self-destroying swiftness,
Intensely, slowly, solemnly roll on,   250
Kindling with mingled sounds, and many tones,
Intelligible words and music wild.
With mighty whirl the multitudinous orb
Grinds the bright brook into an azure mist
Of elemental subtlety, like light;   255
And the wild odour of the forest flowers,
The music of the living grass and air,
The emerald light of leaf-entangled beams
Round its intense yet self-conflicting speed,
Seem kneaded into one aëreal mass   260
Which drowns the sense. Within the orb itself,
Pillowed upon its alabaster arms,
Like to a child o'erwearied with sweet toil,
On its own folded wings, and wavy hair,
The Spirit of the Earth is laid asleep,   265
And you can see its little lips are moving,
Amid the changing light of their own smiles,
Like one who talks of what he loves in dream.
     Ione. 'Tis only mocking the orb's harmony.
     Panthea. And from a star upon its forehead, shoot,   270
Like swords of azure fire, or golden spears
With tyrant-quelling myrtle overtwined,
Embleming heaven and earth united now,
Vast beams like spokes of some invisible wheel
Which whirl as the orb whirls, swifter than thought,   275
Filling the abyss with sun-like lightenings,
And perpendicular now, and now transverse,
Pierce the dark soil, and as they pierce and pass,
Make bare the secrets of the earth's deep heart;
Infinite mines of adamant and gold,   280
Valueless stones, and unimagined gems,
And caverns on crystalline columns poised
With vegetable silver overspread;
Wells of unfathomed fire, and water springs

Whence the great sea, even as a child is fed,   285
Whose vapours clothe earth's monarch mountain-tops
With kindly, ermine snow. The beams flash on
And make appear the melancholy ruins
Of cancelled cycles; anchors, beaks of ships;
Planks turned to marble; quivers, helms, and spears,   290
And gorgon-headed targes, and the wheels
Of scythèd chariots, and the emblazonry
Of trophies, standards, and armorial beasts,
Round which death laughed, sepulchred emblems
Of dead destruction, ruin within ruin!   295
The wrecks beside of many a city vast,
Whose population which the earth grew over
Was mortal, but not human; see, they lie,
Their monstrous works, and uncouth skeletons,
Their statues, homes and fanes; prodigious shapes   300
Huddled in gray annihilation, split,
Jammed in the hard, black deep; and over these,
The anatomies of unknown wingèd things,
And fishes which were isles of living scale,
And serpents, body chains, twisted around   305
The iron crags, or within heaps of dust
To which the torture strength of their last pangs
Had crushed the iron crags; and over these
The jaggèd alligator, and the might
Of earth-convulsing behemoth, which once   310
Were monarch beasts, and on the slimy shores,
And weed-overgrown continents of earth,
Increased and multiplied like summer worms
On an abandoned corpse, till the blue globe
Wrapped deluge round it like a cloak, and they   315
Yelled, gasped, and were abolished; or some God
Whose throne was in a comet, passed and cried,
'Be not!' And like my words they were no more.

The Earth.

The joy, the triumph, the delight, the madness!
The boundless, overflowing, bursting gladness,   320
The vaporous exultation not to be confined!
　　Ha! ha! the animation of delight
　　Which wraps me, like an atmosphere of light,
And bears me as a cloud is borne by its own wind.

The Moon.

Brother mine, calm wanderer,   325
Happy globe of land and air,
Some Spirit is darted like a beam from thee.

Which penetrates my frozen frame,
And passes with the warmth of flame,
With love, and odour, and deep melody   330
　　Through me, through me!

The Earth.

Ha! ha! the caverns of my hollow mountains,
　My cloven fire-crags, sound-exulting fountains
Laugh with a vast and inextinguishable laughter.
　The oceans, and the deserts, and the abysses,   335
　And the deep air's unmeasured wildernesses,
Answer from all their clouds and billows, echoing after.

　They cry aloud as I do. Sceptred curse,
　Who all our green and azure universe
Threatenedst to muffle round with black destruction, sending
　A solid cloud to rain hot thunderstones,   341
　And splinter and knead down my children's bones,
All I bring forth, to one void mass battering and blending,—

　Until each crag-like tower, and storied column,
　Palace, and obelisk, and temple solemn,   345
My imperial mountains crowned with cloud, and snow, and fire;
　My sea-like forests, every blade and blossom
　Which finds a grave or cradle in my bosom,
Were stamped by thy strong hate into a lifeless mire:

　How art thou sunk, withdrawn, covered, drunk up   350
　By thirsty nothing, as the brackish cup
Drained by a desert-troop, a little drop for all;
　And from beneath, around, within, above,
　Filling thy void annihilation, love
Burst in like light on caves cloven by the thunder-ball.   355

The Moon.

　The snow upon my lifeless mountains
　Is loosened into living fountains,
My solid oceans flow, and sing, and shine:
　A spirit from my heart bursts forth,
　It clothes with unexpected birth   360
My cold bare bosom: Oh! it must be thine
　　On mine, on mine!

　Gazing on thee I feel, I know
　Green stalks burst forth, and bright flowers grow,
And living shapes upon my bosom move: 365
　Music is in the sea and air,
　Wingèd clouds soar here and there.

Dark with the rain new buds are dreaming of:
'Tis love, all love!

The Earth.

It interpenetrates my granite mass,   370
Through tangled roots and trodden clay doth pass
Into the utmost leaves and delicatest flowers;
Upon the winds, among the clouds 'tis spread,
It wakes a life in the forgotten dead,
They breathe a spirit up from their obscurest bowers.   375

And like a storm bursting its cloudy prison
With thunder, and with whirlwind, has arisen
Out of the lampless caves of unimagined being:
With earthquake shock and swiftness making shiver
Thought's stagnant chaos, unremoved for ever,   380
Till hate, and fear, and pain, light-vanquished shadows, fleeing,

Leave Man, who was a many-sided mirror,
Which could distort to many a shape of error,
This true fair world of things, a sea reflecting love;
Which over all his kind, as the sun's heaven   385
Gliding o'er ocean, smooth, serene, and even,
Darting from starry depths radiance and life, doth move:

Leave Man, even as a leprous child is left,
Who follows a sick beast to some warm cleft
Of rocks, through which the might of healing springs is poured;
Then when it wanders home with rosy smile,   391
Unconscious, and its mother fears awhile
It is a spirit, then, weeps on her child restored.

Man, oh, not men! a chain of linkèd thought,
Of love and might to be divided not,   395
Compelling the elements with adamantine stress;
As the sun rules, even with a tyrant's gaze,
The unquiet republic of the maze
Of planets, struggling fierce towards heaven's free wilderness.

Man, one harmonious soul of many a soul,   400
Whose nature is its own divine control,
Where all things flow to all, as rivers to the sea;
Familiar acts are beautiful through love;
Labour, and pain, and grief, in life's green grove
Sport like tame beasts, none knew how gentle they could be!

His will, with all mean passions, bad delights,   406
And selfish cares, its trembling satellites,

A spirit ill to guide, but mighty to obey,
  Is as a tempest-wingèd ship, whose helm
Love rules, through waves which dare not overwhelm,   41(?)
Forcing life's wildest shores to own its sovereign sway.

  All things confess his strength. Through the cold mass
  Of marble and of colour his dreams pass;
Bright threads whence mothers weave the robes their children
        wear;
  Language is a perpetual Orphic song,   415
  Which rules with Dædal harmony a throng
Of thoughts and forms, which else senseless and shapeless were.

  The lightning is his slave; heaven's utmost deep
  Gives up her stars, and like a flock of sheep
They pass before his eye, are numbered, and roll on!   420
  The tempest is his steed, he strides the air;
  And the abyss shouts from her depth laid bare,
Heaven, hast thou secrets? Man unveils me; I have none.

The Moon.

  The shadow of white death has passed
  From my path in heaven at last,   425
A clinging shroud of solid frost and sleep;
  And through my newly-woven bowers,
  Wander happy paramours,
Less mighty, but as mild as those who keep
    Thy vales more deep.   430

The Earth.

  As the dissolving warmth of dawn may fold
  A half unfrozen dew-globe, green, and gold,
And crystalline, till it becomes a wingèd mist,
  And wanders up the vault of the blue day,
  Outlives the moon, and on the sun's last ray   435
Hangs o'er the sea, a fleece of fire and amethyst.

The Moon.

  Thou art folded, thou art lying
  In the light which is undying
Of thine own joy, and heaven's smile divine;
  All suns and constellations shower   440
  On thee a light, a life, a power
Which doth array thy sphere; thou pourest thine
    On mine, on mine!

The Earth.

I spin beneath my pyramid of night,
Which points into the heavens dreaming delight,   445

Murmuring victorious joy in my enchanted sleep;
　As a youth lulled in love-dreams faintly sighing,
　Under the shadow of his beauty lying,
Which round his rest a watch of light and warmth doth keep.

The Moon.

　　As in the soft and sweet eclipse,   450
　　When soul meets soul on lovers' lips,
　High hearts are calm, and brightest eyes are dull;
　　So when thy shadow falls on me,
　　Then am I mute and still, by thee
Covered; of thy love, Orb most beautiful,   455
　　　Full, oh, too full!

　　Thou art speeding round the sun
　　Brightest world of many a one;
　　Green and azure sphere which shinest
　　With a light which is divinest   460
　　Among all the lamps of Heaven
　　To whom life and light is given;
　　I, thy crystal paramour
　　Borne beside thee by a power
　　Like the polar Paradise,   465
　　Magnet-like of lovers' eyes;
　　I, a most enamoured maiden
　　Whose weak brain is overladen
　　With the pleasure of her love,
　　Maniac-like around thee move   470
　　Gazing, an insatiate bride,
　　On thy form from every side
　　Like a Mænad, round the cup
　　Which Agave lifted up
　　In the weird Cadmæan forest.   475
　　Brother, wheresoe'er thou soarest
　　I must hurry, whirl and follow
　　Through the heavens wide and hollow,
　　Sheltered by the warm embrace
　　Of thy soul from hungry space,   480
　　Drinking from thy sense and sight
　　Beauty, majesty, and might,
　　As a lover or a chameleon
　　Grows like what it looks upon,
　　As a violet's gentle eye   485
　　Gazes on the azure sky
Until its hue grows like what it beholds,
　　As a gray and watery mist
　　Grows like solid amethyst

Athwart the western mountain it enfolds,   490
  When the sunset sleeps
    Upon its snow—

The Earth.

  And the weak day weeps
    That it should be so.
Oh, gentle Moon, the voice of thy delight   495
Falls on me like thy clear and tender light
Soothing the seaman, borne the summer night,
    Through isles for ever calm;
Oh, gentle Moon, thy crystal accents pierce
The caverns of my pride's deep universe,   500
Charming the tiger joy, whose tramplings fierce
    Made wounds which need thy balm.

Panthea. I rise as from a bath of sparkling water,
A bath of azure light, among dark rocks,
Out of the stream of sound.
  Ione.   Ah me! sweet sister,   505
The stream of sound has ebbed away from us,
And you pretend to rise out of its wave,
Because your words fall like the clear, soft dew
Shaken from a bathing wood-nymph's limbs and hair.
  Panthea. Peace! peace! A mighty Power, which is as
    darkness,   510
Is rising out of Earth, and from the sky
Is showered like night, and from within the air
Bursts, like eclipse which had been gathered up
Into the pores of sunlight: the bright visions,
Wherein the singing spirits rode and shone,   515
Gleam like pale meteors through a watery night.
  Ione. There is a sense of words upon mine ear.
  Panthea. An universal sound like words: Oh, list!

Demogorgon.

Thou, Earth, calm empire of a happy soul,
  Sphere of divinest shapes and harmonies,   520
Beautiful orb! gathering as thou dost roll
  The love which paves thy path along the skies:

The Earth.

I hear: I am as a drop of dew that dies.

Demogorgon.

Thou, Moon, which gazest on the nightly Earth
  With wonder, as it gazes upon thee;   **525**

Whilst each to men, and beasts, and the swift birth
　Of birds, is beauty, love, calm, harmony:

The Moon.

I hear: I am a leaf shaken by thee!

Demogorgon.

Ye Kings of suns and stars, Dæmons and Gods,
　Aetherial Dominations, who possess　　　　　　　530
Elysian, windless, fortunate abodes
　Beyond Heaven's constellated wilderness:

A Voice from above.

Our great Republic hears, we are blest, and bless.

Demogorgon.

Ye happy Dead, whom beams of brightest verse
　Are clouds to hide, not colours to portray,　　　535
Whether your nature is that universe
　Which once ye saw and suffered—

A Voice from beneath.

　　　　　　　　　　　　Or as they
Whom we have left, we change and pass away.

Demogorgon.

Ye elemental Genii, who have homes
　From man's high mind even to the central stone　540
Of sullen lead; from heaven's star-fretted domes
　To the dull weed some sea-worm battens on:

A confused Voice.

We hear: thy words waken Oblivion.

Demogorgon.

Spirits, whose homes are flesh: ye beasts and birds,
　Ye worms, and fish; ye living leaves and buds;　545
Lightning and wind; and ye untameable herds,
　Meteors and mists, which throng air's solitudes:—

A Voice.

Thy voice to us is wind among still woods.

Demogorgon.

Man, who wert once a despot and a slave;
　A dupe and a deceiver; a decay;　　　　　　　550
A traveller from the cradle to the grave
　Through the dim night of this immortal day:

All.

Speak: thy strong words may never pass away.

Demogorgon.

This is the day, which down the void abysm
At the Earth-born's spell yawns for Heaven's despotism,
   And Conquest is dragged captive through the deep: 556
Love, from its awful throne of patient power
In the wise heart, from the last giddy hour
   O dread endurance, from the slippery, steep,
And narrow verge of crag-like agony, springs   560
And folds over the world its healing wings.

Gentleness, Virtue, Wisdom, and Endurance,
These are the seals of that most firm assurance
   Which bars the pit over Destruction's strength;
And if, with infirm hand, Eternity,   565
Mother of many acts and hours, should free
   The serpent that would clasp her with his length;
These are the spells by which to reassume
An empire o'er the disentangled doom.

To suffer woes which Hope thinks infinite;   570
To forgive wrongs darker than death or night;
   To defy Power, which seems omnipotent;
To love, and bear; to hope, till Hope creates
From its own wreck the thing it contemplates;
   Neither to change, nor falter, nor repent;   575
This, like thy glory, Titan, is to be
Good, great and joyous, beautiful and free;
This is alone Life, Joy, Empire, and Victory.

NOTE ON PROMETHEUS UNBOUND, BY MRS. SHELLEY

ON the 12th of March, 1818, Shelley quitted England, never to return.
His principal motive was the hope that his health would be improved by
a milder climate; he suffered very much during the winter previous to his
emigration, and this decided his vacillating purpose. In December, 1817,
he had written from Marlow to a friend, saying:

'My health has been materially worse. My feelings at intervals are of
a deadly and torpid kind, or awakened to such a state of unnatural and
keen excitement that, only to instance the organ of sight, I find the very
blades of grass and the boughs of distant trees present themselves to me
with microscopic distinctness. Towards evening I sink into a state of
lethargy and inanimation, and often remain for hours on the sofa between
sleep and waking, a prey to the most painful irritability of thought. Such,
with little intermission, is my condition. The hours devoted to study are
selected with vigilant caution from among these periods of endurance.

It is not for this that I think of travelling to Italy, even if I knew that Italy would relieve me. But I have experienced a decisive pulmonary attack; and although at present it has passed away without any considerable vestige of its existence, yet this symptom sufficiently shows the true nature of my disease to be consumptive. It is to my advantage that this malady is in its nature slow, and, if one is sufficiently alive to its advances, is susceptible of cure from a warm climate. In the event of its assuming any decided shape, *it would be my duty* to go to Italy without delay. It is not mere health, but life, that I should seek, and that not for my own sake—I feel I am capable of trampling on all such weakness; but for the sake of those to whom my life may be a source of happiness, utility, security, and honour, and to some of whom my death might be all that is the reverse.'

In almost every respect his journey to Italy was advantageous. He left behind friends to whom he was attached; but cares of a thousand kinds, many springing from his lavish generosity, crowded round him in his native country, and, except the society of one or two friends, he had no compensation. The climate caused him to consume half his existence in helpless suffering. His dearest pleasure, the free enjoyment of the scenes of Nature, was marred by the same circumstance.

He went direct to Italy, avoiding even Paris, and did not make any pause till he arrived at Milan. The first aspect of Italy enchanted Shelley; it seemed a garden of delight placed beneath a clearer and brighter heaven than any he had lived under before. He wrote long descriptive letters during the first year of his residence in Italy, which, as compositions, are the most beautiful in the world, and show how truly he appreciated and studied the wonders of Nature and Art in that divine land.

The poetical spirit within him speedily revived with all the power and with more than all the beauty of his first attempts. He meditated three subjects as the groundwork for lyrical dramas. One was the story of Tasso; of this a slight fragment of a song of Tasso remains. The other was one founded on the *Book of Job,* which he never abandoned in idea, but of which no trace remains among his papers. The third was the *Prometheus Unbound.* The Greek tragedians were now his most familiar companions in his wanderings, and the sublime majesty of Æschylus filled him with wonder and delight. The father of Greek tragedy does not possess the pathos of Sophocles, nor the variety and tenderness of Euripides; the interest on which he founds his dramas is often elevated above human vicissitudes into the mighty passions and throes of gods and demi-gods: such fascinated the abstract imagination of Shelley.

We spent a month at Milan, visiting the Lake of Como during that interval. Thence we passed in succession to Pisa, Leghorn, the Baths of Lucca, Venice, Este, Rome, Naples, and back again to Rome, whither we returned early in March, 1819. During all this time Shelley meditated the subject of his drama, and wrote portions of it. Other poems were composed during this interval. and while at the Bagni di Lucca he translated

Plato's *Symposium*. But, though he diversified his studies, his thoughts centred in the *Prometheus*. At last, when at Rome, during a bright and beautiful Spring, he gave up his whole time to the composition. The spot selected for his study was, as he mentions in his preface, the mountainous ruins of the Baths of Caracalla. These are little known to the ordinary visitor at Rome. He describes them in a letter, with that poetry and deli-cacy and truth of description which render his narrated impressions of scenery of unequalled beauty and interest.

At first he completed the drama in three acts. It was not till several months after, when at Florence, that he conceived that a fourth act, a sort of hymn of rejoicing in the fulfilment of the prophecies with regard to Prometheus, ought to be added to complete the composition.

The prominent feature of Shelley's theory of the destiny of the human species was that evil is not inherent in the system of the creation, but an accident that might be expelled. This also forms a portion of Christianity: God made earth and man perfect, till he, by his fall,

'Brought death into the world and all our woe.'

Shelley believed that mankind had only to will that there should be no evil, and there would be none. It is not my part in these Notes to notice the arguments that have been urged against this opinion, but to mention the fact that he entertained it, and was indeed attached to it with fervent enthusiasm. That man could be so perfectionized as to able to expel evil from his own nature, and from the greater part of the creation, was the cardinal point of his system. And the subject he loved best to dwell on was the image of One warring with the Evil Principle, oppressed not only by it, but by all—even the good, who were deluded into considering evil a necessary portion of humanity; a victim full of fortitude and hope and spirit of triumph emanating from a reliance in the ultimate omnipotence of Good. Such he had depicted in his last poem, when he made Laon the enemy and the victim of tyrants. He now took a more idealized image of the same subject. He followed certain classical authorities in figuring Saturn as the good principle, Jupiter the usurping evil one, and Prome theus as the regenerator, who, unable to bring mankind back to primitive innocence, used knowledge as a weapon to defeat evil, by leading man kind, beyond the state wherein they are sinless through ignorance, to that in which they are virtuous through wisdom. Jupiter punished the temerity of the Titan by chaining him to a rock of Caucasus, and causing a vul ture to devour his still-renewed heart. There was a prophecy afloat in heaven portending the fall of Jove, the secret of averting which was known only to Prometheus; and the god offered freedom from torture on condition of its being communicated to him. According to the mytho-logical story, this referred to the offspring of Thetis, who was destined to be greater than his father. Prometheus at last bought pardon for his crime of enriching mankind with his gifts, by revealing the prophecy. Hercules killed the vulture, and set him free; and Thetis was married to Peleus, the father of Achilles.

Shelley adapted the catastrophe of this story to his peculiar views. The son greater than his father, born of the nuptials of Jupiter and Thetis, was to dethrone Evil, and bring back a happier reign than that of Saturn. Prometheus defies the power of his enemy, and endures centuries of torture; till the hour arrives when Jove, blind to the real event, but darkly guessing that some great good to himself will flow, espouses Thetis. At the moment, the Primal Power of the world drives him from his usurped throne, and Strength, in the person of Hercules, liberates Humanity, typified in Prometheus, from the tortures generated by evil done or suffered. Asia, one of the Oceanides, is the wife of Prometheus —she was, according to other mythological interpretations, the same as Venus and Nature. When the benefactor of mankind is liberated, Nature resumes the beauty of her prime, and is united to her husband, the emblem of the human race, in perfect and happy union. In the Fourth Act, the Poet gives further scope to his imagination, and idealizes the forms of creation—such as we know them, instead of such as they appeared to the Greeks. Maternal Earth, the mighty parent, is superseded by the Spirit of the Earth, the guide of our planet through the realms of sky; while his fair and weaker companion and attendant, the Spirit of the Moon, receives bliss from the annihilation of Evil in the superior sphere.

Shelley develops, more particularly in the lyrics of this drama, his abstruse and imaginative theories with regard to the Creation. It requires a mind as subtle and penetrating as his own to understand the mystic meanings scattered throughout the poem. They elude the ordinary reader by their abstraction and delicacy of distinction, but they are far from vague. It was his design to write prose metaphysical essays on the nature of Man, which would have served to explain much of what is obscure in his poetry; a few scattered fragments of observations and remarks alone remain. He considered these philosophical views of Mind and Nature to be instinct with the intensest spirit of poetry.

More popular poets clothe the ideal with familiar and sensible imagery. Shelley loved to idealize the real—to gift the mechanism of the material universe with a soul and a voice, and to bestow such also on the most delicate and abstract emotions and thoughts of the mind. Sophocles was his great master in this species of imagery.

I find in one of his manuscript books some remarks on a line in the *Œdipus Tyrannus*, which show at once the critical subtlety of Shelley's mind, and explain his apprehension of those 'minute and remote distinctions of feeling, whether relative to external nature or the living beings which surround us,' which he pronounces, in the letter quoted in the note to the *Revolt of Islam*, to comprehend all that is sublime in man.

'In the Greek Shakespeare, Sophocles, we find the image,

Πολλὰς δ' ὁδοὺς ἐλθόντα φροντίδος πλάνοις:

a line of almost unfathomable depth of poetry; yet how simple are the images in which it is arrayed!

"Coming to many ways in the wanderings of careful thought."

If the words ὁδοὺς and πλάνοις had not been used, the line might have been explained in a metaphorical instead of an absolute sense, as we say "*ways* and means," and "wanderings" for error and confusion. But they meant literally paths or roads, such as we tread with our feet; and wanderings, such as a man makes when he loses himself in a desert, or roams from city to city—as Œdipus, the speaker of this verse, was destined to wander, blind and asking charity. What a picture does this line suggest of the mind as a wilderness of intricate paths, wide as the universe, which is here made its symbol; a world within a world which he who seeks some knowledge with respect to what he ought to do searches throughout, as he would search the external universe for some valued thing which was hidden from him upon its surface.'

In reading Shelley's poetry, we often find similar verses, resembling, but not imitating the Greek in this species of imagery; for, though he adopted the style, he gifted it with that originality of form and colouring which sprung from his own genius.

In the *Prometheus Unbound*, Shelley fulfils the promise quoted from a letter in the Note on the *Revolt of Islam*.[1] The tone of the composition is calmer and more majestic, the poetry more perfect as a whole, and the imagination displayed at once more pleasingly beautiful and more varied and daring. The description of the Hours, as they are seen in the cave of Demogorgon, is an instance of this—it fills the mind as the most charming picture—we long to see an artist at work to bring to our view the

> 'cars drawn by rainbow-wingèd steeds
> Which trample the dim winds: in each there stands
> A wild-eyed charioteer urging their flight.
> Some look behind, as fiends pursued them there,
> And yet I see no shapes but the keen stars:
> Others, with burning eyes, lean forth, and drink
> With eager lips the wind of their own speed,
> As if the thing they loved fled on before,
> And now, even now, they clasped it. Their bright locks
> Stream like a comet's flashing hair: they all
> Sweep onward.'

Through the whole poem there reigns a sort of calm and holy spirit of love; it soothes the tortured, and is hope to the expectant, till the prophecy is fulfilled, and Love, untainted by any evil, becomes the law of the world.

England had been rendered a painful residence to Shelley, as much by the sort of persecution with which in those days all men of liberal opinions

[1] While correcting the proofsheets of that poem, it struck me that the poet had indulged in an exaggerated view of the evils of restored despotism; which, however injurious and degrading, were less openly sanguinary than the triumph of anarchy, such as it appeared in France at the close of the last century. But at this time a book, *Scenes of Spanish Life*, translated by Lieutenant Crawford from the German of Dr. Huber, of Rostock, fell into my hands. The account of the triumph of the priests and the serviles, after the French invasion of Spain in 1823, bears a strong and frightful resemblance to some of the descriptions of the massacre of the patriots in the *Revolt of Islam*.

were visited, and by the injustice he had lately endured in the Court of
Chancery, as by the symptoms of disease which made him regard a visit
'to Italy as necessary to prolong his life. An exile, and strongly impressed
with the feeling that the majority of his countrymen regarded him with
sentiments of aversion such as his own heart could experience towards
none, he sheltered himself from such disgusting and painful thoughts in
the calm retreats of poetry, and built up a world of his own—with the
more pleasure, since he hoped to induce some one or two to believe that
the earth might become such, did mankind themselves consent. The
charm of the Roman climate helped to clothe his thoughts in greater
beauty than they had ever worn before. And, as he wandered among the
ruins made one with Nature in their decay, or gazed on the Praxitelean
shapes that throng the Vatican, the Capitol, and the palaces of Rome,
his soul imbibed forms of loveliness which became a portion of itself.
There are many passages in the *Prometheus* which show the intense delight he received from such studies, and give back the impression with
a beauty of poetical description peculiarly his own. He felt this, as a
poet must feel when he satisfies himself by the result of his labours;
and he wrote from Rome, 'My *Prometheus Unbound* is just finished,
and in a month or two I shall send it. It is a drama, with characters and
mechanism of a kind yet unattempted; and I think the execution is better
than any of my former attempts.'

I may mention, for the information of the more critical reader, that
the verbal alterations in this edition of *Prometheus* are made from a list
of errata written by Shelley himself.

THE CENCI

A TRAGEDY IN FIVE ACTS

DEDICATION, TO LEIGH HUNT, Esq.

My DEAR FRIEND—I inscribe with your name, from a distant country,
and after an absence whose months have seemed years, this the latest
of my literary efforts.

Those writings which I have hitherto published, have been little else
than visions which impersonate my own apprehensions of the beautiful
and the just. I can also perceive in them the literary defects incidental
to youth and impatience; they are dreams of what ought to be, or may
be. The drama which I now present to you is a sad reality. I lay aside
the presumptuous attitude of an instructor, and am content to paint,
with such colours as my own heart furnishes, that which has been.

Had I known a person more highly endowed than yourself with all
that it becomes a man to possess, I had solicited for this work the
ornament of his name. One more gentle, honourable, innocent and brave;
one of more exalted toleration for all who do and think evil, and yet

himself more free from evil; one who knows better how to receive, and how to confer a benefit, though he must ever confer far more than he can receive; one of simpler, and, in the highest sense of the word, of purer life and manners I never knew: and I had already been fortunate in friendships when your name was added to the list.

In that patient and irreconcilable enmity with domestic and political tyranny and imposture which the tenor of your life has illustrated, and which, had I health and talents, should illustrate mine, let us, comforting each other in our task, live and die.

All happiness attend you! Your affectionate friend,

PERCY B. SHELLEY.

ROME, *May* 29, 1819.

PREFACE

A MANUSCRIPT was communicated to me during my travels in Italy, which was copied from the archives of the Cenci Palace at Rome, and contains a detailed account of the horrors which ended in the extinction of one of the noblest and richest families of that city during the Pontificate of Clement VIII, in the year 1599. The story is, that an old man having spent his life in debauchery and wickedness, conceived at length an implacable hatred towards his children; which showed itself towards one daughter under the form of an incestuous passion, aggravated by every circumstance of cruelty and violence. This daughter, after long and vain attempts to escape from what she considered a perpetual contamination both of body and mind, at length plotted with her mother-in-law and brother to murder their common tyrant. The young maiden, who was urged to this tremendous deed by an impulse which overpowered its horror, was evidently a most gentle and amiable being, a creature formed to adorn and be admired, and thus violently thwarted from her nature by the necessity of circumstance and opinion. The deed was quickly discovered, and, in spite of the most earnest prayers made to the Pope by the highest persons in Rome, the criminals were put to death. The old man had during his life repeatedly bought his pardon from the Pope for capital crimes of the most enormous and unspeakable kind, at the price of a hundred thousand crowns; the death therefore of his victims can scarcely be accounted for by the love of justice. The Pope, among other motives for severity, probably felt that whoever killed the Count Cenci deprived his treasury of a certain and copious source of revenue.[1] Such a story, if told so as to present to the reader all the feelings of those who once acted it, their hopes and fears, their confidences and misgivings, their various interests, passions, and opinions, acting upon and with each other, yet all conspiring to one tremendous end, would be as

---

[1] The Papal Government formerly took the most extraordinary precautions against the publicity of facts which offer so tragical a demonstration of its own wickedness and weakness; so that the communication of the MS. had become, until very lately, a matter of some difficulty.

a light to make apparent some of the most dark and secret caverns of the human heart.

On my arrival at Rome I found that the story of the Cenci was a subject not to be mentioned in Italian society without awakening a deep and breathless interest; and that the feelings of the company never failed to incline to a romantic pity for the wrongs, and a passionate exculpation of the horrible deed to which they urged her, who has been mingled two centuries with the common dust. All ranks of people knew the outlines of this history, and participated in the overwhelming interest which it seems to have the magic of exciting in the human heart. I had a copy of Guido's picture of Beatrice which is preserved in the Colonna Palace, and my servant instantly recognized it as the portrait of *La Cenci*.

This national and universal interest which the story produces and has produced for two centuries and among all ranks of people in a great City, where the imagination is kept for ever active and awake, first suggested to me the conception of its fitness for a dramatic purpose. In fact it is a tragedy which has already received, from its capacity of awakening and sustaining the sympathy of men, approbation and success. Nothing remained as I imagined, but to clothe it to the apprehensions of my countrymen in such language and action as would bring it home to their hearts. The deepest and the sublimest tragic compositions, *King Lear* and the two plays in which the tale of Œdipus is told, were stories which already existed in tradition, as matters of popular belief and interest, before Shakspeare and Sophocles made them familiar to the sympathy of all succeeding generations of mankind.

This story of the Cenci is indeed eminently fearful and monstrous: anything like a dry exhibition of it on the stage would be insupportable. The person who would treat such a subject must increase the ideal, and diminish the actual horror of the events, so that the pleasure which arises from the poetry which exists in these tempestuous sufferings and crimes may mitigate the pain of the contemplation of the moral deformity from which they spring. There must also be nothing attempted to make the exhibition subservient to what is vulgarly termed a moral purpose. The highest moral purpose aimed at in the highest species of the drama, is the teaching the human heart, through its sympathies and antipathies, the knowledge of itself; in proportion to the possession of which knowledge, every human being is wise, just, sincere, tolerant and kind. If dogmas can do more, it is well: but a drama is no fit place for the enforcement of them. Undoubtedly, no person can be truly dishonoured by the act of another; and the fit return to make to the most enormous injuries is kindness and forbearance, and a resolution to convert the injurer from his dark passions by peace and love. Revenge, retaliation, atonement, are pernicious mistakes. If Beatrice had thought in this manner she would have been wiser and better; but she would never have been a tragic character: the few whom such an exhibition would have interested, could never have been sufficiently interested for a dramatic purpose, from the want of finding sympathy in their interest among the mass who surround them. It is in the restless and anatomizing casuistry with which men seek the justification of Beatrice, yet feel that she has done what needs justification; it is in the superstitious horror with which they contemplate alike her wrongs and their revenge, that the dramatic character of what she did and suffered consists.

I have endeavoured as nearly as possible to represent the characters as they probably were, and have sought to avoid the error of making them actuated by my own conceptions of right or wrong, false or true: thus under a thin veil converting names and actions of the sixteenth century into cold impersonations of my own mind. They are represented as Catholics, and as Catholics deeply tinged with religion. To a Protestant apprehension there will appear something unnatural in the earnest and perpetual sentiment of the relations between God and men which pervade the tragedy of the Cenci. It will especially be startled at the combination of an undoubting persuasion of the truth of the popular religion with a cool and determined perseverance in enormous guilt. But religion in Italy is not, as in Protestant countries, a cloak to be worn on particular days; or a passport which those who do not wish to be railed at carry with them to exhibit; or a gloomy passion for penetrating the impenetrable mysteries of our being, which terrifies its possessor at the darkness of the abyss to the brink of which it has conducted him. Religion coexists, as it were, in the mind of an Italian Catholic, with a faith in that of which all men have the most certain knowledge. It is interwoven with the whole fabric of life. It is adoration, faith, submission, penitence, blind admiration; not a rule for moral conduct. It has no necessary connection with any one virtue. The most atrocious villain may be rigidly devout, and without any shock to established faith, confess himself to be so. Religion pervades intensely the whole frame of society, and is according to the temper of the mind which it inhabits, a passion, a persuasion, an excuse, a refuge; never a check. Cenci himself built a chapel in the court of his Palace, and dedicated it to St. Thomas the Apostle, and established masses for the peace of his soul. Thus in the first scene of the fourth act Lucretia's design in exposing herself to the consequences of an expostulation with Cenci after having administered the opiate, was to induce him by a feigned tale to confess himself before death; this being esteemed by Catholics as essential to salvation; and she only relinquishes her purpose when she perceives that her perseverance would expose Beatrice to new outrages.

I have avoided with great care in writing this play the introduction of what is commonly called mere poetry, and I imagine there will scarcely be found a detached simile or a single isolated description, unless Beatrice's description of the chasm appointed for her father's murder should be judged to be of that nature.[1]

In a dramatic composition the imagery and the passion should inter-

_____

[1] An idea in this speech was suggested by a most sublime passage in _El Purgatorio de San Patricio_ of Calderon; the only plagiarism which I have intentionally committed in the whole piece.

penetrate one another, the former being reserved simply for the full development and illustration of the latter. Imagination is as the immortal God which should assume flesh for the redemption of mortal passion. It is thus that the most remote and the most familiar imagery may alike be fit for dramatic purposes when employed in the illustration of strong feeling, which raises what is low, and levels to the apprehension that which is lofty, casting over all the shadow of its own greatness. In other respects, I have written more carelessly; that is, without an over-fastidious and learned choice of words. In this respect I entirely agree with those modern critics who assert that in order to move men to true sympathy we must use the familiar language of men, and that our great ancestors the ancient English poets are the writers, a study of whom might incite us to do that for our own age which they have done for theirs. But it must be the real language of men in general and not that of any particular class to whose society the writer happens to belong. So much for what I have attempted; I need not be assured that success is a very different matter; particularly for one whose attention has but newly been awakened to the study of dramatic literature.

I endeavoured whilst at Rome to observe such monuments of this story as might be accessible to a stranger. The portrait of Beatrice at the Colonna Palace is admirable as a work of art: it was taken by Guido during her confinement in prison. But it is most interesting as a just representation of one of the loveliest specimens of the workmanship of Nature. There is a fixed and pale composure upon the features: she seems sad and stricken down in spirit, yet the despair thus expressed is lightened by the patience of gentleness. Her head is bound with folds of white drapery from which the yellow strings of her golden hair escape, and fall about her neck. The moulding of her face is exquisitely delicate; the eyebrows are distinct and arched: the lips have that permanent meaning of imagination and sensibility which suffering has not repressed and which it seems as if death scarcely could extinguish. Her forehead is large and clear; her eyes, which we are told were remarkable for their vivacity, are swollen with weeping and lustreless, but beautifully tender and serene. In the whole mien there is a simplicity and dignity which, united with her exquisite loveliness and deep sorrow, are inexpressibly pathetic. Beatrice Cenci appears to have been one of those rare persons in whom energy and gentleness dwell together without destroying one another: her nature was simple and profound. The crimes and miseries in which she was an actor and a sufferer are as the mask and the mantle in which circumstances clothed her for her impersonation on the scene of the world.

The Cenci Palace is of great extent; and though in part modernized there yet remains a vast and gloomy pile of feudal architecture in the same state as during the dreadful scenes which are the subject of this tragedy. The Palace is situated in an obscure corner of Rome, near the quarter of the Jews, and from the upper windows you see the immense ruins of Mount Palatine half hidden under their profuse overgrowth of trees. There is a court in one part of the Palace (perhaps that in which Cenci built the Chapel to St. Thomas), supported by granite columns and adorned with antique friezes of fine workmanship, and built up, according to the ancient Italian fashion, with balcony over balcony of open-work. One of the gates of the Palace formed of immense stones and leading through a passage, dark and lofty and opening into gloomy subterranean chambers, struck me particularly.

Of the Castle of Petrella, I could obtain no further information than that which is to be found in the manuscript.

DRAMATIS PERSONÆ

COUNT FRANCESCO CENCI.

GIACOMO, } *his Sons.*
BERNARDO,

CARDINAL CAMILLO.

ORSINO, *a Prelate.*

SAVELLA, *the Pope's Legate.*

OLIMPIO, } *Assassins.*
MARZIO,

ANDREA, *Servant to Cenci.*

Nobles, Judges, Guards, Servants.

LUCRETIA, *Wife of* CENCI, *and Step-mother of his children.*
BEATRICE, *his Daughter.*

The SCENE lies principally in Rome, but changes during the Fourth Act to Petrella, a castle among the Apulian Apennines.

TIME. During the Pontificate of Clement VIII.

ACT I

SCENE I.—*An Apartment in the Cenci Palace.*

Enter COUNT CENCI, *and* CARDINAL CAMILLO.

Camillo. That matter of the murder is hushed up
If you consent to yield his Holiness
Your fief that lies beyond the Pincian gate.—
It needed all my interest in the conclave
To bend him to this point: he said that you   5
Bought perilous impunity with your gold;
That crimes like yours if once or twice compounded
Enriched the Church, and respited from hell
An erring soul which might repent and live:—
But that the glory and the interest   10
Of the high throne he fills, little consist
With making it a daily mart of guilt
As manifold and hideous as the deeds

Which you scarce hide from men's revolted eyes.
    Cenci. The third of my possessions—let it go! **15**
Ay, I once heard the nephew of the Pope
Had sent his architect to view the ground,
Meaning to build a villa on my vines
The next time I compounded with his uncle:
I little thought he should outwit me so! **20**
Henceforth no witness—not the lamp—shall see
That which the vassal threatened to divulge
Whose throat is choked with dust for his reward.
The deed he saw could not have rated higher
Than his most worthless life:—it angers me! **25**
Respited me from Hell!—So may the Devil
Respite their souls from Heaven. No doubt Pope Clement,
And his most charitable nephews, pray
That the Apostle Peter and the Saints
Will grant for their sake that I long enjoy **30**
Strength, wealth, and pride, and lust, and length of days
Wherein to act the deeds which are the stewards
Of their revenue.—But much yet remains
To which they show no title.
    Camillo.   Oh, Count Cenci!
So much that thou mightst honourably live **35**
And reconcile thyself with thine own heart
And with thy God, and with the offended world.
How hideously look deeds of lust and blood
Through those snow white and venerable hairs!—
Your children should be sitting round you now, **40**
But that you fear to read upon their looks
The shame and misery you have written there.
Where is your wife? Where is your gentle daughter?
Methinks her sweet looks, which make all things else
Beauteous and glad, might kill the fiend within you. **45**
Why is she barred from all society
But her own strange and uncomplaining wrongs?
Talk with me, Count,—you know I mean you well.
I stood beside your dark and fiery youth
Watching its bold and bad career, as men **50**
Watch meteors, but it vanished not—I marked
Your desperate and remorseless manhood; now
Do I behold you in dishonoured age
Charged with a thousand unrepented crimes.
Yet I have ever hoped you would amend, **55**
And in that hope have saved your life three times.
    Cenci. For which Aldobrandino owes you now
My fief beyond the Pincian.—Cardinal,
One thing, I pray you, recollect henceforth,

And so we shall converse with less restraint.   60
A man you knew spoke of my wife and daughter—
He was accustomed to frequent my house;
So the next day *his* wife and daughter came
And asked if I had seen him; and I smiled:
I think they never saw him any more.   65
   Camillo. Thou execrable man, beware!—
   Cenci.   Of thee?
Nay this is idle:—We should know each other.
As to my character for what men call crime
Seeing I please my senses as I list,
And vindicate that right with force or guile,   70
It is a public matter, and I care not
If I discuss it with you. I may speak
Alike to you and my own conscious heart—
For you give out that you have half reformed **me**,
Therefore strong vanity will keep you silent   75
If fear should not; both will, I do not doubt.
All men delight in sensual luxury,
All men enjoy revenge; and most exult
Over the tortures they can never feel—
Flattering their secret peace with others' **pain.**   80
But I delight in nothing else. I love
The sight of agony, and the sense of joy,
When this shall be another's, and that **mine.**
And I have no remorse and little fear,
Which are, I think, the checks of other men.   85
This mood has grown upon me, until now
Any design my captious fancy makes
The picture of its wish, and it forms none
But such as men like you would start to **know,**
Is as my natural food and rest debarred   90
Until it be accomplished.
   Camillo.   Art thou not
Most miserable?
   Cenci.   Why, miserable?—
No.—I am what your theologians call
Hardened;—which they must be in impudence,
So to revile a man's peculiar taste.   95
True, I was happier than I am, while yet
Manhood remained to act the thing I thought;
While lust was sweeter than revenge; and now
Invention palls:—Ay, we must all grow old—
And but that there yet remains a deed to act   100
Whose horror might make sharp an appetite
Duller than mine—I'd do—I know not what.
When I was young I thought of nothing else

But pleasure; and I fed on honey sweets:
Men, by St. Thomas! cannot live like bees,   105
And I grew tired:—yet, till I killed a foe,
And heard his groans, and heard his children's groans,
Knew I not what delight was else on earth,
Which now delights me little. I the rather
Look on such pangs as terror ill conceals,   110
The dry fixed eyeball; the pale quivering lip,
Which tell me that the spirit weeps within
Tears bitterer than the bloody sweat of Christ.
I rarely kill the body, which preserves,
Like a strong prison, the soul within my power,   115
Wherein I feed it with the breath of fear
For hourly pain.
    Camillo.   Hell's most abandoned fiend
Did never, in the drunkenness of guilt,
Speak to his heart as now you speak to me;
I thank my God that I believe you not.   120

Enter ANDREA.

    Andrea. My Lord, a gentleman from Salamanca
Would speak with you.
    Cenci.   Bid him attend me in
The grand saloon.   [*Exit* ANDREA.
    Camillo.   Farewell; and I will pray
Almighty God that thy false, impious words
Tempt not his spirit to abandon thee.   [*Exit* CAMILLO.
    Cenci. The third of my possessions! I must use   126
Close husbandry, or gold, the old man's sword,
Falls from my withered hand. But yesterday
There came an order from the Pope to make
Fourfold provision for my cursèd sons;   130
Whom I had sent from Rome to Salamanca,
Hoping some accident might cut them off;
And meaning if I could to starve them there.
I pray thee, God, send some quick death upon them!
Bernardo and my wife could not be worse   135
If dead and damned:—then, as to Beatrice—
                [*Looking around him suspiciously.*
I think they cannot hear me at that door;
What if they should? And yet I need not speak
Though the heart triumphs with itself in words.
O, thou most silent air, that shalt not hear   140
What now I think! Thou, pavement, which I tread
Towards her chamber,—let your echoes talk
Of my imperious step scorning surprise,
But not of my intent!—Andrea!

Enter ANDREA.

Andrea.   My lord?
Cenci. Bid Beatrice attend me in her chamber   145
This evening:—no, at midnight and alone.   [*Exeunt.*

SCENE II.—A *Garden of the Cenci Palace. Enter* BEATRICE *and* ORSINO.
as in conversation.

Beatrice. Pervert not truth,
Orsino. You remember where we held
That conversation;—nay, we see the spot
Even from this cypress;—two long years are past
Since, on an April midnight, underneath   5
The moonlight ruins of mount Palatine,
I did confess to you my secret mind.
　　Orsino. You said you loved me then.
　　Beatrice.   You are a Priest,
Speak to me not of love.
　　Orsino.   I may obtain
The dispensation of the Pope to marry.   10
Because I am a Priest do you believe
Your image, as the hunter some struck deer,
Follows me not whether I wake or sleep?
　　Beatrice. As I have said, speak to me not of love.
Had you a dispensation I have not;   15
Nor will I leave this home of misery
Whilst my poor Bernard, and that gentle lady
To whom I owe my life, and these virtuous thoughts,
Must suffer what I still have strength to share.
Alas, Orsino! All the love that once   20
I felt for you, is turned to bitter pain.
Ours was a youthful contract, which you first
Broke, by assuming vows no Pope will loose.
And thus I love you still, but holily,
Even as a sister or a spirit might;   25
And so I swear a cold fidelity.
And it is well perhaps we shall not marry.
You have a sly, equivocating vein
That suits me not.—Ah, wretched that I am!
Where shall I turn? Even now you look on me   30
As you were not my friend, and as if you
Discovered that I thought so, with false smiles
Making my true suspicion seem your wrong.
Ah, no! forgive me; sorrow makes me seem
Sterner than else my nature might have been;   35
I have a weight of melancholy thoughts,
And they forebode,—but what can they forebode
Worse than I now endure?

Orsino.   All will be well.
Is the petition yet prepared? You know
My zeal for all you wish, sweet Beatrice;   40
Doubt not but I will use my utmost skill
So that the Pope attend to your complaint.
    Beatrice. Your zeal for all I wish;—Ah me, you are cold!
Your utmost skill . . . speak but one word . . . (*aside*) Alas!
Weak and deserted creature that I am,   45
Here I stand bickering with my only friend! [*To* ORSINO.
This night my father gives a sumptuous feast,
Orsino; he has heard some happy news
From Salamanca, from my brothers there,
And with this outward show of love he mocks   50
His inward hate. 'Tis bold hypocrisy,
For he would gladlier celebrate their deaths,
Which I have heard him pray for on his knees:
Great God! that such a father should be mine!
But there is mighty preparation made,   55
And all our kin, the Cenci, will be there,
And all the chief nobility of Rome.
And he has bidden me and my pale Mother
Attire ourselves in festival array.
Poor lady! She expects some happy change   60
In his dark spirit from this act; I none.
At supper I will give you the petition:
Till when—farewell.
    Orsino. Farewell. (*Exit* BEATRICE.) I know the Pope
Will ne'er absolve me from my priestly vow
But by absolving me from the revenue   65
Of many a wealthy see; and, Beatrice,
I think to win thee at an easier rate.
Nor shall he read her eloquent petition:
He might bestow her on some poor relation
Of his sixth cousin, as he did her sister,   70
And I should be debarred from all access.
Then as to what she suffers from her father,
In all this there is much exaggeration:—
Old men are testy and will have their way;
A man may stab his enemy, or his vassal,   75
And live a free life as to wine or women,
And with a peevish temper may return
To a dull home, and rate his wife and children;
Daughters and wives call this foul tyranny.
I shall be well content if on my conscience   80
There rest no heavier sin than what they suffer
From the devices of my love—a net
From which she shall escape not. Yet I fear

Her subtle mind, her awe-inspiring gaze,
Whose beams anatomize me nerve by nerve   85
And lay me bare, and make me blush to see
My hidden thoughts.—Ah, no! A friendless **girl**
Who clings to me, as to her only hope:—
I were a fool, not less than if a panther
Were panic-stricken by the antelope's eye,   90
If she escape me.   [*Exit.*

SCENE III.—*A Magnificent Hall in the Cenci Palace. A Banquet. Enter*
    CENCI, LUCRETIA, BEATRICE, ORSINO, CAMILLO, NOBLES.

    Cenci. Welcome, my friends and kinsmen; welcome ye,
Princes and Cardinals, pillars of the church,
Whose presence honours our festivity.
I have too long lived like an anchorite,
And in my absence from your merry meetings   5
An evil word is gone abroad of me;
But I do hope that you, my noble friends,
When you have shared the entertainment here,
And heard the pious cause for which 'tis given,
And we have pledged a health or two together,   10
Will think me flesh and blood as well as you;
Sinful indeed, for Adam made all so,
But tender-hearted, meek and pitiful.
    First Guest. In truth, my Lord, you seem too light of heart,
Too sprightly and companionable a man,   15
To act the deeds that rumour pins on you.
(*To his Companion.*) I never saw such blithe and open cheer
In any eye!
    Second Guest. Some most desired event,
In which we all demand a common joy,
Has brought us hither; let us hear it, Count.   20
    Cenci. It is indeed a most desired event.
If, when a parent from a parent's heart
Lifts from this earth to the great Father of all
A prayer, both when he lays him down to sleep,
And when he rises up from dreaming it;   25
One supplication, one desire, one hope,
That he would grant a wish for his two sons,
Even all that he demands in their regard—
And suddenly beyond his dearest hope
It is accomplished, he should then rejoice,   30
And call his friends and kinsmen to a feast,
And task their love to grace his merriment,—
Then honour me thus far—for I am he.
    Beatrice (*to* LUCRETIA). Great God! How horrible! Some
        dreadful ill

Must have befallen my brothers.
    Lucretia.   Fear not, Child,   **35**
He speaks too frankly.
    Beatrice.   Ah! My blood runs cold.
I fear that wicked laughter round his eye,
Which wrinkles up the skin even to the hair.
    Cenci. Here are the letters brought from Salamanca;
Beatrice, read them to your mother. God!   **40**
I thank thee! In one night didst thou perform,
By ways inscrutable, the thing I sought.
My disobedient and rebellious sons
Are dead!—Why, dead!—What means this change of cheer?
You hear me not, I tell you they are dead;   **45**
And they will need no food or raiment more:
The tapers that did light them the dark way
Are their last cost. The Pope, I think, will not
Expect I should maintain them in their coffins.
Rejoice with me—my heart is wondrous glad.   **50**
          [LUCRETIA *sinks, half fainting*; BEATRICE *supports her.*
    Beatrice. It is not true!—Dear lady, pray look up.
Had it been true, there is a God in Heaven,
He would not live to boast of such a boon.
Unnatural man, thou knowest that it is false.
    Cenci. Ay, as the word of God; whom here I call   **55**
To witness that I speak the sober truth;—
And whose most favouring Providence was shown
Even in the manner of their deaths. For Rocco
Was kneeling at the mass, with sixteen others,
When the church fell and crushed him to a mummy, **60**
The rest escaped unhurt. Cristofano
Was stabbed in error by a jealous man.
Whilst she he loved was sleeping with his rival;
All in the self-same hour of the same night;
Which shows that Heaven has special care of me.   **65**
I beg those friends who love me, that they mark
The day a feast upon their calendars.
It was the twenty-seventh of December:
Ay, read the letters if you doubt my oath.
    [*The Assembly appears confused; several of the guests rise.*
    First Guest. Oh, horrible! I will depart—
    Second Guest.   And I.—
    Third Guest.   No, stay! **70**
I do believe it is some jest; though faith!
'Tis mocking us somewhat too solemnly.
I think his son has married the Infanta,
Or found a mine of gold in El Dorado;
'Tis but to season some such news; stay, stay!   **75**

I see 'tis only raillery by his smile.
   Cenci (filling a bowl of wine, and lifting it up). Oh, thou
      bright wine whose purple splendour leaps
And bubbles gaily in this golden bowl
Under the lamplight, as my spirits do,
To hear the death of my accursèd sons!   80
Could I believe thou wert their mingled blood,
Then would I taste thee like a sacrament,
And pledge with thee the mighty Devil in Hell,
Who, if a father's curses, as men say,
Climb with swift wings after their children's souls,   85
And drag them from the very throne of Heaven,
Now triumphs in my triumph!—But thou art
Superfluous; I have drunken deep of joy,
And I will taste no other wine to-night.
Here, Andrea! Bear the bowl around.
   A Guest (rising).   Thou wretch!   90
Will none among this noble company
Check the abandoned villain?
   Camillo.   For God's sake
Let me dismiss the guests! You are insane,
Some ill will come of this.
   Second Guest.   Seize, silence him!
   First Guest. I will!
   Third Guest.   And I!
   Cenci (addressing those who rise with a threatening gesture).
     Who moves? Who speaks?
                (turning to the Company)
                   'tis nothing,   95
Enjoy yourselves.—Beware! For my revenge
Is as the sealed commission of a king
That kills, and none dare name the murderer.
   [*The Banquet is broken up; several of the Guests are departing.*
   Beatrice. I do entreat you, go not, noble guests;
What, although tyranny and impious hate   100
Stand sheltered by a father's hoary hair?
What, if 'tis he who clothed us in these limbs
Who tortures them, and triumphs? What, if we,
The desolate and the dead, were his own flesh,
His children and his wife, whom he is bound   105
To love and shelter? Shall we therefore find
No refuge in this merciless wide world?
O think what deep wrongs must have blotted out
First love, then reverence in a child's prone mind,
Till it thus vanquish shame and fear! O think!   110
I have borne much, and kissed the sacred hand

Which crushed us to the earth, and thought its stroke
Was perhaps some paternal chastisement!
Have excused much, doubted; and when no doubt
Remained, have sought by patience, love, and tears   115
To soften him, and when this could not be
I have knelt down through the long sleepless nights
And lifted up to God, the Father of all,
Passionate prayers: and when these were not heard
I have still borne,—until I meet you here,   120
Princes and kinsmen, at this hideous feast
Given at my brothers' deaths. Two yet remain,
His wife remains and I, whom if ye save not,
Ye may soon share such merriment again
As fathers make over their children's graves.   125
O Prince Colonna, thou art near kinsman,
Cardinal, thou art the Pope's chamberlain,
Camillo, thou art chief justiciary,
Take us away!

    Cenci. (*He has been conversing with* CAMILLO *during the first
        part of* BEATRICE's *speech; he hears the conclusion, and
        now advances.*) I hope my good friends here
Will think of their own daughters—or perhaps   130
Of their own throats—before they lend an ear
To this wild girl.

    Beatrice (*not noticing the words of Cenci*). Dare no one look
        on me?
None answer? Can one tyrant overbear
The sense of many best and wisest men?
Or is it that I sue not in some form   135
Of scrupulous law, that ye deny my suit?
O God! That I were buried with my brothers!
And that the flowers of this departed spring
Were fading on my grave! And that my father
Were celebrating now one feast for all!   140

    Camillo. A bitter wish for one so young and gentle;
Can we do nothing?

    Colonna.   Nothing that I see.
Count Cenci were a dangerous enemy:
Yet I would second any one.

    A Cardinal.   And I.

    Cenci. Retire to your chamber insolent girl!   145

    Beatrice. Retire thou, impious man! Ay, hide thyself
Where never eye can look upon thee more!
Wouldst thou have honour and obedience
Who art a torturer? Father, never dream
Though thou mayst overbear this company,   150
But ill must come of ill.—Frown not on me!

Haste, hide thyself, lest with avenging looks
My brothers' ghosts should hunt thee from thy seat!
Cover thy face from every living eye,
And start if thou but hear a human step: 155
Seek out some dark and silent corner, there,
Bow thy white head before offended God,
And we will kneel around, and fervently
Pray that he pity both ourselves and thee.
     Cenci. My friends, I do lament this insane girl   160
Has spoilt the mirth of our festivity.
Good night, farewell; I will not make you longer
Spectators of our dull domestic quarrels.
Another time.—   [*Exeunt all but* CENCI *and* BEATRICE.
                    My brain is swimming round;
Give me a bowl of wine!   [*To* BEATRICE.
                    Thou painted viper!   165
Beast that thou art! Fair and yet terrible!
I know a charm shall make thee meek and tame,
Now get thee from my sight!   [*Exit* BEATRICE.
                    Here, Andrea,
Fill up this goblet with Greek wine. I said
I would not drink this evening; but I must;   170
For, strange to say, I feel my spirits fail
With thinking what I have decreed to do.—
                              [*Drinking the wine.*
Be thou the resolution of quick youth
Within my veins, and manhood's purpose stern,
And age's firm, cold, subtle villainy;   175
As if thou wert indeed my children's blood
Which I did thirst to drink! The charm works well;
It must be done; it shall be done, I swear!   [*Exit.*
                    END OF THE FIRST ACT.

                    ACT II

SCENE I.—*An Apartment in the Cenci Palace. Enter* LUCRETIA *and*
                    BERNARDO.

     Lucretia. Weep not, my gentle boy; he struck but me
Who have borne deeper wrongs. In truth, if he
Had killed me, he had done a kinder deed.
O God, Almighty, do Thou look upon us,
We have no other friend but only Thee!   5
Yet weep not; though I love you as my own,
I am not your true mother.
     Bernardo.   O more, more,
Than ever mother was to any child,
That have you been to me! Had he not been

My father, do you think that I should weep!   10
   Lucretia. Alas! Poor boy, what else couldst thou have done?
Enter BEATRICE.
   Beatrice (*in a hurried voice*). Did he pass this way? Have you
     seen him, brother?
Ah, no! that is his step upon the stairs;
'Tis nearer now; his hand is on the door;
Mother, if I to thee have ever been   15
A duteous child, now save me! Thou, great God,
Whose image upon earth a father is,
Dost Thou indeed abandon me? He comes;
The door is opening now; I see his face;
He frowns on others, but he smiles on me,   20
Even as he did after the feast last night.
Enter a Servant.
Almighty God, how merciful Thou art!
'Tis but Orsino's servant.—Well, what news?
   Servant. My master bids me say, the Holy Father
Has sent back your petition thus unopened.   [*Giving a paper.*
And he demands at what hour 'twere secure   26
To visit you again?
   Lucretia.   At the Ave Mary.   [*Exit Servant.*
So, daughter, our last hope has failed; Ah me!
How pale you look; you tremble, and you stand
Wrapped in some fixed and fearful meditation,   30
As if one thought were over strong for you:
Your eyes have a chill glare; O, dearest child!
Are you gone mad? If not, pray speak to me.
   Beatrice. You see I am not mad: I speak to you.
   Lucretia. You talked of something that your father did   35
After that dreadful feast? Could it be worse
Than when he smiled, and cried, 'My sons are dead!'
And every one looked in his neighbour's face
To see if others were as white as he?
At the first word he spoke I felt the blood   40
Rush to my heart, and fell into a trance;
And when it passed I sat all weak and wild;
Whilst you alone stood up, and with strong words
Checked his unnatural pride; and I could see
The devil was rebuked that lives in him.   45
Until this hour thus have you ever stood
Between us and your father's moody wrath
Like a protecting presence: your firm mind
Has been our only refuge and defence:
What can have thus subdued it? What can now   50
Have given you that cold melancholy look,
Succeeding to your unaccustomed fear?

Beatrice. What is it that you say? I was just thinking
'Twere better not to struggle any more.
Men, like my father, have been dark and bloody,   55
Yet never—Oh! Before worse comes of it
'Twere wise to die: it ends in that at last.
  Lucretia. Oh, talk not so, dear child! Tell me at once
What did your father do or say to you?
He stayed not after that accursèd feast   60
One moment in your chamber.—Speak to me.
  Bernardo. Oh, sister, sister, prithee, speak to us!
  Beatrice (*speaking very slowly with a forced calmness*). It was
          one word, Mother, one little word;
One look, one smile. (*Wildly.*) Oh! He has trampled me
Under his feet, and made the blood stream down   65
My pallid cheeks. And he has given us all
Ditch-water, and the fever-stricken flesh
Of buffaloes, and bade us eat or starve,
And we have eaten.—He has made me look
On my beloved Bernardo, when the rust   70
Of heavy chains has gangrened his sweet limbs,
And I have never yet despaired—but now!
What could I say?   [*Recovering herself.*
          Ah, no! 'tis nothing new.
The sufferings we all share have made me wild:
He only struck and cursed me as he passed;   75
He said, he looked, he did;—nothing at all
Beyond his wont, yet it disordered me.
Alas! I am forgetful of my duty,
I should preserve my senses for your sake.
  Lucretia. Nay, Beatrice; have courage, my sweet girl,   80
If any one despairs it should be I
Who loved him once, and now must live with him
Till God in pity call for him or me.
For you may, like your sister, find some husband,
And smile, years hence, with children round your knees;   85
Whilst I, then dead, and all this hideous coil
Shall be remembered only as a dream.
  Beatrice. Talk not to me, dear lady, of a husband.
Did you not nurse me when my mother died?
Did you not shield me and that dearest boy?   90
And had we any other friend but you
In infancy, with gentle words and looks,
To win our father not to murder us?
And shall I now desert you? May the ghost
Of my dead Mother plead against my soul   95
If I abandon her who filled the place
She left, with more, even, than a mother's love!

Bernardo. And I am of my sister's mind. Indeed
I would not leave you in this wretchedness,
Even though the Pope should make me free to live   100
In some blithe place, like others of my age,
With sports, and delicate food, and the fresh air.
Oh, never think that I will leave you, Mother!
    Lucretia. My dear, dear children!

                 Enter CENCI, *suddenly.*

    Cenci.   What, Beatrice here!
Come hither!   [*She shrinks back, and covers her face.*
           Nay, hide not your face, 'tis fair;   105
Look up! Why, yesternight you dared to look
With disobedient insolence upon me,
Bending a stern and an inquiring brow
On what I meant; whilst I then sought to hide
That which I came to tell you—but in vain.   110
    Beatrice (*wildly, staggering towards the door*). O that the earth
         would gape! Hide me, O God!
    Cenci. Then it was I whose inarticulate words
Fell from my lips, and who with tottering steps
Fled from your presence, as you now from mine.
Stay, I command you—from this day and hour   115
Never again, I think, with fearless eye,
And brow superior, and unaltered cheek,
And that lip made for tenderness or scorn,
Shalt thou strike dumb the meanest of mankind;
Me least of all. Now get thee to thy chamber!   120
Thou too, loathed image of thy cursèd mother,
                            [*To* BERNARDO.
Thy milky, meek face makes me sick with hate!
                 [*Exeunt* BEATRICE *and* BERNARDO.
    (*Aside.*) So much has passed between us as must make
Me bold, her fearful.—'Tis an awful thing
To touch such mischief as I now conceive: 125
So men sit shivering on the dewy bank,
And try the chill stream with their feet; once in . . .
How the delighted spirit pants for joy!
    Lucretia (*advancing timidly towards him*). O husband! Pray
         forgive poor Beatrice.
She meant not any ill.
    Cenci.   Nor you perhaps?   130
Nor that young imp, whom you have taught by rote
Parricide with his alphabet? Nor Giacomo?
Nor those two most unnatural sons, who stirred
Enmity up against me with the Pope?
Whom in one night merciful God cut off: 135
Innocent lambs! They thought not any ill.

You were not here conspiring? You said nothing
Of how I might be dungeoned as a madman;
Or be condemned to death for some offence,
And you would be the witnesses?—This failing,   140
How just it were to hire assassins, or
Put sudden poison in my evening drink?
Or smother me when overcome by wine?
Seeing we had no other judge but God,
And He had sentenced me, and there were none   145
But you to be the executioners
Of His decree enregistered in Heaven?
Oh, no! You said not this?
   Lucretia.   So help me God,
I never thought the things you charge me with!
   Cenci. If you dare speak that wicked lie again   150
I'll kill you. What! It was not by your counsel
That Beatrice disturbed the feast last night?
You did not hope to stir some enemies
Against me, and escape, and laugh to scorn
What every nerve of you now trembles at?   155
You judged that men were bolder than they are;
Few dare to stand between their grave and me.
   Lucretia. Look not so dreadfully! By my salvation
I knew not aught that Beatrice designed;
Nor do I think she designed any thing   150|
Until she heard you talk of her dead brothers.
   Cenci. Blaspheming liar! You are damned for this!
But I will take you where you may persuade
The stones you tread on to deliver you:
For men shall there be none but those who dare   165
All things—not question that which I command.
On Wednesday next I shall set out: you know
That savage rock, the Castle of Petrella:
'Tis safely walled, and moated round about:
Its dungeons underground, and its thick towers   170
Never told tales; though they have heard and seen
What might make dumb things speak.—Why do you linger?
Make speediest preparation for the journey!   [*Exit* LUCRETIA.
The all-beholding sun yet shines; I hear
A busy stir of men about the streets;   17[
I see the bright sky through the window panes:
It is a garish, broad, and peering day;
Loud, light, suspicious, full of eyes and ears,
And every little corner, nook, and hole
Is penetrated with the insolent light.   180
Come darkness! Yet, what is the day to me?
And wherefore should I wish for night, who do

A deed which shall confound both night and day:
'Tis she shall grope through a bewildering mist
Of horror: if there be a sun in heaven   185
She shall not dare to look upon its beams;
Nor feel its warmth. Let her then wish for night;
The act I think shall soon extinguish all
For me: I bear a darker deadlier gloom
Than the earth's shade, or interlunar air,   190
Or constellations quenched in murkiest cloud,
In which I walk secure and unbeheld
Towards my purpose.—Would that it were done!   [*Exit.*

SCENE II.—*A Chamber in the Vatican. Enter* CAMILLO *and* GIACOMO,
                              in conversation.

      Camillo. There is an obsolete and doubtful law
By which you might obtain a bare provision
Of food and clothing—
      Giacomo.   Nothing more? Alas!
Bare must be the provision which strict law
Awards, and agèd, sullen avarice pays.   5
Why did my father not apprentice me
To some mechanic trade? I should have then
Been trained in no highborn necessities
Which I could meet not by my daily toil.
The eldest son of a rich nobleman   10
Is heir to all his incapacities;
He has wide wants, and narrow powers. If you,
Cardinal Camillo, were reduced at once
From thrice-driven beds of down, and delicate food,
An hundred servants, and six palaces,   15
To that which nature doth indeed require?—
      Camillo. Nay, there is reason in your plea; 'twere hard.
      Giacomo. 'Tis hard for a firm man to bear: but I
Have a dear wife, a lady of high birth,
Whose dowry in ill hour I lent my father   20
Without a bond or witness to the deed:
And children, who inherit her fine senses,
The fairest creatures in this breathing world;
And she and they reproach me not. Cardinal,
Do you not think the Pope would interpose   25
And stretch authority beyond the law?
      Camillo. Though your peculiar case is hard, I know
The Pope will not divert the course of law.
After that impious feast the other night
I spoke with him, and urged him then to check   30
Your father's cruel hand; he frowned and said,
'Children are disobedient, and they sting

Their fathers' hearts to madness and despair,
Requiting years of care with contumely.
I pity the Count Cenci from my heart;   35
His outraged love perhaps awakened hate,
And thus he is exasperated to ill.
In the great war between the old and young
I, who have white hairs and a tottering body,
Will keep at least blameless neutrality.'   40

Enter ORSINO.

You, my good Lord Orsino, heard those words.
    Orsino. What words?
    Giacomo.   Alas, repeat them not again!
There then is no redress for me, at least
None but that which I may achieve myself,
Since I am driven to the brink.—But, say,   45
My innocent sister and my only brother
Are dying underneath my father's eye.
The memorable torturers of this land,
Galeaz Visconti, Borgia, Ezzelin,
Never inflicted on the meanest slave   50
What these endure; shall they have no protection?
    Camillo. Why, if they would petition to the Pope
I see not how he could refuse it—yet
He holds it of most dangerous example
In aught to weaken the paternal power,   55
Being, as 'twere, the shadow of his own.
I pray you now excuse me. I have business
That will not bear delay.   [*Exit* CAMILLO.
    Giacomo.   But you, Orsino,
Have the petition: wherefore not present it?
    Orsino. I have presented it, and backed it with   60
My earnest prayers, and urgent interest;
It was returned unanswered. I doubt not
But that the strange and execrable deeds
Alleged in it—in truth they might well baffle
Any belief—have turned the Pope's displeasure   65
Upon the accusers from the criminal:
So I should guess from what Camillo said.
    Giacomo. My friend, that palace-walking devil Gold
Has whispered silence to his Holiness:
And we are left, as scorpions ringed with fire.   70
What should we do but strike ourselves to death?
For he who is our murderous persecutor
Is shielded by a father's holy name,
Or I would—   [*Stops abruptly.
    Orsino.   What? Fear not to speak your thought.

Words are but holy as the deeds they cover: 75
A priest who has forsworn the God he serves;
A judge who makes Truth weep at his decree;
A friend who should weave counsel, as I now,
But as the mantle of some selfish guile;
A father who is all a tyrant seems, 80
Were the profaner for his sacred name.

Giacomo. Ask me not what I think; the unwilling brain
Feigns often what it would not; and we trust
Imagination with such phantasies
As the tongue dares not fashion into words, 85
Which have no words, their horror makes them dim
To the mind's eye.—My heart denies itself
To think what you demand.

Orsino.   But a friend's bosom
Is as the inmost cave of our own mind
Where we sit shut from the wide gaze of day, 90
And from the all-communicating air.
You look what I suspected—

Giacomo.   Spare me now!
I am as one lost in a midnight wood,
Who dares not ask some harmless passenger
The path across the wilderness, lest he, 95
As my thoughts are, should be—a murderer.
I know you are my friend, and all I dare
Speak to my soul that will I trust with thee.
But now my heart is heavy, and would take
Lone counsel from a night of sleepless care. 100
Pardon me, that I say farewell—farewell!
I would that to my own suspected self
I could address a word so full of peace.

Orsino. Farewell!—Be your thoughts better or more bold.
[*Exit* GIACOMO.

I had disposed the Cardinal Camillo 105
To feed his hope with cold encouragement:
It fortunately serves my close designs
That 'tis a trick of this same family
To analyse their own and other minds.
Such self-anatomy shall teach the will 110
Dangerous secrets: for it tempts our powers,
Knowing what must be thought, and may be done,
Into the depth of darkest purposes:
So Cenci fell into the pit; even I,
Since Beatrice unveiled me to myself, 115
And made me shrink from what I cannot shun,
Show a poor figure to my own esteem,
To which I grow half reconciled. I'll do

As little mischief as I can; that thought
Shall fee the accuser conscience.
    (*After a pause.*)   Now what harm   120
If Cenci should be murdered?—Yet, if murdered,
Wherefore by me? And what if I could take
The profit, yet omit the sin and peril
In such an action? Of all earthly things
I fear a man whose blows outspeed his words;   125
And such is Cenci: and while Cenci lives
His daughter's dowry were a secret grave
If a priest wins her.—Oh, fair Beatrice!
Would that I loved thee not, or loving thee
Could but despise danger and gold and all   130
That frowns between my wish and its effect,
Or smiles beyond it! There is no escape . . .
Her bright form kneels beside me at the altar,
And follows me to the resort of men,
And fills my slumber with tumultuous dreams,   135
So when I wake my blood seems liquid fire;
And if I strike my damp and dizzy head
My hot palm scorches it: her very name,
But spoken by a stranger, makes my heart
Sicken and pant; and thus unprofitably   140
I clasp the phantom of unfelt delights
Till weak imagination half possesses
The self-created shadow. Yet much longer
Will I not nurse this life of feverous hours:
From the unravelled hopes of Giacomo   145
I must work out my own dear purposes.
I see, as from a tower, the end of all:
Her father dead; her brother bound to me
By a dark secret, surer than the grave;
Her mother scared and unexpostulating   150
From the dread manner of her wish achieved:
And she!—Once more take courage, my faint heart;
What dares a friendless maiden matched with thee?
I have such foresight as assures success:
Some unbeheld divinity doth ever,   155
When dread events are near, stir up men's minds
To black suggestions; and he prospers best,
Not who becomes the instrument of ill,
But who can flatter the dark spirit, that makes
Its empire and its prey of other hearts   160
Till it became his slave . . . . as I will do.   [*Exit.*

END OF THE SECOND ACT.

ACT III

SCENE I.—*An Apartment in the Cenci Palace.* LUCRETIA, *to her enter*
BEATRICE.

    Beatrice. (*She enters staggering, and speaks wildly.*) Reach me
      that handkerchief!—My brain is hurt;
My eyes are full of blood; just wipe them for me . . .
I see but indistinctly . . .
    Lucretia.   My sweet child,
You have no wound; 'tis only a cold dew
That starts from your dear brow . . . Alas! Alas!   5
What has befallen?
    Beatrice.   How comes this hair undone?
Its wandering strings must be what blind me so,
And yet I tied it fast.—O, horrible!
The pavement sinks under my feet! The walls
Spin round! I see a woman weeping there,   10
And standing calm and motionless, whilst I
Slide giddily as the world reels. . . . My God!
The beautiful blue heaven is flecked with blood!
The sunshine on the floor is black! The air
Is changed to vapours such as the dead breathe   15
In charnel pits! pah! I am choked! There creeps
A clinging, black, contaminating mist
About me . . . 'tis substantial, heavy, thick,
I cannot pluck it from me, for it glues
My fingers and my limbs to one another,   20
And eats into my sinews, and dissolves
My flesh to a pollution, poisoning
The subtle, pure, and inmost spirit of life!
My God! I never knew what the mad felt
Before; for I am mad beyond all doubt!   25
(*More wildly.*) No, I am dead! These putrefying limbs
Shut round and sepulchre the panting soul
Which would burst forth into the wandering air!   (*A pause.*)
What hideous thought was that I had even now?
'Tis gone; and yet its burthen remains here   30
O'er these dull eyes . . . upon this weary heart!
O, world! O, life! O, day! O, misery!
    Lucretia. What ails thee, my poor child? She answers not:
Her spirit apprehends the sense of pain,
But not its cause; suffering has dried away   35
The source from which it sprung . . .
    Beatrice (*franticly*).   Like Parricide . . .
Misery has killed its father: yet its father
Never like mine . . . O, God! What thing am I?

Lucretia. My dearest child, what has your father done?

Beatrice (*doubtfully*). Who art thou, questioner? I have no
    father.   40

(*Aside*.) She is the madhouse nurse who tends on me,
It is a piteous office.   [*To* LUCRETIA, *in a slow, subdued voice*.
                    Do you know
I thought I was that wretched Beatrice
Men speak of, whom her father sometimes hales
From hall to hall by the entangled hair;   45
At others, pens up naked in damp cells
Where scaly reptiles crawl, and starves her there,
Till she will eat strange flesh. This woful story
So did I overact in my sick dreams,
That I imagined . . . no, it cannot be!   50
Horrible things have been in this wide world,
Prodigious mixtures, and confusions strange
Of good and ill; and worse have been conceived
Than ever there was found a heart to do.
But never fancy imaged such a deed   55
As . . .   [*Pauses, suddenly recollecting herself.*
            Who art thou? Swear to me, ere I die
With fearful expectation, that indeed
Thou art not what thou seemest . . . Mother!

Lucretia.   Oh!
My sweet child, know you . . .

Beatrice.   Yet speak it not:
For then if this be truth, that other too   60
Must be a truth, a firm enduring truth,
Linked with each lasting circumstance of life,
Never to change, never to pass away.
Why so it is. This is the Cenci Palace;
Thou art Lucretia; I am Beatrice.   65
I have talked some wild words, but will no more.
Mother, come near me: from this point of time,
I am . . .   [*Her voice dies away faintly.*

Lucretia. Alas! What has befallen thee, child?
What has thy father done?

Beatrice.   What have I done?
Am I not innocent? Is it my crime   70
That one with white hair, and imperious brow,
Who tortured me from my forgotten years,
As parents only dare, should call himself
My father, yet should be!—Oh, what am I?
What name, what place, what memory shall be mine?   75
What retrospects, outliving even despair?

Lucretia. He is a violent tyrant, surely, child:
We know that death alone can make us free;

His death or ours. But what can he have done
Of deadlier outrage or worse injury?   80
Thou art unlike thyself; thine eyes shoot forth
A wandering and strange spirit. Speak to me,
Unlock those pallid hands whose fingers twine
With one another.
    Beatrice.   'Tis the restless life
Tortured within them. If I try to speak   85
I shall go mad. Ay, something must be done;
What, yet I know not . . . something which shall make
The thing that I have suffered but a shadow
In the dread lightning which avenges it;
Brief, rapid, irreversible, destroying   90
The consequence of what it cannot cure.
Some such thing is to be endured or done:
When I know what, I shall be still and calm,
And never anything will move me more.
But now!—O blood, which art my father's blood,   95
Circling through these contaminated veins,
If thou, poured forth on the polluted earth,
Could wash away the crime, and punishment
By which I suffer . . . no, that cannot be!
Many might doubt there were a God above   100
Who sees and permits evil, and so die:
That faith no agony shall obscure in me.
    Lucretia. It must indeed have been some bitter wrong;
Yet what, I dare not guess. Oh, my lost child,
Hide not in proud impenetrable grief   105
Thy sufferings from my fear.
    Beatrice.   I hide them not.
What are the words which you would have me speak?
I, who can feign no image in my mind
Of that which has transformed me: I, whose thought
Is like a ghost shrouded and folded up   110
In its own formless horror: of all words,
That minister to mortal intercourse,
Which wouldst thou hear? For there is none to tell
My misery: if another ever knew
Aught like to it, she died as I will die,   115
And left it, as I must, without a name.
Death! Death! Our law and our religion call thee
A punishment and a reward . . . Oh, which
Have I deserved?
    Lucretia.   The peace of innocence;
Till in your season you be called to heaven.   120
Whate'er you may have suffered, you have done
No evil. Death must be the punishment

Of crime, or the reward of trampling down
The thorns which God has strewed upon the path
Which leads to immortality.
  Beatrice.   Ay, death . . . 125
The punishment of crime. I pray thee, God,
Let me not be bewildered while I judge.
If I must live day after day, and keep
These limbs, the unworthy temple of Thy spirit,
As a foul den from which what Thou abhorrest 130
May mock Thee, unavenged . . . it shall not be!
Self-murder . . . no, that might be no escape,
For Thy decree yawns like a Hell between
Our will and it:—O! In this mortal world
There is no vindication and no law 135
Which can adjudge and execute the doom
Of that through which I suffer.

Enter ORSINO.

(*She approaches him solemnly.*) Welcome, Friend!
I have to tell you that, since last we met,
I have endured a wrong so great and strange,
That neither life nor death can give me rest. 140
Ask me not what it is, for there are deeds
Which have no form, sufferings which have no tongue.
  Orsino. And what is he who has thus injured you?
  Beatrice. The man they call my father: a dread name.
  Orsino. It cannot be . . .
  Beatrice.   What it can be, or not, 145
Forbear to think. It is, and it has been;
Advise me how it shall not be again.
I thought to die; but a religious awe
Restrains me, and the dread lest death itself
Might be no refuge from the consciousness 150
Of what is yet unexpiated. Oh, speak!
  Orsino. Accuse him of the deed, and let the law
Avenge thee.
  Beatrice. Oh, ice-hearted counsellor!
If I could find a word that might make known
The crime of my destroyer; and that done, 155
My tongue should like a knife tear out the secret
Which cankers my heart's core; ay, lay all bare
So that my unpolluted fame should be
With vilest gossips a stale mouthèd story;
A mock, a byword, an astonishment:— 160
If this were done, which never shall be done,
Think of the offender's gold, his dreaded hate,
And the strange horror of the accuser's tale,

Baffling belief, and overpowering speech;
Scarce whispered, unimaginable, wrapped   165
In hideous hints . . . Oh, most assured redress!
 Orsino. You will endure it then?
 Beatrice.   Endure?—Orsino,
It seems your counsel is small profit.
     [*Turns from him, and speaks half to herself.*
         Ay,
All must be suddenly resolved and done.
What is this undistinguishable mist   170
Of thoughts, which rise, like shadow after shadow,
Darkening each other?
 Orsino.   Should the offender live?
Triumph in his misdeed? and make, by use,
His crime, whate'er it is, dreadful no doubt,
Thine element; until thou mayst become   175
Utterly lost; subdued even to the hue
Of that which thou permittest?
 Beatrice (*to herself*).   Mighty death!
Thou double-visaged shadow? Only judge!
Rightfullest arbiter!   [*She retires absorbed in thought.*
 Lucretia.   If the lightning
Of God has e'er descended to avenge . . .   180
 Orsino. Blaspheme not! His high Providence commits
Its glory on this earth, and their own wrongs
Into the hands of men; if they neglect
To punish crime . . .
 Lucretia.   But if one, like this wretch,
Should mock, with gold, opinion, law, and power?   185
If there be no appeal to that which makes
The guiltiest tremble? If because our wrongs,
For that they are unnatural, strange, and monstrous,
Exceed all measure of belief? O God!
If, for the very reasons which should make   190
Redress most swift and sure, our injurer triumphs?
And we, the victims, bear worse punishment
Than that appointed for their torturer?
 Orsino.   Think not
But that there is redress where there is wrong,
So we be bold enough to seize it.
 Lucretia.   How?   195
If there were any way to make all sure,
I know not . . . but I think it might be good
To . . .
 Orsino. Why, his late outrage to Beatrice;
For it is such, as I but faintly guess,
As makes remorse dishonour, and leaves her   200

Only one duty, how she may avenge:
You, but one refuge from ills ill endured;
Me, but one counsel . . .

    Lucretia.   For we cannot hope
That aid, or retribution, or resource
Will arise thence, where every other one   205
Might find them with less need.   [BEATRICE *advances.*

    Orsino.   Then . . .

    Beatrice.   Peace, Orsino!
And, honoured Lady, while I speak, I pray,
That you put off, as garments overworn,
Forbearance and respect, remorse and fear,
And all the fit restraints of daily life,   210
Which have been borne from childhood, but which now
Would be a mockery to my holier plea.
As I have said, I have endured a wrong,
Which, though it be expressionless, is such
As asks atonement; both for what is past,   215
And lest I be reserved, day after day,
To load with crimes an overburthened soul,
And be . . . what ye can dream not. I have prayed
To God, and I have talked with my own heart,
And have unravelled my entangled will,   220
And have at length determined what is right.
Art thou my friend, Orsino? False or true?
Pledge thy salvation ere I speak.

    Orsino.   I swear
To dedicate my cunning, and my strength,
My silence, and whatever else is mine,   225
To thy commands.

    Lucretia.   You think we should devise
His death?

    Beatrice. And execute what is devised,
And suddenly. We must be brief and bold.

    Orsino. And yet most cautious.

    Lucretia.   For the jealous laws
Would punish us with death and infamy   230
For that which it became themselves to do.

    Beatrice. Be cautious as ye may, but prompt. Orsino,
What are the means?

    Orsino.   I know two dull, fierce outlaws,
Who think man's spirit as a worm's, and they
Would trample out, for any slight caprice,   235
The meanest or the noblest life. This mood
Is marketable here in Rome. They sell
What we now want.

Lucretia. To-morrow before dawn,
Cenci will take us to that lonely rock,
Petrella, in the Apulian Apennines. 240
If he arrive there . . .
 Beatrice.   He must not arrive.
 Orsino. Will it be dark before you reach the tower?
 Lucretia. The sun will scarce be set.
 Beatrice.   But I remember
Two miles on this side of the fort, the road
Crosses a deep ravine; 'tis rough and narrow, 245
And winds with short turns down the precipice;
And in its depth there is a mighty rock,
Which has, from unimaginable years,
Sustained itself with terror and with toil
Over a gulf, and with the agony 250
With which it clings seems slowly coming down;
Even as a wretched soul hour after hour,
Clings to the mass of life; yet clinging, leans;
And leaning, makes more dark the dread abyss
In which it fears to fall: beneath this crag 255
Huge as despair, as if in weariness,
The melancholy mountain yawns . . . below,
You hear but see not an impetuous torrent
Raging among the caverns, and a bridge
Crosses the chasm; and high above there grow, 260
With intersecting trunks, from crag to crag,
Cedars, and yews, and pines; whose tangled hair
Is matted in one solid roof of shade
By the dark ivy's twine. At noonday here
'Tis twilight, and at sunset blackest night. 265
 Orsino. Before you reach that bridge make some excuse
For spurring on your mules, or loitering
Until . . .
 Beatrice. What sound is that?
 Lucretia. Hark! No, it cannot be a servant's step
It must be Cenci, unexpectedly 270
Returned . . . Make some excuse for being here.
 Beatrice. (*To* ORSINO, *as she goes out.*) That step we hear
  approach must never pass
The bridge of which we spoke.
        [*Exeunt* LUCRETIA *and* BEATRICE.
 Orsino.   What shall I do?
Cenci must find me here, and I must bear
The imperious inquisition of his looks 275
As to what brought me hither: let me mask
Mine own in some inane and vacant smile.

Enter GIACOMO, *in a hurried manner.*

How! Have you ventured hither? Know you then
That Cenci is from home?
    Giacomo.   I sought him here;
And now must wait till he returns.
    Orsino.   Great God!   280
Weigh you the danger of this rashness?
    Giacomo.   Ay!
Does my destroyer know his danger? We
Are now no more, as once, parent and child,
But man to man; the oppressor to the oppressed;
The slanderer to the slandered; foe to foe: 285
He has cast Nature off, which was his shield,
And Nature casts him off, who is her shame;
And I spurn both. Is it a father's throat
Which I will shake, and say, I ask not gold;
I ask not happy years; nor memories   290
Of tranquil childhood; nor home-sheltered love;
Though all these hast thou torn from me, and more;
But only my fair fame; only one hoard
Of peace, which I thought hidden from thy hate,
Under the penury heaped on me by thee,   295
Or I will . . . God can understand and pardon,
Why should I speak with man?
    Orsino.   Be calm, dear friend
    Giacomo. Well, I will calmly tell you what he did.
This old Francesco Cenci, as you know,
Borrowed the dowry of my wife from me,   300
And then denied the loan; and left me so
In poverty, the which I sought to mend
By holding a poor office in the state.
It had been promised to me, and already
I bought new clothing for my raggèd babes,   305
And my wife smiled; and my heart knew repose.
When Cenci's intercession, as I found,
Conferred this office on a wretch, whom thus
He paid for vilest service. I returned
With this ill news, and we sate sad together   310
Solacing our despondency with tears
Of such affection and unbroken faith
As temper life's worst bitterness; when he,
As he is wont, came to upbraid and curse,
Mocking our poverty, and telling us   315
Such was God's scourge for disobedient sons.
And then, that I might strike him dumb with shame,
I spoke of my wife's dowry; but he coined

A brief yet specious tale, how I had wasted
The sum in secret riot; and he saw   320
My wife was touched, and he went smiling forth.
And when I knew the impression he had made,
And felt my wife insult with silent scorn
My ardent truth, and look averse and cold,
I went forth too: but soon returned again;   325
Yet not so soon but that my wife had taught
My children her harsh thoughts, and they all cried,
'Give us clothes, father! Give us better food!
What you in one night squander were enough
For months!' I looked, and saw that home was hell.   330
And to that hell will I return to more
Until mine enemy has rendered up
Atonement, or, as he gave life to me
I will, reversing Nature's law . . .
    Orsino.   Trust me,
The compensation which thou seekest here   335
Will be denied.
    Giacomo.   Then . . . Are you not my friend?
Did you not hint at the alternative,
Upon the brink of which you see I stand,
The other day when we conversed together?
My wrongs were then less. That word parricide,   340
Although I am resolved, haunts me like fear.
    Orsino. It must be fear itself, for the bare word
Is hollow mockery. Mark, how wisest God
Draws to one point the threads of a just doom,
So sanctifying it: what you devise   345
Is, as it were, accomplished.
    Giacomo.   Is he dead?
    Orsino. His grave is ready. Know that since we met
Cenci has done an outrage to his daughter.
    Giacomo. What outrage?
    Orsino.   That she speaks not, but you may
Conceive such half conjectures as I do,   350
From her fixed paleness, and the lofty grief
Of her stern brow bent on the idle air,
And her severe unmodulated voice,
Drowning both tenderness and dread; and last
From this; that whilst her step-mother and I,   355
Bewildered in our horror, talked together
With obscure hints; both self-misunderstood
And darkly guessing, stumbling, in our talk,
Over the truth, and yet to its revenge,
She interrupted us, and with a look   360
Which told before she spoke it, he must die: . . .

Giacomo. It is enough. My doubts are well appeased;
There is a higher reason for the act
Than mine; there is a holier judge than me,
A more unblamed avenger. Beatrice,   365
Who in the gentleness of thy sweet youth
Hast never trodden on a worm, or bruised
A living flower, but thou hast pitied it
With needless tears! Fair sister, thou in whom
Men wondered how such loveliness and wisdom   370
Did not destroy each other! Is there made
Ravage of thee? O, heart, I ask no more
Justification! Shall I wait, Orsino,
Till he return, and stab him at the door?
    Orsino. Not so; some accident might interpose   375
To rescue him from what is now most sure;
And you are unprovided where to fly,
How to excuse or to conceal. Nay, listen:
All is contrived; success is so assured
That . . .

Enter BEATRICE.

Beatrice. 'Tis my brother's voice! You know me not?
    Giacomo. My sister, my lost sister!
    Beatrice.   Lost indeed!   381
I see Orsino has talked with you, and
That you conjecture things too horrible
To speak, yet far less than the truth. Now, stay not,
He might return: yet kiss me; I shall know   385
That then thou hast consented to his death.
Farewell, farewell! Let piety to God,
Brotherly love, justice and clemency,
And all things that make tender hardest hearts
Make thine hard, brother. Answer not . . . farewell.   390
                          [Exeunt severally.

SCENE II.—*A mean Apartment in* GIACOMO'S *House.* GIACOMO *alone.*

    Giacomo. 'Tis midnight, and Orsino comes not yet.
                [Thunder, and the sound of a storm.
What! can the everlasting elements
Feel with a worm like man? If so, the shaft
Of mercy-wingèd lightning would not fall
On stones and trees. My wife and children sleep: 5
They are now living in unmeaning dreams:
But I must wake, still doubting if that deed
Be just which is most necessary. O,
Thou unreplenishing lamp! whose narrow fire
Is shaken by the wind, and on whose edge   10

Devouring darkness hovers! Thou small flame,
Which, as a dying pulse rises and falls,
Still flickerest up and down, how very soon,
Did I not feed thee, wouldst thou fail and be
As thou hadst never been! So wastes and sinks   15
Even now, perhaps, the life that kindled mine:
But that no power can fill with vital oil
That broken lamp of flesh. Ha! 'tis the blood
Which fed these veins that ebbs till all is cold:
It is the form that moulded mine that sinks   20
Into the white and yellow spasms of death:
It is the soul by which mine was arrayed
In God's immortal likeness which now stands
Naked before Heaven's judgement seat!   [*A bell strikes.*
                                        One! Two!
The hours crawl on; and when my hairs are white,   25
My son will then perhaps be waiting thus,
Tortured between just hate and vain remorse;
Chiding the tardy messenger of news
Like those which I expect. I almost wish
He be not dead, although my wrongs are great;   30
Yet . . . 'tis Orsino's step . . .

                  Enter ORSINO.

                              Speak!
Orsino.   I am come
To say he has escaped.
    Giacomo.   Escaped!
    Orsino.   And safe
Within Petrella. He passed by the spot
Appointed for the deed an hour too soon.
    Giacomo. Are we the fools of such contingencies? 35
And do we waste in blind misgivings thus
The hours when we should act? Then wind and thunder,
Which seemed to howl his knell, is the loud laughter
With which Heaven mocks our weakness! I henceforth
Will ne'er repent of aught designed or done   40
But my repentance.
    Orsino.   See, the lamp is out.
    Giacomo. If no remorse is ours when the dim air
Has drank this innocent flame, why should we quail
When Cenci's life, that light by which ill spirits
See the worst deeds they prompt, shall sink for ever? 45
No, I am hardened.
    Orsino.   Why, what need of this?
Who feared the pale intrusion of remorse
In a just deed? Although our first plan failed,

Doubt not but he will soon be laid to rest.
But light the lamp; let us not talk i' the dark.   50
    Giacomo (*lighting the lamp*). And yet once quenched I cannot
        thus relume
My father's life: do you not think his ghost
Might plead that argument with God?
    Orsino.   Once gone
You cannot now recall your sister's peace;
Your own extinguished years of youth and hope;   55
Nor your wife's bitter words; nor all the taunts
Which, from the prosperous, weak misfortune takes;
Nor your dead mother; nor . . .
    Giacomo.   O, speak no more!
I am resolved, although this very hand
Must quench the life that animated it.   60
    Orsino. There is no need of that. Listen: you know
Olimpio, the castellan of Petrella
In old Colonna's time; him whom your father
Degraded from his post? And Marzio,
That desperate wretch, whom he deprived last year   65
Of a reward of blood, well earned and due?
    Giacomo. I knew Olimpio; and they say he hated
Old Cenci so, that in his silent rage
His lips grew white only to see him pass.
Of Marzio I know nothing.
    Orsino.   Marzio's hate   70
Matches Olimpio's. I have sent these men,
But in your name, and as at your request,
To talk with Beatrice and Lucretia.
    Giacomo. Only to talk?
    Orsino.   The moments which even now
Pass onward to to-morrow's midnight hour   75
May memorize their flight with death: ere then
They must have talked, and may perhaps have done,
And made an end . . .
    Giacomo.   Listen! What sound is that?
    Orsino. The house-dog moans, and the beams crack: nought else.
    Giacomo. It is my wife complaining in her sleep: 80
I doubt not she is saying bitter things
Of me, and all my children round her dreaming
That I deny them sustenance.
    Orsino.   Whilst he
Who truly took it from them, and who fills
Their hungry rest with bitterness, now sleeps   85
Lapped in bad pleasures, and triumphantly
Mocks thee in visions of successful hate
Too like the truth of day.

Giacomo.   If e'er he wakes
Again, I will not trust to hireling hands . . .
    Orsino. Why, that were well. I must be gone; good-night.
When next we meet—may all be done!
    Giacomo.   And all   91
Forgotten: Oh, that I had never been!   [*Exeunt.*

END OF THE THIRD ACT.

ACT IV

SCENE I.—*An Apartment in the Castle of Petrella. Enter* CENCI.

Cenci. She comes not; yet I left her even now
Vanquished and faint. She knows the penalty
Or her delay: yet what if threats are vain?
Am I not now within Petrella's moat?
Or fear I still the eyes and ears of Rome?   5
Might I not drag her by the golden hair?
Stamp on her? Keep her sleepless till her brain
Be overworn? Tame her with chains and famine?
Less would suffice. Yet so to leave undone
What I most seek! No, 'tis her stubborn will   10
Which by its own consent shall stoop as low
As that which drags it down.

Enter LUCRETIA.

                             Thou loathèd wretch!
Hide thee from my abhorrence: fly, begone!
Yet stay! Bid Beatrice come hither.
    Lucretia.   Oh,
Husband! I pray for thine own wretched sake   15
Heed what thou dost. A man who walks like thee
Through crimes, and through the danger of his crimes,
Each hour may stumble o'er a sudden grave.
And thou art old; thy hairs are hoary gray;
As thou wouldst save thyself from death and hell,   20
Pity thy daughter; give her to some friend
In marriage: so that she may tempt thee not
To hatred, or worse thoughts, if worse there be.
    Cenci. What! like her sister who has found a home
To mock my hate from with prosperity?   25
Strange ruin shall destroy both her and thee
And all that yet remain. My death may be
Rapid, her destiny outspeeds it. Go,
Bid her come hither, and before my mood
Be changed, lest I should drag her by the hair.   30
    Lucretia. She sent me to thee, husband. At thy presence

She fell, as thou dost know, into a trance;
And in that trance she heard a voice which said,
'Cenci must die! Let him confess himself!
Even now the accusing Angel waits to hear   35
If God, to punish his enormous crimes,
Harden his dying heart!'
 Cenci.   Why—such things are . . .
No doubt divine revealings may be made.
'Tis plain I have been favoured from above,   39
For when I cursed my sons they died.—Ay . . . so . . .
As to the right or wrong, that's talk . . . repentance . . .
Repentance is an easy moment's work
And more depends on God than me. Well . . . well . . .
I must give up the greater point, which was
To poison and corrupt her soul.
     [*A pause;* LUCRETIA *approaches anxiously, and*
      then shrinks back as he speaks.
        One, two;   45
Ay . . . Rocco and Cristofano my curse
Strangled: and Giacomo, I think, will find
Life a worse Hell than that beyond the grave:
Beatrice shall, if there be skill in hate,
Die in despair, blaspheming: to Bernardo,   50
He is so innocent, I will bequeath
The memory of these deeds, and make his youth
The sepulchre of hope, where evil thoughts
Shall grow like weeds on a neglected tomb.
When all is done, out in the wide Campagna,   55
I will pile up my silver and my gold;
My costly robes, paintings and tapestries;
My parchments and all records of my wealth,
And make a bonfire in my joy, and leave
Of my possessions nothing but my name;   60
Which shall be an inheritance to strip
Its wearer bare as infamy. That done,
My soul, which is a scourge, will I resign
Into the hands of him who wielded it;
Be it for its own punishment or theirs,   65
He will not ask it of me till the lash
Be broken in its last and deepest wound;
Until its hate be all inflicted. Yet,
Lest death outspeed my purpose, let me make
Short work and sure . . .   [*Going.*
 Lucretia. (*Stops him.*) Oh, stay! It was a feint: 70
She had no vision, and she heard no voice.
I said it but to awe thee.
 Cenci.   That is well.

Vile palterer with the sacred truth of God,
Be thy soul choked with that blaspheming lie!
For Beatrice worse terrors are in store   75
To bend her to my will.
   Lucretia.   Oh! to what will?
What cruel sufferings more than she has known
Canst thou inflict?
   Cenci.   Andrea! Go call my daughter,
And if she comes not tell her that I come.
What sufferings? I will drag her, step by step,   80
Through infamies unheard of among men:
She shall stand shelterless in the broad noon
Of public scorn, for acts blazoned abroad,
One among which shall be . . . What? Canst thou guess?
She shall become (for what she most abhors   85
Shall have a fascination to entrap
Her loathing will) to her own conscious self
All she appears to others; and when dead,
As she shall die unshrived and unforgiven,
A rebel to her father and her God,   90
Her corpse shall be abandoned to the hounds;
Her name shall be the terror of the earth;
Her spirit shall approach the throne of God
Plague-spotted with my curses. I will make
Body and soul a monstrous lump of ruin.   95

Enter ANDREA.

   Andrea. The Lady Beatrice . . .
   Cenci.   Speak, pale slave! What
Said she?
   Andrea. My Lord, 'twas what she looked; she said:
'Go tell my father that I see the gulf
Of Hell between us two, which he may pass,
I will not.'

                                     [*Exit* ANDREA.
   Cenci.   Go thou quick, Lucretia,   100
Tell her to come; yet let her understand
Her coming is consent: and say, moreover,
That if she come not I will curse her.

                                   [*Exit* LUCRETIA.
                 Ha!
With what but with a father's curse doth God
Panic-strike armèd victory, and make pale   105
Cities in their prosperity? The world's Father
Must grant a parent's prayer against his child,
Be he who asks even what men call me.
Will not the deaths of her rebellious brothers

Awe her before I speak? For I on them   110
Did imprecate quick ruin, and it came.

Enter LUCRETIA.

Well; what? Speak, wretch!
    Lucretia.   She said, 'I cannot come;
Go tell my father that I see a torrent
Of his own blood raging between us.'
    Cenci (kneeling).   God!
Hear me! If this most specious mass of flesh,   115
Which Thou hast made my daughter; this my blood,
This particle of my divided being;
Or rather, this my bane and my disease,
Whose sight infects and poisons me; this devil
Which sprung from me as from a hell, was meant   120
To aught good use; if her bright loveliness
Was kindled to illumine this dark world;
If nursed by Thy selectest dew of love
Such virtues blossom in her as should make
The peace of life, I pray Thee for my sake,   125
As Thou the common God and Father art
Of her, and me, and all; reverse that doom!
Earth, in the name of God, let her food be
Poison, until she be encrusted round
With leprous stains! Heaven, rain upon her head   130
The blistering drops of the Maremma's dew,
Till she be speckled like a toad; parch up
Those love-enkindled lips, warp those fine limbs
To loathèd lameness! All-beholding sun,
Strike in thine envy those life-darting eyes   135
With thine own blinding beams!
    Lucretia.   Peace! Peace!
For thine own sake unsay those dreadful words.
When high God grants He punishes such prayers.
    Cenci (leaping up, and throwing his right hand towards Heaven).
        He does His will, I mine! This in addition,
That if she have a child . . .
    Lucretia.   Horrible thought!   140
    Cenci. That if she ever have a child; and thou,
Quick Nature! I adjure thee by thy God,
That thou be fruitful in her, and increase
And multiply, fulfilling his command,
And my deep imprecation! May it be   145
A hideous likeness of herself, that as
From a distorting mirror, she may see
Her image mixed with what she most abhors.

Smiling upon her from her nursing breast.
And that the child may from its infancy   150
Grow, day by day, more wicked and deformed,
Turning her mother's love to misery:
And that both she and it may live until
It shall repay her care and pain with hate,
Or what may else be more unnatural.   155
So he may hunt her through the clamorous scoffs
Of the loud world to a dishonoured grave.
Shall I revoke this curse? Go, bid her come,
Before my words are chronicled in Heaven.

                                   [*Exit* LUCRETIA.

I do not feel as if I were a man,   160
But like a fiend appointed to chastise
The offences of some unremembered world.
My blood is running up and down my veins;
A fearful pleasure makes it prick and tingle:
I feel a giddy sickness of strange awe;   165
My heart is beating with an expectation
Of horrid joy.

                    Enter LUCRETIA.

          What? Speak!

     Lucretia.   She bids thee curse;
And if thy curses, as they cannot do,
Could kill her soul . . .

          Cenci.   She would not come. 'Tis well,
I can do both: first take what I demand,   170
And then extort concession. To thy chamber!
Fly ere I spurn thee: and beware this night
That thou cross not my footsteps. It were safer
To come between the tiger and his prey.   [*Exit* LUCRETIA.
It must be late; mine eyes grow weary dim   175
With unaccustomed heaviness of sleep.
Conscience! Oh, thou most insolent of lies!
They say that sleep, that healing dew of Heaven,
Steeps not in balm the foldings of the brain
Which thinks thee an impostor. I will go   180
First to belie thee with an hour of rest,
Which will be deep and calm, I feel: and then . . .
O, multitudinous Hell, the fiends will shake
Thine arches with the laughter of their joy!
There shall be lamentation heard in Heaven   185
As o'er an angel fallen; and upon Earth
All good shall droop and sicken, and ill things
Shall with a spirit of unnatural life
Stir and be quickened . . . even as I am now.   [*Exit*

SCENE II.—*Before the Castle of Petrella. Enter* BEATRICE *and* LUCRETIA
above on the Ramparts.

Beatrice. They come not yet.
Lucretia.   'Tis scarce midnight.
Beatrice.   How slow
Behind the course of thought, even sick with speed,
Lags leaden-footed time!
Lucretia.   The minutes pass . . .
If he should wake before the deed is done?
Beatrice. O, mother! He must never wake again.   5
What thou hast said persuades me that our act
Will but dislodge a spirit of deep hell
Out of a human form.
Lucretia.   'Tis true he spoke
Of death and judgement with strange confidence
For one so wicked; as a man believing   10
In God, yet recking not of good or ill.
And yet to die without confession! . . .
Beatrice.   Oh!
Believe that Heaven is merciful and just,
And will not add our dread necessity
To the amount of his offences.

                Enter OLIMPIO *and* MARZIO, *below.*
Lucretia.   See,   15
They come.
Beatrice.   All mortal things must hasten thus
To their dark end. Let us go down.
                [*Exeunt* LUCRETIA *and* BEATRICE *from above.*
Olimpio. How feel you to this work?
Marzio.   As one who thinks
A thousand crowns excellent market price
For an old murderer's life. Your cheeks are pale.   20
Olimpio. It is the white reflection of your own,
Which you call pale.
Marzio.   Is that their natural hue?
Olimpio. Or 'tis my hate and the deferred desire
To wreak it, which extinguishes their blood.
Marzio. You are inclined then to this business?
Olimpio.   Ay.   25
If one should bribe me with a thousand crowns
To kill a serpent which had stung my child,
I could not be more willing.

                Enter BEATRICE *and* LUCRETIA, *below.*
                        Noble ladies!
Beatrice. Are ye resolved?

Olimpio.   Is he asleep?
Marzio.   Is all
Quiet?
Lucretia. I mixed an opiate with his drink: 30
He sleeps so soundly . . .
Beatrice.   That his death will be
But as a change of sin-chastising dreams,
A dark continuance of the Hell within him,
Which God extinguish! But ye are resolved?
Ye know it is a high and holy deed?   35
Olimpio. We are resolved.
Marzio.   As to the how this act
Be warranted, it rests with you.
Beatrice.   Well, follow!
Olimpio. Hush! Hark! What noise is that?
Marzio.   Ha! some one comes!
Beatrice. Ye conscience-stricken cravens, rock to rest
Your baby hearts. It is the iron gate,   40
Which ye left open, swinging to the wind,
That enters whistling as in scorn. Come, follow!
And be your steps like mine, light, quick and bold.   [*Exeunt.*

SCENE III.—*An Apartment in the Castle. Enter* BEATRICE *and* LUCRETIA.

Lucretia. They are about it now.
Beatrice.   Nay, it is done.
Lucretia. I have not heard him groan.
Beatrice.   He will not groan.
Lucretia. What sound is that?
Beatrice.   List! 'tis the tread of feet
About his bed.
Lucretia.   My God!
If he be now a cold stiff corpse . . .
Beatrice.   O, fear not   5
What may be done, but what is left undone:
The act seals all.

                    Enter OLIMPIO *and* MARZIO.

                        Is it accomplished?
Marzio.   What?
Olimpio. Did you not call?
Beatrice.   When?
Olimpio.   Now.
Beatrice.   I ask if all is over?
Olimpio. We dare not kill an old and sleeping man;
His thin gray hair, his stern and reverend brow,   10
His veinèd hands crossed on his heaving breast,
And the calm innocent sleep in which he lay,

Quelled me. Indeed, indeed, I cannot do it.
    Marzio. But I was bolder; for I chid Olimpio,
And bade him bear his wrongs to his own grave   15
And leave me the reward. And now my knife
Touched the loose wrinkled throat, when the old man
Stirred in his sleep, and said, 'God! hear, O, hear,
A father's curse! What, art Thou not our Father?'
And then he laughed. I knew it was the ghost   20
Of my dead father speaking through his lips,
And could not kill him.
    Beatrice.   Miserable slaves!
Where, if ye dare not kill a sleeping man,
Found ye the boldness to return to me
With such a deed undone? Base palterers!   25
Cowards and traitors! Why, the very conscience
Which ye would sell for gold and for revenge
Is an equivocation: it sleeps over
A thousand daily acts disgracing men;
And when a deed where mercy insults Heaven . . .   30
Why do I talk?
                [*Snatching a dagger from one of them and raising it.*
                    Hadst thou a tongue to say,
'She murdered her own father!'—I must do it!
But never dream ye shall outlive him long!
    Olimpio. Stop, for God's sake!
    Marzio.   I will go back and kill him.
    Olimpio. Give me the weapon, we must do thy will. 35
    Beatrice. Take it! Depart! Return!
                        [*Exeunt* OLIMPIO *and* MARZIO.
                                    How pale thou art!
We do but that which 'twere a deadly crime
To leave undone.
    Lucretia.   Would it were done!
    Beatrice.   Even whilst
That doubt is passing through your mind, the world
Is conscious of a change. Darkness and Hell   40
Have swallowed up the vapour they sent forth
To blacken the sweet light of life. My breath
Comes, methinks, lighter, and the jellied blood
Runs freely through my veins. Hark!

                Enter OLIMPIO *and* MARZIO.

                    He is . . .
    Olimpio.   Dead?
    Marzio. We strangled him that there might be no blood; 45
And then we threw his heavy corpse i' the garden
Under the balcony; 'twill seem it fell.

Beatrice (*giving them a bag of coin*). Here, take this gold, and
 hasten to your homes.
And, Marzio, because thou wast only awed
By that which made me tremble, wear thou this!   50
        [*Clothes him in a rich mantle.*
It was the mantle which my grandfather
Wore in his high prosperity, and men
Envied his state: so may they envy thine.
Thou wert a weapon in the hand of God
To a just use. Live long and thrive! And, mark,   55
If thou hast crimes, repent: this deed is none.
           [*A horn is sounded.*
 Lucretia. Hark, 'tis the castle horn; my God! it sounds
Like the last trump.
 Beatrice.   Some tedious guest is coming.
 Lucretia. The drawbridge is let down; there is a tramp
Of horses in the court; fly, hide yourselves!   60
      [*Exeunt* OLIMPIO *and* MARZIO.
 Beatrice. Let us retire to counterfeit deep rest;
I scarcely need to counterfeit it now:
The spirit which doth reign within these limbs
Seems strangely undisturbed. I could even sleep   64
Fearless and calm: all ill is surely past.   [*Exeunt.*

SCENE IV.—*Another Apartment in the Castle. Enter on one side the*
LEGATE SAVELLA, *introduced by a Servant, and on the other* LUCRE-
TIA *and* BERNARDO.

 Savella. Lady, my duty to his Holiness
Be my excuse that thus unseasonably
I break upon your rest. I must speak with
Count Cenci; doth he sleep?
 Lucretia (*in a hurried and confused manner*). I think he sleeps;
Yet wake him not, I pray, spare me awhile,   5
He is a wicked and wrathful man;
Should he be roused out of his sleep to-night,
Which is, I know, a hell of angry dreams,
It were not well; indeed it were not well.
Wait till day break . . . (*aside*) O, I am deadly sick! 10
 Savella. I grieve thus to distress you, but the Count
Must answer charges of the gravest import,
And suddenly; such my commssion is.
 Lucretia (*with increased agitation*). I dare not rouse him: I
 know none who dare . . .
'Twere perilous; . . . you might as safely waken 15
A serpent; or a corpse in which some fiend
Were laid to sleep.
 Savella.   Lady, my moments here

Are counted. I must rouse him from his sleep,
Since none else dare.
    Lucretia (aside).   O, terror! O, despair!
(*To* BERNARDO.) Bernardo, conduct you the Lord Legate to   20
    Your father's chamber.   [*Exeunt* SAVELLA *and* BERNARDO.

Enter BEATRICE.

Beatrice.   'Tis a messenger
Come to arrest the culprit who now stands
Before the throne of unappealable God.
Both Earth and Heaven, consenting arbiters,
Acquit our deed.
    Lucretia.   Oh, agony of fear!   25
Would that he yet might live! Even now I heard
The Legate's followers whisper as they passed
They had a warrant for his instant death.
All was prepared by unforbidden means
Which we must pay so dearly, having done.   30
Even now they search the tower, and find the body;
Now they suspect the truth; now they consult
Before they come to tax us with the fact;
O, horrible, 'tis all discovered!
    Beatrice.   Mother,
What is done wisely, is done well. Be bold   35
As thou art just. 'Tis like a truant child
To fear that others know what thou hast done,
Even from thine own strong consciousness, and thus
Write on unsteady eyes and altered cheeks
All thou wouldst hide. Be faithful to thyself,   40
And fear no other witness but thy fear.
For if, as cannot be, some circumstance
Should rise in accusation, we can blind
Suspicion with such cheap astonishment,
Or overbear it with such guiltless pride,   45
As murderers cannot feign. The deed is done,
And what may follow now regards not me.
I am as universal as the light;
Free as the earth-surrounding air; as firm
As the world's centre. Consequence, to me,   50
Is as the wind which strikes the solid rock
But shakes it not.   [*A cry within and tumult.*
    Voices.   Murder! Murder! Murder!

Enter BERNARDO *and* SAVELLA.

Savella (to his followers). Go search the castle round; sound
    the alarm;
Look to the gates that none escape!

Beatrice.   What now?   **54**

Bernardo. I know not what to say . . . my father's dead.

Beatrice. How; dead! he only sleeps; you mistake, brother.
His sleep is very calm, very like death;
'Tis wonderful how well a tyrant sleeps.
He is not dead?

Bernardo.   Dead; murdered.

Lucretia (*with extreme agitation*). Oh no, no,
He is not murdered though he may be dead;   **60**
I have alone the keys of those apartments.

Savella. Ha! Is it so?

Beatrice.   My Lord, I pray excuse us;
We will retire; my mother is not well:
She seems quite overcome with this strange horror.

                            [*Exeunt* LUCRETIA *and* BEATRICE.

Savella. Can you suspect who may have murdered him?   **65**

Bernardo. I know not what to think.

Savella.   Can you name any
Who had an interest in his death?

Bernardo.   Alas!
I can name none who had not, and those most
Who most lament that such a deed is done;
My mother, and my sister, and myself.   **70**

Savella. 'Tis strange! There were clear marks of violence.
I found the old man's body in the moonlight
Hanging beneath the window of his chamber,
Among the branches of a pine: he could not
Have fallen there, for all his limbs lay heaped   **75**
And effortless; 'tis true there was no blood . . .
Favour me, Sir; it much imports your house
That all should be made clear; to tell the ladies
That I request their presence.

                            [*Exit* BERNARDO.

Enter GUARDS *bringing in* MARZIO.

Guard.   We have one.

Officer. My Lord, we found this ruffian and another   **80**
Lurking among the rocks; there is no doubt
But that they are the murderers of Count Cenci:
Each had a bag of coin; this fellow wore
A gold-inwoven robe, which shining bright
Under the dark rocks to the glimmering moon   **85**
Betrayed them to our notice: the other fell
Desperately fighting.

Savella.   What does he confess?

Officer. He keeps firm silence; but these lines found on him
May speak.

Savella.   Their language is at least sincere.   [*Reads.*
          '*To the Lady Beatrice.*

'*That the atonement of what my nature sickens to conjecture*
may soon arrive, I send thee, at thy brother's desire, those who will
speak and do more than I dare write . . .
                              '*Thy devoted servant, Orsino.*'

Enter LUCRETIA, BEATRICE, *and* BERNARDO.

Knowest thou this writing, Lady?
          Beatrice.   No.
          Savella.   Nor thou?   95
          Lucretia. (*Her conduct throughout the scene is marked by ex-*
               treme agitation.) Where was it found? What is it? It should
               be
Orsino's hand! It speaks of that strange horror
Which never yet found utterance, but which made
Between that hapless child and her dead father
A gulf of obscure hatred.
          Savella.   Is it so?   100
Is it true, Lady, that thy father did
Such outrages as to awaken in thee
Unfilial hate?
          Beatrice.   Not hate, 'twas more than hate:
This is most true, yet wherefore question me?
          Savella. There is a deed demanding question done;   105
Thou hast a secret which will answer not.
          Beatrice. What sayest? My Lord, your words are bold and rash.
          Savella. I do arrest all present in the name
Of the Pope's Holiness. You must to Rome.
          Lucretia. O, not to Rome! Indeed we are not guilty.   110
          Beatrice. Guilty! Who dares talk of guilt? My Lord,
I am more innocent of parricide
Than is a child born fatherless . . . Dear mother,
Your gentleness and patience are no shield
For this keen-judging world, this two-edged lie,   115
Which seems, but is not. What! will human laws,
Rather will ye who are their ministers,
Bar all access to retribution first,
And then, when Heaven doth interpose to do
What ye neglect, arming familiar things   120
To the redress of an unwonted crime,
Make ye the victims who demanded it
Culprits? 'Tis ye are culprits! That poor wretch
Who stands so pale, and trembling, and amazed,
If it be true he murdered Cenci, was   125
A sword in the right hand of justest God.
Wherefore should I have wielded it? Unless

The crimes which mortal tongue dare never name
God therefore scruples to avenge.
    Savella.   You own
That you desired his death?
    Beatrice.   It would have been   130
A crime no less than his, if for one moment
That fierce desire had faded in my heart.
'Tis true I did believe, and hope, and pray,
Ay, I even knew . . . for God is wise and just,
That some strange sudden death hung over him.   135
'Tis true that this did happen, and most true
There was no other rest for me on earth,
No other hope in Heaven . . . now what of this?
    Savella. Strange thoughts beget strange deeds; and here are both:
I judge thee not.
    Beatrice.   And yet, if you arrest me,   140
You are the judge and executioner
Of that which is the life of life: the breath
Of accusation kills an innocent name,
And leaves for lame acquittal the poor life
Which is a mask without it. 'Tis most false   145
That I am guilty of foul parricide;
Although I must rejoice, for justest cause,
That other hands have sent my father's soul
To ask the mercy he denied to me.
Now leave us free; stain not a noble house   150
With vague surmises of rejected crime;
Add to our sufferings and your own neglect
No heavier sum: let them have been enough:
Leave us the wreck we have.
    Savella.   I dare not, Lady.
I pray that you prepare yourselves for Rome: 155
There the Pope's further pleasure will be known.
    Lucretia. O, not to Rome! O, take us not to Rome!
    Beatrice. Why not to Rome, dear mother? There as here
Our innocence is as an armèd heel
To trample accusation. God is there   160
As here, and with His shadow ever clothes
The innocent, the injured and the weak;
And such are we. Cheer up, dear Lady, lean
On me; collect your wandering thoughts. My Lord,
As soon as you have taken some refreshment,   165
And had all such examinations made
Upon the spot, as may be necessary
To the full understanding of this matter,
We shall be ready. Mother; will you come?
    Lucretia. Ha! they will bind us to the rack, and wrest

Self-accusation from our agony!   171
Will Giacomo be there? Orsino? Marzio?
All present; all confronted; all demanding
Each from the other's countenance the thing
Which is in every heart! O, misery!   175

                              [*She faints, and is borne out.*

Savella. She faints: an ill appearance this.
Beatrice.   My Lord,
She knows not yet the uses of the world.
She fears that power is as a beast which grasps
And loosens not: a snake whose look transmutes
All things to guilt which is its nutriment.   180
She cannot know how well the supine slaves
Of blind authority read the truth of things
When written on a brow of guilelessness:
She sees not yet triumphant Innocence
Stand at the judgement-seat of mortal man,   185
A judge and an accuser of the wrong
Which drags it there. Prepare yourself, my Lord;
Our suite will join yours in the court below.   [*Exeunt.*

END OF THE FOURTH ACT.

ACT V

SCENE I.—*An Apartment in* ORSINO'S *Palace. Enter* ORSINO *and*
GIACOMO.

Giacomo. Do evil deeds thus quickly come to end?
O, that the vain remorse which must chastise
Crimes done, had but as loud a voice to warn
As its keen sting is mortal to avenge!
O, that the hour when present had cast off   5
The mantle of its mystery, and shown
The ghastly form with which it now returns
When its scared game is roused, cheering the hounds
Of conscience to their prey! Alas! Alas!
It was a wicked thought, a piteous deed,   10
To kill an old and hoary-headed father.
Orsino. It has turned out unluckily, in truth.
Giacomo. To violate the sacred doors of sleep;
To cheat kind Nature of the placid death
Which she prepares for overwearied age;   15
To drag from Heaven an unrepentant soul
Which might have quenched in reconciling prayers
A life of burning crimes . . .
Orsino.   You cannot say

I urged you to the deed.
    Giacomo.   O, had I never
Found in thy smooth and ready countenance   20
The mirror of my darkest thoughts; hadst thou
Never with hints and questions made me look
Upon the monster of my thought, until
It grew familiar to desire . . .
    Orsino.   'Tis thus
Men cast the blame of their unprosperous acts   25
Upon the abettors of their own resolve;
Or anything but their weak, guilty selves.
And yet, confess the truth, it is the peril
In which you stand that gives you this pale sickness
Of penitence; confess 'tis fear disguised   30
From its own shame that takes the mantle now
Of thin remorse. What if we yet were safe?
    Giacomo. How can that be? Already Beatrice,
Lucretia and the murderer are in prison.
I doubt not officers are, whilst we speak,   35
Sent to arrest us.
    Orsino.   I have all prepared
For instant flight. We can escape even now,
So we take fleet occasion by the hair.
    Giacomo. Rather expire in tortures, as I may.
What! will you cast by self-accusing flight   40
Assured conviction upon Beatrice?
She, who alone in this unnatural work,
Stands like God's angel ministered upon
By fiends; avenging such a nameless wrong
As turns black parricide to piety;   45
Whilst we for basest ends . . . I fear, Orsino,
While I consider all your words and looks,
Comparing them with your proposal now,
That you must be a villain. For what end
Could you engage in such a perilous crime,   50
Training me on with hints, and signs, and smiles,
Even to this gulf? Thou art no liar? No,
Thou art a lie! Traitor and murderer!
Coward and slave! But, no, defend thyself;   *[Drawing.*
Let the sword speak what the indignant tongue   55
Disdains to brand thee with.
    Orsino.   Put up your weapon.
Is it the desperation of your fear
Makes you thus rash and sudden with a friend,
Now ruined for your sake? If honest anger
Have moved you, know, that what I just proposed   60

Was but to try you. As for me, I think,
Thankless affection led me to this point,
From which, if my firm temper could repent,
I cannot now recede. Even whilst we speak
The ministers of justice wait below: 65
They grant me these brief moments. Now if you
Have any word of melancholy comfort
To speak to your pale wife, 'twere best to pass
Out at the postern, and avoid them so.
    Giacomo. O, generous friend! How canst thou pardon me?
Would that my life could purchase thine!
    Orsino.   That wish   71
Now comes a day too late. Haste; fare thee well!
Hear'st thou not steps along the corridor?

                                                  [Exit GIACOMO.

I'm sorry for it; but the guards are waiting
At his own gate, and such was my contrivance   75
That I might rid me both of him and them
I thought to act a solemn comedy
Upon the painted scene of this new world,
And to attain my own peculiar ends
By some such plot of mingled good and ill   80
As others weave; but there arose a Power
Which grasped and snapped the threads of my device
And turned it to a net of ruin . . . Ha!   *[A shout is heard.*
Is that my name I hear proclaimed abroad?
But I will pass, wrapped in a vile disguise;   85
Rags on my back, and a false innocence
Upon my face, through the misdeeming crowd
Which judges by what seems. 'Tis easy then
For a new name and for a country new,
And a new life, fashioned on old desires,   90
To change the honours of abandoned Rome.
And these must be the masks of that within,
Which must remain unaltered . . . Oh, I fear
That what is past will never let me rest!
Why, when none else is conscious, but myself,   95
Of my misdeeds, should my own heart's contempt
Trouble me? Have I not the power to fly
My own reproaches? Shall I be the slave
Of . . . what? A word? which those of this false world
Employ against each other, not themselves;   100
As men wear daggers not for self-offence.
But if I am mistaken, where shall I
Find the disguise to hide me from myself,
As now I skulk from every other eye?   *[Exit.*

Scene II.—*A Hall of Justice.* Camillo, Judges, *&c., are discovered
seated;* Marzio *is led in.*

First Judge. Accused, do you persist in your denial?
I ask you, are you innocent, or guilty?
I demand who were the participators
In your offence? Speak truth and the whole truth.
Marzio. My God! I did not kill him; I know nothing;   5
Olimpio sold the robe to me from which
You would infer my guilt.
Second Judge.   Away with him!
First Judge. Dare you, with lips yet white from the rack's kiss
Speak false? Is it so soft a questioner,
That you would bandy lover's talk with it   10
Till it wind out your life and soul? Away!
Marzio. Spare me! O, spare! I will confess.
First Judge.   Then speak.
Marzio. I strangled him in his sleep.
First Judge.   Who urged you to it?
Marzio. His own son Giacomo, and the young prelate
Orsino sent me to Petrella; there   15
The ladies Beatrice and Lucretia
Tempted me with a thousand crowns, and I
And my companion forthwith murdered him.
Now let me die.
First Judge. This sounds as bad as truth. Guards, there,
Lead forth the prisoner!

Enter Lucretia, Beatrice, *and* Giacomo, *guarded.*

                              Look upon this man;   20
When did you see him last?
Beatrice.   We never saw him.
Marzio. You know me too well, Lady Beatrice.
Beatrice. I know thee! How? where? when?
Marzio.   You know 'twas I
Whom you did urge with menaces and bribes
To kill your father. When the thing was done   25
You clothed me in a robe of woven gold
And bade me thrive: how I have thriven, you see.
You, my Lord Giacomo, Lady Lucretia,
You know that what I speak is true.
                    [Beatrice *advances towards him; he covers his
                    face, and shrinks back.*
                                        Oh, dart
The terrible resentment of those eyes   30
On the dead earth! Turn them away from me!
They wound: 'twas torture forced the truth. My Lords,

Having said this let me be led to death.

   Beatrice. Poor wretch, I pity thee: yet stay awhile.

   Camillo. Guards, lead him not away.

   Beatrice.   Cardinal Camillo,   35

You have a good repute for gentleness

And wisdom: can it be that you sit here

To countenance a wicked farce like this?

When some obscure and trembling slave is dragged

From sufferings which might shake the sternest heart   40

And bade to answer, not as he believes,

But as those may suspect or do desire

Whose questions thence suggest their own reply:

And that in peril of such hideous torments

As merciful God spares even the damned. Speak now   45

The thing you surely know, which is that you,

If your fine frame were stretched upon that wheel,

And you were told: 'Confess that you did poison

Your little nephew; that fair blue-eyed child

Who was the lodestar of your life:'—and though   50

All see, since his most swift and piteous death,

That day and night, and heaven and earth, and time,

And all the things hoped for or done therein

Are changed to you, through your exceeding grief,

Yet you would say, 'I confess anything:'   55

And beg from your tormentors, like that slave,

The refuge of dishonourable death.

I pray thee, Cardinal, that thou assert

My innocence.

   Camillo (*much moved*). What shall we think, my Lords?

Shame on these tears! I thought the heart was frozen   60

Which is their fountain. I would pledge my soul

That she is guiltless.

   Judge.   Yet she must be tortured.

   Camillo. I would as soon have tortured mine own nephew

(If he now lived he would be just her age;

His hair, too, was her colour, and his eyes   65

Like hers in shape, but blue and not so deep)

As that most perfect image of God's love

That ever came sorrowing upon the earth.

She is as pure as speechless infancy!

   Judge. Well, be her purity on your head, my Lord,   70

If you forbid the rack. His Holiness

Enjoined us to pursue this monstrous crime

By the severest forms of law; nay, even

To stretch a point against the criminals.

The prisoners stand accused of parricide   75

Upon such evidence as justifies
Torture.

   Beatrice. What evidence? This man's?

   Judge.   Even so.

   Beatrice (*to* MARZIO). Come near. And who art thou thus chosen
     forth
Out of the multitude of living men
To kill the innocent?

   Marzio.   I am Marzio,   80
Thy father's vassal.

   Beatrice.   Fix thine eyes on mine;
Answer to what I ask.   [*Turning to the* JUDGES.
                          I prithee mark
His countenance: unlike bold calumny
Which sometimes dares not speak the thing it looks,
He dares not look the thing he speaks, but bends   85
His gaze on the blind earth.
(*To* MARZIO.)   What! wilt thou say
That I did murder my own father?

   Marzio.   Oh!
Spare me! My brain swims round . . . I cannot speak . . .
It was that horrid torture forced the truth.
Take me away! Let her not look on me!   90
I am a guilty miserable wretch;
I have said all I know; now, let me die!

   Beatrice. My Lords, if by my nature I had been
So stern, as to have planned the crime alleged,
Which your suspicions dictate to this slave,   95
And the rack makes him utter, do you think
I should have left this two-edged instrument
Of my misdeed; this man, this bloody knife
With my own name engraven on the heft,
Lying unsheathed amid a world of foes,   100
For my own death? That with such horrible need
For deepest silence, I should have neglected
So trivial a precaution, as the making
His tomb the keeper of a secret written
On a thief's memory? What is his poor life?   105
What are a thousand lives? A parricide
Had trampled them like dust; and, see, he lives!
(*Turning to* MARZIO.) And thou . . .

   Marzio.   Oh, spare me! Speak to me no more!
That stern yet piteous look, those solemn tones,
Wound worse than torture.

   (*To the* JUDGES.)   I have told it all;   110
For pity's sake lead me away to death.

   Camillo. Guards, lead him nearer the Lady Beatrice,

He shrinks from her regard like autumn's leaf
From the keen breath of the serenest north.
   Beatrice. O thou who tremblest on the giddy verge   115
Of life and death, pause ere thou answerest me;
So mayst thou answer God with less dismay:
What evil have we done thee? I, alas!
Have lived but on this earth a few sad years,
And so my lot was ordered, that a father   120
First turned the moments of awakening life
To drops, each poisoning youth's sweet hope; and then
Stabbed with one blow my everlasting soul;
And my untainted fame; and even that peace
Which sleeps within the core of the heart's heart;   125
But the wound was not mortal; so my hate
Became the only worship I could lift
To our great father, who in pity and love,
Armed thee, as thou dost say, to cut him off;
And thus his wrong becomes my accusation;   130
And art thou the accuser? If thou hopest
Mercy in heaven, show justice upon earth:
Worse than a bloody hand is a hard heart.
If thou hast done murders, made thy life's path
Over the trampled laws of God and man,   135
Rush not before thy Judge, and say: 'My maker,
I have done this and more; for there was one
Who was most pure and innocent on earth;
And because she endured what never any
Guilty or innocent endured before: 140
Because her wrongs could not be told, not thought;
Because thy hand at length did rescue her;
I with my words killed her and all her kin.'
Think, I adjure you, what it is to slay
The reverence living in the minds of men   145
Towards our ancient house, and stainless fame!
Think what it is to strangle infant pity,
Cradled in the belief of guileless looks,
Till it become a crime to suffer. Think
What 'tis to blot with infamy and blood   150
All that which shows like innocence, and is,
Iear me, great God! I swear, most innocent,
So that the world lose all discrimination
Between the sly, fierce, wild regard of guilt,
And that which now compels thee to reply   155
To what I ask: Am I or am I not
A parricide?
   Marzio.   Thou art not!
   Judge.   What is this?

Marzio. I here declare those whom I did accuse
Are innocent. 'Tis I alone am guilty.

Judge. Drag him away to torments; let them be   160
Subtle and long drawn out, to tear the folds
Of the heart's inmost cell. Unbind him not
Till he confess.

Marzio.   Torture me as ye will:
A keener pang has wrung a higher truth
From my last breath. She is most innocent!   165
Bloodhounds, not men, glut yourselves well with me;
I will not give you that fine piece of nature
To rend and ruin.

                              [*Exit* Marzio, *guarded.*

Camillo.   What say ye now, my Lords?

Judge. Let tortures strain the truth till it be white
As snow thrice sifted by the frozen wind.   170

Camillo. Yet stained with blood.

Judge (*to* Beatrice.)   Know you this paper, Lady?

Beatrice. Entrap me not with questions. Who stands here
As my accuser? Ha! wilt thou be he,
Who art my judge? Accuser, witness, judge,
What, all in one? Here is Orsino's name;   175
Where is Orsino? Let his eye meet mine.
What means this scrawl? Alas! ye know not what,
And therefore on the chance that it may be
Some evil, will ye kill us?

                    Enter an Officer.

Officer.   Marzio's dead.

Judge. What did he say?

Officer.   Nothing. As soon as we   180
Had bound him on the wheel, he smiled on us,
As one who baffles a deep adversary;
And holding his breath, died.

Judge.   There remains nothing
But to apply the question to those prisoners,
Who yet remain stubborn.

Camillo.   I overrule   185
Further proceedings, and in the behalf
Of these most innocent and noble persons
Will use my interest with the Holy Father.

Judge. Let the Pope's pleasure then be done. Meanwhile
Conduct these culprits each to separate cells;   190
And be the engines ready: for this night
If the Pope's resolution be as grave,
Pious, and just as once, I'll wring the truth
Out of those nerves and sinews, groan by groan.   [*Exeunt.*

SCENE III.—*The Cell of a Prison.* BEATRICE *is discovered asleep on a couch. Enter* BERNARDO.

Bernardo. How gently slumber rests upon her face,
Like the last thoughts of some day sweetly spent
Closing in night and dreams, and so prolonged.
After such torments as she bore last night,
How light and soft her breathing comes. Ay me!   5
Methinks that I shall never sleep again.
But I must shake the heavenly dew of rest
From this sweet folded flower, thus . . . wake! awake!
What, sister, canst thou sleep?
Beatrice (awaking).   I was just dreaming
That we were all in Paradise. Thou knowest   10
This cell seems like a kind of Paradise
After our father's presence.
Bernardo.   Dear, dear sister.
Would that thy dream were not a dream! O God!
How shall I tell?
Beatrice.   What wouldst thou tell, sweet brother?
Bernardo. Look not so calm and happy, or even whilst   15
I stand considering what I have to say
My heart will break.
Beatrice.   See now, thou mak'st me weep:
How very friendless thou wouldst be, dear child,
If I were dead. Say what thou hast to say.
Bernardo. They have confessed; they could endure no more
The tortures . . .
Beatrice.   Ha! What was there to confess?   21
They must have told some weak and wicked lie
To flatter their tormentors. Have they said
That they were guilty? O white innocence,
That thou shouldst wear the mask of guilt to hide   25
Thine awful and serenest countenance
From those who know thee not!

Enter JUDGE *with* LUCRETIA *and* GIACOMO, *guarded.*

                              Ignoble hearts!
For some brief spasms of pain, which are at least
As mortal as the limbs through which they pass,
Are centuries of high splendour laid in dust?   30
And that eternal honour which should live
Sunlike, above the reek of mortal fame,
Changed to a mockery and a byword? What!
Will you give up these bodies to be dragged
At horses' heels, so that our hair should sweep   35
The footsteps of the vain and senseless crowd,

Who, that they may make our calamity
Their worship and their spectacle, will leave
The churches and the theatres as void
As their own hearts? Shall the light multitude 40
Fling, at their choice, curses or faded pity,
Sad funeral flowers to deck a living corpse,
Upon us as we pass to pass away,
And leave . . . what memory of our having been?
Infamy, blood, terror, despair? O thou, 45
Who wert a mother to the parentless,
Kill not thy child! Let not her wrongs kill thee!
Brother, lie down with me upon the rack,
And let us each be silent as a corpse;
It soon will be as soft as any grave. 50
'Tis but the falsehood it can wring from fear
Makes the rack cruel.
    Giacomo.   They will tear the truth
Even from thee at last, those cruel pains:
For pity's sake say thou art guilty now.
    Lucretia. Oh, speak the truth! Let us all quickly die; 55
And after death, God is our judge, not they;
He will have mercy on us.
    Bernardo.   If indeed
It can be true, say so, dear sister mine;
And then the Pope will surely pardon you,
And all be well.
    Judge.   Confess, or I will warp 60
Your limbs with such keen tortures . . .
    Beatrice.   Tortures! Turn
The rack henceforth into a spinning-wheel!
Torture your dog, that he may tell when last
He lapped the blood his master shed . . . not me!
My pangs are of the mind, and of the heart, 65
And of the soul; ay, of the inmost soul,
Which weeps within tears as of burning gall
To see, in this ill world where none are true,
My kindred false to their deserted selves.
And with considering all the wretched life 70
Which I have lived, and its now wretched end,
And the small justice shown by Heaven and Earth
To me or mine; and what a tyrant thou art,
And what slaves these; and what a world we make,
The oppressor and the oppressed . . . such pangs compel
My answer. What is it thou wouldst with me? 76
    Judge. Art thou not guilty of thy father's death?
    Beatrice. Or wilt thou rather tax high-judging God
That He permitted such an act as that

Which I have suffered, and which He beheld;   80
Made it unutterable, and took from it
All refuge, all revenge, all consequence,
But that which thou hast called my father's death?
Which is or is not what men call a crime,
Which either I have done, or have not done;   85
Say what ye will. I shall deny no more.
If ye desire it thus, thus let it be,
And so an end of all. Now do your will;
No other pains shall force another word.

    Judge. She is convicted, but has not confessed.   90
Be it enough. Until their final sentence
Let none have converse with them. You, young Lord,
Linger not here!

    Beatrice.   Oh, tear him not away!

    Judge. Guards, do your duty.

    Bernardo (embracing BEATRICE). Oh! would ye divide
Body from soul?

    Officer.   That is the headsman's business.   95

            [*Exeunt all but* LUCRETIA, BEATRICE, *and* GIACOMO.

    Giacomo. Have I confessed? Is it all over now?
No hope! No refuge! O weak, wicked tongue
Which hast destroyed me, would that thou hadst been
Cut out and thrown to dogs first! To have killed
My father first, and then betrayed my sister;   100
Ay, thee! the one thing innocent and pure
In this black guilty world, to that which I
So well deserve! My wife! my little ones!
Destitute, helpless, and I . . . Father! God!
Canst Thou forgive even the unforgiving,   105
When their full hearts break thus, thus! . . .

                   [*Covers his face and weeps.*

    Lucretia.   O my child!
To what a dreadful end are we all come!
Why did I yield? Why did I not sustain
Those torments? Oh, that I were all dissolved
Into these fast and unavailing tears,   110
Which flow and feel not!

    Beatrice.   What 'twas weak to do,
'Tis weaker to lament, once being done;
Take cheer! The God who knew my wrong, and made
Our speedy act the angel of His wrath,
Seems, and but seems, to have abandoned us.   115
Let us not think that we shall die for this.
Brother, sit near me; give me your firm hand,
You had a manly heart. Bear up! Bear up!
O dearest Lady, put your gentle head

Upon my lap, and try to sleep awhile: 120
Your eyes look pale, hollow and overworn,
With heaviness of watching and slow grief.
Come, I will sing you some low, sleepy tune,
Not cheerful, nor yet sad; some dull old thing,
Some outworn and unused monotony, 125
Such as our country gossips sing and spin,
Till they almost forget they live: lie down!
So, that will do. Have I forgot the words?
Faith! They are sadder than I thought they were.

SONG

False friend, wilt thou smile or weep 130
When my life is laid asleep?
Little cares for a smile or a tear,
The clay-cold corpse upon the bier!
    Farewell! Heigho!
    What is this whispers low? 135
There is a snake in thy smile, my dear;
And bitter poison within thy tear.

Sweet sleep, were death like to thee,
Or if thou couldst mortal be,
I would close these eyes of pain; 140
When to wake? Never again.
    O World! Farewell!
    Listen to the passing bell!
It says, thou and I must part, 144
With a light and a heavy heart.   *[The scene closes.*

SCENE IV.—*A Hall of the Prison. Enter* CAMILLO *and* BERNARDO.

  Camillo. The Pope is stern; not to be moved or bent.
He looked as calm and keen as is the engine
Which tortures and which kills, exempt itself
From aught that it inflicts; a marble form,
A rite, a law, a custom: not a man. 5
He frowned, as if to frown had been the trick
Of his machinery, on the advocates
Presenting the defences, which he tore
And threw behind, muttering with hoarse, harsh voice:
'Which among ye defended their old father 10
Killed in his sleep?' Then to another: 'Thou
Dost this in virtue of thy place; 'tis well.'
He turned to me then, looking deprecation,
And said these three words, coldly: 'They must die.'
  Bernardo. And yet you left him not?

Camillo.   I urged him still;
Pleading, as I could guess, the devilish wrong   16
Which prompted your unnatural parent's death.
And he replied: 'Paolo Santa Croce
Murdered his mother yester evening,
And he is fled. Parricide grows so rife   20
That soon, for some just cause no doubt, the young
Will strangle us all, dozing in our chairs.
Authority, and power, and hoary hair
Are grown crimes capital. You are my nephew,
You come to ask their pardon; stay a moment;   25
Here is their sentence; never see me more
Till, to the letter, it be all fulfilled.'
    Bernardo. O God, not so! I did believe indeed
That all you said was but sad preparation
For happy news. Oh, there are words and looks   30
To bend the sternest purpose! Once I knew them,
Now I forget them at my dearest need.
What think you if I seek him out, and bathe
His feet and robe with hot and bitter tears?
Importune him with prayers, vexing his brain   35
With my perpetual cries, until in rage
He strike me with his pastoral cross, and trample
Upon my prostrate head, so that my blood
May stain the senseless dust on which he treads,
And remorse waken mercy? I will do it!   40
Oh, wait till I return!   [*Rushes out.*
    Camillo.   Alas! poor boy!
A wreck-devoted seaman thus might pray
To the deaf sea.

    Enter LUCRETIA, BEATRICE, *and* GIACOMO, *guarded.*

    Beatrice.   I hardly dare to fear
That thou bring'st other news than a just pardon.
    Camillo. May God in heaven be less inexorable   45
To the Pope's prayers, than he has been to mine.
Here is the sentence and the warrant.
    Beatrice (*wildly*).
My God! Can it be possible I have
To die so suddenly? So young to go
Under the obscure, cold, rotting, wormy ground!   50
To be nailed down into a narrow place;
To see no more sweet sunshine; hear no more
Blithe voice of living thing; muse not again
Upon familiar thoughts, sad, yet thus lost—
How fearful! to be nothing! Or to be . . .   55

What? Oh, where am I? Let me not go mad!
Sweet Heaven, forgive weak thoughts! If there should be
No God, no Heaven, no Earth in the void world;
The wide, gray, lampless, deep, unpeopled world!
If all things then should be . . . my father's spirit,   60
His eye, his voice, his touch surrounding me;
The atmosphere and breath of my dead life!
If sometimes, as a shape more like himself,
Even the form which tortured me on earth,
Masked in gray hairs and wrinkles, he should come   65
And wind me in his hellish arms, and fix
His eyes on mine, and drag me down, down, down!
For was he not alone omnipotent
On Earth, and ever present? Even though dead,
Does not his spirit live in all that breathe,   70
And work for me and mine still the same ruin,
Scorn, pain, despair? Who ever yet returned
To teach the laws of Death's untrodden realm?
Unjust perhaps as those which drive us now,
Oh, whither, whither?
    Lucretia.   Trust in God's sweet love,   75
The tender promises of Christ: ere night,
Think, we shall be in Paradise.
    Beatrice.   'Tis past!
Whatever comes my heart shall sink no more.
And yet, I know not why, your words strike chill:
How tedious, false and cold seem all things. I   80
Have met with much injustice in this world;
No difference has been made by God or man,
Or any power moulding my wretched lot,
'Twixt good or evil, as regarded me.
I am cut off from the only world I know,   85
From light, and life, and love, in youth's sweet prime.
You do well telling me to trust in God,
I hope I do trust in Him. In whom else
Can any trust? And yet my heart is cold.

      [*During the latter speeches* GIACOMO *has retired conversing
          with* CAMILLO, *who now goes out;* GIACOMO *advances.*

    Giacomo. Know you not, Mother . . . Sister, know you not?
Bernardo even now is gone to implore   91
The Pope to grant our pardon.
    Lucretia.   Child, perhaps
It will be granted. We may all then live
To make these woes a tale for distant years:
Oh, what a thought! It gushes to my heart   95
Like the warm blood.

Beatrice.   Yet both will soon be cold.
Oh, trample out that thought! Worse than despair,
Worse than the bitterness of death, is hope:
It is the only ill which can find place
Upon the giddy, sharp and narrow hour   100
Tottering beneath us. Plead with the swift frost
That it should spare the eldest flower of spring:
Plead with awakening earthquake, o'er whose couch
Even now a city stands, strong, fair, and free;
Now stench and blackness yawn, like death. Oh, plead   105
With famine, or wind-walking Pestilence,
Blind lightning, or the deaf sea, not with man!
Cruel, cold, formal man; righteous in words,
In deeds a Cain. No, Mother, we must die:
Since such is the reward of innocent lives;   110
Such the alleviation of worst wrongs.
And whilst our murderers live, and hard, cold men,
Smiling and slow, walk through a world of tears
To death as to life's sleep; 'twere just the grave
Were some strange joy for us. Come, obscure Death,   115
And wind me in thine all-embracing arms!
Like a fond mother hide me in thy bosom,
And rock me to the sleep from which none wake.
Live ye, who live, subject to one another
As we were once, who now . . .

BERNARDO *rushes in.*

Bernardo.   Oh, horrible!   120
That tears, that looks, that hope poured forth in prayer,
Even till the heart is vacant and despairs,
Should all be vain! The ministers of death
Are waiting round the doors. I thought I saw
Blood on the face of one . . . What if 'twere fancy?   125
Soon the heart's blood of all I love on earth
Will sprinkle him, and he will wipe it off
As if 'twere only rain. O life! O world!
Cover me! let me be no more! To see
That perfect mirror of pure innocence   130
Wherein I gazed, and grew happy and good,
Shivered to dust! To see thee, Beatrice,
Who made all lovely thou didst look upon . . .
Thee, light of life . . . dead, dark! while I say, sister,
To hear I have no sister; and thou, Mother,   135
Whose love was as a bond to all our loves . . .
Dead! The sweet bond broken!

Enter CAMILLO *and Guards.*

                              They come! Let me
Kiss those warm lips before their crimson leaves
Are blighted . . . white . . . cold. Say farewell, before
Death chokes that gentle voice! Oh, let me hear   140
You speak!
    Beatrice.   Farewell, my tender brother. Think
Of our sad fate with gentleness, as now:
And let mild, pitying thoughts lighten for thee
Thy sorrow's load. Err not in harsh despair,
But tears and patience. One thing more, my child: 145
For thine own sake be constant to the love
Thou bearest us; and to the faith that I,
Though wrapped in a strange cloud of crime and shame,
Lived ever holy and unstained. And though
Ill tongues shall wound me, and our common name   150
Be as a mark stamped on thine innocent brow
For men to point at as they pass, do thou
Forbear, and never think a thought unkind
Of those, who perhaps love thee in their graves.
So mayest thou die as I do; fear and pain   155
Being subdued. Farewell! Farewell! Farewell!
    Bernardo. I cannot say, farewell!
    Camillo.   Oh, Lady Beatrice!
    Beatrice. Give yourself no unnecessary pain,
My dear Lord Cardinal. Here, Mother, tie
My girdle for me, and bind up this hair   160
In any simple knot; ay, that does well.
And yours I see is coming down. How often
Have we done this for one another; now
We shall not do it any more. My Lord,
We are quite ready. Well, 'tis very well.   165

THE END.

NOTE ON THE CENCI, BY MRS. SHELLEY

THE sort of mistake that Shelley made as to the extent of his own
genius and powers, which led him deviously at first, but lastly into the
direct track that enabled him fully to develop them, is a curious instance
of his modesty of feeling, and of the methods which the human mind
uses at once to deceive itself, and yet, in its very delusion, to make its
way out of error into the path which Nature has marked out as its right
one. He often incited me to attempt the writing a tragedy: he conceived
that I possessed some dramatic talent, and he was always most earnest
and energetic in his exhortations that I should cultivate any talent I

possessed, to the utmost. I entertained a truer estimate of my powers; and above all (though at that time not exactly aware of the fact) I was far too young to have any chance of succeeding, even moderately, in a species of composition that requires a greater scope of experience in, and sympathy with, human passion than could then have fallen to my lot,—or than any perhaps, except Shelley, ever possessed, even at the age of twenty-six, at which he wrote *The Cenci*.

On the other hand, Shelley most erroneously conceived himself to be destitute of this talent. He believed that one of the first requisites was the capacity of forming and following-up a story or plot. He fancied himself to be defective in this portion of imagination: it was that which gave him least pleasure in the writings of others, though he laid great store by it as the proper framework to support the sublimest efforts of poetry. He asserted that he was too metaphysical and abstract, too fond of the theoretical and the ideal, to succeed as a tragedian. It perhaps is not strange that I shared this opinion with himself; for he had hitherto shown no inclination for, nor given any specimen of his powers in framing and supporting the interest of a story, either in prose or verse. Once or twice, when he attempted such, he had speedily thrown it aside, as being even disagreeable to him as an occupation.

The subject he had suggested for a tragedy was Charles I: and he had written to me: 'Remember, remember Charles I. I have been already imagining how you would conduct some scenes. The second volume of *St. Leon* begins with this proud and true sentiment: "There is nothing which the human mind can conceive which it may not execute." Shakespeare was only a human being.' These words were written in 1818, while we were in Lombardy, when he little thought how soon a work of his own would prove a proud comment on the passage he quoted. When in Rome, in 1819, a friend put into our hands the old manuscript account of the story of the Cenci. We visited the Colonna and Doria palaces, where the portraits of Beatrice were to be found; and her beauty cast the reflection of its own grace over her appalling story. Shelley's imagination became strongly excited, and he urged the subject to me as one fitted for a tragedy. More than ever I felt my incompetence; but I entreated him to write it instead; and he began, and proceeded swiftly, urged on by intense sympathy with the sufferings of the human beings whose passions, so long cold in the tomb, he revived, and gifted with poetic language. This tragedy is the only one of his works that he communicated to me during its progress. We talked over the arrangement of the scenes together. I speedily saw the great mistake we had made, and triumphed in the discovery of the new talent brought to light from that mine of wealth (never, alas, through his untimely death, worked to its depths)— his richly gifted mind.

We suffered a severe affliction in Rome by the loss of our eldest child, who was of such beauty and promise as to cause him deservedly to be the idol of our hearts. We left the capital of the world, anxious for a time to escape a spot associated too intimately with his presence and loss.[1] Some friends of ours were residing in the neighbourhood of Leghorn, and we took a small house, Villa Valsovano, about half-way between the town and Monte Nero, where we remained during the summer. Our villa was situated in the midst of a *podere;* the peasants sang as they worked beneath our windows, during the heats of a very hot season, and in the evening the water-wheel creaked as the process of irrigation went on, and the fireflies flashed from among the myrtle hedges: Nature was bright, sunshiny, and cheerful, or diversified by storms of a majestic terror, such as we had never before witnessed.

At the top of the house there was a sort of terrace. There is often such in Italy, generally roofed: this one was very small, yet not only roofed but glazed. This Shelley made his study; it looked out on a wide prospect of fertile country, and commanded a view of the near sea. The storms that sometimes varied our day showed themselves most picturesquely as they were driven across the ocean; sometimes the dark lurid clouds dipped towards the waves, and became waterspouts that churned up the waters beneath, as they were chased onward and scattered by the tempest. At other times the dazzling sunlight and heat made it almost intolerable to every other; but Shelley basked in both, and his health and spirits revived under their influence. In this airy cell he wrote the principal part of *The Cenci.* He was making a study of Calderon at the time, reading his best tragedies with an accomplished lady living near us, to whom his letter from Leghorn was addressed during the following year. He admired Calderon, both for his poetry and his dramatic genius; but it shows his judgement and originality that, though greatly struck by his first acquaintance with the Spanish poet, none of his peculiarities crept into the composition of *The Cenci;* and there is no trace of his new studies, except in that passage to which he himself alludes as suggested by one in *El Purgatorio de San Patricio.*

Shelley wished *The Cenci* to be acted. He was not a playgoer, being of such fastidious taste that he was easily disgusted by the bad filling-up of the inferior parts. While preparing for our departure from England, however, he saw Miss O'Neil several times. She was then in the zenith of her glory; and Shelley was deeply moved by her impersonation of several parts, and by the graceful sweetness, the intense pathos, and sublime vehemence of passion she displayed. She was often in his thoughts as he wrote: and, when he had finished, he became anxious that his tragedy should be acted, and receive the advantage of having this accomplished actress to fill the part of the heroine. With this view he wrote the following letter to a friend in London:

[1] Such feelings haunted him when, in *The Cenci,* he makes Beatrice speak to Cardinal Camillo of

'that fair blue-eyed child
Who was the lodestar of your life:'—

and say—

'All see, since his most swift and piteous death,
That day and night, and heaven and earth, and time,
And all the things hoped for or done therein
Are changed to you, through your exceeding grief.'

'The object of the present letter is to ask a favour of you. I have written a tragedy on a story well known in Italy, and, in my conception, eminently dramatic. I have taken some pains to make my play fit for representation, and those who have already seen it judge favourably. It is written without any of the peculiar feelings and opinions which characterize my other compositions; I have attended simply to the impartial development of such characters as it is probable the persons represented really were, together with the greatest degree of popular effect to be produced by such a development. I send you a translation of the Italian MS. on which my play is founded; the chief circumstance of which I have touched very delicately; for my principal doubt as to whether it would succeed as an acting play hangs entirely on the question as to whether any such a thing as incest in this shape, however treated, would be admitted on the stage. I think, however, it will form no objection; considering, first, that the facts are matter of history, and, secondly, the peculiar delicacy with which I have treated it.[1]

'I am exceedingly interested in the question of whether this attempt of mine will succeed or not. I am strongly inclined to the affirmative at present; founding my hopes on this—that, as a composition, it is certainly not inferior to any of the modern plays that have been acted, with the exception of *Remorse;* that the interest of the plot is incredibly greater and more real; and that there is nothing beyond what the multitude are contented to believe that they can understand, either in imagery, opinion, or sentiment. I wish to preserve a complete incognito, and can trust to you that, whatever else you do, you will at least favour me on this point. Indeed, this is essential, deeply essential, to its success. After it had been acted, and successfully (could I hope for such a thing), I would own it if I pleased, and use the celebrity it might acquire to my own purposes.

'What I want you to do is to procure for me its presentation at Covent Garden. The principal character, Beatrice, is precisely fitted for Miss O'Neil, and it might even seem to have been written for her (God forbid that I should see her play it—it would tear my nerves to pieces); and in all respects it is fitted only for Covent Garden. The chief male character I confess I should be very unwilling that any one but Kean should play. That is impossible, and I must be contented with an inferior actor.'

The play was accordingly sent to Mr. Harris. He pronounced the subject to be so objectionable that he could not even submit the part to Miss O'Neil for perusal, but expressed his desire that the author would write a tragedy on some other subject, which he would gladly accept. Shelley printed a small edition at Leghorn, to ensure its correctness;

[1] In speaking of his mode of treating this main incident, Shelley said that it might be remarked that, in the course of the play, he had never mentioned expressly Cenci's worst crime. Every one knew what it must be, but it was never imaged in words—the nearest allusion to it being that portion of Cenci's curse beginning—

'That, if she have a child,' etc.

as he was much annoyed by the many mistakes that crept into his text when distance prevented him from correcting the press.

Universal approbation soon stamped *The Cenci* as the best tragedy of modern times. Writing concerning it, Shelley said: 'I have been cautious to avoid the introducing faults of youthful composition; diffuseness, a profusion of inapplicable imagery, vagueness, generality, and, as Hamlet says, *words, words.*' There is nothing that is not purely dramatic throughout; and the character of Beatrice, proceeding, from vehement struggle, to horror, to deadly resolution, and lastly to the elevated dignity of calm suffering, joined to passionate tenderness and pathos, is touched with hues so vivid and so beautiful that the poet seems to have read intimately the secrets of the noble heart imaged in the lovely countenance of the unfortunate girl. The Fifth Act is a masterpiece. It is the finest thing he ever wrote, and may claim proud comparison not only with any contemporary, but preceding, poet. The varying feelings of Beatrice are expressed with passionate, heart-reaching eloquence. Every character has a voice that echoes truth in its tones. It is curious, to one acquainted with the written story, to mark the success with which the poet has inwoven the real incidents of the tragedy into his scenes, and yet, through the power of poetry, has obliterated all that would otherwise have shown too harsh or too hideous in the picture. His success was a double triumph; and often after he was earnestly entreated to write again in a style that commanded popular favour, while it was not less instinct with truth and genius. But the bent of his mind went the other way; and, even when employed on subjects whose interest depended on character and incident, he would start off in another direction, and leave the delineations of human passion, which he could depict in so able a manner, for fantastic creations of his fancy, or the expression of those opinions and sentiments, with regard to human nature and its destiny, a desire to diffuse which was the master passion of his soul.

THE MASK OF ANARCHY

WRITTEN ON THE OCCASION OF THE MASSACRE AT MANCHESTER

I

As I lay asleep in Italy
There came a voice from over the
    Sea,
And with great power it forth led
    me
To walk in the visions of Poesy.

II

I met Murder on the way—   5
He had a mask like Castlereagh—
Very smooth he looked, yet grim;
Seven blood-hounds followed him:

III

All were fat; and well they might
Be in admirable plight, 10
For one by one, and two by two,
He tossed them human hearts to
chew
Which from his wide cloak he drew.

IV

Next came Fraud, and he had on,
Like Eldon, an ermined gown; 15
His big tears, for he wept well,
Turned to mill-stones as they fell.

V

And the little children, who
Round his feet played to and fro,
Thinking every tear a gem, 20
Had their brains knocked out by
them.

VI

Clothed with the Bible, as with
light,
And the shadows of the night,
Like Sidmouth, next, Hypocrisy
On a crocodile rode by. 25

VII

And many more destructions
played
In this ghastly masquerade,
All disguised, even to the eyes,
Like Bishops, lawyers, peers, or
spies.

VIII

Last came Anarchy: he rode 30
On a white horse, splashed with
blood;
He was pale even to the lips,
Like Death in the Apocalypse.

IX

And he wore a kingly crown;
And in his grasp a sceptre shone; 35
On his brow this mark I saw—
'I AM GOD, AND KING, AND LAW!'

X

With a pace stately and fast,
Over English land he passed,
Trampling to a mire of blood 40
The adoring multitude.

XI

And a mighty troop around,
With their trampling shook the
ground,
Waving each a bloody sword,
For the service of their Lord. 45

XII

And with glorious triumph, they
Rode through England proud and
gay,
Drunk as with intoxication
Of the wine of desolation.

XIII

O'er fields and towns, from sea to
sea, 50
Passed the Pageant swift and free,
Tearing up, and trampling down;
Till they came to London town.

XIV

And each dweller, panic-stricken,
Felt his heart with terror sicken 55
Hearing the tempestuous cry
Of the triumph of Anarchy.

XV

For with pomp to meet him came,
Clothed in arms like blood and
flame,
The hired murderers, who did
sing 60
'Thou art God, and Law, and King.

XVI

'We have waited, weak and lone
For thy coming, Mighty One!
Our purses are empty, our swords
are cold,
Give us glory, and blood, and
gold.' 65

XVII

Lawyers and priests, a motley
 crowd,
To the earth their pale brows
 bowed;
Like a bad prayer not over loud,
Whispering—'Thou art Law and
 God.'—

XVIII

Then all cried with one accord, 70
'Thou art King, and God, and
 Lord;
Anarchy, to thee we bow,
Be thy name made holy now!'

XIX

And Anarchy, the Skeleton,
Bowed and grinned to every one, 75
As well as if his education
Had cost ten millions to the nation.

XX

For he knew the Palaces
Of our Kings were rightly his;
His the sceptre, crown, and globe,
And the gold-inwoven robe. 81

XXI

So he sent his slaves before
To seize upon the Bank and Tower,
And was proceeding with intent
To meet his pensioned Parlia-
 ment 85

XXII

When one fled past, a maniac maid,
And her name was Hope, she said:
But she looked more like Despair,
And she cried out in the air:

XXIII

'My father Time is weak and
 gray 90
With waiting for a better day;
See how idiot-like he stands,
Fumbling with his palsied hands!

XXIV

'He has had child after child,
And the dust of death is piled 95
Over every one but me—
Misery, oh, Misery!'

XXV

Then she lay down in the street,
Right before the horses' feet,
Expecting, with a patient eye, 100
Murder, Fraud, and Anarchy.

XXVI

When between her and her foes
A mist, a light, an image rose,
Small at first, and weak, and frail
Like the vapour of a vale: 105

XXVII

Till as clouds grow on the blast,
Like tower-crowned giants striding
 fast,
And glare with lightnings as they
 fly,
And speak in thunder to the sky,

XXVIII

It grew—a Shape arrayed in mail
Brighter than the viper's scale, 111
And upborne on wings whose grain
Was as the light of sunny rain.

XXIX

On its helm, seen far away,
A planet, like the Morning's, lay;
And those plumes its light rained
 through 116
Like a shower of crimson dew.

XXX

With step as soft as wind it passed
O'er the heads of men—so fast
That they knew the presence there,
And looked,—but all was empty
 air. 121

XXXI

As flowers beneath May's footstep
   waken,
As stars from Night's loose hair
   are shaken,
As waves arise when loud winds
   call,
Thoughts sprung where'er that step
   did fall.   125

XXXII

And the prostrate multitude
Looked—and ankle-deep in blood,
Hope, that maiden most serene,
Was walking with a quiet mien:

XXXIII

And Anarchy, the ghastly birth, 130
Lay dead earth upon the earth;
The Horse of Death tameless as
   wind
Fled, and with his hoofs did grind
To dust the murderers thronged
   behind.

XXXIV

A rushing light of clouds and splen-
   dour,   135
A sense awakening and yet tender
Was heard and felt—and at its
   close
These words of joy and fear arose

XXXV

As if their own indignant Earth
Which gave the sons of England
   birth   140
Had felt their blood upon her brow,
And shuddering with a mother's
   throe

XXXVI

Had turnèd every drop of blood
By which her face had been be-
   dewed
To an accent unwithstood,—   145
As if her heart had cried aloud:

XXXVII

'Men of England, heirs of Glory,
Heroes of unwritten story,
Nurslings of one mighty Mother,
Hopes of her, and one another; 150

XXXVIII

'Rise like Lions after slumber
In unvanquishable number,
Shake your chains to earth like dew
Which in sleep had fallen on you—
Ye are many—they are few.   155

XXXIX

'What is Freedom?—ye can tell
That which slavery is, too well—
For its very name has grown
To an echo of your own.

XL

' 'Tis to work and have such
   pay   160
As just keeps life from day to day
In your limbs, as in a cell
For the tyrants' use to dwell,

XLI

'So that ye for them are made
Loom, and plough, and sword, and
   spade,   165
With or without your own will bent
To their defence and nourishment.

XLII

' 'Tis to see your children weak
With their mothers pine and peak,
When the winter winds are bleak,—
They are dying whilst I speak. 171

XLIII

' 'Tis to hunger for such diet
As the rich man in his riot
Casts to the fat dogs that lie
Surfeiting beneath his eye;   175

XLIV

' 'Tis to let the Ghost of Gold
Take from Toil a thousandfold
More than e'er its substance could
In the tyrannies of old.

XLV

'Paper coin—that forgery   180
Of the title-deeds, which ye
Hold to something of the worth
Of the inheritance of Earth.

XLVI

' 'Tis to be a slave in soul
And to hold no strong control   185
Over your own wills, but be
All that others make of ye.

XLVII

'And at length when ye complain
With a murmur weak and vain
'Tis to see the Tyrant's crew   190
Ride over your wives and you—
Blood is on the grass like dew.

XLVIII

'Then it is to feel revenge
Fiercely thirsting to exchange
Blood for blood—and wrong for
    wrong—   195
Do not thus when ye are strong.

XLIX

'Birds find rest, in narrow nest
When weary of their wingèd quest;
Beasts find fare, in woody lair   199
When storm and snow are in the
    air.

L

'Asses, swine, have litter spread
And with fitting food are fed;
All things have a home but one—
Thou, Oh, Englishman, hast none!

LI

'This is Slavery—savage men,   205
Or wild beasts within a den
Would endure not as ye do—
But such ills they never knew.

LII

'What art thou Freedom? O! could
    slaves
Answer from their living graves 210
This demand—tyrants would flee
Like a dream's dim imagery:

LIII

'Thou art not, as impostors say,
A shadow soon to pass away,
A superstition, and a name   215
Echoing from the cave of Fame.

LIV

'For the labourer thou art bread,
And a comely table spread
From his daily labour come
In a neat and happy home.   220

LV

'Thou art clothes, and fire, and
    food
For the trampled multitude—
No—in countries that are free
Such starvation cannot be
As in England now we see.   225

LVI

'To the rich thou art a check,
When his foot is on the neck
Of his victim, thou dost make
That he treads upon a snake.

LVII

'Thou art Justice—ne'er for gold
May thy righteous laws be sold 231
As laws are in England—thou
Shield'st alike the high and low.

LVIII

'Thou art Wisdom—Freemen never
Dream that God will damn for ever
All who think those things untrue
Of which Priests make such ado. 237

LIX

'Thou art Peace—never by thee
Would blood and treasure wasted
    be
As tyrants wasted them, when
    all   240
Leagued to quench thy flame in
    Gaul.

LX

'What if English toil and blood
Was poured forth, even as a flood?
It availed, Oh, Liberty,
To dim, but not extinguish thee.

LXI

'Thou art Love—the rich have
    kissed   246
Thy feet, and like him following
    Christ,
Give their substance to the free
And through the rough world fol-
    low thee,

LXII

'Or turn their wealth to arms, and
    make   250
War for thy belovèd sake
On wealth, and war, and fraud—
    whence they
Drew the power which is their
    prey.

LXIII

'Science, Poetry, and Thought
Are thy lamps; they make the lot
Of the dwellers in a cot   256
So serene, they curse it not.

LXIV

'Spirit, Patience, Gentleness,
All that can adorn and bless
Art thou—let deeds, not words,
    express   260
Thine exceeding loveliness.

LXV

'Let a great Assembly be
Of the fearless and the free
On some spot of English ground
Where the plains stretch wide
    around.   265

LXVI

'Let the blue sky overhead,
The green earth on which ye tread,
All that must eternal be
Witness the solemnity.

LXVII

'From the corners uttermost   270
Of the bounds of English coast;
From every hut, village, and town
Where those who live and suffer
    moan
For others' misery or their own,

LXVIII

'From the workhouse and the
    prison
Where pale as corpses newly risen,
Women, children, young and old 277
Groan for pain, and weep for
    cold—

LXIX

'From the haunts of daily life
Where is waged the daily strife 280
With common wants and common
    cares
Which sows the human heart with
    tares—

LXX

'Lastly from the palaces
Where the murmur of distress
Echoes, like the distant sound   285
Of a wind alive around

LXXI

'Those prison halls of wealth and
    fashion,
Where some few feel such compas-
    sion
For those who groan, and toil, and
    wail
As must make their brethren pale—

LXXII

'Ye who suffer woes untold,   291
Or to feel, or to behold
Your lost country bought and sold
With a price of blood and gold—

LXXIII

'Let a vast assembly be,   295
And with great solemnity
Declare with measured words that
    ye
Are, as God has made ye, free—

LXXIV

'Be your strong and simple words
Keen to wound as sharpened
    swords,
And wide as targes let them be,   301
With their shade to cover ye.

LXXV

'Let the tyrants pour around
With a quick and startling sound,
Like the loosening of a sea,   305
Troops of armed emblazonry.

LXXVI

'Let the charged artillery drive
Till the dead air seems alive
With the clash of clanging wheels,
And the tramp of horses' heels.   310

LXXVII

'Let the fixèd bayonet
Gleam with sharp desire to wet
Its bright point in English blood
Looking keen as one for food.

LXXVIII

'Let the horsemen's scimitars   315
Wheel and flash, like sphereless
    stars
Thirsting to eclipse their burning
In a sea of death and mourning.

LXXIX

'Stand ye calm and resolute,
Like a forest close and mute,   320
With folded arms and looks which
    are
Weapons of unvanquished war,

LXXX

'And let Panic, who outspeeds
The career of armèd steeds
Pass, a disregarded shade   325
Through your phalanx undismayed.

LXXXI

'Let the laws of your own land,
Good or ill, between ye stand
Hand to hand, and foot to foot,
Arbiters of the dispute,   330

LXXXII

'The old laws of England—they
Whose reverend heads with age are
    gray,
Children of a wiser day;
And whose solemn voice must be
Thine own echo—Liberty!   335

LXXXIII

'On those who first should violate
Such sacred heralds in their state
Rest the blood that must ensue,
And it will not rest on you.

LXXXIV

'And if then the tyrants dare   340
Let them ride among you there,
Slash, and stab, and maim, and
  hew,—
What they like, that let them do.

LXXXV

'With folded arms and steady
  eyes,
And little fear, and less surprise,
Look upon them as they slay   346
Till their rage has died away.

LXXXVI

'Then they will return with shame
To the place from which they
  came,
And the blood thus shed will speak
In hot blushes on their cheek.   351

LXXXVII

'Every woman in the land
Will point at them as they stand—
They will hardly dare to greet
Their acquaintance in the street.355

LXXXVIII

'And the bold, true warriors
Who have hugged Danger in wars
Will turn to those who would be
  free,
Ashamed of such base company.

LXXXIX

'And that slaughter to the Nation
Shall steam up like inspiration, 361
Eloquent, oracular;
A volcano heard afar.

XC

'And these words shall then become
Like Oppression's thundered doom
Ringing through each heart and
  brain   366
Heard again—again—again—

XCI

'Rise like Lions after slumber
In unvanquishable number—
Shake your chains to earth like
  dew   370
Which in sleep had fallen on you—
Ye are many—they are few.'

NOTE ON THE MASK OF ANARCHY, BY MRS. SHELLEY

THOUGH Shelley's first eager desire to excite his countrymen to resist openly the oppressions existent during 'the good old times' had faded with early youth, still his warmest sympathies were for the people. He was a republican, and loved a democracy. He looked on all human beings as inheriting an equal right to possess the dearest privileges of our nature; the necessaries of life when fairly earned by labour, and intellectual instruction. His hatred of any despotism that looked upon the people as not to be consulted, or protected from want and ignorance, was intense. He was residing near Leghorn, at Villa Valsovano, writing *The Cenci*, when the news of the Manchester Massacre reached us; it roused in him violent emotions of indignation and compassion. The great truth that the many, if accordant and resolute, could control the few, as was shown some years after, made him long to teach his injured countrymen how to resist. Inspired by these feelings, he wrote the *Mask of Anarchy*, which he sent to his friend Leigh Hunt, to be inserted in the *Examiner*, of which he was then the Editor.

'I did not insert it,' Leigh Hunt writes in his valuable and interesting preface to this poem, when he printed it in 1832, 'because I thought that the public at large had not become sufficiently discerning to do justice to the sincerity and kind-heartedness of the spirit that walked in this flaming robe of verse.' Days of outrage have passed away, and with them the exasperation that would cause such an appeal to the many to be injurious. Without being aware of them, they at one time acted on his suggestions, and gained the day. But they rose when human life was respected by the Minister in power; such was not the case during the Administration which excited Shelley's abhorrence.

The poem was written for the people, and is therefore in a more popular tone than usual: portions strike as abrupt and unpolished, but many stanzas are all his own. I heard him repeat, and admired, those beginning

'My Father Time is old and gray,'

before I knew to what poem they were to belong. But the most touching passage is that which describes the blessed effects of liberty; it might make a patriot of any man whose heart was not wholly closed against his humbler fellow-creatures.

PETER BELL THE THIRD

By MICHING MALLECHO, Esq.

Is it a party in a parlour,	Some sipping punch—some sipping tea;
Crammed just as they on earth were crammed,	But, as you by their faces see, All silent, and all—damned!

Peter Bell, by W. WORDSWORTH.

OPHELIA.—What means this, my lord?
HAMLET.—Marry, this is Miching Mallecho; it means mischief.

SHAKESPEARE.

DEDICATION

TO THOMAS BROWN, ESQ., THE YOUNGER, H.F.

DEAR TOM—Allow me to request you to introduce Mr. Peter Bell to the respectable family of the Fudges. Although he may fall short of those very considerable personages in the more active properties which characterize the Rat and the Apostate, I suspect that even you, their historian, will confess that he surpasses them in the more peculiarly legitimate qualification of intolerable dulness.

You know Mr. Examiner Hunt; well—it was he who presented me to two of the Mr. Bells. My intimacy with the younger Mr. Bell naturally sprung from this introduction to his brothers. And in presenting him to you, I have the satisfaction of being able to assure you that he is considerably the dullest of the three.

There is this particular advantage in an acquaintance with any one of the Peter Bells, that if you know one Peter Bell, you know three Peter Bells; they are not one, but three; not three, but one. An awful mystery, which, after having caused torrents of blood, and having been hymned by groans enough to deafen the music of the spheres, is at length illustrated to the satisfaction of all parties in the theological world, by the nature of Mr. Peter Bell.

Peter is a polyhedric Peter, or a Peter with many sides. He changes colours like a chameleon, and his coat like a snake. He is a Proteus of a Peter. He was at first sublime, pathetic, impressive, profound; then dull; then prosy and dull; and now dull—oh so very dull! it is an ultra-legitimate dulness.

You will perceive that it is not necessary to consider Hell and the Devil as supernatural machinery. The whole scene of my epic is in 'this world which is'—so Peter informed us before his conversion to *White Obi*—

> 'The world of all of us, *and where*
> *We find our happiness, or not at all.*'

Let me observe that I have spent six or seven days in composing this sublime piece; the orb of my moonlike genius has made the fourth part of its revolution round the dull earth which you inhabit, driving you mad, while it has retained its calmness and its splendour, and I have been fitting this its last phase 'to occupy a permanent station in the literature of my country.'

Your works, indeed, dear Tom, sell better; but mine are far superior. The public is no judge; posterity sets all to rights.

Allow me to observe that so much has been written of Peter Bell, that the present history can be considered only, like the *Iliad,* as a continuation of that series of cyclic poems, which have already been candidates for bestowing immortality upon, at the same time that they receive it from, his character and adventures. In this point of view I have violated no rule of syntax in beginning my composition with a conjunction; the full stop which closes the poem continued by me being, like the full stops at the end of the *Iliad* and *Odyssey,* a full stop of a very qualified import.

Hoping that the immortality which you have given to the Fudges, you will receive from them; and in the firm expectation, that when London shall be an habitation of bitterns; when St. Paul's and Westminster Abbey shall stand, shapeless and nameless ruins, in the midst of an unpeopled marsh; when the piers of Waterloo Bridge shall become the nuclei of islets of reeds and osiers, and cast the jagged shadows of their broken arches on the solitary stream, some transatlantic commentator will be weighing in the scales of some new and now unimagined system of criticism, the respective merits of the Bells and the Fudges, and their historians. I remain, dear Tom, yours sincerely,

MICHING MALLECHO.

December 1, 1819.

P.S.—Pray excuse the date of place; so soon as the profits of the publication come in, I mean to hire lodgings in a more respectable street.

PROLOGUE

PETER BELLS, one, two and three,
O'er the wide world wandering
    be.—
First, the antenatal Peter,
Wrapped in weeds of the same
    metre,
The so-long-predestined raiment 5
Clothed in which to walk his way
    meant
The second Peter; whose ambition
Is to link the proposition,
As the mean of two extremes—
(This was learned from Aldric's
    themes)   10
Shielding from the guilt of schism
The orthodoxal syllogism;
The First Peter—he who was
Like the shadow in the glass
Of the second, yet unripe,   15
His substantial antitype.—
Then came Peter Bell the Second,
Who henceforward must be reck-
    oned
The body of a double soul,
And that portion of the whole   20
Without which the rest would seem
Ends of a disjointed dream.—
And the Third is he who has
O'er the grave been forced to pass
To the other side, which is,—   25
Go and try else,—just like this.

Peter Bell the First was Peter
Smugger, milder, softer, neater,
Like the soul before it is
Born from *that* world into *this*.   30

The next Peter Bell was he,
Predevote, like you and me,
To good or evil as may come;
His was the severer doom,—
For he was an evil Cotter,   35
And a polygamic Potter.[1]
And the last is Peter Bell,
Damned since our first parents fell,
Damned eternally to Hell—
Surely he deserves it well!   40

PART THE FIRST

DEATH

I

AND Peter Bell, when he had been
    With fresh-imported Hell-fire
    warmed,
Grew serious—from his dress and
    mien
'Twas very plainly to be seen
    Peter was quite reformed.   5

II

His eyes turned up, his mouth
    turned down;
    His accent caught a nasal twang;
He oiled his hair; [2] there might be
    heard
The grace of God in every word
    Which Peter said or sang.   10

III

But Peter now grew old, and had
    An ill no doctor could unravel;

---

[1] The oldest scholiasts read—
                A *dodecagamic* Potter.
This is at once more descriptive and more megalophonous,—but the alliteration of
the text had captivated the vulgar ear of the herd of later commentators.—
[SHELLEY'S NOTE.]

[2] To those who have not duly appreciated the distinction between *Whale*
and *Russia* oil, this attribute might rather seem to belong to the Dandy than the
Evangelic. The effect, when to the windward, is indeed so similar, that it requires
a subtle naturalist to discriminate the animals. They belong, however, to distinct
genera.—[SHELLEY'S NOTE.]

His torments almost drove him
    mad;—
Some said it was a fever bad—
    Some swore it was the gravel. 15

IV

His holy friends then came about,
    And with long preaching and
        persuasion
Convinced the patient that, with-
    out
The smallest shadow of a doubt,
    He was predestined to damna-
        tion. 20

V

They said—'Thy name is Peter
    Bell;
Thy skin is of a brimstone hue;
Alive or dead—ay, sick or well—
The one God made to rhyme with
    hell;
    The other, I think, rhymes with
        you.' 25

VI

Then Peter set up such a yell!—
    The nurse, who with some water
        gruel
Was climbing up the stairs, as well
As her old legs could climb them—
    fell,
    And broke them both—the fall
        was cruel. 30

VII

The Parson from the casement lept
Into the lake of Windermere—
And many an eel—though no adept
In God's right reason for it—
    kept 34
    Gnawing his kidneys half a year.

VIII

And all the rest rushed through the
    door.

And tumbled over one another,
And broke their skulls.—Upon the
    floor
Meanwhile sat Peter Bell, and
    swore,
    And cursed his father and his
        mother; 40

IX

And raved of God, and sin, and
    death,
    Blaspheming like an infidel;
And said, that with his clenchèd
    teeth
He'd seize the earth from under-
    neath,
    And drag it with him down to
        hell. 45

X

As he was speaking came a spasm,
    And wrenched his gnashing teeth
        asunder;
Like one who sees a strange phan-
    tasm
He lay,—there was a silent
        chasm 49
    Between his upper jaw and un-
        der.

XI

And yellow death lay on his face;
    And a fixed smile that was not
        human
Told, as I understand the case,
That he was gone to the wrong
    place:—
    I heard all this from the old
        woman. 55

XII

Then there came down from Lang-
    dale Pike
    A cloud, with lightning, wind
        and hail;
It swept over the mountains like
An ocean,—and I heard it strike
    The woods and crags of Gras-
        mere vale. 60

XIII

And I saw the black storm come
  Nearer, minute after minute; 62
Its thunder made the cataracts
    dumb;
With hiss, and clash, and hollow
    hum,
  It neared as if the Devil was
    in it.   65

XIV

The Devil *was* in it:—he had
    bought
  Peter for half-a-crown; and
    when
The storm which bore him van-
    ished, nought
That in the house that storm had
    caught
  Was ever seen again.   70

XV

The gaping neighbours came next
    day—
  They found all vanished from
    the shore:
The Bible, whence he used to pray,
Half scorched under a hen-coop
    lay;
  Smashed glass—and nothing
    more!   75

PART THE SECOND

THE DEVIL

I

The Devil, I safely can aver,
  Has neither hoof, nor tail, nor
    sting;
Nor is he, as some sages swear,
A spirit, neither here nor there,
  In nothing—yet in everything. 80

II

He is—what we are; for sometimes
  The Devil is a gentleman;
At others a bard bartering rhymes
For sack; a statesman spinning
    crimes;
  A swindler, living as he can; 85

III

A thief, who cometh in the night,
  With whole boots and net pan-
    taloons,
Like some one whom it were not
    right
To mention;—or the luckless
    wight
  From whom he steals nine silver
    spoons.   90

IV

But in this case he did appear
  Like a slop-merchant from Wap-
    ping,
And with smug face, and eye se-
    vere,
On every side did perk and peer 94
  Till he saw Peter dead or nap-
    ping.

V

He had on an upper Benjamin
  (For he was of the driving
    schism)
In the which he wrapped his skin
From the storm he travelled in,
  For fear of rheumatism.   100

VI

He called the ghost out of the
    corse;—
  It was exceedingly like Peter,—
Only its voice was hollow and
    hoarse—
It had a queerish look of course—
  Its dress too was a little
    neater.   105

VII

The Devil knew not his name and
    lot;
    Peter knew not that he was
    Bell:
Each had an upper stream of
    thought,
Which made all seem as it was not;
    Fitting itself to all things
    well. 110

VIII

Peter thought he had parents dear,
    Bothers, sisters, cousins, cro-
    nies,
In the fens of Lincolnshire;
He perhaps had found them there
Had he gone and boldly shown
    his 115

IX

Solemn phiz in his own village;
    Where he thought oft when a
    boy
He'd clomb the orchard walls to
    pillage
The produce of his neighbour's
    tillage,
    With marvellous pride and
    joy. 120

X

And the Devil thought he had,
    'Mid the misery and confusion
Of an unjust war, just made
A fortune by the gainful trade
Of giving soldiers rations bad— 125
    The world is full of strange de-
    lusion—

XI

That he had a mansion planned
    In a square like Grosvenor
    Square,
That he was aping fashion, and

That he now came to Westmore-
    land 130
To see what was romantic there.

XII

And all this, though quite ideal,—
    Ready at a breath to vanish,—
Was a state not more unreal
Than the peace he could not
    feel, 135
    Or the care he could not banish.

XIII

After a little conversation,
    The Devil told Peter, if he chose,
He'd bring him to the world of
    fashion
By giving him a situation 140
    In his own service—and new
    clothes.

XIV

And Peter bowed, quite pleased
    and proud,
    And after waiting some few days
For a new livery—dirty yellow
Turned up with black—the wretch-
    ed fellow 145
    Was bowled to Hell in the
    Devil's chaise.

PART THE THIRD

HELL

I

HELL is a city much like London—
    A populous and a smoky city;
There are all sorts of people un-
    done,
And there is little or no fun
    done: 150
    Small justice shown, and still less
    pity.

II

There is a Castles, and a Canning,
  A Cobbett, and a Castlereagh;
All sorts of caitiff corpses planning
All sorts of cozening for trepan-
      ning   155
  Corpses less corrupt than they.

III

There is a * * * , who has lost
  His wits, or sold them, none
    knows which;
He walks about a double ghost,
And though as thin as Fraud al-
    most—   160
  Ever grows more grim and rich.

IV

There is a Chancery Court; a
    King;
  A manufacturing mob; a set
Of thieves who by themselves are
    sent
Similar thieves to represent;   165
  An army; and a public debt.

V

Which last is a scheme of paper
    money,
  And means—being interpret-
    ed—
'Bees, keep your wax—give us the
    honey,
And we will plant, while skies are
    sunny,   170
  Flowers, which in winter serve
    instead.'

VI

There is a great talk of revolu-
    tion—
  And a great chance of despot-
    ism—
German soldiers—camps—confu-
    sion—
Tumults — lotteries — rage — de-
    lusion—   175
  Gin—suicide—and methodism;

VII

Taxes too, on wine and bread,
  And meat, and beer, and tea, and
    cheese,
From which those patriots pure are
    fed,   179
  Who gorge before they reel to bed
  The tenfold essence of all these.

VIII

There are mincing women, mew-
    ing,
  (Like cats, who *amant miserè*,[1])
Of their own virtue, and pursuing
Their gentler sisters to that ruin,
  Without which—what were chas-
    tity? [2]   186

IX

Lawyers—judges—old hobnobbers
  Are there — bailiffs — chancel-
    lors—
Bishops—great and little robbers—
Rhymesters—pamphleteers—
    stock-jobbers—   190
  Men of glory in the wars,—

[1] One of the attributes in Linnaeus's description of the Cat. To a similar cause the caterwauling of more than one species of this genus is to be referred;—except, indeed, that the poor quadruped is compelled to quarrel with its own pleasures, whilst the biped is supposed only to quarrel with those of others.—[SHELLEY'S NOTE.]

[2] What would this husk and excuse for a virtue be without its kernel prostitution, or the kernel prostitution without this husk of a virtue? I wonder the women of the town do not form an association, like the Society for the Suppression of Vice, for the support of what may be called the 'King, Church, and Constitution' of their order. But this subject is almost too horrible for a joke.—[SHELLEY'S NOTE.]

X

Things whose trade is, over ladies
  To lean, and flirt, and stare, and
    simper,
Till all that is divine in woman
Grows cruel, courteous, smooth, in-
    human,   195
  Crucified 'twixt a smile and
    whimper.

XI

Thrusting, toiling, wailing, moil-
    ing,
  Frowning, preaching — such a
    riot!
Each with never-ceasing labour,
Whilst he thinks he cheats his
    neighbour,   200
  Cheating his own heart of quiet.

XII

And all these meet at levees;—
  Dinners convivial and politi-
    cal;—
Suppers of epic poets;—teas,
Where small talk dies in agonies;—
  Breakfasts professional and crit-
    ical;   206

XIII

Lunches and snacks so aldermanic
  That one would furnish forth ten
    dinners,
Where reigns a Cretan-tonguèd
    panic,
Lest news Russ, Dutch, or Ale-
    mannic   210
  Should make some losers, and
    some winners;—

XIV

At conversazioni—balls—
  Conventicles—and drawing-
    rooms—

Courts of law—committees—calls
Of a morning—clubs—book-
    stalls—
  Churches—masquerades—and
    tombs.   216

XV

And this is Hell—and in this
    smother
All are damnable and damned;
Each one damning, damns the
    other;
They are damned by one another,
By none other are they damned. 221

XVI

'Tis a lie to say, 'God damns [1]!'
  Where was Heaven's Attorney
    General
When they first gave out such
    flams?
Let there be an end of shams,   225
  They are mines of poisonous
    mineral.

XVII

Statesmen damn themselves to be
  Cursed; and lawyers damn their
    souls
To the auction of a fee;
Churchmen damn themselves to
    see
  God's sweet love in burning coals.

XVIII

The rich are damned, beyond all
    cure,   232
  To taunt, and starve, and tram-
    ple on
The weak and wretched; and the
    poor
Damn their broken hearts to endure
  Stripe on stripe, with groan on
    groan.   236

[1] This libel on our national oath, and this accusation of all our countrymen of
being in the daily practice of solemnly asseverating the most enormous falsehood,
I fear deserves the notice of a more active Attorney General than that here alluded
to.—[SHELLEY'S NOTE.]

XIX

Sometimes the poor are damned
    indeed
    To take,—not means for being
        blessed,—
But Cobbett's snuff, revenge; that
    weed
From which the worms that it doth
    feed   240
    Squeeze less than they before
        possessed.

XX

And some few, like we know who,
    Damned—but God alone knows
        why—   243
To believe their minds are given
To make this ugly Hell a Heaven;
    In which faith they live and die.

XXI

Thus, as in a town, plague-stricken,
    Each man be he sound or no
Must indifferently sicken;
As when day begins to thicken, 250
    None knows a pigeon from a
        crow,—

XXII

So good and bad, sane and mad,
    The oppressor and the oppressed;
Those who weep to see what others
Smile to inflict upon their brothers;
    Lovers, haters, worst and best;

XXIII

All are damned—they breathe an
    air,   257
    Thick infected, joy-dispelling:
Each pursues what seems most fair,
Mining like moles, through mind,
    and there   260
Scoop palace-caverns vast, where
    Care
    In thronèd state is ever dwelling.

PART THE FOURTH

SIN

I

Lo, Peter in Hell's Grosvenor
    Square,
    A footman in the Devil's service!
And the misjudging world would
    swear   265
That every man in service there
    To virtue would prefer vice.

II

But Peter, though now damned,
    was not
    What Peter was before damna-
        tion.
Men oftentimes prepare a lot   270
Which ere it finds them, is not
    what
    Suits with their genuine station.

III

All things that Peter saw and felt
    Had a peculiar aspect to him;
And when they came within the
    belt   275
Of his own nature, seemed to melt,
    Like cloud to cloud, into him.

IV

And so the outward world uniting
    To that within him, he became
Considerably uninviting   280
To those who, meditation slighting,
    Were moulded in a different
        frame.

V

And he scorned them, and they
    scorned him;
    And he scorned all they did; and
        they
Did all that men of their own trim

Are wont to do to please their
    whim, 286
Drinking, lying, swearing, play.

VI

Such were his fellow-servants; thus
    His virtue, like our own, was
    built
Too much on that indignant fuss 290
Hypocrite Pride stirs up in us
    To bully one another's guilt.

VII

He had a mind which was somehow
    At once circumference and centre
Of all he might or feel or know; 295
Nothing went ever out, although
    Something did ever enter.

VIII

He had as much imagination
    As a pint-pot;—he never could
Fancy another situation, 300
From which to dart his contem-
    plation,
    Than that wherein he stood.

IX

Yet his was individual mind,
    And new created all he saw
In a new manner, and refined 305
Those new creations, and combined
    Them, by a master-spirit's law.

X

Thus—though unimaginative—
    An apprehension clear, intense,
Of his mind's work, had made alive
The things it wrought on; I believe
    Wakening a sort of thought in
    sense. 312

XI

But from the first 'twas Peter's drift
    To be a kind of moral eunuch,
He touched the hem of Nature's
    shift, 315

Felt faint—and never dared uplift
    The closest, all-concealing tunic.

XII

She laughed the while, with an arch
    smile,
    And kissed him with a sister's
    kiss,
And said—'My best Diogenes, 320
I love you well—but, if you please,
    Tempt not again my deepest
    bliss.

XIII

' 'Tis you are cold—for I, not coy,
    Yield love for love, frank, warm,
    and true;
And Burns, a Scottish peasant
    boy— 325
His errors prove it—knew my joy
    More, learnèd friend, than you.

XIV

'*Bocca bacciata non perde ventura,*
    Anzi rinnuova come fa la luna:—
So thought Boccaccio, whose sweet
    words might cure a 330
Male prude, like you, from what
    you now endure, a
    Low-tide in soul, like a stagnant
    laguna.'

XV

Then Peter rubbed his eyes severe,
    And smoothed his spacious fore-
    head down
With his broad palm;—'twixt love
    and fear, 335
He looked, as he no doubt felt,
    queer,
    And in his dream sate down.

XVI

The Devil was no uncommon
    creature,
    A leaden-witted thief—just hud-
    dled 339

Out of the dross and scum of na-
　　ture;
A toad-like lump of limb and fea-
　　ture,
　　With mind, and heart, and fancy
　　　　muddled.　　　　　　342

XVII

He was that heavy, dull, cold thing,
　　The spirit of evil well may be:
A drone too base to have a sting;
Who gluts, and grimes his lazy
　　wing,
　　And calls lust, luxury.　　347

XVIII

Now he was quite the kind of wight
　　Round whom collect, at a fixed
　　　　aera,
Venison, turtle, hock, and claret,—
Good cheer—and those who come
　　to share it—　　　　　　351
　　And best East Indian madeira!

XIX

It was his fancy to invite
　　Men of science, wit, and learning,
Who came to lend each other light;
He proudly thought that his gold's
　　might　　　　　　　　356
　　Had set those spirits burning.

XX

And men of learning, science, wit,
　　Considered him as you and I
Think of some rotten tree, and sit
Lounging and dining under it,　361
　　Exposed to the wide sky.

XXI

And all the while, with loose fat
　　smile,
　　The willing wretch sat winking
　　　　there,　　　　　　　364
Believing 'twas his power that made
That jovial scene—and that all paid
　　Homage to his unnoticed chair.

XXII

Though to be sure this place was
　　Hell;
　　He was the Devil—and all they—
What though the claret circled well,
And wit, like ocean, rose and fell?—
　　Were damned eternally.　　372

PART THE FIFTH

GRACE

I

AMONG the guests who often stayed
　　Till the Devil's petits-soupers,
A man there came, fair as a
　　maid,　　　　　　　　375
And Peter noted what he said,
　　Standing behind his master's
　　　　chair.

II

He was a mighty poet—and
　　A subtle-souled psychologist;
All things he seemed to understand,
Of old or new—of sea or land—　381
　　But his own mind—which was
　　　　a mist.

III

This was a man who might have
　　turned
　　Hell into Heaven—and so in
　　　　gladness
A Heaven unto himself have
　　earned;
But he in shadows undiscerned　386
　　Trusted,—and damned himself
　　　　to madness.

IV

He spoke of poetry, and how
　　'Divine it was—a light—a love—
A spirit which like wind doth blow
As it listeth, to and fro;　　　391
　　A dew rained down from God
　　　　above;

V

'A power which comes and goes like
      dream,
   And which none can ever trace—
Heaven's light on earth—Truth's
      brightest beam.'   395
And when he ceased there lay the
      gleam
   Of those words upon his face.

VI

Now Peter, when he heard such
      talk,
   Would, heedless of a broken pate,
Stand like a man asleep, or balk   400
Some wishing guest of knife or fork,
   Or drop and break his master's
      plate.

VII

At night he oft would start and
      wake
   Like a lover, and began
In a wild measure songs to make   405
On moor, and glen, and rocky lake,
   And on the heart of man—

VIII

And on the universal sky—
   And the wide earth's bosom
      green,—
And the sweet, strange mystery   410
Of what beyond these things may
      lie,
   And yet remain unseen.

IX

For in his thought he visited
   The spots in which, ere dead and
      damned,
He his wayward life had led;   415
Yet knew not whence the thoughts
      were fed
   Which thus his fancy crammed.

X

And these obscure remembrances
   Stirred such harmony in Peter,
That, whensoever he should please,
He could speak of rocks and trees
   In poetic metre.   422

XI

For though it was without a sense
   Of memory, yet he remembered
      well
Many a ditch and quick-set fence;
Of lakes he had intelligence,   426
   He knew something of heath and
      fell.

XII

He had also dim recollections
   Of pedlars tramping on their
      rounds;
Milk-pans and pails; and odd col-
      lections   430
Of saws, and proverbs; and reflec-
      tions
   Old parsons make in burying-
      grounds.

XIII

But Peter's verse was clear, and
      came
   Announcing from the frozen
      hearth
Of a cold age, that none might
      tame   435
The soul of that diviner flame
   It augured to the Earth:

XIV

Like gentle rains, on the dry plains,
   Making that green which late
      was gray,
Or like the sudden moon, that
      stains
Some gloomy chamber's window-
      panes   441
   With a broad light like day.

XV

For language was in Peter's hand
  Like clay while he was yet a
      potter;
And he made songs for all the
    land,   445
Sweet both to feel and understand,
As pipkins late to mountain Cot-
    ter.

XVI

And Mr. ——, the bookseller,
  Gave twenty pounds for some;—
      then scorning
A footman's yellow coat to wear,
Peter, too proud of heart, I fear, 451
  Instantly gave the Devil warn-
      ing.

XVII

Whereat the Devil took offence,
  And swore in his soul a great
      oath then,   454
'That for his damned impertinence
He'd bring him to a proper sense
  Of what was due to gentlemen!'

PART THE SIXTH

DAMNATION

I

'O THAT mine enemy had written
  A book!'—cried Job:—a fearful
      curse,
If to the Arab, as the Briton,   460
'Twas galling to be critic-bitten:—
  The Devil to Peter wished no
      worse.

II

When Peter's next new book found
    vent,
  The Devil to all the first Reviews
A copy of it slyly sent,   465
With five-pound note as compli-
    ment,
  And this short notice—'Pray
      abuse.'

III

Then *seriatim,* month and quarter,
  Appeared such mad tirades.—
      One said—
'Peter seduced Mrs. Foy's daugh-
    ter,
Then drowned the mother in Ulls-
    water,   471
  The last thing as he went to bed.'

IV

Another—'Let him shave his head!
  Where's Dr. Willis?—Or is he
      joking?
What does the rascal mean or
    hope,   475
No longer imitating Pope,
  In that barbarian Shakespeare
      poking?'

V

One more, 'Is incest not enough?
  And must there be adultery too?
Grace after meat? Miscreant and
    Liar!   480
Thief! Blackguard! Scoundrel!
    Fool! Hell-fire
  Is twenty times too good for you.

VI

'By that last book of yours WE
    think
  You've double damned yourself
      to scorn;
We warned you whilst yet on the
    brink   485
You stood. From your black name
    will shrink
  The babe that is unborn.'

VII

All these Reviews the Devil made
  Up in a parcel, which he had
Safely to Peter's house con-
    veyed.   490
For carriage, tenpence Peter paid—
  Untied them—read them—went
      half mad.

VIII

'What!' cried he, 'this is my reward
  For nights of thought, and days
    of toil?
Do poets, but to be abhorred   495
By men of whom they never heard,
  Consume their spirits' oil?

IX

'What have I done to them?—and
    who
  Is Mrs. Foy? 'Tis very cruel
To speak of me and Betty so!   500
Adultery! God defend me! Oh!
  I've half a mind to fight a duel.

X

'Or,' cried he, a grave look collect-
    ing,
  'Is it my genius, like the moon,
Sets those who stand her face in-
    specting,   505
That face within their brain reflect-
    ing,
Like a crazed bell-chime, out of
    tune?'

XI

For Peter did not know the town,
  But thought, as country readers
    do,
For half a guinea or a crown,   510
He bought oblivion or renown
  From God's own voice [1] in a re-
    view.

XII

All Peter did on this occasion
  Was, writing some sad stuff in
    prose.

It is a dangerous invasion   515
When poets criticize; their station
  Is to delight, not pose.

XIII

The Devil then sent to Leipsic fair
  For Born's translation of Kant's
    book;
A world of words, tail foremost,
    where
Right — wrong — false — true —
    and foul—and fair   521
  As in a lottery-wheel are shook.

XIV

Five thousand crammed octavo
    pages
  Of German psychologics,—he
Who his *furor verborum* as-
    suages   525
Thereon, deserves just seven
    months' wages
  More than will e'er be due to me.

XV

I looked on them nine several days,
  And then I saw that they were
    bad;
A friend, too, spoke in their dis-
    praise,—   530
He never read them;—with amaze
  I found Sir William Drummond
    had.

XVI

When the book came, the Devil
    sent
  It to P. Verbovale,[2] Esquire,
With a brief note of compliment,

---

[1] *Vox populi, vox dei*. As Mr. Godwin truly observes of a more famous saying, *of some merit as a popular maxim, but totally destitute of philosophical accuracy.* —[SHELLEY'S NOTE.]

[2] Quasi, *Qui valet verba:—i. e.* all the words which have been, are, or may be expended by, for, against, with, or on him. A sufficient proof of the utility of this history. Peter's progenitor who selected this name seems to have possessed a *pure anticipated cognition* of the nature and modesty of this ornament of his posterity. — [SHELLEY'S NOTE.]

By that night's Carlisle mail. It
    went,   536
And set his soul on fire.

XVII

Fire, which *ex luce praebens
    fumum,*
Made him beyond the bottom see
Of truth's clear well—when I and
    you, Ma'am,   540
Go, as we shall do, *subter humum,*
We may know more than he.

XVIII

Now Peter ran to seed in soul
    Into a walking paradox;
For he was neither part nor whole,
Nor good, nor bad—nor knave nor
    fool;   546
—Among the woods and rocks

XIX

Furious he rode, where late he
    ran,
    Lashing and spurring his tame
      hobby;
Turned to a formal puritan,   550
A solemn and unsexual man,—
    He half believed *White Obi.*

XX

This steed in vision he would ride,
    High trotting over nine-inch
      bridges,   554
With Flibbertigibbet, imp of pride,
Mocking and mowing by his side—
A mad-brained goblin for a guide—
    Over corn-fields, gates, and
      hedges.

XXI

After these ghastly rides, he came
    Home to his heart, and found
      from thence   560
Much stolen of its accustomed
    flame;

His thoughts grew weak, drowsy,
    and lame
    Of their intelligence.

XXII

To Peter's view, all seemed one
    hue;
    He was no Whig, he was no
      Tory;
No Deist and no Christian he;—566
He got so subtle, that to be
    Nothing, was all his glory.

XXIII

One single point in his belief
    From his organization sprung, 570
The heart-enrooted faith, the chief
Ear in his doctrines' blighted sheaf,
    That 'Happiness is wrong';

XXIV

So thought Calvin and Dominic;
    So think their fierce successors,
      who
Even now would neither stint nor
      stick   576
Our flesh from off our bones to pick,
    If they might 'do their do.'

XXV

His morals thus were under-
    mined:—
    The old Peter—the hard, old
      Potter—   580
Was born anew within his mind;
He grew dull, harsh, sly, unrefined,
    As when he tramped beside the
      Otter.[1]

XXVI

In the death hues of agony   584
    Lambently flashing from a fish,
Now Peter felt amused to see
Shades like a rainbow's rise and
    flee,
    Mixed with a certain hungry
      wish.

---

[1] A famous river in the new Atlantis of the Dynastophylic Pantisocratists.—
[SHELLEY'S NOTE.]

XXVII

So in his Country's dying face
   He looked—and, lovely as she
     lay,
Seeking in vain his last embrace, 591
Wailing her own abandoned case,
   With hardened sneer he turned
     away:

XXVIII

And coolly to his own soul said;—
   'Do you not think that we might
     make   595
A poem on her when she's dead:—
Or no—a thought is in my head—
   Her shroud for a new sheet I'll
     take:

XXIX

'My wife wants one.—Let who will
     bury
   This mangled corpse! And I and
     you,   600
My dearest Soul, will then make
     merry,
As the Prince Regent did with
     Sherry,—'
   'Ay—and at last desert me too.'

XXX

And so his Soul would not be
     gay,
   But moaned within him; like a
     fawn   605
Moaning within a cave, it lay
Wounded and wasting, day by
     day,
   Till all its life of life was gone.

XXXI

As troubled skies stain waters clear,
   The storm in Peter's heart and
     mind
Now made his verses dark and
     queer:
They were the ghosts of what they
     were,   612

Shaking dim grave-clothes in the
     wind.

XXXII

For he now raved enormous folly,
   Of Baptisms, Sunday-schools,
     and Graves,   615
'Twould make George Colman
     melancholy
To have heard him, like a male
     Molly,
   Chanting those stupid staves.

XXXIII

Yet the Reviews, who heaped abuse
   On Peter while he wrote for free-
     dom,   620
So soon as in his song they spy
The folly which soothes tyranny,
   Praise him, for those who feed
     'em.

XXXIV

'He was a man, too great to scan;—
   A planet lost in truth's keen
     rays:—   625
His virtue, awful and prodigious;—
He was the most sublime, religious,
   Pure-minded Poet of these days.'

XXXV

As soon as he read that, cried Peter,
   'Eureka! I have found the way
To make a better thing of metre 631
Than e'er was made by living crea-
     ture
   Up to this blessèd day.'

XXXVI

Then Peter wrote odes to the
     Devil;—
   In one of which he meekly said:
'May Carnage and Slaughter, 636
Thy niece and thy daughter,
May Rapine and Famine,
Thy gorge ever cramming,
   Glut thee with living and dead!

XXXVII

'May Death and Damnation, 641
And Consternation,
Flit up from Hell with pure intent!
Slash them at Manchester,
Glasgow, Leeds, and Chester; 645
Drench all with blood from Avon
to Trent.

XXXVIII

'Let thy body-guard yeomen
Hew down babes and women,
And laugh with bold triumph till
Heaven be rent!
When Moloch in Jewry 650
Munched children with fury,
It was thou, Devil, dining with pure
intent.' [1]

PART THE SEVENTH

DOUBLE DAMNATION

I

THE Devil now knew his proper
cue.—
Soon as he read the ode, he drove
To his friend Lord MacMurder-
chouse's, 655
A man of interest in both houses,
And said:—'For money or for
love,

II

'Pray find some cure or sinecure;
To feed from the superfluous
taxes
A friend of ours—a poet—fewer 660
Have fluttered tamer to the lure
Than he.' His lordship stands
and racks his

III

Stupid brains, while one might
count
As many beads as he had
boroughs,—
At length replies; from his mean
front, 665
Like one who rubs out an account,
Smoothing away the unmeaning
furrows:

IV

'It happens fortunately, dear Sir,
I can. I hope I need require
No pledge from you, that he will
stir 670
In our affairs;—like Oliver,
That he'll be worthy of his hire.'

V

These words exchanged, the news
sent off
To Peter, home the Devil hied,—
Took to his bed; he had no cough,
No doctor,—meat and drink
enough,— 676
Yet that same night he died.

VI

The Devil's corpse was leaded
down;
His decent heirs enjoyed his
pelf,
Mourning-coaches, many a one, 680
Followed his hearse along the
town:—
Where was the Devil himself?

VII

When Peter heard of his promotion,
His eyes grew like two stars for
bliss:

---

[1] It is curious to observe how often extremes meet. Cobbett and Peter use the same language for a different purpose: Peter is indeed a sort of metrical Cobbett. Cobbett is, however, more mischievous than Peter, because he pollutes a holy and now unconquerable cause with the principles of legitimate murder; whilst the other only makes a bad one ridiculous and odious.

If either Peter or Cobbett should see this note, each will feel more indignation at being compared to the other than at any censure implied in the moral perversion laid to their charge.—[SHELLEY'S NOTE.]

There was a bow of sleek devotion
Engendering in his back; each mo-
tion   686
   Seemed a Lord's shoe to kiss.

VIII

He hired a house, bought plate, and
   made
A genteel drive up to his door,
With sifted gravel neatly laid,—690
As if defying all who said,
   Peter was ever poor.

IX

But a disease soon struck into
   The very life and soul of Peter—
He walked about—slept—had the
   hue   695
Of health upon his cheeks—and
   few
   Dug better—none a heartier
   eater.

X

And yet a strange and horrid curse
   Clung upon Peter, night and
   day;
Month after month the thing grew
   worse,   700
And deadlier than in this my verse
   I can find strength to say.

XI

Peter was dull—he was at first
   Dull—oh, so dull—so very dull!
Whether he talked, wrote, or re-
   hearsed—   705
Still with this dulness was he
   cursed—
   Dull—beyond all conception—
   dull.

XII

No one could read his books—no
   mortal,
   But a few natural friends, would
   hear him;

The parson came not near his
   portal;
His state was like that of the immortal   711
   Described by Swift—no man
   could bear him.

XIII

His sister, wife, and children
   yawned,
   With a long, slow, and drear
   ennui,
All human patience far beyond; 715
Their hopes of Heaven each would
   have pawned,
   Anywhere else to be.

XIV

But in his verse, and in his prose,
   The essence of his dulness was
Concentred and compressed so
   close,
   'Twould have made Guatimozin
   doze
   On his red gridiron of brass. 722

XV

A printer's boy, folding those pages,
   Fell slumbrously upon one side;
Like those famed Seven who slept
   three ages.   725
To wakeful frenzy's vigil-rages,
   As opiates, were the same ap-
   plied.

XVI

Even the Reviewers who were hired
   To do the work of his reviewing,
With adamantine nerves, grew
   tired;—   730
Gaping and torpid they retired,
   To dream of what they should be
   doing.

XVII

And worse and worse, the drowsy
   curse

Yawned in him, till it grew a
    pest—
A wide contagious atmosphere, 735
Creeping like cold through all
    things near;
A power to infect and to infest.

XVIII

His servant-maids and dogs grew
    dull;
His kitten, late a sportive elf;
The woods and lakes, so beautiful,
Of dim stupidity were full, 741
All grew dull as Peter's self.

XIX

The earth under his feet—the
    springs,
Which lived within it a quick life,
The air, the winds of many wings,
That fan it with new murmurings,
Were dead to their harmonious
    strife.   747

XX

The birds and beasts within the
    wood,
The insects, and each creeping
    thing,
Were now a silent multitude; 750
Love's work was left unwrought—
    no brood
Near Peter's house took wing.

XXI

And every neighbouring cottager
    Stupidly yawned upon the other:
No jackass brayed; no little cur 755
Cocked up his ears;—no man
    would stir
To save a dying mother.

XXII

Yet all from that charmed dis-
    trict went
But some half-idiot and half-
    knave,
Who rather than pay any rent, 760
Would live with marvellous con-
    tent,
    Over his father's grave.

XXIII

No bailiff dared within that space,
    For fear of the dull charm, to
    enter;
A man would bear upon his face, 765
For fifteen months in any case,
    The yawn of such a venture.

XXIV

Seven   miles   above—below—
    around—
This pest of dulness holds its
    sway;
A ghastly life without a sound; 770
To Peter's soul the spell is bound—
    How should it ever pass away?

NOTE ON PETER BELL THE THIRD, BY MRS. SHELLEY

In this new edition I have added *Peter Bell the Third*. A critique on
Wordsworth's *Peter Bell* reached us at Leghorn, which amused Shelley
exceedingly, and suggested this poem.

I need scarcely observe that nothing personal to the author of *Peter
Bell* is intended in this poem. No man ever admired Wordsworth's poetry
more;—he read it perpetually, and taught others to appreciate its
beauties. This poem is, like all others written by Shelley, ideal. He conceived the idealism of a poet—a man of lofty and creative genius—
quitting the glorious calling of discovering and announcing the beautiful
and good, to support and propagate ignorant prejudices and pernicious

errors; imparting to the unenlightened, not that ardour for truth and spirit of toleration which Shelley looked on as the sources of the moral improvement and happiness of mankind, but false and injurious opinions, that evil was good, and that ignorance and force were the best allies of purity and virtue. His idea was that a man gifted, even as transcendently as the author of *Peter Bell*, with the highest qualities of genius, must, if he fostered such errors, be infected with dulness. This poem was written as a warning—not as a narration of the reality. He was unacquainted personally with Wordsworth, or with Coleridge (to whom he alludes in the fifth part of the poem), and therefore, I repeat, his poem is purely ideal;—it contains something of criticism on the compositions of those great poets, but nothing injurious to the men themselves.

No poem contains more of Shelley's peculiar views with regard to the errors into which many of the wisest have fallen, and the pernicious effects of certain opinions on society. Much of it is beautifully written: and, though, like the burlesque drama of *Swellfoot*, it must be looked on as a plaything, it has so much merit and poetry—so much of *himself* in it— that it cannot fail to interest greatly, and by right belongs to the world for whose instruction and benefit it was written.

OEDIPUS TYRANNUS

OR

SWELLFOOT THE TYRANT

A TRAGEDY IN TWO ACTS

TRANSLATED FROM THE ORIGINAL DORIC

'Choose Reform or Civil War,
When through thy streets, instead of hare with dogs,
A CONSORT-QUEEN shall hunt a KING with hogs,
Riding on the IONIAN MINOTAUR.'

ADVERTISEMENT

THIS Tragedy is one of a triad, or system of three Plays (an arrangement according to which the Greeks were accustomed to connect their dramatic representations), elucidating the wonderful and appalling fortunes of the SWELLFOOT dynasty. It was evidently written by some *learned Theban*, and, from its characteristic dulness, apparently before the duties on the importation of *Attic salt* had been repealed by the Boeotarchs. The tenderness with which he treats the PIGS proves him to have been a *sus Boeotiae;* possibly *Epicuri de grege porcus;* for, as the poet observes,

'A fellow feeling makes us wondrous kind.'

No liberty has been taken with the translation of this remarkable piece of antiquity, except the suppressing a seditious and blasphemous Chorus of the Pigs and Bulls at the last Act. The word Hoydipouse (or more properly Oedipus) has been rendered literally SWELLFOOT, without its having been conceived necessary to determine whether a swelling of the hind or the fore feet of the Swinish Monarch is particularly indicated.

Should the remaining portions of this Tragedy be found, entitled, *Swellfoot in Angaria,* and *Charité,* the Translator might be tempted to give them to the reading Public.

DRAMATIS PERSONAE

TYRANT SWELLFOOT, *King of Thebes.*	*The* GADFLY.
IONA TAURINA, *his Queen.*	*The* LEECH.
MAMMON, *Arch-Priest of Famine.*	*The* RAT.
PURGANAX ⎱ *Wizards, Ministers of*	MOSES, *the Sow-gelder.*
DAKRY ⎰ SWELLFOOT.	SOLOMON, *the Porkman.*
LAOCTONOS	ZEPHANIAH, *Pig-butcher.*

The MINOTAUR.

CHORUS *of the Swinish Multitude.*

GUARDS, ATTENDANTS, PRIESTS, *etc., etc.*

SCENE.—THEBES

ACT I

SCENE I.—*A magnificent Temple, built of thigh-bones and death's-heads, and tiled with scalps. Over the Altar the statue of Famine, veiled; a number of Boars, Sows, and Sucking-Pigs, crowned with thistle, shamrock, and oak, sitting on the steps, and clinging round the Altar of the Temple.*

Enter SWELLFOOT, *in his Royal robes, without perceiving the* PIGS.

Swellfoot. Thou supreme Goddess! by whose power divine
These graceful limbs are clothed in proud array
　　　　　　　[*He contemplates himself with satisfaction.*
Of gold and purple, and this kingly paunch
Swells like a sail before a favouring breeze,
And these most sacred nether promontories　　　　　5
Lie satisfied with layers of fat; and these
Boeotian cheeks, like Egypt's pyramid,
(Nor with less toil were their foundations laid),[1]
Sustain the cone of my untroubled brain,
That point, the emblem of a pointless nothing!　　　10
Thou to whom Kings and laurelled Emperors,

[1] See Universal History for an account of the number of people who died, and the immense consumption of garlic by the wretched Egyptians, who made a sepulchre for the name as well as the bodies of their tyrants.—[SHELLEY'S NOTE.]

Radical-butchers, Paper-money-millers,
Bishops and Deacons, and the entire army
Of those fat martyrs to the persecution
Of stifling turtle-soup, and brandy-devils,   15
Offer their secret vows! Thou plenteous Ceres
Of their Eleusis, hail!
    The Swine. Eigh! eigh! eigh! eigh!
    Swellfoot.   Ha! what are ye,
Who, crowned with leaves devoted to the Furies,
Cling round this sacred shrine?
    Swine. Aigh! aigh! aigh!
    Swellfoot.   What! ye that are
The very beasts that, offered at her altar   20
With blood and groans, salt-cake, and fat, and inwards,
Ever propitiate her reluctant will
When taxes are withheld?
    Swine. Ugh! ugh! ugh!
    Swellfoot.   What! ye who grub
With filthy snouts my red potatoes up
In Allan's rushy bog? Who eat the oats   25
Up, from my cavalry in the Hebrides?
Who swill the hog-wash soup my cooks digest
From bones, and rags, and scraps of shoe-leather,
Which should be given to cleaner Pigs than you?

The Swine.—Semichorus I.

    The same, alas! the same;   30
    Though only now the name
      Of Pig remains to me.

Semichorus II.

    If 'twere your kingly will
    Us wretched Swine to kill,
      What should we yield to thee?   35
Swellfoot. Why, skin and bones, and some few hairs for mortar.

Chorus of Swine.

    I have heard your Laureate sing,
      That pity was a royal thing;
  Under your mighty ancestors, we Pigs
  Were bless'd as nightingales on myrtle sprigs,   40
  Or grasshoppers that live on noonday dew,
  And sung, old annals tell, as sweetly too;
  But now our sties are fallen in, we catch
    The murrain and the mange, the scab and itch;
  Sometimes your royal dogs tear down our thatch,   45
    And then we seek the shelter of a ditch;

Hog-wash or grains, or ruta-baga, none
Has yet been ours since your reign begun.

First Sow.

My Pigs, 'tis in vain to tug.

Second Sow.

I could almost eat my litter.   50

First Pig.

I suck, but no milk will come from the dug.

Second Pig.

Our skin and our bones would be bitter.

The Boars.

We fight for this rag of greasy rug,
Though a trough of wash would be fitter.

Semichorus.

Happier Swine were they than we,   55
Drowned in the Gadarean sea—
I wish that pity would drive out the devils,
Which in your royal bosom hold their revels,
And sink us in the waves of thy compassion!
Alas! the Pigs are an unhappy nation!   60
Now if your Majesty would have our bristles
To bind your mortar with, or fill our colons
With rich blood, or make brawn out of our gristles,
In policy—ask else your royal Solons—
You ought to give us hog-wash and clean straw,   65
And sties well thatched; besides it is the law!

Swellfoot. This is sedition, and rank blasphemy!
Ho! there, my guards!

Enter a GUARD.

Guard.   Your sacred Majesty.
Swellfoot. Call in the Jews, Solomon the court porkman,
Moses the sow-gelder, and Zephaniah   70
The hog-butcher.
Guard.   They are in waiting, Sire.

Enter SOLOMON, MOSES, *and* ZEPHANIAH.

Swellfoot. Out with your knife, old Moses, and spay those Sows
                    [*The* PIGS *run about in consternation.*
That load the earth with Pigs; cut close and deep

Moral restraint I see has no effect,
Nor prostitution, nor our own example, 75
Starvation, typhus-fever, war, nor prison—
This was the art which the arch-priest of Famine
Hinted at in his charge to the Theban clergy—
Cut close and deep, good Moses.

    Moses.   Let your Majesty
Keep the Boars quiet, else——

    Swellfoot.   Zephaniah, cut 80
That fat Hog's throat, the brute seems overfed;
Seditious hunks! to whine for want of grains.

    Zephaniah. Your sacred Majesty, he has the dropsy;—
We shall find pints of hydatids in 's liver,
He has not half an inch of wholesome fat 85
Upon his carious ribs——

    Swellfoot.   'Tis all the same,
He'll serve instead of riot money, when
Our murmuring troops bivouac in Thebes' streets;
And January winds, after a day
Of butchering, will make them relish carrion. 90
Now, Solomon, I'll sell you in a lump
The whole kit of them.

    Solomon.   Why, your Majesty,
I could not give——

    Swellfoot.   Kill them out of the way,
That shall be price enough, and let me hear
Their everlasting grunts and whines no more! 95

                        [Exeunt, driving in the SWINE.

Enter MAMMON, *the Arch-Priest; and* PURGANAX, *Chief of the Council
of Wizards.*

    Purganax. The future looks as black as death, a cloud,
Dark as the frown of Hell, hangs over it—
The troops grow mutinous—the revenue fails—
There's something rotten in us—for the level
Of the State slopes, its very bases topple, 100
The boldest turn their backs upon themselves!

    Mammon. Why what's the matter, my dear fellow, now?
Do the troops mutiny?—decimate some regiments;
Does money fail?—come to my mint—coin paper,
Till gold be at a discount, and ashamed 105
To show his bilious face, go purge himself,
In emulation of her vestal whiteness.

    Purganax. Oh, would that this were all! The oracle!!

    Mammon. Why it was I who spoke that oracle,
And whether I was dead drunk or inspired, 110

I cannot well remember; nor, in truth,
The oracle itself!
    Purganax.   The words went thus:—
'Boeotia, choose reform or civil war!
When through the streets, instead of hare with dogs,
A Consort Queen shall hunt a King with Hogs,   115
Riding on the Ionian Minotaur.'
    Mammon. Now if the oracle had ne'er foretold
This sad alternative, it must arrive,
Or not, and so it must now that it has;
And whether I was urged by grace divine   120
Or Lesbian liquor to declare these words,
Which must, as all words must, be false or true,
It matters not: for the same Power made all,
Oracle, wine, and me and you—or none—
'Tis the same thing. If you knew as much   125
Of oracles as I do——
    Purganax.   You arch-priests
Believe in nothing; if you were to dream
Of a particular number in the Lottery,
You would not buy the ticket?
    Mammon.   Yet our tickets
Are seldom blanks. But what steps have you taken?   130
For prophecies, when once they get abroad,
Like liars who tell the truth to serve their ends,
Or hypocrites who, from assuming virtue,
Do the same actions that the virtuous do,
Contrive their own fulfilment. This Iona——   135
Well—you know what the chaste Pasiphae did,
Wife to that most religious King of Crete,
And still how popular the tale is here;
And these dull Swine of Thebes boast their descent
From the free Minotaur. You know they still   140
Call themselves Bulls, though thus degenerate,
And everything relating to a Bull
Is popular and respectable in Thebes.
Their arms are seven Bulls in a field gules;
They think their strength consists in eating beef,—   145
Now there were danger in the precedent
If Queen Iona——
    Purganax.   I have taken good care
That shall not be. I struck the crust o' the earth
With this enchanted rod, and Hell lay bare!
And from a cavern full of ugly shapes   150
I chose a LEECH, a GADFLY, and a RAT.
The Gadfly was the same which Juno sent

To agitate Io,[1] and which Ezekiel [2] mentions
That the Lord whistled for out of the mountains
Of utmost Aethiopia, to torment   155
Mesopotamian Babylon. The beast
Has a loud trumpet like the scarabee,
His crookèd tail is barbed with many stings,
Each able to make a thousand wounds, and each
Immedicable; from his convex eyes   160
He sees fair things in many hideous shapes,
And trumpets all his falsehood to the world.
Like other beetles he is fed on dung—
He has eleven feet with which he crawls,
Trailing a blistering slime, and this foul beast   165
Has tracked Iona from the Theban limits,
From isle to isle, from city unto city,
Urging her flight from the far Chersonese
To fabulous Solyma, and the Aetnean Isle,
Ortygia, Melite, and Calypso's Rock,   170
And the swart tribes of Garamant and Fez,
Aeolia and Elysium, and thy shores,
Parthenope, which now, alas! are free!
And through the fortunate Saturnian land,
Into the darkness of the West.

    Mammon.   But if   175
This Gadfly should drive Iona hither?

    Purganax. Gods, what an *if!* but there is my gray RAT:
So thin with want, he can crawl in and out
Of any narrow chink and filthy hole,
And he shall creep into her dressing-room,   180
And——

    Mammon. My dear friend, where are your wits? as if
She does not always toast a piece of cheese
And bait the trap? and rats, when lean enough
To crawl through *such* chinks——

    Purganax.   But my LEECH—a leech
Fit to suck blood, with lubricous round rings,   185
Capaciously expatiative, which make
His little body like a red balloon,
As full of blood as that of hydrogen,
Sucked from men's hearts; insatiably he sucks
And clings and pulls—a horse-leech, whose deep maw   190
The plethoric King Swellfoot could not fill,
And who, till full, will cling for ever.

    Mammon.   This

---

[1] The *Prometheus Bound* of Aeschylus.—[SHELLEY'S NOTE.]
[2] And the Lord whistled for the gadfly out of Aethiopia, and for the bee of Egypt, etc.—EZEKIEL.—[SHELLEY'S NOTE.]

For Queen Iona would suffice, and less;
But 'tis the Swinish multitude I fear,
And in that fear I have——
    Purganax.   Done what?
    Mammon.   Disinherited   195
My eldest son Chrysaor, because he
Attended public meetings, and would always
Stand prating there of commerce, public faith,
Economy, and unadulterate coin,
And other topics, ultra-radical;   200
And have entailed my estate, called the Fool's Paradise,
And funds in fairy-money, bonds, and bills,
Upon my accomplished daughter Banknotina,
And married her to the gallows.[1]
    Purganax.   A good match!
    Mammon. A high connexion, Purganax. The bridegroom
Is of a very ancient family,   206
Of Hounslow Heath, Tyburn, and the New Drop,
And has great influence in both Houses;—oh!
He makes the fondest husband; nay, *too* fond,—
New-married people should not kiss in public;   210
But the poor souls love one another so!
And then my little grandchildren, the gibbets,
Promising children as you ever saw,—
The young playing at hanging, the elder learning
How to hold radicals. They are well taught too,   215
For every gibbet says its catechism
And reads a select chapter in the Bible
Before it goes to play.
                        [A most tremendous humming is heard.
    Purganax.   Ha! what do I hear?

                  Enter the GADFLY.

    Mammon. Your Gadfly, as it seems, is tired of gadding.

                      Gadfly.

          Hum! hum! hum!   220
From the lakes of the Alps, and the cold gray scalps
        Of the mountains, I come!
          Hum! hum! hum!
From Morocco and Fez, and the high palaces
        Of golden Byzantium;   225
From the temples divine of old Palestine,
        From Athens and Rome,
        With a ha! and a hum!
        I come! I come!

---

[1] 'If one should marry a gallows, and beget young gibbets, I never saw one so
prone.'—CYMBELINE.—[SHELLEY'S NOTE.]

All inn-doors and windows   230
    Were open to me:
I saw all that sin does,
    Which lamps hardly see
That burn in the night by the curtained bed,—
The impudent lamps! for they blushed not red,   235
    Dinging and singing,
    From slumber I rung her,
Loud as the clank of an ironmonger;
    Hum! hum! hum!

    Far, far, far!   240
With the trump of my lips, and the sting at my hips,
    I drove her—afar!
    Far, far, far!
From city to city, abandoned of pity,
    A ship without needle or star;—   245
Homeless she passed, like a cloud on the blast,
    Seeking peace, finding war;—
    She is here in her car,
    From afar, and afar;—
    Hum! hum!   250

I have stung her and wrung her,
    The venom is working;—
And if you had hung her
    With canting and quirking,
She could not be deader than she will be soon;—   255
I have driven her close to you, under the moon,
    Night and day, hum! hum! ha!
I have hummed her and drummed her
From place to place, till at last I have dumbed her,
    Hum! hum! hum!   260

Enter the LEECH *and the* RAT.

Leech.

    I will suck
    Blood or muck!
The disease of the state is a plethory,
Who so fit to reduce it as I?

Rat.

I'll slily seize and   265
    Let blood from her weasand,—
Creeping through crevice, and chink, and cranny,
With my snaky tail, and my sides so scranny.

Purganax.

Aroint ye! thou unprofitable worm!   [*To the* LEECH.
And thou, dull beetle, get thee back to hell!   270
                                          [*To the* GADFLY.
To sting the ghosts of Babylonian kings,
And the ox-headed Io——

Swine (within).

Ugh, ugh, ugh!
Hail! Iona the divine,
We will be no longer Swine,
But Bulls with horns and dewlaps.

Rat.

For,   275
You know, my lord, the Minotaur——

Purganax (fiercely).

Be silent! get to hell! or I will call
The cat out of the kitchen. Well, Lord Mammon,
This is a pretty business.   [*Exit the* RAT.

Mammon.

I will go
And spell some scheme to make it ugly then.—   [*Exit.*

Enter SWELLFOOT.

Swellfoot. She is returned! Taurina is in Thebes,   281
When Swellfoot wishes that she were in hell!
Oh, Hymen, clothed in yellow jealousy,
And waving o'er the couch of wedded kings
The torch of Discord with its fiery hair;   285
This is thy work, thou patron saint of queens!
Swellfoot is wived! though parted by the sea,
The very name of wife had conjugal rights;
Her cursèd image ate, drank, slept with me,
And in the arms of Adiposa oft   290
Her memory has received a husband's——
        [*A loud tumult, and cries of* 'Iona for ever!—No Swellfoot!'
                                          Hark!
How the Swine cry Iona Taurina;
I suffer the real presence; Purganax,
Off with her head!
    Purganax.   But I must first impanel
A jury of the Pigs.
    Swellfoot.   Pack them then.   295
    Purganax. Or fattening some few in two separate sties,

And giving them clean straw, tying some bits
Of ribbon round their legs—giving their Sows
Some tawdry lace, and bits of lustre glass,
And their young Boars white and red rags, and tails   300
Of cows, and jay feathers, and sticking cauliflowers
Between the ears of the old ones; and when
They are persuaded, that by the inherent virtue
Of these things, they are all imperial Pigs,
Good Lord! they'd rip each other's bellies up,   305
Not to say, help us in destroying her.
    Swellfoot. This plan might be tried too;—where's General
Laoctonos?

Enter LAOCTONOS *and* DAKRY.

              It is my royal pleasure
That you, Lord General, bring the head and body,
If separate it would please me better, hither   310
Of Queen Iona.
    Laoctonos.   That pleasure I well knew,
And made a charge with those battalions bold,
Called, from their dress and grin, the royal apes,
Upon the Swine, who in a hollow square
Enclosed her, and received the first attack   315
Like so many rhinoceroses, and then
Retreating in good order, with bare tusks
And wrinkled snouts presented to the foe,
Bore her in triumph to the public sty.
What is still worse, some Sows upon the ground   320
Have given the ape-guards apples, nuts, and gin,
And they all whisk their tails aloft, and cry,
'Long live Iona! down with Swellfoot!'
    Purganax.   Hark!
    The Swine (without). Long live Iona! down with Swellfoot!
    Dakry.   I
Went to the garret of the swineherd's tower,   325
Which overlooks the sty, and made a long
Harangue (all words) to the assembled Swine,
Of delicacy, mercy, judgement, law,
Morals, and precedents, and purity,
Adultery, destitution, and divorce,   330
Piety, faith, and state necessity,
And how I loved the Queen!—and then I wept
With the pathos of my own eloquence,
And every tear turned to a mill-stone, which
Brained many a gaping Pig, and there was made   335
A slough of blood and brains upon the place,
Greased with the pounded bacon; round and round

The mill-stones rolled, ploughing the pavement up,
And hurling Sucking-Pigs into the air,
With dust and stones.——

Enter MAMMON.

Mammon.   I wonder that gray wizards   340
Like you should be so beardless in their schemes;
It had been but a point of policy
To keep Iona and the Swine apart.
Divide and rule! but ye have made a junction
Between two parties who will govern you   345
But for my art.—Behold this BAG! it is
The poison BAG of that Green Spider huge,
On which our spies skulked in ovation through
The streets of Thebes, when they were paved with dead:
A bane so much the deadlier fills it now   350
As calumny is worse than death,—for here
The Gadfly's venom, fifty times distilled,
Is mingled with the vomit of the Leech,
In due proportion, and black ratsbane, which
That very Rat, who, like the Pontic tyrant,   355
Nurtures himself on poison, dare not touch;—
All is sealed up with the broad seal of Fraud,
Who is the Devil's Lord High Chancellor,
And over it the Primate of all Hell
Murmured this pious baptism:—'Be thou called   360
The GREEN BAG; and this power and grace be thine:
That thy contents, on whomsoever poured,
Turn innocence to guilt, and gentlest looks
To savage, foul, and fierce deformity.
Let all baptized by thy infernal dew   365
Be called adulterer, drunkard, liar, wretch!
No name left out which orthodoxy loves,
Court Journal or legitimate Review!—
Be they called tyrant, beast, fool, glutton, lover
Of other wives and husbands than their own—   370
The heaviest sin on this side of the Alps!
Wither they to a ghastly caricature
Of what was human!—let not man or beast
Behold their face with unaverted eyes!
Or hear their names with ears that tingle not   375
With blood of indignation, rage, and shame!'—
This is a perilous liquor;—good my Lords.—
                [SWELLFOOT *approaches to touch the* GREEN BAG.
Beware! for God's sake, beware!—if you should break
The seal, and touch the fatal liquor——
     Purganax.   There,

Give it to me. I have been used to handle 380
All sorts of poisons. His dread Majesty
Only desires to see the colour of it.

    Mammon. Now, with a little common sense, my Lords,
Only undoing all that has been done
(Yet so as it may seem we but confirm it), 385
Our victory is assured. We must entice
Her Majesty from the sty, and make the Pigs
Believe that the contents of the GREEN BAG
Are the true test of guilt or innocence.
And that, if she be guilty, 'twill transform her 390
To manifest deformity like guilt.
If innocent, she will become transfigured
Into an angel, such as they say she is;
And they will see her flying through the air,
So bright that she will dim the noonday sun; 395
Showering down blessings in the shape of comfits.
This, trust a priest, is just the sort of thing
Swine will believe. I'll wager you will see them
Climbing upon the thatch of their low sties,
With pieces of smoked glass, to watch her sail 400
Among the clouds, and some will hold the flaps
Of one another's ears between their teeth,
To catch the coming hail of comfits in.
You, Purganax, who have the gift o' the gab,
Make them a solemn speech to this effect: 405
I go to put in readiness the feast
Kept to the honour of our goddess Famine,
Where, for more glory, let the ceremony
Take place of the uglification of the Queen.

    Dakry (*to* SWELLFOOT). I, as the keeper of your
        sacred conscience,
Humbly remind your Majesty that the care 411
Of your high office, as Man-milliner
To red Bellona, should not be deferred.

    Purganax. All part, in happier plight to meet again.   [*Exeunt.*

END OF THE FIRST ACT.

ACT II

SCENE I.—*The Public Sty. The* BOARS *in full Assembly.*

Enter PURGANAX.

    Purganax. Grant me your patience, Gentlemen and Boars,
Ye, by whose patience under public burthens
The glorious constitution of these sties
Subsists, and shall subsist. The Lean-Pig rates

Grow with the growing populace of Swine,   5
The taxes, that true source of Piggishness
(How can I find a more appropriate term
To include religion, morals, peace, and plenty,
And all that fit Boeotia as a nation
To teach the other nations how to live?),   10
Increase with Piggishness itself; and still
Does the revenue, that great spring of all
The patronage, and pensions, and by-payments,
Which free-born Pigs regard with jealous eyes,
Diminish, till at length, by glorious steps,   15
All the land's produce will be merged in taxes,
And the revenue will amount to—nothing!
The failure of a foreign market for
Sausages, bristles, and blood-puddings,
And such home manufactures, is but partial;   20
And, that the population of the Pigs,
Instead of hog-wash, has been fed on straw
And water, is a fact which is—you know—
That is—it is a state-necessity—
Temporary, of course. Those impious Pigs,   25
Who, by frequent squeaks, have dared impugn
The settled Swellfoot system, or to make
Irreverent mockery of the genuflexions
Inculcated by the arch-priest, have been whipped
Into a loyal and an orthodox whine.   30
Things being in this happy state, the Queen
Iona——

    [*A loud cry from the* PIGS. 'She is innocent! most innocent!'
  Purganax. That is the very thing that I was saying,
Gentlemen Swine; the Queen Iona being
Most innocent, no doubt, returns to Thebes,   35
And the lean Sows and Boars collect about her,
Wishing to make her think that WE believe
(I mean those more substantial Pigs, who swill
Rich hog-wash, while the others mouth damp straw)
That she is guilty; thus, the Lean-Pig faction   40
Seeks to obtain that hog-wash, which has been
Your immemorial right, and which I will
Maintain you in to the last drop of——
    A Boar (*interrupting him*).   What
Does any one accuse her of?
    Purganax.   Why, no one
Makes *any* positive accusation;—but   45
There were hints dropped, and so the privy wizards
Conceived that it became them to advise
His Majesty to investigate their truth;—

Not for his own sake; he could be content
To let his wife play any pranks she pleased, 50
If, by that suffrance, *he* could please the Pigs;
But then he fears the morals of the Swine,
The Sows especially, and what effect
It might produce upon the purity and
Religion of the rising generation 55
Of Sucking-Pigs, if it could be suspected
That Queen Iona—— [*A pause.*

    First Boar. Well, go on; we long
To hear what she can possibly have done.
    Purganax. Why, it is hinted, that a certain Bull—
Thus much is *known:*—the milk-white Bulls that feed 60
Beside Clitumnus and the crystal lakes
Of the Cisalpine mountains, in fresh dews
Of lotus-grass and blossoming asphodel
Sleeking their silken hair, and with sweet breath
Loading the morning winds until they faint 65
With living fragrance, are so beautiful!—
Well, *I* say nothing;—but Europa rode
On such a one from Asia into Crete,
And the enamoured sea grew calm beneath
His gliding beauty. And Pasiphae, 70
Iona's grandmother,——but *she* is innocent!
And that both you and I, and all assert.
    First Boar. Most innocent!
    Purganax.   Behold this BAG; a bag——
    Second Boar. Oh! no GREEN BAGS!! Jealousy's eyes are green,
Scorpions are green, and water-snakes, and efts, 75
And verdigris, and——
    Purganax.   Honourable Swine,
In Piggish souls can prepossessions reign?
Allow me to remind you, grass is green—
All flesh is grass;—no bacon but is flesh—
Ye are but bacon. This divining BAG 80
(Which is not green, but only bacon colour)
Is filled with liquor, which if sprinkled o'er
A woman guilty of——we all know what—
Makes her so hideous, till she finds one blind
She never can commit the like again. 85
If innocent, she will turn into an angel,
And rain down blessings in the shape of comfits
As she flies up to heaven. Now, my proposal
Is to convert her sacred Majesty
Into an angel (as I am sure we shall do), 90
By pouring on her head this mystic water. [*Showing the Bag.*
I know that she is innocent; I wish

Only to prove her so to all the world.
    First Boar. Excellent, just, and noble Purganax.
    Second Boar. How glorious it will be to see her Majesty   95
Flying above our heads, her petticoats
Streaming like—like—like—
    Third Boar.   Anything.
    Purganax.   Oh no!
But like a standard of an admiral's ship,
Or like the banner of a conquering host,
Or like a cloud dyed in the dying day,   100
Unravelled on the blast from a white mountain;
Or like a meteor, or a war-steed's mane,
Or waterfall from a dizzy precipice
Scattered upon the wind.
    First Boar.   Or a cow's tail.
    Second Boar. Or *anything*, as the learned Boar observed.   105
    Purganax. Gentlemen Boars, I move a resolution,
That her most sacred Majesty should be
Invited to attend the feast of Famine,
And to receive upon her chaste white body
Dews of Apotheosis from this BAG.   110
    [*A great confusion is heard of the* PIGS OUT OF DOORS, *which com-*
       municates itself to those within. During the first Strophe, the
       doors of the Sty are staved in, and a number of exceedingly
       lean PIGS *and* SOWS *and* BOARS *rush in.*

                        Semichorus I.

                        No! Yes!

                        Semichorus II.

                        Yes! No!

                        Semichorus I.

                        A law!

                        Semichorus II.

                        A flaw!

                        Semichorus I.

Porkers, we shall lose our wash,   115
    Or must share it with the Lean-Pigs!

                        First Boar.

Order! order! be not rash!
Was there ever such a scene, Pigs!

An old Sow (*rushing in*).

I never saw so fine a dash
Since I first began to wean Pigs. 120

Second Boar (*solemnly*).

The Queen will be an angel time enough.
I vote, in form of an amendment, that
Purganax rub a little of that stuff
Upon his face.

Purganax (*his heart is seen to beat through his waistcoat*).

Gods! What would ye be at?

Semichorus I.

Purganax has plainly shown a 125
Cloven foot and jackdaw feather.

Semichorus II.

I vote Swellfoot and Iona
Try the magic test together;
Whenever royal spouses bicker,
Both should try the magic liquor. 130

An old Boar (*aside*).

A miserable state is that of Pigs,
For if their drivers would tear caps and wigs,
The Swine must bite each other's ear therefore.

An old Sow (*aside*).

A wretched lot Jove has assigned to Swine,
Squabbling makes Pig-herds hungry, and they dine 135
On bacon, and whip Sucking-Pigs the more.

Chorus.

Hog-wash has been ta'en away:
If the Bull-Queen is divested,
We shall be in every way
Hunted, stripped, exposed, molested; 140
Let us do whate'er we may,
That she shall not be arrested.
QUEEN, we entrench you with walls of brawn,
And palisades of tusks, sharp as a bayonet:
Place your most sacred person here. We pawn 145
Our lives that none a finger dare to lay on it.

Those who wrong you, wrong us;
Those who hate you, hate us;
Those who sting you, sting us;
Those who bait you, bait us; 150
The *oracle* is now about to be
Fulfilled by circumvolving destiny;
Which says: 'Thebes, choose *reform* or *civil war*,
  When through your streets, instead of hare with dogs,
    A CONSORT QUEEN shall hunt a KING with Hogs, 155
Riding upon the IONIAN MINOTAUR.'

Enter IONA TAURINA.

Iona Taurina (*coming forward*). Gentlemen Swine, and gentle
    Lady-Pigs,
The tender heart of every Boar acquits
Their QUEEN, of any act incongruous
With native Piggishness, and she, reposing 160
With confidence upon the grunting nation,
Has thrown herself, her cause, her life, her all,
Her innocence, into their Hoggish arms;
Nor has the expectation been deceived
Of finding shelter there. Yet know, great Boars, 165
(For such whoever lives among you finds you,
And so do I), the innocent are proud!
I have accepted your protection only
In compliment of your kind love and care,
Not for necessity. The innocent 170
Are safest there where trials and dangers wait;
Innocent Queens o'er white-hot ploughshares tread
Unsinged, and ladies, Erin's laureate sings it,[1]
Decked with rare gems, and beauty rarer still,
Walked from Killarney to the Giant's Causeway, 175
Through rebels, smugglers, troops of yeomanry,
White-boys and Orange-boys, and constables,
Tithe-proctors, and excise people, uninjured!
Thus I!——
Lord PURGANAX, I do commit myself 180
Into your custody, and am prepared
To stand the test, whatever it may be!
    Purganax. This magnanimity in your sacred Majesty
Must please the Pigs. You cannot fail of being
A heavenly angel. Smoke your bits of glass, 185
Ye loyal Swine, or her transfiguration
Will blind your wondering eyes.
    An old Boar (*aside*).   Take care, my Lord,

[1] 'Rich and rare were the gems she wore.' See Moore's *Irish Melodies*.—[SHELLEY'S NOTE.]

They do not smoke you first.
    Purganax.   At the approaching feast
Of Famine, let the expiation be.
    Swine. Content! content!
    Iona Taurina (aside).   I, most content of all,   190
Know that my foes even thus prepare their fall!   [*Exeunt omnes.*

SCENE II.—*The interior of the Temple of Famine. The statue of the
Goddess, a skeleton clothed in parti-coloured rags, seated upon a
heap of skulls and loaves intermingled. A number of exceedingly fat
Priests in black garments arrayed on each side, with marrow-bones
and cleavers in their hands.* [SOLOMON, *the Court Porkman.*] *A
flourish of trumpets.*

Enter MAMMON *as arch-priest,* SWELLFOOT, DAKRY, PURGANAX, LAOC-
TONOS, *followed by* IONA TAURINA *guarded. On the other side enter
the* SWINE.

    Chorus of PRIESTS, *accompanied by the* COURT PORKMAN *on
           marrow-bones and cleavers.*

        GODDESS bare, and gaunt, and pale,
        Empress of the world, all hail!
        What though Cretans old called thee
        City-crested Cybele?
            We call thee FAMINE!   5
    Goddess of fasts and feasts, starving and cramming!
    Through thee, for emperors, kings, and priests and lords,
    Who rule by viziers, sceptres, bank-notes, words,
    The earth pours forth its plenteous fruits,
        Corn, wool, linen, flesh, and roots—   10
    Those who consume these fruits through thee grow fat,
        Those who produce these fruits through thee grow lean,
    Whatever change takes place, oh, stick to that!
    And let things be as they have ever been;
        At least while we remain thy priests,   15
        And proclaim thy fasts and feasts.
    Through thee the sacred SWELLFOOT dynasty
    Is based upon a rock amid that sea
    Whose waves are Swine—so let it ever be!

[SWELLFOOT, *etc., seat themselves at a table magnificently covered
at the upper end of the Temple. Attendants pass over the stage
with hog-wash in pails. A number of* PIGS, *exceedingly lean, follow them licking up the wash.*

    Mammon. I fear your sacred Majesty has lost   20
The appetite which you were used to have.
Allow me now to recommend this dish—

A simple kickshaw by your Persian cook,
Such as is served at the great King's second table.
The price and pains which its ingredients cost   25
Might have maintained some dozen families
A winter or two—not more—so plain a dish
Could scarcely disagree.—
    Swellfoot.   After the trial,
And these fastidious Pigs are gone, perhaps
I may recover my lost appetite,—   30
I feel the gout flying about my stomach—
Give me a glass of Maraschino punch.
    Purganax (filling his glass, and standing up). The glorious
        Constitution of the Pigs!
    All. A toast! a toast! stand up, and three times three!
    Dakry. No heel-taps—darken daylights!—
    Laoctonos.   Claret, somehow,   35
Puts me in mind of blood, and blood of claret!
    Swellfoot. Laoctonos is fishing for a compliment,
But 'tis his due. Yes, you have drunk more wine,
And shed more blood, than any man in Thebes.

                               [*To* Purganax.
For God's sake stop the grunting of those Pigs!   40
    Purganax. We dare not, Sire, 'tis Famine's privilege.

Chorus of Swine.

    Hail to thee, hail to thee, Famine!
        Thy throne is on blood, and thy robe is of rags;
    Thou devil which livest on damning;
        Saint of new churches, and cant, and GREEN BAGS,   45
    Till in pity and terror thou risest,
    Confounding the schemes of the wisest;
    When thou liftest thy skeleton form,
        When the loaves and the skulls roll about,
    We will greet thee—the voice of a storm   50
        Would be lost in our terrible shout!

    Then hail to thee, hail to thee, Famine!
        Hail to thee, Empress of Earth!
    When thou risest, dividing possessions;
    When thou risest, uprooting oppressions,   55
        In the pride of thy ghastly mirth;
    Over palaces, temples, and graves,
    We will rush as thy minister-slaves,
    Trampling behind in thy train,
    Till all be made level again!   60

    Mammon. I hear a crackling of the giant **bones**
Of the dread image, and in the black pits

Which once were eyes, I see two livid flames.
These prodigies are oracular, and show
The presence of the unseen Deity.   65
Mighty events are hastening to their doom!
    Swellfoot. I only hear the lean and mutinous **Swine**
Grunting about the temple.
    Dakry.   In a crisis
Of such exceeding delicacy, I think
We ought to put her Majesty, the Queen,   70
Upon her trial without delay.
    Mammon.   THE BAG
Is here.
    Purganax. I have rehearsed the entire scene
With an ox-bladder and some ditchwater,
On Lady P——; it cannot fail. (*Taking up the Bag.*) Your
      Majesty   [*To* Swellfoot.
In such a filthy business had better   75
Stand on one side, lest it should sprinkle you.
A spot or two on me would do no harm,
Nay, it might hide the blood, which the sad **Genius**
Of the Green Isle has fixed, as by a spell,
Upon my brow—which would stain all its seas,   80
But which those seas could never wash away!
    Iona Taurina. My Lord, I am ready—nay, I am impatient
To undergo the test.

[*A graceful figure in a semi-transparent veil passes unnoticed
through the Temple; the word* LIBERTY *is seen through the
veil, as if it were written in fire upon its forehead. Its words
are almost drowned in the furious grunting of the* Pigs, *and
the business of the trial. She kneels on the steps of the Altar,
and speaks in tones at first faint and low, but which ever become louder and louder.*

        Mighty Empress! Death's white wife!
        Ghastly mother-in-law of Life!   85
        By the God who made thee such,
        By the magic of thy touch,
        By the starving and the cramming
Of fasts and feasts! by thy dread self, O Famine!
I charge thee! when thou wake the multitude,   90
Thou lead them not upon the paths of blood.
The earth did never mean her foison
For those who crown life's cup with poison
Of fanatic rage and meaningless revenge—
    But for those radiant spirits, who are still   95
The standard-bearers in the van of Change.
    Be they th' appointed stewards, to fill

The lap of Pain, and Toil, and Age!—
Remit, O Queen! thy accustomed rage!
Be what thou art not! In voice faint and low   100
FREEDOM calls *Famine*,—her eternal foe,
To brief alliance, hollow truce.—Rise now!

[*Whilst the Veiled Figure has been chanting this strophe,* MAM-
MON, DAKRY, LAOCTONOS, *and* SWELLFOOT *have surrounded*
IONA TAURINA, *who, with her hands folded on her breast, and
her eyes lifted to Heaven, stands, as with saint-like resignation, to await the issue of the business, in perfect confidence of
her innocence.*

[PURGANAX, *after unsealing the* GREEN BAG, *is gravely about to
pour the liquor upon her head, when suddenly the whole expression of her figure and countenance changes; she snatches
it from his hand with a loud laugh of triumph, and empties it
over* SWELLFOOT *and his whole Court, who are instantly
changed into a number of filthy and ugly animals, and rush
out of the Temple. The image of* FAMINE *then arises with a
tremendous sound, the* PIGS *begin scrambling for the loaves,
and are tripped up by the skulls; all those who* EAT *the loaves
are turned into* BULLS, *and arrange themselves quietly behind
the altar. The image of* FAMINE *sinks through a chasm in the
earth, and a* MINOTAUR *rises.*

Minotaur. I am the Ionian Minotaur, the mightiest
Of all Europa's taurine progeny—
I am the old traditional Man-Bull;   105
And from my ancestors having been Ionian,
I am called Ion, which, by interpretation,
Is JOHN; in plain Theban, that is to say,
My name's JOHN BULL; I am a famous hunter,
And can leap any gate in all Boeotia,   110
Even the palings of the royal park,
Or double ditch about the new enclosures;
And if your Majesty will deign to mount me,
At least till you have hunted down your game,
I will not throw you.   115
          Iona Taurina. (*During this speech she has been putting on
               boots and spurs, and a hunting-cap, buckishly cocked
               on one side, and tucking up her hair, she leaps nimbly
               on his back.*) Hoa! hoa! tallyho! tallyho! ho! ho!
Come, let us hunt these ugly badgers down,
These stinking foxes, these devouring otters,
These hares, these wolves, these anything but men.
Hey, for a whipper-in! my loyal Pigs,
Now let your noses be as keen as beagles',   120
Your steps as swift as greyhounds', and your cries

More dulcet and symphonious than the bells
Of village-towers, on sunshine holiday;
Wake all the dewy woods with jangling music.
Give them no law (are they not beasts of blood?)   125
But such as they gave you. Tallyho! ho!
Through forest, furze, and bog, and den, and desert,
Pursue the ugly beasts! tallyho! ho!

Full Chorus of IONA *and the* SWINE.

Tallyho! tallyho!
Through rain, hail, and snow,   130
Through brake, gorse, and briar,
Through fen, flood, and mire,
We go! we go!

Tallyho! tallyho!
Through pond, ditch, and slough,   135
Wind them, and find them,
Like the Devil behind them,
Tallyho! tallyho!

[*Exeunt, in full cry;* IONA *driving on the* SWINE, *with the empty*
GREEN BAG.

THE END.

NOTE ON OEDIPUS TYRANNUS, BY MRS. SHELLEY

IN the brief journal I kept in those days, I find recorded, in August,
1820, Shelley 'begins *Swellfoot the Tyrant,* suggested by the pigs at the
fair of San Giuliano.' This was the period of Queen Caroline's landing
in England, and the struggles made by George IV to get rid of her claims;
which failing, Lord Castlereagh placed the '*Green Bag*' on the table of
the House of Commons, demanding in the King's name that an inquiry
should be instituted into his wife's conduct. These circumstances were
the theme of all conversation among the English. We were then at the
Baths of San Giuliano. A friend came to visit us on the day when a fair
was held in the square, beneath our windows: Shelley read to us his *Ode
to Liberty;* and was riotously accompanied by the grunting of a quantity
of pigs brought for sale to the fair. He compared it to the 'chorus of
frogs' in the satiric drama of Aristophanes; and, it being an hour of
merriment, and one ludicrous association suggesting another, he imagined
a political-satirical drama on the circumstances of the day, to which the
pigs would serve as chorus—and *Swellfoot* was begun. When finished,
it was transmitted to England, printed, and published anonymously; but
stifled at the very dawn of its existence by the Society for the Suppression
of Vice, who threatened to prosecute it, if not immediately withdrawn.
The friend who had taken the trouble of bringing it out, of course did

not think it worth the annoyance and expense of a contest, and it was laid aside.

Hesitation of whether it would do honour to Shelley prevented my publishing it at first. But I cannot bring myself to keep back anything he ever wrote; for each word is fraught with the peculiar views and sentiments which he believed to be beneficial to the human race, and the bright light of poetry irradiates every thought. The world has a right to the entire compositions of such a man; for it does not live and thrive by the outworn lesson of the dullard or the hypocrite, but by the original free thoughts of men of genius, who aspire to pluck bright truth

> 'from the pale-faced moon;
> Or dive into the bottom of the deep
> Where fathom-line could never touch the ground,
> And pluck up drowned'

truth. Even those who may dissent from his opinions will consider that he was a man of genius, and that the world will take more interest in his slightest word than in the waters of Lethe which are so eagerly prescribed as medicinal for all its wrongs and woe. This drama, however, must not be judged for more than was meant. It is a mere plaything of the imagination; which even may not excite smiles among many, who will not see wit in those combinations of thought which were full of the ridiculous to the author. But, like everything he wrote, it breathes that deep sympathy for the sorrows of humanity, and indignation against its oppressors, which make it worthy of his name.

CHARLES THE FIRST

DRAMATIS PERSONAE

KING CHARLES I.	ST. JOHN.
QUEEN HENRIETTA.	ARCHY, *the Court Fool.*
LAUD, *Archbishop of Canterbury.*	HAMPDEN.
WENTWORTH, *Earl of Strafford.*	PYM.
LORD COTTINGTON.	CROMWELL.
LORD WESTON.	CROMWELL'S DAUGHTER.
LORD COVENTRY.	SIR HARRY VANE *the younger.*
WILLIAMS, *Bishop of Lincoln.*	LEIGHTON.
Secretary LYTTELTON.	BASTWICK.
JUXON.	PRYNNE.

Gentlemen of the Inns of Court, Citizens, Pursuivants, Marshalsmen,
Law Students, Judges, Clerk.

SCENE I.—*The Masque of the Inns of Court.*

A Pursuivant. Place, for the Marshal of the Masque!

First Citizen. What thinkest thou of this quaint masque which turns,
Like morning from the shadow of the night,

The night to day, and London to a place
Of peace and joy?
   Second Citizen.   And Hell to Heaven.   5
Eight years are gone,
And they seem hours, since in this populous street
I trod on grass made green by summer's rain,
For the red plague kept state within that palace
Where now that vanity reigns. In nine years more   10
The roots will be refreshed with civil blood;
And thank the mercy of insulted Heaven
That sin and wrongs wound, as an orphan's cry,
The patience of the great Avenger's ear.
   A Youth. Yet, father, 'tis a happy sight to see,   15
Beautiful, innocent, and unforbidden
By God or man;—'tis like the bright procession
Of skiey visions in a solemn dream
From which men wake as from a Paradise,
And draw new strength to tread the thorns of life.   20
If God be good, wherefore should this be evil?
And if this be not evil, dost thou not draw
Unseasonable poison from the flowers
Which bloom so rarely in this barren world?
Oh, kill these bitter thoughts which make the present   25
Dark as the future!—

.   .   .   .   .   .

When Avarice and Tyranny, vigilant Fear,
And open-eyed Conspiracy lie sleeping
As on Hell's threshold; and all gentle thoughts
Waken to worship Him who giveth joys   30
With His own gift.
   Second Citizen. How young art thou in this old age of time!
How green in this gray world? Canst thou discern
The signs of seasons, yet perceive no hint
Of change in that stage-scene in which thou art   35
Not a spectator but an actor? or
Art thou a puppet moved by [enginery]?
The day that dawns in fire will die in storms,
Even though the noon be calm. My travel's done,—
Before the whirlwind wakes I shall have found   40
My inn of lasting rest; but thou must still
Be journeying on in this inclement air.
Wrap thy old cloak about thy back;
Nor leave the broad and plain and beaten road,
Although no flowers smile on the trodden dust,   45
For the violent paths of pleasure. This Charles the First
Rose like the equinoctial sun, ...

By vapours, through whose threatening ominous veil
Darting his altered influence he has gained
This height of noon—from which he must decline   50
Amid the darkness of conflicting storms,
To dank extinction and to latest night …
                              There goes
The apostate Strafford; he whose titles
                              whispered aphorisms   55
From Machiavel and Bacon: and, if Judas
Had been as brazen and as bold as he——
    First Citizen.   That
Is the Archbishop.
    Second Citizen.   Rather say the Pope:
London will be soon his Rome: he walks
As if he trod upon the heads of men: 60
He looks elate, drunken with blood and gold;—
Beside him moves the Babylonian woman
Invisibly, and with her as with his shadow,
Mitred adulterer! he is joined in sin,
Which turns Heaven's milk of mercy to revenge.   65
    Third Citizen (lifting up his eyes). Good Lord! rain it down upon
        him! …
Amid her ladies walks the papist queen,
As if her nice feet scorned our English earth.
The Canaanitish Jezebel! I would be
A dog if I might tear her with my teeth!   70
There's old Sir Henry Vane, the Earl of Pembroke,
Lord Essex, and Lord Keeper Coventry,
And others who make base their English breed
By vile participation of their honours
With papists, atheists, tyrants, and apostates.   75
When lawyers masque 'tis time for honest men
To strip the vizor from their purposes.
A seasonable time for masquers this!
When Englishmen and Protestants should sit
                              dust on their dishonoured heads,   80
To avert the wrath of Him whose scourge is felt
For the great sins which have drawn down from Heaven
                              and foreign overthrow.
The remnant of the martyred saints in Rochefort
Have been abandoned by their faithless allies   85
To that idolatrous and adulterous torturer
Lewis of France,—the Palatinate is lost——

Enter LEIGHTON (*who has been branded in the face*) *and* BASTWICK.

Canst thou be—art thou——?
    Leighton.   I *was* Leighton: what

I *am* thou seest. And yet turn thine eyes,
And with thy memory look on thy friend's mind,   90
Which is unchanged, and where is written deep
The sentence of my judge.
    Third Citizen.   Are these the marks with which
Laud thinks to improve the image of his Maker
Stamped on the face of man? Curses upon him,
The impious tyrant!
    Second Citizen.   It is said besides   95
That lewd and papist drunkards may profane
The Sabbath with their
And has permitted that most heathenish custom
Of dancing round a pole dressed up with wreaths
On May-day.   100
A man who thus twice crucifies his God
May well   his brother.—In my mind, friend,
The root of all this ill is prelacy.
I would cut up the root.
    Third Citizen.   And by what means?
    Second Citizen. Smiting each Bishop under the fifth rib.   105
    Third Citizen. You seem to know the vulnerable place
Of these same crocodiles.
    Second Citizen. I learnt it in
Egyptian bondage, sir. Your worm of Nile
Betrays not with its flattering tears like they;
For, when they cannot kill, they whine and weep.   110
Nor is it half so greedy of men's bodies
As they of soul and all; nor does it wallow
In slime as they in simony and lies
And close lusts of the flesh.
    A Marshalsman.   Give place, give place!
You torch-bearers, advance to the great gate,   115
And then attend the Marshal of the Masque
Into the Royal presence.
    A Law Student.   What thinkest thou
Of this quaint show of ours, my agèd friend?
Even now we see the redness of the torches
Inflame the night to the eastward, and the clarions   120
[Gasp?] to us on the wind's wave. It comes!
And their sounds, floating hither round the pageant,
Rouse up the astonished air.
    First Citizen.   I will not think but that our country's wounds
May yet be healed. The king is just and gracious,   125
Though wicked counsels now pervert his will:
These once cast off—
    Second Citizen.   As adders cast their skins
And keep their venom, so kings often change;

Councils and counsellors hang on one another,
Hiding the loathsome   130
Like the base patchwork of a leper's rags.
 The Youth. Oh, still those dissonant thoughts!—List how the music
Grows on the enchanted air! And see, the torches
Restlessly flashing, and the crowd divided
Like waves before an admiral's prow!
 A Marshalsman.   Give place   135
To the Marshal of the Masque!
 A Pursuivant.   Room for the King!
 The Youth. How glorious! See those thronging chariots
Rolling, like painted clouds before the wind,
Behind their solemn steeds: how some are shaped
Like curved sea-shells dyed by the azure depths   140
Of Indian seas; some like the new-born moon;
And some like cars in which the Romans climbed
(Canopied by Victory's eagle-wings outspread)
The Capitolian—See how gloriously
The mettled horses in the torchlight stir   145
Their gallant riders, while they check their pride,
Like shapes of some diviner element
Than English air, and beings nobler than
The envious and admiring multitude.
 Second Citizen. Ay, there they are—   150
Nobles, and sons of nobles, patentees,
Monopolists, and stewards of this poor farm,
On whose lean sheep sit the prophetic crows,
Here is the pomp that strips the houseless orphan,
Here is the pride that breaks the desolate heart.   155
These are the lilies glorious as Solomon,
Who toil not, neither do they spin,—unless
It be the webs they catch poor rogues withal.
Here is the surfeit which to them who earn
The niggard wages of the earth, scarce leaves   160
The tithe that will support them till they crawl
Back to her cold hard bosom. Here is health
Followed by grim disease, glory by shame,
Waste by lame famine, wealth by squalid want,
And England's sin by England's punishment.   165
And, as the effect pursues the cause foregone,
Lo, giving substance to my words, behold
At once the sign and the thing signified—
A troop of cripples, beggars, and lean outcasts,
Horsed upon stumbling jades, carted with dung,   170
Dragged for a day from cellars and low cabins
And rotten hiding-holes, to point the moral
Of this presentment, and bring up the rear

Of painted pomp with misery!
 The Youth.   'Tis but
The anti-masque, and serves as discords do   175
In sweetest music. Who would love May flowers
If they succeeded not to Winter's flaw;
Or day unchanged by night; or joy itself
Without the touch of sorrow?
 Second Citizen.   I and thou——
 A Marshalsman. Place, give place!   180

Scene II.—*A Chamber in Whitehall. Enter the* King, Queen, Laud,
 Lord Strafford, Lord Cottington, *and other Lords;* Archy;
 also St. John, *with some Gentlemen of the Inns of Court.*

 King. Thanks, gentlemen. I heartily accept
This token of your service: your gay masque
Was performed gallantly. And it shows well
When subjects twine such flowers of [observance?]
With the sharp thorns that deck the English crown. 5
A gentle heart enjoys what it confers,
Even as it suffers that which it inflicts,
Though Justice guides the stroke.
Accept my hearty thanks.
 Queen.   And gentlemen,
Call your poor Queen your debtor. Your quaint **pageant** 10
Rose on me like the figures of past years,
Treading their still path back to infancy,
More beautiful and mild as they draw nearer
The quiet cradle. I could have almost wept
To think I was in Paris, where these shows 15
Are well devised—such as I was ere yet
My young heart shared a portion of the burthen,
The careful weight of this great monarchy.
There, gentlemen, between the sovereign's pleasure
And that which it regards, no clamour lifts 20
Its proud interposition.
In Paris ribald censurers dare not move
Their poisonous tongues against these sinless **sports;**
And *his* smile
Warms those who bask in it, as ours would do 25
If . . . Take my heart's thanks: add them, gentlemen,
To those good words which, were he King of France,
My royal lord would turn to golden deeds.
 St. John. Madam, the love of Englishmen can make
The lightest favour of their lawful king 30
Outweigh a despot's.—We humbly take our leaves,
Enriched by smiles which France can never buy.
   [*Exeunt* St. John *and the Gentlemen of the Inns of Court.*

King. My Lord Archbishop,
Mark you what spirit sits in St. John's eyes?
Methinks it is too saucy for this presence.   35

Archy. Yes, pray your Grace look: for, like an unsophisticated [eye]
sees everything upside down, you who are wise will discern the shadow
of an idiot in lawn sleeves and a rochet setting springes to catch wood-
cocks in haymaking time. Poor Archy, whose owl-eyes are tempered to
the error of his age, and because he is a fool, and by special ordinance of
God forbidden ever to see himself as he is, sees now in that deep eye a
blindfold devil sitting on the ball, and weighing words out between king
and subjects. One scale is full of promises, and the other full of protesta-
tions: and then another devil creeps behind the first out of the dark windings [of a] pregnant lawyer's brain, and takes the bandage from the
other's eyes, and throws a sword into the left-hand scale, for all the world
like my Lord Essex's there.   47

Strafford. A rod in pickle for the Fool's back!

Archy. Ay, and some are now smiling whose tears will make the brine;
for the Fool sees——

Strafford. Insolent! You shall have your coat turned and be whipped
out of the palace for this.   52

Archy. When all the fools are whipped, and all the Protestant writers,
while the knaves are whipping the fools ever since a thief was set to
catch a thief. If all turncoats were whipped out of palaces, poor Archy
would be disgraced in good company. Let the knaves whip the fools, and
all the fools laugh at it. [Let the] wise and godly slit each other's noses
and ears (having no need of any sense of discernment in their craft);
and the knaves, to marshal them, join in a procession to Bedlam, to
entreat the madmen to omit their sublime Platonic contemplations, and
manage the state of England. Let all the honest men who lie [pinched?]
up at the prisons or the pillories, in custody of the pursuivants of the
High-Commission Court, marshal them.   63

Enter Secretary LYTTELTON, *with papers.*

King (looking over the papers). These stiff Scots
His Grace of Canterbury must take order
To force under the Church's yoke.—You, Wentworth,
Shall be myself in Ireland, and shall add
Your wisdom, gentleness, and energy,
To what in me were wanting.—My Lord Weston,
Look that those merchants draw not without loss   70
Their bullion from the Tower; and, on the payment
Of shipmoney, take fullest compensation
For violation of our royal forests,
Whose limits, from neglect, have been o'ergrown
With cottages and cornfields. The uttermost   75
Farthing exact from those who claim exemption
From knighthood: that which once was a reward

Shall thus be made a punishment, that subjects
May know how majesty can wear at will
The rugged mood.—My Lord of Coventry, 80
Lay my command upon the Courts below
That bail be not accepted for the prisoners
Under the warrant of the Star Chamber.
The people shall not find the stubbornness
Of Parliament a cheap or easy method 85
Of dealing with their rightful sovereign:
And doubt not this, my Lord of Coventry,
We will find time and place for fit rebuke.—
My Lord of Canterbury.
    Archy.   The fool is here.
    Laud. I crave permission of your Majesty 90
To order that this insolent fellow be
Chastised: he mocks the sacred character,
Scoffs at the state, and—
    King.   What, my Archy?
He mocks and mimics all he sees and hears,
Yet with a quaint and graceful licence—Prithee 95
For this once do not as Prynne would, were he
Primate of England. With your Grace's leave,
He lives in his own world; and, like a parrot
Hung in his gilded prison from the window
Of a queen's bower over the public way, 100
Blasphemes with a bird's mind:—his words, like arrows
Which know no aim beyond the archer's wit,
Strike sometimes what eludes philosophy.—
(*To* ARCHY.) Go, sirrah, and repent of your offence
Ten minutes in the rain; be it your penance 105
To bring news how the world goes there.

                                [*Exit* ARCHY.
                      Poor Archy!
He weaves about himself a world of mirth
Out of the wreck of ours.
    Laud. I take with patience, as my Master did,
All scoffs permitted from above.
    King.   My lord, 110
Pray overlook these papers. Archy's words
Had wings, but these have talons.
    Queen.   And the lion
That wears them must be tamed. My dearest lord,
I see the new-born courage in your eye
Armed to strike dead the Spirit of the Time, 115
Which spurs to rage the many-headed beast.
Do thou persist: for, faint but in resolve,
And it were better thou hadst still remained

The slave of thine own slaves, who tear like curs
The fugitive, and flee from the pursuer; 120
And Opportunity, that empty wolf,
Flies at his throat who falls. Subdue thy actions
Even to the disposition of thy purpose,
And be that tempered as the Ebro's steel;
And banish weak-eyed Mercy to the weak, 125
Whence she will greet thee with a gift of peace,
And not betray thee with a traitor's kiss,
As when she keeps the company of rebels,
Who think that she is Fear. This do, lest we
Should fall as from a glorious pinnacle 130
In a bright dream, and wake as from a dream
Out of our worshipped state.
    King.   Belovèd friend,
God is my witness that this weight of power,
Which He sets me my earthly task to wield
Under His law, is my delight and pride 135
Only because thou lovest that and me.
For a king bears the office of a God
To all the under world; and to his God
Alone he must deliver up his trust,
Unshorn of its permitted attributes. 140
[It seems] now as the baser elements
Had mutinied against the golden sun
That kindles them to harmony, and quells
Their self-destroying rapine. The wild million
Strike at the eye that guides them; like as humours 145
Of the distempered body that conspire
Against the spirit of life throned in the heart,—
And thus become the prey of one another,
And last of death.
    Strafford.   That which would be ambition in a subject
Is duty in a sovereign; for on him, 150
As on a keystone, hangs the arch of life,
Whose safety is its strength. Degree and form,
And all that makes the age of reasoning man
More memorable than a beast's, depend on this—
That Right should fence itself inviolably 155
With Power; in which respect the state of England
From usurpation by the insolent commons
Cries for reform.
Get treason, and spare treasure. Fee with coin
The loudest murmurers; feed with jealousies 160
Opposing factions,—be thyself of none;
And borrow gold of many, for those who lend
Will serve thee till thou payest them; and thus

Keep the fierce spirit of the hour at bay,
Till time, and its coming generations   165
Of nights and days unborn, bring some one chance,

.   .   .   .

Or war or pestilence or Nature's self,—
By some distemperature or terrible sign,
Be as an arbiter betwixt themselves.
     Nor let your Majesty   170
Doubt here the peril of the unseen event.
How did your brother Kings, coheritors
In your high interest in the subject earth,
Rise past such troubles to that height of power
Where now they sit, and awfully serene   175
Smile on the trembling world? Such popular storms
Philip the Second of Spain, this Lewis of France,
And late the German head of many bodies,
And every petty lord of Italy,
Quelled or by arts or arms. Is England poorer   180
Or feebler? or art thou who wield'st her power
Tamer than they? or shall this island be—
[Girdled] by its inviolable waters—
To the world present and the world to come
Sole pattern of extinguished monarchy?   185
Not if thou dost as I would have thee do.
 King. Your words shall be my deeds:
You speak the image of my thought. My friend
(If Kings can have a friend, I call thee so),
Beyond the large commission which [belongs]   190
Under the great seal of the realm, take this:
And, for some obvious reasons, let there be
No seal on it, except my kingly word
And honour as I am a gentleman.
Be—as thou art within my heart and mind—   195
Another self, here and in Ireland:
Do what thou judgest well, take amplest licence,
And stick not even at questionable means.
Hear me, Wentworth. My word is as a wall
Between thee and this world thine enemy—   200
That hates thee, for thou lovest me.
 Strafford.   I own
No friend but thee, no enemies but thine:
Thy lightest thought is my eternal law.
How weak, how short, is life to pay——
 King.   Peace, peace.
Thou ow'st me nothing yet.
(*To* LAUD.)   My lord, what say   205
Those papers?

Laud. Your Majesty has ever interposed,
In lenity towards your native soil,
Between the heavy vengeance of the Church
And Scotland. Mark the consequence of warming　　　210
This brood of northern vipers in your bosom.
The rabble, instructed no doubt
By Loudon, Lindsay, Hume, and false Argyll
(For the waves never menace heaven until
Scourged by the wind's invisible tyranny),　　　215
Have in the very temple of the Lord
Done outrage to His chosen ministers.
They scorn the liturgy of the Holy Church,
Refuse to obey her canons, and deny
The apostolic power with which the Spirit　　　220
Has filled its elect vessels, even from him
Who held the keys with power to loose and bind,
To him who now pleads in this royal presence.—
Let ample powers and new instructions be
Sent to the High Commissioners in Scotland.　　　225
To death, imprisonment, and confiscation,
Add torture, add the ruin of the kindred
Of the offender, add the brand of infamy,
Add mutilation: and if this suffice not,
Unleash the sword and fire, that in their thirst　　　230
They may lick up that scum of schismatics.
I laugh at those weak rebels who, desiring
What we possess, still prate of Christian peace,
As if those dreadful arbitrating messengers
Which play the part of God 'twixt right and wrong,　　　235
Should be let loose against the innocent sleep
Of templed cities and the smiling fields,
For some poor argument of policy
Which touches our own profit or our pride
(Where it indeed were Christian charity　　　240
To turn the cheek even to the smiter's hand);
And, when our great Redeemer, when our God,
When He who gave, accepted, and retained
Himself in propitiation of our sins,
Is scorned in His immediate ministry,　　　245
With hazard of the inestimable loss
Of all the truth and discipline which is
Salvation to the extremest generation
Of men innumerable, they talk of peace!
Such peace as Canaan found, let Scotland now;　　　250
For, by that Christ who came to bring a sword,
Not peace, upon the earth, and gave command
To His disciples at the Passover

That each should sell his robe and buy a sword,—
Once strip that minister of naked wrath,   255
And it shall never sleep in peace again
Till Scotland bend or break.
    King.   My Lord Archbishop,
Do what thou wilt and what thou canst in this.
Thy earthly even as thy heavenly King
Gives thee large power in his unquiet realm.   260
But we want money, and my mind misgives me
That for so great an enterprise, as yet,
We are unfurnished.
    Strafford.   Yet it may not long
Rest on our wills.
    Cottington.   The expenses
Of gathering shipmoney, and of distraining   265
For every petty rate (for we encounter
A desperate opposition inch by inch
In every warehouse and on every farm),
Have swallowed up the gross sum of the imposts;
So that, though felt as a most grievous scourge   270
Upon the land, they stand us in small stead
As touches the receipt.
    Strafford.   'Tis a conclusion
Most arithmetical: and thence you infer
Perhaps the assembling of a parliament.
Now, if a man should call his dearest enemies   275
To sit in licensed judgement on his life,
His Majesty might wisely take that course.
                            [*Aside to* COTTINGTON.
It is enough to expect from these lean imposts
That they perform the office of a scourge,
Without more profit. (*Aloud*.) Fines and confiscations,   280
And a forced loan from the refractory city,
Will fill our coffers: and the golden love
Of loyal gentlemen and noble friends
For the worshipped father of our common country,
With contributions from the catholics,   285
Will make Rebellion pale in our excess.
Be these the expedients until time and wisdom
Shall frame a settled state of government.
    Laud. And weak expedients they! Have we not drained
All, till the   which seemed   290
A mine exhaustless?
    Strafford.   And the love which *is*,
If loyal hearts could turn their blood to gold.
    Laud. Both now grow barren: and I speak it not
As loving parliaments, which, as they have been

In the right hand of bold bad mighty kings   295
The scourges of the bleeding Church, I hate.
Methinks they scarcely can deserve our fear.
  Strafford. Oh! my dear liege, take back the wealth thou gavest:
With that, take all I held, but as in trust
For thee, of mine inheritance: leave me but   300
This unprovided body for thy service,
And a mind dedicated to no care
Except thy safety:—but assemble not
A parliament. Hundreds will bring, like me,
Their fortunes, as they would their blood, before—— 305
  King. No! thou who judgest them art but one. Alas!
We should be too much out of love with Heaven,
Did this vile world show many such as thee,
Thou perfect, just, and honourable man!
Never shall it be said that Charles of England   310
Stripped those he loved for fear of those he scorns;
Nor will he so much misbecome his throne
As to impoverish those who most adorn
And best defend it. That you urge, dear Strafford,
Inclines me rather—
  Queen.   To a parliament?   315
Is this thy firmness? and thou wilt preside
Over a knot of   censurers,
To the unswearing of thy best resolves,
And choose the worst, when the worst comes too soon?
Plight not the worst before the worst must come. 320
Oh, wilt thou smile whilst our ribald foes,
Dressed in their own usurped authority,
Sharpen their tongues on Henrietta's fame?
It is enough! Thou lovest me no more!   *[Weeps.*
  King. Oh, Henrietta!   *[They talk apart.*
  Cottington (to LAUD). Money we have none: 325
And all the expedients of my Lord of Strafford
Will scarcely meet the arrears.
  Laud.   Without delay
An army must be sent into the north;
Followed by a Commission of the Church,
With amplest power to quench in fire and blood, 330
And tears and terror, and the pity of hell,
The intenser wrath of Heresy. God will give
Victory; and victory over Scotland give
The lion England tamed into our hands.
That will lend power, and power bring gold.
  Cottington.   Meanwhile 335
We must begin first where your Grace leaves off.
Gold must give power, or——

Laud.   I am not averse
From the assembling of a parliament.
Strong actions and smooth words might teach them soon
The lesson to obey. And are they not   340
A bubble fashioned by the monarch's mouth,
The birth of one light breath? If they serve no purpose,
A word dissolves them.
    Strafford.   The engine of parliaments
Might be deferred until I can bring over
The Irish regiments: they will serve to assure   345
The issue of the war against the Scots.
And, this game won—which if lost, all is lost—
Gather these chosen leaders of the rebels,
And call them, if you will, a parliament.
    King. Oh, be our feet still tardy to shed blood,   350
Guilty though it may be! I would still spare
The stubborn country of my birth, and ward
From countenances which I loved in youth
The wrathful Church's lacerating hand.
(*To* Laud.) Have you o'erlooked the other articles?   355

                                              [*Re-enter* ARCHY.

    Laud. Hazlerig, Hampden, Pym, young Harry Vane,
Cromwell, and other rebels of less note,
Intend to sail with the next favouring wind
For the Plantations.
    Archy.   Where they think to found
A commonwealth like Gonzalo's in the play,   360
Gynaecocoenic and pantisocratic.
    King. What's that, sirrah?
    Archy.   New devil's politics.
Hell is the pattern of all commonwealths:
Lucifer was the first republican.
Will you hear Merlin's prophecy, how three [posts?]   365
    'In one brainless skull, when the whitethorn is full,
        Shall sail round the world, and come back again:
    Shall sail round the world in a brainless skull,
    And come back again when the moon is at full:'—
When, in spite of the Church,   370
They will hear homilies of whatever length
Or form they please.
    [*Cottington?*] So please your Majesty to sign this order
For their detention.
    Archy. If your Majesty were tormented night and day by fever, gout,
rheumatism, and stone, and asthma, etc., and you found these diseases
had secretly entered into a conspiracy to abandon you, should you think
it necessary to lay an embargo on the port by which they meant to dis-
people your unquiet kingdom of man?   379

King. If fear were made for kings, the Fool mocks wisely;
But in this case——(*writing*). Here, my lord, take the warrant,
And see it duly executed forthwith.——
That imp of malice and mockery shall be punished.   383

[*Exeunt all but* KING, QUEEN, *and* ARCHY.

Archy. Ay, I am the physician of whom Plato prophesied, who was to
be accused by the confectioner before a jury of children, who found him
guilty without waiting for the summing-up, and hanged him without
benefit of clergy. Thus Baby Charles, and the Twelfth-night Queen of
Hearts, and the overgrown schoolboy Cottington, and that little urchin
Laud—who would reduce a verdict of 'guilty, death,' by famine, if it
were impregnable by composition—all impannelled against poor Archy
for presenting them bitter physic the last day of the holidays.   391

Queen. Is the rain over, sirrah?

King.   When it rains
And the sun shines, 'twill rain again to-morrow:
And therefore never smile till you've done crying.   394

Archy. But 'tis all over now: like the April anger of woman, the gentle
sky has wept itself serene.

Queen. What news abroad? how looks the world this morning?

Archy. Gloriously as a grave covered with virgin flowers.
There's a rainbow in the sky. Let your Majesty look at it, for

'A rainbow in the morning   400
Is the shepherd's warning;'

and the flocks of which you are the pastor are scattered among the
mountain-tops, where every drop of water is a flake of snow, and the
breath of May pierces like a January blast.   404

King. The sheep have mistaken the wolf for their shepherd, my poor
boy; and the shepherd, the wolves for their watchdogs.

Queen. But the rainbow was a good sign, Archy: it says that the waters
of the deluge are gone, and can return no more.

Archy. Ay, the salt-water one: but that of tears and blood must yet
come down, and that of fire follow, if there be any truth in lies.—The
rainbow hung over the city with all its shops, . . . and churches, from
north to south, like a bridge of congregated lightning pieced by the
masonry of heaven—like a balance in which the angel that distributes
the coming hour was weighing that heavy one whose poise is now felt
in the lightest hearts, before it bows the proudest heads under the meanest feet.   416

Queen. Who taught you this trash, sirrah?

Archy. A torn leaf out of an old book trampled in the dirt.—But for
the rainbow. It moved as the sun moved, and . . . until the top of the
Tower . . of a cloud through its left-hand tip, and Lambeth Palace
look as dark as a rock before the other. Methought I saw a crown figured
upon one tip, and a mitre on the other. So, as I had heard treasures were
found where the rainbow quenches its points upon the earth, I set off,

and at the Tower—— But I shall not tell your Majesty what I found
close to the closet-window on which the rainbow had glimmered.   425

King. Speak: I will make my Fool my conscience.

Archy. Then conscience is a fool.—I saw there a cat caught in a rat-
trap. I heard the rats squeak behind the wainscots: it seemed to me that
the very mice were consulting on the manner of her death.

Queen. Archy is shrewd and bitter.

Archy.   Like the season,   430
So blow the winds.—But at the other end of the rainbow, where the gray
rain was tempered along the grass and leaves by a tender interfusion of
violet and gold in the meadows beyond Lambeth, what think you that
I found instead of a mitre?

King. Vane's wits perhaps.

Archy.   Something as vain. I saw   435
a gross vapour hovering in a stinking ditch over the carcass of a dead
ass, some rotten rags, and broken dishes—the wrecks of what once administered to the stuffing-out and the ornament of a worm of worms. His
Grace of Canterbury expects to enter the New Jerusalem some Palm
Sunday in triumph on the ghost of this ass.   440

Queen. Enough, enough! Go desire Lady Jane
She place my lute, together with the music
Mari received last week from Italy,
In my boudoir, and——   [*Exit* ARCHY.

King.   I'll go in.

Queen.   My beloved lord,
Have you not noted that the Fool of late   445
Has lost his careless mirth, and that his words
Sound like the echoes of our saddest fears?
What can it mean? I should be loth to think
Some factious slave had tutored him.

King.   Oh, no!
He is but Occasion's pupil. Partly 'tis   450
That our minds piece the vacant intervals
Of his wild words with their own fashioning,—
As in the imagery of summer clouds,
Or coals of the winter fire, idlers find
The perfect shadows of their teeming thoughts: 455
And partly, that the terrors of the time
Are sown by wandering Rumour in all spirits;
And in the lightest and the least, may best
Be seen the current of the coming wind.

Queen. Your brain is overwrought with these deep thoughts.   460
Come, I will sing to you; let us go try
These airs from Italy; and, as we pass
The gallery, we'll decide where that Correggio
Shall hang—the Virgin Mother

With her child, born the King of heaven and earth,   465
Whose reign is men's salvation. And you shall see
A cradled miniature of yourself asleep,
Stamped on the heart by never-erring love;
Liker than any Vandyke ever made,
A pattern to the unborn age of thee,   470
Over whose sweet beauty I have wept for joy
A thousand times, and now should weep for sorrow
Did I not think that after we were dead
Our fortunes would spring high in him, and that
The cares we waste upon our heavy crown   475
Would make it light and glorious as a wreath
Of Heaven's beams for his dear innocent brow.
    King. Dear Henrietta!

SCENE III.—*The Star Chamber,* LAUD, JUXON, STRAFFORD, *and others,*
    as Judges. PRYNNE *as a Prisoner, and then* BASTWICK.

    Laud. Bring forth the prisoner Bastwick: let the clerk
Recite his sentence.
    Clerk.   'That he pay five thousand
Pounds to the king, lose both his ears, be branded
With red-hot iron on the cheek and forehead,
And be imprisoned within Lancaster Castle   5
During the pleasure of the Court.'
    Laud.   Prisoner,
If you have aught to say wherefore this sentence
Should not be put into effect, now speak.
    Juxon. If you have aught to plead in mitigation,
Speak.
    Bastwick. Thus, my lords. If, like the prelates, I   10
Were an invader of the royal power,
A public scorner of the word of God,
Profane, idolatrous, popish, superstitious,
Impious in heart and in tyrannic act,
Void of wit, honesty, and temperance;   15
If Satan were my lord, as theirs,—our God
Pattern of all I should avoid to do:
Were I an enemy of my God and King
And of good men, as ye are;—I should merit
Your fearful state and gilt prosperity,   20
Which, when ye wake from the last sleep, shall turn
To cowls and robes of everlasting fire.
But, as I am, I bid ye grudge me not
The only earthly favour ye can yield,
Or I think worth acceptance at your hands,—   25
Scorn, mutilation, and imprisonment.
              even as my Master did,

Until Heaven's kingdom shall descend on earth,
Or earth be like a shadow in the light
Of Heaven absorbed—some few tumultuous years   30
Will pass, and leave no wreck of what opposes
His will whose will is power.
    Laud. Officer, take the prisoner from the bar,
And be his tongue slit for his insolence.
    Bastwick. While this hand holds a pen——
    Laud.   Be his hands——
    'uxon.   Stop!   35
Forbear, my lord! The tongue, which now can speak
No terror, would interpret, being dumb,
Heaven's thunder to our harm; . . .
And hands, which now write only their own shame,
With bleeding stumps might sign our blood away.   40
    Laud. Much more such 'mercy' among men would be,
Did all the ministers of Heaven's revenge
Flinch thus from earthly retribution. I
Could suffer what I would inflict.

                                       [Exit BASTWICK *guarded.*
                        Bring up
The Lord Bishop of Lincoln.—
(*To* STRAFFORD.)   Know you not   45
That, in distraining for ten thousand pounds
Upon his books and furniture at Lincoln,
Were found these scandalous and seditious letters
Sent from one Osbaldistone, who is fled?
I speak it not as touching this poor person;   50
But of the office which should make it holy,
Were it as vile as it was ever spotless.
Mark, too, my lord, that this expression strikes
His Majesty, if I misinterpret not.

        Enter BISHOP WILLIAMS *guarded.*

    Strafford. 'Twere politic and just that Williams taste   55
The bitter fruit of his connection with
The schismatics. But you, my Lord Archbishop,
Who owed your first promotion to his favour,
Who grew beneath his smile——
    Laud.   Would therefore beg
The office of his judge from this High Court,—   60
That it shall seem, even as it is, that I,
In my assumption of this sacred robe,
Have put aside all worldly preference,
All sense of all distinction of all persons,
All thoughts but of the service of the Church.—   65
Bishop of Lincoln!

Williams.   Peace, proud hierarch!
I know my sentence, and I own it just.
Thou wilt repay me less than I deserve,
In stretching to the utmost

．　　　　　．　　　　　．　　　　　．　　　　　．

SCENE IV.—HAMPDEN, PYM, CROMWELL, *his Daughter, and young*
SIR HARRY VANE.

Hampden. England, farewell! thou, who hast been my cradle,
Shalt never be my dungeon or my grave!
I held what I inherited in thee
As pawn for that inheritance of freedom
Which thou hast sold for thy despoiler's smile: 5
How can I call thee England, or my country?—
Does the wind hold?
    Vane.   The vanes sit steady
Upon the Abbey towers. The silver lightnings
Of the evening star, spite of the city's smoke,
Tell that the north wind reigns in the upper air.   10
Mark too that flock of fleecy-wingèd clouds
Sailing athwart St. Margaret's.
    Hampden.   Hail, fleet herald
Of tempest! that rude pilot who shall guide
Hearts free as his, to realms as pure as thee,
Beyond the shot of tyranny,   15
Beyond the webs of that swoln spider . . .
Beyond the curses, calumnies, and [lies?]
Of atheist priests!   And thou
Fair star, whose beam lies on the wide Atlantic,
Athwart its zones of tempest and of calm,   20
Bright as the path to a belovèd home,
Oh, light us to the isles of the evening land!
Like floating Edens cradled in the glimmer
Of sunset, through the distant mist of years
Touched by departing hope, they gleam! lone regions,   25
Where Power's poor dupes and victims yet have never
Propitiated the savage fear of kings
With purest blood of noblest hearts; whose dew
Is yet unstained with tears of those who wake
To weep each day the wrongs on which it dawns;   30
Whose sacred silent air owns yet no echo
Of formal blasphemies; nor impious rites
Wrest man's free worship, from the God who loves,
To the poor worm who envies us His love!
Receive, thou young   of Paradise.   35
These exiles from the old and sinful world!

．　　　　　．　　　　　．　　　　　．　　　　　．

This glorious clime, this firmament, whose lights
Dart mitigated influence through their veil
Of pale blue atmosphere; whose tears keep green
The pavement of this moist all-feeding earth;　　　　　40
This vaporous horizon, whose dim round
Is bastioned by the circumfluous sea,
Repelling invasion from the sacred towers,
Presses upon me like a dungeon's grate,
A low dark roof, a damp and narrow wall.　　　　　45
The boundless universe
Becomes a cell too narrow for the soul
That owns no master; while the loathliest ward
Of this wide prison, England, is a nest
Of cradling peace built on the mountain tops,—　　　50
To which the eagle spirits of the free,
Which range through heaven and earth, and scorn the storm
Of time, and gaze upon the light of truth,
Return to brood on thoughts that cannot die
And cannot be repelled.　　　　　55
Like eaglets floating in the heaven of time,
They soar above their quarry, and shall stoop
Through palaces and temples thunderproof.

SCENE V

Archy. I'll go live under the ivy that overgrows the terrace, and count
the tears shed on its old [roots?] as the [wind?] plays the song of

　　　　'A widow bird sate mourning
　　　　Upon a wintry bough.'
　　　　　　　[Sings]
　　　'Heigho! the lark and the owl!　　　　　5
　　　　One flies the morning, and one lulls the night:—
　　　Only the nightingale, poor fond soul,
　　　　Sings like the fool through darkness and light.

　　　'A widow bird sate mourning for her love　　　10
　　　　Upon a wintry bough;
　　　The frozen wind crept on above,
　　　　The freezing stream below.

　　　'There was no leaf upon the forest bare,
　　　　No flower upon the ground,
　　　And little motion in the air　　　　　15
　　　　Except the mill-wheel's sound.'

LETTER TO MARIA GISBORNE

LEGHORN, July 1, 1820.

THE spider spreads her webs, whether she be
In poet's tower, cellar, or barn, or tree;
The silk-worm in the dark green mulberry leaves
His winding sheet and cradle ever weaves;
So I, a thing whom moralists call worm,   5
Sit spinning still round this decaying form,
From the fine threads of rare and subtle thought—
No net of words in garish colours wrought
To catch the idle buzzers of the day—
But a soft cell, where when that fades away,   10
Memory may clothe in wings my living name
And feed it with the asphodels of fame,
Which in those hearts which must remember me
Grow, making love an immortality.

Whoever should behold me now, I wist,   15
Would think I were a mighty mechanist,
Bent with sublime Archimedean art
To breathe a soul into the iron heart
Of some machine portentous, or strange gin,
Which by the force of figured spells might win   20
Its way over the sea, and sport therein;
For round the walls are hung dread engines, such
As Vulcan never wrought for Jove to clutch
Ixion or the Titan:—or the quick
Wit of that man of God, St. Dominic,   25
To convince Atheist, Turk, or Heretic,
Or those in philanthropic council met,
Who thought to pay some interest for the debt
They owed to Jesus Chirst for their salvation,
By giving a faint foretaste of damnation   30
To Shakespeare, Sidney, Spenser, and the rest
Who made our land an island of the blest.
When lamp-like Spain, who now relumes her fire
On Freedom's hearth, grew dim with Empire:—
With thumbscrews, wheels, with tooth and spike and jag,
Which fishers found under the utmost crag   36
Of Cornwall and the storm-encompassed isles,
Where to the sky the rude sea rarely smiles
Unless in treacherous wrath, as on the morn
When the exulting elements in scorn,   40

Satiated with destroyed destruction, lay
Sleeping in beauty on their mangled prey,
As panthers sleep;—and other strange and dread
Magical forms the brick floor overspread,—
Proteus transformed to metal did not make   45
More figures, or more strange; nor did he take
Such shapes of unintelligible brass,
Or heap himself in such a horrid mass
Of tin and iron not to be understood;
And forms of unimaginable wood,   50
To puzzle Tubal Cain and all his brood:
Great screws, and cones, and wheels, and groovèd blocks,
The elements of what will stand the shocks
Of wave and wind and time.—Upon the table
More knacks and quips there be than I am able   55
To catalogize in this verse of mine:—
A pretty bowl of wood—not full of wine,
But quicksilver; that dew which the gnomes drink
When at their subterranean toil they swink,
Pledging the demons of the earthquake, who   60
Reply to them in lava—cry halloo!
And call out to the cities o'er their head,—
Roofs, towers, and shrines, the dying and the dead,
Crash through the chinks of earth—and then all quaff
Another rouse, and hold their sides and laugh.   65
This quicksilver no gnome has drunk—within
The walnut bowl it lies, veinèd and thin,
In colour like the wake of light that stains
The Tuscan deep, when from the moist moon rains
The inmost shower of its white fire—the breeze   70
Is still—blue Heaven smiles over the pale seas,
And in this bowl of quicksilver—for I
Yield to the impulse of an infancy
Outlasting manhood—I have made to float
A rude idealism of a paper boat:—   75
A hollow screw with cogs—Henry will know
The thing I mean and laugh at me,—if so
He fears not I should do more mischief.—Next
Lie bills and calculations much perplexed,
With steam-boats, frigates, and machinery quaint   80
Traced over them in blue and yellow paint.
Then comes a range of mathematical
Instruments, for plans nautical and statical;
A heap of rosin, a queer broken glass
With ink in it;—a china cup that was   85
What it will never be again, I think,—
A thing from which sweet lips were wont to drink

The liquor doctors rail at—and which I
Will quaff in spite of them—and when we die
We'll toss up who died first of drinking tea,   90
And cry out,—'Heads or tails?' where'er we be.
Near that a dusty paint-box, some odd hooks,
A half-burnt match, an ivory block, three books,
Where conic sections, spherics, logarithms,
To great Laplace, from Saunderson and Sims,   95
Lie heaped in their harmonious disarray
Of figures,—disentangle them who may.
Baron de Tott's Memoirs beside them lie,
And some odd volumes of old chemistry.
Near those a most inexplicable thing,   100
With lead in the middle—I'm conjecturing
How to make Henry understand; but no—
I'll leave, as Spenser says, with many mo,
This secret in the pregnant womb of time,
Too vast a matter for so weak a rhyme.   105

And here like some weird Archimage sit I,
Plotting dark spells, and devilish enginery,
The self-impelling steam-wheels of the mind
Which pump up oaths from clergymen, and grind
The gentle spirit of our meek reviews   110
Into a powdery foam of salt abuse,
Ruffling the ocean of their self-content;—
I sit—and smile or sigh as is my bent,
But not for them—Libeccio rushes round
With an inconstant and an idle sound,   115
I heed him more than them—the thunder-smoke
Is gathering on the mountains, like a cloak
Folded athwart their shoulders broad and bare;
The ripe corn under the undulating air
Undulates like an ocean;—and the vines   120
Are trembling wide in all their trellised lines—
The murmur of the awakening sea doth fill
The empty pauses of the blast;—the hill
Looks hoary through the white electric rain,
And from the glens beyond, in sullen strain,   125
The interrupted thunder howls; above
One chasm of Heaven smiles, like the eye of Love
On the unquiet world;—while such things are,
How could one worth your friendship heed the war
Of worms? the shriek of the world's carrion jays,   130
Their censure, or their wonder, or their praise?

You are not here! the quaint witch Memory sees,
In vacant chairs, your absent images,

And points where once you sat, and now should be
But are not.—I demand if ever we   135
Shall meet as then we met;—and she replies,
Veiling in awe her second-sighted eyes;
'I know the past alone—but summon home
My sister Hope,—she speaks of all to come.'
But I, an old diviner, who knew well   140
Every false verse of that sweet oracle,
Turned to the sad enchantress once again,
And sought a respite from my gentle pain,
In citing every passage o'er and o'er
Of our communion—how on the sea-shore   145
We watched the ocean and the sky together,
Under the roof of blue Italian weather;
How I ran home through last year's thunder-storm,
And felt the transverse lightning linger warm
Upon my cheek—and how we often made   150
Feasts for each other, where good will outweighed
The frugal luxury of our country cheer,
As well it might, were it less firm and clear
Than ours must ever be;—and how we spun
A shroud of talk to hide us from the sun   155
Of this familiar life, which seems to be
But is not:—or is but quaint mockery
Of all we would believe, and sadly blame
The jarring and inexplicable frame
Of this wrong world:—and then anatomize   160
The purposes and thoughts of men whose eyes
Were closed in distant years;—or widely guess
The issue of the earth's great business,
When we shall be as we no longer are—
Like babbling gossips safe, who hear the war   165
Of winds, and sigh, but tremble not;—or how
You listened to some interrupted flow
Of visionary rhyme,—in joy and pain
Struck from the inmost fountains of my brain,
With little skill perhaps;—or how we sought   170
Those deepest wells of passion or of thought
Wrought by wise poets in the waste of years,
Staining their sacred waters with our tears;
Quenching a thirst ever to be renewed!
Or how I, wisest lady! then endued   175
The language of a land which now is free,
And, winged with thoughts of truth and majesty,
Flits round the tyrant's sceptre like a cloud,
And bursts the peopled prisons, and cries aloud,

'My name is Legion!'—that majestic tongue   180
Which Calderon over the desert flung
Of ages and of nations; and which found
An echo in our hearts, and with the sound
Startled oblivion;—thou wert then to me   185
As is a nurse—when inarticulately
A child would talk as its grown parents do.
If living winds the rapid clouds pursue,
If hawks chase doves through the aethereal way,
Huntsmen the innocent deer, and beasts their prey,
Why should not we rouse with the spirit's blast   190
Out of the forest of the pathless past
These recollected pleasures?
                                  You are now
In London, that great sea, whose ebb and flow
At once is deaf and loud, and on the shore
Vomits its wrecks, and still howls on for more.   195
Yet in its depth what treasures! You will see
That which was Godwin,—greater none than he
Though fallen—and fallen on evil times—to stand
Among the spirits of our age and land,
Before the dread tribunal of *to come*   200
The foremost,—while Rebuke cowers pale and dumb.
You will see Coleridge—he who sits obscure
In the exceeding lustre and the pure
Intense irradiation of a mind,
Which, with its own internal lightning blind,   205
Flags wearily through darkness and despair—
A cloud-encircled meteor of the air,
A hooded eagle among blinking owls.—
You will see Hunt—one of those happy souls
Which are the salt of the earth, and without whom   210
This world would smell like what it is—a tomb;
Who is, what others seem; his room no doubt
Is still adorned with many a cast from Shout,
With graceful flowers tastefully placed about;
And coronals of bay from ribbons hung,   215
And brighter wreaths in neat disorder flung;
The gifts of the most learned among some dozens
Of female friends, sisters-in-law, and cousins.
And there is he with his eternal puns,
Which beat the dullest brain for smiles, like duns   220
Thundering for money at a poet's door;
Alas! it is no use to say, 'I'm poor!'
Or oft in graver mood, when he will look
Things wiser than were ever read in book,

Except in Shakespeare's wisest tenderness.——   225
You will see Hogg,—and I cannot express
His virtues,—though I know that they are great,
Because he locks, then barricades the gate
Within which they inhabit;—of his wit
And wisdom, you'll cry out when you are bit.   230
He is a pearl within an oyster shell,
One of the richest of the deep;—and there
Is English Peacock, with his mountain Fair,
Turned into a Flamingo;—that shy bird
That gleams i' the Indian air—have you not heard   235
When a man marries, dies, or turns Hindoo,
His best friends hear no more of him?—but you
Will see him, and will like him too, I hope,
With the milk-white Snowdonian Antelope
Matched with this cameleopard—his fine wit   240
Makes such a wound, the knife is lost in it;
A strain too learnèd for a shallow age,
Too wise for selfish bigots; let his page,
Which charms the chosen spirits of the time,
Fold itself up for the serener clime   245
Of years to come, and find its recompense
In that just expectation.—Wit and sense,
Virtue and human knowledge; all that might
Make this dull world a business of delight,
Are all combined in Horace Smith.—And these,   250
With some exceptions, which I need not tease
Your patience by descanting on,—are all
You and I know in London.

              I recall
My thoughts, and bid you look upon the night.
As water does a sponge, so the moonlight   255
Fills the void, hollow, universal air—
What see you?—unpavilioned Heaven is fair,
Whether the moon, into her chamber gone,
Leaves midnight to the golden stars, or wan
Climbs with diminished beams the azure steep;   260
Or whether clouds sail o'er the inverse deep,
Piloted by the many-wandering blast,
And the rare stars rush through them dim and fast:—
All this is beautiful in every land.—
But what see you beside?—a shabby stand   265
Of Hackney coaches—a brick house or wall
Fencing some lonely court, white with the scrawl
Of our unhappy politics;—or worse—
A wretched woman reeling by, whose curse

Mixed with the watchman's, partner of her trade, 270
You must accept in place of serenade—
Or yellow-haired Pollonia murmuring
To Henry, some unutterable thing.
I see a chaos of green leaves and fruit
Built round dark caverns, even to the root 275
Of the living stems that feed them—in whose bowers
There sleep in their dark dew the folded flowers;
Beyond, the surface of the unsickled corn
Trembles not in the slumbering air, and borne
In circles quaint, and ever-changing dance, 280
Like wingèd stars the fire-flies flash and glance,
Pale in the open moonshine, but each one
Under the dark trees seems a little sun,
A meteor tamed; a fixed star gone astray
From the silver regions of the milky way;— 285
Afar the Contadino's song is heard,
Rude, but made sweet by distance—and a bird
Which cannot be the Nightingale, and yet
I know none else that sings so sweet as it
At this late hour;—and then all is still— 290
Now—Italy or London, which you will!

Next winter you must pass with me; I'll have
My house by that time turned into a grave
Of dead despondence and low-thoughted care,
And all the dreams which our tormentors are; 295
Oh! that Hunt, Hogg, Peacock, and Smith were there,
With everything belonging to them fair!—
We will have books, Spanish, Italian, Greek;
And ask one week to make another week
As like his father, as I'm unlike mine, 300
Which is not his fault, as you may divine.
Though we eat little flesh and drink no wine,
Yet let's be merry: we'll have tea and toast;
Custards for supper, and an endless host
Of syllabubs and jellies and mince-pies, 305
And other such lady-like luxuries,—
Feasting on which we will philosophize!
And we'll have fires out of the Grand Duke's wood,
To thaw the six weeks' winter in our blood.
And then we'll talk;—what shall we talk about? 310
Oh! there are themes enough for many a bout
Of thought-entangled descant;—as to nerves—
With cones and parallelograms and curves
I've sworn to strangle them if once they dare
To bother me—when you are with me there. 315

And they shall never more sip laudanum,
From Helicon or Himeros [1];—well, come,
And in despite of God and of the devil,
We'll make our friendly philosophic revel
Outlast the leafless time; till buds and flowers   320
Warn the obscure inevitable hours,
Sweet meeting by sad parting to renew;—
'To-morrow to fresh woods and pastures new.'

THE WITCH OF ATLAS

TO MARY

(ON HER OBJECTING TO THE FOLLOWING POEM, UPON THE SCORE OF ITS CONTAINING NO HUMAN INTEREST)

I

How, my dear Mary,—are you critic-bitten
    (For vipers kill, though dead) by some review,
That you condemn these verses I have written,
    Because they tell no story, false or true?
What, though no mice are caught by a young kitten,   5
    May it not leap and play as grown cats do,
Till its claws come? Prithee, for this one time,
Content thee with a visionary rhyme.

II

What hand would crush the silken-wingèd fly,
    The youngest of inconstant April's minions,   10
Because it cannot climb the purest sky,
    Where the swan sings, amid the sun's dominions?
Not thine. Thou knowest 'tis its doom to die,
    When Day shall hide within her twilight pinions
The lucent eyes, and the eternal smile,   15
Serene as thine, which lent it life awhile.

III

To thy fair feet a wingèd Vision came,
    Whose date should have been longer than a day,
And o'er thy head did beat its wings for fame,
    And in thy sight its fading plumes display;   20
The watery bow burned in the evening flame,
    But the shower fell, the swift Sun went his way—
And that is dead.—O, let me not believe
That anything of mine is fit to live!

[1] Ἵμερος, from which the river Himera was named, is, with some slight shade of difference, a synonym of Love.—[SHELLEY'S NOTE.]

IV

Wordsworth informs us he was nineteen years   25
    Considering and retouching Peter Bell;
Watering his laurels with the killing tears
    Of slow, dull care, so that their roots to Hell
Might pierce, and their wide branches blot the spheres
    Of Heaven, with dewy leaves and flowers; this well   30
May be, for Heaven and Earth conspire to foil
The over-busy gardener's blundering toil.

V

My Witch indeed is not so sweet a creature
    As Ruth or Lucy, whom his graceful praise
Clothes for our grandsons—but she matches Peter,   35
    Though he took nineteen years, and she three days
In dressing. Light the vest of flowing metre
    She wears; he, proud as dandy with his stays,
Has hung upon his wiry limbs a dress
Like King Lear's 'looped and windowed raggedness.'   40

VI

If you strip Peter, you will see a fellow
    Scorched by Hell's hyperequatorial climate
Into a kind of a sulphureous yellow:
    A lean mark, hardly fit to fling a rhyme at;
In shape a Scaramouch, in hue Othello.   45
    If you unveil my Witch, no priest nor primate
Can shrive you of that sin,—if sin there be
In love, when it becomes idolatry.

THE WITCH OF ATLAS

I

BEFORE those cruel Twins, whom at one birth
    Incestuous Change bore to her father Time,   50
Error and Truth, had hunted from the Earth
    All those bright natures which adorned its prime,
And left us nothing to believe in, worth
    The pains of putting into learnèd rhyme,
A lady-witch there lived on Atlas' mountain   55
Within a cavern, by a secret fountain.

II

Her mother was one of the Atlantides:
    The all-beholding Sun had ne'er beholden
In his wide voyage o'er continents and seas
    So fair a creature, as she lay enfolden   60

In the warm shadow of her loveliness;—
  He kissed her with his beams, and made all golden
The chamber of gray rock in which she lay—
She, in that dream of joy, dissolved away.

III

'Tis said, she first was changed into a vapour,   65
  And then into a cloud, such clouds as flit,
Like splendour-wingèd moths about a taper,
  Round the red west when the sun dies in it:
And then into a meteor, such as caper
  On hill-tops when the moon is in a fit: 70
Then, into one of those mysterious stars
Which hide themselves between the Earth and Mars.

IV

Ten times the Mother of the Months had bent
  Her bow beside the folding-star, and hidden
With that bright sign the billows to indent   75
  The sea-deserted sand—like children chidden,
At her command they ever came and went—
  Since in that cave a dewy splendour hidden
Took shape and motion: with the living form
Of this embodied Power, the cave grew warm.   80

V

A lovely lady garmented in light
  From her own beauty—deep her eyes, as are
Two openings of unfathomable night
  Seen through a Temple's cloven roof—her hair
Dark—the dim brain whirls dizzy with delight,   85
  Picturing her form; her soft smiles shone afar,
And her low voice was heard like love, and drew
All living things towards this wonder new.

VI

And first the spotted cameleopard came,
  And then the wise and fearless elephant;   90
Then the sly serpent, in the golden flame
  Of his own volumes intervolved;—all gaunt
And sanguine beasts her gentle looks made tame.
  They drank before her at her sacred fount;
And every beast of beating heart grew bold,   95
Such gentleness and power even to behold.

VII

The brinded lioness led forth her young,
    That she might teach them how they should forego
Their inborn thirst of death; the pard unstrung
    His sinews at her feet, and sought to know   100
With looks whose motions spoke without a tongue
    How he might be as gentle as the doe.
The magic circle of her voice and eyes
All savage natures did imparadise.

VIII

And old Silenus, shaking a green stick   105
    Of lilies, and the wood-gods in a crew
Came, blithe, as in the olive copses thick
    Cicadae are, drunk with the noonday dew:
And Dryope and Faunus followed quick,
    Teasing the God to sing them something new;   110
Till in this cave they found the lady lone,
Sitting upon a seat of emerald stone.

IX

And universal Pan, 'tis said, was there,
    And though none saw him,—through the adamant
Of the deep mountains, through the trackless air,   115
    And through those living spirits, like a want,
He passed out of his everlasting lair
    Where the quick heart of the great world doth pant,
And felt that wondrous lady all alone,—
And she felt him, upon her emerald throne.   120

X

And every nymph of stream and spreading tree,
    And every shepherdess of Ocean's flocks,
Who drives her white waves over the green sea,
    And Ocean with the brine on his gray locks,
And quaint Priapus with his company,   125
    All came, much wondering how the enwombèd rocks
Could have brought forth so beautiful a birth;—
Her love subdued their wonder and their mirth.

XI

The herdsmen and the mountain maidens came,
    And the rude kings of pastoral Garamant—   130
Their spirits shook within them, as a flame
    Stirred by the air under a cavern gaunt:

Pigmies, and Polyphemes, by many a name,
  Centaurs, and Satyrs, and such shapes as haunt
Wet clefts,—and lumps neither alive nor dead,   135
Dog-headed, bosom-eyed, and bird-footed.

XII

For she was beautiful—her beauty made
  The bright world dim, and everything beside
Seemed like the fleeting image of a shade:
  No thought of living spirit could abide,   140
Which to her looks had ever been betrayed,
  On any object in the world so wide,
On any hope within the circling skies,
But on her form, and in her inmost eyes.

XIII

Which when the lady knew, she took her spindle   145
  And twined three threads of fleecy mist, and three
Long lines of light, such as the dawn may kindle
  The clouds and waves and mountains with; and she
As many star-beams, ere their lamps could dwindle
  In the belated moon, wound skilfully;   150
And with these threads a subtle veil she wove—
A shadow for the splendour of her love.

XIV

The deep recesses of her odorous dwelling
  Were stored with magic treasures—sounds of air,
Which had the power all spirits of compelling,   155
  Folded in cells of crystal silence there;
Such as we hear in youth, and think the feeling
  Will never die—yet ere we are aware,
The feeling and the sound are fled and gone,
And the regret they leave remains alone.   160

XV

And there lay Visions swift, and sweet, and quaint,
  Each in its thin sheath, like a chrysalis,
Some eager to burst forth, some weak and faint
  With the soft burthen of intensest bliss.
It was its work to bear to many a saint   165
  Whose heart adores the shrine which holiest is,
Even Love's:—and others white, green, gray, and black,
And of all shapes—and each was at her beck.

XVI

And odours in a kind of aviary
  Of ever-blooming Eden-trees she kept,   170
Clipped in a floating net, a love-sick Fairy
  Had woven from dew-beams while the moon yet slept;
As bats at the wired window of a dairy,
  They beat their vans; and each was an adept,
When loosed and missioned, making wings of winds,   175
To stir sweet thoughts or sad, in destined minds.

XVII

And liquors clear and sweet, whose healthful might
  Could medicine the sick soul to happy sleep,
And change eternal death into a night
  Of glorious dreams—or if eyes needs must weep,   180
Could make their tears all wonder and delight,
  She in her crystal vials did closely keep:
If men could drink of those clear vials, 'tis said
The living were not envied of the dead.

XVIII

Her cave was stored with scrolls of strange device,   185
  The works of some Saturnian Archimage,
Which taught the expiations at whose price
  Men from the Gods might win that happy age
Too lightly lost, redeeming native vice;
  And which might quench the Earth-consuming rage   190
Of gold and blood—till men should live and move
Harmonious as the sacred stars above;

XIX

And how all things that seem untameable,
  Not to be checked and not to be confined,
Obey the spells of Wisdom's wizard skill;   195
  Time, earth, and fire—the ocean and the wind,
And all their shapes—and man's imperial will;
  And other scrolls whose writings did unbind
The inmost lore of Love—let the profane
Tremble to ask what secrets they contain.   200

XX

And wondrous works of substances unknown,
  To which the enchantment of her father's power
Had changed those ragged blocks of savage stone,
  Were heaped in the recesses of her bower;

Carved lamps and chalices, and vials which shone 205
  In their own golden beams—each like a flower.
Out of whose depth a fire-fly shakes his light
Under a cypress in a starless night.

XXI

At first she lived alone in this wild home,
  And her own thoughts were each a minister, 210
Clothing themselves, or with the ocean foam,
  Or with the wind, or with the speed of fire,
To work whatever purposes might come
  Into her mind; such power her mighty Sire
Had girt them with, whether to fly or run, 215
Through all the regions which he shines upon.

XXII

The Ocean-nymphs and Hamadryades,
  Oreads and Naiads, with long weedy locks,
Offered to do her bidding through the seas,
  Under the earth, and in the hollow rocks, 220
And far beneath the matted roots of trees,
  And in the gnarlèd heart of stubborn oaks,
So they might live for ever in the light
Of her sweet presence—each a satellite.

XXIII

'This may not be,' the wizard maid replied; 225
  'The fountains where the Naiades bedew
Their shining hair, at length are drained and dried;
  The solid oaks forget their strength, and strew
Their latest leaf upon the mountains wide;
  The boundless ocean like a drop of dew 230
Will be consumed—the stubborn centre must
Be scattered, like a cloud of summer dust.

XXIV

'And ye with them will perish, one by one;—
  If I must sigh to think that this shall be,
If I must weep when the surviving Sun 235
  Shall smile on your decay—oh, ask not me
To love you till your little race is run;
  I cannot die as ye must—over me
Your leaves shall glance—the streams in which ye dwell
Shall be my paths henceforth, and so—farewell!'— 240

XXV

She spoke and wept:—the dark and azure well
  Sparkled beneath the shower of her bright tears,
And every little circlet where they fell
  Flung to the cavern-roof inconstant spheres
And intertangled lines of light:—a knell   245
  Of sobbing voices came upon her ears
From those departing Forms, o'er the serene
Of the white streams and of the forest green.

XXVI

All day the wizard lady sate aloof,
  Spelling out scrolls of dread antiquity,   250
Under the cavern's fountain-lighted roof;
  Or broidering the pictured poesy
Of some high tale upon her growing woof,
  Which the sweet splendour of her smiles could dye
In hues outshining heaven—and ever she   255
Added some grace to the wrought poesy.

XXVII

While on her hearth lay blazing many a piece
  Of sandal wood, rare gums, and cinnamon;
Men scarcely know how beautiful fire is—
  Each flame of it is as a precious stone   260
Dissolved in ever-moving light, and this
  Belongs to each and all who gaze upon.
The Witch beheld it not, for in her hand
She held a woof that dimmed the burning brand.

XXVIII

This lady never slept, but lay in trance   265
  All night within the fountain—as in sleep.
Its emerald crags glowed in her beauty's glance;
  Through the green splendour of the water deep
She saw the constellations reel and dance
  Like fire-flies—and withal did ever keep   270
The tenour of her contemplations calm,
With open eyes, closed feet, and folded palm.

XXIX

And when the whirlwinds and the clouds descended
  From the white pinnacles of that cold hill,
She passed at dewfall to a space extended,   275
  Where in a lawn of flowering asphodel

Amid a wood of pines and cedars blended,
    There yawned an inextinguishable well
Of crimson fire—full even to the brim,
And overflowing all the margin trim.   280

XXX

Within the which she lay when the fierce war
    Of wintry winds shook that innocuous liquor
In many a mimic moon and bearded star
    O'er woods and lawns;—the serpent heard it flicker
In sleep, and dreaming still, he crept afar—   285
    And when the windless snow descended thicker
Than autumn leaves, she watched it as it came
Melt on the surface of the level flame.

XXXI

She had a boat, which some say Vulcan wrought
    For Venus, as the chariot of her star;   290
But it was found too feeble to be fraught
    With all the ardours in that sphere which are,
And so she sold it, and Apollo bought
    And gave it to this daughter: from a car
Changed to the fairest and the lightest boat   295
Which ever upon mortal stream did float.

XXXII

And others say, that, when but three hours old,
    The first-born Love out of his cradle lept,
And clove dun Chaos with his wings of gold,
    And like a horticultural adept,   300
Stole a strange seed, and wrapped it up in mould,
    And sowed it in his mother's star, and kept
Watering it all the summer with sweet dew,
And with his wings fanning it as it grew.

XXXIII

The plant grew strong and green, the snowy flower   305
    Fell, and the long and gourd-like fruit began
To turn the light and dew by inward power
    To its own substance; woven tracery ran
Of light firm texture, ribbed and branching, o'er
    The solid rind, like a leaf's veinèd fan—   310
Of which Love scooped this boat—and with soft motion
Piloted it round the circumfluous ocean.

XXXIV

This boat she moored upon her fount, and lit
  A living spirit within all its frame,
Breathing the soul of swiftness into it.
    Couched on the fountain like a panther tame,
One of the twain at Evan's feet that sit—
  Or as on Vesta's sceptre a swift flame—
Or on blind Homer's heart a wingèd thought,—
In joyous expectation lay the boat.

315

320

XXXV

Then by strange art she kneaded fire and snow
  Together, tempering the repugnant mass
With liquid love—all things together grow
  Through which the harmony of love can pass;
And a fair Shape out of her hands did flow—
  A living Image, which did far surpass
In beauty that bright shape of vital stone
Which drew the heart out of Pygmalion.

325

XXXVI

A sexless thing it was, and in its growth
  It seemed to have developed no defect
Of either sex, yet all the grace of both,—
  In gentleness and strength its limbs were decked
The bosom swelled lightly with its full youth,
  The countenance was such as might select
Some artist that his skill should never die,
Imaging forth such perfect purity.

330

335

XXXVII

From its smooth shoulders hung two rapid wings,
  Fit to have borne it to the seventh sphere,
Tipped with the speed of liquid lightenings,
  Dyed in the ardours of the atmosphere:
She led her creature to the boiling springs
  Where the light boat was moored, and said: 'Sit here!'
And pointed to tne prow, and took her seat
Beside the rudder, with opposing feet.

340

XXXVIII

And down the streams which clove those mountains vast,
  Around their inland islets, and amid
The panther-peopled forests, whose shade cast
  Darkness and odours, and a pleasure hid

346

In melancholy gloom, the pinnace passed;
  By many a star-surrounded pyramid   350
Of icy crag cleaving the purple sky,
And caverns yawning round unfathomably.

XXXIX

The silver noon into that winding dell,
  With slanted gleam athwart the forest tops,
Tempered like golden evening, feebly fell;   355
  A green and glowing light, like that which drops
From folded lilies in which glow-worms dwell,
  When Earth over her face Night's mantle wraps;
Between the severed mountains lay on high,
Over the stream, a narrow rift of sky.   360

XL

And ever as she went, the Image lay
  With folded wings and unawakened eyes;
And o'er its gentle countenance did play
  The busy dreams, as thick as summer flies,
Chasing the rapid smiles that would not stay,   365
  And drinking the warm tears, and the sweet sighs
Inhaling, which, with busy murmur vain,
They had aroused from that full heart and brain.

XLI

And ever down the prone vale, like a cloud
  Upon a stream of wind, the pinnace went: 370
Now lingering on the pools, in which abode
  The calm and darkness of the deep content
In which they paused; now o'er the shallow road
  Of white and dancing waters, all besprent
With sand and polished pebbles:—mortal boat   375
In such a shallow rapid could not float.

XLII

And down the earthquaking cataracts which shiver
  Their snow-like waters into golden air,
Or under chasms unfathomable ever
  Sepulchre them, till in their rage they tear   380
A subterranean portal for the river,
  It fled—the circling sunbows did upbear
Its fall down the hoar precipice of spray,
Lighting it far upon its lampless way.

XLIII

And when the wizard lady would ascend   385
   The labyrinths of some many-winding vale,
Which to the inmost mountain upward tend—
   She called 'Hermaphroditus!'—and the pale
And heavy hue which slumber could extend
   Over its lips and eyes, as on the gale   390
A rapid shadow from a slope of grass,
Into the darkness of the stream did pass.

XLIV

And it unfurled its heaven-coloured pinions,
   With stars of fire spotting the stream below;
And from above into the Sun's dominions   395
   Flinging a glory, like the golden glow
In which Spring clothes her emerald-wingèd minions,
   All interwoven with fine feathery snow
And moonlight splendour of intensest rime,
With which frost paints the pines in winter time.   400

XLV

And then it winnowed the Elysian air
   Which ever hung about that lady bright,
With its aethereal vans—and speeding there,
   Like a star up the torrent of the night,
Or a swift eagle in the morning glare   405
   Breasting the whirlwind with impetuous flight,
The pinnace, oared by those enchanted wings,
Clove the fierce streams towards their upper springs.

XLVI

The water flashed, like sunlight by the prow
   Of a noon-wandering meteor flung to Heaven;   410
The still air seemed as if its waves did flow
   In tempest down the mountains; loosely driven
The lady's radiant hair streamed to and fro:
   Beneath, the billows having vainly striven
Indignant and impetuous, roared to feel   415
The swift and steady motion of the keel.

XLVII

Or, when the weary moon was in the wane,
   Or in the noon of interlunar night,
The lady-witch in visions could not chain
   Her spirit; but sailed forth under the light   420

Of shooting stars, and bade extend amain
   Its storm-outspeeding wings, the Hermaphrodite;
She to the Austral waters took her way,
Beyond the fabulous Thamondocana,—

XLVIII

Where, like a meadow which no scythe has shaven,   425
   Which rain could never bend, or whirl-blast shake,
With the Antarctic constellations paven,
   Canopus and his crew, lay the Austral lake—
There she would build herself a windless haven
   Out of the clouds whose moving turrets make   430
The bastions of the storm, when through the sky
The spirits of the tempest thundered by:

XLIX

A haven beneath whose translucent floor
   The tremulous stars sparkled unfathomably,
And around which the solid vapours hoar,   435
   Based on the level waters, to the sky
Lifted their dreadful crags, and like a shore
   Of wintry mountains, inaccessibly
Hemmed in with rifts and precipices gray,
And hanging crags, many a cove and bay.   440

L

And whilst the outer lake beneath the lash
   Of the wind's scourge, foamed like a wounded thing,
And the incessant hail with stony clash
   Ploughed up the waters, and the flagging wing
Of the housed cormorant in the lightning flash   445
   Looked like the wreck of some wind-wandering
Fragment of inky thunder-smoke—this haven
Was as a gem to copy Heaven engraven,—

LI

On which that lady played her many pranks,
   Circling the image of a shooting star,   450
Even as a tiger on Hydaspes' banks
   Outspeeds the antelopes which speediest are,
In her light boat; and many quips and cranks
   She played upon the water, till the car
Of the late moon, like a sick matron wan,   455
To journey from the misty east began.

LII

And then she called out of the hollow turrets
    Of those high clouds, white, golden and vermilion,
The armies of her ministering spirits—
    In mighty legions, million after million,   460
They came, each troop emblazoning its merits
    On meteor flags; and many a proud pavilion
Of the intertexture of the atmosphere
They pitched upon the plain of the calm mere.

LIII

They framed the imperial tent of their great Queen   465
    Of woven exhalations, underlaid
With lambent lightning-fire, as may be seen
    A dome of thin and open ivory inlaid
With crimson silk—cressets from the serene
    Hung there, and on the water for her tread   470
A tapestry of fleece-like mist was strewn,
Dyed in the beams of the ascending moon.

LIV

And on a throne o'erlaid with starlight, caught
    Upon those wandering isles of aëry dew,
Which highest shoals of mountain shipwreck not,   475
    She sate, and heard all that had happened new
Between the earth and moon, since they had brought
    The last intelligence—and now she grew
Pale as that moon, lost in the watery night—
And now she wept, and now she laughed outright.   480

LV

These were tame pleasures; she would often climb
    The steepest ladder of the crudded rack
Up to some beakèd cape of cloud sublime,
    And like Arion on the dolphin's back
Ride singing through the shoreless air;—oft-time   485
    Following the serpent lightning's winding track,
She ran upon the platforms of the wind,
And laughed to hear the fire-balls roar behind.

LVI

And sometimes to those streams of upper air
    Which whirl the earth in its diurnal round,   490
She would ascend, and win the spirits there
    To let her join their chorus. Mortals found

That on those days the sky was calm and fair,
   And mystic snatches of harmonious sound
Wandered upon the earth where'er she passed,   495
And happy thoughts of hope, too sweet to last.

LVII

But her choice sport was, in the hours of sleep,
   To glide adown old Nilus, where he threads
Egypt and Aethiopia, from the steep
   Of utmost Axumè, until he spreads,   500
Like a calm flock of silver-fleecèd sheep,
   His waters on the plain: and crested heads
Of cities and proud temples gleam amid,
And many a vapour-belted pyramid.

LVIII

By Moeris and the Mareotid lakes,   505
   Strewn with faint blooms like bridal chamber floors,
Where naked boys bridling tame water-snakes,
   Or charioteering ghastly alligators,
Had left on the sweet waters mighty wakes
   Of those huge forms—within the brazen doors   510
Of the great Labyrinth slept both boy and beast,
Tired with the pomp of their Osirian feast.

LIX

And where within the surface of the river
   The shadows of the massy temples lie,
And never are erased—but tremble ever   515
   Like things which every cloud can doom to die,
Through lotus-paven canals, and wheresoever
   The works of man pierced that serenest sky
With tombs, and towers, and fanes, 'twas her delight
To wander in the shadow of the night.   520

LX

With motion like the spirit of that wind
   Whose soft step deepens slumber, her light feet
Passed through the peopled haunts of humankind,
   Scattering sweet visions from her presence sweet,
Through fane, and palace-court, and labyrinth mined   525
   With many a dark and subterranean street
Under the Nile, through chambers high and deep
She passed, observing mortals in their sleep.

LXI

A pleasure sweet doubtless it was to see
  Mortals subdued in all the shapes of sleep.   530
Here lay two sister twins in infancy;
  There, a lone youth who in his dreams did weep;
Within, two lovers linkèd innocently
  In their loose locks which over both did creep
Like ivy from one stem;—and there lay calm   535
Old age with snow-bright hair and folded palm.

LXII

But other troubled forms of sleep she saw,
  Not to be mirrored in a holy song—
Distortions foul of supernatural awe,
  And pale imaginings of visioned wrong;   540
And all the code of Custom's lawless law
  Written upon the brows of old and young:
'This,' said the wizard maiden, 'is the strife
Which stirs the liquid surface of man's life.'

LXIII

And little did the sight disturb her soul,—   545
  We, the weak mariners of that wide lake
Where'er its shores extend or billows roll,
  Our course unpiloted and starless make
O'er its wild surface to an unknown goal:—
  But she in the calm depths her way could take,   550
Where in bright bowers immortal forms abide
Beneath the weltering of the restless tide.

LXIV

And she saw princes couched under the glow
  Of sunlike gems; and round each temple-court
In dormitories ranged, row after row,   555
  She saw the priests asleep—all of one sort—
For all were educated to be so.—
  The peasants in their huts, and in the port
The sailors she saw cradled on the waves,
And the dead lulled within their dreamless graves. 560

LXV

And all the forms in which those spirits lay
  Were to her sight like the diaphanous
Veils, in which those sweet ladies oft array
  Their delicate limbs, who would conceal from us

Only their scorn of all concealment: they   565
    Move in the light of their own beauty thus.
But these and all now lay with sleep upon them,
And little thought a Witch was looking on them.

LXVI

She, all those human figures breathing there,
    Beheld as living spirits—to her eyes   570
The naked beauty of the soul lay bare,
    And often through a rude and worn disguise
She saw the inner form most bright and fair—
    And then she had a charm of strange device,
Which, murmured on mute lips with tender tone,   575
Could make that spirit mingle with her own.

LXVII

Alas! Aurora, what wouldst thou have given
    For such a charm when Tithon became gray?
Or how much, Venus, of thy silver heaven
    Wouldst thou have yielded, ere Proserpina   580
Had half (oh! why not all?) the debt forgiven
    Which dear Adonis had been doomed to pay,
To any witch who would have taught you it?
The Heliad doth not know its value yet.

LXVIII

'Tis said in after times her spirit free   585
    Knew what love was, and felt itself alone—
But holy Dian could not chaster be
    Before she stooped to kiss Endymion,
Than now this lady—like a sexless bee
    Tasting all blossoms, and confined to none,   590
Among those mortal forms, the wizard-maiden
Passed with an eye serene and heart unladen.

LXIX

To those she saw most beautiful, she gave
    Strange panacea in a crystal bowl:—
They drank in their deep sleep of that sweet wave,   595
    And lived thenceforward as if some control,
Mightier than life, were in them; and the grave
    Of such, when death oppressed the weary soul,
Was as a green and overarching bower
Lit by the gems of many a starry flower.   600

LXX

For on the night when they were buried, she
　　Restored the embalmers' ruining, and shook
The light out of the funeral lamps, to be
　　A mimic day within that deathy nook;
And she unwound the woven imagery　　　　　　　605
　　Of second childhood's swaddling bands, and took
The coffin, its last cradle, from its niche,
And threw it with contempt into a ditch.

LXXI

And there the body lay, age after age,
　　Mute, breathing, beating, warm, and undecaying,　　610
Like one asleep in a green hermitage,
　　With gentle smiles about its eyelids playing,
And living in its dreams beyond the rage
　　Of death or life; while they were still arraying
In liveries ever new, the rapid, blind　　　　　　615
And fleeting generations of mankind.

LXXII

And she would write strange dreams upon the brain
　　Of those who were less beautiful, and make
All harsh and crooked purposes more vain
　　Than in the desert is the serpent's wake　　　　620
Which the sand covers—all his evil gain
　　The miser in such dreams would rise and shake
Into a beggar's lap;—the lying scribe
Would his own lies betray without a bribe.

LXXIII

The priests would write an explanation full,　　　625
　　Translating hieroglyphics into Greek,
How the God Apis really was a bull,
　　And nothing more; and bid the herald stick
The same against the temple doors, and pull
　　The old cant down; they licensed all to speak　　630
Whate'er they thought of hawks, and cats, and geese,
By pastoral letters to each diocese.

LXXIV

The king would dress an ape up in his crown
　　And robes, and seat him on his glorious seat,
And on the right hand of the sunlike throne　　　635
　　Would place a gaudy mock-bird to repeat

The chatterings of the monkey.—Every one
　Of the prone courtiers crawled to kiss the feet
Of their great Emperor, when the morning came,
And kissed—alas, how many kiss the same!   640

LXXV

The soldiers dreamed that they were blacksmiths, and
　Walked out of quarters in somnambulism;
Round the red anvils you might see them stand
　Like Cyclopses in Vulcan's sooty abysm,
Beating their swords to ploughshares;—in a band   645
　The gaolers sent those of the liberal schism
Free through the streets of Memphis, much, I wis,
To the annoyance of king Amasis.

LXXVI

And timid lovers who had been so coy,
　They hardly knew whether they loved or not,   650
Would rise out of their rest, and take sweet joy,
　To the fulfilment of their inmost thought;
And when next day the maiden and the boy
　Met one another, both, like sinners caught,
Blushed at the thing which each believed was done   655
Only in fancy—till the tenth moon shone;

LXXVII

And then the Witch would let them take no ill:
　Of many thousand schemes which lovers find,
The Witch found one,—and so they took their fill
　Of happiness in marriage warm and kind.   660
Friends who, by practice of some envious skill,
　Were torn apart—a wide wound, mind from mind!—
She did unite again with visions clear
Of deep affection and of truth sincere.

LXXVIII

These were the pranks she played among the cities   665
　Of mortal men, and what she did to Sprites
And Gods, entangling them in her sweet ditties
　To do her will, and show their subtle sleights,
I will declare another time; for it is
　A tale more fit for the weird winter nights   670
Than for these garish summer days, when we
Scarcely believe much more than we can see.

NOTE ON THE WITCH OF ATLAS, BY MRS. SHELLEY

WE spent the summer of 1820 at the Baths of San Giuliano, four miles from Pisa. These baths were of great use to Shelley in soothing his nervous irritability. We made several excursions in the neighbourhood. The country around is fertile, and diversified and rendered picturesque by ranges of near hills and more distant mountains. The peasantry are a handsome intelligent race; and there was a gladsome sunny heaven spread over us, that rendered home and every scene we visited cheerful and bright. During some of the hottest days of August, Shelley made a solitary journey on foot to the summit of Monte San Pellegrino—a mountain of some height, on the top of which there is a chapel, the object, during certain days of the year, of many pilgrimages. The excursion delighted him while it lasted; though he exerted himself too much, and the effect was considerable lassitude and weakness on his return. During the expedition he conceived the idea, and wrote, in the three days immediately succeeding to his return, the *Witch of Atlas*. This poem is peculiarly characteristic of his tastes—wildly fanciful, full of brilliant imagery, and discarding human interest and passion, to revel in ʹʿe fantastic ideas that his imagination suggested.

The surpassing excellence of *The Cenci* had made me greatly desire that Shelley should increase his popularity by adopting subjects that would more suit the popular taste than a poem conceived in the abstract and dreamy spirit of the *Witch of Atlas*. It was not only that I wished him to acquire popularity as redounding to his fame; but I believed that he would obtain a greater mastery over his own powers, and greater happiness in his mind, if public applause crowned his endeavours. The few stanzas that precede the poem were addressed to me on my representing these ideas to him. Even now I believe that I was in the right. Shelley did not expect sympathy and approbation from the public; but the want of it took away a portion of the ardour that ought to have sustained him while writing. He was thrown on his own resources, and on the inspiration of his own soul; and wrote because his mind overflowed, without the hope of being appreciated. I had not the most distant wish that he should truckle in opinion, or submit his lofty aspirations for the human race to the low ambition and pride of the many; but I felt sure that, if his poems were more addressed to the common feelings of men, his proper rank among the writers of the day would be acknowledged, and that popularity as a poet would enable his countrymen to do justice to his character and virtues, which in those days it was the mode to attack with the most flagitious calumnies and insulting abuse. That he felt these things deeply cannot be doubted, though he armed himself with the consciousness of acting from a lofty and heroic sense of right. The truth burst from his heart sometimes in solitude, and he would write a few unfinished verses that showed that he felt the sting; among such I find the following:—

'Alas! this is not what I thought Life was.
    I knew that there were crimes and evil men,
Misery and hate; nor did I hope to pass
    Untouched by suffering through the ruggèd glen.
In mine own heart I saw as in a glass
    The hearts of others.... And, when
I went among my kind, with triple brass
    Of calm endurance my weak breast I armed,
To bear scorn, fear, and hate—a woful mass!'

I believed that all this morbid feeling would vanish if the chord of sympathy between him and his countrymen were touched. But my persuasions were vain, the mind could not be bent from its natural inclination. Shelley shrunk instinctively from portraying human passion, with its mixture of good and evil, of disappointment and disquiet. Such opened again the wounds of his own heart; and he loved to shelter himself rather in the airiest flights of fancy, forgetting love and hate, and regret and lost hope, in such imaginations as borrow their hues from sunrise or sunset, from the yellow moonshine or paly twilight, from the aspect of the far ocean or the shadows of the woods,—which celebrated the singing of the winds among the pines, the flow of a murmuring stream, and the thousand harmonious sounds which Nature creates in her solitudes. These are the materials which form the *Witch of Atlas:* it is a brilliant congregation of ideas such as his senses gathered, and his fancy coloured, during his rambles in the sunny land he so much loved.

EPIPSYCHIDION

VERSES ADDRESSED TO THE NOBLE AND UNFORTUNATE LADY, EMILIA V———,

NOW IMPRISONED IN THE CONVENT OF ——

L' anima amante si slancia fuori del creato, e si crea nell' infinito un Mondo tutto per essa, diverso assai da questo oscuro e pauroso baratro. HER OWN WORDS

ADVERTISEMENT

THE Writer of the following lines died at Florence, as he was preparing for a voyage to one of the wildest of the Sporades, which he had bought, and where he had fitted up the ruins of an old building, and where it was his hope to have realised a scheme of life, suited perhaps to that happier and better world of which he is now an inhabitant, but hardly practicable in this. His life was singular; less on account of the romantic vicissitudes which diversified it, than the ideal tinge which it received from his own character and feelings. The present Poem, like the *Vita Nuova* of Dante, is sufficiently intelligible to a certain class of readers without a matter-of-fact history of the circumstances to which it relates; and to a certain other class it must ever remain incomprehensible, from a defect of a common organ of perception for the ideas of which it treats. Not but that *gran vergogna sarebbe a colui, che rimasse cosa sotto veste di figura, o di colore rettorico: e domandato non sapesse denudare le sue parole da cotal veste, in guisa che avessero verace intendimento.*

The present poem appears to have been intended by the Writer as the dedication to some longer one. The stanza on the opposite page is almost a literal translation from Dante's famous Canzone

Voi, ch' intendendo, il terzo ciel movete, etc.

The presumptuous application of the concluding lines to his own composition will raise a smile at the expense of my unfortunate friend: be it a smile not of contempt, but pity. S.

My Song, I fear that thou wilt find but few
Who fitly shall conceive thy reasoning,
Of such hard matter dost thou entertain;
Whence, if by misadventure, chance should bring
Thee to base company (as chance may do), 5
Quite unaware of what thou dost contain,
I prithee, comfort thy sweet self again,
My last delight! tell them that they are dull,
And bid them own that thou art beautiful.

EPIPSYCHIDION

SWEET Spirit! Sister of that orphan one,
Whose empire is the name thou weepest on,
In my heart's temple I suspend to thee
These votive wreaths of withered memory.

Poor captive bird! who, from thy narrow cage, 5
Pourest such music, that it might assuage
The ruggèd hearts of those who prisoned thee,
Were they not deaf to all sweet melody;
This song shall be thy rose: its petals pale
Are dead, indeed, my adored Nightingale! 10
But soft and fragrant is the faded blossom,
And it has no thorn left to wound thy bosom.

High, spirit-wingèd Heart! who dost for ever
Beat thine unfeeling bars with vain endeavour,
Till those bright plumes of thought, in which arrayed 15
It over-soared this low and worldly shade,
Lie shattered; and thy panting, wounded breast
Stains with dear blood its unmaternal nest!
I weep vain tears: blood would less bitter be,
Yet poured forth gladlier, could it profit thee. 20

Seraph of Heaven! too gentle to be human,
Veiling beneath that radiant form of Woman
All that is insupportable in thee
Of light, and love, and immortality!
Sweet Benediction in the eternal Curse!   25
Veilèd Glory of this lampless Universe!
Thou Moon beyond the clouds! Thou living Form
Among the Dead! Thou Star above the Storm!
Thou Wonder, and thou Beauty, and thou Terror!
Thou Harmony of Nature's art! Thou Mirror   30
In whom, as in the splendour of the Sun,
All shapes look glorious which thou gazest on!
Ay, even the dim words which obscure thee now
Flash, lightning-like, with unaccustomed glow;
I pray thee that thou blot from this sad song   35
All of its much mortality and wrong,
With those clear drops, which start like sacred dew
From the twin lights thy sweet soul darkens through,
Weeping, till sorrow becomes ecstasy:
Then smile on it, so that it may not die.   40

I never thought before my death to see
Youth's vision thus made perfect. Emily,
I love thee; though the world by no thin name
Will hide that love from its unvalued shame.
Would we two had been twins of the same mother!   45
Or, that the name my heart lent to another
Could be a sister's bond for her and thee,
Blending two beams of one eternity!
Yet were one lawful and the other true,
These names, though dear, could paint not, as is due,   50
How beyond refuge I am thine. Ah me!
I am not thine: I am a part of *thee*.

Sweet Lamp! my moth-like Muse has burned its wings
Or, like a dying swan who soars and sings,
Young Love should teach Time, in his own gray style,   55
All that thou art. Art thou not void of guile,
A lovely soul formed to be blessed and bless?
A well of sealed and secret happiness,
Whose waters like blithe light and music are,
Vanquishing dissonance and gloom? A Star   60
Which moves not in the moving heavens, alone?
A Smile amid dark frowns? a gentle tone
Amid rude voices? a belovèd light?
A Solitude, a Refuge, a Delight?
A Lute, which those whom Love has taught to play   65
Make music on, to soothe the roughest day

And lull fond Grief asleep? a buried treasure?
A cradle of young thoughts of wingless pleasure?
A violet-shrouded grave of Woe?—I measure
The world of fancies, seeking one like thee,   70
And find—alas! mine own infirmity.

She met me, Stranger, upon life's rough way,
And lured me towards sweet Death; as Night by Day,
Winter by Spring, or Sorrow by swift Hope,
Led into light, life, peace. An antelope,   75
In the suspended impulse of its lightness,
Were less aethereally light: the brightness
Of her divinest presence trembles through
Her limbs, as underneath a cloud of dew
Embodied in the windless heaven of June   80
Amid the splendour-winged stars, the Moon
Burns, inextinguishably beautiful:
And from her lips, as from a hyacinth full
Of honey-dew, a liquid murmur drops,
Killing the sense with passion; sweet as stops   85
Of planetary music heard in trance.
In her mild lights the starry spirits dance,
The sunbeams of those wells which ever leap
Under the lightnings of the soul—too deep
For the brief fathom-line of thought or sense.   90
The glory of her being, issuing thence,
Stains the dead, blank, cold air with a warm shade
Of unentangled intermixture, made
By Love, of light and motion: one intense
Diffusion, one serene Omnipresence,   95
Whose flowing outlines mingle in their flowing,
Around her cheeks and utmost fingers glowing
With the unintermitted blood, which there
Quivers, (as in a fleece of snow-like air
The crimson pulse of living morning quiver,)   100
Continuously prolonged, and ending never,
Till they are lost, and in that Beauty furled
Which penetrates and clasps and fills the world;
Scarce visible from extreme loveliness.
Warm fragrance seems to fall from her light dress   105
And her loose hair; and where some heavy tress
The air of her own speed has disentwined,
The sweetness seems to satiate the faint wind;
And in the soul a wild odour is felt,
Beyond the sense, like fiery dews that melt   110
Into the bosom of a frozen bud.—
See where she stands! a mortal shape indued

With love and life and light and deity,
And motion which may change but cannot die;
An image of some bright Eternity;   115
A shadow of some golden dream; a Splendour
Leaving the third sphere pilotless; a tender
Reflection of the eternal Moon of Love
Under whose motions life's dull billows move;
A Metaphor of Spring and Youth and Morning;   120
A Vision like incarnate April, warning,
With smiles and tears, Frost the Anatomy
Into his summer grave.
                 Ah, woe is me!
What have I dared? where am I lifted? how
Shall I descend, and perish not? I know   125
That Love makes all things equal: I have heard
By mine own heart this joyous truth averred:
The spirit of the worm beneath the sod
In love and worship, blends itself with God.

   Spouse! Sister! Angel! Pilot of the Fate
Whose course has been so starless! O too late
Belovèd! O too soon adored, by me!
For in the fields of Immortality
My spirit should at first have worshipped thine,
A divine presence in a place divine;   135
Or should have moved beside it on this earth,
A shadow of that substance, from its birth;
But not as now:—I love thee; yes, I feel
That on the fountain of my heart a seal
Is set, to keep its waters pure and bright   140
For thee, since in those *tears* thou hast delight.
We—are we not formed, as notes of music are,
For one another, though dissimilar;
Such difference without discord, as can make
Those sweetest sounds, in which all spirits shake   145
As trembling leaves in a continuous air?

   Thy wisdom speaks in me, and bids me dare
Beacon the rocks on which high hearts are wrecked.
I never was attached to that great sect,
Whose doctrine is, that each one should select   150
Out of the crowd a mistress or a friend,
And all the rest, though fair and wise, commend
To cold oblivion, though it is in the code
Of modern morals, and the beaten road
Which those poor slaves with weary footsteps tread,   155
Who travel to their home among the dead

By the broad highway of the world, and so
With one chained friend, perhaps a jealous foe,
The dreariest and the longest journey go.

True Love in this differs from gold and clay,   160
That to divide is not to take away.
Love is like understanding, that grows bright,
Gazing on many truths; 'tis like thy light,
Imagination! which from earth and sky,
And from the depths of human fantasy,   165
As from a thousand prisms and mirrors, fills
The Universe with glorious beams, and kills
Error, the worm, with many a sun-like arrow
Of its reverberated lightning. Narrow
The heart that loves, the brain that contemplates,   170
The life that wears, the spirit that creates
One object, and one form, and builds thereby
A sepulchre for its eternity.

Mind from its object differs most in this:
Evil from good; misery from happiness;   175
The baser from the nobler; the impure
And frail, from what is clear and must endure.
If you divide suffering and dross, you may
Diminish till it is consumed away;
If you divide pleasure and love and thought,   180
Each part exceeds the whole; and we know not
How much, while any yet remains unshared,
Of pleasure may be gained, of sorrow spared:
This truth is that deep well, whence sages draw
The unenvied light of hope; the eternal law   185
By which those live, to whom this world of life
Is as a garden ravaged, and whose strife
Tills for the promise of a later birth
The wilderness of this Elysian earth.

There was a Being whom my spirit oft   190
Met on its visioned wanderings, far aloft,
In the clear golden prime of my youth's dawn,
Upon the fairy isles of sunny lawn,
Amid the enchanted mountains, and the caves
Of divine sleep, and on the air-like waves   195
Of wonder-level dream, whose tremulous floor
Paved her light steps;—on an imagined shore,
Under the gray beak of some promontory
She met me, robed in such exceeding glory,
That I beheld her not. In solitudes   200
Her voice came to me through the whispering woods,

And from the fountains, and the odours deep
Of flowers, which, like lips murmuring in their sleep
Of the sweet kisses which had lulled them there,
Breathed but of *her* to the enamoured air;   205
And from the breezes whether low or loud,
And from the rain of every passing cloud,
And from the singing of the summer-birds,
And from all sounds, all silence. In the words
Of antique verse and high romance,—in form,   210
Sound, colour—in whatever checks that Storm
Which with the shattered present chokes the past;
And in that best philosophy, whose taste
Makes this cold common hell, our life, a doom
As glorious as a fiery martyrdom;   215
Her Spirit was the harmony of truth.—

   Then, from the caverns of my dreamy youth
I sprang, as one sandalled with plumes of fire,
And towards the lodestar of my one desire,
I flitted, like a dizzy moth, whose flight   220
Is as a dead leaf's in the owlet light,
When it would seek in Hesper's setting sphere
A radiant death, a fiery sepulchre,
As if it were a lamp of earthly flame.—
But She, whom prayers or tears then could not tame,   225
Passed, like a God throned on a wingèd planet,
Whose burning plumes to tenfold swiftness fan it,
Into the dreary cone of our life's shade;
And as a man with mighty loss dismayed,
I would have followed, though the grave between   230
Yawned like a gulf whose spectres are unseen:
When a voice said:—'O thou of hearts the weakest,
The phantom is beside thee whom thou seekest.'
Then I—'Where?'—the world's echo answered 'where?'
And in that silence, and in my despair,   235
I questioned every tongueless wind that flew
Over my tower of mourning, if it knew
Whither 'twas fled, this soul out of my soul;
And murmured names and spells which have control
Over the sightless tyrants of our fate;   240
But neither prayer nor verse could dissipate
The night which closed on her; nor uncreate
That world within this Chaos, mine and me,
Of which she was the veiled Divinity,
The world I say of thoughts that worshipped her: 245
And therefore I went forth, with hope and fear

And every gentle passion sick to death,
Feeding my course with expectation's breath,
Into the wintry forest of our life;
And struggling through its error with vain strife,   250
And stumbling in my weakness and my haste,
And half bewildered by new forms, I passed,
Seeking among those untaught foresters
If I could find one form resembling hers,
In which she might have masked herself from me.   255
There,—One, whose voice was venomed melody
Sate by a well, under blue nightshade bowers;
The breath of her false mouth was like faint flowers,
Her touch was as electric poison,—flame
Out of her looks into my vitals came,   260
And from her living cheeks and bosom flew
A killing air, which pierced like honey-dew
Into the core of my green heart, and lay
Upon its leaves; until, as hair grown gray
O'er a young brow, they hid its unblown prime   265
With ruins of unseasonable time.

    In many mortal forms I rashly sought
The shadow of that idol of my thought.
And some were fair—but beauty dies away:
Others were wise—but honeyed words betray: 270
And One was true—oh! why not true to me?
Then, as hunted deer that could not flee,
I turned upon my thoughts, and stood at bay,
Wounded and weak and panting; the cold day
Trembled, for pity of my strife and pain.   275
When, like a noonday dawn, there shone again
Deliverance. One stood on my path who seemed
As like the glorious shape which I had dreamed
As is the Moon, whose changes ever run
Into themselves, to the eternal Sun;   280
The cold chaste Moon, the Queen of Heaven's bright isles,
Who makes all beautiful on which she smiles,
That wandering shrine of soft yet icy flame
Which ever is transformed, yet still the same,
And warms not but illumines. Young and fair   285
As the descended Spirit of that sphere,
She hid me, as the Moon may hide the night
From its own darkness, until all was bright
Between the Heaven and Earth of my calm mind,
And, as a cloud charioted by the wind,   290
She led me to a cave in that wild place,
And sate beside me, with her downward face

Illumining my slumbers, like the Moon
Waxing and waning o'er Endymion.
And I was laid asleep, spirit and limb,   295
And all my being became bright or dim
As the Moon's image in a summer sea,
According as she smiled or frowned on me;
And there I lay, within a chaste cold bed:
Alas, I then was nor alive nor dead:—   300
For at her silver voice came Death and Life,
Unmindful each of their accustomed strife,
Masked like twin babes, a sister and a brother,
The wandering hopes of one abandoned mother,
And through the cavern without wings they flew,   305
And cried 'Away, he is not of our crew.'
I wept, and though it be a dream, I weep.

What storms then shook the ocean of my sleep,
Blotting that Moon, whose pale and waning lips
Then shrank as in the sickness of eclipse;—   310
And how my soul was as a lampless sea,
And who was then its Tempest; and when She,
The Planet of that hour, was quenched, what frost
Crept o'er those waters, till from coast to coast
The moving billows of my being fell   315
Into a death of ice, immovable;—
And then—what earthquakes made it gape and split,
The white Moon smiling all the while on it,
These words conceal:—If not, each word would be
The key of staunchless tears. Weep not for me!   320

At length, into the obscure Forest came
The Vision I had sought through grief and shame.
Athwart that wintry wilderness of thorns
Flashed from her motion splendour like the Morn's,
And from her presence life was radiated   325
Through the gray earth and branches bare and dead;
So that her way was paved, and roofed above
With flowers as soft as thoughts of budding love;
And music from her respiration spread
Like light,—all other sounds were penetrated   330
By the small, still, sweet spirit of that sound,
So that the savage winds hung mute around;
And odours warm and fresh fell from her hair
Dissolving the dull cold in the frore air:
Soft as an Incarnation of the Sun,   335
When light is changed to love, this glorious One
Floated into the cavern where I lay,
And called my Spirit, and the dreaming clay

Was lifted by the thing that dreamed below
As smoke by fire, and in her beauty's glow   340
I stood, and felt the dawn of my long night
Was penetrating me with living light:
I knew it was the Vision veiled from me
So many years—that it was Emily.

    Twin Spheres of light who rule this passive **Earth,**   345
This world of love, this *me;* and into birth
Awaken all its fruits and flowers, and dart
Magnetic might into its central heart;
And lift its billows and its mists, and guide
By everlasting laws, each wind and tide   350
To its fit cloud, and its appointed cave;
And lull its storms, each in the craggy grave
Which was its cradle, luring to faint bowers
The armies of the rainbow-wingèd showers;
And, as those marrièd lights, which from the towers   355
Of Heaven look forth and fold the wandering globe
In liquid sleep and splendour, as a robe;
And all their many-mingled influence blend,
If equal, yet unlike, to one sweet end;—
So ye, bright regents, with alternate sway   360
Govern my sphere of being, night and day!
Thou, not disdaining even a borrowed might;
Thou, not eclipsing a remoter light;
And, through the shadow of the seasons three,
From Spring to Autumn's sere maturity,   365
Light it into the Winter of the tomb,
Where it may ripen to a brighter bloom.
Thou too, O Comet beautiful and fierce,
Who drew the heart of this frail Universe
Towards thine own; till, wrecked in that convulsion,   370
Alternating attraction and repulsion,
Thine went astray and that was rent in twain;
Oh, float into our azure heaven again!
Be there Love's folding-star at thy return;
The living Sun will feed thee from its urn   375
Of golden fire; the Moon will veil her horn
In thy last smiles; adoring Even and Morn
Will worship thee with incense of calm breath
And lights and shadows; as the star of Death
And Birth is worshipped by those sisters wild   380
Called Hope and Fear—upon the heart are piled
Their offerings,—of this sacrifice divine
A World shall be the altar.
                                        Lady mine,

Scorn not these flowers of thought, the fading birth
Which from its heart of hearts that plant puts forth   385
Whose fruit, made perfect by thy sunny eyes,
Will be as of the trees of Paradise.

The day is come, and thou wilt fly with me.
To whatsoe'er of dull mortality
Is mine, remain a vestal sister still;   390
To the intense, the deep, the imperishable,
Not mine but me, henceforth be thou united
Even as a bride, delighting and delighted.
The hour is come:—the destined Star has risen
Which shall descend upon a vacant prison.   395
The walls are high, the gates are strong, thick set
The sentinels—but true Love never yet
Was thus constrained: it overleaps all fence:
Like lightning, with invisible violence
Piercing its continents; like Heaven's free breath,   400
Which he who grasps can hold not; liker Death,
Who rides upon a thought, and makes his way
Through temple, tower, and palace, and the array
Of arms: more strength has Love than he or they;
For it can burst his charnel, and make free   405
The limbs in chains, the heart in agony,
The soul in dust and chaos.
                        Emily,
A ship is floating in the harbour now,
A wind is hovering o'er the mountain's brow;
There is a path on the sea's azure floor,   410
No keel has ever ploughed that path before;
The halcyons brood around the foamless isles;
The treacherous Ocean has forsworn its wiles;
The merry mariners are bold and free:
Say, my heart's sister, wilt thou sail with me?   415
Our bark is as an albatross, whose nest
Is a far Eden of the purple East;
And we between her wings will sit, while Night,
And Day, and Storm, and Calm, pursue their flight,
Our ministers, along the boundless Sea,   420
Treading each other's heels, unheededly.
It is an isle under Ionian skies,
Beautiful as a wreck of Paradise,
And, for the harbours are not safe and good,
This land would have remained a solitude   425
But for some pastoral people native there,
Who from the Elysian, clear, and golden air

Draw the last spirit of the age of gold,
Simple and spirited; innocent and bold.
The blue Aegean girds this chosen home, 430
With ever-changing sound and light and foam,
Kissing the sifted sands, and caverns hoar;
And all the winds wandering along the shore
Undulate with the undulating tide:
There are thick woods where sylvan forms abide; 435
And many a fountain, rivulet, and pond,
As clear as elemental diamond,
Or serene morning air; and far beyond,
The mossy tracks made by the goats and deer
(Which the rough shepherd treads but once a year) 440
Pierce into glades, caverns, and bowers, and halls
Built round with ivy, which the waterfalls
Illumining, with sound that never fails
Accompany the noonday nightingales;
And all the place is peopled with sweet airs; 445
The light clear element which the isle wears
Is heavy with the scent of lemon-flowers,
Which floats like mist laden with unseen showers,
And falls upon the eyelids like faint sleep;
And from the moss violets and jonquils peep, 450
And dart their arrowy odour through the brain
Till you might faint with that delicious pain.
And every motion, odour, beam, and tone,
With that deep music is in unison:
Which is a soul within the soul—they seem 455
Like echoes of an antenatal dream.—
It is an isle 'twixt Heaven, Air, Earth, and Sea,
Cradled, and hung in clear tranquillity;
Bright as that wandering Eden Lucifer,
Washed by the soft blue Oceans of young air. 460
It is a favoured place. Famine or Blight,
Pestilence, War and Earthquake, never light
Upon its mountain-peaks; blind vultures, they
Sail onward far upon their fatal way:
The wingèd storms, chanting their thunder-psalm 465
To other lands, leave azure chasms of calm
Over this isle, or weep themselves in dew,
From which its fields and woods ever renew
Their green and golden immortality.
And from the sea there rise, and from the sky 470
There fall, clear exhalations, soft and bright,
Veil after veil, each hiding some delight,
Which Sun or Moon or zephyr draw aside,
Till the isle's beauty, like a naked bride

Glowing at once with love and loveliness,
Blushes and trembles at its own excess:
Yet, like a buried lamp, a Soul no less
Burns in the heart of this delicious isle,
An atom of th' Eternal, whose own smile
Unfolds itself, and may be felt, not seen   480
O'er the gray rocks, blue waves, and forests green,
Filling their bare and void interstices.—
But the chief marvel of the wilderness
Is a lone dwelling, built by whom or how
None of the rustic island-people know: 485
'Tis not a tower of strength, though with its height
It overtops the woods; but, for delight,
Some wise and tender Ocean-King, ere crime
Had been invented, in the world's young prime,
Reared it, a wonder of that simple time,   490
An envy of the isles, a pleasure-house
Made sacred to his sister and his spouse.
It scarce seems now a wreck of human art,
But, as it were Titanic; in the heart
Of Earth having assumed its form, then grown   495
Out of the mountains, from the living stone,
Lifting itself in caverns light and high:
For all the antique and learnèd imagery
Has been erased, and in the place of it
The ivy and the wild-vine interknit   500
The volumes of their many-twining stems;
Parasite flowers illume with dewy gems
The lampless halls, and when they fade, the sky
Peeps through their winter-woof of tracery
With moonlight patches, or star atoms keen,   505
Or fragments of the day's intense serene;—
Working mosaic on their Parian floors.
And, day and night, aloof, from the high towers
And terraces, the Earth and Ocean seem
To sleep in one another's arms, and dream   510
Of waves, flowers, clouds, woods, rocks, and all that we
Read in their smiles, and call reality.

This isle and house are mine, and I have vowed
Thee to be lady of the solitude.—
And I have fitted up some chambers there   515
Looking towards the golden Eastern air,
And level with the living winds, which flow
Like waves above the living waves below.—
I have sent books and music there, and all
Those instruments with which high Spirits call   520

The future from its cradle, and the past
Out of its grave, and make the present last
In thoughts and joys which sleep, but cannot die,
Folded within their own eternity.
Our simple life wants little, and true taste   525
Hires not the pale drudge Luxury, to waste
The scene it would adorn, and therefore still,
Nature with all her children haunts the hill.
The ring-dove, in the embowering ivy, yet
Keeps up her love-lament, and the owls flit   530
Round the evening tower, and the young stars glance
Between the quick bats in their twilight dance;
The spotted deer bask in the fresh moonlight
Before our gate, and the slow, silent night
Is measured by the pants of their calm sleep.   535
Be this our home in Life, and when years heap
Their withered hours, like leaves, on our decay,
Let us become the overhanging day,
The living soul of this Elysian isle,
Conscious, inseparable, one. Meanwhile   540
We two will rise, and sit, and walk together,
Under the roof of blue Ionian weather,
And wander in the meadows, or ascend
The mossy mountains, where the blue heavens bend
With lightest winds, to touch their paramour;   545
Or linger, where the pebble-paven shore,
Under the quick, faint kisses of the sea
Trembles and sparkles as with ecstasy,—
Possessing and possessed by all that is
Within that calm circumference of bliss,   550
And by each other, till to love and live
Be one:—or, at the noontide hour, arrive
Where some old cavern hoar seems yet to keep
The moonlight of the expired night asleep,
Through which the awakened day can never peep;   555
A veil for our seclusion, close as night's,
Where secure sleep may kill thine innocent lights;
Sleep, the fresh dew of languid love, the rain
Whose drops quench kisses till they burn again.
And we will talk, until thought's melody   560
Become too sweet for utterance, and it die
In words, to live again in looks, which dart
With thrilling tone into the voiceless heart,
Harmonizing silence without a sound.
Our breath shall intermix, our bosoms bound,   565
And our veins beat together; and our lips
With other eloquence than words, eclipse

The soul that burns between them, and the wells
Which boil under our being's inmost cells,
The fountains of our deepest life, shall be   570
Confused in Passion's golden purity,
As mountain-springs under the morning sun.
We shall become the same, we shall be one
Spirit within two frames, oh! wherefore two?
One passion in twin-hearts, which grows and grew,   575
Till like two meteors of expanding flame,
Those spheres instinct with it become the same,
Touch, mingle, are transfigured; ever still
Burning, yet ever inconsumable:
In one another's substance finding food,   580
Like flames too pure and light and unimbued
To nourish their bright lives with baser prey,
Which point to Heaven and cannot pass away:
One hope within two wills, one will beneath
Two overshadowing minds, one life, one death,   585
One Heaven, one Hell, one immortality,
And one annihilation. Woe is me!
The wingèd words on which my soul would pierce
Into the height of Love's rare Universe,
Are chains of lead around its flight of fire—   590
I pant, I sink, I tremble, I expire!

Weak Verses, go, kneel at your Sovereign's feet,
And say:—'We are the masters of thy slave;
What wouldest thou with us and ours and thine?'
Then call your sisters from Oblivion's cave,   595
All singing loud: 'Love's very pain is sweet,
But its reward is in the world divine
Which, if not here, it builds beyond the grave.'
So shall ye live when I am there. Then haste
Over the hearts of men, until ye meet   600
Marina, Vanna, Primus, and the rest,
And bid them love each other and be blessed:
And leave the troop which errs, and which reproves,
And come and be my guest,—for I am Love's.

FRAGMENTS CONNECTED WITH EPIPSYCHIDION

THREE EARLY DRAFTS OF THE PREFACE
(ADVERTISEMENT)

PREFACE I

THE following Poem was found amongst other papers in the Portfolio
of a young Englishman with whom the Editor had contracted an intimacy
at Florence, brief indeed, but sufficiently long to render the Catastrophe

by which it terminated one of the most painful events of his life.

The literary merit of the Poem in question may not be considerable; but worse verses are printed every day, &

He was an accomplished & amiable person but his error was, θνητός ὢν μὴ θνητα φρονειν,—his fate is an additional proof that 'The tree of Knowledge is not that of Life.'—He had framed to himself certain opinions, founded no doubt upon the truth of things, but built up to a Babel height; they fell by their own weight, & the thoughts that were his architects, became unintelligible one to the other, as men upon whom confusion of tongues has fallen.

[These] verses seem to have been written as a sort of dedication of some work to have been presented to the person whom they address: but his papers afford no trace of such a work—The circumstances to which [they] the poem allude, may easily be understood by those to whom [the] spirit of the poem itself is [un]intelligible: a detail of facts, sufficiently romantic in [themselves but] their combinations

The melancholy [task] charge of consigning the body of my poor friend to the grave, was committed to me by his desolated family. I caused him to be buried in a spot selected by himself.

PREFACE II

[Epips]   T. E. V. Epipsych
        Lines addressed to
        the Noble Lady
        [Emilia] [E. V.]
            Emilia

[The following Poem was found in the PF. of a young Englishman, who died on his passage from Leghorn to the Levant. He had bought one of the Sporades] He was accompanied by a lady [who might have been] supposed to be his wife, & an effeminate looking youth, to whom he shewed an [attachment] so [singular] excessive an attachment as to give rise to the suspicion, that she was a woman—at his death this suspicion was confirmed;   object speedily found a refuge both from the taunts of the brute multitude, and from the   of her grief in the same grave that contained her lover.—He had bought one of the Sporades, & fitted up a Saracenic castle which accident had preserved in some repair with simple elegance, & it was his intention to dedicate the remainder of his life to undisturbed intercourse with his companions

These verses apparently were intended as a dedication of a longer poem or series of poems

PREFACE III

The writer of these lines died at Florence in [January 1820] while he was preparing * * for one wildest of the of the Sporades, where he bought & fitted up the ruins of some old building—His life was singular, less on account of the romantic vicissitudes which diversified it, than the ideal tinge which they received from his own character & feelings—

The verses were apparently intended by the writer to accompany some longer poem or collection of poems, of which there* [are no remnants in his] * * * remains [in his] portfolio.—

The editor is induced to

The present poem, like the vita Nova of Dante, is sufficiently intelligible to a certain class of readers without a matter of fact history of the circumstances to which it relate, & to a certain other class, it must & ought ever to remain incomprehensible—It was evidently intended to be prefixed to a longer poem or series of poems—but among his papers there are no traces of such a collection.

PASSAGES OF THE POEM, OR CONNECTED THEREWITH

HERE, my dear friend, is a new book for you;
I have already dedicated two
To other friends, one female and one male,—
What you are, is a thing that I must veil;
What can this be to those who praise or rail?   5
I never was attached to that great sect
Whose doctrine is that each one should select
Out of the world a mistress or a friend,
And all the rest, though fair and wise, commend
To cold oblivion—though 'tis in the code   10
Of modern morals, and the beaten road
Which those poor slaves with weary footsteps tread
Who travel to their home among the dead
By the broad highway of the world—and so
With one sad friend, and many a jealous foe,   15
The dreariest and the longest journey go.

Free love has this, different from gold and clay,
That to divide is not to take away.
Like ocean, which the general north wind breaks
Into ten thousand waves, and each one makes   20
A mirror of the moon—like some great glass,
Which did distort whatever form might pass,
Dashed into fragments by a playful child,
Which then reflects its eyes and forehead mild;
Giving for one, which it could ne'er express,   25
A thousand images of loveliness.

If I were one whom the loud world held wise,
I should disdain to quote authorities
In commendation of this kind of love:—
Why there is first the God in heaven above,   30
Who wrote a book called Nature, 'tis to be
Reviewed, I hear, in the next Quarterly;

And Socrates, the Jesus Christ of Greece,
And Jesus Christ Himself, did never cease
To urge all living things to love each other,   35
And to forgive their mutual faults, and smother
The Devil of disunion in their souls.

.   .   .   .

I love you!—Listen, O embodied Ray
Of the great Brightness; I must pass away
While you remain, and these light words must be   40
Tokens by which you may remember me.
Start not—the thing you are is unbetrayed,
If you are human, and if but the shade
Of some sublimer spirit . . . .

.   .   .   .

And as to friend or mistress, 'tis a form;   45
Perhaps I wish you were one. Some declare
You a familiar spirit, as you are;
Others with a   more inhuman
Hint that, though not my wife, you are a woman;
What is the colour of your eyes and hair?   50
Why, if you were a lady, it were fair
The world should know—but, as I am afraid,
The Quarterly would bait you if betrayed;
And if, as it will be sport to see them stumble
Over all sorts of scandals, hear them mumble   55
Their litany of curses—some guess right,
And others swear you're a Hermaphrodite;
Like that sweet marble monster of both sexes,
Which looks so sweet and gentle that it vexes
The very soul that the soul is gone   60
Which lifted from her limbs the veil of stone.

.   .   .   .

It is a sweet thing, friendship, a dear balm,
A happy and auspicious bird of calm,
Which rides o'er life's ever tumultuous Ocean;
A God that broods o'er chaos in commotion;   65
A flower which fresh as Lapland roses are,
Lifts its bold head into the world's frore air,
And blooms most radiantly when others die,
Health, hope, and youth, and brief prosperity;
And with the light and odour of its bloom,   70
Shining within the dungeon and the tomb;

Whose coming is as light and music are
'Mid dissonance and gloom—a star
Which moves not 'mid the moving heavens alone—
A smile among dark frowns—a gentle tone   75
Among rude voices, a belovèd light,
A solitude, a refuge, a delight.
If I had but a friend! Why, I have three
Even by my own confession; there may be
Some more, for what I know, for 'tis my mind   80
To call my friends all who are wise and kind,—
And these, Heaven knows, at best are very few;
But none can ever be more dear than you.
Why should they be? My muse has lost her wings,
Or like a dying swan who soars and sings,   85
I should describe you in heroic style,
But as it is, are you not void of guile?
A lovely soul, formed to be blessed and bless:
A well of sealed and secret happiness;
A lute which those whom Love has taught to play   90
Make music on to cheer the roughest day,
And enchant sadness till it sleeps? . . . .

   .   .   .   .   .   .

To the oblivion whither I and thou,
All loving and all lovely, hasten now
With steps, ah, too unequal! may we meet   95
In one Elysium or one winding-sheet!

    If any should be curious to discover
Whether to you I am a friend or lover,
Let them read Shakespeare's sonnets, taking thence
A whetstone for their dull intelligence   100
That tears and will not cut, or let them guess
How Diotima, the wise prophetess,
Instructed the instructor, and why he
Rebuked the infant spirit of melody
On Agathon's sweet lips, which as he spoke   105
Was as the lovely star when morn has broke
The roof of darkness, in the golden dawn,
Half-hidden, and yet beautiful.
                           I'll pawn
My hopes of Heaven—you know what they are worth—
That the presumptuous pedagogues of Earth,   110
If they could tell the riddle offered here
Would scorn to be, or being to appear
What now they seem and are—but let them chide,
They have few pleasures in the world beside;

Perhaps we should be dull were we not chidden,   115
Paradise fruits are sweetest when forbidden.
Folly can season Wisdom, Hatred Love.

     .   .   .   .

Farewell, if it can be to say farewell
To those who

     .   .   .   .

    I will not, as most dedicators do,   120
Assure myself and all the world and you,
That you are faultless—would to God they were
Who taunt me with your love! I then should wear
These heavy chains of life with a light spirit,
And would to God I were, or even as near it   125
As you, dear heart. Alas! what are we? Clouds
Driven by the wind in warring multitudes,
Which rain into the bosom of the earth,
And rise again, and in our death and birth,
And through our restless life, take as from heaven   130
Hues which are not our own, but which are given,
And then withdrawn, and with inconstant glance
Flash from the spirit to the countenance.
There is a Power, a Love, a Joy, a God
Which makes in mortal hearts its brief abode,   135
A Pythian exhalation, which inspires
Love, only love—a wind which o'er the wires
Of the soul's giant harp
There is a mood which language faints beneath;
You feel it striding, as Almighty Death   140
His bloodless steed . . . .

     .   .   .   .

And what is that most brief and bright delight
Which rushes through the touch and through the sight,
And stands before the spirit's inmost throne,
A naked Seraph? None hath ever known.   145
Its birth is darkness, and its growth desire;
Untameable and fleet and fierce as fire,
Not to be touched but to be felt alone,
It fills the world with glory—and is gone.

     .   .   .   .

It floats with rainbow pinions o'er the stream   150
Of life, which flows, like a   dream
Into the light of morning, to the grave
As to an ocean . . . .

What is that joy which serene infancy
Perceives not, as the hours content them by,   155
Each in a chain of blossoms, yet enjoys
The shapes of this new world, in giant toys
Wrought by the busy   ever new?
Remembrance borrows Fancy's glass, to show
These forms more   sincere   160
Than now they are, than then, perhaps, they were.
When everything familiar seemed to be
Wonderful, and the immortality
Of this great world, which all things must inherit,
Was felt as one with the awakening spirit,   165
Unconscious of itself, and of the strange
Distinctions which in its proceeding change
It feels and knows, and mourns as if each were
A desolation . . . .

.   .   .   .

Were it not a sweet refuge, Emily,   170
For all those exiles from the dull insane
Who vex this pleasant world with pride and pain,
For all that band of sister-spirits known
To one another by a voiceless tone?

.   .   .   .

If day should part us night will mend division   175
And if sleep parts us—we will meet in vision
And if life parts us—we will mix in death
Yielding our mite [?] of unreluctant breath
Death cannot part us—we must meet again
In all in nothing in delight in pain: 180
How, why or when or where—it matters not
So that we share an undivided lot. . . . .

.   .   .   .

And we will move possessing and possessed
Wherever beauty on the earth's bare [?] breast
Lies like the shadow of thy soul—till we   185
Become one being with the world we see. . . .

ADONAIS

AN ELEGY ON THE DEATH OF JOHN KEATS, AUTHOR OF ENDYMION, HYPERION, ETC.

'Αστὴρ πρὶν μὲν ἔλαμπες ἐνὶ ζωοῖσιν 'Εῷος·
νῦν δὲ θανὼν λάμπεις "Εσπερος ἐν φθιμένοις.—PLATO.

PREFACE

Φάρμακον ἦλθε, Βίων, ποτὶ σὸν στόμα, φάρμακον εἶδες.
πῶς τευ τοῖς χείλεσσι ποτέδραμε, κοὐκ ἐγλυκάνθη;
τίς δὲ βροτὸς τοσσοῦτον ἀνάμερος, ἢ κεράσαι τοι,
ἢ δοῦναι λαλέοντι τὸ φάρμακον; ἔκφυγεν ᾠδάν.
—MOSCHUS, EPITAPH. BION.

IT is my intention to subjoin to the London edition of this poem a criticism upon the claims of its lamented object to be classed among the writers of the highest genius who have adorned our age. My known repugnance to the narrow principles of taste on which several of his earlier compositions were modelled prove at least that I am an impartial judge. I consider the fragment of *Hyperion* as second to nothing that was ever produced by a writer of the same years.

John Keats died at Rome of a consumption, in his twenty-fourth year, on the —— of —— 1821; and was buried in the romantic and lonely cemetery of the Protestants in that city, under the pyramid which is the tomb of Cestius, and the massy walls and towers, now mouldering and desolate, which formed the circuit of ancient Rome. The cemetery is an open space among the ruins, covered in winter with violets and daisies. It might make one in love with death, to think that one should be buried in so sweet a place.

The genius of the lamented person to whose memory I have dedicated these unworthy verses was not less delicate and fragile than it was beautiful; and where cankerworms abound, what wonder if its young flower was blighted in the bud? The savage criticism on his *Endymion*, which appeared in the *Quarterly Review*, produced the most violent effect on his susceptible mind; the agitation thus originated ended in the rupture of a blood-vessel in the lungs; a rapid consumption ensued, and the succeeding acknowledgements from more candid critics of the true greatness of his powers were ineffectual to heal the wound thus wantonly inflicted.

It may be well said that these wretched men know not what they do. They scatter their insults and their slanders without heed as to whether the poisoned shaft lights on a heart made callous by many blows or one like Keats's composed of more penetrable stuff. One of their associates is, to my knowledge, a most base and unprincipled calumniator. As to

Endymion, was it a poem, whatever might be its defects, to be treated contemptuously by those who had celebrated, with various degrees of complacency and panegyric, *Paris,* and *Woman,* and a *Syrian Tale,* and Mrs. Lefanu, and Mr. Barrett, and Mr. Howard Payne, and a long list of the illustrious obscure? Are these the men who in their venal good nature presumed to draw a parallel between the Rev. Mr. Milman and Lord Byron? What gnat did they strain at here, after having swallowed all those camels? Against what woman taken in adultery dares the foremost of these literary prostitutes to cast his opprobrious stone? Miserable man! you, one of the meanest, have wantonly defaced one of the noblest speci-mens of the workmanship of God. Nor shall it be your excuse, that, murderer as you are, you have spoken daggers, but used none.

The circumstances of the closing scene of poor Keats's life were not made known to me until the *Elegy* was ready for the press. I am given to understand that the wound which his sensitive spirit had received from the criticism of *Endymion* was exasperated by the bitter sense of un-requited benefits; the poor fellow seems to have been hooted from the stage of life, no less by those on whom he had wasted the promise of his genius, than those on whom he had lavished his fortune and his care. He was accompanied to Rome, and attended in his last illness by Mr. Severn, a young artist of the highest promise, who, I have been informed, 'almost risked his own life, and sacrificed every prospect to unwearied at-tendance upon his dying friend.' Had I known these circumstances before the completion of my poem, I should have been tempted to add my feeble tribute of applause to the more solid recompense which the virtuous man finds in the recollection of his own motives. Mr. Severn can dispense with a reward from 'such stuff as dreams are made of.' His conduct is a golden augury of the success of his future career—may the unextinguished Spirit of his illustrious friend animate the creations of his pencil, and plead against Oblivion for his name!

I

I WEEP for Adonais—he is dead!
O, weep for Adonais! though our tears
Thaw not the frost which binds so dear a head!
And thou, sad Hour, selected from all years
To mourn our loss, rouse thy obscure compeers,   5
And teach them thine own sorrow, say: 'With me
Died Adonais; till the Future dares
Forget the Past, his fate and fame shall be
An echo and a light unto eternity!'

II

Where wert thou, mighty Mother, when he lay,   10
When thy Son lay, pierced by the shaft which flies
In darkness? where was lorn Urania
When Adonais died? With veilèd eyes,

'Mid listening Echoes, in her Paradise
She sate, while one, with soft enamoured breath, 15
Rekindled all the fading melodies,
With which, like flowers that mock the corse beneath,
He had adorned and hid the coming bulk of Death.

III

Oh, weep for Adonais—he is dead!
Wake, melancholy Mother, wake and weep! 20
Yet wherefore? Quench within their burning bed
Thy fiery tears, and let thy loud heart keep
Like his, a mute and uncomplaining sleep;
For he is gone, where all things wise and fair
Descend;—oh, dream not that the amorous Deep 25
Will yet restore him to the vital air;
Death feeds on his mute voice, and laughs at our despair.

IV

Most musical of mourners, weep again!
Lament anew, Urania!—He died,
Who was the Sire of an immortal strain, 30
Blind, old, and lonely, when his country's pride,
The priest, the slave, and the liberticide,
Trampled and mocked with many a loathèd rite
Of lust and blood; he went, unterrified,
Into the gulf of death; but his clear Sprite 35
Yet reigns o'er earth; the third among the sons of light.

V

Most musical of mourners, weep anew!
Not all to that bright station dared to climb;
And happier they their happiness who knew,
Whose tapers yet burn through that night of time 40
In which suns perished; others more sublime,
Struck by the envious wrath of man or god,
Have sunk, extinct in their refulgent prime;
And some yet live, treading the thorny road,
Which leads, through toil and hate, to Fame's serene abode. 45

VI

But now, thy youngest, dearest one, has perished—
The nursling of thy widowhood, who grew,
Like a pale flower by some sad maiden cherished,
And fed with true-love tears, instead of dew;
Most musical of mourners, weep anew! 50

Thy extreme hope, the loveliest and the last,
The bloom, whose petals nipped before they blew
Died on the promise of the fruit, is waste;
The broken lily lies—the storm is overpast.

VII

To that high Capital, where kingly Death   55
Keeps his pale court in beauty and decay,
He came; and bought, with price of purest breath,
A grave among the eternal.—Come away!
Haste, while the vault of blue Italian day
Is yet his fitting charnel-roof! while still   60
He lies, as if in dewy sleep he lay;
Awake him not! surely he takes his fill
Of deep and liquid rest, forgetful of all ill.

VIII

He will awake no more, oh, never more!—
Within the twilight chamber spreads apace   65
The shadow of white Death, and at the door
Invisible Corruption waits to trace
His extreme way to her dim dwelling-place;
The eternal Hunger sits, but pity and awe
Soothe her pale rage, nor dares she to deface   70
So fair a prey, till darkness, and the law
Of change, shall o'er his sleep the mortal curtain draw.

IX

Oh, weep for Adonais!—The quick Dreams,
The passion-wingèd Ministers of thought,
Who were his flocks, whom near the living streams   75
Of his young spirit he fed, and whom he taught
The love which was its music, wander not,—
Wander no more, from kindling brain to brain,
But droop there, whence they sprung; and mourn their lot
Round the cold heart, where, after their sweet pain,   80
They ne'er will gather strength, or find a home again.

X

And one with trembling hands clasps his cold head,
And fans him with her moonlight wings, and cries;
'Our love, our hope, our sorrow, is not dead;
See, on the silken fringe of his faint eyes,   85
Like dew upon a sleeping flower, there lies
A tear some Dream has loosened from his brain.'
Lost Angel of a ruined Paradise!

She knew not 'twas her own; as with no stain
She faded, like a cloud which had outwept its rain.   90

XI

One from a lucid urn of starry dew
Washed his light limbs as if embalming them;
Another clipped her profuse locks, and threw
The wreath upon him, like an anadem,
Which frozen tears instead of pearls begem;   95
Another in her wilful grief would break
Her bow and wingèd reeds, as if to stem
A greater loss with one which was more weak;
And dull the barbèd fire against his frozen cheek.

XII

Another Splendour on his mouth alit,   100
That mouth, whence it was wont to draw the breath
Which gave it strength to pierce the guarded wit,
And pass into the panting heart beneath
With lightning and with music: the damp death
Quenched its caress upon his icy lips;   105
And, as a dying meteor stains a wreath
Of moonlight vapour, which the cold night clips,
It flushed through his pale limbs, and passed to its eclipse.

XIII

And others came ... Desires and Adorations,
Wingèd Persuasions and veiled Destinies,   110
Splendours, and Glooms, and glimmering Incarnations
Of hopes and fears, and twilight Phantasies;
And Sorrow, with her family of Sighs,
And Pleasure, blind with tears, led by the gleam
Of her own dying smile instead of eyes,   115
Came in slow pomp;—the moving pomp might seem
Like pageantry of mist on an autumnal stream.

XIV

All he had loved, and moulded into thought,
From shape, and hue, and odour, and sweet sound,
Lamented Adonais. Morning sought   120
Her eastern watch-tower, and her hair unbound,
Wet with the tears which should adorn the ground,
Dimmed the aëreal eyes that kindle day;
Afar the melancholy thunder moaned,
Pale Ocean in unquiet slumber lay,   125
And the wild Winds flew round, sobbing in their dismay.

XV

Lost Echo sits amid the voiceless mountains,
And feeds her grief with his remembered lay,
And will no more reply to winds or fountains,
Or amorous birds perched on the young green spray,   130
Or herdsman's horn, or bell at closing day;
Since she can mimic not his lips, more dear
Than those for whose disdain she pined away
Into a shadow of all sounds:—a drear
Murmur, between their songs, is all the woodmen hear.   135

XVI

Grief made the young Spring wild, and she threw down
Her kindling buds, as if she Autumn were,
Or they dead leaves; since her delight is flown,
For whom should she have waked the sullen year?
To Phoebus was not Hyacinth so dear   140
Nor to himself Narcissus, as to both
Thou, Adonais: wan they stand and sere
Amid the faint companions of their youth,
With dew all turned to tears; odour, to sighing ruth.

XVII

Thy spirit's sister, the lorn nightingale   145
Mourns not her mate with such melodious pain;
Not so the eagle, who like thee could scale
Heaven, and could nourish in the sun's domain
Her mighty youth with mourning, doth complain,
Soaring and screaming round her empty nest,   150
As Albion wails for thee: the curse of Cain
Light on his head who pierced thy innocent breast,
And scared the angel soul that was its earthly guest!

XVIII

Ah, woe is me! Winter is come and gone,
But grief returns with the revolving year;   155
The airs and streams renew their joyous tone;
The ants, the bees, the swallows reappear;
Fresh leaves and flowers deck the dead Seasons' bier;
The amorous birds now pair in every brake,
And build their mossy homes in field and brere;   160
And the green lizard, and the golden snake,
Like unimprisoned flames, out of their trance awake.

XIX

Through wood and stream and field and hill and Ocean
A quickening life from the Earth's heart has burst
As it has ever done, with change and motion,   165
From the great morning of the world when first
God dawned on Chaos; in its stream immersed,
The lamps of Heaven flash with a softer light;
All baser things pant with life's sacred thirst;
Diffuse themselves; and spend in love's delight,   170
The beauty and the joy of their renewèd might.

XX

The leprous corpse, touched by this spirit tender,
Exhales itself in flowers of gentle breath;
Like incarnations of the stars, when splendour
Is changed to fragrance, they illumine death   175
And mock the merry worm that wakes beneath;
Nought we know, dies. Shall that alone which knows
Be as a sword consumed before the sheath
By sightless lightning?—the intense atom glows
A moment, then is quenched in a most cold repose.   180

XXI

Alas! that all we loved of him should be,
But for our grief, as if it had not been,
And grief itself be mortal! Woe is me!
Whence are we, and why are we? of what scene
The actors or spectators? Great and mean   185
Meet massed in death, who lends what life must borrow.
As long as skies are blue, and fields are green,
Evening must usher night, night urge the morrow,
Month follow month with woe, and year wake year to sorrow.

XXII

'He will awake no more, oh, never more!   190
Wake thou,' cried Misery, 'childless Mother, rise
Out of thy sleep, and slake, in thy heart's core,
A wound more fierce than his, with tears and sighs.'
And all the Dreams that watched Urania's eyes,
And all the Echoes whom their sister's song   195
Had held in holy silence, cried: 'Arise!'
Swift as a Thought by the snake Memory stung,
From her ambrosial rest the fading Splendour sprung.

XXIII

She rose like an autumnal Night, that springs
Out of the East, and follows wild and drear   200
The golden Day, which, on eternal wings,
Even as a ghost abandoning a bier,
Had left the Earth a corpse. Sorrow and fear
So struck, so roused, so rapped Urania:
So saddened round her like an atmosphere   205
Of stormy mist; so swept her on her way
Even to the mournful place where Adonais lay.

XXIV

Out of her secret Paradise she sped,
Through camps and cities rough with stone, and steel,
And human hearts, which to her aery tread   210
Yielding not, wounded the invisible
Palms of her tender feet where'er they fell:
And barbèd tongues, and thoughts more sharp than they,
Rent the soft Form they never could repel,
Whose sacred blood, like the young tears of May,   215
Paved with eternal flowers that undeserving way.

XXV

In the death-chamber for a moment Death,
Shamed by the presence of that living Might,
Blushed to annihilation, and the breath
Revisited those lips, and Life's pale light   220
Flashed through those limbs, so late her dear delight.
'Leave me not wild and drear and comfortless,
As silent lightning leaves the starless night!
Leave me not!' cried Urania: her distress
Roused Death: Death rose and smiled, and met her vain caress.

XXVI

'Stay yet awhile! speak to me once again;   226
Kiss me, so long but as a kiss may live;
And in my heartless breast and burning brain
That word, that kiss, shall all thoughts else survive,
With food of saddest memory kept alive,   230
Now thou art dead, as if it were a part
Of thee, my Adonais! I would give
All that I am to be as thou now art!
But I am chained to Time, and cannot thence depart!

XXVII

'O gentle child, beautiful as thou wert,　　　　　　235
Why didst thou leave the trodden paths of men
Too soon, and with weak hands though mighty heart
Dare the unpastured dragon in his den?
Defenceless as thou wert, oh, where was then
Wisdom the mirrored shield, or scorn the spear?　　240
Or hadst thou waited the full cycle, when
Thy spirit should have filled its crescent sphere,
The monsters of life's waste had fled from thee like deer.

XXVIII

'The herded wolves, bold only to pursue;
The obscene ravens, clamorous o'er the dead;　　245
The vultures to the conqueror's banner true
Who feed where Desolation first has fed,
And whose wings rain contagion;—how they fled,
When, like Apollo, from his golden bow
The Pythian of the age one arrow sped　　　　　250
And smiled!—The spoilers tempt no second blow,
They fawn on the proud feet that spurn them lying low.

XXIX

'The sun comes forth, and many reptiles spawn;
He sets, and each ephemeral insect then
Is gathered into death without a dawn,　　　　255
And the immortal stars awake again;
So is it in the world of living men:
A godlike mind soars forth, in its delight
Making earth bare and veiling heaven, and when
It sinks, the swarms that dimmed or shared its light　　260
Leave to its kindred lamps the spirit's awful night.'

XXX

Thus ceased she: and the mountain shepherds came,
Their garlands sere, their magic mantles rent;
The Pilgrim of Eternity, whose fame
Over his living head like Heaven is bent,　　　　265
An early but enduring monument,
Came, veiling all the lightnings of his song
In sorrow; from her wilds Ierne sent
The sweetest lyrist of her saddest wrong,
And Love taught Grief to fall like music from his tongue.　　270

XXXI

Midst others of less note, came one frail Form,
A phantom among men; companionless
As the last cloud of an expiring storm
Whose thunder is its knell; he, as I guess,
Had gazed on Nature's naked loveliness,   275
Actaeon-like, and now he fled astray
With feeble steps o'er the world's wilderness,
And his own thoughts, along that rugged way,
Pursued, like raging hounds, their father and their prey.

XXXII

A pardlike Spirit beautiful and swift—   280
A Love in desolation masked;—a Power
Girt round with weakness;—it can scarce uplift
The weight of the superincumbent hour;
It is a dying lamp, a falling shower,
A breaking billow;—even whilst we speak   285
Is it not broken? On the withering flower
The killing sun smiles brightly: on a cheek
The life can burn in blood, even while the heart may break.

XXXIII

His head was bound with pansies overblown,
And faded violets, white, and pied, and blue;   290
And a light spear topped with a cypress cone,
Round whose rude shaft dark ivy-tresses grew
Yet dripping with the forest's noonday dew,
Vibrated, as the ever-beating heart
Shook the weak hand that grasped it; of that crew   295
He came the last, neglected and apart;
A herd-abandoned deer struck by the hunter's dart.

XXXIV

All stood aloof, and at his partial moan
Smiled through their tears; well knew that gentle band
Who in another's fate now wept his own,   300
As in the accents of an unknown land
He sung new sorrow; sad Urania scanned
The Stranger's mien, and murmured: 'Who art thou?'
He answered not, but with a sudden hand
Made bare his branded and ensanguined brow,   305
Which was like Cain's or Christ's—oh! that it should be so!

XXXV

What softer voice is hushed over the dead?
Athwart what brow is that dark mantle thrown?
What form leans sadly o'er the white death-bed,
In mockery of monumental stone, 310
The heavy heart heaving without a moan?
If it be He, who, gentlest of the wise,
Taught, soothed, loved, honoured the departed one,
Let me not vex, with inharmonious sighs,
The silence of that heart's accepted sacrifice. 315

XXXVI

Our Adonais has drunk poison—oh!
What deaf and viperous murderer could crown
Life's early cup with such a draught of woe?
The nameless worm would now itself disown:
It felt, yet could escape, the magic tone 320
Whose prelude held all envy, hate, and wrong,
But what was howling in one breast alone,
Silent with expectation of the song,
Whose master's hand is cold, whose silver lyre unstrung.

XXXVII

Live thou, whose infamy is not thy fame! 325
Live! fear no heavier chastisement from me,
Thou noteless blot on a remembered name!
But be thyself, and know thyself to be!
And ever at thy season be thou free
To spill the venom when thy fangs o'erflow; 330
Remorse and Self-contempt shall cling to thee;
Hot Shame shall burn upon thy secret brow,
And like a beaten hound tremble thou shalt—as now.

XXXVIII

Nor let us weep that our delight is fled
Far from these carrion kites that scream below; 335
He wakes or sleeps with the enduring dead;
Thou canst not soar where he is sitting now—
Dust to the dust! but the pure spirit shall flow
Back to the burning fountain whence it came,
A portion of the Eternal, which must glow 340
Through time and change, unquenchably the same,
Whilst thy cold embers choke the sordid hearth of shame.

XXXIX

Peace, peace! he is not dead, he doth not sleep—
He hath awakened from the dream of life—
'Tis we, who lost in stormy visions, keep 345
With phantoms an unprofitable strife,
And in mad trance, strike with our spirit's knife
Invulnerable nothings.—*We* decay
Like corpses in a charnel; fear and grief
Convulse us and consume us day by day, 350
And cold hopes swarm like worms within our living clay.

XL

He has outsoared the shadow of our night;
Envy and calumny and hate and pain,
And that unrest which men miscall delight,
Can touch him not and torture not again; 355
From the contagion of the world's slow stain
He is secure, and now can never mourn
A heart grown cold, a head grown gray in vain;
Nor, when the spirit's self has ceased to burn,
With sparkless ashes load an unlamented urn. 360

XLI

He lives, he wakes—'tis Death is dead, not he;
Mourn not for Adonais.—Thou young Dawn,
Turn all thy dew to splendour, for from thee
The spirit thou lamentest is not gone;
Ye caverns and ye forests, cease to moan! 365
Cease, ye faint flowers and fountains, and thou Air,
Which like a mourning veil thy scarf hadst thrown
O'er the abandoned Earth, now leave it bare
Even to the joyous stars which smile on its despair!

XLII

He is made one with Nature: there is heard 370
His voice in all her music, from the moan
Of thunder, to the song of night's sweet bird;
He is a presence to be felt and known
In darkness and in light, from herb and stone,
Spreading itself where'er that Power may move 375
Which has withdrawn his being to its own;
Which wields the world with never-wearied love
Sustains it from beneath, and kindles it above.

XLIII

He is a portion of the loveliness
Which once he made more lovely: he doth bear   380
His part, while the one Spirit's plastic stress
Sweeps through the dull dense world, compelling there,
All new successions to the forms they wear;
Torturing th' unwilling dross that checks its flight
To its own likeness, as each mass may bear;   385
And bursting in its beauty and its might
From trees and beasts and men into the Heaven's light.

XLIV

The splendours of the firmament of time
May be eclipsed, but are extinguished not;
Like stars to their appointed height they climb,   390
And death is a low mist which cannot blot
The brightness it may veil. When lofty thought
Lifts a young heart above its mortal lair,
And love and life contend in it, for what
Shall be its earthly doom, the dead live there   395
And move like winds of light on dark and stormy air.

XLV

The inheritors of unfulfilled renown
Rose from their thrones, built beyond mortal thought,
Far in the Unapparent. Chatterton
Rose pale,—his solemn agony had not   400
Yet faded from him; Sidney, as he fought
And as he fell and as he lived and loved
Sublimely mild, a Spirit without spot,
Arose; and Lucan, by his death approved:
Oblivion as they rose shrank like a thing reproved.   405

XLVI

And many more, whose names on Earth are dark,
But whose transmitted effluence cannot die
So long as fire outlives the parent spark,
Rose, robed in dazzling immortality.
'Thou art become as one of us,' they cry,   410
'It was for thee yon kingless sphere has long
Swung blind in unascended majesty,
Silent alone amid an Heaven of Song.
Assume thy wingèd throne, thou Vesper of our throng!'

XLVII

Who mourns for Adonais? Oh, come forth,   415
Fond wretch! and know thyself and him aright.
Clasp with thy panting soul the pendulous Earth;
As from a centre, dart thy spirit's light
Beyond all worlds, until its spacious might
Satiate the void circumference: then shrink   420
Even to a point within our day and night;
And keep thy heart light lest it make thee sink
When hope has kindled hope, and lured thee to the brink.

XLVIII

Or go to Rome, which is the sepulchre,
Oh, not of him, but of our joy: 'tis nought   425
That ages, empires, and religions there
Lie buried in the ravage they have wrought;
For such as he can lend,—they borrow not
Glory from those who made the world their prey;
And he is gathered to the kings of thought   430
Who waged contention with their time's decay,
And of the past are all that cannot pass away.

XLIX

Go thou to Rome,—at once the Paradise,
The grave, the city, and the wilderness;
And where its wrecks like shattered mountains rise,   435
And flowering weeds, and fragrant copses dress
The bones of Desolation's nakedness
Pass, till the spirit of the spot shall lead
Thy footsteps to a slope of green access
Where, like an infant's smile, over the dead   440
A light of laughing flowers along the grass is spread;

L

And gray walls moulder round, on which dull Time
Feeds, like slow fire upon a hoary brand;
And one keen pyramid with wedge sublime,
Pavilioning the dust of him who planned   445
This refuge for his memory, doth stand
Like flame transformed to marble; and beneath,
A field is spread, on which a newer band
Have pitched in Heaven's smile their camp of death,
Welcoming him we lose with scarce extinguished breath.   450

LI

Here pause: these graves are all too young as yet
To have outgrown the sorrow which consigned
Its charge to each; and if the seal is set,
Here, on one fountain of a mourning mind,
Break it not thou! too surely shalt thou find   455
Thine own well full, if thou returnest home,
Of tears and gall. From the world's bitter wind
Seek shelter in the shadow of the tomb.
What Adonais is, why fear we to become?

LII

The One remains, the many change and pass;   460
Heaven's light forever shines, Earth's shadows fly;
Life, like a dome of many-coloured glass,
Stains the white radiance of Eternity,
Until Death tramples it to fragments.—Die,
If thou wouldst be with that which thou dost seek!   465
Follow where all is fled!—Rome's azure sky,
Flowers, ruins, statues, music, words, are weak
The glory they transfuse with fitting truth to speak.

LIII

Why linger, why turn back, why shrink, my Heart?
Thy hopes are gone before: from all things here   470
They have departed; thou shouldst now depart!
A light is passed from the revolving year,
And man, and woman; and what still is dear
Attracts to crush, repels to make thee wither.
The soft sky smiles,—the low wind whispers near: 475
'Tis Adonais calls! oh, hasten thither,
No more let Life divide what Death can join together.

LIV

That Light whose smile kindles the Universe,
That Beauty in which all things work and move,
That Benediction which the eclipsing Curse   480
Of birth can quench not, that sustaining Love
Which through the web of being blindly wove
By man and beast and earth and air and sea,
Burns bright or dim, as each are mirrors of
The fire for which all thirst; now beams on me,   485
Consuming the last clouds of cold mortality.

LV

The breath whose might I have invoked in song
Descends on me; my spirit's bark is driven,
Far from the shore, far from the trembling throng
Whose sails were never to the tempest given;   490
The massy earth and sphered skies are riven!
I am borne darkly, fearfully, afar;
Whilst, burning through the inmost veil of Heaven,
The soul of Adonais, like a star,
Beacons from the abode where the Eternal are.   495

CANCELLED PASSAGES OF THE POEM

And ever as he went he swept a lyre
Of unaccustomed shape, and   strings
Now like the   of impetuous fire,
Which shakes the forest with its murmurings,
Now like the rush of the aëreal wings   5
Of the enamoured wind among the treen,
Whispering unimaginable things,
And dying on the streams of dew serene,
Which feed the unmown meads with ever-during green.

.   .   .   .

And the green Paradise which western waves   10
Embosom in their ever-wailing sweep,
Talking of freedom to their tongueless caves,
Or to the spirits which within them keep
A record of the wrongs which, though they sleep,
Die not, but dream of retribution, heard   15
His hymns, and echoing them from steep to steep,
Kept——

.   .   .   .

And then came one of sweet and earnest looks,
Whose soft smiles to his dark and night-like eyes
Were as the clear and ever-living brooks   20
Are to the obscure fountains whence they rise,
Showing how pure they are: a Paradise
Of happy truth upon his forehead low
Lay, making wisdom lovely, in the guise
Of earth-awakening morn upon the brow   25
Of star-deserted heaven, while ocean gleams below.

His song, though very sweet, was low and faint,
A simple strain——

.   .   .

   A mighty Phantasm, half concealed
In darkness of his own exceeding light,   30
Which clothed his awful presence unrevealed,
Charioted on the   night
Of thunder-smoke, whose skirts were chrysolite.

And like a sudden meteor, which outstrips
The splendour-wingèd chariot of the sun,   35
            eclipse
The armies of the golden stars, each one
Pavilioned in its tent of light—all strewn
Over the chasms of blue night——

HELLAS

A LYRICAL DRAMA

ΜΑΝΤΙΣ 'ΕΙΜ' 'ΕΣΘΛΩΝ 'ΑΓΩΝΩΝ.—Oedip. Colon.

TO HIS EXCELLENCY

PRINCE ALEXANDER MAVROCORDATO
LATE SECRETARY FOR FOREIGN AFFAIRS TO THE HOSPODAR OF WALLACHIA

THE DRAMA OF HELLAS IS INSCRIBED AS AN
IMPERFECT TOKEN OF THE ADMIRATION,
SYMPATHY, AND FRIENDSHIP OF
THE AUTHOR

Pisa, *November* 1, 1821.

PREFACE

The poem of *Hellas*, written at the suggestion of the events of the
moment, is a mere improvise, and derives its interest (should it be found
to possess any) solely from the intense sympathy which the Author feels
with the cause he would celebrate.

The subject, in its present state, is insusceptible of being treated otherwise than lyrically, and if I have called this poem a drama from the circumstance of its being composed in dialogue, the licence is not greater
than that which has been assumed by other poets who have called their
productions epics, only because they have been divided into twelve or
twenty-four books.

The *Persae* of Aeschylus afforded me the first model of my conception, although the decision of the glorious contest now waging in Greece being yet suspended forbids a catastrophe parallel to the return of Xerxes and the desolation of the Persians. I have, therefore, contented myself with exhibiting a series of lyric pictures, and with having wrought upon the curtain of futurity, which falls upon the unfinished scene, such figures of indistinct and visionary delineation as suggest the final triumph of the Greek cause as a portion of the cause of civilisation and social improvement.

The drama (if drama it must be called) is, however, so inartificial that I doubt whether, if recited on the Thespian waggon to an Athenian village at the Dionysiaca, it would have obtained the prize of the goat. I shall bear with equanimity any punishment, greater than the loss of such a reward, which the Aristarchi of the hour may think fit to inflict.

The only *goat-song* which I have yet attempted has, I confess, in spite of the unfavourable nature of the subject, received a greater and a more valuable portion of applause than I expected or than it deserved.

Common fame is the only authority which I can allege for the details which form the basis of the poem, and I must trespass upon the forgiveness of my readers for the display of newspaper erudition to which I have been reduced. Undoubtedly, until the conclusion of the war, it will be impossible to obtain an account of it sufficiently authentic for historical materials; but poets have their privilege, and it is unquestionable that actions of the most exalted courage have been performed by the Greeks—that they have gained more than one naval victory, and that their defeat in Wallachia was signalized by circumstances of heroism more glorious even than victory.

The apathy of the rulers of the civilised world to the astonishing circumstance of the descendants of that nation to which they owe their civilisation, rising as it were from the ashes of their ruin, is something perfectly inexplicable to a mere spectator of the shows of this mortal scene. We are all Greeks. Our laws, our literature, our religion, our arts have their root in Greece. But for Greece—Rome, the instructor, the conqueror, or the metropolis of our ancestors, would have spread no illumination with her arms, and we might still have been savages and idolaters; or, what is worse, might have arrived at such a stagnant and miserable state of social institution as China and Japan possess.

The human form and the human mind attained to a perfection in Greece which has impressed its image on those faultless productions, whose very fragments are the despair of modern art, and has propagated impulses which cannot cease, through a thousand channels of manifest or imperceptible operation, to ennoble and delight mankind until the extinction of the race.

The modern Greek is the descendant of those glorious beings whom the imagination almost refuses to figure to itself as belonging to our kind, and he inherits much of their sensibility, their rapidity of conception, their enthusiasm, and their courage. If in many instances he is degraded

by moral and political slavery to the practice of the basest vices it engenders—and that below the level of ordinary degradation—let us reflect
that the corruption of the best produces the worst, and that habits which
subsist only in relation to a peculiar state of social institution may be
expected to cease as soon as that relation is dissolved. In fact, the Greeks,
since the admirable novel of *Anastasius* could have been a faithful picture
of their manners, have undergone most important changes; the flower of
their youth, returning to their country from the universities of Italy, Germany, and France, have communicated to their fellow-citizens the latest
results of that social perfection of which their ancestors were the original
source. The University of Chios contained before the breaking out of the
revolution eight hundred students, and among them several Germans and
Americans. The munificence and energy of many of the Greek princes and
merchants, directed to the renovation of their country with a spirit and a
wisdom which has few examples, is above all praise.

The English permit their own oppressors to act according to their
natural sympathy with the Turkish tyrant, and to brand upon their name
the indelible blot of an alliance with the enemies of domestic happiness,
of Christianity and civilisation.

Russia desires to possess, not to liberate Greece; and is contented to
see the Turks, its natural enemies, and the Greeks, its intended slaves,
enfeeble each other until one or both fall into its net. The wise and generous policy of England would have consisted in establishing the independence of Greece, and in maintaining it both against Russia and the
Turk;—but when was the oppressor generous or just?

Should the English people ever become free, they will reflect upon the
part which those who presume to represent their will have played in the
great drama of the revival of liberty, with feelings which it would become
them to anticipate. This is the age of the war of the oppressed against the
oppressors, and every one of those ringleaders of the privileged gangs of
murderers and swindlers, called Sovereigns, look to each other for aid
against the common enemy, and suspend their mutual jealousies in the
presence of a mightier fear. Of this holy alliance all the despots of the
earth are virtual members. But a new race has arisen throughout Europe,
nursed in the abhorrence of the opinions which are its chains, and she will
continue to produce fresh generations to accomplish that destiny which
tyrants foresee and dread.

The Spanish Peninsula is already free. France is tranquil in the enjoyment of a partial exemption from the abuses which its unnatural and
feeble government are vainly attempting to revive. The seed of blood
and misery has been sown in Italy, and a more vigorous race is arising
to go forth to the harvest. The world waits only the news of a revolution
of Germany to see the tyrants who have pinnacled themselves on its
supineness precipitated into the ruin from which they shall never arise.
Well do these destroyers of mankind know their enemy, when they
impute the insurrection in Greece to the same spirit before which they
tremble throughout the rest of Europe, and that enemy well knows the

power and the cunning of its opponents, and watches the moment of their approaching weakness and inevitable division to wrest the bloody sceptres from their grasp.

PROLOGUE TO HELLAS

Herald of Eternity. It is the day when all the sons of God
Wait in the roofless senate-house, whose floor
Is Chaos, and the immovable abyss
Frozen by His steadfast word to hyaline

.   .   .   .

The shadow of God, and delegate   5
Of that before whose breath the universe
Is as a print of dew.
                    Hierarchs and kings
Who from your thrones pinnacled on the past
Sway the reluctant present, ye who sit
Pavilioned on the radiance or the gloom   10
Of mortal thought, which like an exhalation
Steaming from earth, conceals the   of heaven
Which gave it birth,   assemble here
Before your Father's throne; the swift decree
Yet hovers, and the fiery incarnation   15
Is yet withheld, clothèd in which it shall
                    annul
The fairest of those wandering isles that gem
The sapphire space of interstellar air,
That green and azure sphere, that earth enwrapped   20
Less in the beauty of its tender light
Than in an atmosphere of living spirit
Which interpenetrating all the . . .
          it rolls from realm to realm
And age to age, and in its ebb and flow   25
Impels the generations
To their appointed place,
Whilst the high Arbiter
Beholds the strife, and at the appointed time
Sends His decrees veiled in eternal . . .   30

Within the circuit of this pendent orb
There lies an antique region, on which fell
The dews of thought in the world's golden dawn
Earliest and most benign, and from it sprung
Temples and cities and immortal forms   35
And harmonies of wisdom and of song,
And thoughts, and deeds worthy of thoughts so fair.
And when the sun of its dominion failed,
And when the winter of its glory came,

The winds that stripped it bare blew on and swept   40
That dew into the utmost wildernesses
In wandering clouds of sunny rain that thawed
The unmaternal bosom of the North.
Haste, sons of God,   for ye beheld,
Reluctant, or consenting, or astonished,   45
The stern decrees go forth, which heaped on Greece
Ruin and degradation and despair.
A fourth now waits: assemble, sons of God,
To speed or to prevent or to suspend,
If, as ye dream, such power be not withheld,   50
The unaccomplished destiny.

.   .   .   .

Chorus.

The curtain of the Universe
          Is rent and shattered,
The splendour-wingèd worlds disperse
          Like wild doves scattered.   55

          Space is roofless and bare,
And in the midst a cloudy shrine,
          Dark amid thrones of light.
In the blue glow of hyaline
Golden worlds revolve and shine.   60
          In   flight
From every point of the Infinite,
          Like a thousand dawns on a single night
The splendours rise and spread;
And through thunder and darkness dread   65
Light and music are radiated,
And in their pavilioned chariots led
By living wings high overhead
          The giant Powers move,
Gloomy or bright as the thrones they fill.   70

.   .   .   .   .   .

A chaos of light and motion
Upon that glassy ocean.

.   .   .   .   .   .

The senate of the Gods is met,
Each in his rank and station set;
          There is silence in the spaces—   75
Lo! Satan, Christ, and Mahomet
          Start from their places!

Christ.   Almighty Father!
Low-kneeling at the feet of Destiny

.   .   .   .   .   .

There are two fountains in which spirits weep   80
When mortals err, Discord and Slavery named,
And with their bitter dew two Destinies
Filled each their irrevocable urns; the third,
Fiercest and mightiest, mingled both, and added
Chaos and Death, and slow Oblivion's lymph,   85
And hate and terror, and the poisoned rain

    .   .   .   .   .   .

The Aurora of the nations. By this brow
Whose pores wept tears of blood, by these wide wounds,
By this imperial crown of agony,
By infamy and solitude and death,   90
For this I underwent, and by the pain
Of pity for those who would   for me
The unremembered joy of a revenge,
For this I felt—by Plato's sacred light,
Of which my spirit was a burning morrow—   95
By Greece and all she cannot cease to be.
Her quenchless words, sparks of immortal truth,
Stars of all night—her harmonies and forms,
Echoes and shadows of what Love adores
In thee, I do compel thee, send forth Fate,   100
Thy irrevocable child: let her descend,
A seraph-wingèd Victory [arrayed]
In tempest of the omnipotence of God
Which sweeps through all things.

From hollow leagues, from Tyranny which arms   105
Adverse miscreeds and emulous anarchies
To stamp, as on a wingèd serpent's seed,
Upon the name of Freedom; from the storm
Of faction, which like earthquake shakes and sickens
The solid heart of enterprise; from all   110
By which the holiest dreams of highest spirits
Are stars beneath the dawn . . .
                                She shall arise
Victorious as the world arose from Chaos!
And as the Heavens and the Earth arrayed
Their presence in the beauty and the light   115
Of Thy first smile, O Father,—as they gather
The spirit of Thy love which paves for them
Their path o'er the abyss, till every sphere
Shall be one living Spirit,—so shall Greece—
    Satan. Be as all things beneath the empyrean,   120
Mine! Art thou eyeless like old Destiny,
Thou mockery-king, crowned with a wreath of thorns?

Whose sceptre is a reed, the broken reed
Which pierces thee! whose throne a chair of scorn;
For seest thou not beneath this crystal floor   125
The innumerable worlds of golden light
Which are my empire, and the least of them
       which thou wouldst redeem from me?
Know'st thou not them my portion?
Or wouldst rekindle the   strife   130
Which our great Father then did arbitrate
Which he assigned to his competing sons
Each his apportioned realm?
                 Thou Destiny,
Thou who art mailed in the omnipotence
Of Him who sends thee forth, whate'er thy task,   135
Speed, spare not to accomplish, and be mine
Thy trophies, whether Greece again become
The fountain in the desert whence the earth
Shall drink of freedom, which shall give it strength
To suffer, or a gulf of hollow death   140
To swallow all delight, all life, all hope.
Go, thou Vicegerent of my will, no less
Than of the Father's; but lest thou shouldst faint,
The wingèd hounds, Famine and Pestilence,
Shall wait on thee, the hundred-forkèd snake   145
Insatiate Superstition still shall . . .
The earth behind thy steps, and War shall hover
Above, and Fraud shall gape below, and Change
Shall flit before thee on her dragon wings,
Convulsing and consuming, and I add   150
Three vials of the tears which daemons weep
When virtuous spirits through the gate of Death
Pass triumphing over the thorns of life,
Sceptres and crowns, mitres and swords and snares,
Trampling in scorn, like Him and Socrates.   155
The first is Anarchy; when Power and Pleasure,
Glory and science and security,
On Freedom hang like fruit on the green tree,
Then pour it forth, and men shall gather ashes.
The second Tyranny—
    Christ.   Obdurate spirit!   160
Thou seest but the Past in the To-come.
Pride is thy error and thy punishment.
Boast not thine empire, dream not that thy worlds
Are more than furnace-sparks or rainbow-drops
Before the Power that wields and kindles them.   165
True greatness asks not space, true excellence

Lives in the Spirit of all things that live,
Which lends it to the worlds thou callest thine.

.   .   .   .

 Mahomet. . . . Haste thou and fill the waning crescent
With beams as keen as those which pierced the shadow 170
Of Christian night rolled back upon the West,
When the orient moon of Islam rode in triumph
From Tmolus to the Acroceraunian snow.

.   .   .   .

      Wake, thou Word
Of God, and from the throne of Destiny 175
Even to the utmost limit of thy way
May Triumph

.   .   .   .

  Be thou a curse on them whose creed
Divides and multiplies the most high God.

HELLAS

DRAMATIS PERSONAE

MAHMUD.	DAOOD.
HASSAN.	AHASUERUS, *a Jew.*

CHORUS *of Greek Captive Women.* [*The Phantom of Mahomet II.*]
   Messengers, Slaves, and Attendants.

SCENE, *Constantinople.* TIME, *Sunset.*

SCENE.—*A Terrace on the Seraglio.* MAHMUD *sleeping, an
Indian Slave sitting beside his Couch.*

Chorus of Greek Captive Women.

WE strew these opiate flowers
 On thy restless pillow,—
They were stripped from Orient bowers,
 By the Indian billow.
  Be thy sleep 5
  Calm and deep,
Like theirs who fell—not ours who weep!

Indian.

Away, unlovely dreams!
 Away, false shapes of sleep!
Be his, as Heaven seems, 10
 Clear, and bright, and deep!
Soft as love, and calm as death,
Sweet as a summer night without a breath.

Chorus.

Sleep, sleep! our song is laden
With the soul of slumber;   15
It was sung by a Samian maiden,
Whose lover was of the number
Who now keep
That calm sleep
Whence none may wake, where none shall weep.   20

Indian.

I touch thy temples pale!
I breathe my soul on thee!
And could my prayers avail,
All my joy should be
Dead, and I would live to weep,   25
So thou mightst win one hour of quiet sleep.

Chorus.

Breathe low, low
The spell of the mighty mistress now!
When Conscience lulls her sated snake,
And Tyrants sleep, let Freedom wake.   30
Breathe low—low
The words which, like secret fire, shall flow
Through the veins of the frozen earth—low, low!

Semichorus I.

Life may change, but it may fly not;
Hope may vanish, but can die not;   35
Truth be veiled, but still it burneth;
Love repulsed,—but it returneth!

Semichorus II.

Yet were life a charnel where
Hope lay coffined with Despair;
Yet were truth a sacred lie,   40
Love were lust—

Semichorus I.

If Liberty
Lent not life its soul of light,
Hope its iris of delight,
Truth its prophet's robe to wear,
Love its power to give and bear.   45

Chorus.

In the great morning of the world,
The Spirit of God with might unfurled
The flag of Freedom over Chaos,
    And all its banded anarchs fled,
Like vultures frighted from Imaus,   50
    Before an earthquake's tread.—
So from Time's tempestuous dawn
Freedom's splendour burst and shone:—
Thermopylae and Marathon
Caught, like mountains beacon-lighted,   55
    The springing Fire.—The wingèd glory
On Philippi half-alighted,
    Like an eagle on a promontory.
Its unwearied wings could fan
The quenchless ashes of Milan.   60
From age to age, from man to man,
    It lived; and lit from land to land
    Florence, Albion, Switzerland.

Then night fell; and, as from night,
Reassuming fiery flight,   65
From the West swift Freedom came,
    Against the course of Heaven and doom,
A second sun arrayed in flame,
    To burn, to kindle, to illume.
From far Atlantis its young beams   70
Chased the shadows and the dreams.
France, with all her sanguine steams,
    Hid, but quenched it not: again
    Through clouds its shafts of glory rain
    From utmost Germany to Spain.   75

As an eagle fed with morning
Scorns the embattled tempest's warning,
When she seeks her aerie hanging
    In the mountain-cedar's hair,
And her brood expect the clanging   80
    Of her wings through the wild air,
Sick with famine:—Freedom, so
To what of Greece remaineth now
Returns; her hoary ruins glow
Like Orient mountains lost in day;   85
    Beneath the safety of her wings
Her renovated nurslings prey,
    And in the naked lightenings
Of truth they purge their dazzled eyes.

Let Freedom leave—where'er she flies,   90
A Desert, or a Paradise:
  Let the beautiful and the brave
  Share her glory, or a grave.

Semichorus I.

With the gifts of gladness
  Greece did thy cradle strew;   95

Semichorus II.

With the tears of sadness
  Greece did thy shroud bedew!

Semichorus I.

With an orphan's affection
  She followed thy bier through Time;

Semichorus II.

And at thy resurrection   100
  Reappeareth, like thou, sublime!

Semichorus I.

If Heaven should resume thee,
  To Heaven shall her spirit ascend;

Semichorus II.

If Hell should entomb thee,
  To Hell shall her high hearts bend.   105

Semichorus I.

If Annihilation——

Semichorus II.

Dust let her glories be!
  And a name and a nation
    Be forgotten, Freedom, with thee!

Indian.

His brow grows darker—breathe not—move not!   110
He starts—he shudders—ye that love not,
  With your panting loud and fast,
  Have awakened him at last.

Mahmud (starting from his sleep). Man the Seraglio-guard!
  make fast the gate!
What! from a cannonade of three short hours?   115
'Tis false! that breach towards the Bosphorus

Cannot be practicable yet—who stirs?
Stand to the match; that when the foe prevails
One spark may mix in reconciling ruin
The conqueror and the conquered! Heave the tower   120
Into the gap—wrench off the roof!
    (*Enter* HASSAN.)   Ha! what!
The truth of day lightens upon my dream
And I am Mahmud still.
    Hassan.   Your Sublime Highness
Is strangely moved.
    Mahmud.   The times do cast strange shadows
On those who watch and who must rule their course,   125
Lest they, being first in peril as in glory,
Be whelmed in the fierce ebb:—and these are of them.
Thrice has a gloomy vision hunted me
As thus from sleep into the troubled day;
It shakes me as the tempest shakes the sea,   130
Leaving no figure upon memory's glass.
Would that——no matter. Thou didst say thou knewest
A Jew, whose spirit is a chronicle
Of strange and secret and forgotten things.
I bade thee summon him:—'tis said his tribe   135
Dream, and are wise interpreters of dreams.
    Hassan. The Jew of whom I spake is old,—so old
He seems to have outlived a world's decay;
The hoary mountains and the wrinkled ocean
Seem younger still than he;—his hair and beard   140
Are whiter than the tempest-sifted snow;
His cold pale limbs and pulseless arteries
Are like the fibres of a cloud instinct
With light, and to the soul that quickens them
Are as the atoms of the mountain-drift   145
To the winter wind:—but from his eye looks forth
A life of unconsumèd thought which pierces
The Present, and the Past, and the To-come.
Some say that this is he whom the great prophet
Jesus, the son of Joseph, for his mockery,   150
Mocked with the curse of immortality.
Some feign that he is Enoch: others dream
He was pre-adamite and has survived
Cycles of generation and of ruin.
The sage, in truth, by dreadful abstinence   155
And conquering penance of the mutinous flesh,
Deep contemplation, and unwearied study,
In years outstretched beyond the date of man,
May have attained to sovereignty and science
Over those strong and secret things and thoughts   160

Which others fear and know not.
  Mahmud.   I would talk
With this old Jew.
  Hassan.   Thy will is even now
Made known to him, where he dwells in a sea-cavern
'Mid the Demonesi, less accessible
Than thou or God! He who would question him   165
Must sail alone at sunset, where the stream
Of Ocean sleeps around those foamless isles,
When the young moon is westering as now,
And evening airs wander upon the wave;
And when the pines of that bee-pasturing isle,   170
Green Erebinthus, quench the fiery shadow
Of his gilt prow within the sapphire water,
Then must the lonely helmsman cry aloud
'Ahasuerus!' and the caverns round
Will answer 'Ahasuerus!' If his prayer   175
Be granted, a faint meteor will arise
Lighting him over Marmora, and a wind
Will rush out of the sighing pine-forest,
And with the wind a storm of harmony
Unutterably sweet, and pilot him   180
Through the soft twilight to the Bosphorus:
Thence at the hour and place and circumstance
Fit for the matter of their conference
The Jew appears. Few dare, and few who dare
Win the desired communion—but that shout 185
Bodes——   [*A shout within*.
  Mahmud. Evil, doubtless; like all human sounds.
Let me converse with spirits.
  Hassan.   That shout again.
  Mahmud. This Jew whom thou hast summoned—
  Hassan.   Will be here—
  Mahmud. When the omnipotent hour to which are yoked
He, I, and all things shall compel—enough! 190
Silence those mutineers—that drunken crew,
That crowd about the pilot in the storm.
Ay! strike the foremost shorter by a head!
They weary me, and I have need of rest.
Kings are like stars—they rise and set, they have 195
The worship of the world, but no repose. [*Exeunt severally*.

Chorus.

  Worlds on worlds are rolling ever
    From creation to decay,
  Like the bubbles on a river
    Sparkling, bursting, borne away.   200

But they are still immortal
Who, through birth's orient portal
And death's dark chasm hurrying to and fro,
Clothe their unceasing flight
In the brief dust and light   205
Gathered around their chariots as they go;
New shapes they still may weave,
New gods, new laws receive,
Bright or dim are they as the robes they last
On Death's bare ribs had cast.   210

A power from the unknown God,
A Promethean conqueror, came;
Like a triumphal path he trod
The thorns of death and shame.
A mortal shape to him   215
Was like the vapour dim
Which the orient planet animates with light;
Hell, Sin, and Slavery came,
Like bloodhounds mild and tame,
Nor preyed, until their Lord had taken flight;   220
The moon of Mahomet
Arose, and it shall set:
While blazoned as on Heaven's immortal noon
The cross leads generations on.

Swift as the radiant shapes of sleep   225
From one whose dreams are Paradise
Fly, when the fond wretch wakes to weep,
And Day peers forth with her blank eyes;
So fleet, so faint, so fair,
The Powers of earth and air   230
Fled from the folding-star of Bethlehem:
Apollo, Pan, and Love,
And even Olympian Jove
Grew weak, for killing Truth had glared on them;
Our hills and seas and streams,   235
Dispeopled of their dreams,
Their waters turned to blood, their dew to tears,
Wailed for the golden years.

Enter MAHMUD, HASSAN, DAOOD, *and others.*

Mahmud. More gold? our ancestors bought gold with victory,
And shall I sell it for defeat?
    Daood.   The Janizars   240
Clamour for pay.
    Mahmud.   Go! bid them pay themselves

With Christian blood! Are there no Grecian virgins
Whose shrieks and spasms and tears they may enjoy?
No infidel children to impale on spears?
No hoary priests after that Patriarch   245
Who bent the curse against his country's heart,
Which clove his own at last? Go! bid them kill,
Blood is the seed of gold.
    Daood.   It has been sown,
And yet the harvest to the sicklemen
Is as a grain to each.
    Mahmud.   Then, take this signet,   250
Unlock the seventh chamber in which lie
The treasures of victorious Solyman,—
An empire's spoil stored for a day of ruin.
O spirit of my sires! is it not come?
The prey-birds and the wolves are gorged and sleep;   255
But these, who spread their feast on the red earth,
Hunger for gold, which fills not.—See them fed;
Then, lead them to the rivers of fresh death.   [*Exit* DAOOD.
O miserable dawn, after a night
More glorious than the day which it usurped!   260
O faith in God! O power on earth! O word
Of the great prophet, whose o'ershadowing wings
Darkened the thrones and idols of the West,
Now bright!—For thy sake cursèd be the hour,
Even as a father by an evil child,   265
When the orient moon of Islam rolled in triumph
From Caucasus to White Ceraunia!
Ruin above, and anarchy below;
Terror without, and treachery within;
The Chalice of destruction full, and all   270
Thirsting to drink; and who among us dares
To dash it from his lips? and where is Hope?
    Hassan. The lamp of our dominion still rides high;
One God is God—Mahomet is His prophet.
Four hundred thousand Moslems, from the limits   275
Of utmost Asia, irresistibly
Throng, like full clouds at the Sirocco's cry;
But not like them to weep their strength in tears:
They bear destroying lightning, and their step
Wakes earthquake to consume and overwhelm,   280
And reign in ruin. Phrygian Olympus,
Tmolus, and Latmos, and Mycale, roughen
With horrent arms; and lofty ships even now,
Like vapours anchored to a mountain's edge,
Freighted with fire and whirlwind, wait at Scala   285
The convoy of the ever-veering wind.

Samos is drunk with blood;—the Greek has paid
Brief victory with swift loss and long despair.
The false Moldavian serfs fled fast and far,
When the fierce shout of 'Allah-illa-Allah!'   290
Rose like the war-cry of the northern wind
Which kills the sluggish clouds, and leaves a flock
Of wild swans struggling with the naked storm.
So were the lost Greeks on the Danube's day!
If night is mute, yet the returning sun   295
Kindles the voices of the morning birds;
Nor at thy bidding less exultingly
Than birds rejoicing in the golden day,
The Anarchies of Africa unleash
Their tempest-wingèd cities of the sea,   300
To speak in thunder to the rebel world.
Like sulphurous clouds, half-shattered by the storm,
They sweep the pale Aegean, while the Queen
Of Ocean, bound upon her island-throne,
Far in the West, sits mourning that her sons   305
Who frown on Freedom spare a smile for thee:
Russia still hovers, as an eagle might
Within a cloud, near which a kite and crane
Hang tangled in inextricable fight,
To stoop upon the victor;—for she fears   310
The name of Freedom, even as she hates thine.
But recreant Austria loves thee as the Grave
Loves Pestilence, and her slow dogs of war
Fleshed with the chase, come up from Italy,
And howl upon their limits; for they see   315
The panther, Freedom, fled to her old cover,
Amid seas and mountains, and a mightier brood
Crouch round. What Anarch wears a crown or mitre,
Or bears the sword, or grasps the key of gold,
Whose friends are not thy friends, whose foes thy foes? 320
Our arsenals and our armouries are full;
Our forts defy assault; ten thousand cannon
Lie ranged upon the beach, and hour by hour
Their earth-convulsing wheels affright the city;
The galloping of fiery steeds makes pale   325
The Christian merchant; and the yellow Jew
Hides his hoard deeper in the faithless earth.
Like clouds, and like the shadows of the clouds,
Over the hills of Anatolia,
Swift in wide troops the Tartar chivalry   330
Sweep;—the far flashing of their starry lances
Reverberates the dying light of day.
We have one God, one King, one Hope, one Law;

But many-headed Insurrection stands
Divided in itself, and soon must fall.   335
    Mahmud. Proud words, when deeds come short, are seasonable:
Look, Hassan, on yon crescent moon, emblazoned
Upon that shattered flag of fiery cloud
Which leads the rear of the departing day;
Wan emblem of an empire fading now!   340
See how it trembles in the blood-red air,
And like a mighty lamp whose oil is spent
Shrinks on the horizon's edge, while, from above,
One star with insolent and victorious light
Hovers above its fall, and with keen beams,   345
Like arrows through a fainting antelope,
Strikes its weak form to death.
    Hassan.   Even as that moon
Renews itself——
    Mahmud.   Shall we be not renewed!
Far other bark than ours were needed now
To stem the torrent of descending time: 350
The Spirit that lifts the slave before his lord
Stalks through the capitals of armèd kings,
And spreads his ensign in the wilderness:
Exults in chains; and, when the rebel falls,
Cries like the blood of Abel from the dust;   355
And the inheritors of the earth, like beasts
When earthquake is unleashed, with idiot fear
Cower in their kingly dens—as I do now.
What were Defeat when Victory must appal?
Or Danger, when Security looks pale?—   360
How said the messenger—who, from the fort
Islanded in the Danube, saw the battle
Of Bucharest?—that—
    Hassan.   Ibrahim's scimitar
Drew with its gleam swift victory from Heaven,
To burn before him in the night of battle—   365
A light and a destruction.
    Mahmud.   Ay! the day
Was ours: but how?——
    Hassan.   The light Wallachians,
The Arnaut, Servian, and Albanian allies
Fled from the glance of our artillery
Almost before the thunderstone alit.   370
One half the Grecian army made a bridge
Of safe and slow retreat, with Moslem dead;
The other—
    Mahmud. Speak—tremble not.—
    Hassan.   Islanded

By victor myriads, formed in hollow square
With rough and steadfast front, and thrice flung back 375
The deluge of our foaming cavalry;
Thrice their keen wedge of battle pierced our lines,
Our baffled army trembled like one man
Before a host, and gave them space; but soon,
From the surrounding hills, the batteries blazed, 380
Kneading them down with fire and iron rain:
Yet none approached; till, like a field of corn
Under the hook of the swart sickleman,
The band, intrenched in mounds of Turkish dead,
Grew weak and few.—Then said the Pacha, 'Slaves, 385
Render yourselves—they have abandoned you—
What hope of refuge, or retreat, or aid?
We grant your lives.' 'Grant that which is thine own!'
Cried one, and fell upon his sword and died!
Another—'God, and man, and hope abandon me; 390
But I to them, and to myself, remain
Constant:'—he bowed his head, and his heart burst.
A third exclaimed, 'There is a refuge, tyrant,
Where thou darest not pursue, and canst not harm
Shouldst thou pursue; there we shall meet again.' 395
Then held his breath, and, after a brief spasm,
The indignant spirit cast its mortal garment
Among the slain—dead earth upon the earth!
So these survivors, each by different ways,
Some strange, all sudden, none dishonourable, 400
Met in triumphant death; and when our army
Closed in, while yet wonder, and awe, and shame
Held back the base hyaenas of the battle
That feed upon the dead and fly the living,
One rose out of the chaos of the slain: 405
And if it were a corpse which some dread spirit
Of the old saviours of the land we rule
Had lifted in its anger, wandering by;—
Or if there burned within the dying man
Unquenchable disdain of death, and faith 410
Creating what it feigned;—I cannot tell—
But he cried, 'Phantoms of the free, we come!
Armies of the Eternal, ye who strike
To dust the citadels of sanguine kings,
And shake the souls throned on their stony hearts, 415
And thaw their frostwork diadems like dew;—
O ye who float around this clime, and weave
The garment of the glory which it wears,
Whose fame, though earth betray the dust it clasped,
Lies sepulchred in monumental thought;— 420

Progenitors of all that yet is great,
Ascribe to your bright senate, O accept
In your high ministrations, us, your sons—
Us first, and the more glorious yet to come!
And ye, weak conquerors! giants who look pale   425
When the crushed worm rebels beneath your tread,
The vultures and the dogs, your pensioners tame,
Are overgorged; but, like oppressors, still
They crave the relic of Destruction's feast.
The exhalations and the thirsty winds   430
Are sick with blood; the dew is foul with death;
Heaven's light is quenched in slaughter: thus, where'er
Upon your camps, cities, or towers, or fleets,
The obscene birds the reeking remnants cast
Of these dead limbs,—upon your streams and mountains,   435
Upon your fields, your gardens, and your housetops,
Where'er the winds shall creep, or the clouds fly,
Or the dews fall, or the angry sun look down
With poisoned light—Famine, and Pestilence,
And Panic, shall wage war upon our side!   440
Nature from all her boundaries is moved
Against ye: Time has found ye light as foam.
The Earth rebels; and Good and Evil stake
Their empire o'er the unborn world of men
On this one cast;—but ere the die be thrown,   445
The renovated genius of our race,
Proud umpire of the impious game, descends,
A seraph-wingèd Victory, bestriding
The tempest of the Omnipotence of God,
Which sweeps all things to their appointed doom,   450
And you to oblivion!'—More he would have said,
But—
　　Mahmud. Died—as thou shouldst ere thy lips had painted
Their ruin in the hues of our success.
A rebel's crime, gilt with a rebel's tongue!
Your heart is Greek, Hassan.
　　Hassan.　　　　　　　　　It may be so: 455
A spirit not my own wrenched me within,
And I have spoken words I fear and hate;
Yet would I die for—
　　Mahmud.　　　　　Live! oh live! outlive
Me and this sinking empire. But the fleet—
　　Hassan. Alas!——
　　Mahmud.　　　　　The fleet which, like a flock of clouds   460
Chased by the wind, flies the insurgent banner!
Our wingèd castles from their merchant ships!
Our myriads before their weak pirate bands!

Our arms before their chains! our years of empire
Before their centuries of servile fear! 465
Death is awake! Repulse is on the waters!
They own no more the thunder-bearing banner
Of Mahmud; but, like hounds of a base breed,
Gorge from a stranger's hand, and rend their master.

    Hassan. Latmos, and Ampelos, and Phanae saw 470
The wreck——
    Mahmud. The caves of the Icarian isles
Told each to the other in loud mockery,
And with the tongue as of a thousand echoes,
First of the sea-convulsing fight—and, then,—
Thou darest to speak—senseless are the mountains: 475
Interpret thou their voice!
    Hassan. My presence bore
A part in that day's shame. The Grecian fleet
Bore down at daybreak from the North, and hung
As multitudinous on the ocean line,
As cranes upon the cloudless Thracian wind. 480
Our squadron, convoying ten thousand men,
Was stretching towards Nauplia when the battle
Was kindled.—
First through the hail of our artillery
The agile Hydriote barks with press of sail 485
Dashed:—ship to ship, cannon to cannon, man
To man were grappled in the embrace of war,
Inextricable but by death or victory.
The tempest of the raging fight convulsed
To its crystalline depths that stainless sea, 490
And shook Heaven's roof of golden morning clouds,
Poised on an hundred azure mountain-isles.
In the brief trances of the artillery
One cry from the destroyed and the destroyer
Rose, and a cloud of desolation wrapped 495
The unforeseen event, till the north wind
Sprung from the sea, lifting the heavy veil
Of battle-smoke—then victory—victory!
For, as we thought, three frigates from Algiers
Bore down from Naxos to our aid, but soon 500
The abhorrèd cross glimmered behind, before,
Among, around us; and that fatal sign
Dried with its beams the strength in Moslem hearts,
As the sun drinks the dew.—What more? We fled!—
Our noonday path over the sanguine foam 505
Was beaconed,—and the glare struck the sun pale,—
By our consuming transports; the fierce light
Made all the shadows of our sails blood-red,

And every countenance blank. Some ships lay feeding
The ravening fire, even to the water's level; 510
Some were blown up; some, settling heavily,
Sunk; and the shrieks of our companions died
Upon the wind, that bore us fast and far,
Even after they were dead. Nine thousand perished!
We met the vultures legioned in the air 515
Stemming the torrent of the tainted wind;
They, screaming from their cloudy mountain-peaks,
Stooped through the sulphurous battle-smoke and perched
Each on the weltering carcase that we loved,
Like its ill angel or its damnèd soul, 520
Riding upon the bosom of the sea.
We saw the dog-fish hastening to their feast.
Joy waked the voiceless people of the sea,
And ravening Famine left his ocean cave
To dwell with War, with us, and with Despair. 525
We met night three hours to the west of Patmos,
And with night, tempest——
    Mahmud.   Cease!

Enter a Messenger.

    Messenger.   Your Sublime Highness,
That Christian hound, the Muscovite Ambassador,
Has left the city.—If the rebel fleet
Had anchored in the port, had victory 530
Crowned the Greek legions in the Hippodrome,
Panic were tamer.—Obedience and Mutiny,
Like giants in contention planet-struck,
Stand gazing on each other.—There is peace
In Stamboul.—
    Mahmud.   Is the grave not calmer still? 535
Its ruins shall be mine.
    Hassan.   Fear not the Russian:
The tiger leagues not with the stag at bay
Against the hunter.—Cunning, base, and cruel,
He crouches, watching till the spoil be won,
And must be paid for his reserve in blood. 540
After the war is fought, yield the sleek Russian
That which thou canst not keep, his deserved portion
Of blood, which shall not flow through streets and fields,
Rivers and seas, like that which we may win,
But stagnate in the veins of Christian slaves! 545

Enter second Messenger.

    Second Messenger. Nauplia, Tripolizza, Mothon, Athens,
Navarin, Artas, Monembasia,

Corinth, and Thebes are carried by assault,
And every Islamite who made his dogs
Fat with the flesh of Galilean slaves 550
Passed at the edge of the sword: the lust of blood,
Which made our warriors drunk, is quenched in death;
But like a fiery plague breaks out anew
In deeds which make the Christian cause look pale
In its own light. The garrison of Patras 555
Has store but for ten days, nor is there hope
But from the Briton: at once slave and tyrant,
His wishes still are weaker than his fears,
Or he would sell what faith may yet remain
From the oaths broke in Genoa and in Norway; 560
And if you buy him not, your treasury
Is empty even of promises—his own coin.
The freedman of a western poet-chief
Holds Attica with seven thousand rebels,
And has beat back the Pacha of Negropont: 565
The agèd Ali sits in Yanina
A crownless metaphor of empire:
His name, that shadow of his withered might,
Holds our besieging army like a spell
In prey to famine, pest, and mutiny; 570
He, bastioned in his citadel, looks forth
Joyless upon the sapphire lake that mirrors
The ruins of the city where he reigned
Childless and sceptreless. The Greek has reaped
The costly harvest his own blood matured, 575
Not the sower, Ali—who has bought a truce
From Ypsilanti with ten camel-loads
Of Indian gold.

Enter a third Messenger.

Mahmud. What more?
Third Messenger. The Christian tribes
Of Lebanon and the Syrian wilderness
Are in revolt;—Damascus, Hems, Aleppo 580
Tremble;—the Arab menaces Medina,
The Aethiop has intrenched himself in Sennaar,
And keeps the Egyptian rebel well employed,
Who denies homage, claims investiture
As price of tardy aid. Persia demands 585
The cities on the Tigris, and the Georgians
Refuse their living tribute. Crete and Cyprus,
Like mountain-twins that from each other's veins
Catch the volcano-fire and earthquake-spasm,
Shake in the general fever. Through the city, 590

Like birds before a storm, the Santons shriek,
And prophesyings horrible and new
Are heard among the crowd: that sea of men
Sleeps on the wrecks it made, breathless and still.
A Dervise, learnèd in the Koran, preaches   595
That it is written how the sins of Islam
Must raise up a destroyer even now.
The Greeks expect a Saviour from the West,
Who shall not come, men say, in clouds and glory,
But in the omnipresence of that Spirit   600
In which all live and are. Ominous signs
Are blazoned broadly on the noonday sky:
One saw a red cross stamped upon the sun;
It has rained blood; and monstrous births declare
The secret wrath of Nature and her Lord.   605
The army encamped upon the Cydaris
Was roused last night by the alarm of battle,
And saw two hosts conflicting in the air,
The shadows doubtless of the unborn time
Cast on the mirror of the night. While yet   610
The fight hung balanced, there arose a storm
Which swept the phantoms from among the stars.
At the third watch the Spirit of the Plague
Was heard abroad flapping among the tents;
Those who relieved watch found the sentinels dead.   615
The last news from the camp is, that a thousand
Have sickened, and——

Enter a Fourth Messenger.

Mahmud.   And thou, pale ghost, dim shadow
Of some untimely rumour, speak!
Fourth Messenger.   One comes
Fainting with toil, covered with foam and blood:
He stood, he says, on Chelonites'   620
Promontory, which o'erlooks the isles that groan
Under the Briton's frown, and all their waters
Then trembling in the splendour of the moon,
When as the wandering clouds unveiled or hid
Her boundless light, he saw two adverse fleets   625
Stalk through the night in the horizon's glimmer,
Mingling fierce thunders and sulphureous gleams,
And smoke which strangled every infant wind
That soothed the silver clouds through the deep air.
At length the battle slept, but the Sirocco   630
Awoke, and drove his flock of thunder-clouds
Over the sea-horizon, blotting out
All objects—save that in the faint moon-glimpse

He saw, or dreamed he saw, the Turkish admiral
And two the loftiest of our ships of war,   635
With the bright image of that Queen of Heaven,
Who hid, perhaps, her face for grief, reversed;
And the abhorrèd cross—

Enter an Attendant.

 Attendant.   Your Sublime Highness,
The Jew, who——
  Mahmud. Could not come more seasonably:
Bid him attend. I'll hear no more! too long   640
We gaze on danger through the mist of fear,
And multiply upon our shattered hopes
The images of ruin. Come what will!
To-morrow and to-morrow are as lamps
Set in our path to light us to the edge   645
Through rough and smooth, nor can we suffer aught
Which He inflicts not in whose hand we are.   [*Exeunt.*

Semichorus I.

Would I were the wingèd cloud
Of a tempest swift and loud!
  I would scorn   650
  The smile of morn
And the wave where the moonrise is born!
  I would leave
  The spirits of eve
A shroud for the corpse of the day to weave   655
From other threads than mine!
Bask in the deep blue noon divine.
  Who would? Not I.

Semichorus II.

  Whither to fly?

Semichorus I.

Where the rocks that gird th' Aegean   660
Echo to the battle paean
  Of the free—
  I would flee
A tempestuous herald of victory!
  My golden rain   665
  For the Grecian slain
Should mingle in tears with the bloody main,
  And my solemn thunder-knell
Should ring to the world the passing-bell
  Of Tyranny!   670

Semichorus II.

Ah king! wilt thou chain
The rack and the rain?
Wilt thou fetter the lightning and hurricane?
The storms are free,
But we—   675

Chorus.

O Slavery! thou frost of the world's prime,
Killing its flowers and leaving its thorns bare!
Thy touch has stamped these limbs with crime,
These brows thy branding garland bear,
But the free heart, the impassive soul   680
Scorn thy control!

Semichorus I.

Let there be light! said Liberty,
And like sunrise from the sea,
Athens arose!—Around her born,
Shone like mountains in the morn   685
Glorious states;—and are they now
Ashes, wrecks, oblivion?

Semichorus II.

Go,
Where Thermae and Asopus swallowed
Persia, as the sand does foam;
Deluge upon deluge followed,   690
Discord, Macedon, and Rome:
And lastly thou!

Semichorus I.

Temples and towers,
Citadels and marts, and they
Who live and die there, have been ours,
And may be thine, and must decay;   695
But Greece and her foundations are
Built below the tide of war,
Based on the crystalline sea
Of thought and its eternity;
Her citizens, imperial spirits,   700
Rule the present from the past,
On all this world of men inherits
Their seal is set.

Semichorus II.

Hear ye the blast,
Whose Orphic thunder thrilling calls

From ruin her Titanian walls?
Whose spirit shakes the sapless bones
    Of Slavery? Argos, Corinth, Crete
Hear, and from their mountain thrones
    The daemons and the nymphs repeat
The harmony.

Semichorus I.

I hear! I hear!   710

Semichorus II.

The world's eyeless charioteer,
    Destiny, is hurrying by!
What faith is crushed, what empire bleeds
Beneath her earthquake-footed steeds?
What eagle-wingèd victory sits   715
At her right hand? what shadow flits
    Before? what splendour rolls behind?
    Ruin and renovation cry
'Who but We?'

Semichorus I.

I hear! I hear!
    The hiss as of a rushing wind,   720
The roar as of an ocean foaming,
The thunder as of earthquake coming
    I hear! I hear!
The crash as of an empire falling,
The shrieks as of a people calling   725
'Mercy! mercy!'—How they thrill!
Then a shout of 'kill! kill! kill!'
And then a small still voice, thus—

Semichorus II.

                         For
Revenge and Wrong bring forth their kind,
    The foul cubs like their parents are,   730
Their den is in the guilty mind,
    And Conscience feeds them with despair.

Semichorus I.

In sacred Athens, near the fane
    Of Wisdom, Pity's altar stood:
Serve not the unknown God in vain,   735
But pay that broken shrine again,
    Love for hate and tears for blood.

Enter MAHMUD *and* AHASUERUS.

Mahmud. Thou art a man, thou sayest, even as we.

Ahasuerus. No more!

Mahmud. But raised above thy fellow-men
By thought, as I by power.

Ahasuerus. Thou sayest so. 740

Mahmud. Thou art an adept in the difficult lore
Of Greek and Frank philosophy; thou numberest
The flowers, and thou measurest the stars;
Thou severest element from element;
Thy spirit is present in the Past, and sees 745
The birth of this old world through all its cycles
Of desolation and of loveliness,
And when man was not, and how man became
The monarch and the slave of this low sphere,
And all its narrow circles—it is much— 750
I honour thee, and would be what thou art
Were I not what I am; but the unborn hour,
Cradled in fear and hope, conflicting storms,
Who shall unveil? Nor thou, nor I, nor any
Mighty or wise. I apprehended not 755
What thou hast taught me, but I now perceive
That thou art no interpreter of dreams;
Thou dost not own that art, device, or God,
Can make the Future present—let it come!
Moreover thou disdainest us and ours; 760
Thou art as God, whom thou contemplatest.

Ahasuerus. Disdain thee?—not the worm beneath thy feet!
The Fathomless has care for meaner things
Than thou canst dream, and has made pride for those
Who would be what they may not, or would seem 765
That which they are not. Sultan! talk no more
Of thee and me, the Future and the Past;
But look on that which cannot change—the One,
The unborn and the undying. Earth and ocean,
Space, and the isles of life or light that gem 770
The sapphire floods of interstellar air,
This firmament pavilioned upon chaos,
With all its cressets of immortal fire,
Whose outwall, bastioned impregnably
Against the escape of boldest thoughts, repels them 775
As Calpe the Atlantic clouds—this Whole
Of suns, and worlds, and men, and beasts, and flowers,
With all the silent or tempestuous workings
By which they have been, are, or cease to be,
Is but a vision;—all that it inherits 780
Are motes of a sick eye, bubbles and dreams;

Thought is its cradle and its grave, nor less
The Future and the Past are idle shadows
Of thought's eternal flight—they have no being:
Nought is but that which feels itself to be.   785
    Mahmud. What meanest thou? Thy words stream like a tempest
Of dazzling mist within my brain—they shake
The earth on which I stand, and hang like night
On Heaven above me. What can they avail?
They cast on all things surest, brightest, best,   790
Doubt, insecurity, astonishment.
    Ahasuerus.   Mistake me not! All is contained in each.
Dodona's forest to an acorn's cup
Is that which has been, or will be, to that
Which is—the absent to the present. Thought   795
Alone, and its quick elements, Will, Passion,
Reason, Imagination, cannot die;
They are, what that which they regard appears,
The stuff whence mutability can weave
All that it hath dominion o'er, worlds, worms,   800
Empires, and superstitions. What has thought
To do with time, or place, or circumstance?
Wouldst thou behold the Future?—ask and have!
Knock and it shall be opened—look, and lo!
The coming age is shadowed on the Past   805
As on a glass.
    Mahmud.   Wild, wilder thoughts convulse
My spirit—Did not Mahomet the Second
Win Stamboul?
    Ahasuerus.   Thou wouldst ask that giant spirit
The written fortunes of thy house and faith.
Thou wouldst cite one out of the grave to tell   810
How what was born in blood must die.
    Mahmud.   Thy words
Have power on me! I see——
    Ahasuerus.   What hearest thou?
    Mahmul. A far whisper——
Terrible silence.
    Ahasuerus.   What succeeds?
    Mahmud.   The sound
As of the assault of an imperial city,   815
The hiss of inextinguishable fire,
The roar of giant cannon; the earthquaking
Fall of vast bastions and precipitous towers,
The shock of crags shot from strange enginery,
The clash of wheels, and clang of armèd hoofs,   820
And crash of brazen mail as of the wreck
Of adamantine mountains—the mad blast

Of trumpets, and the neigh of raging steeds,
The shrieks of women whose thrill jars the blood,
And one sweet laugh, most horrible to hear,   825
As of a joyous infant waked and playing
With its dead mother's breast, and now more loud
The mingled battle-cry,—ha! hear I not
''Εν τούτῳ νίκη!' 'Allah-illa-Allah!'?
   Ahasuerus. The sulphurous mist is raised—thou seest—
   Mahmud.   A chasm,   830
As of two mountains, in the wall of Stamboul;
And in that ghastly breach the Islamites,
Like giants on the ruins of a world,
Stand in the light of sunrise. In the dust
Glimmers a kingless diadem, and one   835
Of regal port has cast himself beneath
The stream of war. Another proudly clad
In golden arms spurs a Tartarian barb
Into the gap, and with his iron mace
Directs the torrent of that tide of men,   840
And seems—he is—Mahomet!
   Ahasuerus.   What thou seest
Is but the ghost of thy forgotten dream.
A dream itself, yet less, perhaps, than that
Thou call'st reality. Thou mayest behold
How cities, on which Empire sleeps enthroned,   845
Bow their towered crests to mutability.
Poised by the flood, e'en on the height thou holdest,
Thou mayst now learn how the full tide of power
Ebbs to its depths.—Inheritor of glory,
Conceived in darkness, born in blood, and nourished   850
With tears and toil, thou seest the mortal throes
Of that whose birth was but the same. The Past
Now stands before thee like an Incarnation
Of the To-come; yet wouldst thou commune with
That portion of thyself which was ere thou   855
Didst start for this brief race whose crown is death,
Dissolve with that strong faith and fervent passion
Which called it from the uncreated deep,
Yon cloud of war, with its tempestuous phantoms
Of raging death; and draw with mighty will   860
The imperial shade hither.   [*Exit* AHASUERUS. *The
                Phantom of* MAHOMET THE SECOND *appears.*
   Mahmud.   Approach!
   Phantom.   I come
Thence whither thou must go! The grave is fitter
To take the living than give up the dead;
Yet has thy faith prevailed, and I am here.

The heavy fragments of the power which fell   865
When I arose, like shapeless crags and clouds,
Hang round my throne on the abyss, and voices
Of strange lament soothe my supreme repose,
Wailing for glory never to return.—
  A later Empire nods in its decay: 870
The autumn of a greener faith is come,
And wolfish change, like winter, howls to strip
The foliage in which Fame, the eagle, built
Her aerie, while Dominion whelped below.
The storm is in its branches, and the frost   875
Is on its leaves, and the blank deep expects
Oblivion on oblivion, spoil on spoil,
Ruin on ruin:—Thou art slow, my son;
The Anarchs of the world of darkness keep
A throne for thee, round which thine empire lies   880
Boundless and mute; and for thy subjects thou,
Like us, shalt rule the ghosts of murdered life,
The phantoms of the powers who rule thee now—
Mutinous passions, and conflicting fears,
And hopes that sate themselves on dust, and die!—   885
Stripped of their mortal strength, as thou of thine.
Islam must fall, but we will reign together
Over its ruins in the world of death:—
And if the trunk be dry, yet shall the seed
Unfold itself even in the shape of that   890
Which gathers birth in its decay. Woe! woe!
To the weak people tangled in the grasp
Of its last spasms.
    Mahmud.   Spirit, woe to all!
Woe to the wronged and the avenger! Woe
To the destroyer, woe to the destroyed!   895
Woe to the dupe, and woe to the deceiver!
Woe to the oppressed, and woe to the oppressor!
Woe both to those that suffer and inflict;
Those who are born and those who die! but say,
Imperial shadow of the thing I am,   900
When, how, by whom, Destruction must accomplish
Her consummation!
    Phantom.   Ask the cold pale Hour,
Rich in reversion of impending death,
When _he_ shall fall upon whose ripe gray hairs
Sit Care, and Sorrow, and Infirmity—   905
The weight which Crime, whose wings are plumed with years,
Leaves in his flight from ravaged heart to heart
Over the heads of men, under which burthen
They bow themselves unto the grave: fond wretch!

He leans upon his crutch, and talks of years   910
To come, and how in hours of youth renewed
He will renew lost joys, and——
   Voice without.   Victory! Victory!
                      [The Phantom vanishes.
   Mahmud. What sound of the importunate earth has broken
My mighty trance?
   Voice without.   Victory! Victory!
   Mahmud. Weak lightning before darkness! poor faint smile
Of dying Islam! Voice which art the response   916
Of hollow weakness! Do I wake and live?
Were there such things, or may the unquiet brain,
Vexed by the wise mad talk of the old Jew,
Have shaped itself these shadows of its fear?   920
It matters not!—for nought we see or dream,
Possess, or lose, or grasp at, can be worth
More than it gives or teaches. Come what may,
The Future must become the Past, and I
As they were to whom once this present hour,   925
This gloomy crag of time to which I cling,
Seemed an Elysian isle of peace and joy
Never to be attained.—I must rebuke
This drunkenness of triumph ere it die,
And dying, bring despair. Victory! poor slaves!   930
                    [Exit MAHMUD.
   Voice without. Shout in the jubilee of death! The Greeks
Are as a brood of lions in the net
Round which the kingly hunters of the earth
Stand smiling. Anarchs, ye whose daily food
Are curses, groans, and gold, the fruit of death,   935
From Thule to the girdle of the world,
Come, feast! the board groans with the flesh of men;
The cup is foaming with a nation's blood,
Famine and Thirst await! eat, drink, and die!

Semichorus I.

Victorious Wrong, with vulture scream,   940
Salutes the rising sun, pursues the flying day!
  I saw her, ghastly as a tyrant's dream,
Perch on the trembling pyramid of night,
Beneath which earth and all her realms pavilioned lay
In visions of the dawning undelight.   945
      Who shall impede her flight?
      Who rob her of her prey?

   Voice without. Victory! Victory! Russia's famished eagles
Dare not to prey beneath the crescent's light.

Impale the remnant of the Greeks! despoil!   950
Violate! make their flesh cheaper than dust!

Semichorus II.

Thou voice which art
The herald of the ill in splendour hid!
Thou echo of the hollow heart
Of monarchy, bear me to thine abode   955
When desolation flashes o'er a world destroyed:
Oh, bear me to those isles of jaggèd cloud
Which float like mountains on the earthquake, mid
The momentary oceans of the lightning,
Or to some toppling promontory proud   960
Of solid tempest whose black pyramid,
Riven, overhangs the founts intensely bright'ning
Of those dawn-tinted deluges of fire
Before their waves expire,
When heaven and earth are light, and only light   965
In the thunder-night!

Voice without. Victory! Victory! Austria, Russia, England,
And that tame serpent, that poor shadow, France,
Cry peace, and that means death when monarchs speak.
Ho, there! bring torches, sharpen those red stakes,   970
These chains are light, fitter for slaves and poisoners
Than Greeks. Kill! plunder! burn! let none remain.

Semichorus I.

Alas! for Liberty!
If numbers, wealth, or unfulfilling years,
Or fate, can quell the free!   975
Alas! for Virtue, when
Torments, or contumely, or the sneers
Of erring judging men
Can break the heart where it abides.
Alas! if Love, whose smile makes this obscure world splendid,
Can change with its false times and tides,   981
Like hope and terror,—
Alas for Love!
And Truth, who wanderest lone and unbefriended,
If thou canst veil thy lie-consuming mirror   985
Before the dazzled eyes of Error,
Alas for thee! Image of the Above.

Semichorus II.

Repulse, with plumes from conquest torn,
Led the ten thousand from the limits of the morn

Through many an hostile Anarchy!   990
At length they wept aloud, and cried, 'The Sea! the Sea!'
     Through exile, persecution, and despair,
        Rome was, and young Atlantis shall become
        The wonder, or the terror, or the tomb
Of all whose step wakes Power lulled in her savage lair: 995
     But Greece was as a hermit-child,
        Whose fairest thoughts and limbs were built
     To woman's growth, by dreams so mild,
        She knew not pain or guilt;
And now, O Victory, blush! and Empire, tremble   1000
        When ye desert the free—
        If Greece must be
A wreck, yet shall its fragments reassemble,
And build themselves again impregnably
        In a diviner clime,   1005
To Amphionic music on some Cape sublime,
Which frowns above the idle foam of Time.

Semichorus I.

Let the tyrants rule the desert they have made;
     Let the free possess the Paradise they claim;
Be the fortune of our fierce oppressors weighed   1010
     With our ruin, our resistance, and our name!

Semichorus II.

Our dead shall be the seed of their decay,
     Our survivors be the shadow of their pride,
Our adversity a dream to pass away—
     Their dishonour a remembrance to abide!   1015

Voice without. Victory! Victory! The bought Briton sends
The keys of ocean to the Islamite.—
Now shall the blazon of the cross be veiled,
And British skill directing Othman might,
Thunder-strike rebel victory. Oh, keep holy   1020
This jubilee of unrevengèd blood!
Kill! crush! despoil! Let not a Greek escape!

Semichorus I.

     Darkness has dawned in the East
        On the noon of time:
     The death-birds descend to their feast   1025
        From the hungry clime.
     Let Freedom and Peace flee far
        To a sunnier strand,
     And follow Love's folding-star
        To the Evening land!   1030

Semichorus II.

The young moon has fed
　　Her exhausted horn
　　With the sunset's fire:
The weak day is dead,
　　But the night is not born;   1035
And, like loveliness panting with wild desire
　　While it trembles with fear and delight,
　　Hesperus flies from awakening night,
And pants in its beauty and speed with light
　　Fast-flashing, soft, and bright.   1040
Thou beacon of love! thou lamp of the free!
　　Guide us far, far away,
To climes where now veiled by the ardour of day
　　Thou art hidden
　　From waves on which weary Noon   1045
　　Faints in her summer swoon,
　　Between kingless continents sinless as Eden,
　　Around mountains and islands inviolably
　　　Pranked on the sapphire sea.

Semichorus I.

Through the sunset of hope,   1050
Like the shapes of a dream,
What Paradise islands of glory gleam!
　　Beneath Heaven's cope,
　　Their shadows more clear float by—
The sound of their oceans, the light of their sky,   1055
The music and fragrance their solitudes breathe
Burst, like morning on dream, or like Heaven on death,
　　Through the walls of our prison;
　　And Greece, which was dead, is arisen!

Chorus.

The world's great age begins anew,   1060
　　The golden years return,
The earth doth like a snake renew
　　Her winter weeds outworn:
Heaven smiles, and faiths and empires gleam,
Like wrecks of a dissolving dream.   1065

A brighter Hellas rears its mountains
　　From waves serener far;
A new Peneus rolls his fountains
　　Against the morning star.
Where fairer Tempes bloom, there sleep   1070
Young Cyclads on a sunnier deep.

SHELLEY

A loftier Argo cleaves the main,
    Fraught with a later prize;
Another Orpheus sings again,
    And loves, and weeps, and dies.   1075
A new Ulysses leaves once more
Calypso for his native shore.

Oh, write no more the tale of Troy,
    If earth Death's scroll must be!
Nor mix with Laian rage the joy   1080
    Which dawns upon the free:
Although a subtler Sphinx renew
Riddles of death Thebes never knew.

Another Athens shall arise,
    And to remoter time   1085
Bequeath, like sunset to the skies,
    The splendour of its prime;
And leave, if nought so bright may live,
All earth can take or Heaven can give.

Saturn and Love their long repose   1090
    Shall burst, more bright and good
Than all who fell, than One who rose,
    Than many unsubdued:
Not gold, not blood, their altar dowers,
But votive tears and symbol flowers.   1095

Oh, cease! must hate and death return?
    Cease! must men kill and die?
Cease! drain not to its dregs the urn
    Of bitter prophecy.
The world is weary of the past,   1100
Oh, might it die or rest at last!

NOTES

(1) *The quenchless ashes of Milan* [l. 60, p. 509].

MILAN was the centre of the resistance of the Lombard league against
the Austrian tyrant. Frederic Barbarossa burnt the city to the ground,
but liberty lived in its ashes, and it rose like an exhalation from its ruin.
See Sismondi's *Histoire des Républiques Italiennes,* a book which has
done much towards awakening the Italians to an imitation of their great
ancestors.

(2) *The Chorus* [p. 512].

The popular notions of Christianity are represented in this chorus as
true in their relation to the worship they superseded, and that which in all

probability they will supersede, without considering their merits in a relation more universal. The first stanza contrasts the immortality of the living and thinking beings which inhabit the planets, and to use a common and inadequate phrase, *clothe themselves in matter,* with the transience of the noblest manifestations of the external world.

The concluding verses indicate a progressive state of more or less exalted existence, according to the degree of perfection which every distinct intelligence may have attained. Let it not be supposed that I mean to dogmatise upon a subject, concerning which all men are equally ignorant, or that I think the Gordian knot of the origin of evil can be disentangled by that or any similar assertions. The received hypothesis of a Being resembling men in the moral attributes of His nature, having called us out of non-existence, and after inflicting on us the misery of the commission of error, should superadd that of the punishment and the privations consequent upon it, still would remain inexplicable and incredible. That there is a true solution of the riddle, and that in our present state that solution is unattainable by us, are propositions which may be regarded as equally certain: meanwhile, as it is the province of the poet to attach himself to those ideas which exalt and ennoble humanity, let him be permitted to have conjectured the condition of that futurity towards which we are all impelled by an inextinguishable thirst for immortality. Until better arguments can be produced than sophisms which disgrace the cause, this desire itself must remain the strongest and the only presumption that eternity is the inheritance of every thinking being.

(3) *No hoary priests after that Patriarch* [l. 245, p. 514].

The Greek Patriarch, after having been compelled to fulminate an anathema against the insurgents, was put to death by the Turks.

Fortunately the Greeks have been taught that they cannot buy security by degradation, and the Turks, though equally cruel, are less cunning than the smooth-faced tyrants of Europe. As to the anathema, his Holiness might as well have thrown his mitre at Mount Athos for any effect that it produced. The chiefs of the Greeks are almost all men of comprehension and enlightened views on religion and politics.

(4) *The freedman of a western poet-chief* [l. 563, p. 521].

A Greek who had been Lord Byron's servant commands the insurgents in Attica. This Greek, Lord Byron informs me, though a poet and an enthusiastic patriot, gave him rather the idea of a timid and unenterprising person. It appears that circumstances make men what they are, and that we all contain the germ of a degree of degradation or of greatness whose connection with our character is determined by events.

(5) *The Greeks expect a Saviour from the West* [l. 598, p. 52⁀⁀

It is reported that this Messiah had arrived at a seaport near Lacedaemon in an American brig. The association of names and ideas is irresistibly ludicrous, but the prevalence of such a rumour strongly marks the state of popular enthusiasm in Greece.

(6) *The sound as of the assault of an imperial city* [ll. 814-15, p. 527].

For the vision of Mahmud of the taking of Constantinople in 1453, see Gibbon's *Decline and Fall of the Roman Empire,* vol. xii, p. 223.

The manner of the invocation of the spirit of Mahomet the Second will be censured as over subtle. I could easily have made the Jew a regular conjuror, and the Phantom an ordinary ghost. I have preferred to represent the Jew as disclaiming all pretension, or even belief, in supernatural agency, and as tempting Mahmud to that state of mind in which ideas may be supposed to assume the force of sensations through the confusion of thought with the objects of thought, and the excess of passion animating the creations of imagination.

It is a sort of natural magic, susceptible of being exercised in a degree by any one who should have made himself master of the secret associations of another's thoughts.

(7) *The Chorus* [p. 533].

The final chorus is indistinct and obscure, as the event of the living drama whose arrival it foretells. Prophecies of wars, and rumours of wars, etc., may safely be made by poet or prophet in any age, but to anticipate however darkly a period of regeneration and happiness is a more hazardous exercise of the faculty which bards possess or feign. It will remind the reader 'magno *nec* proximus intervallo' of Isaiah and Virgil, whose ardent spirits overleaping the actual reign of evil which we endure and bewail, already saw the possible and perhaps approaching state of society in which the *'lion shall lie down with the lamb,'* and 'omnis feret omnia tellus.' Let these great names be my authority and my excuse.

(8) *Saturn and Love their long repose shall burst* [l. 1090, p. 534].

Saturn and Love were among the deities of a real or imaginary state of innocence and happiness. *All* those *who fell,* or the Gods of Greece, Asia, and Egypt; the *One who rose,* or Jesus Christ, at whose appearance the idols of the Pagan World were amerced of their worship; and *the many unsubdued,* or the monstrous objects of the idolatry of China, India, the Antarctic islands, and the native tribes of America, certainly have reigned over the understandings of men in conjunction or in succession during periods in which all we know of evil has been in a state of portentous, and, until the revival of learning and the arts, perpetually increasing, activity. The Grecian gods seem indeed to have been personally more innocent, although it cannot be said, that as far as temperance and chastity are concerned, they gave so edifying an example as their successor. The sublime human character of Jesus Christ was deformed by an imputed identification with a Power, who tempted, betrayed, and punished the innocent beings who were called into existence by His sole will; and for the period of a thousand years, the spirit of this most just, wise, and benevolent of men has been propitiated with myriads of hecatombs of those who approached the nearest to His innocence and wisdom, sacrificed under every aggravation of atrocity and variety of torture. The horrors of the Mexican, the Peruvian, and the Indian superstitions are well known.

NOTE ON HELLAS, BY MRS. SHELLEY

THE South of Europe was in a state of great political excitement at the beginning of the year 1821. The Spanish Revolution had been a signal to Italy; secret societies were formed; and, when Naples rose to declare the Constitution, the call was responded to from Brundusium to the foot of the Alps. To crush these attempts to obtain liberty, early in 1821 the Austrians poured their armies into the Peninsula: at first their coming rather seemed to add energy and resolution to a people long enslaved. The Piedmontese asserted their freedom; Genoa threw off the yoke of the King of Sardinia; and, as if in playful imitation, the people of the little state of Massa and Carrara gave the *congé* to their sovereign, and set up a republic.

Tuscany alone was perfectly tranquil. It was said that the Austrian minister presented a list of sixty Carbonari to the Grand Duke, urging their imprisonment; and the Grand Duke replied, 'I do not know whether these sixty men are Carbonari, but I know, if I imprison them, I shall directly have sixty thousand start up.' But, though the Tuscans had no desire to disturb the paternal government beneath whose shelter they slumbered, they regarded the progress of the various Italian revolutions with intense interest, and hatred for the Austrians was warm in every bosom. But they had slender hopes; they knew that the Neapolitans would offer no fit resistance to the regular German troops, and that the overthrow of the constitution in Naples would act as a decisive blow against all struggles for liberty in Italy.

We have seen the rise and progress of reform. But the Holy Alliance was alive and active in those days, and few could dream of the peaceful triumph of liberty. It seemed then that the armed assertion of freedom in the South of Europe was the only hope of the liberals, as, if it prevailed, the nations of the north would imitate the example. Happily the reverse has proved the fact. The countries accustomed to the exercise of the privileges of freemen, to a limited extent, have extended, and are extending, these limits. Freedom and knowledge have now a chance of proceeding hand in hand; and, if it continue thus, we may hope for the durability of both. Then, as I have said—in 1821—Shelley, as well as every other lover of liberty, looked upon the struggles in Spain and Italy as decisive of the destinies of the world, probably for centuries to come. The interest he took in the progress of affairs was intense. When Genoa declared itself free, his hopes were at their highest. Day after day he read the bulletins of the Austrian army, and sought eagerly to gather tokens of its defeat. He heard of the revolt of Genoa with emotions of transport. His whole heart and soul were in the triumph of the cause. We were living at Pisa at that time; and several well-informed Italians, at the head of whom we may place the celebrated Vaccà, were accustomed to seek for sympathy in their hopes from Shelley: they did not find such for the despair they too generally experienced, founded on contempt for their southern countrymen.

While the fate of the progress of the Austrian armies then invading Naples was yet in suspense, the news of another revolution filled him with exultation. We had formed the acquaintance at Pisa of several Constantinopolitan Greeks, of the family of Prince Caradja, formerly Hospodar of Wallachia; who, hearing that the bowstring, the accustomed finale of his viceroyalty, was on the road to him, escaped with his treasures, and took up his abode in Tuscany. Among these was the gentleman to whom the drama of *Hellas* is dedicated. Prince Mavrocordato was warmed by those aspirations for the independence of his country which filled the hearts of many of his countrymen. He often intimated the possibility of an insurrection in Greece; but we had no idea of its being so near at hand, when, on the 1st of April 1821, he called on Shelley, bringing the proclamation of his cousin, Prince Ypsilanti, and, radiant with exultation and delight, declared that henceforth Greece would be free.

Shelley had hymned the dawn of liberty in Spain and Naples, in two odes dictated by the warmest enthusiasm; he felt himself naturally impelled to decorate with poetry the uprise of the descendants of that people whose works he regarded with deep admiration, and to adopt the vaticinatory character in prophesying their success. *Hellas* was written in a moment of enthusiasm. It is curious to remark how well he overcomes the difficulty of forming a drama out of such scant materials. His prophecies, indeed, came true in their general, not their particular, purport. He did not foresee the death of Lord Londonderry, which was to be the epoch of a change in English politics, particularly as regarded foreign affairs; nor that the navy of his country would fight for instead of against the Greeks, and by the battle of Navarino secure their enfranchisement from the Turks. Almost against reason, as it appeared to him, he resolved to believe that Greece would prove triumphant; and in this spirit, auguring ultimate good, yet grieving over the vicissitudes to be endured in the interval, he composed his drama.

Hellas was among the last of his compositions, and is among the most beautiful. The choruses are singularly imaginative, and melodious in their versification. There are some stanzas that beautifully exemplify Shelley's peculiar style; as, for instance, the assertion of the intellectual empire which must be for ever the inheritance of the country of Homer, Sophocles, and Plato:—

> 'But Greece and her foundations are
> Built below the tide of war,
> Based on the crystàlline sea
> Of thought and its eternity.'

And again, that philosophical truth felicitously imaged forth—

> 'Revenge and Wrong bring forth their kind,
>   The foul cubs like their parents are,
> Their den is in the guilty mind,
>   And Conscience feeds them with despair.'

The conclusion of the last chorus is among the most beautiful of his lyrics. The imagery is distinct and majestic; the prophecy, such as poets love to dwell upon, the Regeneration of Mankind—and that regeneration reflecting back splendour on the foregone time, from which it inherits so much of intellectual wealth, and memory of past virtuous deeds, as must render the possession of happiness and peace of tenfold value.

FRAGMENTS OF AN UNFINISHED DRAMA

THE following fragments are part of a Drama undertaken for the amusement of the individuals who composed our intimate society, but left unfinished. I have preserved a sketch of the story as far as it had been shadowed in the poet's mind.

An Enchantress, living in one of the islands of the Indian Archipelago, saves the life of a Pirate, a man of savage but noble nature. She becomes enamoured of him; and he, inconstant to his mortal love, for a while returns her passion; but at length, recalling the memory of her whom he left, and who laments his loss, he escapes from the Enchanted Island, and returns to his lady. His mode of life makes him again go to sea, and the Enchantress seizes the opportunity to bring him, by a spirit-brewed tempest, back to her Island.—[MRS. SHELLEY's NOTE, 1839.]

SCENE.—*Before the Cavern of the Indian Enchantress.*

The ENCHANTRESS *comes forth.*

Enchantress.

HE came like a dream in the dawn of life,
  He fled like a shadow before its noon;
He is gone, and my peace is turned to strife,
  And I wander and wane like the weary moon.
   O, sweet Echo, wake,   5
   And for my sake
Make answer the while my heart shall break!

But my heart has a music which Echo's lips,
  Though tender and true, yet can answer not,
And the shadow that moves in the soul's eclipse 10
  Can return not the kiss by his now forgot;
   Sweet lips! he who hath
   On my desolate path
Cast the darkness of absence, worse than death!

The ENCHANTRESS *makes her spell: she is answered by a Spirit.*

Spirit. Within the silent centre of the earth   15
My mansion is; where I have lived insphered
From the beginning, and around my sleep
Have woven all the wondrous imagery
Of this dim spot, which mortals call the world;
Infinite depths of unknown elements   20
Massed into one impenetrable mask;
Sheets of immeasurable fire, and veins
Of gold and stone, and adamantine iron.
And as a veil in which I walk through Heaven
I have wrought mountains, seas, and waves, and clouds,
And lastly light, whose interfusion dawns   26
In the dark space of interstellar air.

A good Spirit, who watches over the Pirate's fate, leads, in a mysterious manner, the lady of his love to the Enchanted Isle. She is accompanied by a Youth, who loves the lady, but whose passion she returns only
with a sisterly affection. The ensuing scene takes place between them
on their arrival at the Isle. [MRS. SHELLEY'S NOTE, 1839.]

ANOTHER SCENE

INDIAN YOUTH *and* LADY.

Indian. And, if my grief should still be dearer to me
Than all the pleasures in the world beside,
Why would you lighten it?—
        Lady.   I offer only   30
That which I seek, some human sympathy
In this mysterious island.
        Indian.   Oh! my friend,
My sister, my beloved!—What do I say?
My brain is dizzy, and I scarce know whether
I speak to thee or her.
        Lady.   Peace, perturbed heart!   35
I am to thee only as thou to mine,
The passing wind which heals the brow at noon,
And may strike cold into the breast at night,
Yet cannot linger where it soothes the most,
Or long soothe could it linger.
        Indian.   But you said   40
You also loved?
        Lady.   Loved! Oh, I love. Methinks
This word of love is fit for all the world,
And that for gentle hearts another name
Would speak of gentler thoughts than the world owns.
I have loved.

Indian.   And thou lovest not? if so,   45
Young as thou art thou canst afford to weep.
   Lady. Oh! would that I could claim exemption
From all the bitterness of that sweet name.
I loved, I love, and when I love no more
Let joys and grief perish, and leave despair   50
To ring the knell of youth. He stood beside me,
The embodied vision of the brightest dream,
Which like a dawn heralds the day of life;
The shadow of his presence made my world
A Paradise. All familiar things he touched,   55
All common words he spoke, became to me
Like forms and sounds of a diviner world.
He was as is the sun in his fierce youth,
As terrible and lovely as a tempest;
He came, and went, and left me what I am.   60
Alas! Why must I think how oft we two
Have sate together near the river springs,
Under the green pavilion which the willow
Spreads on the floor of the unbroken fountain,
Strewn, by the nurslings that linger there.   65
Over that islet paved with flowers and moss,
While the musk-rose leaves, like flakes of crimson snow,
Showered on us, and the dove mourned in the pine,
Sad prophetess of sorrows not her own?
The crane returned to her unfrozen haunt,,   70
And the false cuckoo bade the spray good morn;
And on a wintry bough the widowed bird,
Hid in the deepest night of ivy-leaves,
Renewed the vigils of a sleepless sorrow.
I, left like her, and leaving one like her,   75
Alike abandoned and abandoning
(Oh! unlike her in this!) the gentlest youth,
Whose love had made my sorrows dear to him,
Even as my sorrow made his love to me!
   Indian. One curse of Nature stamps in the same mould
The features of the wretched; and they are   81
As like as violet to violet,
When memory, the ghost, their odours keeps
Mid the cold relics of abandoned joy.—
Proceed.
   Lady. He was a simple innocent boy.   85
I loved him well, but not as he desired;
Yet even thus he was content to be:—
A short content, for I was——
   Indian [*aside*].   God of Heaven!
From such an islet, such a river-spring——!

I dare not ask her if there stood upon it 90
A pleasure-dome surmounted by a crescent,
With steps to the blue water. [*Aloud*.] It may be
That Nature masks in life several copies
Of the same lot, so that the sufferers
May feel another's sorrow as their own, 95
And find in friendship what they lost in love.
That cannot be; yet it is strange that we,
From the same scene, by the same path to this
Realm of abandonment—— But speak! your breath—
Your breath is like soft music, your words are 100
The echoes of a voice which on my heart
Sleeps like a melody of early days.
But as you said——
    Lady.   He was so awful, yet
So beautiful in mystery and terror,
Calming me as the loveliness of heaven 105
Soothes the unquiet sea:—and yet not so,
For he seemed stormy, and would often seem
A quenchless sun masked in portentous clouds;
For such his thoughts, and even his actions were;
But he was not of them, nor they of him, 110
But as they hid his splendour from the earth.
Some said he was a man of blood and peril,
And steeped in bitter infamy to the lips.
More need was there I should be innocent,
More need that I should be most true and kind, 115
And much more need that there should be found one
To share remorse and scorn and solitude,
And all the ills that wait on those who do
The tasks of ruin in the world of life.
He fled, and I have followed him.
    Indian.   Such a one 120
Is he who was the winter of my peace.
But, fairest stranger, when didst thou depart
From the far hills where rise the springs of India?
How didst thou pass the intervening sea?
    Lady. If I be sure I am not dreaming now, 125
I should not doubt to say it was a dream.
Methought a star came down from heaven,
And rested mid the plants of India,
Which I had given a shelter from the frost
Within my chamber. There the meteor lay, 130
Panting forth light among the leaves and flowers,
As if it lived, and was outworn with speed;
Or that it loved, and passion made the pulse
Of its bright life throb like an anxious heart.

Till it diffused itself, and all the chamber   135
And walls seemed melted into emerald fire
That burned not; in the midst of which appeared
A spirit like a child, and laughed aloud
A thrilling peal of such sweet merriment
As made the blood tingle in my warm feet: 140
Then bent over a vase, and murmuring
Low, unintelligible melodies,
Placed something in the mould like melon-seeds,
And slowly faded, and in place of it
A soft hand issued from the veil of fire,   145
Holding a cup like a magnolia flower,
And poured upon the earth within the vase
The element with which it overflowed,
Brighter than morning light, and purer than
The water of the springs of Himalah.   150
    Indian. You waked not?
    Lady.   Not until my dream became
Like a child's legend on the tideless sand,
Which the first foam erases half, and half
Leaves legible. At length I rose, and went,
Visiting my flowers from pot to pot, and thought   155
To set new cuttings in the empty urns,
And when I came to that beside the lattice,
I saw two little dark-green leaves
Lifting the light mould at their birth, and then
I half-remembered my forgotten dream.   160
And day by day, green as a gourd in June,
The plant grew fresh and thick, yet no one knew
What plant it was; its stem and tendrils seemed
Like emerald snakes, mottled and diamonded
With azure mail and streaks of woven silver;   165
And all the sheaths that folded the dark buds
Rose like the crest of cobra-di-capel,
Until the golden eye of the bright flower,
Through the dark lashes of those veinèd lids,
... disencumbered of their silent sleep,   170
Gazed like a star into the morning light.
Its leaves were delicate, you almost saw
The pulses
With which the purple velvet flower was fed
To overflow, and like a poet's heart   175
Changing bright fancy to sweet sentiment,
Changed half the light to fragrance. It soon fell,
And to a green and dewy embryo-fruit
Left all its treasured beauty. Day by day
I nursed the plant, and on the double flute   18ʋ

Played to it on the sunny winter days
Soft melodies, as sweet as April rain
On silent leaves, and sang those words in which
Passion makes Echo taunt the sleeping strings;
And I would send tales of forgotten love   185
Late into the lone night, and sing wild songs
Of maids deserted in the olden time,
And weep like a soft cloud in April's bosom
Upon the sleeping eyelids of the plant,
So that perhaps it dreamed that Spring was come,   190
And crept abroad into the moonlight air,
And loosened all its limbs, as, noon by noon,
The sun averted less his oblique beam.
    Indian. And the plant died not in the frost?
    Lady.   It grew;
And went out of the lattice which I left   195
Half open for it, trailing its quaint spires
Along the garden and across the lawn,
And down the slope of moss and through the tufts
Of wild-flower roots, and stumps of trees o'ergrown
With simple lichens, and old hoary stones,   200
On to the margin of the glassy pool,
Even to a nook of unblown violets
And lilies-of-the-valley yet unborn,
Under a pine with ivy overgrown.
And there its fruit lay like a sleeping lizard   205
Under the shadows; but when Spring indeed
Came to unswathe her infants, and the lilies
Peeped from their bright green masks to wonder at
This shape of autumn couched in their recess,
Then it dilated, and it grew until   210
One half lay floating on the fountain wave,
Whose pulse, elapsed in unlike sympathies,
Kept time
Among the snowy water-lily buds.
Its shape was such as summer melody   215
Of the south wind in spicy vales might give
To some light cloud bound from the golden dawn
To fairy isles of evening, and it seemed
In hue and form that it had been a mirror
Of all the hues and forms around it and   220
Upon it pictured by the sunny beams
Which, from the bright vibrations of the pool,
Were thrown upon the rafters and the roof
Of boughs and leaves, and on the pillared stems
Of the dark sylvan temple, and reflections   225
Of every infant flower and star of moss

And veined leaf in the azure odorous air.
And thus it lay in the Elysian calm
Of its own beauty, floating on the line
Which, like a film in purest space, divided   230
The heaven beneath the water from the heaven
Above the clouds; and every day I went
Watching its growth and wondering;
And as the day grew hot, methought I saw
A glassy vapour dancing on the pool,   235
And on it little quaint and filmy shapes,
With dizzy motion, wheel and rise and fall,
Like clouds of gnats with perfect lineaments.

.   .   .   .

O friend, sleep was a veil uplift from Heaven—
As if Heaven dawned upon the world of dream—   240
When darkness rose on the extinguished day
Out of the eastern wilderness.
    Indian.   I too
Have found a moment's paradise in sleep
Half compensate a hell of waking sorrow.

THE TRIUMPH OF LIFE

SWIFT as a spirit hastening to his task
Of glory and of good, the Sun sprang forth
Rejoicing in his splendour, and the mask

Of darkness fell from the awakened Earth—   5
The smokeless altars of the mountain snows
Flamed above crimson clouds, and at the birth

Of light, the Ocean's orison arose,
To which the birds tempered their matin lay.
All flowers in field or forest which unclose

Their trembling eyelids to the kiss of day,   10
Swinging their censers in the element,
With orient incense lit by the new ray

Burned slow and inconsumably, and sent
Their odorous sighs up to the smiling air;
And, in succession due, did continent,   15

Isle, ocean, and all things that in them wear
The form and character of mortal mould,
Rise as the Sun their father rose, to bear

Their portion of the toil, which he of old
Took as his own, and then imposed on them: 20
But I, whom thoughts which must remain untold

Had kept as wakeful as the stars that gem
The cone of night, now they were laid asleep
Stretched my faint limbs beneath the hoary stem

Which an old chestnut flung athwart the steep   25
Of a green Apennine: before me fled
The night; behind me rose the day; the deep

Was at my feet, and Heaven above my head,—
When a strange trance over my fancy grew
Which was not slumber, for the shade it spread   30

Was so transparent, that the scene came through
As clear as when a veil of light is drawn
O'er evening hills they glimmer; and I knew

That I had felt the freshness of that dawn
Bathe in the same cold dew my brow and hair,   35
And sate as thus upon that slope of lawn

Under the self-same bough, and heard as there
The birds, the fountains and the ocean hold
Sweet talk in music through the enamoured air,
And then a vision on my brain was rolled.   40

—————————

As in that trance of wondrous thought I lay,
This was the tenour of my waking dream:—
Methought I sate beside a public way

Thick strewn with summer dust, and a great stream
Of people there was hurrying to and fro,   45
Numerous as gnats upon the evening gleam,

All hastening onward, yet none seemed to know
Whither he went, or whence he came, or why
He made one of the multitude, and so

Was borne amid the crowd, as through the sky   50
One of the million leaves of summer's bier;
Old age and youth, manhood and infancy,

Mixed in one mighty torrent did appear,
Some flying from the thing they feared, and some
Seeking the object of another's fear;   55

And others, as with steps towards the tomb,
Pored on the trodden worms that crawled beneath,
And others mournfully within the gloom

Of their own shadow walked, and called it death;
And some fled from it as it were a ghost,   60
Half fainting in the affliction of vain breath:

But more, with motions which each other crossed,
Pursued or shunned the shadows the clouds threw,
Or birds within the noonday aether lost,

Upon that path where flowers never grew,—   65
And, weary with vain toil and faint for thirst,
Heard not the fountains, whose melodious dew

Out of their mossy cells forever burst;
Nor felt the breeze which from the forest told
Of grassy paths and wood-lawns interspersed   70

With overarching elms and caverns cold,
And violet banks where sweet dreams brood, but they
Pursued their serious folly as of old.

And as I gazed, methought that in the way
The throng grew wilder, as the woods of June   75
When the south wind shakes the extinguished day,

And a cold glare, intenser than the noon,
But icy cold, obscured with blinding light
The sun, as he the stars. Like the young moon—

When on the sunlit limits of the night   80
Her white shell trembles amid crimson air,
And whilst the sleeping tempest gathers might—

Doth, as the herald of its coming, bear
The ghost of its dead mother, whose dim form
Bends in dark aether from her infant's chair,—   85

So came a chariot on the silent storm
Of its own rushing splendour, and a Shape
So sate within, as one whom years deform,

Beneath a dusky hood and double cape,
Crouching within the shadow of a tomb;   90
And o'er what seemed the head a cloud-like crape

Was bent, a dun and faint aethereal gloom
Tempering the light. Upon the chariot-beam
A Janus-visaged Shadow did assume

The guidance of that wonder-wingèd team;   95
The shapes which drew it in thick lightenings
Were lost:—I heard alone on the air's soft stream

The music of their ever-moving wings.
All the four faces of that Charioteer
Had their eyes banded; little profit brings   100

Speed in the van and blindness in the rear,
Nor then avail the beams that quench the sun,—
Or that with banded eyes could pierce the sphere

Of all that is, has been or will be done;
So ill was the car guided—but it passed   105
With solemn speed majestically on.

The crowd gave way, and I arose aghast,
Or seemed to rise, so mighty was the trance,
And saw, like clouds upon the thunder-blast,

The million with fierce song and maniac dance   110
Raging around—such seemed the jubilee
As when to greet some conqueror's advance

Imperial Rome poured forth her living sea
From senate-house, and forum, and theatre,
When   upon the free   115

Had bound a yoke, which soon they stooped to bear.
Nor wanted here the just similitude
Of a triumphal pageant, for where'er

The chariot rolled, a captive multitude
Was driven;—all those who had grown old in power   120
Or misery,—all who had their age subdued

By action or by suffering, and whose hour
Was drained to its last sand in weal or woe,
So that the trunk survived both fruit and flower;—

All those whose fame or infamy must grow   125
Till the great winter lay the form and name
Of this green earth with them for ever low;—

All but the sacred few who could not tame
Their spirits to the conquerors—but as soon
As they had touched the world with living flame,   130

Fled back like eagles to their native noon,
Or those who put aside the diadem
Of earthly thrones or gems . . .

Were there, of Athens or Jerusalem,
Were neither mid the mighty captives seen, 135
Nor mid the ribald crowd that followed them,

Nor those who went before fierce and obscene.
The wild dance maddens in the van, and those
Who lead it—fleet as shadows on the green,

Outspeed the chariot, and without repose 140
Mix with each other in tempestuous measure
To savage music, wilder as it grows,

They, tortured by their agonizing pleasure,
Convulsed and on the rapid whirlwinds spun
Of that fierce Spirit, whose unholy leisure 145

Was soothed by mischief since the world begun,
Throw back their heads and loose their streaming hair;
And in their dance round her who dims the sun,

Maidens and youths fling their wild arms in air
As their feet twinkle; they recede, and now 150
Bending within each other's atmosphere,

Kindle invisibly—and as they glow,
Like moths by light attracted and repelled,
Oft to their bright destruction come and go,

Till like two clouds into one vale impelled, 155
That shake the mountains when their lightnings mingle
And die in rain—the fiery band which held

Their natures, snaps—while the shock still may tingle;
One falls and then another in the path
Senseless—nor is the desolation single, 160

Yet ere I can say *where*—the chariot hath
Passed over them—nor other trace I find
But as of foam after the ocean's wrath

Is spent upon the desert shore;—behind,
Old men and women foully disarrayed, 165
Shake their gray hairs in the insulting wind,

And follow in the dance, with limbs decayed,
Seeking to reach the light which leaves them still
Farther behind and deeper in the shade.

But not the less with impotence of will 170
They wheel, though ghastly shadows interpose
Round them and round each other, and fulfil

Their work, and in the dust from whence they rose
Sink, and corruption veils them as they lie,
And past in these performs what   in those. 175

Struck to the heart by this sad pageantry,
Half to myself I said—'And what is this?
Whose shape is that within the car? And why—'

I would have added—'is all here amiss?—'
But a voice answered—'Life!'—I turned, and knew 180
(O Heaven, have mercy on such wretchedness!)

That what I thought was an old root which grew
To strange distortion out of the hill side,
Was indeed one of those deluded crew,

And that the grass, which methought hung so wide 185
And white, was but his thin discoloured hair,
And that the holes he vainly sought to hide,

Were or had been eyes:—'If thou canst, forbear
To join the dance, which I had well forborne!'
Said the grim Feature (of my thought aware). 190

'I will unfold that which to this deep scorn
Led me and my companions, and relate
The progress of the pageant since the morn;

'If thirst of knowledge shall not then abate,
Follow it thou even to the night, but I 195
Am weary.'—Then like one who with the weight

Of his own words is staggered, wearily
He paused; and ere he could resume, I cried:
'First, who art thou?'—'Before thy memory,

'I feared, loved, hated, suffered, did and died, 200
And if the spark with which Heaven lit my spirit
Had been with purer nutriment supplied,

'Corruption would not now thus much inherit
Of what was once Rousseau,—nor this disguise
Stain that which ought to have disdained to wear it; 205

'If I have been extinguished, yet there rise
A thousand beacons from the spark I bore'—
'And who are those chained to the car?'—'The wise,

'The great, the unforgotten,—they who wore
Mitres and helms and crowns, or wreaths of light,   210
Signs of thought's empire over thought—their lore

'Taught them not this, to know themselves; their might
Could not repress the mystery within,
And for the morn of truth they feigned, deep night

'Caught them ere evening.'—'Who is he with chin   215
Upon his breast, and hands crossed on his chain?'—
'The child of a fierce hour; he sought to win

'The world, and lost all that it did contain
Of greatness, in its hope destroyed; and more
Of fame and peace than virtue's self can gain   220

'Without the opportunity which bore
Him on its eagle pinions to the peak
From which a thousand climbers have before

'Fallen, as Napoleon fell.'—I felt my cheek
Alter, to see the shadow pass away,   225
Whose grasp had left the giant world so weak

That every pigmy kicked it as it lay;
And much I grieved to think how power and will
In opposition rule our mortal day,

And why God made irreconcilable   230
Good and the means of good; and for despair
I half disdained mine eyes' desire to fill

With the spent vision of the times that were
And scarce have ceased to be.—'Dost thou behold,'
Said my guide, 'those spoilers spoiled, Voltaire,   235

'Frederick, and Paul, Catherine, and Leopold,
And hoary anarchs, demagogues, and sage—
     names which the world thinks always old,

'For in the battle Life and they did wage,
She remained conqueror. I was overcome   240
By my own heart alone, which neither age,

'Nor tears, nor infamy, nor now the tomb
Could temper to its object.'—'Let them pass,'
I cried, 'the world and its mysterious doom

'Is not so much more glorious than it was,   245
That I desire to worship those who drew
New figures on its false and fragile glass

'As the old faded.'—'Figures ever new
Rise on the bubble, paint them as you may;
We have but thrown, as those before us threw,   250

'Our shadows on it as it passed away.
But mark how chained to the triumphal chair
The mighty phantoms of an elder day;

'All that is mortal of great Plato there
Expiates the joy and woe his master knew not;   255
The star that ruled his doom was far too fair.

'And life, where long that flower of Heaven grew not,
Conquered that heart by love, which gold, or pain,
Or age, or sloth, or slavery could subdue not.

'And near him walk the   twain,   260
The tutor and his pupil, whom Dominion
Followed as tame as vulture in a chain.

'The world was darkened beneath either pinion
Of him whom from the flock of conquerors
Fame singled out for her thunder-bearing minion;   265

'The other long outlived both woes and wars,
Throned in the thoughts of men, and still had kept
The jealous key of Truth's eternal doors,

'If Bacon's eagle spirit had not lept
Like lightning out of darkness—he compelled   270
The Proteus shape of Nature, as it slept

'To wake, and lead him to the caves that held
The treasure of the secrets of its reign.
See the great bards of elder time, who quelled

'The passions which they sung, as by their strain   275
May well be known: their living melody
Tempers its own contagion to the vein

'Of those who are infected with it—I
Have suffered what I wrote, or viler pain!
And so my words have seeds of misery—   280

'Even as the deeds of others, not as theirs.'
And then he pointed to a company,

'Midst whom I quickly recognized the heirs
Of Caesar's crime, from him to Constantine;
The anarch chiefs, whose force and murderous snares   285

Had founded many a sceptre-bearing line,
And spread the plague of gold and blood abroad:
And Gregory and John, and men divine,

Who rose like shadows between man and God;
Till that eclipse, still hanging over heaven,   290
Was worshipped by the world o'er which they strode,

For the true sun it quenched—'Their power was given
But to destroy,' replied the leader:—'I
Am one of those who have created, even

'If it be but a world of agony.'—   295
'Whence camest thou? and whither goest thou?
How did thy course begin?' I said, 'and why?

'Mine eyes are sick of this perpetual flow
Of people, and my heart sick of one sad thought—
Speak!'—'Whence I am, I partly seem to know,   300

'And how and by what paths I have been brought
To this dread pass, methinks even thou mayst guess;—
Why this should be, my mind can compass not;

'Whither the conqueror hurries me, still less;—
But follow thou, and from spectator turn   305
Actor or victim in this wretchedness,

'And what thou wouldst be taught I then may learn
From thee. Now listen:—In the April prime,
When all the forest-tips began to burn

'With kindling green, touched by the azure clime   310
Of the young season, I was laid asleep
Under a mountain, which from unknown time

'Had yawned into a cavern, high and deep;
And from it came a gentle rivulet,
Whose water, like clear air, in its calm sweep   315

'Bent the soft grass, and kept for ever wet
The stems of the sweet flowers, and filled the grove
With sounds, which whoso hears must needs forget

'All pleasure and all pain, all hate and love,
Which they had known before that hour of rest;   320
A sleeping mother then would dream not of

'Her only child who died upon the breast
At eventide—a king would mourn no more
The crown of which his brows were dispossessed

'When the sun lingered o'er his ocean floor　　　325
To gild his rival's new prosperity.
Thou wouldst forget thus vainly to deplore

'Ills, which if ills can find no cure from thee,
The thought of which no other sleep will quell,
Nor other music blot from memory,　　　330

'So sweet and deep is the oblivious spell;
And whether life had been before that sleep
The Heaven which I imagine, or a Hell

'Like this harsh world in which I wake to weep,
I know not. I arose, and for a space　　　335
The scene of woods and waters seemed to keep,

'Though it was now broad day, a gentle trace
Of light diviner than the common sun
Sheds on the common earth, and all the place

'Was filled with magic sounds woven into one　　　340
Oblivious melody, confusing sense
Amid the gliding waves and shadows dun;

'And, as I looked, the bright omnipresence
Of morning through the orient cavern flowed,
And the sun's image radiantly intense　　　345

'Burned on the waters of the well that glowed
Like gold, and threaded all the forest's maze
With winding paths of emerald fire; there stood

'Amid the sun, as he amid the blaze
Of his own glory, on the vibrating　　　350
Floor of the fountain, paved with flashing rays,

'A Shape all light, which with one hand did fling
Dew on the earth, as if she were the dawn,
And the invisible rain did ever sing

'A silver music on the mossy lawn;　　　355
And still before me on the dusky grass,
Iris her many-coloured scarf had drawn:

'In her right hand she bore a crystal glass,
Mantling with bright Nepenthe; the fierce splendour
Fell from her as she moved under the mass　　　360

'Of the deep cavern, and with palms so tender,
Their tread broke not the mirror of its billow,
Glided along the river, and did bend her

'Head under the dark boughs, till like a willow
Her fair hair swept the bosom of the stream   365
That whispered with delight to be its pillow.

'As one enamoured is upborne in dream
O'er lily-paven lakes, mid silver mist,
To wondrous music, so this shape might seem

'Partly to tread the waves with feet which kissed   370
The dancing foam; partly to glide along
The air which roughened the moist amethyst,

'Or the faint morning beams that fell among
The trees or the soft shadows of the trees;
And her feet, ever to the ceaseless song   375

'Of leaves, and winds, and waves, and birds. and bees,
And falling drops, moved in a measure new
Yet sweet, as on the summer evening breeze,

'Up from the lake a shape of golden dew
Between two rocks, athwart the rising moon,   380
Dances i' the wind, where never eagle flew;

'And still her feet, no less than the sweet tune
To which they moved, seemed as they moved to blot
The thoughts of him who gazed on them; and soon

'All that was, seemed as if it had been not;   385
And all the gazer's mind was strewn beneath
Her feet like embers; and she, thought by thought,

'Trampled its sparks into the dust of death;
As day upon the threshold of the east
Treads out the lamps of night, until the breath   390

'Of darkness re-illumine even the least
Of heaven's living eyes—like day she came,
Making the night a dream; and ere she ceased

'To move, as one between desire and shame
Suspended, I said—If, as it doth seem,   395
Thou comest from the realm without a name

'Into this valley of perpetual dream,
Show whence I came, and where I am, and why—
Pass not away upon the passing stream.

'Arise and quench thy thirst, was her reply.   400
And as a shut lily stricken by the wand
Of dewy morning's vital alchemy,

'I rose; and, bending at her sweet command,
Touched with faint lips the cup she raised,
And suddenly my brain became as sand   405

'Where the first wave had more than half erased
The track of deer on desert Labrador;
Whilst the wolf, from which they fled amazed,

'Leaves his stamp visibly upon the shore,
Until the second bursts;—so on my sight   410
Burst a new vision, never seen before,

'And the fair shape waned in the coming light,
As veil by veil the silent splendour drops
From Lucifer, amid the chrysolite

'Of sunrise, ere it tinge the mountain-tops;   415
And as the presence of that fairest planet,
Although unseen, is felt by one who hopes

'That his day's path may end as he began it,
In that star's smile, whose light is like the scent
Of a jonquil when evening breezes fan it,   420

'Or the soft note in which his dear lament
The Brescian [1] shepherd breathes, or the caress
That turned his weary slumber to content;

'So knew I in that light's severe excess
The presence of that Shape which on the stream   425
Moved, as I moved along the wilderness,

'More dimly than a day-appearing dream,
The ghost of a forgotten form of sleep;
A light of heaven, whose half-extinguished beam

'Through the sick day in which we wake to weep   430
Glimmers, for ever sought, for ever lost;
So did that shape its obscure tenour keep

'Beside my path, as silent as a ghost;
But the new Vision, and the cold bright car,
With solemn speed and stunning music, crossed   435

'The forest, and as if from some dread war
Triumphantly returning, the loud million
Fiercely extolled the fortune of her star.

'A moving arch of victory, the vermilion
And green and azure plumes of Iris had   440
Built high over her wind-wingèd pavilion,

---

[1] The favourite song, *Stanco di pascolar le pecorelle*, is a Brescian national air.
—[Mrs. Shelley's Note.]

'And underneath aethereal glory clad
The wilderness, and far before her flew
The tempest of the splendour, which forbade

'Shadow to fall from leaf and stone; the crew   445
Seemed in that light, like atomies to dance
Within a sunbeam;—some upon the new

'Embroidery of flowers, that did enhance
The grassy vesture of the desert, played,
Forgetful of the chariot's swift advance;   450

'Others stood gazing, till within the shade
Of the great mountain its light left them dim;
Others outspeeded it; and others made

'Circles around it, like the clouds that swim
Round the high moon in a bright sea of air;   455
And more did follow, with exulting hymn,

'The chariot and the captives fettered there:—
But all like bubbles on an eddying flood
Fell into the same track at last, and were

'Borne onward.—I among the multitude   460
Was swept—me, sweetest flowers delayed not long;
Me, not the shadow nor the solitude;

'Me, not that falling stream's Lethean song;
Me, not the phantom of that early Form
Which moved upon its motion—but among   465

'The thickest billows of that living storm
I plunged, and bared my bosom to the clime
Of that cold light, whose airs too soon deform.

'Before the chariot had begun to climb
The opposing steep of that mysterious dell,   470
Behold a wonder worthy of the rhyme

'Of him who from the lowest depths of hell,
Through every paradise and through all glory,
Love led serene, and who returned to tell

'The words of hate and awe; the wondrous story   475
How all things are transfigured except Love;
For deaf as is a sea, which wrath makes hoary,

'The world can hear not the sweet notes that move
The sphere whose light is melody to lovers—
A wonder worthy of his rhyme.—The grove   480

'Grew dense with shadows to its inmost covers,
The earth was gray with phantoms, and the air
Was peopled with dim forms, as when there hovers

'A flock of vampire-bats before the glare
Of the tropic sun, bringing, ere evening,   485
Strange night upon some Indian isle;—thus were

'Phantoms diffused around; and some did fling
Shadows of shadows, yet unlike themselves,
Behind them; some like eaglets on the wing

'Were lost in the white day; others like elves   490
Danced in a thousand unimagined shapes
Upon the sunny streams and grassy shelves;

'And others sate chattering like restless apes
On vulgar hands, . . .
Some made a cradle of the ermined capes   495

'Of kingly mantles; some across the tiar
Of pontiffs sate like vultures; others played
Under the crown which girt with empire

'A baby's or an idiot's brow, and made
Their nests in it. The old anatomies   500
Sate hatching their bare broods under the shade

'Of daemon wings, and laughed from their dead eyes
To reassume the delegated power,
Arrayed in which those worms did monarchize,

'Who made this earth their charnel. Others more   505
Humble, like falcons, sate upon the fist
Of common men, and round their heads did soar;

'Or like small gnats and flies, as thick as mist
On evening marshes, thronged about the brow
Of lawyers, statesmen, priest and theorist;—   510

'And others, like discoloured flakes of snow
On fairest bosoms and the sunniest hair,
Fell, and were melted by the youthful glow

'Which they extinguished; and, like tears, they were
A veil to those from whose faint lids they rained   515
In drops of sorrow. I became aware

'Of whence those forms proceeded which thus stained
The track in which we moved. After brief space,
From every form the beauty slowly waned;

'From every firmest limb and fairest face
The strength and freshness fell like dust, and left
The action and the shape without the grace

'Of life. The marble brow of youth was cleft
With care; and in those eyes where once hope shone,
Desire, like a lioness bereft   525

'Of her last cub, glared ere it died; each one
Of that great crowd sent forth incessantly
These shadows, numerous as the dead leaves blown

'In autumn evening from a poplar tree.
Each like himself and like each other were   530
At first; but some distorted seemed to be

'Obscure clouds, moulded by the casual air;
And of this stuff the car's creative ray
Wrought all the busy phantoms that were there,

'As the sun shapes the clouds; thus on the way   535
Mask after mask fell from the countenance
And form of all; and long before the day

'Was old, the joy which waked like heaven's glance
The sleepers in the oblivious valley, died;
And some grew weary of the ghastly dance,   540

'And fell, as I have fallen, by the wayside;—
Those soonest from whose forms most shadows passed,
And least of strength and beauty did abide.

'Then, what is life? I cried.'—

EARLY POEMS [1814, 1815]

STANZA, WRITTEN AT BRACKNELL

THY dewy looks sink in my breast;
Thy gentle words stir poison there;
Thou hast disturbed the only rest
That was the portion of despair!
Subdued to Duty's hard control, 5
I could have borne my wayward lot:
The chains that bind this ruined soul
Had cankered then—but crushed it not.

STANZAS.—APRIL, 1814

AWAY! the moor is dark beneath the moon.
Rapid clouds have drank the last pale beam of even:
Away the gathering winds will call the darkness soon.
And profoundest midnight shroud the serene lights of heaven.

Pause not! the time is past! Every voice cries, Away!   5
  Tempt not with one last tear thy friend's ungentle mood:
Thy lover's eye, so glazed and cold, dares not entreat thy stay:
  Duty and dereliction guide thee back to solitude.

Away, away! to thy sad and silent home;
  Pour bitter tears on its desolated hearth;   10
Watch the dim shades as like ghosts they go and come,
  And complicate strange webs of melancholy mirth.

The leaves of wasted autumn woods shall float around thine head:
  The blooms of dewy spring shall gleam beneath thy feet:
But thy soul or this world must fade in the frost that binds the dead,
  Ere midnight's frown and morning's smile, ere thou and peace may
    meet.

The cloud shadows of midnight possess their own repose,   17
  For the weary winds are silent, or the moon is in the deep:
Some respite to its turbulence unresting ocean knows;
  Whatever moves, or toils, or grieves, hath its appointed sleep.   20

Thou in the grave shalt rest—yet till the phantoms flee
  Which that house and heath and garden made dear to thee erewhile,
Thy remembrance, and repentance, and deep musings are not free
  From the music of two voices and the light of one sweet smile.

TO HARRIET

THY look of love has power to
    calm
  The stormiest passion of my
    soul;
Thy gentle words are drops of
    balm
  In life's too bitter bowl;
No grief is mine, but that alone 5
These choicest blessings I have
    known.

Harriet! if all who long to live
  In the warm sunshine of thine
    eye,
That price beyond all pain must
    give,—
  Beneath thy scorn to die;   10

Then hear thy chosen own too late
His heart most worthy of thy hate.

Be thou, then, one among man-
    kind
  Whose heart is harder not for
    state,
Thou only virtuous, gentle, kind, 15
  Amid a world of hate;
And by a slight endurance seal
A fellow-being's lasting weal.

For pale with anguish is his cheek,
  His breath comes fast, his eyes
    are dim,   20
Thy name is struggling ere he
    speak,
  Weak is each trembling limb;

In mercy let him not endure
The misery of a fatal cure.

Oh, trust for once no erring
    guide!   25

Bid the remorseless feeling flee;
'Tis malice, 'tis revenge, 'tis pride,
    'Tis anything but thee;
Oh, deign a nobler pride to prove,
And pity if thou canst not love.   30

TO MARY WOLLSTONECRAFT GODWIN

I

MINE eyes were dim with tears un-
    shed;
  Yes, I was firm—thus wert not
    thou;—
My baffled looks did fear yet
    dread
  To meet thy looks—I could not
    know
How anxiously they sought to
    shine   5
With soothing pity upon mine.

II

To sit and curb the soul's mute
    rage
  Which preys upon itself alone;
To curse the life which is the cage
  Of fettered grief that dares not
    groan,   10
Hiding from many a careless eye
The scornèd load of agony.

III

Whilst thou alone, then not re-
    garded,
  The   thou alone should be,
To spend years thus, and be re-
    warded,   15
  As thou, sweet love, requited me
When none were near—Oh! I did
    wake

From torture for that moment's
    sake.

IV

Upon my heart thy accents sweet
  Of peace and pity fell like dew   20
On flowers half dead;—thy lips did
    meet
  Mine tremblingly; thy dark eyes
    threw
Their soft persuasion on my brain,
Charming away its dream of pain.

V

We are not happy, sweet! our state
  Is strange and full of doubt and
    fear;   26
More need of words that ills
    abate;—
  Reserve or censure come not
    near
Our sacred friendship, lest there be
No solace left for thee and me.   30

VI

Gentle and good and mild thou art,
  Nor can I live if thou appear
Aught but thyself, or turn thine
    heart
  Away from me, or stoop to wear
The mask of scorn, although it
    be   35
To hide the love thou feel'st for me.

TO ——

YET look on me—take not thine eyes away,
  Which feed upon the love within mine own,
Which is indeed but the reflected ray
  Of thine own beauty from my spirit thrown.

Yet speak to me—thy voice is as the tone   5
Of my heart's echo, and I think I hear
   That thou yet lovest me; yet thou alone
Like one before a mirror, without care
Of aught but thine own features, imaged there;
And yet I wear out life in watching thee;   10
   A toil so sweet at times, and thou indeed
Art kind when I am sick, and pity me.

MUTABILITY

WE are as clouds that veil the midnight moon;
   How restlessly they speed, and gleam, and quiver,
Streaking the darkness radiantly!—yet soon
   Night closes round, and they are lost for ever:

Or like forgotten lyres, whose dissonant strings   5
   Give various response to each varying blast,
To whose frail frame no second motion brings
   One mood or modulation like the last.

We rest.—A dream has power to poison sleep;
   We rise.—One wandering thought pollutes the day;   10
We feel, conceive or reason, laugh or weep;
   Embrace fond woe, or cast our cares away:

It is the same!—For, be it joy or sorrow,
   The path of its departure still is free:
Man's yesterday may ne'er be like his morrow;   15
   Nought may endure but Mutability.

ON DEATH

THERE IS NO WORK, NOR DEVICE, NOR KNOWLEDGE, NOR WISDOM, IN THE GRAVE,
WHITHER THOU GOEST.—*Ecclesiastes.*

THE pale, the cold, and the moony smile
   Which the meteor beam of a starless night
Sheds on a lonely and sea-girt isle,
   Ere the dawning of morn's undoubted light,
Is the flame of life so fickle and wan   5
That flits round our steps till their strength is gone.

O man! hold thee on in courage of soul
   Through the stormy shades of thy worldly way,
And the billows of cloud that around thee roll
   Shall sleep in the light of a wondrous day,   10

Where Hell and Heaven shall leave thee free
To the universe of destiny.

This world is the nurse of all we know,
   This world is the mother of all we feel,
And the coming of death is a fearful blow   15
   To a brain unencompassed with nerves of steel;
When all that we know, or feel, or see,
Shall pass like an unreal mystery.

The secret things of the grave are there,
   Where all but this frame must surely be,   20
Though the fine-wrought eye and the wondrous ear
   No longer will live to hear or to see
All that is great and all that is strange
In the boundless realm of unending change.

Who telleth a tale of unspeaking death?   25
   Who lifteth the veil of what is to come?
Who painteth the shadows that are beneath
   The wide-winding caves of the peopled tomb?
Or uniteth the hopes of what shall be
With the fears and the love for that which we see?   30

A SUMMER EVENING CHURCHYARD

Lechlade, Gloucestershire

The wind has swept from the wide atmosphere
Each vapour that obscured the sunset's ray;
And pallid Evening twines its beaming hair
In duskier braids around the languid eyes of Day:
Silence and Twilight, unbeloved of men,   5
Creep hand in hand from yon obscurest glen.

They breathe their spells towards the departing day,
Encompassing the earth, air, stars, and sea;
Light, sound, and motion own the potent sway,
Responding to the charm with its own mystery.   10
The winds are still, or the dry church-tower grass
Knows not their gentle motions as they pass.

Thou too, aëreal Pile! whose pinnacles
Point from one shrine like pyramids of fire,
Obeyest in silence their sweet solemn spells,   15
Clothing in hues of heaven thy dim and distant spire,
Around whose lessening and invisible height
Gather among the stars the clouds of night.

The dead are sleeping in their sepulchres:
And, mouldering as they sleep, a thrilling sound,   20
Half sense, half thought, among the darkness stirs,
Breathed from their wormy beds all living things around,
And mingling with the still night and mute sky
Its awful hush is felt inaudibly.

Thus solemnized and softened, death is mild   25
And terrorless as this serenest night:
Here could I hope, like some inquiring child
Sporting on graves, that death did hide from human sight
Sweet secrets, or beside its breathless sleep
That loveliest dreams perpetual watch did keep.   30

TO ———

ΔΑΚΡΥΣΙ ΔΙΟΙΣΩ ΠΟΤΜΟΝ 'ΑΠΟΤΜΟΝ.

OH! there are spirits of the air,
  And genii of the evening breeze,
And gentle ghosts, with eyes as fair
  As star-beams among twilight trees:—
Such lovely ministers to meet   5
Oft hast thou turned from men thy lonely feet.

With mountain winds, and babbling springs,
  And moonlight seas, that are the voice
Of these inexplicable things,
  Thou didst hold commune, and rejoice   10
When they did answer thee; but they
Cast, like a worthless boon, thy love away.

And thou hast sought in starry eyes
  Beams that were never meant for thine,
Another's wealth:—tame sacrifice   15
  To a fond faith! still dost thou pine?
Still dost thou hope that greeting hands,
Voice, looks, or lips, may answer thy demands?

Ah! wherefore didst thou build thine hope
  On the false earth's inconstancy?   20
Did thine own mind afford no scope
  Of love, or moving thoughts to thee?
That natural scenes or human smiles
Could steal the power to wind thee in their wiles?

Yes, all the faithless smiles are fled
  Whose falsehood left thee broken-hearted;
The glory of the moon is dead;   25
  Night's ghosts and dreams have now departed;

Thine own soul still is true to thee,
But changed to a foul fiend through misery. 30

This fiend, whose ghastly presence ever
  Beside thee like thy shadow hangs,
Dream not to chase;—the mad endeavour
  Would scourge thee to severer pangs.
Be as thou art. Thy settled fate, 35
Dark as it is, all change would aggravate.

TO WORDSWORTH

POET of Nature, thou hast wept to know
That things depart which never may return:
Childhood and youth, friendship and love's first glow,
Have fled like sweet dreams, leaving thee to mourn.
These common woes I feel. One loss is mine 5
Which thou too feel'st, yet I alone deplore.
Thou wert as a lone star, whose light did shine
On some frail bark in winter's midnight roar:
Thou hast like to a rock-built refuge stood
Above the blind and battling multitude: 10
In honoured poverty thy voice did weave
Songs consecrate to truth and liberty,—
Deserting these, thou leavest me to grieve,
Thus having been, that thou shouldst cease to be.

FEELINGS OF A REPUBLICAN ON THE FALL OF BONAPARTE

I HATED thee, fallen tyrant! I did groan
To think that a most unambitious slave,
Like thou, shouldst dance and revel on the grave
Of Liberty. Thou mightst have built thy throne
Where it had stood even now: thou didst prefer 5
A frail and bloody pomp which Time has swept
In fragments towards Oblivion. Massacre,
For this I prayed, would on thy sleep have crept,
Treason and Slavery, Rapine, Fear, and Lust,
And stifled thee, their minister. I know 10
Too late, since thou and France are in the dust,
That Virtue owns a more eternal foe
Than Force or Fraud: old Custom, legal Crime,
And bloody Faith the foulest birth of Time.

LINES

I

THE cold earth slept below,
  Above the cold sky shone;
And all around, with a chilling
    sound,
From caves of ice and fields of
    snow,
The breath of night like death
    did flow   5
  Beneath the sinking moon.

II

The wintry hedge was black,
  The green grass was not seen,
The birds did rest on the bare
    thorn's breast,
Whose roots, beside the pathway
    track,   10
Had bound their folds o'er many
    a crack
  Which the frost had made be-
    tween.

III

Thine eyes glowed in the glare
  Of the moon's dying light;
As a fen-fire's beam on a sluggish
    stream   15
Gleams dimly, so the moon shone
    there,
And it yellowed the strings of thy
    raven hair,
  That shook in the wind of
    night.

IV

The moon made thy lips pale,
    beloved—
  The wind made thy bosom
    chill—
The night did shed on thy dear
    head   21
Its frozen dew, and thou didst
    lie
Where the bitter breath of the
    naked sky
  Might visit thee at will.

NOTE ON THE EARLY POEMS, BY MRS. SHELLEY

THE remainder of Shelley's Poems will be arranged in the order in which they were written. Of course, mistakes will occur in placing some of the shorter ones; for, as I have said, many of these were thrown aside, and I never saw them till I had the misery of looking over his writings after the hand that traced them was dust; and some were in the hands of others, and I never saw them till now. The subjects of the poems are often to me an unerring guide; but on other occasions I can only guess, by finding them in the pages of the same manuscript book that contains poems with the date of whose composition I am fully conversant. In the present arrangement all his poetical translations will be placed together at the end.

The loss of his early papers prevents my being able to give any of the poetry of his boyhood. Of the few I give as *Early Poems,* the greater part were published with *Alastor;* some of them were written previously, some at the same period. The poem beginning 'Oh, there are spirits in the air' was addressed in idea to Coleridge, whom he never knew; and at whose character he could only guess imperfectly, through his writings, and accounts he heard of him from some who knew him well. He regarded his change of opinions as rather an act of will than conviction, and believed that in his inner heart he would be haunted by what Shelley considered the better and holier aspirations of his youth. The summer evening that suggested to him the poem written in the churchyard of Lechlade occurred during his voyage up the Thames in 1815. He had been advised by a physician to live as much as possible in the open air; and a fortnight of a bright warm July was spent in tracing the Thames to its source. He never spent a season more tranquilly than the summer of 1815. He had just recovered from a severe pulmonary attack; the weather was warm and pleasant. He lived near Windsor Forest; and his life was spent under its shade or on the water, meditating subjects for verse. Hitherto, he had chiefly aimed at extending his political doctrines, and attempted so to do by appeals in prose essays to the people, exhorting them to claim their rights; but he had now begun to feel that the time for action was not ripe in England, and that the pen was the only instrument wherewith to prepare the way for better things.

In the scanty journals kept during those years I find a record of the books that Shelley read during several years. During the years of 1814 and 1815 the list is extensive. It includes, in Greek, Homer, Hesiod, Theocritus, the histories of Thucydides and Herodotus, and Diogenes Laertius. In Latin, Petronius, Suetonius, some of the works of Cicero, a large proportion of those of Seneca and Livy. In English, Milton's poems, Wordsworth's *Excursion,* Southey's *Madoc* and *Thalaba,* Locke *On the Human Understanding,* Bacon's *Novum Organum.* In Italian, Ariosto, Tasso, and Alfieri. In French, the *Rêveries d'un Solitaire* of Rousseau. To these may be added several modern books of travel. He read few novels.

POEMS WRITTEN IN 1816

THE SUNSET

THERE late was One whose subtle being,
As light and wind within some delicate cloud
That fades amid the blue noon's burning sky,
Genius and death contended. None may know
The sweetness of the joy which made his breath   5
Fail, like the trances of the summer air,
When, with the Lady of his love, who then
First knew the unreserve of mingled being,
He walked along the pathway of a field
Which to the east a hoar wood shadowed o'er,   10
But to the west was open to the sky.
There now the sun had sunk, but lines of gold
Hung on the ashen clouds, and on the points
Of the far level grass and nodding flowers
And the old dandelion's hoary beard,   15
And, mingled with the shades of twilight, lay
On the brown massy woods—and in the east
The broad and burning moon lingeringly rose
Between the black trunks of the crowded trees,
While the faint stars were gathering overhead.—   20
'Is it not strange, Isabel,' said the youth,
'I never saw the sun? We will walk here
To-morrow; thou shalt look on it with me.'

That night the youth and lady mingled lay
In love and sleep—but when the morning came   25
The lady found her lover dead and cold.
Let none believe that God in mercy gave
That stroke. The lady died not, nor grew wild,
But year by year lived on—in truth I think
Her gentleness and patience and sad smiles,   30
And that she did not die, but lived to tend
Her agèd father, were a kind of madness,
If madness 'tis to be unlike the world.
For but to see her were to read the tale
Woven by some subtlest bard, to make hard hearts   35
Dissolve away in wisdom-working grief;—
Her eyes were black and lustreless and wan:
Her eyelashes were worn away with tears,
Her lips and cheeks were like things dead—so pale;
Her hands were thin, and through their wandering veins   40
And weak articulations might be seen

Day's ruddy light. The tomb of thy dead self
Which one vexed ghost inhabits, night and day,
Is all, lost child, that now remains of thee!

'Inheritor of more than earth can give,   45
Passionless calm and silence unreproved,
Whether the dead find, oh, not sleep! but rest,
And are the uncomplaining things they seem,
Or live, or drop in the deep sea of Love;
Oh, that like thine, mine epitaph were—Peace!'   50
This was the only moan she ever made.

HYMN TO INTELLECTUAL BEAUTY

I

THE awful shadow of some unseen Power
    Floats though unseen among us,—visiting
    This various world with as inconstant wing
As summer winds that creep from flower to flower,—
Like moonbeams that behind some piny mountain shower, 5
        It visits with inconstant glance
        Each human heart and countenance;
Like hues and harmonies of evening,—
        Like clouds in starlight widely spread,—
        Like memory of music fled,—   10
        Like aught that for its grace may be
Dear, and yet dearer for its mystery.

II

Spirit of BEAUTY, that dost consecrate
    With thine own hues all thou dost shine upon
    Of human thought or form,—where art thou gone?   15
Why dost thou pass away and leave our state,
This dim vast vale of tears, vacant and desolate?
        Ask why the sunlight not for ever
        Weaves rainbows o'er yon mountain-river,
Why aught should fail and fade that once is shown,   20
        Why fear and dream and death and birth
        Cast on the daylight of this earth
        Such gloom,—why man has such a scope
For love and hate, despondency and hope?

III

No voice from some sublimer world hath ever   25
    To sage or poet these responses given—
    Therefore the names of Demon, Ghost, and Heaven,
Remain the records of their vain endeavour,

Frail spells—whose uttered charm might not avail to sever,
    From all we hear and all we see,   30
    Doubt, chance, and mutability.
Thy light alone—like mist o'er mountains driven,
    Or music by the night-wind sent
    Through strings of some still instrument,
    Or moonlight on a midnight stream,   35
Gives grace and truth to life's unquiet dream.

IV

Love, Hope, and Self-esteem, like clouds depart
    And come, for some uncertain moments lent.
    Man were immortal, and omnipotent,
Didst thou, unknown and awful as thou art,   40
Keep with thy glorious train firm state within his heart.
    Thou messenger of sympathies,
    That wax and wane in lovers' eyes—
Thou—that to human thought art nourishment,
    Like darkness to a dying flame!   45
    Depart not as thy shadow came,
    Depart not—lest the grave should be,
Like life and fear, a dark reality.

V

While yet a boy I sought for ghosts, and sped
    Through many a listening chamber, cave and ruin,   50
    And starlight wood, with fearful steps pursuing
Hopes of high talk with the departed dead.
I called on poisonous names with which our youth is fed;
    I was not heard—I saw them not—
    When musing deeply on the lot   55
Of life, at that sweet time when winds are wooing
    All vital things that wake to bring
    News of birds and blossoming,—
    Sudden, thy shadow fell on me;
I shrieked, and clasped my hands in ecstasy!   60

VI

I vowed that I would dedicate my powers
    To thee and thine—have I not kept the vow?
    With beating heart and streaming eyes, even now
I call the phantoms of a thousand hours
Each from his voiceless grave: they have in visioned bowers   65
    Of studious zeal or love's delight
    Outwatched with me the envious night—
They know that never joy illumed my brow

Unlinked with hope that thou wouldst free
This world from its dark slavery,   70
That thou—O awful LOVELINESS,
Wouldst give whate'er these words cannot express.

VII

The day becomes more solemn and serene
    When noon is past—there is a harmony
    In autumn, and a lustre in its sky,   75
Which through the summer is not heard or seen,
As if it could not be, as if it had not been!
        Thus let thy power, which like the truth
        Of nature on my passive youth
    Descended, to my onward life supply   80
        Its calm—to one who worships thee,
        And every form containing thee,
        Whom, SPIRIT fair, thy spells did bind
To fear himself, and love all human kind.

MONT BLANC

LINES WRITTEN IN THE VALE OF CHAMOUNI

I

THE everlasting universe of things
Flows through the mind, and rolls its rapid waves,
Now dark—now glittering—now reflecting gloom—
Now lending splendour, where from secret springs
The source of human thought its tribute brings   5
Of waters,—with a sound but half its own,
Such as a feeble brook will oft assume
In the wild woods, among the mountains lone,
Where waterfalls around it leap for ever,
Where woods and winds contend, and a vast river   10
Over its rocks ceaselessly bursts and raves.

II

Thus thou, Ravine of Arve—dark, deep Ravine—
Thou many-coloured, many-voicèd vale,
Over whose pines, and crags, and caverns sail
Fast cloud-shadows and sunbeams: awful scene,   15
Where Power in likeness of the Arve comes down
From the ice-gulfs that gird his secret throne,
Bursting through these dark mountains like the flame
Of lightning through the tempest;—thou dost lie,
Thy giant brood of pines around thee clinging,   20

Children of elder time, in whose devotion
The chainless winds still come and ever came
To drink their odours, and their mighty swinging
To hear—an old and solemn harmony;
Thine earthly rainbows stretched across the sweep   25
Of the aethereal waterfall, whose veil
Robes some unsculptured image; the strange sleep
Which when the voices of the desert fail
Wraps all in its own deep eternity;—
Thy caverns echoing to the Arve's commotion,   30
A loud, lone sound no other sound can tame;
Thou art pervaded with that ceaseless motion,
Thou art the path of that unresting sound—
Dizzy Ravine! and when I gaze on thee
I seem as in a trance sublime and strange   35
To muse on my own separate fantasy,
My own, my human mind, which passively
Now renders and receives fast influencings,
Holding an unremitting interchange
With the clear universe of things around;   40
One legion of wild thoughts, whose wandering wings
Now float above thy darkness, and now rest
Where that or thou art no unbidden guest,
In the still cave of the witch Poesy,
Seeking among the shadows that pass by   45
Ghosts of all things that are, some shade of thee,
Some phantom, some faint image; till the breast
From which they fled recalls them, thou art there!

III

Some say that gleams of a remoter world
Visit the soul in sleep,—that death is slumber,   50
And that its shapes the busy thoughts outnumber
Of those who wake and live.—I look on high;
Has some unknown omnipotence unfurled
The veil of life and death? or do I lie
In dream, and does the mightier world of sleep   55
Spread far around and inaccessibly
Its circles? For the very spirit fails,
Driven like a homeless cloud from steep to steep
That vanishes among the viewless gales!
Far, far above, piercing the infinite sky,   60
Mont Blanc appears,—still, snowy, and serene—
Its subject mountains their unearthly forms
Pile around it, ice and rock; broad vales between
Of frozen floods, unfathomable deeps,
Blue as the overhanging heaven, that spread   65

And wind among the accumulated steeps;
A desert peopled by the storms alone,
Save when the eagle brings some hunter's bone,
And the wolf tracks her there—how hideously
Its shapes are heaped around! rude, bare, and high,   70
Ghastly, and scarred, and riven.—Is this the scene
Where the old Earthquake-daemon taught her young
Ruin? Were these their toys? or did a sea
Of fire envelop once this silent snow?
None can reply—all seems eternal now.   75
The wilderness has a mysterious tongue
Which teaches awful doubt, or faith so mild,
So solemn, so serene, that man may be,
But for such faith, with nature reconciled;
Thou hast a voice, great Mountain, to repeal   80
Large codes of fraud and woe; not understood
By all, but which the wise, and great, and good
Interpret, or make felt, or deeply feel.

IV

The fields, the lakes, the forests, and the streams,
Ocean, and all the living things that dwell   85
Within the daedal earth; lightning, and rain,
Earthquake, and fiery flood, and hurricane,
The torpor of the year when feeble dreams
Visit the hidden buds, or dreamless sleep
Holds every future leaf and flower;—the bound   90
With which from that detested trance they leap;
The works and ways of man, their death and birth,
And that of him and all that his may be;
All things that move and breathe with toil and sound
Are born and die; revolve, subside, and swell.   95
Power dwells apart in 'ts tranquillity,
Remote, serene, and inaccessible:
And *this*, the naked countenance of earth,
On which I gaze, even these primaeval mountains
Teach the adverting mind. The glaciers creep   100
Like snakes that watch their prey, from their far fountains,
Slow rolling on; there, many a precipice,
Frost and the Sun in scorn of mortal power
Have piled: dome, pyramid, and pinnacle,
A city of death, distinct with many a tower   105
And wall impregnable of beaming ice.
Yet not a city, but a flood of ruin
Is there, that from the boundaries of the sky
Rolls its perpetual stream; vast pines are strewing
Its destined path, or in the mangled soil   110

Branchless and shattered stand; the rocks, drawn down
From yon remotest waste, have overthrown
The limits of the dead and living world,
Never to be reclaimed. The dwelling-place
Of insects, beasts, and birds, becomes its spoil 115
Their food and their retreat for ever gone,
So much of life and joy is lost. The race
Of man flies far in dread; his work and dwelling
Vanish, like smoke before the tempest's stream,
And their place is not known. Below, vast caves 120
Shine in the rushing torrents' restless gleam,
Which from those secret chasms in tumult welling
Meet in the vale, and one majestic River,
The breath and blood of distant lands, for ever
Rolls its loud waters to the ocean-waves, 125
Breathes its swift vapours to the circling air.

V

Mont Blanc yet gleams on high:—the power is there,
The still and solemn power of many sights,
And many sounds, and much of life and death.
In the calm darkness of the moonless nights, 130
In the lone glare of day, the snows descend
Upon that Mountain; none beholds them there,
Nor when the flakes burn in the sinking sun,
Or the star-beams dart through them:—Winds contend
Silently there, and heap the snow with breath 135
Rapid and strong, but silently! Its home
The voiceless lightning in these solitudes
Keeps innocently, and like vapour broods
Over the snow. The secret Strength of things
Which governs thought, and to the infinite dome 140
Of Heaven is as a law, inhabits thee!
And what were thou, and earth, and stars, and sea,
If to the human mind's imaginings
Silence and solitude were vacancy?

July 23, 1816.

FRAGMENT: HOME

DEAR home, thou scene of earliest hopes and joys,
The least of which wronged Memory ever makes
Bitterer than all thine unremembered tears.

FRAGMENT OF A GHOST STORY

A SHOVEL of his ashes took
From the hearth's obscurest nook,
Muttering mysteries as she went.
Helen and Henry knew that Granny
Was as much afraid of Ghosts as any,   5
    And so they followed hard—
But Helen clung to her brother's arm,
And her own spasm made her shake.

NOTE ON POEMS OF 1816, BY MRS. SHELLEY

SHELLEY wrote little during this year. The poem entitled *The Sunset* was written in the spring of the year, while still residing at Bishopsgate. He spent the summer on the shores of the Lake of Geneva. The *Hymn to Intellectual Beauty* was conceived during his voyage round the lake with Lord Byron. He occupied himself during this voyage by reading the *Nouvelle Héloïse* for the first time. The reading it on the very spot where the scenes are laid added to the interest; and he was at once surprised and charmed by the passionate eloquence and earnest enthralling interest that pervade this work. There was something in the character of Saint-Preux, in his abnegation of self, and in the worship he paid to Love, that coincided with Shelley's own disposition; and, though differing in many of the views and shocked by others, yet the effect of the whole was fascinating and delightful.

Mont Blanc was inspired by a view of that mountain and its surrounding peaks and valleys, as he lingered on the Bridge of Arve on his way through the Valley of Chamouni. Shelley makes the following mention of this poem in his publication of the *History of a Six Weeks' Tour, and Letters from Switzerland:* 'The poem entitled *Mont Blanc* is written by the author of the two letters from Chamouni and Vevai. It was composed under the immediate impression of the deep and powerful feelings excited by the objects which it attempts to describe; and, as an undisciplined overflowing of the soul, rests its claim to approbation on an attempt to imitate the untamable wildness and inaccessible solemnity from which those feelings sprang.'

This was an eventful year, and less time was given to study than usual. In the list of his reading I find, in Greek, Theocritus, the *Prometheus* of Aeschylus, several of Plutarch's *Lives*, and the works of Lucian. In Latin, Lucretius, Pliny's *Letters*, the *Annals* and *Germany* of Tacitus. In French, the *History of the French Revolution* by Lacretelle. He read for the first time, this year, Montaigne's *Essays*, and regarded them ever after as one of the most delightful and instructive books in the world. The list is scanty in English works: Locke's *Essay, Political Justice*, and Coleridge's *Lay Sermon*, form nearly the whole. It was his frequent habit to read aloud to me in the evening; in this way we read, this year, the New Testament, *Paradise Lost*, Spenser's *Faery Queen*, and *Don Quixote*.

POEMS WRITTEN IN 1817

MARIANNE'S DREAM

I

A PALE Dream came to a Lady fair,
  And said, A boon, a boon, I pray!
I know the secrets of the air,
  And things are lost in the glare
    of day,
Which I can make the sleeping
  see,   5
If they will put their trust in me.

II

And thou shalt know of things un-
  known,
  If thou wilt let me rest between.
The veiny lids, whose fringe is
  thrown
  Over thine eyes so dark and
    sheen: 10
And half in hope, and half in fright,
The Lady closed her eyes so bright.

III

At first all deadly shapes were
  driven
  Tumultuously across her sleep,
And o'er the vast cope of bending
  heaven   15
  All ghastly-visaged clouds did
    sweep;
And the Lady ever looked to spy
If the golden sun shone forth on
  high.

IV

And as towards the east she turned,
  She saw aloft in the morning air,
Which now with hues of sunrise
  burned,   21
  A great black Anchor rising
    there;

And wherever the Lady turned her
  eyes,
It hung before her in the skies.

V

The sky was blue as the summer
  sea,
  The depths were cloudless over-
    head,   26
The air was calm as it could be,
  There was no sight or sound of
    dread,
But that black Anchor floating still
Over the piny eastern hill.   30

VI

The Lady grew sick with a weight
  of fear
  To see that Anchor ever hanging,
And veiled her eyes; she then did
  hear
  The sound as of a dim low clang-
    ing,
And looked abroad if she might
  know   35
Was it aught else, or but the flow
Of the blood in her own veins, to
  and fro.

VII

There was a mist in the sunless air,
  Which shook as it were with an
    earthquake's shock,
But the very weeds that blossomed
  there   40
  Were moveless, and each mighty
    rock
Stood on its basis steadfastly;
The Anchor was seen no more on
  high.

VIII

But piled around, with summits
    hid
  In lines of cloud at intervals, 45
Stood many a mountain pyramid
  Among whose everlasting walls
Two mighty cities shone, and ever
Through the red mist their domes
    did quiver.

IX

On two dread mountains, from
    whose crest,   50
  Might seem, the eagle, for her
    brood,
Would ne'er have hung her dizzy
    nest,
  Those tower-encircled cities
    stood.
A vision strange such towers to see,
Sculptured and wrought so gor-
    geously   55
Where human art could never be.

X

And columns framed of marble
    white,
  And giant fanes, dome over dome
Piled, and triumphant gates, all
    bright
  With workmanship, which could
    not come   60
From touch of mortal instrument,
Shot o'er the vales, or lustre lent
From its own shapes magnificent.

XI

But still the Lady heard that clang
  Filling the wide air far away; 65
And still the mist whose light did
    hang
  Among the mountains shook
    alway,
So that the Lady's heart beat fast,
As half in joy, and half aghast,
On those high domes her look she
    cast.   70

XII

Sudden, from out that city sprung
  A light that made the earth grow
    red;
Two flames that each with quiver-
    ing tongue
  Licked its high domes, and over-
    head
Among those mighty towers and
    fanes   75
Dropped fire, as a volcano rains
Its sulphurous ruin on the plains.

XIII

And hark! a rush as if the deep
  Had burst its bonds; she looked
    behind
And saw over the western steep 80
  A raging flood descend, and wind
Through that wide vale; she felt
    no fear,
But said within herself, 'Tis clear
These towers are Nature's own, and
    she   84
To save them has sent forth the
    sea.

XIV

And now those raging billows came
  Where that fair Lady sate, and
    she
Was borne towards the showering
    flame
  By the wild waves heaped tumul-
    tuously,
And, on a little plank, the flow 90
Of the whirlpool bore her to and
    fro.

XV

The flames were fiercely vomited
  From every tower and every
    dome,
And dreary light did widely shed
  O'er that vast flood's suspended
    foam,   95

Beneath the smoke which hung its
    night
On the stained cope of heaven's
    light.

XVI

The plank whereon that Lady sate
    Was driven through the chasms,
        about and about,
Between the peaks so desolate   100
    Of the drowning mountains, in
        and out,
As the thistle-beard on a whirlwind
    sails—
While the flood was filling those
    hollow vales.

XVII

At last her plank an eddy crossed,
    And bore her to the city's wall,
Which now the flood had reached
    almost;   106
    It might the stoutest heart appal
To hear the fire roar and hiss
Through the domes of those mighty
    palaces.

XVIII

The eddy whirled her round and
    round   110
    Before a gorgeous gate, which
        stood
Piercing the clouds of smoke which
    bound
    Its aëry arch with light like
        blood;
She looked on that gate of marble
    clear,
With wonder that extinguished
    fear.

XIX

For it was filled with sculptures
    rarest,   116
    Of forms most beautiful and
        strange,
Like nothing human, but the fairest

Of wingèd shapes, whose legions
    range
Throughout the sleep of those that
    are,   120
Like this same Lady, good and fair.

XX

And as she looked, still lovelier
    grew
    Those marble forms;—the sculp-
        tor sure
Was a strong spirit, and the hue
    Of his own mind did there en-
        dure
After the touch, whose power had
    braided   126
Such grace, was in some sad change
    faded.

XXI

She looked, the flames were dim,
    the flood
    Grew tranquil as a woodland
    river
Winding through hills in solitude;
    Those marble shapes then seemed
        to quiver,   131
And their fair limbs to float in
    motion,
Like weeds unfolding in the ocean.

XXII

And their lips moved; one seemed
    to speak,
    When suddenly the mountains
        cracked,   135
And through the chasm the flood
    did break
    With an earth-uplifting cataract:
The statues gave a joyous scream,
And on its wings the pale thin
    Dream
Lifted the Lady from the stream.

XXIII

The dizzy flight of that phantom
    pale   141

Waked the fair Lady from her sleep,
And she arose, while from the veil
Of her dark eyes the Dream did creep,

And she walked about as one who knew   145
That sleep has sights as clear and true
As any waking eyes can view.

TO CONSTANTIA, SINGING

I

Thus to be lost and thus to sink and die,
   Perchance were death indeed!—Constantia, turn!
In thy dark eyes a power like light doth lie,
   Even though the sounds which were thy voice, which burn
Between thy lips, are laid to sleep;   5
   Within thy breath, and on thy hair, like odour, it is yet,
And from thy touch like fire doth leap.
   Even while I write, my burning cheeks are wet,
   Alas, that the torn heart can bleed, but not forget!

II

A breathless awe, like the swift change   10
   Unseen, but felt in youthful slumbers,
Wild, sweet, but uncommunicably strange,
   Thou breathest now in fast ascending numbers.
The cope of heaven seems rent and cloven
   By the enchantment of thy strain,   15
And on my shoulders wings are woven,
   To follow its sublime career
Beyond the mighty moons that wane
   Upon the verge of Nature's utmost sphere,
   Till the world's shadowy walls are past and disappear.   20

III

Her voice is hovering o'er my soul—it lingers
   O'ershadowing it with soft and lulling wings,
The blood and life within those snowy fingers
   Teach witchcraft to the instrumental strings.
My brain is wild, my breath comes quick—   25
   The blood is listening in my frame,
And thronging shadows, fast and thick,
   Fall on my overflowing eyes;
My heart is quivering like a flame;
   As morning dew, that in the sunbeam dies,   30
   I am dissolved in these consuming ecstasies.

IV

I have no life, Constantia, now, but thee,
   Whilst, like the world-surrounding air, thy song
Flows on, and fills all things with melody.—
   Now is thy voice a tempest swift and strong,   35
On which, like one in trance upborne,
   Secure o'er rocks and waves I sweep,
Rejoicing like a cloud of morn.
   Now 'tis the breath of summer night,
Which when the starry waters sleep,
   Round western isles, with incense-blossoms bright,   40
   Lingering, suspends my soul in its voluptuous flight.

TO CONSTANTIA

I

THE rose that drinks the fountain dew
   In the pleasant air of noon,
Grows pale and blue with altered hue—
   In the gaze of the nightly moon;
For the planet of frost, so cold and bright,   5
Makes it wan with her borrowed light.

II

Such is my heart—roses are fair,
   And that at best a withered blossom;
But thy false care did idly wear
   Its withered leaves in a faithless bosom;   10
And fed with love, like air and dew,
Its growth——

FRAGMENT: TO ONE SINGING

MY spirit like a charmèd bark doth swim
   Upon the liquid waves of thy sweet singing,
Far far away into the regions dim

   Of rapture—as a boat, with swift sails winging
Its way adown some many-winding river,   5
Speeds through dark forests o'er the waters swinging . . .

A FRAGMENT: TO MUSIC

SILVER key of the fountain of tears,
   Where the spirit drinks till the brain is wild;
Softest grave of a thousand fears,
   Where their mother, Care, like a drowsy child,
   Is laid asleep in flowers.   5

ANOTHER FRAGMENT TO MUSIC

No, Music, thou art not the 'food of Love,'
Unless Love feeds upon its own sweet self,
Till it becomes all Music murmurs of.

'MIGHTY EAGLE'

SUPPOSED TO BE ADDRESSED TO WILLIAM GODWIN

MIGHTY eagle! thou that soarest
O'er the misty mountain forest,
   And amid the light of morning
Like a cloud of glory hiest,
And when night descends defiest   5
   The embattled tempests' warning!

TO THE LORD CHANCELLOR

I

THY country's curse is on thee, darkest crest
   Of that foul, knotted, many-headed worm
Which rends our Mother's bosom—Priestly Pest!
   Masked Resurrection of a buried Form!

II

Thy country's curse is on thee! Justice sold,   5
   Truth trampled, Nature's landmarks overthrown,
And heaps of fraud-accumulated gold,
   Plead, loud as thunder, at Destruction's throne.

III

And, whilst that sure slow Angel which aye stands
   Watching the beck of Mutability   10
Delays to execute her high commands,
   And, though a nation weeps, spares thine and thee.

IV

Oh, let a father's curse be on thy soul,
   And let a daughter's hope be on thy tomb;
Be both, on thy gray head, a leaden cowl   15
   To weigh thee down to thine approaching doom!

V

I curse thee by a parent's outraged love,
   By hopes long cherished and too lately lost,
By gentle feelings thou couldst never prove,
   By griefs which thy stern nature never crossed;   20

VI

By those infantine smiles of happy light,
  Which were a fire within a stranger's hearth,
Quenched even when kindled, in untimely night
  Hiding the promise of a lovely birth:

VII

By those unpractised accents of young speech,   25
  Which he who is a father thought to frame
To gentlest lore, such as the wisest teach—
  Thou strike the lyre of mind!—oh, grief and shame!

VIII

By all the happy see in children's growth—
  That undeveloped flower of budding years—   30
Sweetness and sadness interwoven both,
  Source of the sweetest hopes and saddest fears—

IX

By all the days, under an hireling's care,
  Of dull constraint and bitter heaviness,—
O wretched ye if ever any were,—   35
  Sadder than orphans, yet not fatherless!

X

By the false cant which on their innocent lips
  Must hang like poison on an opening bloom,
By the dark creeds which cover with eclipse
  Their pathway from the cradle to the tomb—   40

XI

By thy most impious Hell, and all its terror;
  By all the grief, the madness, and the guilt
Of thine impostures, which must be their error—
  That sand on which thy crumbling power is built—

XII

By thy complicity with lust and hate—   45
  Thy thirst for tears—thy hunger after gold—
The ready frauds which ever on thee wait—
  The servile arts in which thou hast grown old—

XIII

By thy most killing sneer, and by thy smile—
  By all the arts and snares of thy black den,   50
And—for thou canst outweep the crocodile—
  By thy false tears—those millstones braining men—

XIV

By all the hate which checks a father's love—
   By all the scorn which kills a father's care—
By those most impious hands which dared remove   55
   Nature's high bounds—by thee—and by despair—

XV

Yes, the despair which bids a father groan,
   And cry, 'My children are no longer mine—
The blood within those veins may be mine own,
   But—Tyrant—their polluted souls are thine;'—   60

XVI

I curse thee—though I hate thee not.—O slave!
   If thou couldst quench the earth-consuming Hell
Of which thou art a daemon, on thy grave
   This curse should be a blessing. Fare thee well!

TO WILLIAM SHELLEY

I

The billows on the beach are leaping around it,
   The bark is weak and frail,
The sea looks black, and the clouds that bound it
   Darkly strew the gale.
Come with me, thou delightful child,   5
Come with me, though the wave is wild,
And the winds are loose, we must not stay,
Or the slaves of the law may rend thee away.

II

They have taken thy brother and sister dear,
   They have made them unfit for thee;   10
They have withered the smile and dried the tear
   Which should have been sacred to me.
To a blighting faith and a cause of crime
They have bound them slaves in youthly prime,
And they will curse my name and thee   15
Because we fearless are and free.

III

Come thou, belovèd as thou art;
   Another sleepeth still
Near thy sweet mother's anxious heart,
   Which thou with joy shalt fill.   20

With fairest smiles of wonder thrown
On that which is indeed our own,
And which in distant lands will be
The dearest playmate unto thee.

IV

Fear not the tyrants will rule for ever,   25
   Or the priests of the evil faith;
They stand on the brink of that raging river,
   Whose waves they have tainted with death.
It is fed from the depth of a thousand dells,
Around them it foams and rages and swells;   30
And their swords and their sceptres I floating see,
Like wrecks on the surge of eternity.

V

Rest, rest, and shriek not, thou gentle child!
   The rocking of the boat thou fearest,
And the cold spray and the clamour wild?—   35
   There, sit between us two, thou dearest—
Me and thy mother—well we know
The storm at which thou tremblest so,
With all its dark and hungry graves,
Less cruel than the savage slaves   40
Who hunt us o'er these sheltering waves.

VI

This hour will in thy memory
   Be a dream of days forgotten long.
We soon shall dwell by the azure sea
Of serene and golden Italy,   45
Or Greece, the Mother of the free;
   And I will teach thine infant tongue
To call upon those heroes old
In their own language, and will mould
Thy growing spirit in the flame
Of Grecian lore, that by such name   50
A patriot's birthright thou mayst claim!

FROM THE ORIGINAL DRAFT OF THE POEM
TO WILLIAM SHELLEY

I

THE world is now our dwelling-place;
Where'er the earth one fading trace
   Of what was great and free does keep,
That is our home! . . .

Mild thoughts of man's ungentle race   5
    Shall our contented exile reap;
For who that in some happy place
His own free thoughts can freely chase
By woods and waves can clothe his face
    In cynic smiles? Child! we shall weep.   10

II

        This lament,
    The memory of thy grievous wrong
Will fade ...
But genius is omnipotent
To hallow ...   15

ON FANNY GODWIN

HER voice did quiver as we parted,
    Yet knew I not that heart was broken
From which it came, and I departed
    Heeding not the words then spoken.
        Misery—O Misery,   5
    This world is all too wide for thee.

LINES

I

THAT time is dead for ever, child!
Drowned, frozen, dead for ever!
    We look on the past
    And stare aghast
At the spectres wailing, pale and ghast,   5
Of hopes which thou and I beguiled
    To death on life's dark river.

II

The stream we gazed on then rolled by;
Its waves are unreturning;
    But we yet stand   10
    In a lone land,
Like tombs to mark the memory
Of hopes and fears, which fade and flee
    In the light of life's dim morning.

DEATH

I

THEY die—the dead return not—Misery
    Sits near an open grave and calls them over,
A Youth with hoary hair and haggard eye--
    They are the names of kindred, friend and lover,
Which he so feebly calls—they all are gone--
Fond wretch, all dead! those vacant names alone,
    This most familiar scene, my pain—
    These tombs—alone remain.

II

Misery, my sweetest friend—oh, weep no more!
  Thou wilt not be consoled—I wonder not!   10
For I have seen thee from thy dwelling's door
  Watch the calm sunset with them, and this spot
Was even as bright and calm, but transitory,
And now thy hopes are gone, thy hair is hoary;
    This most familiar scene, my pain—   15
    These tombs—alone remain.

OTHO

I

THOU wert not, Cassius, and thou couldst not be,
  Last of the Romans, though thy memory claim
From Brutus his own glory—and on thee
  Rests the full splendour of his sacred fame:
Nor he who dared make the foul tyrant quail   5
  Amid his cowering senate with thy name,
Though thou and he were great—it will avail
To thine own fame that Otho's should not fail.

II

'Twill wrong thee not—thou wouldst, if thou couldst feel,
  Abjure such envious fame—great Otho died   10
Like thee—he sanctified his country's steel,
  At once the tyrant and tyrannicide,
In his own blood—a deed it was to bring
  Tears from all men—though full of gentle pride,
Such pride as from impetuous love may spring,   15
    That will not be refused its offering.

FRAGMENTS SUPPOSED TO BE PARTS OF OTHO

I

THOSE whom nor power, nor lying faith, nor toil,
  Nor custom, queen of many slaves, makes blind,
Have ever grieved that man should be the spoil
  Of his own weakness, and with earnest mind
Fed hopes of its redemption; these recur   5
  Chastened by deathful victory now, and find
Foundations in this foulest age, and stir
Me whom they cheer to be their minister.

II

Dark is the realm of grief: but human things
Those may not know who cannot weep for them.   10

    .   .   .   .   .   .

III

Once more descend

The shadows of my soul upon mankind,
For to those hearts with which they never blend,
    Thoughts are but shadows which the flashing mind
From the swift clouds which track its flight of fire,   15
    Casts on the gloomy world it leaves behind.

.   .   .   .

'O THAT A CHARIOT OF CLOUD WERE MINE'

O THAT a chariot of cloud were mine!
    Of cloud which the wild tempest weaves in air,
When the moon over the ocean's line
    Is spreading the locks of her bright gray hair.
O that a chariot of cloud were mine!   5
    I would sail on the waves of the billowy wind
To the mountain peak and the rocky lake,
And the . . .

FRAGMENT: TO A FRIEND RELEASED FROM PRISON

FOR me, my friend, if not that tears did tremble
    In my faint eyes, and that my heart beat fast
With feelings which make rapture pain resemble,
    Yet, from thy voice that falsehood starts aghast,
        I thank thee—let the tyrant keep   5
        His chains and tears, yea, let him weep
        With rage to see thee freshly risen,
        Like strength from slumber, from the prison,
In which he vainly hoped the soul to bind
Which on the chains must prey that fetter humankind.   10

FRAGMENT: SATAN BROKEN LOOSE

A GOLDEN-WINGED Angel stood
    Before the Eternal Judgement-seat:
His looks were wild, and Devil's blood
    Stained his dainty hands and feet.
The Father and the Son   5
Knew that strife was now begun.
They knew that Satan had broken his chain,
And with millions of daemons in his train,
Was ranging over the world again.
Before the Angel had told his tale,   10
    A sweet and a creeping sound
    Like the rushing of wings was heard around;

And suddenly the lamps grew pale—
The lamps, before the Archangels seven,
That burn continually in Heaven.

15

FRAGMENT: *IGNICULUS DESIDERII*

To thirst and find no fill—to wail and wander
With short unsteady steps—to pause and ponder—
To feel the blood run through the veins and tingle
Where busy thought and blind sensation mingle;
To nurse the image of unfelt caresses
Till dim imagination just possesses
The half-created shadow, then all the night
Sick . . .

5

FRAGMENT: *AMOR AETERNUS*

WEALTH and dominion fade into the mass
Of the great sea of human right and wrong,
When once from our possession they must pass;
But love, though misdirected, is among
The things which are immortal, and surpass
All that frail stuff which will be—or which was.

5

FRAGMENT: THOUGHTS COME AND GO IN SOLITUDE

My thoughts arise and fade in solitude,
The verse that would invest them melts away
Like moonlight in the heaven of spreading day:
How beautiful they were, how firm they stood,
Flecking the starry sky like woven pearl!

5

A HATE-SONG

A HATER he came and sat by a ditch,
And he took an old cracked lute;
And he sang a song that was more of a screech
'Gainst a woman that was a brute.

LINES TO A CRITIC

I

HONEY from silkworms who can gather,
Or silk from the yellow bee?
The grass may grow in winter weather
As soon as hate in me.

II

Hate men who cant, and men who pray,
And men who rail like thee;
An equal passion to repay
They are not coy like me.

5

III

Or seek some slave of power and
    gold
  To be thy dear heart's mate; 10
Thy love will move that bigot
    cold
Sooner than me, thy hate.

IV

A passion like the one I prove
  Cannot divided be;
I hate thy want of truth and
    love,
  How should I then hate thee? 16

OZYMANDIAS

I MET a traveller from an antique land
Who said: Two vast and trunkless legs of stone
Stand in the desert . . . Near them, on the sand,
Half sunk, a shattered visage lies, whose frown,
And wrinkled lip, and sneer of cold command,   5
Tell that its sculptor well those passions read
Which yet survive, stamped on these lifeless things,
The hand that mocked them, and the heart that fed:
And on the pedestal these words appear:
'My name is Ozymandias, king of kings: 10
Look on my works, ye Mighty, and despair!'
Nothing beside remains. Round the decay
Of that colossal wreck, boundless and bare
The lone and level sands stretch far away.

NOTE ON POEMS OF 1817, BY MRS. SHELLEY

THE very illness that oppressed, and the aspect of death which had
approached so near Shelley, appear to have kindled to yet keener life
the Spirit of Poetry in his heart. The restless thoughts kept awake by
pain clothed themselves in verse. Much was composed during this year.
The *Revolt of Islam*, written and printed, was a great effort—*Rosalind
and Helen* was begun—and the fragments and poems I can trace to the
same period show how full of passion and reflection were his solitary
hours.

In addition to such poems as have an intelligible aim and shape, many
a stray idea and transitory emotion found imperfect and abrupt expression, and then again lost themselves in silence. As he never wandered without a book and without implements of writing, I find many
such, in his manuscript books, that scarcely bear record; while some of
them, broken and vague as they are, will appear valuable to those who
love Shelley's mind, and desire to trace its workings.

He projected also translating the *Hymns* of Homer; his version of
several of the shorter ones remains, as well as that to Mercury already
published in the *Posthumous Poems*. His readings this year were chiefly
Greek. Besides the *Hymns* of Homer and the *Iliad*, he read the dramas

of Aeschylus and Sophocles, the *Symposium* of Plato, and Arrian's *Historia Indica*. In Latin, Apuleius alone is named. In English, the Bible was his constant study; he read a great portion of it aloud in the evening. Among these evening readings I find also mentioned the *Faerie Queen;* and other modern works, the production of his contemporaries, Coleridge, Wordsworth, Moore, and Byron.

His life was now spent more in thought than action—he had lost the eager spirit which believed it could achieve what it projected for the benefit of mankind. And yet in the converse of daily life Shelley was far from being a melancholy man. He was eloquent when philosophy or politics or taste were the subjects of conversation. He was playful; and indulged in the wild spirit that mocked itself and others—not in bitterness, but in sport. The author of *Nightmare Abbey* seized on some points of his character and some habits of his life when he painted Scythrop. He was not addicted to 'port or madeira,' but in youth he had read of 'Illuminati and Eleutherarchs,' and believed that he possessed the power of operating an immediate change in the minds of men and the state of society. These wild dreams had faded; sorrow and adversity had struck home; but he struggled with despondency as he did with physical pain. There are few who remember him sailing paper boats, and watching the navigation of his tiny craft with eagerness—or repeating with wild energy *The Ancient Mariner,* and Southey's *Old Woman of Berkeley;* but those who do will recollect that it was in such, and in the creations of his own fancy when that was most daring and ideal, that he sheltered himself from the storms and disappointments, the pain and sorrow, that beset his life.

No words can express the anguish he felt when his elder children were torn from him. In his first resentment against the Chancellor, on the passing of the decree, he had written a curse, in which there breathes, besides haughty indignation, all the tenderness of a father's love, which could imagine and fondly dwell upon its loss and the consequences.

At one time, while the question was still pending, the Chancellor had said some words that seemed to intimate that Shelley should not be permitted the care of any of his children, and for a moment he feared that our infant son would be torn from us. He did not hesitate to resolve, if such were menaced, to abandon country, fortune, everything, and to escape with his child; and I find some unfinished stanzas addressed to this son, whom afterwards we lost at Rome, written under the idea that we might suddenly be forced to cross the sea, so to preserve him. This poem, as well as the one previously quoted, were not written to exhibit the pangs of distress to the public; they were the spontaneous outbursts of a man who brooded over his wrongs and woes, and was impelled to shed the grace of his genius over the uncontrollable emotions of his heart. I ought to observe that the fourth verse of this effusion is introduced in *Rosalind and Helen*. When afterwards this child died at Rome, he wrote, *à propos* of the English burying-ground in that city: 'This spot is the repository of a sacred loss, of which the yearnings of a parent's heart are now prophetic; he is rendered immortal by love, as his memory is by death. My beloved child lies buried here. I envy death the body far less than the oppressors the minds of those whom they have torn from me. The one can only kill the body, the other crushes the affections.'

POEMS WRITTEN IN 1818

TO THE NILE

MONTH after month the gathered rains descend
Drenching yon secret Aethiopian dells,
And from the desert's ice-girt pinnacles
Where Frost and Heat in strange embraces blend
On Atlas, fields of moist snow half depend.   5
Girt there with blasts and meteors Tempest dwells
By Nile's aëreal urn, with rapid spells
Urging those waters to their mighty end.
O'er Egypt's land of Memory floods are level
And they are thine, O Nile—and well thou knowest   10
That soul-sustaining airs and blasts of evil
And fruits and poisons spring where'er thou flowest.
Beware, O Man—for knowledge must to thee,
Like the great flood to Egypt, ever be.

PASSAGE OF THE APENNINES

LISTEN, listen, Mary mine,
To the whisper of the Apennine,
It bursts on the roof like the thunder's roar,
Or like the sea on a northern shore,
Heard in its raging ebb and flow   5
By the captives pent in the cave below.
The Apennine in the light of day
Is a mighty mountain dim and gray,
Which between the earth and sky doth lay;
But when night comes, a chaos dread   10
On the dim starlight then is spread,
And the Apennine walks abroad with the storm,
Shrouding . . .

THE PAST

I

WILT thou forget the happy hours
Which we buried in Love's sweet bowers,
Heaping over their corpses cold
Blossoms and leaves, instead of mould?
Blossoms which were the joys that fell,
And leaves, the hopes that yet remain.

II

Forget the dead, the past? Oh, yet
There are ghosts that may take revenge for it,
Memories that make the heart a tomb,
Regrets which glide through the spirit's gloom, 10
   And with ghastly whispers tell
     That joy, once lost, is pain.

TO MARY ———

O MARY dear, that you were here
With your brown eyes bright and
    clear,
And your sweet voice, like a bird
Singing love to its lone mate
In the ivy bower disconsolate; 5
Voice the sweetest ever heard!
And your brow more . . . .
Than the   sky

Of this azure Italy.
Mary dear, come to me soon, 10
I am not well whilst thou art far;
As sunset to the spherèd moon,
As twilight to the western star,
Thou, belovèd, art to me.
O Mary dear, that you were
    here: 15
The Castle echo whispers 'Here!'

ON A FADED VIOLET

I

THE odour from the flower is gone
   Which like thy kisses breathed on me;
The colour from the flower is flown
   Which glowed of thee and only thee!

II

A shrivelled, lifeless, vacant form, 5
   It lies on my abandoned breast,
And mocks the heart which yet is warm,
   With cold and silent rest.

III

I weep,—my tears revive it not!
   I sigh,—it breathes no more on me; 10
Its mute and uncomplaining lot
   Is such as mine should be.

LINES WRITTEN AMONG THE EUGANEAN HILLS
OCTOBER, 1818.

MANY a green isle needs must be
In the deep wide sea of Misery,
Or the mariner, worn and wan,
Never thus could voyage on—

Day and night, and night and day,
Drifting on his dreary way, 6
With the solid darkness black
Closing round his vessel's track:

Whilst above the sunless sky,
Big with clouds, hangs heavily,   10
And behind the tempest fleet
Hurries on with lightning feet,
Riving sail, and cord, and plank,
Till the ship has almost drank   14
Death from the o'er-brimming
   deep;
And sinks down, down, like that
   sleep
When the dreamer seems to be
Weltering through eternity;
And the dim low line before
Of a dark and distant shore   20
Still recedes, as ever still
Longing with divided will,
But no power to seek or shun,
He is ever drifted on
O'er the unreposing wave   25
To the haven of the grave.
What, if there no friends will
   greet;
What, if there no heart will meet
His with love's impatient beat;
Wander wheresoe'er he may.   30
Can he dream before that day
To find refuge from distress
In friendship's smile, in love's
   caress?
Then 'twill wreak him little woe
Whether such there be or no: 35
Senseless is the breast, and cold,
Which relenting love would fold;
Bloodless are the veins and chill
Which the pulse of pain did fill;
Every little living nerve   40
That from bitter words did swerve
Round the tortured lips and brow,
Are like sapless leaflets now
Frozen upon December's bough.

On the beach of a northern sea   45
Which tempests shake eternally,
As once the wretch there lay to
   sleep,
Lies a solitary heap,

One white skull and seven dry
   bones,
On the margin of the stones,   50
Where a few gray rushes stand,
Boundaries of the sea and land:
Nor is heard one voice of wail
But the sea-mews, as they sail
O'er the billows of the gale;   55
Or the whirlwind up and down
Howling, like a slaughtered town,
When a king in glory rides
Through the pomp of fratri-
   cides:
Those unburied bones around   60
There is many a mournful sound;
There is no lament for him,
Like a sunless vapour, dim,
Who once clothed with life and
   thought
What now moves nor murmurs not.

Ay, many flowering islands lie   66
In the waters of wide Agony:
To such a one this morn was led,
My bark by soft winds piloted:
'Mid the mountains Euganean   70
I stood listening to the paean
With which the legioned rooks did
   hail
The sun's uprise majestical;
Gathering round with wings all
   hoar,
Through the dewy mist they soar 75
Like gray shades, till the eastern
   heaven
Bursts, and then, as clouds of even,
Flecked with fire and azure, lie
In the unfathomable sky,
So their plumes of purple grain,   80
Starred with drops of golden rain,
Gleam above the sunlight woods,
As in silent multitudes
On the morning's fitful gale   84
Through the broken mist they sail,
And the vapours cloven and gleam-
   ing

Follow down the dark steep
　　streaming,
Till all is bright, and clear, and
　　still,
Round the solitary hill.

Beneath is spread like a green
　　sea　　　　　　　　　　90
The waveless plain of Lombardy,
Bounded by the vaporous air,
Islanded by cities fair;
Underneath Day's azure eyes
Ocean's nursling, Venice lies, 95
A peopled labyrinth of walls,
Amphitrite's destined halls,
Which her hoary sire now paves
With his blue and beaming waves.
Lo! the sun upsprings behind, 100
Broad, red, radiant, half-reclined
On the level quivering line
Of the waters crystalline;
And before that chasm of light,
As within a furnace bright, 105
Column, tower, and dome, and
　　spire,
Shine like obelisks of fire,
Pointing with inconstant motion
From the altar of dark ocean
To the sapphire-tinted skies; 110
As the flames of sacrifice
From the marble shrines did rise,
As to pierce the dome of gold
Where Apollo spoke of old.

Sun-girt City, thou hast been 115
Ocean's child, and then his queen;
Now is come a darker day,
And thou soon must be his prey,
If the power that raised thee here
Hallow so thy watery bier. 120
A less drear ruin then than now,
With thy conquest-branded brow
Stooping to the slave of slaves
From thy throne, among the waves
Wilt thou be, when the sea-mew 125
Flies, as once before it flew,
O'er thine isles depopulate,

And all is in its ancient state,
Save where many a palace gate
With green sea-flowers overgrown
Like a rock of Ocean's own, 131
Topples o'er the abandoned sea
As the tides change sullenly.
The fisher on his watery way,
Wandering at the close of day, 135
Will spread his sail and seize his
　　oar
Till he pass the gloomy shore,
Lest thy dead should, from their
　　sleep
Bursting o'er the starlight deep,
Lead a rapid masque of death 140
O'er the waters of his path.

Those who alone thy towers behold
Quivering through aëreal gold,
As I now behold them here,
Would imagine not they were 145
Sepulchres, where human forms,
Like pollution-nourished worms,
To the corpse of greatness cling,
Murdered, and now mouldering:
But if Freedom should awake 150
In her omnipotence, and shake
From the Celtic Anarch's hold
All the keys of dungeons cold,
Where a hundred cities lie
Chained like thee, ingloriously, 155
Thou and all thy sister band
Might adorn this sunny land,
Twining memories of old time
With new virtues more sublime;
If not, perish thou and they!— 160
Clouds which stain truth's rising
　　day
By her sun consumed away—
Earth can spare ye: while like
　　flowers,
In the waste of years and hours,
From your dust new nations spring
With more kindly blossoming. 166

Perish—let there only be
Floating o'er thy heartless sea

As the garment of thy sky
Clothes the world immortally,   170
One remembrance, more sublime
Than the tattered pall of time,
Which scarce hides thy visage
        wan;—
That a tempest-cleaving Swan
Of the songs of Albion,   175
Driven from his ancestral streams
By the might of evil dreams,
Found a nest in thee; and Ocean
Welcomed him with such emotion
That its joy grew his, and sprung
From his lips like music flung   181
O'er a mighty thunder-fit,
Chastening terror:—what though
        yet
Poesy's unfailing River,
Which through Albion winds for-
        ever
Lashing with melodious wave   186
Many a sacred Poet's grave,
Mourn its latest nursling fled?
What though thou with all thy dead
Scarce can for this fame repay   190
Aught thine own? oh, rather say
Though thy sins and slaveries foul
Overcloud a sunlike soul?
As the ghost of Homer clings
Round Scamander's wasting
        springs;   195
As divinest Shakespeare's might
Fills Avon and the world with light
Like omniscient power which he
Imaged 'mid mortality;
As the love from Petrarch's urn,   200
Yet amid yon hills doth burn,
A quenchless lamp by which the
        heart
Sees things unearthly;—so thou
        art,
Mighty spirit—so shall be
The City that did refuge thee.   205

Lo, the sun floats up the sky
Like thought-wingèd Liberty,
Till the universal light
Seems to level plain and height;
From the sea a mist has spread,   210
And the beams of morn lie dead
On the towers of Venice now,
Like its glory long ago.
By the skirts of that gray cloud
Many-domèd Padua proud   215
Stands, a peopled solitude,
'Mid the harvest-shining plain,
Where the peasant heaps his grain
In the garner of his foe,
And the milk-white oxen slow   220
With the purple vintage strain,
Heaped upon the creaking wain,
That the brutal Celt may swill
Drunken sleep with savage will;
And the sickle to the sword   225
Lies unchanged, though many a
        lord,
Like a weed whose shade is poison,
Overgrows this region's foison,
Sheaves of whom are ripe to come
To destruction's harvest-home: 230
Men must reap the things they
        sow,
Force from force must ever flow,
Or worse; but 'tis a bitter woe
That love or reason cannot change
The despot's rage, the slave's re-
        venge.
Padua, thou within whose walls
Those mute guests at festivals,
Son and Mother, Death and Sin,
Played at dice for Ezzelin,   239
Till Death cried, "I win, I win!"
And Sin cursed to lose the wager,
But Death promised, to assuage
        her,
That he would petition for
Her to be made Vice-Emperor,
When the destined years were o'er,
Over all between the Po   246
And the eastern Alpine snow,
Under the mighty Austrian.
Sin smiled so as Sin only can,

And since that time, ay, long be-
fore,   250
Both have ruled from shore to
shore,—
That incestuous pair, who follow
Tyrants as the sun the swallow,
As Repentance follows Crime,
And as changes follow Time.   255

In thine halls the lamp of learning,
Padua, now no more is burning;
Like a meteor, whose wild way
Is lost over the grave of day,
It gleams betrayed and to betray:
Once remotest nations came   261
To adore that sacred flame,
When it lit not many a hearth
On this cold and gloomy earth:
Now new fires from antique light
Spring beneath the wide world's
might;   266
But their spark lies dead in thee,
Trampled out by Tyranny.
As the Norway woodman quells,
In the depth of piny dells,   270
One light flame among the brakes,
While the boundless forest shakes,
And its mighty trunks are torn
By the fire thus lowly born:
The spark beneath his feet is dead,
He starts to see the flames it fed 276
Howling through the darkened sky
With a myriad tongues victoriously,
And sinks down in fear: so thou,
O Tyranny, beholdest now   280
Light around thee, and thou hearest
The loud flames ascend, and fear-
est:
Grovel on the earth; ay, hide
In the dust thy purple pride!

Noon descends around me now: 285
'Tis the noon of autumn's glow,
When a soft and purple mist
Like a vaporous amethyst,
Or an air-dissolvèd star
Mingling light and fragrance,
far   290

From the curved horizon's bound
To the point of Heaven's profound,
Fills the overflowing sky;
And the plains that silent lie
Underneath, the leaves unsod-
den   295
Where the infant Frost has trodden
With his morning-wingèd feet,
Whose bright print is gleaming yet;
And the red and golden vines,
Piercing with their trellised lines 300
The rough, dark-skirted wilderness;
The dun and bladed grass no less,
Pointing from this hoary tower
In the windless air; the flower
Glimmering at my feet; the line 305
Of the olive-sandalled Apennine
In the south dimly islanded;
And the Alps, whose snows are
spread
High between the clouds and sun;
And of living things each one; 310
And my spirit which so long
Darkened this swift stream of
song,—
Interpenetrated lie
By the glory of the sky:
Be it love, light, harmony,   315
Odour, or the soul of all
Which from Heaven like dew doth
fall,
Or the mind which feeds this verse
Peopling the lone universe.

Noon descends, and after noon 320
Autumn's evening meets me soon,
Leading the infantine moon,
And that one star, which to her
Almost seems to minister
Half the crimson light she brings 325
From the sunset's radiant springs:
And the soft dreams of the morn
(Which like wingèd winds had
borne
To that silent isle, which lies
Mid remembered agonies,   330
The frail bark of this lone being)
Pass, to other sufferers fleeing,

And its ancient pilot, Pain,
Sits beside the helm again.

Other flowering isles must be   335
In the sea of Life and Agony:
Other spirits float and flee
O'er that gulf: even now, perhaps,
On some rock the wild wave wraps,
With folded wings they waiting sit
For my bark, to pilot it   341
To some calm and blooming cove,
Where for me, and those I love,
May a windless bower be built,
Far from passion, pain, and guilt,
In a dell mid lawny hills,   346
Which the wild-sea murmur fills,
And soft sunshine, and the sound
Of old forests echoing round,
And the light and smell divine   350
Of all flowers that breathe and
    shine:
We may live so happy there,
That the Spirits of the Air,

Envying us, may even entice
To our healing Paradise   355
The polluting multitude;
But their rage would be subdued
By that clime divine and calm,
And the winds whose wings rain
    balm
On the uplifted soul, and leaves 360
Under   which   the   bright   sea
    heaves;
While each breathless interval
In their whisperings musical
The inspired soul supplies
With its own deep melodies,   365
And the love which heals all strife
Circling, like the breath of life,
All things in that sweet abode
With its own mild brotherhood:
They, not it, would change; and
    soon   370
Every sprite beneath the moon
Would repent its envy vain,
And the earth grow young again.

SCENE FROM 'TASSO'

MADDALO, *a Courtier*.   PIGNA, *a Minister*.
MALPIGLIO, *a Poet*.   ALBANO, *an Usher*.

Maddalo. No access to the Duke! You have not said
That the Count Maddalo would speak with him?
    Pigna. Did you inform his Grace that Signor Pigna
Waits with state papers for his signature?
    Malpiglio. The Lady Leonora cannot know   5
That I have written a sonnet to her fame,
In which I   Venus and Adonis.
You should not take my gold and serve me not.
    Albano. In truth I told her, and she smiled and said,
'If I am Venus, thou, coy Poesy,   10
Art the Adonis whom I love, and he
The Erymanthian boar that wounded him.'
O trust to me, Signor Malpiglio,
Those nods and smiles were favours worth the zechin.
    Malpiglio. The words are twisted in some double sense   15
That I reach not: the smiles fell not on me.
    Pigna. How are the Duke and Duchess occupied?
    Albano. Buried in some strange talk. The Duke was leaning,
His finger on his brow, his lips unclosed

The Princess sate within the window-seat,   20
And so her face was hid; but on her knee
Her hands were clasped, veinèd, and pale as snow,
And quivering—young Tasso, too, was there.
    Maddalo. Thou seest on whom from thine own worshipped
        heaven
Thou drawest down smiles—they did not rain on thee.   25
    Malpiglio. Would they were parching lightnings for his sake
On whom they fell!

SONG FOR 'TASSO'

I

I LOVED—alas! our life is love;
But when we cease to breathe and move
I do suppose love ceases too.
I thought, but not as now I do,
Keen thoughts and bright of linkèd lore,   5
Of all that men had thought before,
And all that Nature shows. and more.

II

And still I love and still I think,
But strangely, for my heart can drink
The dregs of such despair, and live,   10
And love; . . .
And if I think, my thoughts come fast,
I mix the present with the past,
And each seems uglier than the last.

III

Sometimes I see before me flee   15
A silver spirit's form, like thee,
O Leonora, and I sit
. . . still watching it,
Till by the grated casement's ledge
It fades, with such a sigh, as sedge   20
Breathes o'er the breezy streamlet's edge.

INVOCATION TO MISERY

I	II
COME, be happy!—sit near me,	Come, be happy!—sit near me:
Shadow-vested Misery:	Sad as I may seem to thee,
Coy, unwilling, silent bride,	I am happier far than thou,
Mourning in thy robe of pride,	Lady, whose imperial brow
Desolation—deified! 5	Is endiademed with woe. 10

III

Misery! we have known each other,
Like a sister and a brother
Living in the same lone home,
Many years—we must live some
Hours or ages yet to come.   15

IV

'Tis an evil lot, and yet
Let us make the best of it;
If love can live when pleasure dies,
We two will love, till in our eyes
This heart's Hell seem Paradise. 20

V

Come, be happy!—lie thee down
On the fresh grass newly mown,
Where the Grasshopper doth sing
Merrily—one joyous thing
In a world of sorrowing!   25

VI

There our tent shall be the willow,
And mine arm shall be thy pillow;
Sounds and odours, sorrowful
Because they once were sweet, shall
    lull
Us to slumber, deep and dull.   30

VII

Ha! thy frozen pulses flutter
With a love thou darest not utter.
Thou art murmuring—thou art
    weeping—
Is thine icy bosom leaping
While my burning heart lies sleep-
    ing?   35

VIII

Kiss me;—oh! thy lips are cold:
Round my neck thine arms en-
    fold—

They are soft, but chill and dead;
And thy tears upon my head
Burn like points of frozen lead.   40

IX

Hasten to the bridal bed—
Underneath the grave 'tis spread:
In darkness may our love be hid,
Oblivion be our coverlid—
We may rest, and none forbid.   45

X

Clasp me till our hearts be grown
Like two shadows into one;
Till this dreadful transport may
Like a vapour fade away,
In the sleep that lasts alway.   50

XI

We may dream, in that long sleep,
That we are not those who weep;
E'en as Pleasure dreams of thee,
Life-deserting Misery,
Thou mayst dream of her with
    me.   55

XII

Let us laugh, and make our mirth,
At the shadows of the earth,
As dogs bay the moonlight clouds,
Which, like spectres wrapped in
    shrouds,
Pass o'er night in multitudes.   60

XIII

All the wide world, beside us,
Show like multitudinous
Puppets passing from a scene;
What but mockery can they mean,
Where I am—where thou hast
    been?   65

STANZAS

WRITTEN IN DEJECTION, NEAR NAPLES

I

THE sun is warm, the sky is clear,
   The waves are dancing fast and bright,
Blue isles and snowy mountains wear
   The purple noon's transparent might,
   The breath of the moist earth is light,   5
Around its unexpanded buds;
   Like many a voice of one delight,
The winds, the birds, the ocean floods,
The City's voice itself, is soft like Solitude's.

II

I see the Deep's untrampled floor   10
   With green and purple seaweeds strown;
I see the waves upon the shore,
   Like light dissolved in star-showers, thrown:
   I sit upon the sands alone,—
The lightning of the noontide ocean   15
   Is flashing round me, and a tone
Arises from its measured motion,
How sweet! did any heart now share in my emotion.

III

Alas! I have nor hope nor health,
   Nor peace within nor calm around,   20
Nor that content surpassing wealth
   The sage in meditation found,
   And walked with inward glory crowned—
Nor fame, nor power, nor love, nor leisure.
   Others I see whom these surround—   25
Smiling they live, and call life pleasure;—
To me that cup has been dealt in another measure.

IV

Yet now despair itself is mild,
   Even as the winds and waters are;
I could lie down like a tired child,
   And weep away the life of care   30
   Which I have borne and yet must bear,
Till death like sleep might steal on me,
   And I might feel in the warm air
My cheek grow cold, and hear the sea   35
Breathe o'er my dying brain its last monotony.

V

Some might lament that I were cold,
  As I, when this sweet day is gone,
Which my lost heart, too soon grown old,
  Insults with this untimely moan;   40
    They might lament—for I am one
Whom men love not,—and yet regret,
  Unlike this day, which, when the sun
Shall on its stainless glory set,
Will linger, though enjoyed, like joy in memory yet.   45

THE WOODMAN AND THE NIGHTINGALE

A woodman whose rough heart was out of tune
(I think such hearts yet never came to good)
Hated to hear, under the stars or moon,

One nightingale in an interfluous wood
Satiate the hungry dark with melody;—   5
And as a vale is watered by a flood,

Or as the moonlight fills the open sky
Struggling with darkness—as a tuberose
Peoples some Indian dell with scents which lie

Like clouds above the flower from which they rose,   10
The singing of that happy nightingale
In this sweet forest, from the golden close

Of evening till the star of dawn may fail,
Was interfused upon the silentness;
The folded roses and the violets pale   15

Heard her within their slumbers, the abyss
Of heaven with all its planets; the dull ear
Of the night-cradled earth; the loneliness

Of the circumfluous waters,—every sphere
And every flower and beam and cloud and wave,   20
And every wind of the mute atmosphere,

And every beast stretched in its ruggèd cave,
And every bird lulled on its mossy bough,
And every silver moth fresh from the grave

Which is its cradle—ever from below   25
Aspiring like one who loves too fair, too far,
To be consumed within the purest glow

Of one serene and unapproachèd star,
As if it were a lamp of earthly light,
Unconscious, as some human lovers are,   30

Itself how low, how high beyond all height
The heaven where it would perish!—and every form
That worshipped in the temple of the night

Was awed into delight, and by the charm
Girt as with an interminable zone,   35
Whilst that sweet bird, whose music was a storm

Of sound, shook forth the dull oblivion
Out of their dreams; harmony became love
In every soul but one.

     .   .   .   .   .

And so this man returned with axe and saw   40
At evening close from killing the tall treen,
The soul of whom by Nature's gentle law

Was each a wood-nymph, and kept ever green
The pavement and the roof of the wild copse,
Chequering the sunlight of the blue serene   45

With jaggèd leaves,—and from the forest tops
Singing the winds to sleep—or weeping oft
Fast showers of aëreal water-drops

Into their mother's bosom, sweet and soft,
Nature's pure tears which have no bitterness;—   50
Around the cradles of the birds aloft

They spread themselves into the loveliness
Of fan-like leaves, and over pallid flowers
Hang like moist clouds:—or, where high branches kiss,

Make a green space among the silent bowers,   55
Like a vast fane in a metropolis,
Surrounded by the columns and the towers

All overwrought with branch-like traceries
In which there is religion—and the mute
Persuasion of unkindled melodies,   60

Odours and gleams and murmurs, which the lute
Of the blind pilot-spirit of the blast
Stirs as it sails, now grave and now acute,

Wakening the leaves and waves, ere it has passed
To such brief unison as on the brain   65
One tone, which never can recur, has cast,
One accent never to return again.

. . . . . .

The world is full of Woodmen who expel
Love's gentle Dryads from the haunts of life,
And vex the nightingales in every dell.   70

MARENGHI [1]

I

LET those who pine in pride or in revenge,
    Or think that ill for ill should be repaid,
Who barter wrong for wrong, until the exchange
    Ruins the merchants of such thriftless trade,
Visit the tower of Vado, and unlearn   5
Such bitter faith beside Marenghi's urn.

II

A massy tower yet overhangs the town,
    A scattered group of ruined dwellings now . . . .

. . . .

III

Another scene ere wise Etruria knew
    Its second ruin through internal strife,   10
And tyrants through the breach of discord threw
    The chain which binds and kills. As death to life,
As winter to fair flowers (though some be poison)
So Monarchy succeeds to Freedom's foison.

IV

In Pisa's church a cup of sculptured gold   15
    Was brimming with the blood of feuds forsworn:
A Sacrament more holy ne'er of old
    Etrurians mingled mid the shades forlorn
Of moon-illumined forests, when . . . .

V

And reconciling factions wet their lips   20
    With that dread wine, and swear to keep each spirit
Undarkened by their country's last eclipse . . . .

. . . .

---

[1] This fragment refers to an event told in Sismondi's *Histoire des Républiques
Italiennes,* which occurred during the war when Florence finally subdued Pisa, and
reduced it to a province.—[MRS. SHELLEY'S NOTE, 1824.]

VI

Was Florence the liberticide? that band
　　Of free and glorious brothers who had planted,
Like a green isle mid Aethiopian sand,　　　　25
　　A nation amid slaveries, disenchanted
Of many impious faiths—wise, just—do they,
　　Does Florence, gorge the sated tyrants' prey?

VII

O foster-nurse of man's abandoned glory,
　　Since Athens, its great mother, sunk in splendour;　　30
Thou shadowest forth that mighty shape in story,
　　As ocean its wrecked fanes, severe yet tender:—
The light-invested angel Poesy
Was drawn from the dim world to welcome thee.

VIII

And thou in painting didst transcribe all taught　　35
　　By loftiest meditations; marble knew
The sculptor's fearless soul—and as he wrought,
　　The grace of his own power and freedom grew.
And more than all, heroic, just, sublime,
Thou wert among the false . . . was this thy crime?　　40

IX

Yes; and on Pisa's marble walls the twine
　　Of direst weeds hangs garlanded—the snake
Inhabits its wrecked palaces;—in thine
　　A beast of subtler venom now doth make
Its lair, and sits amid their glories overthrown,　　45
And thus thy victim's fate is as thine own.

X

The sweetest flowers are ever frail and rare,
　　And love and freedom blossom but to wither;
And good and ill like vines entangled are,
　　So that their grapes may oft be plucked together;—　　50
Divide the vintage ere thou drink, then make
Thy heart rejoice for dead Marenghi's sake.

x a

[Albert] Marenghi was a Florentine;
　　If he had wealth, or children, or a wife
Or friends, [or farm] or cherished thoughts which twine　　55
　　The sights and sounds of home with life's own life
Of these he was despoiled and Florence sent . . . .
　　　.　　　.　　　.　　　.　　　.　　　.　　　.

XI

No record of his crime remains in story,
   But if the morning bright as evening shone,
It was some high and holy deed, by glory   60
   Pursued into forgetfulness, which won
From the blind crowd he made secure and free
The patriot's meed, toil, death, and infamy

XII

For when by sound of trumpet was declared
   A price upon his life, and there was set   65
A penalty of blood on all who shared
   So much of water with him as might wet
His lips, which speech divided not—he went
Alone, as you may guess, to banishment.

XIII

Amid the mountains, like a hunted beast,   70
   He hid himself, and hunger, toil, and cold,
Month after month endured; it was a feast
   Whene'er he found those globes of deep-red gold
Which in the woods the strawberry-tree doth bear,
Suspended in their emerald atmosphere.   75

XIV

And in the roofless huts of vast morasses,
   Deserted by the fever-stricken serf,
All overgrown with reeds and long rank grasses,
   And hillocks heaped of moss-inwoven turf,
And where the huge and speckled aloe made,   80
Rooted in stones, a broad and pointed shade,—

XV

He housed himself. There is a point of strand
   Near Vado's tower and town; and on one side
The treacherous marsh divides it from the land,
   Shadowed by pine and ilex forests wide,   85
And on the other, creeps eternally,
Through muddy weeds, the shallow sullen sea.

XVI

Here the earth's breath is pestilence, and few
   But things whose nature is at war with life—
Snakes and ill worms—endure its mortal dew.   90
   The trophies of the clime's victorious strife—
And ringed horns which the buffalo did wear,
And the wolf's dark gray scalp who tracked him there.

XVII

And at the utmost point . . . stood there
   The relics of a reed-inwoven cot,   95
Thatched with broad flags. An outlawed murderer
   Had lived seven days there: the pursuit was hot
When he was cold. The birds that were his grave
Fell dead after their feast in Vado's wave.

XVIII

There must have burned within Marenghi's breast   100
   That fire, more warm and bright than life and hope,
(Which to the martyr makes his dungeon . . . .
   More joyous than free heaven's majestic cope
To his oppressor), warring with decay,—
Or he could ne'er have lived years, day by day.   105

XIX

Nor was his state so lone as you might think.
   He had tamed every newt and snake and toad,
And every seagull which sailed down to drink
   Those freshes ere the death-mist went abroad.
And each one, with peculiar talk and play,   110
Wiled, not untaught, his silent time away.

XX

And the marsh-meteors, like tame beasts, at night
   Came licking with blue tongues his veinèd feet;
And he would watch them, as, like spirits bright,
   In many entangled figures quaint and sweet   115
To some enchanted music they would dance—
Until they vanished at the first moon-glance.

XXI

He mocked the stars by grouping on each weed
   The summer dew-globes in the golden dawn;
And, ere the hoar-frost languished, he could read   120
   Its pictured path, as on bare spots of lawn
Its delicate brief touch in silver weaves
The likeness of the wood's remembered leaves.

XXII

And many a fresh Spring morn would he awaken—
   While yet the unrisen sun made glow, like iron   125
Quivering in crimson fire, the peaks unshaken
   Of mountains and blue isles which did environ
With air-clad crags that plain of land and sea,—
And feel   liberty.

XXIII

And in the moonless nights, when the dun ocean   130
    Heaved underneath wide heaven, star-impearled,
Starting from dreams . . .
    Communed with the immeasurable world;
And felt his life beyond his limbs dilated,
Till his mind grew like that it contemplated.   135

XXIV

His food was the wild fig and strawberry;
    The milky pine-nuts which the autumn-blast
Shakes into the tall grass; or such small fry
    As from the sea by winter-storms are cast;
And the coarse bulbs of iris-flowers he found   140
Knotted in clumps under the spongy ground.

XXV

And so were kindled powers and thoughts which made
    His solitude less dark. When memory came
(For years gone by leave each a deepening shade),
    His spirit basked in its internal flame,—   145
As, when the black storm hurries round at night,
The fisher basks beside his red firelight.

XXVI

Yet human hopes and cares and faiths and errors,
    Like billows unawakened by the wind,
Slept in Marenghi still; but that all terrors,   150
    Weakness, and doubt, had withered in his mind.
His couch . . .
    .   .   .   .   .

XXVII

And, when he saw beneath the sunset's planet
    A black ship walk over the crimson ocean,—
Its pennon streaming on the blasts that fan it,   155
    Its sails and ropes all tense and without motion,
Like the dark ghost of the unburied even
Striding athwart the orange-coloured heaven,—

XXVIII

The thought of his own kind who made the soul
    Which sped that wingèd shape through night and day,—   160
The thought of his own country . . .

SONNET

LIFT not the painted veil which those who live
Call Life: though unreal shapes be pictured there,
And it but mimic all we would believe
With colours idly spread,—behind, lurk Fear
And Hope, twin Destinies; who ever weave   5
Their shadows, o'er the chasm, sightless and drear.
I knew one who had lifted it—he sought,
For his lost heart was tender, things to love,
But found them not, alas! nor was there aught
The world contains, the which he could approve.   10
Through the unheeding many he did move,
A splendour among shadows, a bright blot
Upon this gloomy scene, a Spirit that strove
For truth, and like the Preacher found it not.

FRAGMENT: TO BYRON

O MIGHTY mind, in whose deep stream this age
Shakes like a reed in the unheeding storm,
Why dost thou curb not thine own sacred rage?

FRAGMENT: APOSTROPHE TO SILENCE

SILENCE! Oh, well are Death and Sleep and Thou
Three brethren named, the guardians gloomy-winged
Of one abyss, where life, and truth, and joy
Are swallowed up—yet spare me, Spirit, pity me,
Until the sounds I hear become my soul,   5
And it has left these faint and weary limbs,
To track along the lapses of the air
This wandering melody until it rests
Among lone mountains in some . . .

FRAGMENT: THE LAKE'S MARGIN

THE fierce beasts of the woods and wildernesses
Track not the steps of him who drinks of it;
For the light breezes, which for ever fleet
Around its margin, heap the sand thereon.

FRAGMENT: 'MY HEAD IS WILD WITH WEEPING'

MY head is wild with weeping for a grief
    Which is the shadow of a gentle mind.
I walk into the air (but no relief
    To seek,—or haply, if I sought, to find;
It came unsought);—to wonder that a chief   5
    Among men's spirits should be cold and blind.

FRAGMENT: THE VINE-SHROUD

FLOURISHING vine, whose kindling clusters glow
Beneath the autumnal sun, none taste of thee;
For thou dost shroud a ruin, and below
The rotting bones of dead antiquity.

NOTE ON POEMS OF 1818, BY MRS. SHELLEY

WE often hear of persons disappointed by a first visit to Italy. This was not Shelley's case. The aspect of its nature, its sunny sky, its majestic storms, of the luxuriant vegetation of the country, and the noble marble-built cities, enchanted him. The sight of the works of art was full enjoyment and wonder. He had not studied pictures or statues before; he now did so with the eye of taste, that referred not to the rules of schools, but to those of Nature and truth. The first entrance to Rome opened to him a scene of remains of antique grandeur that far surpassed his expectations; and the unspeakable beauty of Naples and its environs added to the impression he received of the transcendent and glorious beauty of Italy.

Our winter was spent at Naples. Here he wrote the fragments of *Marenghi* and *The Woodman and the Nightingale,* which he afterwards threw aside. At this time, Shelley suffered greatly in health. He put himself under the care of a medical man, who promised great things, and made him endure severe bodily pain, without any good results. Constant and poignant physical suffering exhausted him; and though he preserved the appearance of cheerfulness, and often greatly enjoyed our wanderings in the environs of Naples, and our excursions on its sunny sea, yet many hours were passed when his thoughts, shadowed by illness, became gloomy,—and then he escaped to solitude, and in verses, which he hid from fear of wounding me, poured forth morbid but too natural bursts of discontent and sadness. One looks back with unspeakable regret and gnawing remorse to such periods; fancying that, had one been more alive to the nature of his feelings, and more attentive to soothe them, such would not have existed. And yet, enjoying as he appeared to do every sight or influence of earth or sky, it was difficult to imagine that any melancholy he showed was aught but the effect of the constant pain to which he was a martyr.

We lived in utter solitude. And such is often not the nurse of cheerfulness; for then, at least with those who have been exposed to adversity, the mind broods over its sorrows too intently; while the society of the enlightened, the witty, and the wise, enables us to forget ourselves by making us the sharers of the thoughts of others, which is a portion of the philosophy of happiness. Shelley never liked society in numbers,—it harassed and wearied him; but neither did he like loneliness, and usually, when alone, sheltered himself against memory and reflection in a book. But, with one or two whom he loved, he gave way to wild and joyous spirits, or in more serious conversation expounded his opinions with vivacity and eloquence. If an argument arose, no man ever argued better. He was clear, logical, and earnest, in supporting his own views; attentive, patient, and impartial, while listening to those on the adverse side. Had not a wall of prejudice been raised at this time between him and his countrymen, how many would have sought the acquaintance of one whom to know was to love and to revere! How many of the more enlightened of his contemporaries have since regretted that they did not seek him! how very few knew his worth while he lived! and, of those few, several were withheld by timidity or envy from declaring their sense of it. But no man was ever more enthusiastically loved—more looked up to, as one superior to his fellows in intellectual endowments and moral worth, by the few who knew him well, and had sufficient nobleness of soul to appreciate his superiority. His excellence is now acknowledged; but, even while admitted, not duly appreciated. For who, except those who were acquainted with him, can imagine his unwearied benevolence, his generosity, his systematic forbearance? And still less is his vast superiority in intellectual attainments sufficiently understood—his sagacity, his clear understanding, his learning, his prodigious memory. All these, as displayed in conversation, were known to few while he lived, and are now silent in the tomb:

> 'Ahi orbo mondo ingrato!
> Gran cagion hai di dever pianger meco;
> Chè quel ben ch' era in te, perdut' hai seco.'

POEMS WRITTEN IN 1819

LINES WRITTEN DURING THE CASTLEREAGH ADMINISTRATION

I

Corpses are cold in the tomb;
Stones on the pavement are dumb;
Abortions are dead in the womb,
And their mothers look pale—like the death-white shore
    Of Albion, free no more.   5

II

Her sons are as stones in the way—
They are masses of senseless clay—
They are trodden, and move not away,—
The abortion with which *she* travaileth
    Is Liberty, smitten to death.   10

III

Then trample and dance, thou Oppressor!
For thy victim is no redresser;
Thou art sole lord and possessor
Of her corpses, and clods, and abortions—they pave
    Thy path to the grave.   15

IV

Hearest thou the festival din
Of Death, and Destruction, and Sin,
And Wealth crying *Havoc!* within?
'Tis the bacchanal triumph that makes Truth dumb,
Thine Epithalamium.   20

V

Ay, marry thy ghastly wife!
Let Fear and Disquiet and Strife
Spread thy couch in the chamber of Life!
Marry Ruin, thou Tyrant! and Hell be thy guide
To the bed of the bride!   25

SONG TO THE MEN OF ENGLAND

I

Men of England, wherefore plough
For the lords who lay ye low?
Wherefore weave with toil and care
The rich robes your tyrants wear?

II

Wherefore feed, and clothe, and save,   5
From the cradle to the grave,
Those ungrateful drones who would
Drain your sweat—nay, drink your blood?

III

Wherefore, Bees of England, forge
Many a weapon, chain, and scourge,
That these stingless drones may spoil   11
The forced produce of your toil?

IV

Have ye leisure, comfort, calm,
Shelter, food, love's gentle balm?
Or what is it ye buy so dear   15
With your pain and with your fear?

V

The seed ye sow, another reaps;
The wealth ye find, another keeps;
The robes ye weave, another wears;
The arms ye forge, another bears.   20

VI

Sow seed,—but let no tyrant reap;
Find wealth,—let no impostor heap;
Weave robes,—let not the idle wear;
Forge arms,—in your defence to bear.

VII

Shrink to your cellars, holes, and cells;   25
In halls ye deck another dwells.
Why shake the chains ye wrought? Ye see
The steel ye tempered glance on ye.

VIII

With plough and spade, and hoe and loom,
Trace your grave, and build your tomb,   30
And weave your winding-sheet, till fair
England be your sepulchre.

SIMILES FOR TWO POLITICAL CHARACTERS OF 1819

I

As from an ancestral oak
  Two empty ravens sound their
    clarion,
Yell by yell, and croak by croak,
When they scent the noonday
    smoke
  Of fresh human carrion:— 5

II

As two gibbering night-birds flit
  From their bowers of deadly
    yew
Through the night to frighten it,
When the moon is in a fit,
  And the stars are none, or
    few:—

III

As a shark and dog-fish wait   11
  Under an Atlantic isle,
For the negro-ship, whose freight
Is the theme of their debate,
  Wrinkling their red gills the
    while—   15

IV

Are ye, two vultures sick for battle,
  Two scorpions under one wet
    stone,
Two bloodless wolves whose dry
    throats rattle,
Two crows perched on the mur-
    rained cattle,
  Two vipers tangled into one. 20

FRAGMENT: TO THE PEOPLE OF ENGLAND

PEOPLE of England, ye who toil and groan,
Who reap the harvests which are not your own,
Who weave the clothes which your oppressors wear,
And for your own take the inclement air;
Who build warm houses . . .   5
And are like gods who give them all they have,
And nurse them from the cradle to the grave . . .

.   .   .   .

FRAGMENT: 'WHAT MEN GAIN FAIRLY'

WHAT men gain fairly—that they should possess,
And children may inherit idleness,
From him who earns it—This is understood;
Private injustice may be general good.
But he who gains by base and armèd wrong,   5
Or guilty fraud, or base compliances,
May be despoiled; even as a stolen dress
Is stripped from a convicted thief, and he
Left in the nakedness of infamy.

A NEW NATIONAL ANTHEM

I

God prosper, speed, and save,
God raise from England's grave
    Her murdered Queen!
Pave with swift victory
The steps of Liberty,   5
Whom Britons own to be
    Immortal Queen.

II

See, she comes throned on high,
On swift Eternity!
    God save the Queen!   10
Millions on millions wait,
Firm, rapid, and elate,
On her majestic state!
    God save the Queen!

III

She is Thine own pure soul   15
Moulding the mighty whole,—
    God save the Queen!
She is Thine own deep love
Rained down from Heaven above,—
Wherever she rest or move,   20
    God save our Queen!

IV

'Wilder her enemies
In their own dark disguise,—
    God save our Queen!
All earthly things that dare   25
Her sacred name to bear,
Strip them, as kings are, bare;
    God save the Queen!

V

Be her eternal throne
Built in our hearts alone—   30
    God save the Queen!
Let the oppressor hold
Canopied seats of gold;
She sits enthroned of old
    O'er our hearts Queen.   35

VI

Lips touched by seraphim
Breathe out the choral hymn
    'God save the Queen!'
Sweet as if angels sang,
Loud as that trumpet's clang   40
Wakening the world's dead gang,—
    God save the Queen!

SONNET: ENGLAND IN 1819

An old, mad, blind, despised, and dying king,—
Princes, the dregs of their dull race, who flow
Through public scorn,—mud from a muddy spring,—
Rulers who neither see, nor feel, nor know,
But leech-like to their fainting country cling,   5
Till they drop, blind in blood, without a blow,—
A people starved and stabbed in the untilled field,—
An army, which liberticide and prey
Makes as a two-edged sword to all who wield,—
Golden and sanguine laws which tempt and slay;   10
Religion Christless, Godless—a book sealed;
A Senate,—Time's worst statute unrepealed,—
Are graves, from which a glorious Phantom may
Burst, to illumine our tempestuous day.

AN ODE

Written October, 1819, before the SPANIARDS had Recovered
their Liberty

Arise, arise, arise!
There is blood on the earth that denies ye bread;
    Be your wounds like eyes
To weep for the dead, the dead, the dead.
What other grief were it just to pay?   **5**
Your sons, your wives, your brethren, were they;
Who said they were slain on the battle day?

    Awaken, awaken, awaken!
The slave and the tyrant are twin-born foes;
    Be the cold chains shaken   **10**
To the dust where your kindred repose, repose:
Their bones in the grave will start and move,
When they hear the voices of those they love,
Most loud in the holy combat above.

    Wave, wave high the banner!   **15**
When Freedom is riding to conquest by:
    Though the slaves that fan her
Be Famine and Toil, giving sigh for sigh.
And ye who attend her imperial car,
Lift not your hands in the banded war,   **20**
But in her defence whose children ye are.

    Glory, glory, glory,
To those who have greatly suffered and done!
    Never name in story
Was greater than that which ye shall have won.   **25**
Conquerors have conquered their foes alone,
Whose revenge, pride, and power they have overthrown:
Ride ye, more victorious, over your own.

    Bind, bind every brow
With crownals of violet, ivy, and pine: **30**
    Hide the blood-stains now
With hues which sweet Nature has made divine:
Green strength, azure hope, and eternity:
But let not the pansy among them be;
Ye were injured, and that means memory.   **35**

CANCELLED STANZA

Gather, O gather,
Foeman and friend in love and peace!
    Waves sleep together
When the blasts that called them to battle, cease.

For fangless Power grown tame and mild   5
Is at play with Freedom's fearless child—
The dove and the serpent reconciled!

ODE TO HEAVEN

CHORUS OF SPIRITS

First Spirit.

PALACE-ROOF of cloudless nights!
Paradise of golden lights!
  Deep, immeasurable, vast,
Which art now, and which wert then
  Of the Present and the Past,   5
Of the eternal Where and When,
  Presence-chamber, temple, home,
  Ever-canopying dome,
  Of acts and ages yet to come!

Glorious shapes have life in thee,   10
Earth, and all earth's company;
  Living globes which ever throng
Thy deep chasms and wildernesses;
  And green worlds that glide along;
And swift stars with flashing tresses;
  And icy moons most cold and bright,   16
  And mighty suns beyond the night,
  Atoms of intensest light.

Even thy name is as a god,
Heaven! for thou art the abode   20
  Of that Power which is the glass
Wherein man his nature sees.
  Generations as they pass
Worship thee with bended knees.
  Their unremaining gods and they
  Like a river roll away: 26
  Thou remainest such—alway!—

Second Spirit.

Thou art but the mind's first chamber,

Round which its young fancies clamber,
  Like weak insects in a cave,   30
Lighted up by stalactites;
  But the portal of the grave,
Where a world of new delights
  Will make thy best glories seem
  But a dim and noonday gleam   35
  From the shadow of a dream!

Third Spirit.

Peace! the abyss is wreathed with scorn
At your presumption, atom-born!
  What is Heaven? and what are ye
Who its brief expanse inherit?   40
  What are suns and spheres which flee
  With the instinct of that Spirit
  Of which ye are but a part?
  Drops which Nature's mighty heart
  Drives through thinnest veins!
    Depart!   45

What is Heaven? a globe of dew,
Filling in the morning new
  Some eyed flower whose young leaves waken
On an unimagined world:
  Constellated suns unshaken,   50
Orbits measureless, are furled
  In that frail and fading sphere,
  With ten millions gathered there,
  To tremble, gleam, and disappear.

CANCELLED FRAGMENTS OF THE ODE TO HEAVEN

THE [living frame which sustains
　　my soul]
Is [sinking beneath the fierce con-
　　trol]
　　Down through the lampless deep
　　　of song
　　I am drawn and driven along—

When a Nation screams aloud　5
Like an eagle from the cloud

When a ...

.　　　.　　　.　　　.

When the night ...

.　　　.　　　.　　　.

Watch the look askance and
　　old—　　　　　　　　　9
See neglect, and falsehood fold...

ODE TO THE WEST WIND [1]

I

O WILD West Wind, thou breath of Autumn's being,
Thou, from whose unseen presence the leaves dead
Are driven, like ghosts from an enchanter fleeing,

Yellow, and black, and pale, and hectic red,
Pestilence-stricken multitudes: O thou,　　　　　　　5
Who chariotest to their dark wintry bed

The wingèd seeds, where they lie cold and low,
Each like a corpse within its grave, until
Thine azure sister of the Spring shall blow

Her clarion o'er the dreaming earth, and fill　　　10
(Driving sweet buds like flocks to feed in air)
With living hues and odours plain and hill:

Wild Spirit, which art moving everywhere;
Destroyer and preserver; hear, oh, hear!

II

Thou on whose stream, mid the steep sky's commotion,　15
Loose clouds like earth's decaying leaves are shed,
Shook from the tangled boughs of Heaven and Ocean,

[1] This poem was conceived and chiefly written in a wood that skirts the Arno, near Florence, and on a day when that tempestuous wind, whose temperature is at once mild and animating, was collecting the vapours which pour down the autumnal rains. They began, as I foresaw, at sunset with a violent tempest of hail and rain, attended by that magnificent thunder and lightning peculiar to the Cisalpine regions.

The phenomenon alluded to at the conclusion of the third stanza is well known to naturalists. The vegetation at the bottom of the sea, of rivers, and of lakes, sympathizes with that of the land in the change of seasons, and is consequently influenced by the winds which announce it.—[SHELLEY'S NOTE.]

Angels of rain and lightning: there are spread
On the blue surface of thine aëry surge,
Like the bright hair uplifted from the head   20

Of some fierce Maenad, even from the dim verge
Of the horizon to the zenith's height,
The locks of the approaching storm. Thou dirge

Of the dying year, to which this closing night
Will be the dome of a vast sepulchre,   25
Vaulted with all thy congregated might

Of vapours, from whose solid atmosphere
Black rain, and fire, and hail will burst: oh, hear!

III

Thou who didst waken from his summer dreams
The blue Mediterranean, where he lay,   30
Lulled by the coil of his crystàlline streams,

Beside a pumice isle in Baiae's bay,
And saw in sleep old palaces and towers
Quivering within the wave's intenser day,

All overgrown with azure moss and flowers   35
So sweet, the sense faints picturing them! Thou
For whose path the Atlantic's level powers

Cleave themselves into chasms, while far below
The sea-blooms and the oozy woods which wear
The sapless foliage of the ocean, know   40

Thy voice, and suddenly grow gray with fear,
And tremble and despoil themselves: oh, hear!

IV

If I were a dead leaf thou mightest bear;
If I were a swift cloud to fly with thee;
A wave to pant beneath thy power, and share   45

The impulse of thy strength, only less free
Than thou, O uncontrollable! If even
I were as in my boyhood, and could be

The comrade of thy wanderings over Heaven,
As then, when to outstrip thy skiey speed   50
Scarce seemed a vision; I would ne'er have striven

As thus with thee in prayer in my sore need.
Oh, lift me as a wave, a leaf, a cloud!
I fall upon the thorns of life! I bleed!

A heavy weight of hours has chained and bowed   55
One too like thee: tameless, and swift, and proud.

V

Make me thy lyre, even as the forest is:
What if my leaves are falling like its own!
The tumult of thy mighty harmonies

Will take from both a deep, autumnal tone,   60
Sweet though in sadness. Be thou, Spirit fierce,
My spirit! Be thou me, impetuous one!

Drive my dead thoughts over the universe
Like withered leaves to quicken a new birth!
And, by the incantation of this verse,   65

Scatter, as from an unextinguished hearth
Ashes and sparks, my words among mankind!
Be through my lips to unawakened earth

The trumpet of a prophecy! O, Wind,
If Winter comes, can Spring be far behind?   70

AN EXHORTATION

CHAMELEONS feed on light and air:
   Poets' food is love and fame:
If in this wide world of care
   Poets could but find the same
With as little toil as they,   5
   Would they ever change their hue
   As the light chameleons do,
Suiting it to every ray
   Twenty times a day?

Poets are on this cold earth,   10
   As chameleons might be,
Hidden from their early birth
   In a cave beneath the sea;
Where light is, chameleons change:
Where love is not, poets do: 15
   Fame is love disguised: if few
Find either, never think it strange
   That poets range.

Yet dare not stain with wealth or
      power   19
   A poet's free and heavenly mind:
If bright chameleons should devour
   Any food but beams and wind,
They would grow as earthly soon
   As their brother lizards are.
   Children of a sunnier star,   25
Spirits from beyond the moon,
   Oh, refuse the boon!

THE INDIAN SERENADE

I

I ARISE from dreams of thee
In the first sweet sleep of night,
When the winds are breathing low,
And the stars are shining bright:
I arise from dreams of thee,   5

And a spirit in my feet
Hath led me—who knows how?
To thy chamber window, Sweet!

II

The wandering airs they faint
On the dark, the silent stream—   10

The Champak odours fail
Like sweet thoughts in a dream;
The nightingale's complaint,
It dies upon her heart;—
As I must on thine,   15
Oh, belovèd as thou art!

Let thy love in kisses rain
On my lips and eyelids pale.   20
My cheek is cold and white, alas!
My heart beats loud and fast;—
Oh! press it to thine own again,
Where it will break at last.

III

Oh lift me from the grass!
I die! I faint! I fail!

CANCELLED PASSAGE

O PILLOW cold and wet with tears!
Thou breathest sleep no more!

TO SOPHIA [MISS STACEY]

I

THOU art fair, and few are fairer
    Of the Nymphs of earth or ocean;
They are robes that fit the wearer—
    Those soft limbs of thine, whose motion
Ever falls and shifts and glances   5
As the life within them dances.

II

Thy deep eyes, a double Planet,
    Gaze the wisest into madness
With soft clear fire,—the winds that fan it
    Are those thoughts of tender gladness   10
Which, like zephyrs on the billow,
Make thy gentle soul their pillow.

III

If, whatever face thou paintest
    In those eyes, grows pale with pleasure,
If the fainting soul is faintest   15
    When it hears thy harp's wild measure,
Wonder not that when thou speakest
Of the weak my heart is weakest.

IV

As dew beneath the wind of morning,
    As the sea which whirlwinds waken,   20
As the birds at thunder's warning,
    As aught mute yet deeply shaken,
As one who feels an unseen spirit
Is my heart when thine is near it.

TO WILLIAM SHELLEY

(With what truth may I say—
Roma! Roma! Roma!
Non è più come era prima!)

I

My lost William, thou in whom
  Some bright spirit lived, and did
That decaying robe consume
  Which its lustre faintly hid,—
Here its ashes find a tomb,   5
  But beneath this pyramid
Thou art not—if a thing divine
Like thee can die, thy funeral
    shrine
Is thy mother's grief and mine.

II

Where art thou, my gentle child? 10
  Let me think thy spirit feeds,
With its life intense and mild,
  The love of living leaves and
    weeds
Among these tombs and ruins
    wild;—
  Let me think that through low
    seeds   15
Of sweet flowers and sunny grass
Into their hues and scents may
    pass
A portion——

TO WILLIAM SHELLEY

THY little footsteps on the sands
  Of a remote and lonely shore;
The twinkling of thine infant hands,
  Where now the worm will feed no more;
Thy mingled look of love and glee   5
When we returned to gaze on thee—

TO MARY SHELLEY

MY dearest Mary, wherefore hast thou gone,
And left me in this dreary world alone?
Thy form is here indeed,—a lovely one—
But thou art fled, gone down the dreary road,
That leads to Sorrow's most obscure abode;   5
Thou sittest on the hearth of pale despair,

                                          Where
For thine own sake I cannot follow thee.

TO MARY SHELLEY

THE world is dreary,
    And I'm weary
Of wandering on without thee, Mary;
    A joy was erewhile
    In thy voice and thy smile,   5
And 'tis gone, when I should be gone too, Mary.

ON THE MEDUSA OF LEONARDO DA VINCI IN THE FLORENTINE GALLERY

I

It lieth, gazing on the midnight sky,
    Upon the cloudy mountain-peak supine;
Below, far lands are seen tremblingly;
    Its horror and its beauty are divine.
Upon its lips and eyelids seems to lie   5
    Loveliness like a shadow, from which shine,
Fiery and lurid, struggling underneath,
The agonies of anguish and of death.

II

Yet it is less the horror than the grace
    Which turns the gazer's spirit into stone,   10
Whereon the lineaments of that dead face
    Are graven, till the characters be grown
Into itself, and thought no more can trace;
    'Tis the melodious hue of beauty thrown
Athwart the darkness and the glare of pain,   15
Which humanize and harmonize the strain.

III

And from its head as from one body grow,
    As   grass out of a watery rock,
Hairs which are vipers, and they curl and flow
    And their long tangles in each other lock,   20
And with unending involutions show
    Their mailèd radiance, as it were to mock
The torture and the death within, and saw
The solid air with many a raggèd jaw.

IV

And, from a stone beside, a poisonous eft   25
    Peeps idly into those Gorgonian eyes;
Whilst in the air a ghastly bat, bereft
    Of sense, has flitted with a mad surprise
Out of the cave this hideous light had cleft,
    And he comes hastening like a moth that hies 30
After a taper; and the midnight sky
Flares, a light more dread than obscurity.

V

'Tis the tempestuous loveliness of terror;
   For from the serpents gleams a brazen glare
Kindled by that inextricable error,   35
   Which makes a thrilling vapour of the air
Become a   and ever-shifting mirror
   Of all the beauty and the terror there—
A woman's countenance, with serpent-locks,
Gazing in death on Heaven from those wet rocks.   40

LOVE'S PHILOSOPHY

I

The fountains mingle with the
      river
And the rivers with the Ocean,
The winds of Heaven mix for ever
   With a sweet emotion;
Nothing in the world is single;   5
   All things by a law divine
In one spirit meet and mingle.
   Why not I with thine?—

II

See the mountains kiss high Heaven
   And the waves clasp one another;
No sister-flower would be for-
      given   11
   If it disdained its brother;
And the sunlight clasps the earth
   And the moonbeams kiss the sea:
What is all this sweet work worth
   If thou kiss not me?   16

FRAGMENT: 'FOLLOW TO THE DEEP WOOD'S WEEDS'

Follow to the deep wood's weeds,
Follow to the wild-briar dingle,
Where we seek to intermingle,
And the violet tells her tale

To the odour-scented gale,   5
For they two have enough to
      do
Of such work as I and you.

THE BIRTH OF PLEASURE

At the creation of the Earth
Pleasure, that divinest birth,
From the soil of Heaven did rise,
Wrapped in sweet wild melodies—
Like an exhalation wreathing   5
To the sound of air low-breathing
Through Aeolian pines, which make
A shade and shelter to the lake

Whence it rises soft and slow;
Her life-breathing [limbs] did
      flow   10
In the harmony divine
Of an ever-lengthening line
Which enwrapped her perfect form
With a beauty clear and warm.

FRAGMENT: LOVE THE UNIVERSE TO-DAY

And who feels discord now or sorrow?
Love is the universe to-day—
These are the slaves of dim to-morrow,
Darkening Life's labyrinthine way.

FRAGMENT: 'A GENTLE STORY OF TWO LOVERS YOUNG'

A GENTLE story of two lovers young,
  Who met in innocence and died in sorrow,
And of one selfish heart, whose rancour clung
  Like curses on them; are ye slow to borrow
    The lore of truth from such a tale?   5
    Or in this world's deserted vale,
    Do ye not see a star of gladness
    Pierce the shadows of its sadness,—
When ye are cold, that love is a light sent
From Heaven, which none shall quench, to cheer the innocent?   10

FRAGMENT: LOVE'S TENDER ATMOSPHERE

THERE is a warm and gentle atmosphere
  About the form of one we love, and thus
As in a tender mist our spirits are
    Wrapped in the   of that which is to us
The health of life's own life—   5

FRAGMENT: WEDDED SOULS

        I AM as a spirit who has dwelt
Within his heart of hearts, and I have felt
His feelings, and have thought his thoughts, and known
The inmost converse of his soul, the tone
Unheard but in the silence of his blood,   5
When all the pulses in their multitude
Image the trembling calm of summer seas.
I have unlocked the golden melodies
Of his deep soul, as with a master-key,
And loosened them and bathed myself therein—   10
Even as an eagle in a thunder-mist
Clothing his wings with lightning.

FRAGMENT: 'IS IT THAT IN SOME BRIGHTER SPHERE'

Is it that in some brighter sphere
We part from friends we meet with
    here?
Or do we see the Future pass
Over the Present's dusky glass?

Or what is that that makes us
    seem   5
To patch up fragments of a dream,
Part of which comes true, and part
Beats and trembles in the heart?

FRAGMENT: SUFFICIENT UNTO THE DAY

Is not to-day enough? Why do I peer
  Into the darkness of the day to come?
Is not to-morrow even as yesterday?
  And will the day that follows change thy doom?

Few flowers grow upon thy wintry way;
And who waits for thee in that cheerless home
Whence thou hast fled, whither thou must return
Charged with the load that makes thee faint and mourn?

FRAGMENT: 'YE GENTLE VISITATIONS OF CALM THOUGHT'

YE gentle visitations of calm thought—
  Moods like the memories of happier earth,
  Which come arrayed in thoughts of little worth,
Like stars in clouds by the weak winds enwrought,—
  But that the clouds depart and stars remain,   5
While they remain, and ye, alas, depart!

FRAGMENT: MUSIC AND SWEET POETRY

How sweet it is to sit and read the tales
  Of mighty poets and to hear the while
Sweet music, which when the attention fails
  Fills the dim pause——

FRAGMENT: THE SEPULCHRE OF MEMORY

AND where is truth? On tombs? for such to thee
Has been my heart—and thy dead memory
Has lain from childhood, many a changeful year,
Unchangingly preserved and buried there.

FRAGMENT: 'WHEN A LOVER CLASPS HIS FAIREST'

I

WHEN a lover clasps his fairest,
Then be our dread sport the rarest.
Their caresses were like the chaff
In the tempest, and be our laugh
His despair—her epitaph!   5

II

When a mother clasps her child,
Watch till dusty Death has piled
His cold ashes on the clay;
She has loved it many a day—
She remains,—it fades away.   10

FRAGMENT: 'WAKE THE SERPENT NOT'

WAKE the serpent not—lest he
Should not know the way to go,—
Let him crawl which yet lies sleeping
Through the deep grass of the meadow!
Not a bee shall hear him creeping,   5
Not a may-fly shall awaken
From its cradling blue-bell shaken,
Not the starlight as he's sliding
Through the grass with silent gliding.

FRAGMENT: RAIN

THE fitful alternations of the rain,
When the chill wind, languid as with pain
Of its own heavy moisture, here and there
Drives through the gray and beamless atmosphere.

FRAGMENT: A TALE UNTOLD

ONE sung of thee who left the tale untold,
  Like the false dawns which perish in the bursting;
Like empty cups of wrought and daedal gold,
  Which mock the lips with air, when they are thirsting.

FRAGMENT: TO ITALY

As the sunrise to the night,
    As the north wind to the clouds,
As the earthquake's fiery flight,
    Ruining mountain solitudes,
Everlasting Italy,   5
Be those hopes and fears on thee.

FRAGMENT: WINE OF THE FAIRIES

I AM drunk with the honey wine
Of the moon-unfolded eglantine,
Which fairies catch in hyacinth bowls.
The bats, the dormice, and the moles
Sleep in the walls or under the sward   5
Of the desolate castle yard;
And when 'tis split on the summer earth
    Or its fumes arise among the dew,
Their jocund dreams are full of mirth,
    They gibber their joy in sleep; for few   10
Of the fairies bear those bowls so new!

FRAGMENT: A ROMAN'S CHAMBER

I

IN the cave which wild weeds cover
Wait for thine aethereal lover;
For the pallid moon is waning,
    O'er the spiral cypress hanging
And the moon no cloud is staining.   5

II

It was once a Roman's chamber,
    Where he kept his darkest revels,
And the wild weeds twine and clamber;
    It was then a chasm for devils.

FRAGMENT: ROME AND NATURE

Rome has fallen, ye see it lying
  Heaped in undistinguished ruin:
Nature is alone undying.

VARIATION OF THE SONG OF THE MOON

(*Pometheus Unbound,* Act iv.)

As a violet's gentle eye
  Gazes on the azure sky
Until its hue grows like what it
    beholds;

As a gray and empty mist
  Lies like solid amethyst   5
Over the western mountain it en-
    folds,

When the sunset sleeps
  Upon its snow;
As a strain of sweetest sound
Wraps itself the wind around   10

Until the voiceless wind be music
  too;
  As aught dark, vain, and dull,
Basking in what is beautiful,
Is full of light and love—

CANCELLED STANZA OF THE MASK OF ANARCHY

(for which stanzas lxviii, lxix have been substituted.)

From the cities where from caves,
Like the dead from putrid graves,
Troops of starvelings gliding come,
Living Tenants of a tomb.

NOTE BY MRS. SHELLEY

Shelley loved the People; and respected them as often more virtuous, as always more suffering, and therefore more deserving of sympathy, than the great. He believed that a clash between the two classes of society was inevitable, and he eagerly ranged himself on the people's side. He had an idea of publishing a series of poems adapted expressly to commemorate their circumstances and wrongs. He wrote a few; but, in those days of prosecution for libel, they could not be printed. They are not among the best of his productions, a writer being always shackled when he endeavours to write down to the comprehension of those who could not understand or feel a highly imaginative style; but they show his earnestness, and with what heartfelt compassion he went home to the direct point of injury—that oppression is detestable as being the parent of starvation, nakedness, and ignorance. Besides these outpourings of compassion and indignation, he had meant to adorn the cause he loved with loftier poetry of glory and triumph: such is the scope of the *Ode to the Assertors of Liberty.* He sketched also a new version of our national anthem, as addressed to Liberty.

POEMS WRITTEN IN 1820

THE SENSITIVE PLANT

PART FIRST

A SENSITIVE Plant in a garden grew,
And the young winds fed it with silver dew,
And it opened its fan-like leaves to the light,
And closed them beneath the kisses of Night.

And the Spring arose on the garden fair,   5
Like the Spirit of Love felt everywhere;
And each flower and herb on Earth's dark breast
Rose from the dreams of its wintry rest.

But none ever trembled and panted with bliss
In the garden, the field, or the wilderness,   10
Like a doe in the noontide with love's sweet want,
As the companionless Sensitive Plant.

The snowdrop, and then the violet,
Arose from the ground with warm rain wet,
And their breath was mixed with fresh odour, sent   15
From the turf, like the voice and the instrument.

Then the pied wind-flowers and the tulip tall,
And narcissi, the fairest among them all,
Who gaze on their eyes in the stream's recess,
Till they die of their own dear loveliness;   20

And the Naiad-like lily of the vale,
Whom youth makes so fair and passion so pale
That the light of its tremulous bells is seen
Through their pavilions of tender green;

And the hyacinth purple, and white, and blue,   25
Which flung from its bells a sweet peal anew
Of music so delicate, soft, and intense,
It was felt like an odour within the sense;

And the rose like a nymph to the bath addressed,
Which unveiled the depth of her glowing breast,   30
Till, fold after fold, to the fainting air
The soul of her beauty and love lay bare:

And the wand-like lily, which lifted up,
As a Maenad its moonlight-coloured cup,
Till the fiery star, which is its eye,   35
Gazed through clear dew on the tender sky;

And the jessamine faint, and the sweet tuberose,
The sweetest flower for scent that blows;
And all rare blossoms from every clime
Grew in that garden in perfect prime.   40

And on the stream whose inconstant bosom
Was pranked, under boughs of embowering blossom,
With golden and green light, slanting through
Their heaven of many a tangled hue,

Broad water-lilies lay tremulously,   45
And starry river-buds glimmered by,
And around them the soft stream did glide and dance
With a motion of sweet sound and radiance.

And the sinuous paths of lawn and of moss,
Which led through the garden along and across,   50
Some open at once to the sun and the breeze,
Some lost among bowers of blossoming trees,

Were all paved with daisies and delicate bells
As fair as the fabulous asphodels,
And flow'rets which, drooping as day drooped too,   55
Fell into pavilions, white, purple, and blue,
To roof the glow-worm from the evening dew.

And from this undefilèd Paradise
The flowers (as an infant's awakening eyes
Smile on its mother, whose singing sweet   60
Can first lull, and at last must awaken it),

When Heaven's blithe winds had unfolded them,
As mine-lamps enkindle a hidden gem,
Shone smiling to Heaven, and every one
Shared joy in the light of the gentle sun;   65

For each one was interpenetrated
With the light and the odour its neighbour shed,
Like young lovers whom youth and love make dear
Wrapped and filled by their mutual atmosphere.

But the Sensitive Plant which could give small fruit   70
Of the love which it felt from the leaf to the root,
Received more than all, it loved more than ever,
Where none wanted but it, could belong to the giver,—

For the Sensitive Plant has no bright flower;
Radiance and odour are not its dower; 75
It loves, even like Love, its deep heart is full,
It desires what it has not, the Beautiful!

The light winds which from unsustaining wings
Shed the music of many murmurings;
The beams which dart from many a star 80
Of the flowers whose hues they bear afar;

The plumèd insects swift and free,
Like golden boats on a sunny sea,
Laden with light and odour, which pass
Over the gleam of the living grass: 85

The unseen clouds of the dew, which lie
Like fire in the flowers till the sun rides high,
Then wander like spirits among the spheres,
Each cloud faint with the fragrance it bears;

The quivering vapours of dim noontide, 90
Which like a sea o'er the warm earth glide,
In which every sound, and odour, and beam,
Move, as reeds in a single stream;

Each and all like ministering angels were
For the Sensitive Plant sweet joy to bear, 95
Whilst the lagging hours of the day went by
Like windless clouds o'er a tender sky.

And when evening descended from Heaven above,
And the Earth was all rest, and the air was all love,
And delight, though less bright, was far more deep, 100
And the day's veil fell from the world of sleep,

And the beasts, and the birds, and the insects were drowned
In an ocean of dreams without a sound;
Whose waves never mark, though they ever impress
The light sand which paves it, consciousness; 105

(Only overhead the sweet nightingale
Ever sang more sweet as the day might fail,
And snatches of its Elysian chant
Were mixed with the dreams of the Sensitive Plant);—

The Sensitive Plant was the earliest 110
Upgathered into the bosom of rest;
A sweet child weary of its delight,
The feeblest and yet the favourite,
Cradled within the embrace of Night.

Part Second

There was a Power in this sweet place,
An Eve in this Eden; a ruling Grace
Which to the flowers, did they waken or dream,
Was as God is to the starry scheme.

A Lady, the wonder of her kind,   5
Whose form was upborne by a lovely mind
Which, dilating, had moulded her mien and motion
Like a sea-flower unfolded beneath the ocean,

Tended the garden from morn to even:
And the meteors of that sublunar Heaven,   10
Like the lamps of the air when Night walks forth,
Laughed round her footsteps up from the Earth!

She had no companion of mortal race,
But her tremulous breath and her flushing face
Told, whilst the morn kissed the sleep from her eyes,   15
That her dreams were less slumber than Paradise:

As if some bright Spirit for her sweet sake
Had deserted Heaven while the stars were awake,
As if yet around her he lingering were,
Though the veil of daylight concealed him from her.   20

Her step seemed to pity the grass it pressed;
You might hear by the heaving of her breast,
That the coming and going of the wind
Brought pleasure there and left passion behind.

And wherever her aëry footstep trod,   25
Her trailing hair from the grassy sod
Erased its light vestige, with shadowy sweep,
Like a sunny storm o'er the dark green deep.

I doubt not the flowers of that garden sweet
Rejoiced in the sound of her gentle feet;   30
I doubt not they felt the spirit that came
From her glowing fingers through all their frame.

She sprinkled bright water from the stream
On those that were faint with the sunny beam;
And out of the cups of the heavy flowers   35
She emptied the rain of the thunder-showers.

She lifted their heads with her tender hands,
And sustained them with rods and osier-bands;
If the flowers had been her own infants, she
Could never have nursed them more tenderly.   40

And all killing insects and gnawing worms,
And things of obscene and unlovely forms,
She bore, in a basket of Indian woof,
Into the rough woods far aloof,—

In a basket, of grasses and wild-flowers full,   45
The freshest her gentle hands could pull
For the poor banished insects, whose intent,
Although they did ill, was innocent.

But the bee and the beamlike ephemeris
Whose path is the lightning's, and soft moths that kiss   50
The sweet lips of the flowers, and harm not, did she
Make her attendant angels be.

And many an antenatal tomb,
Where butterflies dream of the life to come,
She left clinging round the smooth and dark   55
Edge of the odorous cedar bark.

This fairest creature from earliest Spring
Thus moved through the garden ministering
All the sweet season of Summertide,
And ere the first leaf looked brown—she died!   60

Part Third

Three days the flowers of the garden fair,
Like stars when the moon is awakened, were,
Or the waves of Baiae, ere luminous
She floats up through the smoke of Vesuvius.

And on the fourth, the Sensitive Plant   5
Felt the sound of the funeral chant,
And the steps of the bearers, heavy and slow,
And the sobs of the mourners, deep and low;

The weary sound and the heavy breath,
And the silent motions of passing death,   10
And the smell, cold, oppressive, and dank,
Sent through the pores of the coffin-plank;

The dark grass, and the flowers among the grass,
Were bright with tears as the crowd did pass;
From their sighs the wind caught a mournful tone,   15
And sate in the pines, and gave groan for groan.

The garden, once fair, became cold and foul,
Like the corpse of her who had been its soul,
Which at first was lovely as if in sleep,
Then slowly changed, till it grew a heap   20
To make men tremble who never weep.

Swift Summer into the Autumn flowed,
And frost in the mist of the morning rode,
Though the noonday sun looked clear and bright,
Mocking the spoil of the secret night.   25

The rose-leaves, like flakes of crimson snow,
Paved the turf and the moss below.
The lilies were drooping, and white, and wan,
Like the head and the skin of a dying man.

And Indian plants, of scent and hue   30
The sweetest that ever were fed on dew,
Leaf by leaf, day after day,
Were massed into the common clay.

And the leaves, brown, yellow, and gray, and red,
And white with the whiteness of what is dead,   35
Like troops of ghosts on the dry wind passed;
Their whistling noise made the birds aghast.

And the gusty winds waked the wingèd seeds,
Out of their birthplace of ugly weeds,
Till they clung round many a sweet flower's stem,   40
Which rotted into the earth with them.

The water-blooms under the rivulet
Fell from the stalks on which they were set;
And the eddies drove them here and there,
As the winds did those of the upper air.   45

Then the rain came down, and the broken stalks
Were bent and tangled across the walks;
And the leafless network of parasite bowers
Massed into ruin; and all sweet flowers.

Between the time of the wind and the snow   50
All loathliest weeds began to grow,
Whose coarse leaves were splashed with many a speck,
Like the water-snake's belly and the toad's back.

And thistles, and nettles, and darnels rank,
And the dock, and henbane, and hemlock dank,   55
Stretched out its long and hollow shank,
And stifled the air till the dead wind stank.

And plants, at whose names the verse feels loath,
Filled the place with a monstrous undergrowth,
Prickly, and pulpous, and blistering, and blue,   60
Livid, and starred with a lurid dew.

And agarics, and fungi, with mildew and mould
Started like mist from the wet ground cold;
Pale, fleshy, as if the decaying dead
With a spirit of growth had been animated!   65

Spawn, weeds, and filth, a leprous scum,
Made the running rivulet thick and dumb,
And at its outlet flags huge as stakes
Dammed it up with roots knotted like water-snakes.

And hour by hour, when the air was still,   70
The vapours arose which have strength to kill,
At morn they were seen, at noon they were felt,
At night they were darkness no star could melt.

And unctuous meteors from spray to spray
Crept and flitted in broad noonday   75
Unseen; every branch on which they alit
By a venomous blight was burned and bit.

The Sensitive Plant, like one forbid,
Wept, and the tears within each lid
Of its folded leaves, which together grew,   80
Were changed to a blight of frozen glue.

For the leaves soon fell, and the branches soon
By the heavy axe of the blast were hewn;
The sap shrank to the root through every pore
As blood to a heart that will beat no more.   85

For Winter came: the wind was his whip:
One choppy finger was on his lip:
He had torn the cataracts from the hills
And they clanked at his girdle like manacles;

His breath was a chain which without a sound   90
The earth, and the air, and the water bound;
He came, fiercely driven, in his chariot-throne
By the tenfold blasts of the Arctic zone.

Then the weeds which were forms of living death
Fled from the frost to the earth beneath.   95
Their decay and sudden flight from frost
Was but like the vanishing of a ghost!

And under the roots of the Sensitive Plant
The moles and the dormice died for want:
The birds dropped stiff from the frozen air   100
And were caught in the branches naked and bare.

First there came down a thawing rain
And its dull drops froze on the boughs again;
Then there steamed up a freezing dew
Which to the drops of the thaw-rain grew;   105

And a northern whirlwind, wandering about
Like a wolf that had smelt a dead child out,
Shook the boughs thus laden, and heavy, and stiff,
And snapped them off with his rigid griff.

When Winter had gone and Spring came back   110
The Sensitive Plant was a leafless wreck;
But the mandrakes, and toadstools, and docks, and darnels,
Rose like the dead from their ruined charnels.

CONCLUSION

Whether the Sensitive Plant, or that
Which within its boughs like a Spirit sat,   115
Ere its outward form had known decay,
Now felt this change, I cannot say.

Whether that Lady's gentle mind,
No longer with the form combined
Which scattered love, as stars do light,   120
Found sadness, where it left delight,

I dare not guess; but in this life
Of error, ignorance, and strife,
Where nothing is, but all things seem,
And we the shadows of the dream,   125

It is a modest creed, and yet
Pleasant if one considers it,
To own that death itself must be,
Like all the rest, a mockery.

That garden sweet, that lady fair,   130
And all sweet shapes and odours there,
In truth have never passed away:
'Tis we, 'tis ours, are changed; not they.

For love, and beauty, and delight,
There is no death nor change: their might   135
Exceeds our organs, which endure
No light, being themselves obscure.

A VISION OF THE SEA

'TIS the terror of tempest. The rags of the sail
Are flickering in ribbons within the fierce gale:
From the stark night of vapours the dim rain is driven,
And when lightning is loosed, like a deluge from Heaven,

She sees the black trunks of the waterspouts spin   5
And bend, as if Heaven was ruining in,
Which they seemed to sustain with their terrible mass
As if ocean had sunk from beneath them: they pass
To their graves in the deep with an earthquake of sound,
And the waves and the thunders, made silent around,   10
Leave the wind to its echo. The vessel, now tossed
Through the low-trailing rack of the tempest, is lost
In the skirts of the thunder-cloud: now down the sweep
Of the wind-cloven wave to the chasm of the deep
It sinks, and the walls of the watery vale   15
Whose depths of dread calm are unmoved by the gale,
Dim mirrors of ruin, hang gleaming about;
While the surf, like a chaos of stars, like a rout
Of death-flames, like whirlpools of fire-flowing iron,
With splendour and terror the black ship environ,   20
Or like sulphur-flakes hurled from a mine of pale fire
In fountains spout o'er it. In many a spire
The pyramid-billows with white points of brine
In the cope of the lightning inconstantly shine,
As piercing the sky from the floor of the sea.   25
The great ship seems splitting! it cracks as a tree,
While an earthquake is splintering its root, ere the blast
Of the whirlwind that stripped it of branches has passed.
The intense thunder-balls which are raining from Heaven
Have shattered its mast, and it stands black and riven.   30
The chinks suck destruction. The heavy dead hulk
On the living sea rolls an inanimate bulk,
Like a corpse on the clay which is hungering to fold
Its corruption around it. Meanwhile, from the hold,
One deck is burst up by the waters below,   35
And it splits like the ice when the thaw-breezes blow
O'er the lakes of the desert! Who sit on the other?
Is that all the crew that lie burying each other,
Like the dead in a breach, round the foremast? Are those
Twin tigers, who burst, when the waters arose,   40
In the agony of terror, their chains in the hold;
(What now makes them tame, is what then made them bold;)
Who crouch, side by side, and have driven, like a crank,
The deep grip of their claws through the vibrating plank:—
Are these all? Nine weeks the tall vessel had lain   45
On the windless expanse of the watery plain,
Where the death-darting sun cast no shadow at noon,
And there seemed to be fire in the beams of the moon,
Till a lead-coloured fog gathered up from the deep,
Whose breath was quick pestilence; then, the cold sleep   50

Crept, like blight through the ears of a thick field of corn,
O'er the populous vessel. And even and morn,
With their hammocks for coffins the seamen aghast
Like dead men the dead limbs of their comrades cast
Down the deep, which closed on them above and around,   55
And the sharks and the dogfish their grave-clothes unbound,
And were glutted like Jews with this manna rained down
From God on their wilderness. One after one
The mariners died; on the eve of this day,
When the tempest was gathering in cloudy array,   60
But seven remained. Six the thunder has smitten,
And they lie black as mummies on which Time has written
His scorn of the embalmer; the seventh, from the deck
An oak-splinter pierced through his breast and his back,
And hung out to the tempest, a wreck on the wreck.   65
No more? At the helm sits a woman more fair
Than Heaven, when, unbinding its star-braided hair,
It sinks with the sun on the earth and the sea.
She clasps a bright child on her upgathered knee;
It laughs at the lightning, it mocks the mixed thunder   70
Of the air and the sea, with desire and with wonder
It is beckoning the tigers to rise and come near,
It would play with those eyes where the radiance of fear
Is outshining the meteors; its bosom beats high,
The heart-fire of pleasure has kindled its eye,   75
While its mother's is lustreless. 'Smile not, my child,
But sleep deeply and sweetly, and so be beguiled
Of the pang that awaits us, whatever that be,
So dreadful since thou must divide it with me!
Dream, sleep! This pale bosom, thy cradle and bed,   80
Will it rock thee not, infant? 'Tis beating with dread!
Alas! what is life, what is death, what are we,
That when the ship sinks we no longer may be?
What! to see thee no more, and to feel thee no more?
To be after life what we have been before?   85
Not to touch those sweet hands? Not to look on those eyes,
Those lips, and that hair,—all the smiling disguise
Thou yet wearest, sweet Spirit, which I, day by day,
Have so long called my child, but which now fades away
Like a rainbow, and I the fallen shower?'—Lo! the ship   90
Is settling, it topples, the leeward ports dip;
The tigers leap up when they feel the slow brine
Crawling inch by inch on them; hair, ears, limbs, and eyne,
Stand rigid with horror; a loud, long, hoarse cry
Bursts at once from their vitals tremendously,   95
And 'tis borne down the mountainous vale of the wave,
Rebounding, like thunder, from crag to cave,

Mixed with the clash of the lashing rain,
Hurried on by the might of the hurricane:
The hurricane came from the west, and passed on   100
By the path of the gate of the eastern sun,
Transversely dividing the stream of the storm;
As an arrowy serpent, pursuing the form
Of an elephant, bursts through the brakes of the waste.
Black as a cormorant the screaming blast,   105
Between Ocean and Heaven, like an ocean, passed,
Till it came to the clouds on the verge of the world
Which, based on the sea and to Heaven upcurled,
Like columns and walls did surround and sustain
The dome of the tempest; it rent them in twain,   110
As a flood rends its barriers of mountainous crag:
And the dense clouds in many a ruin and rag,
Like the stones of a temple ere earthquake has passed,
Like the dust of its fall, on the whirlwind are cast;
They are scattered like foam on the torrent; and where   115
The wind has burst out through the chasm, from the air
Of clear morning the beams of the sunrise flow in,
Unimpeded, keen, golden, and crystalline,
Banded armies of light and of air, at one gate
They encounter, but interpenetrate.   120
And that breach in the tempest is widening away,
And the caverns of cloud are torn up by the day,
And the fierce winds are sinking with weary wings,
Lulled by the motion and murmurings
And the long glassy heave of the rocking sea,   125
And overhead glorious, but dreadful to see,
The wrecks of the tempest, like vapours of gold,
Are consuming in sunrise. The heaped waves behold
The deep calm of blue Heaven dilating above,
And, like passions made still by the presence of Love,   130
Beneath the clear surface reflecting it slide
Tremulous with soft influence; extending its tide
From the Andes to Atlas, round mountain and isle,
Round sea-birds and wrecks, paved with Heaven's azure smile,
The wide world of waters is vibrating. Where   135
Is the ship? On the verge of the wave where it lay
One tiger is mingled in ghastly affray
With a sea-snake. The foam and the smoke of the battle
Stain the clear air with sunbows: the jar, and the rattle
Of solid bones crushed by the infinite stress   140
Of the snake's adamantine voluminousness;
And the hum of the hot blood that spouts and rains
Where the gripe of the tiger has wounded the veins
Swollen with rage, strength, and effort; the whirl and the splash

As of some hideous engine whose brazen teeth smash   145
The thin winds and soft waves into thunder; the screams
And hissings crawl fast o'er the smooth ocean-streams,
Each sound like a centipede. Near this commotion,
A blue shark is hanging within the blue ocean,
The fin-wingèd tomb of the victor. The other   150
Is winning his way from the fate of his brother
To his own with the speed of despair. Lo! a boat
Advances: twelve rowers with the impulse of thought
Urge on the keen keel,—the brine foams. At the stern
Three marksmen stand levelling. Hot bullets burn   155
In the breast of the tiger, which yet bears him on
To his refuge and ruin. One fragment alone,—
'Tis dwindling and sinking, 'tis now almost gone,—
Of the wreck of the vessel peers out of the sea.
With her left hand she grasps it impetuously.   160
With her right she sustains her fair infant. Death, Fear,
Love, Beauty, are mixed in the atmosphere,
Which trembles and burns with the fervour of dread
Around her wild eyes, her bright hand, and her head,
Like a meteor of light o'er the waters! her child   165
Is yet smiling, and playing, and murmuring; so smiled
The false deep ere the storm. Like a sister and brother
The child and the ocean still smile on each other,
Whilst——

THE CLOUD

I BRING fresh showers for the thirsting flowers,
      From the seas and the streams;
I bear light shade for the leaves when laid
      In their noonday dreams.
From my wings are shaken the dews that waken   5
      The sweet buds every one,
When rocked to rest on their mother's breast,
      As she dances about the sun.
I wield the flail of the lashing hail,
      And whiten the green plains under,   10
And then again I dissolve it in rain,
      And laugh as I pass in thunder.

I sift the snow on the mountains below,
      And their great pines groan aghast;
And all the night 'tis my pillow white,   15
      While I sleep in the arms of the blast.
Sublime on the towers of my skiey bowers,
      Lightning my pilot sits;
In a cavern under is fettered the thunder,
      It struggles and howls at fits;   20

Over earth and ocean, with gentle motion,
    This pilot is guiding me,
Lured by the love of the genii that move
    In the depths of the purple sea;
Over the rills, and the crags, and the hills,   25
    Over the lakes and the plains,
Wherever he dream, under mountain or stream,
    The Spirit he loves remains;
And I all the while bask in Heaven's blue smile,
    Whilst he is dissolving in rains.   30

The sanguine Sunrise, with his meteor eyes,
    And his burning plumes outspread,
Leaps on the back of my sailing rack,
    When the morning star shines dead;
As on the jag of a mountain crag,   35
    Which an earthquake rocks and swings,
An eagle alit one moment may sit
    In the light of its golden wings.
And when Sunset may breathe, from the lit sea beneath,
    Its ardours of rest and of love,   40
And the crimson pall of eve may fall
    From the depth of Heaven above,
With wings folded I rest, on mine aëry nest,
    As still as a brooding dove.

That orbèd maiden with white fire laden,   45
    Whom mortals call the Moon,
Glides glimmering o'er my fleece-like floor,
    By the midnight breezes strewn;
And wherever the beat of her unseen feet,
    Which only the angels hear,   50
May have broken the woof of my tent's thin roof,
    The stars peep behind her and peer;
And I laugh to see them whirl and flee,
    Like a swarm of golden bees,
When I widen the rent in my wind-built tent,   55
    Till the calm rivers, lakes, and seas,
Like strips of the sky fallen through me on high,
    Are each paved with the moon and these.

I bind the Sun's throne with a burning zone,
    And the Moon's with a girdle of pearl;   60
The volcanoes are dim, and the stars reel and swim,
    When the whirlwinds my banner unfurl.
From cape to cape, with a bridge-like shape,
    Over a torrent sea,
Sunbeam-proof, I hang like a roof,—   65
    The mountains its columns be.

The triumphal arch through which I march
　　With hurricane, fire, and snow,
When the Powers of the air are chained to my chair,
　　Is the million-coloured bow;　　　　　　　70
The sphere-fire above its soft colours wove,
　　While the moist Earth was laughing below.

I am the daughter of Earth and Water,
　　And the nursling of the Sky;
I pass through the pores of the ocean and shores;　　75
　　I change, but I cannot die.
For after the rain when with never a stain
　　The pavilion of Heaven is bare,
And the winds and sunbeams with their convex gleams
　　Build up the blue dome of air,　　　　　　80
I silently laugh at my own cenotaph,
　　And out of the caverns of rain,
Like a child from the womb, like a ghost from the tomb,
　　I arise and unbuild it again.

TO A SKYLARK

Hail to thee, blithe Spirit!
　　Bird thou never wert,
That from Heaven, or near it,
　　Pourest thy full heart
In profuse strains of unpremedi-
　　　tated art.　　　　5

Higher still and higher
　　From the earth thou springest
Like a cloud of fire;
　　The blue deep thou wingest,
And singing still dost soar, and
　　soaring ever singest.　　10

In the golden lightning
　　Of the sunken sun,
O'er which clouds are bright-
　　　'ning,
Thou dost float and run;
Like an unbodied joy whose race is
　　just begun.　　　15

The pale purple even
　　Melts around thy flight;
Like a star of Heaven,
　　In the broad daylight
Thou art unseen, but yet I hear thy
　　shrill delight,　　20

Keen as are the arrows
　　Of that silver sphere,
Whose intense lamp narrows
　　In the white dawn clear
Until we hardly see—we feel that
　　it is there.　　　25

All the earth and air
　　With thy voice is loud,
As, when night is bare,
　　From one lonely cloud
The moon rains out her beams, and
　　Heaven is overflowed.　　30

What thou art we know not;
　　What is most like thee?
From rainbow clouds there flow
　　not
Drops so bright to see
As from thy presence showers a
　　rain of melody.　　　35

Like a Poet hidden
　　In the light of thought,
Singing hymns unbidden,
　　Till the world is wrought
To sympathy with hopes and fears
　　it heeded not:　　　40

Like a high-born maiden
In a palace-tower,
Soothing her love-laden
Soul in secret hour
With music sweet as love, which
    overflows her bower: 45

Like a glow-worm golden
In a dell of dew,
Scattering unbeholden
Its aëreal hue
Among the flowers and grass, which
    screen it from the view! 50

Like a rose embowered
In its own green leaves,
By warm winds deflowered,
Till the scent it gives
Makes faint with too much sweet
    those heavy-wingèd
    thieves:

Sound of vernal showers   56
On the twinkling grass,
Rain-awakened flowers,
All that ever was
Joyous, and clear, and fresh, thy
    music doth surpass: 60

Teach us, Sprite or Bird,
What sweet thoughts are
    thine:
I have never heard
Praise of love or wine
That panted forth a flood of rap-
    ture so divine.   65

Chorus Hymeneal,
Or triumphal chant,
Matched with thine would be all
But an empty vaunt,
A thing wherein we feel there is
    some hidden want.   70

What objects are the fountains
Of thy happy strain?

What fields, or waves, or moun-
    tains?
What shapes of sky or plain?
What love of thine own kind? what
    ignorance of pain?   75

With thy clear keen joyance
Languor cannot be:
Shadow of annoyance
Never came near thee:
Thou lovest—but ne'er knew love's
    sad satiety.   80

Waking or asleep,
Thou of death must deem
Things more true and deep
Than we mortals dream,
Or how could thy notes flow in such
    a crystal stream?   85

We look before and after,
And pine for what is not:
Our sincerest laughter
With some pain is fraught;
Our sweetest songs are those that
    tell of saddest thought.   90

Yet if we could scorn
Hate, and pride, and fear;
If we were things born
Not to shed a tear,
I know not how thy joy we ever
    should come near.   95

Better than all measures
Of delightful sound,
Better than all treasures
That in books are found,
Thy skill to poet were, thou scorner
    of the ground!   100

Teach me half the gladness
That thy brain must know,
Such harmonious madness
From my lips would flow
The world should listen then—as
    I am listening now.   105

ODE TO LIBERTY

Yet, Freedom, yet, thy banner, torn but flying,
Streams like a thunder-storm against the wind.—BYRON.

I

A GLORIOUS people vibrated again
    The lightning of the nations: Liberty
From heart to heart, from tower to tower, o'er Spain,
    Scattering contagious fire into the sky,
Gleamed. My soul spurned the chains of its dismay,   5
        And in the rapid plumes of song
        Clothed itself, sublime and strong,
(As a young eagle soars the morning clouds among,)
    Hovering in verse o'er its accustomed prey;
      Till from its station in the Heaven of fame   10
The Spirit's whirlwind rapped it, and the ray
    Of the remotest sphere of living flame
Which paves the void was from behind it flung,
    As foam from a ship's swiftness, when there came
A voice out of the deep: I will record the same.   15

II

The Sun and the serenest Moon sprang forth:
    The burning stars of the abyss were hurled
Into the depths of Heaven. The daedal earth,
    That island in the ocean of the world,
Hung in its cloud of all-sustaining air: 20
        But this divinest universe
        Was yet a chaos and a curse,
For thou wert not: but, power from worst producing worse,
    The spirit of the beasts was kindled there,
      And of the birds, and of the watery forms,   25
    And there was war among them, and despair
      Within them, raging without truce or terms:
The bosom of their violated nurse
    Groaned, for beasts warred on beasts, and worms on worms,
And men on men; each heart was as a hell of storms.   30

III

Man, the imperial shape, then multiplied
    His generations under the pavilion
Of the Sun's throne: palace and pyramid,
    Temple and prison, to many a swarming million
Were, as to mountain-wolves their ragged caves.   35
        This human living multitude
        Was savage, cunning, blind, and rude,
For thou wert not; but o'er the populous solitude,

Like one fierce cloud over a waste of waves,
    Hung Tyranny; beneath, sate deified   40
The sister-pest, congregator of slaves;
    Into the shadow of her pinions wide
Anarchs and priests, who feed on gold and blood
    Till with the stain their inmost souls are dyed,
Drove the astonished herds of men from every side.   45

IV

The nodding promontories, and blue isles,
    And cloud-like mountains, and dividuous waves
Of Greece, basked glorious in the open smiles
    Of favouring Heaven: from their enchanted caves
Prophetic echoes flung dim melody.   50
        On the unapprehensive wild
        The vine, the corn, the olive mild,
Grew savage yet, to human use unreconciled;
    And, like unfolded flowers beneath the sea,
        Like the man's thought dark in the infant's brain,   55
    Like aught that is which wraps what is to be,
        Art's deathless dreams lay veiled by many a vein
Of Parian stone; and, yet a speechless child,
    Verse murmured, and Philosophy did strain
Her lidless eyes for thee; when o'er the Aegean main   60

V

Athens arose: a city such as vision
    Builds from the purple crags and silver towers
Of battlemented cloud, as in derision
    Of kingliest masonry: the ocean-floors
Pave it; the evening sky pavilions it;   65
        Its portals are inhabited
        By thunder-zonèd winds, each head
Within its cloudy wings with sun-fire garlanded,—
    A divine work! Athens, diviner yet,
        Gleamed with its crest of columns, on the will   70
    Of man, as on a mount of diamond, set;
        For thou wert, and thine all-creative skill
Peopled, with forms that mock the eternal dead
    In marble immortality, that hill
Which was thine earliest throne and latest oracle.   75

VI

Within the surface of Time's fleeting river
    Its wrinkled image lies, as then it lay
Immovably unquiet, and for ever
    It trembles, but it cannot pass away!

The voices of thy bards and sages thunder   80
    With an earth-awakening blast
      Through the caverns of the past:
(Religion veils her eyes; Oppression shrinks aghast:)
    A wingèd sound of joy, and love, and wonder,
      Which soars where Expectation never flew,   85
    Rending the veil of space and time asunder!
      One ocean feeds the clouds, and streams, and dew;
One Sun illumines Heaven; one Spirit vast
    With life and love makes chaos ever new,
    As Athens doth the world with thy delight renew.   90

VII

Then Rome was, and from thy deep bosom fairest,
    Like a wolf-cub from a Cadmaean Maenad,[1]
She drew the milk of greatness, though thy dearest
    From that Elysian food was yet unweanèd;
And many a deed of terrible uprightness   95
      By thy sweet love was sanctified;
      And in thy smile, and by thy side,
Saintly Camillus lived, and firm Atilius died.
    But when tears stained thy robe of vestal whiteness,
     And gold profaned thy Capitolian throne,   100
Thou didst desert, with spirit-wingèd lightness,
    The senate of the tyrants: they sunk prone
Slaves of one tyrant: Palatinus sighed
    Faint echoes of Ionian song; that tone
    Thou didst delay to hear, lamenting to disown.   105

VIII

From what Hyrcanian glen or frozen hill,
    Or piny promontory of the Arctic main,
    Or utmost islet inaccessible,
    Didst thou lament the ruin of thy reign,
Teaching the woods and waves, and desert rocks,   110
      And every Naiad's ice-cold urn,
      To talk in echoes sad and stern
Of that sublimest lore which man had dared unlearn?
    For neither didst thou watch the wizard flocks
     Of the Scald's dreams, nor haunt the Druid's sleep.   115
What if the tears rained through thy shattered locks
    Were quickly dried? for thou didst groan, not weep,
When from its sea of death, to kill and burn,
    The Galilean serpent forth did creep,
    And made thy world an undistinguishable heap.   120

[1] See the *Bacchae* of Euripides.—[SHELLEY's NOTE.]

IX

A thousand years the Earth cried, 'Where art thou?'
And then the shadow of thy coming fell
On Saxon Alfred's olive-cinctured brow:
   And many a warrior-peopled citadel,
Like rocks which fire lifts out of the flat deep,   125
      Arose in sacred Italy,
      Frowning o'er the tempestuous sea
Of kings, and priests, and slaves, in tower-crowned majesty;
   That multitudinous anarchy did sweep
      And burst around their walls, like idle foam,   130
   Whilst from the human spirit's deepest deep
      Strange melody with love and awe struck dumb
Dissonant arms; and Art, which cannot die,
   With divine wand traced on our earthly home
Fit imagery to pave Heaven's everlasting dome.   135

X

Thou huntress swifter than the Moon! thou terror
Of the world's wolves! thou bearer of the quiver,
Whose sunlike shafts pierce tempest-wingèd Error,
   As light may pierce the clouds when they dissever
In the calm regions of the orient day!   140
      Luther caught thy wakening glance;
      Like lightning, from his leaden lance
Reflected, it dissolved the visions of the trance
   In which, as in a tomb, the nations lay;
      And England's prophets hailed thee as their queen,   145
   In songs whose music cannot pass away,
      Though it must flow forever: not unseen
Before the spirit-sighted countenance
   Of Milton didst thou pass, from the sad scene
Beyond whose night he saw, with a dejected mien.   150

XI

The eager hours and unreluctant years
   As on a dawn-illumined mountain stood,
Trampling to silence their loud hopes and fears,
   Darkening each other with their multitude,
And cried aloud, 'Liberty!' Indignation   155
      Answered Pity from her cave;
      Death grew pale within the grave,
And Desolation howled to the destroyer, Save!
   When like Heaven's Sun girt by the exhalation
      Of its own glorious light, thou didst arise,   160
      Chasing thy foes from nation unto nation

Like shadows: as if day had cloven the skies
At dreaming midnight o'er the western wave,
 Men started, staggering with a glad surprise,
 Under the lightnings of thine unfamiliar eyes. 165

XII

Thou Heaven of earth! what spells could pall thee then
 In ominous eclipse? a thousand years
Bred from the slime of deep Oppression's den,
 Dyed all thy liquid light with blood and tears,
Till thy sweet stars could weep the stain away; 170
  How like Bacchanals of blood
  Round France, the ghastly vintage, stood
Destruction's sceptred slaves, and Folly's mitred brood!
  When one, like them, but mightier far than they,
  The Anarch of thine own bewildered powers, 175
  Rose: armies mingled in obscure array,
  Like clouds with clouds, darkening the sacred bowers
Of serene Heaven. He, by the past pursued,
 Rests with those dead, but unforgotten hours,
 Whose ghosts scare victor kings in their ancestral towers. 180

XIII

England yet sleeps: was she not called of old?
 Spain calls her now, as with its thrilling thunder
Vesuvius wakens Aetna, and the cold
 Snow-crags by its reply are cloven in sunder:
O'er the lit waves every Aeolian isle 185
  From Pithecusa to Pelorus
  Howls, and leaps, and glares in chorus:
They cry, 'Be dim; ye lamps of Heaven suspended o'er us!'
  Her chains are threads of gold, she need but smile
  And they dissolve; but Spain's were links of steel, 190
  Till bit to dust by virtue's keenest file.
  Twins of a single destiny! appeal
To the eternal years enthroned before us
 In the dim West; impress us from a seal,
 All ye have thought and done! Time cannot dare conceal. 195

XIV

Tomb of Arminius! render up thy dead
 Till, like a standard from a watch-tower's staff,
His soul may stream over the tyrant's head;
 Thy victory shall be his epitaph,
Wild Bacchanal of truth's mysterious wine, 200
  King-deluded Germany,
  His dead spirit lives in thee.

Why do we fear or hope? thou art already free!
  And thou, lost Paradise of this divine
    And glorious world! thou flowery wilderness!   205
  Thou island of eternity! thou shrine
    Where Desolation, clothed with loveliness,
Worships the thing thou wert! O Italy,
  Gather thy blood into thy heart; repress
  The beasts who make their dens thy sacred palaces.   210

XV

Oh, that the free would stamp the impious name
  Of KING into the dust! or write it there,
So that this blot upon the page of fame
  Were as a serpent's path, which the light air
Erases, and the flat sands close behind!   215
    Ye the oracle have heard:
    Lift the victory-flashing sword,
And cut the snaky knots of this foul gordian word,
  Which, weak itself as stubble, yet can bind
    Into a mass, irrefragably firm,   220
  The axes and the rods which awe mankind;
    The sound has poison in it, 'tis the sperm
Of what makes life foul, cankerous, and abhorred;
  Disdain not thou, at thine appointed term,
  To set thine armèd heel on this reluctant worm.   225

XVI

Oh, that the wise from their bright minds would kindle
  Such lamps within the dome of this dim world,
That the pale name of PRIEST might shrink and dwindle
  Into the hell from which it first was hurled,
A scoff of impious pride from fiends impure;   230
    Till human thoughts might kneel alone,
    Each before the judgment-throne
Of its own aweless soul, or of the Power unknown!
  Oh, that the words which make the thoughts obscure
    From which they spring, as clouds of glimmering dew   235
From a white lake blot Heaven's blue portraiture,
  Were stripped of their thin masks and various hue
And frowns and smiles and splendours not their own,
  Till in the nakedness of false and true
  They stand before their Lord, each to receive its due!   240

XVII

He who taught man to vanquish whatsoever
  Can be between the cradle and the grave
Crowned him the King of Life. Oh, vain endeavour!
  If on his own high will, a willing slave,

He has enthroned the oppression and the oppressor. 245
  What if earth can clothe and feed
   Amplest millions at their need,
And power in thought be as the tree within the seed?
  Or what if Art, an ardent intercessor,
   Driving on fiery wings to Nature's throne, 250
  Checks the great mother stooping to caress her,
   And cries: 'Give me, thy child, dominion
Over all height and depth'? if Life can breed
  New wants, and wealth from those who toil and groan,
  Rend of thy gifts and hers a thousandfold for one! 255

XVIII

Come thou, but lead out of the inmost cave
  Of man's deep spirit, as the morning-star
Beckons the Sun from the Eoan wave,
  Wisdom. I hear the pennons of her car
Self-moving, like cloud charioted by flame; 260
   Comes she not, and come ye not,
   Rulers of eternal thought,
To judge, with solemn truth, life's ill-apportioned lot?
  Blind Love, and equal Justice, and the Fame
   Of what has been, the Hope of what will be? 265
  O Liberty! if such could be thy name
   Wert thou disjoined from these, or they from thee:
If thine or theirs were treasures to be bought
  By blood or tears, have not the wise and free
  Wept tears, and blood like tears?—The solemn harmony 270

XIX

Paused, and the Spirit of that mighty singing
  To its abyss was suddenly withdrawn;
Then, as a wild swan, when sublimely winging
  Its path athwart the thunder-smoke of dawn,
Sinks headlong through the aëreal golden light 275
   On the heavy-sounding plain,
   When the bolt has pierced its brain;
As summer clouds dissolve, unburthened of their rain;
  As a far taper fades with fading night,
   As a brief insect dies with dying day,— 280
  My song, its pinions disarrayed of might,
   Drooped; o'er it closed the echoes far away
Of the great voice which did its flight sustain,
  As waves which lately paved his watery way
Hiss round a drowner's head in their tempestuous play. 285

TO ———

I

I FEAR thy kisses, gentle maiden,
    Thou needest not fear mine;
My spirit is too deeply laden
    Ever to burthen thine.

II

I fear thy mien, thy tones, thy motion,   5
    Thou needest not fear mine;
Innocent is the heart's devotion
    With which I worship thine.

ARETHUSA

I

ARETHUSA arose
    From her couch of snows
In the Acroceraunian mountains,—
    From cloud and from crag,
    With many a jag,   5
Shepherding her bright fountains.
    She leapt down the rocks,
    With her rainbow locks
Streaming among the streams;—
    Her steps paved with green   10
    The downward ravine
Which slopes to the western gleams;
    And gliding and springing
    She went, ever singing,
In murmurs as soft as sleep;   15
    The Earth seemed to love her,
    And Heaven smiled above her,
As she lingered towards the deep.

II

    Then Alpheus bold
    On his glacier cold,   20
With his trident the mountains
        strook;
    And opened a chasm
    In the rocks—with the spasm
All Erymanthus shook.
    And the black south wind   25
    It unsealed behind
The urns of the silent snow,

    And earthquake and thunder
    Did rend in sunder
The bars of the springs below.   30
    And the beard and the hair
    Of the River-god were
Seen through the torrent's sweep,
    As he followed the light
    Of the fleet nymph's flight   35
To the brink of the Dorian deep.

III

    'Oh, save me! Oh, guide me!
    And bid the deep hide me,
For he grasps me now by the hair!'
    The loud Ocean heard,   40
    To its blue depth stirred,
And divided at her prayer;
    And under the water
    The earth's white daughter
Fled like a sunny beam;   45
    Behind her descended
    Her billows, unblended
With the brackish Dorian
        stream:—
    Like a gloomy stain
    On the emerald main   50
Alpheus rushed behind,—
    As an eagle pursuing
    A dove to its ruin
Down the streams of the cloudy
        wind.

IV

Under the bowers 55
Where the Ocean Powers
Sit on their pearlèd thrones;
Through the coral woods,
Of the weltering floods,
Over heaps of unvalued stones; 60
Through the dim beams
Which amid the streams
Weave a network of coloured
light;
And under the caves,
Where the shadowy waves 65
Are as green as the forest's night:—
Outspeeding the shark,
And the sword-fish dark,
Under the Ocean's foam,
And up through the rifts 70
Of the mountain clifts
They passed to their Dorian home.

V

And now from their fountains
In Enna's mountains,
Down one vale where the morning
basks, 75
Like friends once parted
Grown single-hearted,
They ply their watery tasks.
At sunrise they leap
From their cradles steep 80
In the cave of the shelving hill;
At noontide they flow
Through the woods below
And the meadows of asphodel;
And at night they sleep 85
In the rocking deep
Beneath the Ortygian shore;—
Like spirits that lie
In the azure sky
When they love but live no more. 90

SONG OF PROSERPINE

WHILE GATHERING FLOWERS ON THE PLAIN OF ENNA

I

Sacred Goddess, Mother Earth,
  Thou from whose immortal bosom
Gods, and men, and beasts have birth,
  Leaf and blade, and bud and blossom,
Breathe thine influence most divine 5
On thine own child, Proserpine.

II

If with mists of evening dew
  Thou dost nourish these young flowers
Till they grow, in scent and hue,
  Fairest children of the Hours,
Breathe thine influence most divine 10
On thine own child, Proserpine.

HYMN OF APOLLO

I

The sleepless Hours who watch me as I lie,
  Curtained with star-inwoven tapestries
From the broad moonlight of the sky,
  Fanning the busy dreams from my dim eyes,—

Waken me when their Mother, the gray Dawn,   5
Tells them that dreams and that the moon is gone.

II

Then I arise, and climbing Heaven's blue dome,
    I walk over the mountains and the waves,
Leaving my robe upon the ocean foam;
    My footsteps pave the clouds with fire; the caves   10
Are filled with my bright presence, and the air
Leaves the green Earth to my embraces bare.

III

The sunbeams are my shafts, with which I kill
    Deceit, that loves the night and fears the day;
All men who do or even imagine ill   15
    Fly me, and from the glory of my ray
Good minds and open actions take new might,
Until diminished by the reign of Night.

IV

I feed the clouds, the rainbows and the flowers
    With their aethereal colours; the moon's globe   20
And the pure stars in their eternal bowers
    Are cinctured with my power as with a robe;
Whatever lamps on Earth or Heaven may shine
Are portions of one power, which is mine.

V

I stand at noon upon the peak of Heaven,   25
    Then with unwilling steps I wander down
Into the clouds of the Atlantic even;
    For grief that I depart they weep and frown:
What look is more delightful than the smile
With which I soothe them from the western isle?   30

VI

I am the eye with which the Universe
    Beholds itself and knows itself divine;
All harmony of instrument or verse,
    All prophecy, all medicine is mine,
All light of art or nature;—to my song   35
Victory and praise in its own right belong.

HYMN OF PAN

I

FROM the forests and highlands
  We come, we come;
From the river-girt islands,
  Where loud waves are dumb
    Listening to my sweet pipings.
The wind in the reeds and the
    rushes,   6
  The bees on the bells of thyme,
The birds on the myrtle bushes,
  The cicale above in the lime,
And the lizards below in the grass,
Were as silent as ever old Timolus
    was,   11
    Listening to my sweet pipings.

II

Liquid Peneus was flowing,
  And all dark Tempe lay
In Pelion's shadow, outgrowing   15
  The light of the dying day,
    Speeded by my sweet pipings.
The Sileni, and Sylvans, and
    Fauns,
  And the Nymphs of the woods
    and the waves,
To the edge of the moist river-
    lawns,   20
  And the brink of the dewy caves,

And all that did then attend and
    follow,
Were silent with love, as you now,
    Apollo,
  With envy of my sweet pip-
    ings.

III

I sang of the dancing stars,   25
  I sang of the daedal Earth,
And of Heaven—and the giant
    wars,
  And Love, and Death, and
    Birth,—
    And then I changed my pip-
    ings,—
Singing how down the vale of Mae-
    nalus   30
  I pursued a maiden and clasped
    a reed.
Gods and men, we are all deluded
    thus!
  It breaks in our bosom and then
    we bleed:
All wept, as I think both ye now
    would,
If envy or age had not frozen your
    blood,
  At the sorrow of my sweet
    pipings.

THE QUESTION

I

I DREAMED that, as I wandered by the way,
  Bare Winter suddenly was changed to Spring,
And gentle odours led my steps astray,
  Mixed with a sound of waters murmuring
Along a shelving bank of turf, which lay
  Under a copse, and hardly dared to fling
Its green arms round the bosom of the stream,
But kissed it and then fled, as thou mightest in dream.

II

There grew pied wind-flowers and violets,
   Daisies, those pearled Arcturi of the earth,   10
The constellated flower that never sets;
   Faint oxslips; tender bluebells, at whose birth
The sod scarce heaved; and that tall flower that wets —
   Like a child, half in tenderness and mirth—
Its mother's face with Heaven's collected tears,   15
When the low wind, its playmate's voice, it hears.

III

And in the warm hedge grew lush eglantine,
   Green cowbind and the moonlight-coloured may,
And cherry-blossoms, and white cups, whose wine
   Was the bright dew, yet drained not by the day;   20
And wild roses, and ivy serpentine,
   With its dark buds and leaves, wandering astray;
And flowers azure, black, and streaked with gold,
Fairer than any wakened eyes behold.

IV

And nearer to the river's trembling edge   25
   There grew broad flag-flowers, purple pranked with white,
And starry river buds among the sedge,
   And floating water-lilies, broad and bright,
Which lit the oak that overhung the hedge
   With moonlight beams of their own watery light;   30
And bulrushes, and reeds of such deep green
As soothed the dazzled eye with sober sheen.

V

Methought that of these visionary flowers
   I made a nosegay, bound in such a way
That the same hues, which in their natural bowers   35
   Were mingled or opposed, the like array
Kept these imprisoned children of the Hours
   Within my hand,—and then, elate and gay,
I hastened to the spot whence I had come,
That I might there present it!—Oh! to whom?   40

THE TWO SPIRITS: AN ALLEGORY

First Spirit.

O THOU, who plumed with strong desire
   Wouldst float above the earth, beware!
A Shadow tracks thy flight of fire—
   Night is coming!

Bright are the regions of the air,   5
  And among the winds and beams
    It were delight to wander there—
      Night is coming!

Second Spirit.

The deathless stars are bright above;
  If I would cross the shade of night,   10
Within my heart is the lamp of love,
    And that is day!
And the moon will smile with gentle light
On my golden plumes where'er they move;
  The meteors will linger round my flight,   15
    And make night day.

First Spirit.

But if the whirlwinds of darkness waken
  Hail, and lightning, and stormy rain;
See, the bounds of the air are shaken—
    Night is coming!   20
The red swift clouds of the hurricane
Yon declining sun have overtaken,
  The clash of the hail sweeps over the plain—
    Night is coming!

Second Spirit.

I see the light, and I hear the sound;   25
I'll sail on the flood of the tempest dark,
With the calm within and the light around
    Which makes night day:
And thou, when the gloom is deep and stark,
Look from thy dull earth, slumber-bound,   30
  My moon-like flight thou then mayst mark
    On high, far away.

Some say there is a precipice
  Where one vast pine is frozen to ruin
O'er piles of snow and chasms of ice   35
    Mid Alpine mountains;
And that the languid storm pursuing
That wingèd shape, for ever flies
  Round those hoar branches, aye renewing
    Its aëry fountains.   40

Some say when nights are dry and clear,
  And the death-dews sleep on the morass,
Sweet whispers are heard by the traveller,

Which make night day:
And a silver shape like his early love doth pass   45
Upborne by her wild and glittering hair,
And when he awakes on the fragrant grass,
He finds night day.

ODE TO NAPLES [1]

EPODE I α

I STOOD within the City disinterred; [2]
And heard the autumnal leaves like light footfalls
Of spirits passing through the streets; and heard
   The Mountain's slumberous voice at intervals
     Thrill through those roofless halls;   5
The oracular thunder penetrating shook
   The listening soul in my suspended blood;
I felt that Earth out of her deep heart spoke—
   I felt, but heard not:—through white columns glowed
     The isle-sustaining ocean-flood,   10
A plane of light between two heavens of azure!
   Around me gleamed many a bright sepulchre
Of whose pure beauty, Time, as if his pleasure
   Were to spare Death, had never made erasure;
     But every living lineament was clear   15
     As in the sculptor's thought; and there
The wreaths of stony myrtle, ivy, and pine,
   Like winter leaves o'ergrown by moulded snow,
     Seemed only not to move and grow
Because the crystal silence of the air   20
   Weighed on their life; even as the Power divine
   Which then lulled all things, brooded upon mine.

EPODE II α

   Then gentle winds arose
   With many a mingled close
Of wild Aeolian sound, and mountain-odours keen;   25
   And where the Baian ocean
   Welters with airlike motion,
Within, above, around its bowers of starry green,
   Moving the sea-flowers in those purple caves,
   Even as the ever stormless atmosphere   30

[1] The Author has connected many recollections of his visit to Pompeii and Baiae with the enthusiasm excited by the intelligence of the proclamation of a Constitutional Government at Naples. This has given a tinge of picturesque and descriptive imagery to the introductory Epodes which depicture these scenes, and some of the majestic feelings permanently connected with the scene of this animating event.—[SHELLEY'S NOTE.]

[2] Pompeii.—[SHELLEY'S NOTE.]

Floats o'er the Elysian realm.
It bore me, like an Angel, o'er the waves
Of sunlight, whose swift pinnace of dewy air
No storm can overwhelm.
I sailed, where ever flows   35
Under the calm Serene
A spirit of deep emotion
From the unknown graves
Of the dead Kings of Melody.[1]
Shadowy Aornos darkened o'er the helm   40
The horizontal aether; Heaven stripped bare
Its depth over Elysium, where the prow
Made the invisible water white as snow;
From that Typhaean mount, Inarime,
There streamed a sunbright vapour, like the standard 45
Of some aethereal host;
Whilst from all the coast,
Louder and louder, gathering round, there wandered
Over the oracular woods and divine sea
Prophesyings which grew articulate—   50
They seize me—I must speak them!—be they fate!

STROPHE I

Naples! thou Heart of men which ever pantest
Naked, beneath the lidless eye of Heaven!
Elysian City, which to calm enchantest
The mutinous air and sea! they round thee, even   55
As sleep round Love, are driven!
Metropolis of a ruined Paradise
Long lost, late won, and yet but half regained!
Bright Altar of the bloodless sacrifice,
Which armèd Victory offers up unstained   60
To Love, the flower-enchained!
Thou which wert once, and then didst cease to be,
Now art, and henceforth ever shalt be, free,
If Hope, and Truth, and Justice can avail,
Hail, hail, all hail!   65

STROPHE II

Thou youngest giant birth
Which from the groaning earth
Leap'st, clothed in armour of impenetrable scale!
Last of the Intercessors!
Who 'gainst the Crowned Transgressors   70
Pleadest before God's love! Arrayed in Wisdom's mail,
Wave thy lightning lance in mirth

[1] Homer and Virgil.—[SHELLEY's NOTE.]

Nor let thy high heart fail,
Though from their hundred gates the leagued Oppressors
    With hurried legions move!   75
    Hail, hail, all hail!

ANTISTROPHE I α

What though Cimmerian Anarchs dare blaspheme
  Freedom and thee? thy shield is as a mirror
To make their blind slaves see, and with fierce gleam
    To turn his hungry sword upon the wearer;   80
      A new Actaeon's error
Shall theirs have been—devoured by their own hounds!
  Be thou like the imperial Basilisk
Killing thy foe with unapparent wounds!
    Gaze on Oppression, till at that dread risk   85
Aghast she pass from the Earth's disk:
Fear not, but gaze—for freemen mightier grow,
And slaves more feeble, gazing on their foe:—
  If Hope, and Truth, and Justice may avail,
    Thou shalt be great—All hail!   90

ANTISTROPHE II α

  From Freedom's form divine,
  From Nature's inmost shrine,
Strip every impious gawd, rend Error veil by veil;
    O'er Ruin desolate,
    O'er Falsehood's fallen state,   95
Sit thou sublime, unawed; be the Destroyer pale!
    And equal laws be thine,
    And wingèd words let sail,
Freighted with truth even from the throne of God:
    That wealth, surviving fate,   100
    Be thine.—All hail!

ANTISTROPHE I β

Didst thou not start to hear Spain's thrilling paean
  From land to land re-echoed solemnly,
Till silence became music? From the Aeaean[1]
    To the cold Alps, eternal Italy   105
    Starts to hear thine! The Sea
Which paves the desert streets of Venice laughs
  In light and music; widowed Genoa wan
By moonlight spells ancestral epitaphs,
    Murmuring, 'Where is Doria?' fair Milan,   110
    Within whose veins long ran

---

[1] Aeaea, the island of Circe.—[SHELLEY'S NOTE.]

The viper's [1] palsying venom, lifts her heel
To bruise his head. The signal and the seal
   (If Hope and Truth and Justice can avail)
Art thou of all these hopes.—O hail!   115

ANTISTROPHE II β

    Florence! beneath the sun,
     Of cities fairest one,
Blushes within her bower for Freedom's expectation:
    From eyes of quenchless hope
    Rome tears the priestly cope,   120
As ruling once by power, so now by admiration,—
    An athlete stripped to run
    From a remoter station
For the high prize lost on Philippi's shore:—
   As then Hope, Truth, and Justice did avail,   125
   So now may Fraud and Wrong! O hail!

EPODE I β

Hear ye the march as of the Earth-born Forms
   Arrayed against the ever-living Gods?
The crash and darkness of a thousand storms
    Bursting their inaccessible abodes   130
     Of crags and thunder-clouds?
See ye the banners blazoned to the day,
   Inwrought with emblems of barbaric pride?
Dissonant threats kill Silence far away,
    The serene Heaven which wraps our Eden wide   135
     With iron light is dyed;
The Anarchs of the North lead forth their legions
   Like Chaos o'er creation, uncreating;
An hundred tribes nourished on strange religions
And lawless slaveries,—down the aëreal regions   140
    Of the white Alps, desolating,
    Famished wolves that bide no waiting,
Blotting the glowing footsteps of old glory,
Trampling our columned cities into dust,
    Their dull and savage lust   145
    On Beauty's corse to sickness satiating—
They come! The fields they tread look black and hoary
With fire—from their red feet the streams run gory!

EPODE II β

    Great Spirit, deepest Love!
    Which rulest and dost move   150

[1] The viper was the armorial device of the Visconti, tyrants of Milan.—[SHELLEY'S NOTE.]

All things which live and are, within the Italian shore;
    Who spreadest Heaven around it,
    Whose woods, rocks, waves, surround it;
Who sittest in thy star, o'er Ocean's western floor;
Spirit of beauty! at whose soft command   155
    The sunbeams and the showers distil its foison
    From the Earth's bosom chill;
Oh, bid those beams be each a blinding brand
Of lightning! bid those showers be dews of poison!
    Bid the Earth's plenty kill!   160
    Bid thy bright Heaven above,
    Whilst light and darkness bound it,
    Be their tomb who planned
    To make it ours and thine!
Or, with thine harmonizing ardours fill   165
And raise thy sons, as o'er the prone horizon
Thy lamp feeds every twilight wave with fire—
Be man's high hope and unextinct desire
The instrument to work thy will divine!
    Then clouds from sunbeams, antelopes from leopards,   170
    And frowns and fears from thee,
    Would not more swiftly flee
Than Celtic wolves from the Ausonian shepherds.—
Whatever, Spirit, from thy starry shrine
    Thou yieldest or withholdest, oh, let be   175
This city of thy worship ever free!

AUTUMN: A DIRGE

I

THE warm sun is failing, the bleak wind is wailing,
The bare boughs are sighing, the pale flowers are dying,
    And the Year
On the earth her death-bed, in a shroud of leaves dead,
    Is lying.   5
    Come, Months, come away,
    From November to May,
    In your saddest array;
    Follow the bier
    Of the dead cold Year,   10
And like dim shadows watch by her sepulchre.

II

The chill rain is falling, the nipped worm is crawling,
The rivers are swelling, the thunder is knelling
    For the Year;
The blithe swallows are flown, and the lizards each gone   15

To his dwelling;
Come, Months, come away;
Put on white, black, and gray;
Let your light sisters play—
Ye, follow the bier   20
Of the dead cold Year,
And make her grave green with tear on tear.

THE WANING MOON

AND like a dying lady, lean and pale,
Who totters forth, wrapped in a gauzy veil,
Out of her chamber, led by the insane
And feeble wanderings of her fading brain,
The moon arose up in the murky East,   5
A white and shapeless mass—

TO THE MOON

I

ART thou pale for weariness
Of climbing heaven and gazing on the earth,
Wandering companionless
Among the stars that have a different birth,—
And ever changing, like a joyless eye   5
That finds no object worth its constancy?

II

Thou chosen sister of the Spirit,
That gazes on thee till in thee it pities . . .

DEATH

I

DEATH is here and death is there,
Death is busy everywhere,
All around, within, beneath,
Above is death—and we are death.

II

Death has set his mark and
        seal   5
On all we are and all we feel,
On all we know and all we fear,

III

First our pleasures die—and then
Our hopes, and then our fears—
        and when
These are dead, the debt is due, 10
Dust claims dust—and we die too.

IV

All things that we love and cherish,
Like ourselves must fade and per-
        ish;
Such is our rude mortal lot—
Love itself would, did they not.   15

LIBERTY

I

THE fiery mountains answer each other;
　Their thunderings are echoed from zone to zone;
The tempestuous oceans awake one another,
　　And the ice-rocks are shaken round Winter's throne,
　　　When the clarion of the Typhoon is blown.   5

II

From a single cloud the lightening flashes,
　Whilst a thousand isles are illumined around,
Earthquake is trampling one city to ashes,
　　An hundred are shuddering and tottering; the sound
　　　Is bellowing underground.   10

III

But keener thy gaze than the lightening's glare,
　And swifter thy step than the earthquake's tramp;
Thou deafenest the rage of the ocean; thy stare
　　Makes blind the volcanoes; the sun's bright lamp
　　　To thine is a fen-fire damp.   15

IV

From billow and mountain and exhalation
　The sunlight is darted through vapour and blast;
From spirit to spirit, from nation to nation,
　　From city to hamlet thy dawning is cast,—
And tyrants and slaves are like shadows of night   20
　　　In the van of the morning light.

SUMMER AND WINTER

IT was a bright and cheerful afternoon,
Towards the end of the sunny month of June,
When the north wind congregates in crowds
The floating mountains of the silver clouds
From the horizon—and the stainless sky   5
Opens beyond them like eternity.
All things rejoiced beneath the sun; the weeds,
The river, and the corn-fields, and the reeds;
The willow leaves that glanced in the light breeze,
And the firm foliage of the larger trees.   10

It was a winter such as when birds die
In the deep forests; and the fishes lie

Stiffened in the translucent ice, which makes
Even the mud and slime of the warm lakes
A wrinkled clod as hard as brick; and when,   15
Among their children, comfortable men
Gather about great fires, and yet feel cold:
Alas, then, for the homeless beggar old!

THE TOWER OF FAMINE

AMID the desolation of a city,
Which was the cradle, and is now the grave
Of an extinguished people,—so that Pity

Weeps o'er the shipwrecks of Oblivion's wave,
There stands the Tower of Famine. It is built   5
Upon some prison-homes, whose dwellers rave

For bread, and gold, and blood: Pain, linked to Guilt,
Agitates the light flame of their hours,
Until its vital oil is spent or spilt.

There stands the pile, a tower amid the towers   10
And sacred domes; each marble-ribbèd roof,
The brazen-gated temples, and the bowers

Of solitary wealth,—the tempest-proof
Pavilions of the dark Italian air,—
Are by its presence dimmed—they stand aloof,   15

And are withdrawn—so that the world is bare;
As if a spectre wrapped in shapeless terror
Amid a company of ladies fair

Should glide and glow, till it became a mirror
Of all their beauty, and their hair and hue,   20
The life of their sweet eyes, with all its error,
Should be absorbed, till they to marble grew.

AN ALLEGORY

I

A PORTAL as of shadowy adamant
  Stands yawning on the highway of the life
Which we all tread, a cavern huge and gaunt;
  Around it rages an unceasing strife
Of shadows, like the restless clouds that haunt   5
The gap of some cleft mountain, lifted high
Into the whirlwinds of the upper sky.

II

And many pass it by with careless tread,
    Not knowing that a shadowy . . .
Tracks every traveller even to where the dead   10
    Wait peacefully for their companion new;
But others, by more curious humour led,
    Pause to examine;—these are very few,
And they learn little there, except to know
That shadows follow them where'er they go.   15

THE WORLD'S WANDERERS

I

TELL me, thou Star, whose wings of light
Speed thee in thy fiery flight,
In what cavern of the night
    Will thy pinions close now?

II

Tell me, Moon, thou pale and gray   5
Pilgrim of Heaven's homeless way,
In what depth of night or day
    Seekest thou repose now?

III

Weary Wind, who wanderest
Like the world's rejected guest,   10
Hast thou still some secret nest
    On the tree or billow?

SONNET

YE hasten to the grave! What seek ye there,
Ye restless thoughts and busy purposes
Of the idle brain, which the world's livery wear?
O thou quick heart, which pantest to possess
All that pale Expectation feigneth fair!   5
Thou vainly curious mind which wouldest guess
Whence thou didst come, and whither thou must go,
And all that never yet was known would know—
Oh, whither hasten ye, that thus ye press,
With such swift feet life's green and pleasant path,   10
Seeking, alike from happiness and woe,
A refuge in the cavern of gray death?
O heart, and mind, and thoughts! what thing do you
Hope to inherit in the grave below?

LINES TO A REVIEWER

ALAS, good friend, what profit can you see
In hating such a hateless thing as me?
There is no sport in hate where all the rage
Is on one side: in vain would you assuage
Your frowns upon an unresisting smile,   5
In which not even contempt lurks to beguile
Your heart, by some fain sympathy of hate.
Oh, conquer what you cannot satiate!
For to your passion I am far more coy
Than ever yet was coldest maid or boy   10
In winter noon. Of your antipathy
If I am the Narcissus, you are free
To pine into a sound with hating me.

FRAGMENT OF A SATIRE ON SATIRE

IF gibbets, axes, confiscations, chains,
And racks of subtle torture, if the pains
Of shame, of fiery Hell's tempestuous wave,
Seen through the caverns of the shadowy grave,
Hurling the damned into the murky air   5
While the meek blest sit smiling; if Despair
And Hate, the rapid bloodhounds with which Terror
Hunts through the world the homeless steps of Error,
Are the true secrets of the commonweal
To make men wise and just; ...   10
And not the sophisms of revenge and fear,
Bloodier than is revenge ...
Then send the priests to every hearth and home
To preach the burning wrath which is to come,
In words like flakes of sulphur, such as thaw   15
The frozen tears ...
If Satire's scourge could wake the slumbering hounds
Of Conscience, or erase the deeper wounds,
The leprous scars of callous Infamy;
If it could make the present not to be,   20
Or charm the dark past never to have been,
Or turn regret to hope; who that has seen
What Southey is and was, would not exclaim,
'Lash on!'   be the keen verse dipped in flame;
Follow his flight with wingèd words, and urge   25
The strokes of the inexorable scourge
Until the heart be naked, till his soul
See the contagion's spots   foul;
And from the mirror of Truth's sunlike shield,

From which his Parthian arrow ...   30
Flash on his sight the spectres of the past,
Until his mind's eye paint thereon—
Let scorn like   yawn below,
And rain on him like flakes of fiery snow.
This cannot be, it ought not, evil still—   35
Suffering makes suffering, ill must follow ill.
Rough words beget sad thoughts,   and, beside,
Men take a sullen and a stupid pride
In being all they hate in others' shame,
By a perverse antipathy of fame.   40
'Tis not worth while to prove, as I could, how
From the sweet fountains of our Nature flow
These bitter waters; I will only say,
If any friend would take Southey some day,
And tell him, in a country walk alone,   45
Softening harsh words with friendship's gentle tone,
How incorrect his public conduct is,
And what men think of it, 'twere not amiss.
Far better than to make innocent ink—

GOOD-NIGHT

I

GOOD-NIGHT? ah! no; the hour is ill
    Which severs those it should unite;
Let us remain together still,
    Then it will be *good* night.

II

How can I call the lone night good,   5
    Though thy sweet wishes wing its flight?
Be it not said, thought, understood—
    Then it will be—*good* night.

III

To hearts which near each other move
    From evening close to morning light,   10
The night is good; because, my love,
    They never *say* good-night.

BUONA NOTTE

I

'BUONA notte, buona notte!'—Come mai
    La notte sarà buona senza te?
Non dirmi buona notte,—chè tu sai,
    La notte sà star buona da per sè.

II

Solinga, scura, cupa, senza speme,   5
    La notte quando Lilla m'abbandona;
Pei cuori chi si batton insieme
    Ogni notte, senza dirla, sarà buona.

III

Come male buona notte si suona
    Con sospiri e parole interrotte!—   10
Il modo di aver la notte buona
    E mai non di dir la buona notte.

ORPHEUS

A. Not far from hence. From yonder pointed hill,
Crowned with a ring of oaks, you may behold
A dark and barren field, through which there flows,
Sluggish and black, a deep but narrow stream,
Which the wind ripples not, and the fair moon   5
Gazes in vain, and finds no mirror there.
Follow the herbless banks of that strange brook
Until you pause beside a darksome pond,
The fountain of this rivulet, whose gush
Cannot be seen, hid by a rayless night   10
That lives beneath the overhanging rock
That shades the pool—an endless spring of gloom,
Upon whose edge hovers the tender light,
Trembling to mingle with its paramour,—
But, as Syrinx fled Pan, so night flies day,   15
Or, with most sullen and regardless hate,
Refuses stern her heaven-born embrace.
On one side of this jagged and shapeless hill
There is a cave, from which there eddies up
A pale mist, like aëreal gossamer,   20
Whose breath destroys all life—awhile it veils
The rock—then, scattered by the wind, it flies
Along the stream, or lingers on the clefts,
Killing the sleepy worms, if aught bide there.
Upon the beetling edge of that dark rock   25
There stands a group of cypresses; not such
As, with a graceful spire and stirring life,
Pierce the pure heaven of your native vale,
Whose branches the air plays among, but not
Disturbs, fearing to spoil their solemn grace;   30
But blasted and all wearily they stand,
One to another clinging; their weak boughs
Sigh as the wind buffets them, and they shake

Beneath its blasts—a weatherbeaten crew!

Chorus. What wondrous sound is that, mournful and faint,   35
But more melodious than the murmuring wind
Which through the columns of a temple glides?

A. It is the wandering voice of Orpheus' lyre,
Borne by the winds, who sigh that their rude king
Hurries them fast from these air-feeding notes;   40
But in their speed they bear along with them
The waning sound, scattering it like dew
Upon the startled sense.

Chorus.   Does he still sing?
Methought he rashly cast away his harp
When he had lost Eurydice.

A.   Ah, no!   45
Awhile he paused. As a poor hunted stag
A moment shudders on the fearful brink
Of a swift stream—the cruel hounds press on
With deafening yell, the arrows glance and wound,—
He plunges in: so Orpheus, seized and torn   50
By the sharp fangs of an insatiate grief,
Maenad-like waved his lyre in the bright air,
And wildly shrieked 'Where she is, it is dark!'
And then he struck from forth the strings a sound
Of deep and fearful melody. Alas!   55
In times long past, when fair Eurydice
With her bright eyes sat listening by his side,
He gently sang of high and heavenly themes.
As in a brook, fretted with little waves
By the light airs of spring—each riplet makes   60
A many-sided mirror for the sun,
While it flows musically through green banks,
Ceaseless and pauseless, ever clear and fresh,
So flowed his song, reflecting the deep joy
And tender love that fed those sweetest notes,   65
The heavenly offspring of ambrosial food.
But that is past. Returning from drear Hell,
He chose a lonely seat of unhewn stone,
Blackened with lichens, a herbless plain.
Then from the deep and overflowing spring   70
Of his eternal ever-moving grief
There rose to Heaven a sound of angry song.
'Tis a mighty cataract that parts
Two sister rocks with waters swift and strong,
And casts itself with horrid roar and din   75
Adown a steep; from a perennial source
It ever flows and falls, and breaks the air
With loud and fierce, but most harmonious roar,

And as it falls casts up a vaporous spray
Which the sun clothes in hues of Iris light.   80
Thus the tempestuous torrent of his grief
Is clothed in sweetest sounds and varying words
Of poesy. Unlike all human works,
It never slackens, and through every change
Wisdom and beauty and the power divine   85
Of mighty poesy together dwell,
Mingling in sweet accord. As I have seen
A fierce south blast tear through the darkened sky,
Driving along a rack of wingèd clouds,
Which may not pause, but ever hurry on,   90
As their wild shepherd wills them, while the stars,
Twinkling and dim, peep from between the plumes.
Anon the sky is cleared, and the high dome
Of serene Heaven, starred with fiery flowers,
Shuts in the shaken earth; or the still moon   95
Swiftly, yet gracefully, begins her walk,
Rising all bright behind the eastern hills.
I talk of moon, and wind, and stars, and not
Of song; but, would I echo his high song,
Nature must lend me words ne'er used before,   100
Or I must borrow from her perfect works,
To picture forth his perfect attributes.
He does no longer sit upon his throne
Of rock upon a desert herbless plain,
For the evergreen and knotted ilexes,   105
And cypresses that seldom wave their boughs,
And sea-green olives with their grateful fruit,
And elms dragging along the twisted vines,
Which drop their berries as they follow fast,
And blackthorn bushes with their infant race   110
Of blushing rose-blooms; beeches, to lovers dear,
And weeping willow trees; all swift or slow,
As their huge boughs or lighter dress permit,
Have circled in his throne, and Earth herself
Has sent from her maternal breast a growth   115
Of starlike flowers and herbs of odour sweet,
To pave the temple that his poesy
Has framed, while near his feet grim lions couch,
And kids, fearless from love, creep near his lair.
Even the blind worms seem to feel the sound.   120
The birds are silent, hanging down their heads,
Perched on the lowest branches of the trees;
Not even the nightingale intrudes a note
In rivalry, but all entranced she listens.

FIORDISPINA

THE season was the childhood of sweet June,
Whose sunny hours from morning until noon
Went creeping through the day with silent feet,
Each with its load of pleasure; slow yet sweet;
Like the long years of blest Eternity   5
Never to be developed. Joy to thee,
Fiordispina and thy Cosimo,
For thou the wonders of the depth canst know
Of this unfathomable flood of hours,
Sparkling beneath the heaven which embowers—   10

    .   .   .   .

They were two cousins, almost like to twins,
Except that from the catalogue of sins
Nature had rased their love—which could not be
But by dissevering their nativity.
And so they grew together like two flowers   15
Upon one stem, which the same beams and showers
Lull or awaken in their purple prime,
Which the same hand will gather—the same clime
Shake with decay. This fair day smiles to see
All those who love—and who e'er loved like thee,   20
Fiordispina? Scarcely Cosimo,
Within whose bosom and whose brain now glow
The ardours of a vision which obscure
The very idol of its portraiture.
He faints, dissolved into a sea of love;   25
But thou art as a planet sphered above;
But thou art Love itself—ruling the motion
Of his subjected spirit: such emotion
Must end in sin and sorrow, if sweet May
Had not brought forth this morn—your wedding-day.   30

    .   .   .   .

'Lie there; sleep awhile in your own dew,
Ye faint-eyed children of the   Hours,'
Fiordispina said, and threw the flowers
Which she had from the breathing—

    .   .   .   .

A table near of polished porphyry.   35
They seemed to wear a beauty from the eye
That looked on them—a fragrance from the touch
Whose warmth   checked their life; a light such
As sleepers wear, lulled by the voice they love,
                which did reprove   40

The childish pity that she felt for them,
And a   remorse that from their stem
She had divided such fair shapes   made
A feeling in the   which was a shade
Of gentle beauty on the flowers: there lay   45
All gems that make the earth's dark bosom gay.
            rods of myrtle-buds and lemon-blooms,
And that leaf tinted lightly which assumes
The livery of unremembered snow—
Violets whose eyes have drunk—   50

.   .   .   .   .   .

Fiordispina and her nurse are now
Upon the steps of the high portico;
Under the withered arm of Media
She flings her glowing arm

.   .   .   .   .   .

            step by step and stair by stair,   55
That withered woman, gray and white and brown—
More like a trunk by lichens overgrown
Than anything which once could have been human.
And ever as she goes the palsied woman

.   .   .   .   .   .

'How slow and painfully you seem to walk,   60
Poor Media! you tire yourself with talk.'
            'And well it may,
Fiordispina, dearest—well-a-day!
You are hastening to a marriage-bed;
I to the grave!'—'And if my love were dead,   65
Unless my heart deceives me, I would lie
Beside him in my shroud as willingly
As now in the gay night-dress Lilla wrought.'
'Fie, child! Let that unseasonable thought
Not be remembered till it snows in June;   70
Such fancies are a music out of tune
With the sweet dance your heart must keep to-night.
What! would you take all beauty and delight
Back to the Paradise from which you sprung,
And leave to grosser mortals?——   75
And say, sweet lamb, would you not learn the sweet
And subtle mystery by which spirits meet?
Who knows whether the loving game is played,
When, once of mortal [vesture] disarrayed,
The naked soul goes wandering here and there   80
Through the wide deserts of Elysian air?
The violet dies not till it'——

TIME LONG PAST

I

LIKE the ghost of a dear friend
dead
    Is Time long past.
A tone which is now forever fled,
A hope which is now forever past,
A love so sweet it could not last, 5
    Was time long past.

II

There were sweet dreams in the
night
    Of Time long past:

And, was it sadness or delight,
Each day a shadow onward cast 10
Which made us wish it yet might
last—
    That Time long past.

III

There is regret, almost remorse,
    For Time long past.
'Tis like a child's belovèd corse 15
A father watches, till at last
Beauty is like remembrance, cast
    From Time long past.

FRAGMENT: THE DESERTS OF DIM SLEEP

I WENT into the deserts of dim sleep—
That world which, like an unknown wilderness,
Bounds this with its recesses wide and deep—

FRAGMENT: 'THE VIEWLESS AND INVISIBLE CONSEQUENCE'

THE viewless and invisible Consequence
Watches thy goings-out, and comings-in,
And ... hovers o'er thy guilty sleep,
Unveiling every new-born deed, and thoughts
More ghastly than those deeds—   5

FRAGMENT: A SERPENT-FACE

HIS face was like a snake's—wrinkled and loose
And withered—

FRAGMENT: DEATH IN LIFE

MY head is heavy, my limbs are weary,
And it is not life that makes me move.

FRAGMENT: 'SUCH HOPE, AS IS THE SICK DESPAIR OF GOOD'

SUCH hope, as is the sick despair of good,
Such fear, as is the certainty of ill,
Such doubt, as is pale Expectation's food
Turned while she tastes to poison, when the will
Is powerless, and the spirit ...   5

FRAGMENT: 'ALAS! THIS IS NOT WHAT I THOUGHT LIFE WAS'

ALAS! this is not what I thought life was.
I knew that there were crimes and evil men,
Misery and hate; nor did I hope to pass
Untouched by suffering, through the rugged glen.
In mine own heart I saw as in a glass   5
The hearts of others   And when
I went among my kind, with triple brass
Of calm endurance my weak breast I armed,
To bear scorn, fear, and hate, a woful mass!

FRAGMENT: MILTON'S SPIRIT

I DREAMED that Milton's spirit rose, and took
    From life's green tree his Uranian lute;
And from his touch sweet thunder flowed, and shook
All human things built in contempt of man,—
And sanguine thrones and impious altars quaked,   5
Prisons and citadels ...

FRAGMENT: 'UNRISEN SPLENDOUR OF THE BRIGHTEST SUN'

UNRISEN splendour of the brightest sun,
To rise upon our darkness, if the star
Now beckoning thee out of thy misty throne
Could thaw the clouds which wage an obscure war
With thy young brightness!   5

FRAGMENT: *PATER OMNIPOTENS*

SERENE in his unconquerable might
Endued[,] the Almighty King, his steadfast throne
Encompassed unapproachably with power
And darkness and deep solitude and awe
Stood like a black cloud on some aëry cliff   5
Embosoming its lightning—in his sight
Unnumbered glorious spirits trembling stood
Like slaves before their Lord—prostrate around
Heaven's multitudes hymned everlasting praise.

FRAGMENT: TO THE MIND OF MAN

THOU living light that in thy rainbow hues
    Clothest this naked world; and over Sea
And Earth and air, and all the shapes that be
    In peopled darkness of this wondrous world

The Spirit of thy glory dost diffuse   5
      truth   thou Vital Flame
Mysterious thought that in this mortal frame
Of things, with unextinguished lustre burnest
      Now pale and faint now high to Heaven upcurled
That eer as thou dost languish still returnest   10
    And ever

Before the   before the Pyramids

So soon as from the Earth formless and rude
One living step had chased drear Solitude
Thou wert, Thought; thy brightness charmed the lids   15
Of the vast snake Eternity, who kept
The tree of good and evil.—

NOTE ON POEMS OF 1820, BY MRS. SHELLEY

WE spent the latter part of the year 1819 in Florence, where Shelley passed several hours daily in the Gallery, and made various notes on its ancient works of art. His thoughts were a good deal taken up also by the project of a steamboat, undertaken by a friend, an engineer, to ply between Leghorn and Marseilles, for which he supplied a sum of money. This was a sort of plan to delight Shelley, and he was greatly disappointed when it was thrown aside.

There was something in Florence that disagreed excessively with his health, and he suffered far more pain than usual; so much so that we left it sooner than we intended, and removed to Pisa, where we had some friends, and, above all, where we could consult the celebrated Vaccà as to the cause of Shelley's sufferings. He, like every other medical man, could only guess at that, and gave little hope of immediate relief; he enjoined him to abstain from all physicians and medicine, and to leave his complaint to Nature. As he had vainly consulted medical men of the highest repute in England, he was easily persuaded to adopt this advice. Pain and ill-health followed him to the end; but the residence at Pisa agreed with him better than any other, and there in consequence we remained.

In the Spring we spent a week or two near Leghorn, borrowing the house of some friends who were absent on a journey to England. It was on a beautiful summer evening, while wandering among the lanes whose myrtle-hedges were the bowers of the fire-flies, that we heard the carolling of the skylark which inspired one of the most beautiful of his poems. He addressed the letter to Mrs. Gisborne from this house, which was hers: he had made his study of the workshop of her son, who was an engineer. Mrs. Gisborne had been a friend of my father in her younger days. She was a lady of great accomplishments, and charming from her frank and affectionate nature. She had the most intense love of knowledge, a delicate and trembling sensibility, and preserved freshness of mind after a life of considerable adversity. As a favourite friend of my father, we had sought her with eagerness; and the most open and cordial friendship was established between us.

Our stay at the Baths of San Giuliano was shortened by an accident. At the foot of our garden ran the canal that communicated between the Serchio and the Arno. The Serchio overflowed its banks, and, breaking its bounds, this canal also overflowed; all this part of the country is below the level of its rivers, and the consequence was that it was speedily flooded. The rising waters filled the Square of the Baths, in the lower part of which our house was situated. The canal overflowed in the garden behind; the rising waters on either side at last burst open the doors, and, meeting in the house, rose to the height of six feet. It was a picturesque sight at night to see the peasants driving the cattle from the plains below to the hills above the Baths. A fire was kept up to guide them across the ford; and the forms of the men and the animals showed in dark relief against the red glare of the flame, which was reflected again in the waters that filled the Square.

We then removed to Pisa, and took up our abode there for the winter. The extreme mildness of the climate suited Shelley, and his solitude was enlivened by an intercourse with several intimate friends. Chance cast us strangely enough on this quiet half-unpeopled town; but its very peace suited Shelley. Its river, the near mountains, and not distant sea, added to its attractions, and were the objects of many delightful excursions. We feared the south of Italy, and a hotter climate, on account of our child; our former bereavement inspiring us with terror. We seemed to take root here, and moved little afterwards; often, indeed, entertaining projects for visiting other parts of Italy, but still delaying. But for our fears on account of our child, I believe we should have wandered over the world, both being passionately fond of travelling. But human life, besides its great unalterable necessities, is ruled by a thousand lilliputian ties that shackle at the time, although it is difficult to account afterwards for their influence over our destiny.

POEMS WRITTEN IN 1821

DIRGE FOR THE YEAR

I

Orphan Hours, the Year is dead,
　Come and sigh, come and weep!
Merry Hours, smile instead,
　For the Year is but asleep.
See, it smiles as it is sleeping,　5
Mocking your untimely weep-
　　　ing.

II

As an earthquake rocks a corse
　In its coffin in the clay,
So White Winter, that rough nurse,
　Rocks the death-cold Year to-
　　　day;　10
Solemn Hours! wail aloud
For your mother in her shroud.

III

As the wild air stirs and sways
   The tree-swung cradle of a
     child,
So the breath of these rude days 15
   Rocks the Year:—be calm and
     mild,
Trembling Hours, she will arise
With new love within her eyes.

IV

January gray is here,
   Like a sexton by her grave;   20
February bears the bier,
   March with grief doth howl and
     rave,
And April weeps—but, O ye
     Hours!
Follow with May's fairest flowers.

TO NIGHT

I

SWIFTLY walk o'er the western
     wave,
     Spirit of Night!
Out of the misty eastern cave,
Where, all the long and lone day-
     light,
Thou wovest dreams of joy and
     fear,   5
Which make thee terrible and
     dear,—
     Swift be thy flight!

II

Wrap thy form in a mantle gray,
     Star-inwrought!
Blind with thine hair the eyes of
     Day;   10
Kiss her until she be wearied out,
Then wander o'er city, and sea, and
     land,
Touching all with thine opiate
     wand—
     Come, long-sought!

III

When I arose and saw the dawn, 15
   I sighed for thee;

When light rode high, and the dew
     was gone,
And noon lay heavy on flower and
     tree,
And the weary Day turned to his
     rest,
Lingering like an unloved guest, 20
   I sighed for thee.

IV

Thy brother Death came, and cried,
     Wouldst thou me?
Thy sweet child Sleep, the filmy-
     eyed,
Murmured like a noontide bee,   25
Shall I nestle near thy side?
Wouldst thou me?—And I replied,
     No, not thee!

V

Death will come when thou art
     dead,
     Soon, too soon—   30
Sleep will come when thou art
     fled;
Of neither would I ask the boon
I ask of thee, belovèd Night—
Swift be thine approaching flight,
     Come soon, soon!   35

TIME

UNFATHOMABLE Sea! whose waves are years,
   Ocean of Time, whose waters of deep woe
Are brackish with the salt of human tears!
   Thou shoreless flood, which in thy ebb and flow

Claspest the limits of mortality, 5
And sick of prey, yet howling on for more,
Vomitest thy wrecks on its inhospitable shore;
Treacherous in calm, and terrible in storm,
Who shall put forth on thee,
Unfathomable Sea? 10

LINES

I

Far, far away, O ye
Halcyons of Memory,
Seek some far calmer nest
Than this abandoned breast!
No news of your false spring 5
To my heart's winter bring,
Once having gone, in vain
Ye come again.

II

Vultures, who build your bowers
High in the Future's towers, 10
Withered hopes on hopes are
spread!
Dying joys, choked by the dead,
Will serve your beaks for prey
Many a day.

FROM THE ARABIC: AN IMITATION

I

My faint spirit was sitting in the light
Of thy looks, my love;
It panted for thee like the hind at noon
For the brooks, my love.
Thy barb whose hoofs outspeed the tempest's flight 5
Bore thee far from me;
My heart, for my weak feet were weary soon,
Did companion thee.

II

Ah! fleeter far than fleetest storm or steed,
Or the death they bear, 10
The heart which tender thought clothes like a dove
With the wings of care;
In the battle, in the darkness, in the need,
Shall mine cling to thee,
Nor claim one smile for all the comfort, love, 15
It may bring to thee.

TO EMILIA VIVIANI

I

Madonna, wherefore hast thou sent to me
Sweet-basil and mignonette?
Embleming love and health, which never yet
In the same wreath might be.

Alas, and they are wet!   5
Is it with thy kisses or thy tears?
  For never rain or dew
  Such fragrance drew
From plant or flower—the very doubt endears
  My sadness ever new,   10
The sighs I breathe, the tears I shed for thee.

II

Send the stars light, but send not love to me,
  In whom love ever made
  Health like a heap of embers soon to fade—

THE FUGITIVES

I

THE waters are flashing,
The white hail is dashing,
The lightnings are glancing,
The hoar-spray is dancing—
        Away!   5

The whirlwind is rolling,
The thunder is tolling,
The forest is swinging,
The minster bells ringing—
        Come away!   10

The Earth is like Ocean,
Wreck-strewn and in motion:
Bird, beast, man and worm
Have crept out of the storm—
        Come away!   15

II

'Our boat has one sail,
And the helmsman is pale;—
A bold pilot I trow,
Who should follow us now,'—
        Shouted he—   20

And she cried: 'Ply the oar!
Put off gaily from shore!'—
As she spoke, bolts of death
Mixed with hail, specked their path
        O'er the sea.   25

And from isle, tower and rock,
The blue beacon-cloud broke,
And though dumb in the blast,
The red cannon flashed fast
        From the lee.   30

III

And 'Fear'st thou?' and 'Fear'st
        thou?'
And 'Seest thou?' and 'Hear'st
        thou?'
And 'Drive we not free
O'er the terrible sea,
        I and thou?'   35

One boat-cloak did cover
The loved and the lover—
Their blood beats one measure,
They murmur proud pleasure
        Soft and low;—   40

While around the lashed Ocean,
Like mountains in motion,
Is withdrawn and uplifted,
Sunk, shattered and shifted
        To and fro.   45

IV

In the court of the fortress
Beside the pale portress,
Like a bloodhound well beaten
The bridegroom stands, eaten
        By shame;   50

On the topmost watch-turret,
As a death-boding spirit,
Stands the gray tyrant father,
To his voice the mad weather
    Seems tame;   55

And with curses as wild
As e'er clung to child,
He devotes to the blast,
The best, loveliest and last
    Of his name!   60

TO ——

Music, when soft voices die,
Vibrates in the memory—
Odours, when sweet violets sicken,
Live within the sense they quicken.

Rose leaves, when the rose is dead,   5
Are heaped for the belovèd bed;
And so thy thoughts, when thou art gone,
Love itself shall slumber on.

SONG

I

Rarely, rarely, comest thou,
  Spirit of Delight!
Wherefore hast thou left me now
  Many a day and night?
Many a weary night and day   5
'Tis since thou art fled away.

II

How shall ever one like me
  Win thee back again?
With the joyous and the free
  Thou wilt scoff at pain.   10
Spirit false! thou hast forgot
  All but those who need thee not.

III

As a lizard with the shade
  Of a trembling leaf,
Thou with sorrow art dismayed; 15
  Even the sighs of grief
Reproach thee, that thou art not
    near,
And reproach thou wilt not hear.

IV

Let me set my mournful ditty
  To a merry measure;   20
Thou wilt never come for pity,
  Thou wilt come for pleasure;

Pity then will cut away
Those cruel wings, and thou wilt
    stay.

V

I love all that thou lovest,   25
  Spirit of Delight!
The fresh Earth in new leaves
    dressed,
  And the starry night;
Autumn evening, and the morn
When the golden mists are born. 30

VI

I love snow, and all the forms
  Of the radiant frost;
I love waves, and winds, and
    storms,
  Everything almost
Which is Nature's, and may be 35
Untainted by man's misery.

VII

I love tranquil solitude,
  And such society
As is quiet, wise, and good;
  Between thee and me   40
What difference? but thou dost
    possess
  The things I seek, not love them
    less.

VIII

I love Love—though he has wings,
  And like light can flee,
But above all other things,   45

Spirit, I love thee—
Thou art love and life! Oh, come,
Make once more my heart thy
  home.

MUTABILITY

I

THE flower that smiles to-day
  To-morrow dies;
All that we wish to stay
  Tempts and then flies.
What is this world's delight?   5
Lightning that mocks the night,
  Brief even as bright.

II

Virtue, how frail it is!
  Friendship how rare!
Love, how it sells poor bliss   10

For proud despair!
But we, though soon they fall,
Survive their joy, and all
  Which ours we call.

III

Whilst skies are blue and bright, 15
  Whilst flowers are gay,
Whilst eyes that change ere night
  Make glad the day;
Whilst yet the calm hours creep,
Dream thou—and from thy sleep 20
  Then wake to weep.

LINES WRITTEN ON HEARING THE NEWS OF THE DEATH OF NAPOLEON

WHAT! alive and so bold, O Earth?
  Art thou not overbold?
  What! leapest thou forth as of old
In the light of thy morning mirth,
The last of the flock of the starry fold?   5
Ha! leapest thou forth as of old?
Are not the limbs still when the ghost is fled,
And canst thou move, Napoleon being dead?

How! is not thy quick heart cold?
  What spark is alive on thy hearth?   10
How! is not *his* death-knell knolled?
  And livest *thou* still, Mother Earth?
Thou wert warming thy fingers old
O'er the embers covered and cold
Of that most fiery spirit, when it fled—   15
What, Mother, do you laugh now he is dead?

'Who has known me of old,' replied Earth,
  'Or who has my story told?
  It is thou who art overbold.'
And the lightning of scorn laughed forth   20
As she sung, 'To my bosom I fold
All my sons when their knell is knolled
And so with living motion all are fed,
And the quick spring like weeds out of the dead.

'Still alive and still bold,' shouted Earth,   25
    'I grow bolder and still more bold.
    The dead fill me ten thousandfold
Fuller of speed, and splendour, and mirth.
I was cloudy, and sullen, and cold,
Like a frozen chaos uprolled,   30
Till by the spirit of the mighty dead
My heart grew warm. I feed on whom I fed.

'Ay, alive and still bold,' muttered Earth,
    'Napoleon's fierce spirit rolled,
    In terror and blood and gold,   35
A torrent of ruin to death from his birth.
Leave the millions who follow to mould
The metal before it be cold;
And weave into his shame, which like the dead
Shrouds me, the hopes that from his glory fled.   40

SONNET: POLITICAL GREATNESS

Nor happiness, nor majesty, nor fame,
Nor peace, nor strength, nor skill in arms or arts,
Shepherd those herds whom tyranny makes tame;
Verse echoes not one beating of their hearts,
History is but the shadow of their shame,   5
Art veils her glass, or from the pageant starts
As to oblivion their blind millions fleet,
Staining that Heaven with obscene imagery
Of their own likeness. What are numbers knit
By force or custom? Man who man would be,   10
Must rule the empire of himself; in it
Must be supreme, establishing his throne
On vanquished will, quelling the anarchy
Of hopes and fears, being himself alone.

THE AZIOLA

I

'Do you not hear the Aziola cry?
    Methinks she must be nigh,'
    Said Mary, as we sate
In dusk, ere stars were lit, or candles brought;
    And I, who thought   5
    This Aziola was some tedious woman,
    Asked, 'Who is Aziola?' How elate
I felt to know that it was nothing human,
    No mockery of myself to fear or hate:
    And Mary saw my soul,   10
And laughed, and said, 'Disquiet yourself not;
    'Tis nothing but a little downy owl.'

II

Sad Aziola! many an eventide
   Thy music I had heard
By wood and stream, meadow and mountain-side,   15
   And fields and marshes wide,—
Such as nor voice, nor lute, nor wind, nor bird,
   The soul ever stirred;
Unlike and far sweeter than them all.
Sad Aziola! from that moment I   20
   Loved thee and thy sad cry.

A LAMENT

I

O WORLD! O life! O time!
On whose last steps I climb,
   Trembling at that where I had stood before;
When will return the glory of your prime?
     No more—Oh, never more!   5

II

Out of the day and night
A joy has taken flight;
   Fresh spring, and summer, and winter hoar,
Move my faint heart with grief, but with delight
     No more—Oh, never more!   10

REMEMBRANCE

I

SWIFTER far than summer's flight—
Swifter far than youth's delight—
Swifter far than happy night,
   Art thou come and gone—
As the earth when leaves are dead,   5
As the night when sleep is sped,
As the heart when joy is fled,
   I am left lone, alone.

II

The swallow summer comes again—
The owlet night resumes her reign—
But the wild-swan youth is fain   11
To fly with thee, false as thou.—
My heart each day desires the morrow;
Sleep itself is turned to sorrow;
Vainly would my winter borrow   15
   Sunny leaves from any bough.

II

Lilies for a bridal bed—
Roses for a matron's head—
Violets for a maiden dead—
   Pansies let *my* flowers be: 20
On the living grave I bear
Scatter them without a tear—
Let no friend, however dear,
   Waste one hope, one fear for me.

TO EDWARD WILLIAMS

I

THE serpent is shut out from Paradise.
    The wounded deer must seek the herb no more
      In which its heart-cure lies:
    The widowed dove must cease to haunt a bower
Like that from which its mate with feignèd sighs   5
      Fled in the April hour.
    I too must seldom seek again
Near happy friends a mitigated pain.

II

Of hatred I am proud,—with scorn content;
    Indifference, that once hurt me, now is grown   10
      Itself indifferent;
But, not to speak of love, pity alone
Can break a spirit already more than bent.
      The miserable one
    Turns the mind's poison into food,—   15
Its medicine is tears,—its evil good.

III

Therefore, if now ι see you seldomer,
    Dear friends, dear *friend!* know that I only fly
      Your looks, because they stir
    Griefs that should sleep, and hopes that cannot die: 20
The very comfort that they minister
      I scarce can bear, yet I,
    So deeply is the arrow gone,
Should quickly perish if it were withdrawn.

IV

When I return to my cold home, you ask   25
    Why I am not as I have ever been.
    You spoil me for the task
Of acting a forced part in life's dull scene,—
Of wearing on my brow the idle mask
      Of author, great or mean,   30
    In the world's carnival. I sought
Peace thus, and but in you I found it not.

V

Full half an hour, to-day, I tried my lot
    With various flowers, and every one still said,
      'She loves me—loves me not.'   35
    And if this meant a vision long since fled—
If it meant fortune, fame, or peace of thought—
      If it meant,—but I dread

To speak what you may know too well:
Still there was truth in the sad oracle.   40

VI

The crane o'er seas and forests seeks her home;
　　No bird so wild but has its quiet nest,
　　　When it no more would roam;
　　The sleepless billows on the ocean's breast
Break like a bursting heart, and die in foam,   45
　　　And thus at length find rest:
　　Doubtless there is a place of peace
Where *my* weak heart and all its throbs will cease.

VII

I asked her, yesterday, if she believed
　　That I had resolution. One who *had*   50
　　　Would ne'er have thus relieved
　　His heart with words,—but what his judgement bade
Would do, and leave the scorner unrelieved.
　　　These verses are too sad
　　To send to you, but that I know,   55
Happy yourself, you feel another's woe.

TO ———

I

One word is too often profaned
　　For me to profane it,
One feeling too falsely disdained
　　For thee to disdain it;
One hope is too like despair   5
　　For prudence to smother,
And pity from thee more dear
　　Than that from another.

II

I can give not what men call love,
　　But wilt thou accept not   10
The worship the heart lifts above
　　And the Heavens reject not,—
The desire of the moth for the star,
　　Of the night for the morrow,
The devotion to something afar   15
　　From the sphere of our sorrow?

TO ———

I

When passion's trance is overpast,
If tenderness and truth could last,
Or live, whilst all wild feelings keep
Some mortal slumber, dark and deep,
I should not weep, I should not weep!   5

II

It were enough to feel, to see,
Thy soft eyes gazing tenderly,

And dream the rest—and burn and be
The secret food of fires unseen,
Couldst thou but be as thou hast been.   10

III

After the slumber of the year
The woodland violets reappear;
All things revive in field or grove,
And sky and sea, but two, which move
And form all others, life and love.   15

A BRIDAL SONG

I

THE golden gates of Sleep unbar
  Where Strength and Beauty, met
    together,
Kindle their image like a star
  In a sea of glassy weather!
Night, with all thy stars look
  down,—   5
  Darkness, weep thy holiest
    dew,—
Never smiled the inconstant moon
  On a pair so true.

Let eyes not see their own delight;—   9
Haste, swift Hour, and thy flight
    Oft renew.

II

Fairies, sprites, and angels, keep
  her!
  Holy stars, permit no wrong!
And return to wake the sleeper,
    Dawn,—ere it be long! 15
O joy! O fear! what will be done
In the absence of the sun!
    Come along!

EPITHALAMIUM

ANOTHER VERSION OF THE PRECEDING

NIGHT, with all thine eyes look
  down!
Darkness shed its holiest dew!
When ever smiled the inconstant
  moon
  On a pair so true?
Hence, coy hour! and quench thy
  light,   5
Lest eyes see their own delight!
Hence, swift hour! and thy loved
  flight
    Oft renew.

Boys.

O joy! O fear! what may be done
In the absence of the sun?   10
    Come along!
The golden gates of sleep unbar!
  When strength and beauty meet
    together,
Kindles their image like a star
  In a sea of glassy weather. 15
Hence, coy hour! and quench thy
  light,
Lest eyes see their own delight!

Hence, swift hour! and thy loved
  flight
    Oft renew.

Girls.

O joy! O fear! what may be done
In the absence of the sun?   21
    Come along!
Fairies! sprites! and angels, keep
  her!
  Holiest powers, permit no
    wrong!
And return, to wake the sleeper, 25
  Dawn, ere it be long.
Hence, swift hour! and quench thy
  light,
Lest eyes see their own delight!
Hence, coy hour! and thy lover
  flight
    Oft renew!   30

Boys and Girls.

O joy! O fear! what will be done
In the absence of the sun?
    Come along!

ANOTHER VERSION OF THE SAME

Boys Sing.

NIGHT! with all thine eyes look
   down!
   Darkness! weep thy holiest dew!
Never smiled the inconstant moon
   On a pair so true.
Haste, coy hour! and quench all
   light,   5
Lest eyes see their own delight!
Haste, swift hour! and thy loved
   flight
   Oft renew!

Girls Sing.

Fairies, sprites, and angels, keep
   her!
   Holy stars! permit no wrong! 10
And return, to wake the sleeper,
   Dawn, ere it be long!
O joy! O fear! there is not one
Of us can guess what may be done
In the absence of the sun:—   15
   Come along!

Boys.

Oh! linger long, thou envious eastern lamp

In the damp
   Caves of the deep!

Girls.

Nay, return, Vesper! urge thy lazy
   car!   20
   Swift unbar
   The gates of Sleep!

Chorus.

The golden gate of Sleep unbar,
   When Strength and Beauty, met
      together,
Kindle their image, like a star   25
   In a sea of glassy weather.
May the purple mist of love
Round them rise, and with them
   move,
Nourishing each tender gem
Which, like flowers, will burst from
   them.   30
As the fruit is to the tree
May their children ever be!

LOVE, HOPE, DESIRE, AND FEAR

. . . . . .
AND many there were hurt by that
   strong boy,
   His name, they said, was Pleas-
      ure,
And near him stood, glorious be-
   yond measure,
Four Ladies who possess all empery
   In earth and air and sea,   5
Nothing that lives from their award
   is free.
   Their names will I declare to
      thee,
   Love, Hope, Desire, and Fear,
   And they the regents are

Of the four elements that frame
   the heart,   10
And each diversely exercised her art
   By force or circumstance or
      sleight
   To prove her dreadful might
   Upon that poor domain.
Desire presented her [false] glass,
   and then   15
   The spirit dwelling there
Was spellbound to embrace what
   seemed so fair
   Within that magic mirror,
   And dazed by that bright
      error,

It would have scorned the [shafts]
   of the avenger,   20
And death, and penitence, and
   danger,
   Had not then silent Fear
   Touched with her palsying
     spear,
So that as if a frozen torrent
The blood was curdled in its cur-
   rent;   25
It dared not speak, even in look or
   motion,
But chained within itself its proud
   devotion.
   Between Desire and Fear thou
     wert
   A wretched thing, poor heart!
Sad was his life who bore thee in
   his breast,   30
   Wild bird for that weak nest.
Till Love even from fierce Desire
   it bought,
And from the very wound of tender
   thought
Drew solace, and the pity of sweet
   eyes
Gave strength to bear those gentle
   agonies,   35

Surmount the loss, the terror, and
   the sorrow.
Then Hope approached, she who
   can borrow
For poor to-day, from rich to-
   morrow,
And Fear withdrew, as night
   when day
Descends upon the orient ray, 40
And after long and vain endur-
   ance
The poor heart woke to her as-
   surance.
—At one birth these four were
   born
With the world's forgotten morn,
And from Pleasure still they hold
All it circles, as of old.   46
When, as summer lures the
   swallow,
Pleasure lures the heart to fol-
   low—
O weak heart of little wit!
The fair hand that wounded it, 50
Seeking, like a panting hare,
Refuge in the lynx's lair,
Love, Desire, Hope, and Fear,
   Ever will be near.

FRAGMENTS WRITTEN FOR HELLAS

I

FAIREST of the Destinies,
Disarray thy dazzling eyes:
Keener far thy lightnings are
   Than the wingèd [bolts] thou
     bearest,
   And the smile thou wearest   5
Wraps thee as a star
   Is wrapped in light.

II

Could Arethuse to her forsaken urn
From Alpheus and the bitter Doris
   run,
   Or could the morning shafts of
   purest light   10

Again into the quivers of the Sun
Be gathered—could one thought
    from its wild flight
Return into the temple of the brain
   Without a change, without a
    stain,—
     Could aught that is, ever
     again   15
Be what it once has ceased to
   be.
       Greece might again be
    free!

III

A star has fallen upon the earth
Mid the benighted nations,

A quenchless atom of immortal
  light,   20
A living spark of Night,
A cresset shaken from the constel-
  lations.
Swifter than the thunder fell
To the heart of Earth, the well
Where its pulses flow and beat, 25
And unextinct in that cold source
Burns, and on   course
Guides the sphere which is its
  prison,

Like an angelic spirit pent
  In a form of mortal birth, 30
Till, as a spirit half-arisen
  Shatters its charnel, it has
   rent,
 In the rapture of its mirth,
The thin and painted garment of
  the Earth,   34
Ruining its chaos—a fierce breath
Consuming all its forms of living
  death.

FRAGMENT: 'I WOULD NOT BE A KING'

I WOULD not be a king—enough
 Of woe it is to love;
The path to power is steep and
 rough,
 And tempests reign above.
I would not climb the imperial
 throne;   5

'Tis built on ice which fortune's sun
 Thaws in the height of noon.
Then farewell, king, yet were I
 one,
 Care would not come so soon.
Would he and I were far away 10
Keeping flocks on Himalay!

GINEVRA

WILD, pale, and wonder-stricken, even as one
Who staggers forth into the air and sun
From the dark chamber of a mortal fever,
Bewildered, and incapable, and ever
Fancying strange comments in her dizzy brain 5
Of usual shapes, till the familiar train
Of objects and of persons passed like things
Strange as a dreamer's mad imaginings,
Ginevra from the nuptial altar went;
The vows to which her lips had sworn assent 10
Rung in her brain still with a jarring din,
Deafening the lost intelligence within.

And so she moved under the bridal veil,
Which made the paleness of her cheek more pale,
And deepened the faint crimson of her mouth,
And darkened her dark locks, as moonlight doth,— 15
And of the gold and jewels glittering there
She scarce felt conscious,—but the weary glare
Lay like a chaos of unwelcome light,
Vexing the sense with gorgeous undelight, 20
A moonbeam in the shadow of a cloud
Was less heavenly fair—her face was bowed,

And as she passed, the diamonds in her hair
Were mirrored in the polished marble stair
Which led from the cathedral to the street;   23
And ever as she went her light fair feet
Erased these images.

The bride-maidens who round her thronging came,
Some with a sense of self-rebuke and shame,
Envying the unenviable; and others   30
Making the joy which should have been another's
Their own by gentle sympathy; and some
Sighing to think of an unhappy home:
Some few admiring what can ever lure
Maidens to leave the heaven serene and pure   35
Of parents' smiles for life's great cheat; a thing
Bitter to taste, sweet in imagining.

But they are all dispersed—and, lo! she stands
Looking in idle grief on her white hands,
Alone within the garden now her own;   40
And through the sunny air, with jangling tone,
The music of the merry marriage-bells,
Killing the azure silence, sinks and swells;—
Absorbed like one within a dream who dreams
That he is dreaming, until slumber seems   45
A mockery of itself—when suddenly
Antonio stood before her, pale as she.
With agony, with sorrow, and with pride,
He lifted his wan eyes upon the bride,
And said—'Is this thy faith?' and then as one   50
Whose sleeping face is stricken by the sun
With light like a harsh voice, which bids him rise
And look upon his day of life with eyes
Which weep in vain that they can dream no more,
Ginevra saw her lover, and forbore   55
To shriek or faint, and checked the stifling blood
Rushing upon her heart, and unsubdued
Said—'Friend, if earthly violence or ill,
Suspicion, doubt, or the tyrannic will
Of parents, chance or custom, time or change,   60
Or circumstance, or terror, or revenge,
Or wildered looks, or words, or evil speech,
With all their stings and venom can impeach
Our love,—we love not:—if the grave which hides
The victim from the tyrant, and divides   65
The cheek that whitens from the eyes that dart
Imperious inquisition to the heart

That is another's, could dissever ours,
We love not.'—'What! do not the silent hours
Beckon thee to Gherardi's bridal bed?   70
Is not that ring'—a pledge, he would have said,
Of broken vows, but she with patient look
The golden circle from her finger took,
And said—'Accept this token of my faith,
The pledge of vows to be absolved by death;   75
And I am dead or shall be soon—my knell
Will mix its music with that merry bell,
Does it not sound as if they sweetly said
"We toll a corpse out of the marriage-bed"?
The flowers upon my bridal chamber strewn   80
Will serve unfaded for my bier—so soon
That even the dying violet will not die
Before Ginevra.' The strong fantasy
Had made her accents weaker and more weak,
And quenched the crimson life upon her cheek,   85
And glazed her eyes, and spread an atmosphere
Round her, which chilled the burning noon with fear,
Making her but an image of the thought
Which, like a prophet or a shadow, brought
News of the terrors of the coming time.   90
Like an accuser branded with the crime
He would have cast on a belovèd friend,
Whose dying eyes reproach not to the end
The pale betrayer—he then with vain repentance
Would share, he cannot now avert, the sentence—   95
Antonio stood and would have spoken, when
The compound voice of women and of men
Was heard approaching; he retired, while she
Was led amid the admiring company
Back to the palace,—and her maidens soon   100
Changed her attire for the afternoon,
And left her at her own request to keep
An hour of quiet and rest:—like one asleep
With open eyes and folded hands she lay,
Pale in the light of the declining day.   105

    Meanwhile the day sinks fast, the sun is set,
And in the lighted hall the guests are met;
The beautiful looked lovelier in the light
Of love, and admiration, and delight
Reflected from a thousand hearts and eyes,   110
Kindling a momentary Paradise.
This crowd is safer than the silent wood,
Where love's own doubts disturb the solitude;

On frozen hearts the fiery rain of wine
Falls, and the dew of music more divine   115
Tempers the deep emotions of the time
To spirits cradled in a sunny clime:—
How many meet, who never yet have met,
To part too soon, but never to forget.
How many saw the beauty, power and wit   120
Of looks and words which ne'er enchanted yet;
But life's familiar veil was now withdrawn,
As the world leaps before an earthquake's dawn,
And unprophetic of the coming hours,
The matin winds from the expanded flowers   125
Scatter their hoarded incense, and awaken
The earth, until the dewy sleep is shaken
From every living heart which it possesses,
Through seas and winds, cities and wildernesses,
As if the future and the past were all   130
Treasured i' the instant;—so Gherardi's hall
Laughed in the mirth of its lord's festival,
Till some one asked—'Where is the Bride?' And then
A bridesmaid went,—and ere she came again
A silence fell upon the guests—a pause   135
Of expectation, as when beauty awes
All hearts with its approach, though unbeheld,
Then wonder, and then fear that wonder quelled;—
For whispers passed from mouth to ear which drew
The colour from the hearer's cheeks, and flew   140
Louder and swifter round the company;
And then Gherardi entered with an eye
Of ostentatious trouble, and a crowd
Surrounded him, and some were weeping loud.

  They found Ginevra dead! if it be death   145
To lie without motion, or pulse, or breath,
With waxen cheeks, and limbs cold, stiff, and white,
And open eyes, whose fixed and glassy light
Mocked at the speculation they had owned.
If it be death, when there is felt around   150
A smell of clay, a pale and icy glare,
And silence, and a sense that lifts the hair
From the scalp to the ankles, as it were
Corruption from the spirit passing forth,
And giving all it shrouded to the earth,   155
And leaving as swift lightning in its flight
Ashes, and smoke, and darkness: in our night
Of thought we know thus much of death,—no more
Than the unborn dream of our life before

Their barks are wrecked on its inhospitable shore.   160
The marriage feast and its solemnity
Was turned to funeral pomp—the company,
With heavy hearts and looks, broke up; nor they
Who loved the dead went weeping on their way
Alone, but sorrow mixed with sad surprise   165
Loosened the springs of pity in all eyes,
On which that form, whose fate they weep in vain,
Will never, thought they, kindle smiles again.
The lamps which, half extinguished in their haste,
Gleamed few and faint o'er the abandoned feast,   170
Showed as it were within the vaulted room
A cloud of sorrow hanging, as if gloom
Had passed out of men's minds into the air.
Some few yet stood around Gherardi there,
Friends and relations of the dead,—and he,   175
A loveless man, accepted torpidly
The consolation that he wanted not;
Awe in the place of grief within him wrought.
Their whispers made the solemn silence seem
More still—some wept, . . .   180
Some melted into tears without a sob,
And some with hearts that might be heard to throb
Leaned on the table, and at intervals
Shuddered to hear through the deserted halls
And corridors the thrilling shrieks which came   185
Upon the breeze of night, that shook the flame
Of every torch and taper as it swept
From out the chamber where the women kept;—
Their tears fell on the dear companion cold
Of pleasures now departed; then was knolled   190
The bell of death, and soon the priests arrived,
And finding Death their penitent had shrived,
Returned like ravens from a corpse whereon
A vulture has just feasted to the bone.
And then the mourning women came.—   195

THE DIRGE

Old winter was gone
In his weakness back to the mountains hoar,
    And the spring came down
From the planet that hovers upon the shore
    Where the sea of sunlight encroaches   200
On the limits of wintry night;—
If the land. and the air, and the sea,

Rejoice not when spring approaches,
  We did not rejoice in thee,
        Ginevra!   205

    She is still, she is cold
        On the bridal couch,
  One step to the white deathbed,
        And one to the bier,
  And one to the charnel—and one, oh where?   210
        The dark arrow fled
          In the noon.

Ere the sun through heaven once more has rolled,
  The rats in her heart
    Will have made their nest,   215
  And the worms be alive in her golden hair,
  While the Spirit that guides the sun,
    Sits throned in his flaming chair,
        She shall sleep.

EVENING: PONTE AL MARE, PISA

I

THE sun is set; the swallows are asleep;
    The bats are flitting fast in the gray air;
The slow soft toads out of damp corners creep,
    And evening's breath, wandering here and there
Over the quivering surface of the stream,   5
Wakes not one ripple from its summer dream.

II

There is no dew on the dry grass to-night,
    Nor damp within the shadow of the trees;
The wind is intermitting, dry, and light;
    And in the inconstant motion of the breeze   10
The dust and straws are driven up and down,
And whirled about the pavement of the town.

III

Within the surface of the fleeting river
    The wrinkled image of the city lay,
Immovably unquiet, and forever   15
    It trembles, but it never fades away;
Go to the . . .
You, being changed, will find it then as now.

IV

The chasm in which the sun has sunk is shut
  By darkest barriers of cinereous cloud,   20
Like mountain over mountain huddled—but
  Growing and moving upwards in a crowd,
And over it a space of watery blue,
Which the keen evening star is shining through.

THE BOAT ON THE SERCHIO

Our boat is asleep on Serchio's stream,
Its sails are folded like thoughts in a dream,
The helm sways idly, hither and thither;
  Dominic, the boatman, has brought the mast,
  And the oars, and the sails; but 'tis sleeping fast,   5
Like a beast, unconscious of its tether.

The stars burnt out in the pale blue air,
And the thin white moon lay withering there;
To tower, and cavern, and rift, and tree,
The owl and the bat fled drowsily.   10
Day had kindled the dewy woods,
  And the rocks above and the stream below,
And the vapours in their multitudes,
  And the Apennine's shroud of summer snow,
And clothed with light of aëry gold   15
The mists in their eastern caves uprolled.

Day had awakened all things that be,
The lark and the thrush and the swallow free,
  And the milkmaid's song and the mower's scythe,
And the matin-bell and the mountain bee: 20
Fireflies were quenched on the dewy corn,
  Glow-worms went out on the river's brim,
  Like lamps which a student forgets to trim:
The beetle forgot to wind his horn,
  The crickets were still in the meadow and hill: 25
Like a flock of rooks at a farmer's gun
Night's dreams and terrors, every one,
Fled from the brains which are their prey
From the lamp's death to the morning ray.

All rose to do the task He set to each,   30
  Who shaped us to His ends and not our own;
The million rose to learn, and one to teach
  What none yet ever knew or can be known.
    And many rose

Whose woe was such that fear became desire;— 35
Melchior and Lionel were not among those;
They from the throng of men had stepped aside,
And made their home under the green hill-side.
It was that hill, whose intervening brow
  Screens Lucca from the Pisan's envious eye, 40
Which the circumfluous plain waving below,
  Like a wide lake of green fertility,
With streams and fields and marshes bare,
  Divides from the far Apennines—which lie
Islanded in the immeasurable air. 45

'What think you, as she lies in her green cove,
Our little sleeping boat is dreaming of?'
'If morning dreams are true, why I should guess
That she was dreaming of our idleness,
And of the miles of watery way 50
We should have led her by this time of day.'—

  'Never mind,' said Lionel,
'Give care to the winds, they can bear it well
  About yon poplar-tops; and see
The white clouds are driving merrily, 55
And the stars we miss this morn will light
More willingly our return to-night.—
How it whistles, Dominic's long black hair!
List, my dear fellow; the breeze blows fair:
Hear how it sings into the air—' 60

—'Of us and of our lazy motions,'
  Impatiently said Melchior,
'If I can guess a boat's emotions;
  And how we ought, two hours before,
To have been the devil knows where.' 65
And then, in such transalpine Tuscan
As would have killed a Della-Cruscan,

.   .   .   .   .   .   °   ₈

So, Lionel according to his art
  Weaving his idle words, Melchior said:
'She dreams that we are not yet out of bed; 70
We'll put a soul into her, and a heart
Which like a dove chased by a dove shall beat.'

.   .   .   .

  'Ay, heave the ballast overboard,
  And stow the eatables in the aft locker.'
'Would not this keg be best a little lowered?' 75
'No, now all's right.' 'Those bottles of warm tea—

(Give me some straw)—must be stowed tenderly;
Such as we used, in summer after six,
To cram in greatcoat pockets, and to mix
Hard eggs and radishes and rolls at Eton, 80
And, couched on stolen hay in those green harbours
Farmers called gaps, and we schoolboys called arbours,
Would feast till eight.'

.   .   .   .

With a bottle in one hand,
As if his very soul were at a stand, 85
Lionel stood—when Melchior brought him steady:—
'Sit at the helm—fasten this sheet—all ready!'

The chain is loosed, the sails are spread,
  The living breath is fresh behind,
As, with dews and sunrise fed, 90
  Comes the laughing morning wind;—
The sails are full, the boat makes head
Against the Serchio's torrent fierce,
Then flags with intermitting course,
  And hangs upon the wave, and stems 95
  The tempest of the . . .
Which fervid from its mountain source
Shallow, smooth and strong doth come,—
Swift as fire, tempestuously
It sweeps into the affrighted sea 100
In morning's smile its eddies coil,
Its billows sparkle, toss and boil,
Torturing all its quiet light
Into columns fierce and bright.

The Serchio, twisting forth 105
Between the marble barriers which it clove
  At Ripafratta, leads through the dread chasm
The wave that died the death which lovers love,
  Living in what it sought; as if this spasm
Had not yet passed, the toppling mountains cling, 110
  But the clear stream in full enthusiasm
Pours itself on the plain, then wandering
  Down one clear path of effluence crystalline
Sends its superfluous waves, that they may fling
  At Arno's feet tribute of corn and wine; 115
Then, through the pestilential deserts wild
  Of tangled marsh and woods of stunted pine,
It rushes to the Ocean.

MUSIC

I

I PANT for the music which is divine,
   My heart in its thirst is a dying flower;
Pour forth the sound like enchanted wine,
   Loosen the notes in a silver shower;
Like a herbless plain, for the gentle rain,   5
I gasp, I faint, till they wake again.

II

Let me drink of the spirit of that sweet sound,
   More, oh more,—I am thirsting yet;
It loosens the serpent which care has bound
   Upon my heart to stifle it;   10
The dissolving strain, through every vein,
   Passes into my heart and brain.

III

As the scent of a violet withered up,
   Which grew by the brink of a silver lake,
When the hot noon has drained its dewy cup,   15
   And mist there was none its thirst to slake—
And the violet lay dead while the odour flew
On the wings of the wind o'er the waters blue—

IV

As one who drinks from a charmèd cup
   Of foaming, and sparkling, and murmuring wine,   20
Whom, a mighty Enchantress filling up,
   Invites to love with her kiss divine . . .

SONNET TO BYRON

[I AM afraid these verses will not please you, but]
If I esteemed you less, Envy would kill
Pleasure, and leave to Wonder and Despair
The ministration of the thoughts that fill
The mind which, like a worm whose life may share   5
A portion of the unapproachable,
Marks your creations rise as fast and fair
As perfect worlds at the Creator's will.
But such is my regard that nor your power
To soar above the heights where others [climb],
Nor fame, that shadow of the unborn hour   10
Cast from the envious future on the time,
Move one regret for his unhonoured name
Who dares these words:—the worm beneath the sod
May lift itself in homage of the God.

FRAGMENT ON KEATS

WHO DESIRED THAT ON HIS TOMB SHOULD BE INSCRIBED—

'HERE lieth One whose name was writ on water.'
But, ere the breath that could erase it blew,
Death, in remorse for that fell slaughter,
Death, the immortalizing winter, flew
Athwart the stream,—and time's printless torrent grew   5
A scroll of crystal, blazoning the name
Of Adonais!

FRAGMENT: 'METHOUGHT I WAS A BILLOW IN THE CROWD'

METHOUGHT I was a billow in the crowd
Of common men, that stream without a shore,
That ocean which at once is deaf and loud;
That I, a man, stood amid many more
By a wayside . . . , which the aspect bore   5
Of some imperial metropolis,
Where mighty shapes—pyramid, dome, and tower—
Gleamed like a pile of crags—

TO-MORROW

WHERE art thou, beloved To-morrow?
When young and old, and strong and weak,
Rich and poor, through joy and sorrow,
Thy sweet smiles we ever seek,—
In thy place—ah! well-a-day!   5
We find the thing we fled—To-day.

STANZA

IF I walk in Autumn's even
While the dead leaves pass,
If I look on Spring's soft heaven,—
Something is not there which was.
Winter's wondrous frost and snow,   5
Summer's clouds, where are they now?

FRAGMENT: A WANDERER

HE wanders, like a day-appearing dream,
Through the dim wildernesses of the mind;
Through desert woods and tracts, which seem
Like ocean, homeless, boundless, unconfined.

FRAGMENT: LIFE ROUNDED WITH SLEEP

THE babe is at peace within the womb;
The corpse is at rest within the tomb:
We begin in what we end.

FRAGMENT: 'I FAINT, I PERISH WITH MY LOVE!'

I FAINT, I perish with my love! I grow
Frail as a cloud whose [splendours] pale
Under the evening's ever-changing glow:
I die like mist upon the gale,
And like a wave under the calm I fail.   5

FRAGMENT: THE LADY OF THE SOUTH

FAINT with love, the Lady of the South
Lay in the paradise of Lebanon
Under a heaven of cedar boughs: the drouth
Of love was on her lips; the light was gone
Out of her eyes—   5

FRAGMENT: ZEPHYRUS THE AWAKENER

COME, thou awakener of the spirit's ocean,
Zephyr, whom to thy cloud or cave
No thought can trace! speed with thy gentle motion!

FRAGMENT: RAIN

THE gentleness of rain was in the wind.

FRAGMENT: 'WHEN SOFT WINDS AND SUNNY SKIES'

WHEN soft winds and sunny skies
With the green earth harmonize,
And the young and dewy dawn,
Bold as an unhunted fawn,
Up the windless heaven is gone,—
Laugh—for ambushed in the day,—
Clouds and whirlwinds watch their prey.

FRAGMENT: 'AND THAT I WALK THUS PROUDLY CROWNED'

AND that I walk thus proudly crowned withal
Is that 'tis my distinction; if I fall,
I shall not weep out of the vital day,
To-morrow dust, nor wear a dull decay.

FRAGMENT: 'THE RUDE WIND IS SINGING'

THE rude wind is singing
   The dirge of the music dead;
The cold worms are clinging
   Where kisses were lately fed.

FRAGMENT: 'GREAT SPIRIT'

GREAT Spirit whom the sea of boundless thought
   Nurtures within its unimagined caves,
In which thou sittest sole, as in my mind,
   Giving a voice to its mysterious waves—

FRAGMENT: 'O THOU IMMORTAL DEITY'

O THOU immortal deity
Whose throne is in the depth of human thought,
   I do adjure thy power and thee
By all that man may be, by all that he is not,
   By all that he has been and yet must be!   5

FRAGMENT: THE FALSE LAUREL AND THE TRUE

'WHAT art thou, Presumptuous, who profanest
   The wreath to mighty poets only due,
Even whilst like a forgotten moon thou wanest?
   Touch not those leaves which for the eternal few
Who wander o'er the Paradise of fame,   5
   In sacred dedication ever grew:
One of the crowd thou art without a name.'
   'Ah, friend, 'tis the false laurel that I wear;
Bright though it seem, it is not the same
   As that which bound Milton's immortal hair;   10
Its dew is poison; and the hopes that quicken
   Under its chilling shade, though seeming fair,
Are flowers which die almost before they sicken.'

FRAGMENT: MAY THE LIMNER

WHEN May is painting with her colours gay
The landscape sketched by April her sweet twin ...

FRAGMENT: BEAUTY'S HALO

THY beauty hangs around thee like
   Splendour around the moon—
Thy voice, as silver bells that strike
   Upon

FRAGMENT: 'THE DEATH KNELL IS RINGING'

THE death knell is ringing
The raven is singing
The earth worm is creeping
The mourners are weeping
Ding dong, bell—   5

FRAGMENT: 'I STOOD UPON A HEAVEN-CLEAVING TURRET'

I STOOD upon a heaven-cleaving turret
    Which overlooked a wide Metropolis—
And in the temple of my heart my Spirit
    Lay prostrate, and with parted lips did kiss
    The dust of Desolations [altar] hearth—   5
    And with a voice too faint to falter
It shook that trembling fane with its weak prayer
'Twas noon,—the sleeping skies were blue
The city

NOTE ON POEMS OF 1821, BY MRS. SHELLEY

MY task becomes inexpressibly painful as the year draws near that
which sealed our earthly fate, and each poem, and each event it records,
has a real or mysterious connexion with the fatal catastrophe. I feel that
I am incapable of putting on paper the history of those times. The heart
of the man, abhorred of the poet, who could

> 'peep and botanize
> Upon his mother's grave,'

does not appear to me more inexplicably framed than that of one who
can dissect and probe past woes, and repeat to the public ear the groans
drawn from them in the throes of their agony.

The year 1821 was spent in Pisa, or at the Baths of San Giuliano. We
were not, as our wont had been, alone; friends had gathered round us.
Nearly all are dead, and, when Memory recurs to the past, she wanders
among tombs. The genius, with all his blighting errors and mighty
powers; the companion of Shelley's ocean-wanderings, and the sharer of
his fate, than whom no man ever existed more gentle, generous, and fearless; and others, who found in Shelley's society, and in his great knowledge and warm sympathy, delight, instruction, and solace; have joined
him beyond the grave. A few survive who have felt life a desert since he
left it. What misfortune can equal death? Change can convert every other
into a blessing, or heal its sting—death alone has no cure. It shakes the
foundations of the earth on which we tread; it destroys its beauty; it
casts down our shelter; it exposes us bare to desolation. When those we
love have passed into eternity, 'life is the desert and the solitude' in which
we are forced to linger—but never find comfort more.

There is much in the *Adonais* which seems now more applicable to Shelley himself than to the young and gifted poet whom he mourned. The poetic view he takes of death, and the lofty scorn he displays towards his calumniators, are as a prophecy on his own destiny when received among immortal names, and the poisonous breath of critics has vanished into emptiness before the fame he inherits.

Shelley's favourite taste was boating; when living near the Thames or by the Lake of Geneva, much of his life was spent on the water. On the shore of every lake or stream or sea near which he dwelt, he had a boat moored. He had latterly enjoyed this pleasure again. There are no pleasure-boats on the Arno; and the shallowness of its waters (except in winter-time, when the stream is too turbid and impetuous for boating) rendered it difficult to get any skiff light enough to float. Shelley, however, overcame the difficulty; he, together with a friend, contrived a boat such as the huntsmen carry about with them in the Maremma, to cross the sluggish but deep streams that intersect the forests,—a boat of laths and pitched canvas. It held three persons; and he was often seen on the Arno in it, to the horror of the Italians, who remonstrated on the danger and could not understand how any one could take pleasure in an exercise that risked life. 'Ma va per la vita!' they exclaimed. I little thought how true their words would prove. He once ventured, with a friend, on the glassy sea of a calm day, down the Arno and round the coast to Leghorn, which, by keeping close in shore, was very practicable. They returned to Pisa by the canal, when, missing the direct cut, they got entangled among weeds, and the boat upset; a wetting was all the harm done, except that the intense cold of his drenched clothes made Shelley faint. Once I went down with him to the mouth of the Arno, where the stream, then high and swift, met the tideless sea, and disturbed its sluggish waters. It was a waste and dreary scene; the desert sand stretched into a point surrounded by waves that broke idly though perpetually around; it was a scene very similar to Lido, of which he had said—

> 'I love all waste
> And solitary places; where we taste
> The pleasure of believing what we see
> Is boundless, as we wish our souls to be:
> And such was this wide ocean, and this shore
> More barren than its billows.'

Our little boat was of greater use, unaccompanied by any danger, when we removed to the Baths. Some friends lived at the village of Pugnano, four miles off, and we went to and fro to see them, in our boat, by the canal; which, fed by the Serchio, was, though an artificial, a full and picturesque stream, making its way under verdant banks, sheltered by trees that dipped their boughs into the murmuring waters. By day, multitudes of ephemera darted to and fro on the surface; at night, the fireflies came out among the shrubs on the banks; the cicale at noon-day kept up their hum; the aziola cooed in the quiet evening. It was a pleasant summer, bright in all but Shelley's health and inconstant spirits; yet he enjoyed himself greatly, and became more and more attached to the part of the country where chance appeared to cast us. Sometimes he projected taking a farm situated on the height of one of the near hills, surrounded by chestnut and pine woods, and overlooking a wide extent of country: or settling still farther in the maritime Apennines, at Massa. Several of his slighter and unfinished poems were inspired by these scenes, and by the companions around us. It is the nature of that poetry, however, which overflows from the soul oftener to express sorrow and regret than joy; for it is when oppressed by the weight of life, and away from those he loves, that the poet has recourse to the solace of expression in verse.

Still, Shelley's passion was the ocean; and he wished that our summers, instead of being passed among the hills near Pisa, should be spent on the shores of the sea. It was very difficult to find a spot. We shrank from Naples from a fear that the heats would disagree with Percy: Leghorn had lost its only attraction, since our friends who had resided there were returned to England; and, Monte Nero being the resort of many English, we did not wish to find ourselves in the midst of a colony of chance travellers. No one then thought it possible to reside at Via Reggio, which latterly has become a summer resort. The low lands and bad air of Maremma stretch the whole length of the western shores of the Mediterranean, till broken by the rocks and hills of Spezia. It was a vague idea, but Shelley suggested an excursion to Spezia, to see whether it would be feasible to spend a summer there. The beauty of the bay enchanted him. We saw no house to suit us; but the notion took root, and many circumstances, enchained as by fatality, occurred to urge him to execute it.

He looked forward this autumn with great pleasure to the prospect of a visit from Leigh Hunt. When Shelley visited Lord Byron at Ravenna, the latter had suggested his coming out, together with the plan of a periodical work in which they should all join. Shelley saw a prospect of good for the fortunes of his friend, and pleasure in his society; and instantly exerted himself to have the plan executed. He did not intend himself joining in the work: partly from pride, not wishing to have the air of acquiring readers for his poetry by associating it with the compositions of more popular writers; and also because he might feel shackled in the free expression of his opinions, if any friends were to be compromised. By those opinions, carried even to their utmost extent, he wished to live and die, as being in his conviction not only true, but such as alone would conduce to the moral improvement and happiness of mankind. The sale of the work might meanwhile, either really or supposedly, be injured by the free expression of his thoughts; and this evil he resolved to avoid.

POEMS WRITTEN IN 1822

THE ZUCCA

I

SUMMER was dead and Autumn was expiring,
   And infant Winter laughed upon the land
All cloudlessly and cold;—when I, desiring
   More in this world than any understand,
Wept o'er the beauty, which, like sea retiring,   5
   Had left the earth bare as the wave-worn sand
Of my lorn heart, and o'er the grass and flowers
Pale for the falsehood of the flattering Hours.

II

Summer was dead, but I yet lived to weep
   The instability of all but weeping;   10
And on the Earth lulled in her winter sleep
   I woke, and envied her as she was sleeping.
Too happy Earth! over thy face shall creep
   The wakening vernal airs, until thou, leaping
From unremembered dreams, shalt   see   15
No death divide thy immortality.

III

I loved—oh, no, I mean not one of ye,
   Or any earthly one, though ye are dear
As human heart to human heart may be;—
   I loved, I know not what—but this low sphere   20
And all that it contains, contains not thee,
   Thou, whom, seen nowhere, I feel everywhere.
From Heaven and Earth, and all that in them are,
Veiled art thou, like a   star.

IV

By Heaven and Earth, from all whose shapes thou flowest, 25
   Neither to be contained, delayed, nor hidden;
Making divine the loftiest and the lowest,
   When for a moment thou art not forbidden
To live within the life which thou bestowest;
   And leaving noblest things vacant and chidden,   30
Cold as a corpse after the spirit's flight,
Blank as the sun after the birth of night.

V

In winds, and trees, and streams, and all things common,
   In music and the sweet unconscious tone
Of animals, and voices which are human,   35
   Meant to express some feelings of their own;
In the soft motions and rare smile of woman,
   In flowers and leaves, and in the grass fresh-shewn,
Or dying in the autumn, I the most
Adore thee present or lament thee lost.   40

VI

And thus I went lamenting, when I saw
   A plant upon the river's margin lie,
Like one who loved beyond his nature's law,
   And in despair had cast him down to die;
Its leaves, which had outlived the frost, the thaw   45
   Had blighted; like a heart which hatred's eye
Can blast not, but which pity kills; the dew
Lay on its spotted leaves like tears too true.

VII

The Heavens had wept upon it, but the Earth
   Had crushed it on her unmaternal breast   50

.   .   .   .

VIII

I bore it to my chamber, and I planted
   It in a vase full of the lightest mould;
The winter beams which out of Heaven slanted
   Fell through the window-panes, disrobed of cold,
Upon its leaves and flowers; the stars which panted   55
   In evening for the Day, whose car has rolled
Over the horizon's wave, with looks of light
Smiled on it from the threshold of the night.

IX

The mitigated influences of air
   And light revived the plant, and from it grew   60
Strong leaves and tendrils, and its flowers fair,
   Full as a cup with the vine's burning dew,
O'erflowed with golden colours; an atmosphere
   Of vital warmth enfolded it anew,
And every impulse sent to every part   65
The unbeheld pulsations of its heart

X

Well might the plant grow beautiful and strong,
    Even if the air and sun had smiled not on it;
For one wept o'er it all the winter long
    Tears pure as Heaven's rain, which fell upon it   **70**
Hour after hour; for sounds of softest song
    Mixed with the stringèd melodies that won it
To leave the gentle lips on which it slept,
Had loosed the heart of him who sat and wept.

XI

Had loosed his heart, and shook the leaves and flowers   **75**
    On which he wept, the while the savage storm
Waked by the darkest of December's hours
    Was raving round the chamber hushed and warm;
The birds were shivering in their leafless bowers,
    The fish were frozen in the pools, the form   **80**
Of every summer plant was dead . . .
Whilst this . . .

.   .   .   .   .   .

THE MAGNETIC LADY TO HER PATIENT

I

'SLEEP, sleep on! forget thy pain;
    My hand is on thy brow,
My spirit on thy brain;
My pity on thy heart, poor friend;
    And from my fingers flow   5
The powers of life, and like a sign,
    Seal thee from thine hour of woe;
And brood on thee, but may not blend
    With thine.

II

'Sleep, sleep on! I love thee not;   10
    But when I think that he
Who made and makes my lot
As full of flowers as thine of weeds,
    Might have been lost like thee;
And that a hand which was not mine   15
    Might then have charmed his agony
As I another's—my heart bleeds
    For thine.

III

'Sleep, sleep, and with the slumber of
    The dead and the unborn   20
Forget thy life and love;
Forget that thou must wake forever;
    Forget the world's dull scorn;
Forget lost health, and the divine
    Feelings which died in youth's brief morn;   25
And forget me, for I can never
    Be thine.

IV

'Like a cloud big with a May shower,
    My soul weeps healing rain
On thee, thou withered flower!   30
It breathes mute music on thy sleep,
    Its odour calms thy brain!
Its light within thy gloomy breast

Spreads like a second youth
   again.
By mine thy being is to its deep 35
   Possessed.

V

'The spell is done. How feel you
   now?'
   'Better—Quite well,' replied
The sleeper.—'What would do 39

You good when suffering and
   awake?
   What cure your head and
   side?—'
'What would cure, that would kill
   me, Jane:
And as I must on earth abide
Awhile, yet tempt me not to break
   My chain.'   45

LINES: 'WHEN THE LAMP IS SHATTERED'

I

When the lamp is shattered
The light in the dust lies dead—
When the cloud is scattered
The rainbow's glory is shed.
   When the lute is broken,   5
Sweet tones are remembered not;
   When the lips have spoken,
Loved accents are soon forgot.

II

As music and splendour
Survive not the lamp and the
   lute,   10
The heart's echoes render
No song when the spirit is mute:—
   No song but sad dirges,
Like the wind through a ruined
   cell,
   Or the mournful surges   15
That ring the dead seaman's knell.

III

When hearts have once mingled
Love first leaves the well-built nest;
   The weak one is singled
To endure what it once pos-
   sessed.   20
   O Love! who bewailest
The frailty of all things here,
   Why choose you the frailest
For your cradle, your home, and
   your bier?

IV

Its passions will rock thee   25
As the storms rock the ravens on
   high;
   Bright reason will mock thee,
Like the sun from a wintry sky.
   From thy nest every rafter
Will rot, and thine eagle home 30
   Leave thee naked to laughter,
When leaves fall and cold winds
   come.

TO JANE: THE INVITATION

Best and brightest, come away!
Fairer far than this fair Day,
Which, like thee to those in sorrow,
Comes to bid a sweet good-morrow
To the rough Year just awake   5
In its cradle on the brake.
The brightest hour of unborn
   Spring,
Through the winter wandering,

Found, it seems, the halcyon Morn
To hoar February born.   10
Bending from Heaven, in azure
   mirth,
It kissed the forehead of the
   Earth,
And smiled upon the silent sea,
And bade the frozen streams be
   free,

And waked to music all their foun-
 tains,   15
And breathed upon the frozen
 mountains,
And like a prophetess of May
Strewed flowers upon the barren
 way,
Making the wintry world appear
Like one on whom thou smilest,
 dear.   20

Away, away, from men and towns,
To the wild wood and the downs—
To the silent wilderness
Where the soul need not repress
Its music lest it should not find 25
An echo in another's mind,
While the touch of Nature's art
Harmonizes heart to heart.
I leave this notice on my door
For each accustomed visitor:— 30
'I am gone into the fields
To take what this sweet hour
 yields,—
Reflection, you may come to-mor-
 row,
Sit by the fireside with Sorrow.—
You with the unpaid bill, De-
 spair,—
You, tiresome verse-reciter,
 Care,—   35
I will pay you in the grave,—
Death will listen to your stave.
Expectation too, be off!

To-day is for itself enough; 40
Hope, in pity mock not Woe
With smiles, nor follow where I go;
Long having lived on thy sweet
 food,
At length I find one moment's good
After long pain—with all your love,
This you never told me of.' 46

Radiant Sister of the Day,
Awake! arise! and come away!
To the wild woods and the plains,
And the pools where winter rains 50
Image all their roof of leaves,
Where the pine its garland weaves
Of sapless green and ivy dun
Round stems that never kiss the
 sun;
Where the lawns and pastures be, 55
And the sandhills of the sea;—
Where the melting hoar-frost wets
The daisy-star that never sets,
And wind-flowers, and violets,
Which yet join not scent to hue, 60
Crown the pale year weak and new;
When the night is left behind,
In the deep east, dun and blind,
And the blue noon is over us,
And the multitudinous 65
Billows murmur at our feet,
Where the earth and ocean meet,
And all things seem only one
In the universal sun.

TO JANE: THE RECOLLECTION

I

Now the last day of many days,
 All beautiful and bright as thou,
 The loveliest and the last, is
  dead,
Rise, Memory, and write its praise!
 Up,—to thy wonted work! come,
  trace   5
  The epitaph of glory fled,—

For now the Earth has changed its
  face,
 A frown is on the Heaven's brow.

II

We wandered to the Pine Forest
 That skirts the Ocean's foam, 10
The lightest wind was in its nest,
 The tempest in its home.

The whispering waves were half
    asleep,
The clouds were gone to play,
And on the bosom of the deep   15
    The smile of Heaven lay;
It seemed as if the hour were one
    Sent from beyond the skies,
Which scattered from above the
    sun
    A light of Paradise.   20

III

We paused amid the pines that
    stood
    The giants of the waste,
Tortured by storms to shapes as
    rude
    As serpents interlaced,
And soothed by every azure breath,
    That under Heaven is blown,   26
To harmonies and hues beneath,
    As tender as its own;
Now all the tree-tops lay asleep,
    Like green waves on the sea,   30
As still as in the silent deep
    The ocean woods may be.

IV

How calm it was!—the silence
    there
    By such a chain was bound
That even the busy woodpecker   35
    Made stiller by her sound
The inviolable quietness;
    The breath of peace we drew
With its soft motion made not less
    The calm that round us grew.   40
There seemed from the remotest
    seat
    Of the white mountain waste,
To the soft flower beneath our feet,
    A magic circle traced,—
A spirit interfused around,   45
    A thrilling, silent life.—
To momentary peace it bound
    Our mortal nature's strife;
And still I felt the centre of

The magic circle there   50
Was one fair form that filled with
    love
    The lifeless atmosphere.

V

We paused beside the pools that lie
    Under the forest bough.—
Each seemed as 'twere a little sky 55
    Gulfed in a world below;
A firmament of purple light
    Which in the dark earth lay,
More boundless than the depth of
    night,
    And purer than the day—   60
In which the lovely forests grew,
    As in the upper air,
More perfect both in shape and hue
    Than any spreading there.
There lay the glade and neighbour-
    ing lawn,   65
    And through the dark green wood
The white sun twinkling like the
    dawn
    Out of a speckled cloud.
Sweet views which in our world
    above
    Can never well be seen,   70
Were imaged by the water's love
    Of that fair forest green.
And all was interfused beneath
    With an Elysian glow,
An atmosphere without a breath, 75
    A softer day below.
Like one beloved the scene had lent
    To the dark water's breast,
Its every leaf and lineament
    With more than truth expressed;
Until an envious wind crept by, 81
    Like an unwelcome thought,
Which from the mind's too faithful
    eye
    Blots one dear image out.
Though thou art ever fair and kind,
    The forests ever green,   86
Less oft is peace in Shelley's mind,
    Than calm in waters, seen.

THE PINE FOREST OF THE CASCINE NEAR PISA

DEAREST, best and brightest,
　　Come away,
To the woods and to the fields!
Dearer than this fairest day
Which, like thee to those in sor-
　　row,　　　　　　　　　5
Comes to bid a sweet good-morrow
To the rough Year just awake
In its cradle in the brake.
The eldest of the Hours of Spring,
Into the Winter wandering,　　10
Looks upon the leafless wood,
And the banks all bare and rude;
Found, it seems, this halcyon Morn
In February's bosom born,
Bending from Heaven, in azure
　　mirth,　　　　　　　　15
Kissed the cold forehead of the
　　Earth,
And smiled upon the silent sea,
And bade the frozen streams be
　　free;
And waked to music all the foun-
　　tains,
And breathed upon the rigid moun-
　　tains,　　　　　　　　20
And made the wintry world appear
Like one on whom thou smilest,
　　Dear.

Radiant Sister of the Day,
Awake! arise! and come away!
To the wild woods and the plains, 25
To the pools where winter rains
Image all the roof of leaves,
Where the pine its garland weaves
Sapless, gray, and ivy dun
Round stems that never kiss the
　　sun—　　　　　　　　30
To the sandhills of the sea,
Where the earliest violets be.

Now the last day of many days,
All beautiful and bright as thou,
The loveliest and the last, is
　　dead,　　　　　　　　35

Rise, Memory, and write its praise!
And do thy wonted work and trace
The epitaph of glory fled;
For now the Earth has changed its
　　face,
A frown is on the Heaven's brow. 40

We wandered to the Pine Forest
　　That skirts the Ocean's foam,
The lightest wind was in its nest,
　　The tempest in its home.

The whispering waves were half
　　asleep,　　　　　　　　45
　　The clouds were gone to play,
And on the woods, and on the deep
　　The smile of Heaven lay.

It seemed as if the day were one
　　Sent from beyond the skies,　50
Which shed to earth above the sun
　　A light of Paradise.

We paused amid the pines that
　　stood,
　　The giants of the waste,
Tortured by storms to shapes as
　　rude　　　　　　　　55
　　With stems like serpents inter-
　　　laced.

How calm it was—the silence there
　　By such a chain was bound,
That even the busy woodpecker
　　Made stiller by her sound　60

The inviolable quietness;
　　The breath of peace we drew
With its soft motion made not less
　　The calm that round us grew.

It seemed that from the remotest
　　seat　　　　　　　　65
　　Of the white mountain's waste
To the bright flower beneath our
　　feet,
　　A magic circle traced;—

A spirit interfused around,
  A thinking, silent life; 70
To momentary peace it bound
  Our mortal nature's strife;—

And still, it seemed, the centre of
  The magic circle there,
Was one whose being filled with
    love
  The breathless atmosphere. 76

Were not the crocuses that grew
  Under that ilex-tree
As beautiful in scent and hue
  As ever fed the bee? 80

We stood beneath the pools that lie
  Under the forest bough,
And each seemed like a sky
  Gulfed in a world below;

A purple firmament of light 85
  Which in the dark earth lay,
More boundless than the depth of
    night,
  And clearer than the day—

In which the massy forests grew
  As in the upper air, 90
More perfect both in shape and hue
  Than any waving there.

Like one beloved the scene had lent
  To the dark water's breast

Its every leaf and lineament 95
  With that clear truth expressed;

There lay far glades and neighbour-
    ing lawn,
  And through the dark green
    crowd
The white sun twinkling like the
    dawn
  Under a speckled cloud. 100

Sweet views, which in our world
    above
  Can never well be seen,
Were imaged by the water's love
  Of that fair forest green.

And all was interfused beneath 105
  With an Elysian air,
An atmosphere without a breath,
  A silence sleeping there.

Until a wandering wind crept by,
  Like an unwelcome thought, 110
Which from my mind's too faithful
    eye
  Blots thy bright image out.

For thou art good and dear and
    kind,
  The forest ever green,
But less of peace in S——'s mind,
  Than calm in waters, seen. 116

WITH A GUITAR, TO JANE

ARIEL to Miranda:—Take
This slave of Music, for the sake
Of him who is the slave of thee,
And teach it all the harmony
In which thou canst, and only thou,
Make the delighted spirit glow, 6
Till joy denies itself again,
And, too intense, is turned to pain;
For by permission and command
Of thine own Prince Ferdinand, 10
Poor Ariel sends this silent token
Of more than ever can be spoken;
Your guardian spirit, Ariel, who,
From life to life, must still pursue

Your happiness;—for thus alone 15
Can Ariel ever find his own.
From Prospero's enchanted cell,
As the mighty verses tell,
To the throne of Naples, he
Lit you o'er the trackless sea, 20
Flitting on, your prow before,
Like a living meteor.
When you die, the silent Moon,
In her interlunar swoon,
Is not sadder in her cell 25
Than deserted Ariel.
When you live again on earth,
Like an unseen star of birth,

Ariel guides you o'er the sea
Of life from your nativity.   30
Many changes have been run
Since Ferdinand and you begun
Your course of love, and Ariel still
Has tracked your steps, and served
    your will;
Now, in humbler, happier lot,   35
This is all remembered not;
And now, alas! the poor sprite is
Imprisoned, for some fault of his,
In a body like a grave;—
From you he only dares to crave,   40
For his service and his sorrow,
A smile to-day, a song to-morrow.

The artist who this idol wrought,
To echo all harmonious thought,
Felled a tree, while on the steep   45
The woods were in their winter
    sleep,
Rocked in that repose divine
On the wind-swept Apennine;
And dreaming, some of Autumn
    past,
And some of Spring approaching
    fast,   50
And some of April buds and show-
    ers,
And some of songs in July bowers,
And all of love; and so this tree,—
O that such our death may be!—
Died in sleep, and felt no pain,   55
To live in happier form again:
From which, beneath Heaven's fair-
    est star,

The artist wrought this loved
    Guitar,
And taught it justly to reply,
To all who question skilfully,   60
In language gentle as thine own;
Whispering in enamoured tone
Sweet oracles of woods and dells,
And summer winds in sylvan cells;
For it had learned all harmonies 65
Of the plains and of the skies,
Of the forests and the mountains,
And the many-voicèd fountains;
The clearest echoes of the hills,
The softest notes of falling rills, 70
The melodies of birds and bees,
The murmuring of summer seas,
And pattering rain, and breathing
    dew,
And airs of evening; and it knew
That seldom-heard mysterious
    sound,   75
Which, driven on its diurnal round,
As it floats through boundless day,
Our world enkindles on its way.—
All this it knows, but will not tell
To those who cannot question well
The Spirit that inhabits it;   81
It talks according to the wit
Of its companions; and no more
Is heard than has been felt before,
By those who tempt it to betray 85
These secrets of an elder day:
But, sweetly as its answers will
Flatter hands of perfect skill,
It keeps its highest, holiest tone
For our belovèd Jane alone.   90

TO JANE: 'THE KEEN STARS WERE TWINKLING'

I

THE keen stars were twinkling,
And the fair moon was rising among
    them,
    Dear Jane!
The guitar was tinkling,

But the notes were not sweet till
    you sung them   5
    Again.

II

As the moon's soft splendour
O'er the faint cold starlight of
    Heaven

Is thrown,
So your voice most tender   10
To the strings without soul had
    then given
Its own.

III

The stars will awaken,
Though the moon sleep a full hour
    later,
To-night;   15
No leaf will be shaken

Whilst the dews of your melody
    scatter
Delight.

IV

Though the sound overpowers,
Sing again, with your dear voice
    revealing   20
A tone
Of some world far from ours,
Where music and moonlight and
    feeling
Are one.

A DIRGE

ROUGH wind, that moanest loud
    Grief too sad for song;
Wild wind, when sullen cloud
    Knells all the night long;

Sad storm, whose tears are vain,   5
Bare woods, whose branches strain,
Deep caves and dreary main,—
    Wail, for the world's wrong!

LINES WRITTEN IN THE BAY OF LERICI

SHE left me at the silent time
When the moon had ceased to climb
The azure path of Heaven's steep,
And like an albatross asleep,
Balanced on her wings of light,   5
Hovered in the purple night,
Ere she sought her ocean nest
In the chambers of the West.
She left me, and I stayed alone
Thinking over every tone   10
Which, though silent to the ear,
The enchanted heart could hear,
Like notes which die when born, but
    still
Haunt the echoes of the hill;
And feeling ever—oh, too much!—
The soft vibration of her touch,   16
As if her gentle hand, even now,
Lightly trembled on my brow;
And thus, although she absent were,
Memory gave me all of her   20
That even Fancy dares to claim:—
Her presence had made weak and
    tame
All passions, and I lived alone
In the time which is our own.

The past and future were forgot,   25
As they had been, and would be,
    not.
But soon, the guardian angel gone,
The daemon reassumed his throne
In my faint heart. I dare not speak
My thoughts, but thus disturbed
    and weak   30
I sat and saw the vessels glide
Over the ocean bright and wide,
Like spirit-wingèd chariots sent
O'er some serenest element
For ministrations strange and
    far;   35
As if to some Elysian star
Sailed for drink to medicine
Such sweet and bitter pain as mine.
And the wind that winged their
    flight
From the land came fresh and light,
And the scent of wingèd flowers,   41
And the coolness of the hours
Of dew, and sweet warmth left by
    day.
Were scattered o'er the twinkling
    day,

And the fisher with his lamp   45
And spear about the low rocks
    damp
Crept, and struck the fish which
    came
To worship the delusive flame.

Too happy they, whose pleasure
    sought
Extinguishes all sense and thought
Of the regret that pleasure leaves, 51
Destroying life alone, not peace!

LINES: 'WE MEET NOT AS WE PARTED'

I

WE meet not as we parted,
    We feel more than all may see;
My bosom is heavy-hearted,
    And thine full of doubt for me:—
    One moment has bound the
        free.   5

II

That moment is gone for ever,
    Like lightning that flashed and
        died—
Like a snowflake upon the river—
    Like a sunbeam upon the tide,
    Which the dark shadows hide. 10

III

That moment from time was singled
    As the first of a life of pain;
The cup of its joy was mingled

—Delusion too sweet though
    vain!
Too sweet to be mine again.   15

IV

Sweet lips, could my heart have
    hidden
    That its life was crushed by you,
Ye would not have then forbidden
    The death which a heart so true
    Sought in your briny dew.   20

V

.   .   .   .   .

.   .   .   .   .

.   .   .   .   .

Methinks too little cost
For a moment so found, so
    lost!   25

THE ISLE

THERE was a little lawny islet
By anemone and violet,
    Like mosaic, paven:
And its roof was flowers and leaves
Which the summer's breath en-
    weaves,   5
Where nor sun nor showers nor
    breeze

Pierce the pines and tallest trees,
    Each a gem engraven;—
Girt by many an azure wave
With which the clouds and moun-
    tains pave   10
    A lake's blue chasm.

FRAGMENT: TO THE MOON

BRIGHT wanderer, fair coquette of
    Heaven,
To whom alone it has been given
To change and be adored for ever,

Envy not this dim world, for
    never
But once within its shadow grew
One fair as ——

EPITAPH

THESE are two friends whose lives were undivided; So let their memory be, now they have glided	Under the grave; let not their bones be parted, For their two hearts in life were single-hearted.

NOTE ON POEMS OF 1822, BY MRS. SHELLEY

THIS morn thy gallant bark
Sailed on a sunny sea:
'Tis noon, and tempests dark
Have wrecked it on the lee.
    Ah woe! ah woe!
By Spirits of the deep
    Thou'rt cradled on the billow
To thy eternal sleep.
Thou sleep'st upon the shore
    Beside the knelling surge,
And Sea-nymphs evermore
    Shall sadly chant thy dirge.
        They come, they come,
The Spirits of the deep,—
    While near thy seaweed pillow
My lonely watch I keep.
From far across the sea
    I hear a loud lament,
By Echo's voice for thee
    From Ocean's caverns sent.
        O list! O list!
The Spirits of the deep!
    They raise a wail of sorrow,
While I forever weep.

WITH this last year of the life of Shelley these Notes end. They are not what I intended them to be. I began with energy, and a burning desire to impart to the world, in worthy language, the sense I have of the virtues and genius of the beloved and the lost; my strength has failed under the task. Recurrence to the past, full of its own deep and unforgotten joys and sorrows, contrasted with succeeding years of painful and solitary struggle, has shaken my health. Days of great suffering have followed my attempts to write, and these again produced a weakness and languor that spread their sinister influence over these notes. I dislike speaking of myself, but cannot help apologizing to the dead, and to the public, for not having executed in the manner I desired the history I engaged to give of Shelley's writings.[1]

---

[1] I at one time feared that the correction of the press might be less exact through my illness; but I believe that it is nearly free from error. Some asterisks occur in a few pages, as they did in the volume of *Posthumous Poems*, either because they refer to private concerns, or because the original manuscript was left imperfect. Did any one see the papers from which I drew that volume, the wonder would be how any eyes or patience were capable of extracting it from so confused a mass, interlined and broken into fragments, so that the sense could only be deciphered and joined by guesses which might seem rather intuitive than founded on reasoning. Yet I believe no mistake was made.

The winter of 1822 was passed in Pisa, if we might call that season winter in which autumn merged into spring after the interval of but few days of bleaker weather. Spring sprang up early, and with extreme beauty. Shelley had conceived the idea of writing a tragedy on the subject of Charles I. It was one that he believed adapted for a drama; full of intense interest, contrasted character, and busy passion. He had recommended it long before, when he encouraged me to attempt a play. Whether the subject proved more difficult than he anticipated, or whether in fact he could not bend his mind away from the broodings and wanderings of thought, divested from human interest, which he best loved, I cannot tell; but he proceeded slowly, and threw it aside for one of the most mystical of his poems, the *Triumph of Life*, on which he was employed at the last.

His passion for boating was fostered at this time by having among our friends several sailors. His favourite companion, Edward Ellerker Williams, of the 8th Light Dragoons, had begun his life in the navy, and had afterwards entered the army; he had spent several years in India, and his love for adventure and manly exercises accorded with Shelley's taste. It was their favourite plan to build a boat such as they could manage themselves, and, living on the sea-coast, to enjoy at every hour and season the pleasure they loved best. Captain Roberts, R.N., undertook to build the boat at Genoa, where he was also occupied in building the *Bolivar* for Lord Byron. Ours was to be an open boat, on a model taken from one of the royal dockyards. I have since heard that there was a defect in this model, and that it was never seaworthy. In the month of February, Shelley and his friend went to Spezia to seek for houses for us. Only one was to be found at all suitable; however, a trifle such as not finding a house could not stop Shelley; the one found was to serve for all. It was unfurnished; we sent our furniture by sea, and with a good deal of precipitation, arising from his impatience, made our removal. We left Pisa on the 26th of April.

The Bay of Spezia is of considerable extent, and divided by a rocky promontory into a larger and smaller one. The town of Lerici is situated on the eastern point, and in the depth of the smaller bay, which bears the name of this town, is the village of San Terenzo. Our house, Casa Magni, was close to this village; the sea came up to the door, a steep hill sheltered it behind. The proprietor of the estate on which it was situated was insane; he had begun to erect a large house at the summit of the hill behind, but his malady prevented its being finished, and it was falling into ruin. He had (and this to the Italians had seemed a glaring symptom of very decided madness) rooted up the olives on the hillside, and planted forest trees. These were mostly young, but the plantation was more in English taste than I ever elsewhere saw in Italy; some fine walnut and ilex trees intermingled their dark massy foliage, and formed groups which still haunt my memory, as then they satiated the eye with a sense of loveliness. The scene was indeed of unimaginable beauty. The blue extent of waters, the almost landlocked bay, the near castle of Lerici shutting it in to the east, and distant Porto Venere to the west; the varied forms of the precipitous rocks that bound in the beach, over which there was only a winding rugged footpath towards Lerici, and none on the other side; the tideless sea leaving no sands nor shingle, formed a picture such as one sees in Salvator Rosa's landscapes only. Sometimes the sunshine vanished when the sirocco raged—the 'ponente' the wind was called on that shore. The gales and squalls that hailed our first arrival surrounded the bay with foam; the howling wind swept round our exposed house, and the sea roared un-remittingly, so that we almost fancied ourselves on board ship. At other times sunshine and calm invested sea and sky, and the rich tints of Italian heaven bathed the scene in bright and ever-varying tints.

The natives were wilder than the place. Our near neighbours of San Terenzo were more like savages than any people I ever before lived among. Many a night they passed on the beach, singing, or rather howling; the women dancing about among the waves that broke at their feet, the men leaning against the rocks and joining in their loud wild chorus. We could get no provisions nearer than Sarzana, at a distance of three miles and a half off, with the torrent of the Magra between; and even there the supply was very deficient. Had we been wrecked on an island of the South Seas, we could scarcely have felt ourselves farther from civiliza-tion and comfort; but, where the sun shines, the latter becomes an unnecessary luxury, and we had enough society among ourselves. Yet I confess housekeeping became rather a toilsome task, especially as I was suffering in my health, and could not exert myself actively.

At first the fatal boat had not arrived, and was expected with great impatience. On Monday, 12th May, it came. Williams records the long-wished-for fact in his journal: 'Cloudy and threatening weather. M. Mag-lian called; and after dinner, and while walking with him on the terrace, we discovered a strange sail coming round the point of Porto Venere, which proved at length to be Shelley's boat. She had left Genoa on Thursday last, but had been driven back by the prevailing bad winds. A Mr. Heslop and two English seamen brought her round, and they speak most highly of her performances. She does indeed excite my sur-prise and admiration. Shelley and I walked to Lerici, and made a stretch off the land to try her: and I find she fetches whatever she looks at. In short, we have now a perfect plaything for the summer.'— It was thus that short-sighted mortals welcomed Death, he having dis-guised his grim form in a pleasing mask! The time of the friends was now spent on the sea; the weather became fine, and our whole party often passed the evenings on the water when the wind promised pleasant sailing. Shelley and Williams made longer excursions; they sailed several times to Massa. They had engaged one of the seamen who brought her round, a boy, by name Charles Vivian; and they had not the slightest apprehension of danger. When the weather was unfavourable, they em-ployed themselves with alterations in the rigging, and by building a boat of canvas and reeds, as light as possible, to have on board the other for the convenience of landing in waters too shallow for the larger vessel. When Shelley was on board, he had his papers with him; and much of the *Triumph of Life* was written as he sailed or weltered on that sea which was soon to engulf him.

The heats set in in the middle of June; the days became excessively hot. But the sea-breeze cooled the air at noon, and extreme heat always put Shelley in spirits. A long drought had preceded the heat; and prayers for rain were being put up in the churches, and processions of relics for the same effect took place in every town. At this time we received letters announcing the arrival of Leigh Hunt at Genoa. Shelley was very eager to see him. I was confined to my room by severe illness, and could not move; it was agreed that Shelley and Williams should go to Leghorn in the boat. Strange that no fear of danger crossed our minds! Living on the sea-shore, the ocean became as a plaything: as a child may sport with a lighted stick, till a spark inflames a forest, and spreads destruction over all, so did we fearlessly and blindly tamper with danger, and make a game of the terrors of the ocean. Our Italian neighbours, even, trusted themselves as far as Massa in the skiff; and the running down the line of coast to Leghorn gave no more notion of peril than a fair-weather inland navigation would have done to those who had never seen the sea. Once, some months before, Trelawny had raised a warning voice as to the difference of our calm bay and the open sea beyond; but Shelley and his friend, with their one sailor-boy, thought themselves a match for the storms of the Mediterranean, in a boat which they looked upon as equal to all it was put to do.

On the 1st of July they left us. If ever shadow of future ill darkened the present hour, such was over my mind when they went. During the whole of our stay at Lerici, an intense presentiment of coming evil brooded over my mind, and covered this beautiful place and genial summer with the shadow of coming misery. I had vainly struggled with these emotions—they seemed accounted for by my illness; but at this hour of separation they recurred with renewed violence. I did not antici-pate danger for them, but a vague expectation of evil shook me to agony, and I could scarcely bring myself to let them go. The day was calm and clear; and, a fine breeze rising at twelve, they weighed for Leghorn. They made the run of about fifty miles in seven hours and a half. The *Bolivar* was in port; and, the regulations of the Health-office not per-mitting them to go on shore after sunset, they borrowed cushions from the larger vessel, and slept on board their boat.

They spent a week at Pisa and Leghorn. The want of rain was severely felt in the country. The weather continued sultry and fine. I have heard that Shelley all this time was in brilliant spirits. Not long before, talking of presentiment, he had said the only one that he ever found infallible was the certain advent of some evil fortune when he felt peculiarly joyous. Yet, if ever fate whispered of coming disaster, such inaudible but not unfelt prognostics hovered around us. The beauty of the place seemed unearthly in its excess; the distance we were at from all signs of civilization, the sea at our feet, its murmurs or its roaring for ever in our ears,—all these things led the mind to brood over strange thoughts, and, lifting it from everyday life, caused it to be familiar with the unreal. A sort of spell surrounded us; and each day, as the voyagers did not return, we grew restless and disquieted, and yet, strange to say, we were not fearful of the most apparent danger.

The spell snapped; it was all over; an interval of agonizing doubt—of days passed in miserable journeys to gain tidings, of hopes that took firmer root even as they were more baseless—was changed to the certainty of the death that eclipsed all happiness for the survivors for evermore.

There was something in our fate peculiarly harrowing. The remains of those we lost were cast on shore; but, by the quarantine-laws of the coast, we were not permitted to have possession of them—the law with respect to everything cast on land by the sea being that such should be burned, to prevent the possibility of any remnant bringing the plague into Italy; and no representation could alter the law. At length, through the kind and unwearied exertions of Mr. Dawkins, our Chargé d'Affaires at Florence, we gained permission to receive the ashes after the bodies were consumed. Nothing could equal the zeal of Trelawny in carrying our wishes into effect. He was indefatigable in his exertions, and full of forethought and sagacity in his arrangements. It was a fearful task; he stood before us at last, his hands scorched and blistered by the flames of the funeral-pyre, and by touching the burnt relics as he placed them in the receptacle prepared for the purpose. And there, in compass of that small case, was gathered all that remained on earth of him whose genius and virtue were a crown of glory to the world—whose love had been the source of happiness, peace, and good,—to be buried with him!

The concluding stanzas of the *Adonais* pointed out where the remains ought to be deposited; in addition to which our beloved child lay buried in the cemetery at Rome. Thither Shelley's ashes were conveyed; and they rest beneath one of the antique weed-grown towers that recur at intervals in the circuit of the massy ancient wall of Rome. He selected the hallowed place himself; there is

> 'the sepulchre,
> Oh, not of him, but of our joy!—
> .   .   .   .   .
> And gray walls moulder round, on which dull Time
> Feeds, like slow fire upon a hoary brand;
> And one keen pyramid with wedge sublime,
> Pavilioning the dust of him who planned
> This refuge for his memory, doth stand
> Like flame transformed to marble; and beneath,
> A field is spread, on which a newer band
> Have pitched in Heaven's smile their camp of death,
> Welcoming him we lose with scarce extinguished breath.'

Could sorrow for the lost, and shuddering anguish at the vacancy left behind, be soothed by poetic imaginations, there was something in Shelley's fate to mitigate pangs which yet, alas! could not be so mitigated; for hard reality brings too miserably home to the mourner all that is lost of happiness, all of lonely unsolaced struggle that remains. Still, though dreams and hues of poetry cannot blunt grief, it invests his fate with a sublime fitness, which those less nearly allied may regard with complacency. A year before he had poured into verse all such ideas about death as give it a glory of its own. He had, as it now seems, almost anticipated his own destiny; and, when the mind figures his skiff wrapped from sight by the thunder-storm, as it was last seen upon the purple sea, and then, as the cloud of the tempest passed away, no sign remained of where it had been [1]—who but will regard as a prophecy the last stanza of the *Adonais?*

> 'The breath whose might I have invoked in song
> Descends on me; my spirit's bark is driven,
> Far from the shore, far from the trembling throng
> Whose sails were never to the tempest given;
> The massy earth and spherèd skies are riven!
> I am borne darkly, fearfully, afar;
> Whilst burning through the inmost veil of Heaven,
> The soul of Adonais, like a star,
> Beacons from the abode where the Eternal are.'

PUTNEY, *May* 1, 1839.

TRANSLATIONS

HYMN TO MERCURY

TRANSLATED FROM THE GREEK OF HOMER

I

SING, Muse, the son of Maia and of Jove,
    The Herald-child, king of Arcadia
And all its pastoral hills, whom in sweet love
    Having been interwoven, modest May
Bore Heaven's dread Supreme. An antique grove   5
    Shadowed the cavern where the lovers lay
In the deep night, unseen by Gods or Men,
And white-armed Juno slumbered sweetly then.

---

[1] Captain Roberts watched the vessel with his glass from the top of the lighthouse of Leghorn, on its homeward track. They were off Via Reggio, at some distance from shore, when a storm was driven over the sea. It enveloped them and several larger vessels in darkness. When the cloud passed onwards, Roberts looked again, and saw every other vessel sailing on the ocean except their little schooner, which had vanished. From that time he could scarcely doubt the fatal truth; yet we fancied that they might have been driven towards Elba or Corsica, and so be saved. The observation made as to the spot where the boat disappeared caused it to be found, through the exertions of Trelawny for that effect. It had gone down in ten fathom water; it had not capsized, and, except such things as had floated from her, everything was found on board exactly as it had been placed when they sailed. The boat itself was uninjured. Roberts possessed himself of her, and decked her; but she proved not seaworthy, and her shattered planks now lie rotting on the shore of one of the Ionian islands, on which she was wrecked.

II

Now, when the joy of Jove had its fulfilling,
    And Heaven's tenth moon chronicled her relief,   **10**
She gave to light a babe all babes excelling,
    A schemer subtle beyond all belief;
A shepherd of thin dreams, a cow-stealing,
    A night-watching, and door-waylaying thief,
Who 'mongst the Gods was soon about to thieve,   **15**
And other glorious actions to achieve.

III

The babe was born at the first peep of day;
    He began playing on the lyre at noon,
And the same evening did he steal away
    Apollo's herds;—the fourth day of the moon   **20**
On which him bore the venerable May,
    From her immortal limbs he leaped full soon,
Nor long could in the sacred cradle keep,
But out to seek Apollo's herds would creep.

IV

Out of the lofty cavern wandering   **25**
    He found a tortoise, and cried out—'A treasure!'
(For Mercury first made the tortoise sing)
    The beast before the portal at his leisure
The flowery herbage was depasturing,
    Moving his feet in a deliberate measure   **30**
Over the turf. Jove's profitable son
Eying him laughed, and laughing thus begun:—

V

'A useful godsend are you to me now,
    King of the dance, companion of the feast,
Lovely in all your nature! Welcome, you   **35**
    Excellent plaything! Where, sweet mountain-beast,
Got you that speckled shell? Thus much I know,
    You must come home with me and be my guest;
You will give joy to me, and I will do
All that is in my power to honour you.   **40**

VI

'Better to be at home than out of door,
    So come with me; and though it has been said
That you alive defend from magic power,
    I know you will sing sweetly when you're dead.'

Thus having spoken, the quaint infant bore,   45
  Lifting it from the grass on which it fed
And grasping it in his delighted hold,
His treasured prize into the cavern old.

VII

Then scooping with a chisel of gray steel,
  He bored the life and soul out of the beast.—   50
Not swifter a swift thought of woe or weal
  Darts through the tumult of a human breast
Which thronging cares annoy—not swifter wheel
  The flashes of its torture and unrest
Out of the dizzy eyes—than Maia's son   53
All that he did devise hath featly done.

VIII

.   .   .   .
  And through the tortoise's hard stony skin
At proper distances small holes he made,
  And fastened the cut stems of reeds within,
And with a piece of leather overlaid   60
  The open space and fixed the cubits in,
Fitting the bridge to both, and stretched o'er all
Symphonious cords of sheep-gut rhythmical.

IX

When he had wrought the lovely instrument,
  He tried the chords, and made division meet,   65
Preluding with the plectrum, and there went
  Up from beneath his hand a tumult sweet
Of mighty sounds, and from his lips he sent
  A strain of unpremeditated wit
Joyous and wild and wanton—such you may   70
Hear among revellers on a holiday.

X

He sung how Jove and May of the bright sandal
  Dallied in love not quite legitimate;
And his own birth, still scoffing at the scandal,
  And naming his own name, did celebrate;   75
His mother's cave and servant maids he planned all
  In plastic verse, her household stuff and state,
Perennial pot, trippet, and brazen pan,—
But singing, he conceived another plan.

XI

. . . .
Seized with a sudden fancy for fresh meat,   80
He in his sacred crib deposited
    The hollow lyre, and from the cavern sweet
Rushed with great leaps up to the mountain's head,
    Revolving in his mind some subtle feat
Of thievish craft, such as a swindler might   85
Devise in the lone season of dun night.

XII

Lo! the great Sun under the ocean's bed has
    Driven steeds and chariot—the child meanwhile strode
O'er the Pierian mountains clothed in shadows,
    Where the immortal oxen of the God   90
Are pastured in the flowering unmown meadows,
    And safely stalled in a remote abode.—
The archer Argicide, elate and proud,
Drove fifty from the herd, lowing aloud.

XIII

He drove them wandering o'er the sandy way,   95
    But, being ever mindful of his craft,
Backward and forward drove he them astray,
    So that the tracks which seemed before, were aft;
His sandals then he threw to the ocean spray,
    And for each foot he wrought a kind of raft   100
Of tamarisk, and tamarisk-like sprigs,
And bound them in a lump with withy twigs.

XIV

And on his feet he tied these sandals light,
The trail of whose wide leaves might not betray
    His track; and then, a self-sufficing wight,   105
Like a man hastening on some distant way,
    He from Pieria's mountain bent his flight;
But an old man perceived the infant pass
Down green Onchestus heaped like beds with grass.

XV

The old man stood dressing his sunny vine: 110
    'Halloo! old fellow with the crooked shoulder!
You grub those stumps? before they will bear wine
    Methinks even you must grow a little older:

Attend, I pray, to this advice of mine,
   As you would 'scape what might appal a bolder— 115
Seeing, see not—and hearing, hear not—and—
If you have understanding—understand.'

XVI

So saying, Hermes roused the oxen vast;
   O'er shadowy mountain and resounding dell,
And flower-paven plains, great Hermes passed; 120
   Till the black night divine, which favouring fell
Around his steps, grew gray, and morning fast
   Wakened the world to work, and from her cell
Sea-strewn, the Pallantean Moon sublime
Into her watch-tower just began to climb. 125

XVII

Now to Alpheus he had driven all
   The broad-foreheaded oxen of the Sun;
They came unwearied to the lofty stall
   And to the water-troughs which ever run
Through the fresh fields—and when with rushgrass tall, 130
   Lotus and all sweet herbage, every one
Had pastured been, the great God made them move
Towards the stall in a collected drove.

XVIII

A mighty pile of wood the God then heaped,
   And having soon conceived the mystery 135
Of fire, from two smooth laurel branches stripped
   The bark, and rubbed them in his palms;—on high
Suddenly forth the burning vapour leaped
   And the divine child saw delightedly.—
Mercury first found out for human weal 140
Tinder-box, matches, fire-irons, flint and steel.

XIX

And fine dry logs and roots innumerous
   He gathered in a delve upon the ground—
And kindled them—and instantaneous
   The strength of the fierce flame was breathed around: 145
And whilst the might of glorious Vulcan thus
   Wrapped the great pile with glare and roaring sound,
Hermes dragged forth two heifers, lowing loud,
Close to the fire—such might was in the God.

XX

And on the earth upon their backs he threw   150
  The panting beasts, and rolled them o'er and o'er,
And bored their lives out. Without more ado
  He cut fat and flesh, and down before
The fire, on spits of wood he placed the two,
  Toasting their flesh and ribs, and all the gore   155
Pursed in the bowels; and while this was done
He stretched their hides over a craggy stone.

XXI

We mortals let an ox grow old, and then
  Cut it up after long consideration,—
But joyous-minded Hermes from the glen   160
  Drew the fat spoils to the more open station
Of a flat smooth space, and portioned them; and when
  He had by lot assigned to each a ration
Of the twelve Gods, his mind became aware
Of all the joys which in religion are.   165

XXII

For the sweet savour of the roasted meat
  Tempted him though immortal. Natheless
He checked his haughty will and did not eat,
  Though what it cost him words can scarce express,
And every wish to put such morsels sweet   170
  Down his most sacred throat, he did repress;
But soon within the lofty portalled stall
He placed the fat and flesh and bones and all.

XXIII

And every trace of the fresh butchery
  And cooking, the God soon made disappear,   175
As if it all had vanished through the sky;
  He burned the hoofs and horns and head and hair,—
The insatiate fire devoured them hungrily;—
  And when he saw that everything was clear,
He quenched the coal, and trampled the black dust,   180
And in the stream his bloody sandals tossed.

XXIV

All night he worked in the serene moonshine—
  But when the light of day was spread abroad
He sought his natal mountain-peaks divine.
  On his long wandering neither Man nor God   185

Had met him, since he killed Apollo's kine,
  Nor house-dog had barked at him on his road;
Now he obliquely through the keyhole passed,
Like a thin mist, or an autumnal blast.

XXV

Right through the temple of the spacious cave   190
  He went with soft light feet—as if his tread
Fell not on earth; no sound their falling gave;
  Then to his cradle he crept quick, and spread
The swaddling-clothes about him; and the knave
  Lay playing with the covering of the bed   195
With his left hand about his knees—the right
Held his belovèd tortoise-lyre tight.

XXVI

There he lay innocent as a new-born child,
  As gossips say; but though he was a God,
The Goddess, his fair mother, unbeguiled,   200
  Knew all that he had done being abroad:
'Whence come you, and from what adventure wild,
  You cunning rogue, and where have you abode
All the long night, clothed in your impudence?
What have you done since you departed hence?   205

XXVII

'Apollo soon will pass within this gate
  And bind your tender body in a chain
Inextricably tight, and fast as fate,
  Unless you can delude the God again,
Even when within his arms—ah, runagate!   210
  A pretty torment both for Gods and Men
Your father made when he made you!'—'Dear mother,'
Replied sly Hermes, 'wherefore scold and bother?

XXVIII

'As if I were like other babes as old,
  And understood nothing of what is what;   215
And cared at all to hear my mother scold.
  I in my subtle brain a scheme have got,
Which whilst the sacred stars round Heaven are rolled
  Will profit you and me—nor shall our lot
Be as you counsel, without gifts or food,   220
To spend our lives in this obscure abode.

XXIX

'But we will leave this shadow-peopled cave
  And live among the Gods, and pass each day
In high communion, sharing what they have
  Of profuse wealth and unexhausted prey;   225
And from the portion which my father gave
  To Phoebus, I will snatch my share away,
Which if my father will not—natheless I,
Who am the king of robbers, can but try.

XXX

'And, if Latona's son should find me out,   230
  I'll countermine him by a deeper plan;
I'll pierce the Pythian temple-walls, though stout,
  And sack the fane of everything I can—
Caldrons and tripods of great worth no doubt,
  Each golden cup and polished brazen pan,   235
All the wrought tapestries and garments gay.'—
So they together talked;—meanwhile the Day

XXXI

Aethereal born arose out of the flood
  Of flowing Ocean, bearing light to men.
Apollo passed toward the sacred wood,   240
  Which from the inmost depths of its green glen
Echoes the voice of Neptune,—and there stood
  On the same spot in green Onchestus then
That same old animal, the vine-dresser,
Who was employed hedging his vineyard there.   245

XXXII

Latona's glorious Son began:—'I pray
  Tell, ancient hedger of Onchestus green,
Whether a drove of kine has passed this way,
  All heifers with crooked horns? for they have been
Stolen from the herd in high Pieria,   250
  Where a black bull was fed apart, between
Two woody mountains in a neighbouring glen,
And four fierce dogs watched there, unanimous as men.

XXXIII

'And what is strange, the author of this theft
  Has stolen the fatted heifers every one,   255
But the four dogs and the black bull are left:—
  Stolen they were last night at set of sun,

Of their soft beds and their sweet food bereft.—
    Now tell me, man born ere the world begun,
Have you seen any one pass with the cows?'— 260
    To whom the man of overhanging brows:

XXXIV

'My friend, it would require no common skill
    Justly to speak of everything I see:
On various purposes of good or ill
    Many pass by my vineyard,—and to me 265
'Tis difficult to know the invisible
    Thoughts, which in all those many minds may be:—
Thus much alone I certainly can say,
I tilled these vines till the decline of day,

XXXV

'And then I thought I saw, but dare not speak 270
    With certainty of such a wondrous thing,
A child, who could not have been born a week,
    Those fair-horned cattle closely following,
And in his hand he held a polished stick:
    And, as on purpose, he walked wavering 275
From one side to the other of the road,
And with his face opposed the steps he trod.'

XXXVI

Apollo hearing this, passed quickly on—
    No wingèd omen could have shown more clear
That the deceiver was his father's son. 280
    So the God wraps a purple atmosphere
Around his shoulders, and like fire is gone
    To famous Pylos, seeking his kine there,
And found their track and his, yet hardly cold,
And cried—'What wonder do mine eyes behold! 285

XXXVII

'Here are the footsteps of the hornèd herd
    Turned back towards their fields of asphodel;—
But *these* are not the tracks of beast or bird,
    Gray wolf, or bear, or lion of the dell,
Or manèd Centaur—sand was never stirred 290
    By man or woman thus! Inexplicable!
Who with unwearied feet could e'er impress
The sand with such enormous vestiges?

XXXVIII

'That was most strange—but this is stranger still!'
    Thus having said, Phoebus impetuously   295
Sought high Cyllene's forest-cinctured hill,
    And the deep cavern where dark shadows lie,
And where the ambrosial nymph with happy will
    Bore the Saturnian's love-child, Mercury—
And a delightful odour from the dew   300
Of the hill pastures, at his coming, flew.

XXXIX

And Phoebus stooped under the craggy roof
    Arched over the dark cavern:—Maia's child
Perceived that he came angry, far aloof,
    About the cows of which he had been beguiled;   305
And over him the fine and fragrant woof
    Of his ambrosial swaddling-clothes he piled—
As among fire-brands lies a burning spark
Covered, beneath the ashes cold and dark.

XL

There, like an infant who had sucked his fill   310
    And now was newly washed and put to bed,
Awake, but courting sleep with weary will,
    And gathered in a lump, hands, feet, and head,
He lay, and his belovèd tortoise still
    He grasped and held under his shoulder-blade.   315
Phoebus the lovely mountain-goddess knew,
Not less her subtle, swindling baby, who

XLI

Lay swathed in his sly wiles. Round every crook
    Of the ample cavern, for his kine, Apollo
Looked sharp; and when he saw them not, he took   320
    The glittering key, and opened three great hollow
Recesses in the rock—where many a nook
    Was filled with the sweet food immortals swallow,
And mighty heaps of silver and of gold
Were piled within—a wonder to behold!   325

XLII

And white and silver robes, all overwrought
    With cunning workmanship of tracery sweet—
Except among the Gods there can be nought
    In the wide world to be compared with it.

Latona's offspring, after having sought
  His herds in every corner, thus did greet
Great Hermes:—'Little cradled rogue, declare
Of my illustrious heifers, where they are!

XLIII

'Speak quickly! or a quarrel between us
  Must rise, and the event will be, that I   335
Shall hurl you into dismal Tartarus,
  In fiery gloom to dwell eternally;
Nor shall your father nor your mother loose
  The bars of that black dungeon—utterly
You shall be cast out from the light of day,   340
To rule the ghosts of men, unblessed as they.'

XLIV

To whom thus Hermes slily answered:—'Son
  Of great Latona, what a speech is this!
Why come you here to ask me what is done
  With the wild oxen which it seems you miss?   345
I have not seen them, nor from any one
  Have heard a word of the whole business;
If you should promise an immense reward,
I could not tell more than you now have heard.

XLV

'An ox-stealer should be both tall and strong,   350
  And I am but a little new-born thing,
Who, yet at least, can think of nothing wrong:—
  My business is to suck, and sleep, and fling
The cradle-clothes about me all day long,—
  Or half asleep, hear my sweet mother sing,   355
And to be washed in water clean and warm,
And hushed and kissed and kept secure from harm.

XLVI

'O, let not e'er this quarrel be averred!
  The astounded Gods would laugh at you, if e'er
You should allege a story so absurd   360
  As that a new-born infant forth could fare
Out of his home after a savage herd.
  I was born yesterday—my small feet are
Too tender for the roads so hard and rough:—
And if you think that this is not enough,   365

XLVII

'I swear a great oath, by my father's head,
   That I stole not your cows, and that I know
Of no one else, who might, or could, or did.—
   Whatever things cows are, I do not know,
For I have only heard the name.'—This said,   370
   He winked as fast as could be, and his brow
Was wrinkled, and a whistle loud gave he,
Like one who hears some strange absurdity.

XLVIII

Apollo gently smiled and said:—'Ay, ay,—
   You cunning little rascal, you will bore   375
Many a rich man's house, and your array
   Of thieves will lay their siege before his door,
Silent as night, in night; and many a day
   In the wild glens rough shepherds will deplore
That you or yours, having an appetite,   380
Met with their cattle, comrade of the night!

XLIX

'And this among the Gods shall be your gift,
   To be considered as the lord of those
Who swindle, house-break, sheep-steal, and shop-lift;—
   But now if you would not your last sleep doze;   385
Crawl out!'—Thus saying, Phoebus did uplift
   The subtle infant in his swaddling clothes,
And in his arms, according to his wont,
A scheme devised, the illustrious Argiphont.

L

. . . .

And sneezed and shuddered—Phoebus on the grass   390
   Him threw, and whilst all that he had designed
He did perform—eager although to pass,
   Apollo darted from his mighty mind
Towards the subtle babe the following scoff:—
'Do not imagine this will get you off,   395

LI

'You little swaddled child of Jove and May!'
   And seized him:—'By this omen I shall trace
My noble herds, and you shall lead the way.'—
   Cyllenian Hermes from the grassy place,

Like one in earnest haste to get away,   400
   Rose, and with hands lifted towards his face
Round both his ears up from his shoulders drew
His swaddling clothes, and—'What mean you to do

LII

'With me, you unkind God?'—said Mercury:
   'Is it about these cows you tease me so?   405
I wish the race of cows were perished!—I
   Stole not your cows—I do not even know
What things cows are. Alas! I well may sigh
   That, since I came into this world of woe,
I should have ever heard the name of one—   410
But I appeal to the Saturnian's throne.'

LIII

Thus Phoebus and the vagrant Mercury
   Talked without coming to an explanation,
With adverse purpose. As for Phoebus, he
   Sought not revenge, but only information,   415
And Hermes tried with lies and roguery
   To cheat Apollo.—But when no evasion
Served—for the cunning one his match had found—
He paced on first over the sandy ground.

LIV

  .   .   .   .   .   .
He of the Silver Bow the child of Jove   420
Followed behind, till to their heavenly Sire
   Came both his children, beautiful as Love,
And from his equal balance did require
   A judgement in the cause wherein they strove.
O'er odorous Olympus and its snows   425
A murmuring tumult as they came arose,—

LV

And from the folded depths of the great Hill,
   While Hermes and Apollo reverent stood
Before Jove's throne, the indestructible
   Immortals rushed in mighty multitude;   430
And whilst their seats in order due they fill,
   The lofty Thunderer in a careless mood
To Phoebus said:—'Whence drive you this sweet prey,
This herald-baby, born but yesterday?—

LVI

'A most important subject, trifler, this   435
  To lay before the Gods!'—'Nay, Father, nay,
When you have understood the business,
  Say not that I alone am fond of prey.
I found this little boy in a recess
  Under Cyllene's mountains far away—   440
A manifest and most apparent thief,
A scandalmonger beyond all belief.

LVII

'I never saw his like either in Heaven
  Or upon earth for knavery or craft:—
Out of the field my cattle yester-even,   445
  By the low shore on which the loud sea laughed,
He right down to the river-ford had driven;
  And mere astonishment would make you daft
To see the double kind of footsteps strange
He has impressed wherever he did range.   450

LVIII

'The cattle's track on the black dust, full well
  Is evident, as if they went towards
The place from which they came—that asphodel
  Meadow, in which I feed my many herds,—
His steps were most incomprehensible—   455
  I know not how I can describe in words
Those tracks—he could have gone along the sands
Neither upon his feet nor on his hands;—

LIX

'He must have had some other stranger mode
  Of moving on: those vestiges immense,   460
Far as I traced them on the sandy road,
  Seemed like the trail of oak-toppings:—but thence
No mark nor track denoting where they trod
  The hard ground gave:—but, working at his fence,
A mortal hedger saw him as he passed   465
To Pylos, with the cows, in fiery haste.

LX

'I found that in the dark he quietly
  Had sacrificed some cows, and before light
Had thrown the ashes all dispersedly
  About the road—then, still as gloomy night,   470

Had crept into his cradle, either eye
  Rubbing, and cogitating some new sleight,
No eagle could have seen him as he lay
Hid in his cavern from the peering day.

LXI

'I taxed him with the fact, when he averred   475
  Most solemnly that he did neither see
Nor even had in any manner heard
  Of my lost cows, whatever things cows be;
Nor could he tell, though offered a reward,
  Not even who could tell of them to me.'   480
So speaking, Phoebus sate; and Hermes then
Addressed the Supreme Lord of Gods and Men:—

LXII

'Great Father, you know clearly beforehand
  That all which I shall say to you is sooth;
I am a most veracious person, and   485
  Totally unacquainted with untruth.
At sunrise Phoebus came, but with no band
  Of Gods to bear him witness, in great wrath,
To my abode, seeking his heifers there,
And saying that I must show him where they are,   490

LXIII

'Or he would hurl me down the dark abyss.
  I know that every Apollonian limb
Is clothed with speed and might and manliness,
  As a green bank with flowers—but unlike him
I was born yesterday, and you may guess   495
  He well knew this when he indulged the whim
Of bullying a poor little new-born thing
That slept, and never thought of cow-driving.

LXIV

'Am I like a strong fellow who steals kine?
  Believe me, dearest Father—such you are—   500
This driving of the herds is none of mine;
  Across my threshold did I wander ne'er,
So may I thrive! I reverence the divine
  Sun and the Gods, and I love you, and care
Even for this hard accuser—who must know   505
I am as innocent as they or you.

LXV

'I swear by these most gloriously-wrought portals
  (It is, you will allow, an oath of might)
Through which the multitude of the Immortals
  Pass and repass forever, day and night,   510
Devising schemes for the affairs of mortals—
  That I am guiltless; and I will requite,
Although mine enemy be great and strong,
His cruel threat—do thou defend the young!'

LXVI

So speaking, the Cyllenian Argiphont   515
  Winked, as if now his adversary was fitted:—
And Jupiter, according to his wont,
  Laughed heartily to hear the subtle-witted
Infant give such a plausible account,
  And every word a lie. But he remitted   520
Judgement at present—and his exhortation
Was, to compose the affair by arbitration.

LXVII

And they by mighty Jupiter were bidden
  To go forth with a single purpose both,
Neither the other chiding nor yet chidden: 525
  And Mercury with innocence and truth
To lead the way, and show where he had hidden
  The mighty heifers.—Hermes, nothing loth,
Obeyed the Aegis-bearer's will—for he
Is able to persuade all easily.   530

LXVIII

These lovely children of Heaven's highest Lord
  Hastened to Pylos and the pastures wide
And lofty stalls by the Alphean ford,
  Where wealth in the mute night is multiplied
With silent growth. Whilst Hermes drove the herd   535
  Out of the stony cavern, Phoebus spied
The hides of those the little babe had slain,
Stretched on the precipice above the plain.

LXIX

'How was it possible,' then Phoebus said,
  'That you, a little child, born yesterday,   540
A thing on mother's milk and kisses fed,
  Could two prodigious heifers ever flay?

Even I myself may well hereafter dread
  Your prowess, offspring of Cyllenian May,
When you grow strong and tall.'—He spoke, and bound   545
Stiff withy bands the infant's wrists around,

LXX

He might as well have bound the oxen wild;
  The withy bands, though starkly interknit,
Fell at the feet of the immortal child,
  Loosened by some device of his quick wit.   550
Phoebus perceived himself again beguiled,
  And stared—while Hermes sought some hole or pit,
Looking askance and winking fast as thought,
Where he might hide himself and not be caught.

LXXI

Sudden he changed his plan, and with strange skill   555
  Subdued the strong Latonian, by the might
Of winning music, to his mightier will;
  His left hand held the lyre, and in his right
The plectrum struck the chords—unconquerable
  Up from beneath his hand in circling flight   560
The gathering music rose—and sweet as Love
The penetrating notes did live and move

LXXII

Within the heart of great Apollo—he
  Listened with all his soul, and laughed for pleasure.
Close to his side stood harping fearlessly   565
  The unabashèd boy; and to the measure
Of the sweet lyre, there followed loud and free
  His joyous voice; for he unlocked the treasure
Of his deep song, illustrating the birth
Of the bright Gods, and the dark desert Earth: 570

LXXIII

And how to the Immortals every one
  A portion was assigned of all that is;
But chief Mnemosyne did Maia's son
  Clothe in the light of his loud melodies;—
And, as each God was born or had begun,   575
  He in their order due and fit degrees
Sung of his birth and being—and did move
Apollo to unutterable love.

LXXIV

These words were wingèd with his swift delight:
  'You heifer-stealing schemer, well do you   580
Deserve that fifty oxen should requite
  Such minstrelsies as I have heard even now.
Comrade of feasts, little contriving wight,
  One of your secrets I would gladly know,
Whether the glorious power you now show forth   585
Was folded up within you at your birth,

LXXV

'Or whether mortal taught or God inspired
  The power of unpremeditated song?
Many divinest sounds have I admired,
  The Olympian Gods and mortal men among;   590
But such a strain of wondrous, strange, untired,
  And soul-awakening music, sweet and strong,
Yet did I never hear except from thee,
Offspring of May, impostor Mercury!

LXXVI

'What Muse, what skill, what unimagined use,   595
  What exercise of subtlest art, has given
Thy songs such power?—for those who hear may choose
  From three, the choicest of the gifts of Heaven,
Delight, and love, and sleep,—sweet sleep, whose dews
  Are sweeter than the balmy tears of even:—   600
And I, who speak this praise, am that Apollo
Whom the Olympian Muses ever follow:

LXXVII

'And their delight is dance, and the blithe noise
  Of song and overflowing poesy;
And sweet, even as desire, the liquid voice   605
  Of pipes, that fills the clear air thrillingly;
But never did my inmost soul rejoice
  In this dear work of youthful revelry
As now. I wonder at thee, son of Jove;
Thy harpings and thy song are soft as love.   610

LXXVIII

'Now since thou hast, although so very small,
  Science of arts so glorious, thus I swear,—
And let this cornel javelin, keen and tall,
  Witness between us what I promise here,—

That I will lead thee to the Olympian Hall, 615
　Honoured and mighty, with thy mother dear,
And many glorious gifts in joy will give thee,
And even at the end will ne'er deceive thee.'

LXXIX

To whom thus Mercury with prudent speech:—
　'Wisely hast thou inquirèd of my skill: 620
I envy thee no thing I know to teach
　Even this day:—for both in word and will
I would be gentle with thee; thou canst reach
　All things in thy wise spirit, and thy sill
Is highest in Heaven among the sons of Jove, 625
Who loves thee in the fulness of his love.

LXXX

'The Counsellor Supreme has given to thee
　Divinest gifts, out of the amplitude
Of his profuse exhaustless treasury;
　By thee, 'tis said, the depths are understood 630
Of his far voice; by thee the mystery
　Of all oracular fates,—and the dread mood
Of the diviner is breathed up; even I—
A child—perceive thy might and majesty.

LXXXI

'Thou canst seek out and compass all that wit 635
　Can find or teach;—yet since thou wilt, come take
The lyre—be mine the glory giving it—
　Strike the sweet chords, and sing aloud, and wake
Thy joyous pleasure out of many a fit
　Of trancèd sound—and with fleet fingers make 640
Thy liquid-voicèd comrade talk with thee,—
It can talk measured music eloquently.

LXXXII

'Then bear it boldly to the revel loud,
　Love-wakening dance, or feast of solemn state,
A joy by night or day—for those endowed 645
　With art and wisdom who interrogate
It teaches, babbling in delightful mood
　All things which make the spirit most elate,
Soothing the mind with sweet familiar play,
Chasing the heavy shadows of dismay. 650

LXXXIII

'To those who are unskilled in its sweet tongue,
    Though they should question most impetuously
Its hidden soul, it gossips something wrong—
    Some senseless and impertinent reply.
But thou who art as wise as thou art strong   655
    Canst compass all that thou desirest. I
Present thee with this music-flowing shell,
Knowing thou canst interrogate it well.

LXXXIV

'And let us two henceforth together feed,
    On this green mountain-slope and pastoral plain,   660
The herds in litigation—they will breed
    Quickly enough to recompense our pain,
If to the bulls and cows we take good heed;—
    And thou, though somewhat over fond of gain,
Grudge me not half the profit.'—Having spoke,   665
The shell he proffered, and Apollo took;

LXXXV

And gave him in return the glittering lash,
    Installing him as herdsman;—from the look
Of Mercury then laughed a joyous flash.
    And then Apollo with the plectrum strook   670
The chords, and from beneath his hands a crash
    Of mighty sounds rushed up, whose music shook
The soul with sweetness, and like an adept
His sweeter voice a just accordance kept.

LXXXVI

The herd went wandering o'er the divine mead,   675
    Whilst these most beautiful Sons of Jupiter
Won their swift way up to the snowy head
    Of white Olympus, with the joyous lyre
Soothing their journey; and their father dread
    Gathered them both into familiar   680
Affection sweet,—and then, and now, and ever,
Hermes must love Him of the Golden Quiver,

LXXXVII

To whom he gave the lyre that sweetly sounded,
    Which skilfully he held and played thereon.
He piped the while, and far and wide rebounded   685
    The echo of his pipings; every one

Of the Olympians sat with joy astounded;
  While he conceived another piece of fun,
One of his old tricks—which the God of Day
Perceiving, said:—'I fear thee, Son of May;—   690

LXXXVIII

'I fear thee and thy sly chameleon spirit,
  Lest thou should steal my lyre and crookèd bow;
This glory and power thou dost from Jove inherit,
  To teach all craft upon the earth below;
Thieves love and worship thee—it is thy merit   695
  To make all mortal business ebb and flow
By roguery:—now, Hermes, if you dare
By sacred Styx a mighty oath to swear

LXXXIX

'That you will never rob me, you will do
  A thing extremely pleasing to my heart.'   700
Then Mercury sware by the Stygian dew,
  That he would never steal his bow or dart,
Or lay his hands on what to him was due,
  Or ever would employ his powerful art
Against his Pythian fane. Then Phoebus swore   705
There was no God or Man whom he loved more.

XC

'And I will give thee as a good-will token,
  The beautiful wand of wealth and happiness;
A perfect three-leaved rod of gold unbroken,
  Whose magic will thy footsteps ever bless;   710
And whatsoever by Jove's voice is spoken
  Of earthly or divine from its recess,
It, like a loving soul, to thee will speak,
And more than this, do thou forbear to seek.

XCI

'For, dearest child, the divinations high   715
  Which thou requirest, 'tis unlawful ever
That thou, or any other deity
  Should understand—and vain were the endeavour;
For they are hidden in Jove's mind, and I,
  In trust of them, have sworn that I would never   720
Betray the counsels of Jove's inmost will
To any God—the oath was terrible.

XCII

'Then, golden-wanded brother, ask me not
　　To speak the fates by Jupiter designed;
But be it mine to tell their various lot　　　　　　　725
　　To the unnumbered tribes of human-kind.
Let good to these, and ill to those be wrought
　　As I dispense—but he who comes consigned
By voice and wings of perfect augury
To my great shrine, shall find avail in me.　　　730

XCIII

'Him will I not deceive, but will assist;
　　But he who comes relying on such birds
As chatter vainly, who would strain and twist
　　The purpose of the Gods with idle words,
And deems their knowledge light, he shall have missed　　735
　　His road—whilst I among my other hoards
His gifts deposit. Yet, O son of May,
I have another wondrous thing to say.

XCIV

'There are three Fates, three virgin Sisters, who
　　Rejoicing in their wind-outspeeding wings,　　740
Their heads with flour snowed over white and new,
　　Sit in a vale round which Parnassus flings
Its circling skirts—from these I have learned true
　　Vaticinations of remotest things.
My father cared not. Whilst they search out dooms,　　745
They sit apart and feed on honeycombs.

XCV

'They, having eaten the fresh honey, grow
　　Drunk with divine enthusiasm, and utter
With earnest willingness the truth they know;
　　But if deprived of that sweet food, they mutter　　750
All plausible delusions;—these to you
　　I give;—if you inquire, they will not stutter;
Delight your own soul with them:—any man
You would instruct may profit if he can.

XCVI

'Take these and the fierce oxen, Maia's child—　　755
　　O'er many a horse and toil-enduring mule,
O'er jaggèd-jawèd lions, and the wild
　　White-tuskèd boars, o'er all, by field or pool,

Of cattle which the mighty Mother mild
   Nourishes in her bosom, thou shalt rule—   760
Thou dost alone the veil from death uplift—
Thou givest not—yet this is a great gift.'

XCVII

Thus King Apollo loved the child of May
   In truth, and Jove covered their love with joy.
Hermes with Gods and Men even from that day   765
   Mingled, and wrought the latter much annoy,
And little profit, going far astray
   Through the dun night. Farewell, delightful Boy,
Of Jove and Maia sprung,—never by me,
Nor thou, nor other songs, shall unremembered be.   770

HOMER'S HYMN TO CASTOR AND POLLUX

Ye wild-eyed Muses, sing the Twins of Jove,
Whom the fair-ankled Leda, mixed in love
With mighty Saturn's Heaven-obscuring Child,
On Taygetus, that lofty mountain wild,
Brought forth in joy: mild Pollux, void of blame,   5
And steed-subduing Castor, heirs of fame.
These are the Powers who earth-born mortals save
And ships, whose flight is swift along the wave.
When wintry tempests o'er the savage sea
Are raging, and the sailors tremblingly   10
Call on the Twins of Jove with prayer and vow,
Gathered in fear upon the lofty prow,
And sacrifice with snow-white lambs,—the wind
And the huge billow bursting close behind,
Even then beneath the weltering waters bear   15
The staggering ship—they suddenly appear,
On yellow wings rushing athwart the sky,
And lull the blasts in mute tranquillity,
And strew the waves on the white Ocean's bed,
Fair omen of the voyage; from toil and dread   20
The sailors rest, rejoicing in the sight,
And plough the quiet sea in safe delight.

HOMER'S HYMN TO THE MOON

Daughters of Jove, whose voice is melody,
Muses, who know and rule all minstrelsy,
Sing the wide-wingèd Moon! Around the earth,
From her immortal head in Heaven shot forth,
Far light is scattered—boundless glory springs;   5
Where'er she spreads her many-beaming wings
The lampless air glows round her golden crown.

But when the Moon divine from Heaven is gone
Under the sea, her beams within abide,
Till, bathing her bright limbs in Ocean's tide,   10
Clothing her form in garments glittering far,
And having yoked to her immortal car
The beam-invested steeds whose necks on high
Curve back, she drives to a remoter sky
A western Crescent, borne impetuously.   15
Then is made full the circle of her light,
And as she grows, her beams more bright and bright
Are poured from Heaven, where she is hovering then,
A wonder and a sign to mortal men.

The Son of Saturn with this glorious Power   20
Mingled in love and sleep—to whom she bore
Pandeia, a bright maid of beauty rare
Among the Gods, whose lives eternal are.

Hail Queen, great Moon, white-armed Divinity,
Fair-haired and favourable! thus with thee   25
My song beginning, by its music sweet
Shall make immortal many a glorious feat
Of demigods, with lovely lips, so well
Which minstrels, servants of the Muses, tell.

HOMER'S HYMN TO THE SUN

OFFSPRING of Jove, Calliope, once more
To the bright Sun, thy hymn of music pour;
Whom to the child of star-clad Heaven and Earth
Euryphaëssa, large-eyed nymph, brought forth;
Euryphaëssa, the famed sister fair   5
Of great Hyperion, who to him did bear
A race of loveliest children; the young Morn,
Whose arms are like twin roses newly born,
The fair-haired Moon, and the immortal Sun,
Who borne by heavenly steeds his race doth run   10
Unconquerably, illuming the abodes
Of mortal Men and the eternal Gods.

Fiercely look forth his awe-inspiring eyes,
Beneath his golden helmet, whence arise
And are shot forth afar, clear beams of light;   15
His countenance, with radiant glory bright,
Beneath his graceful locks far shines around,
And the light vest with which his limbs are bound,
Of woof aethereal delicately twined,
Glows in the stream of the uplifting wind.   20

His rapid steeds soon bear him to the West;
Where their steep flight his hands divine arrest,
And the fleet car with yoke of gold, which he
Sends from bright Heaven beneath the shadowy sea.

HOMER'S HYMN TO THE EARTH: MOTHER OF ALL

O UNIVERSAL Mother, who dost keep
From everlasting thy foundations deep,
Eldest of things, Great Earth, I sing of thee!
All shapes that have their dwelling in the sea,
All things that fly, or on the ground divine   5
Live, move, and there are nourished—these are thine;
These from thy wealth thou dost sustain; from thee
Fair babes are born, and fruits on every tree
Hang ripe and large, revered Divinity!

The life of mortal men beneath thy sway   10
Is held; thy power both gives and takes away!
Happy are they whom thy mild favours nourish;
All things unstinted round them grow and flourish.
For them, endures the life-sustaining field
Its load of harvest, and their cattle yield   15
Large increase, and their house with wealth is filled.
Such honoured dwell in cities fair and free,
The homes of lovely women, prosperously;
Their sons exult in youth's new budding gladness,
And their fresh daughters free from care or sadness,   20
With bloom-inwoven dance and happy song,
On the soft flowers the meadow-grass among,
Leap round them sporting—such delights by thee
Are given, rich Power, revered Divinity.

Mother of gods, thou Wife of starry Heaven,   25
Farewell! be thou propitious, and be given
A happy life for this brief melody,
Nor thou nor other songs shall unremembered be.

HOMER'S HYMN TO MINERVA

I SING the glorious Power with azure eyes,
Athenian Pallas! tameless, chaste, and wise,
Tritogenia, town-preserving Maid,
Revered and mighty; from his awful head
Whom Jove brought forth, in warlike armour dressed,   5
Golden, all radiant! wonder strange possessed
The everlasting Gods that Shape to see,
Shaking a javelin keen, impetuously

Rush from the crest of Aegis-bearing Jove;
Fearfully Heaven was shaken, and did move   10
Beneath the might of the Cerulean-eyed;
Earth dreadfully resounded, far and wide;
And, lifted from its depths, the sea swelled high
In purple billows, the tide suddenly
Stood still, and great Hyperion's son long time   15
Checked his swift steeds, till where she stood sublime
Pallas from her immortal shoulders threw
The arms divine; wise Jove rejoiced to view.
Child of the Aegis-bearer, hail to thee,
Nor thine nor others' praise shall unremembered be.   20

HOMER'S HYMN TO VENUS

[Vv. 1-55, with some omissions.]

MUSE, sing the deeds of golden Aphrodite,
Who wakens with her smile the lulled delight
Of sweet desire, taming the eternal kings
Of Heaven, and men, and all the living things
That fleet along the air, or whom the sea,   5
Or earth, with her maternal ministry,
Nourish innumerable, thy delight
All seek   O crownèd Aphrodite!
Three spirits canst thou not deceive or quell:—
Minerva, child of Jove, who loves too well   10
Fierce war and mingling combat, and the fame
Of glorious deeds, to heed thy gentle flame.
Diana   golden-shafted queen,
Is tamed not by thy smiles; the shadows green
Of the wild woods, the bow, the . . .   15
And piercing cries amid the swift pursuit
Of beasts among waste mountains,—such delight
Is hers, and men who know and do the right.
Nor Saturn's first-born daughter, Vesta chaste,
Whom Neptune and Apollo wooed the last,   20
Such was the will of aegis-bearing Jove;
But sternly she refused the ills of Love,
And by her mighty Father's head she swore
An oath not unperformed, that evermore
A virgin she would live mid deities   25
Divine: her father, for such gentle ties
Renounced, gave glorious gifts—thus in his hall
She sits and feeds luxuriously. O'er all
In every fane, her honours first arise
From men—the eldest of Divinities.   30

These spirits she persuades not, nor deceives,
But none beside escape, so well she weaves
Her unseen toils; nor mortal men, nor gods
Who live secure in their unseen abodes.
She won the soul of him whose fierce delight   35
Is thunder—first in glory and in might.
And, as she willed, his mighty mind deceiving,
With mortal limbs his deathless limbs inweaving,
Concealed him from his spouse and sister fair,
Whom to wise Saturn ancient Rhea bare.   40
　　　　　but in return,
In Venus Jove did soft desire awaken,
That by her own enchantments overtaken,
She might, no more from human union free,
Burn for a nursling of mortality.   45
For once, amid the assembled Deities,
The laughter-loving Venus from her eyes
Shot forth the light of a soft starlight smile,
And boasting said, that she, secure the while,
Could bring at will to the assembled Gods   50
The mortal tenants of earth's dark abodes,
And mortal offspring from a deathless stem
She could produce in scorn and spite of them.
Therefore he poured desire into her breast
Of young Anchises,   55
Feeding his herds among the mossy fountains
Of the wide Ida's many-folded mountains,—
Whom Venus saw, and loved, and the love clung
Like wasting fire her senses wild among.

THE CYCLOPS

A SATYRIC DRAMA

TRANSLATED FROM THE GREEK OF EURIPIDES

| SILENUS. | ULYSSES. |
| CHORUS OF SATYRS. | THE CYCLOPS. |

Silenus. O Bacchus, what a world of toil, both now
And ere these limbs were overworn with age,
Have I endured for thee! First, when thou fled'st
The mountain-nymphs who nursed thee, driven afar
By the strange madness Juno sent upon thee;   5
Then in the battle of the sons of Earth,
When I stood foot by foot close to thy side,
No unpropitious fellow-combatant,
And, driving through his shield my wingèd spear,
Slew vast Enceladus. Consider now,   10

Is it a dream of which I speak to thee?
By Jove, it is not, for you have the trophies!
And now I suffer more than all before.
For when I heard that Juno had devised
A tedious voyage for you, I put to sea   15
With all my children quaint in search of you,
And I myself stood on the beakèd prow
And fixed the naked mast; and all my boys
Leaning upon their oars, with splash and strain
Made white with foam the green and purple sea,—   20
And so we sought you, king. We were sailing
Near Malea, when an eastern wind arose,
And drove us to this waste Aetnean rock;
The one-eyed children of the Ocean God,
The man-destroying Cyclopses, inhabit,   25
On this wild shore, their solitary caves,
And one of these, named Polypheme, has caught us
To be his slaves; and so, for all delight
Of Bacchic sports, sweet dance and melody,
We keep this lawless giant's wandering flocks.   30
My sons indeed, on far declivities,
Young things themselves, tend on the youngling sheep,
But I remain to fill the water-casks,
Or sweeping the hard floor, or ministering
Some impious and abominable meal   35
To the fell Cyclops. I am wearied of it!
And now I must scrape up the littered floor
With this great iron rake, so to receive
My absent master and his evening sheep
In a cave neat and clean. Even now I see   40
My children tending the flocks hitherward.
Ha! what is this? are your Sicinnian measures
Even now the same, as when with dance and song
You brought young Bacchus to Althaea's halls?

Chorus of Satyrs.

STROPHE

Where has he of race divine   45
   Wandered in the winding rocks?
Here the air is calm and fine
   For the father of the flocks;—
Here the grass is soft and sweet,
And the river-eddies meet   50
In the trough beside the cave,
Bright as in their fountain wave.—
Neither here, nor on the dew

Of the lawny uplands feeding?
Oh, you come!—a stone at you 55
    Will I throw to mend your breeding;—
Get along, you hornèd thing,
Wild, seditious, rambling!

EPODE

An Iacchic melody
    To the golden Aphrodite 60
Will I lift, as erst did I
    Seeking her and her delight
With the Maenads, whose white feet
To the music glance and fleet.
Bacchus, O belovèd, where, 65
Shaking wide thy yellow hair,
Wanderest thou alone, afar?
    To the one-eyed Cyclops, we,
Who by right thy servants are,
    Minister in misery, 70
In these wretched goat-skins clad,
    Far from thy delights and thee.

Silenus. Be silent, sons; command the slaves to drive
The gathered flocks into the rock-roofed cave.
    Chorus. Go! But what needs this serious haste, O father?
    Silenus. I see a Grecian vessel on the coast, 76
And thence the rowers with some general
Approaching to this cave.—About their necks
Hang empty vessels, as they wanted food,
And water-flasks.—Oh, miserable strangers! 80
Whence come they, that they know not what and who
My master is, approaching in ill hour
The inhospitable roof of Polypheme,
And the Cyclopian jaw-bone, man-destroying?
Be silent, Satyrs, while I ask and hear 85
Whence coming, they arrive the Aetnean hill.
    Ulysses. Friends, can you show me some clear water-spring,
The remedy of our thirst? Will any one
Furnish with food seamen in want of it?
Ha! what is this? We seem to be arrived 90
At the blithe court of Bacchus. I observe
This sportive band of Satyrs near the caves.
First let me greet the elder.—Hail!
    Silenus.   Hail thou,
O Stranger! tell thy country and thy race.
    Ulysses. The Ithacan Ulysses and the king 95
Of Cephalonia.

Silenus.　　　Oh! I know the man,
Wordy and shrewd, the son of Sisyphus.
　Ulysses. I am the same, but do not rail upon me.—
　Silenus. Whence sailing do you come to Sicily?
　Ulysses. From Ilion, and from the Trojan toils.　　　　　　　　100
　Silenus. How, touched you not at your paternal shore?
　Ulysses. The strength of tempests bore me here by force.
　Silenus. The self-same accident occurred to me.
　Ulysses. Were you then driven here by stress of weather?
　Silenus. Following the Pirates who had kidnapped Bacchus.
　Ulysses. What land is this, and who inhabit it?—　　　　　　　106
　Silenus. Aetna, the loftiest peak in Sicily.
　Ulysses. And are there walls, and tower-surrounded towns?
　Silenus. There are not.—These lone rocks are bare of men.
　Ulysses. And who possess the land? the race of beasts?
　Silenus. Cyclops, who live in caverns, not in houses.　　　　　111
　Ulysses. Obeying whom? Or is the state popular?
　Silenus. Shepherds: no one obeys any in aught.
　Ulysses. How live they? do they sow the corn of Ceres?
　Silenus. On milk and cheese, and on the flesh of sheep.　　　115
　Ulysses. Have they the Bromian drink from the vine's stream?
　Silenus. Ah! no; they live in an ungracious land.
　Ulysses. And are they just to strangers?—hospitable?
　Silenus. They think the sweetest thing a stranger brings
Is his own flesh.
　Ulysses.　　　　What! do they eat man's flesh?　　　　120
　Silenus. No one comes here who is not eaten up.
　Ulysses. The Cyclops now—where is he? Not at home?
　Silenus. Absent on Aetna, hunting with his dogs.
　Ulysses. Know'st thou what thou must do to aid us hence?
　Silenus. I know not: we will help you all we can.　　　　　125
　Ulysses. Provide us food, of which we are in want.
　Silenus. Here is not anything, as I said, but meat.
　Ulysses. But meat is a sweet remedy for hunger.
　Silenus. Cow's milk there is, and store of curdled cheese.
　Ulysses. Bring out:—I would see all before I bargain.　　　130
　Silenus. But how much gold will you engage to give?
　Ulysses. I bring no gold, but Bacchic juice.
　Silenus.　　　　　　　　　　　　　　Oh, joy!
'Tis long since these dry lips were wet with wine.
　Ulysses. Maron, the son of the God, gave it me.
　Silenus. Whom I have nursed a baby in my arms.　　　　　135
　Ulysses. The son of Bacchus, for your clearer knowledge.
　Silenus. Have you it now?—or is it in the ship?
　Ulysses. Old man, this skin contains it, which you see.
　Silenus. Why, this would hardly be a mouthful for me.
　Ulysses. Nay, twice as much as you can draw from thence.　140

Silenus. You speak of a fair fountain, sweet to me.
Ulysses. Would you first taste of the unmingled wine?
Silenus. 'Tis just—tasting invites the purchaser.
Ulysses. Here is the cup, together with the skin.
Silenus. Pour: that the draught may fillip my remembrance.
Ulysses. See!
Silenus.   Papaiapax! what a sweet smell it has!   146
Ulysses. You see it then?—
Silenus.   By Jove, no! but I smell it.
Ulysses. Taste, that you may not praise it in words only.
Silenus. Babai! Great Bacchus calls me forth to dance!
Joy! joy!
Ulysses. Did it flow sweetly down your throat?   150
Silenus. So that it tingled to my very nails.
Ulysses. And in addition I will give you gold.
Silenus. Let gold alone! only unlock the cask.
Ulysses. Bring out some cheeses now, or a young goat.
Silenus. That will I do, despising any master.   155
Yes, let me drink one cup, and I will give
All that the Cyclops feed upon their mountains.

.   .   .   .   .   .

Chorus. Ye have taken Troy and laid your hands on Helen?
Ulysses. And utterly destroyed the race of Priam.

.   .   .   .   .

Silenus. The wanton wretch! she was bewitched to see   160
The many-coloured anklets and the chain
Of woven gold which girt the neck of Paris,
And so she left that good man Menelaus.
There should be no more women in the world
But such as are reserved for me alone.—   165
See, here are sheep, and here are goats, Ulysses,
Here are unsparing cheeses of pressed milk;
Take them; depart with what good speed ye may;
First leaving my reward, the Bacchic dew
Of joy-inspiring grapes.
Ulysses.   Ah me! Alas!   170
What shall we do? the Cyclops is at hand!
Old man, we perish! whither can we fly?
Silenus. Hide yourselves quick within that hollow rock.
Ulysses. 'Twere perilous to fly into the net.
Silenus. The cavern has recesses numberless;   175
Hide yourselves quick.
Ulysses.   That will I never do!
The mighty Troy would be indeed disgraced
If I should fly one man. How many times
Have I withstood, with shield immovable,

Ten thousand Phrygians!—if I needs must die,   180
Yet will I die with glory;—if I live,
The praise which I have gained will yet remain.
    Silenus. What, ho! assistance, comrades, haste, assistance!

        The CYCLOPS, SILENUS, ULYSSES; CHORUS.
    Cyclops. What is this tumult? Bacchus is not here,
Nor tympanies nor brazen castanets.   185
How are my young lambs in the cavern? Milking
Their dams or playing by their sides? And is
The new cheese pressed into the bulrush baskets?
Speak! I'll beat some of you till you rain tears—
Look up, not downwards when I speak to you.   190
    Silenus. See! I now gape at Jupiter himself;
I stare upon Orion and the stars.
    Cyclops. Well, is the dinner fitly cooked and laid?
    Silenus. All ready, if your throat is ready too.
    Cyclops. Are the bowls full of milk besides?
    Silenus.   O'er-brimming;
So you may drink a tunful if you will.   196
    Cyclops. Is it ewe's milk or cow's milk, or both mixed?—
    Silenus. Both, either; only pray don't swallow me.
    Cyclops. By no means.——

        .   .   .   .

What is this crowd I see beside the stalls?   200
Outlaws or thieves? for near my cavern-home
I see my young lambs coupled two by two
With willow bands; mixed with my cheeses lie
Their implements; and this old fellow here
Has his bald head broken with stripes.
    Silenus.   Ah me!   205
I have been beaten till I burn with fever.
    Cyclops. By whom? Who laid his fist upon your head?
    Silenus. Those men, because I would not suffer them
To steal your goods.
    Cyclops.   Did not the rascals know
I am a God, sprung from the race of Heaven?   210
    Silenus. I told them so, but they bore off your things,
And ate the cheese in spite of all I said,
And carried out the lambs—and said, moreover,
They'd pin you down with a three-cubit collar,
And pull your vitals out through your one eye,   215
Furrow your back with stripes, then, binding you,
Throw you as ballast into the ship's hold,
And then deliver you, a slave, to move
Enormous rocks, or found a vestibule.
    Cyclops. In truth? Nay, haste, and place in order quickly

The cooking-knives, and heap upon the hearth, 221
And kindle it, a great faggot of wood.—
As soon as they are slaughtered, they shall fill
My belly, broiling warm from the live coals,
Or boiled and seethed within the bubbling caldron. 225
I am quite sick of the wild mountain game;
Of stags and lions I have gorged enough,
And I grow hungry for the flesh of men.
    Silenus. Nay, master, something new is very pleasant
After one thing forever, and of late 230
Very few strangers have approached our cave.
    Ulysses. Hear, Cyclops, a plain tale on the other side.
We, wanting to buy food, came from our ship
Into the neighbourhood of your cave, and here
This old Silenus gave us in exchange 235
These lambs for wine, the which he took and drank,
And all by mutual compact, without force.
There is no word of truth in what he says,
For slyly he was selling all your store.
    Silenus. I? May you perish, wretch—
    Ulysses.   If I speak false!
    Silenus. Cyclops, I swear by Neptune who begot thee, 241
By mighty Triton and by Nereus old,
Calypso and the glaucous Ocean Nymphs,
The sacred waves and all the race of fishes—
Be these the witnesses, my dear sweet master, 245
My darling little Cyclops, that I never
Gave any of your stores to these false strangers;—
If I speak false may those whom most I love,
My children, perish wretchedly!
    Chorus.   There stop!
I saw him giving these things to the strangers. 250
If I speak false, then may my father perish,
But do not thou wrong hospitality.
    Cyclops. You lie! I swear that he is juster far
Than Rhadamanthus—I trust more in him.
But let me ask, whence have ye sailed, O strangers? 255
Who are you? And what city nourished ye?
    Ulysses. Our race is Ithacan—having destroyed
The town of Troy, the tempests of the sea
Have driven us on thy land, O Polypheme.
    Cyclops. What, have ye shared in the unenvied spoil 260
Of the false Helen, near Scamander's stream?
    Ulysses. The same, having endured a woful toil.
    Cyclops. Oh, basest expedition! sailed ye not
From Greece to Phrygia for one woman's sake?
    Ulysses. 'Twas the Gods' work—no mortal was in fault. 265

But, O great Offspring of the Ocean-King,
We pray thee and admonish thee with freedom,
That thou dost spare thy friends who visit thee,
And place no impious food within thy jaws.
For in the depths of Greece we have upreared   270
Temples to thy great Father, which are all
His homes. The sacred bay of Taenarus
Remains inviolate, and each dim recess
Scooped high on the Malean promontory,
And aëry Sunium's silver veinèd crag,   275
Which divine Pallas keeps unprofaned ever,
The Gerastian asylums, and whate'er
Within wide Greece our enterprise has kept
From Phrygian contumely; and in which
You have a common care, for you inhabit   280
The skirts of Grecian land, under the roots
Of Aetna and its crags, spotted with fire.
Turn then to converse under human laws,
Receive us shipwrecked suppliants, and provide
Food, clothes, and fire, and hospitable gifts;   285
Nor fixing upon oxen-piercing spits
Our limbs, so fill your belly and your jaws.
Priam's wide land has widowed Greece enough;
And weapon-wingèd murder heaped together
Enough of dead, and wives are husbandless,   290
And ancient women and gray fathers wail
Their childless age;—if you should roast the rest—
And 'tis a bitter feast that you prepare—
Where then would any turn? Yet be persuaded;
Forgo the lust of your jaw-bone; prefer   295
Pious humanity to wicked will:
Many have bought too dear their evil joys.
    Silenus. Let me advise you, do not spare a morsel
Of all his flesh. If you should eat his tongue
You would become most eloquent, O Cyclops.   300
    Cyclops. Wealth, my good fellow, is the wise man's God,
All other things are a pretence and boast.
What are my father's ocean promontories,
The sacred rocks whereon he dwells, to me?
Stranger, I laugh to scorn Jove's thunderbolt,   305
I know not that his strength is more than mine.
As to the rest I care not.—When he pours
Rain from above, I have a close pavilion
Under this rock, in which I lie supine,
Feasting on a roast calf or some wild beast,   310
And drinking pans of milk, and gloriously
Emulating the thunder of high Heaven.

And when the Thracian wind pours down the snow,
I wrap my body in the skins of beasts,
Kindle a fire, and bid the snow swirl on. 315
The earth, by force, whether it will or no,
Bringing forth grass, fattens my flocks and herds,
Which, to what other God but to myself
And this great belly, first of deities,
Should I be bound to sacrifice? I well know 320
The wise man's only Jupiter is this,
To eat and drink during his little day,
And give himself no care. And as for those
Who complicate with laws the life of man,
I freely give them tears for their reward. 325
I will not cheat my soul of its delight,
Or hesitate in dining upon you:—
And that I may be quit of all demands,
These are my hospitable gifts;—fierce fire
And yon ancestral caldron, which o'er-bubbling 330
Shall finely cook your miserable flesh.
Creep in!—

.   .   .   .

Ulysses. Ai! ai! I have escaped the Trojan toils,
I have escaped the sea, and now I fall
Under the cruel grasp of one impious man. 335
O Pallas, Mistress, Goddess, sprung from Jove,
Now, now, assist me! Mightier toils than Troy
Are these;—I totter on the chasms of peril;—
And thou who inhabitest the thrones
Of the bright stars, look, hospitable Jove, 340
Upon this outrage of thy deity,
Otherwise be considered as no God!

Chorus (alone).

For your gaping gulf and your gullet wide,
The ravin is ready on every side,
The limbs of the strangers are cooked and done; 345
   There is boiled meat, and roast meat, and meat from the coal,
You may chop it, and tear it, and gnash it for fun,
   An hairy goat's-skin contains the whole.
Let me but escape, and ferry me o'er
The stream of your wrath to a safer shore. 350
The Cyclops Aetnean is cruel and bold,
   He murders the strangers
      That sit on his hearth,
   And dreads no avengers
      To rise from the earth. 355
He roasts the men before they are cold,

He snatches them broiling from the coal,
And from the caldron pulls them whole,
And minces their flesh and gnaws their bone
With his cursèd teeth, till all be gone.   360
    Farewell, foul pavilion:
      Farewell, rites of dread!
    The Cyclops vermilion,
      With slaughter uncloying,
        Now feasts on the dead,   365
        In the flesh of strangers joying!

  Ulysses. O Jupiter! I saw within the cave
Horrible things; deeds to be feigned in words,
But not to be believed as being done.

  Chorus. What! sawest thou the impious Polypheme   370
Feasting upon your loved companions now?

  Ulysses. Selecting two, the plumpest of the crowd,
He grasped them in his hands.—
  Chorus.   Unhappy man!

.   .   .   .

  Ulysses. Soon as we came into this craggy place,
Kindling a fire, he cast on the broad hearth   375
The knotty limbs of an enormous oak,
Three waggon-loads at least, and then he strewed
Upon the ground, beside the red firelight,
His couch of pine-leaves; and he milked the cows,
And pouring forth the white milk, filled a bowl   380
Three cubits wide and four in depth, as much
As would contain ten amphorae, and bound it
With ivy wreaths; then placed upon the fire
A brazen pot to boil, and made red hot
The points of spits, not sharpened with the sickle,   385
But with a fruit tree bough, and with the jaws
Of axes for Aetnean slaughterings.[1]
And when this God-abandoned Cook of Hell
Had made all ready, he seized two of us
And killed them in a kind of measured manner;   390
For he flung one against the brazen rivets
Of the huge caldron, and seized the other
By the foot's tendon, and knocked out his brains
Upon the sharp edge of the craggy stone:
Then peeled his flesh with a great cooking-knife   395
And put him down to roast. The other's limbs
He chopped into the caldron to be boiled.
And I, with the tears raining from my eyes
Stood near the Cyclops, ministering to him;

[1] I confess I do not understand this.—[SHELLEY'S NOTE.]

The rest, in the recesses of the cave,   400
Clung to the rock like bats, bloodless with fear.
When he was filled with my companions' flesh,
He threw himself upon the ground and sent
A loathsome exhalation from his maw.
Then a divine thought came to me. I filled   405
The cup of Maron, and I offered him
To taste, and said:—'Child of the Ocean God,
Behold what drink the vines of Greece produce,
The exultation and the joy of Bacchus.'
He, satiated with his unnatural food,   410
Received it, and at one draught drank it off,
And taking my hand, praised me:—'Thou hast given
A sweet draught after a sweet meal, dear guest.'
And I, perceiving that it pleased him, filled
Another cup, well knowing that the wine   415
Would wound him soon and take a sure revenge.
And the charm fascinated him, and I
Plied him cup after cup, until the drink
Had warmed his entrails, and he sang aloud
In concert with my wailing fellow-seamen   420
A hideous discord—and the cavern rung.
I have stolen out, so that if you will
You may achieve my safety and your own.
But say, do you desire, or not, to fly
This uncompanionable man, and dwell   425
As was your wont among the Grecian Nymphs
Within the fanes of your belovèd God?
Your father there within agrees to it,
But he is weak and overcome with wine,
And caught as if with bird-lime by the cup,   430
He claps his wings and crows in doting joy.
You who are young escape with me, and find
Bacchus your ancient friend; unsuited he
To this rude Cyclops.
    Chorus.   Oh my dearest friend,
That I could see that day, and leave for ever   435
The impious Cyclops.

.   .   .   .

    Ulysses. Listen then what a punishment I have
For this fell monster, how secure a flight
From your hard servitude.
    Chorus.   O sweeter far
Than is the music of an Asian lyre   440
Would be the news of Polypheme destroyed.
    Ulysses. Delighted with the Bacchic drink he goes
To call his brother Cyclops—who inhabit

A village upon Aetna not far off.
  Chorus. I understand, catching him when alone   445
You think by some measure to dispatch him,
Or thrust him from the precipice.
  Ulysses.   Oh no;
Nothing of that kind; my device is subtle.
  Chorus. How then? I heard of old that thou wert wise.
  Ulysses. I will dissuade him from this plan, by saying   450
It were unwise to give the Cyclopses
This precious drink, which if enjoyed alone
Would make life sweeter for a longer time.
When, vanquished by the Bacchic power, he sleeps,
There is a trunk of olive wood within,   455
Whose point having made sharp with this good sword
I will conceal in fire, and when I see
It is alight, will fix it, burning yet,
Within the socket of the Cyclops' eye
And melt it out with fire—as when a man   460
Turns by its handle a great auger round,
Fitting the framework of a ship with beams,
So will I, in the Cyclops' fiery eye
Turn round the brand and dry the pupil up.
  Chorus. Joy! I am mad with joy at your device.   465
  Ulysses. And then with you, my friends, and the old man,
We'll load the hollow depth of our black ship,
And row with double strokes from this dread shore.
  Chorus. May I, as in libations to a God,
Share in the blinding him with the red brand?   470
I would have some communion in his death.
  Ulysses. Doubtless: the brand is a great brand to hold.
  Chorus. Oh! I would lift an hundred waggon-loads,
If like a wasp's nest I could scoop the eye out
Of the detested Cyclops.
  Ulysses.   Silence now!   475
Ye know the close device—and when I call,
Look ye obey the masters of the craft.
I will not save myself and leave behind
My comrades in the cave: I might escape,
Having got clear from that obscure recess,   480
But 'twere unjust to leave in jeopardy
The dear companions who sailed here with me.

Chorus.

Come! who is first, that with his hand
Will urge down the burning brand
Through the lids, and quench and pierce   485
The Cyclops' eye so fiery fierce?

Semichorus I. (*Song within.*)

Listen! listen! he is coming,
A most hideous discord humming.
Drunken, museless, awkward, yelling,
Far along his rocky dwelling;   490
Let us with some comic spell
Teach the yet unteachable.
By all means he must be blinded,
If my counsel be but minded.

Semichorus II.

Happy thou made odorous   495
    With the dew which sweet grapes weep,
To the village hastening thus,
    Seek the vines that soothe to sleep;
Having first embraced thy friend,
Thou in luxury without end,   500
With the strings of yellow hair,
Of thy voluptuous leman fair,
Shalt sit playing on a bed!—
Speak! what door is openèd?

Cyclops.

Ha! ha! ha! I'm full of wine,   505
Heavy with the joy divine,
With the young feast oversated;
Like a merchant's vessel freighted
To the water's edge, my crop
Is laden to the gullet's top.   510
The fresh meadow grass of spring
Tempts me forth thus wandering
    To my brothers on the mountains,
    Who shall share the wine's sweet fountains.
Bring the cask, O stranger, bring!   515

Chorus.

One with eyes the fairest
    Cometh from his dwelling;
Some one loves thee, rarest,
    Bright beyond my telling.
In thy grace thou shinest   520
Like some nymph divinest
In her caverns dewy:—
All delights pursue thee,
Soon pied flowers, sweet-breathing,
Shall thy head be wreathing.   525

Ulysses. Listen, O Cyclops, for I am well skilled
In Bacchus, whom I gave thee of to drink.
　Cyclops. What sort of God is Bacchus then accounted?
　Ulysses. The greatest among men for joy of life.
　Cyclops. I gulped him down with very great delight.　　　530
　Ulysses. This is a God who never injures men.
　Cyclops. How does the God like living in a skin?
　Ulysses. He is content wherever he is put.
　Cyclops. Gods should not have their body in a skin.
　Ulysses. If he gives joy, what is his skin to you?　　　535
　Cyclops. I hate the skin, but love the wine within.
　Ulysses. Stay here now: drink, and make your spirit glad.
　Cyclops. Should I not share this liquor with my brothers?
　Ulysses. Keep it yourself, and be more honoured so.
　Cyclops. I were more useful, giving to my friends.　　　540
　Ulysses. But village mirth breeds contests, broils, and blows.
　Cyclops. When I am drunk none shall lay hands on me.—
　Ulysses. A drunken man is better within doors.
　Cyclops. He is a fool, who drinking, loves not mirth.
　Ulysses. But he is wise, who drunk, remains at home.　　　545
　Cyclops. What shall I do, Silenus? Shall I stay?
　Silenus. Stay—for what need have you of pot companions?
　Cyclops. Indeed this place is closely carpeted
With flowers and grass.
　Silenus.　　　　　　　And in the sun-warm noon
'Tis sweet to drink. Lie down beside me now,　　　550
Placing your mighty sides upon the ground.
　Cyclops. What do you put the cup behind me for?
　Silenus. That no one here may touch it.
　Cyclops.　　　　　　　　　　　Thievish one!
You want to drink;—here place it in the midst.
And thou, O stranger, tell how art thou called?　　　555
　Ulysses. My name is Nobody. What favour now
Shall I receive to praise you at your hands?
　Cyclops. I'll feast on you the last of your companions.
　Ulysses. You grant your guest a fair reward, O Cyclops.
　Cyclops. Ha! what is this? Stealing the wine, you rogue!
　Silenus. It was this stranger kissing me because　　　561
I looked so beautiful.
　Cyclops.　　　　　　You shall repent
For kissing the coy wine that loves you not.
　Silenus. By Jupiter! you said that I am fair.
　Cyclops. Pour out, and only give me the cup full.　　　565
　Silenus. How is it mixed? let me observe.
　Cyclops.　　　　　　　　　　Curse you!
Give it me so.
　Silenus.　　　　Not till I see you wear

That coronal, and taste the cup to you.
   Cyclops. Thou wily traitor!
   Silenus.   But the wine is sweet.
Ay, you will roar if you are caught in drinking.   570
   Cyclops. See now, my lip is clean and all my beard.
   Silenus. Now put your elbow right and drink again.
As you see me drink— . . .
   Cyclops. How now?
   Silenus.   Ye Gods, what a delicious gulp!
   Cyclops. Guest, take it;—you pour out the wine for me.   **575**
   Ulysses. The wine is well accustomed to my hand.
   Cyclops. Pour out the wine!
   Ulysses.   I pour; only be silent.
   Cyclops. Silence is a hard task to him who drinks.
   Ulysses. Take it and drink it off; leave not a dreg.
Oh, that the drinker died with his own draught!   580
   Cyclops. Papai! the vine must be a sapient plant.
   Ulysses. If you drink much after a mighty feast,
Moistening your thirsty maw, you will sleep well;
If you leave aught, Bacchus will dry you up.
   Cyclops. Ho! ho! I can scarce rise. What pure delight!
The heavens and earth appear to whirl about   586
Confusedly. I see the throne of Jove
And the clear congregation of the Gods.
Now if the Graces tempted me to kiss
I would not—for the loveliest of them all   590
I would not leave this Ganymede.
   Silenus.   Polypheme,
I am the Ganymede of Jupiter.
   Cyclops. By Jove, you are; I bore you off from Dardanus.

.   .   .   .

ULYSSES *and the* CHORUS

   Ulysses. Come, boys of Bacchus, children of high race,
This man within is folded up in sleep,   595
And soon will vomit flesh from his fell maw;
The brand under the shed thrusts out its smoke,
No preparation needs, but to burn out
The monster's eye;—but bear yourselves like men.
   Chorus. We will have courage like the adamant rock,   600
All things are ready for you here; go in,
Before our father shall perceive the noise.
   Ulysses. Vulcan, Aetnean king! burn out with fire
The shining eye of this thy neighbouring monster!
And thou, O Sleep, nursling of gloomy Night,   605
Descend unmixed on this God-hated beast,
And suffer not Ulysses and his comrades,
Returning from their famous Trojan toils,

To perish by this man, who cares not either
For God or mortal; or I needs must think   610
That Chance is a supreme divinity,
And things divine are subject to her power.

Chorus.

Soon a crab the throat will seize
    Of him who feeds upon his guest,
Fire will burn his lamp-like eyes   615
    In revenge of such a feast!
A great oak stump now is lying
    In the ashes yet undying.
        Come, Maron, come!
Raging let him fix the doom,   620
    Let him tear the eyelid up
    Of the Cyclops—that his cup
        May be evil!
Oh! I long to dance and revel
    With sweet Bromian, long desired,   625
In loved ivy wreaths attired;
    Leaving this abandoned home—
    Will the moment ever come?

Ulysses. Be silent, ye wild things! Nay, hold your peace,
And keep your lips quite close; dare not to breathe,   630
Or spit, or e'en wink, lest ye wake the monster,
Until his eye be tortured out with fire.
    Chorus. Nay, we are silent, and we chaw the air.
    Ulysses. Come now, and lend a hand to the great stake
Within—it is delightfully red hot.   635
    Chorus. You then command who first should seize the stake
To burn the Cyclops' eye, that all may share
In the great enterprise.
    Semichorus I.   We are too far;
We cannot at this distance from the door
Thrust fire into his eye.
    Semichorus II.   And we just now   640
Have become lame! cannot move hand or foot.
    Chorus. The same thing has occurred to us,—our ankles
Are sprained with standing here, I know not how.
    Ulysses. What, sprained with standing still?
    Chorus.   And there is dust
Or ashes in our eyes, I know not whence.   645
    Ulysses. Cowardly dogs! ye will not aid me then?
    Chorus. With pitying my own back and my back-bone,
And with not wishing all my teeth knocked out,
This cowardice comes of itself—but stay,

I know a famous Orphic incantation   650
To make the brand stick of its own accord
Into the skull of this one-eyed son of Earth.
    Ulysses. Of old I knew ye thus by nature; now
I know ye better.—I will use the aid
Of my own comrades. Yet though weak of hand   655
Speak cheerfully, that so ye may awaken
The courage of my friends with your blithe words.
    Chorus. This I will do with peril of my life,
And blind you with my exhortations, Cyclops.

       Hasten and thrust,   660
       And parch up to dust,
       The eye of the beast
       Who feeds on his guest.
       Burn and blind
       The Aetnean hind!   665
       Scoop and draw,
       But beware lest he claw
       Your limbs near his maw.

    Cyclops. Ah me! my eyesight is parched up to cinders.
    Chorus. What a sweet paean; sing me that again!   670
    Cyclops. Ah me! indeed, what woe has fallen upon me!
But, wretched nothings, think ye not to flee
Out of this rock; I, standing at the outlet,
Will bar the way and catch you as you pass.
    Chorus. What are you roaring out, Cyclops?
    Cyclops.   I perish!   675
    Chorus. For you are wicked.
    Cyclops.   And besides miserable.
    Chorus. What, did you fall into the fire when drunk?
    Cyclops. 'Twas Nobody destroyed me.
    Chorus.   Why then no one
Can be to blame.
    Cyclops.   I say 'twas Nobody
Who blinded me.
    Chorus.   Why then you are not blind.   680
    Cyclops. I wish you were as blind as I am.
    Chorus.   Nay,
It cannot be that no one made you blind.
    Cyclops. You jeer me; where, I ask, is Nobody?
    Chorus. Nowhere, O Cyclops.
    Cyclops. It was that stranger ruined me:—the wretch   685
First gave me wine and then burned out my eye,
For wine is strong and hard to struggle with.
Have they escaped, or are they yet within?
    Chorus. They stand under the darkness of the rock
And cling to it.

Cyclops.   At my right hand or left?   690
Chorus. Close on your right.
Cyclops.   Where?
Chorus.   Near the rock itself.
You have them.
Cyclops.   Oh, misfortune on misfortune!
I've cracked my skull.
Chorus.   Now they escape you—there.
Cyclops. Not there, although you say so.
Chorus.   Not on that side.
Cyclops. Where then?
Chorus.   They creep about you on your left. 695
Cyclops. Ah! I am mocked! They jeer me in my ills.
Chorus. Not there! he is a little there beyond you.
Cyclops. Detested wretch! where are you?
Ulysses.   Far from you
I keep with care this body of Ulysses.
Cyclops. What do you say? You proffer a new name.   700
Ulysses. My father named me so; and I have taken
A full revenge for your unnatural feast;
I should have done ill to have burned down Troy
And not revenged the murder of my comrades.
Cyclops. Ai! ai! the ancient oracle is accomplished;   705
It said that I should have my eye sight blinded
By your coming from Troy, yet it foretold
That you should pay the penalty for this
By wandering long over the homeless sea.
Ulysses. I bid thee weep—consider what I say;   710
I go towards the shore to drive my ship
To mine own land, o'er the Sicilian wave.
Cyclops. Not so, if whelming you with this huge stone,
I can crush you and all your men together;
I will descend upon the shore, though blind,   715
Groping my way adown the steep ravine.
Chorus. And we, the shipmates of Ulysses now,
Will serve our Bacchus all our happy lives.

EPIGRAMS

I.—TO STELLA

FROM THE GREEK OF PLATO

THOU wert the morning star among the living,
    Ere thy fair light had fled;
Now, having died, thou art as Hesperus, giving
    New splendour to the dead.

II.—KISSING HELENA

FROM THE GREEK OF PLATO

KISSING Helena, together
  With my kiss, my soul beside it
    Came to my lips, and there I kept it,—
For the poor thing had wandered thither,
  To follow where the kiss should guide it,   5
    Oh, cruel I, to intercept it!

III.—SPIRT OF PLATO

FROM THE GREEK

EAGLE! why soarest thou above that tomb?
To what sublime and starry-paven home
  Floatest thou?—
I am the image of swift Plato's spirit,
Ascending heaven; Athens doth inherit   5
  His corpse below.

IV.—CIRCUMSTANCE

FROM THE GREEK

A MAN who was about to hang himself,
  Finding a purse, then threw away his rope;
The owner, coming to reclaim his pelf,
  The halter found, and used it. So is Hope
Changed for Despair—one laid upon the shelf,   5
  We take the other. Under Heaven's high cope
Fortune is God—all you endure and do
Depends on circumstance as much as you.

FRAGMENT OF THE ELEGY ON THE DEATH OF ADONIS

FROM THE GREEK OF BION

I MOURN Adonis dead—loveliest Adonis—
Dead, dead Adonis—and the Loves lament.
Sleep no more, Venus, wrapped in purple woof—
  Wake violet-stolèd queen, and weave the crown
Of Death,—'tis Misery calls,—for he is dead.   5

The lovely one lies wounded in the mountains,
His white thigh struck with the white tooth; he scarce
Yet breathes; and Venus hangs in agony there.
The dark blood wanders o'er his snowy limbs,
His eyes beneath their lids are lustreless,   10
The rose has fled from his wan lips, and there
That kiss is dead, which Venus gathers yet.

A deep, deep wound Adonis . . .
A deeper Venus bears upon her heart.
See, his belovèd dogs are gathering round—   15
The Oread nymphs are weeping—Aphrodite
With hair unbound is wandering through the woods,
'Wildered, ungirt, unsandalled—the thorns pierce
Her hastening feet and drink her sacred blood.
Bitterly screaming out, she is driven on   20
Through the long vales; and her Assyrian boy,
Her love, her husband, calls—the purple blood
     From his struck thigh stains her white navel now,
Her bosom, and her neck before like snow.

Alas for Cytherea—the Loves mourn—   25
The lovely, the beloved is gone!—and now
Her sacred beauty vanishes away.
For Venus whilst Adonis lived was fair—
Alas! her loveliness is dead with him.
The oaks and mountains cry, Ai! ai! Adonis!   30
The springs their waters change to tears and weep—
The flowers are withered up with grief . . .

Ai! ai!   Adonis is dead
Echo resounds   Adonis dead.
Who will weep not thy dreadful woe, O Venus?   35
Soon as she saw and knew the mortal wound
Of her Adonis—saw the life-blood flow
From his fair thigh, now wasting,—wailing loud
She clasped him, and cried   'Stay, Adonis!
Stay, dearest one, . . .
                         and mix my lips with thine—   40
Wake yet a while, Adonis—oh, but once,
That I may kiss thee now for the last time—
But for as long as one short kiss may live—
Oh, let thy breath flow from thy dying soul   45
Even to my mouth and heart, that I may suck
That . . .'

FRAGMENT OF THE ELEGY ON THE DEATH OF BION

FROM THE GREEK OF MOSCHUS

Ye Dorian woods and waves, lament aloud,—
Augment your tide, O streams, with fruitless tears,
For the belovèd Bion is no more.
Let every tender herb and plant and flower,
From each dejected bud and drooping bloom,
Shed dews of liquid sorrow, and with breath
Of melancholy sweetness on the wind

Diffuse its languid love; let roses blush,
Anemones grow paler for the loss
Their dells have known; and thou, O hyacinth,   10
Utter thy legend now—yet more, dumb flower,
Than 'Ah! alas!'—thine is no common grief—
Bion the [sweetest singer] is no more.

FROM THE GREEK OF MOSCHUS

Τὰν ἅλα τὰν γλαυκὰν ὅταν ὤνεμος ἀτρέμα βάλλῃ—κ.τ.λ.

WHEN winds that move not its calm surface sweep
The azure sea, I love the land no more;
The smiles of the serene and tranquil deep
Tempt my unquiet mind.—But when the roar
Of Ocean's gray abyss resounds, and foam   5
Gathers upon the sea, and vast waves burst,
I turn from the drear aspect to the home
Of Earth and its deep woods, where, interspersed,
When winds blow loud, pines make sweet melody.
Whose house is some lone bark, whose toil the sea, 10
Whose prey the wandering fish, an evil lot
Has chosen.—But I my languid limbs will fling
Beneath the plane, where the brook's murmuring
Moves the calm spirit, but disturbs it not.

PAN, ECHO, AND THE SATYR

FROM THE GREEK OF MOSCHUS

PAN loved his neighbour Echo—but that child
Of Earth and Air pined for the Satyr leaping;
The Satyr loved with wasting madness wild
The bright nymph Lyda,—and so three went weeping.
As Pan loved Echo, Echo loved the Satyr,   5
The Satyr, Lyda; and so love consumed them.—
And thus to each—which was a woful matter—
To bear what they inflicted Justice doomed them;
For, inasmuch as each might hate the lover,
Each, loving, so was hated.—Ye that love not   10
Be warned—in thought turn this example over,
That when ye love, the like return ye prove not.

FROM VERGIL'S TENTH ECLOGUE

[Vv. 1-26]

MELODIOUS Arethusa, o'er my verse
Shed thou once more the spirit of thy stream:
Who denies verse to Gallus? So, when thou

Glidest beneath the green and purple gleam
Of Syracusan waters, mayst thou flow　　　　　　5
　　Unmingled with the bitter Doric dew!
Begin, and, whilst the goats are browsing now
　　The soft leaves, in our way let us pursue
The melancholy loves of Gallus. List!

　　We sing not to the dead: the wild woods knew　10
His sufferings, and their echoes ...
　　Young Naiads, ... in what far woodlands wild
Wandered ye when unworthy love possessed
　　Your Gallus? Not where Pindus is up-piled,
Nor where Parnassus' sacred mount, nor where　15
　　Aonian Aganippe expands ...
The laurels and the myrtle-copses dim.
　　The pine-encircled mountain, Maenalus,
The cold crags of Lycaeus, weep for him;
　　And Sylvan, crowned with rustic coronals,　　20
Came shaking in his speed the budding wands
　　And heavy lilies which he bore: we knew
Pan the Arcadian.

.　　　.　　　.　　　.　　　.　　　.　　　.

'What madness is this, Gallus? Thy heart's care
With willing steps pursues another there.'　　　25

FROM VERGIL'S FOURTH GEORGIC

[Vv. 360 et seq.]

And the cloven waters like a chasm of mountains
Stood, and received him in its mighty portal
And let him through the deep's untrampled fountains

He went in wonder through the path immortal
Of his great Mother and her humid reign　　　5
And groves profaned not by the step of mortal

Which sounded as he passed, and lakes which rain
Replenished not girt round by marble caves
'Wildered by the watery motion of the main

Half 'wildered he beheld the bursting waves　　10
Of every stream beneath the mighty earth
Phasis and Lycus which the　　　sand paves,

[And] the chasm where old Enipeus has its birth
And father Tyber and Anienas[?] glow
And whence Caicus, Mysian stream, comes forth　15

And rock-resounding Hypanis, and thou
Eridanus who bearest like empire's sign
Two golden horns upon thy taurine brow

Thou than whom none of the streams divine
Through garden-fields and meads with fiercer power,   20
Burst in their tumult on the purple brine.

SONNET

FROM THE ITALIAN OF DANTE

Dante Alighieri to Guido Cavalcanti

GUIDO, I would that Lapo, thou, and I,
Led by some strong enchantment, might ascend
A magic ship, whose charmèd sails should fly
With winds at will where'er our thoughts might wend,
So that no change, nor any evil chance   5
Should mar our joyous voyage; but it might be,
That even satiety should still enhance
Between our hearts their strict community:
And that the bounteous wizard then would place
Vanna and Bice and my gentle love,   10
Companions of our wandering, and would grace
With passionate talk, wherever we might rove,
Our time, and each were as content and free
As I believe that thou and I should be.

THE FIRST CANZONE OF THE CONVITO

FROM THE ITALIAN OF DANTE

I

YE who intelligent the Third Heaven move,
Hear the discourse which is within my heart,
   Which cannot be declared, it seems so new.
The Heaven whose course follows your power and art,
   Oh, gentle creatures that ye are! me drew,   5
   And therefore may I dare to speak to you,
Even of the life which now I live—and yet
   I pray that ye will hear me when I cry,
   And tell of mine own heart this novelty;
How the lamenting Spirit moans in it,   10
And how a voice there murmurs against her
Who came on the refulgence of your sphere.

II

A sweet Thought, which was once the life within
   This heavy heart, many a time and oft
      Went up before our Father's feet, and there   15
   It saw a glorious Lady throned aloft;
And its sweet talk of her my soul did win,

So that I said, 'Thither I too will fare.'
That Thought is fled, and one doth now appear
Which tyrannizes me with such fierce stress,   20
    That my heart trembles—ye may see it leap—
    And on another Lady bids me keep
Mine eyes, and says—Who would have blessedness
Let him but look upon that Lady's eyes,
Let him not fear the agony of sighs.   25

III

This lowly Thought, which once would talk with me
Of a bright seraph sitting crowned on high,
    Found such a cruel foe it died, and so
    My Spirit wept, the grief is hot even now—
And said, Alas for me! how swift could flee   30
That piteous Thought which did my life console!
    And the afflicted one   questioning
        Mine eyes, if such a Lady saw they never,
        And why they would . . .
        I said: 'Beneath those eyes might stand for ever   35
He whom   regards must kill with . . .
To have known their power stood me in little stead,
Those eyes have looked on me, and I am dead.'

IV

'Thou art not dead, but thou hast wanderèd,
    Thou Soul of ours, who thyself dost fret,'   40
A Spirit of gentle Love beside me said;
    For that fair Lady, whom thou dost regret,
Hath so transformed the life which thou hast led,
Thou scornest it, so worthless art thou made.
And see how meek, how pitiful, how staid,   45
Yet courteous, in her majesty she is.
    And still call thou her Woman in thy thought;
    Her whom, if thou thyself deceivest not,
Thou wilt behold decked with such loveliness,
That thou wilt cry [Love] only Lord, lo! here   50
Thy handmaiden, do what thou wilt with her.

V

My song, I fear that thou wilt find but few
    Who fitly shall conceive thy reasoning
    Of such hard matter dost thou entertain.
    Whence, if by misadventure chance should bring   55
Thee to base company, as chance may do,
    Quite unaware of what thou dost contain,
    I prithee comfort thy sweet self again,

My last delight; tell them that they are dull,
And bid them own that thou art beautiful.   60

MATILDA GATHERING FLOWERS

FROM THE PURGATORIO OF DANTE, CANTO XXVIII, ll. 1-51

AND earnest to explore within—around—
The divine wood, whose thick green living woof
Tempered the young day to the sight—I wound

Up the green slope, beneath the forest's roof,
With slow, soft steps leaving the mountain's steep,   5
And sought those inmost labyrinths, motion-proof

Against the air, that in that stillness deep
And solemn, struck upon my forehead bare,
The slow, soft stroke of a continuous ...

In which the   leaves tremblingly were   10
All bent towards that part where earliest
The sacred hill obscures the morning air.

Yet were they not so shaken from the rest,
But that the birds, perched on the utmost spray,
Incessantly renewing their blithe quest,   15

With perfect joy received the early day,
Singing within the glancing leaves, whose sound
Kept a low burden to their roundelay,

Such as from bough to bough gathers around
The pine forest on bleak Chiassi's shore,   20
When Aeolus Sirocco has unbound.

My slow steps had already borne me o'er
Such space within the antique wood, that I
Perceived not where I entered any more,—

When, lo! a stream whose little waves went by,   25
Bending towards the left through grass that grew
Upon its bank, impeded suddenly

My going on. Water of purest hue
On earth, would appear turbid and impure
Compared with this, whose unconcealing dew,   30

Dark, dark, yet clear, moved under the obscure
Eternal shades, whose interwoven looms
The rays of moon or sunlight ne'er endure.

I moved not with my feet, but mid the glooms
Pierced with my charmèd eye, contemplating   35
The mighty multitude of fresh May blooms

Which starred that night, when, even as a thing
That suddenly, for blank astonishment,
Charms every sense, and makes all thought take wing,—

A solitary woman! and she went   40
Singing and gathering flower after flower,
With which her way was painted and besprent.

'Bright lady, who, if looks had ever power
To bear true witness of the heart within,
Dost bask under the beams of love, come lower   45

Towards this bank. I prithee let me win
This much of thee, to come, that I may hear
Thy song: like Proserpine, in Enna's glen,

Thou seemest to my fancy, singing here
And gathering flowers, as that fair maiden when   50
She lost the Spring, and Ceres her, more dear.'

FRAGMENT

ADAPTED FROM THE VITA NUOVA OF DANTE

WHAT Mary is when she a little smiles
I cannot even tell or call to mind,
It is a miracle so new, so rare.

UGOLINO

INFERNO xxxiii. 22-75

Now had the loophole of that dungeon, still
Which bears the name of Famine's Tower from me,
And where 'tis fit that many another will

Be doomed to linger in captivity,
Shown through its narrow opening in my cell   5
Moon after moon slow waning, when a sleep,

*That of the future burst the veil, in dream
Visited me. It was a slumber deep
And evil; for I saw, or I did seem*

To see, *that* tyrant Lord his revels keep,   10
The leader of the cruel hunt to them,
Chasing the wolf and wolf-cubs up the steep

Ascent, that from *the Pisan is the screen*
Of *Lucca;* with him Gualandi came,
Sismondi, and Lanfranchi, *bloodhounds lean,*   15

*Trained to the sport and eager for the game
Wide ranging in his front;* but soon were seen
Though by so short a course, with *spirits tame,*

The father and *his whelps* to flag at once,
And then the sharp fangs gored their bosoms deep   20
Ere morn I roused myself, and heard my sons,

For they were with me, moaning in their sleep,
And begging bread. Ah, for those darling ones!
Right cruel art thou, if thou dost not weep

In thinking of my soul's sad augury;   25
And if thou weepest not now, weep never more!
They were already waked, as wont drew nigh

The allotted hour for food, and in that hour
Each drew a presage from his dream. When I
Heard locked beneath me of that horrible tower   30

*The outlet; then into their eyes alone
I looked to read myself,* without a sign
Or word. I wept not—turned within to stone.

They wept aloud, and little Anselm mine,
Said—'twas my youngest, dearest little one,—   35
'What ails thee, father? Why look so at thine?'

In all that day, and all the following night,
I wept not, nor replied; but when to shine
Upon the world, not us, came forth the light

Of the new sun, and thwart my prison thrown   40
Gleamed through its narrow chink, a doleful sight,
Three faces, each the reflex of my own,

Were imaged by its faint and ghastly ray;
Then I, of either hand unto the bone,
Gnawed, in my agony; and thinking they   45

'Twas done from sudden pangs, in their excess,
All of a sudden raise themselves, and say,
'Father! our woes, so great, were yet the less

Would you but eat of us,—'twas *you who clad
Our bodies in these weeds of wretchedness;
Despoil them.'* Not to make their hearts more sad,   50

I *hushed* myself. That day is at its close,—
Another—still we were all mute. Oh, had
The obdurate earth opened to end our woes!

The fourth day dawned, and when the new sun shone,   55
Outstretched himself before me as it rose
My Gaddo, saying, 'Help, father! hast thou none

For thine own child—is there no help from thee?'
He died—there at my feet—and one by one,
I saw them fall, plainly as you see me.   60

Between the fifth and sixth day, ere 'twas dawn,
I found *myself blind-groping o'er the three.*
Three days I called them after they were gone.

Famine of grief can get the mastery.

SONNET

FROM THE ITALIAN OF CAVALCANTI

GUIDO CAVALCANTI TO DANTE ALIGHIERI

RETURNING from its daily quest, my Spirit
Changed thoughts and vile in thee doth weep to find:
It grieves me that thy mild and gentle mind
Those ample virtues which it did inherit
Has lost. Once thou didst loathe the multitude   5
Of blind and madding men—I then loved thee—
I loved thy lofty songs and that sweet mood
When thou wert faithful to thyself and me.
I dare not now through thy degraded state
Own the delight thy strains inspire—in vain   10
I seek what once thou wert—we cannot meet
And we were wont. Again and yet again
Ponder my words: so the false Spirit shall fly
And leave to thee thy true integrity.

SCENES FROM THE MAGICO PRODIGIOSO

FROM THE SPANISH OF CALDERON

SCENE I.—*Enter* CYPRIAN, *dressed as a Student;* CLARIN *and*
    MOSCON *as poor Scholars, with books.*

Cyprian. In the sweet solitude of this calm place,
This intricate wild wilderness of trees
And flowers and undergrowth of odorous plants,
Leave me; the books you brought out of the house
To me are ever best society.   5
And while with glorious festival and song,
Antioch now celebrates the consecration
Of a proud temple to great Jupiter,
And bears his image in loud jubilee
To its new shrine, I would consume what still   10
Lives of the dying day in studious thought,
Far from the throng and turmoil. You. my friends,
Go, and enjoy the festival; it will

Be worth your pains. You may return for me
When the sun seeks its grave among the billows 15
Which, among dim gray clouds on the horizon,
Dance like white plumes upon a hearse;—and here
I shall expect you.
    Moscon.   I cannot bring my mind,
Great as my haste to see the festival
Certainly is, to leave you, Sir, without 20
Just saying some three or four thousand words.
How is it possible that on a day
Of such festivity, you can be content
To come forth to a solitary country
With three or four old books, and turn your back 25
On all this mirth?
    Clarin.   My master's in the right;
There is not anything more tiresome
Than a procession day, with troops, and priests,
And dances, and all that.
    Moscon.   From first to last,
Clarin, you are a temporizing flatterer; 30
You praise not what you feel but what he does;—
Toadeater!
    Clarin.   You lie—under a mistake—
For this is the most civil sort of lie
That can be given to a man's face. I now
Say what I think.
    Cyprian.   Enough, you foolish fellows! 35
Puffed up with your own doting ignorance,
You always take the two sides of one question.
Now go; and as I said, return for me
When night falls, veiling in its shadows wide
This glorious fabric of the universe. 40
    Moscon. How happens it, although you can **maintain**
The folly of enjoying festivals,
That yet you go there?
    Clarin.   Nay, the consequence
Is clear:—who ever did what he advises
Others to do?—
    Moscon.   Would that my feet were wings, 45
So would I fly to Livia.   [*Exit.*
    Clarin.   To speak truth,
Livia is she who has surprised my heart;
But he is more than half-way there.—Soho!
Livia, I come; good sport, Livia, soho!   [*Exit.*
    Cyprian. Now, since I am alone, let me examine 50
The question which has long disturbed my mind
With doubt, since first I read in Plinius

The words of mystic import and deep sense
In which he defines God. My intellect
Can find no God with whom these marks and signs   55
Fitly agree. It is a hidden truth
Which I must fathom.

[CYPRIAN *reads; the* DAEMON, *dressed in a Court dress, enters.*

Daemon.   Search even as thou wilt,
But thou shalt never find what I can hide.
Cyprian. What noise is that among the boughs? Who moves?
What art thou?—
Daemon.   'Tis a foreign gentleman.   60
Even from this morning I have lost my way
In this wild place; and my poor horse at last,
Quite overcome, has stretched himself upon
The enamelled tapestry of this mossy mountain,
And feeds and rests at the same time. I was   65
Upon my way to Antioch upon business
Of some importance, but wrapped up in cares
(Who is exempt from this inheritance?)
I parted from my company, and lost
My way, and lost my servants and my comrades.   70
Cyprian. 'Tis singular that even within the sight
Of the high towers of·Antioch you could lose
Your way. Of all the avenues and green paths
Of this wild wood there is not one but leads,
As to its centre, to the walls of Antioch;   75
Take which you will, you cannot miss your road.
Daemon. And such is ignorance! Even in the sight
Of knowledge, it can draw no profit from it.
But as it still is early, and as I
Have no acquaintances in Antioch,   80
Being a stranger there, I will even wait
The few surviving hours of the day,
Until the night shall conquer it. I see
Both by your dress and by the books in which
You find delight and company, that you   85
Are a great student;—for my part, I feel
Much sympathy in such pursuits.
Cyprian.   Have you
Studied much?
Daemon.   No,—and yet I know enough
Not to be wholly ignorant.
Cyprian.   Pray, Sir,
What science may you know?—
Daemon.   Many.
Cyprian.   Alas!   90

Much pains must we expend on one alone,
And even then attain it not;—but you
Have the presumption to assert that you
Know many without study.
    Daemon.   And with truth.
For in the country whence I come the sciences   95
Require no learning,—they are known.
    Cyprian.   Oh, would
I were of that bright country! for in this
The more we study, we the more discover
Our ignorance.
    Daemon.   It is so true, that I
Had so much arrogance as to oppose   100
The chair of the most high Professorship,
And obtained many votes, and, though I lost,
The attempt was still more glorious, than the failure
Could be dishonourable. If you believe not,
Let us refer it to dispute respecting   105
That which you know the best, and although I
Know not the opinion you maintain, and though
It be the true one, I will take the contrary.
    Cyprian. The offer gives me pleasure. I am now
Debating with myself upon a passage   110
Of Plinius, and my mind is racked with doubt
To understand and know who is the God
Of whom he speaks.
    Daemon.   It is a passage, if
I recollect it right, couched in these words:
'God is one supreme goodness, one pure essence,   115
One substance, and one sense, all sight, all hands.'
    Cyprian. 'Tis true.
    Daemon.   What difficulty find you here?
    Cyprian. I do not recognize among the Gods
The God defined by Plinius; if he must
Be supreme goodness, even Jupiter   120
Is not supremely good; because we see
His deeds are evil, and his attributes
Tainted with mortal weakness; in what manner
Can supreme goodness be consistent with
The passions of humanity?
    Daemon.   The wisdom   125
Of the old world masked with the names of Gods
The attributes of Nature and of Man;
A sort of popular philosophy.
    Cyprian. This reply will not satisfy me, for
Such awe is due to the high name of God   130
That ill should never be imputed. Then,

Examining the question with more care,
It follows, that the Gods would always will
That which is best, were they supremely good.
How then does one will one thing, one another?   135
And that you may not say that I allege
Poetical or philosophic learning:—
Consider the ambiguous responses
Of their oracular statues; from two shrines
Two armies shall obtain the assurance of   140
One victory. Is it not indisputable
That two contending wills can never lead
To the same end? And, being opposite,
If one be good, is not the other evil?
Evil in God is inconceivable;   145
But supreme goodness fails among the Gods
Without their union.
  Daemon.   I deny your major.
These responses are means towards some end
Unfathomed by our intellectual beam.
They are the work of Providence, and more   150
The battle's loss may profit those who lose,
Than victory advantage those who win.
  Cyprian. That I admit; and yet that God should not
(Falsehood is incompatible with deity)
Assure the victory; it would be enough   155
To have permitted the defeat. If God
Be all sight,—God, who had beheld the truth,
Would not have given assurance of an end
Never to be accomplished: thus, although
The Deity may according to his attributes   160
Be well distinguished into persons, yet
Even in the minutest circumstance
His essence must be one.
  Daemon.   To attain the end
The affections of the actors in the scene
Must have been thus influenced by his voice.   165
  Cyprian. But for a purpose thus subordinate
He might have employed Genii, good or evil,—
A sort of spirits called so by the learned,
Who roam about inspiring good or evil,
And from whose influence and existence we   170
May well infer our immortality.
Thus God might easily, without descent
To a gross falsehood in his proper person,
Have moved the affections by this mediation
To the just point.
  Daemon.   These trifling contradictions   175

Do not suffice to impugn the unity
Of the high Gods; in things of great importance
They still appear unanimous; consider
That glorious fabric, man,—his workmanship
Is stamped with one conception.

Cyprian.   Who made man   180
Must have, methinks, the advantage of the others.
If they are equal, might they not have risen
In opposition to the work, and being
All hands, according to our author here,
Have still destroyed even as the other made?   185
If equal in their power, unequal only
In opportunity, which of the two
Will remain conqueror?

Daemon.   On impossible
And false hypothesis there can be built
No argument. Say, what do you infer   190
From this?

Cyprian.   That there must be a mighty God
Of supreme goodness and of highest grace,
All sight, all hands, all truth, infallible,
Without an equal and without a rival,
The cause of all things and the effect of nothing,   195
One power, one will, one substance, and one essence.
And, in whatever persons, one or two,
His attributes may be distinguished, one
Sovereign power, one solitary essence,
One cause of all cause.   [*They rise.*

Daemon.   How can I impugn   200
So clear a consequence?

Cyprian.   Do you regret
My victory?

Daemon.   Who but regrets a check
In rivalry of wit? I could reply
And urge new difficulties, but will now
Depart, for I hear steps of men approaching,   205
And it is time that I should now pursue
My journey to the city.

Cyprian.   Go in peace!

Daemon. Remain in peace!—Since thus it profits him
To study, I will wrap his senses up
In sweet oblivion of all thought but of   210
A piece of excellent beauty; and, as I
Have power given me to wage enmity
Against Justina's soul, I will extract
From one effect two vengeances.   [*Aside and exit.*

Cyprian.   I never

Met a more learnèd person. Let me now   215
Revolve this doubt again with careful mind.   [*He reads.*

FLORO *and* LELIO *enter.*

Lelio. Here stop. These toppling rocks and tangled boughs,
Impenetrable by the noonday beam,
Shall be sole witnesses of what we——
   Floro.   Draw!
If there were words, here is the place for deeds.   220
   Lelio. Thou needest not instruct me; well I know
That in the field, the silent tongue of steel
Speaks thus,—   [*They fight.*
   Cyprian.   Ha! what is this? Lelio,—Floro,
Be it enough that Cyprian stands between you,
Although unarmed.
   Lelio.   Whence comest thou, to stand   225
Between me and my vengeance?
   Floro.   From what rocks
And desert cells?

Enter MOSCON *and* CLARIN.

   Moscon.   Run! run! for where we left
My master, I now hear the clash of swords.
   Clarin. I never run to approach things of this sort,
But only to avoid them. Sir! Cyprian! sir!   230
   Cyprian. Be silent, fellows! What! two friends who are
In blood and fame the eyes and hope of Antioch,
One of the noble race of the Colalti,
The other son o' the Governor, adventure
And cast away, on some slight cause no doubt,   235
Two lives, the honour of their country?
   Lelio.   Cyprian!
Although my high respect towards your person
Holds now my sword suspended, thou canst not
Restore it to the slumber of the scabbard:
Thou knowest more of science than the duel;   240
For when two men of honour take the field,
No counsel nor respect can make them friends
But one must die in the dispute.
   Floro.   I pray
That you depart hence with your people, and
Leave us to finish what we have begun   245
Without advantage.——
   Cyprian.   Though you may imagine
That I know little of the laws of duel,
Which vanity and valour instituted,
You are in error. By my birth I am
Held no less than yourselves to know the limits 250

Of honour and of infamy, nor has study
Quenched the free spirit which first ordered them;
And thus to me, as one well experienced
In the false quicksands of the sea of honour,
You may refer the merits of the case;　　　　　255
And if I should perceive in your relation
That either has the right to satisfaction
From the other, I give you my word of honour
To leave you.

    Lelio.　　　　Under this condition then
I will relate the cause, and you will cede　　　260
And must confess the impossibility
Of compromise; for the same lady is
Beloved by Floro and myself.

    Floro.　　　　　　　　　It seems
Much to me that the light of day should look
Upon that idol of my heart—but he——　　265
Leave us to fight, according to thy word.

    Cyprian. Permit one question further: is the lady
Impossible to hope or not?

    Lelio.　　　　　　She is
So excellent, that if the light of day
Should excite Floro's jealousy, it were　　　270
Without just cause, for even the light of day
Trembles to gaze on her.

    Cyprian.　　　　Would you for your
Part, marry her?

    Floro.　　　Such is my confidence.

    Cyprian. And you?

    Lelio.　　　　Oh! would that I could lift my hope
So high, for though she is extremely poor,　　275
Her virtue is her dowry.

    Cyprian.　　　And if you both
Would marry her, is it not weak and vain,
Culpable and unworthy, thus beforehand
To slur her honour? What would the world say
If one should slay the other, and if she　　　280
Should afterwards espouse the murderer?

[*The rivals agree to refer their quarrel to* CYPRIAN; *who in
consequence visits* JUSTINA, *and becomes enamoured of her;
she disdains him, and he retires to a solitary sea-shore.*

SCENE II
Cyprian.

O memory! permit it not
That the tyrant of my thought

Be another soul that still
Holds dominion o'er the will,
That would refuse, but can no more,   5
To bend, to tremble, and adore.
Vain idolatry!—I saw,
    And gazing, became blind with error;
Weak ambition, which the awe
    Of her presence bound to terror!   10
So beautiful she was—and I,
Between my love and jealousy,
Am so convulsed with hope and fear,
Unworthy as it may appear;—
So bitter is the life I live,   15
That, hear me, Hell! I now would give
To thy most detested spirit
My soul, for ever to inherit,
To suffer punishment and pine,
So this woman may be mine.   20
Hear'st thou, Hell! dost thou reject it?
My soul is offered!
        Daemon (*unseen*).   I accept it.
                    [*Tempest, with thunder and lightning.*

Cyprian.

What is this? ye heavens for ever pure,
At once intensely radiant and obscure!
    Athwart the aethereal halls   25
The lightning's arrow and the thunder-balls
        The day affright,
    As from the horizon round,
    Burst with earthquake sound,
In mighty torrents the electric fountains;—   30
    Clouds quench the sun, and thunder-smoke
Strangles the air, and fire eclipses Heaven.
    Philosophy, thou canst not even
Compel their causes underneath thy yoke:
From yonder clouds even to the waves below   35
The fragments of a single ruin choke
        Imagination's flight;
For, on flakes of surge, like feathers light,
The ashes of the desolation, cast
        Upon the gloomy blast,   40
    Tell of the footsteps of the storm;
And nearer, see, the melancholy form
Of a great ship, the outcast of the sea,
        Drives miserably!
And it must fly the pity of the port,   45

Or perish, and its last and sole resort
   Is its own raging enemy.
    The terror of the thrilling cry
    Was a fatal prophecy
Of coming death, who hovers now   50
    Upon that shattered prow,
That they who die not may be dying still.
And not alone the insane elements
    Are populous with wild portents,
But that sad ship is as a miracle   55
    Of sudden ruin, for it drives so fast
It seems as if it had arrayed its form
      With the headlong storm.
    It strikes—I almost feel the shock,—
    It stumbles on a jaggèd rock,—   60
Sparkles of blood on the white foam are cast.

                              [*A tempesi*

All exclaim (*within*). We are all lost!
  Daemon (*within*).   Now from this plank will I
Pass to the land and thus fulfil my scheme.

Cyprian.

As in contempt of the elemental rage
  A man comes forth in safety, while the ship's   65
  Great form is in a watery eclipse
Obliterated from the Ocean's page,
And round its wreck the huge sea-monsters sit,
A horrid conclave, and the whistling wave
Is heaped over its carcase, like a grave.   70

  The DAEMON *enters, as escaped from the sea.*

  Daemon (*aside*). It was essential to my purposes
To wake a tumult on the sapphire ocean,
That in this unknown form I might at length
Wipe out the blot of the discomfiture
Sustained upon the mountain, and assail   75
With a new war the soul of Cyprian,
Forging the instruments of his destruction
Even from his love and from his wisdom.—O
Belovèd earth, dear mother, in thy bosom
I seek a refuge from the monster who   80
Precipitates itself upon me.
  Cyprian.   Friend,
Collect thyself; and be the memory
Of thy late suffering, and thy greatest sorrow
But as a shadow of the past,—for nothing
Beneath the circle of the moon, but flows   85

And changes, and can never know repose.
   Daemon.   And who art thou, before whose feet my fate
has prostrated me?
   Cyprian.   One who, moved with pity,
Would soothe its stings.
   Daemon.   Oh, that can never be!
No solace can my lasting sorrows find.   90
   Cyprian. Wherefore?
   Daemon.   Because my happiness is lost.
Yet I lament what has long ceased to be
The object of desire or memory,
And my life is not life.
   Cyprian.   Now, since the fury
Of this earthquaking hurricane is still,   95
And the crystàlline Heaven has reassumed
Its windless calm so quickly, that it seems
As if its heavy wrath had been awakened
Only to overwhelm that vessel,—speak,
Who art thou, and whence comest thou?
   Daemon.   Far more   100
My coming hither cost, than thou hast seen
Or I can tell. Among my misadventures
This shipwreck is the least. Wilt thou hear?
   Cyprian.   Speak.
   Daemon. Since thou desirest, I will then unveil
Myself to thee;—for in myself I am   105
A world of happiness and misery;
This I have lost, and that I must lament
Forever. In my attributes I stood
So high and so heroically great,
In lineage so supreme, and with a genius   110
Which penetrated with a glance the world
Beneath my feet, that, won by my high merit,
A king—whom I may call the King of kings,
Because all others tremble in their pride
Before the terrors of His countenance,   115
In His high palace roofed with brightest gems
Of living light—call them the stars of Heaven—
Named me His counsellor. But the high praise
Stung me with pride and envy, and I rose
In mighty competition, to ascend   120
His seat and place my foot triumphantly
Upon His subject thrones. Chastised, I know
The depth to which ambition falls; too mad
Was the attempt, and yet more mad were now
Repentance of the irrevocable deed:—   125
Therefore I chose this ruin, with the glory

Of not to be subdued, before the shame
Of reconciling me with Him who reigns
By coward cession.—Nor was I alone,
Nor am I now, nor shall I be alone;   130
And there was hope, and there may still be hope,
For many suffrages among His vassals
Hailed me their lord and king, and many still
Are mine, and many more, perchance shall be.
Thus vanquished, though in fact victorious,   135
I left His seat of empire, from mine eye
Shooting forth poisonous lightning, while my words
With inauspicious thunderings shook Heaven,
Proclaiming vengeance, public as my wrong,
And imprecating on His prostrate slaves   140
Rapine, and death, and outrage. Then I sailed
Over the mighty fabric of the world,—
A pirate ambushed in its pathless sands,
A lynx crouched watchfully among its caves
And craggy shores; and I have wandered over   145
The expanse of these wide wildernesses
In this great ship, whose bulk is now dissolved
In the light breathings of the invisible wind,
And which the sea has made a dustless ruin,
Seeking ever a mountain, through whose forests   150
I seek a man, whom I must now compel
To keep his word with me. I came arrayed
In tempest, and although my power could well
Bridle the forest winds in their career,
For other causes I forbore to soothe   155
Their fury to Favonian gentleness;
I could and would not; (thus I wake in him   [Aside.
A love of magic art). Let not this tempest,
Nor the succeeding calm excite thy wonder;
For by my art the sun would turn as pale   160
As his weak sister with unwonted fear;
And in my wisdom are the orbs of Heaven
Written as in a record; I have pierced
The flaming circles of their wondrous spheres
And know them as thou knowest every corner   165
Of this dim spot. Let it not seem to thee
That I boast vainly; wouldst thou that I work
A charm over this waste and savage wood,
This Babylon of crags and agèd trees,
Filling its leafy coverts with a horror   170
Thrilling and strange? I am the friendless guest
Of these wild oaks and pines—and as from thee
I have received the hospitality

Of this rude place, I offer thee the fruit
Of years of toil in recompense; whate'er   175
Thy wildest dream presented to thy thought
As object of desire, that shall be thine.

.   .   .   .   .   .

And thenceforth shall so firm an amity
'Twixt thee and me be, that neither Fortune,
The monstrous phantom which pursues success,   180
That careful miser, that free prodigal,
Who ever alternates, with changeful hand,
Evil and good, reproach and fame; nor Time,
That lodestar of the ages, to whose beam
The wingèd years speed o'er the intervals   185
Of their unequal revolutions; nor
Heaven itself, whose beautiful bright stars
Rule and adorn the world, can ever make
The least division between thee and me,
Since now I find a refuge in thy favour.   190

SCENE III.—*The* DAEMON *tempts* JUSTINA, *who is a Christian.*

Daemon.

Abyss of Hell! I call on thee,
Thou wild misrule of thine own anarchy!
    From thy prison-house set free
    The spirits of voluptuous death,
      That with their mighty breath   5
They may destroy a world of virgin thoughts;
Let her chaste mind with fancies thick as motes
    Be peopled from thy shadowy deep,
    Till her guiltless fantasy
    Full to overflowing be!   10
    And with sweetest harmony,
Let birds, and flowers, and leaves, and all things move
    To love, only to love.
    Let nothing meet her eyes
But signs of Love's soft victories;   15
    Let nothing meet her ear
    But sounds of Love's sweet sorrow,
So that from faith no succour she may borrow,
    But, guided by my spirit blind
    And in a magic snare entwined,   20
      She may now seek Cyprian.
    Begin, while I in silence bind
My voice, when thy sweet song thou hast began.

A Voice (within).

What is the glory far above
All else in human life?

All.

Love! love!   25

[*While these words are sung, the* DAEMON *goes out at one door, and*
JUSTINA *enters at another.*

The First Voice.

There is no form in which the fire
   Of love its traces has impressed not.
Man lives far more in love's desire
   Than by life's breath, soon possessed not.
If all that lives must love or die,   30
All shapes on earth, or sea, or sky,
With one consent to Heaven cry
That the glory far above
All else in life is—

All.

Love! oh, Love!

Justina.

Thou melancholy Thought which art   35
So flattering and so sweet, to thee
When did I give the liberty
   Thus to afflict my heart?
What is the cause of this new Power
   Which doth my fevered being move,   40
Momently raging more and more?
What subtle Pain is kindled now
Which from my heart doth overflow
   Into my senses?—

All.

Love! oh, Love!

Justina.

'Tis that enamoured Nightingale   45
   Who gives me the reply;
He ever tells the same soft tale
   Of passion and of constancy
To his mate, who rapt and fond,
Listening sits, a bough beyond.   50

Be silent, Nightingale—no more
 Make me think, in hearing thee
Thus tenderly thy love deplore,
  If a bird can feel his so,
 What a man would feel for me.   55
  And, voluptuous Vine, O thou
Who seekest most when least pursuing,—
 To the trunk thou interlacest
 Art the verdure which embracest,
And the weight which is its ruin,—   60
 No more, with green embraces, Vine,
  Make me think on what thou lovest,—
 For whilst thus thy boughs entwine,
  I fear lest thou shouldst teach me, sophist,
How arms might be entangled too.   65

Light-enchanted Sunflower, thou
Who gazest ever true and tender
On the sun's revolving splendour!
Follow not his faithless glance
 With thy faded countenance,   70
Nor teach my beating heart to fear,
If leaves can mourn without a tear,
How eyes must weep! O Nightingale,
Cease from thy enamoured tale,—
Leafy Vine, unwreathe thy bower,   75
 Restless Sunflower, cease to move,—
Or tell me all, what poisonous Power
 Ye use against me—

All.

         Love! Love! Love!
 Justina. It cannot be!—Whom have I ever loved?
Trophies of my oblivion and disdain,   80
Floro and Lelio did I not reject?
And Cyprian?—   [*She becomes troubled at the name of Cyprian.*
    Did I not requite him
With such severity, that he has fled
Where none has ever heard of him again?—
Alas! I now begin to fear that this   85
May be the occasion whence desire grows bold,
As if there were no danger. From the moment
That I pronounced to my own listening heart,
'Cyprian is absent!'—O me miserable!
I know not what I feel! [*More calmly.*] It must be pity 90
To think that such a man, whom all the world
Admired, should be forgot by all the world,

And I the cause.   [*She again becomes troubled.*
                    And yet if it were pity,
Floro and Lelio might have equal share,
For they are both imprisoned for my sake.   95
(*Calmly.*) Alas! what reasonings are these? it is
Enough I pity him, and that, in vain,
Without this ceremonious subtlety.
And, woe is me! I know not where to find him now,
Even should I seek him through this wide world.   100

Enter DAEMON.

   Daemon. Follow, and I will lead thee where he is.
   Justina. And who art thou, who hast found entrance hither,
Into my chamber through the doors and locks?
Art thou a monstrous shadow which my madness
Has formed in the idle air?
   Daemon.   No. I am one   105
Called by the Thought which tyrannizes thee
From his eternal dwelling; who this day
Is pledged to bear thee unto Cyprian.
   Justina. So shall thy promise fail. This agony
Of passion which afflicts my heart and soul   110
May sweep imagination in its storm;
The will is firm.
   Daemon.   Already half is done
In the imagination of an act.
The sin incurred, the pleasure then remains;
Let not the will stop half-way on the road.   115
   Justina. I will not be discouraged, nor despair,
Although I thought it, and although 'tis true
That thought is but a prelude to the deed:—
Thought is not in my power, but action is:
I will not move my foot to follow thee.   120
   Daemon. But a far mightier wisdom than thine own
Exerts itself within thee, with such power
Compelling thee to that which it inclines
That it shall force thy step; how wilt thou then
Resist, Justina?
   Justina.   By my free-will.
   Daemon.   I   125
Must force thy will.
   Justina.   It is invincible;
It were not free if thou hadst power upon it.
                                   [*He draws, but cannot move her.*
   Daemon. Come, where a pleasure waits thee.
   Justina.   It were bought
Too dear.

Daemon. 'Twill soothe thy heart to softest peace.
Justina. 'Tis dread captivity.
Daemon.   'Tis joy, 'tis glory.   130
Justina. 'Tis shame, 'tis torment, 'tis despair.
Daemon.   But how
Canst thou defend thyself from that or me,
If my power drags thee onward?
Justina.   My defence
Consists in God.

  [*He vainly endeavours to force her, and at last releases her.*

Daemon.   Woman, thou hast subdued me,
Only by not owning thyself subdued.   135
But since thou thus findest defence in God,
I will assume a feignèd form, and thus
Make thee a victim of my baffled rage.
For I will mask a spirit in thy form
Who will betray thy name to infamy,   140
And doubly shall I triumph in thy loss,
First by dishonouring thee, and then by turning
False pleasure to true ignominy.   [*Exit.*
Justina.   I
Appeal to Heaven against thee; so that Heaven
May scatter thy delusions, and the blot   145
Upon my fame vanish in idle thought,
Even as flame dies in the envious air,
And as the floweret wanes at morning frost;
And thou shouldst never—But, alas! to whom
Do I still speak?—Did not a man but now   150
Stand here before me?—No, I am alone,
And yet I saw him. Is he gone so quickly?
Or can the heated mind engender shapes
From its own fear? Some terrible and strange
Peril is near. Lisander! father! lord!   155
Livia!—

Enter LISANDER *and* LIVIA.

Lisander. Oh, my daughter! What?
Livia.   What!
Justina.   Saw you
A man go forth from my apartment now?—
I scarce contain myself!
Lisander.   A man here!
Justina. Have you not seen him?
Livia.   No, Lady.
Justina. I saw him.
Lisander.   'Tis impossible; the doors   160
Which led to this apartment were all locked.

Livia (*aside*). I daresay it was Moscon whom she saw,
For he was locked up in my room.
    Lisander.   It must
Have been some image of thy fantasy. 165
Such melancholy as thou feedest is
Skilful in forming such in the vain air
Out of the motes and atoms of the day.
    Livia. My master's in the right.
    Justina.   Oh, would it were
Delusion; but I fear some greater ill.
I feel as if out of my bleeding bosom 170
My heart was torn in fragments; ay,
Some mortal spell is wrought against my frame;
So potent was the charm that, had not God
Shielded my humble innocence from wrong,
I should have sought my sorrow and my shame 175
With willing steps.—Livia, quick, bring my cloak,
For I must seek refuge from these extremes
Even in the temple of the highest God
Where secretly the faithful worship.
    Livia.   Here.
    Justina (*putting on her cloak*). In this, as in a shroud of snow, may I
Quench the consuming fire in which I burn, 181
Wasting away!
    Lisander.   And I will go with thee.
    Livia. When I once see them safe out of the house
I shall breathe freely.
    Justina.   So do I confide
In thy just favour, Heaven!
    Lisander.   Let us go. 185
    Justina. Thine is the cause, great God! turn for my sake,
And for Thine own, mercifully to me!

STANZAS FROM CALDERON'S CISMA DE INGLATERRA

I

Hast thou not seen, officious with delight,
    Move through the illumined air about the flower
The Bee, that fears to drink its purple light,
    Lest danger lurk within that Rose's bower?
Hast thou not marked the moth's enamoured flight 5
    About the Taper's flame at evening hour,
Till kindle in that monumental fire
His sunflower wings their own funereal pyre?

II

My heart, its wishes trembling to unfold,
   Thus round the Rose and Taper hovering came,   10
And Passion's slave, Distrust, in ashes cold,
   Smothered awhile, but could not quench the flame,—
Till Love, that grows by disappointment bold,
   And Opportunity, had conquered Shame;
And like the Bee and Moth, in act to close,   15
I burned my wings, and settled on the Rose.

SCENES FROM THE FAUST OF GOETHE

Scene I.—Prologue in Heaven. *The* Lord *and the* Host *of*
Heaven.

Enter three Archangels.

Raphael.

The sun makes music as of old
   Amid the rival spheres of Heaven,
On its predestined circle rolled
   With thunder speed: the Angels even
Draw strength from gazing on its glance,   5
   Though none its meaning fathom may:—
The world's unwithered countenance
   Is bright as at Creation's day.

Gabriel.

And swift and swift, with rapid lightness,
   The adornèd Earth spins silently,   10
Alternating Elysian brightness
   With deep and dreadful night; the sea
Foams in broad billows from the deep
   Up to the rocks, and rocks and Ocean,
Onward, with spheres which never sleep,   15
   Are hurried in eternal motion.

Michael.

And tempests in contention roar
   From land to sea, from sea to land;
And, raging, weave a chain of power,
   Which girds the earth, as with a band.—   20
A flashing desolation there,
   Flames before the thunder's way;
But Thy servants, Lord, revere
   The gentle changes of Thy day.

Chorus of the Three.

The Angels draw strength from Thy glance,   25
    Though no one comprehend Thee may;—
Thy world's unwithered countenance
    Is bright as on Creation's day.[1]

Enter MEPHISTOPHELES.

Mephistopheles. As thou, O Lord, once more art kind enough
To interest Thyself in our affairs,   30
And ask, 'How goes it with you there below?'
And as indulgently at other times
Thou tookest not my visits in ill part,
Thou seest me here once more among Thy household.
Though I should scandalize this company,   35
You will excuse me if I do not talk
In the high style which they think fashionable;
My pathos certainly would make You laugh too,
Had You not long since given over laughing.
Nothing know I to say of suns and worlds;   40
I observe only how men plague themselves;—

[1] *Raphael.* The sun sounds, according to ancient custom,
In the song of emulation of his brother-spheres.
And its fore-written circle
Fulfils with a step of thunder.
Its countenance gives the Angels strength
Though no one can fathom it.
The incredible high works
Are excellent as at the first day.
    Gabriel. And swift, and inconceivably swift
The adornment of earth winds itself round,
And exchanges Paradise-clearness
With deep dreadful night.
The sea foams in broad waves
From its deep bottom, up to the rocks,
And rocks and sea are torn on together
In the eternal swift course of the spheres.
    Michael. And storms roar in emulation
From sea to land, from land to sea,
And make, raging, a chain
Of deepest operation round about.
There flames a flashing destruction
Before the path of the thunderbolt.
But Thy servants, Lord, revere
The gentle alternations of Thy day.
    Chorus. Thy countenance gives the Angels strength,
Though none can comprehend Thee:
And all Thy lofty works
Are excellent as at the first day.

Such is a literal translation of this astonishing chorus; it is impossible to represent in another language the melody of the versification; even the volatile strength
and delicacy of the ideas escape in the crucible of translation, and the reader is
surprisd to find a *caput mortuum.*—[SHELLEY'S NOTE.]

The little god o' the world keeps the same stamp,
As wonderful as on creation's day:—
A little better would he live, hadst Thou
Not given him a glimpse of Heaven's light   45
Which he calls reason, and employs it only
To live more beastlily than any beast.
With reverence to Your Lordship be it spoken,
He's like one of those long-legged grasshoppers,
Who flits and jumps about, and sings for ever   50
The same old song i' the grass. There let him lie,
Burying his nose in every heap of dung.
  The Lord. Have you no more to say? Do you come here
Always to scold, and cavil, and complain?
Seems nothing ever right to you on earth?   55
  Mephistopheles. No, Lord! I find all there, as ever, bad at best.
Even I am sorry for man's days of sorrow;
I could myself almost give up the pleasure
Of plaguing the poor things.
  The Lord.   Knowest thou Faust?
  Mephistopheles. The Doctor?
  The Lord.   Ay; My servant Faust.
  Mephistopheles.   In truth   60
He serves You in a fashion quite his own;
And the fool's meat and drink are not of earth.
His aspirations bear him on so far
That he is half aware of his own folly,
For he demands from Heaven its fairest star,   65
And from the earth the highest joy it bears,
Yet all things far, and all things near, are vain
To calm the deep emotions of his breast.
  The Lord. Though he now serves Me in a cloud of error,
I will soon lead him forth to the clear day.   70
When trees look green, full well the gardener knows
That fruits and blooms will deck the coming year.
  Mephistopheles. What will You bet?—now I am sure of winning—
Only, observe You give me full permission
To lead him softly on my path.
  The Lord.   As long   75
As he shall live upon the earth, so long
Is nothing unto thee forbidden—Man
Must err till he has ceased to struggle.
  Mephistopheles.   Thanks.
And that is all I ask; for willingly
I never make acquaintance with the dead.   80
The full fresh cheeks of youth are food for me,
And if a corpse knocks, I am not at home.
For I am like a cat—I like to play

A little with the mouse before I eat it.

The Lord. Well, well! it is permitted thee. Draw thou   85
His spirit from its springs; as thou find'st power,
Seize him and lead him on thy downward path;
And stand ashamed when failure teaches thee
That a good man, even in his darkest longings,
Is well aware of the right way.

    Mephistopheles.   Well and good.   90
I am not in much doubt about my bet,
And if I lose, then 'tis Your turn to crow;
Enjoy Your triumph then with a full breast.
Ay; dust shall he devour, and that with pleasure,
Like my old paramour, the famous Snake.   95

    The Lord. Pray come here when it suits you; for I never
Had much dislike for people of your sort.
And, among all the Spirits who rebelled,
The knave was ever the least tedious to Me.
The active spirit of man soon sleeps, and soon   100
He seeks unbroken quiet; therefore I
Have given him the Devil for a companion,
Who may provoke him to some sort of work,
And must create forever.—But ye, pure
Children of God, enjoy eternal beauty;—   105
Let that which ever operates and lives
Clasp you within the limits of its love;
And seize with sweet and melancholy thoughts
The floating phantoms of its loveliness.

           [Heaven closes; the Archangels exeunt.

    Mephistopheles. From time to time I visit the old fellow,
And I take care to keep on good terms with Him.   111
Civil enough is the same God Almighty,
To talk so freely with the Devil himself.

SCENE II.—MAY-DAY NIGHT. *The Hartz Mountain, a desolate
Country.* FAUST, MEPHISTOPHELES.

    Mephistopheles. Would you not like a broomstick? As for me
I wish I had a good stout ram to ride;
For we are still far from the appointed place.

    Faust. This knotted staff is help enough for me,
Whilst I feel fresh upon my legs. What good   5
Is there in making short a pleasant way?
To creep along the labyrinths of the vales,
And climb those rocks, where ever-babbling springs,
Precipitate themselves in waterfalls,
Is the true sport that seasons such a path.   10
Already Spring kindles the birchen spray,
And the hoar pines already feel her breath:

Shall she not work also within our limbs?
Mephistopheles. Nothing of such an influence do I feel.
My body is all wintry, and I wish   15
The flowers upon our path were frost and snow.
But see how melancholy rises now,
Dimly uplifting her belated beam,
The blank unwelcome round of the red moon,
And gives so bad a light, that every step   20
One stumbles 'gainst some crag. With your permission,
I'll call an Ignis-fatuus to our aid:
I see one yonder burning jollily.
Halloo, my friend! may I request that you
Would favour us with your bright company?   25
Why should you blaze away there to no purpose?
Pray be so good as light us up this way.
    Ignis-fatuus. With reverence be it spoken, I will try
To overcome the lightness of my nature;
Our course, you know, is generally zigzag.   30
    Mephistopheles. Ha, ha! your worship thinks you have to deal
With men. Go straight on, in the Devil's name,
Or I shall puff your flickering life out.
    Ignis-fatuus.   Well,
I see you are the master of the house;
I will accommodate myself to you.   35
Only consider that to-night this mountain
Is all enchanted, and if Jack-a-lantern
Shows you his way, though you should miss your own,
You ought not to be too exact with him.

FAUST, MEPHISTOPHELES, *and* IGNIS-FATUUS, *in alternate Chorus.*

            The limits of the sphere of dream,   40
                The bounds of true and false, are past.
            Lead us on, thou wandering Gleam,
                Lead us onward, far and fast,
                To the wide, the desert waste.

            But see, how swift advance and shift   45
                Trees behind trees, row by row,—
            How, clift by clift, rocks bend and lift
                Their frowning foreheads as we go.
                The giant-snouted crags, ho! ho!
                How they snort, and how they blow!   50

            Through the mossy sods and stones,
                Stream and streamlet hurry down—
                    A rushing throng! A sound of song
                Beneath the vault of Heaven is blown!
            Sweet notes of love, the speaking tones   55

Of this bright day, sent down to say
  That Paradise on Earth is known,
Resound around, beneath, above.
All we hope and all we love
Finds a voice in this blithe strain,   60
    Which wakens hill and wood and rill,
      And vibrates far o'er field and vale,
      And which Echo, like the tale
Of old times, repeats again.

To-whoo! to-whoo! near, nearer now   65
The sound of song, the rushing throng!
Are the screech, the lapwing, and the jay,
All awake as if 'twere day?
See, with long legs and belly wide,
    A salamander in the brake!   70
    Every root is like a snake,
And along the loose hillside,
With strange contortions through the night,
Curls, to seize or to affright;
And, animated, strong, and many,   75
They dart forth polypus-antennae,
To blister with their poison spume
The wanderer. Through the dazzling gloom
The many-coloured mice, that thread
The dewy turf beneath our tread,   80
In troops each other's motions cross,
Through the heath and through the moss;
And, in legions intertangled,
    The fire-flies flit, and swarm, and throng,
Till all the mountain depths are spangled.   85

Tell me, shall we go or stay?
    Shall we onward? Come along!
    Everything around is swept
Forward, onward, far away!
Trees and masses intercept   90
The sight, and wisps on every side
Are puffed up and multiplied.

Mephistopheles. Now vigorously seize my skirt, and gain
This pinnacle of isolated crag.
One may observe with wonder from this point,   95
How Mammon glows among the mountains.
    Faust.   Ay—
And strangely through the solid depth below
A melancholy light, like the red dawn,
Shoots from the lowest gorge of the abyss
Of mountains, lightning hitherward: there rise   100

Pillars of smoke, here clouds float gently by;
Here the light burns soft as the enkindled air,
Or the illumined dust of golden flowers;
And now it glides like tender colours spreading;
And now bursts forth in fountains from the earth;   105
And now it winds, one torrent of broad light,
Through the far valley with a hundred veins;
And now once more within that narrow corner
Masses itself into intensest splendour.
And near us, see, sparks spring out of the ground,   110
Like golden sand scattered upon the darkness;
The pinnacles of that black wall of mountains
That hems us in are kindled.
 Mephistopheles.   Rare: in faith!
Does not Sir Mammon gloriously illuminate
His palace for this festival?—it is   115
A pleasure whch you had not known before.
I spy the boisterous guests already.
 Faust.   How
The children of the wind rage in the air!
With what fierce strokes they fall upon my neck!

Mephistopheles.

Cling tightly to the old ribs of the crag.   120
 Beware! for if with them thou warrest
In their fierce flight towards the wilderness,
Their breath will sweep thee into dust, and drag
 Thy body to a grave in the abyss.
A cloud thickens the night.   125
 Hark! how the tempest crashes through the forest!
 The owls fly out in strange affright;
The columns of the evergreen palaces
 Are split and shattered;
The roots creak, and stretch, and groan;   130
And ruinously overthrown,
 The trunks are crushed and shattered
By the fierce blast's unconquerable stress.
Over each other crack and crash they all
In terrible and intertangled fall;   135
And through the ruins of the shaken mountain
 The airs hiss and howl—
It is not the voice of the fountain,
 Nor the wolf in his midnight prowl.
 Dost thou not hear?   140
  Strange accents are ringing
 Aloft, afar, anear?
  The witches are singing!

The torrent of a raging wizard song
 Streams the whole mountain along. 145

Chorus of Witches.

The stubble is yellow, the corn is green,
 Now to the Brocken the witches go;
The mighty multitude here may be seen
 Gathering, wizard and witch, below.
Sir Urian is sitting aloft in the air; 150
 Hey over stock! and hey over stone!
 'Twixt witches and incubi, what shall be done?
Tell it who dare! tell it who dare!

A Voice.

Upon a sow-swine, whose farrows were nine,
 Old Baubo rideth alone. 155

Chorus.

Honour her, to whom honour is due,
Old mother Baubo, honour to you!
An able sow, with old Baubo upon her,
Is worthy of glory, and worthy of honour!
The legion of witches is coming behind, 160
Darkening the night, and outspeeding the wind—

A Voice.

Which way comest thou?

A Voice.

Over Ilsenstein;
The owl was awake in the white moonshine;
 I saw her at rest in her downy nest,
And she stared at me with her broad, bright eyne. 165

Voices.

And you may now as well take your course on to Hell,
Since you ride by so fast on the headlong blast.

A Voice.

She dropped poison upon me as I passed.
Here are the wounds——

Chorus of Witches.

Come away! come along!
The way is wide, the way is long, 170
But what is that for a Bedlam throng?
Stick with the prong, and scratch with the broom.

The child in the cradle lies strangled at home,
And the mother is clapping her hands.—

Semichorus of Wizards I.

We glide in
Like snails when the women are all away;   175
And from a house once given over to sin
Woman has a thousand steps to stray.

Semichorus II.

A thousand steps must a woman take,
Where a man but a single spring will make.

Voices above.

Come with us, come with us, from Felsensee.   180

Voices below.

With what joy would we fly through the upper sky!
We are washed, we are 'nointed, stark naked are we;
But our toil and our pain are forever in vain.

Both Choruses.

The wind is still, the stars are fled,
The melancholy moon is dead;   185
The magic notes, like spark on spark,
Drizzle, whistling through the dark.
Come away!

Voices below.

Stay, Oh, stay!

Voices above.

Out of the crannies of the rocks   190
Who calls?

Voices below.

Oh, let me join your flocks!
I, three hundred years have striven
To catch your skirt and mount to Heaven,—
And still in vain. Oh, might I be
With company akin to me!   195

Both Choruses.

Some on a ram and some on a prong,
On poles and on broomsticks we flutter along;
Forlorn is the wight who can rise not to-night.

A Half-Witch below.

I have been tripping this many an hour:
Are the others already so far before?   200
No quiet at home, and no peace abroad!
And less methinks is found by the road.

Chorus of Witches.

Come onward, away! aroint thee, aroint!
A witch to be strong must anoint—anoint—
Then every trough will be boat enough;   205
With a rag for a sail we can sweep through the sky,
Who flies not to-night, when means he to fly?

Both Choruses.

We cling to the skirt, and we strike on the ground;
Witch-legions thicken around and around;
Wizard-swarms cover the heath all over.   [*They descend.*

Mephistopheles.

What thronging, dashing, raging, rustling;   211
What whispering, babbling, hissing, bustling;
What glimmering, spurting, stinking, burning,
As Heaven and Earth were overturning.
There is a true witch element about us;   215
Take hold on me, or we shall be divided:—
Where are you?
     Faust (from a distance). Here!
        Mephistopheles.   What!
I must exert my authority in the house.
Place for young Voland! pray make way, good people.
Take hold on me, doctor, and with one step   220
Let us escape from this unpleasant crowd:
They are too mad for people of my sort.
Just there shines a peculiar kind of light—
Something attracts me in those bushes. Come
This way: we shall slip down there in a minute.   225
     Faust. Spirit of Contradiction! Well, lead on—
'Twere a wise feat indeed to wander out
Into the Brocken upon May-day night,
And then to isolate oneself in scorn,
Disgusted with the humours of the time.   230
     Mephistopheles. See yonder, round a many-coloured flame
A merry club is huddled altogether:
Even with such little people as sit there
One would not be alone.
     Faust.   Would that I were

Up yonder in the glow and whirling smoke,   235
Where the blind million rush impetuously
To meet the evil ones; there might I solve
Many a riddle that torments me!
    Mephistopheles.   Yet
Many a riddle there is tied anew
Inextricably. Let the great world rage!   240
We will stay here safe in the quiet dwellings.
'Tis an old custom. Men have ever built
Their own small world in the great world of all.
I see young witches naked there, and old ones
Wisely attired with greater decency.   245
Be guided now by me, and you shall buy
A pound of pleasure with a dram of trouble.
I hear them tune their instruments—one must
Get used to this damned scraping. Come, I'll lead you
Among them; and what there you do and see,   250
As a fresh compact 'twixt us two shall be.
How say you now? this space is wide enough—
Look forth, you cannot see the end of it—
An hundred bonfires burn in rows, and they
Who throng around them seem innumerable: 255
Dancing and drinking, jabbering, making love,
And cooking, are at work. Now tell me, friend,
What is there better in the world than this?
    Faust. In introducing us, do you assume
The character of Wizard or of Devil?   260
    Mephistopheles. In truth, I generally go about
In strict incognito; and yet one likes
To wear one's orders upon gala days.
I have no ribbon at my knee; but here
At home, the cloven foot is honourable.   265
See you that snail there?—she comes creeping up,
And with her feeling eyes hath smelt out something.
I could not, if I would, mask myself here.
Come now, we'll go about from fire to fire:
I'll be the Pimp, and you shall be the Lover.   270
[*To some old Women, who are sitting round a heap of glimmering coals.*
Old gentlewomen, what do you do out here?
You ought to be with the young rioters
Right in the thickest of the revelry—
But every one is best content at home.

General.

Who dare confide in right or a just claim?   275
    So much as I had done for them! and now—
With women and the people 'tis the same,

Youth will stand foremost ever,—age may go
To the dark grave unhonoured.

Minister.

Nowadays
People assert their rights: they go too far;   280
But as for me, the good old times I praise;
Then we were all in all—'twas something worth
One's while to be in place and wear a star;
That was indeed the golden age on earth.

Parvenu.

We too are active, and we did and do   285
What we ought not, perhaps; and yet we now
Will seize, whilst all things are whirled round and round,
A spoke of Fortune's wheel, and keep our ground.

Author.

Who now can taste a treatise of deep sense
And ponderous volume? 'tis impertinence   290
To write what none will read, therefore will I
To please the young and thoughtless people try.

Mephistopheles (who at once appears to have grown very old). I
find the people ripe for the last day,
Since I last came up to the wizard mountain;
And as my little cask runs turbid now,   295
So is the world drained to the dregs.

Pedlar-witch.   Look here,
Gentlemen; do not hurry on so fast;
And lose the chance of a good pennyworth.
I have a pack full of the choicest wares
Of every sort, and yet in all my bundle   300
Is nothing like what may be found on earth;
Nothing that in a moment will make rich
Men and the world with fine malicious mischief—
There is no dagger drunk with blood; no bowl
From which consuming poison may be drained   305
By innocent and healthy lips; no jewel,
The price of an abandoned maiden's shame;
No sword which cuts the bond it cannot loose,
Or stabs the wearer's enemy in the back;
No——

Mephistopheles. Gossip, you know little of these times.   310
What has been, has been; what is done, is past,
They shape themselves into the innovations
They breed, and innovation drags us with it.
The torrent of the crowd sweeps over us:
You think to impel, and are yourself impelled.   315

Faust. What is that yonder?

Mephistopheles. Mark her well. It is Lilith.

Faust. Who?

Mephistopheles. Lilith, the first wife of Adam.
Beware of her fair hair, for she excels
All women in the magic of her locks;
And when she winds them round a young man's neck, 320
She will not ever set him free again.

Faust.

There sit a girl and an old woman—they
Seem to be tired with pleasure and with play.

Mephistopheles.

There is no rest to-night for any one:
When one dance ends another is begun; 325
Come, let us to it. We shall have rare fun.

[FAUST *dances and sings with a girl, and* MEPHISTOPHELES *with an old Woman.*

Faust.

I had once a lovely dream
In which I saw an apple-tree,
Where two fair apples with their gleam
To climb and taste attracted me. 330

The Girl.

She with apples you desired
From Paradise came long ago:
With you I feel that if required,
Such still within my garden grow.

. . . . .

Procto-Phantasmist. What is this cursèd multitude about?
Have we not long since proved to demonstration 336
That ghosts move not on ordinary feet?
But these are dancing just like men and women.

The Girl. What does he want then at our ball?

Faust. Oh! he
Is far above us all in his conceit: 340
Whilst we enjoy, he reasons of enjoyment;
And any step which in our dance we tread,
If it be left out of his reckoning,
Is not to be considered as a step.
There are few things that scandalize him not: 345
And when you whirl round in the circle now,
As he went round the wheel in his old mill,
He says that you go wrong in all respects,
Especially if you congratulate him

Upon the strength of the resemblance.

    Procto-Phantasmist.   **Fly!**   350

Vanish! Unheard-of impudence! What, still there!
In this enlightened age too, since you have been
Proved not to exist!—But this infernal brood
Will hear no reason and endure no rule.
Are we so wise, and is the *pond* still haunted?   355
How long have I been sweeping out this rubbish
Of superstition, and the world will not
Come clean with all my pains!—it is a case
Unheard of!

    The Girl.   Then leave off teasing us so.

    Procto-Phantasmist. I tell you, spirits, to your faces now,   360
That I should not regret this despotism
Of spirits, but that mine can wield it not.
To-night I shall make poor work of it,
Yet I will take a round with you, and hope
Before my last step in the living dance   365
To beat the poet and the devil together.

    Mephistopheles. At last he will sit down in some foul puddle;
That is his way of solacing himself;
Until some leech, diverted with his gravity,
Cures him of spirits and the spirit together.   370

               [*To* FAUST, *who has seceded from the dance.*

Why do you let that fair girl pass from you,
Who sung so sweetly to you in the dance?

    Faust. A red mouse in the middle of her singing
Sprung from her mouth.

    Mephistopheles.   That was all right, my friend:
Be it enough that the mouse was not gray.   375
Do not disturb your hour of happiness
With close consideration of such trifles.

    Faust. Then saw I——

    Mephistopheles.   **What?**

    Faust.   Seest thou not a pale,
Fair girl, standing alone, far, far away?
She drags herself now forward with slow steps,   380
And seems as if she moved with shackled feet:
I cannot overcome the thought that she
Is like poor Margaret.

    Mephistopheles.   Let it be—pass on—
No good can come of it—it is not well
To meet it—it is an enchanted phantom,   385
A lifeless idol; with its numbing look,
It freezes up the blood of man; and they
Who meet its ghastly stare are turned to stone,
Like those who saw Medusa.

Faust.   Oh, too true!
Her eyes are like the eyes of a fresh corpse   390
Which no belovèd hand has closed, alas!
That is the breast which Margaret yielded to me—
Those are the lovely limbs which I enjoyed!
    Mephistopheles. It is all magic, poor deluded fool!
She looks to every one like his first love.   395
    Faust. Oh, what delight! what woe! I cannot turn
My looks from her sweet piteous countenance.
How strangely does a single blood-red line,
Not broader than the sharp edge of a knife,
Adorn her lovely neck!
    Mephistopheles.   Ay, she can carry   400
Her head under her arm upon occasion;
Perseus has cut it off for her. These pleasures
End in delusion.—Gain this rising ground,
It is as airy here as in a . . .
And if I am not mightily deceived,   405
I see a theatre.—What may this mean?
    Attendant. Quite a new piece, the last of seven, for 'tis
The custom now to represent that number.
'Tis written by a Dilettante, and
The actors who perform are Dilettanti;   410
Excuse me, gentlemen; but I must vanish.
I am a Dilettante curtain-lifter.

JUVENILIA

QUEEN MAB

A PHILOSOPHICAL POEM, WITH NOTES

ECRASEZ L'INFAME!—*Correspondance de Voltaire.*
Avia Pieridum poragro loca, nullius ante
Trita solo; juvat integros accedere fonteis;
Atque haurire: juvatque novos decerpere flores.

     .   .   .   .

Unde prius nulli velarint tempora musae.
Primum quod magnis doceo de rebus; et arctis
Religionum animos nodis exsolvere pergo.—*Lucret.* lib. iv.
Δος πॖ στω, καὶ κοσμον κινησω.—*Archimedes.*

TO HARRIET * * * * *

WHOSE is the love that gleaming
    through the world,
Wards off the poisonous arrow of
    its scorn?
Whose is the warm and partial
    praise,

Virtue's most sweet reward?

Beneath whose looks did my reviv-
    ing soul   5
Riper in truth and virtuous daring
    grow?

Whose eyes have I gazed fondly
    on,
And loved mankind the more?

HARRIET! on thine:—thou wert
    my purer mind;
Thou wert the inspiration of my
    song;   10
  Thine are these early wilding
    flowers,
  Though garlanded by me.

Then press into thy breast this
    pledge of love;
And know, though time may change
    and years may roll,
  Each floweret gathered in my
    heart   15
  It consecrates to thine.

QUEEN MAB

I

How wonderful is Death,
Death and his brother Sleep!
One, pale as yonder waning moon
  With lips of lurid blue;
The other, rosy as the morn   5
When throned on ocean's wave
It blushes o'er the world:
Yet both so passing wonderful!

Hath then the gloomy Power
Whose reign is in the tainted sepul-
    chres   10
  Seized on her sinless soul?
Must then that peerless form
Which love and admiration cannot
    view
Without a beating heart, those
    azure veins
Which steal like streams along a
    field of snow,   15
  That lovely outline, which is fair
    As breathing marble, perish?
  Must putrefaction's breath
Leave nothing of this heavenly
    sight

But loathsomeness and ruin?
Spare nothing but a gloomy
    theme,   21
On which the lightest heart might
    moralize?
Or is it only a sweet slumber
    Stealing o'er sensation,
Which the breath of roseate
    morning   25
  Chaseth into darkness?
  Will Ianthe wake again,
And give that faithful bosom joy
Whose sleepless spirit waits to
    catch
Light, life and rapture from her
    smile?   30

Yes! she will wake again,
Although her glowing limbs are
    motionless,
  And silent those sweet lips,
  Once breathing eloquence,
That might have soothed a
    tiger's rage,   35
Or thawed the cold heart of a
    conqueror.
  Her dewy eyes are closed,
And on their lids, whose texture
    fine
Scarce hides the dark blue orbs
    beneath,
  The baby Sleep is pillowed: 40
  Her golden tresses shade
  The bosom's stainless pride,
Curling like tendrils of the para-
    site
Around a marble column.

Hark! whence that rushing
    sound?
'Tis like the wondrous strain 46
That round a lonely ruin swells,
Which, wandering on the echo-
    ing shore,
  The enthusiast hears at eve-
    ning:
'Tis softer than the west wind's
    sigh;   50

'Tis wilder than the unmeasured notes
Of that strange lyre whose strings
The genii of the breezes sweep:
Those lines of rainbow light
Are like the moonbeams when they fall   55
Through some cathedral window, but the tints
Are such as may not find
Comparison on earth.

Behold the chariot of the Fairy Queen!
Celestial coursers paw the unyielding air;   60
Their filmy pennons at her word they furl,
And stop obedient to the reins of light:
These the Queen of Spells drew in,
She spread a charm around the spot,
And leaning graceful from the aethereal car,   65
Long did she gaze, and silently,
Upon the slumbering maid.

Oh! not the visioned poet in his dreams,
When silvery clouds float through the 'wildered brain,
When every sight of lovely, wild and grand   70
Astonishes, enraptures, elevates,
When fancy at a glance combines
The wondrous and the beautiful,—
So bright, so fair, so wild a shape
Hath ever yet beheld,   75
As that which reined the coursers of the air,
And poured the magic of her gaze
Upon the maiden's sleep.

The broad and yellow moon
Shone dimly through her form—   80
That form of faultless symmetry;
The pearly and pellucid car
Moved not the moonlight's line:
'Twas not an earthly pageant:
Those who had looked upon the sight,   85
Passing all human glory,
Saw not the yellow moon,
Saw not the mortal scene,
Heard not the night-wind's rush,
Heard not an earthly sound,   90
Saw but the fairy pageant,
Heard but the heavenly strains
That filled the lonely dwelling.

The Fairy's frame was slight, yon fibrous cloud,
That catches but the palest tinge of even,   95
And which the straining eye can hardly seize
When melting into eastern twilight's shadow,
Were scarce so thin, so slight; but the fair star
That gems the glittering coronet of morn,
Sheds not a light so mild, so powerful,   100
As that which, bursting from the Fairy's form,
Spread a purpureal halo round the scene,
Yet with an undulating motion,
Swayed to her outline gracefully.

From her celestial car   105
The Fairy Queen descended,
And thrice she waved her wand

Circled with wreaths of
   amaranth:
Her thin and misty form 109
Moved with the moving air,
And the clear silver tones,
As thus she spoke, were such
As are unheard by all but gifted
   ear.

Fairy.

'Stars! your balmiest influ-
   ence shed!   114
Elements! your wrath sus-
   pend!
Sleep, Ocean, in the rocky
   bounds
   That circle thy domain!
Let not a breath be seen to stir
Around yon grass-grown ruin's
   height,   119
Let even the restless gossamer
Sleep on the moveless air!
Soul of Ianthe! thou,
Judged alone worthy of the envied
   boon,
That waits the good and the sin-
   cere; that waits
Those who have struggled, and
   with resolute will   125
Vanquished earth's pride and mean-
   ness, burst the chains,
The icy chains of custom, and have
   shone
The day-stars of their age;—Soul
   of Ianthe!
   Awake! arise!'
   Sudden arose   130
Ianthe's Soul; it stood
All beautiful in naked purity,
The perfect semblance of its bodily
   frame.
Instinct with inexpressible beauty
   and grace,
   Each stain of earthliness 135
Had passed away, it reassumed
Its native dignity, and stood
   Immortal amid ruin.

Upon the couch the body lay

Wrapped in the depth of slum-
   ber: 140
Its features were fixed and mean-
   ingless,
Yet animal life was there,
And every organ yet performed
Its natural functions: 'twas a
   sight
Of wonder to behold the body and
   soul.   145
The self-same lineaments, the
   same
Marks of identity were there:
Yet, oh, how different! One aspires
   to Heaven,
Pants for its sempiternal heritage,
And ever-changing, ever-rising still,
   Wantons in endless being. 151
The other, for a time the unwilling
   sport
Of circumstance and passion, strug-
   gles on;
Fleets through its sad duration
   rapidly:
Then, like an useless and worn-out
   machine,   155
   Rots, perishes, and passes.

Fairy.

'Spirit! who hast dived so
   deep;
Spirit! who hast soared so
   high;
Thou the fearless, thou the
   mild,
Accept the boon thy worth hath
   earned,   160
   Ascend the car with me.'

Spirit.

'Do I dream? Is this new feeling
But a visioned ghost of slumber?
   If indeed I am a soul,
A free, a disembodied soul,   165
   Speak again to me.'

Fairy.

'I am the Fairy MAB: to me 'tis
   given

The wonders of the human world
    to keep:
The secrets of the immeasurable
    past,
In the unfailing consciences of
    men,
Those stern, unflattering chron-
    iclers, I find: 171
The future, from the causes which
    arise
In each event, I gather: not the
    sting
Which retributive memory im-
    plants
In the hard bosom of the selfish
    man;
Nor that ecstatic and exulting
    throb
Which virtue's votary feels when
    he sums up   177
The thoughts and actions of a well-
    spent day,
Are unforeseen, unregistered by me:
And it is yet permitted me, to
    rend   180
The veil of mortal frailty, that the
    spirit,
Clothed in its changeless purity,
    may know
How soonest to accomplish the
    great end
For which it hath its being, and
    may taste
That peace, which in the end all
    life will share.   185
This is the meed of virtue; happy
    Soul,
    Ascend the car with me!'

The chains of earth's immure-
    ment
    Fell from Ianthe's spirit;
They shrank and brake like ban-
    dages of straw   190
    Beneath a wakened giant's
    strength.
    She knew her glorious change,

    And felt in apprehension uncon-
      trolled   193
    New raptures opening round:
Each day-dream of her mortal
    life,
Each frenzied vision of the slum-
    bers
    That closed each well-spent
    day,
    Seemed now to meet reality.

The Fairy and the Soul pro-
    ceeded;
    The silver clouds disparted;
And as the car of magic they as-
    cended,   201
Again the speechless music
    swelled,
Again the coursers of the air
Unfurled their azure pennons, and
    the Queen
    Shaking the beamy reins   205
    Bade them pursue their way.

    The magic car moved on.
The night was fair, and countless
    stars
Studded Heaven's dark blue
    vault,—
    Just o'er the eastern wave   210
Peeped the first faint smile of
    morn:—
    The magic car moved on—
From the celestial hoofs
The atmosphere in flaming sparkles
    flew,
    And where the burning wheels
Eddied above the mountain's lofti-
    est peak,   216
Was traced a line of lightning.
Now it flew far above a rock,
    The utmost verge of earth,
The rival of the Andes, whose
    dark brow   220
    Lowered o'er the silver sea.

Far, far below the chariot's path,
    Calm as a slumbering babe,
Tremendous Ocean lay.

The mirror of its stillness showed
The pale and waning stars, 226
The chariot's fiery track,
And the gray light of morn
Tinging those fleecy clouds
That canopied the dawn. 230
Seemed it, that the chariot's way
Lay through the midst of an im-
mense concave,
Radiant with million constella-
tions, tinged
With shades of infinite colour,
And semicircled with a belt 235
Flashing incessant meteors.

The magic car moved on.
As they approached their goal
The coursers seemed to gather
speed;
The sea no longer was distin-
guished; earth 240
Appeared a vast and shadowy
sphere;
The sun's unclouded orb
Rolled through the black con-
cave;
Its rays of rapid light
Parted around the chariot's swifter
course, 245
And fell, like ocean's feathery
spray
Dashed from the boiling surge
Before a vessel's prow.

The magic car moved on.
Earth's distant orb appeared
The smallest light that twinkles in
the heaven; 251
Whilst round the chariot's way
Innumerable systems rolled,
And countless spheres diffused
An ever-varying glory. 255
It was a sight of wonder: some
Were hornèd like the crescent
moon;
Some shed a mild and silver
beam

Like Hesperus o'er the western
sea;
Some dashed athwart with trains
of flame, 260
Like worlds to death and ruin
driven;
Some shone like suns, and, as the
chariot passed,
Eclipsed all other light.

Spirit of Nature! here!
In this interminable wilderness 265
Of worlds, at whose immensity
Even soaring fancy staggers,
Here is thy fitting temple.
Yet not the lightest leaf
That quivers to the passing breeze
Is less instinct with thee: 271
Yet not the meanest worm
That lurks in graves and fattens on
the dead
Less shares thy eternal breath.
Spirit of Nature! thou! 275
Imperishable as this scene,
Here is thy fitting temple.

II

IF solitude hath ever led thy steps
To the wild Ocean's echoing
shore,
And thou hast lingered there,
Until the sun's broad orb
Seemed resting on the burnished
wave, 5
Thou must have marked the
lines
Of purple gold, that motionless
Hung o'er the sinking sphere:
Thou must have marked the bil-
lowy clouds
Edged with intolerable radiancy
Towering like rocks of jet 11
Crowned with a diamond
wreath.
And yet there is a moment,
When the sun's highest point

Peeps like a star o'er Ocean's west-
　　　ern edge,　　　　　　　　　15
When those far clouds of feathery
　　　gold,
Shaded with deepest purple,
　　　gleam
Like islands on a dark blue sea;
Then has thy fancy soared above
　　　the earth,
　　　And furled its wearied wing 20
　　　Within the Fairy's fane.

Yet not the golden islands
Gleaming in yon flood of light,
Nor the feathery curtains
Stretching o'er the sun's bright
　　　couch,　　　　　　　　　　25
Nor the burnished Ocean
　　　waves
　　　Paving that gorgeous dome,
So fair, so wonderful a sight
As Mab's aethereal palace could
　　　afford.
Yet likest evening's vault, that
　　　faery Hall!　　　　　　　30
As Heaven, low resting on the
　　　wave, it spread
　　　Its floors of flashing light,
　　　Its vast and azure dome,
　　　Its fertile golden islands
　　　Floating on a silver sea; 35
Whilst suns their mingling beam-
　　　ings darted
Through clouds of circumambient
　　　darkness,
And pearly battlements around
Looked o'er the immense of
　　　Heaven.

The magic car no longer
　　　moved.
　　　The Fairy and the Spirit 41
　　　Entered the Hall of Spells:
　　　Those golden clouds
That rolled in glittering bil-
　　　lows
Beneath the azure canopy 45

With the aethereal footsteps trem-
　　　bled not:
　　　The light and crimson mists,
Floating to strains of thrilling mel-
　　　ody
　　　Through that unearthly dwell-
　　　ing,
Yielded to every movement of the
　　　will.
Upon their passive swell the Spirit
　　　leaned,　　　　　　　　　51
And, for the varied bliss that
　　　pressed around,
　　　Used not the glorious privilege
　　　Of virtue and of wisdom.

'Spirit!' the Fairy said, 55
And pointed to the gorgeous
　　　dome,
　　　'This is a wondrous sight
　　　And mocks all human gran-
　　　deur;
But, were it virtue's only meed, to
　　　dwell
In a celestial palace, all resigned 60
To pleasurable impulses, immured
Within the prison of itself, the will
Of changeless Nature would be un-
　　　fulfilled.
Learn to make others happy. Spirit,
　　　come!
This is thine high reward:—the
　　　past shall rise;　　　　　65
Thou shalt behold the present; I
　　　will teach
　　　The secrets of the future.'

The Fairy and the Spirit
Approached the overhanging bat-
　　　tlement.—
　　　Below lay stretched the uni-
　　　verse!
There, far as the remotest line
That bounds imagination's
　　　flight,　　　　　　　　　72
　　　Countless and unending
　　　orbs

In mazy motion intermingled,
Yet still fulfilled immutably
Eternal Nature's law. 76
Above, below, around,
The circling systems formed
A wilderness of harmony;
Each with undeviating aim,
In eloquent silence, through the
depths of space 81
Pursued its wondrous way.

There was a little light
That twinkled in the misty distance:
None but a spirit's eye 85
Might ken that rolling orb;
None but a spirit's eye
And in no other place
But that celestial dwelling, might behold
Each action of this earth's inhabitants. 90
But matter, space and time
In those aëreal mansions cease to act;
And all-prevailing wisdom, when it reaps
The harvest of its excellence, o'erbounds
Those obstacles, of which an earthly soul 95
Fears to attempt the conquest.

The Fairy pointed to the earth.
The Spirit's intellectual eye
Its kindred beings recognized.
The thronging thousands, to a passing view, 100
Seemed like an ant-hill's citizens.
How wonderful! that even
The passions, prejudices, interests,
That sway the meanest being, the weak touch
That moves the finest nerve,
And in one human brain 106

Causes the faintest thought, becomes a link
In the great chain of Nature.

'Behold,' the Fairy cried,
'Palmyra's ruined palaces!— 110
Behold! where grandeur frowned;
Behold! where pleasure smiled;
What now remains?—the memory
Of senselessness and shame—
What is immortal there? 115
Nothing—it stands to tell
A melancholy tale, to give
An awful warning: soon
Oblivion will steal silently
The remnant of its fame. 120
Monarchs and conquerors there
Proud o'er prostrate millions trod—
The earthquakes of the human race;
Like them, forgotten when the ruin
That marks their shock is past.

'Beside the eternal Nile, 126
The Pyramids have risen.
Nile shall pursue his changeless way:
Those Pyramids shall fall;
Yea! not a stone shall stand to tell 130
The spot whereon they stood!
Their very site shall be forgotten, 132
As is their builder's name!

'Behold yon sterile spot;
Where now the wandering Arab's tent 135
Flaps in the desert-blast.

There once old Salem's haughty
 fane
Reared high to Heaven its thou-
 sand golden domes,
 And in the blushing face of day
 Exposed its shameful glory.
Oh! many a widow, many an
 orphan cursed   141
The building of that fane; and
 many a father,
Worn out with toil and slavery,
 implored
The poor man's God to speed it
 from the earth,
And spare his children the detested
 task   145
Of piling stone on stone, and poi-
 soning
 The choicest days of life,
 To soothe a dotard's vanity.
There an inhuman and uncultured
 race
Howled hideous praises to their
 Demon-God;   150
They rushed to war, tore from the
 mother's womb
The unborn child,—old age and
 infancy,
Promiscuous perished; their vic-
 torious arms
Left not a soul to breathe. Oh! they
 were fiends:
But what was he who taught them
 that the God   155
Of nature and benevolence hath
 given
A special sanction to the trade of
 blood?
His name and theirs are fading, and
 the tales
Of this barbarian nation, which im-
 posture
Recites till terror credits, are pur-
 suing   160
 Itself into forgetfulness.

'Where Athens, Rome, and
 Sparta stood,

There is a moral desert now:
 The mean and miserable huts,
 The yet more wretched pal-
  aces,   165
 Contrasted with those ancient
  fanes,
Now crumbling to oblivion;
The long and lonely colonnades,
Through which the ghost of
 Freedom stalks,
 Seem like a well-known
  tune,
Which in some dear scene we have
 loved to hear,   171
 Remembered now in sad-
  ness.
 But, oh! how much more
  changed,
 How gloomier is the con-
  trast
 Of human nature there!   175
Where Socrates expired, a tyrant's
 slave,
A coward and a fool, spreads death
 around—
 Then, shuddering, meets his
  own.
Where Cicero and Antoninus
 lived,
A cowled and hypocritical
 monk   180
 Prays, curses and deceives.

'Spirit, ten thousand years
 Have scarcely passed away,
Since, in the waste where now the
 savage drinks
His enemy's blood, and aping Eu-
 rope's sons,   185
 Wakes the unholy song of war,
 Arose a stately city,
Metropolis of the western conti-
 nent:
 There, now, the mossy column-
  stone,   189
Indented by Time's unrelaxing
 grasp,

Which once appeared to brave
All, save its country's ruin;
There the wide forest scene,
Rude in the uncultivated loveliness
Of gardens long run wild,
Seems, to the unwilling sojourner,
whose steps 196
Chance in that desert has delayed,
Thus to have stood since earth was
what it is.
Yet once it was the busiest haunt,
Whither, as to a common centre,
flocked 200
Strangers, and ships, and merchandise:
Once peace and freedom blessed
The cultivated plain:
But wealth, that curse of man,
Blighted the bud of its prosperity:
Virtue and wisdom, truth and
liberty, 206
Fled, to return not, until man shall
know
That they alone can give the bliss
Worthy a soul that claims
Its kindred with eternity. 210

'There's not one atom of yon earth
But once was living man;
Nor the minutest drop of rain,
That hangeth in its thinnest cloud, 214
But flowed in human veins:
And from the burning plains
Where Libyan monsters yell,
From the most gloomy glens

Of Greenland's sunless clime, 219
To where the golden fields
Of fertile England spread
Their harvest to the day,
Thou canst not find one spot
Whereon no city stood. 224

'How strange is human pride!
I tell thee that those living things,
To whom the fragile blade of grass,
That springeth in the morn
And perisheth ere noon,
Is an unbounded world; 230
I tell thee that those viewless beings,
Whose mansion is the smallest particle
Of the impassive atmosphere,
Think, feel and live like man;
That their affections and antipathies,
Like his, produce the laws 236
Ruling their moral state;
And the minutest throb
That through their frame diffuses
The slightest, faintest motion,
Is fixed and indispensable 241
As the majestic laws
That rule yon rolling orbs.'

The Fairy paused. The Spirit,
In ecstasy of admiration, felt 245
All knowledge of the past revived;
the events
Of old and wondrous times,
Which dim tradition interruptedly
Teaches the credulous vulgar, were
unfolded
In just perspective to the view;
Yet dim from their infinitude. 251
The Spirit seemed to stand
High on an isolated pinnacle;
The flood of ages combating below,
The depth of the unbounded universe

Above, and all around   256
Nature's unchanging harmony.

III

'FAIRY!' the Spirit said,
And on the Queen of Spells
Fixed her aethereal eyes,
'I thank thee. Thou hast
    given
A boon which I will not resign,
    and taught   5
A lesson not to be unlearned. I
    know
The past, and thence I will essay
    to glean
A warning for the future, so that
    man
May profit by his errors, and derive
    Experience from his folly: 10
For, when the power of imparting
    joy
Is equal to the will, the human soul
Requires no other Heaven.'

Mab.

'Turn thee, surpassing Spirit!
Much yet remains unscanned.
Thou knowest how great is
    man,   16
Thou knowest his imbecility:
Yet learn thou what he is:
Yet learn the lofty destiny
Which restless time prepares
For every living soul.   21

'Behold a gorgeous palace, that,
    amid
Yon populous city rears its thou-
    sand towers
And seems itself a city. Gloomy
    troops
Of sentinels, in stern and silent
    ranks,
Encompass it around: the dweller
    there   26
Cannot be free and happy; hearest
    thou not

The curses of the fatherless, the
    groans
Of those who have no friend? He
    passes on:
The King, the wearer of a gilded
    chain
That binds his soul to abjectness,
    the fool   31
Whom courtiers nickname mon-
    arch, whilst a slave
Even to the basest appetites—that
    man
Heeds not the shriek of penury; he
    smiles
At the deep curses which the desti-
    tute   35
Mutter in secret, and a sullen joy
Pervades his bloodless heart when
    thousands groan
But for those morsels which his
    wantonness
Wastes in unjoyous revelry, to save
All that they love from famine:
    when he hears   40
The tale of horror, to some ready-
    made face
Of hypocritical assent he turns,
Smothering the glow of shame,
    that, spite of him,
Flushes his bloated cheek.
                    Now to the meal
Of silence, grandeur, and excess,
    he drags   45
His palled unwilling appetite. If
    gold,
Gleaming around, and numerous
    viands culled
From every clime, could force the
    loathing sense
To overcome satiety,—if wealth
The spring it draws from poisons
    not,—or vice,   50
Unfeeling, stubborn vice, convert-
    eth not
Its food to deadliest venom; then
    that king

Is happy; and the peasant who fulfils
His unforced task, when he returns at even,
And by the blazing faggot meets again
Her welcome for whom all his toil is sped,   56
Tastes not a sweeter meal.
                        Behold him now
Streched on the gorgeous couch; his fevered brain
Reels dizzily awhile: but ah! too soon
The slumber of intemperance subsides,   60
And conscience, that undying serpent, calls
Her venomous brood to their nocturnal task.
Listen! he speaks! oh! mark that frenzied eye—
Oh! mark that deadly visage.'

King.
                    'No cessation!
Oh! must this last for ever? Awful Death,   65
I wish, yet fear to clasp thee!—Not one moment
Of dreamless sleep! O dear and blessèd peace!
Why dost thou shroud thy vestal purity
In penury and dungeons? wherefore lurkest
With danger, death, and solitude; yet shunn'st   70
The palace I have built thee? Sacred peace!
Oh visit me but once, but pitying shed
One drop of balm upon my withered soul.'

The Fairy.
'Vain man! that palace is the virtuous heart,

And Peace defileth not her snowy robes
In such a shed as thine. Hark! yet he mutters;   76
His slumbers are but varied agonies,
They prey like scorpions on the springs of life.
There needeth not the hell that bigots frame
To punish those who err: earth in itself   80
Contains at once the evil and the cure;
And all-sufficing Nature can chastise
Those who transgress her law,— she only knows
How justly to proportion to the fault
The punishment it merits.
                            Is it strange 85
That this poor wretch should pride him in his woe?
Take pleasure in his abjectness, and hug
The scorpion that consumes him?
                            Is it strange
That, placed on a conspicuous throne of thorns,
Grasping an iron sceptre, and immured   90
Within a splendid prison, whose stern bounds
Shut him from all that's good or dear on earth,
His soul asserts not its humanity?
That man's mild nature rises not in war
Against a king's employ? No—'tis not strange.   95
He, like the vulgar, thinks, feels, acts and lives
Just as his father did; the unconquered powers
Of precedent and custom interpose

Between a *king* and virtue. Stran-
    ger yet,
To those who know not Nature, nor
    deduce   100
The future from the present, it may
    seem,
That not one slave, who suffers
    from the crimes
Of this unnatural being; not one
    wretch,
Whose children famish, and whose
    nuptial bed
Is earth's unpitying bosom, rears
    an arm
To dash him from his throne!
          Those gilded flies 106
That, basking in the sunshine of a
    court,
Fatten on its corruption!—what
    are they?
—The drones of the community;
    they feed
On the mechanic's labour: the
    starved hind   110
For them compels the stubborn
    glebe to yield
Its unshared harvest; and yon
    squalid form,
Leaner than fleshless misery, that
    wastes
A sunless life in the unwholesome
    mine,
Drags out in labour a protracted
    death,
To glut their grandeur; many
    faint with toil,   116
That few may know the cares and
    woe of sloth.

'Whence, think'st thou, kings and
    parasites arose?
Whence that unnatural line of
    drones, who heap
Toil and unvanquishable penury
On those who build their palaces,
    and bring   121
Their daily bread?—From vice,
    black loathsome vice;

From rapine, madness, treachery,
    and wrong;
From all that 'genders misery, and
    makes
Of earth this thorny wilderness;
    from lust,   125
Revenge, and murder. . . . And
    when Reason's voice,
Loud as the voice of Nature, shall
    have waked
The nations; and mankind per-
    ceive that vice
Is discord, war, and misery; that
    virtue
Is peace, and happiness and har-
    mony;   130
When man's maturer nature shall
    disdain
The playthings of its childhood;—
    kingly glare
Will lose its power to dazzle; its
    authority
Will silently pass by; the gorgeous
    throne
Shall stand unnoticed in the regal
    hall,   135
Fast falling to decay; whilst false-
    hood's trade
Shall be as hateful and unprofitable
As that of truth is now.
          Where is the fame
Which the vainglorious mighty of
    the earth
Seek to eternize? Oh! the faintest
    sound   140
From Time's light footfall, the mi-
    nutest wave
That swells the flood of ages,
    whelms in nothing
The unsubstantial bubble. Ay! to-
    day
Stern is the tyrant's mandate, red
    the gaze
That flashes desolation, strong the
    arm   145
That scatters multitudes. To-mor-
    row comes!

That mandate is a thunder-peal
   that died
In ages past; that gaze, a transient
   flash
On which the midnight closed, and
   on that arm
The worm has made his meal.
   The virtuous man, 150
Who, great in his humility, as kings
Are little in their grandeur; he
   who leads
Invincibly a life of resolute good,
And stands amid the silent dun-
   geon-depths
More free and fearless than the
   trembling judge, 155
Who, clothed in venal power,
   vainly strove
To bind the impassive spirit;—
   when he falls,
His mild eye beams benevolence
   no more:
Withered the hand outstretched
   but to relieve;
Sunk Reason's simple eloquence,
   that rolled 160
But to appal the guilty. Yes! the
   grave
Hath quenched that eye, and
   Death's relentless frost
Withered that arm: but the unfad-
   ing fame
Which Virtue hangs upon its vo-
   tary's tomb;
The deathless memory of that man,
   whom kings 165
Call to their mind and tremble;
   the remembrance
With which the happy spirit con-
   templates
Its well-spent pilgrimage on earth,
Shall never pass away.

'Nature rejects the monarch, not
   the man; 170
The subject, not the citizen: for
   kings

And subjects, mutual foes, forever
   play
A losing game into each other's
   hands,
Whose stakes are vice and misery.
   The man
Of virtuous soul commands not,
   nor obeys. 175
Power, like a desolating pestilence,
Pollutes whate'er it touches; and
   obedience,
Bane of all genius, virtue, freedom,
   truth,
Makes slaves of men, and, of the
   human frame,
A mechanized automaton.
   When Nero, 180
High over flaming Rome, with sav-
   age joy
Lowered like a fiend, drank with
   enraptured ear
The shrieks of agonizing death, be-
   held
The frightful desolation spread,
   and felt
A new-created sense within his
   soul
Thrill to the sight, and vibrate to
   the sound; 186
Think'st thou his grandeur had not
   overcome
The force of human kindness? and,
   when Rome,
With one stern blow, hurled not
   the tyrant down,
Crushed not the arm red with her
   dearest blood, 190
Had not submissive abjectness de-
   stroyed
Nature's suggestions?
   Look on yonder earth:
The golden harvests spring; the
   unfailing sun
Sheds light and life; the fruits, the
   flowers, the trees,
Arise in due succession; all things
   speak 195

Peace, harmony, and love. The universe,
In Nature's silent eloquence, declares
That all fulfil the works of love and joy,—
All but the outcast, Man. He fabricates
The sword which stabs his peace; he cherisheth　　200
The snakes that gnaw his heart; he raiseth up
The tyrant, whose delight is in his woe,
Whose sport is in his agony. Yon sun,
Lights it the great alone? Yon silver beams,
Sleep they less sweetly on the cottage thatch　　205
Than on the dome of kings? Is mother Earth
A step-dame to her numerous sons, who earn
Her unshared gifts with unremitting toil;
A mother only to those puling babes
Who, nursed in ease and luxury, make men　　210
The playthings of their babyhood, and mar,
In self-important childishness, that peace
Which men alone appreciate?

'Spirit of Nature! no.
The pure diffusion of thy essence throbs　　215
Alike in every human heart.
Thou, aye, erectest there
Thy throne of power unappealable:
Thou art the judge beneath whose nod
Man's brief and frail authority　　220
Is powerless as the wind
That passeth idly by.

Thine the tribunal which surpasseth
The show of human justice,
As God surpasses man.　225

'Spirit of Nature; thou
Life of interminable multitudes;
Soul of those mighty spheres
Whose changeless paths through Heaven's deep silence lie;
Soul of that smallest being,　230
The dwelling of whose life
Is one faint April sun-gleam;—
Man, like these passive things,
Thy will unconsciously fulfilleth:
Like theirs, his age of endless peace,　235
Which time is fast maturing,
Will swiftly, surely come;
And the unbounded frame, which thou pervadest,
Will be without a flaw
Marring its perfect symmetry.　240

IV

'How beautiful this night! the balmiest sigh,
Which vernal zephyrs breathe in evening's ear,
Were discord to the speaking quietude
That wraps this moveless scene. Heaven's ebon vault,
Studded with stars unutterably bright,　5
Through which the moon's unclouded grandeur rolls,
Seems like a canopy which love had spread
To curtain her sleeping world. Yon gentle hills,
Robed in a garment of untrodden snow;

Yon darksome rocks, whence icicles
    depend, 10
So stainless, that their white and
    glittering spires
Tinge not the moon's pure beam;
    yon castled steep,
Whose banner hangeth o'er the
    time-worn tower
So idly, that rapt fancy deemeth
    it
A metaphor of peace;—all form a
    scene
Where musing Solitude might love
    to lift 16
Her soul above this sphere of earth-
    liness;
Where Silence undisturbed might
    watch alone,
So cold, so bright, so still.
                The orb of day,
In southern climes, o'er ocean's
    waveless field 20
Sinks sweetly smiling: not the
    faintest breath
Steals o'er the unruffled deep; the
    clouds of eve
Reflect unmoved the lingering
    beam of day;
And vesper's image on the western
    main
Is beautifully still. To-morrow
    comes:
Cloud upon cloud, in dark and
    deepening mass, 26
Roll o'er the blackened waters;
    the deep roar
Of distant thunder mutters aw-
    fully;
Tempest unfolds its pinion o'er the
    gloom
That shrouds the boiling surge; the
    pitiless fiend, 30
With all his winds and lightnings,
    tracks his prey;
The torn deep yawns,—the vessel
    finds a grave

Beneath its jaggèd gulf.
            Ah! whence yon glare
That fires the arch of Heaven?—
    that dark red smoke
Blotting the silver moon? The stars
    are quenched 35
In darkness, and the pure and
    spangling snow
Gleams faintly through the gloom
    that gathers round!
Hark to that roar, whose swift and
    deaf'ning peals
In countless echoes through the
    mountains ring,
Startling pale Midnight on her
    starry throne! 40
Now swells the intermingling din;
    the jar
Frequent and frightful of the burst-
    ing bomb;
The falling beam, the shriek, the
    groan, the shout,
The ceaseless clangour, and the
    rush of men
Inebriate with rage:—loud, and
    more loud 45
The discord grows; till pale Death
    shuts the scene,
And o'er the conqueror and the
    conquered draws
His cold and bloody shroud.—Of
    all the men
Whom day's departing beam saw
    blooming there,
In proud and vigorous health; of
    all the hearts 50
That beat with anxious life at sun-
    set there;
How few survive, how few are
    beating now!
All is deep silence, like the fearful
    calm
That slumbers in the storm's por-
    tentous pause;
Save when the frantic wail of
    widowed love 55

Comes shuddering on the blast, or
    the faint moan
With which some soul bursts from
    the frame of clay
Wrapped round its struggling pow-
    ers.
               The gray morn
Dawns on the mournful scene; the
    sulphurous smoke
Before the icy wind slow rolls
    away,
And the bright beams of frosty
    morning dance   61
Along the spangling snow. There
    tracks of blood
Even to the forest's depth, and
    scattered arms,
And lifeless warriors, whose hard
    lineaments
Death's self could change not,
    mark the dreadful path 65
Of the outsallying victors: far be-
    hind,
Black ashes note where their proud
    city stood.
Within yon forest is a gloomy
    glen—
Each tree which guards its dark-
    ness from the day,
Waves o'er a warrior's tomb.
             I see thee shrink, 70
Surpassing Spirit!—wert thou hu-
    man else?
I see a shade of doubt and horror
    fleet
Across thy stainless features: yet
    fear not;
This is no unconnected misery,
Nor stands uncaused and irretriev-
    able.   75
Man's evil nature, that apology
Which kings who rule, and cowards
    who crouch, set up
For their unnumbered crimes,
    sheds not the blood
Which desolates the discord-wasted
    land.

From kings, and priests, and states-
    men, war arose,   80
Whose safety is man's deep unbet-
    tered woe,
Whose grandeur his debasement.
    Let the axe
Strike at the root, the poison-tree
    will fall;
And where its venomed exhalations
    spread
Ruin, and death, and woe, where
    millions lay   85
Quenching the serpent's famine,
    and their bones
Bleaching unburied in the putrid
    blast,
A garden shall arise, in loveliness
Surpassing fabled Eden.
               Hath Nature's soul,
That formed this world so beauti-
    ful, that spread   90
Earth's lap with plenty, and life's
    smallest chord
Strung to unchanging unison, that
    gave
The happy birds their dwelling in
    the grove,
That yielded to the wanderers of
    the deep
The lovely silence of the unfath-
    omed main,   95
And filled the meanest worm that
    crawls in dust
With spirit, thought, and love; on
    Man alone,
Partial in causeless malice, wan-
    tonly
Heaped ruin, vice, and slavery; his
    soul
Blasted with withering curses;
    placed afar   100
The meteor-happiness, that shuns
    his grasp,
But serving on the frightful gulf to
    glare,
Rent wide beneath his footsteps?
               Nature!—no!

Kings, priests, and statesmen, blast
    the human flower
Even in its tender bud; their influ-
    ence darts   105
Like subtle poison through the
    bloodless veins
Of desolate society. The child,
Ere he can lisp his mother's sacred
    name,
Swells with the unnatural pride of
    crime, and lifts
His baby-sword even in a hero's
    mood.   110
This infant-arm becomes the blood-
    iest scourge
Of devastated earth; whilst spe-
    cious names,
Learned in soft childhood's unsus-
    pecting hour,
Serve as the sophisms with which
    manhood dims
Bright Reason's ray, and sanctifies
    the sword   115
Upraised to shed a brother's inno-
    cent blood.
Let priest-led slaves cease to pro-
    claim that man
Inherits vice and misery, when
    Force
And Falsehood hang even o'er the
    cradled babe,
Stifling with rudest grasp all natu-
    ral good.   120
Ah! to the stranger-soul, when
    first it peeps
From its new tenement, and looks
    abroad
For happiness and sympathy, how
    stern
And desolate a tract is this wide
    world!
How withered all the buds of natu-
    ral good!   125
No shade, no shelter from the
    sweeping storms
Of pitiless power! On its wretched
    frame,

Poisoned, perchance, by the disease
    and woe
Heaped on the wretched parent
    whence it sprung
By morals, law, and custom, the
    pure winds   130
Of Heaven, that renovate the in-
    sect tribes,
May breathe not. The untainting
    light of day
May visit not its longings. It is
    bound
Ere it has life: yea, all the chains
    are forged
Long ere its being: all liberty and
    love   135
And peace is torn from its defence-
    lessness;
Cursed from its birth, even from
    its cradle doomed
To abjectness and bondage!

'Throughout this varied and eternal
    world
Soul is the only element: the
    block   140
That for uncounted ages has re-
    mained
The moveless pillar of a mountain's
    weight
Is active, living spirit. Every grain
Is sentient both in unity and
    part,
And the minutest atom compre-
    hends   145
A world of loves and hatreds; these
    beget
Evil and good: hence truth and
    falsehood spring;
Hence will and thought and action,
    all the germs
Of pain or pleasure, sympathy or
    hate,
That variegate the eternal uni-
    verse.   150
Soul is not more polluted than the
    beams

Of Heaven's pure orb, ere round
    their rapid lines
The taint of earth-born atmos-
    pheres arise.
'Man is of soul and body, formed
    for deeds
Of high resolve, on fancy's boldest
    wing   155
To soar unwearied, fearlessly to
    turn
The keenest pangs to peacefulness,
    and taste
The joys which mingled sense and
    spirit yield.
Or he is formed for abjectness and
    woe,
To grovel on the dunghill of his
    fears,   160
To shrink at every sound, to quench
    the flame
Of natural love in sensualism, to
    know
That hour as blessed when on his
    worthless days
The frozen hand of Death shall set
    its seal,
Yet fear the cure, though hating the
    disease.   165
The one is man that shall hereafter
    be;
The other, man as vice has made
    him now.

'War is the statesman's game, the
    priest's delight,
The lawyer's jest, the hired assas-
    sin's trade,
And, to those royal murderers,
    whose mean thrones 170
Are bought by crimes of treachery
    and gore,
The bread they eat, the staff on
    which they lean.
Guards, garbed in blood-red livery,
    surround
Their palaces, participate the
    crimes

That force defends, and from a na-
    tion's rage   175
Secure the crown, which all the
    curses reach
That famine, frenzy, woe and
    penury breathe.
These are the hired bravos who de-
    fend
The tyrant's throne—the bullies of
    his fear:
These are the sinks and channels
    of worst vice,   180
The refuse of society, the dregs
Of all that is most vile: their cold
    hearts blend
Deceit with sternness, ignorance
    with pride,
All that is mean and villanous, with
    rage
Which hopelessness of good, and
    self-contempt,   185
Alone might kindle; they are
    decked in wealth,
Honour and power, then are sent
    abroad
To do their work. The pestilence
    that stalks
In gloomy triumph through some
    eastern land
Is less destroying. They cajole with
    gold,   190
And promises of fame, the thought-
    less youth
Already crushed with servitude: he
    knows
His wretchedness too late, and
    cherishes
Repentance for his ruin, when his
    doom
Is sealed in gold and blood!   195
Those too the tyrant serve, who,
    skilled to snare
The feet of Justice in the toils of
    law,
Stand, ready to oppress the weaker
    still;

And right or wrong will vindicate
   for gold,
Sneering at public virtue, which
   beneath   200
Their pitiless tread lies torn and
   trampled, where
Honour sits smiling at the sale of
   truth.

'Then grave and hoary-headed
   hypocrites,
Without a hope, a passion, or a
   love,
Who, through a life of luxury and
   lies,   205
Have crept by flattery to the seats
   of power,
Support the system whence their
   honours flow. . . .
They have three words:—well ty-
   rants know their use,
Well pay them for the loan, with
   usury
Torn from a bleeding world!—God,
   Hell, and Heaven.   210
A vengeful, pitiless, and almighty
   fiend,
Whose mercy is a nickname for the
   rage
Of tameless tigers hungering for
   blood.
Hell, a red gulf of everlasting fire,
Where poisonous and undying
   worms prolong   215
Eternal misery to those hapless
   slaves
Whose life has been a penance for
   its crimes.
And Heaven, a meed for those who
   dare belie
Their human nature, quake, be-
   lieve, and cringe
Before the mockeries of earthly
   power   220

'These tools the tyrant tempers to
   his work,

Wields in his wrath, and as he wills
   destroys,
Omnipotent in wickedness: the
   while
Youth springs, age moulders, manhood tamely does
His bidding, bribed by short-lived
   joys to lend   225
Force to the weakness of his trembling arm.

'They rise, they fall; one generation
   comes
Yielding its harvest to destruction's
   scythe.
It fades, another blossoms: yet behold!
Red glows the tyrant's stamp-mark
   on its bloom,   230
Withering and cankering deep its
   passive prime.
He has invented lying words and
   modes,
Empty and vain as his own coreless
   heart;
Evasive meanings, nothings of
   much sound,
To lure the heedless victim to the
   toils   235
Spread round the valley of its paradise.

'Look to thyself, priest, conqueror,
   or prince!
Whether thy trade is falsehood, and
   thy lusts
Deep wallow in the earnings of the
   poor,
With whom thy Master was:—or
   thou delight'st   240
In numbering o'er the myriads of
   thy slain,
All misery weighing nothing in the
   scale
Against thy short-lived fame: or
   thou dost load

With cowardice and crime the
    groaning land,
A pomp-fed king. Look to thy
    wretched self!   245
Ay, art thou not the veriest slave
    that e'er
Crawled on the loathing earth?
    Are not thy days
Days of unsatisfying listless-
    ness?
Dost thou not cry, ere night's long
    rack is o'er,
"When will the morning come?" Is
    not thy youth   250
A vain and feverish dream of sen-
    sualism?
Thy manhood blighted with unripe
    disease?
Are not thy views of unregretted
    death
Drear, comfortless, and horrible?
    Thy mind,
Is it not morbid as thy nerveless
    frame,   255
Incapable of judgment, hope, or
    love?
And dost thou wish the errors to
    survive
That bar thee from all sympathies
    of good,
After the miserable interest
Thou hold'st in their protraction?
    When the grave   260
Has swallowed up thy memory and
    thyself,
Dost thou desire the bane that
    poisons earth
To twine its roots around thy
    coffined clay,
Spring from thy bones, and blossom
    on thy tomb,
That of its fruit thy babes may
    eat and die?   265

V

'Thus do the generations of the
    earth

Go to the grave, and issue from the
    womb,
Surviving still the imperishable
    change
That renovates the world; even as
    the leaves
Which the keen frost-wind of the
    waning year   5
Has scattered on the forest soil,
    and heaped
For many reasons there—though
    long they choke,
Loading with loathsome rottenness
    the land,
All germs of promise, yet when the
    tall trees
From which they fell, shorn of their
    lovely shapes,   10
Lie level with the earth to moulder
    there,
They fertilize the land they long
    deformed,
Till from the breathing lawn a for-
    est springs
Of youth, integrity, and loveliness,
Like that which gave it life, to
    spring and die,   15
Thus suicidal selfishness, that
    blights
The fairest feelings of the opening
    heart,
Is destined to decay, whilst from
    the soil
Shall spring all virtue, all delight,
    all love,
And judgment cease to wage un-
    natural war   20
With passion's unsubduable array.
Twin-sister of religion, selfishness!
Rival in crime and falsehood, aping
    all
The wanton horrors of her bloody
    play;
Yet frozen, unimpassioned, spirit-
    less,   25
Shunning the light, and owning not
    its name,

Compelled, by its deformity, to screen
With flimsy veil of justice and of right,
Its unattractive lineaments, that scare
All, save the brood of ignorance: at once   30
The cause and the effect of tyranny;
Unblushing, hardened, sensual, and vile;
Dead to all love but of its abjectness,
With heart impassive by more noble powers
Than unshared pleasure, sordid gain, or fame;   35
Despising its own miserable being,
Which still it longs, yet fears to disenthrall.

'Hence commerce springs, the venal interchange
Of all that human art or nature yield;
Which wealth should purchase not, but want demand,   40
And natural kindness hasten to supply
From the full fountain of its boundless love,
For ever stifled, drained, and tainted now.
Commerce! beneath whose poison-breathing shade
No solitary virtue dares to spring,   45
But Poverty and Wealth with equal hand
Scatter their withering curses, and unfold
The doors of premature and violent death,
To pining famine and full-fed disease,
To all that shares the lot of human life,   50
Which poisoned, body and soul, scarce drags the chain,
That lengthens as it goes and clanks behind.

'Commerce has set the mark of selfishness,
The signet of its all-enslaving power
Upon a shining ore, and called it gold: 55
Before whose image bow the vulgar great,
The vainly rich, the miserable proud,
The mob of peasants, nobles, priests, and kings,
And with blind feelings reverence the power
That grinds them to the dust of misery.   60
But in the temple of their hireling hearts
Gold is a living god, and rules in scorn
All earthly things but virtue.

'Since tyrants, by the sale of human life,
Heap luxuries to their sensualism, and fame   65
To their wide-wasting and insatiate pride,
Success has sanctioned to a credulous world
The ruin, the disgrace, the woe of war.
His hosts of blind and unresisting dupes
The despot numbers; from his cabinet   70
These puppets of his schemes he moves at will,
Even as the slaves by force or famine driven,

Beneath a vulgar master, to perform
A task of cold and brutal drudgery;—
Hardened to hope, insensible to fear, 75
Scarce living pulleys of a dead machine,
Mere wheels of work and articles of trade,
That grace the proud and noisy pomp of wealth!

'The harmony and happiness of man
Yields to the wealth of nations; that which lifts 80
His nature to the heaven of its pride,
Is bartered for the poison of his soul;
The weight that drags to earth his towering hopes,
Blighting all prospect but of selfish gain,
Withering all passion but of slavish fear, 85
Extinguishing all free and generous love
Of enterprise and daring, even the pulse
That fancy kindles in the beating heart
To mingle with sensation, it destroys,—
Leaves nothing but the sordid lust of self, 90
The grovelling hope of interest and gold,
Unqualified, unmingled, unredeemed
Even by hypocrisy.
                    And statesmen boast
Of wealth! The wordy eloquence, that lives
After the ruin of their hearts, can gild 95

The bitter poison of a nation's woe,
Can turn the worship of the servile mob
To their corrupt and glaring idol, Fame,
From Virtue, trampled by its iron tread,
Although its dazzling pedestal be raised 100
Amid the horrors of a limb-strewn field,
With desolated dwellings smoking round.
The man of ease, who, by his warm fireside,
To deeds of charitable intercourse,
And bare fulfilment of the common laws 105
Of decency and prejudice, confines
The struggling nature of his human heart,
Is duped by their cold sophistry; he sheds
A passing tear perchance upon the wreck
Of earthly peace, when near his dwelling's door 110
The frightful waves are driven,—when his son
Is murdered by the tyrant, or religion
Drives his wife raving mad. But the poor man,
Whose life is misery, and fear, and care;
Whom the morn wakens but to fruitless toil; 115
Who ever hears his famished offspring's scream,
Whom their pale mother's uncomplaining gaze
For ever meets, and the proud rich man's eye
Flashing command, and the heartbreaking scene

Of thousands like himself;—he
little heeds 120
The rhetoric of tyranny; his hate
Is quenchless as his wrongs; he
laughs to scorn
The vain and bitter mockery of
words,
Feeling the horror of the tyrant's
deeds,
And unrestrained but by the arm of
power, 125
That knows and dreads his enmity.

'The iron rod of Penury still com-
pels
Her wretched slave to bow the knee
to wealth,
And poison, with unprofitable toil,
A life too void of solace to con-
firm 130
The very chains that bind him to
his doom.
Nature, impartial in munificence,
Has gifted man with all-subduing
will.
Matter, with all its transitory
shapes,
Lies subjected and plastic at his
feet, 135
That, weak from bondage, tremble
as they tread.
How many a rustic Milton has
passed by,
Stifling the speechless longings of
his heart,
In unremitting drudgery and
care!
How many a vulgar Cato has com-
pelled 140
His energies, no longer tameless
then,
To mould a pin, or fabricate a nail!
How many a Newton, to whose pas-
sive ken
Those mighty spheres that gem in-
finity

Were only specks of tinsel, fixed in
Heaven 145
To light the midnights of his native
town!

'Yet every heart contains perfec-
tion's germ:
The wisest of the sages of the earth,
That ever from the stores of reason
drew
Science and truth, and virtue's
dreadless tone, 150
Were but a weak and inexperienced
boy,
Proud, sensual, unimpassioned, un-
imbued
With pure desire and universal love,
Compared to that high being, of
cloudless brain,
Untainted passion, elevated will, 155
Which Death (who even would
linger long in awe
Within his noble presence, and be-
neath
His changeless eyebeam) might
alone subdue.
Him, every slave now dragging
through the filth
Of some corrupted city his sad
life, 160
Pining with famine, swoln with
luxury,
Blunting the keenness of his spir-
itual sense
With narrow schemings and un-
worthy cares,
Or madly rushing through all vio-
lent crime,
To move the deep stagnation of his
soul,— 165
Might imitate and equal.
But mean lust
Has bound its chains so tight
around the earth,
That all within it but the virtuous
man

Is venal: gold or fame will surely
    reach
The price prefixed by selfishness,
    to all   170
But him of resolute and unchanging
    will;
Whom, nor the plaudits of a servile
    crowd,
Nor the vile joys of tainting luxury,
Can bribe to yield his elevated
    soul
To Tyranny or Falsehood, though
    they wield   175
With blood-red hand the sceptre of
    the world.

'All things are sold: the very light
    of Heaven
Is venal; earth's unsparing gifts of
    love,
The smallest and most despicable
    things
That lurk in the abysses of the
    deep,   180
All objects of our life, even life
    itself,
And the poor pittance which the
    laws allow
Of liberty, the fellowship of man,
Those duties which his heart of hu-
    man love
Should urge him to perform instinc-
    tively,   185
Are bought and sold as in a public
    mart
Of undisguising selfishness, that
    sets
On each its price, the stamp-mark
    of her reign.
Even love is sold; the solace of all
    woe
Is turned to deadliest agony, old
    age   190
Shivers in selfish beauty's loathing
    arms,
And youth's corrupted impulses
    prepare

A life of horror from the blighting
    bane
Of commerce; whilst the pestilence
    that springs
From unenjoying sensualism, has
    filled   195
All human life with hydra-headed
    woes.

'Falsehood demands but gold to
    pay the pangs
Of outraged conscience; for the
    slavish priest
Sets no great value on his hireling
    faith:
A little passing pomp, some servile
    souls,   200
Whom cowardice itself might safely
    chain,
Or the spare mite of avarice could
    bribe
To deck the triumph of their lan-
    guid zeal,
Can make him minister to tyranny.
More daring crime requires a loftier
    meed: 205
Without a shudder, the slave-
    soldier lends
His arm to murderous deeds, and
    steels his heart,
When the dread eloquence of dying
    men,
Low mingling on the lonely field
    of fame,
Assails that nature, whose applause
    he sells   210
For the gross blessings of a patriot
    mob,
For the vile gratitude of heartless
    kings,
And for a cold world's good word,
    —viler still!

'There is a nobler glory, which sur-
    vives
Until our being fades, and, solac-
    ing   215

All human care, accompanies its
  change;
Deserts not virtue in the dungeon's
  gloom,
And, in the precincts of the palace,
  guides
Its footsteps through that labyrinth
  of crime;
Imbues his lineaments with daunt-
  lessness,   220
Even when, from Power's avenging
  hand, he takes
Its sweetest, last and noblest title
  —death;
—The consciousness of good, which
  neither gold,
Nor sordid fame, nor hope of heav-
  enly bliss
Can purchase; but a life of resolute
  good,   225
Unalterable will, quenches desire
Of universal happiness, the heart
That beats with it in unison, the
  brain,
Whose ever wakeful wisdom toils to
  change
Reason's rich stores for its eternal
  weal.   230

'This commerce of sincerest virtue
  needs
No mediative signs of selfishness,
No jealous intercourse of wretched
  gain,
No balancings of prudence, cold
  and long;
In just and equal measure all is
  weighed,   235
One scale contains the sum of human weal,
And one, the good man's heart.
            How vainly seek
The selfish for that happiness denied
To aught but virtue! Blind and
  hardened, they,

Who hope for peace amid the
  storms of care,   240
Who covet power they know not
  how to use,
And sigh for pleasure they refuse
  to give,—
Madly they frustrate still their own
  designs;
And, where they hope that quiet to
  enjoy
Which virtue pictures, bitterness of
  soul,   245
Pining regrets, and vain repent-
  ances,
Disease, disgust, and lassitude, pervade
Their valueless and miserable lives.

'But hoary-headed Selfishness has
  felt
Its death-blow, and is tottering to
  the grave: 250
A brighter morn awaits the human
  day,
When every transfer of earth's
  natural gifts
Shall be a commerce of good words
  and works;
When poverty and wealth, the
  thirst of fame,
The fear of infamy, disease and
  woe,   255
War with its million horrors, and
  fierce hell
Shall live but in the memory of
  Time,
Who, like a penitent libertine, shall
  start,
Look back, and shudder at his
  younger years.'

VI

ALL touch, all eye, all ear,
The Spirit felt the Fairy's burning
  speech.
O'er the thin texture of its frame,
The varying periods painted chang-
  ing glows,

As on a summer even,   5
When soul-enfolding music floats
    around,
The stainless mirror of the lake
Re-images the eastern gloom,
Mingling convulsively its purple
    hues
    With sunset's burnished
    gold.   10

Then thus the Spirit spoke:
'It is a wild and miserable world!
Thorny, and full of care,
Which every fiend can make his
    prey at will.
O Fairy! in the lapse of years, 15
Is there no hope in store?
Will yon vast suns roll on
Interminably, still illuming
The night of so many wretched
    souls,
    And see no hope for
    them?   20
Will not the universal Spirit e'er
Revivify this withered limb of
    Heaven?'

The Fairy calmly smiled
In comfort, and a kindling gleam
    of hope
Suffused the Spirit's linea-
    ments.   25
'Oh! rest thee tranquil; chase those
    fearful doubts,
Which ne'er could rack an ever-
    lasting soul,
That sees the chains which bind it
    to its doom.
Yes! crime and misery are in yon-
    der earth,
    Falsehood, mistake, and
    lust;   30
    But the eternal world
Contains at once the evil and the
    cure.
Some eminent in virtue shall start
    up,
Even in perversest time:

The truths of their pure lips, that
    never die,   35
Shall bind the scorpion falsehood
    with a wreath
    Of ever-living flame,
Until the monster sting itself to
    death.

'How sweet a scene will earth be-
    come!
Of purest spirits a pure dwelling-
    place,   40
Symphonious with the planetary
    spheres;
When man, with changeless Nature
    coalescing,
Will   undertake   regeneration's
    work,
When its ungenial poles no longer
    point
    To the red and baleful sun 45
    That faintly twinkles there.

'Spirit! on yonder earth,
Falsehood now triumphs; deadly
    power
Has fixed its seal upon the lip of
    truth!
Madness and misery are there! 50
The happiest is most wretched! Yet
    confide,
Until pure health-drops, from the
    cup of joy,
Fall like a dew of balm upon the
    world.
Now, to the scene I show, in silence
    turn,
And read the blood-stained charter
    of all woe,   55
Which Nature soon, with re-creat-
    ing hand,
Will blot in mercy from the book
    of earth.
How bold the flight of Passion's
    wandering wing,
How swift the step of Reason's
    firmer tread,

How calm and sweet the victories
    of life,   60
How terrorless the triumph of the
    grave!
How powerless were the mightiest
    monarch's arm,
Vain his loud threat, and impotent
    his frown!
How ludicrous the priest's dog-
    matic roar!
The weight of his exterminating
    curse   65
How light! and his affected char-
    ity,
To suit the pressure of the changing
    times,
What palpable deceit!—but for thy
    aid,
Religion! but for thee, prolific
    fiend,
Who peoplest earth with demons,
    Hell with men,   70
And Heaven with slaves!

'Thou taintest all thou look'st
    upon!—the stars,
Which on thy cradle beamed so
    brightly sweet,
Were gods to the distempered play-
    fulness
Of thy untutored infancy: the
    trees,   75
The grass, the clouds, the moun-
    tains, and the sea,
All living things that walk, swim,
    creep, or fly,
Were gods: the sun had homage,
    and the moon
Her worshipper. Then thou be-
    cam'st, a boy,
More daring in thy frenzies: every
    shape,   80
Monstrous or vast, or beautifully
    wild,
Which, from sensation's relics,
    fancy culls;

The spirits of the air, the shudder-
    ing ghost,
The genii of the elements, the pow-
    ers
That give a shape to Nature's
    varied works,   85
Had life and place in the corrupt
    belief
Of thy blind heart: yet still thy
    youthful hands
Were pure of human blood. Then
    manhood gave
Its strength and ardour to thy
    frenzied brain;
Thine eager gaze scanned the stu-
    pendous scene,   90
Whose wonders mocked the knowl-
    edge of thy pride:
Their everlasting and unchanging
    laws
Reproached thine ignorance.
    Awhile thou stoodst
Baffled and gloomy; then thou
    didst sum up
The elements of all that thou didst
    know;   95
The changing seasons, winter's
    leafless reign,
The budding of the Heaven-breath-
    ing trees,
The eternal orbs that beautify the
    night,
The sunrise, and the setting of the
    moon,
Earthquakes and wars, and poisons
    and disease,   100
And all their causes, to an abstract
    point
Converging, thou didst bend and
    called it God!
The self-sufficing, the omnipo-
    tent,
The merciful, and the avenging
    God!
Who, prototype of human misrule,
    sits   105

High in Heaven's realm, upon a
    golden throne,
Even like an earthly king; and
    whose dread work,
Hell, gapes for ever for the un-
    happy slaves
Of fate, whom He created, in his
    sport,
To triumph in their torments when
    they fell!   110
Earth heard the name; Earth trem-
    bled, as the smoke
Of His revenge ascended up to
    Heaven,
Blotting the constellations; and
    the cries
Of millions, butchered in sweet
    confidence
And unsuspecting peace, even
    when the bonds   115
Of safety were confirmed by wordy
    oaths
Sworn in His dreadful name, rung
    through the land;
Whilst innocent babes writhed on
    thy stubborn spear,
And thou didst laugh to hear the
    mother's shriek
Of maniac gladness, as the sacred
    steel   120
Felt cold in her torn entrails!

'Religion! thou wert then in man-
    hood's prime:
But age crept on: one God would
    not suffice
For senile puerility; thou framedst
A tale to suit thy dotage, and to
    glut   125
Thy misery-thirsting soul, that the
    mad fiend
Thy wickedness had pictured might
    afford
A plea for sating the unnatural
    thirst
For murder, rapine, violence, and
    crime,

That still consumed thy being, even
    when   130
Thou heardst the step of Fate;—
    that flames might light
Thy funeral scene, and the shrill
    horrent shrieks
Of parents dying on the pile that
    burned
To light their children to thy paths,
    the roar
Of the encircling flames, the ex-
    ulting cries   135
Of thine apostles, loud commingling
    there,
    Might sate thine hungry ear
    Even on the bed of death!

'But now contempt is mocking thy
    gray hairs;
Thou art descending to the dark-
    some grave,   140
Unhonoured and unpitied, but by
    those
Whose pride is passing by like
    thine, and sheds,
Like thine, a glare that fades be-
    fore the sun
Of truth, and shines but in the
    dreadful night
That long has lowered above the
    ruined world.   145

'Throughout these infinite orbs of
    mingling light,
Of which yon earth is one, is wide
    diffused
A Spirit of activity and life,
That knows no terms, cessation, or
    decay;
That fades not when the lamp of
    earthly life,   150
Extinguished in the dampness of the
    grave,
Awhile there slumbers, more than
    when the babe
In the dim newness of its being feels
The impulses of sublunary things,

And all is wonder to unpractised
    sense: 155
But, active, steadfast, and eternal,
    still
Guides the fierce whirlwind, in the
    tempest roars,
Cheers in the day, breathes in the
    balmy groves,
Strengthens in health, and poisons
    in disease;
And in the storm of change, that
    ceaselessly 160
Rolls round the eternal universe,
    and shakes
Its undecaying battlement, pre-
    sides,
Apportioning with irresistible law
The place each spring of its ma-
    chine shall fill;
So that when waves on waves tu-
    multuous heap 165
Confusion to the clouds, and
    fiercely driven
Heaven's lightnings scorch the up-
    rooted ocean-fords,
Whilst, to the eye of shipwrecked
    mariner,
Lone sitting on the bare and shud-
    dering rock,
All seems unlinked contingency and
    chance: 170
No atom of this turbulence fulfils
A vague and unnecessitated task,
Or acts but as it must and ought to
    act.
Even the minutest molecule of light,
That in an April sunbeam's fleet-
    ing glow 175
Fulfils its destined, though invisi-
    ble work,
The universal Spirit guides; nor
    less,
When merciless ambition, or mad
    zeal,
Has led two hosts of dupes to bat-
    tle-field,

That, blind, they there may dig
    each other's graves, 180
And call the sad work glory, does it
    rule
All passions: not a thought, a will,
    an act,
No working of the tyrant's moody
    mind,
Nor one misgiving of the slaves who
    boast
Their servitude, to hide the shame
    they feel, 185
Nor the events enchaining every
    will,
That from the depths of unre-
    corded time
Have drawn all-influencing virtue,
    pass
Unrecognized, or unforeseen by
    thee,
Soul of the Universe! eternal
    spring 190
Of life and death, of happiness and
    woe,
Of all that chequers the phantas-
    mal scene
That floats before our eyes in
    wavering light,
Which gleams but on the darkness
    of our prison,
    Whose chains and massy
      walls 195
    We feel, but cannot see.

'Spirit of Nature! all-sufficing
    Power,
Necessity! thou mother of the
    world!
Unlike the God of human error,
    thou
Requir'st no prayers or praises;
    the caprice 200
Of man's weak will belongs no
    more to thee
Than do the changeful passions of
    his breast
To thy unvarying harmony: the
    slave,

Whose horrible lusts spread misery
    o'er the world,
And the good man, who lifts, with
    virtuous pride,   205
His being, in the sight of happiness,
That springs from his own works;
    the poison-tree,
Beneath whose shade all life is
    withered up,
And the fair oak, whose leafy
    dome affords
A temple where the vows of happy
    love   210
Are registered, are equal in thy
    sight:
No love, no hate thou cherishest:
    revenge
And favouritism, and worst desire
    of fame
Thou know'st not: all that the wide
    world contains
Are but thy passive instruments,
    and thou   215
Regard'st them all with an impar-
    tial eye,
Whose joy or pain thy nature can-
    not feel,
  Because thou hast not human
    sense,
  Because thou art not human
    mind.

'Yes! when the sweeping storm
    of time   220
Has sung its death-dirge o'er the
    ruined fanes
And broken altars of the almighty
    Fiend
Whose name usurps thy honours,
    and the blood
Through centuries clotted there, has
    floated down
The tainted flood of ages, shalt
    thou live   225
Unchangeable! A shrine is raised
    to thee,
  Which, nor the tempest-breath
    of time,

Nor the interminable flood,
Over earth's slight pageant
    rolling,
  Availeth to destroy,—   230
The sensitive extension of the
    world.
That wondrous and eternal
    fane,
Where pain and pleasure, good and
    evil join,
To do the will of strong necessity,
And life, in multitudinous shapes,
Still pressing forward where no
    term can be,   236
  Like hungry and unresting
    flame
Curls round the eternal columns of
    its strength.'

VII

Spirit.

'I was an infant when my mother
    went
To see an atheist burned. She took
    me there:
The dark-robed priests were met
    around the pile;
The multitude was gazing silently;
And as the culprit passed with
    dauntless mien,   5
Tempered disdain in his unaltering
    eye,
Mixed with a quiet smile, shone
    calmly forth:
The thirsty fire crept round his
    manly limbs;
His resolute eyes were scorched to
    blindness soon;
His death-pang rent my heart! the
    insensate mob   10
Uttered a cry of triumph, and I
    wept.
"Weep not, child!" cried my
    mother, "for that man
Has said, There is no God."'

Fairy.

'There is no God!
Nature confirms the faith his death-
          groan sealed:
Let heaven and earth, let man's
          revolving race,   15
His ceaseless generations tell their
          tale;
Let every part depending on the
          chain
That links it to the whole, point to
          the hand
That grasps its term! let every seed
          that falls
In silent eloquence unfold its
          store   20
Of argument; infinity within,
Infinity without, belie creation;
The exterminable spirit it contains
Is nature's only God; but human
          pride   24
Is skilful to invent most serious
          names
To hide its ignorance.
                    The name of God
Has fenced about all crime with
          holiness,
Himself the creature of His wor-
          shippers,
Whose names and attributes and
          passions change,
Seeva, Buddh, Foh, Jehovah, God,
          or Lord,   30
Even with the human dupes who
          build His shrines,
Still serving o'er the war-polluted
          world
For desolation's watchword;
          whether hosts
Stain His death-blushing chariot-
          wheels, as on
Triumphantly they roll, whilst
          Brahmins raise   35
A sacred hymn to mingle with the
          groans;
Or countless partners of His power
          divide

His tyranny to weakness; or the
          smoke
Of burning towns, the cries of fe-
          male helplessness,
Unarmed old age, and youth, and
          infancy,   40
Horribly massacred, ascend to
          Heaven
In honour of His name; or, last and
          worst,
Earth groans beneath religion's iron
          age,
And priests dare babble of a God
          of peace,
Even whilst their hands are red
          with guiltless blood,   45
Murdering the while, uprooting
          every germ
Of truth, exterminating, spoiling
          all,
Making the earth a slaughter-
          house!

          'O Spirit! through the sense
By which thy inner nature was ap-
          prised   50
    Of outward shows, vague dreams
          have rolled,
    And varied reminiscences have
          waked
          Tablets that never fade;
    All things have been imprinted
          there,
    The stars, the sea, the earth, the
          sky,   55
    Even the unshapeliest lineaments
          Of wild and fleeting visions
          Have left a record there
          To testify of earth.

'These are my empire, for to me is
          given   60
The wonders of the human world
          to keep,
And Fancy's thin creations to
          endow
With manner, being, and reality;

Therefore a wondrous phantom,
    from the dreams
Of human error's dense and pur-
    blind faith,   65
I will evoke, to meet thy question-
    ing.
    Ahasuerus, rise!'

        A strange and woe-worn
            wight
    Arose beside the battlement,
        And   stood   unmoving
            there.   70
His inessential figure cast no shade
    Upon the golden floor;
His port and mien bore mark of
    many years,
And chronicles of untold ancient-
    ness
Were legible within his beamless
    eye: 75
    Yet his cheek bore the mark of
        youth;
Freshness and vigour knit his
    manly frame;
The wisdom of old age was min-
    gled there
    With youth's primaeval daunt-
        lessness;
        And inexpressible woe,   80
Chastened by fearless resignation,
    gave
An awful grace to his all-speaking
    brow.

Spirit.

'Is there a God?'

Ahasuerus.

'Is there a God!—ay, an almighty
    God,
And vengeful as almighty! Once
    His voice   85
Was heard on earth; earth shud-
    dered at the sound;
The fiery-visaged firmament ex-
    pressed

Abhorrence, and the grave of
    Nature yawned
To swallow all the dauntless and
    the good
That dared to hurl defiance at His
    throne,   90
Girt as it was with power. None but
    slaves
Survived, — cold-blooded slaves,
    who did the work
Of tyrannous omnipotence; whose
    souls
No honest indignation ever urged
To elevated daring, to one deed   95
Which gross and sensual self did
    not pollute.
These slaves built temples for the
    omnipotent Fiend,
Gorgeous and vast: the costly
    altars smoked
With human blood, and hideous
    paeans rung
Through all the long-drawn aisles.
    A murderer heard   100
His voice in Egypt, one whose gifts
    and arts
Had raised him to his eminence in
    power,
Accomplice of omnipotence in
    crime,
And confidant of the all-knowing
    one.
    These were Jehovah's words:—

'From an eternity of idleness   106
I, God, awoke; in seven days' toil
    made earth
From nothing; rested, and created
    man:
I placed him in a Paradise, and
    there
Planted the tree of evil, so that he
Might eat and perish, and My soul
    procure   111
Wherewith to sate its malice, and
    to turn,
Even like a heartless conqueror of
    the earth,

All misery to My fame. The race
of men
Chosen to My honour, with impunity   115
May sate the lusts I planted in
their heart.
Here I command thee hence to
lead them on,
Until, with hardened feet, their conquering troops
Wade on the promised soil through
woman's blood,
And make My name be dreaded
through the land.   120
Yet ever-burning flame and ceaseless woe
Shall be the doom of their eternal
souls,
With every soul on this ungrateful
earth,
Virtuous or vicious, weak or strong,
—even all
Shall perish, to fulfil the blind revenge   125
(Which you, to men, call justice)
of their God.'

              The murderer's brow
Quivered with horror.
                  'God omnipotent,
Is there no mercy? must our pun-
ishment
Be endless? will long ages roll
away   130
And see no term? Oh! wherefore
hast Thou made
In mockery and wrath this evil
earth?
Mercy becomes the powerful—be
but just:
O God! repent and save.'

           'One way remains:
I will beget a Son, and He shall
bear   135
The sins of all the world; He shall
arise

In an unnoticed corner of the
earth,
And there shall die upon a cross,
and purge
The universal crime; so that the
few
On whom My grace descends,
those who are marked 140
As vessels to the honour of their
God,
May credit this strange sacrifice,
and save
Their souls alive: millions shall live
and die,
Who ne'er shall call upon their
Saviour's name,
But, unredeemed, go to the gaping
grave.   145
Thousands shall deem it an old
woman's tale,
Such as the nurses frighten babes
withal:
These in a gulf of anguish and of
flame
Shall curse their reprobation end-
lessly,
Yet tenfold pangs shall force them
to avow,   150
Even on their beds of torment,
where they howl,
My honour, and the justice of their
doom.
What then avail their virtuous
deeds, their thoughts
Of purity, with radiant genius
bright,
Or lit with human reason's earthly
ray?   155
Many are called, but few will I
elect.
Do thou My bidding, Moses!'
              Even the murderer's cheek
Was blanched with horror, and his
quivering lips
Scarce faintly uttered — 'O al-
mighty One,
I tremble and obey!'   160

'O Spirit! centuries have set their
    seal
On this heart of many wounds, and
    loaded brain,
Since the Incarnate came: humbly
    He came,
Veiling His horrible Godhead in
    the shape
Of man, scorned by the world, His
    name unheard,   165
Save by the rabble of His native
    town,
Even as a parish demagogue. He
    led
The crowd; He taught them jus-
    tice, truth, and peace,
In semblance; but He lit within
    their souls
The quenchless flames of zeal, and
    blessed the sword   170
He brought on earth to satiate with
    the blood
Of truth and freedom His malig-
    nant soul.
At length His mortal frame was led
    to death.
I stood beside Him: on the tortur-
    ing cross
No pain assailed His unterrestrial
    sense;   175
And yet He groaned. Indignantly I
    summed
The massacres and miseries which
    His name
Had sanctioned in my country, and
    I cried,
"Go! Go!" in mockery.
A smile of godlike malice reillumed
His fading lineaments.—"I go,"
    He cried,   181
"But thou shalt wander o'er the
    unquiet earth
Eternally."—The dampness of the
    grave
Bathed my imperishable front. I
    fell,

And long lay tranced upon the
    charmèd soil.   185
When I awoke Hell burned within
    my brain,
Which staggered on its seat; for all
    around
The mouldering relics of my kin-
    dred lay,
Even as the Almighty's ire arrested
    them,
And in their various attitudes of
    death   190
My murdered children's mute and
    eyeless skulls
Glared ghastlily upno me.
                    But my soul,
From sight and sense of the pollut-
    ing woe
Of tyranny, had long learned to
    prefer
Hell's freedom to the servitude of
    Heaven.   195
Therefore I rose, and dauntlessly
    began
My lonely and unending pil-
    grimage,
Resolved to wage unweariable war
With my almighty Tyrant, and to
    hurl
Defiance at His impotence to harm
Beyond the curse I bore. The very
    hand   201
That barred my passage to the
    peaceful grave
Has crushed the earth to misery,
    and given
Its empire to the chosen of His
    slaves.
These have I seen, even from the
    earliest dawn   205
Of weak, unstable and precarious
    power,
Then preaching peace, as now they
    practise war;
So, when they turned but from the
    massacre

Of unoffending infidels, to quench
Their thirst for ruin in the very
  blood   210
That flowed in their own veins,
  and pitiless zeal
Froze every human feeling, as the
  wife
Sheathed in her husband's heart
  the sacred steel,
Even whilst its hopes were dream-
  ing of her love;
And friends to friends, brothers to
  brothers stood   215
Opposed in bloodiest battle-field,
  and war,
Scarce satiable by fate's last death-
  draught, waged,
Drunk from the winepress of the
  Almighty's wrath;
Whilst the red cross, in mockery of
  peace,
Pointed to victory! When the fray
  was done,   220
No remnant of the exterminated
  faith
Survived to tell its ruin, but the
  flesh,
With putrid smoke poisoning the
  atmosphere,
That rotted on the half-extin-
  guished pile.

'Yes! I have seen God's worship-
  pers unsheathe 225
The sword of His revenge, when
  grace descended,
Confirming all unnatural impulses,
To sanctify their desolating deeds;
And frantic priests waved the ill-
  omened cross
O'er the unhappy earth: then shone
  the sun   230
On showers of gore from the up-
  flashing steel
Of safe assassination, and all crime
Made stingless by the Spirits of the
  Lord,

And blood-red rainbows canopied
  the land.

'Spirit, no year of my eventful be-
  ing   235
Has passed unstained by crime and
  misery,
Which flows from God's own faith.
  I've marked His slaves
With tongues whose lies are venom-
  ous, beguile
The insensate mob, and, whilst one
  hand was red
With murder, feign to stretch the
  other out   240
For brotherhood and peace; and
  that they now
Babble of love and mercy, whilst
  their deeds
Are marked with all the narrow-
  ness and crime
That Freedom's young arm dare
  not yet chastise,
Reason may claim our gratitude,
  who now   245
Establishing the imperishable
  throne
Of truth, and stubborn virtue,
  maketh vain
The unprevailing malice of my Foe,
Whose bootless rage heaps tor-
  ments for the brave,
Adds impotent eternities to pain,
Whilst keenest disappointment
  racks His breast 251
To see the smiles of peace around
  them play,
To frustrate or to sanctify their
  doom.

'Thus have I stood,—through a
  wild waste of years
Struggling with whirlwinds of mad
  agony,   255
Yet peaceful, and serene, and self-
  enshrined,
Mocking my powerless Tyrant's
  horrible curse

With stubborn and unalterable will,
Even as a giant oak, which Heav-
    en's fierce flame
Had scathèd in the wilderness, to
    stand   260
A monument of fadeless ruin there;
Yet peacefully and movelessly it
    braves
The midnight conflict of the win-
    try storm,
    As in the sunlight's calm it
    spreads
Its worn and withered arms on
    high   265
To meet the quiet of a summer's
    noon.'
    The Fairy waved her wand:
    Ahasuerus fled
Fast as the shapes of mingled shade
    and mist,
That lurk in the glens of a twilight
    grove,   270
    Flee from the morning
    beam:
The matter of which dreams are
    made
Not more endowed with actual
    life
Than this phantasmal portrai-
    ture
Of wandering human thought. 275

VIII

The Fairy.

'THE Present and the Past thou
    hast beheld:
It was a desolate sight. Now,
    Spirit, learn
    The secrets of the Future.—
    Time!
Unfold the brooding pinion of thy
    gloom,
Render thou up thy half-devoured
    babes,   5
And from the cradles of eternity,
Where millions lie lulled to their
    portioned sleep

By the deep murmuring stream of
    passing things,
Tear thou that gloomy shroud.—
    Spirit, behold
    Thy glorious destiny!'   10

    Joy to the Spirit came.
Through the wide rent in Time's
    eternal veil,
Hope was seen beaming through
    the mists of fear:
    Earth was no longer Hell;
    Love, freedom, health, had
    given   15
Their ripeness to the manhood of
    its prime,
    And all its pulses beat
Symphonious to the planetary
    spheres:
    Then dulcet music swelled
Concordant with the life-strings of
    the soul;   20
It throbbed in sweet and languid
    beatings there,
Catching new life from transitory
    death,—
Like the vague sighings of a wind
    at even,
That wakes the wavelets of the
    slumbering sea
And dies on the creation of its
    breath,   25
And sinks and rises, fails and
    swells by fits:
    Was the pure stream of feel-
    ing
    That sprung from these
    sweet notes,
And o'er the Spirit's human sym-
    pathies
With mild and gentle motion
    calmly flowed.   30

    Joy to the Spirit came,—
Such joy as when a lover sees
The chosen of his soul in happiness,
    And witnesses her peace

Whose woe to him were bitterer
   than death,   35
      Sees her unfaded cheek
Glow mantling in first luxury of
   health,
      Thrills with her lovely eyes,
Which like two stars amid the
   heaving main
      Sparkle through liquid bliss.

Then in her triumph spoke the
   Fairy Queen: 41
'I will not call the ghost of ages
   gone
To unfold the frightful secrets of
   its lore;
      The present now is past,
And those events that desolate the
   earth   45
Have faded from the memory of
   Time,
Who dares not give reality to that
Whose being I annul. To me is
   given
The wonders of the human world
   to keep,
Space, matter, time, and mind.
   Futurity   50
Exposes now its treasure; let the
   sight
Renew and strengthen all thy fail-
   ing hope.
O human Spirit! spur thee to the
   goal
Where virtue fixes universal peace,
And midst the ebb and flow of hu-
   man things,   55
Show somewhat stable, somewhat
   certain still,
A lighthouse o'er the wild of dreary
   waves.

'The habitable earth is full of bliss;
Those wastes of frozen billows
   that were hurled
By everlasting snowstorms round
   the poles,   60

Where matter dared not vegetate
   or live,
But ceaseless frost round the vast
   solitude
Bound its broad zone of stillness,
   are unloosed;
And fragrant zephyrs there from
   spicy isles
Ruffle the placid ocean-deep, that
   rolls   65
Its broad, bright surges to the
   sloping sand,
Whose roar is wakened into echoings sweet
To murmur through the Heaven-
   breathing groves
And melodize with man's blest nature there.

'Those deserts of immeasurable
   sand,   70
Whose age - collected fervours
   scarce allowed
A bird to live, a blade of grass to
   spring,
Where the shrill chirp of the green
   lizard's love
Broke on the sultry silentness
   alone,
Now teem with countless rills and
   shady woods,   75
Cornfields and pastures and white
   cottages;
And where the startled wilderness
   beheld
A savage conqueror stained in kindred blood,
A tigress sating with the flesh of
   lambs
The unnatural famine of her toothless cubs,   80
Whilst shouts and howlings through
   the desert rang,
Sloping and smooth the daisy-
   spangled lawn,
Offering sweet incense to the sunrise, smiles

To see a babe before his mother's
door,
    Sharing his morning's meal 85
With the green and golden bas-
    ilisk
    That comes to lick his feet.

'Those trackless deeps, where many
    a weary sail
Has seen above the illimitable
    plain,
Morning on night, and night on
    morning rise,   90
Whilst still no land to greet the
    wanderer spread
Its shadowy mountains on the sun-
    bright sea,
Where the loud roarings of the
    tempest-waves
So long have mingled with the
    gusty wind
In melancholy loneliness, and
    swept   95
The desert of those ocean soli-
    tudes,
But vocal to the sea-bird's harrow-
    ing shriek,
The bellowing monster, and the
    rushing storm,
Now to the sweet and many-min-
    gling sounds
Of kindliest human impulses re-
    spond.   100
Those lonely realms bright garden-
    isles begem,
With lightsome clouds and shining
    seas between,
And fertile valleys, resonant with
    bliss,
Whilst green woods overcanopy the
    wave,
Which like a toil-worn labourer
    leaps to shore,   105
To meet the kisses of the flow'rets
    there.

'All things are recreated, and the
    flame

Of consentaneous love inspires all
    life:
The fertile bosom of the earth gives
    suck
To myriads, who still grow be-
    neath her care,   110
Rewarding her with their pure per-
    fectness:
The balmy breathings of the wind
    inhale
Her virtues, and diffuse them all
    abroad:
Health floats amid the gentle at-
    mosphere,
Glows in the fruits, and mantles on
    the stream: 115
No storms deform the beaming
    brow of Heaven,
Nor scatter in the freshness of its
    pride
The foliage of the ever-verdant
    trees;
But fruits are ever ripe, flowers
    ever fair,
And Autumn proudly bears her
    matron grace,   120
Kindling a flush on the fair cheek
    of Spring,
Whose virgin bloom beneath the
    ruddy fruit
Reflects its tint, and blushes into
    love.

'The lion now forgets to thirst for
    blood:
There might you see him sporting
    in the sun   125
Beside the dreadless kid; his claws
    are sheathed,
His teeth are harmless, custom's
    force has made
His nature as the nature of a lamb.
Like passion's fruit, the night-
    shade's tempting bane
Poisons no more the pleasure it be-
    stows: 130
All bitterness is past; the cup of
    joy

Unmingled mantles to the goblet's
    brim,
And courts the thirsty lips it fled
    before.

'But chief, ambiguous Man, he
    that can know
More misery, and dream more joy
    than all;   135
Whose keen sensations thrill within
    his breast
To mingle with a loftier instinct
    there,
Lending their power to pleasure
    and to pain,
Yet raising, sharpening, and refin-
    ing each;
Who stands amid the ever-varying
    world,   140
The burthen or the glory of the
    earth;
He chief perceives the change, his
    being notes
The gradual renovation, and de-
    fines
Each movement of its progress on
    his mind.

'Man, where the gloom of the long
    polar night   145
Lowers o'er the snow-clad rocks
    and frozen soil,
Where scarce the hardiest herb that
    braves the frost
Basks in the moonlight's ineffectual
    glow,
Shrank with the plants, and dark-
    ened with the night;
His chilled and narrow energies,
    his heart,   150
Insensible to courage, truth, or
    love,
His stunted stature and imbecile
    frame,
Marked him for some abortion of
    the earth,
Fit compeer of the bears that
    roamed around,

Whose habits and enjoyments were
    his own: 155
His life a feverish dream of stag-
    nant woe,
Whose meagre wants, but scantily
    fulfilled,
Apprised him ever of the joyless
    length
Which his short being's wretched-
    ness had reached;
His death a pang which famine,
    cold and toil   160
Long on the mind, whilst yet the
    vital spark
Clung to the body stubbornly, had
    brought:
All was inflicted here that Earth's
    revenge
Could wreak on the infringers of
    her law;
One curse alone was spared—the
    name of God.   165

'Nor where the tropics bound the
    realms of day
With a broad belt of mingling cloud
    and flame,
Where blue mists through the un-
    moving atmosphere
Scattered the seeds of pestilence,
    and fed
Unnatural vegetation, where the
    land
Teemed with all earthquake, tem-
    pest and disease,   171
Was Man a nobler being; slavery
Had crushed him to his country's
    blood-stained dust;
Or he was bartered for the fame of
    power,
Which all internal impulses de-
    stroying,
Makes human will an article of
    trade;
Or he was changed with Christians
    for their gold,   177
And dragged to distant isles, where
    to the sound

Of the flesh-mangling scourge, he
    does the work
Of all-polluting luxury and wealth,
Which doubly visits on the ty-
    rants' heads   181
The long-protracted fulness of
    their woe;
Or he was led to legal butchery,
To turn to worms beneath that
    burning sun,
Where kings first leagued against
    the rights of men,   185
And priests first traded with the
    name of God.

'Even where the milder zone af-
    forded Man
A seeming shelter, yet contagion
    there,
Blighting his being with unnum-
    bered ills,
Spread like a quenchless fire; nor
    truth till late   190
Availed to arrest its progress, or
    create
That peace which first in bloodless
    victory waved
Her snowy standard o'er this fa-
    voured clime:
There man was long the train-
    bearer of slaves,   194
The mimic of surrounding misery,
The jackal of ambition's lion-rage,
The bloodhound of religion's hun-
    gry zeal.

'Here now the human being stands
    adorning
This loveliest earth with taintless
    body and mind;
Blessed from his birth with all
    bland impulses,   200
Which gently in his noble bosom
    wake
All kindly passions and all pure de-
    sires.
Him, still from hope to hope the
    bliss pursuing

Which from the exhaustless lore of
    human weal
Dawns on the virtuous mind, the
    thoughts that rise   205
In time-destroying infiniteness, gift
With self-enshrined eternity, that
    mocks
The unprevailing hoariness of age,
And man, once fleeting o'er the
    transient scene
Swift as an unremembered vision,
    stands   210
Immortal upon earth: no longer
    now
He slays the lamb that looks him
    in the face,
And horribly devours his mangled
    flesh,
Which, still avenging Nature's
    broken law,
Kindled all putrid humours in his
    frame,   215
All evil passions, and all vain belief,
Hatred, despair, and loathing in
    his mind,
The germs of misery, death, dis-
    ease, and crime.
No longer now the wingèd habi-
    tants,
That in the woods their sweet lives
    sing away,   220
Flee from the form of man; but
    gather round,
And prune their sunny feathers on
    the hands
Which little children stretch in
    friendly sport
Towards these dreadless partners
    of their play.
All things are void of terror: Man
    has lost   225
His terrible prerogative, and stands
An equal amidst equals: happiness
And science dawn though late upon
    the earth;
Peace cheers the mind, health reno-
    vates the frame;

Disease and pleasure cease to
    mingle here,   230
Reason and passion cease to com-
    bat there;
Whilst each unfettered o'er the
    earth extend
Their all-subduing energies, and
    wield
The sceptre of a vast dominion
    there;
Whilst every shape and mode of
    matter lends   235
Its force to the omnipotence of
    mind,
Which from its dark mine drags the
    gem of truth
To decorate its Paradise of peace.'

IX

'O HAPPY Earth! reality of
    Heaven!
To which those restless souls that
    ceaselessly
Throng through the human uni-
    verse, aspire;
Thou consummation of all mortal
    hope!
Thou glorious prize of blindly-
    working will!   5
Whose rays, diffused throughout
    all space and time,
Verge to one point and blend for
    ever there:
Of purest spirits thou pure dwell-
    ing place!
Where care and sorrow, impotence
    and crime,
Languor, disease, and ignorance
    dare not come: 10
O happy Earth, reality of Heaven!

'Genius has seen thee in her pas-
    sionate dreams,
And dim forebodings of thy love-
    liness
Haunting the human heart, have
    there entwined

Those rooted hopes of some sweet
    place of bliss   15
Where friends and lovers meet to
    part no more.
Thou art the end of all desire and
    will,
The product of all action; and
    the souls
That by the paths of an aspiring
    change
Have reached thy haven of per-
    petual peace,   20
There rest from the eternity of toil
That framed the fabric of thy per-
    fectness.

'Even Time, the conqueror, fled
    thee in his fear;
That hoary giant, who, in lonely
    pride,
So long had ruled the world, that
    nations fell,   25
Beneath his silent footstep. Pyra-
    mids,
That for millenniums had with-
    stood the tide
Of human things, his storm-breath
    drove in sand
Across that desert where their
    stones survived
The name of him whose pride had
    heaped them there.   30
Yon monarch, in his solitary pomp,
Was but the mushroom of a sum-
    mer day,
That his light-wingèd footstep
    pressed to dust:
Time was the king of earth: all
    things gave way
Before him, but the fixed and vir-
    tuous will,   35
The sacred sympathies of soul and
    sense,
That mocked his fury and pre-
    pared his fall.

'Yet slow and gradual dawned the
    morn of love;

Long lay the clouds of darkness
o'er the scene,
Till from its native Heaven they
rolled away: 40
First, Crime triumphant o'er all
hope careered
Unblushing, undisguising, bold and
strong;
Whilst Falsehood, tricked in Vir-
tue's attributes,
Long sanctified all deeds of vice
and woe,
Till done by her own venomous
sting to death,   45
She left the moral world without
a law,
No longer fettering Passion's fear-
less wing,
Nor searing Reason with the brand
of God.
Then steadily the happy ferment
worked;
Reason was free; and wild though
Passion went   50
Through tangled glens and wood-
embosomed meads,
Gathering a garland of the strang-
est flowers,
Yet like the bee returning to her
queen,
She bound the sweetest on her
sister's brow,
Who meek and sober kissed the
sportive child,   55
No longer trembling at the broken
rod.

'Mild was the slow necessity of
death:
The tranquil spirit failed beneath
its grasp,
Without a groan, almost without
a fear,
Calm as a voyager to some distant
land,   60
And full of wonder, full of hope as
he.

The deadly germs of languor and
disease
Died in the human frame, and
Purity
Blessed with all gifts her earthly
worshippers.
How vigorous then the athletic
form of age!   65
How clear its open and unwrinkled
brow!
Where neither avarice, cunning,
pride, nor care,
Had stamped the seal of gray de-
formity
On all the mingling lineaments of
time.
How lovely the intrepid front of
youth!   70
Which meek-eyed courage decked
with freshest grace;
Courage of soul, that dreaded not
a name,
And elevated will, that journeyed
on
Through life's phantasmal scene in
fearlessness,
With virtue, love, and pleasure,
hand in hand.   75

'Then, that sweet bondage which
is Freedom's self,
And rivets with sensation's softest
tie
The kindred sympathies of human
souls,
Needed no fetters of tyrannic
law: 79
Those delicate and timid impulses
In Nature's primal modesty arose,
And with undoubted confidence
disclosed
The growing longings of its dawn-
ing love,
Unchecked by dull and selfish
chastity,
That virtue of the cheaply vir-
tuous.   85

Who pride themselves in senseless-
    ness and frost.
No longer prostitution's venomed
    bane
Poisoned the springs of happiness
    and life;
Woman and man, in confidence and
    love,
Equal and free and pure together
    trod   90
The mountain-paths of virtue,
    which no more
Were stained with blood from
    many a pilgrim's feet.

'Then, where, through distant
    ages, long in pride
The palace of the monarch-slave
    had mocked
Famine's faint groan, and Penury's
    silent tear,   95
A heap of crumbling ruins stood,
    and threw
Year after year their stones upon
    the field,
Wakening a lonely echo; and the
    leaves
Of the old thorn, that on the top-
    most tower
Usurped the royal ensign's gran-
    deur, shook   100
In the stern storm that swayed
    the topmost tower
And whispered strange tales in the
    Whirlwind's ear.

'Low through the lone cathedral's
    roofless aisles
The melancholy winds a death-
    dirge sung: 104
It were a sight of awfulness to see
The works of faith and slavery, so
    vast,
So sumptuous, yet so perishing
    withal!
Even as the corpse that rests be-
    neath its wall.

A thousand mourners deck the
    pomp of death
To-day, the breathing marble glows
    above   110
To decorate its memory, and
    tongues
Are busy of its life: to-morrow,
    worms
In silence and in darkness seize
    their prey.

'Within the massy prison's moulder-
    ing courts,
Fearless and free the ruddy chil-
    dren played,   115
Weaving gay chaplets for their in-
    nocent brows
With the green ivy and the red
    wall-flower,
That mock the dungeon's unavail-
    ing gloom;
The ponderous chains, and grat-
    ings of strong iron,
There rusted amid heaps of broken
    stone   120
That mingled slowly with their
    native earth:
There the broad beam of day,
    which feebly once
Lighted the cheek of lean Cap-
    tivity
With a pale and sickly glare, then
    freely shone
On the pure smiles of infant play-
    fulness: 125
No more the shuddering voice of
    hoarse Despair
Pealed through the echoing vaults,
    but soothing notes
Of ivy-fingered winds and glad-
    some birds
And merriment were resonant
    around.

'These ruins soon left not a wreck
    behind: 130
Their elements, wide scattered o'er
    the globe,

To happier shapes were moulded,
    and became
Ministrant to all blissful impulses:
Thus human things were perfected,
    and earth,
Even as a child beneath its mother's
    love,   135
Was strengthened in all excellence,
    and grew
Fairer and nobler with each pass-
    ing year.

'Now Time his dusky pennons o'er
    the scene
Closes in steadfast darkness, and
    the past
Fades from our charmèd sight. My
    task is done: 140
Thy lore is learned. Earth's won-
    ders are thine own,
With all the fear and all the hope
    they bring.
My spells are passed: the present
    now recurs.
Ah me! a pathless wilderness re-
    mains
Yet unsubdued by man's reclaim-
    ing hand.   145

'Yet, human Spirit, bravely hold
    thy course,
Let virtue teach thee firmly to
    pursue
The gradual paths of an aspiring
    change:
For birth and life and death, and
    that strange state
Before the naked soul has found its
    home,   150
All tend to perfect happiness, and
    urge
The restless wheels of being on their
    way,
Whose flashing spokes, instinct
    with infinite life,
Bicker and burn to gain their
    destined goal:

For birth but wakes the spirit to
    the sense   155
Of outward shows, whose unexpe-
    rienced shape
New modes of passion to its frame
    may lend;
Life is its state of action, and the
    store
Of all events is aggregated there
That variegate the eternal uni-
    verse;   160
Death is a gate of dreariness and
    gloom,
That leads to azure isles and beam-
    ing skies
And happy regions of eternal hope.
Therefore, O Spirit! fearlessly bear
    on:
Though storms may break the
    primrose on its stalk, 165
Though frosts may blight the
    freshness of its bloom,
Yet Spring's awakening breath will
    woo the earth,
To feed with kindliest dews its
    favourite flower,
That blooms in mossy banks and
    darksome glens,
Lighting the greenwood with its
    sunny smile.   170

'Fear not then, Spirit, Death's dis-
    robing hand,
So welcome when the tyrant is
    awake
So welcome when the bigot's hell-
    torch burns;
'Tis but the voyage of a darksome
    hour,
The transient gulf-dream of a
    startling sleep.   175
Death is no foe to Virtue: earth
    has seen
Love's brightest roses on the scaf-
    fold bloom,
Mingling with Freedom's fadeless
    laurels there,

And presaging the truth of vi-
    sioned bliss.
Are there not hopes within thee,
    which this scene   180
Of linked and gradual being has
    confirmed?
Whose stingings bade thy heart
    look further still,
When, to the moonlight walk by
    Henry led,
Sweetly and sadly thou didst talk
    of death?
And wilt thou rudely tear them
    from thy breast,   185
Listening supinely to a bigot's
    creed,
Or tamely crouching to the tyrant's
    rod,
Whose iron thongs are red with
    human gore?
Never: but bravely bearing on, thy
    will
Is destined an eternal war to wage
With tyranny and falsehood, and
    uproot   191
The germs of misery from the hu-
    man heart.
Thine is the hand whose piety
    would soothe
The thorny pillow of unhappy
    crime,
Whose impotence an easy pardon
    gains,   195
Watching its wanderings as a
    friend's disease:
Thine is the brow whose mildness
    would defy
Its fiercest rage, and brave its
    sternest will,
When fenced by power and master
    of the world.
Thou art sincere and good; of reso-
    lute mind,   200
Free from heart-withering custom's
    cold control,
Of passon lofty, pure and unsub-
    dued.

Earth's pride and meanness could
    not vanquish thee,
And therefore art thou worthy of
    the boon
Which thou hast now received:
    Virtue shall keep   205
Thy footsteps in the path that
    thou hast trod,
And many days of beaming hope
    shall bless
Thy spotless life of sweet and
    sacred love.
Go, happy one, and give that
    bosom joy
Whose sleepless spirit waits to
    catch   210
Light, life and rapture from thy
    smile.'

The Fairy waves her wand of
    charm.
Speechless with bliss the Spirit
    mounts the car,
That rolled beside the battle-
    ment,
Bending her beamy eyes in thank-
    fulness.   215
Again the enchanted steeds were
    yoked,
Again the burning wheels inflame
The steep descent of Heaven's un-
    trodden way.
Fast and far the chariot flew:
The vast and fiery globes that
    rolled   220
Around the Fairy's palace-gate
Lessened by slow degrees and soon
    appeared
Such tiny twinklers as the planet
    orbs
That there attendant on the solar
    power
With borrowed light pursued their
    narrower way.   225

Earth floated then below:
The chariot paused a moment
    there;

The Spirit then descended:
The restless coursers pawed the
ungenial soil,
Snuffed the gross air, and then,
their errand done,   230
Unfurled their pinions to the winds
of Heaven.

The Body and the Soul united
then,
A gentle start convulsed Ianthe's
frame:

Her veiny eyelids quietly unclosed;
Moveless awhile the dark blue orbs
remained: 235
She looked around in wonder and
beheld
Henry, who kneeled in silence by
her couch,
Watching her sleep with looks of
speechless love,
And the bright beaming stars
That through the casement
shone.   240

NOTE ON QUEEN MAB, BY MRS. SHELLEY

SHELLEY was eighteen when he wrote *Queen Mab;* he never published it. When it was written, he had come to the decision that he was too young to be a 'judge of controversies'; and he was desirous of acquiring 'that sobriety of spirit which is the characteristic of true heroism.' But he never doubted the truth or utility of his opinions; and, in printing and privately distributing *Queen Mab,* he believed that he should further their dissemination, without occasioning the mischief either to others or himself that might arise from publication. It is doubtful whether he would himself have admitted it into a collection of his works. His severe classical taste, refined by the constant study of the Greek poets, might have discovered defects that escape the ordinary reader; and the change his opinions underwent in many points would have prevented him from putting forth the speculations of his boyish days. But the poem is too beautiful in itself, and far too remarkable as the production of a boy of eighteen, to allow of its being passed over: besides that, having been frequently reprinted, the omission would be vain. In the former edition certain portions were left out, as shocking the general reader from the violence of their attack on religion. I myself had a painful feeling that such erasures might be looked upon as a mark of disrespect towards the author, and am glad to have the opportunity of restoring them.

A series of articles was published in the *New Monthly Magazine* during the autumn of the year 1832, written by a man of great talent, a fellow-collegian and warm friend of Shelley: they describe admirably the state of his mind during his collegiate life. Inspired with ardour for the acquisition of knowledge, endowed with the keenest sensibility and with the fortitude of a martyr, Shelley came among his fellow-creatures, congregated for the purposes of education, like a spirit from another sphere; too delicately organized for the rough treatment man uses towards man, especially in the season of youth, and too resolute in carrying out his own sense of good and justice, not to become a victim. To a devoted attachment to those he loved he added a determined resistance to oppression. Refusing to fag at Eton, he was treated with revolting cruelty by masters and boys: this roused instead of taming his spirit, and he rejected the duty of obedience when it was enforced by menaces and punishment. To aversion to the society of his fellow-creatures, such as he found them when collected together in societies, where one egged-on the other to acts of tyranny, was joined the deepest sympathy and compassion; while the attachment he felt for individuals, and the admiration with which he regarded their powers and their virtues, led him to entertain a high opinion of the perfectibility of human nature; and he believed that all could reach the highest grade of moral improvement, did not the customs and prejudices of society foster evil passions and excuse evil actions.

The oppression which, trembling at every nerve yet resolute to heroism, it was his ill-fortune to encounter at school and at college, led him to dissent in all things from those whose arguments were blows, whose faith appeared to engender blame and hatred. 'During my existence,' he wrote to a friend in 1812, 'I have incessantly speculated, thought, and read.' His readings were not always well chosen; among them were the works of the French philosophers: as far as metaphysical argument went, he temporarily became a convert. At the same time, it was the cardinal article of his faith that, if men were but taught and induced to treat their fellows with love, charity, and equal rights, this earth would realize paradise. He looked upon religion, as it is professed, and above all practised, as hostile instead of friendly to the cultivation of those virtues which would make men brothers.

Can this be wondered at? At the age of seventeen, fragile in health and frame, of the purest habits in morals, full of devoted generosity and universal kindness, glowing with ardour to attain wisdom, resolved at every personal sacrifice to do right, burning with a desire for affection and sympathy,—he was treated as a reprobate, cast forth as a criminal.

The cause was that he was sincere; that he believed the opinions which he entertained to be true. And he loved truth with a martyr's love; he was ready to sacrifice station and fortune, and his dearest affections, at its shrine. The sacrifice was demanded from, and made by, a youth of seventeen. It is a singular fact in the history of society in the civilized nations of modern times that no false step is so irretrievable as one made in early youth. Older men, it is true, when they oppose their fellows and transgress ordinary rules, carry a certain prudence or hypocrisy as a shield along with them. But youth is rash; nor can it imagine, while asserting what it believes to be true, and doing what it believes to be right, that it should be denounced as vicious, and pursued as a criminal.

Shelley possessed a quality of mind which experience has shown me to be of the rarest occurrence among human beings: this was his *unworldliness*. The usual motives that rule men, prospects of present or future advantage, the rank and fortune of those around, the taunts and censures, or the praise, of those who were hostile to him, had no influence whatever over his actions, and apparently none over his thoughts. It is difficult even to express the simplicity and directness of purpose that adorned him. Some few might be found in the history of mankind, and some one at least among his own friends, equally disinterested and scornful, even to severe personal sacrifices, of every baser motive. But no one, I believe, ever joined this noble but passive virtue to equal active endeavours for the benefit of his friends and mankind in general, and to equal power to produce the advantages he desired. The world's brightest gauds and its most solid advantages were of no worth in his eyes, when compared to the cause of what he considered truth, and the good of his fellow-creatures. Born in a position which, to his inexperienced mind, afforded the greatest facilities to practise the tenets he espoused, he boldly declared the use he would make of fortune and station, and enjoyed the belief that he should materially benefit his fellow-creatures by his actions; while, conscious of surpassing powers of reason and imagination, it is not strange that he should, even while so young, have believed that his written thoughts would tend to disseminate opinions which he believed conducive to the happiness of the human race.

If man were a creature devoid of passion, he might have said and done all this with quietness. But he was too enthusiastic, and too full of hatred of all the ills he witnessed, not to scorn danger. Various disappointments tortured, but could not tame, his soul. The more enmity he met, the more earnestly he became attached to his peculiar views, and hostile to those of the men who persecuted him.

He was animated to greater zeal by compassion for his fellow-creatures. His sympathy was excited by the misery with which the world is burning. He witnessed the sufferings of the poor, and was aware of the evils of ignorance. He desired to induce every rich man to despoil himself of superfluity, and to create a brotherhood of property and service, and was ready to be the first to lay down the advantages of his birth. He was of too uncompromising a disposition to join any party. He did not in his youth look forward to gradual improvement: nay, in those days of intolerance, now almost forgotten, it seemed as easy to look forward to the sort of millennium of freedom and brotherhood which he thought the proper state of mankind as to the present reign of moderation and improvement. Ill-health made him believe that his race would soon be run; that a year or two was all he had of life. He desired that these years should be useful and illustrious. He saw, in a fervent call on his fellow-creatures to share alike the blessings of the creation, to love and serve each other, the noblest work that life and time permitted him. In this spirit he composed *Queen Mab*.

He was a lover of the wonderful and wild in literature, but had not fostered these tastes at their genuine sources—the romances and chivalry of the middle ages—but in the perusal of such German works as were current in those days. Under the influence of these he, at the age of fifteen, wrote two short prose romances of slender merit. The sentiments and language were exaggerated, the composition imitative and poor. He wrote also a poem on the subject of Ahasuerus—being led to it by a German fragment he picked up, dirty and torn, in Lincoln's Inn Fields. This fell afterwards into other hands, and was considerably altered before it was printed. Our earlier English poetry was almost unknown to him. The love and knowledge of Nature developed by Wordsworth —the lofty melody and mysterious beauty of Coleridge's poetry—and the wild fantastic machinery and gorgeous scenery adopted by Southey —composed his favourite reading; the rhythm of *Queen Mab* was founded on that of *Thalaba*, and the first few lines bear a striking resemblance in spirit, though not in idea, to the opening of that poem. His fertile imagination, and ear tuned to the finest sense of harmony, preserved him from imitation. Another of his favourite books was the poem of *Gebir* by Walter Savage Landor. From his boyhood he had a wonderful facility of versification, which he carried into another language; and his Latin school-verses were composed with an ease and correctness that procured for him prizes, and caused him to be resorted to by all his friends for help. He was, at the period of writing *Queen Mab*, a great traveller within the limits of England, Scotland, and Ireland. His time was spent among the loveliest scenes of these countries. Mountain and lake and forest were his home; the phenomena of Nature were his favourite study. He loved to inquire into their causes, and was addicted to pursuits of natural philosophy and chemistry, as far as they could be carried on as an amusement. These tastes gave truth and vivacity to his descriptions, and warmed his soul with that deep admiration for the wonders of Nature which constant association with her inspired.

He never intended to publish *Queen Mab* as it stands; but a few years after, when printing *Alastor,* he extracted a small portion which he entitled *The Daemon of the World*. In this he changed somewhat the versification, and made other alterations scarcely to be called improvements.

Some years after, when in Italy, a bookseller published an edition of *Queen Mab* as it originally stood. Shelley was hastily written to by his friends, under the idea that, deeply injurious as the mere distribution of the poem had proved, the publication might awaken fresh persecutions. At the suggestion of these friends he wrote a letter on the subject, printed in the *Examiner* newspaper—with which I close this history of his earliest work.

To the Editor of the 'Examiner.'

'Sir,

'Having heard that a poem entitled *Queen Mab* has been surreptitiously published in London, and that legal proceedings have been instituted against the publisher, I request the favour of your insertion of the following explanation of the affair, as it relates to me.

'A poem entitled *Queen Mab* was written by me at the age of eighteen,

I daresay in a sufficiently intemperate spirit—but even then was not intended for publication, and a few copies only were struck off, to be distributed among my personal friends. I have not seen this production for several years. I doubt not but that it is perfectly worthless in point of literary composition; and that, in all that concerns moral and political speculation, as well as in the subtler discriminations of metaphysical and religious doctrine, it is still more crude and immature. I am a devoted enemy to religious, political, and domestic oppression; and I regret this publication, not so much from literary vanity, as because I fear it is better fitted to injure than to serve the sacred cause of freedom. I have directed my solicitor to apply to Chancery for an injunction to restrain the sale; but, after the precedent of Mr. Southey's *Wat Tyler* (a poem written, I believe, at the same age, and with the same unreflecting enthusiasm), with little hope of success.

'Whilst I exonerate myself from all share in having divulged opinions hostile to existing sanctions, under the form, whatever it may be, which they assume in this poem, it is scarcely necessary for me to protest against the system of inculcating the truth of Christianity or the excellence of Monarchy, however true or however excellent they may be, by such equivocal arguments as confiscation and imprisonment, and invective and slander, and the insolent violation of the most sacred ties of Nature and society.

'SIR,

'I am your obliged and obedient servant,

'Pisa, June 22, 1821.' 'PERCY B. SHELLEY.

VERSES ON A CAT

I

A CAT in distress,
Nothing more, nor less;
Good folks, I must faithfully tell ye,
As I am a sinner,
It waits for some dinner 5
To stuff out its own little belly.

II

You would not easily guess
All the modes of distress
Which torture the tenants of earth;
And the various evils, 10
Which like so many devils,
Attend the poor souls from their
birth.

III

Some a living require,
And others desire

An old fellow out of the way; 15
And which is the best
I leave to be guessed,
For I cannot pretend to say.

IV

One wants society,
Another variety, 20
Others a tranquil life;
Some want food,
Others, as good,
Only want a wife.

V

But this poor little cat 25
Only wanted a rat,
To stuff out its own little maw;
And it were as good
Some people had such food,
To make them *hold their jaw!* 30

FRAGMENT: OMENS

HARK! the owlet flaps his wings
In the pathless dell beneath;
Hark! 'tis the night-raven sings
Tidings of approaching death.

EPITAPHIUM

[LATIN VERSION OF THE EPITAPH
IN GRAY'S ELEGY.]

I

HIC sinu fessum caput hospitali
Cespitis dormit juvenis, nec illi
Fata ridebant, popularis ille
      Nescius aurae.

II

Musa non vultu genus arroganti 5
Rustica natum grege despicata,
Et suum tristis puerum notavit
      Sollicitudo.

III

Indoles illi bene larga, pectus
Veritas sedem sibi vindicavit, 10
Et pari tantis meritis beavit
      Munere coelum.

IV

Omne quod moestis habuit miserto
Corde largivit lacrimam, recepit
Omne quod coelo voluit, fidelis 15
      Pectus amici.

V

Longius sed tu fuge curiosus
Caeteras laudes fuge suspicari,
Caeteras culpas fuge velle tractas
      Sede tremenda. 20

VI

Spe tremescentes recubant in illa
Sede virtutes pariterque culpae,
In sui Patris gremio, tremenda
      Sede Deique.

IN HOROLOGIUM

INTER marmoreas Leonorae pen-
    dula colles
Fortunata nimis Machina dicit
    horas.
Quas *manibus* premit illa duas
    insensa papillas
Cur mihi sit *digito* tangere, amata,
    nefas?

A DIALOGUE

Death.

FOR my dagger is bathed in the
    blood of the brave,
I come, care-worn tenant of life,
    from the grave,
Where Innocence sleeps 'neath the
    peace-giving sod,
And the good cease to tremble at
    Tyranny's nod;
I offer a calm habitation to thee,—
Say, victim of grief, wilt thou slum-
    ber with me? 6
My mansion is damp, cold silence
    is there,
But it lulls in oblivion the fiends of
    despair;
Not a groan of regret, not a sigh,
    not a breath,
Dares dispute with grim Silence the
    empire of Death. 10
I offer a calm habitation to thee,—
Say, victim of grief, wilt thou slum·
    ber with me?

Mortal.

Mine eyelids are heavy; my soul
    seeks repose,
It longs in thy cells to embosom its
    woes,
It longs in thy cells to deposit its
    load, 15
Where no longer the scorpions of
    Perfidy goad,—
Where the phantoms of Prejudice
    vanish away,
And Bigotry's bloodhounds lose
    scent of their prey.
Yet tell me, dark Death, when
    thine empire is o'er,

What awaits on Futurity's mist-
covered shore?   20

Death.

Cease, cease, wayward Mortal! I
dare not unveil
The shadows that float o'er Eternity's vale;
Nought waits for the good but a
spirit of Love,
That will hail their blest advent to
regions above.
For Love, Mortal, gleams through
the gloom of my sway,   25
And the shades which surround me
fly fast at its ray.
Hast thou loved?—Then depart
from these regions of hate,
And in slumber with me blunt the
arrows of fate.
I offer a calm habitation to
thee,—
Say, victim of grief, wilt thou slumber with me?   30

Mortal.

Oh! sweet is thy slumber! oh!
sweet is the ray
Which after thy night introduces
the day;
How concealed, how persuasive,
self-interest's breath,
Though it floats to mine ear from
the bosom of Death!
I hoped that I quite was forgotten
by all,   35
Yet a lingering friend might be
grieved at my fall,
And duty forbids, though I languish to die,
When departure might heave Virtue's breast with a sigh.
O Death! O my friend! snatch this
form to thy shrine,
And I fear, dear destroyer, I shall
not repine.   40

TO THE MOONBEAM

I

MOONBEAM, leave the shadowy
vale,
To bathe this burning brow.
Moonbeam, why art thou so pale,
As thou walkest o'er the dewy
dale,
Where humble wild-flowers
grow?   5
Is it to mimic me?
But that can never be;
For thine orb is bright,
And the clouds are light,
That at intervals shadow the star-
studded night.   10

II

Now all is deathly still on earth;
Nature's tired frame reposes;
And, ere the golden morning's
birth
Its radiant hues discloses,
Flies forth its balmy
breath.   15
But mine is the midnight
of Death,
And Nature's morn
To my bosom forlorn
Brings but a gloomier night, im-
plants a deadlier thorn.

III

Wretch! Suppress the glare of
madness   20
Struggling in thine haggard
eye,
For the keenest throb of sadness,
Pale Despair's most sickening
sigh,
Is but to mimic me;
And this must ever be, 25
When the twilight of care,
And the night of despair,
Seem in my breast but joys to the
pangs that rankle there.

THE SOLITARY

I

DAR'ST thou amid the varied multi-
tude
To live alone, an isolated thing?
To see the busy beings round
thee spring,
And care for none; in thy calm
solitude,
A flower that scarce breathes in the
desert rude 5
To Zephyr's passing wing?

II

Not the swart Pariah in some Indian grove,
Lone, lean, and hunted by his
brother's hate,
Hath drunk so deep the cup of
bitter fate
As that poor wretch who cannot,
cannot love: 10
He bears a load which nothing can
remove,
A killing, withering weight.

III

He smiles—'tis sorrow's deadliest
mockery;
He speaks—the cold words flow
not from his soul;
He acts like others, drains the
genial bowl,— 15
Yet, yet he longs—although he
fears—to die;
He pants to reach what yet he
seems to fly,
Dull life's extremest goal.

TO DEATH

DEATH! where is thy victory?
To triumph whilst I die,
To triumph whilst thine ebon
wing
Enfolds my shuddering soul?
O Death! where is thy sting? 5
Not when the tides of murder
roll,
When nations groan, that kings
may bask in bliss.

Death! canst thou boast a victory
such as this—
When in his hour of pomp and
power
His blow the mightiest mur-
derer gave, 10
Mid Nature's cries the sacrifice
Of millions to glut the grave;
When sunk the Tyrant Desolation's
slave;
Or Freedom's life-blood streamed
upon thy shrine;
Stern Tyrant, couldst thou boast a
victory such as mine? 15

To know in dissolution's void
That mortals' baubles sunk
decay;
That everything, but Love, de-
stroyed
Must perish with its kindred
clay,—
Perish Ambition's crown, 20
Perish her sceptred sway;
From Death's pale front fades
Pride's fastidious frown.
In Death's damp vault the lurid
fires decay,
That Envy lights at heaven-born
Virtue's beam—
That all the cares subside, 25
Which lurk beneath the tide
Of life's unquiet stream;—
Yes! this is victory!
And on yon rock, whose dark form
glooms the sky,
To stretch these pale limbs, when
the soul is fled; 30
To baffle the lean passions of
their prey,
To sleep within the palace of the
dead!
Oh! not the King, around whose
dazzling throne
His countless courtiers mock the
words they say,
Triumphs amid the bud of glory
blown. 35

As I in this cold bed, and faint
    expiring groan!

Tremble, ye proud, whose grandeur
    mocks the woe
Which props the column of un-
    natural state!
You the plainings, faint and
    low,
    From Misery's tortured soul
      that flow,   40
    Shall usher to your fate.
Tremble, ye conquerors, at whose
    fell command
The war-fiend riots o'er a peaceful
    land!
You Desolation's gory throng
Shall bear from Victory
    along   45
    To that mysterious strand.

. . . . . .

LOVE'S ROSE

I

HOPES, that swell in youthful
    breasts,
    Live not through the waste of
    time!
Love's rose a host of thorns invests;
    Cold, ungenial is the clime,
    Where its honours blow.   5
Youth says, 'The purple flowers are
    mine,'
    Which die the while they glow.

II

Dear the boon to Fancy given,
    Retracted whilst it's granted:

Sweet the rose which lives in
    Heaven,   10
    Although on earth 'tis planted,
    Where its honours blow,
While by earth's slaves the leaves
    are riven
    Which die the while they glow.

III

Age cannot Love destroy,   15
    But perfidy can blast the flower,
    Even when in most unwary hour
    It blooms in Fancy's bower.
Age cannot Love destroy,
But perfidy can rend the shrine   20
In which its vermeil splendours
    shine.

EYES: A FRAGMENT

    How eloquent are eyes!
Not the rapt poet's frenzied lay
When the soul's wildest feelings
    stray
    Can speak so well as they.
    How eloquent are eyes!   5
Not music's most impassioned note
On which Love's warmest fervours
    float
    Like them bids rapture rise.
    Love, look thus again,—
That your look may light a waste
    of years,   10
Darting the beam that conquers
    cares
    Through the cold shower of
    tears.
    Love, look thus again!

. . . . . .

ORIGINAL POETRY
BY VICTOR AND CAZIRE

*A Person complained that whenever he began to write, he never could
arrange his ideas in grammatical order. Which occasion suggested the
idea of the following lines:*

I

HERE I sit with my paper, my pen
    and my ink,

First of this thing, and that thing,
    and t'other thing think;
Then my thoughts come so pell-
    mell all into my mind,

That the sense or the subject I
never can find:
This word is wrong placed,—no
regard to the sense,   5
The present and future, instead of
past tense,
Then my grammar I want; O dear!
what a bore,
I think I shall never attempt to
write more,
With patience I then my thoughts
must arraign,
Have them all in due order like
mutes in a train,   10
Like them too must wait in due
patience and thought,
Or else my fine works will all come
to nought.
My wit too 's so copious, it flows
like a river,
But disperses its waters on black
and white never;
Like smoke it appears independent
and free,   15
But ah luckless smoke! it all passes
like thee—
Then at length all my patience entirely lost,
My paper and pens in the fire are
tossed;
But come, try again—you must
never despair,
Our Murray's or Entick's are not
all so rare,   20
Implore their assistance—they'll
come to your aid,
Perform all your business without
being paid,
They'll tell you the present tense,
future and past,
Which should come first, and which
should come last,
This Murray will do—-then to Entick repair,   25
To find out the meaning of any
word rare.

This they friendly will tell, and
ne'er make you blush,
With a jeering look, taunt, or an
O fie! tush!
Then straight all your thoughts in
black and white put,
Not minding the if's, the be's, and
the but,   30
Then read it all over, see how it
will run,
How answers the wit, the retort,
and the pun,
Your writings may then with old
Socrates vie,
May on the same shelf with Demos-
thenes lie,
May as Junius be sharp, or as Plato
be sage,   35
The pattern or satire to all of the
age;
But stop—a mad author I mean not
to turn,
Nor with thirst of applause does my
heated brain burn,
Sufficient that sense, wit, and gram-
mar combined,
My letters may make some slight
food for the mind;   40
That my thoughts to my friends I
may freely impart,
In all the warm language that flows
from the heart.
Hark! futurity calls! it loudly
complains,
It bids me step forward and just
hold the reins,
My excuse shall be humble, and
faithful, and true,   45
Such as I fear can be made but by
few—
Of writers this age has abundance
and plenty,
Three score and a thousand, two
millions and twenty,
Three score of them wits who all
sharply vie,

To try what odd creature they best
   can belie,   50
A thousand are prudes who for
   Charity write,
And fill up their sheets with spleen,
   envy, and spite[,]
One million are bards, who to
   Heaven aspire,
And stuff their works full of bom-
   bast, rant, and fire,
T'other million are wags who in
   Grub-street attend,   55
And just like a cobbler the old writ-
   ings mend,
The twenty are those who for pul-
   pits indite,
And pore over sermons all Saturday
   night.
And now my good friends—who
   come after I mean,
As I ne'er wore a cassock, or dined
   with a dean,   60
Or like cobblers at mending I never
   did try,
Nor with poets in lyrics attempted
   to vie;
As for prudes these good souls I
   both hate and detest,
So here I believe the matter must
   rest.—
I've heard your complaint—my
   answer I've made,   65
And since to your calls all the
   tribute I've paid,
Adieu my good friend; pray never
   despair,
But grammar and sense and everything dare,
Attempt but to write dashing, easy,
   and free,
Then take out your grammar and
   pay him his fee,   70
Be not a coward, shrink not to a
   tense,
But read it all over and make it
   out sense.

What a tiresome girl!—pray soon
   make an end,
Else my limited patience you'll
   quickly expend.
Well adieu, I no longer your patience will try—   75
So swift to the post now the letter
   shall fly.

                JANUARY, 1810.

II

TO MISS —— [HARRIET GROVE]
  FROM MISS —— [ELIZABETH
               SHELLEY]

FOR your letter, dear —— [Hattie],
   accept my best thanks,
Rendered long and amusing by
   virtue of franks,
Though concise they would please,
   yet the longer the better,
The more news that's crammed in,
   more amusing the letter,
All excuses of etiquette nonsense I
   hate,   5
Which only are fit for the tardy and
   late,
As when converse grows flat, of the
   weather they talk,
How fair the sun shines—a fine day
   for a walk,
Then to politics turn, of Burdett's
   reformation,
One declares it would hurt, t'other
   better the nation,   10
Will ministers keep? sure they've
   acted quite wrong,
The burden this is of each morning-
   call song.
So —— is going to —— you say,
I hope that success her great efforts
   will pay [——]
That [the Colonel] will see her, be
   dazzled outright,   15
And declare he can't bear to be out
   of her sight.
Write flaming epistles with love's
   pointed dart,

Whose sharp little arrow struck
    right on his heart,
Scold poor innocent Cupid for mis-
    chievous ways,
He knows not how much to laud
    forth her praise,   20
That he neither eats, drinks or
    sleeps for her sake,
And hopes her hard heart some
    compassion will take,
A refusal would kill him, so des-
    perate his flame,
But he fears, for he knows she is
    not common game,
Then praises her sense, wit, dis-
    cernment and grace,   25
He's not one that's caught by a sly
    looking face,
Yet that's *too* divine—such a black
    sparkling eye,
At the bare glance of which near a
    thousand will die;
Thus runs he on meaning but one
    word in ten,
More than is meant by most such
    kind of men,   30
For they're all alike, take them one
    with another,
Begging pardon—with the excep-
    tion of my brother.
Of the drawings you mention much
    praise I have heard,
Most opinion's the same, with the
    difference of word,
Some get a good name by the voice
    of the crowd,   35
Whilst to poor humble merit small
    praise is allowed,
As in parliament votes, so in pic-
    tures a name,
Oft determines a fate at the altar
    of fame.—
So on Friday this City's gay vortex
    you quit,
And no longer with Doctors and
    Johnny cats sit—   40

Now your parcel's arrived ——
    [Bysshe's] letter shall go,
I hope all your joy mayn't be
    turned into woe,
Experience will tell you that pleas-
    ure is vain,
When it promises sunshine how
    often comes rain.
So when to fond hope every bless-
    ing is nigh,   45
How oft when we smile it is
    checked with a sigh,
When Hope, gay deceiver, in pleas-
    ure is dressed,
How oft comes a stroke that may
    rob us of rest.
When we think ourselves safe, and
    the goal near at hand,
Like a vessel just landing, we're
    wrecked near the strand,   50
And though memory forever the
    sharp pang must feel,
'Tis our duty to bear, and our hard-
    ship to steel—
May misfortunes dear Girl, ne'er
    thy happiness cloy,
May the days glide in peace, love,
    comfort and joy,
May thy tears with soft pity for
    other woes flow,   55
Woes, which thy tender heart
    never may know,
For hardships our own, God has
    taught us to bear,
Though sympathy's soul to a friend
    drops a tear.
Oh dear! what sentimental stuff
    have I written,
Only fit to tear up and play with a
    kitten.   60
What sober reflections in the midst
    of this letter!
Jocularity sure would have suited
    much better;
But there are exceptions to all com-
    mon rules,

For this is a truth by all boys
    learned at schools.
Now adieu my dear —— [Hattie]
    I'm sure I must tire,   65
For if I do, you may throw it into
    the fire,
So accept the best love of your cou-
    sin and friend,
Which brings this nonsensical
    rhyme to an end.
              April 30, 1810.

III. SONG

COLD, cold is the blast when De-
    cember is howling,
    Cold are the damps on a dying
    man's brow,——
Stern are the seas when the wild
    waves are rolling,
    And sad is the grave where a
    loved one lies low;
But colder is scorn from the being
    who loved thee,   5
More stern is the sneer from the
    friend who has proved thee,
More sad are the tears when their
    sorrows have moved thee,
    Which mixed with groans, an-
    guish and wild madness
    flow—
And ah! poor —— has felt all this
    horror,
    Full long the fallen victim con-
    tended with fate: 10
'Till a destitute outcast abandoned
    to sorrow,
    She sought her babe's food at her
    ruiner's gate—
Another had charmed the remorse-
    less betrayer,
He turned laughing aside from her
    moans and her prayer,
She said nothing, but wringing the
    wet from her hair,   15
Crossed the dark mountain side,
    though the hour it was late.
'Twas on the wild height of the
    dark Penmanmawr,

That the form of the wasted ——
    reclined;
She shrieked to the ravens that
    croaked from afar,
    And she sighed to the gusts of
    the wild sweeping wind.—
'I call not yon rocks where the
    thunder peals rattle,   21
I call not yon clouds where the
    elements battle,
    But thee, cruel —— I call thee
    unkind!'—

Then she wreathed in her hair the
    wild flowers of the moun-
    tain,
    And deliriously laughing, a gar-
    land entwined,   25
She bedewed it with tears, then she
    hung o'er the fountain,
    And leaving it, cast it a prey
    to the wind.
'Ah! go,' she exclaimed, 'when the
    tempest is yelling,
'Tis unkind to be cast on the sea
    that is swelling,
But I left, a pitiless outcast, my
    dwelling,   30
    My garments are torn, so they
    say is my mind—'
Not long lived ——, but over her
    grave
    Waved the desolate form of a
    storm-blasted yew,
Around it no demons or ghosts dare
    to rave,
    But spirits of peace steep her
    slumbers in dew.   35
Then stay thy swift steps mid the
    dark mountain heather,
Though chill blow the wind and
    severe is the weather,
For perfidy, traveller! cannot be-
    reave her,
    Of the tears, to the tombs of the
    innocent due.—
              JULY, 1810.

IV. SONG

Come [Harriet]! sweet is the hour,
  Soft Zephyrs breathe gently
    around,
The anemone's night-boding flower,
  Has sunk its pale head on the
    ground.

'Tis thus the world's keenness hath
    torn,   5
  Some mild heart that expands
    to its blast,
'Tis thus that the wretched for-
    lorn,
  Sinks poor and neglected at
    last.—

The world with its keenness and
    woe,
  Has no charms or attraction for
    me,   10
Its unkindness with grief has laid
    low,
  The heart which is faithful to
    thee.

The high trees that wave past the
    moon,
  As I walk in their umbrage with
    you,
All declare I must part with you
    soon,   15
  All bid you a tender adieu!—

Then [Harriet]! dearest farewell,
  You and I love, may ne'er meet
    again;
These woods and these meadows
    can tell
  How soft and how sweet was the
    strain.—   20
                    APRIL, 1810.

V. SONG

DESPAIR

Ask not the pallid stranger's woe,
  With beating heart and throb-
    bing breast,

Whose step is faltering, weak, and
    slow,
  As though the body needed
    rest.—
Whose 'wildered eye no object
    meets,   5
  Nor cares to ken a friendly
    glance,
With silent grief his bosom beats,—
  Now fixed, as in a deathlike
    trance.

Who looks around with fearful eye,
  And shuns all converse with
    mankind,   10
As though some one his griefs
    might spy,
  And soothe them with a kindred
    mind.

A friend or foe to him the same,
  He looks on each with equal eye;
The difference lies but in the
    name,   15
  To none for comfort can he fly.—
'Twas deep despair, and sorrow's
    trace,
  To him too keenly given,
Whose memory, time could not ef-
    face—
  His peace was lodged in
    Heaven.—   20

He looks on all this world be-
    stows,
  The pride and pomp of power,
As trifles best for pageant shows
  Which vanish in an hour.
When torn is dear affection's tie,
  Sinks the soft heart full low; 26
It leaves without a parting sigh,
  All that these realms bestow.
                     JUNE, 1810.

VI. SONG

SORROW

To me this world's a dreary blank,
  All hopes in life are gone and
    fled,

My high strung energies are sank,
   And all my blissful hopes lie
      dead.—

The world once smiling to my
      view,   5
   Showed scenes of endless bliss
      and joy;
The world I then but little knew,
   Ah! little knew how pleasures
      cloy;

All then was jocund, all was gay,
   No thought beyond the present
      hour,   10
I danced in pleasure's fading ray,
   Fading alas! as drooping flower.

Nor do the heedless in the throng,
   One thought beyond the morrow
      give[,]
They court the feast, the dance,
      the song,   15
   Nor think how short their time
      to live.

The heart that bears deep sorrow's
      trace,
   What earthly comfort can con-
      sole,
It drags a dull and lengthened
      pace,
   'Till friendly death its woes en-
      roll.—   20

The sunken cheek, the humid eyes,
   E'en better than the tongue can
      tell;
In whose sad breast deep sorrow
      lies,
   Where memory's rankling traces
      dwell.—

The rising tear, the stifled sigh, 25
   A mind but ill at ease display,
Like blackening clouds in stormy
      sky,
   Where fiercely vivid lightnings
      play.

Thus when souls' energy is dead,
   When sorrow dims each earthly
      view,   30
When every fairy hope is fled,
   We bid ungrateful world adieu.
          August, 1810.

VII. SONG

HOPE

And said I that all hope was fled,
   That sorrow and despair were
      mine,
That each enthusiast wish was
      dead,
   Had sank beneath pale Misery's
      shrine.—

Seest thou the sunbeam's yellow
      glow,   5
   That robes with liquid streams
      of light;
Yon distant Mountain's craggy
      brow.
   And shows the rocks so fair,—
      so bright ——

Tis thus sweet expectation's ray,
   In softer view shows distant
      hours,   10
And portrays each succeeding day,
   As dressed in fairer, brighter
      flowers,—

The vermeil tinted flowers that
      blossom;
   Are frozen but to bud anew,
Then sweet deceiver calm my
      bosom,   15
   Although thy visions be not
      true,—

Yet true they are,—and I'll believe,
   Thy whisperings soft of love and
      peace,
God never made thee to deceive,
   'Tis sin that bade thy empire
      cease.   20

Yet though despair my life should
    gloom,
Though horror should around me
    close,
With those I love, beyond the
    tomb,
Hope shows a balm for all my
    woes.

AUGUST, 1810.

VIII. SONG

TRANSLATED FROM THE ITALIAN

OH! what is the gain of restless
    care,
    And what is ambitious treasure?
And what are the joys that the
    modish share,
    In their sickly haunts of pleas-
      sure?

My husband's repast with delight
    I spread,   5
    What though 'tis but rustic fare,
May each guardian angel protect
    his shed,
    May contentment and quiet be
    there.

And may I support my husband's
    years,
    May I soothe his dying pain, 10
And then may I dry my fast fall-
    ing tears,
    And meet him in Heaven again.

JULY, 1810.

IX. SONG

TRANSLATED FROM THE GERMAN

AH! grasp the dire dagger and
    couch the fell spear,
    If vengeance and death to thy
    bosom be dear,
The dastard shall perish, death's
    torment shall prove,
For fate and revenge are decreed
    from above.

Ah! where is the hero, whose
    nerves strung by youth, 5
Will defend the firm cause of jus-
    tice and truth;
With insatiate desire whose bosom
    shall swell,
To give up the oppressor to judge-
    ment and Hell—

For him shall the fair one twine
    chaplets of bays,
To him shall each warrior give
    merited praise,   10
And triumphant returned from the
    clangour of arms,
He shall find his reward in his
    loved maiden's charms.

In ecstatic confusion the warrior
    shall sip,
The kisses that glow on his love's
    dewy lip,
And mutual, eternal, embraces shall
    prove,   15
The rewards of the brave are the
    transports of love.

OCTOBER, 1809.

X

THE IRISHMAN'S SONG

THE stars may dissolve, and the
    fountain of light
May sink into ne'er ending chaos
    and night,
Our mansions must fall, and earth
    vanish away,
But thy courage O Erin! may
    never decay.

See! the wide wasting ruin extends
    all around,   5
Our ancestors' dwellings lie sunk
    on the ground,
Our foes ride in triumph through-
    out our domains,
And our mightiest heroes lie
    stretched on the plains.

Ah! dead is the harp which was
    wont to give pleasure,
Ah! sunk is our sweet country's
    rapturous measure,   10
But the war note is waked, and the
    clangour of spears,
The dread yell of Sloghan yet
    sounds in our ears.

Ah! where are the heroes! tri-
    umphant in death,
Convulsed they recline on the
    blood sprinkled heath,
Or the yelling ghosts ride on the
    blast that sweeps by,   15
And 'my countrymen! vengeance!'
    incessantly cry.
                OCTOBER, 1809.

XI. SONG

FIERCE roars the midnight
    storm
    O'er the wild mountain,
Dark clouds the night deform,
    Swift rolls the fountain—

See! o'er yon rocky height,   5
    Dim mists are flying—
See by the moon's pale light,
    Poor Laura's dying!

Shame and remorse shall howl,
    By her false pillow—   10
Fiercer than storms that roll,
    O'er the white billow;

No hand her eyes to close,
    When life is flying,
But she will find repose,   15
    For Laura's dying!

Then will I seek my love,
    Then will I cheer her,
Then my esteem will prove.
    When no friend is near her.   20

On her grave I will lie,
    When life is parted,
On her grave I will die,
    For the false hearted.
             DECEMBER, 1809.

XII. SONG

To ——— [HARRIET]

AH! sweet is the moonbeam that
    sleeps on yon fountain,
And sweet the mild rush of the
    soft-sighing breeze,
And sweet is the glimpse of yon
    dimly-seen mountain,
'Neath the verdant arcades of
    yon shadowy trees.

But sweeter than all was thy tone
    of affection,   5
Which scarce seemed to break on
    the stillness of eve,
Though the time it is past!—yet
    the dear recollection,
For aye in the heart of thy
    [Percy] must live.

Yet he hears thy dear voice in the
    summer winds sighing,
Mild accents of happiness lisp
    in his ear,   10
When the hope-wingèd moments
    athwart him are flying,
And he thinks of the friend to
    his bosom so dear.—

And thou dearest friend in his
    bosom for ever
Must reign unalloyed by the fast
    rolling year,
He loves thee, and dearest one
    never, Oh! never   15
Canst thou cease to be loved by
    a heart so sincere.
              AUGUST, 1810.

XIII. SONG

To ——— [HARRIET]

STERN, stern is the voice of fate's
    fearful command,
When accents of horror it
    breathes in our ear,
Or compels us for aye bid adieu to
    the land,

Where exists that loved friend to
    our bosom so dear,
'Tis sterner than death o'er the
    shuddering wretch bending,
And in skeleton grasp his fell
    sceptre extending,   6
Like the heart-stricken deer to that
    loved covert wending,
    Which never again to his eyes
    may appear—
And ah! he may envy the heart-
    stricken quarry,
    Who bids to the friend of affec-
    tion farewell,   10
He may envy the bosom so bleed-
    ing and gory,
    He may envy the sound of the
    drear passing knell,
Not so deep is his grief on his
    death couch reposing,
    When on the last vision his dim
    eyes are closing!
As the outcast whose love-raptured
    senses are losing,   15
    The last tones of thy voice on the
    wild breeze that swell!

Those tones were so soft, and so
    sad, that ah! never,
    Can the sound cease to vibrate
    on Memory's ear,
In the stern wreck of Nature for
    ever and ever,
    The remembrance must live of a
    friend so sincere.   20
            AUGUST, 1810.

XIV

SAINT EDMOND'S EVE

OH! did you observe the Black
    Canon pass,
    And did you observe his frown?
He goeth to say the midnight mass,
    In holy St. Edmond's town.

He goeth to sing the burial chaunt,
    And to lay the wandering sprite,

Whose shadowy, restless form doth
    haunt,   7
    The Abbey's drear aisle this
    night.

It saith it will not its wailing cease,
    'Till that holy man come near, 10
'Till he pour o'er its grave the
    prayer of peace,
    And sprinkle the hallowed tear.

The Canon's horse is stout and
    strong
    The road is plain and fair,
But the Canon slowly wends along,
    And his brow is gloomed with
    care.   16

Who is it thus late at the Abbey-
    gate?
    Sullen echoes the portal bell,
It sounds like the whispering voice
    of fate,
    It sounds like a funeral knell. 20

The Canon his faltering knee thrice
    bowed,
    And his frame was convulsed
    with fear,
When a voice was heard distinct
    and loud,
    'Prepare! for thy hour is near.'

He crosses his breast, he mutters a
    prayer,   25
    To Heaven he lifts his eye,
He heeds not the Abbot's gazing
    stare,
    Nor the dark Monks who mur-
    mured by.

Bare-headed he worships the sculp-
    tured saints
    That frown on the sacred walls,
His face it grows pale,—he trem-
    bles, he faints,   31
    At the Abbot's feet he falls.

And straight the father's robe he
    kissed,

Who cried, 'Grace dwells with
    thee,
The spirit will fade like the morn-
    ing mist,   35
    At your benedicite.

'Now haste within! the board is
    spread,
Keen blows the air, and cold,
The spectre sleeps in its earthy bed,
'Till St. Edmond's bell hath
    tolled,—   40

'Yet rest your wearied limbs to-
    night,
You've journeyed many a mile,
To-morrow lay the wailing sprite,
That shrieks in the moonlight
    aisle.

'Oh! faint are my limbs and my
    bosom is cold,   45
Yet to-night must the sprite be
    laid,
Yet to-night when the hour of hor-
    ror's told,
Must I meet the wandering
    shade.

'Nor food, nor rest may now de-
    lay,—
For hark! the echoing pile,   50
A bell loud shakes!—Oh haste
    away,
O lead to the haunted aisle.'

The torches slowly move before,
    The cross is raised on high,
A smile of peace the Canon wore, 55
    But horror dimmed his eye—

And now they climb the footworn
    stair,
    The chapel gates unclose,
Now each breathed low a fervent
    prayer,   59
    And fear each bosom froze——

Now paused awhile the doubtful
    band

And viewed the solemn scene,—
Full dark the clustered columns
    stand,
The moon gleams pale be-
    tween—

'Say father, say, what cloisters'
    gloom   65
Conceals the unquiet shade,
Within what dark unhallowed
    tomb,
The corse unblessed was laid.'

'Through yonder drear aisle alone
    it walks,
And murmurs a mournful plaint,
Of thee! Black Canon, it wildly
    talks,   71
And call on thy patron saint—

'The pilgrim this night with won-
    dering eyes,
As he prayed at St. Edmond's
    shrine,
From a black marble tomb hath
    seen it rise,   75
And under yon arch recline.'—

'Oh! say upon that black marble
    tomb,
What memorial sad appears.'—
'Undistinguished it lies in the chan-
    cel's gloom,
No memorial sad it bears'—   80

The Canon his paternoster reads,
    His rosary hung by his side,
Now swift to the chancel doors he
    leads,
    And untouched they open wide,

Resistless, strange sounds his steps
    impel,   85
To approach to the black marble
    tomb,
'Oh! enter, Black Canon,' a whis-
    per fell,
'Oh! enter, thy hour is come.'

He paused, told his beads, and the
    threshold passed,

Oh! horror, the chancel doors
   close,   90
A loud yell was borne on the rising
   blast,
   And a deep, dying groan arose.

The Monks in amazement shud-
   dering stand,
   They burst through the chan-
      cel's gloom,
From St. Edmond's shrine, lo! a
   skeleton's hand,   95
   Points to the black marble tomb.

Lo! deeply engraved, an inscription
   blood red,
   In characters fresh and clear—
'The guilty Black Canon of Elm-
   ham's dead,   99
   And his wife lies buried here!'

In Elmham's tower he wedded a
   Nun,
   To St. Edmond's his bride he
      bore,
On this eve her noviciate here was
   begun,
   And a Monk's gray weeds she
      wore;—

O! deep was her conscience dyed
   with guilt,   105
   Remorse she full oft revealed,
Her blood by the ruthless Black
   Canon was spilt,
   And in death her lips he sealed;

Her spirit to penance this night was
   doomed,
   'Till the Canon atoned the deed,
Here together they now shall rest
   entombed,   111
   'Till their bodies from dust are
      freed—

Hark! a loud peal of thunder
   shakes the roof,
   Round the altar bright light-
      nings play,
Speechless with horror the Monks
   stand aloof,   115

And the storm dies sudden
   away—

The inscription was gone! a cross
   on the ground,
   And a rosary shone through the
      gloom,
But never again was the Canon
   there found,
   Or the Ghost on the black mar-
      ble tomb.   120

XV. REVENGE

'AH! quit me not yet, for the wind
   whistles shrill,
Its blast wanders mournfully over
   the hill,
The thunder's wild voice rattles
   madly above,
You will not then, cannot then,
   leave me my love.—'

I must dearest Agnes, the night is
   far gone—   5
I must wander this evening to
   Strasburg alone,
I must seek the drear tomb of my
   ancestors' bones,
And must dig their remains from
   beneath the cold stones.

'For the spirit of Conrad there
   meets me this night,
And we quit not the tomb 'till dawn
   of the light,   10
And Conrad's been dead just a
   month and a day!
So farewell dearest Agnes for I
   must away,—

'He bid me bring with me what
   most I held dear,
Or a month from that time should
   I lie on my bier,
And I'd sooner resign this false
   fluttering breath,   15
Than my Agnes should dread either
   danger or death,

'And I love you to madness my
  Agnes I love,
My constant affection this night
  will I prove,
This night will I go to the sepul-
  chre's jaw,
Alone will I glut its all conquering
  maw'—   20

'No! no loved Adolphus thy Agnes
  will share,
In the tomb all the dangers that
  wait for you there,
I fear not the spirit,—I fear not the
  grave,
My dearest Adolphus I'd perish to
  save'—

'Nay seek not to say that thy love
  shall not go,   25
But spare me those ages of horror
  and woe,
For I swear to thee here that I'll
  perish ere day,
If you go unattended by Agnes
  away'—

The night it was bleak the fierce
  storm raged around,
The lightning's blue fire-light
  flashed on the ground, 30
Strange forms seemed to flit,—and
  howl tidings of fate,
As Agnes advanced to the sepulchre gate.—

The youth struck the portal,—the
  echoing sound
Was fearfully rolled midst the
  tombstones around,
The blue lightning gleamed o'er the
  dark chapel spire,   35
And tinged were the storm clouds
  with sulphurous fire.

Still they gazed on the tombstone
  where Conrad reclined,
Yet they shrank at the cold chilling blast of the wind,

When a strange silver brilliance
  pervaded the scene,
And a figure advanced—tall in
  form—fierce in mien.   40

A mantle encircled his shadowy
  form,
As light as a gossamer borne on
  the storm,
Celestial terror sat throned in his
  gaze,
Like the midnight pestiferous meteor's blaze.—

Spirit.

Thy father, Adolphus! was false,
  false as hell,   45
And Conrad has cause to remember
  it well,
He ruined my Mother, despised me
  his son,
I quitted the world ere my vengeance was done.

I was nearly expiring—'twas close
  of the day,—
A demon advanced to the bed
  where I lay,   50
He gave me the power from whence
  I was hurled,
To return to revenge, to return to
  the world,—

Now Adolphus I'll seize thy best
  loved in my arms,
I'll drag her to Hades all blooming
  in charms,
On the black whirlwind's thundering pinion I'll ride,   55
And fierce yelling fiends shall exult
  o'er thy bride—

He spoke, and extending his
  ghastly arms wide,
Majestic advanced with a swift
  noiseless stride,
He clasped the fair Agnes—he
  raised her on high,

And cleaving the roof sped his way
    to the sky—   60
All was now silent,—and over the
    tomb,
Thicker, deeper, was swiftly ex-
    tended a gloom,
Adolphus in horror sank down on
    the stone,
And his fleeting soul fled with a
    harrowing groan.
           DECEMBER, 1809.

XVI. GHASTA

OR, THE AVENGING DEMON!!!

*The idea of the following tale
was taken from a few unconnected
German Stanzas.—-The principal
Character is evidently the Wandering Jew, and although not mentioned by name, the burning Cross
on his forehead undoubtedly alludes to that superstition, so preva-
lent in the part of Germany called
the Black Forest, where this scene
is supposed to lie.*

HARK! the owlet flaps her wing,
    In the pathless dell beneath,
Hark! night ravens loudly sing,
    Tidings of despair and death.—

Horror covers all the sky,   5
    Clouds of darkness blot the
        moon,
Prepare! for mortal thou must die,
    Prepare to yield thy soul up
        soon—

Fierce the tempest raves around,
    Fierce the volleyed lightnings
        fly,   10
Crashing thunder shakes the
    ground,
    Fire and tumult fill the sky.—

Hark! the tolling village bell,
    Tells the hour of midnight come,
Now can blast the powers of Hell,

Fiend-like goblins now can
    roam—   16

See! his crest all stained with rain,
    A warrior hastening speeds his
        way,
He starts, looks round him, starts
    again,
    And sighs for the approach of
        day.   20

See! his frantic steed he reins,
    See! he lifts his hands on high,
Implores a respite to his pains,
    From the powers of the sky.—

He seeks an Inn, for faint from
    toil,   25
    Fatigue had bent his lofty form,
To rest his wearied limbs awhile,
    Fatigued with wandering and the
        storm.

   .   .   .   .   .
    .   .   .   .   .

Slow the door is opened wide—
    With trackless tread a stranger
        came,   30
His form Majestic, slow his stride,
    He sate, nor spake,—nor told his
        name—

Terror blanched the warrior's
    cheek,
    Cold sweat from his forehead
        ran,
In vain his tongue essayed to
    speak,—   35
    At last the stranger thus be-
        gan:

'Mortal! thou that saw'st the sprite,
    Tell me what I wish to know,
Or come with me before 'tis light,
    Where cypress trees and man-
        drakes grow.   40

'Fierce the avenging Demon's ire,
    Fiercer than the wintry blast,
Fiercer than the lightning's fire,
    When the hour of twilight's
        past'—

The warrior raised his sunken
    eye,   45
It met the stranger's sullen scowl,
'Mortal! Mortal! thou must die,'
In burning letters chilled his soul.

Warrior.

Stranger! whoso'er you are,
    I feel impelled my tale to tell— 50
Horrors stranger shalt thou hear,
    Horrors drear as those of Hell.

O'er my Castle silence reigned,
    Late the night and drear the
        hour,
When on the terrace I observed, 55
    A fleeting shadowy mist to
        lower.—

Light the cloud as summer fog,
    Which transient shuns the morn-
        ing beam;
Fleeting as the cloud on bog,
    That hangs or on the mountain
        stream.—   60

Horror seized my shuddering brain,
    Horror dimmed my starting eye,
In vain I tried to speak,—In vain
    My limbs essayed the spot to
        fly—

At last the thin and shadowy
    form,   65
    With noiseless, trackless foot-
        steps came,—
Its light robe floated on the storm,
    Its head was bound with lambent
        flame.

In chilling voice drear as the breeze
    Which sweeps along th' autum-
        nal ground,   70
Which wanders through the leafless
    trees,
    Or the mandrake's groan which
        floats around.

'Thou art mine and I am thine,
    'Till the sinking of the world,

I am thine and thou art mine,   75
    'Till in ruin death is hurled ——

'Strong the power and dire the fate,
    Which drags me from the depths
        of Hell,
Breaks the tomb's eternal gate,
    Where fiendish shapes and dead
        men yell,   80

'Haply I might ne'er have shrank
    From flames that rack the guilty
        dead,
Haply I might ne'er have sank
    On pleasure's flow'ry, thorny
        bed—

—'But stay! no more I dare dis-
        close,   85
Of the tale I wish to tell,
On Earth relentless were my woes,
    But fiercer are my pangs in
        Hell—

'Now I claim thee as my love,
    Lay aside all chilling fear, 90
My affection will I prove
    Where sheeted ghosts and spec-
        tres are!

'For thou art mine, and I am thine,
    'Till the dreaded judgement day,
I am thine, and thou art mine—   95
    Night is past— I must away.'

Still I gazed, and still the form
    Pressed upon my aching sight,
Still I braved the howling storm,
    When the ghost dissolved in
        night.—

Restless, sleepless fled the night, 101
    Sleepless as a sick man's bed,
When he sighs for morning light,
    When he turns his aching
        head,—

Slow and painful passed the day, 105
    Melancholy seized my brain,
Lingering fled the hours away,
    Lingering to a wretch in pain.—

At last came night, ah! horrid hour,
  Ah! chilling time that wakes the
    dead,   110
When demons ride the clouds that
  lower,
  —The phantom sat upon my
    bed.

In hollow voice, low as the sound
  Which in some charnel makes its
    moan,
What floats along the burying
    ground,   115
  The phantom claimed me as her
    own.

Her chilling finger on my head,
  With coldest touch congealed my
    soul—
Cold as the finger of the dead,
  Or damps which round a tomb-
    stone roll—   120

Months are passed in lingering
    round,
  Every night the spectre comes,
With thrilling step it shakes the
    ground,
  With thrilling step it round me
    roams—

Stranger! I have told to thee, 125
  All the tale I have to tell—
Stranger! canst thou tell to me,
  How to 'scape the powers of
    Hell?—

Stranger.

Warrior! I can ease thy woes,
  Wilt thou, wilt thou, come with
    me—   130
Warrior! I can all disclose,
  Follow, follow, follow me.

Yet the tempest's duskiest wing,
  Its mantle stretches o'er the sky,
Yet the midnight ravens sing, 135
  'Mortal! Mortal! thou must die.'

At last they saw a river clear,
  That crossed the heathy path
    they trod,
The Stranger's look was wild and
    drear,
  The firm Earth shook beneath
    his nod—   140

He raised a wand above his head,
  He traced a circle on the plain,
In a wild verse he called the dead,
  The dead with silent footsteps
    came.

A burning brilliance on his head, 145
  Flaming filled the stormy air,
In a wild verse he called the dead,
  The dead in motley crowd were
    there.—

'Ghasta! Ghasta! come along,
  Bring thy fiendish crowd with
    thee,
Quickly raise th' avenging Song, 151
  Ghasta! Ghasta! come to me.'

Horrid shapes in mantles gray,
  Flit athwart the stormy night,
'Ghasta! Ghasta! come away, 155
  Come away before 'tis light.'

See! the sheeted Ghost they bring,
  Yelling dreadful o'er the heath,
Hark! the deadly verse they sing,
  Tidings of despair and death! 160

The yelling Ghost before him
    stands,
  See! she rolls her eyes around,
Now she lifts her bony hands,
  Now her footsteps shake the
    ground.

Stranger.

Phantom of Theresa say, 165
  Why to earth again you came,
Quickly speak, I must away!
  Or you must bleach for aye in
    flame,—

Phantom.

Mighty one I know thee now,
　　Mightiest power of the sky,　170
Know thee by thy flaming brow,
　　Know thee by thy sparkling eye.

That fire is scorching! Oh! I came,
　　From the caverned depth of Hell,
My fleeting false Rodolph to claim,
　　Mighty one! I know thee
　　　　well.—　　　　　　176

Stranger.

Ghasta! seize yon wandering sprite,
　　Drag her to the depth beneath,
Take her swift, before 'tis light,
　　Take her to the cells of death! 180

Thou that heardst the trackless
　　　　dead,
　　In the mouldering tomb must lie,
Mortal! look upon my head,
　　Mortal! Mortal! thou must die.

Of glowing flame a cross was there
　　Which threw a light around his
　　　　form,　　　　　　　186
Whilst his lank and raven hair,
　　Floated wild upon the storm.—

The warrior upwards turned his
　　　　eyes,
　　Gazed upon the cross of fire,　190
There sat horror and surprise,
　　There sat God's eternal ire.—

A shivering through the Warrior
　　　　flew,
　　Colder than the nightly blast,
Colder than the evening dew,　195
　　When the hour of twilight 's
　　　　past.—

Thunder shakes th' expansive sky,
　　Shakes the bosom of the heath,
'Mortal! Mortal! thou must die'—
　　The warrior sank convulsed in
　　　　death.　　　　　　200
　　　　　　JANUARY, 1810.

XVII. FRAGMENT,

OR THE TRIUMPH OF CONSCIENCE

'TWAS dead of the night when I
　　sate in my dwelling,
　　One glimmering lamp was ex-
　　　　piring and low,—
Around the dark tide of the tem-
　　pest was swelling,
Along the wild mountains night-
　　ravens were yelling,
　　They bodingly presaged destruc-
　　　　tion and woe!　　　　　5

'Twas then that I started, the wild
　　storm was howling,
　　Nought was seen, save the light-
　　　　ning that danced on the sky,
Above me the crash of the thunder
　　was rolling,
　　And low, chilling murmurs the
　　　　blast wafted by.—

My heart sank within me, unheeded
　　the jar　　　　　　　　10
　　Of the battling clouds on the
　　　　mountain-tops broke,
Unheeded the thunder-peal crashed
　　in mine ear,
This heart hard as iron was stran-
　　ger to fear,
　　But conscience in low noiseless
　　　　whispering spoke.

'Twas then that her form on the
　　whirlwind uprearing,　　15
The dark ghost of the murdered
　　Victoria strode,
Her right hand a blood reeking dag-
　　ger was bearing,
　　She swiftly advanced to my lone-
　　　　some abode.—
I wildly then called on the tempest
　　to bear me!

　.　　.　　.　　.　　.　　.　　.

　.　　.　　.　　.　　.　　.　　.

POEMS FROM ST. IRVYNE, OR, THE ROSICRUCIAN

I.—VICTORIA

[Another version of *The Triumph of Conscience* immediately preceding.]

I

'TWAS dead of the night, when I
    sat in my dwelling;
  One glimmering lamp was expir-
    ing and low;
Around, the dark tide of the tem-
    pest was swelling,
Along the wild mountains night-
    ravens were yelling,—
  They bodingly presaged destruc-
    tion and woe.   5

II

'Twas then that I started!—the
    wild storm was howling,
  Nought was seen, save the light-
    ning, which danced in the
    sky;
Above me, the crash of the thunder
    was rolling,
  And low, chilling murmurs, the
    blast wafted by.

III

My heart sank within me—un-
    heeded the war   10
  Of the battling clouds, on the
    mountain-tops, broke;—
Unheeded the thunder-peal crashed
    in mine ear—
This heart, hard as iron, is stranger
    to fear;
  But conscience in low, noiseless
    whispering spoke.

IV

'Twas then that her form on the
    whirlwind upholding,   15

The ghost of the murdered Vic-
    toria strode;
In her right hand, a shadowy
    shroud she was holding,
  She swiftly advanced to my lone-
    some abode.

V

I wildly then called on the tempest
    to bear me—

.   .   .   .

II.—'ON THE DARK HEIGHT OF JURA'

I

GHOSTS of the dead! have I not
    heard your yelling
  Rise on the night-rolling breath
    of the blast,
When o'er the dark aether the tem-
    pest is swelling,
  And on eddying whirlwind the
    thunder-peal passed?

II

For oft have I stood on the dark
    height of Jura,   5
  Which frowns on the valley that
    opens beneath;
Oft have I braved the chill night-
    tempest's fury,
  Whilst around me, I thought,
    echoed murmurs of death.

III

And now, whilst the winds of the
    mountain are howling,
  O father! thy voice seems to
    strike on mine ear;   10
In air whilst the tide of the night-
    storm is rolling,
  It breaks on the pause of the ele-
    ments' jar.

IV

On the wing of the whirlwind which
 roars o'er the mountain
Perhaps rides the ghost of my
 sire who is dead:
On the mist of the tempest which
 hangs o'er the fountain, 15
Whilst a wreath of dark vapour
 encircles his head.

III.—SISTER ROSA: A BALLAD

I

THE death-bell beats!—
The mountain repeats
The echoing sound of the knell;
 And the dark Monk now
 Wraps the cowl round his brow, 5
As he sits in his lonely cell.

II

And the cold hand of death
Chills his shuddering breath,
As he lists to the fearful lay
 Which the ghosts of the sky, 10
 As they sweep wildly by,
Sing to departed day.
 And they sing of the hour
 When the stern fates had power
To resolve Rosa's form to its
 clay. 15

III

But that hour is past;
And that hour was the last
Of peace to the dark Monk's brain.
 Bitter tears, from his eyes,
 gushed silent and fast;
And he strove to suppress them in
 vain.

IV

Then his fair cross of gold he
 dashed on the floor, 21
When the death-knell struck on his
 ear.—
 'Delight is in store

For her evermore;
But for me is fate, horror, and
 fear.' 25

V

Then his eyes wildly rolled,
When the death-bell tolled,
And he raged in terrific woe.
 And he stamped on the ground,—
 But when ceased the sound, 30
Tears again began to flow.

VI

And the ice of despair
Chilled the wild throb of care,
And he sate in mute agony still;
 Till the night-stars shone
 through the cloudless air, 35
And the pale moonbeam slept on
 the hill.

VII

Then he knelt in his cell:—
And the horrors of hell
Were delights to his agonized pain,
 And he prayed to God to dissolve
 the spell, 40
Which else must for ever remain.

VIII

And in fervent pray'r he knelt on
 the ground,
Till the abbey bell struck One:
His feverish blood ran chill at the
 sound:
A voice hollow and horrible murmured around— 45
 'The term of thy penance is
 done!'

IX

Grew dark the night;
The moonbeam bright
Waxed faint on the mountain high;
 And, from the black hill, 50
 Went a voice cold and still,—
'Monk! thou art free to die.'

X

Then he rose on his feet,
And his heart loud did beat,
And his limbs they were palsied
    with dread; 55
Whilst the grave's clammy dew
O'er his pale forehead grew;
And he shuddered to sleep with the
    dead.

XI

And the wild midnight storm
Raved around his tall form, 60
As he sought the chapel's gloom:
And the sunk grass did sigh
To the wind, bleak and high,
As he searched for the new-made
    tomb.

XII

And forms, dark and high, 65
Seemed around him to fly,
And mingle their yells with the
    blast:
And on the dark wall
Half-seen shadows did fall,
As enhorrored he onward passed. 70

XIII

And the storm-fiends wild rave
O'er the new-made grave,
And dread shadows linger around.
The Monk called on God his soul
    to save,
And, in horror, sank on the
    ground. 75

XIV

Then despair nerved his arm
To dispel the charm,
And he burst Rosa's coffin asunder.
And the fierce storm did swell
More terrific and fell, 80
And louder pealed the thunder.

XV

And laughed, in joy, the fiendish
    throng,

Mixed with ghosts of the mould-
    ering dead:
And their grisly wings, as they
    floated along,
Whistled in murmurs dread. 85

XVI

And her skeleton form the dead
    Nun reared
    Which dripped with the chill dew
    of hell.
In her half-eaten eyeballs two pale
    flames appeared,
And triumphant their gleam on the
    dark Monk glared,
    As he stood within the cell. 90

XVII

And her lank hand lay on his shud-
    dering brain;
    But each power was nerved by
    fear.—
'I never henceforth, may breathe
    again;
Death now ends mine anguished
    pain.—
    The grave yawns,—we meet
    there.' 95

XVIII

And her skeleton lungs did utter the
    sound,
    So deadly, so lone, and so fell,
That in long vibrations shuddered
    the ground;
And as the stern notes floated
    around,
    A deep groan was answered from
    hell. 100

IV.—St. Irvyne's Tower

I

How swiftly through Heaven's wide
    expanse
    Bright day's resplendent colours
    fade!

How sweetly does the monbeam's
glance
  With silver tint St. Irvyne's
glade!

II

No cloud along the spangled air, 5
  Is borne upon the evening
breeze;
How solemn is the scene! how fair
  The moonbeams rest upon the
trees!

III

Yon dark gray turret glimmers
white,
  Upon it sits the mournful owl;
Along the stillness of the night, 11
  Her melancholy shriekings roll.

IV

But not alone on Irvyne's tower,
  The silver moonbeam pours her
ray;
It gleams upon the ivied bower, 15
  It dances in the cascade's spray.

V

'Ah! why do dark'ning shades con-
ceal
  The hour, when man must cease
to be?
Why may not human minds unveil
  The dim mists of futurity?   20

VI

'The keenness of the world hath
torn
  The heart which opens to its
blast;
Despised, neglected, and forlorn,
  Sinks the wretch in death at
last.'

V.—BEREAVEMENT

I

How stern are the woes of the
desolate mourner,

As he bends in still grief o'er
  the hallowèd bier,
As enanguished he turns from the
  laugh of the scorner,
And drops, to Perfection's remembrance, a tear;
When floods of despair down his
  pale cheek are streaming, 5
When no blissful hope on his bosom
  is beaming,
Or, if lulled for awhile, soon he
  starts from his dreaming,
  And finds torn the soft ties to
affection so dear.

II

Ah! when shall day dawn on the
  night of the grave,
Or summer succeed to the winter
  of death?   10
Rest awhile, hapless victim, and
  Heaven will save
  The spirit, that faded away with
the breath.
Eternity points in its amaranth
  bower,
Where no clouds of fate o'er the
  sweet prospect lower,
Unspeakable pleasure, of goodness
  the dower,   15
  When woe fades away like the
mist of the heath.

VI.—THE DROWNED LOVER

I

AH! faint are her limbs, and her
  footstep is weary,
  Yet far must the desolate wanderer roam;
Though the tempest is stern, and
  the mountain is dreary,
  She must quit at deep midnight
her pitiless home.
I see her swift foot dash the dew
  from the whortle,   5
As she rapidly hastes to the green
  grove of myrtle;

And I hear, as she wraps round
   her figure the kirtle,
'Stay thy boat on the lake,—
   dearest Henry, I come.'

II

High swelled in her bosom the
   throb of affection,
As lightly her form bounded over
   the lea,   10
And arose in her mind every dear
   recollection;
'I come, dearest Henry, and wait
   but for thee.'
How sad, when dear hope every
   sorrow is soothing,
When sympathy's swell the soft
   bosom is moving,
And the mind the mild joys of affection is proving,   15

Is the stern voice of fate that
   bids happiness flee!

III

Oh! dark lowered the clouds on
   that horrible eve,
And the moon dimly gleamed
   through the tempested air;
Oh! how could fond visions such
   softness deceive?
Oh! how could false hope rend
   a bosom so fair?   20
Thy love's pallid corse the wild
   surges are laving,
O'er his form the fierce swell of
   the tempest is raving;
But, fear not, parting spirit; thy
   goodness is saving,
In eternity's bowers, a seat for
   thee there.

POSTHUMOUS FRAGMENTS
OF MARGARET NICHOLSON

Being Poems found amongst the Papers of that noted Female who
attempted the life of the King in 1786. Edited by John Fitzvictor.

ADVERTISEMENT

THE energy and native genius of these Fragments must be the only
apology which the Editor can make for thus intruding them on the public
notice. The first I found with no title, and have left it so. It is intimately
connected with the dearest interests of universal happiness; and much
as we may deplore the fatal and enthusiastic tendency which the ideas
of this poor female had acquired, we cannot fail to pay the tribute of
unequivocal regret to the departed memory of genius, which, had it
been rightly organized, would have made that intellect, which has since
become the victim of frenzy and despair, a most brilliant ornament to
society.

In case the sale of these Fragments evinces that the public have any
curiosity to be presented with a more copious collection of my unfortunate Aunt's poems, I have other papers in my possession which shall,
in that case, be subjected to their notice. It may be supposed they
require much arrangement; but I send the following to the press in the
same state in which they came into my possession.   J. F.

WAR

AMBITION, power, and avarice, now
 have hurled
Death, fate, and ruin, on a bleed-
 ing world.
See! on yon heath what countless
 victims lie,
Hark! what loud shrieks ascend
 through yonder sky;
Tell then the cause, 'tis sure the
 avenger's rage   5
Has swept these myriads from
 life's crowded stage:
Hark to that groan, an anguished
 hero dies,
He shudders in death's latest
 agonies;
Yet does a fleeting hectic flush his
 cheek,
Yet does his parting breath essay
 to speak—   10
'Oh God! my wife, my children—
 Monarch thou
For whose support this fainting
 frame lies low;
For whose support in distant lands
 I bleed,
Let his friends' welfare be the war-
 rior's meed.
He hears me not—ah! no—kings
 cannot hear,   15
For passion's voice has dulled their
 listless ear.
To thee, then, mighty God, I lift
 my moan,
Thou wilt not scorn a suppliant's
 anguished groan.
Oh! now I die—but still is death's
 fierce pain—
God hears my prayer—we meet,
 we meet again,'   20
He spake, reclined him on death's
 bloody bed,
And with a parting groan his spirit
 fled.

Oppressors of mankind to *you*
 we owe
The baleful streams from whence
 these miseries flow;
For you how many a mother weeps
 her son,   25
Snatched from life's course ere
 half his race was run!
For you how many a widow drops
 a tear,
In silent anguish, on her husband's
 bier!
'Is it then Thine, Almighty
 Power,' she cries,
'Whence tears of endless sorrow
 dim these eyes?   30
Is this the system which Thy
 powerful sway,
Which else in shapeless chaos sleep-
 ing lay,
Formed and approved?—it cannot
 be—but oh!
Forgive me, Heaven, my brain is
 warped by woe.'
'Tis not—He never bade the war-
 note swell,   35
He never triumphed in the work of
 hell—
Monarchs of earth! thine is the
 baleful deed,
Thine are the crimes for which thy
 subjects bleed.
Ah! when will come the sacred
 fated time,
When man unsullied by his leaders'
 crime,   40
Despising wealth, ambition, pomp,
 and pride,
Will stretch him fearless by his foemen's side?
Ah! when will come the time, when
 o'er the plain
No more shall death and desolation
 reign?
When will the sun smile on the
 bloodless field,   45

And the stern warrior's arm the
    sickle wield?
Not whilst some King, in cold am-
    bition's dreams,
Plans for the field of death his
    plodding schemes;
Not whilst for private pique the
    public fall,
And one frail mortal's mandate
    governs all.   50
Swelled with command and mad
    with dizzying sway;
Who sees unmoved his myriads
    fade away.
Careless who lives or dies—so that
    he gains
Some trivial point for which he
    took the pains.
What then are Kings?—I see the
    trembling crowd,   55
I hear their fulsome clamours
    echoed loud;
Their stern oppressor pleased ap-
    pears awhile,
But April's sunshine is a Mon-
    arch's smile—
Kings are but dust—the last event-
    ful day
Will level all and make them lose
    their sway;   60
Will dash the sceptre from the
    Monarch's hand,
And from the warrior's grasp wrest
    the ensanguined brand.
  Oh! Peace, soft Peace, art thou
    for ever gone,
Is thy fair form indeed for ever
    flown?
And love and concord hast thou
    swept away,   65
As if incongruous with thy parted
    sway?
Alas, I fear thou hast, for none
    appear.
Now o'er the palsied earth stalks
    giant Fear,

With War, and Woe, and Terror, in
    his train;
List'ning he pauses on the embat-
    tled plain,   70
Then speeding swiftly o'er the en-
    sanguined heath,
Has left the frightful work to Hell
    and Death.
See! gory Ruin yokes his blood-
    stained car,
He scents the battle's carnage from
    afar;
Hell and Destruction mark his mad
    career,   75
He tracks the rapid step of hurry-
    ing Fear;
Whilst ruined towns and smoking
    cities tell,
That thy work, Monarch, is the
    work of Hell.
'It is thy work!' I hear a voice
    repeat,
Shakes the broad basis of thy
    blood-stained seat;   80
And at the orphan's sigh, the
    widow's moan,
Totters the fabric of thy guilt-
    stained throne—
'It is thy work, O Monarch;' now
    the sound
Fainter and fainter, yet is borne
    around,
Yet to enthusiast ears the murmurs
    tell   85
That Heaven, indignant at the
    work of Hell,
Will soon the cause, the hated cause
    remove,
Which tears from earth peace, in-
    nocence, and love.

FRAGMENT

SUPPOSED TO BE AN EPITHALAMIUM
OF FRANCIS RAVAILLAC AND
CHARLOTTE CORDAY

'TIS midnight now—athwart the
    murky air,

Dank lurid meteors shoot a livid
  gleam;
From the dark storm-clouds flashes
  a fearful glare,
  It shows the bending oak, the
    roaring stream.

I pondered on the woes of lost man-
  kind,   5
  I pondered on the ceaseless rage
    of Kings;
My rapt soul dwelt upon the ties
  that bind
  The mazy volume of commin-
    gling things,
When fell and wild misrule to man
  stern sorrow brings.

I heard a yell—it was not the knell,
  When the blasts on the wild lake
    sleep,   11
That floats on the pause of the sum-
  mer gale's swell,
  O'er the breast of the waveless
    deep.

I thought it had been death's ac-
  cents cold
  That bade me recline on the
    shore;   15
I laid mine hot head on the surge-
  beaten mould,
  And thought to breathe no more.

    But a heavenly sleep
    That did suddenly steep
      In balm my bosom's pain, 20
    Pervaded my soul,
    And free from control,
      Did mine intellect range
        again.

Methought enthroned upon a sil-
  very cloud,
  Which floated mid a strange and
    brilliant light;   25
My form upborne by viewless
  aether rode,
  And spurned the lessening realms
    of earthly night.

What heavenly notes burst on my
  ravished ears,
  What beauteous spirits met my
    dazzled eye!
Hark! louder swells the music of
  the spheres,   30
  More clear the forms of speech-
    less bliss float by,
And heavenly gestures suit aethe-
  real melody.

But fairer than the spirits of the air,
  More graceful than the Sylph of
    symmetry,
Than the enthusiast's fancied love
  more fair,   35
  Were the bright forms that swept
    the azure sky.
Enthroned in roseate light, a heav-
  enly band
  Strewed flowers of bliss that
    never fade away;
They welcome virtue to its native
  land,
  And songs of triumph greet the
    joyous day   40
When endless bliss the woes of fleet-
  ing life repay.

Congenial minds will seek their
  kindred soul,
  E'en though the tide of time has
    rolled between;
They mock weak matter's impotent
  control,
  And seek of endless life the eter-
    nal scene.   45
At death's vain summons *this* will
  never die,
  In Nature's chaos *this* will not
    decay—
These are the bands which closely,
  warmly, tie
  Thy soul, O Charlotte, 'yond this
    chain of clay,
To him who thine must be till time
  shall fade away.   50

Yes, Francis! thine was the dear
    knife that tore
A tyrant's heart-strings from his
    guilty breast,
Thine was the daring at a tyrant's
    gore,
    To smile in triumph, to contemn
      the rest;
And thine, loved glory of thy sex!
    to tear   55
    From its base shrine a despot's
      haughty soul,
To laugh at sorrow in secure de-
    spair,
    To mock, with smiles, life's lin-
      gering control,
And triumph mid the griefs that
    round thy fate did roll.

Yes! the fierce spirits of the aveng-
    ing deep   60
    With endless tortures goad their
      guilty shades.
I see the lank and ghastly spectres
    sweep
    Along the burning length of yon
      arcades;
And I see Satan stalk athwart the
    plain;
    He hastes along the burning soil
      of Hell.   65
'Welcome, ye despots, to my dark
    domain,
    With maddening joy mine an-
      guished senses swell
To welcome to their home the
    friends I love so well.'

    .   .   .   .

Hark! to those notes, how sweet,
    how thrilling sweet
They echo to the sound of angels'
    feet.   70

    .   .   .   .

Oh haste to the bower where roses
    are spread,
For there is prepared thy nuptial
    bed.

Oh haste—hark! hark!—they're
    gone.

    .   .   .   .

Chorus of Spirits.

Stay, ye days of contentment and
    joy,   74
    Whilst love every care is erasing,
Stay ye pleasures that never can
    cloy,
    And ye spirits that can never
      cease pleasing.

And if any soft passion be near,
    Which mortals, frail mortals, can
      know,
Let love shed on the bosom a tear,
    And dissolve the chill ice-drop of
      woe.   81

SYMPHONY.

Francis.

'SOFT, my dearest angel, stay,
Oh! you suck my soul away;
Suck on. suck on, I glow, I glow!
Tides of maddening passion roll, 85
And streams of rapture drown my
    soul.
Now give me one more billing kiss,
Let your lips now repeat the bliss,
Endless kisses steal my breath,
No life can equal such a death.' 90

Charlotte.

'Oh! yes I will kiss thine eyes so
    fair,
    And I will clasp thy form;
Serene is the breath of the balmy
    air,
    But I think, love, thou feelest me
      warm
And I will recline on thy marble
    neck   95
    Till I mingle into thee;
And I will kiss the rose on thy
    cheek,
    And thou shalt give kisses to me.

For here is no morn to flout our delight,
    Oh! dost thou not joy at this? 100
And here we may lie an endless
night,
    A long, long night of bliss.'

Spirits! when raptures move,
Say what it is to love,
When passion's tear stands on the
    cheek,   105
    When bursts the unconscious
    sigh;
And the tremulous lips dare not
speak
    What is told by the soul-felt eye.
But what is sweeter to revenge's ear
Than the fell tyrant's last expir-
    ing yell?   110
Yes! than love's sweetest blisses 'tis
    more dear
    To drink the floatings of a des-
    pot's knell.
I wake—'tis done—'tis over.

.   .   .   .   .

DESPAIR

AND canst thou mock mine agony,
    thus calm
    In cloudless radiance, Queen of
    silver night?
Can you, ye flow'rets, spread your
    perfumed balm
    Mid pearly gems of dew that
    shine so bright?
And you wild winds, thus can you
    sleep so still   5
    Whilst throbs the tempest of my
    breast so high?
Can the fierce night-fiends rest on
    yonder hill,
    And, in the eternal mansions of
    the sky,
Can the directors of the storm in
    powerless silence lie?

Hark! I hear music on the zephyr's
    wing,   10

    Louder it floats along the un-
    ruffled sky;
Some fairy sure has touched the
    viewless string—
    Now faint in distant air the mur-
    murs die.
Awhile it stills the tide of agony.
    Now—now it loftier swells—
    again stern woe   15
Arises with the awakening melody.
    Again fierce torments, such as
    demons know,
In bitterer, feller tide, on this torn
    bosom flow.

Arise ye sightless spirits of the
    storm,
    Ye unseen minstrels of the aëreal
    song,   20
Pour the fierce tide around this
    lonely form,
    And roll the tempest's wildest
    swell along.
Dart the red lightning, wing the
    forkèd flash,
    Pour from thy cloud-formed hills
    the thunder's roar;
Arouse the whirlwind—and let
    ocean dash   25
    In fiercest tumult on the rocking
    shore,—
Destroy this life or let earth's fab-
    ric be no more.

Yes! every tie that links me here is
    dead;
    Mysterious Fate, thy mandate I
    obey,
Since hope and peace, and joy, for
    aye are fled,   30
    I come, terrific power, I come
    away.
Then o'er this ruined soul let spirits
    of Hell,
    In triumph, laughing wildly,
    mock its pain;
And though with direst pangs mine
    heart-strings swell,

I'll echo back their deadly yells
   again,   35
Cursing the power that ne'er made
   aught in vain.

FRAGMENT

YES! all is past—swift time has
   fled away,
   Yet its swell pauses on my sick-
      ening mind;
How long will horror nerve this
   frame of clay?
I'm dead, and lingers yet my soul
   behind.

Oh! powerful Fate, revoke thy
   deadly spell,   5
   And yet that may not ever, ever
      be,
Heaven will not smile upon the
   work of Hell;
Ah! no, for Heaven cannot smile
   on me;
Fate, envious Fate, has sealed my
   wayward destiny.

I sought the cold brink of the mid-
   night surge,   10
   I sighed beneath its wave to hide
      my woes,
The rising tempest sung a funeral
   dirge,
   And on the blast a frightful yell
      arose.

Wild flew the meteors o'er the mad-
   dened main,
   Wilder did grief athwart my
      bosom glare;   15
Stilled was the unearthly howling,
   and a strain,
   Swelled mid the tumult of the
      battling air,
'Twas like a spirit's song, but yet
   more soft and fair.

I met a maniac—like he was to me,
   I said—'Poor victim, wherefore
      dost thou roam?   20
And canst thou not contend with
   agony,

That thus at midnight thou dost
   quit thine home?'
'Ah there she sleeps: cold in her
   bloodless form,
   And I will go to slumber in her
      grave;
And then our ghosts, whilst raves
   the maddened storm,   25
Will sweep at midnight o'er the
   wildered wave;
Wilt thou our lowly beds with tears
   of pity lave?'

'Ah! no, I cannot shed the pitying
   tear,
   This breast is cold, this heart can
      feel no more;
But I can rest me on thy chilling
   bier,   30
   Can shriek in horror to the tem-
      pest's roar.'

. . . . .

THE SPECTRAL HORSEMAN

WHAT was the shriek that struck
   Fancy's ear
As it sate on the ruins of time that
   is past?
Hark! it floats on the fitful blast of
   the wind,
And breathes to the pale moon a
   funeral sigh.
It is the Benshie's moan on the
   storm,   5
Or a shivering fiend that thirsting
   for sin,
Seeks murder and guilt when virtue
   sleeps,
Winged with the power of some
   ruthless king,
And sweeps o'er the breast of the
   prostrate plain.
It was not a fiend from the regions
   of Hell   10
That poured its low moan on the
   stillness of night:

It was not a ghost of the guilty
　　dead,
Nor a yelling vampire reeking with
　　gore;
But aye at the close of seven years'
　　end,
That voice is mixed with the swell
　　of the storm,　　　　　　　15
And aye at the close of seven
　　years' end,
A shapeless shadow that sleeps on
　　the hill
Awakens and floats on the mist of
　　the heath.
It is not the shade of a murdered
　　man,
Who has rushed uncalled to the
　　throne of his God,　　　　20
And howls in the pause of the eddy-
　　ing storm.
This voice is low, cold, hollow, and
　　chill,
'Tis not heard by the ear, but is felt
　　in the soul.
'Tis more frightful far than the
　　death-daemon's scream,
Or the laughter of fiends when they
　　howl o'er the corpse　　25
Of a man who has sold his soul to
　　Hell.
It tells the approach of a mystic
　　form,
A white courser bears the shadowy
　　sprite;
More thin they are than the mists
　　of the mountain,
When the clear moonlight sleeps on
　　the waveless lake.　　　30
More pale *his* cheek than the snows
　　of Nithona,
When winter rides on the northern
　　blast,
And howls in the midst of the leaf-
　　less wood.
Yet when the fierce swell of the
　　tempest is raving,

And the whirlwinds howl in the
　　caves of Inisfallen,　　　35
Still secure mid the wildest war of
　　the sky,
The phantom courser scours the
　　waste,
And his rider howls in the thunder's
　　roar.
O'er him the fierce bolts of avenging
　　Heaven
Pause, as in fear, to strike his
　　head.　　　　　　　　40
The meteors of midnight recoil
　　from his figure,
Yet the 'wildered peasant, that oft
　　passes by,
With wonder beholds the blue flesh
　　through his form:
And his voice, though faint as the
　　sighs of the dead,
The startled passenger shudders to
　　hear,　　　　　　　　45
More distinct than the thunder's
　　wildest roar.
Then does the dragon, who, chained
　　in the caverns
To eternity, curses the champion
　　of Erin,
Moan and yell loud at the lone
　　hour of midnight,
And twine his vast wreaths round
　　the forms of the daemons;
Then in agony roll his death-swim-
　　ming eyeballs,　　　　51
Though 'wildered by death, yet
　　never to die!
Then he shakes from his skeleton
　　folds the nightmares,
Who, shrieking in agony, seek the
　　couch
Of some fevered wretch who courts
　　sleep in vain;　　　　55
Then the tombless ghosts of the
　　guilty dead
In horror pause on the fitful gale.
They float on the swell of the eddy-
　　ing tempest.

And scared seek the caves of gigantic ...
Where their thin forms pour unearthly sounds   60
On the blast that sweeps the breast
 of the lake,
And mingles its swell with the
 moonlight air.

MELODY TO A SCENE OF
FORMER TIMES

ART thou indeed forever gone,
 Forever, ever, lost to me?
Must this poor bosom beat alone,
 Or beat at all, if not for thee?
Ah! why was love to mortals
 given,   5
To lift them to the height of
 Heaven,
Or dash them to the depths of Hell?
Yet I do not reproach thee, dear!
Ah, no! the agonies that swell
 This panting breast, this fren-
  zied brain,   10
 Might wake my ——'s slumb-
  b'ring tear.
Oh! Heaven is witness I did love,
And Heaven does know I love thee
 still,
Does know the fruitless sick'ning
 thrill,
 When reason's judgment vainly
  strove   15
To blot thee from my memory;
But which might never, never be.
Oh! I appeal to that blest day
When passion's wildest ecstasy
Was coldness to the joys I knew, 20
When every sorrow sunk away.
Oh! I had never lived before,
But now those blisses are no more.
 And now I cease to live again,
I do not blame thee, love; ah,
 no!   25
The breast that feels this anguished
   —ne

Throbs for thy happiness alone.
Two years of speechless bliss are
 gone,
I thank thee, dearest, for the dream.
'Tis night—what faint and distant
 scream   30
Comes on the wild and fitful blast?
It moans for pleasures that are past,
It moans for days that are gone by.
Oh! lagging hours, how slow you
 fly!
 I see a dark and lengthened
  vale,   35
The black view closes with the
 tomb;
But darker is the lowering gloom
 That shades the intervening
  dale.
In visioned slumber for awhile
I seem again to share thy smile, 40
I seem to hang upon thy tone.
 Again you say, 'Confide in me,
For I am thine, and thine alone,
 And thine must ever, ever be.'
But oh! awak'ning still anew, 45
Athwart my enanguished senses
 flew
 A fiercer, deadlier agony!
[End of *Posthumous Fragments
of Margaret Nicholson.*]

STANZA FROM A TRANSLA-
TION OF THE MARSEIL-
LAISE HYMN

TREMBLE, Kings despised of man!
 Ye traitors to your Country,
Tremble! Your parricidal plan
 At length shall meet its des-
  tiny ...
We all are soldiers fit to fight, 5
But if we sink in glory's night
Our mother Earth will give ye new
The brilliant pathway to pursue
 Which leads to Death or Vic-
  tory ...

BIGOTRY'S VICTIM

I

Dares the lama, most fleet of the
    sons of the wind,
    The lion to rouse from his skull-
        covered lair?
When the tiger approaches can the
    fast-fleeting hind
    Repose trust in his footsteps of
        air?
No! Abandoned he sinks in a trance
    of despair,   5
    The monster transfixes his
        prey,
    On the sand flows his life-
        blood away;
Whilst India's rocks to his death-
    yells reply,
Protracting the horrible harmony.

II

Yet the fowl of the desert, when
    danger encroaches,   10
Dares fearless to perish defend-
    ing her brood,
Though the fiercest of cloud-pierc-
    ing tyrants approaches
    Thirsting—ay, thirsting for
        blood;
And demands, like mankind, his
    brother for food;
    Yet more lenient, more gen-
        tle than they;   15
    For hunger, not glory, the
        prey
Must perish. Revenge does not howl
    in the dead.
Nor ambition with fame crown the
    murderer's head.

III

Though weak as the lama that
    bounds on the mountains,
    And endued not with fast-fleet-
    ing footsteps of air,   20

Yet, yet will I draw from the purest
    of fountains,
    Though a fiercer than tiger is
    there.
Though, more dreadful than death,
    it scatters despair,
    Though its shadow eclipses
    the day,
    And the darkness of deepest
    dismay   25
Spreads the influence of soul-chill-
    ing terror around,
And lowers on the corpses, that rot
    on the ground.

IV

They came to the fountain to draw
    from its stream
    Waves too pure, too celestial, for
    mortals to see;
They bathed for awhile in its sil-
    very beam,   30
    Then perished, and perished like
    me.
For in vain from the grasp of the
    Bigot I flee;
    The most tenderly loved of
    my soul
    Are slaves to his hated con-
    trol.
He pursues me, he blasts me! 'Tis
    in vain that I fly: 35
What remains, but to curse him,—
    to curse him and die?

ON AN ICICLE THAT CLUNG
TO THE GRASS OF A GRAVE

I

Oh! take the pure gem to where
    southerly breezes,
    Waft repose to some bosom as
    faithful as fair,
In which the warm current of love
    never freezes,
    As it rises unmingled with selfish-
    ness there,

Which, untainted by pride, unpolluted by care,   5
Might dissolve the dim icedrop,
   might bid it arise,
Too pure for these regions, to gleam
   in the skies.

II

Or where the stern warrior, his
   country defending,
   Dares fearless the dark-rolling
     battle to pour.
Or o'er the fell corpse of a dread
   tyrant bending,   10
   Where patriotism red with his
     guilt-reeking gore
Plants Liberty's flag on the slave-
   peopled shore,
With victory's cry, with the shout
   of the free,
Let it fly, taintless Spirit, to mingle
   with thee.

III

For I found the pure gem, when
   the daybeam returning,   15
   Ineffectual gleams on the snow-
     covered plain,
When to others the wished-for ar-
   rival of morning
   Brings relief to long visions of
     soul-racking pain;
   But regret is an insult—to grieve
     is in vain:
And why should we grieve that a
   spirit so fair   20
Seeks Heaven to mix with its own
   kindred there?

IV

But still 'twas some Spirit of kindness descending
   To share in the load of mortal-
     ity's woe,
Who over thy lowly-built sepulchre
   bending

Bade sympathy's tenderest tear-
   drop to flow.   25
Not for *thee* soft compassion
   celestials did know,
But if *angels* can weep, sure *man*
   may repine,
May weep in mute grief o'er thy
   low-laid shrine.

V

And did I then say, for the altar of
   glory,
   That the earliest, the loveliest of
     flowers I'd entwine,   30
Though with millions of blood-
   reeking victims 'twas gory,
   Though the tears of the widow
     polluted its shrine,
   Though around it the orphans,
     the fatherless pine?
Oh! Fame, all thy glories I'd yield
   for a tear
To shed on the grave of a heart so
   sincere.   35

LOVE

WHY is it said thou canst not live
   In a youthful breast and fair,
Since thou eternal life canst give,
   Canst bloom for ever there?
Since withering pain no power pos-
   sessed,   5
   Nor age, to blanch thy vermeil
     hue,
Nor time's dread victor, death, con-
   fessed,
   Though bathed with his poison
     dew,
Still thou retain'st unchanging
   bloom,
Fixed tranquil, even in the tomb. 10
And oh! when on the blest, reviv-
   ing,
   The day-star dawns of love,
Each energy of soul surviving
   More vivid, soars above,

Hast thou ne'er felt a rapturous
    thrill,   15
  Like June's warm breath,
    athwart thee fly,
O'er each idea then to steal,
  When other passions die?
Felt it in some wild noonday dream,
When sitting by the lonely stream,
Where Silence says, 'Mine is the
    dell';   21
  And not a murmur from the
    plain,
And not an echo from the fell,
  Disputes her silent reign.

ON A FETE AT CARLTON
HOUSE: FRAGMENT

        By the mossy brink,
With me the Prince shall sit and
  think;
Shall muse in visioned Regency,
Rapt in bright dreams of dawning
  Royalty.

TO A STAR

SWEET star, which gleaming o'er
  the darksome scene
Through fleecy clouds of silvery
  radiance fliest,
Spanglet of light on evening's
  shadowy veil,
Which shrouds the day-beam from
  the waveless lake,
Lighting the hour of sacred love;
  more sweet   5
Than the expiring morn-star's paly
  fires:—
Sweet star! When wearied Nature
  sinks to sleep,
And all is hushed,—all, save the
  voice of Love,
Whose broken murmurings swell
  the balmy blast
Of soft Favonius, which at inter-
  vals   10
Sighs in the ear of stillness, art
  thou aught but

Lulling the slaves of interest to re-
  pose
With that mild, pitying gaze? Oh,
  I would look
In thy dear beam till every bond of
  sense
Became enamoured——   15

TO MARY, WHO DIED IN
THIS OPINION

I

MAIDEN, quench the glare of sor-
  row
  Struggling in thine haggard eye:
Firmness dare to borrow
  From the wreck of destiny;
For the ray morn's bloom reveal-
  ing   5
Can never boast so bright an hue
  As that which mocks concealing,
And sheds its loveliest light on you.

II

  Yet is the tie departed
Which bound thy lovely soul to
  bliss?   10
  Has it left thee broken-hearted
In a world so cold as this?
  Yet, though, fainting fair one,
Sorrow's self thy cup has given,
  Dream thou'lt meet thy dear
  one,   15
Never more to part, in Heaven.

III

  Existence would I barter
  For a dream so dear as thine,
  And smile to die a martyr
On affection's bloodless shrine.   20
  Nor would I change for pleas-
  ure
That withered hand and ashy
  cheek,
  If my heart enshrined a treasure
Such as forces thine to break.

A TALE OF SOCIETY AS IT IS: FROM FACTS, 1811

I

SHE was an agèd woman; and the years
  Which she had numbered on her toilsome way
  Had bowed her natural powers to decay.
She was an agèd woman; yet the ray
  Which faintly glimmered through her starting tears,   5
  Pressed into light by silent misery,
Hath soul's imperishable energy.
    She was a cripple, and incapable
  To add one mite to gold-fed luxury:
    And therefore did her spirit dimly feel   10
  That poverty, the crime of tainting stain,
Would merge her in its depths, never to rise again.

II

One only son's love had supported her.
    She long had struggled with infirmity,
  Lingering to human life-scenes; for to die,   15
  When fate has spared to rend some mental tie,
Would many wish, and surely fewer dare.
But, when the tyrant's bloodhounds forced the child
  For his cursed power unhallowed arms to wield—
    Bend to another's will—become a thing   20
  More senseless than the sword of battlefield—

Then did she feel keen sorrow's keenest sting;
And many years had passed ere comfort they would bring.

III

For seven years did this poor woman live
  In unparticipated solitude.   25
  Thou mightst have seen her in the forest rude
  Picking the scattered remnants of its wood.
If human, thou mightst then have learned to grieve.
The gleanings of precarious charity
  Her scantiness of food did scarce supply.   30
  The proofs of an unspeaking sorrow dwelt
  Within her ghastly hollowness of eye:
    Each arrow of the season's change she felt.
Yet still she groans, ere yet her race were run,
One only hope: it was—once more to see her son.   35

IV

It was an eve of June, when every star
  Spoke peace from Heaven to those on earth that live.
  She rested on the moor. 'Twas such an eve
  When first her soul began indeed to grieve:
Then he was here; now he is very far.   40
The sweetness of the balmy evening
  A sorrow o'er her agèd soul did fling,
    Yet not devoid of rapture's mingled tear:

A balm was in the poison of the
    sting.
This agèd sufferer for many a
    year   45
Had never felt such comfort. She
    suppressed
A sigh—and turning round, clasped
    William to her breast!

V

And, though his form was wasted
    by the woe
Which tyrants on their victims
    love to wreak,
Though his sunk eyeballs and
    his faded cheek   50
Of slavery's violence and scorn
    did speak,
Yet did the agèd woman's bosom
    glow.
The vital fire seemed re-illumed
    within
By this sweet unexpected wel-
    coming.
Oh, consummation of the fond-
    est hope   55
That ever soared on Fancy's
    wildest wing!
Oh, tenderness that foundst so
    sweet a scope!
Prince who dost pride thee on
    thy mighty sway,
When *thou* canst feel such love,
    thou shalt be great as they!

VI

Her son, compelled, the country's
    foes had fought,   60
Had bled in battle; and the
    stern control
Which ruled his sinews and
    coerced his soul
Utterly poisoned life's unmin-
    gled bowl,
And unsubduable evils on him
    brought.

He was the shadow of the lusty
    child   65
Who, when the time of summer
    season smiled,
Did earn for her a meal of
    honesty,
And with affectionate discourse
    beguiled
The keen attacks of pain and
    poverty;
Till Power, as envying her this
    only joy,   70
From her maternal bosom tore the
    unhappy boy.

VII

And now cold charity's unwel-
    come dole
Was insufficient to support the
    pair;
And they would perish rather
    than would bear
The law's stern slavery, and
    the insolent stare   75
With which law loves to rend the
    poor man's soul—
The bitter scorn, the spirit-sink-
    ing noise
Of heartless mirth which women,
    men, and boys
Wake in this scene of legal
    misery.

.   .   .   .   .

TO THE REPUBLICANS OF NORTH AMERICA

I

BROTHERS! between you and me
    Whirlwinds sweep and billows
    roar:
Yet in spirit oft I see
    On thy wild and winding shore
Freedom's bloodless banners
    wave,—   5
Feel the pulses of the brave

Unextinguished in the grave,—
　　See them drenched in sacred
　　　gore,—
Catch the warrior's gasping breath
Murmuring 'Liberty or death!'　10

II

Shout aloud! Let every slave,
　　Crouching at Corruption's
　　　throne,
Start into a man, and brave
　　Racks and chains without a
　　　groan;
And the castle's heartless glow,　15
And the hovel's vice and woe,
Fade like gaudy flowers that
　　blow—
　　Weeds that peep, and then are
　　　gone
Whilst, from misery's ashes risen,
Love shall burst the captive's
　　prison.　20

III

Cotopaxi! bid the sound
　　Through thy sister mountains
　　　ring,
Till each valley smile around
　　At the blissful welcoming!
And, O thou stern Ocean deep,　25
Thou whose foamy billows sweep
Shores where thousands wake to
　　weep
　　Whilst they curse a villain king,
On the winds that fan thy breast
Bear thou news of Freedom's rest!

IV

Can the daystar dawn of love,　31
　　Where the flag of war unfurled
Floats with crimson stain above
　　The fabric of a ruined world?
Never but to vengeance driven　35
When the patriot's spirit shriven
Seeks in death its native Heaven!
　　There, to desolation hurled,
Widowed love may watch thy bier,
Balm thee with its dying tear　40

TO IRELAND

I

Bear witness, Erin! when thine in-
　　jured isle
Sees summer on i　verd at pas-
　　tures smile,
Its cornfields waving in the winds
　　that sweep
The billowy surface of thy circling
　　deep!
Thou tree whose shadow o'er the
　　Atlantic gave
Peace, wealth and beauty, to its
　　friendly wave,
　　　Its blossoms fade,
And blighted are the leaves that
　　cast its shade;
Whilst the cold hand gathers its
　　scanty fruit,
Whose chillness struck a canker to
　　its root.　10

II

　　　I could stand
Upon thy shores, O Erin, and could
　　count
The billows that, in their unceasing
　　swell,
Dash on thy beach, and every wave
　　might seem
An instrument in Time the giant's
　　grasp,　15
To burst the barriers or Eternity.
Proceed, thou giant, conquering and
　　to conquer;
March on thy lonely way! The
　　nations fall
Beneath thy noiseless footstep;
　　pyramids
That for millenniums have defied
　　the blast,　20
And laughed at lightnings, thou
　　dost crush to nought.
Yon monarch, in his solitary pomp,
Is but the fungus of a winter day
That thy light footstep presses into
　　dust.

Thou art a conqueror, Time; all
    things give way   25
Before thee but the 'fixed and vir-
    tuous will';
The sacred sympathy of soul which
    was
When thou wert not, which shall be
    when thou perishest.

·   ·   ·   ·   ·

ON ROBERT EMMET'S GRAVE

·   ·   ·   ·   ·

VI

No trump tells thy virtues—the
    grave where they rest
    With thy dust shall remain un-
        polluted by fame,
Till thy foes, by the world and by
    fortune caressed,
    Shall pass like a mist from the
        light of thy name.

VII

When the storm-cloud that lowers
    o'er the day-beam is gone, 5
Unchanged, unextinguished its
    life-spring will shine;
When Erin has ceased with their
    memory to groan,
    She will smile through the tears
    of revival on thine.

THE RETROSPECT: CWM
ELAN, 1812

A SCENE, which 'wildered fancy
    viewed
In the soul's coldest solitude,
With that same scene when peace-
    ful love
Flings rapture's colour o'er the
    grove,
When mountain, meadow, wood
    and stream   5
With unalloying glory gleam,
And to the spirit's ear and eye
Are unison and harmony.

The moonlight was my dearer day;
Then would I wander far away, 10
And, lingering on the wild brook's
    shore
To hear its unremitting roar,
Would lose in the ideal flow
All sense of overwhelming woe;
Or at the noiseless noon of night 15
Would climb some heathy moun-
    tain's height,
And listen to the mystic sound
That stole in fitful gasps around.
I joyed to see the streaks of day
Above the purple peaks decay, 20
And watch the latest line of light
Just mingling with the shades of
    night;
For day with me was time of woe
When even tears refused to flow;
Then would I stretch my languid
    frame   25
Beneath the wild woods' gloomiest
    shade,
And try to quench the ceaseless
    flame
That on my withered vitals preyed;
Would close mine eyes and dream I
    were
On some remote and friendless
    plain,   30
And long to leave existence there,
If with it I might leave the pain
That with a finger cold and lean
Wrote madness on my withering
    mien.

It was not unrequited love   35
That bade my 'wildered spirit rove;
'Twas not the pride disdaining life,
That with this mortal world at
    strife
Would yield to the soul's inward
    sense,
Then groan in human impotence, 40
And weep because it is not given
To taste on Earth the peace of
    Heaven.
'Twas not that in the narrow sphere

Where Nature fixed my wayward
    fate
There was no friend or kindred dear
Formed to become that spirit's
    mate,   46
Which, searching on tired pinion,
    found
Barren and cold repulse around;
Oh, no! yet each one sorrow gave
New graces to the narrow grave. 50
For broken vows had early quelled
The stainless spirit's vestal flame;
Yes! whilst the faithful bosom
    swelled,
Then the envenomed arrow came,
And Apathy's unaltering eye   55
Beamed coldness on the misery;
And early I had learned to scorn
The chains of clay that bound a
    soul
Panting to seize the wings of morn,
And where its vital fires were born
To soar, and spur the cold control
Which the vile slaves of earthly
    night   62
Would twine around its struggling
    flight.

Oh, many were the friends whom
    fame
Had linked with the unmeaning
    name,   65
Whose magic marked among man-
    kind
The casket of my unknown mind,
Which hidden from the vulgar glare
Imbibed no fleeting radiance there.
My darksome spirit sought — it
    found   70
A friendless solitude around.
For who that might undaunted
    stand,
The saviour of a sinking land,
Would crawl, its ruthless tyrant's
    slave,
And fatten upon Freedom's grave,
Though doomed with her to perish,
    where   76

The captive clasps abhorred de-
    spair.

They could not share the bosom's
    feeling,
Which, passion's every throb re-
    vealing,
Dared force on the world's notice
    cold   80
Thoughts of unprofitable mould,
Who bask in Custom's fickle ray,
Fit sunshine of such wintry day!
They could not in a twilight walk
Weave an impassioned web of talk,
Till mysteries the spirits press   86
In wild yet tender awfulness,
Then feel within our narrow sphere
How little yet how great we are!
But they might shine in courtly
    glare,   90
Attract the rabble's cheapest stare,
And might command where'er they
    move
A thing that bears the name of
    love;
They might be learnèd, witty, gay,
Foremost in fashion's gilt array, 95
On Fame's emblazoned pages
    shine,
Be princes' friends, but never
    mine!

Ye jagged peaks that frown sub-
    lime,
Mocking the blunted scythe of
    Time,
Whence I would watch its lustre
    pale   100
Steal from the moon o'er yonder
    vale
Thou rock, whose bosom black and
    vast,
Bared to the stream's unceasing
    flow,
Ever its giant shade doth cast
On the tumultuous surge below: 105
Woods, to whose depths retires to
    die

The wounded Echo's melody,
And whither this lone spirit bent
The footstep of a wild intent:
Meadows! whose green and span-
   gled breast   110
These fevered limbs have often
 pressed,
Until the watchful fiend Despair
Slept in the soothing coolness there!
Have not your varied beauties seen
The sunken eye, the withering
 mien,   115
Sad traces of the unuttered pain
That froze my heart and burned my
 brain.
How changed since Nature's sum-
 mer form
Had last the power my grief to
 charm,
Since last ye soothed my spirit's
 sadness,   120
Strange chaos of a mingled mad-
 ness!
Changed!—not the loathsome
 worm that fed
In the dark mansions of the dead,
Now soaring through the fields of
 air,
And gathering purest nectar there,
A butterfly, whose million hues 126
The dazzled eye of wonder views,
Long lingering on a work so strange,
Has undergone so bright a change.
How do I feel my happiness? 130
I cannot tell, but they may guess
Whose every gloomy feeling gone,
Friendship and passion feel alone;
Who see mortality's dull clouds
Before affection's murmur fly, 135
Whilst the mild glances of her eye
Pierce the thin veil of flesh that
 shrouds
The spirit's inmost sanctuary.
O thou! whose virtues latest
 known,
First in this heart yet claim'st a
 throne;   140

Whose downy sceptre still shall
 share
The gentle sway with virtue there;
Thou fair in form, and pure in
 mind,
Whose ardent friendship rivets
 fast
The flowery band our fates that
 bind,   145
Which incorruptible shall last
When duty's hard and cold control
Has thawed around the burning
 soul,—
The gloomiest retrospects that
 bind
With crowns of thorn the bleeding
 mind,   150
The prospects of most doubtful
 hue
That rise on Fancy's shuddering
 view,—
Are gilt by the reviving ray
Which thou hast flung upon my
 day.

FRAGMENT OF A SONNET

TO HARRIET

EVER as now with Love and Virtue's glow
May thy unwithering soul not
 cease to burn,
Still may thine heart with those
 pure thoughts o'erflow
Which force from mine such quick
 and warm return.

TO HARRIET

IT is not blasphemy to hope that
 Heaven
More perfectly will give those
 nameless joys
Which throb within the pulses of
 the blood
And sweeten all that bitterness
 which Earth

Infuses in the heaven-born soul. O
   thou   5
Whose dear love gleamed upon the
   gloomy path
Which this lone spirit travelled,
   drear and cold,
Yet swiftly leading to those awful
   limits
Which mark the bounds of Time
   and of the space
When Time shall be no more; wilt
   thou not turn   10
Those spirit-beaming eyes and look
   on me,
Until I be assured that Earth is
   Heaven,
And Heaven is Earth?—will not
   thy glowing cheek,
Glowing with soft suffusion, rest
   on mine,
And breathe magnetic sweetness
   through the frame   15
Of my corporeal nature, through
   the soul
Now knit with these fine fibres?
   I would give
The longest and the happiest day
   that fate
Has marked on my existence but
   to feel
One soul-reviving kiss... O thou
   most dear,   20
'Tis an assurance that this Earth
   is Heaven,
And Heaven the flower of that un-
   tainted seed
Which springeth here beneath such
   love as ours.
Harriet! let death all mortal ties
   dissolve,
But ours shall not be mortal! The
   cold hand   25
Of Time may chill the love of
   earthly minds
Half frozen now; the frigid inter-
   course

Of common souls lives but a sum-
   mer's day;
It dies, where it arose, upon this
   earth.
But ours! oh, 'tis the stretch of
   Fancy's hope   30
To portray its continuance as now,
Warm, tranquil, spirit-healing;
   nor when age
Has tempered these wild ecstasies,
   and given
A soberer tinge to the luxurious
   glow
Which blazing on devotion's pin-
   nacle   35
Makes virtuous passion supersede
   the power
Of reason; nor when life's aestival
   sun
To deeper manhood shall have
   ripened me;
Nor when some years have added
   judgement's store
To all thy woman sweetness, all
   the fire   40
Which throbs in thine enthusiast
   heart; not then
Shall holy friendship (for what
   other name
May love like ours assume?), not
   even then
Shall Custom so corrupt, or the
   cold forms
Of this desolate world so harden
   us,   45
As when we think of the dear
   love that binds
Our souls in soft communion, while
   we know
Each other's thoughts and feelings,
   can we say
Unblushingly a heartless compliment,
Praise, hate, or love with the un-
   thinking world,   50
Or dare to cut the unrelaxing nerve

That knits our love to virtue. Can
those eyes,
Beaming with mildest radiance on
my heart
To purify its purity, e'er bend
To soothe its vice or consecrate its
fears?   55
Never, thou second Self! Is confidence
So vain in virtue that I learn to
doubt
The mirror even of Truth? Dark
flood of Time,
Roll as it listeth thee; I measure
not
By month or moments thy am-
biguous course.   60
Another may stand by me on thy
brink,
And watch the bubble whirled be-
yond his ken,
Which pauses at my feet. The sense
of love,
The thirst for action, and the im-
passioned thought
Prolong my being; if I wake no
more,   65
My life more actual living will contain
Than some gray veteran's of the
world's cold school,
Whose listless hours unprofitably
roll
By one enthusiast feeling unredeemed,
Virtue and Love! unbending Forti-
tude,   70
Freedom, Devotedness and Purity!
That life my Spirit consecrates to
you.

SONNET

TO A BALLOON LADEN WITH
KNOWLEDGE

BRIGHT ball of flame that through
the gloom of even

Silently takest thine aethereal
way,
And with surpassing glory
dimm'st each ray
Twinkling amid the dark blue
depths of Heaven,—
Unlike the fire thou bearest, soon
shalt thou   5
Fade like a meteor in surround-
ing gloom,
Whilst that, unquenchable, is
doomed to glow
A watch-light by the patriot's
lonely tomb;
A ray of courage to the oppressed
and poor;
A spark, though gleaming on the
hovel's hearth,   10
Which through the tyrant's gilded
domes shall roar;
A beacon in the darkness of the
Earth;
A sun which, o'er the renovated
scene,
Shall dart like Truth where False-
hood yet has been.

SONNET

ON LAUNCHING SOME BOTTLES
FILLED WITH KNOWLEDGE
INTO THE BRISTOL CHANNEL

VESSELS of heavenly medicine! may
the breeze
Auspicious waft your dark green
forms to shore;
Safe may ye stem the wide surrounding roar
Of the wild whirlwinds and the raging seas;
And oh! if Liberty e'er deigned to
stoop   5
From yonder lowly throne her
crownless brow,
Sure she will breathe around your
emerald group

The fairest breezes of her West
    that blow.
Yes! she will waft ye to some free-
    born soul
Whose eye-beam, kindling as it
    meets your freight,   10
Her heaven-born flame in suffer-
    ing Earth will light,
Until its radiance gleams from pole
    to pole,
And tyrant-hearts with power-
    less envy burst
To see their night of ignorance
    dispersed.

THE DEVIL'S WALK

A BALLAD

I

ONCE, early in the morning,
    Beelzebub arose,
With care his sweet person adorn-
    ing,
    He put on his Sunday clothes.

II

He drew on a boot to hide his
    hoof,   5
    He drew on a glove to hide his
        claw,
His horns were concealed by a *Bras
    Chapeau,*
And the Devil went forth as natty
    a *Beau*
    As Bond-street ever saw.

III

He sate him down, in London
    town,   10
    Before earth's morning ray;
With a favourite imp he began to
    chat,
On religion, and scandal, this and
    that,
    Until the dawn of day.

IV

And then to St. James's Court he
    went,   15
    And St. Paul's Church he took on
        his way;
He was mighty thick with every
    Saint,
    Though they were formal and he
        was gay.

V

The Devil was an agriculturist,
    And as bad weeds quickly
        grow,   20
In looking over his farm, I wist,
    He wouldn't find cause for
        woe.

VI

He peeped in each hole, to each
    chamber stole,
    His promising live-stock to
        view;
Grinning applause, he just showed
    them his claws,   25
And they shrunk with affright from
    his ugly sight,
    Whose work they delighted to
        do.

VII

Satan poked his red nose into
    crannies so small
    One would think that the inno-
        cents fair,
Poor lambkins! were just doing
    nothing at all   30
But settling some dress or arrang-
    ing some ball,
    But the Devil saw deeper
    there.

VIII

A Priest, at whose elbow the Devil
    during prayer
    Sate familiarly, side by side,

Declared that, if the Tempter were
  there, 35
   His presence he would not
  abide.
Ah! ah! thought Old Nick, that's a
  very stale trick,
For without the Devil, O favourite
  of Evil,
   In your carriage you would
  not ride.

IX

Satan next saw a brainless King, 40
   Whose house was as hot as his
  own;
Many Imps in attendance were
  there on the wing,
They flapped the pennon and
  twisted the sting,
   Close by the very Throne.

X

Ah! ah! thought Satan, the pasture
  is good, 45
   My Cattle will here thrive better
  than others;
They dine on news of human blood,
They sup on the groans of the dying and dead,
And supperless never will go to
  bed;
   Which will make them fat as
  their brothers. 50

XI

Fat as the Fiends that feed on
  blood,
   Fresh and warm from the fields
  of Spain,
     Where Ruin ploughs her gory
  way,
Where the shoots of earth are
  nipped in the bud,
   Where Hell is the Victor's
  prey, 55
Its glory the meed of the slain.

XII

Fat—as the Death-birds on Erin's
  shore,
That glutted themselves in her
  dearest gore,
   And flitted round Castlereagh,
When they snatched the Patriot's
  heart, that *his* grasp 60
Had torn from its widow's maniac
  clasp,
   And fled at the dawn of day.

XIII

Fat—as the Reptiles of the tomb,
   That riot in corruption's spoil,
That fret their little hour in
  gloom, 65
   And creep, and live the while.

XIV

Fat as that Prince's maudlin brain,
   Which, addled by some gilded
  toy,
Tired, gives his sweetmeat, and
  again
   Cries for it, like a humoured
  boy. 70

XV

For he is fat,—his waistcoat gay,
When strained upon a levee day,
   Scarce meets across his princely
  paunch;
And pantaloons are like half-moons
   Upon each brawny haunch. 75

XVI

How vast his stock of calf! when
  plenty
   Had filled his empty head and
  heart,
Enough to satiate foplings twenty,
   Could make his pantaloon seams
  start.

XVII

The Devil (who sometimes is called
    Nature),   80
  For men of power provides thus
    well,
Whilst every change and every fea-
    ture,
  Their great original can tell.

XVIII

Satan saw a lawyer a viper slay,
  That crawled up the leg of his
    table,   85
It reminded him most marvellously
  Of the story of Cain and Abel.

XIX

The wealthy yeoman, as he wan-
    ders
  His fertile fields among,
And on his thriving cattle pon-
    ders,   90
  Counts his sure gains, and hums
    a song;
Thus did the Devil, through earth
    walking,
  Hum low a hellish song.

XX

For they thrive well whose garb of
    gore
  Is Satan's choicest livery,   95
And they thrive well who from the
    poor
  Have snatched the bread of
    penury,
And heap the houseless wanderer's
    store
  On the rank pile of luxury.

XXI

The Bishops thrive, though they
    are big;   100
  The Lawyers thrive, though they
    are thin;

For every gown, and every wig,
  Hides the safe thrift of Hell
    within.

XXII

Thus pigs were never counted
    clean,
  Although they dine on finest
    corn;   105
And cormorants are sin-like lean,
  Although they eat from night to
    morn.

XXIII

Oh! why is the Father of Hell in
    such glee,
  As he grins from ear to ear?
Why does he doff his clothes joy-
    fully,   110
  As he skips, and prances, and
    flaps his wing,
As he sidles, leers, and twirls his
    sting,
  And dares, as he is, to appear?

XXIV

A statesman passed—alone to him,
  The Devil dare his whole shape
    uncover,   115
To show each feature, every limb,
  Secure of an unchanging lover.

XXV

At this known sign, a welcome
    sight,
  The watchful demons sought
    their King,
And every Fiend of the Stygian
    night,   120
  Was in an instant on the wing.

XXVI

Pale Loyalty, his guilt-steeled
    brow,
  With wreaths of gory laurel
    crowned:

The hell-hounds, Murder, Want and Woe,
   Forever hungering, flocked around;   125
From Spain had Satan sought their food,
'Twas human woe and human blood!

XXVII

Hark! the earthquake's crash I hear,—
   Kings turn pale, and Conquerors start,
Ruffians tremble in their fear,   130
   For their Satan doth depart.

XVIII

This day Fiends give to revelry
   To celebrate their King's return,
And with delight its Sire to see
   Hell's adamantine limits burn.

XXIX

But were the Devil's sight as keen
   As Reason's penetrating eye, 137
His sulphurous Majesty I ween,
   Would find but little cause for joy.

XXX

For the sons of Reason see   140
   That, ere fate consume the Pole,
The false Tyrant's cheek shall be
   Bloodless as his coward soul.

FRAGMENT OF A SONNET

FAREWELL TO NORTH DEVON

.   .   .   .   .

Where man's profane and tainting hand
Nature's primaeval loveliness has marred,
And some few souls of the high bliss debarred

Which else obey her powerful command;
   . . . mountain piles 5
That load in grandeur Cambria's emerald vales.

ON LEAVING LONDON FOR WALES

HAIL to thee, Cambria; for the unfettered wind
Which from thy wilds even now methinks I feel,
Chasing the clouds that roll in wrath behind,
And tightening the soul's laxest nerves to steel;
True mountain Liberty alone may heal 5
The pain which Custom's obduracies bring,
And he who dares in fancy even to steal
One draught from Snowdon's ever sacred spring
Blots out the unholiest rede of worldly witnessing.

And shall that soul, to selfish peace resigned, 10
So soon forget the woe its fellows share?
Can Snowdon's Lethe from the free-born mind
So soon the page of injured penury tear?
Does this fine mass of human passion dare
To sleep, unhonouring the patriot's fall, 15
Or life's sweet load in quietude to bear
While millions famish even in Luxury's hall,
And Tyranny, high raised, stern lowers on all?

No, Cambria! never may thy matchless vales

A heart so false to hope and vir-
    tue shield; 20
Nor ever may thy spirit-breath-
    ing gales
Waft freshness to the slaves who
    dare to yield.
For me! . . . the weapon that I
    burn to wield
I seek amid thy rocks to ruin
    hurled,
That Reason's flag may over
    Freedom's field, 25
Symbol of bloodless victory,
    wave unfurled,
A meteor-sign of love effulgent o'er
    the world.

. . . . .

Do thou, wild Cambria, calm
    each struggling thought;
Cast thy sweet veil of rocks and
    woods between,
That by the soul to indignation
    wrought 30
Mountains and dells be mingled
    with the scene;
Let me forever be what I have
    been,
But not forever at my needy door
Let Misery linger speechless, pale
    and lean;
I am the friend of the unfriended
    poor,— 35
Let me not madly stain their
    righteous cause in gore.

THE WANDERING JEW'S
SOLILOQUY

Is it the Eternal Triune, is it He
Who dares arrest the wheels of
    destiny
And plunge me in the lowest Hell
    of Hells?
Will not the lightning's blast de-
    stroy my frame?
Will not steel drink the blood-life
    where it swells? 5

No—let me hie where dark De-
    struction dwells,
To rouse her from her deeply cav-
    erned lair,
And, taunting her cursed sluggish-
    ness to ire,
Light long Oblivion's death-torch
    at its flame
And calmly mount Annihilation's
    pyre. 10
Tyrant of Earth! pale Misery's
    jackal Thou!
Are there no stores of vengeful vio-
    lent fate
Within the magazines of Thy fierce
    hate?
No poison in the clouds to bathe
    a brow
That lowers on Thee with desperate
    contempt? 15
Where is the noonday Pestilence
    that slew
The myriad sons of Israel's fa-
    voured nation?
Where the destroying Minister that
    flew
Pouring the fiery tide of desolation
Upon the leagued Assyrian's at-
    tempt? 20
Where the dark Earthquake-
    daemon who engorged
At the dread word Korah's uncon-
    scious crew?
Or the Angel's two-edged sword of
    fire that urged
Our primal parents from their
    bower of bliss
(Reared by Thine hand) for errors
    not their own 25
By Thine omniscient mind fore-
    doomed, foreknown?
Yes! I would court a ruin such as
    this,
Almighty Tyrant! and give thanks
    to Thee—
Drink deeply—drain the cup of
    hate; remit this—I may die.

EVENING

TO HARRIET

O THOU bright Sun! beneath the
    dark blue line
Of western distance that sublime
    descendest,
And, gleaming lovelier as thy
    beams decline,
Thy million hues to every vapour
    lendest,
And, over cobweb lawn and grove
    and stream   5
    Sheddest the liquid magic of thy
    light,
Till calm Earth, with the parting
    splendour bright,
Shows like the vision of a
    beauteous dream;
What gazer now with astronomic
    eye
    Could coldly count the spots
    within thy sphere?   10
Such were thy lover, Harriet,
    could he fly
The thoughts of all that makes his
    passion dear,
And, turning senseless from thy
    warm caress,
Pick flaws in our close-woven
    happiness.

TO IANTHE

I LOVE thee, Baby! for thine own
    sweet sake;
Those azure eyes, that faintly
    dimpled cheek,
Thy tender frame, so eloquently
    weak,
Love in the sternest heart of hate
    might wake;
But more when o'er thy fitful slum-
    ber bending   5
Thy mother folds thee to her
    wakeful heart,
Whilst love and pity, in her
    glances blending,

All that thy passive eyes can feel
    impart:
More, when some feeble lineaments
    of her,
Who bore thy weight beneath her
    spotless bosom,   10
As with deep love I read thy
    face, recur,—
More dear art thou, O fair and
    fragile blossom;
Dearest when most thy tender
    traits express
The image of thy mother's love-
    liness.

SONG FROM
THE WANDERING JEW

SEE yon opening flower
    Spreads its fragrance to the
    blast;
It fades within an hour,
    Its decay is pale—is fast.
Paler is yon maiden;   5
    Faster is her heart's decay;
Deep with sorrow laden,
    She sinks in death away.

FRAGMENT FROM THE
WANDERING JEW

THE Elements respect their Mak-
    er's seal!
    Still like the scathèd pine tree's
    height,
    Braving the tempests of the
    night
Have I 'scaped the flickering flame.
Like the scathed pine, which a
    monument stands   5
Of faded grandeur, which the
    brands
    Of the tempest-shaken air
Have riven on the desolate heath;
    Yet it stands majestic even in
    death,
    And rears its wild form there.   10

TO THE QUEEN OF MY HEART

I

SHALL we roam, my love,
To the twilight grove,
When the moon is rising bright;
Oh, I'll whisper there,
In the cool night-air,   5
What I dare not in broad daylight!

II

I'll tell thee a part
Of the thoughts that start
To being when thou art nigh;
And thy beauty, more bright   10
Than the stars' soft light,
Shall seem as a weft from the sky.

III

When the pale moonbeam
On tower and stream
Sheds a flood of silver sheen,   15
How I love to gaze
As the cold ray strays
O'er thy face, my heart's throned queen!

IV

Wilt thou roam with me
To the restless sea,   20
And linger upon the steep,
And list to the flow
Of the waves below
How they toss and roar and leap?

V

Those boiling waves,   25
And the storm that raves
At night o'er their foaming crest,
Resemble the strife
That, from earliest life,
The passions have waged in my
breast.   30

VI

Oh, come, then, and rove
To the sea or the grove,
When the moon is rising bright;
And I'll whisper there,
In the cool night-air,   35
What I dare not in broad daylight.

INDEX OF FIRST LINES

907